D1399864

DIRECTORY OF
MILITARY AIRCRAFT OF THE WORLD

DIRECTORY OF
MILITARY AIRCRAFT OF THE WORLD

Peter R. March

CASSELL&CO

Cassell & Co
Wellington House
125 Strand
London WC2R 0BB

First published in Great Britain in 2001 by Cassell & Co
in association with the Royal Air Force Benevolent Fund

Text copyright © Peter R. March 2001
Design and layout copyright © Cassell & Co 2001

The right of Peter R. March to be identified as the author of this work has been
asserted in accordance with the Copyright, Designs and Patents Act of 1988.

All rights reserved. No part of this publication may be reproduced, stored in a retrieval system,
or transmitted, in any form or by any means, electronic, mechanical, photocopying, recording,
or otherwise, without the prior written permission of both the copyright holder and the
publisher of this book.

Britsh Library Cataloguing-in-Publication Data
A catalogue record for this book is available from the British Library
ISBN 1-85409-527-7

Distribution in the USA by
Sterling Publishing Co Inc
387 Park Avenue South
New York, NY 10016-8810

Book design by Graham Finch
Printed in Slovenia

CONTENTS

ACKNOWLEDGEMENTS

This Directory would not have been possible without the considerable efforts of a large team of contributing editors and photographers. I am very grateful to Sue Bushell, Ben Dunnell, Malcolm Lowe, Daniel March, Lindsay Peacock, Robby Robinson and Brian Strickland for the many hours of painstaking research that went into providing the individual aircraft profiles. In addition Brian Strickland and Robby Robinson undertook a comprehensive review of the text before publication. The World Air Arms Inventory was prepared with the help of Ben Dunnell and Daniel March.

I was assisted in the formidable task of locating over 700 suitable photographs to illustrate the 412 aircraft in the Directory by many photographers, but I would particularly like to thank Peter Foster, Daniel March, Rod Simpson and Brian Pickering/Military Aviation Photographs for their outstanding contributions. I am also very grateful to Gordon Bartley of BAE Systems for providing a large number of images from his files, and the other aerospace companies that helped with the coverage.

The services of one of the UK's leading aviation illustrators has considerably enhanced the presentation and uniqueness of the Directory. Some 212 high quality digital artworks were specially prepared by Pete West to illustrate over half of the types of military aircraft currently in use around the world.

Last but by no means least I must thank Graham Finch for his meticulous attention to detail in his layout and design of the book overall. His knowledge of the subject and a determination to 'get it right' has helped me to avoid a number of pitfalls in completing this major task.

To all the above and the many other contributors to the text and illustrations who have not been mentioned individually, thank you for your help.

Peter R March

INTRODUCTION

This first all-colour *Directory of Military Aircraft of the World* provides a comprehensive guide to over 400 types of aircraft that are believed to be in service with the world's military air arms at the beginning of 2001. It presents a broad description of each type of aircraft, detailing its development, current service, special features and major variants. The technical data for a major variant of the type is presented in a quick reference panel. This includes details of the aircraft's powerplant(s), the vital statistics in metric units with imperial conversion, its range and endurance, weapon load, and concludes with the type's first flight and service entry dates, where known.

Two colour illustrations are provided for each of the 412 types, including 212 artworks specially prepared for the Directory. Where possible, the photographs and artwork show a side view and an alternative angle of representative aircraft recently in service.

The aircraft are presented in alphabetical order under the name of the manufacturer that is currently building them for military service, or the company mainly responsible for production of the aircraft described. When there are several important variants of a design that are significantly different or are used for alternative roles, or are manufactured in another country under license, these are given a separate page entry. Where this occurs, a cross-reference is shown at the end of the text. The country of origin is clearly identified on each page, as is the principal role of the specific type of aircraft in military service.

In addition, there is an extensively illustrated fifty-page World Air Arms Inventory that lists the principal types of aircraft that are believed to be currently in service with each of the world's air arms, from Afghanistan to Zimbabwe. The listing under each air arm is broken down under four sub-headings: combat, combat support, training and miscellaneous, according to the aircraft's main role with that force. The miscellaneous category covers communications, transport and VIP aircraft, and includes some aircraft operated exclusively by the government of that country.

To assist readers in finding a specific aircraft or variant, manufacturer, aero engine or weapon, there is a comprehensive index listed under these four headings.

Aermacchi MB.326

EMB.326 Xavante Paraguayan Air Force

TECHNICAL DATA

Aermacchi MB.326GB

Powerplant: One Rolls-Royce (Bristol Siddeley)
Viper 20 Mk540 turbojet
Developing: 15.3kN (3,410lb st)
Span: 10.85m (35ft 7in)
Length: 10.67m (35ft 0in)
Height: 3.72m (12ft 2in)
All-up weight: 5,216kg (11,500lb)
Maximum speed: 871km/h (541mph)
Cruise speed: 797km/h (495mph)
Operational ceiling: 39,000ft
Maximum range: 2,445km (1,520 miles)
Mission range: 1,296km (806 miles)
Endurance: up to 3 hours
Accommodation: Instructor and trainee pilot
(instructor in rear seat)
Warload: up to 1,814kg (4,000lb) of external
stores on six underwing pylons/attachments for
various gun, cannon and unguided rocket pods,
light bombs, two Aérospatiale AS.12 missiles,
reconnaissance pods, or external fuel tanks.
First flown: 10 December 1957;
Spring 1967 (MB.326G)
Entered service: January 1962 (Italian MB.326)

DEVELOPMENT

Inspired by the then-developing all-through jet-
training philosophy, the MB.326 was conceived in the
mid-1950s and first flew in December 1957. Italian Air
Force interest led to eventual orders for over 100 basic
trainer MB.326 aircraft which first entered service in
early 1962; Italy also procured several armed trainer
MB.326E models. An early export customer was
Australia, where Commonwealth (CAC) carried out
local manufacture from 1967 of the CA-30 (MB.326H)
for the Royal Australian Air Force (87) and Navy (10).
Armed trainer MB.326B were bought by Tunisia in
1965, and Ghana (MB.326F). Aermacchi duly developed
the strengthened and more powerful MB.326G, which
first flew in the spring of 1967. This longer span,
better equipped, and more capable model became
the MB.326GB, ordered by the Argentine Navy (eight
Pelicanos), Congo (Zaïre, 17 Sukisas 1969-70), and
Zambia. The type was licence-produced in Brazil by
Embraer from 1970/1971 as the EMB-326GB Xavante,
including 166 for the Brazilian Air Force (as the AT-26),
six for Togo and 10 for Paraguay. The MB.326K single-
seat light attack derivative was first flown by Aermacchi
in August 1970, and was exported to Dubai, Ghana,
Tunisia, and Zaïre. A two-seat version of the more
powerful 'K, the MB.326L, was supplied to Tunisia and
Dubai. South African-built derivatives are described
separately. Aermacchi states that 761 MB.326 of all

types were built, of which Aermacchi itself made some
321. The final MB.326 (a Xavante) was delivered by
Embraer in February 1983.

CURRENT SERVICE

All of the Italian Air Force's MB.326s have now been
retired. Australian MB.326Hs are due for replacement
by the BAE Systems Hawk 127, and currently serve
with No 79 Squadron at Pearce, and No 76 Squadron
at Williamstown. A few surviving Argentine Navy
MB.326GBs (supplemented by 11 or 12 EMB-326GBs
from Brazil in 1983 after the Falkland Islands conflict)
continue as operational trainers within FAE 1 at
Comandante Espora AB. Brazilian Xavantes remain
in service with several ground attack/reconnaissance
units including 10° Grupo de Aviação at Santa Maria,
and for fast-jet operational conversion with 2°/5° GAv
at Natal. In addition to these operators, MB.326s or
EMB-326s continue in service in Dubai, Ghana,
Paraguay, Tunisia, Togo, and Zambia. The status of
Zaïre's aircraft is unknown following the recent
turmoil in that country.

SPECIAL FEATURES

The all-metal straight-winged subsonic MB.326 is of
simple but rugged design, but does not feature a
raised rear seat for the instructor as normally found
on this type of aircraft. The basic layout did however

lend itself easily to successful redesign for single-seat
ground attack/COIN models.

VARIANTS

The single-seat **MB.326K** simply had the second crew
station removed and faired over, and like the **MB.326B**
and **'E** has internal lower fuselage guns fitted (in this
case two 30mm DEFA 553 cannons), with provision for
up to 1,814kg (4,000lb) of external stores including
two Matra R550 Magic air-to-air missiles. Power is
provided by a 17.79kN (4,000lb st) Viper Mk632-43
turbojet. Brazilian-built **EMB.326 Xavantes** carry
mainly Brazilian-produced or designed weapons and
avionics.

SEE ALSO: ATLAS/DENEL IMPALA

Aermacchi MB.326KD
United Emirates Air Force

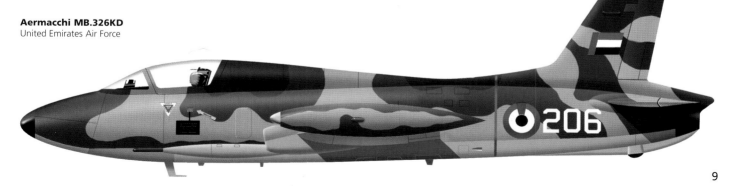

Aermacchi MB.339

SINGLE TURBOJET TWO-SEAT ADVANCED LEAD-IN FIGHTER/LIGHT ATTACK AIRCRAFT

Aermacchi MB.339CB Royal New Zealand Air Force

TECHNICAL DATA

Aermacchi MB.339CD

Powerplant: One Rolls-Royce Viper Mk 632-43 turbojet

Developing: 17.79kN (4,000lb st)

Span: 11.22m (36ft 9.75in)

Length: 11.24m (36ft 10.5in)

Height: 3.99m (13ft 1in)

All-up weight: 6,350kg (14,000lb)

Maximum speed: 926km/h (575mph)

Cruise speed: 815km/h (508mph)

Operational Ceiling: 46,000ft

Maximum range: 2,037km (1,266 miles)

Mission range: 944km (587 miles)

Endurance: up to 3 hours 50 minutes

Accommodation: Instructor and trainee pilot (instructor in rear seat)

Warload: up to 1,814kg (4,000lb) of external stores on six underwing pylons/attachments for various gun, cannon and light bombs, unguided rocket pods, cannon and gun pods including AN/SUU-11A/A Minigun 7.62mm machine-gun packs, two Matra R550 Magic or AIM-9 Sidewinder air-to-air missiles, two AGM-65 Maverick guided missiles, reconnaissance pods, or external fuel tanks.

First flown: 12 August 1976 (prototype MB.339X); 24 April 1996 (MB.339CD)

Entered service: 8 August 1979 (MB.339A); 18 December 1996 (MB.339CD)

DEVELOPMENT

A logical successor to the successful MB.326, the higher performance and redesigned MB.339 first flew in prototype form during August 1976. Initial production deliveries to the Italian Air Force were made in August 1979, this service eventually ordering just over 100 MB.339As (including several MB.339RM calibration examples, and MB.339PANs for the Italian Air Force's aerobatic team the *Frecce Tricolori*). The MB.339A gained several export successes, including the Argentine Navy (from 1980; several were lost during the Falkland Islands conflict), Ghana, Malaysia, Nigeria, Peru and Dubai. Similar to the MB.326, the MB.339 was developed into a single-seat light attack model, the MB.339K Veltro 2, but this version did not achieve any orders; neither did the T-Bird II derivative, which Aermacchi and Lockheed entered unsuccessfully in the US JPATS trainer competition. The uprated and better equipped MB.339C lead-in advanced trainer and ground-attack derivative first flew in December 1985; this model was ordered in 1990 by the Royal New Zealand Air Force (18 MB.339CBs), and later 15 for the Italian Air Force (MB.339CDs, delivered from December 1996). Six MB.339CEs (MB.339FDs) were ordered by Eritrea in November 1995, with deliveries starting in 1997; one was lost in combat during 1998. By early 2000, 208 production MB.339s had been built, plus five prototype/development aircraft.

CURRENT SERVICE

Italian Air Force MB.339As operate principally within the 61° Stormo at Lecce on basic training duties, with others assigned to various units for continuation training and related tasks. The Italian MB.339CDs also serve mainly in the 61° Stormo on more advanced pilot training/weapons training. Italian MB.339s have a secondary close support and anti-helicopter role, including the Rivolto-based MB.339PANs of the *Frecce Tricolori*. RNZAF MB.339CBs serve with No 14 Squadron at Ohakea for advanced training/light attack duties. MB.339s also continue to serve in Dubai, Eritrea, Ghana, Malaysia, Nigeria, and Peru. The Italian Air Force is expected to acquire further MB.339CDs.

SPECIAL FEATURES

The all-metal airframe of the MB.339 is similar to the MB.326 but with revised vertical tail, and a re-designed fuselage forward of the wing with a stepped-up rear cockpit, improved avionics and other changes. Italian licence-built Viper engines are used, as pioneered in the MB.326.

VARIANTS

MB.339As are powered by the Viper Mk632-43 turbojet, while the **MB.339C** has the more powerful Viper Mk.680-43 (19.57kN (4,400lb st)), although Italian **MB.339CDs** have the Mk 632-43. The *Frecce*

Tricolori **MB.339PANs** carry smoke-generating pods for air display performances, and omit the MB.339's usual wingtip fuel tanks. The **MB.339C** series features improved avionics including a digital nav/attack system, head-up displays (HUD), and HOTAS controls, and many other refinements (including optional provision for an in-flight refuelling probe), plus a lengthened nose. The **MB.339AM** is an anti-ship model of the MB.339C armed with OTO Melara Marte Mk 2A anti-ship missiles. The **MB.339FD** is an export version of the MB.339CD with the Viper Mk.680-43 engine.

Aermacchi MB.339A
Italian Air Force

SINGLE ENGINE LIGHTWEIGHT MULTI-ROLE FIGHTER   **TAIWAN**

A-1 Ching-Kuo Republic of China Air Force

TECHNICAL DATA

AIDC/IDF A-1 Ching-Kuo

Powerplants: Two ITEC (AlliedSignal/AIDC)
TFE 1042-70 (F-25) afterburning turbofans
Developing: 26.8kN (6,025lb st) dry;
41.8kN (9,400lb st) with afterburning
Span: 8.53m (28ft 0in)
Length: 14.21m (46ft 7in) – including nose probe
Height: 4.65m (15ft 3in)
All-up weight: 12,245kg (27,000lb)
Maximum speed: 1,295km/h (804mph)
Operational ceiling: 54,000ft
Accommodation: Pilot only
(two in tandem in trainer)
Warload: One 20mm M61A1 cannon. Six underwing
hardpoints. Can operate with a variety of missiles,
bombs, guided bombs and cluster munitions –
including the GBU-12, CBU-87 Rockeye, AGM-65B
TV Maverick ASM, AIM-9P Sidewinder, together
with indigenous Sky Sword I and Sky Sword II
radar-guided AAMs. For the anti-shipping role it
may be equipped with indigenous Hsiung Feng II
sea-skimming anti-ship missiles.
First flown: 28 May 1989 (single seat);
10 July 1990 (two-seat)
Entered service: 10 February 1993

DEVELOPMENT

In 1982, Taiwan launched an ambitious programme
to develop an advanced fighter to replace its fleet of
F-5s and F-104s after the US placed an embargo on the
sale of the F-16 and F-20, or other comparable fighters.
However, the same restrictions were not placed on
technical assistance, allowing US aerospace companies
to collaborate closely with AIDC in the development
of an indigenous fighter and weapons system. The
initial plans to deliver 256 Ching-Kuos – also known
as the Indigenous Defence Fighter (IDF) – was halved
in the mid-1990s when the arms embargo was lifted,
which enabled Taiwan to purchase F-16s and Mirage
2000-5s. The aircraft is named after a former President
of Taiwan, Chiang Ching-Kuo.

CURRENT SERVICE

Deliveries of the IDF were completed in January 2000,
and AIDC is now seeking permission to export the
aircraft as an advanced trainer. The majority of the
130 aircraft bought by the Taiwanese Air Force are
single-seaters – only 28 are two-seaters. The type
equips the 1st Tactical Fighter Wing (443rd TFW) –
1st Tactical Fighter Squadron, 3rd TFS and 9th TFS at
Tainan and the 3rd TFW (427th TFW) – 7th TFS, 8th
TFS and 28th TFS at Chin Chuang Kang.

SPECIAL FEATURES

The IDF bears a resemblance to the F-16, but has twin
F/A-18 Hornet-style intakes. Like the Fighting Falcon
it has a cockpit sidestick rather than the conventional
controls. General Dynamics (now Lockheed Martin)
was involved in the airframe design and Honeywell
was a partner in the ITEC joint venture with AIDC to
supply the engine. The GD-53 multi-mode radar is a
variant of Lockheed Martin's APG-67. Leading edge
root extensions give the aircraft the appearance of a
scaled down F/A-18.

VARIANTS

The **A-1** is the basic version of the Ching-Kuo and the
proposed development version, fitted with improved
performance engines, was cancelled. The '**Derivative
IDF**' advanced trainer is now being developed. This
design removes the cannon to make room for 700kg
extra fuel and modifies the belly missile recess to
allow use of an external, centreline fuel tank. The
avionics will be simplified, but the wingtip missile
rails and four underwing hardpoints
will be retained. A prototype is
expected to fly in 2002.

A-1 Ching-Kuo
Republic of China Air Force

Aero Industry Development Corporation (AIDC) AT-3 Tsu-Chiang

AT-3B Tsu-Chiang Republic of China Air Force

DEVELOPMENT

The AT-3 was the first military jet development in Taiwan to achieve series production. Developing its own advanced trainer represented a considerable achievement for the Taiwanese aerospace industry, and the aircraft was AIDC's second indigenous design to enter Taiwanese military service. Known in service with the Republic of China Air Force as the Tsu-Chiang, the AT-3 basic trainer provides the initial 120-hour jet course at the Service's academy at Kang Shau, Taiwan. Contracts were placed on behalf of the air force for 60 production aircraft, the last of which was delivered by early 1990. In the late 1980s, Smiths Industries was appointed prime contractor for a programme to convert 20 AT-3s for the close-air support role. The AT-3 replaced the piston-powered T-CH-1 Chung Tsing.

CURRENT SERVICE

The AT-3 is in service only in Taiwan. In addition to the service's academy, the AT-3B equips one RoCAF unit – No 71 Squadron of the 443rd TFW at Tainan. The type also equips the air force's display team.

SPECIAL FEATURES

The AT-3B has a sophisticated weapons system for light strike duties and has Westinghouse AN/APG-66 radar. Provision is also made for an aerial target system to be carried on the fuselage centre-line and on outboard wing pylons.

VARIANTS

The basic training version of the Tsu-Chiang was retrospectively designated **AT-3A** and the converted close-air support variant became the **AT-3B**. An attack version designated **A-3 Lui Ming** was developed in the late 1980s, and featured similar armament to the AT-3B, but with a single-seat cockpit. Two prototypes were built, but development was halted in favour of the AT-3B. AIDC is considering a developed AT-3 for export if it does not win the necessary approvals for the 'Derivative IDF'.

TECHNICAL DATA

AIDC AT-3 Tsu-Chiang

Powerplants: Two Garrett (AlliedSignal) TFE732-2-2C non-afterburning turbofans
Developing: 15.57kN (3,500lb st)
Span: 10.46m (34ft 3.75in)
Length: 12.90m (42ft 4in)
Height: 4.83m (15ft 10in)
All-up weight: 7,938kg (17,500lb)
Maximum speed: 904km/h (561mph)
Operational ceiling: 48,000ft
Maximum range: 2,280km (1,416 miles)
Endurance: 3hr 12min
Accommodation: Two in tandem; pilot only in AT-3A
Warload: AT-3A – internal weapons bay can be fitted with a gun pod. Centreline pylon and four underwing hardpoints and two wingtip launch rails. Maximum ordnance of 2,721kg (6,000lb) includes bombs, training bombs, rockets and wingtip-mounted AAMs.
First flown: 16 September 1980
Entered service: March 1984

AT-3A Tsu-Chiang Republic of China Air Force

Aero L-29 Delfin

SINGLE TURBOJET TWO-SEAT BASIC TRAINER/LIGHT ATTACK AIRCRAFT

L-29 Delfin Czech Air Force

TECHNICAL DATA

Aero L-29 Delfin
Powerplant: One Motorlet M 701-c500 turbojet
Developing: 890kg (1,960lb st)
Span: 10.29m (33ft 9in)
Length: 10.81m (35ft 5in)
Height: 3.13m (10ft 3in)
All-up weight: 3,540kg (7,804lb)
Maximum speed: 655km/h (407mph)
Cruise speed: 547km/h (340mph)
Operational ceiling: 36,090ft
Maximum range: 894km (555miles)
Mission range: 640km (397 miles)
Endurance: 2 hours 30 minutes
Accommodation: Instructor and trainee pilot
(instructor in rear seat)
Warload: Two main weapon attachments under
wings for up to eight light air-to-ground rockets,
two 7.62mm or similar machine-gun pods, two
bombs up to 100kg (220lb), or two fuel tanks.
No internal gun.
First flown: 5 April 1959
Entered service: 1963

DEVELOPMENT

The increasingly important concept of 'all-through' jet training gained favour in the West during the 1950s, and eventually in the Soviet Bloc as well. In 1961 a fly-off was held to determine a standard all-through jet trainer for the Soviet Union and its satellites in Europe, and the winner was adjudged to be Czechoslovakia's Aero L-29 Delfin (Dolphin). This type had first flown in April 1959 powered by a British Viper turbojet, but production aircraft were equipped with the Czech Motorlet M 701 powerplant. The first production machine was completed in the spring of 1963, and manufacture continued into the mid-1970s. By far the largest customer was the Soviet Union, which acquired over 2,000 examples, and the Delfin also served with all Soviet Bloc air forces – except Poland. Receiving the NATO code-name 'Maya', the L-29 was also exported to countries sympathetic to the Soviet Union. L-29s were airlifted by Aeroflot to Nigeria in 1967 for use in the conflict against Biafra. Approximately 3,600 Delfins of all types were built.

CURRENT SERVICE

The veteran L-29 remains in service in amazingly large (albeit now decreasing) numbers. In its country of origin, the Czech Republic's Air Force still uses the type in small numbers for continuation and refresher training, as unit 'hacks', and for limited test purposes. The Russian Federation continues to employ a number of the Delfins supplied to the former Soviet Union, using the type mainly for test purposes, as pilotless drones, and in the paramilitary aeroclub organisation ROSTO, for introductory and elementary training from airfields such as Vyaz'ma. Slovakia, Romania and Bulgaria also continue to use the L-29 in some numbers, as does Cuba, Syria, Egypt and Iraq. Mali (in the early 1980s) and Ghana (in 1989, from Nigerian stocks) are the most recent new users of Delfins, while Azerbaijan may have some ex-Soviet examples still serviceable.

SPECIAL FEATURES

Of simple all-metal construction and very easy to maintain, the Delfin has excellent flying qualities and can operate easily from grass strips and partly-prepared airfields. It has the classic 1950s/1960s jet trainer layout of tandem seating on early ejector seats and straight wing design. The L-29's docility and easy maintenance has led to large numbers persisting in service.

VARIANTS

Delfins were designed to carry various light weapons for introductory weapons training, but a dedicated reconnaissance version, the **L-29R**, was also built with wingtip fuel tanks, a reconnaissance fairing beneath the fuselage, as well as weapons carrying capability. A single-seat model, the **L-29A Akrobat** aerobatic aircraft, with the rear crew position removed and faired over, also existed during the later 1960s, but in very small numbers. Some contemporary Russian-operated Delfins have been converted into pilotless drones with radio command from ground and possibly airborne transmitters.

L-29 Delfin Slovak Air Force

Aero L-39/L-59 Albatros

SINGLE TURBOFAN SINGLE-SEAT CLOSE-SUPPORT/LIGHT ATTACK AIRCRAFT

L-39 Albatros Russian Air Force

TECHNICAL DATA

Aero L-39ZA Albatros

Powerplant: One Progress (Ivchenko) AI-25 TL turbofan
Developing: 16.87kN (3,792lb st)
Span: 9.46m (31ft 0.5in)
Length: 12.13m (39ft 9.5in)
Height: 4.77m (15ft 7.75in)
All-up weight: 5,670kg (12,500lb)
Maximum speed: 755km/h (469mph)
Cruise speed: 630km/h (391mph)
Operating Ceiling: 11,000m (36,090ft)
Maximum range: 1,800km (1,119 miles)
Mission range: 1,000km (621 miles)
Endurance: 4 hours
Accommodation: Instructor and trainee pilot (instructor in rear seat)
Warload: No internal gun. Detachable underfuselage centreline gun pod with twin-barrel 23mm GSh-23 gun. Four underwing weapons pylons (two per wing) for up to 1,000kg (2,205lb) of Western or Soviet-origin weapons, including bombs, rocket launchers (for CRV7, 2.75in FFAR rockets, or equivalent), fuel tanks (on inboard pylons only), or air-to-air missiles such as AIM-9 Sidewinder or Soviet equivalent.
First flown: 4 November 1968
Entered service: early 1974

DEVELOPMENT

One of the world's most successful and numerous jet trainer and light attack aircraft, the L-39 Albatros was developed as a logical successor to the L-29 Delfin, able to fulfil a wider range of training requirements and with a genuine light strike capability. The first L-39 flew in November 1968 and the initial production pilot training L-39C model entered service with the Czechoslovak Air Force in 1974 after some re-design of the original layout. The type duly went on to serve in large numbers with the Soviet Union's Air Force (2,080 examples) and various other Soviet-aligned countries. Continued development led to the L-39V target facilities aircraft, the L-39ZO armed trainer, and the L-39ZA ground attack and reconnaissance version in the mid-1970s. The Westernised L-139 (avionics and powerplant) has yet to find a customer. However, further refinement has led to the updated and more powerful L-39MS, and thence to the new-generation L-59. This model first flew in September 1986 and the first L-59 delivery was in January 1993 to Egypt. L-39 and L-59 production continues as required, the most recent order being in February 1999 for 12 L-39Cs from the Yemen. The single-seat L-159 (see separate entry) is a direct L-39/L-59 development. Aero states that a total of 2,854 L-39s has been built (excluding the Yemen order), plus five L-39MS models and 60 L-59s.

CURRENT SERVICE

The Czech Republic's now comparatively small force of L-39s (L-39C, L-39ZA and L-39MS versions), serve with several units for training purposes, including the 341st Training Squadron at Pardubice. By far the largest user is the Russian Federation which still employs the L-39 in substantial numbers (over 1,200 remain) as its main advanced/weapons trainer. In addition to these operators, the L-39 in various models continues to serve in the following countries: Afghanistan (with government and rebel forces), Algeria, Azerbaijan, Bangladesh, Bulgaria, Cambodia (ex-Czech, refurbished in Israel), Cuba, Egypt (ex-Libya), Ethiopia, Hungary (ex-East Germany/Germany), Iraq, North Korea, Kyrgyzstan, Libya, Lithuania, Nigeria, Romania, Slovakia, Syria, Thailand, Turkmenistan, Uganda (ex-Libya), Ukraine, Uzbekistan, and Vietnam. The Slovak and Russian Federation Air Forces' aerobatic teams each fly the L-39. Users of the L-59 are Tunisia (L-59T) and Egypt (L-59E).

SPECIAL FEATURES

Of mainly all-metal construction, the L-39 family feature simple modular construction, ease of maintenance and the ability to operate from austere landing strips. Newer models have considerably improved Western avionics.

VARIANTS

Many **L-39Cs** have a single weapons pylon beneath each wing. The **L-39ZO** introduced reinforced wings with four weapons stations for weapons training, while the **L-39ZA** introduced the under-fuselage gun pack. A more powerful Progress DV-2 turbofan of 21.58kN (4,850lb st) powers the L-59, which also has a very slightly larger dimensionally reinforced structure, and Western avionics to customer choice.

L-39ZA Albatros Czech Air Force

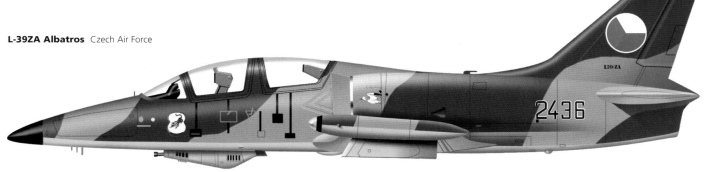

Aero L-159

Aero L-159

TECHNICAL DATA

Aero L-159
Powerplant: One AlliedSignal/ITEC F124-GA-100 turbofan
Thrust: 28.0kN (6,300lb st)
Span: 9.54m (31ft 3in) (including wingtip fuel tanks)
Length: 12.73m (41ft 9in)
Height: 4.77m (15ft 7in)
All-up weight: 8,000kg (17,637lb)
Maximum speed: 960km/h (596mph)
Operational ceiling: 43,300ft
Maximum range: 2,530km (1,572miles)
Mission range: 1,560km (969 miles)
Accommodation: Single pilot
Warload: No internal gun. Up to 2,340kg (5,159lb) of external stores on one centreline and six wing pylons, including laser-guided and free-fall 'iron' bombs; rocket, gun and reconnaissance pods; air-to-surface missiles such as AGM-65 Maverick, AIM-9L Sidewinder or similar air-to-air missiles. Also AMS Brimstone missile and BAE Systems TIALD pod.
First flown: 2 August 1997:
13 August 1998 (single-seat)
Entered service: late 2000

DEVELOPMENT

The outstanding success of the L-39 Albatros family prompted Aero Vodochody to examine, during the early 1990s, the growth potential of the basic L-39/ L-59 layout. At the same time the new Czech Republic (created on 1 January 1993) was studying a complete military re-equipment programme to replace many Soviet-imposed types then in service and to bring the country's air force in line with NATO standards and inter-operability. This created the requirement for a light and affordable multi-role combat aircraft, and in July 1997 a contract was formally signed for 72 L-159 ALCA (Advanced Light Combat Aircraft) for the Czech Air Force. The first prototype flew in August 1997, followed more importantly during August 1998 by the first L-159 in full single-seat configuration approximating to production standard. From the outset the L-159 programme has included considerable Western input, which has been an important desire for the Czechs. A Boeing-led consortium has recently been accepted by the Czech government to take a roughly one-third stake in Aero Vodochody itself, making the L-159 not only the first new production

combat aircraft to come from the former 'Eastern Bloc' since the fall of communism, but also currently the most important East-West collaborative military aviation programme.

CURRENT SERVICE

The Czech Republic's requirement for 72 L-159s is being constructed in several specific batches. The slightly delayed first batch of five was scheduled for delivery during 2000, followed by 16 intended for delivery in 2000, 26 in 2001, and the final 25 in 2002. Initial deliveries are to the LZO test establishment for service evaluation and clearance. The L-159 will form the backbone of the Czech Republic's future combat aircraft strength – in the close support, air defence, tactical reconnaissance, border patrol, and lead-in fighter and weapons training roles – together with a yet to be procured pure fighter type of Western origin.

SPECIAL FEATURES

The Aero L-159 is a major collaborative programme with several Western companies. In addition to the AlliedSignal powerplant, the L-159's radar is an Italian

FIAR Grifo-L multi-mode pulse doppler unit, and its avionics are provided by Bendix/King and Honeywell in a package integrated by Boeing. Significantly for the Czechs, who joined NATO in 1999, the new aircraft is also fully compatible with Western weapons systems.

VARIANTS

The majority of the Czech L-159s will be single-seat aircraft, with several **L-159B** two-seat trainers also possibly included. Aero also needs export orders and a potential customer is Poland, which may require around 40 lead-in trainers due to continuing problems with its indigenous PZL I-22 Iryda jet trainer. A Polish procurement deal could see the transfer of part of the L-159's production to Poland if this deal takes place, with detail changes to suit Polish requirements.

Aero L-159 Czech Air Force

Aérospatiale (Sud) SA 313/318 Alouette II

SINGLE TURBOSHAFT MULTI-ROLE HELICOPTER

Alouette II German Army

TECHNICAL DATA

Aérospatiale SA 318C Alouette II

Powerplant: One Turboméca Astazou IIA turboshaft
Developing: 395kW (530eshp) downrated to 268kW (360eshp)
Driving: three-blade main and two-blade tail rotors
Main rotor diameter: 10.20m (33ft 5.6 in)
Fuselage length: 9.75m (31ft 11.75in)
Height: 2.75m (9ft 0in)
Maximum take-off weight: 1,650kg (3,638lb)
Maximum speed: 205km/h (127mph)
Maximum cruise speed: 180km/h (112mph)
Operational ceiling: 17,715ft
Range: 720km (447 miles)
Endurance: 5hr 18min
Accommodation: Two crew and three passengers or one pilot and four passengers. Can carry two stretchers in the medevac role.
Warload: A wide variety of rockets, guns or air-to-surface missiles including the AS-11 anti-armour missile
First flown: 12 March 1955 (SE 3120); 31 January 1961 (SA 318C Alouette)
Entered service: 1957

DEVELOPMENT

The SA 313B Alouette II originated from the piston-engined SE 3120 light general-purpose helicopter of 1952 designed and built by the Société Nationale de Constructions Aéronautique du Sud-Est (SNCASE). Aimed chiefly at the civilian agricultural market, the aircraft was quickly identified as being suitable for development to incorporate one of the new turbine engines which were becoming available for rotary-wing designs. Fitted with a Turboméca Artouste turboshaft, the resultant SE 313B Alouette II was delivered in significant numbers to both military and civil operators. Further evolution of the design resulted in the Alouette II Astazou which was delivered as the SA 318C from 1965. By 1970 the company had become part of Aérospatiale and production continued until 1975, by which time a total of 1,305 Alouette IIs had been built. The aircraft achieved such sales thanks to

its tremendous versatility. The 'bug-eye' glazed cabin offered unprecedented visibility and its lightweight structure offered class-winning performance. Military Alouette IIs have been used in the liaison, observation, training, air ambulance and attack roles.

CURRENT SERVICE

Alouette IIs remain in military service with air arms of the following countries: Belgium, Cameroon, Congo, Djibouti, Dominican Republic, France, Germany, Guinea-Bissau, Indonesia, Lebanon, Senegal, Tunisia and Turkey.

SPECIAL FEATURES

The Alouette II's bug-eye cabin gives excellent all-round vision for the pilot and/or observers. It has an open fuselage structure with a fuel tank behind the cabin, and a skid-type landing gear with retractable

wheels or pneumatic floats as an option. A rescue hoist can be fitted.

VARIANTS

The **SE 3130** was the first production model (designation later changed to **SA 313B**). The **SE 3140** version had a Turboméca Turmo II engine, although no production examples were built. The definitive **SA 318C** variant was powered by the Turboméca Astazou IIA. See separate entry for **SA 315 (Lama)**, developed for the Indian Army.

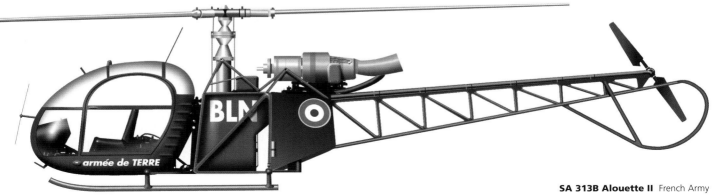

SA 313B Alouette II French Army

Aérospatiale (Sud) SA 316/319 Alouette III

SINGLE TURBOSHAFT UTILITY TRANSPORT AND MULTI-ROLE HELICOPTER

FRANCE

Alouette III *French Gendarmerie*

TECHNICAL DATA

Aérospatiale SA 319B Alouette III
Powerplant: One Turboméca Astazou XIV turboshaft
Developing: 649kW (870eshp) derated to 447kW (600eshp)
Driving: Three-blade main and tail rotors
Main rotor diameter: 11.02m (36ft 1.75 in)
Fuselage length: 10.03m (32ft 10.75in)
Height: 3.00m (9ft 10in)
Maximum take-off weight: 2250kg (4,960lb)
Maximum speed: 220km/h (136mph)
Maximum cruise speed: 197km/h (122mph)
Hover ceiling (IGE): 10,170ft
Range: 605km (375 miles) with normal passenger load
Accommodation: One pilot, six equipped troops or two stretchers and two attendants or up to 750 kg (1,653 lb) of cargo
Warload: A wide range of armament which can include a 7.62-mm (0.3-in) machine-gun or 20-mm cannon firing through the port side cabin door, one or two MATRA 155H rocket pods, Euromissile HOT or AS11 anti-armour missiles or two Mk 44 torpedoes
First flown: 31 July 1951 (piston-powered prototype); 28 February 1959 (Alouette III)
Entered service: 1961

DEVELOPMENT

A natural development of the Alouette II, the Alouette III was initially designated SE 3160 and differed from its predecessor in featuring a widened and extensively-glazed cabin which could accommodate up to seven, a tricycle-type undercarriage and a covered tail boom with a three-bladed tail rotor. The chosen powerplant for the new aircraft was the more powerful Artouste III turboshaft and the aircraft entered production as the SA 316A in 1961. The early promise of the design prompted Hindustan Aeronautics Ltd (HAL) of India to acquire a licence for production for the Indian armed forces and given the local name Chetak. The main production version, the SA 316B, was introduced into service in 1970 fitted with the more powerful Artouste IIIB turboshaft giving greater load-carrying capability and performance. Licence-production of the SA 316B was carried out in Switzerland and, more significantly in Romania where 230 examples of the locally-designated IAR 316B were produced. The final production version built by Aérospatiale, the SA 319B, was powered by an Astazou XIV turboshaft and again

offered increased performance combined with a 25 per cent reduction in fuel consumption. Production of the Alouette III ended in 1983 after a production run of 1,455 units, by which time the aircraft had entered service with air arms in over 60 countries.

CURRENT SERVICE

Albania, Angola, Argentina, Austria, Belgium, Bolivia, Burkina Faso, Burundi, Cameroon, Chad, Congo, Congo (Zaïre), Ecuador, France, Gabon, Ghana, Greece, Guinea-Bissau, Indonesia, Iraq, Ireland, South Korea, Lebanon, Libya, Malaysia, Malta, Mexico, Myanmar, Pakistan, Portugal, Senegal, South Africa, Surinam, Switzerland, Tunisia, Venezuela, Zimbabwe. The HAL licence-produced Chetak is in service in India, Namibia, Nepal and Seychelles.

SPECIAL FEATURES

The powerful engine gives excellent hot-and-high performance. Large side doors allow qick and easy ingress and egress of troops. A hoist may be mounted on the port side for air-sea rescue

operations. Able to be converted for a wide-range of roles including air ambulance and gunship.

VARIANTS

SA 316A: first production model with Artouste III turboshaft; **SA 316B:** main production version with Artouste IIIB turboshaft and improved main and tail rotor transmission: **SA 316C:** built in small numbers with more powerful Artouste IIID; **SA 319B:** Astazou XIV powerplant and a wide range of weapons options; **HAL Chetak:** licence-built version tailored to needs of the Indian armed forces.

SA 316B Alouette III *Portuguese Air Force*

Aérospatiale (Sud) SA 315 Lama

SINGLE TURBOSHAFT HIGH-PERFORMANCE MULTI-ROLE HELICOPTER

HAL Cheetah Indian Army

DEVELOPMENT

Designed initially to meet an Indian armed forces requirement for a high-performance multi-role helicopter, the Lama is basically a hot-and-high variant of the SA 313B Alouette II. Reinforcing the Alouette II's airframe allowed its rotor system (including the transmission) and the Artouste IIIB powerplant to be incorporated into the new design. Production was initiated simultaneously in both France and India (where the aircraft was built under licence as the HAL Cheetah) and over 650 examples have subsequently been produced. The aircraft's excellent power-to-weight ratio helped it to establish a number of world records in the 1970s, including the helicopter absolute height record of 40,820ft. In military service, the Lama is used in a variety of roles that include liaison, obervation, training, photographic, transport, rescue and air ambulance.

CURRENT SERVICE

Argentina, Chile, Ecuador, Morocco, Pakistan, Peru, and Togo all currently operate Lamas. HAL Cheetahs are in Indian service with the Air Force Academy at Hakimpet and 114HU at Siachen Glacier. The type is also operated by the Indian Army with Nos 3, 6, 18, 22, 23 and 31 Reconnaissance and Observation Flights and No 655 Squadron at Nasik. Four Lamas serve as utility helicopters with the Namibia Defence Force, following independence from South Africa in 1991. The HB 315B Gavião is in Bolivian service with Grupo Aéreo Mixto at Cochabamba and Grupo Aéreo 51 at Santa Cruz de la Sierra.

SPECIAL FEATURES

Its high-performance powerplant makes the Lama ideal for hot-and-high operations. It has provision for underslung loads of up to 1135 kg (2,500 lb). A glazed cabin gives excellent visibility, and pneumatic floats are available for water operations.

VARIANTS

The Aérospatiale production version was the **SA 315B**. The type was also built under licence in India as the **HAL Cheetah**. In Brazil, Helibras-assembled versions were designated **HB 315 Gavião**.

SEE ALSO: AEROSPATIALE (SUD) SA 313/318 ALOUETTE II

TECHNICAL DATA

Aérospatiale SA 315B Lama
Powerplant: One Turboméca Artouste IIIB turboshaft
Developing: 650kW (870eshp) derated to 410kW (550eshp)
Driving: three-blade main and tail rotors
Main rotor diameter: 11.02m (36ft 1.75in)
Fuselage length: 10.23m (33ft 6.25in)
Height: 3.09m (10ft 1.75in)
Maximum take-off weight: 2300kg (5,071lb)
Maximum speed: 210km/h (130mph)
Maximum cruise speed: 192km/h (119mph)
Operational ceiling: 17,715ft
Range: 515km (320 miles)
Accommodation: One pilot and up to four passengers or two stretchers with one attendant
Warload: Normally none
First flown: 12 March 1955 (SE 3120); 17 March 1969 (SA 315B)
Entered service: 1970

HAL Cheetah Indian Army

Aérospatiale SA 321 Super Frelon

THREE TURBOSHAFT MULTI-ROLE HELICOPTER

SA 321G Super Frelon *French Navy*

TECHNICAL DATA

Aérospatiale SA 321G Super Frelon
Powerplants: Three Turboméca Turmo IIIC7 turboshafts
Developing: 1,201kW (1,610shp)
Driving: Six-blade main rotor, five-blade tail rotor
Main rotor diameter: 18.90m (62ft 0in)
Fuselage length: 19.40m (63ft 7.5in)
Height: 6.76m (22ft 2.5in)
All-up weight: 13,000kg (28,660lb)
Maximum speed: 275km/h (171mph)
Cruise speed: 248km/h (154mph)
Operational ceiling: 10,170ft
Maximum ferry range: 1,020km (633 miles)
Mission range: 815km (506 miles)
Endurance: 4hr
Accommodation: Two crew on flight deck, three other crew as required; provision for up to 27/30 troops, or some 5,000kg (11,023lb) of internal or external cargo
Warload: when fitted, up to four Mk 46 anti-submarine homing torpedoes, or two AM39 Exocet anti-shipping missiles.
First flown: 7 December 1962
Entered service: 1966 (France); 1967 (Israel)

DEVELOPMENT

Arising from the smaller SE 3200 Frelon medium transport helicopter that first flew in 1959, the SA 321 was developed in conjunction with Sikorsky and Fiat and fulfilled a French Navy requirement for an anti-submarine/anti-ship platform. The first of six prototype/pre-production Super Frelons flew in December 1962; 24 SA 321Gs were ordered for the French Navy (five Ga transport, 17 Gb maritime models), and entered service with Escadrille 27S in 1966 in the Pacific, for transport duties at French nuclear test sites. Full French service entry was in 1970 with Flottille 32F, providing anti-submarine cover for French nuclear submarines entering and leaving port, plus deployments on French aircraft/helicopter-carriers. An early export customer was Israel (12 SA 321Ks in two specific versions); some served in the 1967 'Six Day War'. Israeli machines were later re-engined with three 1,413kW (1,895shp) General Electric T58-16 turboshafts. Other export customers included South Africa (16 SA 321Ls, which were not amphibious, lacking the outrigger sponsons); Iraq (16 SA 321GVs, Exocet-equipped, which served with distinction in the 1980s Iran-Iraq War); Libya (eight SA 321Ms transport, six navalised SA 321GMs); 16 SA 321Ja for the Communist Chinese Navy; and a single SA 321Ja for VIP use by President Mobutu of Zaïre. Production ended in 1983, when 99 military Super Frelons had been built. Manufacture continues in China, where Changhe Aircraft Industries Corporation is building the Z-8 copy. French Navy machines lost their anti-submarine and anti-ship roles in the early 1980s, and now generally operate unarmed.

CURRENT SERVICE

The French Navy's Flottilles 32F at Lanvéoc-Poulmic and 33F at Saint-Mandrier (Toulon) currently fly the SA 321G on search and rescue, commando assault, vertical replenishment of ships, and 'service public' (pollution control, disaster relief) missions. Several were deployed aboard the French aircraft-carrier *Foch* during NATO *Allied Force* operations over Kosovo and Serbia in 1999. They will be replaced in 2005 by the new NH 90 helicopter. The South African and Israeli Super Frelons have been withdrawn. The type remains in service in Iraq and Libya, and is current with the Communist Chinese Navy which additionally continues to receive the indigenous Changhe Z-8. Former President Mobutu's VIP Super Frelon is believed to still exist, as a part of the Democratic Republic of Congo's fledgling air arm.

SPECIAL FEATURES

Possessing a considerable internal volume and external load-carrying capability, the Super Frelon has a rear loading door/ramp similar to that of military transport aircraft. The basically all-metal helicopter has a boat hull-type fuselage, and is fully amphibious when fitted with the outrigger sponsons common to most versions. The main rotors fold and the tailplane hinges to allow stowage aboard ship.

VARIANTS

The prototype **Changhe Z-8** first flew on 11 December 1985, and is almost identical to the amphibious Super Frelon. It is powered by three 1,156kW (1,550shp) Changzhou WZ6 turboshafts, and can carry torpedoes, anti-ship missiles or mines.

SA 321G Super Frelon *French Navy*

Aérospatiale (SOCATA) TB30B Epsilon

SINGLE PISTON-ENGINED BASIC TRAINER

DEVELOPMENT

The success of SOCATA's TB10 Tobago series of light touring aircraft prompted design work to begin in 1977 on a two-seat basic trainer based on the same airframe. At this time, the Armée de l'Air was drawing up its own specification for a new basic training aircraft and, when this was officially announced, Aérospatiale modified its designs into two proposals – the TB30A and TB30B, with 194kW (260hp) and 224kW (300hp) engines respectively. A development contract was issued in 1979, and two prototypes conducted flight trials before the first two production contracts were awarded in 1982. With retractable tricycle undercarriage, a large backward-sliding canopy and cockpit ergonomics designed to prepare the student for the Dassault Alpha Jet, the production TB30B differed from the first prototype in having rounded wings, increased span and a redesigned

TB30B Epsilon French Air Force

TECHNICAL DATA

Aérospatiale TB30B Epsilon

Powerplant: One Textron Lycoming AEIO-540-L1B5D piston engine
Developing: 224kW (300hp)
Driving: Two-blade propeller
Span: 7.92m (25ft 11.75in)
Length: 7.59m (24ft 10.75in)
Height: 2.66m (8ft 8.75in)
Maximum weight: 1,250kg (2,755lb)
Maximum speed: 378km/h (236mph)
Cruising speed: 358km/h (222mph)
Operational ceiling: 23,000ft
Range: 1,250km (777 miles)
Accommodation: Instructor and student in tandem
Warload: Togolese aircraft only – up to 300kg (660lb) of ordnance
First flown: 22 December 1979 (TB30A); October 1980 (TB30B)
Entered service: July 1983

fuselage, upswept winglets and new tail unit. The fuel injection system allows for up to two minutes of continuous inverted flight and the airframe is fully stressed for aerobatics. The Armée de l'Air ordered a total of 150 examples, all of which had been delivered by 1989, and are now France's standard basic trainer. The only export customers have been the Portuguese Air Force which received 18 examples, assembled locally by OGMA, and the Togolese Air Force, which ordered an armed version, that can either be flown by a single pilot in this role or by a pilot and student in the training role.

CURRENT SERVICE

The major Epsilon operator is France which has over 140 examples in current service with Air Force Education and Training Command (CEAA). Portugal operates 16 of 18 OGMA-assembled TB30Bs with 101

Squadron at BA11 Beja, and Togo operates three of four delivered in 1986/87 as armed basic trainers.

SPECIAL FEATURES

The Epsilon has excellent visibility from the cockpit thanks to the large 'wrap around' canopy. The airframe is stressed to +6.7 and -3.35 g, thus allowing both negative and positive aerobatic manoeuvres. The armed variant for the Togolese Air Force is equipped with four underwing hardpoints which can carry air-to-surface rockets and machine-guns.

VARIANTS

The **TB30B** is the standard production trainer; the **TB30B (Togo)** an armed basic trainer with underwing hardpoints. The TB30 formed the basis of the **TB31 Omega** with a Turboméca Arries turboprop. This flew in 1985 but lack of orders prevented production.

TB30B Epsilon French Air Force

Aérospatiale/Westland SA330 Puma

TWIN TURBOSHAFT MEDIUM TRANSPORT AND UTILITY HELICOPTER

FRANCE/UK

Puma HC1 Royal Air Force

TECHNICAL DATA

Aérospatiale SA330B Puma

Powerplants: Two Turboméca Turmo IIIC turboshafts
Developing: 984kW (1,320shp)
Driving: Four-blade main and five-blade tail rotors
Main rotor diameter: 15.0m (49ft 2.5in)
Fuselage length: 14.06m (46ft 1.5in)
Height: 5.14m (16ft 10.5in)
All-up weight: 6,400kg (14,109lb)
Maximum speed: 280km/h (174mph)
Cruise speed: 271km/h (168mph)
Operational ceiling: 19,685ft
Maximum ferry range: 572km (354 miles)
Accommodation: Two crew and up to 15-20 fully-equipped troops; maximum payload 3,200kg (7,055lb)
First flown: 15 April 1965 (SA330 prototype); 25 November 1970 (RAF Puma HC1)
Entered service: March 1969 (French Army SA330B); June 1971 (RAF)

DEVELOPMENT

The SA330 Puma was originally designed to meet a French Army requirement for an all-weather utility helicopter, though the Royal Air Force's need for a replacement for the Whirlwind and Belvedere saw the type being included in the terms of the 1967 Anglo-French helicopter agreement which also took in the Gazelle and Lynx. Initial development was undertaken by Sud Aviation, before responsibility passed to the newly-formed Aérospatiale. In fact, the desired all-weather capability was not achieved until later in the type's production life, while 'hot and high' modifications would also follow. The Puma was to be developed through several versions before major modifications produced the AS332 Super Puma (later AS532 Cougar, described under Eurocopter).

CURRENT SERVICE

The French Air Force and French Army Light Aviation are the major users of the basic Puma, in its SA330B guise (this designation also covering more powerful versions, otherwise designated SA330H – see below), while the Westland-built Puma HC1 remains in RAF service with three squadrons. Other SA330 operators are the air forces of Cameroon, Ethiopia, Gabon, Indonesia, Iraq (current status unknown), Ivory Coast, Kuwait, Lebanon, Malawi, Morocco, Nepal, Nigeria, Portugal, Senegambia, South Africa, Spain, Togo, the United Arab Emirates and Zaire, as well as the Army aviation arms of Chile, Ecuador, Pakistan and Spain. In addition, numerous quasi-military agencies and organisations fly Pumas, among them the Argentine Coast Guard and German Federal Border Guards.

SPECIAL FEATURES

A number of French Army SA330B Pumas are fitted with OMERA ORB-37 radar, mounted in the nose and distinguishable by the fitment's bulging radome. In addition, all French Army and RAF Pumas are capable of carrying a pintle-mounted machine gun in the cabin door. Portuguese Air Force examples used for search and rescue duties are distinctive, with the radome for their ORB-31 radar on the nose, and the flotation gear fitted to their wheel fairings and nose. It was also significant that the Puma, from its SA330L version onwards, was the first Western helicopter to be certified for all-weather operations.

VARIANTS

The initial three military production Puma variants offered were the French military **SA330B**, export **SA330C** and the **SA330E** which was the designation given to the RAF **Puma HC1**. When the more powerful Turmo IVC engines came on stream in 1974, delivering 1,174kW (1,575shp) each, the **SA330H** was produced – confusingly, those purchased by the French services were designated **SA330Ba**. From 1977 onwards, glass-fibre rotors were added, producing the **SA330L** for new production although these items were retrofitted to older Pumas. Foreign licence-built examples and upgrades produced by Romania's IAR and South Africa's Atlas (the latter including the improved **Oryx** variant) are described separately. Five Portuguese Air Force Pumas were converted locally to **SA330S** standard by OGMA in the late 1980s, entailing the fitment of glass-fibre rotors, new avionics and the Super Puma's Makila engines. IPTN produced 11 **SA330Js** (locally designated NSA-330) from Aérospatiale kits during the early 1980s, these going to the Indonesian Air Force.

SEE ALSO: IAR-330 PUMA AND ATLAS/DENEL ORYX

Puma HC1 Royal Air Force

Aérospatiale/Westland SA341/342 Gazelle

SINGLE TURBOSHAFT ANTI-TANK, SCOUT AND TRAINING HELICOPTER

FRANCE

SA341F/M Gazelle French Army Light Aviation

TECHNICAL DATA

Aérospatiale SA341F Gazelle

Powerplant: One Turboméca Astazou IIIA turboshaft
Developing: 440kW (590eshp)
Driving: Three-blade main and fenestron tail rotors
Main rotor diameter: 10.5m (34ft 5.5in)
Fuselage length: 9.53m (31ft 3.2in)
Height: 3.18m (10ft 5.3in)
All-up weight: 1,800kg (3,968lb)
Maximum speed: 264km/h (164mph)
Cruise speed: 233km/h (144mph)
Operational ceiling: 16,405ft
Maximum range: 710km/h (441 miles)
Mission range: 670km (415miles)
Accommodation: Pilot and up to four passengers
First flown: 12 April 1968 (SA340 prototype);
2 August 1968 (pre-production SA341);
11 May 1973 (SA342)
Entered service: 1969 (France); 1973 (UK)

DEVELOPMENT

A French Army requirement for a new light observation helicopter led to Aérospatiale producing its SA340 prototype, originally proposed to use Turboméca's Oredon turboshaft engine then under development. In the event, this unit was abandoned and the existing Astazou II adopted. The new machine was to have a fully-enclosed fuselage, rigid main rotor and the then-new fenestron tail rotor unit. British involvement alongside Aérospatiale was finalised in 1967, and two SA340 prototypes were flown, before the helicopter was revised as the SA341 and officially named Gazelle in July 1969. Further refinements, including provision of a longer cabin, large access doors, bigger tail surfaces and the use of the Astazou IIIA engine, occurred before the first full production-standard SA341 was flown by Aérospatiale on 6 August 1971. The first Westland-built example flew on 31 January 1972, entering service the following year. Also in 1973, the more powerful SA342 made its maiden flight; it would subsequently be produced in three military variants.

CURRENT SERVICE

French Army Light Aviation remains the biggest user of the basic Gazelle, with SA341F/Ms and SA342L/Ms equipping elements of all five helicopter regiments as well as training/liaison squadrons and other smaller units. The Army Air Corps retains Gazelle AH1s for training and scout purposes; the RAF still has one HT3 on strength and the Royal Marines also use AH1s. Other Gazelle operators are the air forces of Angola, Cameroon, Gabon, Guinea Republic, Iraq (status unknown), Jordan, Kenya, Kuwait, Lebanon, Libya, Morocco, Rwanda, Senegambia, Serbia, Syria, Trinidad & Tobago, Tunisia and the UAE, as well as the Irish Air Corps, the armies of Ecuador and Egypt, and the Cyprus National Guard.

SPECIAL FEATURES

The fenestron tail unit is the most distinctive feature of the Gazelle's design, this having been the first production helicopter to adopt such an arrangement. In-service examples have been equipped with various different target-locating sights, notably those of the French ALAT, which can utilise the Athos scouting sight also used on the Cougar. Anti-tank Gazelles carry their weapon loads on short stub pylons fitted just behind the cabin doors on both sides.

VARIANTS

The Astazou IIIN powerplant was fitted to British-built Westland Gazelle variants, the Army Air Corps AH1 (manufacturer's designation SA341B), Royal Navy HT2 trainer (SA341C), RAF HT3 trainer (SA341D) and HCC4 VIP transport (SA341E). Some 294 Gazelles were built by Westland between 1972 and 1984, of which 282 went to the UK armed forces. French Army SA341Fs used the Astazou IIIC, as did the military export SA341H. The SA341M, as used by the ALAT, was an upgraded SA341F capable of carrying the Euromissile HOT anti-tank weapon (40 were thus equipped) and the SA341F/Canon has a GIAT 20mm cannon fitment. Meanwhile, the Astazou XIVH engine delivering 640kW (858shp) powers the SA342, first built for military export sales as the SA342K but then modified with an improved design of fenestron tail. This produced the SA342L, and subsequently the SA342M bought by the French ALAT – in addition, a batch of 30 SA342L1s destined for China were diverted into ALAT service. Gazelles were built under licence by SOKO in Yugoslavia, who produced the SA341H Partizan before the civil war broke out, and were in the throes of supplying the Yugoslav military with both the SA341L HERA scout and SA342L GAMA anti-tank variants. 48 SA342Ls were also built in Egypt from Aérospatiale kits for the country's Army aviation arm.

Westland Gazelle AH1 Royal Marines

Aerostar Iak-52/Yakovlev Yak-52

SINGLE PISTON-ENGINED TANDEM TWO-SEAT BASIC/PRIMARY TRAINER

DEVELOPMENT

In effect one component of a family of light aircraft that also includes the Yak-50 and Yak-53 single-seat aerobatic aircraft, the two-seat Yak-52 trainer is unique in being built in Romania, having been designed and developed in the Soviet Union. Design work began in 1975, and the type owed much to the Yak-50 which immediately preceded it. The Yak-50 was a tailwheel undercarriage design which drew on experience with the highly successful Yak-18 family of training and aerobatic aircraft (described separately). The Yak-52 is essentially a replacement for the two-seat trainers in the Yak-18 series, but it embodies some of the design changes introduced for the Yak-50, including a new wing design; it also utilises a similar retractable tricycle undercarriage type to that used on many Yak-18As. Following design work by Yakovlev, production of the Yak-52 was entrusted to the Romanian aircraft industry under the Comecon agreement within the Eastern Bloc. Construction of the first Romanian-built machine began at IAv's facilities in Bacau during 1977 and it first flew in May 1978. Series manufacture began in 1979 and the 500th example was delivered in 1983; over 1,780 had been built by late 1996 when production had virtually ceased. For some years the aircraft has also been called the Iak-52, reflecting the Romanian input in the whole programme; IAv Bacau became known as Aerostar in the early 1990s. Flight-testing has now been completed of a 'westernised' model, the Iak-52W, on which the future of the type depends. An armed military version, the Yak-54, previously existed in very small numbers. Most military-operated Yak-52s currently in service are trainers or are flown by paramilitary organisations, although Georgian-operated examples may have seen combat during the early/mid-1990s.

Aerostar Iak-52W

CURRENT SERVICE

By far the largest user of the Yak-52 is the Russian Federation, which mainly employs the type within its paramilitary aeroclub organisation ROSTO (formerly DOSAAF). A similar body exists in the Ukraine and this also operates the Yak-52 in some numbers. Yak-52s additionally serve within Lithuania's national guard. The type operates in a training capacity in its country of manufacture, Romania, and until recently did so in Hungary, although the Hungarian aircraft are now temporarily withdrawn from use. Yak-52s also operate in Georgia. There are currently no known military users of the single-seat Yak-50 and Yak-53.

SPECIAL FEATURES

Of all-metal construction but with fabric-covered main control surfaces, the Yak-52 has the completely revised (compared to the Yak-18A) wing planform devised for the Yak-50 aerobatic single-seater. It has, however, a similar retractable tricycle undercarriage layout to that of most of the production Yak-18A models, its undercarriage legs/wheels being exposed when retracted.

VARIANTS

The armed **Yak-54** had underwing weapons pylons; only three appear to have been built. The **Iak-52W** has greater internal fuel capacity that increases its maximum range to 1,200km (746 miles), and has metal-covered main control surfaces. It also has a much higher input of Western equipment and avionics, improved brakes, and a three-bladed propeller.

TECHNICAL DATA

Aerostar (Yakovlev) Iak-52

Powerplant: One Aerostar-built VOKBM (Bakanov) M-14P radial engine
Developing: 269kW (360hp)
Driving: Two-blade propeller
Span: 9.30m (30ft 6.25in)
Length: 7.75m (25ft 5in)
Height: 2.70m (8ft 10.25in)
All-up weight: 1,305kg (2,877lb)
Maximum speed: 285km/h (177mph)
Cruise speed: 190km/h (118mph)
Operational ceiling: 13,120ft
Maximum range: 550km (341 miles)
Mission range: 480km (298 miles)
Endurance: Approximately 2.5 hours
Accommodation: Instructor and pupil pilot in tandem (instructor in rear seat)
Warload: None
First flown: May 1978 (IAv Bacau prototype)
Entered service: 1979/1980 (Romanian-built examples)

Aerostar Iak-52 Hungarian Air Force

Aérostructure (Fournier) RF-10

TWO-SEAT MOTOR GLIDER FOR INITIAL PILOT TRAINING

Aérostructure (Fournier) RF-10 Portuguese Air Force

DEVELOPMENT

Fournier developed a range of motor gliders in the 1960s, based on classic sailplane design. These were completely new aircraft, designed from the start as motor gliders, to enable the aircraft to take off under their own power, and then operate at height as a conventional sailplane. The RF-1 to RF-7 range were successfully produced throughout the 1960s and 70s, and versions were built by other manufacturers. A completely new range was subsequently developed, and the RF-8 was an all-metal tandem two-seater. The RF-9 followed, which had side-by-side seating, and a total of 14 of this model was produced. It featured folding wings, a retractable tailwheel undercarriage and a 50kW (68hp) Limbach SL1700E engine. From this was developed the plastics-composite model designated RF-10. Because of financial problems at the Société Fournier, the RF-10 was built by Société Aérostructure at Marmande in south-west France –

13 examples were built. The prototype was lost during flight tests involving spinning and the subsequent production versions featured an enlarged fin and rudder and a T-tail configuration. The company found the complex construction of the aircraft difficult to cope with and the design passed to AeroMot in Porto Alegra in Brazil, who continued production as the AMT-100 Ximango.

CURRENT SERVICE

Four were delivered to the Portuguese Air Force and serve with No 802 Squadron at the Air Force Academy at Sintra. They are used for career officers to go solo prior to embarking on their flying course. Several air arms operate motor gliders for initial training, but the RF-10 only received orders from Portugal.

SPECIAL FEATURES

The RF-10 introduced an all-composite structure with

a carbon fibre main spar. The wings can be detached from the fuselage for transportation. Outer portions of each wing can also be folded inwards for storage, without disconnecting aileron controls. The aircraft has a steerable tailwheel and retractable mainwheels. Upper surface airbrakes are installed, and the one-piece cockpit canopy opens upwards and rearward. Dual controls are standard.

VARIANTS

The two prototypes featured a low-mounted tailplane, but the production versions had the T-tail. Otherwise there were no other variations.

TECHNICAL DATA

Aérostructure (Fournier) RF-10

Powerplant: One Limbach L2000-EO-I flat-four piston engine
Developing: 59.5kW (80hp)
Driving: Two-blade propeller
Span: 17.47m (57ft 3.75in)
Length: 7.89m (25ft 10.75in)
Height: 1.03m (6ft 4in)
All-up weight: 800kg (1,764lb)
Maximum speed: 200km/h (124mph)
Cruising speed: 180km/h (112mph)
Maximum range: 1,000km (621 miles)
Operational ceiling: 13,125ft
Accommodation: Two, side-by-side
Warload: None
First flown: 6 March 1981 (prototype); 10 May 1984 (first production)
Entered service: Late 1980s

Aérostructure (Fournier) RF-10 Portuguese Air Force

Aerotech T-23 Uirapuru

SINGLE-ENGINED TWO-SEAT PRIMARY TRAINER

T-23 Uirapuru Paraguayan Air Force

DEVELOPMENT

Aerotech was a small São Paulo-based company, formed in 1962. It designed its A-122 Uirapuru in the early 1960s as a private venture and the earlier civil version had an O-320 or O-320-A engine. The first military version flew in 1968. The Brazilian Air Force placed an order for 30 under the designation T-23. Subsequent orders raised the Brazilian total to 100, and these were used for primary training by the Air Force Academy at Piras-Sununga, São Paulo, where it replaced the Fokker S.11 and S.12 as the basic trainer.

Aerotech also exported military Uirapurus to the Air Forces of Bolivia (18) and Paraguay (8). In addition some 20 civil examples were supplied to Brazilian state-supported flying clubs. Production came to an end in 1977 after 155 of the two models had been built.

CURRENT SERVICE

The T-23 is now out of service with the Brazilian Air Force. It was retired as a primary trainer in 1980, but a limited number remained on strength and were used for miscellaneous duties until well into the 1990s. It continues in service with the Bolivian Air Force's Escuadrón Priario at Base Aéreo El Trompillo, Santa Cruz de la Sierra and with the Paraguayan Air Force's Escuadrón Aerotech, Grupo Aéreo de Instruction at

BAM Nhu Guazu, Campo Grande.

SPECIAL FEATURES

The Uirapuru's airframe is of light alloy, and it has a non-retractable undercarriage with a steerable nosewheel. Dual controls are standard.

VARIANTS

The **A-122A** was the military model and the **A-122B** was the civil version. The **A-132 Uirapuru II** was a subsequent development that was later renamed the **A-132 Tangará**. It first flew on 26 February 1981, and was a fully aerobatic version of the A-122 with a more powerful Avco Lycoming engine, increased wingspan and improved cockpit canopy.

TECHNICAL DATA

Aerotech T-23 Uirapuru

Powerplant: One Textron Lycoming O-320-B2B piston engine
Developing: 119.5kW (160hp)
Driving: Two-blade propeller
Span: 8.50m (27ft 10.75in)
Length: 6.60m (21ft 8in)
Height: 2.70m (8ft 10in)
All-up weight: 840kg (1,852lb)
Maximum speed: 225km/h (140mph)
Operational ceiling: 14,765ft
Maximum range: 800km (497miles)
Endurance: 4 hours
Accommodation: Two, side-by-side
Warload: None
First flown: 2 June 1965 (civil version); January 1968 (military version)
Entered service: 1969

T-23 Uirapuru Paraguayan Air Force

Agusta A 109

TWO-TURBOSHAFT LIGHT OBSERVATION/MULTI-ROLE HELICOPTER

Agusta A 109HA Belgian Army

TECHNICAL DATA

Agusta A 109EOA
Powerplants: Two Rolls-Royce Allison 250-C20R/1 turboshafts
Developing: 335.5 kW (450 shp)
Driving: Four-blade main rotor, two-blade tail rotor
Main rotor diameter: 11.0m (36ft 1in)
Fuselage length: 11.45m (37ft 6.75in)
Height: 3.50m (11ft 5.75in)
All-up weight: 2,720 kg (5,996 lb)
Maximum speed: 278km/h (172mph)
Cruise speed: 252km/h (156mph)
Operational ceiling: 15,000ft
Maximum ferry range: 820km (510 miles)
Mission range: 615km (382 miles)
Endurance: 4hr
Accommodation: One or two flight crew; seating for up to seven lightly equipped troops including on-board gunner if required
Warload: one 7.62mm machine-gun in cabin (pintle-mounted); one 12.7mm machine-gun in door gunner position. External armament options for gun pods of 7.62mm or 12.7mm; 70mm twelve-round rocket pods or combined gun/rocket pods; some Italian machines can carry TOW anti-tank missiles with chin or roof-mounted sights.
First flown: 4 August 1971
Entered service: 1976/1977 (first civil deliveries); 1988 (A 109EOA)

DEVELOPMENT

Developed as a private venture, the A 109 prototype flew in August 1971, and deliveries to civil customers of initial production A 109As began in 1976/1977. The Italian Army Aviation evaluated five A 109As armed with four TOW missiles on simple mountings beside the lower fuselage and a chin-mounted sight. The A 109A Mk II followed in the early 1980s, and the A 109C in the later 1980s. The re-engined A 109K first flew in April 1983 and also has military applications; it continues in production in several specific versions. The Italian Army Aviation's most numerous model is the A 109EOA armed scout, 24 being delivered from 1988. The Belgian Army ordered 28 anti-armour (HA) and 18 scout (HO) A 109CM(BA)s in 1988/1989, for assembly in Belgium by SABCA. The major South African arms procurement package announced in 1998, will include 40 South African-assembled A 109Ms.

CURRENT SERVICE

The Italian Army Aviation's mixed fleet of A 109s serve the army aviation centre at Viterbo and in independent units including the 28° and 30° Gruppo Squadroni; other A 109EOAs operate within the 7° Reggimento Elicotteri d'Attacco 'Vega'. The Italian Police also operates the A 109. Belgian Army A 109HAs serve with 17 and 18 BnHATk at Liège-Bierset and A 109HOs with the SLV at Brasschaat. Other operators are Argentina (A 109A, Army); Dubai (A 109K2, Police); Ghana (A 109A, Air Force, ex-Uganda); Libya (Air Force); Malaysia (A 109C, Air Force); Paraguay (A 109A, Air Force); Peru (A 109K2 (KM), Army); Venezuela (A 109C, Army; A 109A, National Guard). Two Argentine Army A 109As captured during the Falklands War in 1982 operate covertly with Britain's special forces, alongside two A 109As acquired separately. They are operated by the Army Air Corps' No 8 Flight at Netheravon.

SPECIAL FEATURES

Highly-successful in civil and military service, the A 109 is produced in a wide variety of different versions. Some civil models feature a retractable undercarriage but this is not included on many military examples, which instead have fixed mountings beside the main undercarriage legs for weapons carriage. More recent models feature advanced avionics, while some have a widened cabin interior.

VARIANTS

The formidable Belgian **A 109HA** anti-armour models have a Saab HeliTOW sighting/firing system and can carry four or eight TOW, TOW 2 or TOW 2A anti-tank missiles. The Belgian machine-gun armed scouts have a Saab Helios observation system. Agusta offers alternative engine options; the powerful **A 109K** series normally have two 575kW (771shp) Turboméca Arriel 1K/1 turboshafts.

Agusta A 109HO Belgian Army

Agusta A 129 Mangusta

TWIN-TURBOSHAFT LIGHT ANTI-ARMOUR AND ESCORT/SCOUT HELICOPTER

A 129 Mangusta Italian Army Aviation

TECHNICAL DATA

Agusta A 129 Mangusta
Powerplants: Two Rolls-Royce Gem Mk.2 1004D turboshafts (licence-built by Piaggio)
Developing: 657kW (881shp)
Driving: Four-blade main rotor, two-blade tail rotor
Main rotor diameter: 11.90m (39ft 0.5in)
Fuselage length: 12.28m (40ft 3.25in)
Wing span: 3.20m (10ft 6in)
Height: 3.35m (11ft 0in)
All-up weight: 4,070kg (8,973lb)
Maximum speed: 294km/h (183mph)
Cruise speed: 250km/h (155mph)
Operational ceiling: 15,500ft
Maximum ferry range: 1,000km (621miles)
Mission range: over 200km (124miles)
Endurance: 3hr 5min
Accommodation: Two crew (gunner/co-pilot in front, pilot behind and above)
Warload: Maximum of 1,200kg (2,645lb) on four hardpoints beneath helicopter's stub wings. Up to eight TOW, Improved-TOW or TOW2/2A wire-guided anti-tank missiles. Secondary armament SNIA BPD 81mm Medusa rocket pods (12- or seven-round system) and/or Mk 66 Hydra 70mm rocket pods in various configurations, plus gun pods (7.62mm, 12.7mm or 20mm guns).
First flown: 11 September 1983
Entered service: October 1990

DEVELOPMENT

The Italian Army requirement for an indigenous anti-tank helicopter that led to the Mangusta (Mongoose) was issued in 1972, but a protracted gestation resulted in project go-ahead only in 1978, and the prototype first flew on 11 September 1983, (officially, four days later). Six prototypes eventually flew, and deliveries to the Italian Army of initial 'Batch 1' production helicopters began in October 1990. Fifteen austere 'Batch 1' Mangustas were built with day-capable Saab/HeliTOW missile armament system featuring a nose-mounted sight, followed by 30 'Batch 2' A 129s with night-fighting capability (Saab HeliTOW system with FLIR incorporating laser range-finder/designator). Italian Army Mangustas saw action during 1993/94 as part of Operation *Ibis* during the UN relief mission in Somalia, and also covered the foreign withdrawal from the same country in 1995 during Operation *Ibis II*. Combat in Somalia illustrated the need for Mangustas to have a nose mounted gun, GPS and night vision goggles for the crew; some of these requirements are now addressed in the A 129 International, the final 15 of Italy's total Mangusta procurement of 60 being partially to International standard (but retaining the Gem powerplant).

CURRENT SERVICE

'Batch 1' and 'Batch 2' Mangustas were delivered to the Italian Army Aviation between 1990 and 1996. Current front-line service is with units of the 7° Reggimento Elicotteri d'Attacco 'Vega' at Casarsa in north-eastern Italy with one element at nearby Belluno. Some Mangustas are also attached to the army aviation centre at Viterbo.

SPECIAL FEATURES

Europe's first operational anti-tank helicopter, the Mangusta's classic anti-armour helicopter layout combines strength (it can withstand hitting the ground at up to 11.2-metres per second) with lightweight construction (45% of the basic airframe weight is comprised of lightweight composite materials). The considerable development potential within the comparatively simple basic Mangusta design is exploited in the A 129 International.

VARIANTS

Projected A 129 variants such as maritime anti-ship and utility models have so far not reached production, nor did the Mangusta-based Tonal multi-national anti-tank helicopter programme of the late 1980s.

The most important development of the basic **A 129** is the all-weather multi-mission **A 129 International**. A more powerful model, re-engined with two Allison/Allied Signal LHTEC CTS800-2 turboshafts of 1,016kW (1,362shp), it has a chin turret-mounted 20mm cannon (Lockheed Martin M167), a five-blade main rotor, upgraded avionics and provision for increased armament – including Stinger air-to-air missiles and Hellfire anti-tank missiles. A specific development of it is the **A 129 Scorpion**, directed at the Australian Army's AIR 87 armed reconnaissance helicopter requirement.

A 129 Mangusta Italian Army Aviation

Agusta (SIAI-Marchetti) S.211

SINGLE TURBOFAN BASIC TRAINER AND LIGHT ATTACK AIRCRAFT

Agusta S.211 Phillipine Air Force

DEVELOPMENT

Developed by SIAI-Marchetti as a private venture project for a lightweight, low-cost basic trainer and light attack aircraft, the S.211 was one of a large crop of basic jet trainers to hit the market during the mid-1980s. Unfortunately, like several of its competitors in this somewhat overcrowded field, it did not achieve great sales success and only four nations adopted the type (one has already retired its fleet). However, the S.211 boasted some advanced design features such as its wing configuration and low gross weight, while also being suitable for light strike duties. It was heavily touted for the US military's JPATS requirement, the bid being put forward in conjunction with Grumman, but was ultimately unsuccessful.

CURRENT SERVICE

The major users of the S.211 are the Republic of Singapore Air Force (to whom 30 were delivered, including 24 examples locally-assembled by Singapore Aerospace) whose aircraft are used for basic training with No 130 'Eagle' Squadron at RAAF Pearce in Australia, and the Philippine Air Force, which received 18 (14 of which were built by PADC from kits supplied by Agusta), these serving with the 105th Combat

Crew Training Squadron at Basa and the 103rd Pilot Training Squadron at Fenando. They are used for both training and ground attack, but the fleet has suffered high attrition and is grounded regularly. The S.211's only other operator is the Royal Brunei Air Wing, those used by Haiti having been sold to the USA.

SPECIAL FEATURES

One of the more advanced features for a basic jet trainer which was incorporated into the S.211 was the shoulder-wing design, which is of supercritical section. At the time of its initial production, the type had the lowest gross weight of any jet trainer with the exception of the Promavia Jet Squalus, mainly due to 61% of the external surfaces being made from composite materials. It has an air-conditioned cockpit and one piece framed canopy.

VARIANTS

An uprated S.211A proposed by Agusta in the early 1990s, with a more powerful JT15D-5C turbofan of 14.2kN (3,190lb), new avionics and a stretched fuselage (developed in conjunction with Singapore Aircraft Industries) was never built or ordered.

TECHNICAL DATA

Agusta S.211

Powerplant: One Pratt & Whitney JT15D-4C turbofan

Developing: 11.12kN (2,500lb st)

Span: 8.43m (27ft 8in)

Length: 9.31m (30ft 6.5in)

Height: 3.80m (12ft 5.5in)

All-up weight: 3,150kg (6,944lb)

Maximum speed: 740km/h (460mph)

Cruise speed: 667km/h (414mph)

Operational ceiling: 40,000ft

Maximum range: 2,483km (1,541miles)

Mission range: 556km (345miles)

Endurance: 3hr 24min

Accommodation: Two in tandem

Warload: Four underwing hardpoints. Maximum external ordnance 600kg (1,320lb) – gunpods, four AL-18-50, Matra F2, LAU-32 or AL-6-80 rocket launchers, bombs or napalm containers.

First flown: 10 April 1981

Entered service: 1983

Agusta S.211 Phillipine Air Force

Airbus A310

Airbus A310-304MRT German Air Force

DEVELOPMENT

Following on from its initial product, the Airbus A300, Airbus Industrie recognised the potential market need for a shorter-range variant (originally designated A300B-10). Three airlines – namely Eastern Airlines, Lufthansa and Swissair – expressed interest in the type, which was officially launched by Airbus as the A310 during 1978. Its cabin has the same cross-section measurements as the A300, but the A310 is some 26ft shorter than its predecessor. It featured a new higher aspect ratio wing, and new and smaller horizontal tail surfaces. The A310-200 was the first production variant (the -100 regional version not being built), followed by the longer-range A310-300. Although the basic A310 is no longer in production, the type has gained numerous military orders through the acquisition of 'off-the-shelf' ex-civil examples for a variety of roles. The most notable of these are the Canadian Forces' CC-150 Polaris, a 'combi' passenger/cargo transport, and the German Luftwaffe's similar A310-304 MRTs (Multi-Role Transports). A tanker/transport variant of the latter is being planned at the time of writing.

CURRENT SERVICE

The first military A310 customer was the Royal Thai Air Force, which obtained a new-build A310-324 during 1991 for government VIP transport duties. That same year, the German Luftwaffe received three A310-304s from the former East German state airline Interflug, and these remain in use as VIP transports. Between 1996 and 1999, four further examples of the same sub-type were acquired from Lufthansa, and are now in service as A310-304MRTs. All the German aircraft are based at Köln/Bonn with the FBS special transport squadron. With the Canadian Forces, the aircraft is known as the CC-150 Polaris and five are in use with 8 Wing, No 437 Squadron, based at CFB Trenton, Ontario – all ex-civil A310-304s. Other military customers have been the French Air Force (a pair of A310-304s, bought from Royal Jordanian Airlines and in service with ET 03.060 at Paris-Charles de Gaulle for VIP transport taskings) and the Belgian Air Force (two A310-222s, again VIP-configured and based with 21 Smaldeel at Brussels-Melsbroek).

SPECIAL FEATURES

The A310-300 series, as used by the Canadians, French, Germans and Thais, is almost identical to the A310-200 as purchased by Belgium but for the fitment of small winglets. The planned MRTT (Multi-Role Tanker/Transport) derivative of the A310-304, which will be used by the Luftwaffe, incorporates not only the large cargo door of the MRT version but will also be equipped with a pair of underwing-mounted air-to-air refuelling pods.

VARIANTS

Only the Belgian Air Force uses the **A310-200**, in its **-222** guise. This variant is powered by the Pratt & Whitney JT9D-7R4E1 engine, as opposed to the GE CF6 as used on the -304 models, and the PW4152 on the Royal Thai Air Force **A310-324s**. Of the Luftwaffe's A310s, the initial three ex-Interflug aircraft are operated as VIP and staff transports with a mainly white colour scheme, while the quartet acquired from Lufthansa are operated currently as MRTs and have been painted in a new grey livery. Raytheon E-Systems has offered Australia the A310 as an AEW & C platform fitted with Elta's phased array radar. The **A310-200C** convertible is available as a conversion of an existing A310.

TECHNICAL DATA

Airbus A310-304/CC-150 Polaris

Powerplants: Two General Electric CF6-80C2A2 turbofans
Thrust: 237.98kN (53,000lb st)
Span: 43.89m (144ft 0in)
Length: 46.66m (153ft 1in)
Height: 15.80m (51ft 10in)
All-up weight: 164,000kg (361,650lb)
Maximum speed: 897km/h (566mph)
Cruise speed: 850km/h (527mph)
Operational ceiling: 40,000ft
Maximum range: 9,850km (5,953 miles)
Accommodation: Flight crew of two. With a standard passenger interior fitment, up to 270 people can be accommodated.
First flown: 3 April 1982 (A310 prototype)
Entered service: September 1991
(Royal Thai Air Force)

CC-150 Polaris Canadian Armed Forces

Airbus A340

FOUR-TURBOFAN LONG-RANGE VIP/GOVERNMENT AIRCRAFT

Airbus A340 Government of Saudi Arabia

DEVELOPMENT

The Airbus A330/A340, launched in 1987, is one aircraft initially produced in three versions – one twin and two four-engined models. Seating capacity ranges from 240 to 440. The aircraft share the same airframe, with the differences being engines, engine-related and fuselage length. The A340 is a third-generation wide-body aircraft from Airbus Industrie, and it is offered in two sizes, allowing operators to tailor capacity and capability to demand. The larger A340-300 has seat-mile costs on a level with those of the largest four-engined airliners, while the smaller A340-200 has the longest range of any commercial airliner available. The flexibility of four engines – the optimum number for long-range aircraft, ensuring freedom from all ETOPS-related constraints – provides operational benefits not available with twin-engined aircraft, while offering levels of efficiency not possible with tri-jet designs, due to their in-built aerodynamic and weight penalties. The A340 incorporates more extensive use of composites than any other airliner.

CURRENT SERVICE

It is in service as a government aircraft in Brunei and some Gulf states.

SPECIAL FEATURES

The A340 has an all-new highly advanced wing mated to a twin-aisle fuselage with the same cross section as that of the Airbus A310, A300-600 and A330. By incorporating many of the technological advances developed for the smaller A320, the A340 has a level of technical excellence unsurpassed by any other aircraft. Is fitted with an advanced 'glass' flight deck incorporating sidestick controllers, together with a digital fly-through-computer flight control system.

Seating is eight-abreast within the classic 222in Airbus wide-body fuselage. The A340 is unique in having efficient high-lift devices root to tip, reducing power requirements and improving low-speed performance.

VARIANTS

Offering the flexibility to convert between main deck 'passenger plus cargo' configuration to all-passenger configuration, the **A340 Combi** offers the ability to satisfy a wide range of needs in one aircraft. The **A340-300** has the same fuselage length as the twin-engined A330-300. Airbus has since launched the **A340-500** and **A340-600** – with up to 9.07m (35ft 1in) stretch as direct competition to the Boeing 747-400 and powered by 249kN (56,000lb st) Rolls-Royce Trent 556 turbofans. First flight is scheduled for 2001. A modified tanker version of the Airbus A330 is proposed for the UK Future Strategic Tanker Aircraft (FSTA) Private Finance Initiative (PFI), in competition with the Boeing 767 and others.

Airbus A340-200

Powerplants: Four CFM International CFM56-5C or -5C3 turbofans
Developing: 138.8kN (31,200lb st) or 145kN (32,500lb st)
Span: 60.30m (197ft 10in)
Length: 59.39m (194ft 10in)
Height: 16.8m (55ft 3in)
All-up weight: 250,404kg (558,900lb)
Maximum speed: 914km/h (573mph)
Economical cruising speed: 880km/h (545mph)
Operational ceiling: 41,000ft
Maximum range: 13,805km (8,578 miles)
Accommodation: Flight crew of two. Airliner version up to 440 passengers
Warload: Nil
First Flown: 25 October 1991 (A340-300); 1 April 1992 (A340-200)
Entered service: March 1993 (airline service)

Airbus A340 Government of Saudi Arabia

Airtech (CASA-IPTN) CN-235

TWIN-TURBOPROP GENERAL PURPOSE TRANSPORT/CARGO AIRCRAFT

SPAIN/INDONESIA

CN-235MP Persuader Irish Air Corps

TECHNICAL DATA

Airtech CN-235M
Powerplants: Two General Electric CT7-9C turboprops
Developing: 1,394.5kW (1,870 shp) (automatic power reserve rating)
Driving: four blade propellers
Span: 25.81m (84ft 8in)
Length: 21.40m (70ft 2.5in)
Height: 8.18m (26ft 10in)
All-up weight: 16,000kg (35,273lb)
Maximum speed: 460km/h (286mph)
Cruise speed: 445km/h (276mph)
Operational ceiling: 22,500ft
Maximum range: 4,445km (2,762 miles)
Mission range: 1,528km (950 miles)
Endurance: over 3.5 hours
Accommodation: Two crew on flight deck; loadmaster or jumpmaster as required, up to 48 fully-equipped troops, or up to 46 paratroops, or cargo as required
Warload: Three attachments beneath each wing; maritime versions can carry guided anti-ship missiles such as Harpoon or AM 39 Exocet, or Mk46 torpedoes
First flown: 11 November 1983
Entered service: 9 February 1987 (Saudi Arabia)

DEVELOPMENT

The considerable success of the CASA C-212 Aviocar and the co-operation between CASA and IPTN (formerly Nurtanio) of Indonesia over production of that aircraft, led both companies to look into a larger development to suit both civil and military transport roles. Airtech, a joint CASA-IPTN company, was established in 1980/81, and the resulting CN-235 first flew in November 1983 in Spain (CASA built), and in December 1983 (IPTN-built prototype). Production has subsequently been shared between the two countries with final assembly lines in both; a third production source was established by Turkish Aerospace Industries (TAI) to manufacture Turkish-ordered examples, plus some export models. The CN-235 exists in civil and military versions. The initial Series 10 were mainly civil models, as are the more powerful Series 100/Series 200 (Spanish-built) and Series 110/220 (Indonesian-built); the standard military CN-235M transport model exists alongside most of these versions – the first military CN-235s to be delivered to Saudi Arabia in February 1987 were Series 10 models. Several special-mission military developments exist, including maritime patrol models – the CN-235MP Persuader (built in Spain and Turkey), and the Indonesian CN-235MPA. A further development, being pursued solely by CASA, is the stretched C-295, which first flew on 28 November 1997 and has secured several orders from the Spanish Air Force (C-295M). Production/outstanding orders for

military models of the CN-235 currently total 204 plus several prototypes/trials aircraft.

CURRENT SERVICE

The Spanish Air Force's CN-235s comprise transport (18 T.19B) and VIP-configured (two T.19A) examples, operated with Ala 35 at Madrid/Getafe. The Royal Saudi Air Force's No 1 Squadron at Al Kharj operates four Series 10 CN-235Ms, two being VIP-configured. The Indonesian Air Force's CN-235s serve with SkU 2 at Halim-Perdanakusuma, while the Indonesian Navy's SkU (RON) 800 at Surabaya/Lanudal Juanda is just receiving CN-235MPA models. In addition to these users, CN-235s of various versions currently serve with some 19 other military operators, including the US Air Force, and the air force, army, navy, paramilitary police or coast guards of the following : Abu Dhabi, Botswana, Brunei, Chile, Colombia, Ecuador, France, Gabon, Ireland, Malaysia, Morocco, Oman, Panama, Papua New Guinea, South Africa, South Korea, Thailand, Turkey.

SPECIAL FEATURES

Of classic high-wing cargo transport layout with a payload capacity of 6,000kg (13,227lb), the CN-235 features mainly metal construction with some use of composites. The fuselage is pressurised and has a rear loading ramp/door, the aircraft being able to operate from semi-prepared airstrips.

VARIANTS

The initial **Series 10** featured CT7-7A turboprops, while the **Series 100** introduced the CT7-9C powerplant and the **Series 200** includes various improvements including structural reinforcement. The **CN-235MP Persuader** includes a Litton AN/APS-504(V)5 search radar and forward-looking infrared. The Indonesian **CN-235MPA** has various sea-search radar options with a modified nose shape including the Marconi Seaspray 4000 or Thomson-CSF Ocean Master 100, can carry Mk46 torpedoes and has two mission crew stations in the capacious fuselage and seating for six passengers.

CASA CN-235 Spanish Air Force

Alenia G222

TWIN-TURBOPROP TACTICAL TRANSPORT/CARGO AIRCRAFT

Alenia G222TCM Italian Air Force

TECHNICAL DATA

Alenia G222TCM
Powerplants: Two Fiat-built General Electric T64-GE-P4D turboprops
Developing: 2,535 kW (3,400 shp)
Driving: Three-blade propellers
Span: 28.70m (94ft 2in)
Length: 22.70m (74ft 5.5in)
Height: 10.57m (34ft 8.25in)
All-up weight: 28,000kg (61,730lb)
Maximum speed: 487km/h (303mph)
Cruise speed: 437km/h (272mph)
Operational ceiling: 24,935ft
Maximum range: 4,685km (2,911miles)
Mission range: 1,260km (783 miles)
Endurance: Approx 3.75hr
Accommodation: Pilot, co-pilot, and flight engineer. Loadmaster or jumpmaster as required; up to 46 fully-equipped troops, or up to 40 fully-equipped paratroops, or cargo as required
Warload: None
First flown: 18 July 1970
Entered service: November 1976 (Dubai); April 1978 (Italy)

DEVELOPMENT

Conceived from an early 1960s NATO requirement for a V/STOL tactical transport, the G222 was originally a Fiat project with several unusual configurations. Fiat's most conventional proposal later gained official Italian interest; two unpressurised prototype G222s were ordered in 1968, with the first flying in July 1970. Most major Italian aerospace companies were eventually involved in the production of the G222, with the type being under the Alenia grouping from 1990. The first production-standard aircraft flew in late 1975, and deliveries began in 1976 with a single aircraft for Dubai. Italian orders totalled 46 in several versions (plus five for the Italian Ministry of Civil Defence), and the type has gained export orders from Dubai (one), the Congo (three), the Argentine Army (three), Libya (20 G222Ts with 3,635 kW (4,860 shp) Rolls-Royce Tyne Mk801 turboprops; two VIP-configured), Nigeria (five), Somalia (two delivered), Thailand (six), and Venezuela (six Air Force, two Army). In the early 1990s, the US Air Force ordered ten G222s (plus eight options not taken up) under the designation C-27A Spartan, primarily for use in Central America with mission equipment installed by Chrysler Technologies Airborne Systems. These aircraft served with the 310th Airlift Squadron, 24th Wing at Howard Air Force Base, Panama, but were withdrawn by early 1999 and stored. As a joint venture in conjunction with Lockheed Martin, Alenia has developed an upgraded model, the C-27J Spartan II

under the grouping Lockheed Martin Alenia Tactical Transport Systems. The C-27J prototype first flew on 25 September 1999.

CURRENT SERVICE

The Italian Air Force's G222TCM cargo and transport fleet serves principally with the 2° and 98° Gruppi of the 46th Brigata Aerea at Pisa. The two G222VSs serve with the 71° Gruppo/14° Stormo at Pratica di Mare, where the 8° Gruppo/14° Stormo's four G222RM calibration aircraft are also based, plus two aircraft with the RSV. The Dubai and Somali G222s have now been withdrawn. The type is still active in Argentina, Libya, Nigeria, Thailand and Venezuela. The latter's remaining airworthy G222s now all serve with the Venezuelan Air Force's Grupo Aéreo de Transporte 6 at El Libertador; the Royal Thai Air Force's G222s are with 603 Squadron of 6 Wing at Don Muang.

SPECIAL FEATURES

The pressurised G222 possesses an excellent short-field performance, even from grass and unprepared surfaces, aided by spoilers and double-slotted wing flaps. The conventional high-wing tactical transport layout has large rear-loading doors and an integral ramp. The main undercarriage height is adjustable on the ground for ease of loading or unloading.

VARIANTS

The **G222VS** is an electronic warfare model carrying up to ten additional crew with onboard detection, recording and signal processing equipment; it has two external radomes, on the fin top and beneath the nose. The **G222RM** is a calibration aircraft and the **G222SAA** is a firefighting version with a modular dispersal system for water or fire retardant. The new **C-27J** has common flight deck features of the C-130J as offered to the Italian Air Force, with two 3,132kW (4,200shp) Rolls-Royce Allison AE 2100D3 turboprops and Dowty six-bladed propellers.

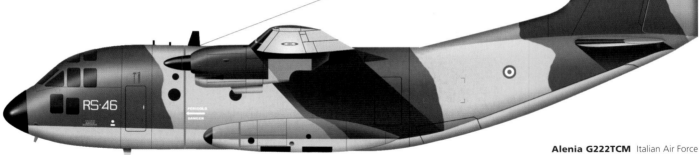

Alenia G222TCM Italian Air Force

AMX International AMX

AMX International AMX Italian Air Force

TECHNICAL DATA

AMX International AMX
Powerplant: One Rolls-Royce RB168-807 Spey non-afterburning turbofan (licence-built)
Developing: 49.1kN (11,030lb st)
Span: 8.87m (29ft 1in) (excluding wingtip missiles/rails)
Length: 13.23m (43ft 5in)
Height: 4.55m (14ft 11in)
All-up weight: 13,000kg (28,660lb)
Maximum speed: 914km/h (568mph)
Operational ceiling: 42,650ft
Maximum range: 3,333km (2,071 miles)
Mission range: 1,778km (1,106 miles)
Accommodation: Single pilot (AMX-T two)
Warload: one internal M61A1 Vulcan multi-barrel 20mm cannon (Italian aircraft); two internal DEFA 554 30mm cannon (Brazilian aircraft). Four underwing, one centreline, and one wingtip (each wing) pylons for up to 3,800kg (8,377lb) of external ordnance, including free fall 'iron' bombs, cluster bombs, rockets, and reconnaissance pods; air-to-surface ordnance (with related guidance systems fitted) including Exocet and Martel missiles, and laser-guided bombs; wingtip air-to-air missiles (AIM-9L Sidewinder or similar for Italian, and MAA-1 Piranha for Brazilian aircraft)
First flown: 15 May 1984
Entered service: April 1989

DEVELOPMENT

Derived from a 1977 Italian Air Force requirement for a tactical fighter-bomber replacement for the Fiat G.91R/Y and F-104G Starfighter, the AMX became an important co-operative programme between Italy and Brazil. Initial co-operation between Aermacchi and Embraer on the A-X (as a replacement for the Brazilian EMB-326 Xavantes) eventually led to the AMX and the setting-up of AMX International by Aeritalia (now Alenia) and Aermacchi of Italy, and Embraer of Brazil. Eventual requirements for the two countries grew to over 300 examples, plus six to seven prototypes. The first aircraft was flown on 15 May 1984 in Italy, and initial deliveries were made to the Italian Air Force in April 1989 and to the Brazilian Air Force in October 1989. Work is shared on a roughly 70:30 split between Italy and Brazil, with final assembly lines in both countries. The AMX's engine is licence-built by a consortium of Italian companies with Brazilian input. The combat-capable AMX-T two-seat trainer version first flew in Italy on 14 March 1990. In 1997, the last of 110 Italian single-seat AMXs of those definitely on order had been delivered, while production for the Brazilian Air Force continues. The first AMX export order was confirmed in 1999, comprising eight aircraft for Venezuela in AMX-ATA (Advanced Trainer/Attack)

configuration. The Italian government has approved an upgrade of 70 aircraft.

CURRENT SERVICE

A total of 238 AMXs were delivered to the Italian Air Force and 79 to the Brazilian Air Force. Current Italian units include elements of the 2° Stormo at Rivolto, the 32° Stormo (Amendola), and the 51° Stormo (Istrana), plus some test aircraft at the RSV (Pratica di Mare). Brazilian Air Force AMXs operate within the 16° Grupo de Aviação at Santa Cruz.

SPECIAL FEATURES

Sometimes called a 'pocket Tornado', the diminutive AMX is genuinely multi-role, although Brazilian single-seat AMXs (known as A-1s) have different armament, weapon delivery systems and avionics from Italian aircraft. In-flight refuelling is provided via an external refuelling probe. The two-seat AMX-T (known as the TA-1 in Brazil) is the same size as the single-seat aircraft, but with reduced fuel.

VARIANTS

The main proposed derivatives of the basic **AMX** and **AMX-T** centre on the two-seater. The **AMX-ATA** is a considerably uprated model with improved avionics

and radar, and increased weapons envelope. A two-seat defence-suppression variant, the **AMX-E**, has also been proposed. Re-engining with a more powerful, non-afterburning model of the Eurojet EJ200 turbofan has also been studied, and may be a part of the Venezuelan AMX-ATA deal. Italian-operated aircraft, which have already received some upgrading, may incorporate some of the AMX-ATA improvements (the so-called 'Super AMX') in future upgrades.

AMX International AMX
Italian Air Force

Antonov An-2

DEVELOPMENT

Designed for agricultural use in the immediate post-WWII era, Antonov's An-2 appeared anachronistic even at this time and was expected to have only a short-term service life. The aircraft has, in fact, become one of the great success stories of post-war Soviet aviation and during a production run of some 50 years, over 18,000 examples have been built. Although the age of the biplane was considered over by the late-1940s, Antonov deliberately chose a biplane layout to achieve excellent low-speed handling, STOL performance and strong structure. The resulting aircraft was not only durable enough for operations from the many rough landing strips in the wastes of Russia but was adaptable enough to be applied to tasks never envisaged. The Soviet military and the air arms of its allies accepted the aircraft in large numbers. Although mainly utilised in the light transport and communications roles, the An-2 has also been utlised as a paratroop transport, glider tug, air ambulance, trainer, surveillance platform, fire-bomber and even a light bomber. The An-2 remains in service in Russia and with many other air arms, and the availabilty of low-cost airframes and spares will ensure it continues for many more years. The prevalence of the type, particularly in politically unstable countries, prompted the US Army to acquire three examples for threat simulation as part of the Operational Test and Evaluation Command (OPTEC). Responsibility for An-2 production was transferred to Poland's PZL Mielec which, since 1960, has produced over 12,000 examples. Licence-production has been undertaken in China as the Harbin Y-5 of which some 1,500 were produced. A turbine-engine version, designated An-3 and developed in the late 1980s, never reached production.

CURRENT SERVICE

An-2s serve with the air arms of the following nations: Afghanistan, Albania, Angola, Armenia, Azerbaijan, Benin, Bulgaria, Croatia, Cuba, Egypt, Estonia, Georgia, Laos, Latvia, Lithuania, Mali, Moldova, Mongolia, Nicaragua, Poland, Romania, Russia, Ukraine, USA, Vietnam and Yugoslavia.

Antonov An-2 Romanian Air Force

SPECIAL FEATURES

To give the aircraft its STOL performance, full-span leading-edge slats and electrically-actuated double-slotted trailing edge flaps are fitted which, combined with the large wing area and robust undercarriage, allow operations from almost any terrain. Skis can be fitted for operations from snow and the large loading door on the port side can be removed for paradropping.

VARIANTS

To meet the many roles to which the type has been applied a large number of variants have been produced. The main transport variants are the **An-2P**, **An-2T** and **An-2TP**. The **PZL An-2TD** is a freight/paratroop version and the **PZL An-2S** was adapted for the air ambulance and glider-towing roles. Meteorological research, survey, and training versions of the An-2 are more usually designated **An-2ZA**.

TECHNICAL DATA

PZL Mielec (Antonov) An-2P 'Colt'

Powerplant: One PZL Kalisz ASz-621R radial piston engine
Developing: 746kW (1,000hp)
Driving: Four-blade propeller
Span: upper wing 18.18m (59ft 7.25in); lower wing 14.24m (46ft 8.5in)
Length: 12.74m (41ft 9.5in)
Height: 6.10m (20ft 0in)
Maximum take-off weight: 5500kg (12,125lb)
Maximum speed: 258km/h (160mph)
Cruising speed: 185km/h (115mph)
Operational ceiling: 14,425ft
Accommodation: Flight crew of one or two pilots and up to 12 passengers
Warload: None – although some aircraft have been modified to carry a small bomb load
Range: 900km (560 miles) with average payload
First flown: 31 August 1947; 23 October 1960 (PZL Mielec)
Entered service: 1948

Antonov An-2 Polish Air Force

Antonov An-12

FOUR-TURBOPROP MEDIUM-LIFT CARGO/FREIGHT TRANSPORT

USSR

Antonov An-12BP Russian Air Force

DEVELOPMENT

The An-12 is a freight-carrying derivative of the long retired An-10 airliner, itself derived from the smaller, twin-engined An-8. For many years the An-12 was the Soviet Bloc's main medium-lift cargo transport, a Soviet C-130 Hercules equivalent. The prototype first flew in 1958, the type entering service with the Soviet Air Force's Military Transport Aviation (VTA) in 1959. The basic freighter An-12BP (NATO code name 'Cub') was followed by several electronic-warfare derivatives for Soviet use; the basic transport An-12 was widely exported to Soviet-aligned and non-aligned countries. A major early operator was India. Altogether 1,243 An-12s of all types were built, production ending in 1972. The type is still widely used, despite partial replacement by the Ilyushin Il-76 in Soviet/Russian Federation service. A major derivative is the Shaanxi (SAC) Y-8, currently in production in Communist China, which first flew in December 1974 and operates with Chinese military forces and several export customers, at least 60 to 65 having so far been delivered.

CURRENT SERVICE

Over 150 An-12BPs remain in Russian service, plus over 20 electronic-warfare variants and several test and trials aircraft. Most Russian An-12BPs are assigned

to VTA units and transport echelons in other air force branches and commands; some electronic-warfare aircraft and transports remain in Russian Federation Naval Aviation service. Current export operators include Algeria, Ethiopia and Iraq; Yemen and Angola (possibly withdrawn); Afghanistan (including possibly rebel forces); and former Soviet republics including Belarus, Kazakhstan, Turkmenistan, Uzbekistan, and Ukraine. Communist Chinese Y-8s serve with PLANAF (naval) and principally PLAAF (air force) units. Y-8D export models were supplied to Myanmar (four), Sudan (one), and Sri Lanka (three) – including two configured as makeshift bombers.

SPECIAL FEATURES

The all-metal An-12 has pressurised crew and passenger areas; it can carry up to 20,000kg (44,092lb) of payload, including small AFVs and APCs, or 60 paratroops, in its unpressurised cargo hold. No integral loading ramp is fitted, a separate ramp being used to load and offload vehicles. The An-12 can operate from austere landing strips, and use skis for operations on snow or ice.

VARIANTS

The electronic-warfare versions of the An-12 have many sensors and aerials around their airframes, sometimes

in large fairings, plus redesigned interiors for EW operators and their work stations and electronics. They include the **'Cub-A'** and **'Cub-B'** Elint aircraft; **'Cub-C'** and **'Cub-D'** ECM and jamming aircraft. The **Shaanxi Y-8** is longer, has four 3,169 kW (4,250 shp) SAEC (Zhuzhou) WJ6 turboprops, and a redesigned rear fuselage freight door which acts as an integral loading ramp. Variants are the **Y-8A** helicopter/ freight carrier; **Y-8D** export model; **Y-8E** drone carrier (one Chang Hong 1 UAV under each wing); and **Y-8X** maritime patrol aircraft with Western (principally Collins and Litton Canada) avionics and radar.

TECHNICAL DATA

Antonov An-12BP

Powerplants: Four Progress (Ivchenko) AI-20K turboprops
Developing: 2,985kW (4,000shp)
Driving: Four-blade propellers
Span: 38.0m (124ft 8in)
Length: 33.10m (108ft 7in)
Height: 10.53m (34ft 6in)
Maximum weight: 61,000kg (134,480lb)
Maximum speed: 777km/h (483mph)
Cruise speed: 670km/h (416mph)
Operational ceiling: 33,465ft
Maximum range: 5,700kg (3,542 miles)
Mission range: 3,600km (2,237 miles)
Endurance: approximately 7 hours
Accommodation: Flight crew of five or six (two pilots, flight engineer and radio operator in cockpit, navigator in nose, air-drop observer/ gunner in tail); up to 14 passengers in cabin behind flight deck; large cargo capacity
Warload: Two Nudelman Richter NR-23 23mm cannons in tail turret on some aircraft
First flown: 1958
Entered service: 1959

Antonov An-12BP Ukraine Air Force

Antonov An-22

Antonov An-22 Russian Air Force

TECHNICAL DATA

Antonov An-22 'Cock'
Powerplants: Four Kuibyshev (Kuznetsov)
NK-12MA turboprops
Developing: 11,186kW (15,000shp)
Driving: Eight-blade contra-rotating propellers
Span: 64.40m (211ft 4in)
Length: 57.80m (189ft 7in)
Height: 12.53m (41ft 1.5in)
Maximum weight: 250,000kg (551,160lb)
Maximum speed: 740km/h (460mph)
Cruise speed: 600km/h (373mph)
Operational ceiling: 32,800ft
Maximum range: 10,950km (6,800 miles)
Mission range: 5,000km (3,100 miles)
Endurance: between 8 and approximately
14.5 hours
Accommodation: Flight crew of five or six (two
pilots, navigator, flight engineer, radio operator
or loadmaster); up to 29 passengers in cabin
behind flight deck; large cargo capacity as
required
Warload: None
First flown: 27 February 1965
Entered service: 1966-1967 (civil and military
operations)

DEVELOPMENT
The world's largest turboprop-powered aircraft so far produced, the An-22 Antei (Antheus) was developed to meet a Soviet military requirement for a long-range heavy transport/freighter, and first flew in February 1965. Some five prototypes/pre-production examples were followed by approximately 100 (possibly slightly less) production aircraft; production ended in 1974. Entering Aeroflot and initial Soviet military service in 1966-1967, many have subsequently flown in Aeroflot colours although performing military tasks. In full-scale service from 1969 with the Soviet Air Force's Military Transport Aviation (VTA) , the An-22 (NATO code name 'Cock') has served only with Soviet/Russian forces during its operational military career. The type broke a wide selection of world records from as early as 1967 onwards, and featured prominently in the Soviet invasion of Afghanistan in late 1979.

CURRENT SERVICE
Although intended to be largely replaced in service by the turbofan-powered An-124 Ruslan, the An-22 remains in service in larger numbers than the Ruslan;

some 45 still serve the Russian Federation Air Force's Military Transport Aviation (VTA), principally with 8 VTAP (military transport aviation regiment) at Tver and 81 VTAP at Ivanovo. The VTA itself is currently undergoing some reorganisation. Many, if not all, Aeroflot-painted An-22s are available for military service as required.

SPECIAL FEATURES
Of all-metal construction, the massive An-22 has a unique 14-wheel landing gear with tyres whose pressure can be altered in flight or on the ground to suit different runway surfaces, and an undercarriage design for rough field operations. The unpressurised main cargo hold is 33m (108ft 4in) long and is accessed via a retractable rear loading ramp/lower rear fuselage; up to 80,000kg (176,368lb) of cargo can be carried, including tanks, self-propelled guns, tracked SAM launchers, and many other military vehicles and loads. Overhead moveable winches and gantries in the roof of the main cargo hold can manoeuvre loads within the fuselage. Up to 29 passengers can be seated in a pressurised compartment behind the pressurised

flight deck. Paratroops can also be carried, and loads can be paradropped in flight if necessary. Large double-slotted flaps help the An-22's good rough field capabilities, and the type's powerful Kuznetsov turboprops drive massive contra-rotating propeller assemblies that provide a huge slipstream over these flap surfaces.

VARIANTS
No specific derivatives of the **An-22** have emerged, but a general upgrading of the type has seen the introduction of prominent forward fuselage/nose bulges containing various radars. An all-passenger derivative was studied but never proceeded with.

Antonov An-22 Russian Air Force

Antonov An-26/An-30

TWIN-TURBOPROP SHORT/MEDIUM-RANGE FREIGHT/CARGO TRANSPORT, AND SPECIALIST SURVEY PLATFORM   **UKRAINE**

Antonov An-26 Polish Air Force

TECHNICAL DATA

Antonov An-26B

Powerplants: Two ZMKB Progress (Ivchenko) AI-24VT turboprops
Deceloping: 2,074kW (2,780shp)
Driving: four-blade propellers
Span: 29.20m (95ft 2in)
Length: 23.80m (78ft 1in)
Height: 8.58m (28ft 2in)
All-up weight: 24,000kg (52,911lb)
Maximum speed: 540km/h (335mph)
Cruise speed: 435km/h (270mph)
Maximum range: 2,660km (1,652 miles)
Mission range: 1,100km (683 miles)
Accommodation: Flight crew of five (pilot, co-pilot, radio operator, flight engineer, and navigator), plus optional loadmaster; up to 5,500kg (12,125lb) of freight, or 38 to 40 passengers/lightly-armed troops
Warload: normally none; provision on some aircraft for a rack on each side of the fuselage for small bomb or air-drop container
First flown: 1968 (An-26); September 1969 (An-28); 1974 (An-30)
Entered service: 1969 (An-26); 1975 (An-30)

DEVELOPMENT

A logical development of the successful An-24 civil and military passenger transport, the An-26 was designed by Antonov as a dedicated military cargo derivative and includes some features of the cargo-configured An-24 models. In particular it features a complete re-design of the rear fuselage to make the type into a true cargo carrier. The first example flew in 1968 and deliveries began in 1969, with the type subsequently entering very widespread service with Warsaw Pact air forces and Soviet-aligned air arms. Code-named 'Curl' by NATO, the baseline An-26 was later followed by several specialised developments including the An-26B ('Curl-A') with palletised cargo handling capability, and the An-26RTR electronic-warfare signals intelligence model ('Curl-B'). A total of some 1,410 An-26 of all versions was built in Kiev before production switched in the later 1980s to the An-32 (described separately). The long-range An-26D conversion of the An-26B, was announced during 1997. Very limited manufacture has also been undertaken by Xian (XAC) in China as the Y7H and Y7H-500, the first flight being made in late 1988. An An-24/An-26 derivative is the An-30 (code-name 'Clank', specifically for aerial survey/mapping duties and earth resources reconnaissance (with a secondary transport capability), and now used by several air forces for 'Open Skies' verification missions. The type first flew in 1974.

CURRENT SERVICE

An-26s of various versions serve with some 35 air arms world-wide, including Afghanistan, Angola, Azerbaijan, Belarus, Benin, Bulgaria, Cambodia, Cape Verde Islands, China, Cuba, Czech Republic, Ethiopia, Hungary, Iraq, Kazakhstan, Laos, Libya, Lithuania, Madagascar, Mali, Mongolia, Mozambique, Nicaragua, Niger, Poland, Romania, the Russian Federation, Slovakia, Syria, Ukraine, Uzbekistan, Vietnam, Yemen, Yugoslavia, and Zambia. Specialist An-30s fly in Afghanistan, Bulgaria, China, Czech Republic, Kazakhstan, Romania, the Russian Federation, and Ukraine. Many Russian 'civil' Aeroflot examples are available for military use. The Angolan and Mozambique An-26s are armed.

SPECIAL FEATURES

An-26s have a single 7.85kN (1,765lb st) Soyuz (Tumansky) RU-19A-300 auxiliary turbojet fitted in the rear of the right-hand engine nacelle for extra take-off thrust and as an APU (introduced in the An-24RT freighter). The An-26's fully pressurised cargo hold has a rear-loading ramp/door, which can, if required, be retracted forwards on rails beneath the fuselage to facilitate direct loading from trucks, or for air-dropping freight. Most An-26s have a prominent bulged window in the left-hand forward fuselage, and the versatility to have their interior layouts altered for specific mission types.

VARIANTS

The **An-26D** long-range model (up to 3,600km, 2,236 miles) has conformal fuel tanks fitted along its fuselage sides. Various VIP-configured, calibration and ambulance An-26 versions also exist with specific interior/equipment layouts. The pressurised **An-30** has a fully glazed nose for its navigator/sensors operator, and a raised cockpit for easier access into the nose. It carries a variety of photographic or survey equipment and related electronics or processing equipment, plus two extra crew members. The Chinese **Y7H/Y7H-500** models have Dongan (DEMC) WJ5E turboprops (of 2,274kW, 3,050shp) and the obligatory single nacelle-mounted RU-19A-300 turbojet.

Antonov An-30 Czech Air Force

Antonov An-32

TWIN-TURBOPROP SHORT/MEDIUM-RANGE FREIGHT/CARGO TRANSPORT

DEVELOPMENT

Derived directly from the widely-used An-26, the An-32 was a re-engined development primarily for 'hot and high' operations with redesigned high-lift control surfaces. The type eventually replaced altogether the An-26 in production, with the initial prototype/development aircraft (including a converted An-26) first flying in 1975. In 1979, Antonov intimated that a production go-ahead for the new aircraft would depend on securing export orders, and these were duly forthcoming with a substantial order from India in 1980. Initially, Indian plans included the assembly/production of An-32s in India, but eventually this idea was dropped and all Indian-operated examples were produced in the then-Soviet Union. Total Indian procurement amounted to 123 examples, and this major boost for the An-32 programme led to export orders from a variety of other air arms around the world, as well as production for the Soviet armed forces. The type received the NATO code name 'Cline'. The ending of the Soviet Union and its European influence saw a considerable decline in orders, and An-32 production had almost completely ended by 1998/99, by which time some 346 examples (excluding prototype/development aircraft) had been built. Production is still available to special order, recent deliveries being made to the Peruvian Army.

Antonov An-32 Indian Air Force

TECHNICAL DATA

Antonov An-32

Powerplants: Two ZMKB Progress (Ivchenko) AI-20D Series 5 turboprops
Developing: 3,810kW (5,109shp)
Driving: four-blade propellers
Span: 29.20m (95ft 9.5in)
Length: 23.68m (77ft 8.25in)
Height: 8.75m (28ft 8.5in)
All-up weight: 27,000kg (59,525lb)
Maximum speed: 530km/h (329mph)
Cruise speed: 470km/h (292mph)
Operational Ceiling: 30,400ft
Maximum range: 2,000km (1,242 miles)
Mission range: 850km (528 miles)
Endurance: approximately 2 hours
Accommodation: Flight crew of three (pilot, co-pilot and navigator) with provision for flight engineer or optional loadmaster; up to 42 paratroops with jumpmaster, or 50 passengers; up to approximately 6,700kg (14,770lb) of freight
Warload: normally none; provision on some aircraft for two racks on each side of the fuselage for small bombs or air-drop containers of up to 500kg (1,102lb) each.
First flown: 1975
Entered service: July 1984

CURRENT SERVICE

Named 'Sutlej' in Indian service, deliveries to India of the An-32 began in July 1984. The type equips six Indian Air Force short/medium-range transport squadrons (currently in the process of some reorganisation), plus some examples used for paratroop and multi-engine pilot conversion training. Military An-32s also serve in differing quantities in the following countries: Afghanistan, Angola, Bangladesh, Croatia, Cuba, Equatorial Guinea, Ethiopia, Peru (including some armed examples), the Russian Federation, and Sri Lanka.

SPECIAL FEATURES

The An-32's more powerful (compared to the An-26) ZMKB Progress turboprops are housed in completely new nacelles with a much higher thrust line giving ground and fuselage clearance for the type's larger propellers. The auxiliary RU-19 turbojet of the An-26 is deleted in the An-32, but an APU is fitted for autonomous operation at austere landing strips. An electrically-powered mobile winch that moves along a rail in the cargo cabin roof is fitted (as also found in An-26 models). Various high-lift devices include triple-slotted wing trailing-edge flaps with automatic leading-edge slats, and a full-span slotted tailplane. The An-26's rear fuselage ventral fins are enlarged on the An-32, and it can operate from unpaved airstrips.

VARIANTS

Most production **An-32s** are to baseline An-32 layout (with provision for various interior configurations to customer choice), although Antonov did reveal a developed and more powerful **An-32B** derivative in the early 1990s, in an attempt to gain further export orders. An **An-32P** fire-bomber has also been marketed. Indian Air Force **'Sutlej'** are very specifically fitted to customer specification, with a high level of Indian-supplied equipment.

Antonov An-32P

Antonov An-72/An-74

TWIN-TURBOFAN STOL TRANSPORT AND MARITIME PATROL AIRCRAFT

An-72 'Coaler'

where the airflow is trapped by the extended flaps and rapidly increases the available lift, giving the An-72 an exceptional STOL performance. Another positive effect of the high-mounted engine is the minimalisation of FOD ingestion from loose semi-prepared runways, for which the undercarriage is optimised with low-pressure types and a twin-wheel nose unit.

VARIANTS

An-72A – the main production freighter version; **An-72P** – the armed maritime patrol version; **An-74** – the freighter version optimised for cold weather operations; **An-72S** – the VIP transport version; **An-72AT** – fitted with internal standard containers; **An-72KT** – the convertible passenger/freight model. Israeli Aircraft Industries are offering an improved An-72P with a glass cockpit, Elta EC/M 2022A radar, Electro Optical observation system and Elisia electronic warfare suite.

DEVELOPMENT

In the mid-1970s, the Antonov design bureau was tasked with designing a STOL aircraft to replace the An-26 in the light/medium tactical transport role. Eight pre-production An-72 'Coaler-A's were produced at the Antonov factory in Kiev. The new aircraft incorporated a high-wing, a T-tail and high-mounted turbofan engines discharging over the upper surface of the wing. The An-72's rear cargo ramp was adapted to that fitted to the An-32, with telescopic struts folding down from the rear of the undercarriage fairing to support the rear fuselage when loading. The high-set wing provided an obstruction-free freight hold, which could also be configured to carry passengers. The first production version, designated An-72A 'Coaler-C' (appearing in the West after the later An-74 'Coaler-B'), had a longer span wing and fuselage compared to the 'Coaler-A' and sold mainly to civilian cargo operators, although a number of aircraft allocated to Aeroflot were actually flown by military crews. Several differnt variants of the 'Coaler-C' were built including a dedicated freighter, an executive transport, air ambulance and a maritime reconnaissance aircraft. This latter variant, designated An-72P, features advanced avionics, a 23-mm cannon in the starboard undercarriage, wing-mounted pylons for air-launched rockets and can also be adapted to carry torpedoes, bombs or mines. The Russian Border

Guards are the sole operator of this variant. The An-74 'Coaler-B' was initially intended as a polar version for operations in the Arctic and Antarctic. Flying in the high-visibility red colour scheme of the Aeroflot Polar Directorate, the aircraft have been used to resupply research stations and for monitoring ice flows. The aircraft can be differentiated from the An-72 by the two observation blisters aft of the flight deck and a larger nose radome. The basic An-74 has spawned a number of variants including a combi passenger/freight version and a VIP transport, none of which has yet attracted a military order. The most radical development was the An-74 'Madcap' AEW platform which flew in prototype form with a rotordome mounted on top of a forward-swept fin and rudder. The aircraft was touted as a lower-cost AWACS system before the project was abandoned in the early 1990s.

CURRENT SERVICE

Transport An-72s serve with the Russian Air Force. The Ukrainian Air Force operates a small number of An-72s and An-74s for dedicated transport tasks. The only other military operator is the Peruvian Air Force, which operates the An-74 'Coaler-B'.

SPECIAL FEATURES

The jet efflux from the high-mounted engines passes over the upper wing instigating the 'Coanda' effect,

---

TECHNICAL DATA

Antonov An-72A 'Coaler-C'

Powerplants: Two ZMDB Progress (Lotarev) D-36 turbofans
Developing: 73.62kN (16,550lb st)
Span: 31.89m (104ft 7.5in)
Length: 28.07m (92ft 1in)
Height: 8.65m (28ft 5in)
Maximum weight: 34,500kg (76,058lb)
Maximum speed: 705km/h (438mph)
Cruising speed: 600km/h (373mph)
Operational ceiling: 38,715ft
Maximum range: 4800km (2,980 miles)
Mission range: 800km (497 miles) with maximum payload
Maximum payload: 10,000kg (22,046lb)
Warload: The An 72P can carry one 23mm gun pod, a UB-23M rocker launcher under each wing and four 100kg (220lb) bombs
First flown: 22 December 1977
Entered service: 1985

Antonov An-72 'Coaler'
Russian Air Force

Antonov An-124 Ruslan

FOUR-TURBOFAN HEAVY-LIFT LONG-RANGE CARGO/FREIGHT TRANSPORT

Antonov An-124 Ruslan

DEVELOPMENT

Developed to provide a long-range heavy-lift cargo capability for Aeroflot and for the Soviet Air Force's long-range transport aviation elements, mainly to replace the turboprop-powered An-22 Antheus, the An-124 grew into the world's largest production

TECHNICAL DATA

Antonov An-124 Ruslan

Powerplants: Four ZMKB Progress (Ivchenko (Lotarev)) D-18T turbofans
Developing: 229.5kN (51,590lb st)
Span: 73.30m (240ft 5in)
Length: 69.10m (226ft 8in)
Height: 21.08m (69ft 2in)
All-up weight: 405,000kg (892,875lb)
Maximum speed: 865km/h (537mph)
Cruise speed: 800km/h (497mph)
Operational ceiling: 31,170ft
Maximum range: 15,700km (9,755miles)
Mission range: 4,500km (2,795 miles)
Endurance: Maximum 20 hours
Accommodation: Pilot and co-pilot, two flight engineers, navigator and radio/communications operator; up to 88 passengers in various seating configurations, and large cargo capacity
Warload: None
First flown: 26 December 1982
Entered service: January 1986 (civil); 1987 (military)

aircraft and first flew in December 1982. Military operations began in 1987 and approximately 27 are believed to have been delivered to what is now the Russian Federation Air Force's Military Transport Aviation (VTA). Some (but not all) of these aircraft wear military markings, while Aeroflot's fleet of civil An-124-100s are available for military tasks. The type received the NATO code name 'Condor' and the Russian name Ruslan, and has broken several world records. It has been very successful in both civil (sometimes in conjunction with Western companies) and military service, but a VTA example crashed into a suburban area of Irkutsk in December 1997 with considerable loss of life, whilst carrying a cargo of Sukhoi Su-27s. Approximately 45 An-124s of all types have been built, and the type has featured in proposals to meet the RAF's Short Term Strategic Airlifter requirement.

CURRENT SERVICE

VTA An-124s serve principally with 566 VTAP (military transport aviation regiment) at Seshcha. The VTA itself is undergoing some reorganisation; between 20 and 25 An-124s are believed to be in VTA service. Two An-124-100s of the Rossiya division of Aeroflot are used on Russian state transport missions as required.

SPECIAL FEATURES

Larger (except in fuselage length) and with more capacity than the USAF's Lockheed C-5 Galaxy, the An-124 can carry up to 150,000kg (330,700lb) internally.

A wide variety of cargo can be carried, including Main Battle Tanks or a complete SS-20 ICBM system. The aircraft's nose hinges upwards around the flight deck for frontal access, via an integral folding ramp, to the huge unobstructed main cargo hold, which also has rear access from ramp-equipped rear-loading fuselage doors. The rear cargo door and whole fuselage attitude can be adjusted on the ground to facilitate loading/unloading directly from vehicles. The passenger cabin is to the rear of the wing attachment in the upper fuselage, and is pressurised – as are the crew stations; the cargo hold is also semi-pressurised. The multi-wheel landing gear allows for operations from semi-prepared surfaces, and the aircraft has full fly-by-wire control systems. Composite materials are used in the aircraft's structure for strength and weight-saving.

VARIANTS

In addition to the standard Russian military **An-124** and the civil derivative (sometimes called the **An-124-100**), several upgraded models have been proposed by Antonov including the provision of Western avionics or re-engining with General Electric turbofans – or even turboprops. A satellite launcher modification and a fire-bomber derivative have also been proposed.

Antonov An-124
Russian Air Force

ASTA Nomad/Searchmaster

TWIN-TURBOPROP STOL MULTI-ROLE LIGHT TRANSPORT AIRCRAFT

DEVELOPMENT

The then Government Aircraft Factory (GAF) concern in Australia, later renamed Aerospace Technologies of Australia (ASTA), began work on the Nomad utility aircraft – with short take-off and landing capabilities – during the mid-1960s. It was to be built in two versions with different fuselage lengths, intended for both civil and military use – the 12-seater N22, and the 17-seat N24. The type's production run lasted until 1984, with a maritime surveillance derivative named Searchmaster and the military-optimised Missionmaster having been added to the range. The N22 formed the basis for the Searchmaster coastal patrol aircraft. Production of the type totalled 172 of all versions.

N24A Searchmaster Royal Thai Navy

CURRENT SERVICE

The Royal Australian Army Aviation Corps uses the N22 Nomad, the fleet being used for both training and utility transport duties, while two further N22s and a single N24A remain on strength with the Royal Australian Air Force's trials unit as utility aircraft. N22B Missionmasters and Searchmasters are flown by the Philippine Air Force; the Indonesian Navy uses 18 Searchmasters, and the Royal Thai Air Force operates the Missionmaster as a counter-insurgency platform. The Papua New Guinea Defence Force is another operator of Nomads and Searchmasters. Numerous Australian civil operators have also adopted the Nomad, among them the legendary Royal Flying Doctors Service and the Coastguard.

SPECIAL FEATURES

The type's impressive STOL capabilities are provided by full-span double-slotted flaps, giving a take-off roll of

only 183m (600ft). All Nomads, Missionmasters and Searchmasters have the same distinctive undercarriage layout, the wheels retracting into sizeable under-fuselage-mounted fairings from which sturdy struts provide extra rigidity for the slab-shaped wing. Also noteworthy is the cockpit's large glazed area. The Searchmaster L is fitted with a distinctive under-fuselage radome that houses the maritime search radar, while the Missionmaster can carry underwing weapon hardpoints. One other notable feature of the type is that it was the first fixed-wing aircraft to incorporate the Allison 250-B powerplant, an engine normally utilised only by helicopters, including the Bell JetRanger.

VARIANTS

The N22 was developed into the strengthened N22B with a higher payload, while the N24 Commuterliner

added a further five seats. Versions of the N24 have included the Cargomaster freighter and Medicmaster aerial ambulance. Two derivatives of the basic design have been produced – the Missionmaster military transport with drop doors in the cabin floor, and wing hardpoints which can carry up to 909kg (2,000lb) of stores such as rocket pods or gun packs; and the Searchmaster, built in two different versions. The Searchmaster B uses a Bendix RDR-1400 surveillance radar mounted in the nose, while the Searchmaster L is equipped with a Litton APS-504(V)2 radar giving 360 deg coverage from an under-belly radome.

TECHNICAL DATA

ASTA N22B Searchmaster L

Powerplants: Two Allison 250-B17C turboprops
Developing: 313kW (420eshp)
Driving: Three-blade propellers
Span: 16.52m (54ft 2.3in)
Length: 12.56m (41ft 2.4in)
Height: 5.52m (18ft 1.5in)
All-up weight: 3,855kg (8,500lb)
Maximum speed: 311km/h (193mph)
Cruise speed: 258km/h (161mph)
Operational ceiling: 21,000ft
Maximum range: 1,353km (840 miles)
Endurance: Up to 8 hours
Accommodation: Two crew and 12 passengers or a cargo load of up to 1,931kg (4,250lb). Normal crew complement of one or two pilots, a tactical navigator and one or two observers.
Warload: Four underwing hardpoints can carry up to 910kg (2,000lb) between them – although this capability is rarely used. Royal Thai Air Force aircraft have been armed with pintle-mounted machine guns as mini-gunships.
First flown: 23 July 1971 (N24A)
Entered service: 1975

N22 Missionmaster Royal Thai Air Force

Atlas Cheetah

SINGLE TURBOJET SINGLE-SEAT STRIKE FIGHTER AND TWO-SEAT CONVERSION/OPERATIONAL TRAINER — SOUTH AFRICA

DEVELOPMENT

The Atlas Cheetah project began as a South African rebuild/upgrade of several different marks of French-built Dassault Mirage III. The programme arose when South Africa was subject to UN arms embargo and forced to upgrade existing weapons, or make its own; it included upgrades to Mirage III single and two-seat models previously supplied from France. Still shrouded in secrecy, the programme eventually also seemingly included Israeli-built Kfirs – themselves derived from the Mirage III – which Atlas (now Denel) rebuilt to Cheetah standard. The Cheetah programme was revealed in 1986 and the type became operational in 1987, initially with two-seat Cheetah Ds (assumed to be ex-Mirage IIIDZ and D2Z) and later included the single-seat Cheetah E (ex-Mirage IIIEZ) fighter and Cheetah R (ex-Mirage IIIRZ/R2Z) reconnaissance aircraft. After a period of SAAF service, some of these models are now mainly withdrawn from service. Currently

Cheetah E South African Air Force

operational with the SAAF are single-seat Cheetah C fighters and Cheetah D two-seaters. The Cheetah Cs have apparently originated from elsewhere, and it appears that the 38 Cheetah Cs that were produced are either IAI Kfirs rebuilt in South Africa and delivered between 1992 and 1995, or former Mirages from other sources. Some current Cheetah Ds may also be former Kfirs. A proposed Cheetah ACW (Advanced Combat Wing) derivative with wingtip-mounted air-to-air missiles was not proceeded with.

CURRENT SERVICE

Most currently-active SAAF Cheetahs serve with No 2 'Flying Cheetahs' Squadron at Louis Trichardt. This nominally includes a strength of some 36 Cheetah Cs, plus a number of Cheetah Ds, possibly a single Cheetah R and again possibly some Cheetah Es. One Cheetah C is usually operated by the SAAF's Test Flight and Development Centre at Bredasdorp. The SAAF Cheetah fleet will be retired from approximately 2002 and replaced by the Saab/BAE Systems JAS 39 Gripen.

SPECIAL FEATURES

The Cheetah has the classic tailless delta layout of the Mirage III family, but the current operational Cheetah is an amalgam of South African and Israeli experience

in upgrading and improving the basic Mirage III design, including Israeli knowledge from its Kfir programme.

VARIANTS

The basic, original extensive **Cheetah** upgrade programme included lower wing re-skinning and possibly re-sparring; the addition of a new, drooped, dog-tooth wing leading edge and small wing fences; and the addition of fixed canard foreplanes to the intake sides. The nose was lengthened to allow room for avionics equipment (and drooped, with long strakes added, on the two-seater), and a starboard-side removable in-flight refuelling probe was added beside the cockpit. About 50% of the airframe was re-built and zero-lifed. Mainly Israeli avionics were fitted, including Elbit HUD and nav/attack system with inertial navigation, plus provision for HOTAS operation and sighting via a South African-produced helmet-mounted sight. Some Cheetahs have an Israeli Elta radar; upgraded/two-seat models have the more powerful Atar 09 K-50 turbojet.

SEE ALSO: ENAER PANTERA, DASSAULT MIRAGE III/V/50, IAI DAGGER & IAI KFIR

TECHNICAL DATA

Atlas Cheetah E

Powerplant: One SNECMA Atar 09 C-3 turbojet
Developing: 60.8kN (13,670lb st) with afterburning
Span: 8.22m (26ft 11.5in)
Length: 15.65m (51ft 4.25in) (including nose probe)
Height: 4.55m (14ft 11.25in)
Maximum speed: 2,338km/h (1,453mph)
Cruise speed: 956km/h (594mph)
Operational ceiling: 55,775ft
Maximum range: undisclosed
Mission range: undisclosed
Endurance: undisclosed
Accommodation: Single pilot in Cheetah E and C; instructor (in rear seat) and trainee pilot in Cheetah D
Warload: Two internal DEFA 30mm cannons in lower fuselage/intakes. Approximately 4,000kg (8,818lb) of external stores on up to seven removable underwing/underfuselage attachments for two fuel tanks, up to eight 227kg (500lb) free-fall bombs, laser-guided bombs or AS.30 air-to-surface missiles; outer underwing pylons can carry Armscor V3B Kukri, or V3C Darter air-to-air infra-red homing missiles.
First flown: 1986 (Cheetah D)
Entered service: July/August 1987 (Cheetah D)

Cheetah E South African Air Force

847

42

Atlas Impala

SINGLE TURBOJET TWO-SEAT BASIC TRAINER, AND ADVANCED TRAINER/LIGHT ATTACK AIRCRAFT — **SOUTH AFRICA**

Atlas Impala Mk1 South African Air Force

DEVELOPMENT

A licence-built derivative of the Aermacchi MB.326 (described separately), the Impala was built by the Atlas Aircraft Corporation in South Africa in two distinct models: the Impala Mk1 (MB.326M), which approximated to the basic trainer models of the two-seat MB.326, but with light attack capability; and the Impala Mk2, a close derivative of the single-seat

TECHNICAL DATA

Atlas Impala Mk1

Powerplant: One Rolls-Royce (Bristol Siddeley) Viper 11 Mk22 turbojet
Developing: 11.12kN (2,500lb st)
Span: 10.56m (34ft 8in)
Length: 10.67m (35ft 0in)
Height: 3.72m (12ft 2.5in)
All-up weight: 3,450kg (7,600lb)
Maximum speed: 806km/h (501mph)
Cruise speed: 770km/h (478mph)
Operational Ceiling: 41,000ft
Maximum range: 1,665km (1,035 miles)
Mission range: 920km (572 miles)
Endurance: up to 2.25 hours
Accommodation: Instructor and trainee pilot (instructor in rear seat)
Warload: up to approximately 907kg (2,000lb) of external stores on up to six underwing attachments for various gun, cannon and unguided rocket pods (including two AN/SUU-11A/A General Electric Minigun 7.62mm machine-gun packs, or two Matra 361 37mm FFAR rocket packs), light bombs up to 227kg (500lb), two Nord/Aérospatiale AS.11 missiles, reconnaissance pods, two Del Mar towed targets, or napalm tanks
First flown: 10 December 1957 (original MB.326); 11 May 1966 (Atlas-built)
Entered service: 3 June 1966 (Mk1); 22 April 1974 (Mk2)

armed light attack MB.326K. South Africa selected the MB.326 for indigenous production in 1964 by the then-new Atlas Aircraft Corporation at Kempton Park, Transvaal, and the first deliveries were made to the South African Air Force in June 1966. Sixteen Aermacchi component 'kits' initiated production, followed by some 40 aircraft with part-Italian, part-South African components, after which production mainly included South African parts. The final Impala Mk1 was delivered in August 1974, 151 having been built. One hundred Impala Mk2s were also produced, starting with seven complete aircraft supplied by Aermacchi (MB.326KCs), followed by 15 'kits' of parts leading to full indigenous production by Atlas. Impala Mk2 production ended in the early 1980s. Around six SAAF squadrons plus several training schools operated the Impala, the type seeing considerable action over Angola and what is now Namibia. Cameroon recently became the second country to operate Impalas.

CURRENT SERVICE

Although the South African Air Force's Impala Mk1s are being increasingly edged out by the Pilatus PC-7 MkII Astra, the type continues in the pilot training role with No 85 Combat Flying School at Hoedspruit. This unit also has some Impala Mk2s on strength for advanced training and combat indoctrination/weapons

training. Impala Mk2s (plus some Mk1s) also equip the SAAF's No 8 Squadron at Bloemspruit in the light attack role. Between 20 and 30 Mk2s are believed to remain in service. Surplus South African Impalas were supplied to Cameroon in 1996 and 1997. Included were two two-seat Impala Mk1s, and four Impala Mk2s.

SPECIAL FEATURES

Ideally suited to pilot training/weapons training and light attack missions, the simple but rugged Impala has excellent handling characteristics and is able to sustain substantial combat damage yet return safely to base.

VARIANTS

Early **Impala Mk1s** were powered by the Viper 11 Mk22 turbojet, but later machines appear to have received the more powerful (15.17kN/3,410lb st) Viper 20 Mk540 as fitted in the Aermacchi MB.326G series. **Impala Mk2s** also utilised this powerplant rather than the Viper Mk632-43 turbojet of the MB.326K. The single-seat Impala Mk2s have different avionics from their Italian-made counterparts and can carry a wide variety of weapons on their six underwing pylons (up to a maximum of 1,814kg (4,000lb)), some of these being of South African design or manufacture.

SEE ALSO: AERMACCHI MB.326

Atlas Impala Mk2 South African Air Force

Atlas/Denel Oryx

TWO-TURBOSHAFT MULTI-ROLE TRANSPORT HELICOPTER

TP-1 Oryx South African Air Force

TECHNICAL DATA

Atlas/Denel Oryx

Powerplants: Two Topaz (licence-built Turboméca Makila 1A1) turboshafts
Developing: 1,400 kW (1,877 shp), emergency rating
Driving: Four-blade main rotor, five-blade tail rotor
Main rotor diameter: 15.0m (49ft 2.5in)
Fuselage length: 14.06m (46ft 1.5in)
Height: 5.14m (16ft 10.25in)
All-up weight: 8,400 kg (18,518 lb)
Maximum speed: 305km/h (189mph)
Cruise speed: 263km/h (163mph)
Operational ceiling: 23,500ft
Maximum ferry range: 830km (515 miles)
Mission range: 561km (348 miles)
Endurance: up to 3.25 hours
Accommodation: Three crew (pilot, co-pilot and flight engineer); up to 16 fully equipped troops in main cabin, or freight as required
Warload: None; provision for armed versions as required – using detachable weapons pylons.
First flown: 1986 (XTP-1 Beta programme)
Entered service: 1991

DEVELOPMENT

Created during the UN arms embargo on South Africa, which caused the South Africans to develop their own weapons systems, the Oryx (originally called Gemsbok) was designed as a medium-lift transport helicopter partly to replace South African Air Force Super Frelon and (later) Puma helicopters. The Oryx is effectively a Eurocopter Puma/Super Puma derivative, with engine and transmission similar to the indigenously-designed Atlas/Denel Rooivalk combat support/attack helicopter. The Gemsbok project commenced in the late 1980s and existed alongside the Rooivalk programme. The Puma-derived Atlas XTP-1 Beta project provided important data for the Gemsbok/Oryx as well as being a significant part of the whole Rooivalk development effort. Atlas was eventually contracted for 50 production Oryx plus one actual prototype, and production Oryx were possibly based on Romanian-manufactured Puma components. The Oryx entered SAAF service in

1991, and the final production aircraft was delivered in May 1996. The type serves mainly in the tactical transport and SAR roles, but can also be based on warships and has been used by the South Africans in support of ship-based Antarctic operations. The Oryx has been offered for export and as a Puma upgrade programme, a possible export/indigenous production contender being Malaysia.

CURRENT SERVICE

South African Air Force Oryx (sometimes called TP-1 Oryx) partly equip four squadrons, alongside other types: No 15 at Durban, No 17 at Swartkort, No 19 at Louis Trichardt and No 22 at Ysterplaat (Cape Town) in the tactical role. The latter has a secondary fire-fighting/civil defence role and for providing helicopters to naval ships and SAR missions. SAAF Oryx were heavily involved in the rescue of civilians during the massive flooding in Mozambique during early 2000.

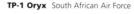

TP-1 Oryx South African Air Force

SPECIAL FEATURES

The Oryx is basically a re-engineered Puma with Super Puma/Cougar features, and excellent hot and high performance. The tailplane is of a new design and composites are used where possible throughout construction. Increased fuel can be carried in the main undercarriage sponsons or within the fuselage, and for ship-borne operations the main rotor blades fold and full corrosion protection is included. Modernised/updated avionics package options include a night vision goggle-capable layout, and provision for single-pilot operation. A 2,500 litre (550 Imp gal) fire-fighting 'bucket' can be carried beneath the fuselage. Similarly, a 272 kg (600lb) hydraulic rescue hoist can be fitted to the fuselage side as required.

VARIANTS

Several armament package options have been tested, partly a throw-back to the XTP-1 development/test programme. These include a 20mm cannon turret in the forward fuselage/nose, with unguided rockets, anti-tank missiles, and air-to-air missiles mounted on short wings/pylons extending from the fuselage sides. Related guidance systems would be fitted for these weapons, and if required a specific weapons officer station would be included with related avionics and an extra crew member.

SEE ALSO: AEROSPATIALE SA330 PUMA, IAR-330 PUMA & WESTLAND PUMA

Atlas/Denel Rooivalk

TWO-TURBOSHAFT COMBAT SUPPORT/ATTACK HELICOPTER

SOUTH AFRICA

AH-2A Rooivalk South African Air Force

TECHNICAL DATA

Atlas/Denel AH-2A Rooivalk
Powerplants: Two Turboméca Makila 1K2 turboshafts
Developing: 1,573kW (2,109shp) each, emergency rating
Driving: Four-blade main rotor, five-blade tail rotor
Main rotor diameter: 15.58m (51ft 1.5in)
Fuselage length: 16.39m (53ft 9.25in) (including tail rotor))
Height: 5.185m (17ft 0.25in)
Maximum weight: 8,750kg (19,290lb)
Maximum speed: 309km/h (192mph)
Cruise speed: 278km/h (173mph)
Operational ceiling: 20,000ft
Maximum ferry range: 1,335km (829 miles)
Mission range: 940km (584 miles)
Endurance: up to 5hr
Accommodation: Two crew (weapons officer/co-pilot in front, pilot behind and above)
Warload: One 20mm Armscor F2 cannon in steerable chin mounting linked to gunner's helmet-mounted sight display. Maximum of 2,032kg (4,480lb) on six hardpoints beneath helicopter's stub wings. Up to 16 Denel ZT6 Mokopa laser-guided anti-tank missiles on inner four pylons, or two or four M159 19-round rocket pods for Forges de Zeebrugge FZ90 70-mm rockets. Two or four air-to-air missiles (eg. Mistral or other IR homing) on outer pylons.
First flown: 27 February 1986 (XH-1); 11 February 1990 (XH-2); November 1996 (EDM)
Entered service: November 1998/January 1999

DEVELOPMENT

Conceived when South Africa was subject to UN arms embargo, the Rooivalk was designed to meet a South African Air Force need for a combat support/attack helicopter, mainly to succeed Alouette III gunships then in service. Design of the XH-2 Rooivalk (Red Kestrel) started in 1984, and drew on experience with two initial South African attack helicopter projects, the Alouette III-based Atlas XH-1 Alpha and the Puma-derived Atlas XTP-1 Beta. The Rooivalk project used similar engines, rotor system and transmission to the SA 330 Puma, but was otherwise an all-new design. The prototype first flew in February 1990. The ending of conflict with South Africa's neighbours led to defence cutbacks and a temporary curtailment to the Rooivalk project. Atlas (Denel Aviation from 1996) continued with the venture, and flew a second prototype (for avionics and weapons development) in 1992 and later a third. An SAAF order was finally placed, in July 1996, for 12 CSH-2 Rooivalks (re-designated AH-2A in 1998). A long-term need for 36 exists, with the possibility of extending the initial production run to 20 examples.

CURRENT SERVICE

The SAAF's No 16 Squadron at Bloemspruit was re-activated in January 1999 to operate the Rooivalk, and received its first example that month. Initial deliveries had been made to the SAAF in November 1998. The squadron is due to be fully operational in late 2000, with the possibility of a second squadron forming.

SPECIAL FEATURES

The Rooivalk has a classic attack helicopter layout with a narrow, armoured tandem-seating fuselage and a strong, high impact absorption main landing gear. The rotor blades and part of the fuselage structure are made from composite materials, and heat/IR signature suppressors are fitted to the exhausts with particle separators on the intakes. Originally intended to have locally-produced Topaz engines, production examples have Turboméca Makila 1K2 turboshafts as standard. The nose-mounted gyro-stabilised turret contains forward-looking infrared, a low-light television camera and a laser range-finder. Crew helmet-mounted sights are standard.

VARIANTS

A possible maritime version was unveiled in 1998 with chin-mounted search radar and navalisation features including folding main rotor blades, plus anti-ship missiles including Penguin or Exocet. Submissions based on the basic Rooivalk layout have been made to meet attack helicopter requirements in Britain, Malaysia, Australia (RedHawk), Singapore and Turkey.

AH-2A Rooivalk South African Air Force

ZU - AHC

Avions de Transport Régional ATR-42/72

TWIN-TURBOPROP TRANSPORT AND PATROL AIRCRAFT

DEVELOPMENT

In October 1981, Aeritalia (now Alenia) of Italy and France's Aérospatiale joined forces to develop and build a new series of twin-turboprop regional airliners, under the Avions de Transport Régional banner. The ATR-42 (so named owing to its seating capacity) was the first, being followed by the 64-74 seat stretched ATR-72, powered by the PW124 engine, which first flew in 1989. Both have proved extremely successful, the high wing layout allowing for a capacious, high-roofed cabin. ATR has proposed several variants of interest to military operators, but only recently has the type received any orders for service applications. Most significant of these is the ATR-42MP Surveyor maritime patrol aircraft, which is based on the ATR-42-400 platform.

CURRENT SERVICE

Two ATR-42s are currently in service with the Italian Guardia di Finanza, with 2 Gruppo Aereo Esplorazione Aeromarittima at Practica di Mare, the first production ATR-42MP Surveyor having been received by the GdiF during December 1999. This has been specially modified for long-range maritime patrol. A second aircraft, a standard transport version, was already in use by the service, but is now to re-enter service following conversion to Surveyor standard. In addition, a single ATR-42F freighter was sold to the Gabonaise Air Force.

SPECIAL FEATURES

A wide array of sensor equipment is carried by the ATR Surveyor, including a long-range 360° surveillance radar mounted in the aircraft's belly (distinguishable by a small black radome), a TV/infrared turret on the back of the starboard main gear sponson (steerable by a crew operator) and, forward of that, a searchlight

ATR-42MP Surveyor

sponson. Large bubble windows are fitted for lookout purposes, and cameras can be mounted in these windows. In addition, the port main gear sponson can carry a 23mm gun pod. A large forward cargo door and aft para/supply-dropping door are also fitted, and the interior is of 'quick-change' configuration to allow operation in such roles as troop transport, medical evacuation and even VIP transport. Belly radome and FLIR turret are fitted on the starboard side of the main undercarriage fairing.

VARIANTS

The **Surveyor** was not the first version to be offered for military use. Prior to that, an earlier maritime

patrol derivative of both the ATR-42 and 72 was proposed, named **Petrel**, but it received no orders. Likewise, the **ATR-52C Milfreighter**, developed from the ATR-72 platform and featuring a rear loading door and ramp, was never purchased. However, a single **ATR-42F** freighter, this version having a strengthened floor, was purchased for military use by Gabon, fitted with a port side cargo door.

TECHNICAL DATA

**Avions de Transport Régional
ATR-42MP Surveyor**

Powerplants: Two Pratt & Whitney Canada PW127E turboprops
Developing: 1,789kW (2,400shp)
Driving: Six-blade propellers
Span: 24.57m (80ft 7.5in)
Length: 22.67m (74ft 4.5in)
Height: 7.6m (24ft 10.75in)
All-up weight: 17,900kg (39,462lb)
Maximum cruising speed: 490km/h (303mph)
Operational ceiling: 25,000ft
Maximum range: 1,612km (1.002 miles)
Endurance: Up to 8 hours
Accommodation: Flight crew of three plus additional workstations
Warload: Provision for external load attachments on the fuselage. Weapons and stores for anti-ship and anti-submarine roles.
First flown: 16 August 1984 (ATR-42 prototype); 27 October 1989 (ATR-72)
Entered service: 15 December 1999 (ATR-42MP)

ATR-42 French Air Force

BAC One-Eleven

TWIN-ENGINED SHORT/MEDIUM-RANGE TRANSPORT

DEVELOPMENT

The BAC One-Eleven dates back to a 1956 Hunting Aircraft project for a 32-seat transport with turbojet propulsion. Hunting was eventually acquired by the British Aircraft Corporation (BAC) and the aircraft was later put into production as the BAC 111 – later named One-Eleven. The first commercial flights were flown on 9 April 1965 with British United Airways, followed by Braniff on 25 April 1965. The 500 Series entered regular service with British European Airways on 1 November 1968. In the early 1980s, British Aerospace (BAe) concluded arrangements for the type to be built in Romania as the Rombac (later Romaero) One-Eleven for both export and domestic markets, but the programme fell short of expectations – only 19 were built before production terminated in the mid-1990s. Almost all One-Eleven production went to commercial operators, but some went to the Royal Australian Air Force and the Brazilian Air Force. Northrop used a One-Eleven for system development on the YF-23 Advanced Tactical Fighter programme in the early 1990s.

BAC One-Eleven UK DERA

CURRENT SERVICE

The only current military operators are Oman and the UK. Three One-Eleven 485GDs serve as transports with the Royal Air Force of Oman. A handful of former One-Eleven airliners have been acquired by DERA for work with the Empire Test Pilots School (ETPS) and for various test requirements at Boscombe Down.

SPECIAL FEATURES

The One-Eleven has a low-set wing incorporating Fowler-type flaps on its trailing edge and air brakes/spoilers on its upper surfaces forward of the flaps, with rear-mounted pod engines and a T-tail. The Oman Series 485s have forward freight doors, quick change interiors and rough field capability. Integral

rear stairs are a standard fitting. An APU is fitted in the tailcone.

VARIANTS

Series 200 – original short version, of which 56 were built; **Series 300** – with Spey 511 turbofans, increased payload and range (nine aircraft built); **Series 400** – incorporated modifications to meet US requirements with more powerful engines and an increase in gross weight, 69 being produced; **Series 500** – with fuselage stretch of 2.45m (8ft 4in), increased wingspan, more powerful engines and able to accommodate up to 119 passengers, 87 being built; **Series 475** – the final

variant intended for operations to and from smaller airports or in 'hot and high' conditions. Two special variants were built as executive aircraft, but many earlier versions were subsequently converted with VIP interiors. A Romanian development – the **Romaero Airstar 2500**, with Rolls-Royce Tay turbofans – did not come to fruition.

BAC One-Eleven UK DERA

TECHNICAL DATA

BAC One-Eleven Series 475/500

Powerplants: Two Rolls-Royce Spey 512DW turbofans
Developing: 55.83kN (12,550lb st)
Span: 28.50m (93ft 6in)
Length: 32.61m (107ft 0in)
Height: 7.47m (24ft 6in)
All-up weight: 47,400kg (104,500lb)
Maximum speed: 871km/h (541mph)
Cruise speed: 742km/h (461mph)
Operational ceiling: 35,000ft
Maximum range: 2,745km (1,705 miles)
Accommodation: Crew of two and up to 89 passengers (119 in 500 Series)
Warload: None
First flown: 20 August 1963 (Series 200); 9 June 1964 (Series 203); 19 July 1965 (Series 400); 7 February 1968 (Series 500)
Entered service: 9 April 1965 (BUA); 1969 (Brazilian Air Force)

BAC Strikemaster

SINGLE JET ADVANCED TRAINER AND LIGHT ATTACK AIRCRAFT

Strikemaster Mk 82 Sultan of Oman Air Force

DEVELOPMENT

The BAC Strikemaster was the ultimate development of the Hunting Jet Provost, which began life as a jet development of the piston-engined Percival Provost. The Jet Provost proved to be a highly successful trainer, selling in large numbers to the RAF and overseas air arms. As a private venture, BAC developed the Jet Provost into the Strikemaster – a tactical multi-role aircraft able to fly both pilot and weapon training sorties, in addition to performing light-attack and reconnaissance roles. The BAC Strikemaster was virtually an armed version of the RAF's Jet Provost

T5, which had a redesigned longer nose and a larger and deeper canopy. A more powerful version of the Viper engine was fitted. The airframe was reinforced for operations in rigorous environments. Side-by-side Martin Baker Mk PB4 ejector seats were installed and a comprehensive suite of navigation/communications equipment – including VOR/ILS, DME and TACAN – was fitted. The Strikemaster appealed to smaller air arms because of its ability to conduct light attack missions, counter-insurgency combat operations and reconnaissance, in addition to advanced pilot training. It was exported to Ecuador, Kenya, Kuwait, New Zealand, Oman, Saudi Arabia, Singapore, Sudan and South Yemen. Total production was 146, all but ten of which were built as Mk 80s. Sudan took delivery of ten Mk 90s in 1984. Many Strikemasters have seen prolonged active service – the 20 in service in Oman have sustained substantial battle damage.

CURRENT SERVICE

Strikemasters now only survive in service with the

Ecuadorean Air Force's Escuadrón de Combat at ALA 23, HQ Base Aérea 'Alfaro' at Manta and with No 1 Squadron, the Royal Air Force of Oman, at Misirah.

SPECIAL FEATURES

The Strikemaster has a short landing gear suitable for operations from rough strips, fixed wingtip tanks (of 48 Imp Gal – 218 litres) and a pressurised and air-conditioned cockpit. Its armament made it particularly suitable for counter-insurgency combat operations, for which it can be fitted with self-sealing fuel tanks and armour plate. It can be equipped with two Beagle reconnaissance pods, each containing a Vinten F.95 70mm camera.

VARIANTS

Strikemasters were supplied to Ecuador (**Mk 89**), Kenya (**Mk 87**), Kuwait (**Mk 83**), New Zealand (**Mk 88**), Oman (**Mks 82/82A**), Saudi Arabia (**Mks 80/80A**), Singapore (**Mk 84**) and Sudan (**Mk 55**) – but all versions were basically identical.

TECHNICAL DATA

BAC Strikemaster Mk 80

Powerplant: One Rolls-Royce (Bristol Siddeley) Viper 535 turbojet
Developing: 15.2kN (3,413lb st)
Span: 11.23m (36ft 10in)
Length: 10.27m (33ft 9in)
Height: 3.10m (10ft 2in)
All-up weight: 5,215kg (11,500lb)
Maximum speed: 775km/h (480mph)
Operational ceiling: 40,000ft
Maximum range: 2,224km (1,382 miles)
Mission range: 445km (277 miles)
Accommodation: Crew of two, side-by-side
Warload: Two internal 7.62mm FN machine guns. External ordnance up to 1,360kg (3,000lb) on four underwing hardpoints – including rockets, bombs, gun and cannon pods and reconnaissance pods
First flown: 26 October 1967
Entered service: 1968 (Saudi Arabia)

Strikemaster Mk 82 Sultan of Oman Air Force

BAC VC10

BAC VC10 C1K Royal Air Force

DEVELOPMENT

Design of the VC10 began in 1956, resulting from a British Overseas Airways Corporation (BOAC) requirement for a jet airliner capable of serving on its routes to Africa, the Far East and Australia. The new airliner featured four rear-mounted Conway turbofans, a T-tail, and an advanced wing with complex high-lift features. The modification of the Vickers (BAC) VC10 airliner into a military transport gave the RAF useful passenger and long-range cargo-carrying capacity, and 14 were ordered by the RAF, produced at a lower cost compared with the development of a new aircraft. By the late 1960s, the RAF was flying 27 VC10 flights a month to the Far East, via the Persian Gulf. In 1978, a programme commenced to convert VC10s to tankers, to augment the existing Victor tanker fleet. Five ex-Gulf Air standard VC10s were converted to VC10 K2s and four Super VC10 Series 1154s from East African Airways to VC10 K3 standard. In the late 1980s, five ex-British Airways Super VC10s were converted to short-range K4s. All conversion work was undertaken by BAe at Filton, Bristol. In the early 1990s, the RAF decided to convert 13 C1s to C1K configuration.

CURRENT SERVICE

Eleven BAC VC10 C1Ks serve with No 10 Squadron at RAF Brize Norton and nine VC10 K3/K4s with No 101 Squadron, also at Brize Norton. Some of the fleet are deployed in support of operations in the Gulf and based at Muharraq, Bahrain, and one with 1312 Flight at Mount Pleasant, Falkland Islands for the refuelling of RAF Tornado F3s.

SPECIAL FEATURES

The VC10 K2/3 conversion involved the installation of extra fuel tanks in the cabin, with three hose drum units – two under the wings, and one under the rear fuselage. A closed circuit TV system is fitted to enable the flight crew to monitor refuelling operations. The K4 is similar to the K3 with the standard wing and fin fuel tankage, but without cabin fuel tanks. The C1Ks are fitted with Loral Matador IRCMs. All marks have a nose refuelling probe to enable them to take on additional fuel whilst in the air.

VARIANTS

The **VC10 C1K**, with primary transport and secondary tanker roles, has a standard VC10 fuselage, with the refinements of the Super VC10. The **VC10 K2** is a tanker conversion of the standard airliner, whilst the **K3** is a Super VC10 conversion, having a 3.96m (13ft) longer fuselage. The **K4s** are five additional Super

TECHNICAL DATA

BAC VC10 C1K

Powerplants: Four Rolls-Royce Conway 301 turbofans
Developing: 96.67kN (21,800lb st)
Span: 44.55m (146ft 2in)
Length: 48.36m (158ft 8in)
Height: 12.04m (39ft 6in)
All-up weight: 146,510kg (323,000lb)
Maximum speed: 953km/h (581mph)
Cruise speed: 885km/h (548mph)
Operational ceiling: 42,000ft
Maximum range: 6,275km (3,900 miles)
Accommodation: Flight crew of two pilots and flight engineer and up to 150 passengers or cargo
Warload: None
First flown: 29 June 1962; 26 November 1965 (RAF)
Entered service: 7 June 1966 (C1); May 1984 (K2); 1985 (K3); 1993 (K4)

VC10s, converted in the early 1990s, which do not have main deck fuel tanks.

BAC VC10 K3 Royal Air Force

BAE Systems (Hawker Siddeley) Hawk/ Hawk 100

TWO-SEAT ADVANCED TRAINER AND LIGHT ATTACK AIRCRAFT

Hawk 127 Royal Australian Air Force

TECHNICAL DATA

BAE Systems Hawk 100

Powerplant: One Rolls-Royce Turboméca Adour 871 turbofan
Developing: 27.0kN (6,030lb st)
Span: 9.94m (32ft 7in)
Length: 12.43m (40ft 7in)
Height: 3.98m (13ft 1in)
All-up weight: 9,100kg (20,062lb)
Maximum speed: 1,038km/h (645mph)
Operational ceiling: 44,500ft
Maximum range: 1,495km (928 miles)
Mission range: 510km (316 miles)
Accommodation: Crew of two, in tandem
Warload: Centreline 30mm Aden cannon (optional). AIM-9 Sidewinder AAMs. Up to 3,000kg (4,828lb) of external ordnance - including rocket pods, bombs and cluster bombs.
First flown: 21 August 1974 (Hawk T1)
Entered service: October 1976 (Hawk T1, RAF); 11 April 1980 (Hawk 100, Kenya)

DEVELOPMENT

Since entering service with the Royal Air Force, the Hawk has become a global success story and it has benefitted from an ongoing development programme to enhance its capabilities. The Hawk T1/T1A is the RAF's principal Advanced Flying and Tactical Weapons Training aircraft, and of 176 T1s delivered to the RAF, 88 were modified for the secondary air defence role (as the T1A) and these can be equipped with AIM-9 Sidewinders. The Hawk 100 is a two-seat lightweight fighter and advanced weapons system training aircraft with ground attack capability, suitable for Lead-In Fighter Training, Navigator, and Weapons System Operator training. Equipped with a seven-station combat wing, and a state-of-the-art avionics system, the Hawk 100 can perform operational missions comparable to those of more sophisticated front line combat aircraft, but at a fraction of the cost. An upgrade programme is underway on the Hawk T1, which involves the replacement of the rear and central fuselage (Mod 2010). The new fuselage section (Mk 65A) incorporates all the fatigue enhancements made by BAE Systems from the experience gained in developing its later series of Hawks. The weapons training role of the aircraft has been enhanced with

the addition of a Gun Sight Video Recording System (GRVS). The system comprises a video camera that films the view through the pilot's Head-Up Display (HUD) and records onto video tape instead of 'wet' film, as is currently used.

CURRENT SERVICE

Hawk 100 Series aircraft serve with the air arms of Brunei, Finland, India, Indonesia, Kenya, Kuwait, Malaysia, Oman, South Korea, Switzerland, United Arab Emirates and Zimbabwe. It is shortly to enter service with the Royal Australian Air Force, the Canadian Government – for NATO Flying Training in Canada (NFTC) – and the South African Air Force.

SPECIAL FEATURES

The Hawk 100 has a seven-station combat wing with combat manoeuvre flaps; an advanced cockpit layout with Multi-Function Displays (MFD) and Hands-on-Throttle and Stick (HOTAS); optional nose-mounted FLIR and/or laser sensors and a fin-mounted Radar Warning Receiver (RWR). Its long endurance and excellent fuel economy make the Hawk 100 an ideal aircraft for patrolling shipping lanes and offshore oil and gas installations.

VARIANTS

The **Hawk T1** was the initial version of the Hawk; the **Hawk 50**, first flown on 17 May 1976, fully exploited the basic Hawk design and introduced a limited ground attack capability of the type; the **Hawk 60**, first flown on 1 April 1982, incorporated further design refinements, increased weight and uprated Mk861 Adour turbofan; the **Hawk 100** is a lightweight fighter and advanced weapons system trainer; **Hawk LIFT** is a further subsequent change to the avionics suite and associated aircraft system of the Hawk 100 series – this being the Hawk Lead-In Fighter Trainer (LIFT), a cost-effective pilot training system, capable of producing high calibre aircrew for future front line operational service.

SEE ALSO: BAE SYSTEMS HAWK 200 AND MCDONNELL DOUGLAS T-45 GOSHAWK

Hawk T1 Royal Air Force

BAE Systems Hawk 200

SINGLE-SEAT LIGHTWEIGHT MULTI-ROLE COMBAT AIRCRAFT

Hawk 208 Royal Malaysian Air Force

TECHNICAL DATA

BAE Systems Hawk 200

Powerplant: One Rolls-Royce/Turboméca Adour Mk871 turbofan
Developing: 26.85kN (6,030lb st)
Span: 9.39m (30ft 9.75in);
9.94m (32ft 7in) with missiles
Length: 11.35m (37ft 3in)
Height: 3.98m (13ft 1in)
All-up weight: 9,100kg (20,061lb)
Maximum speed: 1,065km/h (661mph)
Cruise speed: 1,021km/h (633mph)
Operational ceiling: 45,000ft
Maximum range: 2,390km (1820 miles)
Mission range: 1,335km (829 miles)
Accommodation: Pilot only
Warload: Four underwing pylons capable of 3,495kg (7,700lb) of ordnance. Centreline 30mm Aden cannon. Wingtip rails allow carriage of four Sidewinder or similar AAMs.
First flown: 19 May 1986; February 1992 (200 RDA)
Entered service: 15 August 1994 (Oman)

DEVELOPMENT

The international success of the two-seat Hawk variants enabled British Aerospace to develop a single-seat version which would attract new customers, especially smaller air arms that required a relatively cheap air superiority fighter and ground attack aircraft – often to replace ageing Hunters. Large drop-tanks, each holding 130 Imp gal, eliminated the need for costly structural changes to increase fuel capacity within the fuselage. The Hawk 200 also benefitted from the aerodynamic and structural changes developed for the Hawk 60 Series. With the design of the Hawk's fuselage to accommodate a single cockpit and the addition of a modern radar, there is room to fit a pair of integral 25mm Aden cannon under the cockpit floor – which represents a significant increase in its combat capability. The Hawk 200 has about 80% commonality with the two-seat models. It has air-to-air refuelling capability, an extensive air-to-air and air-to-surface weaponry, and is now equipped with state-of-the-art avionics systems – which includes the Northrop Grumman APG-66H multi-mode radar in a

new nose – similar to those being fitted to more expensive front line combat aircraft. The excellent performance combines high levels of manoeuvrability with care-free handling in all regimes of flight, even when heavily armed. It can operate in the maritime support role in excess of 300nm. The Hawk 200's versatile weapons carrying capability makes it ideally suited for close air support.

CURRENT SERVICE

The Hawk 200 is in service with the following air arms: Indonesia – Hawk 209s with Squadron Udara 1 at Abdulrachman Saleh and Udara 12 at Pekanbaru; Malaysia – Hawk 208s for the advanced/weapons training role (replacing A-4PTMs) with Nos 6, 9 and 15 Squadrons at Kuantan, Lubuan and Butterworth respectively; and Oman – 12 Hawk 203s with No 6 Squadron at Masirah.

SPECIAL FEATURES

Enlarged nose to accommodate nose-mounted radar. Chaff/flare dispenser at base of fin. Fin is taller than

on other Hawk variants. The Hawk 200 has fuselage-mounted tailplane vanes or SMURFS (Side-Mounted Unit, horizontal tail Root Fins) as developed for the US Navy's T-45 Goshawk. It has an advanced wing with leading edge droop for improved manoeuvrability and combat manoeuvre flap setting, full-span flaps and wing-tip rails for air-to-air missiles. The advanced cockpit layout with Multi-function Displays (MFD) and Hands-on-Throttle-and-Stick (HOTAS) controls.

VARIANTS

The different mark numbers refer to the countries to which the Hawk 200 has been exported. The Radar Development Aircraft (RDA) version is fitted with the APG-66H radar – as used in the F-16 Fighting Falcon.

SEE ALSO HAWKER SIDDELEY/BAE SYSTEMS HAWK 100 AND MCDONNELL DOUGLAS/BAE SYSTEMS T-45 GOSHAWK

Hawk 203 Sultan of Oman Air Force

١٢١ 131

Beech 33/35/36 Bonanza

SINGLE PISTON-ENGINED TRAINING/ COMMUNICATIONS AIRCRAFT

F33C Bonanza Mexican Air Force

DEVELOPMENT

To meet the projected growth in the general aviation market, particularly in the USA, in the immediate post-war period, Beech designed an all-metal low-wing four-seat monoplane designated Model 35 Bonanza. The aircraft featured a distinctive V-tail and embodied much of the advances in aviation technology gained during the war years. The initial design spawned a whole family which included the conventionally tailed Model 33 Bonanza/Debonair and also the Model 36 Bonanza. These variants offered improvements over the initial Model 35 – whether in range, performance or capacity (some variants are configured for six persons). The most popular variant in military service has been the Model 33 in both F33A standard and F33C aerobatic forms. Most operators have now retired

the Bonanza but the aircraft remains in service with a small number of air arms, mainly in the training and ad hoc communications role.

CURRENT SERVICE

Bolivia: the College of Military Aviation operates a number of different types of aircraft including V35/36 Bonanzas. The aircraft have generally been acquired following confiscation in drug-related prosecutions; Colombia: the Colombian Navy operates two B33 Bonanzas in the general communications role; Cote d'Ivoire: operates four aerobatic F33C Bonanzas for basic training and liaison duties; Germany: Deutsche Luftwaffen Ausbildungsstaffel, based in the USA at Tuscon, Arizona, undertakes primary training for future Luftwaffe pilots on civilian-registered F33 Bonanzas; Indonesia: F33A Bonanzas are operated by Skwadron Udara (RON) 200 of the Naval Aviation Service as basic trainers; Iran: around 26 F33A/C Bonanzas remain in service as trainers with the Iranian Air Force's Flying

Training School; Mexico: 40 F33C Bonanzas are currently utilised by the Mexican Air Force Flying School for basic training; Spain: Grupo 42 of the Spanish Air Force operates 25 F33A/C Bonanzas as refresher trainers and communications aircraft, known locally as E.24As and Bs.

SPECIAL FEATURES

The original Model 35 set new standards in terms of quality of build and production when it entered service in the late 1940s. The F33C is strengthened to allow basic aerobatic manoeuvres to be flown.

VARIANTS

The **QU-22B** had special avionics equipment under the USAF's 'Pave Eagle' program and was deployed in Vietnam to pick up and relay to a ground station the data transmitted from acoustic sensors. The **Model PD249** was a close-support two-seat armed version of the A36 to meet the requirements of the USAF's 'Pave Coin' competition - but did not enter production.

TECHNICAL DATA

Beech F33A Bonanza

Powerplant: One Teledyne Continental IO-520-B flat-six piston engine
Developing: 213kW (285hp)
Driving: Two-blade propeller
Span: 10.20m (33ft 5.5in)
Length: 7.77m (25ft 6in))
Height: 2.51m (8ft 3in)
All up weight: 1,452kg (3,400lb)
Maximum speed: 336km/h (209mph)
Economical cruise speed: 253km/h (157mph)
Operational ceiling: 17,500ft
Range: 803km (499 miles)
Accommodation: Student and instructor, or pilot and three passengers
First flown: 22 December 1945 (Model 35 prototype)
Entered service: 1946 (Spain)

F33A/E.24A Bonanza Spanish Air Force

Beech T-34 Mentor & Turbo Mentor

SINGLE PISTON-ENGINED/TURBOPROP BASIC AND PRIMARY TRAINER/LIGHT ATTACK AIRCRAFT

T-34C Turbo Mentor Indonesian Air Force

TECHNICAL DATA

Beech T-34C Turbo Mentor
Powerplant: One Pratt & Whitney Canada PT6A-25 turboprop
Developing: 533kW (715shp) (torque limited to 298kW – 400shp)
Driving: three-blade propeller
Span: 10.16m (33ft 4in)
Length: 8.75m (28ft 8.5in)
Height: 3.02m (9ft 11in)
All-up weight: 1,950kg (4,300lb)
Maximum speed: 414km/h (256mph)
Cruise speed: 396km/h (246mph)
Operational ceiling: 30,000ft plus
Maximum range: 1,311km (814miles)
Mission range: 790km (491miles)
Endurance: approximately 3.5 hours
Accommodation: Instructor and pupil in tandem
Warload: up to 544kg (1,200lb) of ordnance
First flown: 2 December 1948 (Model 45 Mentor); 21 September 1973 (first YT-34C prototype)
Entered service: November 1977 (T-34C)

DEVELOPMENT

Developed as a private venture from the ultimately highly successful Beech Bonanza light civil aircraft, the prototype Model 45 (later called Mentor) first flew in December 1948, and three service test examples were ordered by the US Air Force for delivery in 1950. Designated T-34A, and powered by the 167.8kW (225hp) Continental O-470-13 piston-engine, the USAF eventually ordered 450 production examples, 100 being Canadian-built. Deliveries began in 1953/1954. During 1954, the US Navy also selected the Mentor for its basic training needs, and 423 were delivered from 1954/1955 as the similarly-powered T-34B. The Mentor was also a major export success, and production licences were granted to Canada (Canadian Car and Foundry Ltd), Argentina (FMA), and Japan (Fuji). Surplus USAF aircraft were also assigned to other countries in the early 1960s. Fuji subsequently developed its own versions of the Mentor, including the KM, KM-2 and further models. In 1972/1973, the US Navy initiated a study into the possible development of the basic T-34. The turboprop-powered T-34C Turbo Mentor resulted, with updated avionics, increased fuel and various airframe changes. The first prototype flew in September 1973, and 353 were built for the US Navy, with the last being delivered in 1990. An armed export derivative for

armament system and tactical strike training, plus forward air control and counter-insurgency operations, the T-34C-1, was also produced. Some 1,533 Mentors and Turbo Mentors of all types were built.

CURRENT SERVICE

Piston-engined Mentors still serve in several countries, including Argentina (T-34A, Air Force – 30 being modernised locally by LMSA); Colombia (T-34A/B, Air Force); Dominican Republic (T-34B); Japan (Air Self-Defence Force – Fuji-built derivative); Uruguay (T-34A and B, Air Force and Navy); and Venezuela (VT-34A, Air Force). The US Navy's large fleet of T-34C Turbo Mentors serve with VT-27 and VT-28 at Naval Air Station Corpus Christi, Texas; VT-2, VT-3 and VT-6 at NAS Whiting Field, Florida; and VT-4 and VT-10 at NAS Pensacola, Florida. The US Army and US Marine Corps also operate a small number of T-34Cs. Export Turbo Mentors (including the T-34C-1) serve with the Argentine Navy (several were lost during the Falklands Conflict in 1982); Algeria; Ecuador (Air Force and Navy); the Gabonese Presidential Guard; Indonesia (Air Force); Morocco (Air Force); Peru (Navy); Uruguay (Navy); and Taiwan - the latter's Air Force operating around 40 examples in its Air Academy at Kangshan. Fuji-built T-5 turboprop-powered derivatives serve with Japan's naval forces.

SPECIAL FEATURES

Differing from the civil four-seat Bonanza, from which it grew by having a slimmer fuselage with the classic tandem two-seat dual-control military primary trainer layout, the Mentor also adopted a conventional tail rather than the Bonanza's original famous 'V'-tail. Basically all metal in construction, Mentors were stressed for aerobatic manoeuvres up to +10g, and the later Turbo Mentors featured much structural strengthening compared to the piston-engined Mentor.

VARIANTS

The **T-34C-1** armed Turbo Mentor has four underwing pylons for up to 544kg (1,200lb) of ordnance, and a gunsight and weapons controls in the front cockpit. Weapons include small bombs, minigun and rocket pods, incendiary bombs, or AGM-22A anti-tank missiles. The type can also tow targets.

Beech T-34C Turbo Mentor
United States Navy

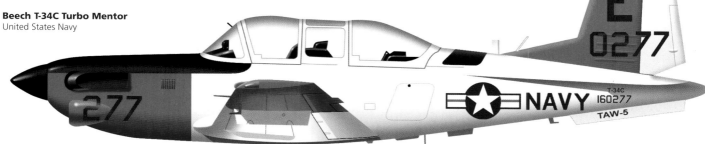

Beech 55 Baron/T-42A Cochise

TWIN PISTON-ENGINED LIGHT TRANSPORT AND MILITARY TRAINER

Beech E.20 Spanish Air Force

DEVELOPMENT

Launched in 1960, the highly-successful Model 95-55 Baron was derived from the Beech Model 95 Travel Air of the mid/late 1950s. The prototype Model 95-55 flew in February 1960, and the type gained immediate civil sales success, leading to a variety of gradually developed and improved models, beginning with the Model 95-A55 Baron of 1962. In February 1965, the US Army selected the Model 95-B55 Baron as the winner of its competition for an 'off-the-shelf' design to fulfil a requirement for a twin-engined fixed-wing instrument trainer. Produced as the Model 95-B55B, 65 were procured as the T-42A Cochise, with deliveries commencing to the US Army in September 1965. In 1971, a further five T-42As were ordered for delivery to the Turkish Army under US Military Assistance Programme (MAP) arrangements. Turkey also later received three further T-42As, these being ex-US Army machines. Seven T-42As were supplied to the Spanish Air Force in 1972, where the type became known as the E.20; these are believed to be ex-US Army aircraft, but 12 Model 95-B55 Barons were also later supplied to Spain (the latter eventually joining the Spanish civil register). Manufacture of the final Model 95-55 Baron (a Model 95-E55) was completed in the early 1980s, when 3,726 Barons of the Model

55 series had been built. Continuing development of the Baron family led to the Model 56 series (93 delivered), and thence to the Model 58 Baron which was introduced in 1969. This new model included pressurised and turbo-supercharged derivatives, with the basic Model 58 continuing in production well into the 1990s – more than 1,700 of this version being built.

CURRENT SERVICE

The US Army's surviving T-42As were finally retired some years ago. However, the Spanish Air Force's E.20 fleet currently numbers four active T-42As, which operate on refresher training, light communications and liaison tasks with 421 Escuadrón at Getafe. The Turkish Army's equally long-lived T-42A fleet currently numbers four or five examples, operated at the Army's aviation school near Ankara for twin-engine and instrument training, plus light VIP transport duties. Very small numbers of Barons of various different types also currently serve with the military or with paramilitary organisations in Bolivia, Chile, Mexico, Pakistan, Paraguay and Venezuela.

SPECIAL FEATURES

Of simple and robust all-metal construction, the Beech Baron series was one of the longest-standing and most

successful of US light-twin civil types; its suitability as a military light transport and trainer has been proven in the longevity of the T-42As still in service.

VARIANTS

The **Model 95-55 Baron**, a more powerful derivative of the Model 95 Travel Air, benefited from aerodynamic improvements and more advanced avionics, including full blind-flying instrumentation. The US Army's **T-42A Cochise** had customer-specified avionics, including a comprehensive nav-aids fit for its intended primary role. Later models introduced successively more powerful engines and many detail improvements, leading to the considerably altered **Model 58 Baron** series.

TECHNICAL DATA

Beech T-42A Cochise

Powerplants: Two Continental IO-470-L piston engines
Developing: 194kW (260hp)
Driving: Three-blade propellers
Span: 11.53m (37ft 10in)
Length: 8.31m (27ft 3in)
Height: 2.92m (9ft 7in)
All-up weight: 2,313kg (5,100lb)
Maximum speed: 380km/h (236mph)
Cruise speed: 314km/h (195mph)
Operational ceiling: 19,700ft
Maximum range: 1,970km (1,225 miles)
Mission range: approximately 644km (400 miles)
Endurance: 2.5 hours
Accommodation: Pilot and co-pilot (or instructor pilot and pupil) side-by-side, with seating for two other occupants side-by-side behind front seats
Warload: None
First flown: 29 February 1960 (original Model 95-55 prototype)
Entered service: 2 September 1965 (T-42A)

Beech Baron 58 Paraguayan Air Force

Beech 65 / 80 Queen Air

TWIN PISTON-ENGINED LIGHT TRANSPORT AND MILITARY TRAINER

DEVELOPMENT

The successful and long-running Queen Air family of civil piston-engined transports was developed to meet increasing demands in the US for a well-equipped twin-piston-engined business/executive aircraft. The type was derived from the already-successful Beech Model 50 Twin Bonanza, and the first prototype flew in August 1958. The initial basic Model 65 was followed by the improved Model A65 (introduced in 1967), while the first example of the refined and more powerful Model 80 had by then already flown (in August 1961). The latter led to the related Models A80 and B80. With rearrangement of the basic interior layout, a number of Queen Airliner derivatives were also produced, with up to ten/eleven seats. The Model 88 was a piston-engined pressurised equivalent of the initial turboprop Model 90 King Air, a type that was itself derived from the success of the Queen Air line. Specific military models of the Queen Air included the L-23F Seminole light transport, over 70 of which were built for the US Army up to 1963; these were redesignated as U-8Fs in 1962. The Queen Air also gave rise to the initial models of the Beech U-21 family of light transport/cargo and special mission aircraft for the US Army, these being a hybrid with the Model 90 King Air. In addition, many Queen Airs of various different versions entered military service as virtual 'off-the-shelf' purchases, an early military customer being Japan. Production of the final Model B80s was completed in 1977/1978, by which time well over 1,000 Queen Airs (including military models) had been built.

CURRENT SERVICE

The US Army's U-8F Seminoles and early U-21 Queen Air derivatives were withdrawn from service some time ago. Amongst the oldest current military Queen Airs are the surviving two or three Queen Air Model A65s of the Uruguayan Air Force's Escuela Militar de

Beech Queen Air 65 Uruguayan Air Force

Aeronáutica at Pando. In addition, military/paramilitary Queen Airs of a wide variety of models are currently active in Algeria, Argentina, Colombia, the Dominican Republic, Ecuador, Peru and Venezuela. Recent reports suggest that the last Japanese Queen Airs have now been retired. Israeli aircraft were due for replacement by Socata TB.20 Trinidads, although a number of U-21A/ RU-21As are believed to remain in service.

SPECIAL FEATURES

One of a number of successful 1950s & 1960s designs that established Beech as one of the USA's premier aircraft manufacturers, the all-metal Queen Air introduced airliner standards to the small transport/business type of civil aircraft with such refinements as full all-weather instrumentation and a range of optional equipment. The type has proven eminently suitable for light transport and training with its varied military operators.

VARIANTS

The early **Model 65 Queen Airs** retained a layout similar to the Model 50 Twin Bonanza, with a distinctive rounded fin/rudder shape. Aerodynamic improvements led to the swept vertical tail surfaces of all later models, and some changes in exterior dimensions. A wide variety of internal seating arrangements, equipment levels and powerplants were included in the Queen Air line.

TECHNICAL DATA

Beech Model A65 Queen Air

Powerplants: Two Lycoming IGSO-480-A1E6 piston engines
Developing: 254kW (340hp)
Driving: Three-blade propellers
Span: 13.98m (45ft 10in)
Length: 10.82m (35ft 6in)
Height: 4.34m (14ft 3in)
All-up weight: 3,493kg (7,700lb)
Maximum speed: 385km/h (239mph)
Cruise speed: 275km/h (171mph)
Operational ceiling: 31,300ft
Maximum range: 2,670km (1,660 miles)
Mission range: approximately 1,287km (800 miles)
Endurance: approximately 4.5 hours
Accommodation: Crew of one or two on flight deck, four to seven passengers depending on required seating arrangements
Warload: None
First flown: 28 August 1958 (original Model 65 prototype)
Entered service: late 1959 (Model 65); 1967/1968 (Model A65)

Beech Queen Air Ecuadorean Air Force

Beech 90 King Air & T-44A Pegasus

TWIN-TURBOPROP LIGHT TRANSPORT AND MULTI-ENGINE PILOT TRAINER

TC-90 King Air Japanese Maritime Self-Defence Force

TECHNICAL DATA

Beech T-44A Pegasus
Powerplants: Two Pratt & Whitney Canada PT6A-34B turboprops
Developing: 410 kW (550shp) (flat-rated)
Driving: Three-blade propellers
Span: 15.32m (50ft 3in)
Length: 10.82m (35ft 6in)
Height: 4.33m (14ft 2in)
All-up weight: 4,377kg (9,650lb)
Maximum speed: 445km/h (276mph)
Cruise speed: 401km/h (249mph)
Operational ceiling: 29,500ft
Maximum range: 2,344km (1,456 miles)
Mission range: approximately 1,471km (914 miles)
Endurance: 3 hours
Accommodation: Pilot and trainee pilot on flight deck with full dual controls; seating for between four and eight passengers in main cabin depending on specific variants
Warload: None
First flown: January 1964 (initial true King Air prototype)
Entered service: 5 April 1977 (T-44A)

DEVELOPMENT

The pressurised, turboprop-powered Model 90 King Air was a logical follow-on to the successful Model 65 Queen Air family. The original Queen Air-derived development aircraft first flew in 1963, and the initial Model 90-type King Air first flew in January 1964. American military procurement began with an NU-8F development aircraft, leading to the unpressurised Queen Air-derived U-21 Ute King Air derivatives, which served with the US Army from 1967 in light transport and electronic-warfare roles, in numerous versions. The main US military user now is the US Navy, which selected the Model 90 in 1976 to fulfil its VTAM(X) multi-engine pilot trainer requirement; sometimes called the H90 King Air and designated T-44A, this version is a hybrid Model C90/E90, and 61 were procured from 1977. The Japanese also use a Model C90 derivative, the TC-90, for multi-engine and instrument training. Various King Air Models have been used by a variety of other countries for

many transport and training tasks. Continuing development of the King Air line led to the Model 100 King Air which first flew in March 1969. The US Army procured five advanced pressurised Model A100s during 1971 as the U-21F. The type has similarly gained a number of overseas military export sales. Over 1,864 Model 90 King Airs of all types had been built by the mid-1990s, plus some 388 Model 100 King Airs.

CURRENT SERVICE

Approximately 57 surviving US Navy T-44A Pegasus aircraft serve with VT-31 'Wise Owls' at Naval Air Station Corpus Christi, Texas, on multi-engine pilot training for the US Navy and the other US armed services. The Japanese Maritime Self Defence Force operates 27 TC-90 King Airs with the 202nd Kokutai at Tokushima; several naval UC-90/LC-90 King Airs perform liaison duties. A Bombardier-led private consortium uses eight Model C90As for contract multi-engine flying training for the Canadian Armed

Forces' Air Command at the Southport Aerospace Centre, Manitoba. Model 90 King Airs of various different marks additionally serve with the armed forces of Bolivia, Chile, Colombia, Mexico, Paraguay, Peru, and Venezuela. Military-operated Model 100 King Airs fly in Chile, Ecuador, Jamaica, Morocco and Tanzania. The US Army's handful of U-21Fs have recently been loaned to the US Navy at NAS Patuxent River, Maryland, for test pilot training.

SPECIAL FEATURES

The basically all-metal, pressurised (except for US Army U-21s) Model 90 King Airs and their later developments share generally similar construction and configuration, with various different engine power-ratings options and equipment levels. The type is well suited to light military transport and training requirements.

VARIANTS

The hybrid **T-44A** includes a near-standard commercial avionics package but with customer-specified additions including UHF and TACAN. Its PT6A-34B turboprops are flat-rated from 559kW (750shp). Some military King Airs are configured as VIP transports. The pressurised **Model 100 King Air** (compared to the **Model 90**) has increased internal capacity, a lengthened fuselage, reduced wingspan, altered tail surfaces and twin-wheel main undercarriage. A choice of engines was available (as in the Model 90 family).

C90 King Air 300 Colombian Air Force

Beech/Raytheon 200/300/350 Super King Air & C-12

TWIN-TURBOPROP LIGHT TRANSPORT/VIP AND ELECTRONIC-WARFARE AIRCRAFT

USA

Beech RC-12K United States Army

TECHNICAL DATA

Beech C-12F (Model B200C)

Powerplants: Two Pratt & Whitney Canada PT6A-42 turboprops
Developing: 634 kW (850shp)
Driving: three-blade propellers
Span: 16.61m (54ft 6in)
Length: 13.34m (43ft 9in)
Height: 4.57m (15ft 0in)
All-up weight: 5,670kg (12,500lb)
Maximum speed: 545km/h (339mph)
Cruise speed: 523km/h (325mph)
Operational ceiling: 35,000ft
Maximum range: 3,658km (2,273 miles)
Mission range: 2,205km (1,370 miles)
Endurance: approximately 4 hours
Accommodation: Pilot and co-pilot on flight deck; seating for six to eight passengers in main cabin, up to a maximum of 13
Warload: None
First flown: 27 October 1972
Entered service: July 1975 (C-12A); May 1984 (C-12F)

DEVELOPMENT

Derived from the outstandingly successful Model 90 King Air family and the later Model 100 King Air, the first prototype Model 200 layout first flew in October 1972. In addition to becoming a highly successful civil aircraft in business use and with commuter airlines, the type has found world-wide military use. The first military operator was the US Army in 1974 with the RU-21J (Model 200); this were the first of a major series of electronic-warfare derivatives of several distinct Model 200 versions for the US Army under the later RC-12 designation. In July 1975, the first C-12A (Model A200) joined the US military, the start of a long line of transport derivatives of different Model 200 versions including the important C-12F and related models. Several specialist versions of the Model 200 have also been marketed, including the radar-equipped Model B200T Maritime Patrol derivative. The most recent Model 200 development is the improved Model 300 and the Raytheon Beech Model 350, ordered by the US Army as the C-12S (Model 350) and several overseas customers. US military procurement of the Model 200 Super King Air currently totals 380 of all versions.

CURRENT SERVICE

The US Air Force's C-12 transports continue to serve various diverse operators including some US Embassy

flights, but a large batch of them was transferred to the US Army in 1995. The US Navy and Marine Corps Super King Airs serve on various communications, transport, base flight, and missile range surveillance duties; several US Navy UC-12Bs (unofficially TC-12Bs) serve alongside Beech T-44A Pegasus aircraft with VT-31 'Wise Owls' at Naval Air Station Corpus Christi, Texas, on multi-engine pilot training for the US services. US Army RC-12 electronic-warfare models are mainly operated within the US Army's Intelligence and Security Command, and with units such as the 1st Military Intelligence Battalion at Wiesbaden, Germany with RC-12D and RC-12K 'Guardrail' aircraft. Model 200, 300 or 350 Super King Airs are also operated in a variety of military versions in Algeria, Argentina, Australia, Bolivia, Cambodia, Chile, Colombia, Ecuador, Egypt, France, Germany, Guatemala, India, Ireland, Israel, Japan (including Model 350/LR-2 transport/ reconnaissance), Macedonia, Malaysia, Morocco, New Zealand, Papua New Guinea, Peru, Saudi Arabia, South Africa, Sri Lanka, Sweden, Thailand, Togo, Turkey, Uruguay, and Venezuela.

SPECIAL FEATURES

The 'top of the range' in turboprop business and executive aircraft, the Super King Air is a major departure from the previous King Airs, with increased

wingspan, lengthened and altered fuselage, 'T'-tail, increased fuel capacity, improved pressurisation, and higher specification performance.

VARIANTS

There are detail changes between individual **Model 200** versions, including more powerful PT6A turboprops and provision for cargo doors. The latest **C-12S** (Model 350) is a slightly stretched and more powerful derivative with winglets, and seating for up to 15 passengers in a quick-change cargo/transport layout. The extensively modified US Army **RC-12** family, including the **'Guardrail'** and **'Guardrail Common Sensor'** models, carry many external dipole and blade antennae and wingtip pods, and are packed with electronics for communications interception and battlefield signals intelligence.

Beech C-12R United States Army

Beech/Raytheon 1900

Beech C-12J US Army

DEVELOPMENT

An enlarged derivative of the highly successful King Air/Super King Air family, design of the 19-seat Beech 1900 pressurised civil commuter airliner commenced in 1979, and the first prototype flew in September 1982. The basic production model was the 1900C (sometimes called 'Airliner'); initial civil deliveries were made in February 1984. It was followed by the 1900C-1 with altered fuel capacity. Approximately 248 total production examples of both types were built. These were followed by the 1900D which first flew in March 1990 and is the current production model, featuring a deeper fuselage with greater internal headroom and volume, more power and various other changes. In the late 1980s, the USAF began replacing transport/support Air National Guard-operated Convair C-131 Samaritans with the Fairchild C-26 under the ANG Support Turboprop Aircraft (ANGOSTA) programme, and also acquired six Beech 1900Cs, designated C-12Js, within this plan. The first examples were obtained in autumn/winter 1987. These duly served with various ANG squadrons as required, but some have recently been assigned to regular USAF units and two to the US Army. Military

export orders include 12 1900C-1s for Taiwan, all delivered during 1988, and eight specially-configured 1900C-1s for Egypt: the latter comprising six Elint and two maritime patrol aircraft, delivered from October 1988. More recently, two 1900C-1s were acquired by the Royal Thai Army. The 1900D is available in transport and special mission models; the US Army acquired one 1900D in early 1997.

CURRENT SERVICE

The original six-aircraft US military C-12J fleet continues to be reshuffled as required. Recent USAF deployments include one aircraft with the 46th Test Wing at Eglin AFB, Florida, and three assigned to Pacific Air Forces (3rd Wing at Elmendorf AFB, Alaska, and the 51st Fighter Wing at Osan Air Base, South Korea). One of the two US Army C-12Js has flown for HQ US European Command at Stuttgart, Germany. The sole US Army C-12J/1900D-model recently served with the Chemical and Biological Defense Command at the Aberdeen Proving Ground in the US. The Thai and most of the Egyptian 1900C-1s remain in regular service, while the 11 surviving Taiwanese Air Force 1900C-1s (one was written off in August 1990) are

split between the Air Force's VIP squadron (usually based at Sungshan) and the transport training element of the Air Academy at Kangshan.

SPECIAL FEATURES

The basically all-metal, pressurised 1900 has a classic low-wing twin-engine commuter airliner layout, with considerable versatility in interior layout for different seating/cargo designs to customer choice. The type is a suitable basis for a low-cost but effective Elint and maritime patrol platform, with sufficient space and on-board power for the equipment and crew to perform those missions.

VARIANTS

Most Beech 1900s in military service are in a standard configuration. The Egyptian-operated maritime patrol **1900C-1s** have Litton sea-search radar and various ESM equipment; the Elint equipment aboard the other Egyptian aircraft is undisclosed.

TECHNICAL DATA

Beech C-12J (Model 1900C/C-1)
Powerplants: Two Pratt & Whitney Canada PT6A-65B turboprops
Developing: 820 kW (1,100shp)
Driving: Four-blade propellers
Span: 16.61m (54ft 5in)
Length: 17.63m (57ft 10in)
Height: 4.54m (14ft 10in)
All-up weight: 7,530kg (16,600lb)
Maximum speed: 474km/h (295mph)
Cruise speed: 435km/h (271mph)
Operating ceiling: 25,000ft
Maximum range: 2,775km (1,725 miles)
Mission range: 1,471km (914 miles)
Endurance: approx 3.5 hours
Accommodation: Pilot and co-pilot, and up to 19 passengers in standard seating arrangement, 12 to 15 in VIP style layout, or cargo configuration, depending upon mission requirements
Warload: None
First flown: 3 September 1982 (first Model 1900 prototype)
Entered service: September 1987

Beech C-12J United States Army

Beech/Raytheon T-1A Jayhawk/Beechjet 400T

TWIN-ENGINED BUSINESS JET AND TRAINER

T-1A Jayhawk United States Air Force

DEVELOPMENT

In December 1985, the Diamond II executive jet (which first flew in August 1978) was acquired from Mitsubishi by the Beech Aircraft Corporation, initially built as the Beech 400 it was made from kits supplied by the

TECHNICAL DATA

Beech T-1A Jayhawk

Powerplants: Two Pratt & Whitney Canada JT15D-5B turbofans
Developing: 12.9kN (2,900lb st)
Span: 13.25m (43ft 6in)
Length: 14.75m (48ft 4in)
Height: 4.24m (13ft 11in)
All-up weight: 7,157kg (15,780lb)
Maximum speed: 854km/h (531mph)
Cruising speed: 835km/h (517mph)
Operational ceiling: 41,000ft
Maximum range: 3,575km (2,222 miles)
Accommodation: Two crew plus instructor seat and a further four seats for students in the cabin
First flown: September 1989
Entered service: January 1992

Japanese company. The aircraft was entered by Beech for the USA SUPT (specialised undergraduate pilot training) system competition for a tanker/transport training system (TTTS). The jet pilot was previously trained on the T-37 followed by the T-38, but this process involved all single pilot/one man flying, with no crew participation. The use of the TTTS system gives a training system more representative of the flying that the pilot will experience operationally. Pilots then go on to fly transports such as the C-17, C-141, C-5, KC-10 and KC-135. For this role, the executive jet was beefed up in some areas to be able to withstand bird strikes at low-level and to counter low-level flying stresses. Manufacture of the range is now undertaken by Raytheon.

CURRENT SERVICE

The Jayhawk first entered service with the USAF in January 1992 and the last of 180 was delivered on 23 July 1997. The following are the main operators:-
12th Flying Training Wing (FTW), 99th Flying Training Squadron (FTS) at Randolph AFB; 14th FTW/48th FTS at Columbus AB, 47th FTW/86th FTS at Laughlin, the 71st FTW with 32th FTS at Vance AFB, and finally the

340th Flying Training Group with four squadrons, the 5th, 43rd, 96th & 97th. The Japan Air Self Defence Force has also taken delivery of a number of 400Ts (equivalent to the T-1A), as a basis for a transport aircrew trainer (designated T-400).

SPECIAL FEATURES

An off-the-shelf basic small executive jet which has been adapted to the TTTS role to replace the T-38 and other single seat aircraft as part of the training package. The redesign to the training role has permitted the avionics and systems to be cabin mounted so that they are easy to maintain. The cabin now only seats four, usually students awaiting their turn at instruction.

VARIANTS

Beechjet 400T: equivalent to the J-1A Jayhawk for Japan Self Defence Force to train pilots and refresh other multi engine crews; **Beech T-1A Jayhawk:** the USAF TTTS trainer for transport and bomber crews.

T-1A Jayhawk United States Air Force

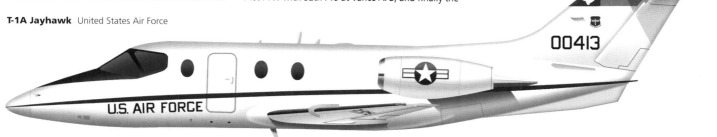

Bell 47 Sioux

SINGLE PISTON-ENGINED UTILITY HELICOPTER

Bell 47G Hellenic Air Force

DEVELOPMENT

The first truly mass-produced helicopter, the Bell Model 47 entered production shortly after the end of World War II and remained in continuous production by Bell for 28 years, before the last example was built in 1973. A classic design, the Model 47 was the first helicopter to obtain an Approved Type Certificate and a total of over 5,000 were eventually built in a wide range of military and civil variants. Characterised by its large glass 'bubble' fuselage and open structure tailboom, the Model 47 entered service with the USAAF in 1947 as the Model 47A. Subsequently ordered in large numbers by the US Army as the H-13 Sioux, the type was adapted for a plethora of roles that included observation, light transport, communications, training, VIP transport and casualty evacuation. It gained particular fame in the latter role during the Korean War, operating as H-13C/Ds, with an external litter

mounted on either side of the fuselage. The aircraft was also deployed by the US Army as an observation aircraft during the Vietnam War. The definitive helicopter of its era, the Model 47 was operated by all the US air arms and also by the air arms of over 40 other nations. Agusta of Italy, Kawasaki of Japan and Westlands of Great Britain all licence-built the type (the latter under sub-licence from Agusta) and the aircraft remains in service (albeit in much reduced numbers) around the world.

CURRENT SERVICE

Bell 47s remain in service with some 12 air arms around the world today the majority of which are engaged in the training and communications roles. The current operators are: Colombia, Dominican Republic, Greece, Lesotho, Libya, Malta, New Zealand, Pakistan, Paraguay, Tanzania, Uruguay and Zambia.

SPECIAL FEATURES

The Bell Model 47 offers both crew members superb visibility as the cockpits is almost entirely surrounded by glass. Later versions incorporated a whole host of improvements and modifications including more powerful engines, float-equipment, solid tail booms and wheeled undercarriage.

VARIANTS

Model 47: prototype and 11 service test aircraft for USAAF evaluation, powered by Franklin O-335-1 engine; **YR-13**: 28 test and evaluation aircraft for the USAAF and US Navy; **YR-13A**: Three YR-13s modified for cold weather operations; **H-13B**: US Army variant similar to Model 47D with four-wheeled undercarriage; **H-13C**: modified H-13Bs with skid undercarriage and external stretcher carriers; **H-13D**: similar to H-13C but with more powerful Franklin O-335-5 engine; **H-13E**: dual-control version with new tail and rotor gear box; **XH-13F**: experimental version with Turboméca Artouste turbine engine; **H-13G**: military version of Model 47G with improved elevator surfaces and increased fuel capacity; **H-13H**: more powerful Lycoming VO-435-23 engine, new skid undercarriage and all-metal rotor blades – equivalent to Model 47G-2; **H-13J**: VIP version of Model 47J with three-seat interior and enclosed tail boom; **H-13K**: fitted with Franklin 6VS-O-335 engine and larger diameter rotor; **OH-13S**: three-seat observation version with extended tail boom and rotor blades; **TH-13T**: two-seat trainer with additional avionics and tinted plastic 'bubble'; **HTL-1**: US Navy designation for transferred YR-13s; **HTL-2**: US Navy equivalent of H-13B; **HTL-3**: trainer equivalent of Model 47E; **HTL-4**: Higher payload version of Model 47D; **HTL-5**: similar to the HTL-4 but powered by Franklin O-335-5 engine; **HTL-6**: US Navy version of H-13G, which could be fitted with float kits; **HTL-7**: US Navy training version of Model 47J with all-weather instruments, covered tail boom and modified engine; **HUL-1**: Model 47J for utility and ice-breaker patrol duties; **HUL-1G**: US Coast Guard version for SAR duties; **HUL-1M**: experimental version of HUL-1 powered by Allison YT-63-A-3 turbine engine. Other air arms operated a host of 'civilian' variants including the **Model 47D**, **Model 47G** and **Model 47J**. Many second-hand ex-US armed forces examples were also acquired by a number of military operators. Agusta-built versions were designated **AB-47** and Westland assembled a number of these for the British Army as the **Sioux AH1**.

TECHNICAL DATA

Bell 47G-5

Powerplant: One Avco Lycoming VO-435-B1A six-cylinder piston engine
Developing: 198kW (265 hp)
Driving: Twin-blade main and tail rotors
Main rotor diameter: 11.32m (37ft 1.5in)
Fuselage length: 9.90m (32ft 6in)
Height: 2.82m (9ft 3in)
All up weight: 1,293kg (2,850lb)
Maximum speed: 196km/h (105mph) at sea level
Cruise speed: 137km/h (85mph)
Operational ceiling: 10,500ft
Range: 412km (256 miles)
Accommodation: Crew of one/two plus up to two stretchers
First flown: 8 December 1945
Entered service: March 1946 (commercial); 1947 (military)

Bell 47G Royal New Zealand Air Force

Bell 204/205

SINGLE TURBOSHAFT MULTI-ROLE HELICOPTER

UH-1H Iroquois United States Army

TECHNICAL DATA

Bell 205

Powerplant: One Textron Lycoming T53-L-13 turboshaft
Developing: 1,044kW (1,400shp)
Driving: Two-blade main and two-blade tail rotors
Main rotor diameter: 14.63m (48ft 0 in)
Fuselage length: 12.77m (41ft 10.25in)
Height: 4.41m (14ft 5.5in)
All up weight: 4,309kg (9,500lb)
Maximum speed: 204km/h (127mph)
Operational ceiling: 12,600ft
Range: 511km (318 miles)
Accommodation: One pilot and 12-14 troops
Warload: A wide variety of rockets, guns or air to surface ordnance
First flown: 22 October 1956 (XH-40); 16 August 1961 (YUH-1D)
Entered service: 9 August 1963 (UH-1D)

DEVELOPMENT

Bell's (Model 204) XH-40, which made its first flight in October 1956 powered by a Lycoming XT53-L-1 turboshaft, was the first turbine-powered helicopter acquired by the US Army, entering production as the HU-1A (the 'HU' prefix giving rise to the Huey nickname.) The Huey soon became the US Army's standard transport helicopter, and other variants equipped the USMC, USN and USAF. The Model 204 was built under licence in both Italy (by Agusta) and Japan (by Fuji). An improved version of the UH-1, the Model 205 was proposed to the US Army in 1960. Over 2,000 were built for the service and many more for export. The UH-1D was later replaced on the production line by the UH-1H, with the more powerful T53-L-13 turbine. Over 3,500 UH-1Hs were built for the US Army, with wide scale exports also taking place. Like the earlier Model 204, Agusta licence-built the Model 205, and designed and produced anti-submarine warfare versions of both. The last UH-1H left the production line in 1986.

CURRENT SERVICE

Model 204s/205s serve in Argentina, Austria, Australia, Bolivia, Bosnia-Herzegovinia, Brazil, Chile, Columbia, Cyprus, Dominica, Ethiopia, Germany, Greece, Guatemala, Honduras, Indonesia, Iran, Italy, Jamaica, Jordan, South Korea, Lebanon, Mexico, Morocco, Myanmar, New Zealand, Oman, Panama, Papua New Guinea, Pakistan, Paraguay, Peru, Philippines, Saudi Arabia, El Salvador, Singapore, Spain, Sweden, Taiwan, Tanzania, Thailand, Tunisia, Turkey, Uruguay, US Army, Venezuela and NASA.

SPECIAL FEATURES

The Bell Huey is one of the world's most successful helicopters in terms of numbers built, operators, and length of service. Large numbers retired from US Army service in the 1990s are now starting second lives with other air arms, police departments and civil operators.

VARIANTS

XH-40: model 204 prototype for US Army; **HU-1A**: production version of the YH-40, became the **UH-1A**; **HU-1B**: HU-1A with an enlarged cabin and revised rotor blades, redesignated **UH-1B** in 1962; **UH-1C**: improved HU-1B; **UH-1D**: production for US Army and export; **UH-1E**: USMC Model 204; **TH-1E**: USMC trainer version of the UH-1E; **UH-1F**: USAF Model 204 for ICBM site support; **TH-1F**: USAF trainer version of UH-1F;

UH-1H: upgraded UH-1D with T53-L-13 turboshaft; **UH-1HP Huey II**: upgraded Huey offered by Bell with the T53-703; **EH-1H**: ECM conversion of UH-1D, fitted with early 'Quickfix' systems; **JUH-1H**; SOTAS testbeds and 'aggressor Hueys', painted as Russian 'Hinds'; **HH-1H**: USAF base rescue helicopter; **UH-1J**: JGSDF version of UH-1H fitted with the T53-703 turboshaft; **HH-1K**: USN Model 204 for base SAR missions; **UH-1L**: USN version of TH-1L; **TH-1L**: USN Model 204 for helicopter pilot training; **UH-1M**: US Army Model 204 with low-level-light TV equipment; **UH-1P**: psychological warfare version of UH-1F; **UH-1V**: medevac version of UH-1H; **EH-1X**: electronic jammer; **AB 204**: Agusta licence-built version; **AB 204AS**: anti-submarine warfare version of the AB 204; **AB 205**: licence production version built by Agusta; **CH-118**: Canadian UH-1Hs; **Fuji-Bell 204B-2**: Fuji developed version for JGSDF; **Huey 800**: Global Helicopter conversion fitted with T800-800 engine; **UH-1/T700 Ultras Huey**: UNC Helicopter upgrade fitted with T700-GE-701C engine.

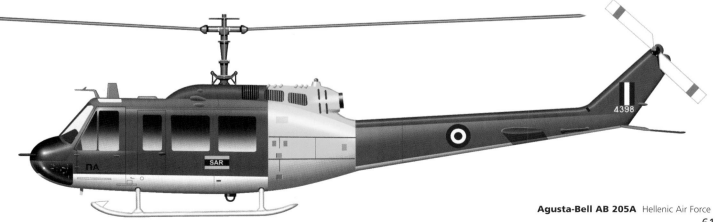

Agusta-Bell AB 205A Hellenic Air Force

Bell 206 JetRanger & TH-57/TH-67

SINGLE TURBOSHAFT LIGHT TRANSPORT/TRAINING HELICOPTER

Bell TH-67C SeaRanger United States Navy

TECHNICAL DATA

Bell TH-67A Creek

Powerplant: One Rolls-Royce Allison 250-C20JN or 250-C20J turboshaft

Developing: 313kW (420shp)

Driving: Two-blade main and tail rotors

Main rotor diameter: 10.16m (33ft 4in)

Fuselage length: 9.50m (31ft 2in) (including tailskid)

Height: 2.89m (9ft 6in)

All-up weight: 1,428kg (3,149lb)

Maximum speed: 225km/h (140mph)

Cruise speed: 214km/h (133mph)

Operational ceiling: 13,500ft

Maximum ferry range: 732km (455 miles)

Mission range: 605km (376 miles)

Endurance: approximately 3 hours

Accommodation: Instructor and pupil pilot in front seats with full dual controls; seating for up to three occupants on bench seat in rear of cabin

Warload: Usually none, but can be fitted with pintle-mounted machine guns

First flown: 8 December 1962 (original YOH-4/YHO-4A); 10 January 1966 (Model 206A)

Entered service: 15 October 1993 (TH-67A Creek)

DEVELOPMENT

Originally conceived to compete in the US Army's early 1960's Light Observation Helicopter (LOH) competition, Bell's original YHO-4/YOH-4A was unsuccessful in that contest, but Bell subsequently refined the basic design; the resulting civil-orientated Model 206A JetRanger first flew in January 1966. The increasingly successful type was further developed as the more powerful and refined Model 206B JetRanger II (available from 1971) and the stretched seven-seat Model 206L LongRanger (first flown in 1974). Further power and detail changes led to the Model 206B-3 JetRanger III, deliveries of which began from 1977. Production by Bell Helicopter in the USA of JetRangers/LongRangers was transferred to Bell Helicopter Textron Canada in 1986/87. Current types include the Model 206B-3 JetRanger III and the Model 206L-4 LongRanger IV. JetRangers and LongRangers have been produced for many years under licence in Italy by Agusta. In 1968, the US Navy took delivery of an initial batch of TH-57A SeaRanger dual-control trainers, later supplanted by TH-57B and TH-57C versions, deliveries of which were completed in the mid-1980s. In March 1993, the JetRanger was chosen by the US Army for its New Training Helicopter (NTH) requirement; deliveries began in October 1993

of 157 TH-67A Creeks. In total, over 7,700 JetRangers/LongRangers have so far been built (including OH-58 derivatives, described separately).

CURRENT SERVICE

US Army TH-67A Creeks serve primarily with training units 1-212 AVN (Training) and 1-223 AVN (Training) at Fort Rucker, Alabama; US Navy TH-57C SeaRangers (plus some TH-57Bs) principally serve with training squadrons HT-8 and HT-18 at NAS Whiting Field, Florida. Military or police-operated Model 206 JetRangers serve in Brazil, Brunei, Bulgaria, Canada, Chile, Croatia, Djibouti, Dubai, Ecuador, Guatemala, Guyana, Indonesia, Israel, Jamaica, Mexico, Morocco, Oman, Pakistan, Peru, Slovenia, Spain, Sri Lanka, Taiwan, Thailand and Venezuela. Military users of LongRangers include Algeria, Bangladesh, Cameroon, Colombia, Dubai, Guatemala, Israel, Mexico, Nepal, and Venezuela. Italian Agusta-built JetRangers serve in Austria, Finland, Greece, Iran (plus locally-assembled models), Israel, Italy, Libya, Macedonia, Saudi Arabia, Tanzania (LongRangers), Turkey (also including LongRangers), Uganda, Yemen, and Zambia.

SPECIAL FEATURES

Arguably the most successful light helicopter design

yet created, the JetRanger and its derivatives are of principally all-metal construction.

VARIANTS

Most JetRangers and LongRangers are powered by variants of the ubiquitous Rolls-Royce Allison 250-C20 turboshaft or its T63 military equivalent (Model 206As had the 250-C18 engine). Although many examples in military service are used for transport, liaison or training duties, some are armed (such as the Swedish Navy's anti-submarine Agusta-built depth charge carrying **Hkp 6** models). The US Army's **TH-67A Creeks** are divided into VFR trainers and differently equipped IFR trainers.

SEE ALSO: BELL OH-58D KIOWA WARRIOR

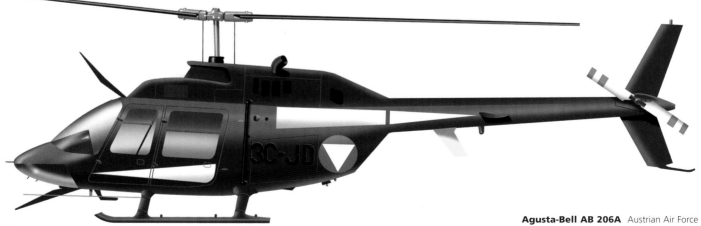

Agusta-Bell AB 206A Austrian Air Force

Bell OH-58 Kiowa/Kiowa Warrior series

SINGLE TURBOSHAFT LIGHT OBSERVATION/ATTACK HELICOPTER

OH-58D Kiowa Warrior United States Army

TECHNICAL DATA

Bell OH-58D(I) Kiowa Warrior
Powerplant: One Rolls-Royce Allison 250-C30R/3 or 250-C30R (T703-AD-700) turboshaft
Developing: 485 kW (650 shp)
Driving: Four-blade main rotor, two-blade tail rotor
Main rotor diameter: 10.67m (35ft 0in)
Fuselage length: 10.44m (34ft 3in) (incl tailskid)
Height: 3.93m (12ft 10.5in)
All-up weight: 2,495kg (5,500lb)
Maximum speed: 237km/h (147mph)
Cruise speed: 204km/h (127mph)
Operational ceiling: 15,000ft
Maximum ferry range: 496km (308 miles)
Mission range: 463km (288 miles)
Endurance: 3hr 5min
Accommodation: Pilot and co-pilot/observer
Warload: Outriggers on fuselage sides for various loads including up to four AGM-114 Hellfire laser-guided anti-tank missiles; up to four Stinger air-to-air missiles; two seven-round 2.75in Hydra 70 rocket pods; one 0.5in machine-gun pod (left-hand outrigger only). Combat Scout options include four TOW 2 anti-tank missiles, two GIAT 20mm cannon pods, 7.62mm gun pods.
First flown: 1968 (OH-58A); 6 October 1983 (OH-58D)
Entered service: 23 May 1969 (OH-58A); December 1985 (OH-58D); May/June 1991 (Kiowa Warrior)

DEVELOPMENT

Initially unsuccessful in the US Army's early 1960s Light Observation Helicopter (LOH) competition, Bell won the re-opened competition in March 1968 with a derivative of the commercial Model 206A JetRanger. Subsequently procured as the OH-58A Kiowa, 2,200 were built, deliveries starting in May 1969. A total of 74 similar COH-58As was built for the Canadian Armed Forces as the CH-136; twelve minigun-armed OH-58Bs were built for Austria, and some 56 Model 206B-1s were constructed for Australia as the CA-32. A total of 585 US Army OH-58As were later converted to the more powerful and improved OH-58C standard. In September 1981, Bell's considerably upgraded, OH-58A-based, Model 406 proposal to meet the Army Helicopter Improvement Programme (AHIP) to support AH-64 Apaches, was successful. This created a close combat reconnaissance helicopter for the support of attack helicopters and artillery spotting, fitted with a McDonnell Douglas/Northrop mast-mounted sight. At least 201 OH-58A were converted to the new OH-58D standard, and in 1987 – under the 'Prime Chance' programme – 15 were heavily armed for

operations against Iranian high-speed attack craft in the Persian Gulf. This helped lead to the fully-armed OH-58D(I) Kiowa Warrior, the standard to which all OH-58A conversions are now being made. The first was completed/delivered in 1991. At least 192 are planned, with many OH-58Ds also being brought to this level. All Kiowa Warriors are planned to have Multi-Purpose Light Helicopter (MPLH) knock-down capability, with quick-folding rotors, for air transportation. An austere armed OH-58D version, the Model 406CS Combat Scout, was also marketed; 15 were delivered to Saudi Arabia (as MH-58Ds) from mid-1990. Taiwan received 26 new-build OH-58Ds from July 1993.

CURRENT SERVICE

Australian Army and Navy Kiowas (Kalkadoons), armed Austrian OH-58Bs, Taiwanese OH-58Ds, and Saudi Arabian Combat Scouts, all continue in service. US Army unmodified OH-58A/Cs still serve (many with the Army National Guard) but in dwindling numbers.

The growing US Army Kiowa Warrior force operates with air cavalry units within several Army commands, in the US and elsewhere.

SPECIAL FEATURES

The Kiowa Warrior uses the JetRanger/Kiowa design layout, but with full weapons provision, more power, and advanced avionics. Fully air-portable, with folding rotor blades and removable mast-mounted sight.

VARIANTS

The **Model 406CS Combat Scout**, a downgraded export version, has a roof-mounted sight, slightly different power, less advanced avionics and different armament provision than the **Kiowa Warrior**. The **OH-58D(I) Kiowa Warrior MPLH** has a cargo hook (907kg, 2,000lb capacity), and provision for six externally-carried troops. A stealth **OH-58X** demonstrator was also created.

SEE ALSO: BELL MODEL 206 JETRANGER & TH-57/TH-67

Bell OH-58D Kiowa Warrior United States Army

Bell AH-1 HueyCobra/SuperCobra

SINGLE OR TWIN-TURBOSHAFT CLOSE SUPPORT/ATTACK HELICOPTER

AH-1T SeaCobra United States Marines Corps

TECHNICAL DATA

Bell AH-1W SuperCobra
Powerplants: Two General Electric T700-GE-401 turboshafts
Developing: 1,286kW (1,725 shp)
Driving: Two-blade main and tail rotors
Main rotor diameter: 14.63m (48ft 0in)
Fuselage length: 13.87m (45ft 6in)
Height: 4.44m (14ft 7in)
All-up weight: 6,690 kg (14,750 lb)
Maximum speed: 315km/h (196mph)
Cruise speed: 245km/h (152mph)
Operating ceiling: 17,500ft
Maximum ferry range: undisclosed
Mission range: 518km (322 miles)
Endurance: 3hr
Accommodation: Two crew (gunner/co-pilot in front, pilot behind and above)
Warload: One 20mm M197 three-barrel cannon in General Electric undernose turret linked to crewmembers' helmet-mounted sight display. Two hardpoints beneath each stub wing for up to eight TOW missiles, eight AGM-114 Hellfire missiles, up to four 19-round or seven-round 2.75in Hydra 70 rocket pods, two CBU-55B fuel-air explosive weapons, two M118 grenade dispensers, two AGM-122A Sidearm missiles or two AIM-9L air-to-air missiles
First flown: 7 September 1965 (Model 209 prototype); 16 November 1983 (AH-1T+/AH-1W prototype)
Entered service: June 1967 (AH-1G); 27 March 1986 (AH-1W)

DEVELOPMENT

Intended to meet the US Army's AAFSS requirement and the pressing need for an attack helicopter for service in Vietnam, Bell created – in record time – a Model 209 prototype which first flew in September 1965. Initial US Army deliveries (as the AH-1G) were made in mid-1967, and some 1,119 were eventually built. The US Marine Corps procured its own AH-1J SeaCobras (67 examples) from 1969/70, with altered armament options and fitted with a different, 'twin-pac' powerplant. US Army AH-1Gs were later rebuilt or modified to different equipment, armament and powerplant options under various designations including AH-1P, AH-1Q, AH-1R and AH-1S, plus the Up-gun AH-1S (now AH-1E) and Modernized AH-1S (now AH-1F); the latter is the US Army's main current version. Many of these models also include new-build machines, and several versions have been exported. Fuji in Japan licence-built the AH-1F for Japan's Army Aviation. All these models were single-engined. For the US Marine Corps, the initial AH-1J was followed by the 'twin-pac'-powered AH-1T Improved SeaCobra from 1976/77 (57 built). These led, from 1980, to the re-engined twin-engine AH-1T+ which first flew in 1983 and became the current AH-1W SuperCobra. Surviving AH-1Ts were rebuilt to AH-1W standard and new-build procurement of 169 for the US Marine Corps was completed in 1998. Ten were built for

Turkey, and up to 63 are being procured by Taiwan. Marine Corps models are being continually upgraded, with a major Phase II modernisation planned to turn them into AH-1Zs (sometimes called KingCobra).

CURRENT SERVICE

The US Army announced in April 2000 that its remaining 343 AH-1s will be withdrawn from service by October 2001. The US Marine Corps' AH-1W fleet will be active for many years, although the AH-1J is now withdrawn. Marine Corps AH-1W deployment currently includes six active force and two reserve force light helicopter attack squadrons and a detachment, plus a training squadron. This model also continues to serve in Turkey and Taiwan. In addition, single-engine AH-1s of various marks currently serve in Bahrain, Israel, Japan, Jordan, Pakistan, South Korea, and Thailand. Survivors of Iran's AH-1J-equivalent fleet are also still active.

SPECIAL FEATURES

The HueyCobra introduced the now classic attack helicopter layout of a narrow fuselage with stepped tandem seating for its two crew members, a chin-mounted cannon and heavy armament on stub wings.

VARIANTS

Single-engine models of the AH-1 are powered by

versions of the Avco Lycoming T53 turboshaft. The US Marine Corps **AH-1J SeaCobra** and **AH-1T Improved SeaCobra** were powered by models of the Pratt & Whitney Canada T400 twin-turboshaft 'twin-pac' engine. The **AH-1Z** is planned to have a four-blade main and tail rotor, new stub wings with greater weapons-carrying capacity, and a new transmission and advanced targeting system.

Bell AH-1F HueyCobra Israeli Defence Force/Air Force

Bell 212/UH-1N

TWIN-TURBINE MULTI-ROLE HELICOPTER

Agusta-Bell AB 212 Italian Air Force

A 14-passenger civil version, known as the Twin Two-Twelve, was developed alongside the initial military version. The enhanced safety margin provided by the powerplant made the type ideal for off-shore platform support. It was the first helicopter of US manufacture to be bought by the Civil Air Authority of China. Like the majority of Bell's designs, Agusta of Italy acquired a licence and manufactured the type as the Agusta-Bell AB 212. The company developed the AB 212ASW anti-submarine warfare version, initial deliveries of which were made to the Iranian Navy.

CURRENT SERVICE

Versions of the Bell 212 serve the air arms of Argentina, Austria, Bahrain, Bangladesh, Brunei, Columbia, Ecuador, Gabon, Ghana, Greece, Guatemala, Italy, Jamaica, South Korea, Lebanon, Libya, Macedonia, Mexico, Oman, Palestine, Panama, Peru, Philippines, Sri Lanka, Thailand, UK, United Arab Emirates, Uruguay, USAF, USN, USMC, Venezuela, Yemen and Zaire.

SPECIAL FEATURES

The combining of the airframe of the UH-1H with the increased power of the PWAC PT6T Twin-Pac created a helicopter with a surplus of power and excellent high and dry performance.

DEVELOPMENT

After gaining experience with the twin-turbine Bell Model 208 Twin Delta, Bell designed the Model 212 to meet a Canadian requirement for a higher powered version of the Bell UH-1H. The Model 212 was a joint venture between Bell, the Canadian government and Pratt & Whitney Aircraft of Canada. The latter's PT6T Twin-Pac, which consisted of two turboshaft engines mounted side-by-side driving a single output shaft via a combining gearbox, was to power the new

helicopter. The airframe was generally similar to the UH-1H. Initial deliveries were to the USAF in 1970, who designated the type the UH-1N. Deliveries to the US Navy and US Marine Corps started in 1971 of UH-1Ns and VIP configured VH-1Ns, the latter being used for Presidential transport with HMX-1. The Canadian Armed Forces, for which the type had been designed, gained its first CH-135 on 3 May 1971. A total of 38 UH-1Ns and VH-1Ns were later redesignated as base rescue helicopters and became HH-1Ns. Although the Canadians have retired their CH-135s, the USMC's UH-1Ns are the subject of a rebuild programme which will add, amongst other improvements, a four-bladed rotor. The upgraded UH-1Ns will emerge as UH-1Ys.

VARIANTS

AB 212: Agusta licence built version of the Bell 212; **AB 212ASW**: anti-submarine warfare version built by Agusta; **UH-1N**: base-line utility version for USAF (79) and USMC (221); **HH-1N**: base rescue designation of UH-1Ns and VH-1Ns; **VH-1N**: eight VIP models for the USMC; **UH-1Y**: upgraded four blade UH-1N for the USMC; **CH-135**: Canadian version, initially designated CUN-1N – since retired; **Twin-Two Twelve**: commercial version for off-shore gas/oil platform support.

TECHNICAL DATA

Bell 212

Powerplant: One Pratt & Whitney Canada T400-CP-400 Turbo Twin-Pac
Developing: 1,342kW (1,800shp)
Driving: Two-blade main and two-blade tail rotors
Main rotor diameter: 14.69m (48ft 2.25 in)
Fuselage length: 12.92m (42ft 4.75in)
Height: 4.53m (14ft 10.25in)
All up weight: 5,080kg (11,200lb)
Maximum speed: 259km/h (161mph)
Maximum cruise speed: 230km/h (142mph)
Operational ceiling: 14,200ft
Range: 420km (261 miles)
Accommodation: Pilot and up to 14 passengers
Warload: Includes a 0.30 in MAG pod machine gun system, 2.75 in air-to-ground rocket launchers (7 or 19 rounds), side-mounted 0.50in or 0.30in machine guns
First flown: April 1969
Entered service: 1970 (USAF)

Bell UH-1N United States Navy

Bell 214 / 214ST

SINGLE/TWIN-TURBOSHAFT TROOP TRANSPORT/ARMED ASSAULT HELICOPTER

USA

Bell 214ST Iraqi Air Force

DEVELOPMENT

The Iranian armed forces' requirement for a version of the ubiquitous 'Huey' with a more powerful engine for improved 'hot and high' operations led Bell to develop its 'Huey Plus' (itself a development of the Model 205) into the improved 16-seat Model 214A. Additional power was provided by a single Textron Lycoming T5508D rated at 2,185kW (2,930shp), giving the aircraft much improved performance at high ambient temperatures. A total of 287 Model 214As were delivered to Iran in the mid-1970s under the local name Isfahan. A further 400 examples had been ordered at the time of the 1978 Islamic revolution, which caused the cancellation of this and any further orders. The aircraft were heavily involved in the first Gulf War with Iraq in the 1980s as utility and assault transports, and today around 90 are believed to be still in service. Iran also received 39 Model 214Cs that were equipped for SAR duties. The commercial version which evolved from the Model 214A was the 214B 'BigLifter', which was purchased in small numbers by several minor air arms. The demand by the Iranians for even better performance and increased payload/ capacity led to the development of the Bell Model 214ST (ST for Stretched Twin) which, despite sharing the same Model number, bears little relation to its

predecessor. The 214A's single engine was replaced by two General Electric CT7-2A engines, the fuselage was stretched and re-profiled, the rotor blades were of increased diameter and constructed of composite materials, and numerous other smaller modifications were incorporated. Production was to have been under licence in Iran with an initial order of 350 examples. However, the Islamic revolution forced an end to this programme before the first example flew in July 1979. Bell pursued the project itself and launched limited series production of 100 examples. Ironically, by far the biggest order for the type came from Iraq, which ordered 45 examples, ostensibly for the civilian Ministry of Communications and Transport. However, the aircraft were operated by the Iraqi Air Force and saw active combat, equipped as gunships, against Iranian Isfahans during the first Gulf War. Small numbers were also purchased by a handful of other air arms, the most significant of which is the Thai armed forces which acquired nine examples.

CURRENT SERVICE

Bell Model 214/214STs are operated by the air arms of the following nations: Brunei, Cambodia, Iran, Iraq, South Korea, Oman, Peru, Philippines, Thailand, United Arab Emirates and Venezuela.

SPECIAL FEATURES

The Model 214A's extra power gives a significant improvement in performance over the earlier single engine 'Hueys'. External winches may be mounted for SAR operations and a number have been equipped as gunships. The Model 214ST's more capacious cabin and twin engines allow an extra four fully-equipped soldiers to be carried, and the aircraft can be fitted with skid or wheeled undercarriage

VARIANTS

Model 214A/Isfahan: initial utility version initially designed for the Iranian armed forces; **Model 214B 'BigLifter'**: intended mainly for civilian market although some military operators; **Model 214C**: SAR version for the Iranian armed forces; **Model 214ST**: stretched twin-engined variant with improved performance and capacity.

TECHNICAL DATA

Bell Model 214ST

Powerplants: Two General Electric CT7-2A turboshafts
Developing: 1,212kW (1,625shp)
Driving: Two-blade main and two-blade tail rotors
Main rotor diameter: 15.85m (52ft 0in)
Fuselage length: 15.02m (49ft 3.5in)
Height: 4.84m (15ft 10.5in)
All up weight: 7,938kg (17,500lb)
Maximum cruise speed: 259km/h (161mph)
Hover ceiling (IGE): 6,400ft
Range: 858km (533 miles)
Accommodation: Crew of 2/3 and 16-20 fully-equipped troops
Maximum payload: more than 3493kg (7,700lb)
First flown: 13 March 1974 (Bell 214A) 21 July 1979 (Bell 214ST)
Entered service: Mid-1970s

Bell 214ST Venezuelan Air Force

Bell/Agusta-Bell 412/AB412

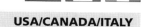

TWIN-TURBOSHAFT UTILITY TRANSPORT/ARMED SCOUT/SAR HELICOPTER

USA/CANADA/ITALY

DEVELOPMENT

In an effort to increase both range and cruising speed performance of its highly successful Model 212 series, Bell began design work in the mid-1970s on an improved version featuring the introduction of a new advanced-technology foldable four-bladed main rotor of composite construction. This new arrangement, plus the introduction of the PT6T-3B-1 engine and an increase in standard fuel capacity, was tested on two Bell 212s which became the prototypes for the new helicopter. The first production helicopters were delivered to the civilian market in 1981 – and military orders soon followed, the most significant of which was Canada which, in 1992, ordered 100 examples under the designation CH-146 Griffon. Indeed, in 1989 Bell transferred its production of the aircraft to Quebec in Canada, where the improved Bell 412SP and 412HP have also been produced, these variants

Griffin HT1 UK DFHS

TECHNICAL DATA

Agusta-Bell AB 412 Grifone

Powerplant: One Pratt & Whitney Canada PT6T-3B Turbo Twin Pac turboshaft
Developing: 1342kW (1,800shp)
Driving: Four-blade main and two-blade tail rotors
Main rotor diameter: 14.02m (46ft 0in)
Fuselage length: 12.92m (42ft 4.75in)
Height: 4.32m (14ft 2.25in)
All up weight: 5,400kg (11,905lb)
Maximum speed: 259km/h (161mph)
Maximum Cruise speed: 226km/h (140mph)
Operational ceiling: 17,000ft
Range: 805km (500 miles)
Endurance: 4hr 12min
Accommodation: Crew of 2/3 plus up to 14 fully-equipped troops
Maximum payload: 2,291kg (5,050lb)
First flown: August 1979 (Bell 412)
Entered service: 1980

offering improved transmission, gross weight and fuel capacity. The Indonesian company IPTN has undertaken licence production of the type as the NBell-412. Having long been associated with production of Bell designs, Agusta-Bell of Italy began producing the civilian AB 412 before launching its own military variant named Grifone. Designed for roles as diverse as fire-support, reconnaissance, combat assault and SAR, the Grifone can be fitted with twin side-mounted cannon, rocket pods a 360° search radar, FLIR, TV sensors and armour protection. IR emission-reduction devices have also been fitted to the engine exhausts.

CURRENT SERVICE

Bell 412s are in service with the air arms or agencies of the following nations: Bahrain, Botswana, Canada, Colombia, Cyprus, Czech Republic, Ecuador, Gabon, Guatemala, Guyana, Honduras, Indonesia, Lesotho, Norway, Peru, Poland, Slovenia, Sri Lanka, Thailand, Uganda, United Kingdom and Venezuela. AB 412s operate in Finland, Ghana, Italy, Lesotho, Netherlands,

Saudi Arabia, Sweden, Turkey, Uganda, United Arab Emirates, Venezuela and Zimbabwe.

SPECIAL FEATURES

The type's excellent four-bladed composite main rotors reduce cabin vibration and noise and the aircraft offers improved range, payload and speed over its predecessor. Strengthened undercarriage skids and energy-absorbing seats can be fitted for both crew and passengers, thus increasing safety in the result of a heavy/crash landing. An external hoist may be fitted to the starboard side above the cabin for SAR operations.

VARIANTS

Progressive development of the 412 led to the **412P** (Special performance), **412HP** (High Performance) and the current **412EP** (Enhanced Performance) – this also forms the basis for the **CH-146 Griffon**. In the UK, nine 412EPs equip the civilian-operated Defence Helicopter Flying School and these are designated **Griffin HT1s**.

Agusta-Bell AB 412SP Royal Netherlands Air Force

Bell/Boeing V-22 Osprey

TWIN-TURBOSHAFT TILT-ROTOR MULTI-MISSION AIRCRAFT

MV-22B Osprey United States Marine Corps

TECHNICAL DATA

Bell/Boeing MV-22B Osprey

Powerplants: Two Rolls-Royce Allison T406-AD-400 turboshafts
Developing: 4,586kW (6,150shp)
Driving: Three-blade proprotors
PropRotor diameter: 11.61m (38ft 1in)
Fuselage length: 17.47m (57ft 4in) (excluding in-flight refuelling probe when fitted)
Wing span: 15.52m (50ft 11in) (including engine nacelles)
Height: 6.73m (22ft 1in) (nacelles vertical)
All-up weight: 27,442kg (60,500lb)
Max speed: 565km/h (351mph) (in aircraft mode)
Cruise speed: 509km/h (316mph) (in aircraft mode)
Operational ceiling: 26,000ft
Maximum ferry range: 3,335km (2,072miles)
Mission range: 953km (592miles)
Endurance: 5.2 hours
Accommodation: Pilot, co-pilot and crew chief in USMC version; up to 24 combat-equipped Marines
Warload: None; possible future provision for nose-mounted gun or cannon, possibly turret-mounted
First flown: 19 March 1989
Entered service: May 1999 (initial USMC delivery)

DEVELOPMENT

The roots of the ground-breaking V-22 programme lie within experiments in tilt-wing and tilt-propulsion craft which culminated in the successful Bell XV-15 tilt-rotor. First flown in May 1977, an XV-15 was re-activated in the early 1990s to assist with the Osprey flight test and development programme. The Osprey originated from the US DoD's early-1980s Joint Services Advanced Vertical Lift Aircraft (JVX) programme. The project eventually encompassed Bell and Boeing through a joint programme office and collaborative departments within both companies. Initial design began in 1983 and the first of five flying prototypes flew in March 1989. Four production representative engineering and manufacturing development (EMD) aircraft flew in 1997 and 1998. The first of the initial production block of five aircraft, a US Marine Corps MV-22B, was delivered in May 1999 for service evaluation and testing. The USMC currently requires 360 MV-22Bs (initially 552 examples), the USAF 50 CV-22Bs, and the US Navy 48 HV-22Bs.

CURRENT SERVICE

The first USMC unit to operate the type was planned to be the training squadron VMMT-204 at Marine Corps Air Station New River, North Carolina. Some test aircraft are based at Naval Air Station Patuxent River, Maryland, for development and service evaluation.

SPECIAL FEATURES

The Osprey can fly like an aircraft but land and take-off like a helicopter due to its rotatable engine pods and huge proprotors. Automatic control of configuration change when commanded by the pilot, and fly-by-wire controls give safe flight and transition between helicopter and aircraft modes. A cross-shaft layout allows both proprotors to safely remain turning even after the loss of one engine; failure of a nacelle rotation actuator automatically reverts the machine to helicopter mode to allow a safe landing. The entire wing can be slewed to lie along the top of the fuselage and the proprotors folded to allow stowage aboard ship.

VARIANTS

The USAF's **CV-22B** will be a long-range special operations and combat rescue machine able to carry up to 12 specially-equipped troops or cargo, with a combat radius of some 964km (599miles). The US Navy's **HV-22Bs** will be combat SAR, fleet logistics supply and special warfare machines. A requirement for a US Navy anti-submarine warfare model also exists. There is currently no funding for a US Army combat assault, medevac and special operations version based on the standard Marine Corps transport/assault **MV-22B**.

MV-22B Osprey United States Marines Corps

Bellanca (Champion) Citabria

SINGLE ENGINE TWO-SEAT TRAINER AND AEROBATIC AIRCRAFT

Bellanca 7GCBC Citabria Turkish Army

DEVELOPMENT

The Citabria has its origins in the WW2 Aeronca L-3 Grasshopper, by way of the Champion. Acquisition by Bellanca of the assets of the 7AC Champion Aircraft Corporation in September 1970, led to the production of aircraft derived from that company's Model 7AC Champ – of which more than 7,000 had been built. The most enduring of these derivatives were the Bellanca 7GCBC Citabria ('airbatic' reversed) and the Bellanca 8GCBC Scout. These combined a modest aerobatic facility with a good cruising performance and a roomy cabin for the two occupants, in tandem. A total of 1,215 7GCBC Citabrias and 736 Decathlons had been built when production ended in 1980, following the closure of Bellanca's production line.

CURRENT SERVICE

In 1979, the Turkish Army ordered 40 to serve in the primary training role and the aircraft is also used to screen potential students. Thirty examples still serve at the Turkish Army Aviation School base at Ankara-Güverncinilik. A Bellanca 8KCAB Decathlon serves with the Guatemalan Air Force at BA La Aurora for aerobatic training. In 1999, a Citabria was acquired by Tonga for training purposes.

SPECIAL FEATURES

A braced high-wing monoplane with NASA-1412 aerofoil section aerobatic wing, the Citabria was a modified version of the 7EC Traveler, by way of the 7ECA, with a modified fin and increased all-up-weight. Its wing is of mixed construction while the fuselage and tail unit has a steel-tube basic structure with fabric covered surfaces. As with most of the Champion

products the Citabria's undercarriage is of the fixed tailwheel type. The enclosed cabin provides seating for two in tandem – and because of the aircraft's aerobatic capability (with limits of +5g and -2g), the cabin door is jettisonable in an emergency.

VARIANTS

The Citabria was produced in three versions: the **7ECA Citabria** with a 74kW (100hp) Continental O-200C engine; the **7GCBC Citabria 160** with a 118.4kW (160hp) Lycoming O-320-D2A and the **7KCAB Citabria 150S** which had a new NASA-1412 aerofoil section aerobatic wing, a modified undercarriage and is powered by a 112kW (150hp) Lycoming IO-320-E2A. The **Model 8GCBC Scout** was a 7KCAB with a strengthened airframe and 134kW (180hp) 0-360-C1E engine. The **8KCAB Decathlon** was a further aerobatic development of the Scout fitted with a 112kW (150hp) Lycoming AEIO-320-E2B.

TECHNICAL DATA

Bellanca (Champion) Model 7GCBC Citabria

Powerplant: One Avco Lycoming 0-320-D2A piston engine
Developing: 118.4kW (160hp)
Driving: Two-blade propeller
Span: 10.19m (33ft 5in)
Length: 6.92m (22ft 8.5in)
Height: 2.35m (7ft 8.5in)
All-up weight: 748kg (1,650lb)
Maximum speed: 209km/h (130mph)
Cruising speed: 189km/h (117mph)
Operational ceiling: 17,000ft
Maximum range: 845km (525 miles)
Accommodation: Two, in tandem
Warload: None
First flown: 30 May 1965 (Model 7GCAA)
Entered service: 1979 (Turkish Army)

Bellanca 7GCBC Citabria

Beriev Be-12 Tchaika

TWIN-TURBOPROP MARITIME PATROL/SAR AMPHIBIAN

Beriev Be-12P

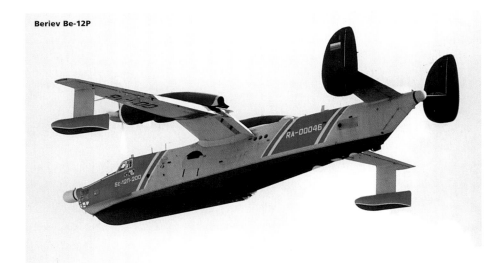

TECHNICAL DATA

Beriev Be-12 Tchaika
Powerplants: Two Ivchenko (Progress) AI-20D or AI-20M turboprops
Developing: 3,124kW (4,190shp)
Span: 29.71m (97ft 5.75in)
Length: 30.17m (99ft 0in)
Height: 7.00m (22ft 11.75in)
All-up weight: 31,000kg (68,345lb)
Maximum speed: 608km/h (378mph)
Cruise speed: 320km/h (199mph)
Operational Ceiling: 37,000ft
Maximum range: 7,500km (4,660miles)
Mission range: 1,000km (621 miles)
Accommodation: Five or six according to role, including pilot and co-pilot, navigator, main electronics operator, one or two ASW sensor operators or observers
Warload: Approximately 3,000kg (6,614lb), in an internal fuselage weapons bay behind the lower hull 'step', and on four underwing pylons (two beneath each wing, outboard of the engines). Internal carriage of sonobuoys, flares and markers, plus depth charges and possibly torpedoes; external provision for unguided bombs and rockets, and guided anti-ship missiles
First flown: 18 October 1960
Entered service: Late 1964

DEVELOPMENT

Designed from a 1957 requirement as a successor to the earlier piston-engined Beriev Be-6 anti-submarine/maritime patrol flying boat of the late 1940s, the Be-12 (NATO code name 'Mail') incorporates the general layout of the Be-6, but is larger with more powerful turboprop engines for its original anti-submarine mission. Successful flight testing from 1960 led to a production run of some 132 aircraft, and the type entered service with the Soviet Union's naval air force (AV-MF) as the M-12 in late 1964. As well as their primary coastal anti-submarine role, Be-12s also performed anti-shipping coastal surveillance, photographic survey and reconnaissance, and search and rescue tasks; the latter gained in significance for the Be-12 from the late 1960s as Soviet long-range shore-based anti-submarine aircraft and shipborne helicopters progressively took over the type's ASW mission. The Be-12 served with units of the AV-MF's Northern, Baltic, Black Sea and Pacific fleets, surviving aircraft becoming part of the Russian Federation's Naval Aviation forces from 1992. During the Cold War from around 1968 to the early 1970s, Soviet-operated Be-12s were deployed to Egypt (and possibly also Syria) for surveillance duties and flew in Egyptian

military markings. Soviet Be-12s also operated from Vietnam in Vietnamese markings from 1980; these aircraft were later passed to the Vietnamese military.

CURRENT SERVICE

Western sources believe that over 50 Be-12s still serve with Russian Naval Aviation forces, principally in surveillance and SAR roles with the Northern, Baltic and Black Sea Fleets. The status of the Vietnamese-operated Be-12s is unclear. Several are operated by the Ukraine following the Soviet Union's break-up and the giving-up to the Ukraine of some ex-Soviet equipment, and now transferred to Air Force control at Mikolayiv (Nickolaev).

SPECIAL FEATURES

The distinctive high-mounted gull wing (causing the Be-12's semi-official name of Tchaika or gull) mounts the turboprop engines as high as possible away from the water. For ASW operations the Be-12 carries magnetic anomaly detector (MAD) equipment in a prominent tailboom, and sea-search radar in a nose radome above several observation windows. A retractable tailwheel undercarriage allows the aircraft to operate from land as well as water.

VARIANTS

No major production variants are known to exist. The Soviet/Russian-operated aircraft have had several equipment upgrades during their service careers; original AI-20D turboprops were replaced in some Be-12s by AI-20M powerplants in a separate re-engining programme. The reversion of some aircraft to the SAR role caused the removal of the internal weapons bay and MAD gear, giving these aircraft a revised designation to of **Be-12PS**. The recent **Be-12P** fire bomber and a proposed cargo-carrying version, have been heavily promoted to the military. Specially-prepared Be-12s broke many world records in their class during the 1960s to the early 1980s.

Be-12 Tchaika Russian Naval Aviation

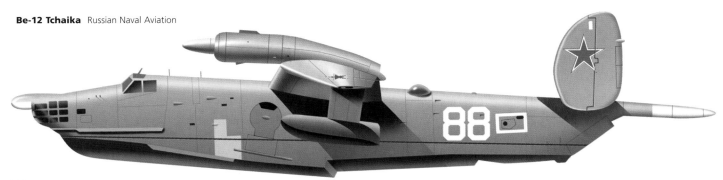

Boeing B-52 Stratofortress

EIGHT-TURBOFAN HEAVY BOMBER

B-52H Stratofortress United States Air Force

TECHNICAL DATA

Boeing B-52H Stratofortress

Powerplants: Eight Pratt & Whitney TF33-P-3 turbofans
Developing: 75.62kN (17,000lb st)
Span: 56.39m (185ft 0in)
Length: 49.05m (160ft 11in)
Height: 12.40m (40ft 8in)
All-up weight: 221,353kg (488,000lb) take-off; 229,088kg (505,000lb) with in-flight refuelling
Maximum speed: 957km/h (595mph)
Cruise speed: 819km/h (509mph)
Operational ceiling: 55,000ft
Maximum range: exceeds 16,093km (10,000 miles)
Accommodation: Two pilots, navigator, radar navigator and electronic warfare officer
Warload: about 22,680kg (50,000lb), with weapon options including maximum of 20 AGM-86B Air Launched Cruise Missiles or AGM-129 Advanced Cruise Missiles, both with nuclear warheads. B61 and B83 nuclear bombs can also be carried. Non-nuclear ordnance includes AGM-86C Conventional Air Launched Cruise Missile or AGM-142 Have Nap tactical attack missile or AGM-84 Harpoon missile. Also compatible with extensive array of bombs, including up to 51 M117 750lb weapons or heavier items and is gaining ability to operate with modern weapons such as JDAM (Joint Direct Attack Munition), JSOW (Joint Stand-Off Weapon) and WCMD (Wind Corrected Munitions Dispenser).
First flown: 15 April 1952 (YB-52 prototype), July 1960 (engine testbed conversion of B-52G), 6 March 1961 (production B-52H)
Entered service: June 1955 (B-52B); May 1961 (B-52H)

DEVELOPMENT

Development of the mighty Stratofortress was launched in the late 1940s, with Boeing being one of several companies that submitted proposals to the US Army Air Force for a new intercontinental bomber aircraft. The company's Model 464 provided the basis for the B-52 and was selected by the USAAF in June 1946, but further redesign ensued before the YB-52 ventured aloft for the first time in April 1952. Even then, yet more configuration changes followed and it was not until the summer of 1955 that SAC accepted its first B-52B. This marked the start of a production run that continued until October 1962, when the 744th and final Stratofortress was delivered to the USAF. The USAF intends to keep updating the aircraft as part of its bomber master plan up to 2034.

CURRENT SERVICE

The US Air Force presently retains 90 examples of the B-52H. The majority are assigned to regular force units, which consist of the 2nd Bomb Wing at Barksdale AFB, Louisiana with three squadrons and the 5th Bomb Wing at Minot AFB, North Dakota with one squadron. Nine examples are assigned to one squadron of the Air Force Reserve Command's 917th Wing, also at Barksdale, while Air Force Materiel Command's 412th Test Wing has one at Edwards AFB, California for test duties. The only other flyable Stratofortress is the NB-52B used as an airborne launch platform by NASA.

SPECIAL FEATURES

The most notable feature of the Stratofortress is the undercarriage, which comprises four twin-wheeled main units arranged in tandem pairs and housed within the fuselage fore and aft of the internal weapons bay, plus single-wheel outriggers beneath each wing, inboard of the auxiliary fuel tanks. Another distinctive attribute is the shoulder-mounted wing, from which podded pairs of engines are suspended.

VARIANTS

Following on from two prototypes and three **B-52As**, production of the Stratofortress for the now-defunct Strategic Air Command began with the **B/RB-52B** (50 built) and extended through the **B-52C** (35), **B-52D** (170), **B-52E** (100), **B-52F** (89) and **B-52G** (193). All were fitted with versions of the J57 turbojet, while the **B-52H** (102 built) was the only model with turbofan engines. The USAF is considering a proposal to create a limited number of **EB-52s**.

B-52H Stratofortress United States Air Force

Boeing 707

FOUR-TURBOJET OR TURBOFAN PASSENGER/VIP TRANSPORT AND SPECIALIST ELECTRONIC-WARFARE PLATFORM   USA

Boeing EC-707 Israeli Defence Force Air Force

TECHNICAL DATA

Boeing 707-320C
Powerplants: Four Pratt & Whitney JT3D-3 turbofans
Developing: 80.07kN (18,000lb st)
Span: 44.42m (145ft 9in)
Length: 46.61m (152ft 11in)
Height: 12.93m (42ft 5in)
All-up weight: 148,325kg (327,000lb)
Maximum speed: 1,010km/h (627mph)
Cruise speed: 886km/h (550mph)
Operational ceiling: 38,500ft
Maximum range: 12,086km (7,510 miles)
Mission range: 6,317km (3,925 miles)
Endurance: over 7 hours
Accommodation: Normally three or four-man crew on flight deck; many different seating arrangements in military 707s, including special VIP interiors, or provision for specialist flight crews in electronic-warfare equipped models
Warload: None
First flown: 20 December 1957 (first production 707 airliner); 4 April 1959 (first USAF VC-137A)
Entered service: 4 May 1959 (VC-137A)

DEVELOPMENT

Derived from the company-sponsored Model 367-80 which first flew in July 1954, the Boeing 707 was effectively an enlarged civil derivative of the Model 717 Stratotanker/Stratoliner which preceded it. With a larger diameter fuselage, greater length and span, the Boeing 707 was the world's most successful jet-powered airliner of its day; it has also been procured (either as new-build or ex-civil) by many military operators for a variety of duties including transport/ VIP work, in-flight refuelling (sometimes using add-on refuelling pods), and electronic-warfare. The first military models were three VC-137As for the USAF in 1959. Small-scale USAF procurement also included two VC-137C for Presidential use, and two EC-137D development aircraft for the E-3 Sentry programme. Altogether, 1,010 Model 707s was built, the final military examples being derived from the civil 707-320 type series as the E-3 Sentry and E-6 Mercury (see separate entries). Most, if not all, the current military Model 707s in service world-wide are converted 707-320B or -320C civil models, which were the most important final major versions of the civil Model 707. New-build procurement was however made for Canada (five CC-137s in 1970-1971), Iran (from 1974) and West Germany (four in 1968).

CURRENT SERVICE

Although most USAF C-137 type transports are now being retired and replaced in service by C-32s (Boeing 757s), odd Model 707 derivatives remain, such as an EC-137D transport with US Central Command, while some EC-18B ARIA and EC-18D CMMCA tracking and instrumentation examples serve with the Air Force Flight Test Centre (AFFTC) at Edwards AFB, California. The US Navy uses two ex-civil 707s as TC-18Fs for E-6 Mercury flight crew training with the Navy Training Support Unit at Tinker AFB, Oklahoma. The NATO Airborne Early Warning Force (NAEWF) employs six Luxembourg-registered Model 707s for crew training and transport duties alongside its E-3 Sentry fleet from Geilenkirchen in Germany. In addition, 707s in various roles serve with the military of the following countries: Argentina, Australia, Brazil, Chile (including one Phalcon, locally named Condor), Colombia, Egypt, India, Indonesia, Iran, Israel (including several EW aircraft), Italy, Morocco, Pakistan, Paraguay, Peru, Qatar, Romania, Saudi Arabia, South Africa (including several EW aircraft), Spain, Togo, and Venezuela.

SPECIAL FEATURES

The classic four-jet swept-wing Model 707 design lends itself to military transport/VIP use; it has ample on-board space for the electronics and extra crew needed for specialist electronic-warfare models, or the capacity needed for in-flight refuelling conversions.

VARIANTS

Electronic-warfare Model 707 conversions include those by E-Systems of the US, and IAI Bedek/Elta in Israel. The most-modified EW Model 707 is the **Phalcon** AEW/COMINT/ELINT aircraft from IAI's Bedek/Elta subsidiary, with a bulbous nose radar and conformal cheek antennae arrays along the forward fuselage. Some 707s converted for in-flight refuelling employ the Beech Model 1080 'probe and drogue' wingtip pod refuelling system, although several other add-on in-flight refuelling systems have been used.

SEE ALSO: BOEING E-3 SENTRY, BOEING E-6 MERCURY, & NORTHROP GRUMMAN/BOEING E-8 J-STARS

Boeing 707-329C NATO

LX-N
20199

NATO ✈ OTAN

Boeing KC-135 Stratotanker

USA

C-135FR Stratotanker French Air Force

which serve principally with units of the regular Air Force's Air Mobility Command, Pacific Air Forces and USAFE (100th Air Refueling Wing at Mildenhall), and with the Air Force Reserve and Air National Guard. Various examples also serve with other specialised units. The fleet has a global refueling role/ capability, often deploying to forward bases for UN or NATO operations. The 11 surviving French C-135FR Stratotankers plus three recently-delivered ex-USAF KC-135Rs serve with ERV 00.093 'Bretagne' at Istres. Turkish KC-135Rs serve with the Tanker Filo at Incirlik. The first Singapore Air Force Stratotanker was delivered in autumn 1999; at least two will be retained in the US for training purposes. Surviving Stratoliners in the 1990s included a C-135C (ex-C-135B) used by the USAF's own C-in-C.

DEVELOPMENT

In July 1954 Boeing's private venture Model 367-80 first flew, as an intended new-generation transport with potential as a military tanker and cargo transport. Boeing hoped it would attract military orders, leading to a possible civil airliner spin-off deriving from the basic four-jet swept-wing layout. The USAF ordered the type later in 1954, fitted with Boeing's 'flying boom' type in-flight refuelling system. The first KC-135A flew in August 1956, with the type designation Boeing Model 717. Between 1956 and the mid-1960s, some 820 Model 717s were built. Approximately 724 of these were KC-135A Stratotanker dedicated tankers with passenger and cargo-carrying capacity and powered by Pratt & Whitney J57-P-59W turbojets with water-injection; others were C-135 Stratoliner military cargo/passenger models without in-flight refuelling provision. All these are smaller than the Model 707 airliner which was developed later from the same basic Model 367-80 layout. The USAF received its first KC-135A in June 1957; there have since been many upgrades and re-engining of the KC-135 fleet, and the whole KC-135/C-135 series has included many electronic-warfare and communications/reconnaissance/test aircraft modifications and conversions which are usually re-designated RC-135 or EC-135. Twelve C-135F tanker/transports were built for France. Recent export customers for upgraded Stratotankers include Turkey and Singapore.

CURRENT SERVICE

The USAF's current fleet of some 550 Stratotankers mainly includes KC-135E, KC-135R, and KC-135T models,

SPECIAL FEATURES

With a maximum fuel load of 92,210 kg (203,288lb), the KC-135R is typical of all Stratotankers in carrying its fuselage fuel load in lower fuselage fuel tanks, leaving the upper 'deck' for cargo, equipment or passengers. Experience in the Gulf War led to some Stratotankers being fitted with a cargo roller system in this upper area for ease of handling large loads.

VARIANTS

Apart from wing re-skinning, provision of larger tail surfaces, avionics and other updates, upgrades have included re-engine modifications using ex-civil Pratt & Whitney JT3D (TF33) turbofans to create the **KC-135E**, or later with CFM International F108-CF-100 turbofans making the **KC-135R**, which can itself be refuelled in flight. The **KC-135Q** was a tanker conversion specifically for the USAF's now-retired SR-71 Blackbirds. The most recent upgrade is the **KC-135T** (including some former **KC-135Q**) for operations with the USAF's F-117s. French **C-135F** tanker/transports have a modification to allow 'probe and drogue' refuelling from the USAF-type 'flying boom' fitted; they were re-engined with CFM International F108-CF-100 turbofans.

SEE ALSO: BOEING C-135 STRATOLIFTER VARIANTS & BOEING RC-135

TECHNICAL DATA

Boeing KC-135R Stratotanker

Powerplants: Four CFM International F108-CF-100 turbofans
Developing: 97.86kN (22,000lb st)
Span: 39.88m (130ft 10in)
Length: 41.53m (136ft 3in)
Height: 12.70m (41ft 8in)
All-up weight: 146,286kg (322,500lb)
Maximum speed: 981km/h (610mph)
Cruise speed: 853km/h (530mph)
Operational ceiling: 45,000ft
Maximum range: undisclosed
Mission range: 9,265km (5,758 miles)
Endurance: approximately 10.5 hours unrefuelled
Accommodation: Normally three-man crew on flight deck, plus boom refuelling operator in rear fuselage; up to 80 passengers or cargo in upper compartment of fuselage
Warload: None
First flown: 31 August 1956
Entered service: June 1957

KC-135R Stratotanker United States Air Forces Europe

Boeing C-135 Stratolifter variants

FOUR-TURBOFAN TRANSPORT AIRCRAFT

Boeing OC-135B United States Air Force Open Skies

DEVELOPMENT

Despite being one of the world's most potent air arms, the US Air Force transport fleet was predominantly made up of piston-engined aircraft at the dawn of the 1960s, when it was acknowledged that an urgent need existed for jet-powered aircraft. Boeing's KC-135 Stratotanker was then in series production for Strategic Air Command and it was decided in 1960 that a number of suitably modified aircraft should be purchased for the Military Air Transport Service (MATS) as the C-135 Stratolifter. This would, however, be purely an interim solution, giving MATS jet experience pending delivery of the Lockheed C-141 StarLifter, development of which was launched at about the same time. In the event, a total of 48 C-135s was obtained by MATS, which operated them for several years.

CURRENT SERVICE

Only one of the 48 aircraft supplied to MATS retains its original designation, this being a C-135B assigned to the New Jersey Air National Guard. However, this machine features satellite communications antennae and numerous other aerials and may well function as a command post. Nine other former MATS aircraft also

remain in use, but these have all been redesignated over the years. Two are known as OC-135Bs and perform 'Open Skies' surveillance duties with the 55th Reconnaissance Wing (a third OC-135B is held in storage). Two more are ostensibly engaged on weather reconnaissance as WC-135Ws, although one is probably used to evaluate electronic reconnaissance equipment since it is based at Majors Field, Greenville, Texas. Others have become C-135C (one still in use), C-135E (three in use) and EC-135N (one in use) and now undertake staff transport and test duties.

SPECIAL FEATURES

Basically similar to the KC-135 from which it evolved, the C-135 lacked in-flight refuelling equipment. The C-135A version was fitted with Pratt & Whitney J57 turbojets, while the C-135B was the first version to use TF33 turbofans.

VARIANTS

Two basic transport versions were originally built for MATS in the early 1960s, specifically the turbojet-powered **C-135A** and the turbofan-powered **C-135B**. Delivery of the first aircraft was expedited by the

conversion of three KC-135As to C-135A configuration on the production line and the first of these was handed over in June 1961. Subsequently, 15 more C-135As were built as such and they were followed by 30 examples of the C-135B. Service with MATS (and its successor, Military Airlift Command) came to an end in 1967. However, almost all these aircraft found new leases of life with other USAF organisations and commands and many were extensively modified. Such adaptations have included the **WC-135B** weather reconnaissance version, **EC-135N ARIA** (Advanced Range Instrumentation Aircraft), **VC-135B** executive transport, various types of **RC-135** for electronic reconnaissance missions (described separately) and the **TC-135** for crew training.

SEE ALSO: BOEING KC-135 STRATOTANKER & BOEING RC-135

TECHNICAL DATA

Boeing C-135B Stratolifter

Powerplants: Four Pratt & Whitney TF33-P-5 turbofans
Developing: 80.07kN (18,000lb st)
Span: 39.88m (130ft 10in)
Length: 41.00m (134ft 6in)
Height: 12.70m (41ft 8in)
All-up weight: 132,449kg (292,000lb)
Maximum speed: 966km/h (600mph)
Cruise speed: 850km/h (528mph)
Operational ceiling: 50,000ft
Maximum range: 7,443km (4,625 miles)
Accommodation: Flight crew plus up to 60 passengers, depending on configuration
First flown: 20 December 1961
Entered service: March 1962

Boeing C-135B United States Air Force

Boeing RC-135 variants

FOUR-TURBOFAN ELECTRONIC RECONNAISSANCE AIRCRAFT

Boeing RC-135V United States Air Force

DEVELOPMENT

Basic development of the Boeing KC-135 Stratotanker – from which a number of aircraft were modified for strategic reconnaissance duties – is described elsewhere. However, ten aircraft were purpose-built for this duty as RC-135Bs in the mid-1960s, although they did not see operational service. Instead, they were flown to Martin Aircraft at Baltimore to be fitted out for the reconnaissance and intelligence gathering role, which eventually culminated with delivery of the first RC-135C

TECHNICAL DATA

Boeing RC-135V

Powerplants: Four Pratt & Whitney TF33 turbofans
Developing: 80.07kN (18,000lb st)
Span: 39.88m (130ft 10in)
Length: 42.82m (140ft 6in)
Height: 12.70m (41ft 8in)
All-up weight: approx 136,077kg (300,000lb)
Maximum speed: 966km/h (600mph)
Operational ceiling: 41,750ft
Maximum range: 9,100km (5,650 miles)
Endurance: 11 hours (without in-flight refuelling)
Accommodation: Flight crew of four and 25 to 35 mission crew
First flown: 18 May 1964 (as RC-135B)
Entered service: 27 January 1967 (first delivery as RC-135C); April 1967 (first operational sortie)

Boeing RC-135V United States Air Force

to the 55th Strategic Reconnaissance Wing in January 1967. Further upgrading resulted in these aircraft being converted to RC-135U and RC-135V standard, while the RC-135S and RC-135W models began life as pure transport C-135Bs, before being modified for reconnaissance tasks.

CURRENT SERVICE

All 22 RC-135s currently on the USAF inventory are assigned to the 55th Reconnaissance Wing at Offutt AFB, Nebraska. From there, they routinely deploy to other bases, with major overseas operating locations including RAF Mildenhall in England and Kadena, Okinawa.

SPECIAL FEATURES

The configuration of these aircraft varies markedly depending upon the mission that is performed. 'Rivet Joint' RC-135Vs and RC-135Ws feature the classic extended 'hog nose' and large cheek fairings on the forward fuselage that contain antennae associated with intelligence gathering. They also have a large antennae 'farm' on the fuselage undersides that forms part of the multiple communications emitter locator system (MUCELS). 'Combat Sent' RC-135Us have cheek fairings, but lack the 'hog nose', although they are fitted with numerous other fairings at the nose, tail and wingtips. Finally, the RC-135S has the 'hog nose', but has only small cheeks in conjunction with three

tube-like fairings. Other distinguishing features of the RC-135S include a teardrop-shaped fairing on the aft fuselage and additional windows for infrared and optical sensors used to track missiles and re-entry vehicles. Plans are in hand to re-engine the entire fleet with the CFM International F108 turbofan.

VARIANTS

Four reconnaissance-dedicated versions of the C-135 presently exist, although many others have seen service since the early 1960s, when suitably modified Stratotankers were first assigned to electronic intelligence gathering duty. Versions in use today comprise the **RC-135S 'Cobra Ball'** (three aircraft in two different configurations), **RC-135U 'Combat Sent'** (two aircraft), **RC-135V 'Rivet Joint'** (eight aircraft) and **RC-135W 'Rivet Joint'** (nine aircraft). Training and operational support tasks are performed by single examples of the **TC-135S** and **TC-135W**. These are similar in appearance to their operational counterparts, with the TC-135S having a black-painted wing and 'hog nose' even though it lacks mission equipment. The TC-135W also incorporates the 'hog nose' and is fitted with cheek fairings, but it too has no mission equipment.

Boeing E-3 Sentry

FOUR-TURBOFAN AWACS AIRBORNE RADAR AND COMMAND PLATFORM

E-3A Sentry NATO

TECHNICAL DATA

Boeing E-3C Sentry
Powerplants: Four Pratt & Whitney
TF33-PW-100/100A turbofans
Developing: 93.4kN (21,000lb st)
Span: 44.42m (145ft 9in)
Length: 46.61m (152ft 11in)
Height: 12.73m (41ft 9in)
All-up weight: 150,820kg (332,500lb)
Maximum speed: 853km/h (530mph)
Operational ceiling: over 29,000ft
Maximum range: undisclosed
Mission range: over 3,218km (2,000 miles)
Endurance: approximately 11 hours unrefuelled
Accommodation: Four-man crew on flight deck;
up to 18 AWACS specialists/system operators
Warload: None; inboard underwing hardpoints
on some aircraft, but usually employed for
additional mission related pods. Could carry
self-defence AAMs
First flown: 5 February 1972 (EC-137D);
31 October 1975 (E-3A)
Entered service: 24 March 1977

DEVELOPMENT

Boeing was contracted in 1970 to develop a new generation airborne long-endurance AWACS (Airborne Warning And Control System) platform partly to replace existing radar-equipped Lockheed EC-121 Warning Stars. Two Boeing 707-320 airframes were converted into EC-137D testbeds, initially flying in 1972. The rotating-radome mounted Westinghouse AN/APY-1 airborne surveillance radar was later selected, and the first genuine E-3A layout first flew in October 1975; initial service deliveries were made in March 1977 to the USAF's 552nd Airborne Warning and Control Wing. The USAF eventually contracted for some 34 E-3 Sentries, finished or upgraded to several marks including Core E-3A, E-3B, NATO Standard E-3A, and the recent upgraded E-3C. The last was delivered in 1984. In 1978, NATO member countries agreed to the establishment of a NATO AEW force; 18 E-3A NATO Standard aircraft were ordered, and delivered from 1982. All are civil registered in Luxembourg. The failed Nimrod AEW3 programme led Britain to contract in 1986 for six (later seven) AWACS to E-3D Sentry AEW1 standard, the first being delivered to the RAF in 1991. In 1987, France ordered four AWACS to E-3F SDA standard, with official delivery to the French Air Force in 1991 and 1992. Under the 'Peace Sentinel' programme, Saudi Arabia received five E-3A from mid-1986, plus eight unique KE-3A air refuelling

tanker/transports. Boeing states that 68 E-3 of all marks were built (excluding the Saudi KE-3As).

CURRENT SERVICE

The USAF's Sentry fleet is concentrated at Tinker AFB, Oklahoma, with the three squadrons (963rd, 964th, 965th ACSs) of the 552nd Airborne Control Wing of Air Combat Command; the 962nd ACS at Elmendorf AFB, Alaska, and 961st ACS at Kadena AB, Okinawa, operate within Pacific Air Forces. USAF Sentries operate from overseas bases as required during times of NATO or UN operations. The 17 surviving Sentries of NATO's Airborne Early Warning Force (NAEWF) are based at Geilenkirchen in Germany, with forward operating bases in a number of member countries. The RAF's Sentry force, a component of the NAEWF, is based at Waddington with Nos 8 and 23 Squadrons. French Sentries fly with EDCA 00.036 at Bourges-Avord. Royal Saudi Air Force E-3A and KE-3A aircraft operate with No 18 Squadron at Prince Sultan AB, Riyadh.

SPECIAL FEATURES

The E-3 is based on the Boeing 707-320 layout but strengthened and 'hardened', and with the addition of the rotating radome and its support structure. The fuselage contains multiple consoles and workstations for the AWACS specialists and systems operators, and various equipment bays.

VARIANTS

USAF and NATO Sentries are 'flying boom' in-flight refuelled, while RAF aircraft are 'probe and drogue' refuelled. RAF aircraft have increased span due to wingtip-mounted ESM pods. RAF and French aircraft are powered by CFM International CFM56-2A-3 turbofans of 106.8kN (24,000lb st). Upgrades to US aircraft have introduced more powerful computers, and other improvements including GPS, upgraded radar and a limited maritime surveillance capability, in addition to the air surveillance main role. All later aircraft have AN/APY-2 radar. Other upgrades include JTIDS (Joint Tactical Information Distribution System). USAF and NATO E-3s are being fitted with ESM sensors in side-mounted canoe fairings. **E-3Ds** have wing-tip mounted Loral ESM pods.

SEE ALSO: BOEING 707, BOEING E-6 MERCURY & NORTHROP GRUMMAN/BOEING E-8 J-STARS

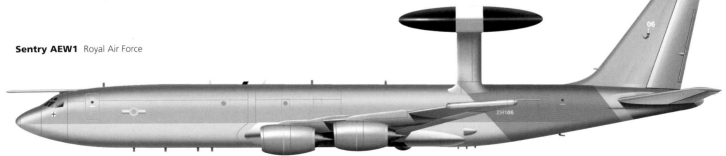

Sentry AEW1 Royal Air Force

Boeing E-6 Mercury

FOUR-TURBOFAN LONG ENDURANCE COMMUNICATIONS RELAY AIRCRAFT

E-6B Mercury United States Navy

TECHNICAL DATA

Boeing E-6A Mercury

Powerplants: Four CFM International F108-CF-100 turbofans

Developing: 106.8kN (24,000lb st)

Span: 45.16m (148ft 2in)

Length: 46.61m (152ft 11in)

Height: 12.93m (42ft 5in)

All-up weight: 155,128kg (342,000lb)

Maximum speed: 981km/h (610mph)

Cruise speed: 842km/h (523mph)

Operational ceiling: 42,000ft

Maximum range: undisclosed

Mission range: 11,760km (7,307 miles)

Endurance: up to 15 hours 24 minutes unrefuelled

Accommodation: Four-man crew on flight deck; up to five communications operators, or increased mission crew for extended or remote deployment assignments

Warload: None

First flown: 19 February 1987

Entered service: 2 August 1989

DEVELOPMENT

One of several important military derivatives of the Boeing 707, the E-6 Mercury (originally named Hermes) was developed as a new generation airborne long-endurance communications relay platform, providing the link between the US national command authority and the US Navy's nuclear submarines (particularly the Trident ballistic nuclear submarine fleet). Previously this communications task had been performed by US Navy Lockheed EC-130Q Hercules, and is known by the Americanism TACAMO (TAke Charge And Move Out). The E-6 prototype/systems development aircraft first flew in February 1987 (with the first full test flight in June 1987). A total of 16 E-6As was built, including the prototype. With a similar basic airframe to the E-3 Sentry, these new-build machines of Boeing 707 layout had CFM International powerplants. The first two examples were delivered to US Navy Squadron VQ-3 at Naval Air Station Barber's Point, Hawaii, in August 1989 for Pacific area coverage; VQ-4 at NAS Patuxent River, Maryland, received its first E-6A in January 1991 for Atlantic/Mediterranean coverage. Reduced East-West tension led to the previous continuous TACAMO airborne alert being ended in 1991. The E-6A force was duly concentrated at Tinker AFB, Oklahoma, but with detachments elsewhere. An upgrade to E-6B standard (by Raytheon) has seen the Mercury fleet taking over the USAF's EC-135C 'Looking Glass' airborne command post role in support

of the US ground-based ICBM force. E-6B airborne command post operations began in early 1998, and the final Mercury conversion/upgrade is contracted for 2001.

CURRENT SERVICE

The US Navy's E-6A/E-6B force, comprising VQ-3 'Ironmen' and VQ-4 'Shadows', is based at Tinker AFB, Oklahoma, under the USAF's Strategic Communications Wing One. Detachments are maintained at Travis AFB, California, Offutt AFB, Nebraska, and NAS Patuxent River, Maryland. The Offutt detachment specifically continues the 'Looking Glass' airborne command post role.

SPECIAL FEATURES

Similar to the Sentry but without that type's rotating radome and support structure, the E-6 also has the E-3's nuclear and electromagnetic pulse 'hardening', but with corrosion protection, other detail differences and various pods and antennae around the airframe including satellite communications/ESM pods at the wingtips. Highly sophisticated and classified on-board avionics include airborne very low frequency (AVLF) equipment, VHF and UHF communications equipment with secure voice capability, and sophisticated airborne navigation and GPS avionics. AVLF communication with submerged submarines is achieved using a 7,925m (26,000 ft) long trailing wire aerial, with a 41 kg (90lb)

drogue at its end, which the E-6 deploys and flies in tight circuits to make the aerial hang vertically for maximum effectiveness. Advanced communications equipment is similarly carried for links with other components (airborne or ground-based) of the US national command authority.

VARIANTS

Most if not all of the Mercury fleet will be modified to E-6B standard. This includes the installation of airborne national command post (ABNCP) communications and related equipment to allow the E-6B to relay command and communications to the land-based US ICBM force, in addition to continuing the role of communications relay platform with the US Navy's nuclear submarines.

SEE ALSO: BOEING 707, BOEING E-3 SENTRY & NORTHROP GRUMMAN/BOEING E-8 J-STARS

E-6B Mercury United States Navy

Boeing 727/C-22

THREE-TURBOFAN PASSENGER TRANSPORT AIRCRAFT

Boeing C-22B United States Air Force

DEVELOPMENT

The 727 was Boeing's first attempt to satisfy airline demand for a jet-powered aircraft designed specifically for short-to-medium haul routes. It was undoubtedly one of the most important products to originate from

TECHNICAL DATA

Boeing 727-200

Powerplants: Three Pratt & Whitney JT8D-9A turbofans
Developing: 64.50kN (14,500lb st)
Span: 32.92m (108ft 0in)
Length: 46.69m (153ft 2in)
Height: 10.36m (34ft 0in)
All-up weight: 95,027kg (209,500lb)
Maximum speed: 1,001km/h (622mph)
Cruise speed: 871km/h (541mph)
Maximum range: 4,392km (2,720 miles) with 12,474kg (27,500lb) payload
Accommodation: Flight crew of four, plus four cabin crew; passenger numbers dependent on cabin layout
Payload: 18,144kg (40,000lb)
First flown: 9 February 1963 (prototype commercial 727-100); 27 July 1967 (727-200)
Entered service: February 1964 (commercial 727-100); December 1967 (commercial 727-200)

Boeing's prolific drawing office in the 1960s. Design work was undertaken at the very start of that decade and roll-out of the prototype in late November 1962 revealed that Boeing had opted for a radical rethink, in choosing to press ahead with a tri-jet concept. The prototype 727 flew for the first time in early February 1963 and paved the way for a particularly successful era in Boeing history, for it turned out to be the progenitor of no fewer than 1,830 aircraft.

CURRENT SERVICE

Although never widely used by military air arms, the number has declined in recent years and less than 10 examples of the Boeing 727 remain active in military service. With the US Air Force, the Air National Guard has three C-22Bs (727-100) that serve as staff transports from Andrews AFB, while there is also one C-22C (727-200) that is believed to be assigned to the 486th Flight Test Squadron. Other purely military operators comprise the Mexican Air Force and the Royal New Zealand Air Force, each of which possesses a pair of aircraft. In Latin America, the military-run airlines SATENA of Colombia and TAME of Ecuador use the 727 in limited quantities, while others are utilised for VIP airlift duties by several governments, including those of Bahrain, Burkina Faso, Congo, Nigeria, Saudi Arabia, Taiwan and the Yemen.

SPECIAL FEATURES

The most distinctive single characteristic of the Boeing 727 is the engine installation, which was possibly influenced by the French Caravelle airliner. It was certainly identical to the de Havilland DH 121 Trident in that it features single podded engines attached to each aft fuselage side, with a third engine buried in the aft fuselage and fed by an inlet that extends forward from the base of the fin. Like the British Trident, it also made use of a high-set tailplane.

VARIANTS

Numerous derivatives of the basic Model 727 emerged during the course of a lengthy production run, but none were built specifically for military operators. The original **727-100** series remained in production until 1972, by which time almost 600 had been built, but that number was handsomely exceeded by the stretched **727-200** which had greater passenger capacity and, as a direct consequence, increased earning power. When production of the 727-200 series finally ended in September 1984, more than 1,250 had emerged from the factory in Seattle.

Boeing 727-109 Republic of China Air Force

Boeing 737/C-40 & T-43

Boeing T-43A United States Air Force

DEVELOPMENT

Easily the world's most successful jet airliner, with more than 4,250 examples sold to date and no sign of a drop in demand, the Boeing 737 emerged in the mid-1960s and was intended specifically to undertake short-haul, high-frequency services. Flown for the first time in prototype form during April 1967, it was certified by the US Federal Aviation Agency in December 1967

TECHNICAL DATA

Boeing T-43A

Powerplants: Two Pratt & Whitney JT8D turbofans
Developing: 64.4kN (14,500lb st)
Span: 28.35m (93ft 0in)
Length: 30.48m (100ft 0in)
Height: 11.28m (37ft 0in)
All-up weight: 52,391kg (115,500lb)
Maximum speed: 1,010km/h (628mph)
Cruise speed: 927km/h (576mph)
Maximum range: 4,818km (2,994 miles)
Endurance: 6hr
Accommodation: Flight deck crew plus up to 16 students and three instructors
First flown: 9 April 1967 (Boeing 737 prototype)
Entered service: 1968 (commercial operations); July 1973 (T-43A)

and entered passenger-carrying service with United Airlines in early 1968. Since then, stretched and re-engined models have appeared and the latest 'Next Generation' 737s bear only a superficial resemblance to the original prototype.

CURRENT SERVICE

The major operator of variations on the Boeing 737 theme is the US Air Force, which acquired 19 T-43As in the first half of the 1970s as replacements for piston-powered T-29s in the navigation training role. At the present time, ten T-43As still serve with the 12th Flying Training Wing at Randolph AFB, Texas, while two more are in store. Seven others used for transport tasks were redesignated as CT-43As, although only six survive, with one assigned to Central Command as a staff transport, while the other five operate in civilian guise on so-called 'Janet' flights between Las Vegas and the test base at Groom Lake, Nevada. A version of the 737-700 known as the C-40A Clipper is on order by the US Navy to replace C-9 and DC-9 Skytrain II aircraft with Reserve transport squadrons from late 2000. Versions of the 737 have also been purchased for the air arms of Brazil, Chile, India, Mexico, South Korea, Taiwan, Thailand and Venezuela, mainly for VIP airlift tasks, while Indonesia has a trio of maritime surveillance versions and Australia has selected an

AEW derivative. Several governments use 737s in civil markings, including Iran, Niger, Pakistan, Saudi Arabia, Sharjah and Turkmenistan.

SPECIAL FEATURES

The 737 features the characteristic low-wing, podded engine layout introduced by the Boeing 367-80 in the mid-1950s and used in every Boeing airliner design since. Intended to complement the 707 and 727 by filling the short-to-medium haul market niche, the 737 has an identical fuselage cross section. The T-43 has navigation stations fitted along the starboard side of the fuselage.

VARIANTS

Numerous derivatives have emerged and production continues of the 'Next Generation' versions, with current models comprising the **737-600, 737-700, 737-800** and **737-900** series. Purely military aircraft are the **T-43A** navigation trainer and **CT-43A** transport of the USAF; the **C-40A** Clipper transport for the US Navy and the **737AEW&C** ordered by Australia.

Boeing 737 Surveiller
Indonesian Air Force

Boeing VC-25A United States Air Force

DEVELOPMENT

Conceived in the latter half of the 1960s, the Boeing 747 revolutionised the airline business and was almost solely responsible for bringing air travel within the reach of a wider public. When its development was launched in July 1966, following an order for 25 from the now defunct Pan American World Airways, it was undoubtedly a most risky venture, and became a great technical achievement. Flown for the first time in February 1969, flight testing was accomplished in a remarkably short time, and Pan Am took delivery of its first aircraft on 12 December 1969, with the first revenue-earning service being flown on 21 January 1970. Since then, numerous improvements have been incorporated in the basic design and the 747 remains in demand for long-haul operators today.

CURRENT SERVICE

Although well over 1,000 examples of the Boeing 747 have been built, the majority has been for airline customers and very few have ever donned military battledress. Nevertheless, three air forces are presently operating versions of the basic type. The US Air Force has a total of six aircraft at the moment, comprising a pair of VC-25A Presidential transports and four E-4B National Emergency Airborne Command Post (NEACP) aircraft and will eventually possess a small fleet of AL-1As, armed with a powerful laser for the destruction of ballistic missiles. Executive airlift duties are also performed by two Boeing 747-47Cs that serve with the Japan Air Self-Defence Force's 701 Squadron, while Iran retains some of the 16 aircraft received prior to the overthrow of the Shah. Several other luxuriously appointed 747s and 747SPs are employed as Government transports by Brunei, Oman, Qatar, Saudi Arabia and the United Arab Emirates.

SPECIAL FEATURES

The first wide-bodied airliner to be conceived, the first to fly and the first to enter service, the 747 nevertheless retained standard Boeing features. Most noteworthy among these is the low-wing, podded-engine, layout that was perfected by earlier aircraft from the Seattle company, such as the KC-135 and 707/720 series. However, the 747 was on a rather greater scale than anything previously undertaken by Boeing.

VARIANTS

Numerous commercial derivatives have been produced over the years, including the shortened **747SP**, but only the **747-400** series is now in production, with Boeing currently offering all-passenger or combi passenger/cargo versions, and specialist freighters. Purely military versions acquired by the USAF comprise the **VC-25A** executive transport, the **E-4** airborne command post and the forthcoming **AL-1A** anti-ballistic missile defence aircraft.

TECHNICAL DATA

Boeing E-4B

Powerplants: Four General Electric F103-GE-100 turbofans
Developing: 233.53kN (52,500lb st)
Span: 59.64m (195ft 8in)
Length: 70.51m (231ft 4in)
Height: 19.33m (63ft 5in)
All-up weight: 362,874kg (800,000lb)
Maximum speed: 969km/h (602mph)
Cruise speed: 933km/h (580mph)
Operational ceiling: 45,000ft
Maximum range: 12,600km (7,830 miles)
Endurance: 12 hours (without in-flight refuelling); 72 hours (with in-flight refuelling)
Accommodation: Four crew plus reserve crew, battle staff and mission specialists
First flown: 9 February 1969 (Boeing 747); 13 June 1973 (E-4A)
Entered service: 1974 (E-4A); 1980 (E-4B)

Boeing E-4B United States Air Force

Boeing 757/C-32

TWIN-TURBOFAN EXECUTIVE TRANSPORT AIRCRAFT

Boeing C-32A United States Air Force

DEVELOPMENT

Designed to satisfy the market for a medium-range turbofan-powered airliner with modern avionics equipment, the decision to proceed with the Boeing 757 was made public in early 1978, and development was launched immediately thereafter, with Eastern Airlines and British Airways placing orders in August of that year. Utilising the same fuselage cross section as the earlier 707/727/737 airliners, manufacture of a prototype was undertaken in the early 1980s and this duly flew for the first time in February 1982. At that time, it was powered by Rolls-Royce RB535C engines, but alternative Pratt & Whitney PW2037 or PW2040 turbofans were subsequently offered. Certification for passenger operations was awarded shortly before the end of 1982, with the first revenue-earning services being flown on 1 January 1983 by Eastern Airlines. By

the start of 1999, almost 1,000 examples of the Boeing 757 had been ordered, with production continuing at a rate of about 48 per year from 2000 onwards.

CURRENT SERVICE

Several air arms presently operate variations on the Boeing 757 theme, with the US Air Force having purchased four examples that were delivered in 1998-1999. Given the military designation C-32A in USAF service, these are engaged in executive air transport tasks with the 89th Airlift Wing at Andrews AFB, on the outskirts of Washington. Other military operators are Argentina and Mexico, which each possess single examples for similar duties. Kazakhstan, Saudi Arabia and Turkmenistan also use Boeing 757s as government transports, although these aircraft are all operated in civilian guise.

SPECIAL FEATURES

The Boeing 757 incorporates established design characteristics associated with other products from this manufacturer, such as the podded underslung

engines, married to a low-wing configuration that features sophisticated high-lift devices to ensure good field performance at all weights. Alternative powerplants are available to satisfy varying customer requirements, with options currently comprising the Rolls-Royce 535E4/E4B, Pratt & Whitney PW2037 and Pratt & Whitney PW2040.

VARIANTS

Several versions of the basic **Boeing 757-200** airliner have emerged since the type entered service in the early 1980s, including the **757-200PF Package Freighter** optimised for the carriage of freight by United Parcel Service, the **757-200 Freighter** conversion and the **757-200M Combi**, which is a mixed cargo/passenger derivative. A more recent development is the **757-300**, which is a stretched version with increased passenger seating. The only purely military model to emerge to date has been the **C-32A** for the USAF executive airlift role. Powered by PW2040 engines, the C-32A is essentially similar to the basic 757-200 as delivered to civilian customers, although it has a VIP cabin interior.

TECHNICAL DATA

Boeing 757-200

Powerplants: Two Pratt & Whitney PW2040 turbofans
Developing: 185.49kN (41,700lb st)
Span: 38.05m (124ft 10in)
Length: 47.32m (155ft 3in)
Height: 13.56m (44ft 6in)
All-up weight: 115,666kg (255,000lb)
Cruise speed: 850km/h (527mph)
Cruise altitude: 41,000ft
Maximum range: 7,277km (4,522 miles)
Accommodation: 16 crew and 45 passengers
First flown: 19 February 1982 (757 prototype); 11 February 1998 (C-32A)
Entered service: January 1983 (commercial 757); June 1998 (C-32A)

Boeing C-32A United States Air Force

Boeing 767 AWACS

TWIN-TURBOFAN AIRBORNE WARNING AND CONTROL AIRCRAFT

Boeing E-767 AWACS Japanese Air Self-Defence Force

DEVELOPMENT
Development of the Boeing 767-200 airliner on which the 767 AWACS is based began in the latter half of the 1970s, and a decision to go-ahead was taken in July 1978, following receipt of an order for 30 aircraft from United Airlines. Assembly of the 767 prototype commenced in July 1979 and this flew for the first time in late September 1981, powered by Pratt & Whitney JT9D turbofans; subsequently, the first flight of an aircraft fitted with General Electric CF6-80A engines took place on 19 February 1982. In December 1991, Boeing revealed that the 767 had been chosen as a potential replacement platform for the E-3 Sentry

in the airborne command and control mission. Detail design studies were undertaken and in November 1993 Japan ordered two aircraft as E-767s. The maiden flight took place in October 1994 without the rotodome, which was not installed until 1996. Initial flight with the rotodome took place on 9 August 1996.

CURRENT SERVICE
The only air arm that has purchased the 767 AWACS to date is Japan, which has received four, although a requirement is understood to exist for another four. The initial pair of aircraft was handed over at Boeing's Seattle factory on 11 March 1998 and they arrived in Japan on 23 March 1998, being joined by the second pair at the beginning of 1999. All four are currently assigned to 601 Squadron, operating from Hamamatsu Air Base. Several other air arms have expressed interest in acquiring the 767 AWACS, but no orders have been placed.

SPECIAL FEATURES
The basic Model 767 incorporates classic Boeing design

features such as podded engines suspended from a low-wing configuration. The 767 AWACS variant is most easily identifiable by the prominent rotodome which is mounted on struts above the aft fuselage section and contains the Westinghouse AN/APY-2 E/F-band surveillance radar (as on the E-3). Internally it is configured with stations for communications, data processing, eight multi-function operator consoles in two rows, equipment bays, gallery and crew rest area.

VARIANTS
Although Boeing has proposed tanker/transport and ground surveillance derivatives of the 767, military use of this type is limited to the quartet of aircraft used by Japan for airborne command and control. However, the Brunei government possesses one VIP-configured 767-200 and the US Army has been using the original prototype as an airborne sensor testbed, although this is still owned by Boeing and flown in civil markings under contract. Numerous versions have also been developed for airline service, with total sales now approaching the 1,000 mark.

TECHNICAL DATA

Boeing E-767 AWACS

Powerplants: Two General Electric CF6-80C2B6FA turbofans
Developing: 273.6kN (61,500lb st)
Span: 47.57m (156ft 1in)
Length: 48.51m (159ft 2in)
Height: 15.85m (52ft 0in)
All-up weight: 174,635kg (385,000lb)
Cruise speed: exceeds 805km/h (500mph)
Operational ceiling: 43,000ft
Maximum range: 8,334-9,260km
(5,178-5,754 miles)
Endurance: 13 hours (at 556km; 345 mile radius)
Accommodation: Two flight crew and up to 19 mission specialists
First flown: 26 September 1981 (767 prototype); 10 October 1994 (767 AWACS)
Entered service: 8 September 1982 (767 airliner); 23 March 1998 (767 AWACS delivery to Japan)

Boeing E-767 AWACS Japanese Air Self-Defence Force

Boeing (McDonnell Douglas) F-15 Eagle

TWIN-TURBOFAN HIGH-PERFORMANCE AIR SUPERIORITY FIGHTER

F-15C Eagle United States Air Force

TECHNICAL DATA

McDonnell Douglas F-15C Eagle

Powerplants: Two Pratt & Whitney F100-PW-220 turbofans
Developing: 65.26kN (14,670lb st) dry and 106.0 kN (23,830lb st) with afterburning
Span: 13.05m (42ft 9.75in)
Length: 19.43m (63ft 9in)
Height: 5.63m (18ft 5.5in)
All up weight: 68,000kg (30,845lb)
Maximum speed: 2,655km/h (1,650mph))
Operational ceiling: 60,000ft
Range: 5,745km (3,570 miles) with drop tanks
Endurance: 5hr 15min
Accommodation: One pilot (two in F-15B/D)
Warload: One M61A1 20mm cannon. Maximum ordnance 7,257 or 10,705kg (16,000lb or 23,000lb) with and without conformal fuel tanks, usually four AIM-9s and four AIM-7s, with the AIM-7s replaced by AIM-120s in the F-15C MSIP version.
First flown: 27 July 1972 (F-15A);
26 February 1979 (F-15C)
Entered service: January 1976 (F-15A);
September 1979 (F-15C)

DEVELOPMENT

Incorporating all the lessons learned from air-to-air combat during the Vietnam War, the McDonnell Douglas Eagle arose from the USAF's FX requirement, for a long-range air superiority fighter to replace the F-4 Phantom II. The first of ten single-seat F-15A development aircraft flew in July 1972; the first of two two-seat development F-15Bs on 7 July 1973. Early problems involved the Pratt & Whitney F100-PW-100 engine and the Hughes APG-63 radar, but these were overcome, allowing the Eagle to first enter service with the 1st TFW based at Langley AFB, Virginia. In April 1977, the first Eagles arrived in Europe with the 36th Tactical Fighter Wing based at Bitburg, Germany. Continual development of the type resulted in the emergence of the improved F-15C and F-15D, fitted with an improved APG-63 and the ability to carry Conformal Fuel Tanks (CFT), adding 750 US gallons (2389 litres) of fuel. An upgrade of the flight software increase the flight envelope to 9g, while later F-15C/Ds gained the more powerful P&W F100-PW-220 engine. The first unit with the improved Eagles was the 18th TFW at Kadena AB, in September 1979. The first export Eagles arrived in Israel in December 1976, with the IDF/AF christening them the Baz (Falcon), while later F-15C/D deliveries become known as the Akef (Buzzard). Japan decided to licence produce the Eagle as the F-15J to replace its F-104Js with the JASDF, and plans to acquire a total of 224. Saudi Arabia procured F-15C/D aircraft under Project *Peace Sun*, with the first

arriving on 11 August 1981. A Multi-Stage Improvement Program (MSIP) was designed for the USAF's F-15A/Bs and F-15C/Ds that featured radar and other avionics improvements. The first operator of MSIP F-15C/Ds was the 33rd TFW at Eglin AFB, which was responsible for the bulk of Eagle 'kills' during the Gulf War.

CURRENT SERVICE

Israel (38 F-15A, 6 F-15B, 16 F-15C, 11 F-15D); Japan (166 F-15J, 45 F-15DJ); Saudi Arabia (87 F-15C/D); USAF (103 F-15A, 21 F-15B, 348 F-15C, 51 F-15D), serving with Air Combat Command, Air National Guard, Air Force Reserve Command, Air Educational and Training Command, Air Force Systems Command, USAF Europe, Pacific Air Forces and NASA.

SPECIAL FEATURES

With a thrust-to-weight ratio beyond unity and a large warload contained within an extremely agile airframe, the Eagle is still one of the world's best dog-fighters, even nearly 30 years after its first flight.

VARIANTS

F-15A – first production version for the USAF; **TF-15A** – initial designation of the **F-15B** conversion trainer; **F-15A/B MSIP** Multi-Stage Improvement Program upgrade of F-15A and F-15Bs featuring some portions of the MSIP II for F-15C/Ds, including Dash 220E F100 engines, 9g capability, and improvements to the original APG-63; **NF-15B** – an early TF-15A fitted with

canards used as the STOL/Manoeuvre Technology Demonstrator (S/MTD), before becoming the ACTIVE (Advanced Control Technology for Integrated Vehicles) aircraft fitted with thrust vectoring nozzles; **F-15C** – improved air superiority fighter, fitted with upgraded APG-63 and able to carry CFTs; **F-15C/D MSIP-II** Multi-Stage Improvement Program II which included an upgrade of the APG-63 radar to APG-70 standard, giving the F-15C/D the ability to fire the AIM-120; **F-15D** – two-seat conversion trainer version of the F-15C; **F-15DJ** – two-seat conversion trainers for the JASDF, original aircraft built by McDonnell Douglas, later examples by Mitsubishi; **F-15J** – F-15C version for the JASDF, all but two built by Mitsubishi.

SEE ALSO: BOEING (McDONNELL DOUGLAS) F-15 STRIKE EAGLE

F-15J Eagle Japanese Air Self Defence Force

Boeing (McDonnell Douglas) F-15E Strike Eagle

TWIN-TURBOFAN HIGH-PERFORMANCE TWO-SEAT MULTI-ROLE STRIKE FIGHTER

F-15E Strike Eagle United States Air Force

TECHNICAL DATA

McDonnell Douglas F-15E Strike Eagle

Powerplants: Two Pratt & Whitney F100-PW-220 turbofans (later F100-PW-229)
Developing: 79.2kN (17,800lb st) and 129.4kN (29,100lb st) with afterburning
Span: 13.05m (42ft 9.75in)
Length: 19.43m (63ft 9in)
Height: 5.63m (18ft 5.5in)
All up weight: 3,6741kg (81,000lb)
Maximum speed: 2,655 km/h (1,650mph)
Cruise speed: 917km/h (568mph)
Operational ceiling: 60,000ft
Range: 5,745km (3,570 miles) with CFTs and drop tanks
Accommodation: One pilot and one Weapon Systems Operator (WSO), in tandem
Warload: One M61A1 20mm Vulcan cannon. Maximum ordnance 11,000kg (24,250lb), including Mk 82 227kg (500lb) bombs (26 of), Mk 84 907kg (2,000lb) bombs (7 of), BGU-10 (7), GBU-12 (15) or GBU-15 (2) guided munitions all with an AN/AXQ-14 datalink pod. Other munitions include CBU-52, -58, -71, -87, -89, -90, -92 or -93 bombs, AGM-65 Mavericks, AGM-88 HARM or B57 or B61 nuclear bombs. AIM-7M, AIM-9 and AIM-120s can be carried for self-defence.
First flown: 11 December 1986 (1st production)
Entered service: 1988

DEVELOPMENT

Although the original F-15 Eagle was developed for the air superiority role, the ability of the type to perform strike missions was not lost on McDonnell Douglas. They privately funded a development of the F-15B as the Enhanced Tactical Fighter, using the second pre-production aircraft. Fitted with an AAQ-26 Pave Tack laser range finding/designator, a modified APG-63 radar and carrying a weapon systems officer (WSO) in the rear seat, the Strike Eagle first flew on 8 July 1980, and was the winner of Tactical Air Command's Dual-Role Fighter programme for an F-111 replacement in February 1984, beating the rival General Dynamics F-16XL, with the USAF ordering the type as the F-15E. The Pave Tack pod was replaced by the Low-Altitude Navigation and Targeting for Night (LANTIRN) pod on the production aircraft. The radar was a modified APG-70 with a new SAR capability, allowing accurate radar maps of the target area to be produced. The first F-15E was flown in December 1986, with the first operator being the 405th Tactical Training Wing at Luke AFB. The unit was called up for duty in the Persian Gulf in August 1990, and during *Desert Storm* the

radar was found to be useful for 'Scud-hunting'. The USAF has ordered a total of 229 aircraft, the latest three having been ordered in May 2000. Israel ordered the Strike Eagle in May 1994, initially ordering 21 F-15Is under the *Peace Sun V* programme, followed by four further aircraft within the *Peace Sun VI* programme. Saudi Arabia ordered 72 slightly down-graded Strike Eagles as F-15Ss, the first of which flew on 19 June 1995.

CURRENT SERVICE

Israel – 25 F-15Is with 69 Tayeset, Bacha 8 at Tel Norf; Saudi Arabia – 72 F-15Ss with No 55 Squadron at King Khalid AB, Khamis Mushart; USAF – 202 F-15Es, serving with Air Combat Command, Air Educational and Training Command, Air Force Systems Command, USAF Europe and Pacific Air Forces.

SPECIAL FEATURES

The Strike Eagle is able to penetrate sophisticated air defences, identify and designate a target and then destroy it with guided munitions. Its ability to carry a wide range of munitions makes it one of the most

versatile aircraft in the USAF inventory, while its Eagle ancestry means the type is also capable of air-to-air engagements.

VARIANTS

F-15E – standard USAF 'Strike Eagle'; **F-15I** – long range interdictor version for the Israeli Defence Force/Air Force, who have christened it the Ra'am (Thunder); **F-15S** – slightly downgraded F-15E for the Royal Saudi Air Force.

SEE ALSO: BOEING (McDONNELL DOUGLAS) F-15 EAGLE

F-15E Strike Eagle United States Air Force

Boeing (McDonnell Douglas) F/A-18 Hornet

TWIN-TURBOFAN HIGH-PERFORMANCE MULTI-ROLE STRIKE FIGHTER

USA

F/A-18D Hornet Swiss Air Force

TECHNICAL DATA

McDonnell Douglas F/A-18C Hornet

Powerplants: Two General Electric
F404-GE-402 EPE turbofans
Developing: 78.7kN (17,700lb st) with afterburning
Span: 11.43m (37ft 6in) without wingtip
mounted AAMs
Length: 17.07m (56ft 0in)
Height: 4.66m (15ft 3.5in)
All up weight: 2,5401kg (56,000lb)
Maximum speed: more than 1915km/h (1,190mph)
Operational ceiling: 50,000ft
Range: 3,336km (2,073 miles) with drop tanks
Accommodation: One pilot, or two in tandem in
F/A-18B/D
Warload: One M61A1 Vulcan 20mm cannon.
AIM-7, AIM-9 and AIM-120s can be carried for
the fighter role or for self defence. For strike
missions precision guided munitions, such as the
AGM-65 Maverick, AGM-84E SLAM, AGM-62
Walleye, GBU-10/12/16 laser guided bombs, or
unguided Mk 80 series of munitions and CBU-59
can be carried. AGM-84 Harpoon missiles can be
carried for anti-shipping strikes.
First flown: 18 November 1978 (pre-production
F/A-18A); 3 September 1986 (F/A-18C)
Entered service: August 1982

DEVELOPMENT

Developed from the Northrop YF-17A, which won the US Navy's Air Combat Fighter competition against the YF-16, the McDonnell Douglas F/A-18 Hornet was selected to replace the US Navy's A-7 Corsair IIs and the US Marine Corps' fleet of F-4 Phantom IIs. Originally dedicated fighter (F-18) and attack variants (A-18) were planned, but both missions were combined into the one airframe design, leading to the adoption of the unusual F/A-18 designation. First flying in November 1978, nine pre-production F/A-18As and two TF-18A two-seat operational conversion trainers were used in the development process. The first production aircraft started to join the US Navy in May 1980, but the first operational squadron to use the type was the US Marine Corps' VMFA-314, declared operational on 7 January 1983. In both the attack and the fighter role the type proved to be outstanding, in part due to the effectiveness of its AN/APG-65 radar. After 371 F/A-18As (and 40 F/A-18Bs) were produced, production switched to the improved F/A-18C, the first Hornet variant capable of firing the AIM-120 AMRAAM and imaging infrared Maverick missiles. Alongside the 'C, the F/A-18D two-seater was acquired by the USMC as a replacement for the A-6 Intruder. Later versions of the F/A-18D featured a night attack capability. Other F/A-18Ds have been modified to undertake the recce mission as F/A-18D(RC)s, being capable of operating the ATARS pod. Amongst those countries that bought the type, Australia, Finland and Switzerland chose to assemble the type in their own country. One of the problems with the original generation Hornet was a lack of range. Development of an enlarged version,

featuring a 86cm (2ft 10in) stretch in fuselage length and a 25% increase in wing area, started in the early 1990s. Ordered as the F/A-18E (single-seat) and F/A-18F (two seater), the 'Super Hornet' is due to replace older Hornet versions and the US Navy's F-14 Tomcat fighter. The US fiscal year 2000 budget called for a multi-year contract for 222 F/A-18E/Fs. An electronic warfare version, the EF/A-18G has also been proposed as an EA-6B Prowler replacement.

CURRENT SERVICE

Australia (54 AF-18A, 16 ATF-18A); Canada (82 CF-188A, 37 CF-188B); Finland (57 F/A-18C, 7 F/A-18D); Kuwait (32 KAF-18C, 8 KAF-18D); Spain (93 C.15, 16 CE.15); Switzerland (26 F/A-18C, 7 F/A-18D); US Navy and US Marine Corps (203 F/A-18A, 31 F/A-18B, 420 F/A-18C, 65 F/A-18D, 13 F/A-18E, 4 F/A-18F) and NASA.

SPECIAL FEATURES

The multi-role nature of the Hornet has made it attractive to many countries that require a range of capabilities but cannot afford to operate separate types for different tasks.

VARIANTS

F/A-18A – initial production version for US Navy and US Marine Corps; **TF-18A** – two-seat conversion trainer version of the F/A-18A, redesignated **F/A-18B**; **F/A-18C** – upgraded single-seat version, featuring increased weapons capability, improved avionics, with later production examples being delivered with night attack capabilities; **F/A-18D** – two-seat attack aircraft developed for the US Marines, later versions being

night attack capable **(F/A-18D+)**; **F/A-18E** – Super Hornet, enlarged version of the Hornet ordered by the US Navy to replace older generation Hornets; **F/A-18F** – two-seat Super Hornet, destined to replace the F-14 Tomcat as the US Navy's carrier borne fighter; **EF/A-18G** – proposed EW variant of the Super Hornet; **AF-18A** – version of the F/A-18A for the RAAF, assembled by ASTA; **ATF-18A** – version of the F/A-18B for the RAAF; **CF-18A & CF-18B** – versions of the F/A-18A and F/A-18B for the Canadian Armed Forces, known locally as CF-188A and CF-188B; **EF-18A & EF-18B** – versions of the F/A-18A and F/A-18B for the Spanish Air Force, known locally as the C.15 and CE.15, with upgraded versions being known as the EF-18A+ and EF-18B+; **KAF-18C** – F/A-18C for the Kuwait Air Force; **KAF-18D** – F/A-18D for the Kuwait Air Force.

F/A-18C Hornet
United States Navy

Boeing (McDonnell Douglas) C-17 Globemaster III

FOUR-TURBOFAN STRATEGIC/TACTICAL TRANSPORT AIRCRAFT

C-17A Globemaster III United States Air Force

DEVELOPMENT

Programme go-ahead occurred in August 1981, when McDonnell Douglas (since merged with Boeing) was selected by the USAF to develop the C-17 in response to the C-X cargo aircraft requirement. Subsequent progress was far from swift, however, and it was not until November 1987 that work began on manufacture of a prototype. This was eventually completed in December 1990, but it did not make its maiden flight until September 1991, being one of several aircraft used for testing that presaged deliveries to the USAF's Air Mobility Command (AMC) in summer 1993.

CURRENT SERVICE

Approximately half of the USAF's planned fleet of 120 C-17As has been delivered, progressively replacing long-serving C-141 StarLifters. The first deliveries were made to the 437th Airlift Wing at Charleston AFB, South Carolina, which is now almost fully equipped, and conversion of the 62nd Airlift Wing at McChord AFB, Washington began in 1999. In addition, Air Education and Training Command has received eight aircraft for use with the 97th Air Mobility Wing at Altus AFB, Oklahoma, while the prototype still serves with the test force at Edwards AFB, California. Four C-17s are due to join the Royal Air Force on a lease basis in Summer 2001, as a temporary measure pending the availability of the proposed Airbus A400M.

SPECIAL FEATURES

The C-17A incorporates a number of classic cargo aircraft features. Foremost amongst these is the choice of a high wing configuration, with podded underslung engines, that allows unobstructed access to the cargo hold, as well as a rear ramp that combines with a sharply upswept aft fuselage to offer good clearance for bulky and outsize loads. It also has a T-tail and winglets, as well as flap-blowing to enhance short-field performance.

VARIANTS

To date, only one version of the Globemaster III has been produced, this being the basic **C-17A** transport. However, design studies of a tanker/transport version known as the **KC-17** have been undertaken. This would have extra fuel capacity and an interchangeable cargo door containing 'flying boom' and/or hose drum unit refuelling equipment, as well as a palletised operator's station in the hold. No orders have resulted and efforts to market the proposed civil MD-17 cargo aircraft have also been unsuccessful. Additional studies have looked at the possibility of stretching the design by inserting fuselage 'plugs', but this proposal has not been taken up by the USAF.

TECHNICAL DATA

Boeing C-17A Globemaster III

Powerplants: Four Pratt & Whitney F117-PW-100 turbofans
Developing: 181.0kN (40,700lb st)
Span: 50.29m (165ft 0in) wings only; 51.76m (169ft 10in) including winglets
Length: 53.04m (174ft 0in)
Height: 16.79m (55ft 1in)
All-up weight: 265,350kg (585,000lb)
Cruise speed: 648km/h (403mph)
Operational ceiling: 45,000ft
Maximum range: 7,630km (4,741 miles) with 36,287kg (80,000lb) payload
Ferry range: 9,432km (5,860 miles)
Accommodation: Crew comprising pilot, co-pilot and loadmaster, plus up to 102 paratroops
Payload: 76,655kg (169,000lb)
First flown: 15 September 1991 (prototype); 18 May 1992 (first production aircraft)
Entered service: 14 June 1993 (first delivery to operational unit)

C-17A Globemaster III RAF No99 Sqn

MD520MG Defender Phillipine Air Force

DEVELOPMENT

The successful evolution of the famous 'Loach' series of aircraft resulted in a new family of variants based on the tried and tested MD500E. The first variant in the new series emerged in 1982 and was intended for the civil market designated MD530F Lifter. The MD530F incorporated a number of new features including a fully articulated five-blade main rotor driven by the 484kw (650shp) Allison 250-C30 turboshaft. Military applications of the design were a consideration from the beginning, and in May 1984 the first MD530MG Defender made its maiden flight. Based on the 530F, the MD530MG is lightweight and highly versatile and

can perform roles as diverse as anti-armour, day and night surveillance, cargo carrying and light attack. The fully integrated cockpit includes a multi-function display, hands-on lever and stick (HOLAS) weapon delivery. Weapons can include machine-guns, anti-armour missiles, rockets, and in the future, air-to-air missiles. The similarly configured MD520MG version is operated by the Philippines. Other military variants comprise the MD530 Nightfox, with night vision goggles and a thermal imager for night surveillance, and the Paramilitary MD530MG Defender, which is a lower cost version suitable for police or patrol work. The US Army's Special Operations Command also operates several MD500 variants with original rounded nose contours, equipped to a similar standard to the MD530MG. These include AH-6G gunships and the MH-6H which is believed to be used for the covert insertion of special forces. MD Helicopters has also developed NOTAR versions of both the MD520 and MD530, of which the MD520N Defender is aimed at the military market. No military operator has placed orders for NOTAR-equipped variants as yet.

CURRENT SERVICE

Argentina (MD530); Chile (MD530); Colombia (MD 530); Iraq (MD530); Mexico (MD530); US Army (AH-/MH-6) and the Philippines (MD520).

SPECIAL FEATURES

Developed from the combat proven H-6 series, the MD520/530 retains the former's excellent visibility from the cockpit, making it ideal for observation duties. Reduced noise and good maximum speed make armed versions potent in the light attack/anti-armour roles. An optional cargo hook has 907kg (2,000lb) capacity.

VARIANTS

MD520/530: original versions intended for civilian operators although can be applied to military duties; **MD520/530MG Defender:** armed light attack or utility military variant; **MD530MG Paramilitary MG Defender:** low-cost variant mainly for security forces; **MD520N/530N:** NOTAR versions primarily for civilian market; **MD520N Defender:** armed military NOTAR variant currently under development.

TECHNICAL DATA

Boeing (McDonnell Douglas Helicopters) MD520N

Powerplant: One Rolls-Royce Allison 250-C20R turboshaft
Developing: 317kW (425shp) for take-off
Driving: Five-blade main rotor and NOTAR system
Main rotor diameter: 8.36m (27ft 5in)
Fuselage length: 7.77m (25ft 6in)
Height: 3.01m (9ft 10.75in) with extended skids
All up weight: 1,519kg (3,350lb)
Maximum speed: 281km/h (175mph)
Maximum Cruise speed: 249km/h (155mph)
Operational ceiling: 14,175ft
Range: 424km (263 miles)
Endurance: 2hr 24min
Accommodation: Pilot plus up to four passengers or crew
First flown: 1 May 1990
Entered service: October 1991

Boeing (MDH) MD530FF Colombian Air Force

Boeing (McDonnell Douglas Helicopters) MD900 Explorer

TWIN-TURBOSHAFT UTILITY/LIGHT ATTACK HELICOPTER

MD900 Explorer Belgian Gendarmerie

DEVELOPMENT

The successful development of the NOTAR system, first tested on an OH-6A NOTAR testbed in the early 1980s, was integrated into a larger eight seat design initially known as the MDX. In conjunction with partner firms including Hawker de Havilland, Canadian Marconi, Kawasaki, IAI and Lucas Aerospace ten prototype and trials aircraft were constructed before FAA certification was approved in December 1994. The MD900 Explorer integrates a host of modern technology including the NOTAR anti-torque system, five-blade main rotor of composite materials with titanium leading edges, a largely carbon fibre cockpit cabin and tail structure and modern avionics including full IFR capability an optional weather radar and an integrated LCD instrumentation display system. Deliveries to civilian operators began in 1994, and in 1996 the Belgian Gendarmerie received two MD900s in law enforcement configuration which have replaced the SA 330H Puma in service. The other military operator is the US Coast

Guard which leases two MD902 Enhanced Explorers under the Operation *New Frontier* programme. These operate from Coast Guard cutters armed with a door-mounted 7.62-mm machine gun and are used on anti-drug smuggling operations. Up to 12 examples may be acquired in the future. A dedicated combat version named Combat Explorer was displayed at the 1995 Paris Air Salon. Capable of utility, medevac or combat missions, the Combat Explorer can be armed with rocket pods or machine-gun pods combined with FLIR and a roof-mounted surveillance/targeting system – however, no orders have yet been announced.

CURRENT SERVICE

Currently serves only with the Belgian Gendarmerie and the US Coast Guard. The Slovakian Police has also placed an order for the MD902.

SPECIAL FEATURES

The NOTAR system helps reduce noise and increase

efficiency and combined with the largely composite construction gives the aircraft excellent fuel economy. An external hook may be fitted to the aircraft with a 1,361kg (3,000lb) capacity. In addition a personnel hoist, wire strike kit and emergency floats can all be added as an optional extra.

VARIANTS

MD900 Explorer: initial civilian utility version; **MD902 Enhanced Explorer**: improved version with increased range and endurance; **MH-90 Enforcer**: designation for two leased MD 900s for US Coast Guard (now replaced by two MD 902 Enhanced Explorers); **Combat Explorer**: military attack, medevac or utility version.

TECHNICAL DATA

Boeing (McDonnell Douglas Helicopters) MD900 Explorer

Powerplants: Two Pratt & Whitney Canada PW206E turboshafts
Developing: 463kW (621shp)
Driving: Five-blade main rotor and NOTAR system
Main rotor diameter: 10.31m (33ft 10 in)
Fuselage length: 9.85m (32ft 4in)
Height: 3.66m (12ft 0in)
All up weight: 2,835kg (6,250lb)
Maximum speed: 259km/h (161mph)
Maximum cruise speed: 248km/h (154mph)
Operational ceiling: 17,500ft
Maximum range: 542km (337 miles)
Endurance: 2hr 54min
Accommodation: One/two crew and up to six passengers
First flown: 18 December 1992
Entered service: 1996 (Military service)

MD900 Explorer Belgian Gendarmerie

Boeing (McDonnell Douglas)/BAE Systems T-45 Goshawk

SINGLE TURBOFAN JET TRAINER AIRCRAFT

T-45A Goshawk United States Navy

TECHNICAL DATA

Boeing/BAE Systems T-45A Goshawk

Powerplant: One Rolls-Royce/Turboméca Adour Mk 871 turbofan
Thrust: 26.00kN (5,845lb st)
Span: 9.39m (30ft 9.75in)
Length: 11.98m (39ft 4in) including nose probe
Height: 4.26m (14ft 0in)
Maximum weight: 5,787Kg (12,758lb)
Maximum speed: 1,006km/h (625mph)
Operational ceiling: 40,000ft
Ferry range: 1,532km (952 miles)
Accommodation: Instructor and student
Warload: No integral armament provided; one hardpoint under each wing can carry practice bombs and rockets for training in weapon delivery techniques
First flown: 16 April 1988
Entered service: June 1992 (instructor training); January 1994 (student training)

DEVELOPMENT

Selected on 18 November 1981 to satisfy the US Navy's VTXTS competition for a new jet trainer to replace the TA-4J Skyhawk and T-2C Buckeye, two full-scale development aircraft were initially ordered from McDonnell Douglas, both of which flew during 1988. Although deliveries were expected to begin in late 1989, considerable delays were encountered due to a significant number of airframe and powerplant changes. In consequence, it was not until the first half of 1992 that aircraft began to reach Naval Air Training Command, following extensive testing at Patuxent River, Maryland throughout 1990-91.

CURRENT SERVICE

Introduced to the US Navy/Marine Corps training role in 1992, the McDonnell Douglas (now Boeing) Goshawk has now supplanted the long-serving TA-4J Skyhawk with training units in the southern USA. Initial deliveries were to Training Wing Two (TW-2) at Kingsville, Texas and the two squadrons of this

unit (VT-21 and VT-22) are both fully equipped with the T-45A. The second organisation to receive the Goshawk was Training Wing One at Meridian, Mississippi, which accepted its first T-45C in 1997, initially allocating the new type to VT-23 squadron, which was renumbered as VT-7 in 1999. Eventually, the T-45C will also replace T-2C Buckeyes with VT-9 at the same base.

SPECIAL FEATURES

The T-45 is basically similar in appearance to the BAE Systems Hawk trainer, but extensively modified for carrier training. The most obvious alterations are the provision of an arrester hook beneath the aft fuselage and a modified twin-wheel nose undercarriage unit incorporating a tow link for catapult launch; other changes include a redesign of the forward fuselage, which is deeper and longer, as well as strengthening to cope with the additional stress of carrier operations. The tailplane span and height of the fin have also been increased slightly, with the rudder being modified

and a single ventral fin added. Twin air brakes are fitted on the fuselage sides in place of the single air brake on British-built aircraft.

VARIANTS

The original intention was to purchase just over 300 Goshawks, production starting with 54 examples of the purely land-based **T-45B** version, followed by 253 carrier-capable **T-45As**. This idea was shelved in 1984, when it was decided to instead acquire exactly 300 T-45As, although further changes have occurred and the current plan anticipates a total buy of 169 aircraft. More than half have been delivered, with the initial 83 completed as T-45As, but recent production has been of the **T-45C** version which has digital 'Cockpit 21' avionics, and all subsequent aircraft will be to this standard. Eventually, it is planned to upgrade surviving T-45As to the same configuration between 2002 and 2007, allowing the Navy to have a standardised fleet of T-45Cs.

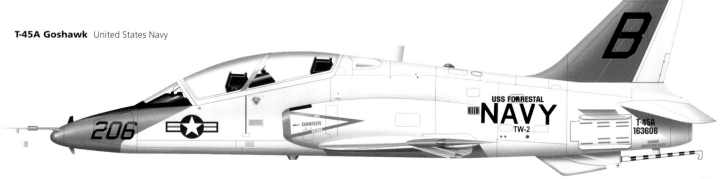

T-45A Goshawk United States Navy

Boeing (McDonnell Douglas)/GKN Westland AH-64 Apache 🇺🇸 🇬🇧

TWIN-TURBOSHAFT ANTI-ARMOUR ATTACK HELICOPTER

USA/UK

WAH-64 Apache Longbow UK Army Air Corps

TECHNICAL DATA

McDonnell Douglas AH-64A Apache
Powerplants: Two General Electric
T700-GE-701C turboshafts
Developing: 1,410 kW (1,890 eshp)
Driving: Four-blade main and tail rotors
Main rotor diameter: 14.63 m (48 ft 0 in)
Fuselage length: 14.97 m (49 ft 1.5 in)
Wing span: 5.23 m (17 ft 2 in)
Height: 4.66 m (15 ft 4 in)
All-up weight: 9,525 kg (21,000 lb)
Maximum speed: 293 km/h (181 mph)
Cruise speed: 278 km/h (173 mph)
Operating ceiling: 21,000 ft
Maximum ferry range: 1,900 km (1,178 miles)
Mission range: 480 km (299 miles)
Endurance: 3 hr 10 min
Accommodation: Two crew (co-pilot/gunner in
front, pilot behind and above)
Warload: Single nose-mounted 30-mm (1,200
rounds) M230 Bushmaster Chain Gun; four
hardpoints on stub wings to carry 16 AGM-114
Hellfire laser-guided anti-armour missiles or up
to 74 2.75 in rockets. Also capability for unguided
rockets, Sidewinder, Stinger and Mistral air-to-
air and Sidearm anti-radiation missiles.
First flown: 30 September 1975
Entered service: February 1984

DEVELOPMENT
Conceived by Hughes helicopters in 1973 and later taken over by McDonnell Douglas, and more recently Boeing, the YAH-64 was designed to meet the US Army's Advanced Attack Helicopter requirement. First flown on 30 September 1975, it was successful in competition with the Bell YAH-63, but production approval was not given until March 1982, and the first machine entered service nearly two years later. Since that time, over 800 AH-64As have been supplied to the US Army and five overseas air arms, including the first for the UK. Upgraded in the light of operational experience, the improved AH-64D – first flown on 15 April 1992 – has enhanced avionics, while the AH-64D Apache Longbow, fitted with a mast-mounted millimetre wave radar, followed into service in March 1997. Over 500 of the US Army's AH-64As are being modified to AH-64Ds, 227 of which will be to full Longbow standard. The UK has ordered 67 WAH-64s for the Army Air Corps, the first of which was handed over in March 2000. Powered by Rolls-

Royce Turboméca RTM322 turboshafts, they are being built by GKN Westland at Yeovil.

CURRENT SERVICE
Over 800 with the US Army, and also the air forces of Egypt, Greece, Israel, Netherlands, Saudi Arabia, Singapore and the United Arab Emirates (Abu Dhabi).

SPECIAL FEATURES
The Apache is designed to survive hits from 23mm cannon and the cockpit can withstand hitting the ground at up to 13 metres per second. It is fitted with a super-heated ceramic block to deceive heat-seeking missiles. Digital technology is used to pinpoint targets for commanders, other helicopters, tanks and other vehicles. Its Hellfire missiles can destroy a tank up to 20km away. The 30-mm cannon is linked to the helmets, aiming where the pilot or gunner is looking. Key parts of the helicopter and engines are armour-protected. The four-blade main rotor is of laminated steel, glass reinforced plastic and composite materials.

VARIANTS
The **AH-64A** was the initial and main production model, used by the US Army and all the above overseas operators. The current production **AH-64D** is readily identified by its mast-mounted Lockheed Martin/Westinghouse **Longbow** millimetre-wave radar. The US Army began modifying its AH-64As to Longbow standard in March 1997 as part of a ten-year programme, with Kuwait and the Royal Netherlands Air Force both due to receive the new version. The GKN Westland-built **WAH-64s** for the UK Army Air Corps are Longbow-configured.

AH-64D Apache Longbow
United States Army

Boeing-Vertol CH-46 Sea Knight

TWIN-TURBOSHAFT TRANSPORT/UTILITY HELICOPTER

CH-113 Labrador Canadian Armed Forces

TECHNICAL DATA

Boeing (Vertol) CH-46E Sea Knight
Powerplants: Two General Electric T58-GE-16 turboshafts
Developing: 1,394kW (1,870shp)
Driving: Tandem three-blade rotors
Main rotor diameter: 15.24m (50ft 0in)
Fuselage length: 13.66m (44ft 10in)
Height: 5.09m (16ft 8.5in)
All-up weight: 11,022kg (24,300lb)
Maximum speed: 267km/h (166mph)
Maximum ferry range: 1,112km (691 miles)
Range: 1,019km (633 miles) with 1,088kg (2,400lb) payload
Accommodation: Crew of three plus up to 25 fully equipped troops
Payload: 3,175kg (7,000lb)
First flown: 22 April 1958 (commercial Model 107); 16 October 1962 (CH-46A); 1975 (CH-46E)
Entered service: June 1964 (CH-46A); 1977 (CH-46E)

DEVELOPMENT

A militarised version of the commercial Vertol 107, the Sea Knight emerged in the late 1950s when both the US Army and the US Marine Corps expressed interest in this turbine-powered machine. The Army eventually selected the Chinook following evaluation of the Model 107, but the Marines purchased the Sea Knight to replace the piston-powered Sikorsky HUS-1 Seahorse. Initially designated HRB-1, the Sea Knight had become the CH-46A by the time of its maiden flight in late 1962 and it began to enter service with the Marines just under two years later, remaining in production for about a decade.

CURRENT SERVICE

Approximately half of the 624 Sea Knights that were completed by early 1971 remain active with the US Navy and Marine Corps today, albeit in extensively modernised form, for they have been subjected to various upgrade programmes. The most numerous version is the CH-46E, some 225 examples of which

equip Marine Corps medium helicopter squadrons, to be replaced by the MV-22 Osprey tilt-rotor during the next decade or so. Other versions are flown by combat support squadrons and base rescue flights of the US Navy, which presently has about 80 Sea Knights. Missions undertaken include vertical replenishment support of fleet activities (CH-46D and UH-46D) and search and rescue (HH-46D). Overseas operators of the Vertol 107 are Canada (designated as CH-113 Labradors) and Sweden, though neither country is likely to retain these elderly helicopters for much longer.

SPECIAL FEATURES

The most notable attribute of the Sea Knight family is the twin-rotor configuration that was conceived by Vertol. Although similar in appearance to the Chinook, the Sea Knight is smaller and lighter and makes use of a slightly different undercarriage layout, consisting of mainwheel units attached to small sponsons on the aft fuselage sides and a single nosewheel assembly beneath the forward fuselage.

VARIANTS

Numerous versions of the Sea Knight have served with Navy and Marine Corps units. These include the **CH-46A**, **HH-46A**, **UH-46A** and **CH-46F**, which have all disappeared as a result of modernisation and upgrade projects. In consequence, only four versions remain in use, with the **CH-46E** being the principal version and unique to the Marine Corps. The US Navy's 80-strong fleet is composed of just over two dozen **CH-46Ds**, about 12 **UH-46Ds** and approximately 40 **HH-46Ds**. US Army interest in the type resulted in the evaluation of three **YHC-1As** (later redesignated **YCH-46C**) in the late 1950s, but this service eventually opted for the larger and more powerful Chinook.

SEE ALSO: KAWASAKI-VERTOL KV-107

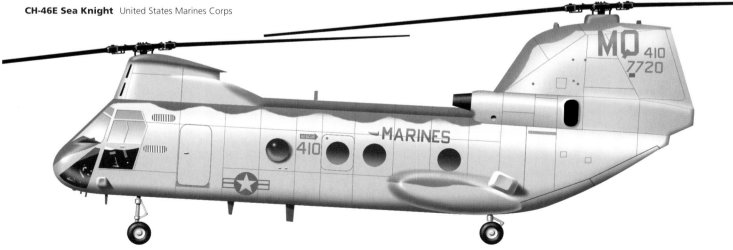

CH-46E Sea Knight United States Marines Corps

Boeing/Kawasaki-Vertol KV-107

Kawasaki-Vertol KV-107
Swedish Navy

TECHNICAL DATA

Kawasaki-Vertol KV-107-IIA
Powerplants: Two Ishikawajima-Harima (General
Electric) CT58-IHI-140-1 turboshafts
Developing: 932kW (1,250shp)
Driving: Three-blade tandem main rotors
Main rotor diameter: 15.24m (50ft 0in) each
Fuselage length: 13.59m (44ft 7in)
Height: 5.13m (16ft 10in)
Maximum weight: 9,706kg (21,400lb)
Maximum speed: 270km/h (168mph)
Cruise speed: 241km/h (150mph)
Operational ceiling: 17,000ft
Maximum range: 1,097km (682 miles)
Normal range: 357km (222 miles)
Accommodation: Three crew and up to 26 troops
Payload: 3,172kg (6,993lb)
Warload: None
First flown: April 1958 (Boeing-built);
May 1962 (Kawasaki-built)
Entered service: 1966 (Kawasaki military versions)

DEVELOPMENT

Development of the Model 107 tandem-rotor medium
helicopter was launched by Vertol in the USA in the
mid-1950s and a variation on the basic design was
built in considerable numbers for the US Navy and
Marine Corps as the H-46 Sea Knight. in the early
1960s, Kawasaki acquired a manufacturing licence
from Boeing Vertol and subsequently flew the first
locally-built example in May 1962. Initially, the
agreement with Boeing Vertol only covered production
for domestic markets, with KV-107s being procured
by all three elements of the armed forces. By 1965,
further negotiations resulted in Kawasaki being
granted worldwide marketing rights.

CURRENT SERVICE

Military examples of the KV-107 still serve with the
Japanese Air Self-Defence Force, which received 52
during 1967-90. Most have now been replaced by
Chinooks, but about 20 examples of the KV-107-IIA
version are assigned to search-and-rescue tasks. Until
quite recently, the Ground Self-Defence Force still
had a handful of survivors of 60 KV-107s delivered
from 1966 onwards, but these could now have been
withdrawn from service. The only other KV-107s are
in Swedish military service, with the navy air arm
operating seven of the eight delivered during 1972-74,

alongside a similar quantity of Boeing Vertol 107s. The
Saudi government has about a dozen KV-107-IIAs that
perform various duties, including medical evacuation/
SAR, fire fighting and conventional transport.

SPECIAL FEATURES

The Kawasaki KV-107 possesses the characteristic
tandem rotor layout that was pioneered by Vertol and
used to greatest effect in the Boeing Vertol Chinook
heavy-lift helicopter. SAR-configured KV-107s of the
JASDF have enlarged sponsons that contain extra
fuel in addition to the twin-wheeled aft undercarriage
units. Other special features of SAR versions include
domed observation windows on each side, four

searchlights for night operations, a rescue hoist and
additional navigation/communications equipment.

VARIANTS

Relatively few variants exist, but original Japanese
production concentrated on the **KV-107-II**, fitted
with CT58-110-1 engines rated at 932kW (1,250shp).
Examples were supplied to the JASDF, JGSDF and
JMSDF, but all have now been withdrawn from use.
Subsequent installation of more powerful engines
resulted in the **KV-107-IIA**, with improved performance
and the limited number of helicopters that still equip
JASDF rescue detachments are all to this standard.
Aircraft delivered to Sweden are basically to KV-107-II
standard, but are powered by Rolls-Royce Gnome
H.1200 turboshaft engines and have Decca navigation
systems; they are known locally as the **Hkp 4C**.

SEE ALSO: BOEING-VERTOL CH-46 SEA KNIGHT

Kawasaki-Vertol KV-107
Swedish Navy

Boeing CH-47 Chinook

TWIN-TURBOSHAFT TRANSPORT HELICOPTER

Chinook HC2 Royal Air Force

TECHNICAL DATA

Boeing CH-47SD Chinook

Powerplants: Two Honeywell T55-L-714A turboshafts
Developing: 3,039kW (4,075shp)
Driving: Tandem three-blade rotors
Rotor diameter: 18.29m (60ft 0in)
Fuselage length: 15.87m (52ft 1in)
Height: 5.70m (18ft 8.5in)
All-up weight: 24,494kg (54,000lb)
Maximum speed: 287km/h (178mph)
Cruise speed: 259km/h (161mph)
Service ceiling: 22,100ft
Range: 1,207km (750 miles) with 12,558kg (27,686lb) payload
Accommodation: Crew of two pilots and loadmaster, plus up to 55 troops
Payload: 12,944kg (28,537lb)
First flown: 21 September 1961 (YCH-47A prototype); February 1982 (CH-47D); 26 August 1999 (CH-47SD)
Entered service: 16 August 1962 (first CH-47A delivered)

DEVELOPMENT

The origins of the Chinook can be traced back to the late 1950s when the US Army began searching for a new turbine-powered medium/heavy lift helicopter to replace the piston-powered CH-37 Mojave. The resultant design bore a marked resemblance to the Vertol 107 commercial helicopter, but was much more utilitarian and significantly more powerful. A contract was awarded to Boeing Vertol in fiscal year 1959 for five prototype YHC-1B helicopters (later redesignated YCH-47As). After successful testing of these, the first of a succession of orders for production Chinooks was placed in the following year, with entry into service occurring in summer 1962. Subsequent development has resulted in improved versions, and this process continues. The CH-47F ICH (Improved Cargo Helicopter) is due to fly in prototype form in early 2001.

CURRENT SERVICE

The major Chinook operator has always been the US Army, which took delivery of almost 750 and which still possesses more than 400 examples of the CH-47D variant, at least 300 of which are destined for further upgrading to CH-47F standard. The Chinook has also been widely exported, with customers for helicopters built by Boeing and licensees in both Italy and Japan comprising Argentina, Australia, Canada, Egypt, Greece, Holland, Iran, Italy, Japan, Libya, Morocco, Singapore, South Korea, Spain, Taiwan, Thailand and the UK. With the exception of Canada, all still use the Chinook.

SPECIAL FEATURES

The most distinctive single attribute of the CH-47 is the twin-rotor layout that was pioneered by Vertol in the latter half of the 1950s and which has proved so successful. This allows unobstructed access to the cabin via a rear loading ramp and enables the Chinook to carry troops, cargo or small vehicles with equal facility. Bulbous sponsons on the fuselage side accommodate fuel and provide mounting points for the Chinook's undercarriage, which consists of twin wheel units at the front and single wheel units at the rear.

VARIANTS

Quantity production of the Chinook began in the early 1960s and is continuing, with nearly 1,200 examples having been built by Boeing (formerly Boeing Vertol) in the USA, by Meridionali in Italy and by Kawasaki in Japan. New-build US Army versions were the **CH-47A** (349 delivered), **CH-47B** (108) and **CH-47C** (281). An improvement programme subsequently led to the **CH-47D**. Three new-build examples of this version were purchased by the US Army, but the majority resulted from remanufacture of older models, with nearly 500 being upgraded. Most emerged as CH-47Ds, but the total includes 25 **MH-47Es** for special forces operations. Export aircraft are basically similar to those of the US Army, but the latest version is the **CH-47SD** 'Super D' which has been ordered by Singapore and Taiwan.

CH-47C Chinook Egyptian Air Force

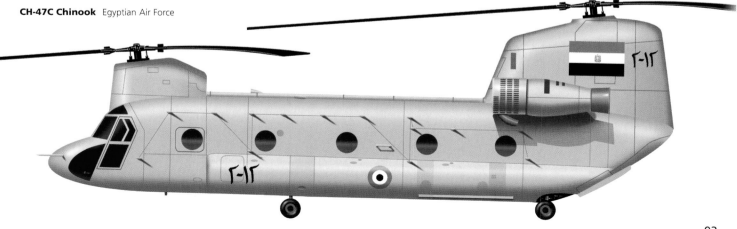

Bombardier (de Havilland Canada) DHC-8 Dash 8

TWIN-TURBOPROP STOL TRANSPORT, NAVIGATION TRAINING AND RANGE SUPPORT AIRCRAFT **CANADA**

Bombardier E-9A United States Air Force

DEVELOPMENT

To fit a requirement for a short-haul transport with capacity between de Havilland Canada's smaller Twin Otter and larger Dash 7, the company began design work in the late 1970s on a twin-turboprop powered transport for the commuter airliner market. Although not quite possessing the STOL performance of its larger brother, the Dash 8 does incorporate a similar high-set wing and large T-tail and is in many respects a scaled-down version of the Dash 7. Typically rugged, the Dash 8 can operate from unpaved runways and offers much increased economy over the four-engined Dash 7. The aircraft entered commercial service in the mid-1980s and sold sufficiently well for the company to develop the increased speed/payload Series 200 and, in the 1990s, the Q300/Q400 stretched variants produced by Bombardier, which absorbed DHC. It is now a successful regional airliner and has found a

growing market with the military. Following the Dash 7 into service, the Canadian Armed Forces ordered the CC-142 transport (Dash 8M Series 100) for service in support of Canadian forces in Germany. The aircraft were withdrawn to Canada in the early 1990s and two currently serve with No 402 Squadron at Manitoba alongside four CT-142 navigation trainers. This variant is distinguished by its prominent mapping radar in an extended nose. Both the CC-142 and the CT-142 are fitted with long-range fuel tanks, low-pressure tyres, reinforced cabin floors and mission avionics. Two Dash 8 Series 100s are operated by the USAF's 475th WEG as E-9A missile range control aircraft. These specially modified examples are fitted with a large electronically-steered phased-array radar in the fuselage and an AN/APS-128D surveillance radar in a ventral dome. The E-9A is used to relay telemetry, voice, and drone and fighter control data whilst observing the range with its radar. Dash 8s in military service are mainly limited to variants of the Dash 8-100.

CURRENT SERVICE

No 402 Squadron, Canadian Armed Forces operates two CC-142 transports and four CT-142 navigation

trainers ; 475th WEG of Air Combat Command, USAF operates two for missile range control – designated E-9As; four Dash 8-200s are fitted with search radar and FLIR for Australian Customs use; the Kenyan Air Force operates three Dash 8 Series 100s for VIP and utility transport duties.

SPECIAL FEATURES

A high-lift wing and two-section full-length slotted Fowler trailing edge flaps give good STOL performance.

VARIANTS

Triton, the Maritime surveillance version based on the Q300 with weapons pylons, radar, MAD and wingtip ESM, has yet to receive any orders. The **Series 100** was the original model and the **100A** followed in 1990; the **Series 100B** was introduced in 1992 with more powerful PW121 engines for better climb and airfield performance. The **Series 200** entered service in 1994 and has a higher cruising speed and greater commonality with the stretched **Dash 8-300**; The-300 has 50 seats and is 3.43m (11ft 3in) longer with PW123 turboprops; the **Dash 8-400** is a 70-seat regional airliner that came into service in 1999.

TECHNICAL DATA

Bombardier DHC-8 Dash 8M Series 100 (CC-142)

Powerplants: Two Pratt & Whitney Canada PW120A turboprops
Developing: 1,491kW (2,000shp)
Driving: Four-blade propellers
Span: 25.91m (85ft 0in)
Length: 22.25m (73ft 0in)
Height: 7.49m (24ft 7in)
All up weight: 15,649kg (34,500lb)
Maximum cruise speed: 497km/h (308mph)
Operational ceiling: 25,000ft
Range: 1,520km (944 miles)
Accommodation: Two crew and up to 39 passengers
Warload: None
First flown: 20 June 1983
Entered service: 23 October 1984 (airline service)

Bombardier CC-142 Canadian Armed Forces

Breguet (Dassault) Br 1050 Alizé

SINGLE TURBOPROP CARRIER-BORNE MARITIME RECONNAISSANCE/UTILITY AIRCRAFT

Br 1050 Alizé French Navy

TECHNICAL DATA

Breguet Br 1050 Alizé
Powerplant: One Rolls-Royce Dart R.Da.7
Mk 21 turboprop
Developing: 1,473kW (1,975shp)
Driving; four-blade propeller
Span: 15.60m (51ft 2in)
Length: 13.86m (45ft 6in)
Height: 5.00m (16ft 5in)
All-up weight: 8,200kg (18,078lb)
Maximum speed: 520km/h (323mph)
Cruise speed: 370km/h (230mph)
Operational ceiling: 20,500ft
Maximum range: 2,870km (1,785miles)
Mission range: 1,890km (1,174 miles)
Endurance: 5hours 10minutes
Accommodation: Pilot and co-pilot/systems
operator, third crew member as required
Warload: Currently none, provision for internal
or underwing stores as required
First flown: 6 October 1956
Entered service: 20 May 1959

DEVELOPMENT

Derived from the mixed-powerplant prototype Breguet Vultur of late 1940s/early 1950s-vintage, the Br 1050 was developed as a carrier-based anti-submarine hunter-killer platform, the prototype flying in October 1956. Named Alizé (trade wind), the five prototype/pre-production machines were followed by 75 production aircraft for the French Navy and 12 for India, official deliveries beginning to the French Navy in May 1959 and to the Indian Navy during early 1961. In the anti-submarine role, the Alizé was carrier-based and included retractable Thomson-CSF search radar, and sonar equipment in the main undercarriage fairings for submarine-hunting. It was armed with various internally-carried weapons including a homing torpedo, depth charges, or bombs; and depth charges, rockets or two SS.11 (or similar) missiles under the wings. Three crew were carried, a pilot, radar operator and sensors operator. The type initially served with Flottilles 4F, 6F, and 9F of the French Navy and some second-line units; the Indian Navy's No 310 'Cobras' Squadron also operated the type, sometimes deploying aboard the Indian aircraft-carrier Vikrant. Never intended to last in

service for over 40 years, the Alizé now only operates for the French in the surface maritime surveillance role and usually flies unarmed; Alizés were carried aboard the aircraft-carrier Foch during the French Navy's contribution to NATO Allied Force operations against the Serbs in 1999.

CURRENT SERVICE

The last remaining French Navy Alizé unit is Flottille 6F, home-based at Nîmes-Garons and sometimes embarked when required aboard the aircraft-carrier Foch. Its nine aircraft will remain in service until the Foch is retired, towards the middle of the decade. The Indian Navy's Alizés were recently withdrawn, and replaced in No 310 squadron by Dornier 228s; it is believed that some of the aircraft are stored in flyable condition.

SPECIAL FEATURES

The Alizé was designed for aircraft-carrier operations, featuring folding wings and an arrester hook beneath the tail. The type's Thomson-CSF DRAA 2A search radar was in a retractable under-fuselage mounted assembly behind the wing trailing edge. A lower

fuselage weapons bay with hinged doors carried the Alizé's internal armament, and wing hardpoints under the outer (folding) wing sections mounted the external armament.

VARIANTS

No major variants of the Alizé have existed, but several upgrades of French aircraft have taken place starting in the mid-1960s and again in the 1970s. In the early 1980s, a major upgrade to 28 aircraft included the addition of new Thomson-CSF Iguane radar, improved communications and navigation provision, and ESM equipment. In the early 1990s, some 24 examples received datalink and other minor modifications, and between 1995 and 1998 a few aircraft received a number of updates to extend their service lives beyond 2000.

Br 1050 Alizé French Navy

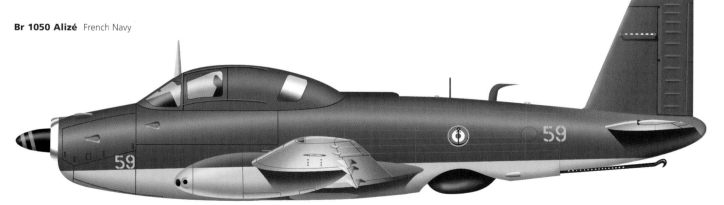

British Aerospace (Hawker Siddeley) 125/Dominie

TWIN-TURBOJET/TURBOFAN TRANSPORT/NAVIGATION TRAINING/SAR/UTILITY AIRCRAFT

DEVELOPMENT

As one of the world's first executive jets, the then de Havilland 125 was quickly identified by the RAF as suitable to replace the Meteor NF(T)14 as the RAF's standard navigation trainer for advanced students destined for fast jet operations. As with many of its contemporaries, the 125 incorporated a low-mounted wing and mid-mounted tailplane to keep the control surfaces clear of the jet efflux from the rear fuselage-mounted Rolls-Royce Viper turbojet engines. The aircraft entered RAF service as the Dominie T1 with No 1 Air Navigation School in late 1965 and a total of 20 was delivered. The eleven remaining in service today with No 55(R) Squadron received an upgrade in the late 1990s, allowing the aircraft to continue in service well into the new century. In addition to the navigation training role, the RAF have operated the 125 in the communications/transport role. Four Viper-powered HS125 CC1s (similar to the civilian Series 400) were procured in 1971, followed by two CC2s (similar to the Series 600) and were operated by No 32 Squadron before these variants were retired in 1994. Today, the squadron operates six Garrett TFE731-powered CC3s which offer much improved range,

Dominie T1 Royal Air Force

economy, climb performance and maximum speed. These aircraft operate in a low-visibility grey colour scheme and are fitted with infrared countermeasures in an extended tail fairing. The UK has also operated the 125 as a test aircraft for a number of roles including one as a radar testbed fitted with Blue Vixen radar and Sea Harrier FA2 weapons systems. Other operators of the 125 family have included Brazil with the VC-93 VIP transport version and the EC-93 radar calibration aircraft; the US Air Force, which operated Series 800 aircraft as C-29As for combat flight inspection and navigation duties before the responsibility was handed over to the FAA in 1991; and the JASDF which operates two versions of the Series 800; the U-125 calibration aircraft and the U-125A which is utilised in the SAR role fitted with a 360deg scan radar and a FLIR sensor, as well as rescue equipment.

CURRENT SERVICE

RAF – Dominie T1 at Cranwell; BAe 125 CC3 with No 32 (The Royal) Squadron at Northolt; Brazil – VC-93 (VIP transport) & EC-93 (radar calibration); Japan – U-125 (calibration) & U-125A (SAR); Malawi – BAe 125 Series 800 (government transport); Saudi Arabia – BAe 125 Series 800 (VIP transport); South Africa – BAe 125 Series 400 (VIP transport); Turkmenistan – BAe 125 Series 1000 (government transport).

SPECIAL FEATURES

The 125/Dominie has found particular use by military air arms as a VIP transport thanks to the type's roomy cabin of constant circular cross-section allowing a wide range of VIP interior layouts. A robust undercarriage allows operations from unpaved strips without special modification and constant re-design and upgrading has resulted in a long production life and excellent performance in relation to today's contemporary types.

VARIANTS

The **Series 1,1A** and **1B** were the original versions; the similar **Series 2** was the basis for the RAF **Dominie T1**; subsequent Viper-powered 125 models were the **Series 3** and **4** (which became **Series 400** when de Havilland merged into Hawker Siddeley; the **Series 600** followed with a stretched fuselage and seating for eight; the Garrett-powered **125-700** was introduced in the late 1970s and the **Series 800** followed in 1983. The 125-800 became the Raytheon **Hawker 800** from 1993 (described separately).

SEE ALSO: RAYTHEON HAWKER 800

TECHNICAL DATA

BAe 125 Series 800 (U-125)

Powerplants: Two Garrett TFE731-5R-1H turbofans
Developing: 19.13kN (4,300lb st))
Span: 15.66m (51ft 4.5in)
Length: 15.60m (51ft 2in)
Height: 5.36m (17ft 7in)
All up weight: 12,429kg (27,400lb)
Maximum speed: 845km/h (523mph)
Economical cruise speed: 741km/h (461mph)
Operational ceiling: 43,000ft
Range: 5,560km (3,454 miles)
Accommodation: Two crew and up to 14 passengers
Warload: None
First flown: 13 August 1962 (DH125 prototype); 1976 (125-700); May 1983 (125-800)
Entered service: December 1965 (Dominie T1)

BAe 125 CC3 Royal Air Force

ZE395

British Aerospace Harrier T4, T8 & T60

SINGLE TURBOFAN TWO-SEAT V/STOL OPERATIONAL TRAINER

Harrier T8 Royal Navy

DEVELOPMENT

Genesis of the two-seat Harrier dates back to 1960 when, before the first P.1127 had even flown, Sydney Camm directed his project engineer to investigate alternative schemes by which a second pilot might be accommodated. The two-seat Hunter had proved reasonably straightforward, but the very nature of vectored jet lift on the Harrier imposed critical design considerations, not the least of which were airframe weight, weight distribution, low-speed roll and pitch control, and the singular engine configuration with its critical hot gas recirculation characteristics. As the Pegasus engine was developed to produce over 15,000lb st, it became evident that a conventional tandem cockpit could be incorporated in a lengthened nose with relatively little alteration. The fin height was increased by some 46cm (18in). The two-seat Harrier T2 possessed all the weapon carrying and aiming capabilities of the GR1. The last of the original batch were completed as T2As – equivalent to the modified GR1As. With the introduction of the Pegasus 103, LRMTS and RWR the designation was changed to T4. A total of 25 two-seaters was built for the RAF and Fleet Air Arm – two were completed as T2As, nine as T4s and three as T4Ns. Nine of the original T2s were progressively modified to T4 standard. It was not until 1975 that the United States Marine Corps obtained funding to purchase eight two-seaters – these being designated TAV-8As. The T8 version was developed incorporating equipment and system upgrading to be compatible with the Sea Harrier FA2.

CURRENT SERVICE

The Harrier T4 no longer serves in the RAF, having been replaced by the T10 from 1995, but one T4 mod is used as a VAAC (Vectored thrust Advanced Aircraft flight Control) aircraft by DPA/AFD, DERA at Boscombe

Down. Four Harrier T8s are operative with 899 NAS at RNAS Yeovilton, used for Sea Harrier operational conversion duties. The Indian Navy originally obtained two Harrier T60s (former RAF T4s) which have been in service for nearly 20 years – and two further ex-RAF T4s were refurbished in the UK and delivered to India in 1999.

SPECIAL FEATURES

The T8 has similar avionics to the Sea Harrier FA2, but without the Blue Vixen radar

VARIANTS

The **Harrier T2** was the original version and was upgraded to the **T4** when a more powerful Pegasus engine became available. The envisaged Harrier T6 was not developed. The two-seaters in Royal Navy service remain as Harriers, without the Sea Harrier nomenclature. The **T8** was developed to be compatible with the second generation Sea Harrier. The ultimate development is the **T10**, which is described separately.

TECHNICAL DATA

BAe Harrier T8

Powerplant: One Rolls-Royce Bristol Pegasus 103 vectored thrust turbofan
Developing: 95.74kN (21,500lb st)
Span: 7.67m (25ft 2in)
Length: 17.06m (56ft 0.2in)
Height: 3.71m (12ft 2in)
All-up weight: 11,455kg (25,200lb)
Maximum speed: 1,194km/h (740mph)
Operational ceiling: 51,250ft
Endurance: 3 hours
Accommodation: Two in tandem
Warload: As for Sea Harrier FA2
First Flown: 22 April 1969 (T4)
Entered service: Mid-1970 (T4)

SEE ALSO: BRITISH AEROSPACE/McDONNELL DOUGLAS HARRIER T10/TAV-8B

Harrier T60 Indian Navy

British Aerospace Sea Harrier

SINGLE TURBOFAN V/STOL NAVAL MULTI-ROLE FIGHTER

Sea Harrier FA2 Royal Navy

DEVELOPMENT

Developed from the RAF's Harrier, it originally filled the gap left by the phase-out of the Phantom FGR2 and the decommissioning of HMS *Ark Royal* in 1979, the Royal Navy's last carrier. This coincided with the introduction of the new smaller 20,000 ton ASW carriers. The Sea Harrier is one of the most important types ever to enter FAA service, and the Falklands conflict of 1982 proved the prudence in adopting the V/STOL type. Naval interest in the concept was late in materialising until was it accepted that no further fixed-wing aircraft could be ordered. In 1975, 24 FRS1s and a single T4A trainer were ordered, and a further ten FRS1s were ordered three years later. Following the South Atlantic operations, 14 Sea Harrier FRS1s were ordered as attrition replacements and in 1984 nine more FRS1s, together with T4(N)s, were added, bringing RN procurement of the original version up to 57 single-seaters and four trainers. The FA2 was the mid-life upgrade of the FRS1, with changes to the airframe, cockpit, avionics, radar and armament. Thirty-four FRS1 were converted and 18 new-build FA2s were delivered between 1993 and 1997. The wingspan was slightly increased and the upgrade to the cockpit involved HOTAS controls and multi-function CRT displays. It has beyond visual-range capability with the AIM-120 AMRAAM and BAe Blue Vixen pulse-Doppler multi-mode radar. It is likely that the more

powerful Pegasus 11-61 engine (which is standard on the AV-8B) will be introduced as a broader upgrade.

CURRENT SERVICE

Sea Harriers currently equip the Royal Navy (FA2s) and the Indian Navy (FRS51s). RN FA2s are new build or converted aircraft. Following the Strategic Defence Review of 1998, the integration of RAF and FAA V/STOL aircraft will mean that in 2003, 28 Sea Harriers and seven two-seat Harriers will move out of their present location at RNAS Yeovilton and into the joint base of Wittering/Cottesmore, to operate with their RAF colleagues as Joint Force Harrier.

SPECIAL FEATURES

The main difference between the Royal Navy's Sea Harrier and RAF's Harrier GR7 is the latter's front fuselage contours, with a bulbous radome covering a Ferranti Blue Fox pulse-modulated radar and its associated weapons bay. The cockpit is raised to give the pilot an improved view.

VARIANTS

The **FRS1** was the initial version for the Royal Navy, and the Indian Navy export version – the **FRS51** – is similar. The **FA2** is slightly stretched, with a 35cm (1ft 2in) plug behind the wing, and it also has a larger, rounded nose.

TECHNICAL DATA

BAe Sea Harrier FA2

Powerplant: One Rolls-Royce Pegasus 104/106 vectored thrust turbofan
Developing: 95.6kN (21,500lb st)
Span: 7.70m (25ft 3in)
Length: 14.17m (46ft 6in)
Height: 3.71m (12ft 2in)
All-up weight: 9,843kg (21,700lb)
Maximum speed: 1,185km/h (734mph)
Cruise speed: 840km/h (520mph)
Operational ceiling: 51,000ft
Maximum range: 970km (602 miles)
Mission range: 370km (230 miles)
Accommodation: Pilot only
Warload: Up to four AIM-120 AMRAAMS on outboard and under-fuselage station, or two AIM-120s and four AIM-9 Sidewinders. Can also carry two 30mm Aden cannon. Other weapons include Sea Eagle anti-shipping missile, bombs and rockets.
First flown: September 1979 (FRS1); 2 April 1993 (FRS2/FA2).
Entered service: 31 March 1980

Sea Harrier FA2 Royal Navy

British Aerospace/McDonnell Douglas Harrier GR7

SINGLE TURBOFAN SINGLE-SEAT V/STOL DAY/NIGHT GROUND ATTACK AIRCRAFT

DEVELOPMENT

British Aerospace initiated independent development of an advanced Harrier during the late 1970s to succeed the GR3. This 'big wing' Harrier was often known as the 'tin wing' Harrier, due to the wing being made of conventional alloy and not incorporating carbon fibre. By the early 1980s, the US became involved and a partnership between BAe and McDonnell Douglas ensued to proceed with development of the aircraft. BAe consequently abandoned its own GR5 and used the designation for its licence-built version of the McDonnell Douglas AV-8B Harrier II. Later production aircraft became GR5As, which had provision for GR7 avionics. Surviving GR5s were converted to GR7s. The Harrier GR7 is basically the equivalent of the night attack AV-8B, using much of the same equipment and avionics, and has the same overnose bulge housing the GEC Sensors FLIR. One hundred were delivered to the RAF before manufacture of the GR7 ended in December 1997. The first GR7s replaced front-line Harrier GR3 squadrons in Germany.

Harrier GR7 Royal Air Force

CURRENT SERVICE

The RAF's Nos 1, 3 and 4 Squadrons are based at RAF Cottesmore as part of the new Joint Force Harrier. No 20(R) Squadron is based at RAF Wittering. At times the Harriers have been deployed in Operation *Bolton*, monitoring the No Fly Zone over Southern Iraq, and as part of Operation *Warden*, protecting Kurdish settlements in Northern Iraq. The RAF's Harrier force was also involved in Operation *Allied Force* during the Kosovo crisis in 1999, with aircraft operating from the Italian base at Gioia del Colle.

SPECIAL FEATURES

The GR7 has a Marconi Zeus ECM system and Plessey MAWS. It features an NVG compatible cockpit, which allows use of Ferranti Night Owl NVGs. Later Harriers have a 100% LERX, which further delays the onset of wing rock and improves turn performance. Fitted with a TIALD pod the GR7 can also automatically launch laser-guided PGMs. Provision of a dedicated Sidewinder pylon allows adequate defence capability even when carrying a full offensive load.

VARIANTS

Improvement and modification has been a continuing process since the aircraft entered service. The **GR7** is to be upgraded to **GR9** standard, including a new, more powerful, Pegasus 11-61 engine and this will allow the Harrier to operate Storm Shadow and Brimstone missiles.

SEE ALSO AV-8A & AV-8B HARRIER, HARRIER T4/T8, HARRIER T10/TAV-8B AND SEA HARRIER

TECHNICAL DATA

British Aerospace Harrier GR7

Powerplant: One Rolls-Royce Pegasus Mk 105 vectored thrust turbofan
Developing: 95.74kN (21,500lb st)
Span: 9.25m (30ft 4in)
Length: 14.35m (47ft 1in)
Height: 3.55m (11ft 7.75in)
All-up weight: 14,515Kg (32,000lb) for STO; 8,595kg (18,950lb) for VTO
Maximum speed: 1,061km/h (661mph))
Operational ceiling: Over 50,000ft
Maximum range: 3,243km (2,015 miles)

Mission range: 1,162km (722 miles)
Accommodation: Pilot only
Warload: Two 25mm Royal Ordnance Factories cannon on under-fuselage station. Nine weapons pylons with 4,900kg (10,800lb) payload. Range of freefall and retarded bombs, including 1,000lb laser-guided, cluster and practice. Alternatively, or as a mix, rocket launchers, ASMs, Sidewinder/ Magic AAMs or other stores. Additional pods can be carried.
Endurance: Three hours
First flown: 30 April 1985 (GR5); 18 May 1990 (GR7)
Entered service: 1 July 1987 (GR5); 20 July 1990 (GR7)

Harrier GR7 Royal Air Force

British Aerospace/McDonnell Douglas Harrier T10/TAV-8B

SINGLE TURBOFAN TWO-SEAT V/STOL TRAINER/GROUND ATTACK AIRCRAFT

McDonnell Douglas TAV-8B United States Marines Corps

TECHNICAL DATA

BAe Harrier T10

Powerplant: One Rolls-Royce Pegasus Mk 105
vectored thrust turbofan
Developing: 95.75kN (21,750lb st)
Span: 9.25m (30ft 4in)
Length: 15.79m (51ft 9.5in)
Height: 3.55m (11ft 7.5in)
All-up weight: 14,515Kg (32,000lb) for STO;
8,518Kg (18,780lb) for VTO
Maximum speed: 1,061km/h (661mph))
Operational ceiling: Over 50,000ft
Maximum range: 3,035km (2,263 miles)
Endurance: 3 hours
Accommodation: Two in tandem
Warload: As for Harrier GR7
First flown: 21 October 1986 (TAV-8B);
7 April 1994 (T10)
Entered service: 9 Dec 1986 (TAV-8B-7); 1995 (T10)

DEVELOPMENT

The further development in the USA of the single-seat AV-8B – and in the UK of the GR7 – saw the most ambitious design changes for the two-seat equivalents, the TAV-8B and Harrier T10 respectively. The RAF decided it needed a Harrier II trainer. In April 1988, the UK MoD stated that Britain would not buy the TAV-8B, as the expense could not be justified – but in 1990 it was agreed that the RAF would receive 14 new Harrier operational training aircraft, rather than adapt the ageing T4 into a T6. Based on the TAV-8B, the T10 has the FLIR equipment of the Harrier GR7, and, unlike the TAV-8B, it is a fully operational aircraft with a wartime attack role, although lacking the Hughes ARBS. The USMC initially decided not to ask for a trainer version of the AV-8B, since V/STOL

training could satisfactorily be provided on existing TAV-8As, which would be supplemented by a further purchase from the BAe production line. However, it later became clear that the handling characteristics of the Harrier II were so different from those of the AV-8A that the expense of developing a TAV-8B was justified.

CURRENT SERVICE

Each operational RAF Harrier squadron has its own two-seaters, and a total of 13 T10s were delivered. The TAV-8B is used by a Harrier training squadron with the US Marine Corps (24 were received) and it is scheduled for an upgrade with the F402-RR-408A engine. The Royal Thai Navy took over two ex-Spanish Navy TAV-8S Matadors for use from a new light

aircraft carrier when Spain purchased a single TAV-8B as a Matador II. Italy has two TAV-8Bs, equipped with -408 engines – the only Harrier trainers fitted with this engine. The Indian Naval Aviation operates the aircraft carrier INS *Viraat* (ex-HMS *Hermes*) and uses the Sea Harrier and Harrier T60. They are shore-based at Goa-Dablomin with INAS 551 when not at sea.

SPECIAL FEATURES

The T10 differs from the TAV-8 in having eight underwing pylons (not two) and FLIR. It is fully combat-capable with standard avionics and an ability to use a variety of combat weapons. Its US counterpart carries only training armament.

VARIANTS

There are no variants of the RAF's **Harrier T10**. The **TAV-8B Harrier II** has a shorter fuselage (0.47m – 1ft 6.5in) than the T10. The USMC TAV-8Bs are receiving an engine upgrade.

SEE ALSO BRITISH AEROSPACE/McDONNELL DOUGLAS HARRIER GR7, AV-8A, AV-8B AND HARRIER T4/T8

Harrier T10 Royal Air Force

British Aerospace 146

FOUR-TURBOFAN STOL VIP TRANSPORT

BAe 146 CC2 Royal Air Force

DEVELOPMENT

The BAe 146/RJ Series originates from a 1973 proposal by Hawker Siddeley for a new short-range, low-noise civil transport as the HS146. Shortly afterwards the nationalisation of British aviation under the British Aerospace name led to a shelving of the proposal, before design work resumed in July 1978 involving risk sharing partners Avco in the USA and Saab-Scania in Sweden. The first Series 100 was rolled out in May 1981 and several further civilian developments of the type followed. The Series 200 had a lengthened fuselage for up to 112 passengers plus an increase in take-off weight; the Series 300 was further extended and had accommodation for 128 passengers in a high-density layout; and there were several cargo versions – including the 146-QT Quiet Trader ordered by TNT Aviation Services. In 1990, the aircraft was relaunched as the Avro RJ Series (RJ70, RJ85, RJ100 and RJ115)

with various passenger capacities, plus freighter versions, and production of this series continued until 1997. Proposed military versions of the aircraft as a multi-role transport were announced in 1987 and included the BAe 146STA (Small Tactical Airlifter), BAe 146MT (Military Tanker), BAe 146MRL (Military Rear Loader) and BAe 146MSL (Military Side Loader). The BAe 146STA was the only one of these to reach prototype form, but despite extensive sales tours no orders were forthcoming. The only air arm to operate the type is the RAF, which uses the BAe 146 CC2 as a VIP transport aircraft, operated by No 32 (The Royal) Squadron. After evaluating two BAe 146 Series 100s (146 CC1s) in 1983-84, two 146 Series 200s (146 CC2s) were acquired in mid-1986, followed by a third in 1991, replacing the Andover CC2 in RAF service.

CURRENT SERVICE

Three BAe 146 CC2s serve with No 32 (The Royal) Squadron at RAF Northolt.

SPECIAL FEATURES

The BAe 146 is characterised by its low-noise signature offered by the Textron ALF502R engines. The high lift high-mounted wing has large Fowler-type trailing edge flaps giving the aircraft the ability to operate from short or semi-prepared strips with minimal ground facilities. Distinctive large petal airbrakes close to form the tailcone of the aircraft and are utilised during low-speed operations. RAF 146 CC2s have been fitted with Loral Matador infrared jamming systems offering an ECM capability.

VARIANTS

The 146 series is now marketed as the **Avro RJ** series, with improved engines and other systems. The 146-100 version is now the **RJ70**, the 146-200 the **RJ85** and the 146-300 the **RJ100**. The **146QT-Quiet Trader** is the freighter version. The **CC2** is the current VIP transport version and is the only variant in current military service.

TECHNICAL DATA

BAe 146 CC2

Powerplants: Four Textron Lycoming ALF502R-5 turbofans
Developing: 31.0kN (6,970lb st)
Span: 26.21m (86ft 0in)
Length: 28.60m (93ft 10in)
Height: 8.59m (28ft 2in)
All up weight: 42,184kg (93,000lb)
Maximum cruise speed: 801km/h (498mph)
Operational ceiling: 30,000ft
Range: 2,909km (1,808 miles)
Accommodation: Two crew and up to 94 passengers or VIP interior on CC2s
First flown: 3 September 1981 (Series 100 prototype)
Entered service: June 1983 (CC1); 1986 (CC2)

BAe 146 CC2 Royal Air Force

Canadair CL-41 Tutor

SINGLE TURBOJET TRAINER AIRCRAFT

DEVELOPMENT

One of a number of jet trainers that entered service in the late 1950s and early 1960s, the CL-41 Tutor was conceived by Canadair as a private venture and made its first flight in prototype form in January 1960. At that time, the Royal Canadian Air Force (RCAF) needed a new basic trainer, but did not immediately opt for Canadair's Tutor, choosing to evaluate competing Western designs before settling on the home-grown machine. The first production example was handed over to the RCAF on 16 December 1963, but student training did not commence until February 1965. Deliveries were completed in 1966.

CURRENT SERVICE

Following retirement of the Malaysian aircraft in the mid-1980s, Canada is now the only air arm to operate the CL-41, which is known as the CT-114 Tutor in Canadian service. About 120 aircraft survive, although 20 of these are normally held in storage. Of the 100 or so operational aircraft, the majority equip units of No 15 Wing at Moose Jaw, Saskatchewan. These comprise No 2 Canadian Forces Flying Training School

CT-114 Tutor Canadian Armed Forces

and the Flight Instructor School, plus No 431 *Snowbirds* Squadron, the national aerobatic team. A few are also assigned to the Central Flying School, which is part of No 17 Wing at Winnipeg, Manitoba, while the Aerospace Engineering and Test Establishment at Cold Lake, Alberta, normally has a couple of Tutors assigned. After primary training, pupils complete some 200 hours on the CT-114 to gain their 'wings' before proceeding to specialised training for combat jets, multi-engine types or helicopters.

SPECIAL FEATURES

Similar in many respects to the Cessna T-37 and Hunting Jet Provost trainers, the CL-41 Tutor incorporated the side-by-side seating arrangement for instructor and student used by both of those types. Other similarities include the low-set, straight wing configuration, with air inlets in the wing root adjacent to the cockpit, and an upward-hinging canopy, but it differs in having a T-tail arrangement. Twin lateral door-type airbrakes are also positioned on the fuselage sides, aft of the wing.

VARIANTS

Three versions of the Tutor have existed. Following the two prototypes, quantity production of the basic **CL-41** was undertaken during 1963-66 to satisfy an RCAF order for 190. This later changed identity to Air Command, but the **CT-114 Tutor** continues to give good service today, almost four decades after entering service. An upgrade was undertaken in the 1970s to improve the avionics. With production for the RCAF complete, Canadair then built 20 aircraft to satisfy the only export order. This came from Malaysia, which took delivery of a version known as the **CL-41G** in 1967; in Malaysian service, the name **Tebuan** (Wasp) was adopted and these aircraft fulfilled dual trainer/ light attack duties for almost 20 years. They had six suspension points capable of carrying up to 1,590kg (3,500lb) of gun pods, bombs, rockets, Sidewinder missiles and soft landing gear. The second Tutor prototype was converted to **CL-41R** configuration, fitted with an avionics suite similar to that of the CF-104 Starfighter. In this guise, it functioned as an experimental systems trainer.

TECHNICAL DATA

Canadair CT-114 Tutor

Powerplant: One Orenda (General Electric) J85-CAN-J4 turbojet
Developing: 13.12kN (2,950lb st)
Span: 11.13m (36ft 6in)
Length: 9.75m (32ft 0in)
Height: 2.84m (9ft 3.75in)
All-up weight: 3,532kg (7,788lb)
Maximum speed: 782km/h (486mph)
Operational ceiling: 43,000ft
Normal range: 1,002km (623 miles)
Accommodation: Instructor and student
Warload: Normally nil, but CL-41G had six hardpoints for up to 1,590kg (3,500lb) of ordnance, including bombs and rockets
First flown: 13 January 1960 (CL-41A); June 1964 (CL-41G)
Entered service: 29 October 1963

CT-114 Tutor Canadian Armed Forces

Canadair CL-215 and CL-415

TWIN-ENGINED FIREFIGHTING/MULTI-MISSION AMPHIBIAN

Canadair CL-215 Yugoslav Air Force

TECHNICAL DATA

Canadair CL-415

Powerplants: Two Pratt & Whitney Canada PW123AF turboprops
Developing: 1,775kW (2,380shp)
Driving: Four-blade propellers
Span: 28.63m (93ft 11in)
Length: 19.82m (65ft 0.5in)
Height: 8.98m (29ft 5.5in) on land;
6.88m (22ft 7in) on water
Maximum weight: 19,890kg (43,850lb) on land;
17,168kg (37,850lb) on water
Maximum cruise speed: 376km/h (234mph)
Patrol speed: 241km/h (150mph)
Ferry range: 2,426km (1,507 miles)
Accommodation: Normally two crew, plus third cockpit member, two observers and mission specialist
Payload: 6,123kg (13,500lb) in firefighting configuration; 3,789kg (8,353lb) in utility configuration
Warload: None
First flown: 23 October 1967 (CL-215);
8 June 1989 (CL-215T conversion);
6 December 1993 (CL-415)
Entered service: 1995 (CL-415)

DEVELOPMENT

Conceived from the outset for the aerial firefighting role and later adapted for other tasks such as search and rescue, transport and maritime surveillance, the initial version was the CL-215, which was fitted with radial piston engines and flew for the first time in late 1967. Production of this model continued until 1990, but by then, the first turbine-powered derivative had appeared as the CL-215T, which is basically a CL-215 modified to take Pratt & Whitney Canada PW123 engines. The same powerplant is also installed on the new-build CL-415 SuperScooper, which was officially launched in 1991 with an order from the French government.

CURRENT SERVICE

Military use of the Canadair machine is by no means widespread, but at least four countries are known to currently operate piston and turbine-engined versions. One of the first military customers for the original CL-215 was Greece, which accepted the first of 20 aircraft in 1973 of which approximately 15 are still in service with the Hellenic Air Force today, while

Croatia's Air Force and the Royal Thai Naval Air Arm each have two. Another early military operator of the original CL-215 was Spain, which received 30, although attrition and disposal of some reduced the fleet by half, with all 15 survivors being modified to CL-215T standard in the early 1990s. The first of four new-build CL-415 entered service with Croatia in 1997, and the only other military customer for this model is Greece, which purchased ten in January 1999.

SPECIAL FEATURES

Although the powerplant installation may vary, all members of the family are boat-type amphibians with a high-wing configuration employed to lift the engines clear of the spray thrown up when operating from water. In addition, both the CL-215T and CL-415 have wingtip endplates and auxiliary finlets for added stability in flight. For operation from land, all versions feature a retractable tricycle undercarriage.

VARIANTS

Production commenced in the late 1960s of the original **CL-215**, with Pratt & Whitney R-2800 radial

piston engines, and some 125 had been completed by 1990, when the last example was handed over to Greece. Re-engining with the PW123 turboprop in 1989 resulted in the **CL-215T** and a number of aircraft have been modified to this standard, including 15 for Spain. Since 1995, however, new-build production has been of **CL-415** variants, including the **CL-415M** for maritime, SAR and other missions and the **CL-415GR** for Greece.

Canadair CL-215 Spanish Air Force

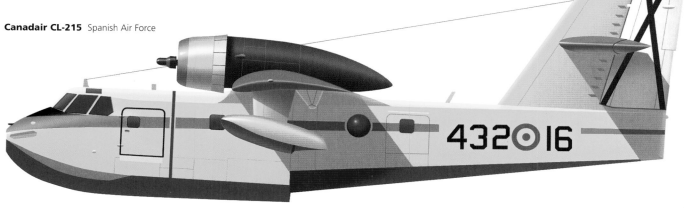

Canadair CL-600 Challenger

TWIN-TURBOFAN EXECUTIVE TRANSPORT AIRCRAFT

CL601-1A Challenger German Air Force

DEVELOPMENT

In April 1976, Canadair acquired rights from Bill Lear to design, manufacture and market the proposed LearStar 600. This was originally to be a twin-turbofan business aircraft with an advanced technology wing and Canadair began its development programme in September of that year, revealing major design changes including a T-tail layout in March 1977, when the name Challenger was adopted. In this guise, and powered by AlliedSignal ALF 502L-2 turbofans, the prototype made its initial flight in November 1978, with delivery of production aircraft starting in late 1980. Subsequent development led to the Challenger 601 with General Electric's CF34 engine, which is now the standard powerplant of the Challenger 604.

CURRENT SERVICE

At least 30 examples of the Challenger have seen military service and most remain in use today. Canada was the first nation to purchase the type, receiving 12 Challenger 600s and four Challenger 601s. No 434 Squadron operated ten CC-144s for combat support until 31 May 2000. Two of these joined No 412 Squadron at Trenton for medevac and general transport duties alongside six other Challengers. Other operators include Croatia, with one Challenger 601 and one Challenger 604 for VIP airlift. Germany uses a fleet of seven VIP-configured Challenger 601s,

while the Czech Republic has one. Other military users include China, Denmark (with two Challenger 604s for communications and exclusive economic zone patrol tasks) and Malaysia.

SPECIAL FEATURES

Low-wing design with high-set T-tail configuration and twin turbofan engines mounted on pylons attached to the aft fuselage section. Initial production aircraft lacked winglets, but these were added commencing with the Challenger 601 and subsequently retrofitted to many early Challengers.

VARIANTS

The initial production version was the **Challenger 600**, with AlliedSignal ALF 502 turbofan engines. Some 84 were built by mid-1983, by which time the **Challenger 601** had appeared, the first version to be fitted with General Electric CF34 engines. Three variations were successively produced between May 1983 and early 1996, these being the basic Model **601-1A** (66 built), the Model **601-3A** with 'glass' cockpit (134 built) and the Model **601-3R** extended-range version (59 built). Since then, the only version available has been the **Challenger 604**, which introduced a number of refinements such as a modified and strengthened tail section, revised landing gear, and General Electric CF34-3B engines.

TECHNICAL DATA

Canadair CL-600 Challenger 601

Powerplants: Two General Electric CF34-1A turbofans
Thrust: 38.48kN (8,650lb st) without automatic power reserve (APR);
40.66kN (9,140lb st) with APR
Span: 19.61m (64ft 4in) including winglets
Length: 20.85m (68ft 5in)
Height: 6.30m (20ft 8in)
All-up weight: 19,950kg (43,100lb)
Maximum cruise speed: 851km/h (529mph)
Normal cruise speed: 819km/h (509mph)
Operational ceiling: 45,000ft
Maximum range: 6,371km (3,959 miles)
Accommodation: Two crew and maximum of 19 passengers
Maximum payload: 2,229kg (4,915lb)
First flown: 8 November 1978 (prototype); 17 September 1982 (first production Challenger 601)
Entered service: December 1980 (Challenger 600 first delivery); 1983 (Challenger 601)

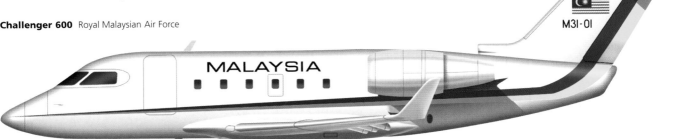

Challenger 600 Royal Malaysian Air Force

CASA C-101 Aviojet

SINGLE TURBOFAN TWO-SEAT BASIC TRAINER, AND ADVANCED TRAINER/LIGHT ATTACK AIRCRAFT **SPAIN**

C-101CC Aviojet Royal Jordanian Air Force

TECHNICAL DATA

CASA C-101CC Aviojet

Powerplant: One Garrett (AlliedSignal) TFE731-5-1J non-afterburning turbofan
Developing: 20.91kN (4,700lb st) (military power reserve rating)
Span: 10.60m (34ft 9.375in)
Length: 12.50m (41ft 0in)
Height: 4.25m (13ft 11.25in)
All-up weight: 6,300kg (13,890lb)
Maximum speed: 834km/h (518mph)
Cruise speed: 612km/h (379mph)
Operational Ceiling: 42,000ft
Maximum range: 3,706km (2,303 miles)
Mission range: 1,038km (644 miles)
Endurance: up to 7 hours
Accommodation: Instructor and trainee pilot (instructor in rear seat)
Warload: internal weapons bay below rear cockpit for optional packages including single 30mm DEFA 553 cannon pod or twin 12.7mm (0.5in) Browning M3 machine gun pod, or reconnaissance pod; six underwing pylons (three per wing) for total external stores load of 2,250 kg (4,960 lb). Armament options include LAU-3/A 2.75in rocket pods, LAU-10 5in rocket pods, 125 kg BR125 bombs and/or 250 kg BR250 or similar bombs, two AGM-65 Maverick guided missiles (with related guidance systems fitted), and napalm bombs.
First flown: 27 June 1977
Entered service: March 1980

DEVELOPMENT

Designed by CASA, with technical expertise from Northrop and MBB, the C-101 Aviojet was intended specifically to replace the Spanish Air Force's ageing Hispano HA-200 Saetas and Lockheed T-33s. Design work began in 1974 with official go-ahead in 1975, and the first prototype flew in June 1977. The initial production aircraft flew in November 1979, and an order for 60 for the Spanish Air Force was increased later by another 28. Initial service Aviojet deliveries began to the Spanish Air Force's Academia General del Aire (AGA) at San Javier in March 1980, Spain's C-101EB-01 models being known locally as the E.25 Mirlo (Blackbird). Four of the armed trainer derivative of the C-101EB, the C-101BB, were ordered in 1983 by Honduras, and Jordan ordered 14 (later 16) C-101CC export light attack models in 1986. Chile is the most important export customer, having ordered examples of the C-101BB and C-101CC and then producing the type locally (initially with parts supplied by CASA) as the ENAER T-36 Halcon (Hawk) and A-36 Halcon. Orders for 14 and 23 respectively have been made, with initial deliveries in 1982, but completion of the order has progressed slowly. CASA developed the Aviojet as the export C-101DD with advanced avionics

and weapons capability, including AIM-9 Sidewinders and Matra Magic AAMs, but no orders resulted.

CURRENT SERVICE

Some 76 of Spain's E.25 Mirlos still serve, principally with the Ejército del Aire's AGA at San Javier; or with Grupo 74 at Matacán, mainly for refresher training, and Grupo 54 at Torrejón. The E.25 is also flown by Spain's national aerobatic team, the *Patrulla Aguila*, at San Javier. The Royal Jordanian Air Force's 12 or 13 surviving C-101CCs fly with No 11 Squadron of the King Hussein Air College, Mafraq. The Chilean Air Force's Halcón fleet serves with Grupo 1 at Iquique, and Grupo 3 at Temuco. The Honduran C-101BBs that serve with the Honduran Air Force's Academia Militar de Aviación at La Palmerola were apparently added to recently by some A-36 Halcóns from Chile.

SPECIAL FEATURES

Built along modular lines and fully aerobatic, the simple but versatile and capable C-101 has ample on-board fuel capacity and a fuel-effecient engine (a high-bypass turbofan – an engine widely used on business jets and known for its reliability) to give an excellent endurance for this type of aircraft.

VARIANTS

The Spanish-operated **C-101EB-01** model has a Garrett TFE731-2-2J turbofan of 15.57kN (3,500lb st) and is the basic Aviojet variant, although partially upgraded in the early 1990s. The Chilean **C-101BB-02s** and Honduran **C-101BB-03s** have a slightly more powerful TFE731, but have a less powerful and less comprehensive avionics package than the **C-101CC-04** of Jordan and the **C-101CC-02** of Chile, and the related Chilean-made examples (which were recently upgraded).

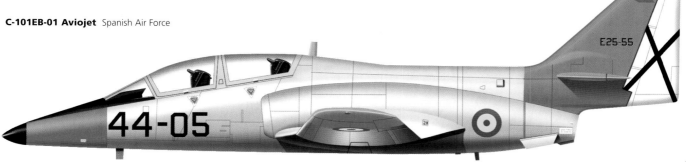

C-101EB-01 Aviojet Spanish Air Force

CASA C-212 Aviocar

TWIN-TURBOPROP GENERAL PURPOSE TRANSPORT/CARGO AIRCRAFT

C-212-200 Aviocar Spanish Air Force

TECHNICAL DATA

CASA C-212-300

Powerplants: Two AlliedSignal TPE331-10R-513C turboprops
Developing: 670kW (900shp) (automatic power reserve rating)
Driving: three-blade propellers
Span: 20.28m (66ft 6.5in)
Length: 16.15m (52ft 11.75in)
Height: 6.60m (21ft 7.75in)
All-up weight: 8,000kg (17,637lb)
Maximum speed: 370km/h (230mph)
Cruise speed: 300km/h (186mph)
Operational ceiling: 26,000ft
Maximum range: 2,600km (1,616 miles)
Mission range: 1,682km (1,045 miles)
Endurance: approximately 8 hours
Accommodation: Pilot and co-pilot; loadmaster or jumpmaster as required, up to 24 fully-equipped paratroops, or up to 25 fully-equipped troops, or cargo as required
Warload: Optional provision for two machine gun pods or two small rocket launchers on hardpoints under wings or on fuselage sides; Patroller models can carry Mk46 or Stingray torpedoes, or unguided rockets, or anti-ship missiles such as Aérospatiale AS15TT or Sea Skua
First flown: 26 March 1971;
30 April 1978 (Srs 200); 1984 (Srs 300)
Entered service: March 1974

DEVELOPMENT

To replace Spanish-operated locally-produced Ju 52/3m transports and other ageing types, CASA began design studies in 1964 and received the official go-ahead in 1967-68 for the C-212 Aviocar. The first flight of this light utility STOL transport was made in March 1971 and early production examples began reaching the Spanish Air Force in 1974. The type has subsequently proved highly successful in military and civil guise for many operators world-wide in a number of versions. The initial production models (now generically called Series 100) were followed by the improved Series 200 from 1979-80, with more powerful TPE331 engines and increased carrying capability. From 1987 the Series 300 became available, this model having structural improvements and improved TPE331 engines with increased range and payload capabilities. The newest model is the Series 400, developed from 1995; it has more powerful TPE331 turboprops, improved avionics and capability. Specialised adaptations of the Series 300 and 400 models are called Patroller, including anti-submarine and maritime patrol versions. IPTN of Indonesia has licence-manufactured 100 and 200 Series Aviocar models, although this Indonesian production has now virtually ended. Some 460 C-212s of all types have been built so far.

CURRENT SERVICE

The Spanish Air Force's sizeable C-212 fleet comprises various specific models known locally under several T.12 designations, plus the radar-equipped D.3 SAR version. Cargo Aviocars serve with units such as Ala 37 at Villanubla, and 461 Escuadrón at Gando in the Canary Islands. SAR D.3 Aviocars operate mainly with 801 and 803 Escuadróns. Several Aviocars serve with the USAF's Special Operations Command, including the 6th Special Operations Squadron at Hurlburt Field, Florida. In addition to these users, Aviocars of various versions currently serve with some 26 other military operators, including the air force, army, navy, coast guard or paramilitary police of the following: Angola, Argentina, Bolivia, Bosnia-Hertzegovia, Botswana, Chad, Chile, Colombia, Dominican Republic, France, Indonesia, Jordan, Lesotho, Mexico, Myanmar, Panama, Papua New Guinea, Paraguay, Portugal, South Africa, Surinam, Sweden, Thailand, United Arab Emirates, Uruguay, Venezuela, and Zimbabwe.

SPECIAL FEATURES

The all-metal, unpressurised Aviocar has a fixed tricycle undercarriage and a two-section rear loading door/ramp which can be opened in flight for paratroop egress. The Aviocar's simple but rugged layout has been adapted to special mission configurations, or can carry up to 2,700 kg (5,952lb) of freight including light vehicles.

VARIANTS

The **Series 300** C-212 introduced winglets for improved climb performance and stability, and a reshaped nose. Some **Series 300** maritime reconnaissance/**Patroller** models have a large 'platypus' nose with a scanning radar. The recent **Series 400** has a redesigned nose, with Patroller options for a 360° search radar, forward-looking infra-red, and other mission equipment, and a re-designed interior with consoles for extra crew to work the aircraft's additional sensors/avionics. Specially equipped electronic-warfare versions are also being marketed.

C-212-300 Aviocar Royal Thai Air Force

Cessna 150/152

SINGLE PISTON-ENGINED TRAINER/LIAISON AIRCRAFT

Cessna 150M Paraguay Navy

DEVELOPMENT

Originally conceived as a light trainer/tourer aircraft for use by civilian flying clubs and private individuals, the Cessna 150 was one of a number of single-engined aircraft that emerged from the design offices of the Wichita-based company in the 1950s. Broadly similar in basic appearance to the Model 172 and 182, it was smaller and lighter and could only accommodate two occupants. The prototype made its maiden flight in Autumn 1957 and quantity production got underway in August 1958. In addition to US-built aircraft, Reims Aviation obtained manufacturing rights in the 1960s and produced the type in France for many years.

CURRENT SERVICE

Despite finding ready acceptance with commercial flying schools, military use of the Cessna 150 has been much less widespread. Today, examples of the Cessna 150 serve in fairly limited numbers with the air arms of Colombia, Ecuador, Paraguay, Peru, Sri Lanka and

Thailand, while similar aircraft produced in France by Reims Aviation as the F 150 and FRA 150 are flown by Burundi, Congo Democratic Republic and the Seychelles. Duties undertaken include primary training and liaison/communications tasks. The only country known to operate the slightly more powerful Cessna 152 is Venezuela, where two or three are used by the National Guard Air Co-Operation Fleet for training purposes.

SPECIAL FEATURES

Classic Cessna features such as the high-positioned, strut-braced wing are evident on both the Model 150 and 152, although they were also among the first of the American company's products to make use of a tricycle-undercarriage layout. Early Model 150s were fitted with a straight fin, but a continual process of enhancement resulted in the adoption of a swept tail with effect from the Model 150F, which entered production in 1966.

VARIANTS

At least 14 different versions of the basic **Model 150** were produced by the parent company, these being the **150A** to **150N**, with Reims Aviation also building large numbers of the **150F** to **150M** under licence in France. Differences introduced on the **Model 152**, which entered production in 1977, mainly concern the engine, with this type using the Textron Lycoming O-235, rated at 82kW (110hp). As with the 150, the Model 152 was built under licence in France, also starting in 1977. Additionally, both Cessna and Reims Aviation produced versions of the two basic types which featured a strengthened airframe; these are known as the **A150** and **A152 Aerobat (FA/FRA 150/152** for French aircraft), by virtue of possessing full aerobatic capability.

Cessna FRA150L Somali Air Force

TECHNICAL DATA

Cessna 150

Powerplant: One Teledyne Continental O-200-A piston engine
Developing: 74.5kW (100hp)
Driving: Two-blade propeller
Span: 9.97m (32ft 8.5in)
Length: 7.29m (23ft 11in)
Height: 2.59m (8ft 6in)
All-up weight: 726kg (1,600lb)
Maximum speed: 261km/h (162mph)
Cruise speed: 153km/h (95mph)
Operational ceiling: 14,000ft
Ferry range: 1,361km (846 miles)
Normal range: 779km (484 miles)
Accommodation: Pilot and passenger/student
First flown: 15 September 1957
Entered service: 1958

Cessna 172 Skyhawk & T-41 Mescalero

SINGLE PISTON-ENGINED TRAINER/LIAISON AIRCRAFT

Cessna T-41D Peruvian Air Force

DEVELOPMENT

Put into quantity production by Cessna in November 1955, the Model 172 was essentially a Model 170 with a redesigned fin and a tricycle undercarriage layout instead of the original tailwheel configuration. The Model 172A of 1960 introduced swept tail surfaces, this being one of many new features incorporated over time. Given the name Skyhawk in the early 1960s, the Model 172 had huge commercial success, with almost 36,000 built by the parent company by 1985, when production was suspended (although it restarted in the mid-1990s). As with several other Cessna designs, Reims Aviation of France secured manufacturing rights, producing it as the F 172 and FR 172 from 1963 onwards.

CURRENT SERVICE

Model 172s are currently used by Bolivia, Burkina Faso, Chile, Greece, Guatemala, Indonesia, Madagascar, Nicaragua, Pakistan, Peru, Surinam, Trinidad and Tobago, Uruguay and Venezuela, while Reims Aviation equivalents serve with Ireland and Saudi Arabia. T-41s are just as widely used, with nations known to utilise variants of this derivative being Argentina, Colombia, Dominican Republic, Ecuador, Greece,

Honduras, Indonesia, South Korea, Paraguay, Peru, Philippines, El Salvador, Thailand, Turkey, Uruguay and the USA.

SPECIAL FEATURES

The basic configuration embodies strut-braced, high-wing layout, with tricycle undercarriage units. The initial 172 model of 1955 had a straight fin, replaced by swept tail surfaces with effect from the Model 172A in 1960. A cut-down rear cabin layout was first incorporated on the Model 172D in 1963, which allowed a wrap-around rear window to be adopted for enhanced all-round visibility. Military T-41s lack the spatted undercarriage of their civil counterparts.

VARIANTS

A long-lasting process of refinement resulted in the basic civilian Model 172 being produced in an almost bewildering number of versions, these using suffix letters as a means of differentiation. By 1985, when production was suspended, Cessna had progressed as far as the **Model 172Q**. Versions that have emerged since manufacture restarted comprise the **172R** and **172S**. Purely military derivatives began with the **T-41A**, purchased for flight screening by the USAF in 1964.

TECHNICAL DATA

Cessna T-41D Mescalero

Powerplant: One Teledyne Continental IO-360-D piston engine
Developing: 156.5kW (210hp)
Driving: Two-blade propeller
Span: 10.92m (35ft 10in)
Length: 8.20m (26ft 11in)
Height: 2.68m (8ft 9.5in)
All-up weight: 1,156kg (2,550lb)
Maximum speed: 246km/h (153mph)
Cruise speed: 233km/h (145mph)
Operational ceiling: 17,000ft
Ferry range: 1,030km (640 miles)
Normal range: 990km (615 miles)
Accommodation: Pilot and up to three passengers
First flown: 12 June 1955
Entered service: 1956 (commercial Model 172)

The US Army acquired over 250 **T-41Bs** in 1967 for training and light utility duties; the USAF buying about 50 **T-41Cs** for training with the Academy at Colorado Springs. More than 200 **T-41Ds** were also built for friendly nations under the Military

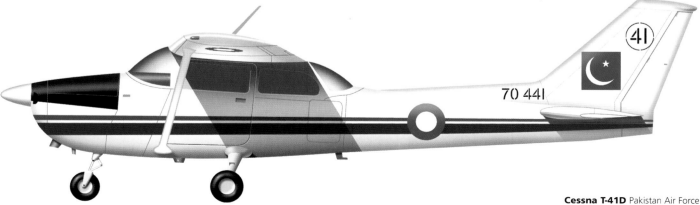

Cessna T-41D Pakistan Air Force

Cessna 180, 182, 185 & U-17

SINGLE PISTON-ENGINED LIGHT UTILITY AIRCRAFT

Cessna 182 Argentine Navy

DEVELOPMENT

The first of this family of versatile and utilitarian light aircraft to appear was the Model 180, which made its maiden flight in the first half of 1952, with deliveries commencing in early 1953. Subsequent refinement of the basic design culminated in the Model 182 of 1956. Although it looked significantly different, by virtue of its tricycle undercarriage, it retained the same airframe and engine. However, as with many other Cessna types, swept tail surfaces were introduced in the early 1960s, the first version to embody this refinement being the Model 182C. By then, the Model 185 had also entered production, this being an improved 180 with a strengthened

TECHNICAL DATA

Cessna U-17B

Powerplant: One Continental IO-520-D piston engine
Developing: 224kW (300hp)
Driving: Two-blade propeller
Span: 11.02m (36ft 2in)
Length: 7.7m (25ft 6in)
Height: 2.36m (7ft 9in)
All-up weight: 1,520kg (3,350lb)
Maximum speed: 283km/h (176mph)
Cruise speed: 208km/h (129mph)
Operational ceiling: 17,150ft
Ferry range: 1,730km (1,075 miles)
Normal range: 1,328km (825 miles)
Accommodation: Pilot and three passengers (180/182); pilot and five passengers (185)
First flown: 26 May 1952 (Model 180 prototype)
Entered service: February 1953 (Model 180); 1956 (Model 182); 1961 (Model 185)

cargo pack beneath the belly. Today, only the Model 182 is still being built, having been re-instated in production in the mid-1990s.

CURRENT SERVICES

Versions of the Model 180 are presently used by Indonesia, Myanmar, Nicaragua and Thailand, while the Model 182 was recently reported in service with Argentina, Belgium, Bolivia, Guatemala, Lesotho, Mexico, Uruguay, the USA and Venezuela. Versions of the Model 185 are presently used by Honduras, Indonesia, Iran, Paraguay and South Africa. Turning to specifically military models, a small number of Cessna 180s was produced for the US Military Assistance Program as U-17Cs, but none are believed to survive in military service today. However, almost 500 U-17A/B versions were also funded for the MAP during 1963-73 and quite a few of these are still flying in Argentina, Greece, Nicaragua, Thailand, Turkey and Uruguay.

SPECIAL FEATURES

Configuration varies according to version, but all incorporate the classic Cessna strut-braced, high-wing layout, in conjunction with either a tailwheel (Model 180/185 and U-17 series) or a tricycle undercarriage (Model 182) layout. The latter derivative is less 'agricultural' in appearance and often incorporates embellishments such as spats over wheel assemblies.

VARIANTS

With production of all three basic sub-types continuing for at least a decade, it is not surprising that many variants exist. In each case, these adhere to Cessna conventions, with sequential versions being identified by suffix letter. Thus, at least nine different derivatives of the **Model 180** were built, these being the **180** and **180A** to **180H**. However, the **Model 182** is by far the most prolific member of the family, with the current production version being the **182S**. Military models were the **U-17A/B** (based on the Cessna 185) and the **U-17C** (Cessna 180).

Cessna U-17A Uruguayan Air Force

Cessna 206, 207 & 210

SINGLE PISTON-ENGINED COMMUNICATIONS/LIAISON AIRCRAFT

Cessna U206H Uruguayan Air Force

DEVELOPMENT

Evolution of this family of Cessna singles began with the Model 210, which was essentially an improved Model 182, introducing retractable landing gear and with a more powerful engine. Flown for the first time at the beginning of 1957, subsequent testing seems to have been a fairly leisurely process, with deliveries of production aircraft not getting underway until 1960. Further development led to the Model 205, basically a Model 210 with a fixed undercarriage, which in turn paved the way for the Model 206 in 1964 and, ultimately, the Model 207 in 1969.

CURRENT SERVICE

Variants of the Model 206, variously known as the Skywagon, Turbo Skywagon, Stationair and Turbo Stationair depending on configuration and production date, currently serve with military forces in Argentina, Bolivia, Chile, Colombia, Djibouti, Ecuador, Guatemala, Mexico, Paraguay, Peru, Tanzania, Thailand, Uruguay and Venezuela, while the Model 207 (Skywagon, Turbo Skywagon and Stationair 8) is operated by Argentina,

Dominican Republic, Indonesia and Venezuela. With regard to the Model 210 (Centurion, Pressurised Centurion and Turbo Centurion), this is known to serve with Bolivia, Colombia, Croatia, Dominican Republic, Guatemala, Jamaica, Mexico, Paraguay, Philippines and Uruguay. Other variants in military service are conversions of basic models, comprising the Robertson STOL 210 which is used by Bolivia and the Soloy U206G Stationair which serves with Costa Rica. In most cases, the number of aircraft operated is relatively small.

SPECIAL FEATURES

All three basic sub-types (206, 207 and 210) feature the high-wing, tricycle undercarriage layout that has been such a classic attribute of single-engined aircraft from the Cessna line since the late 1950s. Initially, the Model 210 did incorporate strut-bracing, but a fully cantilever wing was developed in the mid-1960s and this was adopted as standard with effect from the Model 210G of 1967, obviating the need for struts. This version is also unusual in having retractable

landing gear, whereas Model 206 and 207 aircraft are somewhat less complex and possess fixed undercarriage units as well as strut-braced wings.

VARIANTS

Numerous versions of all three types exist, with Cessna allocating suffix letters to identify them. In many cases, detailed design changes are far from obvious, but major differences such as the provision of cabin pressurisation and addition of turbo-supercharging are also indicated by prefix letters. Thus, the **P210N** and **P210R** are Pressurised Centurions, while the **TU206G**, **T207** and **T210** are variants that are fitted with a turbo-supercharged engine.

TECHNICAL DATA

Cessna Model 206 Stationair

Powerplant: One Teledyne Continental IO-520-F piston engine
Developing: 224kW (300hp)
Driving: Three-blade propeller
Span: 11.15m (36ft 7in)
Length: 8.53m (28ft 0in)
Height: 2.92m (9ft 6.75in)
All-up weight: 1,633kg (3,600lb)
Maximum speed: 280km/h (174mph)
Cruise speed: 211km/h (131mph)
Operational ceiling: 14,800ft
Ferry range: 1,641km (1,020 miles)
Normal range: 1,287km (800 miles)
Accommodation: Pilot and five passengers (Model 206/210); pilot and seven passengers (Model 207)
First flown: 25 February 1957 (Model 210); 1964 (Model 206)
Entered service: 1960 (Model 210); 1964 (Model 206); 1969 (Model 207)

Cessna T210N Bolivian Air Force

Cessna 208 Caravan I

SINGLE TURBOPROP UTILITY AIRCRAFT

Cessna 208 Caravan I South African Air Force

DEVELOPMENT

Claimed by the manufacturer to be the first purpose-built single-engine turboprop utility aircraft for the general aviation market, development of the Caravan I dates back to the start of the 1980s, with the prototype flying for the first time shortly before the end of 1982. US certification was achieved in October 1984, with series production from 1985. Subsequent development resulted in the stretched Model 208B, in response to a request from Federal Express, which has a fleet of almost 300 Caravan Is.

CURRENT SERVICE

Although more than 1,000 Caravan I have been built to date, military use is by no means extensive, with just a handful of nations having purchased this type. The Brazilian Air Force was the first military customer, acquiring eight for utility transport tasks in 1987. A year later, the South African Air Force obtained the first of 12, while the Chilean Army received eight Grand Caravans in 1998. In addition, a small number of aircraft are active with paramilitary organisations

in Colombia and Thailand. Those in Colombia include one with the military airline SATENA and two with the national police force. Finally, Thailand's KASET agricultural aviation command is believed to possess eight examples.

SPECIAL FEATURES

Rugged utilitarian aircraft with high, strut-braced, wing, tricycle undercarriage layout and single turboprop engine; large upward and downward hinging split cargo door on port side of fuselage aft of wing. Optional equipment includes a ventral cargo pannier and colour weather radar in a pod fitted to the leading edge of the starboard wing.

VARIANTS

The basic utility model is the **208**. This launched production, although as already noted, a number of other versions have appeared. Foremost among these is the **Model 208B**, which first flew in March 1986 and which is easily the most numerous version, accounting for about 70 per cent of production to date. The **Grand**

Caravan is similar in appearance, but is a quick-change passenger version, with cabin windows and seating for up to 14 occupants. Aircraft for military customers are basically similar to commercial Model 208s, but a version known as the **U-27A** is available for utility/special mission tasks. This has provisions for carriage of armament, but optional equipment includes observation and bubble windows for surveillance and a reconnaissance pod on the centreline station.

TECHNICAL DATA

Cessna 208A Caravan I

Powerplant: One Pratt & Whitney Canada PT6A-114 turboprop
Developing: 447kW (600shp)
Driving: Three-blade propeller
Span: 15.88m (52ft 1in)
Length: 11.46m (37ft 7in)
Height: 4.52m (14ft 10in)
Maximum weight: 3,629kg (8,000lb)
Cruise speed: 341km/h (212mph)
Operational ceiling: 27,600ft
Maximum range: 2,539km (1,578miles)
Accommodation: Pilot and up to nine passengers
Payload: 1,360kg (3,000lb)
Warload: U-27A version has provision for three hardpoints under each wing and one on fuselage centreline for carriage of bombs and/or rocket pods or auxiliary fuel tanks; pintle-mounted 12.7mm machine gun can be positioned in door on port side
First flown: 9 December 1982
Entered service: 1985 (commercial operators); 1987 (military operators)

Cessna 208B Caravan I Chilean Army

Cessna 305 / O-1 Bird Dog

SINGLE PISTON-ENGINED OBSERVATION AIRCRAFT

DEVELOPMENT

Based on the Cessna 170 and known as the Model 305 by its manufacturer, the Bird Dog began as a company-funded private venture, but emerged victorious in a 1950 US Army competition for a new light observation/liaison aircraft and was subsequently ordered into production for that service. More than 3,500 Bird Dogs were eventually built, the majority of which went to the US Army, but some were also acquired by the US Marine Corps. In addition, just over 20 were built by Fuji in Japan, while an unknown number were assembled at Dhamial in Pakistan using a mixture of spare parts and locally fabricated components.

CURRENT SERVICE

Although once extensively used for the observation role, the advent of the more versatile helicopter has progressively led to a decline in the number of Bird Dog operators and today it remains in use with just a handful of countries, namely Chile, South Korea, Libya, Pakistan and Thailand. In each case, the number of aircraft operated is small and final withdrawal is probably fairly imminent. The only models currently in use are the O-1A and O-1E.

SPECIAL FEATURES

The Bird Dog has a high-wing, strut-braced design with tailwheel undercarriage and a slender fuselage accommodating two occupants in a tandem seating arrangement. The extensively glazed cockpit offers good all-round vision for the observation role. Underwing hardpoints can be used to accommodate smoke rockets for target marking when used in the forward air control role.

VARIANTS

The initial production version of the Bird Dog was the **L-19A** (redesignated as the **O-1A** in 1962), which

Cessna O-1E Bird Dog *Chilean Air Force*

accounted for almost 2,500 aircraft, virtually all of which went to the US Army. They were followed by just over 300 **TL-19Ds** (later **TO-1D**) for the Army, which also received close to 500 examples of the final **L-19E** (later **O-1E**) production version. A number of aircraft were diverted from Army contracts to the US Marine Corps, these comprising the **OE-1** (later **O-1B**) and the **OE-2** (later **O-1C**). The only other new-build examples consisted of experimental turboprop-powered versions ordered in 1952. The first of these was the sole **XL-19B**, which was followed by two **XL-19Cs** – however, no orders for production aircraft were forthcoming. In

addition to new-build machines, a number of versions came about through conversion programmes. These included the **TL-19A** (later **TO-1A**) trainer derivative with dual controls for the Army and three versions that were used for forward air control duties with the US Air Force in Southeast Asia during the 1960s, namely the **O-1D**, **O-1F** and **O-1G**.

TECHNICAL DATA

Cessna O-1E Bird Dog

Powerplant: One Continental O-470-11 piston engine
Developing: 159kW (213hp)
Driving: Two-blade propeller
Span: 10.97m (36ft 0in)
Length: 7.85m (25ft 9in)
Height: 2.22m (7ft 3.5in)
All-up weight: 1,087kg (2,400lb)
Maximum speed: 243km/h (151mph)
Cruise speed: 167km/h (104mph)
Operational ceiling: 18,500ft
Normal range: 853km (530 miles)
Accommodation: Pilot and observer/passenger
Warload: Normally nil, but can carry smoke rockets on two underwing hardpoints for target marking, or unguided rockets.
First flown: December 1949
Entered service: 1951

Cessna O-1E Bird Dog *Chilean Air Force*

Cessna 310

Cessna 310R Colombian Air Force

DEVELOPMENT

The first in a long line of hugely successful twin-engined executive aircraft, development of the Model 310 was undertaken at the dawn of the 1950s, with the prototype making its maiden flight in January 1953 and deliveries commencing in 1954. Although aimed primarily at the commercial market, the US Air Force was an important customer, buying both the Model 310A and the Model 310D. In common with many other Cessna products, progressive refinement of the basic design ensured that it enjoyed a long production run, with the last examples being completed in 1981.

CURRENT SERVICE

Good performance characteristics and relatively low cost made the Model 310 an attractive proposition

as a staff transport and communications aircraft from the outset and it has been extensively used by air arms around the world. Although it once possessed a fleet of more than 200 aircraft, the US Air Force no longer operates the type, but it is still used by around ten nations. These include Colombia, Congo Democratic Republic, France, Honduras, Mexico, Paraguay, Surinam, Thailand, Trinidad and Tobago, and Venezuela. In most cases, the number on charge is modest, but France has more than a dozen which fulfil communications tasks and some test duties with the Centre d'Essais en Vol (Flight Research Centre).

SPECIAL FEATURES

The Model 310 is a neat and compact twin-engined low-wing monoplane with retractable undercarriage and wing-tip auxiliary fuel tanks. Early production aircraft had straight vertical tail surfaces, but with the introduction of the Model 310D in 1960 these gave way to a more rakish swept fin and rudder. One other notable change was the adoption of upturned 'stabila-tip' wing tanks on the Model 310G in 1962,

while a turbocharged version became available in the late 1960s.

VARIANTS

Numerous derivatives were built during the course of a 27-year production run, these adhering to normal Cessna practice by using sequential suffix letters up to and including the **Model 310R**. Basically similar, but fitted with turbocharged engines from the outset, the **Model 320 Skyknight** was a variant that enjoyed a relatively short production run by Cessna standards, but several hundred were completed between 1962 and 1968, when it gave way to the turbocharged **Model T310**. Also based on the 310, the **Model 340** differed mainly in having a pressurised cabin, but even fewer were completed and no examples of the Model 320 or 340 are currently in military service. US Air Force procurement began with 160 **L-27As** in 1957-58, these being equivalent to the Model 310A, while the 35 **L-27Bs** purchased in 1960 were comparable with the Model 310D. In 1962, they were respectively redesignated as the **U-3A** and **U-3B**.

TECHNICAL DATA

Cessna 310

Powerplants: Two Continental IO-520-M piston engines
Developing: 212.5kW (285hp)
Driving: Three-blade propellers
Span: 11.25m (36ft 11in)
Length: 9.74m (31ft 11.5in)
Height: 3.25m (10ft 8in)
All-up weight: 2,495kg (5,500lb)
Maximum speed: 383km/h (238mph)
Cruise speed: 267km/h (166mph)
Operational ceiling: 19,750ft
Maximum range: 2,097km (1,303 miles)
Normal range: 916km (569 miles)
Accommodation: Pilot and up to five passengers
First flown: 3 January 1953
Entered service: 1954

Cessna 310Q French Air Force

Cessna 337 & O-2 Super Skymaster

TWIN-ENGINED OBSERVATION/LIAISON AIRCRAFT

Cessna FTB 337G Milirole Portuguese Air Force

DEVELOPMENT

The evolutionary process that culminated in the military Cessna O-2 Super Skymaster began with the Model 336 Skymaster, which first flew in prototype form on 28 February 1961. The original design was only a four-seater aircraft, but flight-testing revealed some shortcomings and a number of revisions were incorporated. These included increasing the size of the vertical tail surfaces and other changes were also made to the cooling system for the rear engine, which displayed a tendency to overheat. In addition, the cabin was enlarged to accommodate up to six occupants, with a pre-production prototype featuring these alterations flying in August 1962. Deliveries began in 1963, but the inadequate performance of the Model 336 prompted further redesign, with the most important revision introduced by the Model 337 of 1964 being the retractable undercarriage. Subsequently, a suitably modified version was ordered by the USAF for forward air control duty as the O-2A.

CURRENT SERVICE

Although the USAF received about 500 examples of the O-2, only two are understood to be in service with the US armed forces today, with the Army using them for communications duties. Other O-2As taken from surplus stocks are flown by Botswana, Chile, Costa Rica, South Korea, Namibia and El Salvador, while a few US-built Model 337s serve with Burkina Faso, Chile and Mexico. Another US-built version of the aircraft that was adapted by Summit Aviation as the Sentry O2-337 is used by Haiti and Thailand in limited quantities. In addition, Reims Aviation produced a considerable number of aircraft as the F 337, which is still used by Madagascar and Togo. An armed French-built version known as the FTB 337G Milirole serves with Guinea-Bissau, Mauritania, Portugal and Zimbabwe.

SPECIAL FEATURES

Undoubtedly the most novel single feature of the Cessna Model 337 series is the engine arrangement, with one powerplant installed in the nose as a conventional tractor and the second, at the rear of the fuselage, acting as a pusher. This highly unusual configuration in turn necessitated the adoption of twin tail-booms married to a strut-braced, high-wing layout that gave it a distinct overall appearance.

VARIANTS

Purely military versions originating from Cessna comprised the **O-2A** forward air control aircraft, with additional glazing in the door structure to provide better downward vision, and the **O-2B**, optimised for psychological warfare duties with loudspeakers and provision for leaflet dropping. Reims Aviation also conceived the armed **FTB 337 Milirole**, which had four underwing stores stations for 7.62mm machine gun pods and rocket launchers.

Cessna O-2A Super Skymaster

TECHNICAL DATA

Cessna O-2A Super Skymaster

Powerplants: Two Teledyne Continental IO-360C/D piston engines
Developing: 157kW (210hp)
Driving: Two-blade propellers
Span: 11.58m (38ft 0in)
Length: 9.07m (29ft 9in)
Height: 2.84m (9ft 4in)
All-up weight: 2,449kg (5,400lb)
Maximum speed: 320km/h (199mph)
Cruise speed: 232km/h (144mph)
Operational ceiling: 19,800ft
Normal range: 1,706km (1,060 miles)
Accommodation: Pilot and up to five passengers
Warload: Provisions for underwing carriage of smoke markers, rocket pods and gun pods
First flown: 30 March 1964 (prototype Model 337)
Entered service: April 1967 (first O-2A delivery)

Cessna 400 Series/Reims Aviation F 406 Caravan II

TWIN-ENGINED LIGHT UTILITY/SPECIAL MISSION AIRCRAFT

F 406 Caravan II French Army

DEVELOPMENT

In the early 1960s, following on from the successful twin-engined Model 310, Cessna began to develop a range of even larger aircraft, starting with the Model 411 of 1962 and eventually expanding to encompass such types as the Model 401, 402, 404 Titan, 421 Golden Eagle and 441 Conquest. None of these types are now in production, but Reims Aviation has developed and is currently manufacturing the F 406 Caravan II. Evolved from the Model 441 Conquest airframe, design of the F 406 was revealed in mid-1982, with a prototype flying for the first time just over a year later and close to 100 have now been completed, mainly for civilian customers.

CURRENT SERVICE

Twin-engined aircraft originating from Cessna in the USA are still widely used, with examples of the Model 401, 402, 404 Titan, 421 Golden Eagle and 441 Conquest all currently in military service. The Reims Aviation

F 406 Caravan II has also found limited acceptance with military customers. Operators include the French Army, which has two for target towing and liaison duties, while some are also used for paramilitary tasks by Namibia and the Seychelles Coast Guard. More recently, South Korea has purchased five target tugs for service with the Naval air arm and the Greek Coast Guard is due to receive two F 406 Surmar maritime surveillance aircraft by the end of 2000.

SPECIAL FEATURES

All versions of the Cessna family of medium-sized twins incorporate a low wing, tricycle undercarriage, configuration, with either turbocharged piston (401, 402, 404 and 421) or turboprop (441) engines. The same basic characteristics are inherent in the F 406 Caravan II, although the horizontal tail surfaces of this are affixed to the fin, rather than the fuselage, and also feature marked dihedral. The F 406 Caravan II can be fitted with a ventral pod for additional cargo.

VARIANTS

The only aircraft of this type in current production is the **F 406 Caravan II**, available in several versions, tailored to meet specific mission requirements. Most of the aircraft built thus far have been standard utility transports, but Reims Aviation has developed five variations on the maritime patrol theme, differing in detail although all feature a ventrally-mounted radar able to provide 360 degree coverage. The basic version is the **Vigilant** for surveillance of land and/or sea, while more specialised models comprise the **Vigilant Frontier** for border patrol; the **Vigilant Polmar II** for pollution monitoring; the maritime surveillance **Vigilant Surmar**; and the **Vigilant-Comint** intelligence-gathering derivative with airborne ECM and direction-finding antennae in a ventral radome. Vigilant-Comint can also be fitted with wing pylons for carriage of stores such as gun or rocket pods.

TECHNICAL DATA

Reims Aviation F 406 Caravan II

Powerplants: Two Pratt & Whitney Canada PT6A-112 turboprops
Developing: 373kW (500shp)
Driving: Three-blade propellers
Span: 15.08m (49ft 5.5in)
Length: 11.89m (39ft 0.25in)
Height: 4.01m (13ft 2in)
Maximum weight: 4,468kg (9,850lb)
Maximum speed: 424km/h (263mph)
Economic cruise speed: 370km/h (230mph)
Operational ceiling: 30,000ft
Maximum range: 2,135km (1,327 miles)
Accommodation: Crew of two and up to 12 passengers
Payload: 2,219kg (4,892lb)
First flown: 22 September 1983
Entered service: 1985

F 406 Caravan II French Army

Cessna T-37

Cessna T-37B United States Air Force

DEVELOPMENT

Design of the T-37 was undertaken in response to a 1952 USAF requirement for a new primary jet trainer, with the resulting Model 318 being selected as the most suitable candidate. At that time, three prototype XT-37s were ordered and the first of these flew in October 1954. Following successful trials, the type was ordered into production for Air Training Command,

TECHNICAL DATA

Cessna T-37B

Powerplants: Two Teledyne Continental J69-T-25 turbojets
Developing: 4.56kN (1,025lb st)
Span: 10.29m (33ft 9in)
Length: 8.92m (29ft 3in)
Height: 2.79m (9ft 2in)
All-up weight: 2,993kg (6,600lb)
Maximum speed: 684km/h (425mph)
Cruise speed: 612km/h (380mph)
Operational ceiling: 39,200ft
Normal range: 1,500km (932 miles)
Accommodation: Pilot and student
First flown: 12 October 1954 (T-37); 27 September 1955 (T-37A)
Entered service: 1957

which eventually took delivery of almost 1,000, while many more were completed for export.

CURRENT SERVICE

Although long since phased out of production, several hundred examples of the Cessna T-37 are still used for basic jet training by some ten air arms. At one time, it looked as if the Fairchild T-46 would take over in this role with the US Air Force, but it was cancelled in 1988 and the trusty T-37B continues to provide sterling service. However, its days are numbered, for it will be replaced by the Raytheon Beech T-6A Texan II during the current decade. Other air arms that continue to rely on Cessna's long-serving trainer are those of Bangladesh (T-37B), Chile (T-37B/C), Colombia (T-37C), Germany (T-37B), Greece (T-37B/C), South Korea (T-37C), Morocco (T-37B), Pakistan (T-37B/C) and Turkey (T-37B/C).

SPECIAL FEATURES

One of the first jet trainers to enter service, the T-37 is of conventional design, with straight wings and horizontal tail surfaces, with the latter positioned midway up the fin to lift them clear of the jet efflux. Twin engines offer additional safety, with these buried in the wing root area and fed by small intakes adjacent to the cockpit. Like many comparable trainers of its time, a side-by-side seating layout was adopted for

student and instructor. One of the T-37's most striking features its squat appearance when on the ground.

VARIANTS

Production of more than 530 examples of the **T-37A** had been completed by 1959, when manufacture switched to the **T-37B**. This had a more powerful version of the J69 turbojet engine and also featured improved navigation and communications equipment. Eventually, virtually all surviving T-37As were upgraded to T-37B standard. The only other version to enter production was the **T-37C**, supplied to friendly nations under the Military Assistance Program in the 1960s and 1970s. Although mainly for basic training, it could undertake weapons training, for it was fitted with a hardpoint beneath each wing as well as a gunsight and could carry bombs, gun pods or rocket pods. Somewhat more formidable in terms of firepower, the **YAT-37D** was an armed derivative powered by different engines that was optimised for light attack and counter-insurgency missions. Two aircraft were converted for trials in 1963 and these paved the way for the **A-37 Dragonfly** series (see separate entry).

SEE ALSO: CESSNA A-37 DRAGONFLY

Cessna T-37B United States Air Force

Cessna A-37B Dragonfly

TWIN-TURBOJET LIGHT ATTACK AIRCRAFT

Cessna A-37B Uruguayan Air Force

DEVELOPMENT

Optimised for counter-insurgency duties, the origins of the Dragonfly date back to 1963, when two T-37B trainers were modified to YAT-37D standard for trials. Able to carry a respectable weapons load, these very quickly proved the soundness of the concept and it was decided to modify further aircraft to A-37A configuration, for operational use by Air Commando units of the US Air Force. Subsequently, the brand new A-37B, which was stressed to 6g, entered production in the mid-1960s.

TECHNICAL DATA

Cessna A-37B Dragonfly

Powerplants: Two General Electric J85-GE-17A turbojets
Developing: 12.68kN (2,850lb st)
Span: 10.93m (35ft 10.5in)
Length: 8.93m (29ft 3.5in) excluding probe
Height: 2.70m (8ft 10.5in)
Maximum weight: 6,350kg (14,000lb)
Maximum speed: 843km/h (524mph)
Cruise speed: 787km/h (489mph)
Operational ceiling: 41,765ft
Maximum range: 1,628km (1,012 miles)
Mission range: 740km (460 miles) with maximum warload
Accommodation: Two pilots or pilot and observer
Warload: Maximum ordnance load 2,270kg (5,000lb) on eight underwing stores stations; weaponry can include bombs and rockets, plus fixed 7.62mm GAU-2B/A minigun in nose section
First flown: 22 October 1963 (YAT-37D development aircraft)
Entered service: 1967 (A-37A); May 1968 (A-37B)

CURRENT SERVICE

Relatively inexpensive to produce and operate, the A-37 was made available by the USA under the Military Assistance Program and was extensively used by a number of Latin American air arms. Today, several of them continue to utilise the A-37B variant, which is active in Chile, Colombia, the Dominican Republic, Ecuador, Guatemala, Honduras, Peru, El Salvador and Uruguay. Other examples continue to serve with Asian countries, notably South Korea and Thailand, both of which acquired the Dragonfly after South Vietnam collapsed in 1975, when many aircraft were flown out of the country by escaping Vietnamese airmen.

SPECIAL FEATURES

Similar in appearance to the T-37 trainer, the A-37 differed in a number of ways. Most beneficial, but perhaps least obvious, was a change of engine, with the more powerful General Electric J85 adopted as standard by all versions. Armour plating was also added to provide an extra measure of protection for pilots, but the most visible alterations were the eight underwing stores stations. These could be used to carry ordnance or jettisonable fuel tanks, and the

A-37 also had fixed wingtip tanks and internal gun armament. Ground attack avionics were provided and modifications were also made to the landing gear, which used larger wheels and tyres.

VARIANTS

Following on from the pair of **YAT-37D** development aircraft, 39 early production **T-37As** were converted to **A-37As**, although none of these are active today. Thereafter, production of the **A-37B** was launched, this version being instantly recognisable by virtue of having a fixed in-flight refuelling probe extending forward from the extreme nose section. Almost 600 A-37Bs were produced by 1975. Some were for the USAF, but many more went to friendly nations, with a particularly large number being supplied to South Vietnam, where they saw extensive combat action. At a later date, at least 130 A-37Bs were assigned to forward air control tasks with additional radio communications equipment as the **OA-37B**. These saw service with second-line elements of the USAF until 1992.

SEE ALSO: CESSNA T-37

Cessna A-37B Peruvian Air Force

Cessna Citation 500/550/551/560 & 650

TWIN-TURBOFAN EXECUTIVE AIRCRAFT

Cessna UC-35A United States Army

DEVELOPMENT

In October 1968, Cessna announced its intention to develop and market a turbofan-powered executive aircraft. Initially known as the Fanjet 500, this flew in prototype form in September 1969, at which time the name Citation was adopted. Deliveries began during 1971, but production of this version ended long ago. However, subsequent development resulted in the appearance of numerous improved versions, and the Citation remains in production today.

CURRENT SERVICE

The Citation family has met with reasonable success in the military market, with at least a dozen air arms operating various versions. The numbers involved are usually small, seldom involving more than one or two examples. The original Model 500 Citation I is still used by Argentina, Ecuador and Venezuela, while the Model 550/551 Citation II is flown by Bosnia, Chile, Colombia, Ecuador, Myanmar, Paraguay, South Africa, Spain, Sweden, Turkey and Venezuela. Morocco, Pakistan and Spain utilise the Model 560 Citation V, improved versions of which serve with the US armed forces. Finally, Chile has one Model 650 Citation III and Turkey has two Model 650 Citation VIIs.

SPECIAL FEATURES

A low-wing monoplane design was adopted for all

Citation versions, with podded turbofan engines attached to the aft fuselage sides. The Model 500, 550/551 and 560 versions all have straight wings and horizontal tail surfaces, with a slightly swept vertical tail. The Model 650 series is radically different in appearance, incorporating moderate sweep on the wings and horizontal tail surfaces, with the latter being positioned at the top of the fin.

VARIANTS

Production of the Citation series began with the **Model 500 Citation I**, but further development soon led to the **Model 550 Citation II**, with a longer fuselage and increased span, as well as more fuel and baggage capacity. Initial deliveries of the Citation II were made in 1978. Also known as the Citation II, the **Model 551** is basically similar, whereas the **Model 560** featured yet another stretch in length and a new version of the JT15D engine. Further refinement of the **Model 560 Citation V** led to the **Citation Ultra** and today's **Citation Ultra Encore**, both of which have been acquired by the US forces. In the case of the US Army, the Citation Ultra is designated **UC-35A**, while the US Marine Corps operates it as the **UC-35B**. Both services are now receiving the Citation Ultra Encore as the **UC-35C** and **UC-35D** respectively. Turning to the US Air Force, a handful of Citation Ultra aircraft were fitted with AN/APG-66 radar and infrared tracking

systems before being delivered in 1997. Known as the **OT-47B**, they are believed to assist with interdiction of drug-runners. The **Model 650** is also in limited military service.

TECHNICAL DATA

Cessna 560 Citation Ultra

Powerplants: Two Pratt & Whitney Canada JT15D-5D turbofans
Developing: 13.55kN (3,045lbst)
Span: 15.90m (52ft 2in)
Length: 14.90m (48ft 10.75in)
Height: 4.57m (15ft 0in)
Maximum weight: 7,393kg (16,300lb)
Maximum cruise speed: 796km/h (495mph)
Operational ceiling: 45,000ft
Maximum range: 3,630km (2,255 miles) with five passengers, maximum fuel and reserves
Accommodation: Two crew and up to eight passengers
First flown: 15 September 1969 (Citation I prototype); August 1987 (Citation V prototype)
Entered service: 1971 (Citation I); April 1989 (Citation V)

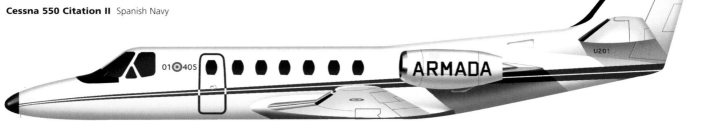

Cessna 550 Citation II Spanish Navy

Chengdu Aircraft Industrial Corporation JJ-5/FT-5

SINGLE TURBOJET FIGHTER TRAINER AIRCRAFT

Chengdu FT-5 Pakistan Air Force

DEVELOPMENT

Based on the J-5A, which itself was a derivative of the Soviet MiG-17PF, development of the Chengdu Jianjiji Jiaolianji-5 (Fighter Training Aircraft 5) began during 1965 and culminated in a successful maiden flight in the first half of 1966. On the completion of flight testing, it was ordered into quantity production for the People's Liberation Army Air Force (PLAAF) and soon became the standard advanced jet trainer with that air arm, replacing the old and obsolescent MiG-15UTI 'Midget'.

CURRENT SERVICE

Although fundamentally of 1950s vintage, the JJ-5 is still widely used by the PLAAF as a fighter trainer, with several hundred examples currently believed to remain in service, although it is likely that these will ultimately be replaced by the indigenous Hongdu K-8 Karakorum. Manufacture for export was also undertaken, with at least six air arms still possessing

some examples of the FT-5 export equivalent. These comprise Albania, which has about eight; North Korea, with at least a couple of dozen; Pakistan, with about 30 survivors of more than 50 received from 1974; Sri Lanka, which has two (both now grounded); Sudan, also with two; and Zimbabwe, which has two in storage. Others have seen service with Bangladesh and Tanzania, although they have now been retired.

SPECIAL FEATURES

Similar in appearance to the MiG-17 series, from which it evolved, the JJ-5/FT-5 retains the basic mid-position, swept-wing, configuration of the Russian fighter, with high-set horizontal tail surfaces. However, it differs by virtue of being a two-seater, with a slightly longer fuselage to accommodate a second cockpit in tandem. It also retains the familiar lipped air inlet of the MiG-17, which is believed to house a radar-ranging gunsight, but detail changes have been made to the nose air inlet and the jetpipe.

Twin airbrakes are situated on the aft fuselage sides.

VARIANTS

The basic variant, as used in large numbers by the People's Republic of China, is the JJ-5. A total of 1,061 was eventually built in the course of a production run that spanned approximately two decades, while a modest number were supplied to export customers. In overseas service, although these aircraft adopted the designation FT-5, they were essentially identical to the Chinese machines in virtually every respect.

SEE ALSO: MIKOYAN-GUREVICH MIG-17

TECHNICAL DATA

Chengdu JJ-5

Powerplant: One Xian (XAE) Wopen WP5D turbojet
Developing: 26.48kN (5,952lb st)
Span: 9.63m (31ft 7in)
Length: 11.50m (37ft 9in)
Height: 3.80m (12ft 5.75in)
Maximum weight: 6,215kg (13,700lb)
Maximum speed: 1,048km/h (651mph)
Normal operating speed: 775km/h (482mph)
Operational ceiling: 46,900ft
Maximum range: 1,230km (764 miles)
Endurance: 2hrs 38mins
Accommodation: Pilot and student
Warload: Normally nil, but can be used as a gunnery trainer, with single Type 23-1 23mm gun in a removable belly pack
First flown: 8 May 1966 (JJ-5);
11 November 1964 (J-5A)
Entered service: 1967

Chengdu FT-5 Zimbabwe Air Force

Chengdu Aircraft Industrial Corporation J-7/F-7

SINGLE TURBOJET FIGHTER AIRCRAFT

Chengdu F-7P Pakistan Air Force

DEVELOPMENT

Award of a licence to manufacture the MiG-21F-13 version and its Tumansky R-11F-300 engine occurred as long ago as 1961. Subsequent adoption as the J-7 (Jianjiji or Fighter Aircraft 7) led to assembly of the first locally fabricated example beginning in early 1964. At that time, responsibility was entrusted to the Shenyang factory, where the first flight took place in 1966. Thereafter, a few examples of the basic J-7 were completed, before quantity production was launched at Chengdu with the J-7 I in 1967. Since then, Chengdu has progressively improved on the basic design – the latest version being the J-7E, which has a distinctive double-delta wing planform resembling that of the Saab Draken.

CURRENT SERVICE

Several hundred examples of the J-7 are in service with the People's Liberation Army Air Force and Navy, these being mainly used as interceptors. Considerable success has also been achieved on the export market, with overseas air arms that operate versions of the F-7 comprising: Albania (F-7A), Bangladesh (F-7M), Egypt (F-7B), Iran (F-7M), Iraq (F-7B), Myanmar (F-7M), Pakistan (F-7P and F-7MP), Sri Lanka (F-7BS), Sudan (F-7B), Tanzania (F-7A) and Zimbabwe (F-7B). Pakistan is reportedly planning to buy at least 50 examples of the F-7MG, although these may adopt the designation

F-7PG. Two-seat trainer equivalents, built by Guizhou, are designated JJ-7 (China) and FT-7 (export).

SPECIAL FEATURES

In its original form, the J-7 (and the export F-7 equivalents) was basically identical in appearance to the hugely successful MiG-21 series, from which it evolved. The tailed delta configuration was retained by most versions, but with the advent of the J-7E (and the F-7MG export counterpart), this gave way to a double-delta planform, with a tapered outboard trailing edge.

VARIANTS

Numerous versions of the Chengdu J-7 have emerged during more than three decades of production. In the case of aircraft for China's own forces, progressive developments were at first identified by suffix numbers, as exemplified by the **J-7 I**, **J-7 II** and **J-7 III**, but the newest double-delta model is known as the **J-7E**. Production for export began with the **F-7A** and **F-7B**, which are basically equivalent to the J-7 I and J-7 II respectively, while the **F-7M** is an improved version of the J-7 II with western avionics. The **F-7P** Airguard is a variant of the F-7M that was tailored to Pakistan's requirements, with some 24 modifications that include a Martin-Baker Mk 10L ejection seat and the ability to operate with the AIM-9 Sidewinder.

TECHNICAL DATA

Chengdu J-7 III

Powerplant: One Liyang WP13 turbojet
Developing: 43.2kN (9,700lb st) dry; 59.8kN (13,448lb st) with afterburner
Span: 7.15m (23ft 5.5in)
Length: 14.885m (48ft 10in) including probe
Height: 4.105m (13ft 5.5in)
Maximum weight: 8,150kg (17,967lb)
Maximum operating Mach number: Mach 2.1
Operational ceiling: 59,060ft
Maximum range: 1,900km (1,180 miles)
Normal range: 960km (596 miles)
Accommodation: Pilot only
Warload: Single 23mm Type 23-3 cannon in ventral pack; five external stores stations provided for carriage of PL-2 or PL-5 IR-homing air-to-air missiles, unguided rockets and bombs or additional fuel
First flown: 17 January 1966 (J-7); 26 April 1984 (J-7 III)
Entered service: 1992 (J-7 III)

SEE ALSO: MIKOYAN-GUREVICH MiG-21 & GUIZHOU/GAIC JJ-7/FT-7

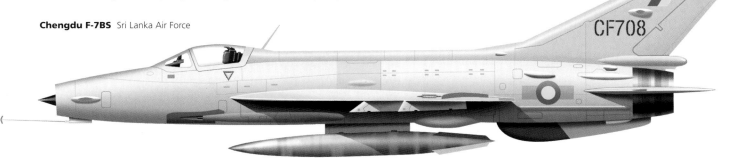

Chengdu F-7BS Sri Lanka Air Force

Convair 580/C-131H

TWIN-TURBOPROP TRANSPORT AIRCRAFT

Convair CV-580 Colombian Army

DEVELOPMENT

Trials of a turbine-powered version of this highly successful design began in 1954, when the US Air Force evaluated a pair of Convair 340 airliners. Allocated the designation YC-131C, they were fitted with Allison YT56-A-3 engines (military versions of the Allison 501-D13) and proved the basic soundness of the idea. However, it was not until the late 1950s that serious consideration was given to marketing the conversion more widely. Following the award of FAA certification in 1960, Pacific Airmotive of Burbank, California launched a conversion production line and a large number of Convair 580s were eventually produced.

CURRENT SERVICE

Only a handful of examples of this turboprop-powered transport remain in military use today and all are to be found in service with Latin American air arms. Peru's paramilitary national police force may still be operating a single former USAF C-131H, while the Convair 580 is known to be active with three countries. The Bolivian Air Force's paramilitary airline, Transportes Aéreos Militar, has a total of five, although only two are thought to remain in regular service, while both

the Colombian Army and the Mexican Air Force have single examples for VIP transport and communications duties.

SPECIAL FEATURES

A twin-engined, low-wing monoplane design, with tricycle undercarriage configuration. The original piston engines of the Convair 340/400 were replaced by turboprops on the Convair 580, with conversion being a relatively straightforward procedure. The modification necessitated slightly increasing the horizontal and vertical tail surface area to provide adequate control in the event of engine failure on take-off, and to maintain centre of gravity range.

VARIANTS

Numerous turbine-engined versions of the Convair 240/340/440 transport aircraft were developed in the 1950s and 1960s, with the most successful model being the Allison-powered Convair 580. Although mainly aimed at the civilian airliner market, with which it achieved considerable success, a reasonable number of military aircraft were also converted. These included the **VC-131H** (later redesignated **C-131H**), which was

initially delivered to the USAF's elite Washington-based executive transport unit, before eventually being passed on to the US Navy Reserve. Canada also undertook production of 10 Convair 440 aircraft as the **CC-109 Cosmopolitan**. These were initially fitted with the Napier Eland Mk504 turboprop, although several were later upgraded to basic **Convair 580** standard, with more powerful Allison engines. General Dynamics also undertook a conversion programme, which utilised the Rolls-Royce Dart turboprop engine; **Convair 240s** modified by this company became known as the **Convair 600**, while **Convair 340/440** aircraft were redesignated as the **Convair 640**, but no Dart-engined aircraft survive.

TECHNICAL DATA

Convair 580

Powerplants: Two Allison 501-D13H turboprops
Developing: 2,796kW (3,750shp)
Driving: Four-blade propellers
Span: 32.11m (105ft 4in)
Length: 24.84m (81ft 6in)
Height: 8.89m (29ft 2in)
Maximum weight: 24,948kg (55,000lb)
Cruise speed: 550km/h (342mph)
Ferry range: 3,660km (2,274 miles) with crew and 25 passengers (CC-109)
Normal range: 1,996km (1,244 miles) with crew and 48 passengers (CC-109)
Accommodation: Crew and maximum of 56 passengers, depending upon internal layout
Payload: 6,486kg (14,300lb)
First flown: 1954 (YC-131C testbed); 1959 (Convair 580)
Entered service: September 1960 (FAA certification of Convair 580)

Convair CV-580 Mexican Air Force

Dassault Etendard/Super Etendard

CARRIER-BORNE NAVAL STRIKE FIGHTER

Super Etendard French Navy

TECHNICAL DATA

Dassault Super Etendard

Powerplant: One SNECMA Atar 8K-50 turbojet
Developing: 49.03kN (11,023lb st)
Span: 9.60m (31ft 6in)
Length: 14.31m (46ft 11.5in)
Height: 3.86m (12ft 8in)
All up weight: 12,000kg (26,455lb)
Maximum speed: 1380km/h (857mph)
Combat radius: 850km (528 miles)
Operational ceiling: over 45,000ft
Warload: Maximum ordnance 2,100kg (4,630lb) and for the anti-ship role the Super Etendard carries two AM39 Exocet missiles or a variety of other stores on two fuselage and four underwing pylons. These additional weapons may include tactical nuclear bombs, stand-off missiles, rocket pods, laser-guided-missiles, AAMs, dumb bombs or ECM pods
Accommodation: Pilot only
First flown: 21 May 1958 (Etendard); 29 October 1974 (Super Etendard)
Entered service: June 1978 (Super Etendard)

DEVELOPMENT

The Etendard was originally designed by Dassault as its entry into the 1955 NATO competition to find a light strike fighter able to operate from unpaved strips. While the Aeritalia G91 ultimately won that contest, Dassault pressed ahead on its own, giving the Etendard the more powerful SNECMA Atar 08 engine and renaming the aircraft the Etendard IV, and this aircraft underwent a series of modifications to meet Aèronavale requirements for a carrier-based attack and reconnaissance aircraft. Two versions were built, the first being the IVM which first flew on 21 May 1958 and which joined the French Navy in 1962 and which was used in the attack role. In 1960, the first Etendard IVP reconnaissance/tanker aircraft flew, equipped with OMERA reconnaissance cameras, inflight-refuelling capability and a 'buddy-pack' for Etendard to Etendard refuelling. The IVPs were officially retired from service in July 2000, although they saw subsequent service over Bosnia and Kosovo acting as tankers for Super Etendards and performing reconnaissance duties. In the mid-1970s, France was seeking 100 new-carrier-based strike fighters and it was eventually decided that an upgraded Etendard IV would fill the criteria. The upgraded Super Etendard has a SNECMA Atar 8K-50 engine, improved weapon and navigation systems and air refuelling probe. The first examples joined the Aèronavale in 1978, but it was the sole export customer, Argentina, who were

the first to use them in combat, launching Exocet attacks against British ships during the Falklands conflict in 1982. Three examples have been lost since but the surviving examples remain in service with the Argentine Navy. Iraq leased five 'SuEs' from France in 1983 for use in the war against Iran. One was lost, and the remainder were returned to France. During the mid-1980s, the SEM upgrade extended the long-range strike and anti-ship capability of the aircraft, and the upgraded aircraft, of which 52 remain in French service, went to war as part of **Allied Force** against the Serbs over Kosovo in 1999, attacking targets with bombs and AS30L missiles. Currently, 'SuEs' are being modified for the reconnaissance role to replace the Etendard IVPs and the strike variants of the Super Etendard will eventually be replaced by the Rafale M.

CURRENT SERVICE

Etendard IVP/IVPM: French Navy, possibly still in limited numbers with 16 Flottille (16F) at Landivisiau; Super Etendard: French Navy, with 11 Flottille (11F) and 17 Flottille (17F) at Landivisiau; Argentina, with Escaudron Aéronavale 3 at BA Comandante Espora.

SPECIAL FEATURES

Swept-wing carrier fighter/strike/reconnaissance aircraft which, despite being in service for 30 years, continues to play an important part in French naval aviation.

VARIANTS

Etendard: lightweight proposed NATO fighter, proposal unsuccessful; **Etendard IVM**: Aéronavale strike aircraft with all-weather radar, with nose-mounted underfin blade for AS20 guidance; **Etendard IVP**: Aéronavale reconnaissance/tanker with five camera ports and improved navigation systems; **Super Etendard**: only one major variant but **Super Etendard Modernisée** (SEM) five-stage modernisation project has allowed the 'SuE' to use the latest weapons or designators. Next stage of upgrade will see aircraft being able to carry LGBs and equipment to designate the weapons themselves. As part of this step, the ability to carry a new reconnaissance pod is being undertaken. The final upgrade step will deliver a night precision attack capability.

Super Etendard French Navy

Dassault Falcon/Mystère 10

TWIN-JET VIP TRANSPORT AND ECM TRAINER

Dassault Falcon 10MER French Navy

DEVELOPMENT
Following the success of their Falcon 20, Dassault revealed at the 1969 Paris Air Salon that a smaller and faster variant would be built. Named the Mystère 10 MiniFalcon, this scaled down bizjet differed in several ways from its predecessor. Namely, Garrett turbofans replaced General Electric turbojets, the wings were of a higher aspect ratio, and accommodation would now be for 4-7 people rather than 8-12. During test flying, the aircraft set an FAI 1,000km (621 mile) closed circuit speed record of 926km/h (575 mph). Airframe components were constructed at several different factories, namely Potez (fuselage), CASA of Spain (wings), IAM of Italy (nose assembly and tail units) and Latècoére (doors, fins and other small components); final assembly took place at Avions Marcel Dassault's Istres plant. The majority of Falcon 10s were sold to commercial operators though small numbers were sold to governments as VIP transports. The French Aèronavale took delivery of six specially-equipped Mystère-Falcon 10MER aircraft which act as ECM, test, trainer, communication and VIP aircraft. They were also used for the training of pilots of the Dassault Super Etendard carrier-based fighter and as a mock intruder for ground control radar crew training. Production terminated in 1990 after 226 had been produced.

CURRENT SERVICE
The only military user is the French Navy, whose Falcon 10MER fleet serves with Aèronavale 57 Escadrille de Servitude at Landivisiau.

SPECIAL FEATURES
The Falcon 10 is a neat looking, high-aspect ratio bizjet, most commonly seen in the VIP transport role. It can be equipped for aerial photography, ambulance duties, navigator/attack systems training and radio navigation and calibration. It has full-span slats and double-slotted flaps.

VARIANTS
Falcon 10 – the standard small capacity business jet; **Mystère-Falcon 100** – later production aircraft with minor adjustments; **Mystère-Falcon 10MER** – naval variant employed as air defence target, trainer, calibration aircraft, transport, VIP communication, casevac and ECM aircraft.

TECHNICAL DATA

Dassault Falcon 10

Powerplants: Two Garrett TFE731-2 turbofans
Developing: 14.37kN (3,230lb st)
Span: 13.08m (42ft 11in)
Length: 13.86m (45ft 5.75in)
Height: 4.61m (15ft 1.5in)
Maximum weight: 8500kg (18,740lb)
Maximum cruising speed: 912km/h (566mph)
Service ceiling: 45,000 ft
Accommodation: Crew of two and up to seven passengers
Warload: None
First flown: 1 December 1970 (turbojet-powered); April 1973 (turbofan-powered)
Entered service: November 1973

Dassault Falcon 10MER French Navy

Dassault Falcon/Mystère 20/200

TWIN-JET VIP TRANSPORT, ECM TRAINER AND MARITIME PATROL AIRCRAFT

Dassault Mystère 20 French Air Force

TECHNICAL DATA

Dassault Falcon 200

Powerplants: Two Garrett ATF3-6A-4C turbofans
Developing: 23.13kN (5,200lb st)
Span: 16.32m (53ft 7in)
Length: 17.15m (56ft 3in)
Height: 5.32m (17ft 5in)
Maximum weight: 14515kg (32,000lb)
Maximum cruising speed: 870km/h (541mph)
Economical cruising speed: 780km/h (485mph)
Operational ceiling: 45,000ft
Range: 4,650km (2,889 miles)
Accommodation: Crew of two and up to ten passengers or three stretchers
Warload: The Gardian was offered with the capability of carrying two AM39 Exocet anti-shipping missiles
First flown: 4 May 1963 (Falcon 20)
Entered service: July 1965 (civil); 1977 (military)

DEVELOPMENT

Progenitor of the famed Falcon family, the Mystère 20 began life as a concept as a light twin-jet incorporating aerodynamic features of the Mirage IV fighter. Work began in December 1961, with the first flight taking place two years later. Originally equipped with Pratt & Whitney JT12A-6 turbojets (pending delivery of the General Electric CF700), the aircraft was aimed at the US business jet market and links with PanAm saw the creation of the Business Jet Sales Division which oversaw the marketing and selling of the aircraft. By July 1963, 40 aircraft had been ordered, with options on a further 120. The name Mystère 20 was predominantly used in France while Fan Jet Falcon evolved into Falcon 20 in the USA. The original model was superseded by the 20D, and then the 20F with improved engines, fuel capacity, maximum take-off weights and the introduction of full-span leading-edge slats for enhanced take-off and landing performance. 1977 saw the first military order, the US Coast Guard ordering a total of 41 aircraft under the designation HU-25A (see separate entry). The aircraft were used for a number of roles including all-weather SAR, maritime surveillance, environmental protection and communications. A series of upgrades to the type has seen variants capable of pollution monitoring and

interception duties. The French Aèronavale purchased the Falcon 20H Gardian for maritime surveillance and this variant possesses improved Thomson-CSF Varan radar and navigation features. Further variants have been offered for a host of duties and several examples have been fitted with fighter radar for training while others conduct EW/ECM training and target towing. More than 500 have been built.

CURRENT SERVICE

Falcon 20s currently serve with the air arms of Belgium, Cambodia, Egypt, France (Aèronavale and Armée de l'Air), Iran, Lebanon, Morocco, Norway, Oman, Pakistan, Peru, Portugal, Spain, Syria and Venezuela, the majority serving as VIP transports. The French Navy operates five maritime patrol Gardians in its New Caledonia and Tahiti territories in the Pacific. The Armée de l'Air uses the type to train crews for the Mirage IV, 2000 and F1CR.

SPECIAL FEATURES

Multi-purpose light business jet able to fulfil a wide range of duties from transport to fighter radar trainer and target tug to pollution monitoring. A number are equipped with Motorola SLAR and Texas Instruments linescan for maritime pollution detection.

VARIANTS

Falcon 20C – original production type incorporating General Electric CF700-C engines; **Falcon 20D** – uprated CF700-2D engine, increased fuel capacity and increased take off weight to 12,400kg (27,337lb); **Falcon 20E** – engines delivering 19.2kN (4,315lb st) and 13,000kg (28,660lb) maximum take-off weight; **Falcon 20F** – introduced full-span leading edge slats and further increased fuel capacity; **Falcon 20G/200** – new three-spool ATF3 turbofans; **Falcon 20H Gardian** – maritime surveillance variant operated by the Aèronavale for SAR and patrol. Typified by extra-large observation window on port side of fuselage; **Falcon 200 Gardian 2** – an unbuilt variant marketed for Exocet attack, ESM/ECM, target designation and target towing; **Falcon 20 SNA** – equipped with Mirage radar and electronics for training in low-level attack.

SEE ALSO: DASSAULT HU-25 GUARDIAN

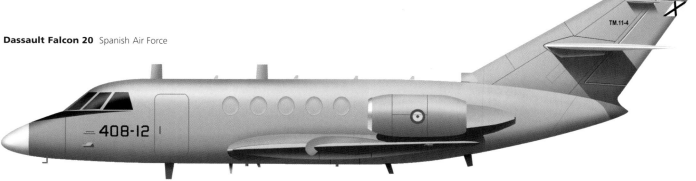

Dassault Falcon 20 Spanish Air Force

Dassault HU-25 Guardian

TWIN-JET MARITIME PATROL AIRCRAFT

HU-25 Guardian United States Coast Guard

TECHNICAL DATA

Dassault HU-25 Guardian

Powerplants: Two Garrett ATF-3-6-2C turbofans
Developing: 24.20kN (5,440lb st)
Span: 16.30m (53ft 6in)
Length: 17.15m (56ft 3in)
Height: 5.32m (17ft 5in)
All-up weight: 15,200kg (33,510lb)
Maximum speed: 855km/h (531mph)
Cruise speed: 764km/h (475mph)
Operational ceiling: 45,000ft
Range: 4,170km (2,591 miles))
Accommodation: Two pilots, two observers and
a Surveillance System Operator (SSO)
Warload: None. Four fuselage hardpoints can
carry rescue packs and four underwing hardpoints
for sensor pods
First flown: 4 May 1963 (Falcon 20);
1980 (HU-25A Guardian)
Entered service: 1981 (HU-25A); May 1988 (HU-25C)

DEVELOPMENT

The US Coast Guard opted to purchase 41 Falcon 20Gs in early 1977, initially for medium-range, all-weather SAR duties. Differing from earlier versions, they had the more powerful Garrett AirResearch ATF3-6-2C turbofans. With the designation HU-25A, these aircraft have a sophisticated array of equipment, including comprehensive navigation and communications gear, together with APS-127 radar so they can perform overwater search and rescue, maritime surveillance and environmental protection tasks. It incorporated a drop hatch through which rescue supplies could be delivered by parachute. It did not enter service until 1981, replacing the long-serving Grumman HU-16E Albatross amphibian. Since delivery a number of Guardians have been subjected to further modifications and less than half remain in the original configuration.

CURRENT SERVICE

Operated from the main Coast Guard Stations at Cape Cod, Massachusetts; Sacramento, California; San Diego, California; Corpus Christi, Texas; Miami, Florida; Mobile, Alabama; Astoria, Oregan and Elizabeth City, North Carolina. They undertake surveillance duties connected with the detection of maritime pollution and the identification of the vessels responsible.

SPECIAL FEATURES

The HU-25B has a Motorola AN/APS-131 side-looking airborne radar (SLAR) in a fuselage pod which is slightly offset to starboard. A Texas Industries RS-18C linescan unit is in another pod under the starboard wing and a laser-illuminated TV is fitted under the port wing. The HU-25C Interceptor was developed for a high-performance aircraft for use in interdiction of drug smuggling activities, fitted with Westinghouse AN/APG-66 radar in the nose and a turret-mounted Texas Industries WF-360 FLIR sensor. Also installed in this version is a complex suite of secure HF, UHF and VHF-FM communications equipment to co-ordinate operations with law enforcement agencies.

VARIANTS

HU-25A was the original configuration; the **HU-25B** is the initial updated version; **HU-25C** – further upgrade as the **Interceptor** for pursuit and identification of suspicious air and sea traffic.

SEE ALSO: DASSAULT FALCON 20/200

HU-25 Guardian United States Coast Guard

Dassault Falcon/Mystère 50

VIP TRANSPORT AND MARITIME PATROL AIRCRAFT

Dassault Falcon 50 Surmar French Navy

DEVELOPMENT

The Falcon 50 was designed by Dassault as a tri-jet to complement the Falcon 20, but offering far greater range. Aimed at the trans-USA and transcontinental flight markets, the Falcon 50 shares the same cabin cross-section as its predecessor, but has been extensively redesigned and it has an advanced supercritical new wing with compound leading edge sweep. It was decided to fit three engines, the choice being the uprated version of the TFE731 turbofan used in the Falcon 10 and 100 and this version has secured military orders as a VIP transport. Most serve as government transports and are fitted with four or five cabin seats. Some are converted to an ambulance configuration. The Falcon 50EX (Extended performance) version was launched offering improvement in performance and giving an increased range. The Falcon 50 Surmar is a maritime surveillance and SAR variant for the French Navy. By mid-2000 over 250 examples had been sold.

CURRENT SERVICE

Falcon 50s currently equip the air arms of France, Iran, Italy, Morocco, Portugal, South Africa, Spain and Switzerland.

SPECIAL FEATURES

The third engine duct extends well forward above the rear fuselage, the inlet being faired into a vertical tail less acutely swept than previous Falcons. When used for maritime surveillance, the Falcon 50 Surmars have Thomson CSF Ocean Master radar and Thomson TTD Chlio FLIR.

VARIANTS

The **Falcon 50** is the standard version; the extended range **50EX**, which features a new EFIS flightdeck, made its maiden flight in 1996. It has TFE731-40 turbofans of 16.46kN (3,700lb st); **Falcon 50 retrofit** – upgrade to existing Falcon 50s with Rockwell Collins ProLine 4 flight deck with the advanced avionics of the Falcon EX; **Falcon 50 Evasan** is the Falcon 50/50EX fitted with a medevac module. The **Falcon 50 Surmar** is a maritime surveillance/SAR variant.

SEE ALSO: DASSAULT FALCON 900

TECHNICAL DATA

Dassault Falcon 50

Powerplants: Three AlliedSignal TFE731-3C turbofans
Developing: 16.46kN (3,700lb st)
Span: 18.86m (61ft 11in)
Length: 18.52m (60ft 9.25in)
Height: 6.97m (22ft 10.5in)
All up weight: 18,500kg (40,780lb)
Maximum cruising speed: 880km/h (497mph)
Operational Ceiling: 49,000ft
Accommodation: Flight crew of two and up to 12 passengers
Warload: None
Range: 6,840km (4,027 miles)
First flown: 7 November 1976 (Falcon 50); 10 April 1996 (50EX)
Entered service: July 1979 (Falcon 50); February 1997 (Falcon 50EX)

Dassault Falcon 50 Swiss Air Force

Dassault Falcon/Mystère 900

THREE-TURBOFAN VIP TRANSPORT AND MARITIME PATROL AIRCRAFT

Falcon 900 Belgian Air Force

DEVELOPMENT

A stretched version of the Falcon 50, the Falcon 900 has a greater fuselage cross-section and an additional 8cm (3in) of passenger headroom, uprated powerplants and slightly modified wing. Designed primarily for civilian use, the first prototype flew in 1984, with certification being granted two years later. Over 235 examples had been sold by mid-2000 with production continuing. The basic model was succeeded by the 900B, and most recently the 900EX. The first of two VIP Mystère 900s was delivered to the Armée de l'Air's Groupe de Liaison Aériennes Ministérielles (GLAM) in 1987 and similarly tasked aircraft have gone to several other nations. Japan's Maritime Safety Agency has modified two examples for long range maritime surveillance duties.

CURRENT SERVICE

Falcon 900s equip the air arms of Algeria, Australia, Belgium, France, Gabon, Italy, Japan, Malaysia, Qatar, South Africa and Spain (as the T.18).

SPECIAL FEATURES

The aircraft's structure incorporates a high degree of composite materials. Surveillance aircraft are fitted with US search radar, an operational control station, special communications radar, HU-25A Guardian-style observation windows and a drop hatch for sonobuoys, fares and markers. The cabin may be divided into three sections. Double-slotted flaps and leading edge slats are fitted.

VARIANTS

Falcon 900: the standard military and civilian variant; **Falcon 900B:** powered by uprated engines (TFE731-5BRs of 21.1kN (4,750lb st)) and cleared for operations from unpaved runways, also slight improvement in range – introduced in 1991; **Falcon 900C:** combines airframe, powerplant and cabin of 900B with several systems of the Falcon 900EX, and entered service in 2000; **Falcon 900EX:** long range development (8,335km/5,180 miles) of the Falcon 900B, re-engined with TFE731-60 turbofans, Honeywell Primus 20000 avionics, colour EFIS and entered service in 1996; **Falcon 900B/EX Evasan:** is fitted with medical evacuation modules. and can also have an operating unit/trauma room arrangement for on-site treatment – satellite links are able to be installed for two-way communications with hospitals; **Falcon 900 Multirole:** version for the Japanese Maritime Safety Agency. A laminar flow wing was tested on the Falcon 900 in 1994.

SEE ALSO: DASSAULT FALCON/MYSTERE 50

Falcon 900 Spanish Air Force

TECHNICAL DATA

Dassault Falcon/Mystère 900B

Powerplants: Three AlliedSignal TFE731-5AR-1C turbofans
Developing: 20.02kN (4,500lb st)
Span: 19.33m (63ft 5in)
Length: 20.21m (66ft 3.75in)
Height: 7.55m (24ft 9.25in)
All up weight: 20,640kg (45,503lb)
Maximum cruising speed: 893km/h (555 mph)
Operational ceiling: 51,015ft
Accommodation: Flight crew of two and up to 18 passengers
Warload: None
Range: 7,227km (4,491 miles)
First flown: 21 September 1984 (Falcon 900); 1 June 1995 (Falcon 900EX)
Entered service: November 1987 (French Air Force)

Dassault Mirage III, V & 50

SINGLE-ENGINED MULTI-ROLE FIGHTER

Mirage IIIEX

TECHNICAL DATA

Dassault Mirage 50M

Powerplant: One SNECMA Atar 9K-50 turbojet
Developing: 49.03kN (11,023lb st) dry and
70.82kN (15,873lb st) with afterburning
Span: 8.20m (26ft 11.6in)
Length: 15.56m (51ft 0.6in)
Height: 4.50m (14ft 9in)
All up weight: 14,000kg (32,407lb)
Maximum speed: 2,338km/h (1,453mph)
Cruising speed: 956km/h (594mph)
Combat radius: 1,315km (817 miles)
Operational ceiling: 59,055ft
Accommodation: Pilot only (two in tandem in
two-seaters)
Warload: Two 30mm DEFA 552A fixed forward-
firing cannon plus up to 4,000kg (8,818lb) of
disposable stores carried on three underfuselage
and four underwing hardpoints. Weapons
include one Matra R350 AAM, Matra R550 Magic
or AIM-9 Sidewinder AAMs, AS30 and AS37
ASMs, bombs and rockets.
First flown: 17 November 1956 (Mirage III);
15 April 1979 (Mirage 50)
Entered service: July 1961

DEVELOPMENT

Genesis of the Mirage III family can be traced back to early 1953 with an Armée de l'Air requirement for a light fighter. Dassault designed a number of systems, culminating in the Mystère Delta, later renamed the Mirage I, which was more a proof of concept aircraft than an actual production type. However, on the drawing board as successors to this initial design were the Mirage II, III and IV. While the II was ignored, work proceeded at a formidable rate on the III, the first aircraft flying on 17 November 1956. The impressive speed of the new aircraft was demonstrated on 24 October 1958, when a Mirage IIIA became the first European aircraft to reach Mach 2, beating the British Lightning by a month. The aircraft was well received by the French Air Force and the first operational squadron of Mirage IIIC interceptors was formed in July 1961. Shortly afterwards, these aircraft were supplemented by the 'stretched' Mirage IIIE, which offered a ground attack capability, and the Mirage IIIR reconnaissance aircraft. The aircraft did well on the export market, being sold to Spain, Switzerland, Israel, Argentina, Brazil, Venezuela, Australia, South Africa and Pakistan. Many of these operators have taken their aircraft to war, usually with great success, though Argentina's Mirage IIIEAs suffered at the hands of Royal Navy Sea Harriers during the Falklands Conflict. Israel then requested a simplified aircraft, which would have much in common with the Mirage IIIs already in service, yet which would have some equipment removed and which would be cheaper and have a faster turnaround. The resultant Mirage 5 was instantly recognisable by its sharper nose cone.

However, an embargo on Israel meant the aircraft went elsewhere instead, though other nations bought the type. Israel responded by developing its own non-licensed aircraft. To boost the power of the Mirage III family, it was decided to refit early aircraft with the Atar 9K-50 powerplant. Chile was the first official recipient of Mirage 50s, though several other aircraft such as the Milan and the IIIR2Z possessed similar capabilities. The myriad versions of the Mirage III/5/50 make identification difficult, especially when operators added equipment that had been previously deleted by others; for example, adding radar to the Mirage 5.

CURRENT SERVICE

France has retired its Mirage IIIs, but the type is still operational with the following air arms: Mirage III – Argentina, Brazil, Pakistan, Switzerland; Mirage 5 – Argentina, Chile, Colombia, Congo, Egypt, Gabon, Libya, Pakistan, Peru, UAE; Mirage 50 – Chile, Venezuela.

SPECIAL FEATURES

Sleek delta-winged aircraft that established Dassault as a world-class jet manufacturer. The Mirage III family has been modified into dozens of sub-variants and exported to many nations and despite the fact the first prototype flew nearly 50 years ago, the aircraft remains in service.

VARIANTS

Mirage IIIC: original radar-equipped fighter, now retired; **Mirage IIIB:** two-seat trainer; **Mirage IIIE:** multi-role strike/attack aircraft with modest engine upgrade and additional avionics; **Mirage IIIBE:** two-

seat trainer version of the Mirage IIIE; **Mirage IIIR:** reconnaissance variant of the IIIE; **Mirage 5:** simplified version of the Mirage IIIE, optimised for daytime ground attack and without radar, recognised by slimmer nose profile; **Mirage 5D:** two-seat trainer of the Mirage 5; **Mirage 5R:** reconnaissance variant of Mirage 5; **Mirage 50:** Mirage III or 5 aircraft with uprated Atar 9K-50 engine. While these examples represent the major variant of the family, there have been dozens of sub variants produced by individual operators. A typical upgrade feature is the addition of canard foreplanes as adopted by the Dagger, Finger, Milan, MirSip, Pantera and several other nations whose aircraft merely have designations, not names. The Israeli **Kfir** and the South African **Cheetah** represent total independent rebuilds which bear little resemblance to their French predecessors.

SEE ALSO: ENAER PANTERA, IAI DAGGER & KFIR,
ATLAS/DENEL CHEETAH

Mirage IIID-BR Colombian Air Force

Dassault Mirage IV

STRATEGIC NUCLEAR BOMBER AND RECONNAISSANCE AIRCRAFT

Mirage IVP French Air Force

DEVELOPMENT

In 1954, the French government decided to create its own nuclear deterrent (Force de Frappe), one element of which would be a manned bomber which would carry the AN22 free-fall nuclear bomb. Dassault had been working on the Mirage IV heavy fighter which was ultimately discarded yet its frame in the shape of the Mirage IVC was retained and when this was built up in terms of size, weight, speed and range, the Mirage IVA was the finished article. Equipped with the Atar 9C engine and aided by RATO pods, the Mirage IVA is a two-man, delta wing and was designed to penetrate enemy airspace at high speeds, delivering its weapon and then egressing the area. By 1968, the aircraft was fully operational with six squadrons operating a total of 62 aircraft spread around France so as to minimise the risk of simultaneous destruction of the entire fleet. By the 1980s, the Mirage IVA's capability to penetrate enemy airspace was felt to be insufficient, and the remaining 18 aircraft were upgraded to IVP standard, which gave the aircraft

updated avionics and the ability to carry the Mach 3 ASMP stand-off nuclear missile. However, by 1996 it was decided to retire the majority of the aircraft, leaving only five which were modified for the photo-recce role. The aircraft, whose reconnaissance gear is mounted in a belly-mounted pod, proved their worth over Somalia, Rwanda, Chad, Zaire – and later Bosnia and Kosovo in 1999, flying hundreds of sorties and gathering vital data. The remaining aircraft are scheduled to remain in service until 2005.

CURRENT SERVICE

Five active (and five stored) remain to provide a long-range strategic reconnaissance capability and are based with Escaudron de Reconnaissance Strategique 01.091 'Gascogne' at BA 118 Mont-de-Marsan. These have the CT52 photo pod carried in place of the former AN22 free-fall atomic bombs.

SPECIAL FEATURES

Ageing, yet very efficient, Dassault delta whose

supreme speed allowed safe penetration of enemy airspace to deliver nuclear payload or to obtain reconnaissance data. Twelve booster rockets (six under each wing) could be used to improve field performance.

VARIANTS

Mirage IVA: original bomber variant, designed to drop free-fall AN22 nuclear bomb; **Mirage IVP**: modified aircraft with updated avionics, radar warning receivers and the ability to carry the stand-off ASMP missile; **Mirage IVP (photo)**: reconnaissance variant with four pod mounted cameras and an infrared suite.

TECHNICAL DATA

Dassault Mirage IV

Powerplants: Two SNECMA Atar 9K-50 turbojets
Developing: 49.03kN (11,023lb st) dry and 70.61kN (15,873lb st) with afterburning
Span: 11,85m (38ft 10.5in)
Length: 23.50m (77ft 1.2in)
Height: 5.65m (18ft 6.4in)
All up weight: 31,600kg (69,666lb)
Maximum speed: 2,338km/h (1,453 mph)
Ferry range: 4,000km (2,486 miles)
Combat radius: 1,240km (771 miles)
Operational ceiling: 65,615ft
Accommodation: Two
Warload: Now usually none. Was able to carry up to 7,200kg (15,873lb) of disposable stores including ASMP, AS397 Martel anti-radiation missiles and free-fall bombs on one underfuselage or four underwing hardpoints.
First flown: 17 June 1959
Entered service: 1964

Mirage IVP French Air Force

Dassault Mirage F1

Mirage F1C Spanish Air Force

TECHNICAL DATA

Dassault Mirage F1C

Powerplant: One SNECMA Atar 9K-50 turbojet
Developing: 49.0kn (11,025lb st) dry,
70.21kN (15,785lb st) with afterburning
Span: 8.40m (27ft 7in)
Length: 15.30m (50ft 2in)
Height: 4.50m (14ft 9in)
All up weight: 16,200kg (35,715lb)
Maximum speed: 2,335 km/h (1,453 mph)
Combat radius: 600km (373 miles)
Operational ceiling: 65,615 ft
Accommodation: Pilot only (two in-tandem in F1B)
Warload: Up to 6,300kg (13,889lb) of disposable
stores with standard air-to-air configuration of
either two AIM-9 or Magic infrared missiles on
wingtip rails and either one MATRA R530 or
Super 530F radar-guided AAMs, rockets, bombs
and ASMs including AM39 Exocet or Armat anti-
radiation missile on centreline or on wing pylons.
Additionally there are two 30mm DEFA 553 fixed
forward-firing cannon in the underside of the
forward fuselage.
First flown: 23 December 1966
Entered service: December 1973

DEVELOPMENT

Despite its designation, the Mirage F1 was designed as the successor to the Mirage III/5 family. It was decided to forsake the delta-wing of the previous Mirages for a high-mounted wing and conventional tail surfaces, and the first company prototype flew on 23 December 1966. It was officially adopted by the French Air Force the following year, with three prototypes ordered. Designed as an all-weather interceptor, the F1C offered a host of improvements over its predecessor, the Mirage III, and was equipped with the Thomson-CSF Cyrano IV radar. The first examples entered service with the first squadron of the 30 Wing at Reims and the Armée de l'Air eventually acquired a total of 83 examples of this type equipping three wings of three squadrons each. Twenty F1B tandem-seat trainers were subsequently ordered to equip an OCU. By the 1990s, availability of the Mirage 2000 meant the retirement of three F1C squadrons and these displaced aircraft were modified to F1CT ground attack standard. These aircraft remain in service, performing well over Kosovo in 1999. When it was clear that the Mirage F1 would definitely go ahead, Dassault produced a dedicated reconnaissance variant, the F1CR, which carries a number of systems, both internally and externally. Mirage F1CRs fought successfully in *Desert Storm*, Bosnia and Kosovo, even fulfilling their secondary role of dropping bombs on Iraqi SAM sites. It is expected that the French F1 fleet – in the shape of

10 F1C/Bs, 20 F1CRs and 20 F1CTs – will soldier on until retirement in 2015. The basic F1C did well on the export market, being sold to six countries. South Africa, Morocco and Kuwait have all used their aircraft operationally, with the South Africans most notably tangling (successfully) with MiG-21s. As well as the F1Cs, the SAAF also bought the simplified ground-attack F1A, used in ground attack missions in Angola and against guerrillas. A further export variant was the F1E, which was a dedicated fighter/attack aircraft sold to several nations including Ecuador, Iraq and Libya.

CURRENT SERVICE

Mirage F1s equip the air arms of Ecuador, France, Greece, Iraq, Jordan, Kuwait, Libya, Morocco and Spain.

SPECIAL FEATURES

For the F1, Dassault dispensed with the traditional delta wing in lieu of a swept wing. Built in a number of variants, the F1 never achieved the sales success of its predecessor but continues to be used by a number of air forces. The F1CRs are fitted with infrared linescan installed in place of the cannon, optical cameras in a small nose fairing and various centreline recce pods.

VARIANTS

Mirage F1C: all-weather interceptor with two cannon and later AAMs, supplemented by **F1C-200** variant

with fixed inflight refuelling probe; **F1B**: fully combat capable two-seat trainer; **F1CR**: dedicated recce variant with internal reconnaissance equipment supplemented by a centreline pods carrying sensor equipment; **F1CT**: tactical air-to-ground variant with new radar, attack systems, RWR and provision for a wide range of weapons; **F1A**: South African variant of the F1C designed for attack missions and equipped with Aôda radar, inflight refuelling probe. AZ variant has a laser rangefinder. **F1E**: new aircraft powered by the new SNEMCA M53 turbofan, failed to win any export orders – the designation was used for an upgraded multi-role fighter/attack version with turbojet engine and more capable nav/attack system. This variant did sell, with several nations buying the type; **F1D**: two-seat combat-capable trainer variant based on the F1E.

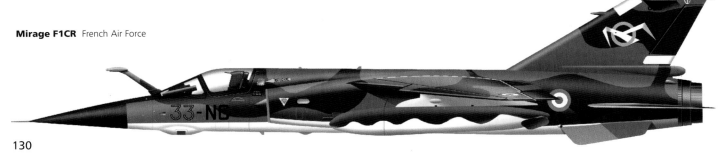

Mirage F1CR French Air Force

Dassault Mirage 2000

SINGLE TURBOFAN MULTIROLE FIGHTER

Dassault Mirage 2000-5 French Air Force

TECHNICAL DATA

Dassault Mirage 2000C

Powerplant: One SNECMA M53-P2 afterburning turbofan
Developing: 64.33kN (14,462lb st) dry and 95.12kN (21,384lb st) afterburning
Span: 9.13m (30ft 0in)
Length: 14.36m (47ft 1.25in)
Height: 5.20m (17ft 0.75in)
Maximum weight: 17,000kg (37,478lb)
Maximum speed: 2,338km/h (1,453mph)
Operational ceiling: 59,055ft
Combat range: with two drop tanks – 1,850km (1,150 miles)
Accommodation: One pilot (C,E,R,-5 variants), pilot and WSO/Instructor (B D,N,S)
Warload: Two internal 30mm DEFA 554 cannon, two MATRA Magic 2 and two MATRA MICA Super 530D air-to-air missiles for aerial combat. Ground attack versions carry a wide range of weaponry ranging from AM39 Exocet anti-ship missiles to the ASMP stand off nuclear missile. Up to 6,300kg (13,890lb) of ordnance
First flown: 10 March 1978
Entered service: April 1983

DEVELOPMENT

Born out of the cancelled Avion de Combat Futur (ACF) Super Mirage project in 1975, the Mirage 2000 is the latest in a long line of aircraft to bear the Mirage name. A return to the proven delta wing configuration and a rapid, yet successful design process led to a powerful interceptor with a big high-lift wing and large internal volume. Service entry commenced in 1983 with 2 Escadre de Chasse (EC 2) being the first recipients of the Mirage 2000C. Accompanying the C model is the Mirage 2000B trainer which is only 19cm (7.5in) longer and retains full combat capability. The superb performance of the Mirage quickly led to international interest. The first country to order the Mirage 2000 was Egypt, but India was the first to actually receive its aircraft. India's Mirages were given the designation 2000H and earned the local nickname Vajra, which is loosely translated as Thunderbolt. However, the Indians were never totally satisfied with the expensive Dassault product and seized the chance to buy MiG-29 'Fulcrums' when they were offered. During the Mirage 2000's design process, it was envisaged that the type would one day have a nuclear capability. A two-seat B model, designated 2000N (Nuclèaire), had its structure strengthened and received advanced avionics in the shape of terrain-following, ground-mapping and air-to-ground radars. Weaponry comes in the shape of the ASMP (Air-Sol

Moyenne Portèe – Air-to-Ground Medium range missile). To provide a modern attack aircraft, Dassault took the 2000N and modified it to carry conventional equipment such as Aèrospatiale's AS30L laser-guided missile and the MATRA/BAe BGL 1000 bomb. Precision dropping is achieved by the use of the Thomson CSF PDLCT (Pod de Dèsignation Laser & Camèra Thermique) TV/thermal imaging pod. This laser designator pod with infra-red camera is used to direct weapons to their targets. In order to re-establish the Mirage 2000 in the highly competitive export market, Dassault created the 2000-5 bringing together the Thomson-CSF RDM radar, the APSI cockpit, MATRA/BAe Mica missiles and the ICMS Mk 2 self-defence suite in a major update of the original interceptor variant. The first 2000-5 flew on 27 April 1991 and has since entered limited French service. It has also been exported to Abu Dhabi, Qatar and Taiwan.

CURRENT SERVICE

Mirage 2000s in different versions equip the air arms of Abu Dhabi, Egypt, France, Greece, India, Peru, Qatar and Taiwan.

SPECIAL FEATURES

The Mirage 2000's delta-wing design offers excellent lift, ensuring superb agility. High speed and low-level ability ensures the lethality of the Nuclèaire variant.

It has fly-by-wire controls and inherent instability, and leading edge slats improve manoeuvrability.

VARIANTS

Mirage 2000B – standard two-seat trainer; **Mirage 2000C** – single-seat interceptor; **Mirage 2000D** – two-seat conventional attack aircraft; **Mirage 2000E** – early export designation for C model multi-role version; **Mirage 2000ED** – export designation for B model trainer; **Mirage 2000N** – two- seat nuclear attack aircraft, armed with ASMP missile; **Mirage 2000S** – export designation for D model (no longer on offer); **Mirage 2000-5 Mk2**: interceptor with advanced avionics and improved weapon options and night-attack capability (same as the 2000-9 developed for the UAE).

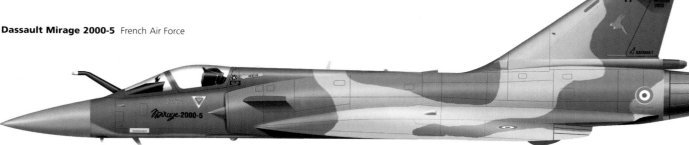

Dassault Mirage 2000-5 French Air Force

Dassault Rafale

Rafale B French Air Force

TECHNICAL DATA

Dassault Rafale D

Powerplants: Two SNECMA M88-3 turbofans
Developing: 48.7kN (10,950lb st) dry, 75kN (16,861lb st) with afterburning
Span: 10.90m (35ft 9in)
Length: 15.27m (50ft 1in)
Height: 5.34m (17ft 6in)
All up weight: 21,500kg (47,400lb)
Maximum speed: 2,125km/h (1,317mph)
Operational ceiling: 55,000ft
Combat radius: 1,760km (1,094 miles)
Warload: One 30mm GIAT/DEFA 791B cannon plus up to 6,000kg (13,230lb) of disposable air-to-air and air-to-ground stores on a total of 14 underfuselage, underwing and wingtip hardpoints. Weapons include ASMP nuclear stand-off missile, up to eight Matra Mica AAMs, AM39 Exocets, laser-guided bombs, AS 30L laser-guided ASMs or Apache dispensers with anti-armour or anti-runway munitions.
First flown: ACX (Avion de Combat Experimentale) 4 July 1986; 19 May 1991 (Rafale C)
Entered service: Armèe de l'Air squadron entry set for 2005. First Aéronavale unit set for June 2001

DEVELOPMENT

France was originally part of the European Fighter Aircraft project, which led to the Eurofighter Typhoon, until August 1985 when withdrawal was caused by the French desire for a fighter smaller than was being designed by the project. The ACX (Avion de Combat Experimentale) had been designed by Dassault, but the withdrawal prompted further development, with the first example flying in 1986. The ACX helped to establish the aerodynamic design, performance and systems that resulted in the Rafale. Both the Armèe de l'Air and Aéronavale were involved in the project and the ACX, later renamed Rafale, made 460 test sorties, including touch-and-go landings on the carrier *Clemenceau*. Between 1991 and 1993, the first Rafale C and B (single and two-seat respectively) prototypes flew and it was soon determined that the dual-control B, originally envisaged as a combat-capable trainer would instead be the main Armèe de l'Air operational variant, manned by a pilot, with or without a weapon systems operator. The Rafale will be able to carry a range of weapons on 14 hardpoints and used in conjunction with the REB2 radar. Planned Armèe de l'Air procurement is currently 212 aircraft (reduced from 250 and then 234), with 130 two-seat examples and the first unit is due to be declared operational at

Saint-Dizier in 2005. In the Air Force it will replace Jaguars and Mirage F1s, and in the Navy will replace Super Etendards and Crusaders (the latter having already been retired). Aéronavale procurement has remained unchanged at 86 single-seat attack aircraft with delivery starting in 2001.

CURRENT SERVICE

French Armèe de l'Air (Rafale B) and Aèronavale (Rafale M) will be the first Rafale operators. As yet, there has been no firm export orders although China expressed interest in 1996/97 but an order now seems unlikely.

SPECIAL FEATURES

Fifth-generation delta-winged semi-stealthy fighter and attack aircraft. Along with late-model Mirage 2000s, the Rafale will spearhead France's offensive aviation forces well into the 21st Century. The Rafale has some stealth measures and composite materials in its construction, a fly-by-wire control system and the comprehensive Spectra integrated defensive aids subsystem.

VARIANTS

Rafale B: two-seat, (pilot and WSO) dual-control fully operational Armèe de l'Air fighter. The B will be the

predominant version of the type in Air Force service; **Rafale C:** single-seat combat version for the Armèe de l'Air; **Rafale D** (a generic term): original configuration from which current production versions are derived. The D stands for 'Rafale Discret' (stealthy). **Rafale M:** single seat carrier-borne fighter – a strengthened undercarriage and reduced take-off weight, coupled with the loss of one hardpoint and the addition of a catapult bar and tailhook are all modifications needed for carrier operations. A two-seat fighter/trainer is also currently being discussed. **Rafale R:** possible future reconnaissance variant which would incorporate a stealthy sensor pod and which would replace the Mirage F1CR and naval Super Etendards in this role.

Rafale M French Navy

Dassault-Breguet Atlantic/Atlantique

TWIN-TURBOPROP MARITIME PATROL, ANTI-SUBMARINE AND SAR AIRCRAFT

FRANCE

Br.1150 Atlantic German Navy

TECHNICAL DATA

Dassault-Breguet Atlantique 2
Powerplants: Two Rolls-Royce Tyne RTy.20 Mk 21 turboprops
Developing: 4,549 kW (6,100 shp)
Driving: four-blade propellers
Span: 37.42m (122ft 9.25in)
Length: 33.63m (110ft 4in)
Height: 10.89m (35ft 8.75in)
All-up weight: 46,200kg (101,850lb)
Maximum speed: 648km/h (402mph)
Cruise speed: 555km/h (345mph)
Operational ceiling: 30,000ft
Maximum range: 9,075km (5,635 miles)
Mission range: 3,700km (2,300 miles)
Endurance: up to 18 hours
Accommodation: Pilot, co-pilot and flight engineer on flight deck; nine further mission crew for the aircraft's avionics and systems plus observers
Warload: Maximum internal weapons load 2,500kg (5,511lb) in main weapons bay in unpressurised lower fuselage for bombs, depth charges, up to eight Mk 46 or seven Murène torpedoes, two air-to-surface missiles such as AM 39 Exocet or AS 37 Martel ASMs; four underwing pylons for up to 3,500kg (7,716lb) of bombs, depth charges or air-to-surface missiles; compartment aft of weapons bay carries over 100 sonobuoys with Alkan pneumatic launchers.
First flown: 21 October 1961; 8 May 1981 (ATL 2)
Entered service: 10 December 1965; February 1991 (ATL 2)

DEVELOPMENT

Breguet's Br.1150 design won a late 1950s NATO requirement for a long-range maritime patrol aircraft. The first, short-fuselage prototype flew in October 1961; altogether, four prototypes and 87 production aircraft were built by a Breguet-led multi-national consortium, comprising 40 for France, 20 for West Germany, 18 for Italy, and nine for the Netherlands. Initial deliveries were made in December 1965. Five of the German aircraft have served as electronic-warfare platforms, while the Dutch aircraft were withdrawn in 1984. Three former French Atlantics transferred in the mid-1970s to Pakistan were later augmented by others; one was shot down by Indian forces in August 1999 during renewed tension between both countries. An updated and more capable replacement for the original Atlantics was created by Dassault-Breguet as the Atlantique 2, originally called ANG (Atlantic Nouvelle Génération) or ATL 2. The prototype flew in May 1981 and the type became operational during February 1991. Only France has ordered this new model, the French Navy's requirement for 42 having now been cut to 28. A re-engined, third generation model called the Atlantique 3 has been marketed by Dassault, but has not gained production orders.

CURRENT SERVICE

The French Navy's Atlantique 2 force is divided between Flottilles 21F at Nîmes-Garons, and 23F at Lann-Bihoué; the final Atlantique 2 was delivered in early 1998. Original Atlantics continue to serve with the German Navy's 1st Staffel of Marinefliegergeschwader 3 'Graf von Zeppelin' at Nordholz. Italian Atlantics are operated jointly by the Italian Air Force and Navy with joint crews aboard; they fly with 86° Gruppo of 30° Stormo at Cagliari-Elmas in Sardinia, and 88° Gruppo of 41° Stormo at Catania-Sigonella in Sicily. Surviving Pakistan Navy Atlantics serve with No 29 Squadron at Karachi/Drigh Road (Mehran).

SPECIAL FEATURES

Of basically all-metal construction, the Atlantic has a 'double bubble' fuselage cross-section which has a pressurised upper area for the crew. A CSF search radar was originally fitted in the Atlantic, within a retractable underfuselage radome, with a magnetic anomaly detector (MAD) in the lengthened tailboom and electronics pod atop the tail.

VARIANTS

The **Atlantique 2** features considerable structural detail refinement compared to the **Atlantic**, with completely new avionics including the Thomson-CSF Iguane sea-search radar, new Sextant MAD receiver in the tailboom, nose-mounted forward-looking infrared, wingtip electronics pods and many improvements in mission avionics. Existing Italian and German Atlantics have been considerably upgraded, the German aircraft having a significant KWS upgrade including a new Texas Instruments AN/APS-134(V) radar and many other improvements. The German electronic warfare Atlantics have mission avionics by E-Systems under the 'Peace Peek' programme, including a large fixed ventral radome.

Dassault-Breguet Atlantique 2 French Navy

Dassault-Breguet/Dornier Alpha Jet

TWIN-TURBOFAN TWO-SEAT BASIC/ADVANCED TRAINER, AND LIGHT ATTACK AIRCRAFT

FRANCE/GERMANY

Alpha Jet E French Air Force

TECHNICAL DATA

Dassault-Breguet/Dornier Alpha Jet E

Powerplants: Two SNECMA/Turboméca Larzac 04-C6 turbofans
Developing: 13.24kN (2,976lb st)
Span: 9.11m (29ft 10.75 in)
Length: 12.29m (40ft 3.5 in)
Height: 4.19m (13ft 9in)
All-up weight: 7,250kg (15,983lb)
Maximum speed: 1,000km/h (621mph)
Cruise speed: 916km/h (569mph)
Operational ceiling: 48,000ft
Maximum range: approximately 2,600km (1,616 miles)
Mission range: 1,130km (702 miles)
Endurance: approximately 3.5 hours
Accommodation: Instructor and trainee pilot (instructor in rear seat)
Warload: optional removable gun pod below fuselage centreline for single 30mm DEFA 553 cannon; four underwing pylons (two per wing) for total external stores load of 2,500 kg (5,512 lb). Armament options include various gun and rocket pods, bombs or fuel tanks.
First flown: 26 October 1973
Entered service: May 1979 (Alpha Jet E); April 1978 (Alpha Jet E); April 1982 (Alpha Jet NGEA)

DEVELOPMENT

The joint Franco-German Alpha Jet programme of the late 1960s was intended as a basic/advanced and lead-in trainer. Changing German requirements caused a switch to light attack and anti-helicopter combat roles for that country's subsequent Alpha Jet procurement. The first of four Alpha Jet prototypes flew in October 1973, and final assembly lines were established in both France and Germany. The first French Air Force Alpha Jets were delivered in 1978 and the type entered French service in May 1979. Both France (Alpha Jet E trainers) and Germany (the differently-configured Alpha Jet A light attack aircraft) each procured 175 examples. The first of 33 Alpha Jet B for Belgium was completed in 1978, with most being locally assembled (by SABCA). Trainer Alpha Jets have been exported to several countries; local assembly of the majority of 30 for Egypt (designated MS-1) was performed by the Arab Organisation for Industrialisation (AOI) in Helwan. Dassault-Breguet/Dornier subsequently developed the better-equipped Alpha Jet NGEA for lead-in/weapons training and light attack; the first example flew in April 1982, and the majority of at least 15 for Egypt (designated MS-2) were assembled by AOI. An all-weather/attack Alpha Jet development called Lancier was also devised but not produced; Dassault continues to promote the Alpha Jet ATS (Advanced Training System). In early 2000, talks began with Hindustan Aeronautics for the transfer of Alpha Jet production

tooling to India for possible manufacture and service there. Redundant ex-German Alpha Jet A models were passed to Portugal starting in 1993, and in 2000 approximately 12 including spares were supplied to Britain, with a large batch also destined for Thailand.

CURRENT SERVICE

The French Air Force's sizeable Alpha Jet E fleet serves mainly as pilot trainers (EAC 00.314 at Tours), test pilot trainers (EPNER at Istres), or as operational transition and weapons trainers (ETO 1/8 'Saintonge' and ETO 2/8 'Nice' at Cazaux). The French Air Force's aerobatic team, the *Patrouille de France* flies Alpha Jet Es from Salon de Provence. Alpha Jets of various different versions also operate with the air forces of Belgium, Cameroon, Côte d'Ivoire, Egypt, Morocco, Nigeria, Portugal (including that country's *Asas de Portugal* aerobatic team), Qatar and Togo. A handful of former Luftwaffe Alpha Jets were delivered to the UK early in 2000 to replace Hunters and Hawks with DERA on test and trials duties at Boscombe Down and Llanbedr.

SPECIAL FEATURES

Alpha Jets have the classic tandem two-seat trainer layout with raised rear (instructors') seat, but unusually feature a shoulder-mounted wing. Most Alpha Jets are dual-control trainers, but many of the German aircraft were operated with a single crew

member aboard in their now defunct close air support/light strike/anti-helicopter roles.

VARIANTS

The pointed-nose German **Alpha Jet As** have different equipment, avionics, weapons-aiming and armament options compared to the blunt-nose trainer models. The **Alpha Jet NGEA** has more powerful 14.1kN (3,175lb st) Larzac 04-C20 turbofans, improved avionics and equipment including a laser range-finder in its re-shaped nose, and expanded underwing armament options including infrared air-to-air missiles with related weapon-aiming equipment.

Dassault-Breguet Alpha Jet
Qatar Air Force

De Havilland Canada DHC-1 Chipmunk

SINGLE PISTON-ENGINED TWO-SEAT TANDEM TRAINER

DHC-1 Chipmunk

DEVELOPMENT

The de Havilland Canada Chipmunk was developed as a primary trainer immediately after World War II and first flew on 22 May 1946. With a fixed tailwheel undercarriage and a single-piece sliding canopy, it was initially ordered into production for the Royal Canadian Air Force. A total of 735 examples was subsequently delivered to the Royal Air Force under the designation T10. These differed from the Canadian T1 by having a multi-panel sliding canopy and being fully aerobatic. Export Chipmunks were produced in the UK as the T20 and T21, with over 230 examples going to ten foreign air forces. In addition, licence-production was also undertaken for the Portuguese Air Force by OGMA in Portugal, producing 60 more examples. Canadian export production centered on the DHC-1B and the T30 which were sold to Chile, Colombia, Egypt, Lebanon, Thailand and Uruguay.

A few Chipmunks of No 114 Squadron were pressed into service in Cyprus on internal security flights during the EOKA troubles of the late 1950s/early 1960s. The first Chipmunks to wear RAF roundels were flown by Oxford UAS from February 1950 and thereafter replaced the Tiger Moth with all 17 University Air Squadrons, as well as equipping many RAF Volunteer Reserve flying schools in the early 1950s. National Service pilots underwent their initial training on the 'Chippie', which served intermittently with the RAF College, Cranwell.

CURRENT SERVICE

A small number of T20s still serve with Grupo Operativo 12 of the Portuguese Air Force, based at BA1 Sintra.

SPECIAL FEATURES

The Chipmunk's all-metal stressed-skin construction allows the aircraft to be fully aerobatic, with excellent visibility from both front and rear seats.

VARIANTS

Royal Canadian Air Force variants comprised the **T1** and the Gipsy 10-engined **T2**: the Royal Air Force, Royal Navy and the Army Air Corps operated the British-built **T10** and export versions included the **DHC-1B** (equivalent to the T2), **T20**, **T21** and **T30**: the Mk 21 was British-built, as the Mk 20, but to civil requirements (28 completed). The **Mk 22** was the conversion of T10s to civil standard with the Mk 20 powerplant. The **Mk 20** was the British-built export version of the T10, but with the Gipsy Major 10 Series 2 engine.

TECHNICAL DATA

De Havilland DHC-1 Chipmunk T10

Powerplant: One de Havilland Gipsy Major 8 piston engine
Developing: 108kW (145 hp)
Driving: Two-blade propeller
Span: 10.45m (34ft 4in)
Length: 7.75m (25ft 5in)
Height: 2.13m (7ft 0in)
Maximum weight: 914kg (2,014lb)
Maximum speed: 222km/h (138mph)
Cruise speed: 187km/h (116mph)
Operational ceiling: 15,800ft
Range: 451km (280 miles)
Accommodation: pilot and student, in tandem
Warload: None
First flown: 22 May 1946
Entered service: February 1950 (RAF)

DHC-1 Chipmunk

De Havilland Canada DHC-2 Beaver

SINGLE PISTON-ENGINED STOL UTILITY TRANSPORT AND LIAISON AIRCRAFT

U-6A Beaver United States Navy

DEVELOPMENT

As de Havilland Canada's first dedicated STOL aircraft, the DHC-2 was designed in the late 1940s to appeal as an effective, rugged and reliable utility aircraft to both civil and military customers. The first and most important military contract was awarded after six evaluation DHC-2s under the designation YL-20 won a joint US Army/USAF contest for a communications and light transport aircraft. A total of 959 examples were delivered under the designation L-20, and the type subsequently played an important role in the Korean War. A number of US Army Beavers were modified to allow operations on skis, and in 1962 the remaining examples were redesignated U-6A. In the 1960s, DHC produced a turboprop version designated DHC-2 Mk III, which incorporated a 410kW (550shp) Pratt & Whitney Canada PT6A-6A engine, together with a lengthened fuselage (allowing the carriage of two additional passengers), a square-cut fin and a ventral strake. Production of the DHC-2 totalled 1,691 plus 59 DHC-2 Mk IIIs. At the height of its career, the Beaver was to be found in over 50 countries, where

it won universal acclaim for its performance, ground stability conferred by its wide-track tailwheel landing gear, and its versatility.

CURRENT SERVICE

The oldest design still in service (operated by the US Navy) is the U-6A, three of which operate with the US Naval Test Pilot School. Small numbers of military Beavers also serve with the air arms of Colombia, Haiti and South Korea.

SPECIAL FEATURES

A strut-supported high wing with large trailing-edge flaps gives the Beaver an exceptional short-field performance. Great flexibility was bestowed on the type by its ability to operate on wheel, ski, float or amphibious float landing gear.

VARIANTS

The main military production variant of the Beaver was the **DHC-2/L-20**, whilst the enlarged turboprop-powered version was produced as the **DHC-2 Mk III**.

TECHNICAL DATA

De Havilland DHC-2 Beaver I

Powerplant: One Pratt & Whitney R-985 Wasp Junior piston engine
Developing: 336kW (450hp)
Driving: Three-blade propeller
Span: 14.63m (48ft 0in)
Length: 9.25m (30ft 4in)
Height: 2.74m (9ft 0in)
Maximum take-off weight: 2313kg (5,100lb)
Maximum speed: 257km/h (160mph)
Economical cruising speed: 209km/h (130mph)
Operational ceiling: 18,000ft
Maximum range: 1252km (778 miles)
Mission range: 777km (483 miles)
Accommodation: One or two crew and up to seven passengers
Warload: None.
First flown: 16 August 1947
Entered service: 1952

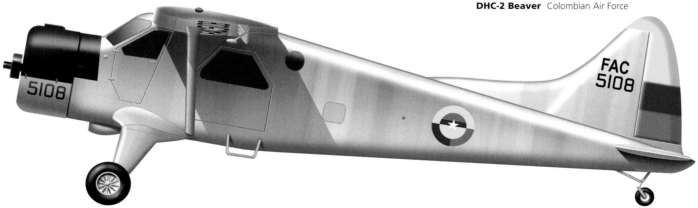

DHC-2 Beaver Colombian Air Force

De Havilland Canada DHC-4 Caribou

TWIN PISTON-ENGINED STOL TROOP/CARGO TRANSPORT OR CASEVAC AIRCRAFT

DEVELOPMENT

Designed as a STOL-performance replacement for the ubiquitous Douglas DC-3/C-47, the DHC-4 Caribou was evaluated by the US Army in the late 1950s as the YAC-1. It combined the payload of the DC-3 with the STOL performance of the earlier single-engined DHC Beaver and Otter. The basic version was subsequently ordered as the AC-1 (later CV-2A) tactical airlifter, and 159 were delivered – becoming the largest type ever operated by the US Army. The US Secretary of Defense had to waive a restriction which limited US Army aircraft to fixed-wing aircraft with an empty weight less than 2,268kg (6,720lb). A higher gross weight version designated CV-2A had entered service by the time the US became embroiled in the Vietnam War, and here the aircraft's ability to deliver light infantry and light vehicles to forward landing strips was utilised. In 1967, the remaining aircraft were transferred to the US Air Force and redesignated as C-7As. The Canadian Armed Forces operated the type (as the CC-108) in limited numbers, but these were replaced once the Buffalo entered service. The STOL capabilities of the DHC-4 won favour with several other air forces, particularly for operations in rugged or mountainous terrain such as Colombia, Cameroon, Malaysia and Oman. Two were loaned to the Indian Air Force by the USAF. Australian Caribous also saw extensive service in Vietnam. Production of all variants totalled 307 by the time production ended in 1973. Relatively few reached the civil market.

CURRENT SERVICE

The main operator is the RAAF, whose aircraft serve in the transport role with Nos 35 and 38 Squadrons,

DHC-4 Caribou Royal Australian Air Force

86 Wing at Townsville and Amberley. The Malaysian Air Force introduced the type in 1966 and a dozen still serve with No 1 Squadron, Markas Banduan Udara at Kuching, but are due to be replaced by CN235s. The Costa Rican Air Force received three, but only one remains airworthy with Base Aérea No 2 at San José – Juan Santamaria International Airport.

SPECIAL FEATURES

The DHC-4 features a shoulder-mounted high-aspect ratio wing with full-span double slotted flaps giving the aircraft an exceptional STOL performance. It is well suited to demanding conditions, and the STOL performance (unmatched by few types, previously or

since) saw it operate into areas otherwise considered the domain of the helicopter. The main (retractable) landing gear was designed to be robust enough for operations from rough strips, and a rear ramp facilitates rear-loading of troops or vehicles and can also be opened in flight for dispatching paratroops.

VARIANTS

The **DHC-4/CV-2A** was the original transport version for the US Army; the **DHC-4A/CV-2B** supplanted it on the production line from aircraft No 24 and was the higher gross weight version and main export variant.

DHC-4 Caribou Royal Australian Air Force

TECHNICAL DATA

De Havilland Canada DHC-4A Caribou

Powerplants: Two Pratt & Whitney R-2000-7M2 Twin Wasp radial piston engines
Developing: 1,081kW (1,450hp)
Driving: Three-blade propellers
Span: 29.15m (95ft 7.5in)
Length: 22.13m (72ft 7in)
Height: 9.70m (31ft 9in)
Maximum weight: 14197kg (31,300lb)
Maximum speed: 347km/h (216mph)
Cruise speed: 293km/h (182mph)
Operational ceiling: 24,800ft
Maximum range: 2103km (1,307 miles)
Mission range: 780km (484 miles)
Accommodation: Two crew and 32 troops or 22 stretcher cases
Payload: 3,636kg (8,000lb)
Warload: None.
First flown: 30 July 1958
Entered service: 1960 (US Army)

De Havilland Canada DHC-5 Buffalo

TWIN-TURBOPROP STOL TROOP/CARGO TRANSPORT AIRCRAFT

CC-115 Buffalo Canadian Armed Forces

TECHNICAL DATA

De Havilland Canada DHC-5A Buffalo

Powerplants: Two General Electric CT64-820-1 turboprops
Developing: 2,278kW (3,055shp)
Driving: Three-blade propellers
Span: 29.26m (96ft 0in)
Length: 24.08m (79ft 0in)
Height: 8.73m (28ft 8in)
Maximum weight: 22,315kg (49,200lb)
Maximum speed: 435km/h (271mph)
Cruise speed: 335km/h (208mph)
Operational ceiling: 30,000ft
Maximum range: 3,493km (2,171 miles)
Mission range: 815km (507 miles) with maximum payload
Accommodation: Two crew, plus loadmaster, and up to 41 fully-equipped troops
Payload: 6,279kg (13,843lb) including trucks, artillery or palleted loads
Warload: None
First flown: 9 April 1964
Entered service: 1968

DEVELOPMENT

In response to a 1962 US Army requirement for a turboprop-powered replacement for the DHC-4 Caribou, de Havilland Canada evolved and refined the design into the DHC-5 Buffalo. Originally termed Caribou II, the Buffalo was larger in terms of length, span and internal volume, with a T-tail, and did not feature its predecessor's anhedral centre-section. It was designed to meet the requirement to carry loads such as the Pershing missile, a 105mm howitzer or a 15cwt truck. The most important change, however, was the introduction of the General Electric CT64 turbine engine which more than doubled the available power. In 1967, the US Army's large fixed-wing assets were transferred to the USAF (as C-8s) which had no requirement for the DHC-5. Production orders were received from the Canadian Armed Forces which acquired 15 under the designation CC-115, and Brazil with 18 C-115Bs. The only significant development was

the DHC-5D with improved General Electric CT64-820-4 engines which prompted renewed interest and orders including ten examples for Egypt featuring LAPES (low-altitude parachute extraction system) and DHC reopened the Buffalo production line in 1974. A total of 123 DHC-5s had been delivered when the production line was shut down in 1986.

CURRENT SERVICE

The Canadian Armed Forces continues to operate six CC-115 Buffalos in the Search and Rescue role. Other countries retaining the type for transport and training purposes are Brazil, Cameroon, Congo (Zaïre), Ecuador, Egypt, Indonesia, Kenya, Peru, Sudan, Tanzania, Togo and Zambia.

SPECIAL FEATURES

Full-span double slotted flaps and powerful engines provide excellent STOL performance. The large tailfin,

rudder and T-tail configuration help ensure adequate directional stability. The Buffalo's rugged twin-wheel retractable tricycle undercarriage allows rough-field operations.

VARIANTS

The **DHC-5A/CC-115** was the original production variant, and the **DHC-5D** was the more powerful CT64-820-4 engined version with higher maximum take-off weight. A proposed version with Rolls-Royce Dart turboprops did not materialise.

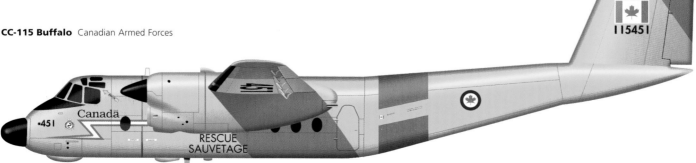

CC-115 Buffalo Canadian Armed Forces

De Havilland Canada DHC-6 Twin Otter

TWIN-TURBOPROP STOL UTILITY TRANSPORT OR SAR AIRCRAFT

DHC-6 Twin Otter 300 Royal Norwegian Air Force

TECHNICAL DATA

De Havilland Canada DHC-6 Twin Otter Series 300 (landplane)

Powerplants: Two Pratt & Whitney Canada PT6A-27 turboprops
Developing: 462kW (620hp)
Driving: Three-blade propellers
Span: 19.81m (65ft 0in)
Length: 15.77m (51ft 9in)
Height: 5.94m (19ft 6in)
Maximum take-off weight: 5670kg (12,500lb)
Maximum cruising speed: 338km/h (210mph)
Operational ceiling: 26,700ft
Mission range: 1297km (806 miles) with a 1134kg (2,500-lb) payload
Accommodation: Two crew and up to 20 passengers
Maximum payload: 1941kg (4,280lb)
Warload: None
First flown: 20 May 1965
Entered service: 1966

DEVELOPMENT

The success of de Havilland Canada's DHC-3 Otter STOL utility transport aircraft in the 1950s prompted DHC, in the early 1960s, to develop a twin-turboprop powered successor based on the same high-lift wing and principles of cost-effectiveness, reliability and the ability to operate from short unprepared strips. Launched as the DHC-6 Series 100 (of which 115 were built) with a distinctive short nose and PT6A-20 engines, the Twin Otter was initially more successful in the civilian market, with the sole military operator being the Canadian Armed Forces, which received eight CC-138s for the SAR role. The following Series 200 featured a lengthened nose (increasing baggage capacity) and attracted small numbers of military orders before production switched to the definitive Series 300. The DHC-6-300 has the more powerful PT6A-27 engines, increasing maximum take-off weight by 10%, and has been by far the most successful of the Twin Otter series, attracting a host of military

customers – including the USA, which ordered the type as the UV-18. Military operators employ the Twin Otter in a variety of roles including SAR, maritime patrol, troop transport, air ambulance or for paradropping.

CURRENT SERVICE

The DHC-6 has seen fairly wide use with air forces and government agencies. Military operators currently operating the type include Argentina, Australia, Benin, Canada, Chile, Colombia, Ecuador, Ethiopia, France, Haiti, Norway, Paraguay, Peru, Sudan and the United States (USAF and US Army).

SPECIAL FEATURES

The DHC-6 retains the Otter's basic high-aspect ratio high-mounted wing with full-span double-slotted flaps and ailerons, which can be drooped simultaneously with the flaps to enhance STOL performance. The fixed tricycle undercarriage gear can have optional

floats or ski installations, as well as the standard low pressure tyres for rough terrain. High-capacity brakes are fitted, and the rugged airframe coupled with its STOL performance gives the Twin Otter a 'fly from anywhere' capability.

VARIANTS

The original production version was the **DHC-6-100**. The subsequent **DHC-6-200** model featured a longer nose that provided greater cargo capacity. The main production version, the **DHC-6-300**, is fitted with more powerful engines, giving increased performance and payload. Some have been fitted with an expendable fabric membrane tank holding 1,818 litres (400 Imp gal) for water bombing fire-fighting operations.

DHC-6 Twin Otter 300 French Air Force

De Havilland Canada DHC-7 Dash 7

FOUR-TURBOPROP STOL TRANSPORT, MARITIME PATROL OR SURVEILLANCE AIRCRAFT

De Havilland Canada DHC-7 Dash 7 Venezuelan Navy

DEVELOPMENT

The Dash 7 was developed primarily for the civilian market as a medium capacity STOL airliner for smaller regional airlines. In keeping with the rest of the DHC family, the Dash 7 was endowed with a high-mounted high-lift wing. Four PT6A engines are mounted on the wing, and feature large-diameter propellers that help to reduce propeller tip noise. The Canadian Armed Forces operated two CC-132s (a 30-seat VIP aircraft and mixed cargo/passenger transport) with No 412 Squadron at Lahr in Germany in the 1980s, before they were replaced in service by the Dash 8. The only remaining operators are the Venezuelan Navy, which has a single DHC-7-100 modified for maritime patrol duties, and the US Army, which has six highly secretive aircraft used for drug interdiction, battlefield surveillance and reconnaissance under the Airborne Reconnaissance Low (ARL) programme. These six aircraft (variously designated as O-5A, OE-5B and RC-7) were acquired from civilian operators and continue to be operated with civilian registrations and liveries, with discrete US Army titles. They are fitted with a wide variety of sensors, avionics and intelligence gathering equipment and are flown under a mission configuration known as 'Crazyhawk'. All six are due to be brought up to full RC-7B multi-mission capability. At one time, USAF Dash 7s provided support for the strategic radar base at Thule, Greenland.

CURRENT SERVICE

US Army (six); Venezuelan Navy (one) with Grupo de Transporte Táctico at 'Simon Bolivar' International Airport at Maiqueti.

SPECIAL FEATURES

Four turboprop engines allow for good engine-out safety during STOL operations. The high-mounted high aspect ratio wing is equipped with large-area double slotted flaps and also has a pair of inboard spoilers for lift-dumping. The large propellers are driven at lower speeds, keeping both engine and propeller noise to a minimum. The Dash 7 features a circular fuselage and T-tail, and its STOL performance, that includes a very steep approach, allows it to operate from many small airfields denied to aircraft of comparable size.

VARIANTS

The **Dash 7 Series 100** was the main production passenger carrying model; the **Dash 7 Series 101** was the cargo/passenger carrying model, with a large access door in the forward port fuselage; the **Dash 7 Series 150** was the late production model with increased weights and increased fuel capacity; two **CC-132** military models were built for the Canadian Armed Forces for VIP/transport duties. It was also offered by the manufacturer as the **Dash 7R Ranger** reconnaissance and surveillance aircraft, but this was not put into production.

TECHNICAL DATA

De Havilland Canada DHC-7 Dash 7 Series 100

Powerplants: Four Pratt & Whitney Canada PT6A-50 turboprops
Developing: 835kW (1,120shp)
Driving: Four-blade propellers
Span: 28.35m (93ft 0in)
Length: 24.58m (80ft 7.5in)
Height: 7.98m (26ft 2in)
Maximum weight: 19,958kg (44,000lb)
Cruising speed: 428km/h (266mph)
Operational ceiling: 21,000ft
Mission range: 2,168km (1,347 miles)
Accommodation: Two crew and up to 50 passengers
Maximum payload: 5,284kg (11,600lb)
Warload: None
First flown: 27 March 1975
Entered service: 1978 (Canadian Armed Forces)

DHC-7 **Dash 7** United States Army

Dornier Do 27

Dornier Do 27/C-127 Spanish Air Force

DEVELOPMENT

The first post-WW2 aircraft to be designed and built by the Dornier company was actually designed by Claudius Dornier in Madrid working in the Oficinas Tecnicas Dornier. The Do 27 was developed from the Do 25 prototype which first flew in June 1954 and was powered by a 112kW (150hp) ENMA Tigre G4B piston engine. To improve performance and load carrying ability the 205kW (275hp) Lycoming GO-480-B1A6 engine was fitted and the new aircraft was designated Do 27. Production was initially undertaken by CASA in Spain and the first order was for 50 aircraft for the Spanish Air Force, designated C-127s, to fulfill a requirement for a light communications aircraft. Following their success in Spain, the German Army and Air Force ordered the Do 27 in large numbers. Production in Germany was initiated in 1956, and of the 571 examples produced at the Dornier factory, over 400 were placed into service by the Luftwaffe, including a number of dual control Do 27B-1s which were used for training purposes, but which are now

all retired. At one time, Do 27s were in service with around 20 air arms (many being ex-German Air Force aircraft), including Portugal, Nigeria, Israel, Sudan and Turkey. Other second-hand Do 27s were delivered to a number of African nations. Most Do 27s were retired in the 1980s, leaving just a handful of operators.

CURRENT SERVICE

The Spanish Air Force currently operates around 30 C-127/Do 27s on general communications and station 'hack' duties. The only other remaining operators are Guinea-Bissau with two Do 27As, and Burundi with a single Do 27Q-4.

SPECIAL FEATURES

With a long high-aspect ratio wing and a good power-to-weight ratio, the Do 27 has excellent short-field performance, and a large fixed tailwheel-type undercarriage allows operations from unprepared strips. The cockpit canopy hinges in the centre to allow port and starboard entry and the large expanse of

glass allows good all-round visibility. The Do 27's STOL performance was ideal for use in underdeveloped countries with mountains and rough terrain.

VARIANTS

Do 27/C-127 – the CASA production version for the Spanish Air Force; **Do 27A-1** – initial basic Dornier military variant; **Do 27A-3** – increased gross weight version; **Do 27A-4** – with wide track undercarriage and increased gross weight; **Do 27B-1** – dual control version for German forces; **Do 27B-2** – higher gross weight and dual control; **Do 27H** – was based on the A-4 with a more powerful engine and three-blade propeller; **Do 27Q-5** – fitted with a 200kW (270hp) GSO-480-B1A6 engine driving a two-blade propeller.

TECHNICAL DATA

Dornier Do 27H-2

Powerplant: One Lycoming GSO-480-B1B6 piston engine
Developing: 255kW (340hp)
Driving: Three-blade propeller
Span: 12.00m (39ft 5in)
Length: 9.60m (31ft 6in)
Height: 2.80m (9ft 2in)
Maximum weight: 1,848kg (4,065lb)
Maximum speed: 245km/h (152mph)
Cruising speed: 180km/h (112mph)
Operational ceiling: 22,000ft
Range: 1,360km (845 miles)
Accommodation: Pilot and up tp six passengers. Can be configured for stretchers or freight.
Warload: Usually none
First flown: June 1954
Entered service: Mid-1950s

Dornier Do 27/C-127 Spanish Air Force

Dornier Do 28D/128 Skyservant

Do 28D Skyservant Hellenic Air Force

DEVELOPMENT

The Dornier Do 28D Skyservant was a development of the Do 28, which flew in 1959 and was itself a twin-engined evolution of the Do 27. Although bearing a family resemblance, the Do 28D was actually a very different aircraft incorporating a host of changes from the Do 28. A larger flat-sided fuselage allowed a greater capacity of cargo and was readily adaptable for any number of specialised roles. New systems, avionics and equipment were also fitted, as was a new larger and more squared-off tail unit. The initial production Do 28D-1s had the wingspan increased by 50cm (1ft 7in) over that of the prototypes and 54 were built, including four VIP versions for the Luftwaffe, before production shifted to the Do 28D-2 model, which became the main production version and was adopted by air arms around the world. Improvements to the Do 28D-2 included a lengthened internal cabin and increased fuel capacity. The biggest operator was the Luftwaffe, which operated over 100 examples for light transport and communications duties. Other significant operators included the Bundesmarine, which

operated 20 examples, including two Skyservants that were converted to carry SLAR, IR/UV scanners and cameras in the pollution control role, designated as Do 282OUs. In the 1980s, Dornier introduced the Model 128-2 which, having incorporated a number of minor refinements, sold in small numbers, and the Model 128-6 Turbo-Skyservant (designated Do 28D-5X) fitted with 300kW (400shp) Pratt & Whitney Canada PT6A-110 turboprops. Nigeria and Cameroon were the only customers for the Turbo-Skyservant – the latter's being fitted with a MEL Marea search radar in a chin installation for maritime patrol.

CURRENT SERVICE

The type serves with the air arms of Benin, Cameroon, Greece, Israel, Kenya, Morocco, Niger, Nigeria, Peru, Yugoslavia and Zambia.

SPECIAL FEATURES

The Skyservant retains the same wing layout as the Do 27 and Do 28, giving excellent STOL performance. Large cabin doors allow bulky loads to be carried.

A transverse beam through the lower front fuselage carries the twin engines, beneath which the faired mainwheels of the fixed tricycle undercarriage are mounted.

VARIANTS

Do 28D-1 – the original production version: **Do 28D-2** – the improved production version with greater fuel capacity and gross weight; **Do 28D-2T** – conversion of Do 28D-2 with TIGO-540 supercharged engines, applied to all remaining German examples in the early 1980s; **Do 28D-2OU** – Pollution control modification; **Model 128-2** – Do 28D-2 with more modern equipment and avionics; **Model 128-6 (D-5X) Turbo-Skyservant** – turbine-engined variant with improved performance and maximum take-off weight – 16 supplied to Peru.

TECHNICAL DATA

Dornier Do 28D-2 Skyservant

Powerplants: Two Textron Lycoming IGSO-540-A1E piston engines
Developing: 283kW (380hp)
Driving: Three-blade propellers
Span: 15.50m (50ft 10.25in)
Length: 12.00m (39ft 4.5in)
Height: 3.90m (12ft 10in)
Maximum weight: 3650kg (8,047lb)
Maximum speed: 320km/h (199mph)
Cruise speed: 230km/h (143mph)
Operational ceiling: 24,280ft
Range: 1810km (1,124 miles)
Accommodation: One or two pilots and up to 13 troops
Maximum payload: 805kg (1,774lb)
Warload: None
First flown: 23 February 1966; April 1978 (D-5X)
Entered service: 1968

Do 28D Skyservant Royal Moroccan Air Force

Dornier 228

TWIN-TURBOPROP UTILITY TRANSPORT, MARITIME PATROL AND SURVEILLANCE AIRCRAFT

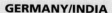

Dornier 228-212 German Navy

TECHNICAL DATA

Dornier 228 Maritime Patrol Version A

Powerplants: Two Garrett (Allied Signal) TPE331-5-252D turboprops
Developing: 533ekW (715shp)
Driving: Four-blade propellers
Span: 16.97m (55ft 8in)
Length: 15.04m (49ft 4.2in)
Height: 4.86m (15ft 11.5in)
Maximum take-off weight: 6,400kg (14,110lb)
Maximum speed: 432km/h (267mph)
Economical cruising speed: 305km/h (190mph)
Operational ceiling: 28,000ft
Range: 1740km (1,982 miles)
Maximum endurance: 10 hours
Accommodation: Two crew and up to 19 passengers (three with a radar operator for maritime patrol version)
Warload: None
Maximum payload: 2117kg (4,667lb)
First flown: 28 March 1981 (228-100); 9 May 1981 (228-200)
Entered service: 1983

DEVELOPMENT

Utilising the same fuselage cross-section as the Do 28D Skyservant, the Dornier 228 was initially designated Do 28E. The aircraft is, however, a much more modern design featuring a new, more efficient supercritical 'crescent' wing, turboprop engines, a retractable tricycle undercarriage, and modern systems and equipment. The 228 has been produced in two major variants – the 228-100 and the longer-fuselage 228-200 – as a regional airliner, light military transport and in various maritime patrol configurations. Since 1996, when Fairchild acquired Dornier, all production of the 228 has been undertaken by HAL in India – who have built the type under licence since 1991 – in what has been by far the most important military contract for the type. The Indian Air Force currently operates two squadrons of HAL 228-201s (capable of carrying 19 passengers or freight) in the transport role. In addition, the Indian Navy operates 15 HAL 228-101 Maritime Patrol Versions fitted with surveillance radar, sensors and probably short-range air-to-surface missiles. The Indian Coast Guard has also acquired 25 HAL 228-101s, which are used for maritime patrol of Indian territorial waters and for SAR. Dornier has incorporated a wide variety of different sensors and radars to meet particular customer needs and both -100s and -200s are used in a wide variety of roles. The German Marineflieger operates two 228-212s specially modified for pollution control carrying Forward-Looking and Sideways-Looking Airborne Radar (FLAR, SLAR), laser sensors, IR/UV sensors, video and still cameras and a live datalink. Finland and Thailand have SLAR-equipped versions for maritime patrol, while other roles include VIP transport, troop/cargo transport and policing duties.

CURRENT SERVICE

228s equip the air arms or paramilitary police forces of the following countries: Bhutan, Cape Verde, Finland, Germany, India, Italy, Malawi, Maldives, Mauritius, Niger, Nigeria, Oman and Thailand.

SPECIAL FEATURES

The improved 'crescent' wing gives more economical performance compared to the earlier Do 28D. Its box-like fuselage gives the 228 good internal capacity for a range of internal layouts. The Maritime Patrol version is available with MEL Marea II search radar and linescan equipment.

VARIANTS

228-100 – the shorter fuselage production version capable of carrying 15 passengers: **228-200** – the longer fuselage production version capable of carrying 19 passengers. **228 Maritime Patrol** versions are based on either the -100 or -200 airframe and are fitted with customers' choice of sensors and radar.

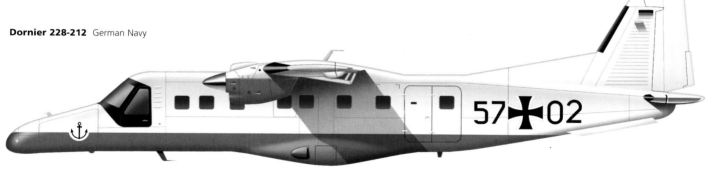

Dornier 228-212 German Navy

Douglas DC-3/C-47 & Basler Turbo Dakota

TWIN PISTON- OR TURBOPROP-POWERED TROOP/CARGO TRANSPORT

Douglas C-47A Paraguayan Air Force

TECHNICAL DATA

Douglas C-47A

Powerplants: Two Pratt & Whitney R-1830-92 Twin Wasp radial piston engines
Developing: 895kW (1,200hp)
Driving: Three-blade propellers
Span: 28.96m (95ft 0in)
Length: 19.66m (64ft 6in)
Height: 5.16m (16ft 11.5in)
Maximum weight: 13,290kg (29,300lb)
Maximum speed: 346km/h (215mph)
Cruising speed: 266km/h (165mph)
Operational ceiling: 21,900ft
Maximum range: 2,430km (1,510 miles)
Accommodation: Two crew and up to 28 fully-equipped troops
Maximum payload: 2994kg (6,600lb)
First flown: 17 December 1935
Entered service: October 1938

DEVELOPMENT

One of the most famous aircraft of all time, and the only pre-World War II design still in military service, the DC-3/C-47 family re-defined air transport and was the first truly modern monoplane airliner to enter service. Although designed for the civilian market, military applications for the aircraft were readily apparent. A number of DC-2s (and subsequently DC-3s) were 'militarised' and entered service with the USAAC. By the time that the USA was drawn into World War II in December 1941, plans for a definitive military version, designated C-47, had already been laid and the first production example was delivered in February 1942. Production continued until 1946, by which time 10,655 of the DC-3/C-47 family had been built, with the vast majority going to the USAAF and the US Navy. The aircraft was used in every wartime theatre in numerous different roles leading to a plethora of designations. In the USSR, it was built in quantity as the Lisunov Li-2. The most important basic variants were the C-47 basic troop or cargo transport, the C-53 dedicated troop transport, and the C-117 passenger transport with airline-style seats. The RAF adopted the type as the Dakota and a number of other nations adopted this name during and in the post-war period. During the late 1940s, the USAAF disposed of the

majority of its C-47s and many of the aircraft were purchased by other air arms. In the post-war era, the USAF did develop the dedicated AC-47 gunship, which was used operationally in the Vietnam War. Many hundreds of C-47/DC-3s remained in widespread service into the 1970s, and despite the gradual decline in numbers since that time the type still remains in service with around 20 air arms. The most successful amongst a number of programmes to enhance the performance and prolong the service life of the type were the turboprop installations carried out by Basler Turbo Conversions to produce the Basler Turbo-67. Installation of 1,060kW (1,425shp) Pratt & Whitney PT6A-67R turboprops and lengthening of the fuselage increased the troop capacity to 40 and allowed a 20% increase in payload. The South African Air Force has introduced a similar conversion into service known as the C-47TP Super Dakota.

CURRENT SERVICE

DC-3/C-47s serve in Colombia, Congo, Congo (Zaïre), Dominican Republic, Greece, Guatemala, Haiti, Honduras, Israel, Laos, Madagascar, Mexico, Paraguay, El Salvador, Thailand; Turboprop versions are used by Bolivia, Colombia, Guatemala, Malawi, Mali, El Salvador, South Africa, Thailand.

SPECIAL FEATURES

The all-metal stressed skin design was a revolution when the DC-2, and subsequently the DC-3, entered service prior to World War II. The aircraft's excellent handling, durability and ability to fulfill a wide variety of roles account for the aircraft's ongoing popularity.

VARIANTS

C-47A – basic configuration for the USAAF Skytrain; all production versions were of a similar pattern. Post-war surplus C-47s became the standard equipment of almost all of the world's airlines. This glut of surplus transports severely inhibited the development of new types for many years. The two notable turboprop conversions of the DC-3 are the **Basler Turbo-67** and the **Professional Aviation Jet Prop DC-3**.

SEE ALSO: LISUNOV Li-2

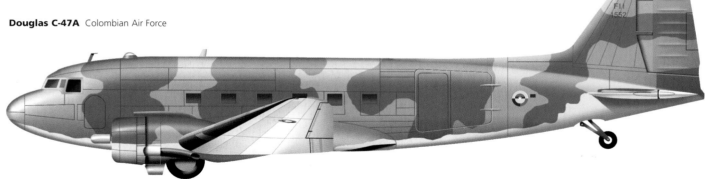

Douglas C-47A Colombian Air Force

Douglas DC-8

FOUR-TURBOJET/TURBOFAN TRANSPORT OR ELECTRONIC WARFARE PLATFORM

Douglas DC-8-72CF French Air Force

DEVELOPMENT

Although launched as a direct competitor to Boeing's revolutionary Model 707, the Douglas DC-8 never sold in the same numbers to airlines, either in the USA or around the world. This trend was also reflected in military sales, with the 707 in its C-135 and E-3 guises being sold in hundreds, whereas only a handful of air arms adopted the DC-8 into service. Containing a typical two-class layout of 120 seats, the DC-8 Series 10 entered airline service in 1959, and the type was subsequently offered with various combinations of engine, fuel capacity and gross weights, culminating in the popular Series 50. To meet the demand for increased capacity, Douglas 'stretched' the airframe to produce the Series 60 which was capable of holding 259 passengers in a single-class layout. The proliferation of fuel-efficient turbofan engines prompted the Series 70, which were Series 60 airframes retrofitted with

CFM56 turbofans replacing the Pratt & Whitney JT3D turbojets. Over 550 DC-8s were built in a number of different variants and two distinct fuselage lengths. The US Navy converted an-ex-airline DC-8-54F with specialised electronic warfare equipment for use as an electronic aggressor on fleet exercises. Designated EC-24A, the aircraft was operated by Raytheon Systems on behalf of the US Navy, and was retired into storage in January 1999. The Armée de L'Air converted a single DC-8-53 SARIGUE for electronic and communications intelligence gathering and this is fitted with SLAR radar and specialised equipment. The aircraft is due to be replaced in this role by a CFM56-powered DC-8-72 during 2000.

CURRENT SERVICE

France has operated a single DC-8-53 SARIGUE since 1977 in the ECM/Elint reconnaissance role at Escuadron Electronique 00.52 'Aubrac' at BA105 Evereux. This features wingtip pods and a dorsal fairing. It also fulfils the tasks of CASSIC. Two re-engined ex-civil airliner DC-8-72CFs are used for long-range transport.

The other remaining operators are the Gabonese government with a single DC-8-73F, and the Peruvian Air Force, whose Presidential squadron operates two VIP-equipped DC-8-62CFs with Escadrille Presidential, Grupo Aéreo de Transporte 8 at Lima-Callao.

SPECIAL FEATURES

The DC-8's fuselage was found to be ideal for cargo/combi operations and the fuselage adaptability was utilised in producing specialised electronic versions. CFM56-powered versions have increased capacity and longer range and are identified by the broader engine intakes.

VARIANTS

DC-8 Series 10 to 50 – short-fuselage production versions available in with cargo or passenger layouts
DC-8 Series 60 – turbojet-powered stretched variant
DC-8 Series 70 – turbofan-powered conversions offering increased gross weight and improved fuel economy. Electronic variants comprise the **EC-24A** threat simulator and **DC-8-54F SARIGUE**.

TECHNICAL DATA

Douglas DC-8 Series 70

Powerplants: Four CFM International CFM56-2-C5 turbofans
Developing: 97.9kN (22,000lb)
Span: 43.41m (142ft 5in)
Length: 57.12m (187ft 5in)
Height: 12.91m (42ft 4in)
Maximum weight: 162,065kg (355,000lb)
Cruising speed: 933km/h (578mph)
Range: 8,950km (5,561 miles)
Accommodation: Flight crew of three and up to 220 passengers in high density configuration.
Warload: None
First flown: 30 May 1958 (DC-8)
Entered service: September 1959 (civil airlines)

Douglas DC-8-62CF Peruvian Air Force

EH Industries EH.101 Merlin

THREE-ENGINED NAVAL AND TRANSPORT HELICOPTER

Merlin HM1 *Royal Navy*

TECHNICAL DATA

EH Industries EH.101 Merlin HM1

Powerplants: Three Rolls-Royce/Turboméca RTM322-01 turboshafts
Developing: 1,724kW (2,312shp)
Driving: Five-blade main and four-blade tail rotors
Main rotor diameter: 18.59m (61ft 0in)
Fuselage length: 22.80m (74ft 9.6in)
Height: 6.65m (21ft 10in)
All up weight: 13,559kg (29,830lb)
Maximum speed: 309km/h (193mph)
Maximum cruise speed: 296km/h (184mph)
Operational ceiling: 15,000ft
Range: 1,853km (1,152 miles)
Endurance: 5 hours on station with maximum weapon load
Accommodation: One or two pilots, observer and acoustic systems operator
Warload: Four homing torpedoes (eg Sting Ray, or Mk 46), or two air-to-surface missiles in the ASV role
First flown: 9 October 1987 (EH.101); 6 December 1995 (first production Merlin HM1)
Entered service: 1998 (HM1 with No 700M NAS, the IFTU)

DEVELOPMENT

EH Industries was formed by Westland Helicopters and Agusta in June 1980 to develop a new anti-submarine warfare helicopter for the Royal Navy and the Italian navy to replace the Sea King. A family of helicopters was to be produced using this design as a basis, which were to include army, navy and civil variants. Nine prototypes were built by the two firms, with PP1, a Westland-built 'generic' airframe, making the type's first flight in October 1987. All prototypes had flown by the end of January 1991. Deliveries began to 700M Naval Air Squadron in the last quarter of 1998, the unit being responsible for the intensive flight trials. The Royal Navy is expecting to get 44 Merlin HM1s, which are due to be upgraded to HM2s with the ability to fire anti-shipping missiles. About half of the HM1s had been delivered by mid-2000. The RAF has ordered 22 Merlin HC3 support helicopters, the first joining No 28 Squadron in autumn 2000. The Italian Navy is due to get eight Series 100 ASW/ASuW helicopters, four more for airborne early warning and four Series

400 utility transports versions. Originally they hoped to get 36 examples. In 1992, the type was selected to replace the Sea King and Labrador in service with the Canadian Armed Forces as the CH-148 and CH-149, but this contract was cancelled a year later. Ironically, Canada later selected the EH.101 as the AW.320 Cormorant to replace the Labradors for a second time, and the first of 15 are due to be delivered from October 2000. A single Series 510 has also been delivered to the Police Department in Tokyo.

CURRENT SERVICE

Versions are on order or in service with Canada, Italy, and the UK (FAA and RAF).

SPECIAL FEATURES

The Merlin has been designed to land on any naval vessel that can accommodate the smaller Westland Lynx, requiring great agility to accomplish this task. Extra power and safety is provided by the use of its three engines.

VARIANTS

EH.101 – nine prototypes built to prove and develop the various versions for the UK and Italy; **AW.320 Cormorant** – Canadian Labrador replacement, ordered after cancellation of the CH-149 ; **CH-148 Petrel** – Canadian Sea King replacement, order later cancelled; **CH-149 Chimo** – Canadian Labrador replacement, ordered but later cancelled; **Heliliner** - Civil airliner version of the transport EH.101; Italian Navy versions – the Italian Navy has ASW/ASuW, AEW and a utility transport version under development ; **Merlin HM1** – FAA anti-submarine warfare version; **Merlin HM2** – FAA anti-surface vessel capable upgrade of the HM1; **Merlin HC3** – RAF support helicopter version.

Merlin HM1 *Royal Navy*

Embraer EMB-110 Bandeirante/EMB-111 Bandeirulha

TWIN-TURBOPROP TRANSPORT/UTILITY, SPECIAL MISSIONS AND MARITIME PATROL AIRCRAFT

P-95 Bandeirulha Brazilian Air Force

TECHNICAL DATA

Embraer EMB-111A (P-95/P-95A) Bandeirulha

Powerplants: Two Pratt & Whitney Canada PT6A-34 turboprops
Developing: 559 kW (750 shp)
Driving: Three-blade propellers
Span: 15.95m (52ft 4in)
Length: 14.91m (48ft 11in)
Height: 4.91m (16ft 1in)
Maximum weight: 7,000kg (15,432lb)
Maximum speed: 434km/h (270mph)
Cruise speed: 352km/h (218mph)
Operational ceiling: 25,500ft
Maximum range: 2,945km (1,830 miles)
Mission range: up to 2,280km (1,417 miles)
Endurance: 5 to 6 hours
Accommodation: Pilot and co-pilot, seating for up to five mission crew including radar/radio operators and observers
Warload: Four underwing pylons/weapons stations (up to 1,000kg (2,205lb) capacity) for eight 5in HVAR rockets or up to four rocket pods containing 2.75in FFAR rockets, small bombs, smoke grenades or flares. Ventral fuselage outlet for smoke markers, flares or chaff. One starboard wing pylon can be replaced by a wing leading edge-mounted 50 million candlepower searchlight.
First flown: 26 October 1968 (YC-95); 15 August 1977 (prototype EMB-111)
Entered service: February 1973 (C-95); 11 April 1978 (EMB-111)

DEVELOPMENT

Originally designed by the Brazilian Air Ministry's technical department under Frenchman Max Holste, the Bandeirante (Pioneer) became an Embraer project when that company was formed in 1969. The first prototype YC-95 had flown in October 1968, and the newly-designated EMB-110 has since enjoyed considerable success in military and civil operation. The first production short-fuselage EMB-110 flew in August 1972. The type entered Brazilian Air Force service in February 1973 as the C-95; stretched C-95A (EMB-110K1) cargo/transports, C-95B (EMB-110P1K) convertible transports, EC-95 (EMB-110A) navaids calibration aircraft, R-95 (EMB-110B) reconnaissance/survey aircraft, SC-95B (EMB-110P1K) SAR aircraft, and more recently C-95C transports, have all also served with the Brazilian Air Force. Some models have also been exported. Continuing development led to the EMB-111 Bandeirante Patrulha (P-95 Bandeirulha in Brazilian service) which first flew in August 1977. This armed maritime and coastal patrol model has also seen limited export success, and two Brazilian Air Force P-95s were loaned to Argentina in 1982 during the Falkland Islands conflict. Bandeirante production ceased in the early 1990's, when some 500 EMB-110/EMB-111 of all models (civil and military) had been built.

CURRENT SERVICE

The Brazilian Air Force's very active Bandeirante fleet

numbers well over one hundred examples. Various transport squadrons operate the type including 1°/15° GAv at Campo Grande in south-western Brazil; SAR SC-95Bs also operate from Campo Grande with 2°/10° GAv. The R-95 Bandeirantes fly with 1°/6° GAv at Recife. The Brazilian Air Force's P-95 fleet serves with 1° GAE, 1°/7° GAv at Salvador, 2°/7° GAv at Florianópolis, and 3°/7° GAv at Belém. The Brazilian Army also operates three transport C-95s. Transport Bandeirantes are additionally flown by the air forces of Colombia, Gabon, and Uruguay (plus a survey/reconnaissance example), by the Chilean Navy, and a modified patrol model with the Cape Verde Coast Guard. EMB-111 Bandeirante Patrulhas are operated by the Chilean Navy and the Gabonese Air Force.

SPECIAL FEATURES

The mainly all-metal, unpressurised Bandeirante has various possible seating arrangements depending on mission requirements and specific model. Continuing development saw the aircraft gradually grow in size and available power compared to the original YC-95 of 1968. Later examples of the Bandeirante have a dihedral horizontal tail.

VARIANTS

The **C-95A** and **C-95B** transport/cargo Bandeirantes have a payload capacity of 1,650kg (3,638lb) and a rear cargo door. The survey/reconnaissance **R-95** has a

large under-fuselage camera fairing; the SAR **SC-95B** carries medical crew/equipment, up to six stretchers, can air-drop emergency supplies, and has domed fuselage windows for greater visual search capability. The **EMB-111 Bandeirulha** has a bulbous nose that contains search radar (AIL (Cutler-Hammer/Eaton) AN/APS-128), and avionics that are more sophisticated than its military transport and civilian counterparts; it also has wingtip fuel tanks for increased range.

C-95B Bandeirante Brazilian Air Force

Embraer EMB-120/VC-97 Brasilia

TWIN-TURBOPROP VIP TRANSPORT AIRCRAFT

VC-97 Brasilia Brazilian Air Force

DEVELOPMENT

Success with the EMB-110 Bandeirante in the civil commuter airliner market prompted EMBRAER, in the late 1970s, to begin design work on a much improved and higher capacity development. Finalised as a twin-turboprop low-wing design, the EMB-120 utilised a semi-monocoque fuselage and a T-tail and could carry up to 30 passengers with a flight deck crew of two. The aircraft received Brazilian certification in May 1985 and the first delivery was made to a US commuter airline the following month. It became one of the first of the 1980s 'new generation' of commuter aircraft, designed for two-crew operations. Despite being undeniably successful in the commuter airline market, the Brasilia failed to emulate the military sales of the EMB-110/111 Bandeirante family and has

so far only attracted one military customer. Five VIP transport versions were delivered to the Brazilian Air Force between 1987 and 1988 as VC-97s. The aircraft, basically the equivalent of the EMB-110RT, features a special VIP luxury interior layout. One of the VC-97s was destroyed in a training accident in 1988.

CURRENT SERVICE

The Brazilian Air Force has four VC-97s (EMB-120RTs) with 6 Esquadrão de Transporte Aéreo Regional at Brasilia AB.

SPECIAL FEATURES

The Brasilia's low-mounted unswept wing and high-mounted swept T-tail bestowed much improved performance over the earlier EMB-110 Bandeirante.

A distinctive fin fillet gives the aircraft good lateral stability. Weather radar and emergency locator transmitters are fitted as standard.

VARIANTS

The **EMB-120** is the basic original version; the extended range **EMB-120ER**, **EMB-120 Combi**, **EMB-120 Convertible** and **EMB-120ER Advanced** subsequently followed. The planned **EMB-120AEW** and **EMB-120SR** versions were dropped in 1996 when the EMB-145 (described separately) was chosen as the platform for its Amazon Surveillance System programme.

EMB-120 Brasilia Brazilian Air Force

TECHNICAL DATA

Embraer EMB-120RT (VC-97) Brasilia

Powerplants: Two Pratt & Whitney Canada PW118 or PW118A turboprops
Developing: 1,342kW (1,800shp)
Driving: Four-blade propellers
Span: 19.78m (64ft 10.75in)
Length: 20.07m (65ft 10in)
Height: 6.35m (20ft 10in)
All up weight: 11,990kg (26,433lb)
Maximum speed: 606km/h (377mph)
Maximum cruise speed: 555km/h (345mph)
Operational ceiling: 32,000ft
Range: 1,575km (979 miles)
Accommodation: Two crew and up to 30 passengers or 6-12 passengers with VIP interior
First flown: 27 July 1983
Entered service: June 1985 (civil); 1987 (VC-97)

Embraer EMB-121 Xingu

TWIN-TURBOPROP LIGHT TRANSPORT AND MULTI-ENGINE TRAINER

EMB-121AN Xingu French Navy

TECHNICAL DATA

Embraer EMB-121A Xingu I

Powerplants: Two Pratt & Whitney Canada
PT6A-28 turboprops
Developing: 507kW (680shp)
Driving: Three-blade propellers
Span: 14.45m (47ft 5in)
Length: 12.25m (40ft 2.25in)
Height: 4.74m (15ft 6.5in)
Maximum weight: 5,670kg (12,500lb)
Maximum speed: 450km/h (280mph)
Cruise speed: 376km/h (234mph)
Operational ceiling: 26,000ft
Maximum range: 2,352km (1,461 miles)
Mission range: 1,666km (1,035 miles)
Endurance: approximately 4.5hr
Accommodation: Pilot and co-pilot, seating for
six to nine passengers
Warload: None
First flown: 10 October 1976 (Xingu I);
4 September 1981 (Xingu II)
Entered service: 1978/1979 (Brazil); 1982 (France)

DEVELOPMENT

The success of the EMB-110 Bandeirante prompted Embraer to evolve the type's basic design into a family of transports using a similar wing and power source but with different fuselage sizes. The most successful of these initially planned developments was the smaller EMB-121 Xingu. It first flew in October 1976, but development problems delayed certification. The Brazilian Air Force ordered six examples and several of the early production Xingus were delivered from 1978 onwards. Known as the VU-9, they flew on VIP transport and liaison duties with the GTE and the 6° ETA. By far the largest single military user has been France, which ordered the type in 1981 as a liaison aircraft and multi-engine pilot trainer in preference to competing US designs. Twenty five were ordered for the French Air Force, and 16 for the French Navy, although 43 serial numbers have been noted for French-operated Xingus, possibly suggesting two additional acquisitions from elsewhere. The first French Air Force examples were delivered early in 1982. The Brazilian Air Force later acquired several further Xingus, sometimes called EC-9. A developed Xingu version, the EMB-121A1 Xingu II was marketed by Embraer and first flew in September 1981 although it is not clear if any of the military deliveries were to

this standard or were upgraded as such (most if not all the French aircraft were not). A stretched Xingu III proposal was never proceeded with. Some 105 Xingus of all types were eventually built.

CURRENT SERVICE

French Air Force and Navy Xingus have served with a variety of second-line transport and liaison units over the years, but the principal French user has been and remains the French Air Force's multi-engine transport pilot training unit, the Ecole de l'Aviation de Transport 00.319 at Bourges-Avord. This unit additionally recently received several Xingus from the French Navy, whose own Xingu fleet has been reshuffled in recent times; the most recent Navy second-line unit to use the type being 2S at Lann-Bihoué, with 28F expected to form on the Xingu and Nord 262E at Hyères. Xingus continue to serve with the Brazilian Air Force's 6° ETA at Brasilia, and as required with the GTE (government VIP and transport unit) also at Brasilia.

SPECIAL FEATURES

The diminutive Xingu has a pressurised fuselage much shorter than the Bandeirante, with the Xingu II being certificated for single-pilot operation. Up to nine passenger seats can be installed although a more

normal arrangement is for six seats; the aircraft is well suited to liaison and general VIP transport duties over comparatively short distances.

VARIANTS

The **Xingu II** has more powerful PT6A-135 turboprops and four-bladed propellers plus increased fuel capacity. Operationally, the Brazilian VIP Xingus have a special internal cabin layout, and the French Air Force's multi-engine trainers are equipped as school aircraft for their pilot training role with full dual controls, in conjunction with a ground-based Xingu simulator at Avord; they have customer-specified military avionics including VOR-ILS, TACAN, radio altimeter and weather radar.

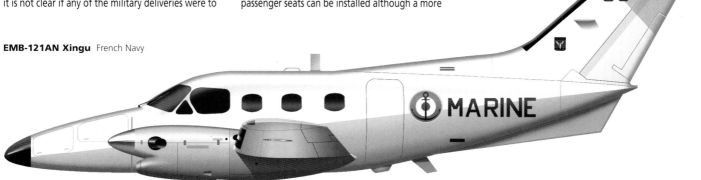

EMB-121AN Xingu French Navy

Embraer EMB-145 & ERJ-135

TWIN-TURBOFAN SPECIAL MISSIONS AIRCRAFT AND VIP TRANSPORT

Embraer R-99A Brazilian Air Force

TECHNICAL DATA

Embraer EMB-145SA

Powerplants: Two Rolls-Royce Allison AE3007A turbofans
Thrust: 33.0kN (7,426lb st)
Span: 20.04m (65ft 9in)
Length: 29.87m (98ft 0in)
Height: 6.75m (22ft 2in)
All-up weight: 22,600kg (45,415lb)
Maximum cruising speed: 833km/h (516mph)
Operational ceiling: 37,000ft
Maximum range: 2,445km (1,519 miles)
Accommodation: Five-man crew for longer missions comprising pilot, co-pilot and three systems operators
Warload: None
First flown: 4 July 1998 (ERJ-135); 22 May 1999 (EMB-145SA); 17 December 1999 (EMB-145RS)
Entered service: EMB-145 variants currently undergoing trials, set to enter Brazilian Air Force service in 2001; first ERJ-135 delivered to Hellenic Air Force during January 2000

DEVELOPMENT

In 1997, the Brazilian government awarded Embraer a contract to develop special missions variants of its ERJ-145 regional jet for an official requirement. This was called SIVAM – Brazil's Surveillance System for the Amazon, which requires an airborne platform for natural resources surveys, environmental research, border surveillance and to carry out flights in support of Amazonian development. Two such designs have thus far been built, comprising the EMB-145SA, an airborne early warning and control aircraft (designated EMB-145 AEW&C for potential export customers), and the EMB-145RS, for remote sensing operations. The EMB-145SA (AEW&C) has been developed by Embraer in conjunction with Ericsson, who have produced the type's mission equipment. At the centre of this is the Ericsson PS-890 Erieye radar system, which has many different applications: apart from the AEW and the command and control roles, it can undertake several other missions such as SAR co-ordination and maritime

reconnaissance. The Erieye radar can detect aircraft of fighter size at a range of up to 350km, and has an instrumented range of 450km. It also has the ability to vector multiple fighters onto a target, and the aircraft's mission system can be integrated into ground command assets via satellite or radio-based data links. Both the EMB-145RS and SA carry additional COMINT and ELINT equipment. The 3.54m-shorter ERJ-135 was launched by Embraer in September 1997, and the new regional airliner type was certified during 1999. Its first military purchase was by the Hellenic Air Force, who have also ordered an example of the new ECJ-135 Legacy.

CURRENT SERVICE

Five examples of the EMB145-SA (locally designated as the R-99A) and three EMB-145RSs (designated as R-99Bs) have been ordered by the Brazilian Air Force, to be operated by 2/6 Grupo de Aviacao at Anapolis. These will monitor the vast and remote areas of the

Amazon basin for drug trafficking, illegal mining and logging – plus the unauthorised destruction of rain forests. They will also be tasked with providing early warning, air defence and air traffic control facilities. Deliveries should commence in 2001. Meanwhile, the Hellenic Air Force is to procure four EMB-145 AEW&C aircraft for its AWACS requirement; it already has two ERJ-135s on strength with its new VIP Flight, plus an ECJ-135 Legacy on order for the same unit.

SPECIAL FEATURES

Embraer and Ericsson elected to use a dorsal flat plate antenna for the Erieye radar system on the EMB-145SA, in order to reduce aerodynamic drag and allowing for volumetric coverage at all altitudes. This fitment is much the same as that on the Saab 340 AEW&C which also uses the Erieye radar. Its systems can process real-time information, with three operator consoles being situated within the fuselage. The EMB-145RS uses a MacDonald Dettwiler Integrated Radar Imaging System synthetic aperture radar which is mounted in an underfuselage protrusion. Further antennae for the equipment is located under the wing roots.

VARIANTS

Apart from the **EMB-145RS** and **SA (AEW&C)** versions of the ERJ-145, Embraer also offers the **EMB-145MP/ASW** for maritime surveillance. The shorter-fuselage **ERJ-135** is now being marketed as the **ECJ-135 Legacy** for corporate use, this aircraft having been launched in July 2000. Its primary distinguishing feature is the addition of winglets.

Embraer ERJ-135

Embraer EMB-312 Tucano

SINGLE TURBOPROP TWO-SEAT BASIC/ADVANCED AND WEAPONS TRAINER/LIGHT ATTACK AIRCRAFT   **BRAZIL**

EMB-312F Tucano French Air Force

TECHNICAL DATA

Embraer EMB-312 Tucano

Powerplant: One Pratt & Whitney Canada PT6A-25C turboprop
Developing: 559 kW (750 shp)
Driving: three-blade propeller
Span: 11.14m (36ft 6.5in)
Length: 9.86m (32ft 4.25in)
Height: 3.40m (11ft 1.75in)
All-up weight: 3,175kg (7,000lb)
Maximum speed: 448km/h (278mph)
Cruise speed: 411km/h (255mph)
Operational ceiling: 30,000ft
Maximum range: 3,330km (2,069 miles)
Mission range: 1,843km (1,145 miles)
Ferry range: 3,330km (2,069 miles)
Endurance: approximately 5 hours
Accommodation: Instructor and trainee pilot (instructor in rear seat)
Warload: Two weapons attachments beneath each wing of 250 kg (551lb) capacity each, including 7.62mm C2 or similar machine-gun pods, four practice bombs or up to four 250lb Mk81 bombs, seven-round rocket launchers such as LM-37/7A
First flown: 16 August 1980
Entered service: September 1983

DEVELOPMENT

Responding to Brazilian Air Force requirements for a Cessna T-37 replacement, Brazil's indigenous aircraft designer/manufacturer Embraer began studies in 1978 that led to the EMB-312 Tucano (Toucan); the prototype first flew in August 1980. The Brazilian Air Force eventually received 133 T-27 and AT-27 Tucanos from September 1983. Highly successful from the start, the type duly gained export orders for both trainer and armed trainer/light attack examples. In 1983, Egypt ordered Tucanos for itself and Iraq; following delivery of an initial ten Embraer-built complete aircraft from October 1984, local assembly commenced in Egypt by the Arab Organisation for Industrialisation (AOI) at Helwan, with the PT6A engines for these aircraft also assembled in Egypt. Egypt eventually received 54 Tucanos and Iraq 80. Notable export orders included 50 Embraer-built examples for France; licence production also existed in Northern Ireland as the Shorts Tucano (described separately). Total Embraer/AOI Tucano production so far amounts to some 492 examples. A modified Tucano layout was entered unsuccessfully in the 1990s US JPATS trainer competition. The latest development is the EMB-314 (formerly EMB-312H) Super Tucano, an advanced/weapons trainer and light attack aircraft. Brazilian-operated Super Tucano ALX will perform patrol and general aviation aircraft interception/anti-smuggling operations over Brazil's

Amazon Basin within the new SIVAM Amazon surveillance programme, in conjunction with ERJ-145 AEW&C (R-99) surveillance aircraft. The first ALX-configured prototype flew in May 1996 and 99 single-seat A-29 and two-seat AT-29 ALX have been ordered.

CURRENT SERVICE

Brazilian Air Force Tucanos operate with a number of training and light attack units. Significant amongst these is 1° Esquadrão of the Academia da Força Aérea at Pirassununga and its fleet of trainer T-27 Tucanos for advanced flying training. The Brazilian Air Force's aerobatic team, the *Esquadrilha da Fumaça*, is equipped with Tucanos at Pirassununga. The French Air Force's EMB-312F fleet is centred on GI 00.312 of the Ecole de l'Air at Salon de Provence, which received its first Tucanos in 1994/1995. Other current Embraer or AOI-built Tucano operators are Argentina, Colombia, Egypt, Honduras, Iran, Iraq, Peru, and Venezuela.

SPECIAL FEATURES

One of the highest specification and best appointed of current turboprop trainers, the standard trainer Tucano has ejector seats, can be fitted with avionics to suit customer requirement including a gunsight/weapons aiming sight for light strike and weapons training, and has the classic raised tandem rear seat arrangement for increased instructor vision.

VARIANTS

The French **EMB-312F** has unique specification equipment and features, including an increased fatigue life airframe, ventral airbrake and French avionics. The **EMB-314/ALX Super Tucano** is stronger, longer (11.42m/37ft 5in), and more powerful (one 930kW/1,250 shp PT6A-68/1 or PT6A-68-5 turboprop) than the EMB-312, with a five-blade propeller and five weapons attachments (four underwing) for gun or rocket pods, air-to-air missiles, fuel tanks and bombs. The cockpit cover is altered in shape and the armoured cockpit has zero/zero ejector seats, glass cockpit displays which are night-vision goggles compatible, and has a HUD and relevant weapons-aiming systems and equipment.

SEE ALSO: SHORTS TUCANO

EMB-312 T-27 Tucano Brazilian Air Force

ENAER T-35 Pillan

T-35 Pillan Chilean Air Force

design from Piper's original PA-28R configuration, along with the use of an aerobatics-capable wing design. This has produced an aircraft with a longer fuselage than the Piper Arrow it is based on.

VARIANTS

The **T-35A** primary and **T-35B** instrument trainers are currently in Chilean service, while the **T-35C** (which is equivalent to the A model) is used by Spain, and the **T-35D** by Panama and Paraguay. ENAER hoped to cash in on the apparently burgeoning market for turboprop trainers in the mid-1980s by developing the **T-35TX Aucan**, powered by a 313kW (420eshp) Allison 250-B17D turboprop, which first flew in 1986. The aircraft was modified by ENAER the following year, featuring a one-piece sideways-opening canopy, and three years further on agreement was reached with the Soloy Corporation to provide kits for a turboprop conversion. In March 1991, the **T-35DT Turbo Pillan** flew for the first time, but no orders have been forthcoming.

DEVELOPMENT

Following construction by ENAER (Empresa Nacional de Aeronautica de Chile) of 27 Piper PA-28 Dakotas for the Chilean Air Force and local flying clubs from 1980 onwards, it was decided by the former that a fully aerobatic trainer was required. It was to be based on the Piper Arrow, but incorporating a re-designed fuselage centre section and wing assembly, and a Lycoming powerplant delivering 300hp. Re-designated as the T-35 Pillan (meaning 'devil'), the first two prototype aircraft were built by Piper and flew during 1981, to be followed in due course by ENAER's initial trio of examples. The Pillan was to be used for *ab initio*, intermediate and instrument flying training by the Chilean Air Force, and deliveries commenced in the summer of 1985 of 60 T-35A primary and 20 T-35B instrument trainers. Forty-one T-35C variants were subsequently built for the Spanish

Air Force by CASA, and these are flown under the local designation of E.26 Tamiz.

CURRENT SERVICE

The main Chilean Air Force user of the Pillan is the Escuela de Aviación Capitán Avalos, based at El Bosque AB, Santiago – this is also the factory airfield where ENAER built the aircraft. It currently flies around 30 T-35A/Bs, while others are used for refresher training and liaison at other bases. The Spanish Air Force Tamiz fleet is entirely concentrated with Ala 79, the Academia del Aire at San Javier, which flies 37 of the 41 aircraft delivered. Pillans were also supplied to Panama (10), Paraguay (15), Guatemala and El Salvador.

SPECIAL FEATURES

The Pillan's large bubble canopy is particularly distinctive, this being one of the features of the re-

TECHNICAL DATA

ENAER T-35A Pillan

Powerplant: One Textron Lycoming IO-540-K1K5 piston engine
Developing: 224kW (300hp)
Driving: Three-blade propeller
Span: 8.84m (29ft 0in)
Length: 8.0m (26ft 3in)
Height: 2.64m (8ft 8in)
All-up weight: 1,338kg (2,950lb)
Maximum speed: 446km/h (277mph)
Cruise speed: 266km/h (166mph)
Operational ceiling: 19,160ft
Maximum range: 1,204km (748miles)
Mission range: 1,093km (679miles)
Endurance: 5hr 36m
Accommodation: Two in tandem
First flown: 6 March 1981 (Piper-built T-35 prototype)
Entered service: 31 July 1985

T-35 Pillan Chilean Air Force

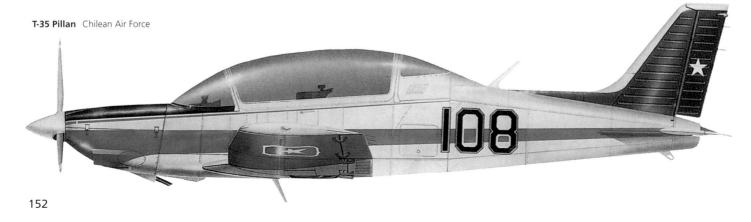

ENAER (Dassault) Mirage/Pantera 50CN

SINGLE TURBOJET SINGLE-SEAT FIGHTER-BOMBER

Pantera 50CN Chilean Air Force

DEVELOPMENT

The Pantera (Panther) is an upgrade of the Chilean Air Force's original Mirage 50FC fleet. The basic type was developed by Dassault-Breguet as an uprated Mirage 5, using the Atar 9K-50 powerplant developed for the Mirage F1, in order to provide greater operational flexibility by virtue of a better take-off performance, improved acceleration and greater agility with a heavier and more varied weapon load. Dassault's initial Mirage 50 flew for the first time on 15 April 1979, with Chile being the first customer (following delivery of three initial Mirage IIIR2Zs from South Africa, similarly equipped with 9K-50 engines). Both Mirage IIIs and 5s were able to be converted to Mirage 50 standard. The ENAER Pantera upgrade was developed with technical assistance of Israeli Aircraft Industries (IAI) and launched in the mid-1980s.

CURRENT SERVICE

A total of 13 Pantera 50CH/FCH single-seaters are operated by Grupo 4 of the Chilean Air Force, and are based at Punta Arenas (Carlos Ibanez AB) in southern Chile. The air arm's two-seat Mirage 50DC has also been upgraded to Pantera standard.

SPECIAL FEATURES

The Pantera upgrade has added IAI-designed, non-moveable canard foreplanes, shoulder-mounted on the engine intake trunks to the basic Mirage 50 shape, and the aircraft also has a reshaped nose, with a forward fuselage extension of approximately 1m (3ft 3.3in) inserted immediately ahead of the windscreen. This nose configuration is somewhat reminiscent of that on the IAI Kfir, which also owes its origins to the Mirage. Radar warning receivers were mounted on the tail fins, and the fleet is equipped with in-flight refuelling probes.

VARIANTS

The single-seat operational version is the **Pantera 50CN**, equipped with Israeli avionics as a major part of the ENAER/IAI upgrade. The reshaped nose of the Pantera houses Elta EL/M-2001B ranging radar, while other new features include INS, a computerised HUD, and modified control systems for the weapons fit, electrical and hydraulic systems, while Caiquen III radar warning receivers are fin-mounted. The only other variant is the sole two-seat **Pantera 50DC**.

TECHNICAL DATA

ENAER Pantera 50CN

Powerplant: One SNECMA Atar 9K-50 turbojet
Thrust: 49.03kN (11,023lb st) dry, 70.82kN (15,873lb st) with afterburner
Span: 8.22m (26ft 11.6in)
Length: 15.56m (51ft 1in)
Height: 4.50m (14ft 9in)
All-up weight: 14,700kg (32,407lb)
Maximum speed: 2,338km/h (1,453mph)
Cruise speed: 956km/h (594mph)
Operational ceiling: 59,055ft
Maximum range: 1,315km (816 miles)
Mission range: 1,260km (782 miles)
Accommodation: Pilot only
Warload: Seven attachment points for external loads are fitted, with multiple launchers permitting a maximum load of four tonnes.
First flown: Late 1988
Entered service: 1990

SEE ALSO: DASSAULT MIRAGE III/V/50 & ATLAS CHEETAH

Pantera 50CN Chilean Air Force

English Electric Canberra

TWIN-TURBOJET MULTI-MISSION AIRCRAFT

Canberra PR9 Royal Air Force

TECHNICAL DATA

English Electric Canberra PR9

Powerplants: Two Rolls-Royce Avon 206 non-afterburning turbojets
Thrust: 50.10kN (11,250lb st)
Span: 20.6m (67ft 10in)
Length: 20.2m (66ft 8in)
Height: 4.7m (15ft 7in)
All-up weight: 24,925kg (54,950lb)
Maximum speed: 822km/h (547mph)
Operational ceiling: 70,000ft plus
Maximum range: 8,167km (5,075 miles)
Accommodation: Pilot and navigator
Warload: None
First flown: 13 May 1949 (Canberra prototype); 8 July 1955 (PR9 prototype)
Entered service: May 1951 (B2); January 1960 (PR9)

DEVELOPMENT

The first prototype of Britain's first jet bomber, then designated as the English Electric A1, first took to the air from Warton on 13 May 1949 and heralded the start of an exceptionally long, varied and successful operational career for the type, subsequently named the Canberra. The B2 was first into service two years later, followed by the T4 conversion trainer. Later, more powerful Avon Mk109 engines produced the B6, and the addition of a dorsal gun pack as well as a modified nose with offset canopy saw Canberras operating in the interdiction role, primarily as B(I)8s. Initial photo-recce Canberras were PR3s, then PR7s and finally the 'ultimate' Canberra, the Shorts-built high-altitude PR9 with Mk206 Avons. Other British service derivatives over the years have included the E15 for electronic countermeasures duties, and the TT18 target tug, that saw both RAF and Royal Navy service. Many test and trials Canberras were used by the research establishments in the UK, and various designations were given to export aircraft. Many ex-

RAF Canberras were purchased by overseas customers after their retirement, refurbished by BAC/BAe and flown to pastures new. The type's most significant foreign user was however the US Air Force, who selected the Canberra for low-level intruder operations as the licence-built Martin B-57.

CURRENT SERVICE

The RAF has five Canberra PR9s and two T4 conversion trainers on strength, all with No 39 (1 PRU) Squadron at Marham. The PR9s are used primarily for survey and mapping duties. Two more, both modified B2s, serve as target tugs/drone-launchers with DERA at Llanbedr. Meanwhile, remaining overseas Canberra operators are Argentina, India and Peru, where they continue as active bombers.

SPECIAL FEATURES

The PR9's most distinguishing features when compared with other serving Canberras are the fighter-style tear drop cockpit canopy, which is offset to port, and its

longer nose. The navigator enters his position, located in the nose of the aircraft, through the hinged nose. PR9s have an extended-chord inner wing, and the outer wing panels have been extended. The ailerons are hydraulically boosted. The standard camera fitment until recent upgrades (described below) comprised a Zeiss RMK survey camera, three nose-mounted cameras for low-level work and a single oblique camera to port.

VARIANTS

The RAF's **Canberra PR9s** have had their equipment progressively updated down the years, and look set to continue in service well into the 21st century with no potential replacement in sight. A new sensor fit has recently been introduced, comprising a Recon Optical KA-93 panoramic wet-film camera on all five aircraft, and a digital EO LOROP camera on two of them. The latter is carried in the former flare-bay under the PR9's fuselage, and uses a much larger camera port than previous Canberra fitments. It is believed to effectively be similar to the U-2's SYERS (Senior Year Electro Optical Relay System).

Canberra PR9 Royal Air Force

Enstrom F-28, 280 & 480

SINGLE PISTON-ENGINED PRIMARY TRAINING HELICOPTER

Enstrom F-28F Colombian Air Force

DEVELOPMENT

The first flight of the prototype Enstrom F-28 light utility helicopter in May 1962 heralded the start of a long and immensely successful production run for the type in its many variants. The F-28F version appeared in 1981, and used a new turbo-supercharged Textron Lycoming piston powerplant, giving an improved performance. Further refinements produced the 280FX four years later – this model incorporated new landing skids, a tail rotor guard and a new tailplane design, and it was in this guise that Enstrom's helicopters would see their first service with a military air arm. A four-seater version, the 480FX, was to be developed from the 280 and made its initial flight in October 1989. The new variant provided the basis for the TH-28, a contender for the US Army's New Training Helicopter (NTH) requirement. Certified in 1992, the helicopter (Enstrom's first to be specifically designed for a military need) was eventually beaten to the order by the Bell Jet Ranger.

CURRENT SERVICE

The first military Enstrom purchaser was the Chilean Army, which uses the 280FX, a total of 15 of which were ordered in 1989. These are used for helicopter training with the 1st 'Independencia' Aviation Brigade at Rancagua. The Peruvian and Colombian armies fly F-28F derivatives, also for basic helicopter training – nine serve with Aviación del Ejército Peruano at 'Jorges Chavez' International Airport, Lima-Callao; the Columbian ones with 514 Escudión Entrenamiento at Base Aéreo 'Luis F. Pinto' at Melgar.

SPECIAL FEATURES

The 280FX has various design improvements over the standard 280 model, intended to provide better aerodynamics. Most noticeable is the fact that the rear rotor driveshaft is faired over, rather than being left 'open' as with the F-28F and 280. The skid landing gear is also fully-faired, while F-28Fs and all 280s have endplate tail fins.

VARIANTS

The basic **Enstrom F-28** design has spawned a host of different individual modified variants as described in the description of the type's development above, headed by the turbo-supercharged **F-28F** and its subsequent development, the further refined **280FX**. Turning the helicopter into a four-seater produced the **480**, and the (ultimately unsuccessful) military **TH-28** version for the US Army's training requirement incorporated fuel tanks and seating designed to meet military crashworthiness requirements. Another change to this porposed version was the addition of instrument flying equipment for easier operation in inclement weather – the TH-28 could also have been used as a light patrol helicopter.

TECHNICAL DATA

Enstrom 280FX

Powerplant: One Textron Lycoming HIO-360-F1AD turbocharged piston engine
Developing: 168kW (225hp)
Driving: Three-blade main and two-blade tail rotors
Main rotor diameter: 9.75m (32ft 0in)
Fuselage length: 8.92m (29ft 3in)
Height: 2.79m (9ft 2in)
All-up weight: 1,179kg (2,600lb)
Maximum speed: 180km/h (112mph)
Cruise speed: 165km/h (102mph)
Operational ceiling: 12,000ft
Maximum range: 423km (262miles)
Endurance: 3hr 30min
Accommodation: Two side-by-side
First flown: May 1962 (F-28 prototype); 1985 (280FX)
Entered service: 1989

Enstrom 280FX Chilean Army

Eurocopter (Aérospatiale) SA365 Dauphin/HH-65 Dolphin

TWIN-ENGINED MULTI-ROLE HELICOPTER

FRANCE

HH-65A Dolphin United States Coast Guard

DEVELOPMENT
In the early 1970s, Aérospatiale (now Eurocopter) commenced development of a helicopter to supersede the Alouette III. The initial version was the SA360 Dauphin, which had a single engine and a tailwheel undercarriage, making its first flight on 2 June 1972. It soon became apparent that the Dauphin's military potential lay with a twin-engined helicopter and the SA365C Dauphin II was introduced, with a retractable tricycle undercarriage and greater use of composites. Aérospatiale developed three dedicated military versions including the AS365F. Under the designation SA366G1, Aérospatiale developed a variant of the Dauphin to fulfil a US Coast Guard requirement to

replace its ageing Sikorsky HH-52s, but this required an American powerplant to be installed. Produced as the HH-65A Dolphin, a total of 96 examples was delivered. The Dolphin has been the subject of much controversy for being underpowered – especially as more equipment has been added. Re-engining options, have, so far, not come to fruition – but the USCG is keen to reduce the number of helicopter types it uses and is seeking a replacement for the HH-65A.

CURRENT SERVICE
The Z-9/Z-9A, the version of the Dauphin produced in China, serves with the AFPLA and Navy. Two US Coast Guard trials aircraft were purchased by Israel for use from its naval patrol boats. Two are in service with the US Navy Test Pilot's School at Patuxent River. The remaining 94 (some of which are in store) are distributed to Coast Guard Air stations around the US and serve from shore bases, ice breakers and cutters. Five AS365Fs serve with the Irish Air Corps, two for

naval support and three for search and rescue.

SPECIAL FEATURES
Inflatable flotation bags are provided for waterborne operations of the type up to sea state 5. A nose-mounted Northrop See Hawk FLIR sensor aids night and poor weather rescue operations. For all-weather operations, equipment includes a starboard-side rescue hoist and searchlight. It has an automatic control system and an omnidirectional airspeed system able to provide information while the aircraft is hovering.

VARIANTS
The **AS365F** was the first military Dauphin version. In the 1980s a batch of **Harbin (HAMC) Z-9 Haituns** (Dolphins) were assembled in China. The **Z-9A-100**, with more indigenous components followed in the early 1990s. The **HH-65A** was intended to operate from the SRR (short-range recovery) missions from both shore bases and Coast Guard vessels.

TECHNICAL DATA

Aérospatiale HH-35A Dolphin (AS366G1)
Powerplants: Two Textron Lycoming LTS101-750A-1 turboshafts
Developing: 507kW (680shp)
Driving: Four-blade main rotor and 11-bladed fenestron shrouded tail rotor
Main Rotor Diameter: 11.94m (39ft 2in)
Fuselage Length: 11.63m (38ft 1.75in)
Height: 3.98m (13ft 1in)
All-up weight: 4,040kg (8,928lb)
Maximum speed: 324km/h (201mph)
Cruising speed: 257km/h (160mph)
Operational ceiling: 7,510ft
Maximum range: 760km (471 miles)
Endurance: 4 hours
Accommodation: Pilot, co-pilot and hoist operator
Warload: None
First flown: 24 January 1975 (SA365); 23 July 1980 (HH-65A)
Entered service: 1 February 1987

AS365F Dauphin Irish Air Corps

Eurocopter (Aérospatiale) AS332 Super Puma

TWIN-TURBOSHAFT MULTI-ROLE MEDIUM UTILITY HELICOPTER

AS332M Super Puma Swedish Air Force

DEVELOPMENT

The AS332 Super Puma was initially intended as a primarily civil helicopter, but soon found sales among military customers. With improved survivability when compared against the SA330 Puma (described under Aerospatiale), and fitted with more powerful Makila turboshafts, the improvements over its successful predecessor were significant. The type was to be extensively developed under the Super Puma designation and, after 1990, as the AS532 Cougar, which introduced further separate versions.

CURRENT SERVICE

AS332s are operated by Abu Dhabi, Brazil, Cameroon, the Chilean Army, China, the Democratic Republic of Congo, Ecuador, French Army Light Aviation, Gabon, the Indonesian Navy, Japan, Jordan, Malaysia, Mexico, Nepal, Nigeria, Oman, Panama, Qatar, Singapore, South Korea, the Spanish Army, Swedish Air Force, Swiss Air Force, Togo and Venezuela. Over 500 had been delivered by early 2000.

SPECIAL FEATURES

More visible than the new glass-fibre rotors is the prominent ventral fin which was added to the Puma airframe for the Super Puma, and the longer nose to house weather radar (either Bendix/King RDR 1400 or Honeywell Primus 500 equipment).

VARIANTS

The **AS332B** was the basic short-fuselage utility version, later joined by the **AS332M**, which has a stretched fuselage 76cm (30in) longer, allowing for an increased payload, and its 'civil' counterparts, the **AS332C** and **AS332L**, that also found military purchasers. Maritime **AS332Fs** retained the shorter fuselage, no stretched naval derivatives being produced until after the type became the AS532 Cougar in 1990. Only then was the fuselage extended for a third time on production examples. The **AS332L2** is the later Mk2, integrating modern technology and composites with a fuselage 'plug'. It is the first helicopter that has a certified 'super-contingency' operation capability.

TECHNICAL DATA

Eurocopter (Aérospatiale) AS332M Super Puma

Powerplants: Two Turboméca Makila 1A1 turboshafts
Developing: 1,357kW (1,819eshp)
Driving: Four-blade main and five-blade tail rotors
Main rotor diameter: 16.20m (53.20ft)
Fuselage length: 16.79m (55.00ft)
Height: 4.97m (16.30ft)
All-up weight: 9,350kg (20,615lb)
Maximum speed: 315km/h (195mph)
Cruise speed: 280km/h (174mph)
Operational ceiling: 17,000ft
Maximum ferry range: 800km (497miles)
Mission range: 618km (384miles)
Endurance: 3hr 20min
Accommodation: Two crew and 24 passengers
First flown: 13 September 1978 (AS332 prototype)
Entered service: 1981 (AS332B)

SEE ALSO: EUROCOPTER (AÉROSPATIALE) AS532 COUGAR

AS332 Super Puma Brazilian Air Force

Eurocopter (Aérospatiale) AS350 Ecureuil & AS550 Fennec

SINGLE TURBOSHAFT LIGHT MULTI-PURPOSE HELICOPTER

TECHNICAL DATA

Eurocopter AS550C-3 Fennec
Powerplant: One Turboméca Arriel 2B turboshaft
Developing: 632kW (847eshp)
Driving: Three-blade main and two-blade tail rotors
Main rotor diameter: 10.69m (35ft 1in)
Fuselage length: 10.93m (35ft 11in)
Height: 3.24m (10ft 7in)
All-up weight: 2,250kg (4,960lb)
Maximum speed: 287km/h (178mph)
Cruise speed: 245km/h (153mph)
Operational ceiling: 15,750ft
Maximum range: 666km (414miles)
Maximum endurance: 4hr (no reserve)
Accommodation: One pilot and five passengers
Warload: Single 20mm M621cannon; two 7.62mm machine guns; a light torpedo; launchers for 12 68mm rockets or seven 2.75in rockets or HeliTOW anti-tank system
First flown: 27 June 1974 (AS350 prototype – Lycoming LTS101 turboshaft); 14 February 1975 (Turboméca Arriel)
Entered service: 1975

DEVELOPMENT

Designed and originally produced by Aerospatiale in France, the AS350/550 has subsequently been built by the successor company Eurocopter, and under licence by Helibras in Brazil. The AS350 Ecureuil prototype was powered by a Textron Lycoming LTS101 turboshaft, but the Turboméca Arriel unit appeared in the second aircraft which made its initial flight on 14 February 1975. Only the AS350C, optimised as the A-Star for the US market, continued to use the former engine. Designed as a successor to the highly successful family of Alouette II and III helicopters, the Ecureuil spawned an armed version that was first designated AS350L and later AS550 Fennec. A total of over 2,100 AS350/AS550s had been built for civil and military customers by the end of 1999.

CURRENT SERVICE

Current military AS350 and AS550 operators include: Abu Dhabi, Albania, Algeria, Argentina, the Royal Australian Army and Navy, Benin, Botswana, Brazil, Central African Republic, Royal Danish Army, Ecuador, Djibouti, French Army, Gabon, Guinea, Jamaica, Mali, Paraguay, Peru, Singapore, Tunisia, UK armed forces' Defence Helicopter Flying School and Venezuela.

SPECIAL FEATURES

A tadpole-shaped fuselage is a particularly distinctive feature of the Ecureuil, as are the short stub wings fitted to armed Fennec versions which can carry TOW or Mistral missiles. Other possible fitments include a 20mm gun and a side-mounted machine gun.

VARIANTS

The standard AS350 Ecureuil and subsequent AS350B are in service with several air arms for light utility, transport/liaison and training duties. A variety of military AS550 Fennec versions have been offered, namely the AS550U-2 unarmed utility helicopter; the AS550A-2 with cannon and rocket armament, which has not been ordered by any customer; the AS550C-2 anti-tank variant, as used by the Royal Danish Army with Hughes TOW missiles; and two naval derivatives, the unarmed utility AS550M-2 and anti-shipping AS550S-2, neither of which have yet been produced. Helibras has built the type in Brazil, in unarmed HB350B/B-1 and HB350L-1 types, for the Brazilian Army, Navy and Air Force. The UK's tri-service Defence Helicopter Flying School uses the AS350BA and BB, the only difference being that the former – Squirrel HT2s – are fitted with winches, while the latter are 'standard' Squirrel HT1 trainers. Eurocopter currently offers the AS550C-3 Fennec, an updated anti-tank version. Other military versions were offered as AS55U2s (unarmed, utility). The Ecureuil has been assembled under licence in Brazil by Helibras and is similar to AS350B standard.

HB350B Ecureuil Brazilian Navy

Eurocopter (Aérospatiale) AS355 Twin Squirrel & AS555 Fennec

TWIN-TURBOSHAFT LIGHT MULTI-PURPOSE HELICOPTER

AS355F-1 Twin Squirrel UK DERA

DEVELOPMENT

The twin-engined version of the AS350 Ecureuil was launched by Aérospatiale in mid-1978. The initial production version was the S355E with 313kW (420hp) Allison 250-C20F turboshafts, followed by the AS335F with wide-chord rotor blades and other refinements. The first production AS355 versions of the twin-engined Ecureuil, known as the Twin Squirrel or Ecureuil 2, were powered by Allison turboshafts, but the later AS555s have switched to the Turboméca Arrius unit. Commonality between the single- and twin-engined Ecureuils was found in many areas, with alterations being made to the powerplant and fuel system, apart from the obvious changes to the fuselage design. The AS355M military version had its designation changed to AS555 Fennec in 1990.

CURRENT SERVICE

Principal user of the military version is the French Air Force. The French Army (ALAT) took delivery of ten AS555UN Fennecs for IFR training. AS355s and AS555s of various sub-types are also used by Benin, Brazil (Air Force and Navy), Djibouti, Fiji, Malawi, Sierra Leone and the Royal Air Force.

SPECIAL FEATURES

Apart from a redesigned fuselage to accommodate the extra engine, there are few external differences between the twin- and single-engined Ecureuils. Cannon-armed versions carry this weapon either under the fuselage centreline or in the side doors.

VARIANTS

The basic Allison 250-powered **AS355F** is used for various tasks by a number of operators, including the RAF, who fly three hired VIP transport versions, and the French Air Force, which flies five with door-mounted machine guns (these are based in French Guyana). Of the specifically military derivatives, the **AS555UN** is the reconnaissance/observation and training helicopter, while the **AS555AN** is the armed variant capable of carrying 20mm GIAT cannon. The latter is used by the French Army Light Aviation component. Once again, Helibras has produced the type under licence as the **HB355F-2 Esquilo**, which takes various local designations in Brazilian service. Eurocopter has proposed two naval versions, the **AS555MN** with a 360-degree radar for surveillance and the torpedo-armed **AS555SN**, but they have not found any customers. Aérospatiale has demonstrated an **AS555SR** naval version of the Fennec carrying a Bendix 1500 radar under the nose, a Crouzet MAD and armament of two homing torpedoes.

TECHNICAL DATA

Eurocopter AS555AN Fennec

Powerplants: Two Turboméca Arrius 1A turboshafts
Developing: 296kW (397eshp)
Driving: Three-blade main and two-blade tail rotors
Main rotor diameter: 10.69m (35ft 0.75in)
Fuselage length: 10.93m (35ft 10.5in)
Height: 3.24m (10.63ft)
All-up weight: 2,600kg (5,732lb)
Maximum speed: 278km/h (172mph)
Cruise speed: 221km/h (138mph)
Operational ceiling: 13,125ft
Maximum ferry range: 722km (448 miles)
Endurance: 2hr 20min
Accommodation: One pilot and five passengers
First flown: 28 September 1979 (AS355 prototype)
Entered service: 19 January 1990 (AS555AN)

AS355 Twin Squirrel HCC1 Royal Air Force

Eurocopter (Aérospatiale) AS532 Cougar

TWIN-TURBOSHAFT MULTI-ROLE MEDIUM UTILITY HELICOPTER

FRANCE

AS532 Cougar Royal Saudi Air Force

DEVELOPMENT

From January 1990 onwards, military versions of the AS332 series (described separately) were renamed as the AS532 Cougar family, with new designations for the individual variants. Since then, numerous further derivatives have been developed (notably the AS532U-2 and A-2 Cougar Mk2) and the type is now available with three different configurations of fuselage length.

CURRENT SERVICE

Operators of the AS532 Cougar series are the Argentine Army, Chilean Navy, French Air Force, French Army Light Aviation, German Air Force, Kuwait Navy, Royal Netherlands Air Force, Royal Saudi Air Force, Spanish Army and Turkish Army. Twelve AS532s have been ordered by the Swiss Air Force to supplement its

earlier AS332 Super Pumas, and ten of these are to be licence-built at Emmen.

SPECIAL FEATURES

As with the previous Super Puma, the Cougar has a distinctive dorsal fin when compared with the original SA330 Puma design. The design is basically the same as that of the Super Puma, incorporating features to increase the survivability of the helicopter and its crew, including glass-fibre rotors which can withstand small arms fire and still operate for up to 40 hours. The naval AS532SC has large sponsons containing flotation gear.

VARIANTS

Since the change from AS332 Super Puma to AS532 Cougar, the variety of versions produced has increased. The **AS532UC** and armed **AC** versions have the shortest fuselage of 15.53m (50.95ft), the latter being able to carry side-mounted machine guns and pods holding 20mm guns or 68mm SNEB rocket launchers. From

these, the **AS532SC** naval version was developed, armed with either two AM39 Exocet missiles or homing torpedoes. Next up in size are the **AS532UE, UL** and **AL** derivatives – the former is a 'basic' option with minimum levels of radio and navigation equipment, while the UL version (used by the French Army as the **AS532UL Horizon** as the platform for its Orchidee battlefield surveillance radar) has a higher specification, and the AL is an armed option. The latest additions to the family are the **AS532U-2** and the armed **A-2**, with a longer fuselage of 16.79m (55.08ft), uprated Makila 1A2 engines delivering 1,236kW (1,657eshp) and a glass cockpit with 4-axis autopilot. Both the AS532UL and U-2 have been ordered by several air arms, including the German Air Force, as VIP transports. The armed AS532A-2 is now being delivered to the French Air Force for use in the combat search and rescue role.

SEE ALSO: EUROCOPTER (AEROSPATIALE) AS332 SUPER PUMA

TECHNICAL DATA

Eurocopter (Aérospatiale) AS532UL Cougar

Powerplants: Two Turboméca Makila 1A1 turboshafts
Developing: 1,263kW (1,657eshp)
Driving: Four-blade main and five-blade tail rotors
Main rotor diameter: 15.60m (51.18ft)
Fuselage length: 16.29m (53.44ft)
Height: 4.92m (16.14ft)
All-up weight: 9,350kg (20,615lb)
Maximum speed: 278km/h (173mph)
Cruise speed: 258 km/h (159mph)
Operational ceiling: 11,319ft
Maximum ferry range: 800km (496miles)
Mission range: 618km (384miles)
Endurance: 3hr 20min
Accommodation: Two crew and 29 passengers
First flown: 13 September 1978 (AS332 prototype); 6 February 1987 (Cougar Mk2)
Entered service: 1981 (AS332); 1992 (Cougar Mk2); 24 June 1996 (AS532UL)

AS532UL Cougar French Army Light Aviation

Eurocopter (Aérospatiale) AS565 Panther & EC155B

TWIN-TURBOSHAFT MULTI-ROLE MEDIUM HELICOPTER

AS565 Panther

DEVELOPMENT

The SA365 Dauphin II, described under Aérospatiale, spawned a further-developed, dedicated military multi-role variant initially known as the SA365K – this first appeared in early 1986, and under the AS565 Panther designation (since 1990) has been offered in a number of variants. More recently, the EC155B has become the latest in the line.

CURRENT SERVICE

The largest user of the AS565 Panther (as opposed to the earlier SA365 variants described separately) is the French Navy, which has 15 on strength. Other Panther operators are the Brazilian Army, Chilean Navy and the Royal Saudi Naval Force, while the Hong Kong Government Flying Service has ordered five EC155Bs.

SPECIAL FEATURES

Basically similar to dedicated military variants of the SA365 Dauphin II, the Panther has the same longer radar nose as military Dauphins, and those used for SAR work with the French Navy, and some of the Saudi examples, are fitted with a winch. The new EC155B has new digital avionics, a five-bladed main rotor of advanced construction and with variable speed options for a lower noise footprint, and a redesigned fenestron.

VARIANTS

The French Navy was the first purchaser of the **AS565MA Panther** (since bought by Chile), which is used for SAR work. The Saudis procured the equivalent **AS565SC** and the anti-shipping **AS565SA** armed with four Aerospatiale AS15TT missiles; the French Navy now has two of the latter. Currently being marketed by Eurocopter are the **AS565UB** utility helicopter and the armed shipborne **AS565SB**, as well as the new 12-place **EC155B** with increased cargo capacity.

TECHNICAL DATA

AS565MA Panther

Powerplants: Two Turboméca Arriel 2C turboshafts
Developing: 597kW (800eshp)
Driving: Four-blade main and fenestron tail rotors
Main rotor diameter: 11.94m (39.17ft)
Fuselage length: 12.08m (39.63ft)
Height: 4.06m (13.32ft)
All-up weight: 4,300kg (9,480lb)
Maximum speed: 296km/h (184mph)
Cruise speed: 275km/h (172mph)
Operational ceiling: 13,780ft
Mission range: 814km (506miles)
Endurance: 4.6hr with auxiliary tanks
Accommodation: Two crew and ten passengers
First flown: 29 February 1984 (Panther AS365M prototype); 17 June 1997 (EC155)
Entered service: November 1998 (EC155)

AS565UA Panther Brazilian Army

Eurocopter (MBB) BO105

TWIN-TURBOSHAFT LIGHT ANTI-TANK SCOUT/UTILITY HELICOPTER

MBB BO105M German Army

TECHNICAL DATA

MBB BO105CB

Powerplants: Two Allison 250-C20B turboshafts
Developing: 320kW (429eshp)
Driving: Four-blade main and two-blade tail rotors
Main rotor diameter: 9.84m (32ft 3.5in)
Fuselage length: 8.56m (28ft 1in)
Height: 3.00m (9ft 10.25in)
All-up weight: 2,500kg (5,511lb)
Maximum speed: 270km/h (167mph)
Cruise speed: 242km/h (150mph)
Operational ceiling: 17,000ft
Maximum range: 1,112km (690miles)
Mission range: 658km (408miles)
Accommodation: One pilot and five passengers
Warload: Can carry six Euromissile HOT anti-tank weapons; armament on other anti-tank BO105s can include a single 20mm Rheinmetall cannon and two 7.62mm machine guns.
First flown: 16 February 1967 (BO105 prototype)
Entered service: 1970

DEVELOPMENT

Messerschmitt Bolkow-Blohm first flew its initial BO105 prototype in 1967, following three years of development. Production BO105C and BO105CB variants were to follow, the latter in 1975. The German Army became the first military customer of the type, purchasing both unarmed scout and armed anti-tank variants – the latter with a roof-mounted stabilised sight. An update of the German Army's armed BO105Ps, locally designated as PAH-1s (Panzerabwehr-Hubschrauber-1), included the fitment of new main rotor blades and improved cooling equipment in order to extend the type's service life until the arrival of the Eurocopter Tiger. Other armed derivatives of the type were produced under licence by CASA for the Spanish Army. Among the BO105's other roles are aeromedical evacuation, light utility transport and short-range search and rescue.

CURRENT SERVICE

The German Army remains the largest single BO105 operator, with 97 BO105Ms and 208 BO105Ps used by elements of eight regiments and the training unit, as well as two BO105Cs with the WTD-61 military trials unit. Iraq did have 75 BO105Cs on strength, but this total is now uncertain, so the Spanish Army is probably the next largest user of the type with 68 licence-produced examples. Other BO105 operators are Bahrain, Brunei, Chile, Czech Republic, Colombia, Dubai, Indonesia (34 licence-built NBO105s with the Navy and Army), Jordan, Kenya, Lesotho, Mexico, the Netherlands (27 BO105CBs, soon to be retired), Peru, the Phillippines, Sierra Leone, Sudan, Sweden (a mixture of armed and unarmed BO105CBs), Trinidad & Tobago, and the United Emirates.

SPECIAL FEATURES

The BO105 has a rigid main rotor constructed from GRP, which gives this helicopter an outstanding aerobatic performance for such a machine, and extra agility for its operational roles. Armed versions can carry HOT anti-tank missiles in horizontal tubes mounted on the fuselage sides, used in conjunction with the roof-mounted sight. Mast-mounted sight equipment has been trialled. When used for light SAR work, emergency flotation gear is often fitted to the landing skids – this is a feature on the Swedish Army and Mexican Navy BO105s thus employed.

VARIANTS

Over the years there have been many different versions of this versatile and popular helicopter. The **BO105C** and **CB** were the initial basic utility versions, with armed modifications available. Derivatives of these include the slightly-stretched **BO105CBS** with accommodation for six people, and the **BO105LS** built by Eurocopter Canada with improved 'hot and high' capability from its Allison 250-C28C turboshafts. The German Army uses **BO105M** scouts and **BO105P** anti-tank helicopters, while the Spanish Army has HOT-equipped **BO105ATHs**, cannon-armed **BO105GSHs** and unarmed **BO105LOHs**. Those built in Indonesia by IPTN are known as **NBO105s**.

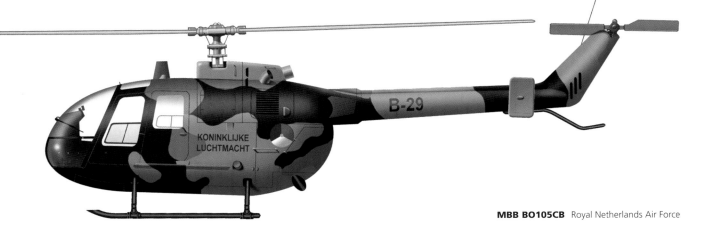

MBB BO105CB Royal Netherlands Air Force

Eurocopter/Kawasaki BK117

TWIN-TURBOSHAFT UTILITY HELICOPTER

Eurocopter/Kawasaki BK117A South African Air Force

DEVELOPMENT

The BK117A, a joint venture between MBB of Germany and Kawasaki of Japan, was intended as a larger, more powerful BO105 primarily for the civil market – but it achieved few military sales. With its sizeable fuselage capacity, however, the type has proved popular with civil air ambulance operators including Germany's ADAC in the aeromedical evacuation role.

CURRENT SERVICE

Sixteen examples of the BK117B-1 were delivered to the Iraqi Air Force, to be used for SAR tasks, between September 1988 and March 1989, though the current status of this fleet is unclear. Other military users of the type are the defence forces of the former South African provinces of Ciskei, Bophuthatswana, Transkei and Venda, as well as the UAE (in Sharjah) and the Japanese Air Self Defence Force's Technical Research and Development Institute. The sole armed BK117AVT trials version flies with Germany's WTD-61 test unit.

SPECIAL FEATURES

A particularly distinctive feature of the BK117 is the provision of clamshell rear loading doors, ideal for medevac or SAR tasks.

VARIANTS

The sole 'radical' variant on the basic design theme of this helicopter was the **BK117A-3M**, also known as the **BK117AVT**, which was mooted by MBB between 1985-88 as a dedicated military anti-tank version, which could carry eight HOT anti-armour missiles in conjunction with a roof-mounted sight, and had new electronic cockpit displays, amongst other refinements. A number of other weapons fits were also trialled. However, it was not purchased by any air arm, and the prototype now flies with the German WTD-61 trials establishment. The **BK117C-1** is a German development with a new cockpit and Turboméca Arriel engines. Indonesia has constructed a few licence-built examples known as **NBK117s**.

TECHNICAL DATA

Eurocopter/Kawasaki BK117B-2
Powerplants: Two Textron Lycoming LTS 101-750B-1 turboshafts
Developing: 516kW (692eshp)
Driving: Four-blade main and two-blade tail rotors
Main rotor diameter: 11.00m (36ft 1in)
Fuselage length: 9.91m (32ft 6in)
Height: 3.85m (12ft 8in)
All-up weight: 3,350kg (7,385lb)
Maximum speed: 278km/h (172mph)
Cruise speed: 250km/h (155mph)
Operational ceiling: 15,000ft
Mission range: 541km (336miles)
Accommodation: One pilot and ten passengers
Warload: Usually none, but can be offered with eight HOT 2 or four TOW anti-tank missiles
First flown: 13 June 1979 (prototype)
Entered service: September 1988

Kawasaki BK117 Japanese Air Self-Defence Force

163

Eurocopter Tiger

TWIN-TURBOSHAFT AIR-TO-AIR COMBAT, FIRE SUPPORT AND ANTI-TANK HELICOPTER

Eurocopter Tiger UHT

DEVELOPMENT

In 1984, the French and German governments decided to proceed with the joint development of a new anti-tank helicopter, to meet the requirements of both their armies' aviation components. These were to be known as the PAH-2 Tiger for Germany, and Tigre HAC (Hélicoptère Anti-Char) to the French. An armed escort version was added to the drawing board three years later, designated the Gerfaut HAP (Hélicoptère d'Appui et de Protection) for the French Army. However, the PAH-2 requirement was dropped by the German Army in favour of the broader specification, since renamed Tiger UHT. The specially-developed, multinational, MTR 390 engines began flight testing in a modified AS565 Panther in February 1991, and two months later the first Tiger prototype, PT1, was ready for initial flight tests. The first true HAP version took to the air on 22 April 1993, and by autumn 1999 four prototypes had flown in France and one in Germany.

CURRENT SERVICE

The first Tigers are scheduled for delivery in 2002, with contracts having been placed for initial production of 80 units for Germany and France. A total of 212 are on order for Germany, with 75 HAP and 140 HAC Tigres due for delivery to the French Army's Light Aviation component.

SPECIAL FEATURES

The Tiger has a semi-rigid main rotor of advanced composite construction, helping to make for superb manoeuvrability when combined with the helicopter's light weight. Anhedral stub wings carry the machine's weapon load, apart from the 30mm GIAT cannon, which is mounted under the Tiger's nose. Its tailplane has endplate fins, while armour plating is used to protect the crew and key parts of the airframe. Low observability by visual, radar and IR means is a feature of the design, increasing its survivability.

VARIANTS

For the French Army, the **Tigre HAP** has been ordered as an air-to-air combat and battlefield fire support helicopter with day and night capability. The German Army **Tiger UHT** and French **HAC** derivatives are much the same, being the multi-role fire support and anti-tank versions, with German examples carrying Stinger AAMs and Mistral AAMs for the French. These Tigers carry a mast-mounted sight.

TECHNICAL DATA

Eurocopter Tigre HAP

Powerplants: Two MTU/Turboméca/Rolls-Royce MTR 390 turboshafts
Developing: 873kW (1,171eshp)
Driving: Four-blade main and three-blade tail rotors
Main rotor diameter: 13.00m (42.65ft)
Fuselage length: 14.08m (46.22ft)
Wing span: 4.52m (14.83ft)
Height: 3.83m (12.56ft)
Maximum weight: 6,000kg (13,230lb)
Maximum speed: 280km/h (174mph)
Cruise speed: 250km/h (155mph)
Operational ceiling: 10,500ft
Maximum ferry range: 800km (497 miles)
Mission range: 752km (460 miles)
Endurance: 3hr 25min
Accommodation: Two crew (gunner in front, pilot behind and above)
Warload: 30mm GIAT cannon in chin turret, two 68mm SNEB rocket pods and four Mistral AAMs on pylons under stub wings. UHT version can carry eight HOT or Trigat anti-tank weapons, four Stinger 2 AAMs and a 12.7mm gun pod.
First flown: 29 April 1991 (prototype PT1); 15 December 1994 (PT4)
Entered service: First Tiger deliveries to French and German Armies expected in 2002

Eurocopter Tiger UHT

Eurocopter EC135 & EC635

TWIN-TURBOSHAFT LIGHT UTILITY AND TRAINING HELICOPTER

DEVELOPMENT

The EC135 was very significant as the first Eurocopter helicopter development programme to be started under the company's common management structure. In 1988, the then MBB began flight trials of its Bö108 helicopter technology demonstrator, with innovations such as a hingeless main rotor, new vibration-absorbing materials and an airframe constructed almost entirely of composites. Following a successful test programme, it was announced by MBB in January 1991 that the type would be developed into a production Bö105 successor, and in June that year a second Bö108 flew with a stretched fuselage and other modifications. MBB was merged into the Eurocopter combine in January 1992, whereupon the new helicopter was renamed the EC135. It was subsequently decided to offer a seven-seat layout and to use a fenestron tail arrangement. After some two years of flight tests from Eurocopter's German facilities, series production of the type commenced in mid-1996. It quickly became the police helicopter of choice, with many forces around the world adopting the EC135 for their law enforcement duties. The German Army aviation component, the Heeresflieger, became the initial military customer for this highly-successful helicopter.

CURRENT SERVICE

First deliveries of the EC135 T1 to the German Army are starting to occur during 2000 – the type will replace the Alouette II in the training role and features NVG compatible cockpit lighting. In addition, the military-

Eurocopter EC135

optimised EC635 T1 has gained its first customer with the Portuguese Army, with nine examples ordered. The first Portuguese EC635s will be delivered in 2001, powered by the more powerful Arrius 2B1A engines. Most EC135s delivered to date have been to police forces and law enforcement agencies, among them the German Bundesgrenzschutz (Federal Border Guards).

SPECIAL FEATURES

This 'new generation' light utility/training helicopter utilises the latest technology in rotary-wing aircraft design to help produce excellent performance. The EC135 and military EC635 are built using composite materials for lightness and strength, and the seats and fuel system are among the most crashworthy of any small helicopter. The hingeless, bearingless main

rotor (the first such design ever to be used on a production helicopter) is high-set, and combined with its advanced construction and the fenestron tail, makes for a quiet machine. It has large sliding side doors and two clamshell rear doors for ease of loading – a popular feature with civil air ambulance operators and police forces, who have enthusiastically adopted the EC135.

VARIANTS

There are two versions of both the EC135 and military-optimised EC635, each with the same designation suffix. The P1 variants use Pratt & Whitney PW206B turboshafts, while the T1 is powered by Turboméca Arrius units. Both deliver the same power output, though in both cases there is a slight power increase when fitted to the EC635.

TECHNICAL DATA

Eurocopter EC635 T1

Powerplants: Two Turboméca Arrius 2B1 turboshafts

Developing: 435kW (583eshp)

Driving: Four-blade main and fenestron tail rotors

Main rotor diameter: 10.2m (33.5ft)

Fuselage length: 10.21m (33.5ft)

Height: 3.62m (11.9ft)

All-up weight: 2,900kg (6,400lb)

Maximum speed: 277km/h (172mph)

Cruise speed: 260km/h (161mph)

Operational ceiling: 20,000ft

Maximum ferry range: 925km (574 miles)

Endurance: 4hr 10min

Accommodation: One pilot and 7/8 passengers, or two pilots and 6/7 passengers.

First flown: 15 February 1994

Entered service: Civil deliveries commenced during the latter half of 1996. The EC135 T1 is entering German Army service during 2000, the first recipient being the Heeresfliegerwaffenschule (Army Weapons School) at Bückeburg.

Eurocopter EC135

Eurofighter Typhoon

TWIN-TURBOFAN SINGLE-SEAT MULTI-ROLE COMBAT AIRCRAFT

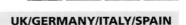

Eurofighter Typhoon

TECHNICAL DATA

Eurofighter Typhoon

Powerplants: Two Eurojet EJ200 afterburning turbofans
Developing: 60.0kN (13,490lb st); 90.0kN (20,227lb st) with afterburner
Span: 10.95m (36ft 0in)
Length: 15.96m (52ft 5in)
Height: 5.28m (17ft 4in)
All-up weight: 21,000kg (46,297lb)
Maximum speed: Mach 2; 2,125km/h (1,324mph)
Maximum range: 3,705km (2,300miles)
Mission range: 1,852km (1,151 miles)
Endurance: Over 3.25hr
Accommodation: Pilot only
Warload: Up to 6,500kg (14,300lb) including BVRAAMs, ASRAAMs, AIM-9L Sidewinders, 454kg (1,000lb bombs, BL755 cluster bombs, laser-guided bombs (GBU-24 and Paveway III) and ALARMs in the air-to-surface role; and a wide range of other stores due to be added in the future including Storm Shadow, Brimstone, JDAMs and Harpoon.
First flown: 27 March 1994 (DA1-Germany); 6 April 1994 (DA2-England); 31 August 1996 (DA6-two-seater)
Entered service: Service operational evaluation units due to be formed in 2002; first operational squadrons will receive the Typhoon in 2004.

DEVELOPMENT

The Eurofighter consortium of British Aerospace (now BAE Systems), Germany's MBB (today Daimler-Chrysler Aerospace) and Aeritalia (later Alenia) of Italy, joined soon by Spain's CASA, was established in June 1986 in order to develop and produce a new-generation air superiority fighter which was then scheduled to enter service by the late 1990s. BAe's EAP (Experimental Aircraft Programme) demonstrator provided much valuable data input for the programme between 1986 and 1991, during which time the Eurofighter's design requirements had been finalised by the four governments involved. Part of this was to be the development of the Eurojet EJ200 powerplants, by Rolls-Royce, MTU, Fiat Avio and ITP. Contracts for the provision of eight prototypes and subsequent testing were signed in November 1988. However, German worries about funding led to detail design changes in an effort to cut costs, resulting in the final Eurofighter 2000 variant, and each nation scaled down its purchasing requirements. The initial two prototypes, DA1 built by DASA in Germany and then DA2 from BAe Warton, finally made their maiden flights during March and April 1994 respectively, powered by interim Rolls-Royce RB199 turbofans. Alenia's DA3 was the first Eurofighter to be equipped with the definitive EJ200 engines, getting airborne in June 1995; in August 1996, the first Spanish prototype, DA6, became the first two-seater to fly. All aircraft

have subsequently been re-engined. In September 1998, the aircraft was named the Eurofighter Typhoon.

CURRENT SERVICE

Typhoons are on the strength of the manufacturers' own trials fleets, forming part of the German armed forces' WTD-61, Italian RSV and Spanish Grupo 54/CLAEX trials units, and the UK's Defence Procurement Agency/BAE Systems at Warton. Procurement will total 232 aircraft for the RAF, 180 for the Luftwaffe, 121 for the Italian Air Force and 87 for the Spanish Air Force. The Hellenic Air Force seems set to receive between 60 and 90 examples from around 2006.

SPECIAL FEATURES

From the outset the Eurofighter Typhoon was designed to have an unstable aerodynamic configuration for increased agility in both the beyond visual range (BVR) and close-in spheres of air combat, the design incorporating prominent canard foreplanes and an active digital fly-by-wire system. The ECR 90 radar allows automatic assessment and prioritisation of targets at over 70 miles away, while the EJ200 engines' ability for employment in the 'supercruise' mode, at high speed without recourse to afterburning, will enable the Typhoon to quickly close on adversaries. In close-range combat, the pilot can make use of Directive Voice Input (DVI) and Voice Throttle and Stick (VTAS) technology, allowing various functions

to be undertaken automatically. German and Italian Typhoons will only be flown in the air-to-air role, but those of the UK and Spain will have a multi-role capability for operation in the air-to-surface mode.

VARIANTS

So far, only two basic variants have been produced, the single- and two-seat Typhoons, but varying weapons fits will of course allow a whole range of different individual roles to be undertaken including SEAD and maritime attack alongside the 'basic' air-to-air and air-to-ground taskings.

Eurofighter Typhoon

Extra EA300

SINGLE PISTON-ENGINED AEROBATIC AIRCRAFT

Extra EA300 Jordan

TECHNICAL DATA

Extra EA300S

Powerplant: One Textron Lycoming AEIO-540-L1B5 flat-six piston engine
Developing: 224kW (300hp)
Driving: Three or four-blade (on EA303S) propeller
Span: 8.00m (26ft 3in)
Length: 7.12m (23ft 4.25in)
Height: 2.62m (8ft 7.25in)
All-up weight: 950kg (2,094lb)
Aerobatic weight: 870kg (1,918lb)
Maximum speed: 342km/h (213mph)
Cruise speed: 315km/h (196mph)
Operational ceiling: 16,000ft
Maximum range: 974km (605miles)
Accommodation: One pilot and one passenger
First flown: 14 July 1983 (Extra 230); 4 May 1988 (EA300); 4 March 1992 (EA300S)
Entered service: 1989 (Chile)

DEVELOPMENT

To compete with the increasing range of capable Russian aerobatic aircraft, Walter Extra in Germany, began the design of his first single-seat monoplane in the early 1980s – the Extra 230, which featured wooden wings. Based mainly on the Stephens Akro with a raised rear fuselage and faired-in cockpit, it was initially known as a Stephens Akro Laser EA230, and first flew in July 1983. After the formation of Extra Flugzeubau GmbH, the EA230 was put into production at Dinslaken, and a new manufacturing facility was completed in 1995. The single-seat design led to the tandem two-seat EAS300, which features a composite wing.

CURRENT SERVICE

Extra EA300s serve with the Chilean Air Force, who took delivery of six during 1989 and 1990, as equipment for Escuadeilla de Alta Acróbacia (*Los Halcones*), the national aerobatic team based with Brigada Aérea II at Santiago-Los Cerrillos. They replaced the team's Pitts S-2A/S Specials between 1989-90, and are also used for aerobatic training. The quasi-military *Royal Jordanian Falcons* aerobatic team operates Extra 300s at the Al Matar Air Base, Amman/Marka. The French Air Force's 'Equipe de Voltige' has purchased an Extra 300 and an Extra 300S for aerobatic use at Salon de Provence.

SPECIAL FEATURES

A distinctive feature is the long canopy, the cockpit being able to accommodate a seat for a passenger as well as the pilot. When flying alone, the pilot usually sits at the rear of the cockpit. It has a cantilever composite arch main wheel undercarriage with wheel spats and steerable tailwheel. As it was designed for unlimited competition aerobatics it features additional transparencies to the lower sides of the cockpit.

VARIANTS

No other versions of the Extra 300 are in military service apart from those used by the Chileans, French and Jordanians. The Extra 300S is the single-seat version of the 300 with the same powerplant, but with a shortened wing by 50cm (19.5in) and more powerful ailerons, but as yet, none are in military service. The Extra 300L is a low-wing version (instead of mid-wing) with deeper ailerons, and the fuselage is shortened by 25cm (10in). The more recent 330 is a modified version of the 300, fitted with a Lycoming AEIO-580 engine.

Extra EA300 Chilean Air Force *Los Halcones*

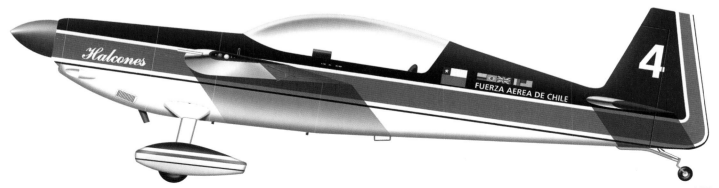

Fairchild C-123 Provider

TWIN PISTON/JET-ENGINED MEDIUM TRANSPORT AND MULTI-MISSION AIRCRAFT

C-123K Provider Honduran Air Force

TECHNICAL DATA

Fairchild C-123K Provider
Powerplants: Two Pratt & Whitney R-2800-99W
Double Wasp piston engines and two General
Electric J85-GE-17 turbojets
Developing: 1,715kW (2,300hp) and 12.69kN
(2,850lb st) each respectively
Span: 33.53m (110ft 0in)
Length: 23.92m (76ft 3in)
Height: 10.39m (34ft 1in)
All-up weight: 18,288kg (60,000lb)
Maximum speed: 367km/h (228mph)
Cruise speed: 278km/h (173mph)
Operational ceiling: 29,000ft
Maximum range: 5,279km (3,390miles)
Mission range: 1,666km (1,033miles) with max payload
Accommodation: Two pilots and up to 61 fully-
equipped troops or 50 stretchers
First flown: 1 September 1954 (C-123B);
 27 May 1966 (C-123K)
Entered service: 1956 (C-123B); 1967 (C-123K)

DEVELOPMENT

Almost uniquely, the C-123 Provider was developed from a glider transport design – the little-known, all-metal Chase XG-20. An example of this machine was fitted with two Pratt & Whitney R-2800 piston engines, and was put into production by Fairchild as the C-123B Provider, with 302 aircraft forming an initial USAF order. Production later switched to the C-123K with dual piston/jet power. Providers saw very extensive service during the Vietnam campaign, being used as tactical transports and also for numerous other duties such as the dropping of Agent Orange, to defoliate the North Vietnamese forest canopy. AC-123K gunships were also adapted from standard transports during the war.

CURRENT SERVICE

Nowadays, the venerable Provider is a rare bird, but one which still flies with three nations – albeit with a total of only seven aircraft between them, all C-123Ks. One is used by the Honduran Air Force's Escuadron Transporte, while two are flown by No 602 Squadron of the Royal Thai Air Force for cloud-seeding duties. The paramilitary Peruvian National Police, quite an extensive air arm, has four aircraft on charge with Escuadron 500 at Jorge Chavez International Airport, Lima, to assist in the struggle against the narcotics trade and terrorist activities.

SPECIAL FEATURES

The most distinctive feature of the C-123K version

that remains in service today are the two J85 turbojet engines mounted in underwing pods just outboard of the R-2800 pistons. This yielded a welcome boost in performance, especially in 'hot and high' conditions, or when the aircraft were especially heavily-laden.

VARIANTS

Of all those produced, only the **C-123K** is still in use. Those of the Royal Thai Air Force carry cloud-seeding equipment but are otherwise standard transports.

C-123K Provider Honduran Air Force

Fairchild A-10 Thunderbolt II

TWIN-TURBOFAN CLOSE AIR SUPPORT AIRCRAFT

USA

A-10A Thunderbolt II US Air Force

TECHNICAL DATA

Fairchild A-10A Thunderbolt II

Powerplants: Two General Electric TF34-GE-100 turbofans
Developing: 40.32kN (9,065lb st)
Span: 17.53m (57ft 6in)
Length: 16.26m (53ft 4in)
Height: 4.47m (14ft 8in)
All-up weight: 22,680kg (50,000lb)
Maximum speed: 834km/h (518mph)
Cruise speed: 706km/h (439mph)
Operational ceiling: 30,500ft
Maximum range: 3949km (2,451miles)
Mission range: 1,000km (621miles)
Accommodation: Pilot only
Warload: One General Electric GAU-8/A Avenger 30mm seven-barrelled cannon contaning up to 1,350 rounds of either high explosive or armour-piercing ammunition; up to ten AGM-65 Maverick anti-armour missiles and an AIM-9L Sidewinder for self-defence, or various types of bombs including CBU-52, CBU-71 or CBU-87 cluster munitions. OA-10s are normally equipped with an LAU-68 rocket pod for their FAC role.
First flown: 10 May 1972 (YA-10A); 1 October 1975 (production A-10A)
Entered service: March 1977

DEVELOPMENT

The USAF's AX requirement for a new, dedicated, highly-survivable counter-insurgency and close air support aircraft, building on lessons learned during the Vietnam conflict, brought two final contenders for this important order – the Northrop A-9 and Fairchild A-10. Two prototype YA-10As were flown, subsequently beating the competition after evaluation was completed; one was converted afterwards to two-seat YA-10B configuration, although this all-weather variant (carrying a weapons systems officer) was cancelled. The type's most important deployment began in early 1978, when the 81st Tactical Fighter Wing at RAF Bentwaters and Woodbridge in the UK received their first Thunderbolt IIs. Its role, had the Cold War escalated, would have been the destruction of the Warsaw Pact's advancing armour, operating from forward bases in Germany. It took until Operation *Desert Storm* in 1991 for the A-10 to earn its combat spurs, when 144 aircraft from wings normally based in the UK and USA deployed to Saudi Arabia. During the conflict, they shot down two helicopters and destroyed countless Iraqi military vehicles, air defence

installations and *Scud* missile launch sites.

CURRENT SERVICE

The USAF has remained the sole operator of the A-10A throughout its service career, though its fleet (707 were delivered) has been steadily reduced in recent years following the end of the Cold War and the subsequent drawdown of forces, especially in Europe. Three operational Wings of Air Combat Command (the 23rd, 347th and 355th Wings) now fly the type along with the 81st Fighter Wing, USAF Europe. In addition, three Air Force Reserve Command and six Air National Guard squadrons also fly the type.

SPECIAL FEATURES

High battlefield survivability was a particularly important feature of the A-10's design from the outset, with more emphasis being placed on this attribute and on low-level agility than on outright performance. The two TF34 turbofans are mounted high on the rear fuselage in order to lessen the risk of their being hit by small arms fire, while both the pilot and ammunition are protected by a bathtub-

type titanium shield. The strong structure enables multiple hits to be taken with the aircraft remaining airborne, and fast maintenance at base or at Forward Operating Locations is aided by the A-10's relatively simple structure and ease of component replacement.

VARIANTS

Apart from the two-seat **YA-10B** there has only been one other Thunderbolt II variant. This is the **OA-10A**, used in the Forward Air Control role without any modification to the aircraft, except to carry smoke rockets and Sidewinder AAMs for self defence. Various detail improvements have been made to the A-10A fleet over the years, including the addition of autopilot.

A-10A Thunderbolt II US Air Force

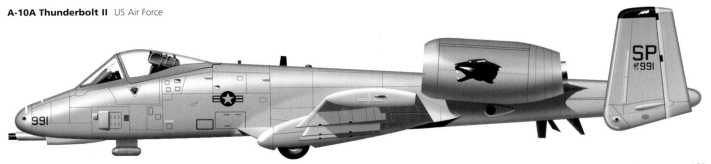

Fairchild (Swearingen) Metro, Merlin & C-26

TWIN-TURBOPROP LIGHT TRANSPORT AND MULTI-MISSION AIRCRAFT

Fairchild C-26A United States Air Force

DEVELOPMENT

Initial production of this twin-turboprop executive transport series began with the Swearingen Merlin II in 1966. Four years later, the Merlin III appeared, with a re-designed tail layout being the major external alteration. In 1981, Swearingen was purchased by Fairchild, under whose banner the line continued thereafter. The stretched Metro III formed the basis for the C-26A selected by the USAF for the Air National Guard's Operational Support Aircraft (ANGOSA) requirement, and various versions of this Metro and the equivalent Merlin IV have been purchased as VIP transports. Fairchild has also developed the Multi-Mission Surveillance Aircraft (MMSA) as a quickly-convertible ELINT/recce/survey and standard transport aircraft, although no sales have yet been achieved.

CURRENT SERVICE

The Argentine Army Corps flies four Merlin IIIAs and a trio of IVAs for communications and VIP duties at Córdoba and Bahia Blanca, while the Belgian Air Force does likewise with its five Merlin IIIAs with 15 Wing Tpt Aè at Melsbroek, and also the Mexican Air Force, using a single IVA. The three Merlin IVAs of the Royal Thai Air Force are flown on survey sorties with Wing 6 at Don Muang, and four Metro IIIs equip a unit of the Chilean Police (Carabineros de Chile). The US military is by far the largest single user

of the type with C-26A/Bs initially used by 26 Air National Guard squadrons, and 11 Army National Guard flight detachments. More recently seven of these have been transferred to the US Navy as C-26Ds, three being allocated for use in the Pacific theatre and four in Europe. A civil-registered Merlin IV, designated Tp88, is operated by the Swedish Air Force trials unit.

SPECIAL FEATURES

Compared with the earlier Merlin III, the subsequent Metro III and Merlin IV have a significantly-lengthened, more slender fuselage and smaller fin area. C-26A/Bs are equipped with quick-change 'combi' interiors enabling cargo, passengers or stretcher cases to be carried with ease at short notice.

VARIANTS

Only the **Merlin III** as used by Argentina and Belgium represents the earlier members of this family in military service. The **Metro III** and **Merlin IV** are basically equivalent to one another as the stretched VIP/ general transports, from which the MMSA and an earlier Swedish Air Force **Tp88** AEW development platform (not adopted for service) were developed. US military **C-26As** were later followed into service by the improved **C-26B**, incorporating GPS and a microwave landing system.

TECHNICAL DATA

Fairchild Metro III/C-26A
Powerplants: Two Garrett (Allied Signal) TPE331-121UAR turboprops
Developing: 834kW (1,119eshp)
Driving: four-blade propellers
Span: 17.37m (57ft 0in)
Length: 18.09m (59ft 4.25in)
Height: 5.08m (16ft 8in)
All-up weight: 6,577kg (14,500lb)
Maximum speed: 517km/h (321mph)
Cruise speed: 467km/h (290mph)
Operational ceiling: 27,500ft
Maximum range: 1,970km (1,222 miles)
Mission range: 711km (400 miles)
Accommodation: Two crew and up to 19 passengers
First flown: 1981 (Metro III)
Entered service: 1988 (C-26A)

Merlin IIIA Belgian Air Force

Fairchild Dornier 328

TWIN-TURBOPROP VIP TRANSPORT

Dornier 328 Colombian Air Force

DEVELOPMENT

Following on from the proven 19-seat Dornier 228, it was decided by Dornier to progress with a new, more advanced, 30 seat regional airliner successor. It differs substantially in appearance from its predecessor, with a rounded fuselage and T-tail, but retains a high-wing layout. Production is undertaken by Fairchild Aerospace in Germany with the collaboration of a number of international partners, notably OGMA in Portugal, which was recently selected as the supplier of Do 328 fuselage shells, while Aermacchi (cockpit shells) and DaimlerChrysler Aerospace (wing, empennage and tail components) are among the other groups involved.

CURRENT SERVICE

Only one military customer has been found for the Dornier 328 to date – this is Colombia's para-military passenger and cargo carrier SATENA, which uses six examples of the 328-120.

SPECIAL FEATURES

The Dornier 328 is equipped with a Honeywell Primus 2000 EFIS cockpit, including five colour multi-function screen displays and a full-colour weather radar. Composites make up 25% of the structural weight.

VARIANTS

The basic production variant is the **328-110**, using the Pratt & Whitney PW119B powerplant. Also available is the 328-120, powered by the PW119C, which adds an extra 5% of thermodynamic power and thus boasts an improved 'hot and high' performance. Adding to the type's short-field capabilities, the **328-130** has improved flaps and ground spoilers. The **328 Utility** is a projected version suited to several different roles, from quick-change cargo carrying to flying sensors platform. The **328-210** is a high-density variant of the 328-100, with four-abreast seating for up to 99 passengers. The **328-220** is a high-density variant of the 328-130. In addition Fairchild Aerospace offers a range of jet developments, of which the **328JET** is the sole current production derivative, with P&W PW306/9 turbofans of 26.9kN (6,050lb st). It will however be followed by the 70-seat **728JET**, which might well be offered by Northrop Grumman as an airborne early warning platform to sit alongside the smaller E-2 Hawkeye in their 'range' of such aircraft.

Dornier 328

TECHNICAL DATA

Fairchild Dornier 328-110

Powerplants: Two Pratt & Whitney PW119B turboprops
Developing: 1,625kW (2,180shp)
Span: 20.98m (68ft 10in)
Length: 21.28m (69ft 10in)
Height: 7.24m (23ft 9in)
All-up weight: 13,990kg (30,843lb)
Maximum speed: 620km/h (386mph)
Operational ceiling: 28,000ft
Maximum range: 1,853km (1,151 miles)
Accommodation: Crew of two and up to 34 passengers
Warload: None
First flown: 6 December 1991
Entered service: First civil use with Air Engiadina from 21 October 1993; entered SATENA service during 1994

FAMA/FMA IA-50 Guaraní II

TWIN-TURBOPROP TRANSPORT AND UTILITY AIRCRAFT

FMA IA-50 Guaraní II Argentine Air Force

DEVELOPMENT

The original DINFIA Guaraní I was a twin-turboprop light transport designed and built by the Fábrica Militaire de Avions State Aircraft Factory. It used some structural components of the earlier IA35 Huanquero and first flew on 6 February 1962. The IA-50 (originally known as the FA2) was subsequently developed with more powerful (693kW/930shp) Turboméca Bastan VI-A turboprops. The new type featured modified wings with de-icing boots, a single swept fin and rudder and had a lighter, shorter fuselage. Two prototypes were built, the first flying on 23 April 1963, followed by a pre-production aircraft that was modified to meet FAA requirements. Production was initiated in 1964 with an initial contract for 21 aircraft. Subsequently

this total was increased to 38 aircraft with deliveries to the Argentinean Air Force for communications, photographic (with the Military Geographic Institute) and executive transport duties. The Argentinean Navy also received one as a staff transport.

CURRENT SERVICE

Forty-one were built, including prototypes, and all served with the Argentine forces. Only a handful now remain in service with 11 Brigade Aérea at Base Aérea General Urguiza at Parana. The type has gradually been replaced, from the mid-1990s, by surplus US C-12 Hurons.

SPECIAL FEATURES

The Guaraní has a fuselage door with built-in steps at the rear on the port side. It has a low-set wing and a

large sharply swept tail. The passenger executive version had two rows of three inward facing seats. The utility and paratroop had seven inward facing seats on the port side of the cabin and eight on the starboard side, while the navigation trainer had six seats with three equipment consoles. One Guaraní was fitted with a ski undercarriage for Antarctic operations.

VARIANTS

One was furnished as an executive transport for use by the President of Argentina. A navigator and radar training version was also built and four were configured for photo-survey work. Three were adapted for navaid and landing system calibration flights. Some were used as air ambulances and could carry six stretchers and two attendants.

TECHNICAL DATA

FMA IA-50 Guaraní II

Powerplants: Two Turboméca Bastan VI-A turboprops
Developing: 693kW (930shp)
Driving: Three-blade propellers
Span: 19.59m (64ft 3.25in)
Length: 15.30m (50ft 2.5in)
Height: 5.61m (18ft 5in)
All-up weight: 7,750kg (17,055lb)
Maximum speed: 500km/h (311mph)
Cruising speed: 450km/h (280mph)
Operational ceiling: 41,000ft
Maximum range: 2,575km (1,600 miles)
Accommodation: Crew of two and up to 15 passengers
Warload: None
First flown: 23 April 1963
Entered service: 1965

FMA IA-50 Guaraní II Argentine Air Force

FFA AS202 Bravo

SINGLE PISTON-ENGINED PRIMARY/BASIC TRAINER

AS202/18A-4 Bravo Omani Air Force

DEVELOPMENT
SIAI-Marchetti designed the type in the late 1960s as the S202, and it was officially launched as a joint venture between the Italian concern and Flug und Fahrzeugwerke AG (FFA) of Switzerland. Prototypes were flown in both countries during 1969, and four years later the project was taken over entirely by FFA. Since then, various engine sizes have been offered, as well as variants with differing individual fitments. Its relatively high cost, coupled with good performance and agility, is the main reason that the Bravo has sold better to the military than to civilian customers.

CURRENT SERVICE
The largest Bravo user is the Indonesian Air Force with 25 AS202/18A-3s in service with its primary flying school – Skwadron Pendidikan 101 at Adisumarmo. Some 20 AS202/18A-2s are still used by the Iraqi Air Force, while ten 18A-1 examples are flown by the Royal Moroccan Air Force for Initial Selection at Marrakech, and a single aircraft by the Ugandan Air Force. Four 18A-4s equip part of No 1 Squadron, Omani Air Force at Misirah for primary training.

SPECIAL FEATURES
It is possible for the Bravo to be fitted out as a three-seater, with the instructor sitting to the left and two students on a wider seat to the right under the wide bubble canopy. It is a fairly conventional light aircraft, with non-retractable landing gear and side-by-side seating.

VARIANTS
The main production **AS202/18A** has spawned four sub-types. The **18A-1** has the lightest gross weight of these, at 950kg for aerobatics; this was increased by 30kg on the **A-2**, which also has a bigger canopy and electric trim. On the lower-cost **A-3**, the trim is operated mechanically and this aircraft has a simpler electrical system. Only the Omani Royal Flight uses the **A-4**, which has a gross weight of 1,010kg and improved instruments. The **Bravo 32TP** is a turbine-powered (240kW/320shp) Allison 250-B17C version, that flew in 1991, but this has not been further developed. The utility version has space for 100kg (221lb) of baggage in lieu of the rear seat. In 1990, FFA transferred all its aviation activities to FFT and the **Eurotrainer 2000A** was developed – a four-seat aircraft based on the Bravo, but of composite construction and featuring retractable landing gear, the first of which was flown on 29 April 1991.

TECHNICAL DATA

FFA AS202/18A-2 Bravo

Powerplant: One Textron Lycoming AEIO-360-B1F piston engine
Developing: 134kW (180hp)
Driving: two-blade propeller
Span: 9.75m (31ft 11.75in)
Length: 7.50m (24ft 7.25in)
Height: 2.81m (9ft 2.75in)
All-up weight: 1,080kg (2,381lb)
Maximum speed: 240km/h (148mph)
Cruise speed: 226km/h (141mph)
Operational ceiling: 18,000ft
Maximum range: 1,140km (707miles)
Accommodation: Two/three side-by-side
First flown: 7 March 1969 (Swiss); 7 May 1969 (SIAI-built)
Entered service: 1972

AS202/18A-3 Bravo Indonesian Air Force

FMA (FAMA) IA-58 Pucará

TWIN-TURBOPROP CLOSE AIR SUPPORT AND COUNTER-INSURGENCY AIRCRAFT

IA-58A Pucará Uruguayan Air Force

TECHNICAL DATA

FMA IA-58A Pucará

Powerplants: Two Turboméca Astazou XVIG turboprops
Developing: 729kW (978eshp) each
Span: 14.50m (47ft 6.8in)
Length: 14.25m (46ft 9in)
Height: 5.36m (17ft 7in)
All-up weight: 6,800kg (14,991lb)
Maximum speed: 500km/h (311mph)
Cruise speed: 430km/h (267mph)
Operational ceiling: 32,800ft
Maximum range: 3,710km (2,305 miles)
Mission range: 400km (248 miles)
Accommodation: Two in tandem
Warload: Two 20mm Hispano HS-284 cannon, four 7.62mm Browning machine guns in forward fuselage and up to 1500kg (3,307lb) of external stores including cannon, rockets and iron bombs.
First flown: 20 August 1969 (prototype);
8 November 1974 (IA-58A)
Entered service: 1976

DEVELOPMENT

Recognising the likelihood of the Argentine Air Force becoming involved in counter-insurgency and anti-guerilla warfare operations, the FMA concern (then part of the air arm's Support Command) began design studies in the 1960s on the twin-turboprop IA-58 optimised for these roles. The first prototype flew with Garrett TPE331 engines, but these were replaced by the Astazou for all subsequent examples. Only the IA-58A Pucara has been produced, updated versions with improved cannon armament and increased survivability having both been shelved.

CURRENT SERVICE

Only one Argentine Air Force unit, Grupo 3, now flies the Pucara, with 40 on operational strength and some 25 in storage, out of 108 built for the Argentine Air Force. Three are operated by the Sri Lankan Air Force with No 1 Flying Training Wing at Anuradhapura, and four more by the Uruguayan Air Force. A trio of Pucaras were donated to the Colombian Air Force in 1989 by the Argentine Air Force.

SPECIAL FEATURES

When optmised for short-field operations, the IA-58A can be equipped with three JATO bottles to provide a better take-off performance. The stalky undercarriage facilitates not only the carriage of a good weapons load, but also easier operation from unprepared strips. Only the front cockpit is armoured, as Pucaras rarely fly with a second crew member in combat.

VARIANTS

While only the **IA-58A** has ever seen service, three modified prototypes have since flown between 1979-85. The **IA-58B** was equipped with two 30mm DEFA cannon and improved avionics, while the **IA-58C**, which first flew in May 1979, altered the design to include a single bubble canopy and an increased range of weaponry including Matra Magic AAMs. Finally, the **IA-66** returned to the Garrett TPE331 to provide power, but as with its two predecessors, no orders were forthcoming.

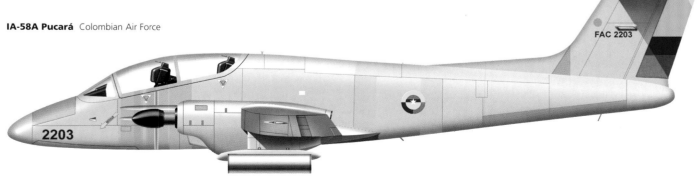

IA-58A Pucará Colombian Air Force

FMA (FAMA) IA-63 Pampa

SINGLE TURBOFAN ADVANCED AND WEAPONS TRAINER

IA-63 Pampa Argentine Air Force

DEVELOPMENT

Intended as a replacement for Morane Saulnier MS.760 Paris armed jet trainers (built under licence by FMA), design work on the IA-63 Pampa began in 1979. Dornier assisted in the process, following on from the success of the Alpha Jet, and a distinct similarity between the two aircraft can be discerned. The TFE731 engine was selected at the outset – plans to power a later prototype with a Pratt & Whitney JT15D-5 unit falling by the wayside.

CURRENT SERVICE

Sole operator of the IA-63 Pampa is the Argentine Air Force. Eighteen examples are flown by Grupo 4 de Caza, Escuadrón I, BAM El Plumerillo, Mendoza, to provide advanced training and weapons instruction. They are also used by Commando de Material, Centro de Ensayos en Vuelo BAM Códoba. Funding cuts have severely delayed or curtailed further procurement plans for front-line units. However, the fleet has now virtually been fully upgraded for the operational light attack role, apart from its primary purpose as a weapons trainer.

SPECIAL FEATURES

While the Pampa does resemble the Alpha Jet in many ways, the use of an unswept wing configuration does distinguish the Argentine aircraft from its European counterpart in one important respect. The IA-63's primary control system is operated by a dual-system hydraulic servo unit, backed up by an auxiliary ram-air turbine, and hydraulics are likewise used for the undercarriage, flap and airbrake mechanisms.

VARIANTS

The standard IA-63 has been the only version to see production thus far, but the improved **Pampa 2000** was offered to the US military as a contender for its joint-service JPATS trainer requirement. Marketed in conjunction with Vought, this aircraft would have featured American avionics, but it failed to gain the JPATS order.

IA-63 Pampa Argentine Air Force

TECHNICAL DATA

FMA IA-63 Pampa

Powerplant: One Garrett TFE731-2-2N turbofan
Developing: 15.57kN (3,500lb st)
Span: 9.69m (31ft 9.25in)
Length: 10.93m (35ft 10.25in)
Height: 4.29m (14ft 1in)
All-up weight: 5,000kg (11,023lb)
Maximum speed: 819km/h (509mph)
Cruise speed: 747km/h (464mph)
Operational ceiling: 42,325ft
Maximum range: 1,853km (1,150 miles)
Mission range: 440km (272 miles)
Endurance: 3hr 48min
Accommodation: Two in tandem
Warload: Up to 3,417lb (1,550kg) of external stores including a 30mm DEFA cannon in a ventral pod, and various iron bomb fitments.
First flown: 6 October 1984
Entered service: March 1988

Fokker F-27

Fokker F-27-400M Finnish Air Force

DEVELOPMENT

The success of the basic F-27 Friendship commuter airliner design led Fokker to offer the type for military customers as the F-27-300M Troopship, equipped with a strengthened floor and cargo doors. The Royal Netherlands Air Force became the first customer of the specifically military version, after an earlier purchase of three F-27-100s for VIP transport. The F-27-400M which followed used an uprated version of the Dart turboprop. Later, Fokker offered a new maritime reconnaissance derivative, with various F-27 Maritime sub-types going into production. Many air arms acquired ex-civil examples for military use.

CURRENT SERVICE

Multiple examples of the military F-27 are flown by the Argentine Air Force (twelve in total comprising F-27-400s, 500s and 600s), Bolivian Air Force (six 400Ms), Finnish Air Force (two 100s and a 400M),

Ghana Air Force (three 400Ms and a 600), Indonesian Air Force (seven 400Ms), Iranian Air Force, Army and Navy (sixteen aircraft, mostly 400Ms), Myanmar Air Defence Force (four FH-227s), Nigerian Air Force (two 200MPAs), Pakistan Air Force, Army and Navy (200s and 400Ms), Peruvian Navy (a dozen 200s), Senegalese Air Force (eight 200s and six 400s), Spanish Air Force (three 200MPAs) and the Royal Thai Navy (three 200 Maritime Enforcers and two 400Ms). Operators of single F-27s are Guatemala, the Icelandic and Indian Coast Guards, the Phillippines and Uruguay.

SPECIAL FEATURES

All F-27M Troopship versions were fitted with quick-change interiors, allowing for an easy switch between the passenger and cargo-carrying roles. The Maritime derivatives use an underfuselage Litton APS-504 search radar, bulged observation windows, and nose-mounted Bendix weather radar.

VARIANTS

The **F-27-100** is primarily a VIP transport, while the **F-27-300M** and **400M Troopships** were dedicated military types. Later updates included the **F-27-500** with a fuselage stretch and capacity for 60 passengers. Most F-27 Maritimes are of **F-27-200MPA** standard, though Thailand flies the armed Maritime Enforcer on anti-shipping and armed ASW duties. FH-227s were licence-built by Fairchild-Hiller in the USA.

TECHNICAL DATA

Fokker F-27-400M

Powerplants: Two Rolls-Royce Dart RDa.7 Mk532-7 turboprops
Developing: 1,528kW (2,050eshp)
Driving: four-blade propellers
Span: 29.00m (95ft 2in)
Length: 23.56m (77ft 3.5in)
Height: 8.70m (28ft 7in)
All-up weight: 20,412kg (45,000lb)
Maximum speed: 474km/h (293mph)
Cruise speed: 463km/h (287mph)
Operational ceiling: 25,000ft
Maximum range: 1,807km (1,125miles)
Mission range: 1,241km (770miles)
Endurance: up to eight hours
Accommodation: Two crew and 46 paratroops or 6,025kg (13,283lb) of cargo
Warload: None, though a Maritime Enforcer was offered
First flown: 24 November 1955; 1965 (F-27-400M)
Entered service: 1957

Fokker F-27-200MPA Spanish Air Force

Fokker F-28 Fellowship

F-28 3000C Fellowship Argentine Air Force

DEVELOPMENT

Following the success of the turboprop F-27 series, Fokker decided to embark upon an entry into the twin-jet small medium-range airliner market. The F-28 soon found favour with numerous commuter and 'feeder' carriers worldwide, and likewise became popular with several air arms and governments as a comfortable VIP transport with a short/rough-field capability that proved particularly popular in Africa and South America, as evidenced by the list of nations that fly it. Apart from the different marks detailed below, the F-28 was later developed into the Fokker 100 (described separately).

CURRENT SERVICE

Argentina is the main military F-28 operator, its air force flying two Mk1000s with its Presidential Flight and four Mk1000s, and the Navy using three Mk3000s. Fellowships are also in service in Cambodia, Colombia, Ecuador, Ghana, Indonesia, Malaysia, Peru, the

Philippines, Tanzania and Togo. Most of these are with Government, Presidential and VIP units, and some are civil-registered or flown by para-military airlines (the latter being SATENA in Colombia and TAME in Ecuador).

SPECIAL FEATURES

The F-28 was developed with a short/rough-field capability, and various different marks are equipped with such as side-loading freight doors and quick-change 'combi' passenger-cargo interior fitments.

VARIANTS

The standard **Mk1000** normally carries 65 seats, but this total is obviously reduced in the VIP transport role. A variation is the **Mk1000C** with its side-loading cargo door, while the **Mk3000** and **3000C** are equivalent versions with uprated Spey engines and a greater wingspan. The **Mk4000** stretched the basic F-28 fuselage to accommodate 79 seats.

TECHNICAL DATA

Fokker F-28 3000C Fellowship
Powerplants: Two RB183-2 Rolls-Royce Spey Mk555-15P turbofans
Developing: 44.04kN (9,990lb st)
Span: 25.07m (82ft 3in)
Length: 27.40m (89ft 10.75in)
Height: 8.47m (27ft 9.5in)
All-up weight: 33,113kg (73,000lb)
Maximum speed: 843km/h (523mph)
Cruise speed: 678km/h (421mph)
Operational ceiling: 35,000ft
Maximum range: 3,169km (1,969miles)
Accommodation: Two crew and 65 passengers
First flown: 9 May 1967 (Mk1000 prototype)
Entered service: 1969

F-28 3000C Fellowship Colombian Air Force

Fokker 50 & 60

DEVELOPMENT

An improved, modernised development of the successful F-27 Friendship/Troopship series, the first prototype Fokker 50 (also known by the manufacturer's designation of F-27-050) first took to the air three days before the end of 1985. It is a 46-68-passenger twin-turboprop transport, and is also in service with many civil airlines worldwide. Apart from sales of 'stock' aircraft as VIP transports and other proposed special missions versions, the main military derivative is the Fokker 60UTA-N which was selected by the Royal Netherlands Air Force as a replacement for its long-serving F-27-300Ms in 1994 – the new aircraft was delivered from 1996 onwards, and has proved a great success as a utility and support transport, platform for paradropping and medical evacuation aircraft.

CURRENT SERVICE

The Royal Netherlands Air Force is a primary user of the two types, with two Fokker 50s for VIP transport purposes and four 60UTA-Ns all on the strength of No 334 Squadron at Eindhoven. The Republic of Singapore Air Force operates the largest number of F50s, four being 50UTA-B utility transports while the other four are Maritime Enforcer 2 derivatives – all are in service with No 121 Squadron. Other military or quasi-military F50 customers are the Republic of China (Taiwanese) Air Force, with three VIP-configured examples; the Tanzanian People's Defence Force Air Wing, using a single civil-registered aircraft; and the Royal Thai Border Police, with one aircraft for VIP duties.

SPECIAL FEATURES

The modifications to the basic Fokker 50 design which produced the 60UTA-N are numerous. A 1.62m (5ft 4in) fuselage stretch was incorporated, along with the provision of a 3.05 x 1.78m cargo door – this enables an F-16's F100 engine to be easily loaded for transport. A fitment of radar warning receivers (RWRs) was added, along with wingtip-mounted ESM pods.

Fokker 50 Royal Netherlands Air Force

All of these changes have produced an excellent, versatile military transport which is well-liked by its Dutch pilots and has been heavily utilised.

VARIANTS

Many special-purpose Fokker 50 variants were proposed by the manufacturer in the late 1980s and early 1990s, most of them being maritime patrol derivatives. However, only one such version actually flew and was ordered: this is the **Maritime Enforcer 2**, which took to the air for the first time in January 1993. The Enforcers in service with the Republic of Singapore Air Force have a 360° Texas Instruments APS-134 search radar, an internal ASQ-504 magnetic anomaly detector and GEC FLIR equipment amongst other additions for the role. The fall of Fokker into bankruptcy in early 1996 put a stop to any further development. Forward Aircraft, that took over the production rights to the Fokker turboprops, hopes to sell three surveillance-equipped 60UTA-Ns to the Royal Netherlands Air Force.

TECHNICAL DATA

Fokker 60UTA-N

Powerplants: Two Pratt & Whitney PW127B turboprops
Developing: 2,050kW (2,750shp)
Driving: Six-blade propellers
Span: 29.00m (95ft 1in)
Length: 26.87m (88ft 2in)
Height: 8.34m (27ft 3in)
All-up weight: 22,950kg (50,596lb)
Maximum speed: 565km/h (352mph)
Cruise speed: 522km/h (325mph)
Operational ceiling: 25,000ft
Maximum range: 2,900km (1,799miles)
Accommodation: Three crew and up to 50 passengers or 7.3 tonnes of freight
First flown: 28 December 1985 (Fokker 50); 2 November 1995 (60UTA-N)
Entered service: June 1996

Fokker 60UTA-N Royal Netherlands Air Force

Fouga (Potez/Aérospatiale) CM170 Magister

TWIN-TURBOJET ADVANCED TRAINER

FRANCE

IAI Tzukit Israeli Air Force

DEVELOPMENT

A French Air Force specification for a new advanced trainer led to the Fouga concern building three CM170 Magister prototypes, the type subsequently becoming the first jet trainer to enter service with any air arm. Fouga was taken over by Potez in 1958, becoming part of Sud Aviation in 1967, and then eventually Aérospatiale. However, it is by the original maker's name that the Magister is best known. 622 were to be built in France, and 299 under licence by Flugzeug-Union-Süd in Germany, Israel's IAI (as the Tzukit) and Valmet in Finland. The CM175 Zéphyr was a hook-equipped variant for the French Navy used for inital carrier training, but this version has now been retired.

CURRENT SERVICE

The Algerian and Royal Moroccan Air Forces each have 20 CM170s, the former's aircraft being used for light attack duties. Eleven remain in Belgian Air Force service for refresher training and base flight operations, while Magisters are also flown by the Cameroon Air Force, Gabonese Air Force and Presidential Guard, Lebanese Air Force, El Salvadorean Air Force and the Senegalese Air Force. Their roles are either advanced training or COIN. All French CM170s have now been phased out, along with the Super Magisters of the Irish Air Corps.

SPECIAL FEATURES

The CM170's butterfly tail configuration remains its most unique and distinctive feature. Also notable is the very short undercarriage and large cockpit canopy. A small tailwheel can be seen in the tailskid 'bumper', while all Magisters are fitted with tip-tanks.

VARIANTS

The **CM170-1** was the initial production variant, followed by the **CM170-2** with Marboré IVC turbojets. Modifications on the **CM170-3** included fitment of Martin-Baker ejector seats and larger fuel tanks, this version becoming known as the **Super Magister**.

TECHNICAL DATA

Fouga CM170-1 Magister

Powerplants: Two Turboméca Marboré IIA turbojets
Developing: 3.92kN (882lb st)
Span: 11.40m (37ft 5in)
Length: 10.06m (33ft 0in)
Height: 2.80m (9ft 2in)
All-up weight: 3,200kg (7,055lb)
Maximum speed: 715km/h (444mph)
Cruise speed: 650km/h (403mph)
Operational ceiling: 36,090ft
Maximum range: 1,200km (745miles)
Mission range: 925km (573miles)
Endurance: 2hr 40min
Accommodation: Two in tandem
First flown: 23 July 1952
Entered service: 1956

CM170 Magister
Belgian Air Force

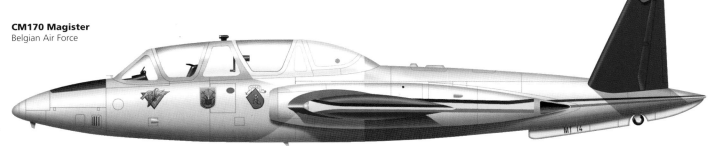

Fuji T-1

SINGLE TURBOJET ADVANCED TRAINER

Fuji T-1A Japanese Air Self-Defence Force

DEVELOPMENT

The T-1 is a very significant aeroplane in one sense, having been the first indigenous jet-powered design to be produced by the Japanese aircraft industry. It was designed to meet a Japanese Defence Agency requirement for a replacement for the North American T-6G basic trainer. Originally, the intention had been for the powerplant of all production T-1s to be of Japanese origin as well, namely an Ishikawajima-Harima J3-IHI-3 turbojet delivering 11.8kN (2,645lb st). However, it was the Bristol Siddeley (later Rolls-Royce) Orpheus engine that powered the first prototypes and the initial (and largest) production batch of T-1As. The type was originally named Hatsutaka (Young Hawk) but this name is not now used. Deliveries of the T-1 were completed in 1963.

CURRENT SERVICE

The numbers of T-1s in service with the JASDF have steadily dwindled since the arrival of the Kawasaki T-4, but the type remains in use with 13 Hiko Kyoiku-

dan (Air Training Wing) at Ashiya AB for pilot training and with Hiko Kaihatsu Jikken-dan (Air Development and Test Wing) at Gifu AB. It is gradually being replaced by the Kawasaki T-4.

SPECIAL FEATURES

A particularly distinctive feature of the T-1 is the nose air intake, which is vertically split down its centre. Also noticeable is the long cockpit canopy, while the wings have moderate sweepback, and a ventral airbrake is mounted at a point just aft of the front seat.

VARIANTS

While the **T-1A** using the Orpheus engine proved to be the main production variant, the Japanese J3 unit did see use in the **T-1B**, of which 20 were built, fitted with a 11.79kN (2,645lb st) Ishikawajima-Harima J3-IHI-3 turbojet. The **T-1C** used an uprated version of the J3 powerplant (13.8kN (3,085lb st) J3-IHI-7) and first flew during 1965, although today only T-1As and T-1Bs remain in JASDF service.

TECHNICAL DATA

Fuji T-1A

Powerplant: One Rolls-Royce (Bristol Siddeley) Orpheus Mk805 turbojet
Developing: 17.79kN (4,000lb st)
Span: 10.49m (34ft 5in)
Length: 12.12m (39ft 9.2in)
Height: 4.08m (13ft 4.6in)
All-up weight: 5,000kg (11,023lb)
Maximum speed: 925km/h (575mph)
Cruise speed: 620km/h (385mph)
Operational ceiling: 47,245ft
Maximum range: 1,860km (1,156 miles)
Mission range: 1,300km (807 miles)
Accommodation: Two in tandem
First flown: 19 January 1958 (T-1A);
17 May 1960 (T-1B); April 1965 (T-1C)
Entered service: 1959 (T-1A); September 1962 (T-1B)

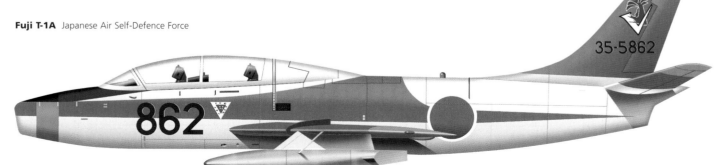

Fuji T-1A Japanese Air Self-Defence Force

Fuji T-3

Fuji T-3 Japanese Air Self-Defence Force

DEVELOPMENT

The initial KM-2 version was born out of the Beech T-34 Mentor design, a type that had already been produced under licence by Fuji Heavy Industries for the Japanese military. It incorporated numerous improvements over the American design, among them the engine – the 168kW (225hp) Continental O-470 of the T-34 was replaced by Fuji with a more powerful 253.5kW (340hp Lycoming). KM-2s were delivered to the Japanese Maritime Self-Defence Force (JMSDF), and a later order by the Japanese Air Self-Defence Force (JASDF) saw production of the equivalent T-3 derivative. Delivery was relatively slow, 50 being built for the JASDF between 1978 and 1992. The KM-2B was a modification of the

KM-2, combining the airframe and powerplant of the KM-2 with the two-seat cockpit installation of the T-34A, and first flew on 26 September 1974.

CURRENT SERVICE

All the earlier KM-2s have now been retired from service in favour of the Fuji T-5, but the more recent T-3 remains in use with the 4th Air Wing, DAI 11 and 12 Hiko Kyoku-dans at Shizuhama and Hofu-Kita ABs – the JASDF's primary training wings. It provides the first 75 hours of primary pilot training in the JASDF, prior to progressing to the Kawasaki T-4.

SPECIAL FEATURES

Except for the more powerful engine, the Fuji T-3 has many small detail differences when compared with its Beech T-34A/B precursor. The Japanese version has a slightly longer fuselage and wingspan, and a higher

maximum take-off weight. The heated and ventilated cabin has a frame canopy, with a rearward-sliding section over each seat. Dual controls and blind-flying instrumentation are standard fitments. However, the T-3's internal fuel capacity is some 76 litres (20 US gallons) less than that of the Mentor.

VARIANTS

Only the one basic version of the JASDF's T-3 has been produced by Fuji, while all the JMSDF **KM-2s** have now been retired to make way for the T-5 turboprop development(described separately). Also no longer in use is the sole sub-type of the KM-2, the **TL-1**; two were produced as basic fixed-wing trainers for the Japanese Ground Self-Defence Force (JGSDF). A modified **T-3Kai** has been developed as the prototype **T-7**, powered by a 298kW (400shp) Rolls-Royce Allison 250 turboprop, with alterations to the cowling, tail and wings.

TECHNICAL DATA

Fuji T-3

Powerplant: One Textron Lycoming IGSO-480-A1A6 piston engine
Developing: 254kW (340hp)
Driving: three-blade propeller
Span: 10.04m (32ft 11.25in)
Length: 8.04m (26ft 4.25in)
Height: 3.02m (9ft 11in)
All-up weight: 1,510kg (3,329lb)
Maximum speed: 413km/h (257mph)
Cruise speed: 254km/h (158mph)
Operational ceiling: 26,800ft
Mission range: 965km (599miles)
Accommodation: Two in tandem
First flown: July 1962 (KM-2); 17 January 1978 (T-3)
Entered service: September 1962 (KM-2); 1978 (T-3)

Fuji T-3 Japanese Air Self-Defence Force

Fuji T-5

Fuji T-5 Japanese Maritime Self-Defence Force

DEVELOPMENT

Just as the US forces replaced their piston-engined Beech T-34 Mentors with the Turbo Mentor, so the Japanese Maritime Self-Defence Force (JMSDF) wished to likewise phase out its Fuji KM-2s, developed from the American design, in favour of an all-metal light alloy turboprop successor. The KM-2D was the initial prototype of a converted derivative, but the JMSDF requirement laid down in 1987 for a further-modified KM-2 successor led to the KM-2Kai – later designated as the T-5 in Japanese service. It has an electrically retractable tricycle undercarriage.

CURRENT SERVICE

Deliveries to the JMSDF of T-5s are continuing at a steady pace, with 40 being the total order on Fuji's books. The type serves with 201 Kyoiku Kokutai of the DAI 4 Koku-dan (4th Air Wing) at Matsushima AB for basic training.

SPECIAL FEATURES

The T-5 is a very major upgrade of the T-34-derived KM-2 in all respects. Apart from the fitment of the Allison 250 turboprop, the conversion also involves modifying the cockpit to a side-by-side arrangement with a rearward-sliding blister canopy replacing the earlier aircraft's side doors. The cockpit is large enough to accommodate four seats if desired (in utility version). The T-5 has a new, rearward-swept tail fin of increased area. The tainer has dual controls and is fully aerobatic.

VARIANTS

So far, only the basic **T-5** (still designated **KM-2Kai** by the manufacturer) has been produced, and only for the JMSDF. The utility version, with a further two seats, also can be used as a military transport.

TECHNICAL DATA

Fuji KM-2 Kai (T-5)

Powerplant: One Rolls-Royce Allison 250-B17D turboprop
Developing: 261kW (350eshp)
Driving: three-blade propeller
Span: 10.04m (32ft 11.25in)
Length: 8.44m (27ft 8.25in)
Height: 2.96m (9ft 8.5in)
All-up weight: 1,805kg (3,979lb)
Maximum speed: 357km/h (222mph)
Cruise speed: 287km/h (178mph)
Operational ceiling: 25,000ft
Maximum range: 945km (587 miles)
Accommodation: Two side-by-side, with room for two further seats behind (utility version)
First flown: 28 June 1984 (KM-2D prototype); 27 April 1988 (production T-5)
Entered service: August 1988

Fuji T-5 Japanese Maritime Self-Defence Force

General Dynamics F-111

TWIN-TURBOFAN LONG-RANGE INTERDICTOR AND RECONNAISSANCE AIRCRAFT

USA

DEVELOPMENT

The gestation of the F-111 in its various forms was often a fraught one, but resulted eventually in a very capable long-range interdictor which has given sterling service, including in combat. It was developed as a result of the US Navy's need for a long-range interceptor and the USAF's TFX (Tactical Fighter Experimental) requirement, calling for a highly-capable strike aircraft able to penetrate deep into enemy territory. The USN requirement was cancelled in 1968 as the F-111B developed as a fighter was much too heavy, but the USAF received its initial F-111As during 1967. Almost immediately, the 'Aardvark' (as the type was soon nicknamed) was bloodied in combat with early series aircraft being sent to Vietnam. The RAF and Royal Australian Air Force became the first

General Dynamics F-111C Royal Australian Air Force

TECHNICAL DATA

General Dynamics F-111C

Powerplants: Two Pratt & Whitney TF30-P-103 afterburning turbofans

Developing: 82.29kN (18,500lb st) each with afterburner

Span: 21.34m (70.00ft) wings spread

Length: 22.40m (73ft 6in)

Height: 5.22m (17ft 1.4in)

All-up weight: 49,895kg (110,000lb)

Maximum speed: 2,655km/h (1,650mph)

Cruise speed: 780km/h (483mph)

Operational ceiling: 60,000ft

Maximum range: In excess of 5,950km (3,215miles)

Accommodation: Pilot and navigator/weapons systems operator

Warload: Primary weapons load is 2,000lb GBU-10/500lb GBU-12 Paveway II LGBs used in conjunction with Pave Tack laser designators. For the anti-shipping role they can carry AGM-84 Harpoon, and also have AGM-88 HARM capability. Two AIM-9P Sidewinders can be carried for self-defence. It's capability will be enhanced with the introduction of the AGM-142 RAPTOR in 2000.

First flown: 21 December 1964 (prototype)

Entered service: 1967 (F-111A); 1973 (F-111C)

---

export customers, but the British order was cancelled and the RAAF examples were only delivered after ten years of wrangling over various technical maladies. However, they soon proved their worth, and remain in Australian service. Once the teething troubles had been rectified, the USAF's F-111s were soon recognised as highly-capable aeroplanes – in 1986, F-111Fs of the 48th TFW undertook the *El Dorado Canyon* raid on Libya, while five years later the type saw significant action during the Gulf campaign. Only on the day of its retirement from active USAF service was the F-111 officially named as the Aardvark.

CURRENT SERVICE

The USAF has now retired all of its F-111s and EF-111s, leaving the Royal Australian AF as the sole operator of the type, with F-111C/G and RF-111Cs. No 82 Wing, comprising Nos 1 (strike/recce) and 6 (strike/training) Squadrons, is based at RAAF Amberley, Queensland and has 32 examples of the type on strength. The wartime task of the Strike and Reconnaissance Group would be to fly interdiction sorties within Australia's maritime approaches, and provide precision strike capability with guided weapons.

SPECIAL FEATURES

On entry into service in 1967, the F-111 became the world's first combat aircraft to use variable-geometry wing technology. The wing sweeps between 16° and 72.5°, allowing for a substantial weapons payload and an impressive low-level performance. Another unique feature is the cockpit escape capsule housing the two crew, which detaches from the aircraft as a single unit.

VARIANTS

Four **F-111As** purchased as attrition replacements remain with the Royal Australian AF, this having been the initial production version. The **F-111E** incorporated improved avionics, and those on the **D**-model that followed were more advanced still. These two variants have now all been phased out, while the nuclear-capable **FB-111A** soldiers on with the RAAF after the conversion of some to **F-111G** standard. The RAAF's **F-111Cs** are basically A-models but with the FB-111's longer-span wings, some also being recce-configured. All the Australian aircraft have recently gone through a 'digital' Avionics Upgrade Programme. Last of the production variants was the **F-111F**, which combined the FB-111's avionics with the E's weapons systems.

General Dynamics F-111C Royal Australian Air Force

Grob G102 & G103 Astir/Acro/Viking

G103 Viking T1 Royal Air Force

DEVELOPMENT

The Burkhard Grob firm's first sailplane to enter series production was the G102 Astir CS (Club Standard), of composite construction and using the company's now trademark T-tail arrangement. Various developments of the Astir line were to follow, among them the two-seat Twin Astir, before production switched to the improved G103A Twin II and Twin II Acro – the latter being the basis for the Viking TX1 ordered by the Royal Air Force.

CURRENT SERVICE

The main military user of Grob sailplanes is the Royal Air Force, which operates 91 G103As designated as Viking TX1s from its Volunteer Gliding Schools, for the training of air cadets. The Argentine Air Force uses the Astir CS and Twin Astir, while the Belgian Air Cadets fly G102 Astirs and G103A Twin IIs, and the Hellenic Air Force has five Twin Astirs. The Italian Air Force operates the Twin Astir as well.

SPECIAL FEATURES

Composite glass-fibre/resin construction was used by Grob from the outset, and has been a feature of all its products, as has the T-tail configuration. Individual variants have each incorporated detail differences over one another.

VARIANTS

The initial **G102 Astir CS**, a standard class glider, was followed into production by the **Astir CS-77** with a modified-profile fuselage, and then the **Standard III** version with the initial fuselage but of particularly lightweight design (an example of this type took the absolute world altitude record for a sailplane in 1986). On the **G102 Astir CS Jeans**, equivalent to the CS-77, the mainwheel is fixed rather than being retractable, while the **G103 Twin Astir** is a two-seat development with retractable gear ahead of the centre of gravity and no nosewheel. The fixed mainwheel was moved aft and a nosewheel added on the **G103A Twin II**, another two-seater, which then spawned the **Twin II Acro** with detail modifications and which was ordered by the RAF as the **Viking**. A new wing design and cockpit modifications were adopted for the **G103C Twin III Acro**, of which a self-launching powered version, the **Twin III SL**, was developed with a mast-mounted retractable engine and a steerable nosewheel for ease of operation.

G103 Viking T1 Royal Air Force

TECHNICAL DATA

Grob G103A Twin II Acro/Viking T1

Span: 17.5m (57ft 4in)
Length: 8.18m (26ft 10in)
Height: 1.55m (5ft 1in)
All-up weight: 580kg (1,279lb)
Maximum speed: 110km/h (68mph)
First flown: 6 December 1991
Entered service: 1992

Grob G109 & G109B Vigilant

SINGLE-ENGINED POWERED SAILPLANE

G109B Vigilant T1 Royal Air Force

DEVELOPMENT

Another self-launching sailplane from the Burkhard Grob stable, the G-109, with its initial 60kW (80hp) Limbach L2000 EB1A powerplant, was capable of a much-improved performance. Grob-Werke KG was formed in 1971 at Mindelheim in Germany and its initial products were glass-fibre sailplanes. In 1980, the powered glider G-109 was launched, which is a side-by-side two-seater, featuring an upward hinged canopy, a T-tail, non-retractable tailwheel landing gear and hydraulic brakes. It made its maiden flight on 14 March 1980 and series production began in the summer of 1981. From 1983, the generally enlarged G-109B was also available with its more powerful in-house Grob engine and modified canopy – it was this version which the RAF purchased as the Vigilant T1 for air cadet training. Production, which had ended in 1986, was resumed in 1990 to meet an RAF order for 53 aircraft.

TECHNICAL DATA

Grob G109B/Vigilant T1

Powerplant: One Grob GVW 2500 piston engine
Developing: 71kW (95hp)
Driving: two-blade propeller
Span: 17.4m (57ft 1in)
Length: 7.80m (25ft 7in)
Height: 1.80m (5ft 10.75in)
All-up weight: 850kg (1,874lb)
Maximum speed: 240km/h (149mph)
Cruising speed: 190km/h (118mph)
Operational ceiling: 14,435ft
Accommodation: two, side-by-side
First flown: 18 March 1983 (as powered sailplane)
Entered service: March 1990 (Vigilant T1)

CURRENT SERVICE

Vigilants serve with the RAF's Volunteer Gliding Schools at the self-launching schools of the Air Training Cadets and Combined Cadet Force (No 612 at Abingdon; No 613 at Halton; No 616 at Henlow; No 624 at Chivenor; No 632 at Ternhill; No 633 at Cosford; No 635 at Samlesbury; No 637 at Little Rissington; No 642 at Linton-on-Ouse; No 663 at Kinloss and No 664 at Belfast) and at the Air Cadets Central Gliding School. It was introduced into service as a replacement for the Slingsby Venture. It is also used by the quasi-military Royal Thai Aero Club at Don Muang.

SPECIAL FEATURES

The Grob G109 has a glass-fibre (Gfk) airframe and was selected to replace a long-serving fleet of wooden motor-gliders used by the Volunteer Gliding Schools of the Air Training Corps.

VARIANTS

Only the two versions described above have been produced – the basic **G109** and the improved **G109B**. The G-109B has longer span wings, fixed windshield, larger sliding cockpit and Hoffman wooden variable pitch propeller.

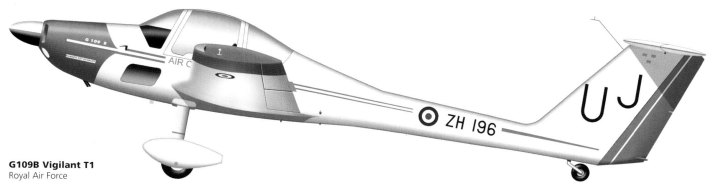

G109B Vigilant T1
Royal Air Force

Grob G115 Tutor

SINGLE-ENGINED AEROBATIC AND PRIMARY TRAINER AIRCRAFT

DEVELOPMENT

The G115 was developed by Burkhart Grob in Germany in the early 1980s as an aerobatic and utility aircraft. Grob was formed in 1928 and aviation activities were introduced in 1971, and over 3,500 aircraft have been constructed to date, including sailplanes and powered aircraft. Selection of the Grob G115 by the RAF as a replacement for the Bulldog trainer was announced in 1998. The specification had included a requirement that the new aircraft should be selected from an already proven design available 'off the peg', with consequent savings over a 'new' design. The Grob was selected on the basis that it best fitted the design criteria with particular emphasis placed on the cockpit space and ergonomics. The production of the G115 had ceased in 1993, but the line was opened up again for the RAF order. Cost-effective and reliable, with a spacious cockpit that is able to accommodate two large pilots wearing full military equipment, the Tutor has excellent handling characteristics. These include a full-range of aerobatic and spinning manoeuvres, with excellent all-round vision, enabling the touchdown point to be constantly visible during approach. The Tutor has almost double the fuel efficiency of the Bulldog and significantly lower noise levels.

CURRENT SERVICE

Five examples are in service with the Naval Grading Flight at Plymouth-Roborough Airport as the Grob G115D Heron. The Belfast-based arm of Bombardier Services was chosen as the preferred bidder in the RAF Light Aircraft Flying Task (LAFT) competition. The Private Finance Initiative (PFI) multi-million pound contract called for the supply of both aircraft (99 ordered) and training services over a ten-year period at the RAF's 13 UAS and AEF bases. The final aircraft are due for delivery in September 2001. RAF Tutors have been allocated civil registrations from G-BYUA to G-BYYB (with the exception of G-BYXU,XV & XW). The G115TA variant is in service with the United Arab Emirates (UAE).

G115E Tutor Royal Air Force

SPECIAL FEATURES

The G115 is made mainly of composites, has a fixed nosewheel undercarriage and is fitted with Bendix King avionics and a state-of-the-art Differential Global Positioning System (DGPS). The latter enables flight characteristics to be down-linked via satellite to each University Air Squadron airfield – information that includes altitude, heading and exact position is available for de-briefing and also down-loading onto students' personal computers.

VARIANTS

The **G115C** is the original utility version, not intended for aerobatic training, with a 119kW (160hp) O-320-DIA engine and two-blade propeller; the **G115D** has a 134kW (180hp) AEIO-360-B1F engine and three-blade propeller; the **G115TA** is the aerobatic and utility version, designed to meet the special requirements of commercial flying schools or military training establishments. The RAF **G115E** differs from the naval Heron in having an increased payload and instrument layout.

TECHNICAL DATA

Grob 115E Tutor

Powerplant: One Textron Lycoming AEIO-540-D4D5 piston engine
Developing: 194kW (260hp)
Driving: Three-blade propeller
Span: 10.19m (33ft 5.7in)
Length: 8.06m (26ft 5.5in)
Height: 2.57m (8ft 5in)
All-up weight: 1,440kg (3,175lb); 1,350kg (2,976lb) for aerobatics
Maximum speed: 320km/h (199mph))
Maximum range: 1,310km (814 miles)
Accommodation: Two, side-by-side
Warload: None
First flown: November 1985 (G115C)
Entered service: Early 1994 (G115D Heron – Royal Navy); August 1999 (G115E Tutor – RAF/CFS)

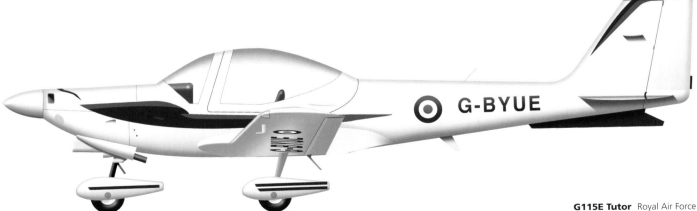

G115E Tutor Royal Air Force

Grumman S-2 Tracker

TWIN RADIAL PISTON- OR TURBOPROP-ENGINED ANTI-SUBMARINE WARFARE AIRCRAFT

USA

S-2E Tracker Argentine Navy

DEVELOPMENT

Upon entering US Navy service as the S-2F Tracker in 1954, the S-2 began a long and exceptionally successful career as a maritime patrol aircraft and,

TECHNICAL DATA

Grumman S-2E Tracker

Powerplants: Two Wright R-1820-82WA Cyclone radial piston engines
Developing: 1,137kW (1,525hp)
Driving: Three-blade propellers
Span: 22.13m (72ft 7in)
Length: 13.26m (43ft 6in)
Height: 5.06m (16ft 7in)
All-up weight: 13,222kg (29,150lb)
Maximum speed: 426km/h (265mph)
Cruise speed: 333km/h (207mph)
Operational ceiling: 21,000ft
Maximum range: 2,094km (1,300 miles)
Mission range: 1,853km (1,150 miles)
Endurance: 9hr
Accommodation: crew of four
First flown: 4 December 1952 (S2F)
Entered service: February 1954 (S2F)

thanks to many upgrades, will fly on for many years yet in military and civil hands. Apart from the various US Navy operational versions, there were conversions to utility US-2 and trainer TS-2 derivatives, while it is surplus American examples that form the majority of the remaining Tracker fleets today. Some of these are currently being updated with turboprop engines.

CURRENT SERVICE

The Argentine Navy flies one last piston S-2E and four S-2T Turbo Trackers with Escuadrillo Aeronaval Anti-submarine at BA Commandante Espora, while the Republic of China Air Force (Taiwan) operates a fleet of 32 S-2Ts with 33 and 34 ASS (6th ASW Group) at Pingtung South. The only other remaining military Tracker operator is the Royal Thai Navy Air Division with seven remaining utility US-2Cs and Fs with No 101 Squadron, Wing 1, at U-Tapao. Many more, mostly Turbo Trackers, are in service worldwide with civilian and governmental operators (such as the French Sécurité Civile) for firebombing duties.

SPECIAL FEATURES

This relatively short, 'dumpy' aircraft has quite a

squat appearance, with its stubby nose, fairly short-looking mainwheel legs and large tail fin. All Trackers are fitted with a small 'bumper' tailwheel, and have a short magnetic anomaly detector (MAD) visible at the extremity of the rear fuselage. The turboprop conversions alter the engine nacelle shape quite substantially.

VARIANTS

The basic **S-2E** has now been largely supplanted by the turboprop-powered **S-2T Turbo Tracker** conversions. Conversions undertaken by Israel's IAI/Bedek using the Garrett TPE331-15 powerplant, and installed by Marsh Aviation of the USA, have been adopted by Argentina and Taiwan. Meanwhile, the Royal Thai Navy's remaining **US-2C/Fs** are utility transports with the ASW equipment removed.

S-2E Tracker
Republic of China Air Force

Grumman OV-1 Mohawk

TWIN-TURBOPROP BATTLEFIELD RECONNAISSANCE AND OBSERVATION AIRCRAFT

OV-1B Mohawk Argentine Army

DEVELOPMENT

The OV-1 Mohawk was the first turboprop aircraft to see widespread US Army service upon introduction in 1961. It became the service's primary fixed-wing battlefield surveillance and intelligence-gathering platform – the OV-1D and RV-1D being the definitive versions, with improved radar and infrared sensor equipment. A total of 111 Mohawks saw US Army service, some being converted for ELINT duties

TECHNICAL DATA

Grumman OV-1D Mohawk

Powerplants: Two Textron Lycoming T53-L-15 turboprops
Developing: 820kW (1,100eshp)
Driving: Three-blade propellers
Span: 14.63m (48ft 0in)
Length: 12.50m (41ft 0in)
Height: 3.86m (12ft 8in)
All-up weight: 8,722kg (19,230lb)
Maximum speed: 478km/h (297mph)
Cruise speed: 443km/h (275mph)
Operational ceiling: 30,300ft
Maximum range: 1,980km (1,217miles)
Ferry range: 1,980km (1,230miles)
Endurance: four hours plus
Accommodation: Pilot and observer side-by-side
Warload: Usually none – but guns and rocket pods can be carried on the two underwing hardpoints.
First flown: 14 April 1959 (YOV-1A)
Entered service: April 1961 (OV-1B)

(including the secretive EV-1E variant (Quick Look III Mohawks), capable of monitoring hostile emissions along national borders).

CURRENT SERVICE

Following long US Army operation in the European, Southeast Asian, Far Eastern and Central American theatres amongst others, the OV-1 and RV-1 were phased out of front-line service after some 35 years – its last user within the US forces having been the Army National Guard. In addition, those operated by Israel have also now been retired, but ex-US Army OV-1Ds remain in service with the Argentine Army, with Escuela de Aviación del Ejército and Esc de Air de Exploración y Reconocimiento 601 at Campo de Mayo. Mohawks also equip the Republic of Korea Air Force, with examples having been 'left' in South Korea after a US Army unit deployed there was disbanded.

OV-1B Mohawk Argentine Army

SPECIAL FEATURES

This very distinctive aeroplane has a number of notable features. Starting at the front, the pilot and observer are housed under a sturdy, braced canopy with a large glass area all round. The side cockpit glass is bulged outwards to improve downward visibility. Both crew members have Martin-Baker ejector seats. The two T53 powerplants are overwing-mounted, while large drop-tanks are fitted on the outboard underwing attachments. The triple fin arrangement is the Mohawk's most notable external feature.

VARIANTS

The **OV-1B** is the only serving variant today, and is equipped with AN/AAS-24 IR scanners, the AN/APD-7 radar surveillance fitment, and KS-60 recce cameras – carried in a large pod under the fuselage. The **OV-1C** had an AAS-24 infrared surveillance system.

Grumman EA-6 Prowler

TWIN-TURBOFAN ELECTRONIC WARFARE AIRCRAFT

DEVELOPMENT

The first Prowlers to be built were 27 initial EA-6A derivatives of the A-6A Intruder, the first of which flew in 1963. They were used by three US Marine Corps units operating in the reconnaissance and electronic warfare roles, later seeing service as EW aggressors for training purposes, but now retired. The definitive EA-6B which followed added two extra crew members, and its EW systems have been steadily upgraded over its long US Navy and USMC service career. Early examples were only configured to monitor and jam hostile signals across four frequency bands, but updates to the ALQ-99 Tactical Jamming System have since been undertaken to improve this coverage, while also enabling the Prowler to itself attack hostile installations using AGM-88A HARM anti-radiation missiles.

CURRENT SERVICE

US Navy Prowlers now also provide the USAF's primary tactical EW and jamming capability since the

EA-6B Prowler US Marine Corps

withdrawal of the latter's EF-111s, operating with sixteen units (all shore-based) at NAS Whidbey Island, WA. The US Marine Corps' Prowlers now equip four units, one at NAS Iwakuni in Japan, while the other three are home-based at MCAS Cherry Point, NC when not on deployment. Both the USN and USMC recently deployed aircraft to the Adriatic and to Italy in support of NATO operations in Bosnia and Kosovo. EA-6B squadrons are responsible for all US EW jamming missions – escorting both US Navy and USAF strike aircraft packages.

SPECIAL FEATURES

When compared with the now-retired A-6 Intruder, on which it was based, the main distinguishing external feature of the Prowler is the prominent fin-top 'football' fairing containing System Integration Receivers, the aircraft's EW antennae. Further SIRs are housed in smaller fairings lower down the tail fin. Under the fuselage is the TJS (Tactical Jamming

System) pod, housing the tracking receiver and two noise jammers, which are powered by a windmilling external turbine generator at the front of this fitment. The EA-6B's refuelling probe has at its base the forward antenna for the aircraft's self-protection deception jamming equipment. Another important feature is the two-cabin cockpit, with the pilot in the port front seat and the three ECM operatives occupying the other positions. The Prowler's fuselage is some 1.37m (4ft 6in) longer than that of the A-6 Intruder from which it was developed.

VARIANTS

The current standard of all in-service **EA-6Bs** with both the USN and US Marine Corps is the ICAP-II configuration, allowing for HARM-equipped SEAD sorties to be undertaken. A further update, known as ADVCAP/ Block 91, has new avionics and further improved the transmission capability of the EA-6B's jamming suite.

TECHNICAL DATA

Grumman EA-6B Prowler

Powerplants: Two Pratt & Whitney J52-P-408 turbofans
Developing: 49.8kN (11,200lb st)
Span: 16.15m (53ft 0in)
Length: 18.24m (59ft 10in)
Height: 4.95m (16ft 3in)
All-up weight: 29,484kg (65,000lb)
Maximum speed: 928km/h (608mph)
Cruise speed: 774km/h (481mph)
Operational ceiling: 38,000ft
Maximum range: 3,861km (2,398miles)
Mission range: 1,769km (1,098miles)
Accommodation: Pilot and three electronic countermeasures officers
Warload: Up to four (usually two) AGM-88A HARM anti-radar defence suppression missiles can be carried on a pair of inboard underwing pylons.
First flown: 1963 (EA-6A); 25 May 1968 (EA-6B)
Entered service: 1971

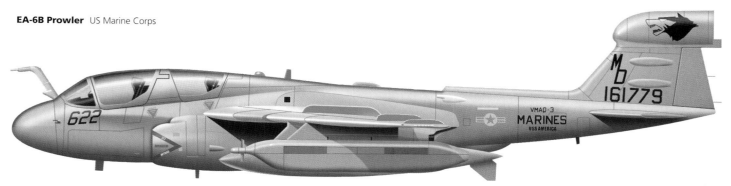

EA-6B Prowler US Marine Corps

Grumman C-2A Greyhound

TWIN-TURBOPROP CARRIER ON-BOARD DELIVERY AIRCRAFT

C-2A Greyhound United States Navy

DEVELOPMENT

A US Navy requirement for a new carrier on-board delivery (COD) aircraft, to be used for transporting important cargo and personnel between shore bases and aircraft carriers, led to Grumman proposing the C-2A Greyhound for the role – a derivative of the E-2 Hawkeye AEW platform (likewise, the C-1A Trader which the Greyhound was to replace had been developed from the S-2 Tracker). Nineteen were initially purchased, of which seven were lost by the mid-1970s, and the veteran Trader continued in service. However, a further 39 C-2As were then built when the production line re-opened in 1982.

CURRENT SERVICE

Two operational US Navy squadrons (VRC-30, at NAS North Island, CA and VRC-40, headquartered at NAS Oceana but detached to Norfolk, VA) continue to fly 36 Greyhounds for COD duties. Six more are used by VAW-120, also based at NAS Norfolk, for training crews destined for the COD role, while a final C-2A

flies with the Naval Force Aircraft Test Squadron (NFATS) from Patuxent River as a support aircraft. Units based at Cubi Point in the Philippines and NAS Sigonella, Spain, have now been disbanded.

SPECIAL FEATURES

Obviously, the C-2A has a much wider and deeper fuselage than the E-2 on which it was based in order to undertake its transport role, with an upswept rear section. This incorporates the loading doors and rear ramp. In addition, it is noticeable that the Greyhound's four tail fins are not canted inwards as on the E-2 Hawkeye, due to the change in airflow patterns caused by removal of the rotating AEW radome. The C-2A also has a strengthened nosewheel unit to cope with the transport payloads being carried.

VARIANTS

Only the **C-2A** has ever been in service, aircraft being produced in two batches – initially between 1965 and 1968, then again from 1982 to 1989.

TECHNICAL DATA

Grumman C-2A Greyhound

Powerplants: Two Allison T56-A-425 turboprops
Developing: 3,663kW (4,912eshp)
Driving: four-blade propellers
Span: 24.56m (80ft 7in)
Length: 17.32m (56ft 10in)
Height: 4.84m (15ft 10.5in)
All-up weight: 26,081kg (57,500lb)
Maximum speed: 574km/h (357mph)
Cruise speed: 482km/h (299mph)
Operational ceiling: 33,500ft
Maximum range: 2,891km (1,794miles)
Mission range: 1,930km (1,196miles)
Accommodation: Two crew and 39 passengers, 20 stretchers and 4 attendants, or up to 4,540kg (10,000lb) of freight.
First flown: 18 November 1964 (YC-2A)
Entered service: early 1966

C-2A Greyhound United States Navy

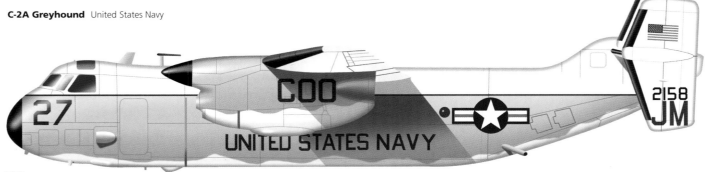

Grumman F-14 Tomcat

F-14B Tomcat United States Navy

TECHNICAL DATA

Grumman F-14B Tomcat

Powerplants: Two General Electric F100-GE-400 afterburning turbofans
Developing: 102.75kN (23,000lb) with afterburner
Span: 19.54m (64ft 1.5in) wings spread
Length: 19.10m (62ft 8in)
Height: 4.88m (16ft 0in)
All-up weight: 33,724kg (74,349lb)
Maximum speed: 1,997km/h (1,241mph)
Cruise speed: 764km/h (475mph)
Operational ceiling: Over 53,000ft
Maximum range: 2,965km (1,840miles)
Accommodation: Pilot and radar intercept officer in tandem
Warload: Two AIM-9M Sidewinders are carried for close-range combat purposes, while up to six (but more usually two-four) AIM-54C Phoenix or AIM-7M Sparrow AAMs are used for longer-range engagements. An M61A1 Vulcan 20mm six-barrelled cannon is mounted to port in the lower forward fuselage. The F-14 can also be fitted with bomb racks in its semi-recessed missile bays, which normally carry four of the Phoenix or Sparrow missiles, to deliver various free-fall general purpose stores.
First flown: 21 December 1970 (F-14 prototype); September 1986 (F-14A(plus))
Entered service: October 1972 (F-14A); 1988 (F-14B)

DEVELOPMENT

After the navalised F-111B was cancelled, the US Navy's requirement for a new long-range fleet interceptor to replace the F-4 Phantom remained unfulfilled. Having gained experience in variable-geometry wing design in co-operation with General Dynamics on the F-111B, Grumman subsequently developed its Model G-303 fighter, selected by the USN as its new fighter in January 1969. The first development F-14 Tomcat flew during late December 1970, with deliveries commencing two years later, and the type embarked on its first operational US Navy cruise in 1974. Early maladies suffered by the TF30 powerplant, including disintegrating fan blades and compressor stalls during hard manoeuvring were soon rectified, and the Tomcat became an outstanding interceptor. Much later, in the late 1980s, rebuilds of some F-14As to A(Plus) standard with new engines were undertaken, along with new-build aircraft – all re-designated as F-14Bs. The F-14D also added new avionics, but is only in relatively limited service compared with other variants.

CURRENT SERVICE

Thirteen US Navy fighter squadrons are currently equipped with F-14s of all types, but mostly F-14As and -Bs. All are now shore-based at NAS Oceana, VA, apart from one located at NAS Atsugi in Japan. Other Tomcats are on strength with the Naval Force Aircraft Test Squadron, the Naval Weapons Test Squadrons at Point Mugu and China Lake, the Naval Strike Air Warfare Center and the Navy Test Pilots School. The only other F-14 customer is the Islamic Republic of Iran Air Force, though its Tomcat operations have been curtailed somewhat in recent years by the US arms embargo against Iran restricting spare parts and technical expertise. Of 79 F-14As delivered, 50-55 remain on strength with two squadrons, of which some 30 aircraft are active.

SPECIAL FEATURES

The F-14's wings can be swept between 20° and 68° in flight, being controlled by a computer to provide optimum performance according to the aircraft's flight attitude and airflow data. Its twin fins are distinctive, as are the outward-canted engine air intakes. The Tactical Air Reconnaissance Pod System (TARPS) equipment, when carried, is mounted on a starboard rear underfuselage position.

VARIANTS

A substantial number of **F-14As** were upgraded to **F-14B** standard, with an improved fire-control system and the F100-GE-400 turbofan replacing the earlier Pratt & Whitney TF30-P-412/414. It was planned to then carry out a final update to **F-14D** configuration incorporating digital avionics and digital radar processing linked to AWG-9 radar and improved radar warning fitments amongst other refinements, but only some four USN units (including VF-101, the type conversion outfit which flies all three derivatives) have received them, leaving both -As and -Bs in widespread service.

Grumman F-14B Tomcat United States Navy

Grumman (Schweizer) G-164 Ag-Cat

G-164 Ag-Cat Hellenic Air Force

DEVELOPMENT

A rather unusual member of the Grumman family of 'feline' military aircraft, the Ag-Cat was developed by the company during the early-mid 1950s as a sturdy platform for crop-spraying duties. However, the entire production run was undertaken however by Schweizer Aircraft of Elmira, New York, who acquired full design rights from Grumman in 1981. Schweizer's largest powered-aircraft (their previous work had been glider business), the Ag-Cat was constructed of steel tubing, with numerous aluminium panels, and it was initially powered by a Continental or Jacobs radial engine. When production finally ceased in 1988, some 2,621 Ag-Cats had been produced.

CURRENT SERVICE

The Hellenic Air Force is the only military air arm to operate the Ag-Cat. In 1968, the Greek government's Ministry of Works transferred its crop-dusting duties to the Air Force in an arrangement unique in Europe. Of the 23 aircraft acquired in 1968, 19 remain in service with 126 SM/359 MAEDY based at Dekelia. During the spraying season, aircraft are deployed all over Greece.

SPECIAL FEATURES

The Ag-Cat is one of the most distinctive-looking aircraft in service with any air arm in the world, and is one of the last remaining machines of biplane configuration still serving. The angular tail-fin with its large rudder for increased agility is notable, along with the sizeable, squared-off cockpit canopy which is a feature of the Hellenic Air Force examples, and of course the uncowled R-985 radial powerplant. The hopper containing the fertiliser being sprayed is situated behind and underneath the pilot, with spray bars along the trailing edges of the lower wings.

VARIANTS

The basic **G-164 Ag-Cat** is in Hellenic Air Force service, although the Greeks opted for an enclosed cockpit configuration. The **G-164B/C Ag-Cat Super B** and **C** were later developments. Early Ag-Cats had open cockpits but this was subsequently changed to an enclosed cabin. Some were built under licence in Ethiopia by Adams Air Service and known as 'Eshets'. The **G-164D Ag-Cat**, of which 24 were produced, had a lengthened forward fuselage and a PT6A turboprop.

TECHNICAL DATA

Grumman (Schweizer) G-164 Ag-Cat
Powerplants: One Pratt & Whitney R-985-AN1 radial piston engine
Developing: 336kW (450hp)
Driving: two-blade propeller
Span: 10.95km (35ft 11in)
Length: 7.42km (24ft 4in)
Height: 3.28km (10ft 9in)
All-up weight: 1,701kg (3,750lb)
Maximum speed: 177km/h (110mph)
Cruise speed: 137km/h (85mph)
Maximum range: 400km (250miles)
Accommodation: Pilot only
First flown: 27 April 1957
Entered service: 1968

G-164 Ag-Cat Hellenic Air Force

Guizhou (GAIC) JJ-7 & FT-7

SINGLE TURBOJET TWO-SEAT FIGHTER TRAINER

Guizhou (GAIC) FT-7BZ Air Force of Zimbabwe

DEVELOPMENT

After Chengdu had itself carried out a redesign of the basic MiG-21F-13, which it built under licence in China, thus producing the J-7 II fighter, the Guizhou Aviation Industry Corporation (GAIC) went on to develop a supersonic lead-in/fighter conversion trainer, with combat capability. This process spawned the JJ-7 (Jianjiao-7), which, as one would expect given its parentage, bears a strong resemblance to the two-seat MiG-21U series. It initially entered service with the People's Republic of China Air Force; for export, the type was subsequently offered as the FT-7. In 1994, development began of a lengthened two-seat operational combat version of the FT-7P, which was 'stretched' by means of a 60cm (23.6in) fuselage plug, and this version entered Pakistani Air Force service.

CURRENT SERVICE

The JJ-7 is used in some numbers by the Air Force of the People's Liberation Army, with around 50 being in service. Usage of export FT-7s basically corresponds to the list of countries which fly the Chengdu J-7 and F-7 in their various forms – the operational trainer serves with the Bangladesh Defence Force Air Wing, Myanmar Air Force, Pakistani Air Force, Sri Lankan Air Force and the Air Force of Zimbabwe.

SPECIAL FEATURES

Under the rearward of the twin-opening canopies, a retractable periscope is fitted (as on many MiG-21 trainers) and the cockpit is equipped with duplicated instrumentation and controls. When compared with its Soviet forebear, the JJ-7/FT-7 series is basically externally very similar, the medium-chord tail-fin and large ventral fins of angular shape being essentially as fitted to MiG-21PFs, and its more direct relative, the Chengdu F-7 series.

VARIANTS

The only difference between the JJ-7 (the Chinese designation for the domestic forces) in service with the People's Republic of China and the export FT-7 is the latter's avionics fitment, provided by GEC. Two nations use local designations, namely Pakistan (FT-7P) and Zimbabwe (FT-7Z) but the aircraft are unchanged.

TECHNICAL DATA

Guizhou (GAIC) JJ-7/FT-7

Powerplant: One Liyang (LMC) Wopen WP-7B afterburning turbojet
Developing: 59.82kN (13,448lb st) with afterburner
Span: 7.15m (23ft 5.4in)
Length: 14.87m (48ft 9.5in)
Height: 4.103m (13ft 5.5in)
All-up weight: 8,600kg (18,959lb)
Maximum speed: 2,175km/h (1,350mph)
Operational ceiling: 56,760ft
Maximum range: 1,300km (806 miles)
Mission range: 1,010km (627 miles)
Accommodation: Two in tandem
Warload: A 23mm twin-barrelled 23-3 cannon can be fitted in a ventral pack, along with two PL-2B AAMs, two 250kg free-fall bombs or a pair of 57mm rocket pods on underwing pylons. FT-7P has a fixed internal gun.
First flown: 5 July 1985 (JJ-7); Late 1987 (FT-7); 9 November 1990 (FT-7P)
Entered service: 1987 (JJ-7); 1996 (FT-7P)

Guizhou (GAIC) FT-7P

Gulfstream Aerospace (Grumman) Gulfstream I/VC-4A

TWIN-TURBOPROP EXECUTIVE/VIP TRANSPORT

Gulfstream VC-4A United States Coast Guard

DEVELOPMENT

Grumman (subsequently Grumman American, then Gulfstream Aerospace after Grumman sold its interest in 1978) began design in the mid-1950s of a twin-turboprop executive transport which was intended for a crew of two and 10-14 passengers in typical configuration, but with a high density layout that could seat a maximum of 24 passengers. It was a conventional low-wing monoplane with pressurised accommodation and retractable undercarriage. It combined high power (but low operating costs) with a capacious fuselage and considerable fuel tankage – this made it a remarkable long-range corporate

aircraft that also appealed to several military customers. 200 Gulfstream Is were built, among them a number produced for the US Navy and Marine Corps as the TC-4 Academe to train bombardiers and navigators for the A-6 Intruder fleet. These were distinguished from standard Gulfstreams by having a bulbous nose radome. They were regularly updated in tune with the latest A-6 upgrades, having a simulated Intruder cockpit and four radar/navigator operator consoles in the aft of the cabin. However, when the A-6 was retired, the TC-4's career also ended.

CURRENT SERVICE

The US Coast Guard operates a single VC-4A VIP/executive transport, based at Coast Guard Air Station Miami. A Gulfstream I is used by the Venezuelan Air

Force as a VIP transport with Commando Aéro Logístico, Escaudrón 41 at La Carlota, Caracas.

SPECIAL FEATURES

The two Rolls-Royce Dart turboprops are overwing-mounted, the unswept wings themselves having noticeable dihedral. The folding airstair is situated just aft of the cockpit on the port side.

VARIANTS

The **Gulfstream I-C** had a fuselage stretch of 3.25m (10ft 8in) to provide seating for a maximum of 37 passengers, but otherwise is similar to the original **Gulfstream I**. Only a single VIP-configured US Coast Guard **VC-4A** and Venezuela's standard Gulfstream I remain in military service.

TECHNICAL DATA

Grumman Gulfstream I/VC-4A

Powerplants: Two Rolls-Royce Dart RDa.7/2 Mk529-8X turboprops
Developing: 1,648kW (2,210eshp)
Driving: four-blade propellers
Span: 23.88m (78ft 4in)
Length: 20.69m (67ft 10.75in)
Height: 7.11m (23ft 4in)
All-up weight: 16,330kg (36,000lb)
Maximum speed: 587km/h (365mph)
Cruise speed: 480km/h (298mph)
Operational ceiling: 33,600ft
Maximum range: 3,186km (1,978miles)
Mission range: 1,843km (1,144miles)
Accommodation: Two crew and ten VIP passengers
First flown: 14 August 1958 (Gulfstream I)
Entered service: December 1966

Gulfstream I

Gulfstream Aerospace (Grumman) Gulfstream II/C-20J

TWIN-TURBOFAN EXECUTIVE/VIP TRANSPORT

Gulfstream Aerospace Gulfstream II NASA

DEVELOPMENT

Like the turboprop Gulfstream I, the Gulfstream II was initially a Grumman product before Gulfstream Aerospace itself took over in 1978. This first aircraft in the series to be jet-powered can truthfully be said to have spawned the long line of executive and VIP transports that have followed, 258 being produced between 1966 and 1980, of which only one was built for a military operator. This was the US Coast Guard, which used a single VC-11A from July 1968 onwards (the USCG's first jet equipment). This aircraft has now been retired, but other 'used' Gulfstream IIs have been purchased by service and Government operators, among them the US Army.

CURRENT SERVICE

Gulfstream IIs are used by a number of air arms and paramilitary operators as VIP transports, several with

civil registrations – those on strength with the Bahrain Amiri Air Force, Libyan Arab Republic Air Force, Royal Moroccan Air Force, Panamanian National Air Service and Royal Saudi Air Force falling into this category. Two are flown by the quasi-military Saudi Armed Forces Medical Services for medevac duties, and one by the Russian Air Force for communications, while the Venezuelan Air Force has a single example in military colours. The US Army used to fly two VC-11As, but now possesses only a single Gulfstream II version (re-designated as a C-20J in line with later Gulfstream IIIs and IVs) with its Priority Air Transport Detachment. The USCG operates C-20s.

SPECIAL FEATURES

As the first jet in the family lineage, the Gulfstream II introduced the basic configuration of a swept wing and T-tail, which has become so familiar in this series

of aircraft. The twin Spey turbofans are pod-mounted on the rear fuselage, just forward of the tailfin which is itself swept back.

VARIANTS

The standard civil Gulfstream II and, as ordered 'after-market' by several operators listed above, has naturally been available with a variety of different interior specifications depending on the individual operator, but all GIIs are basically identical. The only one with a particular designation still in service is the US Army **C-20J**. Gulfstream **11Bs** are GIIs retrofitted with the GIII's wing.

TECHNICAL DATA

Gulfstream Aerospace Gulfstream II/C-20J

Powerplants: Two Rolls-Royce RB168 Spey Mk511-8 turbofans
Developing: 50.71kN (11,400lb st)
Span: 20.98m (68ft 10in)
Length: 24.36m (79ft 11in)
Height: 7.47m (24ft 6in)
All-up weight: 29,710kg (65,500lb)
Maximum speed: 941km/h (585mph)
Cruise speed: 909km/h (565mph)
Operational ceiling: 43,000ft
Maximum range: 5,568km (3,456miles)
Accommodation: Crew of two and up to 19 passengers (8/12 in VIP configuration)
First flown: 2 October 1966
Entered service: July 1968 (US Coast Guard VC-11A)

Gulfstream Aerospace Gulfstream II Bahrain Amiri Air Force

Gulfstream Aerospace Gulfstream III/C-20 & SRA-1

TWIN-TURBOFAN EXECUTIVE/VIP TRANSPORT AND MULTI-MISSION AIRCRAFT

Gulfstream Aerospace C-20B United States Air Force

DEVELOPMENT

An improved development of the Gulfstream II, the stretched Gulfstream III was the last of this series of executive transports to be developed and initially marketed by Grumman before Gulfstream Aerospace took over in 1978. It was also the first of the line to receive truly significant orders from air arms around the world, among them the US military with whom it was designated as the C-20, for various roles that include search-and-rescue, fishery patrol and ELINT taskings.

CURRENT SERVICE

By far the largest users of the Gulfstream III are the US armed forces, of which the Air Force (C-20A, B, C and E), Army (C-20E), Navy (C-20D) and Coast Guard (C-20B) fly various sub-types of the C-20 family. The USAF is the biggest operator, with 12 aircraft in all, of which three are C-20As used by the 86th Airlift Wing at Ramstein, Germany, six C-20Bs and a C-20C are on the strength of the 89th AW at Andrews AFB, Maryland, and a C-20E is flown by the Pacific Flight Detachment. However, all the US military examples are used for VIP and staff transport duties. The same is true for GIIIs with the Algerian Government, and the air forces of Bahrain, Chile (designated C-20B), Egypt, Gabon, Italy, Ivory Coast, Jordan, Morocco, Saudi Arabia and Venezuela. The two remaining Royal Danish Air Force examples are used for fishery protection and SAR support, while the Indian Air Force flies two GIIIs on ELINT duties as well as one for test purposes.

TECHNICAL DATA

Gulstream Aerospace Gulfstream GIII
Powerplants: Two Rolls-Royce RB168 Spey Mk511-8 turbofans
Developing: 50.71kN (11,400lb st)
Span: 23.72m (77ft 10in)
Length: 25.32m (83ft 1in)
Height: 7.43m (24ft 4.5in)
All-up weight: 31,615kg (69,700lb)
Maximum speed: 929km/h (577mph)
Cruise speed: 840km/h (522mph)
Operational ceiling: 45,000ft
Maximum range: 7,600km (4,726miles)
Accommodation: Two crew and up to 21 passengers
First flown: 2 December 1979 (Gulfstream III)
Entered service: 16 September 1983 (C-20A)

SPECIAL FEATURES

The GIII is externally similar to the II, but several important changes were made, including a 61cm (24in) fuselage stretch, while the Gulfstream III/C-20 also has a wing of increased span and with winglets.

VARIANTS

All of the US military C-20s are effectively similar, the only major difference apart from individual cabin fitments being the fact that the **C-20B** and **C** have simpler electrical systems than other variants. The Royal Danish Air Force **Gulfstream IIIs** were built to SMA-3 multi-mission standard with quick-change interiors for the fishery protection, SAR support and VIP transport roles, while the **SRA-1** is a surveillance and recce platform whose systems were adopted by the Indian Air Force for two of its aircraft that fly on ELINT-gathering duties.

SEE ALSO: GULSTREAM AEROSPACE (GRUMMAN) GULFSTREAM II, GULFSTREAM AEROSPACE GULFSTREAM IV & GULFSTREAM V

Gulfstream III Royal Danish Air Force

Gulfstream Aerospace Gulfstream IV/C-20

TWIN-TURBOFAN EXECUTIVE/VIP TRANSPORT AND MULTI-MISSION AIRCRAFT

Gulfstream Aerospace C-20G United States Navy

DEVELOPMENT

As a development of the GIII, the Gulfstream IV added a 1.37m (54in) fuselage stretch over its predecessor, and featured a change of powerplant from the Rolls-Royce Spey to the Tay, offering greater economy of operation and better outright performance. Greater fuel capacity and more advanced avionics were among the other improvements, and like the new aircraft would soon also find favour as its forebears had done as a military VIP transport. The US forces continued the C-20 series of designations for the GIV.

CURRENT SERVICE

The USAF flies two C-20Hs, used by the 89th AW at Andrews AFB, while the US Navy's C-20Gs are split between VR-48 and VR-51, and the US Army Priority Air Transport Detachment uses a single C-20F. Other

operators of the Gulfstream IV as VIP transports only are the Botswana Defence Force Air Wing, Egyptian Air Force, Irish Air Corps, Cote d'Ivoire Air Force, Indian Air Force, Royal Netherlands Air Force, Royal Air Force of Oman, Royal Saudi Air Force, Turkish Air Force and Venezuelan Air Force. The Swedish Air Force has two GIV-SPs, locally designated S102B Korpen, on the strength of F16M, which operates them in the ELINT role, as well as a sole Tp102 transport example.

SPECIAL FEATURES

The Gulfstream IV incorporates all of the external features of the GIII before it, though the fuselage stretch does make for an even more sleek appearance. With the switch to Tay engines, the nacelles of the GIV are of an increased size compared with those of the Spey-powered II and III.

VARIANTS

Of the US military Gulfstream IVs, the **C-20G** is the only significantly different version – they are equipped with a quick-change passenger/cargo interior, and also cargo doors, for their role with the US Navy. The others are all standard VIP and staff transports. The Swedish Air Force's two **S102B Korpen** conversions of the Gulfstream IV-SP provide ELINT facilities, while the **SRA-4** is a multi-mission (EW, maritime patrol, ASW, quick-change transport and recce) development which flew in demonstrator form during 1988 but has not yet found any customers.

TECHNICAL DATA

Gulfstream Aerospace Gulfstream IV

Powerplants: Two Rolls-Royce Tay Mk611-8 turbofans
Developing: 61.61kN (13,850lb st)
Span: 23.72m (77ft 10in)
Length: 26.92m (88ft 4in)
Height: 7.45m (24ft 5in)
All-up weight: 33,203kg (73,200lb)
Maximum cruising speed: 943km/h (586mph) at 31,000ft
Cruise speed: 841km/h (523mph)
Operational ceiling: 45,000ft
Maximum range: 7,820km (4,859miles)
Accommodation: Two crew and up to 19 passengers
Warload: SRA-4: two anti-shipping missiles on two underwing hardpoints
First flown: 19 September 1985
Entered service: 1986

Gulfstream Aerospace C-20H United States Air Force

Gulfstream Aerospace Gulfstream V/C-37

TWIN-TURBOFAN STAFF/VIP TRANSPORT

Gulfstream V

DEVELOPMENT

The Gulfstream V is the ultimate development of the company's long line of T-tailed business/executive/VIP jet transports. Many significant improvements over its predecessors, notably in terms of aerodynamics, range, refinement and outright performance, have been incorporated - a new wing design, featuring the use of winglets, is one of these while the BMW Rolls-Royce BR710 turbofans deliver much greater range, fuel efficiency and higher speeds. The GV is eight feet longer than the Gulfstream IV it replaces.

CURRENT SERVICE

Only the USAF has so far ordered the Gulfstream V as a military VIP/staff transport, designating it the C-37A. Four aircraft are in service with the 1st Airlift Squadron/89th Airlift Wing at Andrews AFB, Maryland.

SPECIAL FEATURES

The Gulfstream V boasts an especially advanced Honeywell SPZ-8500 avionics fitment, which can be integrated with a head-up display system. Its BR710 turbofans are fitted with Full Authority Digital Engine Controls (FADEC) for ease and safety of operation. Like commercial airliners, the GV is certified for ETOPS (Extended-Range Two-Engined Operations) flying over long stretches of water, and boasts a particularly impressive maximum range of some 6,500nm. All GVs and C-37s are equipped with a fresh-air control system in the cabin, and have a baggage capacity of 2,500lb. A particular priority has been cabin insulation, with the engines being set well back from the cabin bulkheads, the incorporation of titanium 'muffling' equipment, and re-engineered windows for further quietness.

VARIANTS

So far only the USAF's **C-37A** is in military service, but special missions versions are likely to follow. The Gulfstream V was proposed as a platform for the UK Ministry of Defence's ASTOR (Airborne Stand-Off Radar) programme, but lost out to the Bombardier Global Express. However, similar versions are likely to appear in the future for various roles.

Gulfstream V

TECHNICAL DATA

Gulfstream Aerospace Gulfstream V/C-37A

Powerplants: Two BMW Rolls-Royce BR710A1-10 turbofans
Developing: 65.6kN (14,750lb st)
Span: 28.5m (93ft 6in)
Length: 29.4m (96ft 5in)
Height: 7.9m (25ft 10in)
All-up weight: 40,370kg (89,000lb)
Maximum speed: Mach 0.9
Cruise speed: Mach 0.8
Operational ceiling: 51,000ft
Maximum range: 12,046km (7,485 miles)
Endurance: 14hr 38min
Accommodation: Two crew and up to 19 passengers
First flown: 28 November 1995
Entered service: 15 July 1998 (C-37A)

HAL (Hindustan Aeronautics) HJT-16 Kiran I & II

SINGLE TURBOJET BASIC JET TRAINER

HAL Kiran II Indian Air Force

TECHNICAL DATA

HAL Kiran II

Powerplant: One HAL licence-built Rolls-Royce Orpheus Mk701-01 turbojet
Developing: 18.4kN (4,130lb st)
Span: 10.70m (35ft 1.25in)
Length: 10.60m (34ft 9.5in)
Height: 3.635m (11ft 11in)
All-up weight: 5,000kg (11,023lb)
Maximum speed: 780km/h (484mph)
Cruise speed: 417km/h (259mph)
Operational ceiling: 39,375ft
Maximum range: 615km (381 miles)
Accommodation: Two side-by-side
Warload: The Kiran IA can carry up to 227kg (500lb) of stores on two underwing pylons, consisting of either iron bombs or rocket pods. Two 7.62mm machine guns mounted in the nose are a feature of the Kiran II, which also has four hardpoints providing for a load up to 1,000kg (2,200lb).
First flown: 4 September 1964 (Kiran I); 30 July 1976 (Kiran II)
Entered service: March 1968 (Kiran I); March 1985 (Kiran II)

DEVELOPMENT

The first jet product of Hindustan Aeronautics, the Kiran was ordered as a replacement for the Indian Air Force's ageing DH Vampires. The initial Viper-engined Kiran Is and IAs, of which deliveries began in 1968, were followed into production by the improved Orpheus-powered Kiran II for which the go-ahead was given in September 1972. However, the Indian Air Force refused to accept the type after the first prototype had performed poorly in trials. The second aircraft flew in February 1979, but it took another four years for the type to be satisfactorily completed and deliveries only commenced early in 1985. However, the Kiran II has since proved a popular and successful basic jet trainer for the Indian Air Force and Navy, 61 having rolled off the HAL line.

CURRENT SERVICE

The Indian Air Force Academy at Training Command HQ, Bangalore operates some 160 Kirans of all three marks, from three different bases – Bidar for the Kiran Is, Dundigal for the IAs, and Hakimpet for the Kiran IIs. Apart from that, Indian Naval Aviation has been the only other customer with six each of Kiran Is and IIs flown by INAS 551 at Cochin, providing lead-in jet training for Sea Harrier pilots.

SPECIAL FEATURES

The Kiran was intended from the outset to be a jet trainer in the mould of the Hunting/BAC Jet Provost. The engine of the Kiran I, the Rolls-Royce Viper, was the same as that of the British design. However, there were several more advanced features on the Kiran, notably the pressurised cockpit. It is of fairly conventional jet trainer design for the period, with an unswept wing and half-moon engine air intakes situated just aft of the canopy. The Kiran II can be distinguished by the two 7.62mm machine guns in the nose and undernose-mounted blade antennae.

VARIANTS

Developed from the basic Viper-engined **Kiran I**, the **IA** was an armed trainer capable of carrying 227kg (500lb) of stores, either bombs or rocket pods, on two underwing pylons. The **Kiran II** introduced the more powerful Orpheus powerplant, as well as a wing stressed to carry stores or drop tanks on four underwing hardpoints, the two nose-mounted machine guns and more modern avionics. It is to be replaced by the HJT-36, which is likely to enter service in 2004.

HAL Kiran IA Indian Air Force

HAL (Hindustan Aeronautics) HPT-32 Deepak & HTT-35

SINGLE PISTON-ENGINED PRIMARY TRAINER

INDIA

HAL HPT-32 Deepak Indian Air Force

TECHNICAL DATA

HAL HPT-32 Deepak

Powerplant: One Textron Lycoming AEIO-540-D4B5 piston engine
Developing: 194kW (260hp)
Driving: two-blade propeller
Span: 9.50m (31ft 2in)
Length: 7.72m (25ft 4in)
Height: 2.88m (9ft 5.5in)
All-up weight: 1,250kg (2,756lb)
Maximum speed: 265km/h (164mph)
Cruise speed: 213km/h (132mph)
Operational ceiling: 18,045ft
Maximum range: 744km (461miles)
Accommodation: Two side-by-side
First flown: 6 January 1977
Entered service: 1985

DEVELOPMENT

Rather like the Kiran II jet trainer, HAL's HPT-32 Deepak piston-powered ab initio trainer suffered a somewhat lengthy development process. It was intended to replace the Indian Air Force's long-serving HT-2, the Hindustan company's first powered aircraft product, and changed from the older type's tandem seating arrangement to a side-by-side configuration. Originally, HAL planned for the Deepak to be able to be operated in other roles apart from in the training sphere, such as target-towing and observation, but this intention was somewhat overtaken by the long gestation period for the type. The first HPT-32 flew in early 1977, but it took over two years for the second Deepak to do likewise, and then the aircraft was deemed to be unacceptable by the Indian Air Force and various aerodynamic, weight-saving and other modifications had to be made. 1985 saw initial deliveries to the air arm, and three years further on Air Force Academy courses on the Deepak commenced.

CURRENT SERVICE

As with the Kiran, only the Indian armed forces have adopted the Deepak. The Air Force has 130 aircraft, split between the Training Command Elementary Flying School at Allahabad and the Flying Instructors' School at Tambaram. Eight are operated as primary trainers by Indian Naval Aviation, being used by INAS 550 based at Cochin.

SPECIAL FEATURES

Apart from the standard two seats in a side-by-side arrangement, the Deepak can carry an optional extra seat located in a position aft in the cockpit (normally covered over). This enables the type to undertake a secondary liaison role in addition to its various training duties. The aircraft is of basically unremarkable appearance for a primary trainer, save perhaps for its very large tail fin, incorporating a similarly sizeable rudder. The Deepak also features a fixed tricycle undercarriage.

VARIANTS

Only the basic production variant of the **HPT-32** has been built, in two batches totalling some 138 aircraft. The first 88 included the eight Indian Navy examples, with the second batch being delivered from 1993 onwards. A turboprop variant, the **HTT-34** propelled by an Allison 250-B17D unit delivering 313kW (420eshp) was proposed by HAL, making its maiden flight on 17 June 1984 and re-appearing in a slightly modified form during 1989. It incorporated a 0.35m (1ft 1.75in) fuselage stretch and had a smaller tail fin, but was not ordered for series production. The prototypes have been used by the Indian Air Force Aircraft and Systems Testing Establishment.

HAL HPT-32 Deepak Indian Air Force

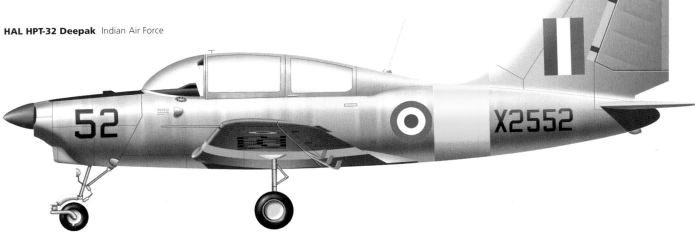

200

HAL (Hindustan Aeronautics) Advanced Light Helicopter

TWIN-ENGINED MULTI-ROLE HELICOPTER

HAL ALH Indian Army

DEVELOPMENT

The first indigenous helicopter to be built in India, the Advanced Light Helicopter is being built in different versions for the Indian Army, Navy, Air Force and Coast Guard. It was designed and developed by HAL in partnership with Eurocopter Deutschland (formerly MBB). Design work commenced in November 1984, and it was built as a multi-role civil and military helicopter for a variety of tasks such as commuter and VIP transport, medevac, offshore support, SAR and firefighting. The armed military version is for anti-tank, close-air support, anti-ship and anti-submarine roles. The unarmed military version is for observation, casualty evacuation, assault, logistic support and training. An initial order for 100 has been placed.

CURRENT SERVICE

The Indian Army Aviation was the first to receive the ALH, as the Army has been insistent on having its own dedicated anti-tank helicopter units. The Indian Air

Force is in the process of receiving its first ALHs.

SPECIAL FEATURES

The ALH features a hingeless main rotor system with swept back tips and composite construction main and tail rotor blades. The ALH demonstrates a good hot and high performance and flight handling qualities. With a tricycle undercarriage it is capable of deck landing operations, and it features two clamshell rear doors for access to the cargo compartment and rear loading. The ALH has optional weather radar and Doppler navigation, depending on the mission. The Army ALH can be fitted with a Lockheed Martin turreted three-barrel 20mm chin gun.

VARIANTS

The naval version has a wheeled undercarriage (twin-nose wheels and single main wheels) and has nose sea-search radar installation; other versions have a skid undercarriage. Higher rated engines are also an

option. A two-seat dedicated attack version, which would feature the ALH's dynamic systems and a new fuselage, is under development.

TECHNICAL DATA

HAL Advanced Light Helicopter (ALH)

Powerplants: Two Turboméca TM333-2B turboshafts
Developing: 745kW (1,000shp)
Driving: Four-blade main and tail rotors
Rotor Diameter: 13.20m (43ft 4in)
Fuselage Length: 12.89m (42ft 4in)
Height: 4.91m (16ft 1.5in)
All-up weight: 5,000kg (11,023lb) – Army version; 5,500kg (12,125lb) – Naval version
Maximum speed: 280km/h (173mph)
Cruising speed: 245km/h (152mph)
Operational ceiling: 19,685ft
Maximum range: 800km (499 miles)
Duration: 3hr 48min
Accommodation: Crew of two and up to 14 passengers
Warload: Two stub wings can carry a variety of ordnance. Army version can be fitted with a 20mm chin gun turret, rockets, anti-armour missiles and AAMs. Naval version can carry up to four torpedoes and depth charges. Various hardpoint stations for underslung loads.
First flown: 20 August 1992 (first prototype); 28 May 1994 (Army/Air Force prototype); 23 December 1995 (Navy prototype)
Entered service: Late 1998 (Indian Army); 1999 (Indian Air Force)

HAL ALH Indian Navy

Harbin Y-11 & Y-12

TWIN PISTON- OR TURBOPROP-ENGINED UTILITY TRANSPORT

Harbin Y-12 II Peruvian Air Force

DEVELOPMENT

It was decided to select an indigenous product with which to replace the Harbin Y-5s (licence-produced Antonov An-2s) in service in the People's Republic of China. The resulting piston-engined Harbin Y-11 was later replaced on the production line by the turboprop-powered Y-12 (initially referred to as the Y-11T1) with a stretched fuselage offering the carriage of a greater payload over longer ranges. International certification was achieved by the Y-12 II, using PT6A turboprops, and this version has gained some overseas military orders. It is sometimes referred to as the 'Turbo Panda'.

CURRENT SERVICE

Some 15 Y-11s are flown in the People's Republic of China by the Air Force of the People's Liberation Army. The Royal Cambodian Air Force uses Y-12s, as do the quasi-military Peruvian National Police and the Sri Lankan Air Force. Meanwhile, Y-12 IIs are on the inventories of the Eritrean Air Force, Mauritanian

Islamic Air Force, Malaysian Air Force, Mongolian Air Force, Pakistan Air Force, Peruvian Air Force, Sri Lanka Air Force, Tanzanian People's Defence Force Air Wing and the Zambian Air Force.

SPECIAL FEATURES

The basic configuration of both the piston Y-11 and turboprop Y-12 is relatively familiar in many ways as being that of a short-field utility transport. It is a high-wing design braced at mid-span, with a sturdy non-retractable undercarriage on small stub-wings for rough strip operations, and an upswept tail incorporating the rear loading ramp. The tail fin itself is tall and angular, with a dorsal 'fillet' extension and small ventral fin under the tail cone.

VARIANTS

The initial **Y-11** was powered by two SMPC (Zhuzhou) HS-6A radial piston engines each delivering 213kW (285hp), though it was also available with uprated

HS-6D units. It was supplanted from 1992 onwards by the **Y-11B** with improved asymmetric performance from its 261kW (350hp) Continental TSIO-550-B engines, while the **Y-11B I** incorporated more modern avionics. With an increased-capacity, stretched fuselage as well as PT6A turboprops, the **Y-12 I** has mostly been used by Chinese civil operators on geosurvey and mineral exploration work; production then switched to the **Y-12 II** with more powerful engines and other detail refinements to smooth the path towards international airworthiness acceptance. A stretched version is under consideration, as is a pressurised version.

TECHNICAL DATA

Harbin Y-12 II

Powerplants: Two Pratt & Whitney PT6A-27 turboprops
Developing: 507kW (680eshp) (flat-rated)
Driving: Three-blade propellers
Span: 17.24m (56ft 6.5in)
Length: 14.86m (48ft 9in)
Height: 5.58m (18ft 3.5in)
All-up weight: 5,300kg (11,684lb)
Maximum speed: 328km/h (204mph)
Cruise speed: 292km/h (181mph)
Operational ceiling: 22,960ft
Maximum range: 1,340km (831 miles)
Accommodation: Two crew and up to 17 passengers (or 16 parachutists) or 1,700kg (3,748lb) freight, when in all-cargo configuration
First flown: 1975 (Y-11); 14 July 1982 (Y-12); 16 August 1984 (Y-12 II)
Entered service: 1975 (Y-11)

Harbin Y-12 II Peruvian Air Force

Hawker Hunter

SINGLE TURBOJET FIGHTER/GROUND ATTACK, ADVANCED TRAINER AND TRIALS AIRCRAFT

Hawker Hunter T7 Zimbabwean Air Force

DEVELOPMENT

In the early 1950s, the Royal Air Force was searching for a replacement for the Gloster Meteor in the day-fighter role, a requirement admirably filled by the Sydney Camm-designed Hawker P1067 – later to be renamed as the Hunter. The RAF's initial F1s and F2s handled superbly but were beset by a lack of range, this being rectified by the F4, with increased fuel tankage. Equipping the Hunter with the Avon 203 engine gave it a superb performance for its day in its F6 guise, and the type was put into licence production and service with many NATO and other air arms around the world, while seeing extensive RAF service at home and abroad. The T7 trainer remained on the RAF's

inventory from 1958 until 1994, the same year that the Swiss Air Force retired its faithful F58s and T68s. Military usage of this classic fighter continues, but only small numbers remain in active service.

CURRENT SERVICE

Two air arms retain Hunters in front-line service – the Lebanese Air Force, with five FGA70s and FGA70As for air defence and attack duties along with a T66C conversion trainer at Al Quwwat Al Jawwiya Al Lubnaniya, and the Air Force of Zimbabwe, which flies six FGA9s and a T81 with No 1 Squadron at Thornhill/Gwern. In the UK, a T7 is used by the Air Fleet Department of the Defence Evaluation & Research Agency (DERA) at Boscombe Down, and a T7 remains on the strength of the Empire Test Pilots' School – mainly for inverted spin training, for which it is the only swept-wing type deemed suitable – but the remaining service life of these aircraft is limited.

SPECIAL FEATURES

The Hunter must surely be classed as one of the most graceful combat aircraft of all time in appearance. All of those in service today have the 'dogtooth' wing leading edge configuration and all-flying tail arrangement adopted from the F6 onwards.

VARIANTS

The remaining front-line Hunters – Lebanon's **FGA70s & 70As**, and Zimbabwe's **FGA9s** – are all basically of the same configuration – equivalent to the RAF's FGA9. This dedicated fighter-bomber carried a much-increased weapons load and fuel tankage compared with the earlier fighter variants, and was thus fitted with a braking parachute and stronger undercarriage. DERA's Hunter FGA9 is often fitted with equipment for NBC chemical spray trials. The export two-seat Hunters were powered by the Avon Mk200 series engines, like their fighter/strike counterparts.

TECHNICAL DATA

Hawker Hunter FGA9

Powerplant: One Rolls-Royce Avon RA28 Mk207 turbojet
Developing: 45.15kN (10,150lb st)
Span: 10.26m (33ft 8in)
Length: 13.98m (45ft 10.5in)
Height: 4.01m (13ft 2in)
All-up weight: 11,158kg (24,600lb)
Maximum speed: 1,144km/h (710mph)
Cruise speed: 740km/h (460mph)
Operational ceiling: 50,000ft
Maximum range: 2,961km (1,834 miles)
Mission range: 713km (442 miles)
Accommodation: Pilot only
Warload: A pack containing four 30mm Aden cannon in the lower fuselage is standard equipment. Four underwing pylons can carry up to 3,355kg (7,400lb) of ordnance, including bombs and rockets. Some are wired for AA-9 AAMs.
First flown: 20 July 1951 (P1067 prototype)
Entered service: July 1954 (F1)

Hawker Hunter T7 UK DERA

Hawker Siddeley (BAe) 748 & Andover

TWIN-TURBOPROP MEDIUM-RANGE TRANSPORT AND SPECIAL MISSIONS AIRCRAFT

UK

Andover C1(PR) UK DERA Open Skies

DEVELOPMENT

The Avro 748 was the last new production aircraft to originate from that famous company, being soon re-designated as the Hawker Siddeley HS748 after Avro was absorbed into that company, then later as the BAe 748. The last development of the basic 748 passenger aircraft by BAe was the Super 748 with uprated Dart turboprops; the 748 Coastguarder variant failed to win any orders. However, the Andover military freighter design (the first prototype of which first flew in 1963, converted from the first Avro 748) had been more successful, with 31 seeing RAF service in various forms, and also being ordered by the Royal New Zealand Air Force. Most of the RAF aircraft were Andover C1 transports; other versions including the E3 and E3A runway navigation aid calibration aircraft. Six Andover CC2s saw service with the the Queen's Flight, No 32 Squadron and other communications units, but were not 'true' Andovers, but 748 Series 2s without the rear loading ramp and redesigned tail section. However, all the RAF and RNZAF aircraft are now retired.

CURRENT SERVICE

British use of the Andover is now confined to the Defence Evaluation & Research Agency at Boscombe Down, where single examples of the C1(PR) and HS748 Series 107 are on the strength of the Air Fleet Department, while the Empire Test Pilots School has a standard C1. There are however many 748s in service worldwide, with the Royal Australian Air Force (ten aircraft, HS748/228s and 229s), Royal Australian Navy (two Series 268s for electronic warfare training), and the air forces of Belgium, Brazil, Burkina Faso, Ecuador, India (the largest user, with 50 examples licence-built by HAL), Republic of Korea, Madagascar, Nepal (its Royal Flight aircraft), Sri Lanka and Thailand.

SPECIAL FEATURES

The Andover (apart from those designated CC2 by the RAF) re-designed the 748's tail section to incorporate an upswept rear fuselage with a rear loading ramp, and a new tailplane with dihedral. A 'kneeling' undercarriage was fitted for ease of operation.

VARIANTS

DERA's now unique **C1(PR)** is used as the United Kingdom's contribution to the multi-national Open Skies programme. It is operated with an underfuselage camera on overflights of military installations at home and abroad, with observers from different nations on board verifying enforcement of arms control measures. It was one of two originally modified for the RAF for use by No 60 Squadron at Wildenrath in Germany for reconnaissance duties. Military HS(BAe) 748s are almost all from the **Series 2** family, with varying designations. Those built by HAL in India included 20 **748(M)s** with a large cargo door, while one Indian example was converted as an AEW testbed with a large fuselage-mounted rotodome, but this has recently crashed.

TECHNICAL DATA

Hawker Siddeley (BAe) Andover C1(PR)

Powerplant: Two Rolls-Royce Dart RDa.12 Mk201C turboprops
Developing: 2,420kW (3,245eshp)
Driving: four-blade propellers
Span: 29.87m (98ft 0in)
Length: 23.75m (77ft 1in)
Height: 8.97m (29ft 5in)
All-up weight: 22,680kg (50,000lb)
Maximum speed: 490km/h (303mph)
Cruise speed: 415km/h (258mph)
Operational ceiling: 24,000ft
Maximum range: 1,891km (1,173 miles)
Accommodation: crew of two-four and up to 52 troops (or 40 paratroops)
First flown: 20 June 1960 (Avro 748); 9 July 1965 (Andover C1)
Entered service: June 1966

HS748 Series 2A Belgian Air Force

Hawker Siddeley Nimrod R1

Nimrod R1 Royal Air Force

DEVELOPMENT

In May 1974, three Nimrod R1s replaced Comet R2s (and before that Canberras) for electronic reconnaissance duties with No 51 Squadron at RAF Wyton. One ditched in the Moray Firth in May 1995 whilst on a test flight after an overhaul. It was subsequently replaced by the conversion of an existing surplus MR2 airframe to R1 configuration. Its large number of crew members are responsible for tuning the R1's receivers and recording and analysing collected signals. The aircraft have been progressively modified since they were introduced, gaining more and more antennas above and below the fuselage, and Loral ARI 18240/1 wingtip ESM pods. Wingtip pods and FR probes were added from 1982.

CURRENT SERVICE

The Nimrod R1 gained its first battle honours during the Falklands conflict. During the Gulf War of 1991 they were actively monitoring Iraqi radar and radio communications and made a notable contribution to the highly successful air operations. They were also in use over Kosovo in 1999, working with similarly equipped allied air arms (such as the USAF's RC-135 'Rivet Joints' and US Navy's EP-3E Aries IIs).

SPECIAL FEATURES

The R1 is externally distinguishable from the maritime MR2 version by the absence of the magnetic anomaly detection (MAD) tail boom, no searchlight and a distinctive pod on the leading edge of the port wing. It has radomes mounted on its tailcone and external wing tank fairings, antenna pods on each wingtip and hook antenna arrays on top of the fuselage. Under the cabin floor, in what was the weapons bay of the MR2, a wide range of special equipment is housed. Nimrod R1s now have Embodiment of Service Radio Installation Modification (SRIM) 6029 and other cockpit and radar modifications. Recently SRIM 6113 (codenamed *Starwindow*) is a new fit to all three R1 airframes, and was developed by E-Systems Melpar Division in Virginia USA. A 'special signals' intercept facility upgrade has been incorporated to boost the R1's communications and electronic-inteligence sub systems. This includes a poled network of 22 digital intercept receivers, a wideband, digital direction-finding system; an intercept capability against frequency-agile transmitters and in-flight analysis. The 'special signals' upgrade is believed to involve a digital recording and playback suite; a multi-channel digital data demodulator and enhanced pulser signal processing capability.

VARIANTS

As outlined above.

SEE ALSO: HAWKER SIDDELEY NIMROD MR2

TECHNICAL DATA

Hawker Siddeley Nimrod R1

Powerplants: Four Rolls-Royce RB168-20 Spey Mk250 turbofans
Developing: 54.0kN (12,140lb st)
Span: Approx 35.02m (115ft) over pods
Length: (excluding noseprobe) 35.66m (117ft)
Height: 9.08m (29ft 8.5in)
All-up weight: Not available
Maximum speed: Not available
Cruise speed: Not available
Operational ceiling: Not available
Maximum range: Not available
Mission range: Not available
Accommodation: Normal crew complement 28
Warload: None
First flown: 23 May 1967 (MR1); 2 April 1997 (last conversion)
Entered service: First delivery (XW664) was to RAF Wyton on 7 July 1971 in a 'green' state. Modified to R1 and reflown on 30 October 1973. First operation was on 3 May 1974 and formal commissioning took place on 10 May 1974.

Nimrod R1 Royal Air Force

Hawker Siddeley Nimrod MR2

FOUR-TURBOFAN MARITIME PATROL AIRCRAFT

DEVELOPMENT

The Nimrod has its origins in the de Havilland DH106 Comet, the world's first operational jet airliner, that made its maiden flight on 27 July 1949. From the Comet design, the Hawker Siddeley HS801 maritime reconnaissance variant was developed as a contender for the RAF's requirement to replace its ageing Avro Shackletons in the role, and successfully secured the order, with two Comet 4Cs being converted as the initial prototypes. The first of these was re-engined with Rolls-Royce Speys, the chosen powerplant for production examples, while the second retained its existing Avon units, being used as the avionics and

Nimrod MR2 Royal Air Force

TECHNICAL DATA

Hawker Siddeley Nimrod MR2

Powerplants: Four Rolls-Royce RB168-20 Spey Mk250 turbofans
Developing: 54.0kN (12,140lb st)
Span: 35.00m (114ft 10in)
Length: 38.63m (126ft 9in)
Height: 9.08m (29ft 8.5in)
All-up weight: 80,514kg (177,500lb)
Maximum speed: 926km/h (575mph)
Cruise speed: 787km/h (490mph)
Operational ceiling: 42,000ft
Maximum range: 9,266km (5,750miles)
Mission range: Over 1,609km (1,000miles)
Endurance: 12hr
Accommodation: Currently 13 - pilot, co-pilot and flight engineer, navigator and tactical navigator, main air electronics officer, seven radio, radar and sonic systems operators/observers and stores loaders.
Warload: Maximum ordnance 6,124kg(13,500lb), in main lower fuselage weapons bay and smaller rear sonobuoy bay; one pylon beneath each wing. Weapons include six or nine air-drop Marconi StingRay torpedoes, AGM-84 Harpoon anti-ship missiles, air-drop mines, depth charges, and 'iron bombs'. Each underwing pylon can carry one Harpoon missile, or two AIM-9 Sidewinder air-to-air missiles for self-defence.
First flown: 23 May 1967 (MR1)
Entered service: October 1969 (MR1); August 1979 (MR2)

---

systems testbed only. No 236 Operational Conversion Unit received its first Nimrod MR1s during October 1969, and five squadrons were operational at the type's peak in service. Eleven examples were selected for conversion in the late 1970s to Nimrod AEW3 standard, but the cancellation of this project saw ten being put into storage and one used as a ground instructional airframe – all have now been scrapped. The whole remaining MR1 fleet was converted from 1979 onwards to MR2 standard with new avionics and mission equipment, apart from the three new-build aircraft that had been ordered as R1s (see separate entry) or electronic intelligence-gathering operations, and which had entered service in 1974.

CURRENT SERVICE

The Nimrod has only ever been operated by the RAF. The entire fleet of MR2s is based at RAF Kinloss on the Moray Firth in Scotland, where the Kinloss Wing has 24 aircraft pooled within four squadrons. No 51 Squadron flies the three ELINT-gathering R1 variants from RAF Waddington in Lincolnshire.

SPECIAL FEATURES

All Nimrods are now refuelling probe-equipped, the first 16 conversions having been undertaken during the 1982 Falklands War in which the type was heavily involved. The MR2's Thorn EMI Searchwater maritime

search radar is mounted in the nose radome, while the magnetic anomaly detector (MAD) boom is prominent at the tail. The fin-top 'football' radome houses ESM equipment. The addition of the large underfuselage weapons bay to the original Comet design produced the distinctive 'double-bubble' fuselage shape when viewed in cross-section – this and other modifications requiring a dorsal fin extension. A powerful searchlight is fitted in the starboard pod mounted outboard on the wing, while those on the wingtips contain Loral ESM pods; a fitment which has necessitated the addition of tailplane finlets for aerodynamic purposes.

VARIANTS

Twenty-one **MR2s** are being updated to Nimrod **MRA4** standard by BAE Systems at Woodford. This rebuild/ update programme involves complete reconstruction – including a new, larger wing and BMW Rolls-Royce BR710 turbofans. After the installation of a Boeing missions system and other avionics, delivery to the RAF is expected by the middle of the decade. BAE Systems and the UK Government have proposed the Nimrod MR4 to Japan for its MP-X requirement, as the order is potentially large enough to restart fuselage production.

SEE ALSO: HAWKER SIDDELEY NIMROD R1

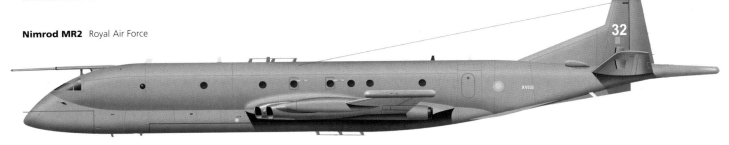

Nimrod MR2 Royal Air Force

Heliopolis Gomhouria

SINGLE PISTON-ENGINED PRIMARY TRAINER

Heliopolis Gomhouria

DEVELOPMENT

There are few serving military aircraft today whose origins can be traced quite as far back as those of the Heliopolis Gomhouria. Its forebear is the Bücker Bü181 Bestmann, which following its first flight in early 1939 had been produced in quantity as an advanced trainer for the wartime Luftwaffe, and had been used by the Egyptian Air Force during the war years. Apart from Czechoslovakia's Zlin concern, the other licence-builder of the Bestmann after WW2 was the Heliopolis company, established by the Egyptian Government at Heliopolis near Cairo. Based with the National General Aero Organisation, it produced 300 examples of several marks of the type named as the Gomhouria, before production ceased in 1979. They saw extensive service in Egypt and with other air forces in the region, incorporating various modifications to the original German design.

CURRENT SERVICE

The Egyptian Air Force currently still operates some 35 Gomhourias, of Mks 6 and 8R, as primary trainers with the Air Force Academy at the Primary Training Brigade at Biberis and the Flying Training Squadron at Khatamia.

SPECIAL FEATURES

Among the modifications undertaken by Heliopolis to the original Bestmann design were the fitment of a bubble canopy and the provision of additional fuel tankage. The Gomhouria is now obviously of somewhat dated design, being of tailwheel configuration with non-retractable undercarriage.

VARIANTS

The **Gomhouria Mks 1 and 5** were powered by the 78.3kW (105hp) Walter Minor 4-III engine, while the Mks 2, 3 and 4 used a 109.2kW (145hp) Continental C145 unit – the same powerplant in it's later Continental O-300 form which equips the **Mks 6** and **8R** in current service with the Egyptian Air Force. The Gomhouria Mk 6 version has a limited aerobatic capability. Surprisingly, 1999 saw the announcement that an American concern is to re-develop the Gomhouria for the civil market and put it back into series production.

TECHNICAL DATA

Heliopolis Gomhouria Mk6

Powerplant: One Teledyne Continental O-300-A piston engine
Developing: 108kW (145hp)
Driving: Two-blade propeller
Span: 10.60m (34ft 9.3in)
Length: 7.85m (25ft 9in)
Height: 2.05m (6ft 8.7in)
All-up weight: 800kg (1,764lb)
Maximum speed: 225km/h (140mph)
Cruise speed: 205km/h (127mph)
Operational ceiling: 19,685ft
Maximum range: 780km (484 miles)
Accommodation: Two side-by-side
First flight: early 1950s
Entered service: mid 1950s

Heliopolis Gomhouria Mk 6

Hiller UH-12

SINGLE PISTON-ENGINED LIGHT UTILITY AND BASIC TRAINING HELICOPTER

H-23 Raven

TECHNICAL DATA

Hiller UH-12E
Powerplant: One Textron Lycoming VO-540A1B piston engine
Developing: 241kW (323hp)
Driving: Two-blade main rotor and two-blade tail rotor
Main rotor diameter: 10.80m (35ft 5in)
Fuselage length: 8.89m (28ft 6in)
Height: 3.08m (10ft 1.25in)
All-up weight: 1,270kg (2,800lb)
Maximum speed: 154km/h (96mph)
Cruise speed: 145km/h (90mph)
Operational ceiling: 15,200ft
Maximum range: 676km (420miles)
Mission range: 330km (205miles)
Accommodation: Three, side-by-side
First flown: 1958 (UH-12E)
Entered service: 1959

DEVELOPMENT

Stanley Hiller's original design for a light utility and training helicopter dates back to 1948, and a total of over 2,000 examples of the type in its various forms were later produced by the Hiller concern. Among these were H-23 Ravens of numerous sub-types used by the US forces, mainly for liaison and training, as well as UH-12s supplied to the Royal Navy for basic helicopter instruction.

CURRENT SERVICE

Standard piston-engined UH-12Es are currently used by the Egyptian Air Force with the Helicopter Training Brigade at El Minya (with eighteen examples, making it the largest single Hiller user). The Mexican Navy and Paraguayan Navy at Sajonia Naval Air Force Base also use UH-12Es for communications duties. Eight turbine-powered Hiller (Soloy) UH-12E.4s are flown by the Argentine Army Corps with Escuela de Aviación del Ejército at Campo de Mayo.

SPECIAL FEATURES

The Hiller UH-12 helicopter is of very distinctive design, with its thin, upswept tailboom. The large glass area of the three-place cockpit is also noteworthy, giving good all-round vision.

VARIANTS

Aside from the standard piston UH-12E, Hiller also developed (in conjunction with Soloy) a three-seat turbine-powered derivative. Known as the UH-12T or UH-12E.4, it is this version which serves with the Argentine Army. It is powered by an Allison 250-C20B turboshaft. In 1992, the new Rogerson Hiller company resumed production of the UH-12 as the civil UH-12E Hauler, and also offered the UH-12ET for the US Army's New Training Helicopter (NTH) requirement, but was unsuccessful.

H-23 Raven

Hoffman H36 Dimona

SINGLE-ENGINED MOTOR-GLIDER

Hoffman H36 Dimona

DEVELOPMENT

The German Hoffman firm developed this popular motor-glider for basic flying training and sport flying purposes. It is built by Hoffman Flugzeugbau GmbH at Friesach in Austria, and it is probably the most popular of current motor gliders, successfully bridging the gap between the original motorised sailplanes and full-scale light aircraft. It has conventional landing gear with brakes and full instrumentation for touring.

CURRENT SERVICE

Ten Dimonas are in service with the Royal Thai Air Force and are used for flight experience and primary training, out of 14 originally purchased. They are based with No 1 Flying Training School at Kamphaeng Saen.

SPECIAL FEATURES

The Dimona has a T-tail arrangement, spatted mainwheels, and low-set wings which can be folded backwards along the fuselage sides for ease of road transport and storage. Though of gliding design concept, through the high-aspect ratio wings that are incorporated in its layout, the Dimona has a conventional light aircraft cockpit and fixed tailwheel landing gear. It is constructed entirely of composites.

VARIANTS

Only the one basic version of the **Dimona** has been produced. Hoffman left the firm in the mid-1980s to form a new company, Wolff Hoffman Flugzeubau KG that produced a lighter version of the Dimona. This features a shorter span forward-swept wing and a tricycle undercarriage. Its powerplant is a Limbach L2400 engine. The HK-36R Super Dimona is a major redesign of the H36 with a Rotax 912A engine and improved undercarriage.

TECHNICAL DATA

Hoffman H36 Dimona

Powerplant: One Limbach SL2000-EB1C engine
Developing: 59.7kW (80hp)
Span: 16.0m (52ft 6in)
Length: 6.85m (22ft 6in)
Height: 1.62m (5ft 4in)
All-up weight: 740kg (1,631lb)
Maximum speed: 210km/h (130mph)
Cruising speed: 180km/h (112mph)
Operational ceiling: 19,680ft
Maximum range: 1,000km (621miles)
Accommodation: Two side-by-side
First flown: 9 October 1980

Hoffman H36 Dimona

Hongdu (Nanchang) Q-5/A-5 Fantan

TWIN-TURBOJET ATTACK AIRCRAFT

Nanchang A-5-III 'Fantan' Pakistan Air Force

DEVELOPMENT

Based on the J-6 fighter, which was itself a licence-built MiG-19, the Q-5 began life in 1958, when Shenyang conceived a proposal for a close air support and ground attack derivative of the J-6, with limited air-to-air capability. Project leadership was then allocated to Nanchang (now Hongdu), only to be abandoned in 1961. Despite this, limited work continued and the Q-5 was officially resurrected in 1963. Thereafter, the pace quickened and a prototype flew for the first time in 1965, with authority to build a small batch of pre-production aircraft following by the end of that year. Trials with the prototype and pre-production examples revealed that further improvement was necessary and testing of two extensively modified aircraft resumed in October 1969. In this form, the Q-5 was ordered into production at the end of 1969, with deliveries to the Chinese Air Force commencing in 1970.

CURRENT SERVICE

Almost 1,000 examples of the Fantan have been built, with the majority going to the People's Liberation Army Air Force and Navy. In addition, at least 140 have been delivered to Bangladesh (A-5C), North Korea (Q-5 IA), Myanmar (A-5C) and Pakistan (A-5-III).

SPECIAL FEATURES

Although it evolved from the MiG-19 via the J-6, the Q-5 differs markedly in overall physical appearance, having two fuselage-mounted air intakes adjacent to the cockpit in place of the original nose intake. Other features include mid-mounted sharply swept wings and an area ruled fuselage, which breaks just behind the wing to facilitate engine changes.

VARIANTS

The basic **Q-5** had an internal weapons bay able to take two 500kg (1,100lb) bombs. Subsequently, this was replaced by the **Q-5 I**, which was a longer ranged version with extra fuel in the sealed-off weapons bay and additional hardpoints. The **Q-5 IA**, essentially a Q-5 I with an extra station on each wing, plus new gun/bomb sighting systems, pressure refuelling and additional ECM equipment. The final domestic version is the **Q-5 II**, essentially similar to the Q-5 IA, but with a radar warning receiver. Export aircraft for Bangladesh, Myanmar and Pakistan use the designation **A-5C** (although Pakistan calls them **A-5-IIIs**) and feature enhanced avionics, Martin-Baker Mk 10 ejection seats and modified stores stations to accommodate Western weapons like the Sidewinder missile.

TECHNICAL DATA

Hongdu (Nanchang) Q-5 IA Fantan

Powerplants: Two LM (Liming) WP6 turbojets
Thrust: 25.5kN (5,730lb st) dry; 31.9kN (7,165lb st) with afterburner
Span: 9.68m (31ft 9in)
Length: 15.65m (51ft 4.25in) including probe
Height: 4.335m (14ft 2.75in)
Maximum weight: 11,830kg (26,080lb)
Maximum speed: 1,220km/h (758mph)
Operational ceiling: 52,000ft
Maximum range: 1,820km (1,130 miles)
Combat radius: 600km (373 miles) hi-lo-hi with maximum external stores and without afterburner
Accommodation: Pilot only
Warload: Maximum external stores load of 2,000kg (4,410lb) on 10 stations; weapons options include bombs, cluster bombs, rockets, C-801 anti-ship attack missile and IR-homing air-to-air missiles such as PL-2, PL-2B, PL-7, AIM-9 Sidewinder and R550 Magic. Internal armament of one Norinco Type 23 23mm cannon with 100 rounds in each wing root.
First flown: 4 June 1965
Entered service: 1970

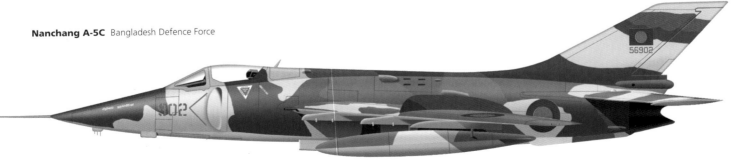

Nanchang A-5C Bangladesh Defence Force

Hongdu/PAC K-8 Karakorum

SINGLE TURBOFAN BASIC TRAINER/LIGHT ATTACK AIRCRAFT

K-8 Karakorum

TECHNICAL DATA

Hongdu/PAC K-8 Karakorum

Powerplant: One AlliedSignal TFE731-2A-2 turbofan
Developing: 16.01kN (3,600lb st)
Span: 9.63m (31ft 7.25in)
Length: 11.60m (38ft 0.75in) including nose probe
Height: 4.21m (13ft 9.75in)
All-up weight: 4,330kg (9,546lb)
Maximum speed: 950km/h (590mph)
Operational ceiling: 42,660ft
Maximum range: 2,250km (1,398 miles)
Endurance: 4hr 25min
Accommodation: Two pilots
Warload: Maximum external stores load of 943kg (2,080lb) on four underwing stations. Weapon options include bombs, cluster bombs, rockets and PL-7 IR-homing air-to-air missiles. Centreline stores station can accommodate a 23mm gun pod
First flown: 21 November 1990
Entered service: November 1994 (for evaluation by Pakistan)

DEVELOPMENT

First knowledge of the existence of this Chinese trainer came to Western attention at the 1987 Paris Air Show, when the Nanchang Aircraft Manufacturing Company announced it was seeking an international partner to share in development. At that time, it was known as the L-8, but a subsequent co-development agreement with Pakistan saw a change in designation to K-8. The original intention was to create production centres in both countries, but in 1994, Pakistan decided against this, although its 25 per cent share of sub-contract work rose to 45 per cent. In the meantime, assembly of three flying prototypes and a static/fatigue test airframe began in January 1989, with the first flight following shortly before the end of 1990. The K-8 is now being jointly produced by Hongdu and Pakistan Aeronautical Complex (PAC).

CURRENT SERVICE

By late 2000, deliveries had been made to China, Pakistan, Myanmar and Zambia. Exact numbers are not known, but the latter two nations have

displayed their new aircraft to the public. Pakistan has revealed a requirement for up to 100 to replace the T-37, while China is known to require several hundred. It is also under consideration by Bangladesh, Eritrea, Laos and Sri Lanka, although no firm orders have yet been placed.

SPECIAL FEATURES

Of largely conventional design and construction, the K-8 is a low-wing monoplane design with a slightly swept vertical tail. It has a tricycle undercarriage arrangement, with single wheels on each unit. Pilot and student are housed in tandem. Although primarily intended as a trainer, it could be utilised as a light ground attack aircraft.

VARIANTS

The basic model, as supplied to China and Pakistan in pre-production form, is the **K-8**, which is powered by engines of Western manufacture and also incorporates Western avionics equipment. However, the **K-8J** is reportedly the designation allocated to a version for

Chinese service, that is expected to be powered by the 16.87kN (3,792lb st) Progress ZMKB AI-25TL turbofan, although the 21.58kN (4,852lb st) PS/ZMK DV-2 engine has been reported as an alternative choice. Another one-off version is designated **K-8VSA**, which is a variable stability test aircraft assigned to the Chinese Flight Test Establishment. It is fitted with a fly-by-wire automatic flight control system as well as a data acquisition system.

K-8 Karakorum

Hughes 369/Kawasaki OH-6

SINGLE TURBINE OBSERVATION HELICOPTER

Hughes OH-6A Colombian Air Force

TECHNICAL DATA

Hughes OH-6A Cayuse

Powerplant: One Allison T63-A-5A turboshaft
Developing: 236.5kW (317shp) derated to 160kw (214.5shp) for continuous operation
Driving: Four-blade main and two-blade tail rotors
Main rotor diameter: 8.03m (26ft 4in)
Fuselage length: 7.01m (23ft 0in)
Height: 2.48m (8ft 1.4in)
Maximum weight: 1,225kg (2,700lb)
Maximum speed: 241km/h (150mph)
Cruise speed: 216km/h (134mph)
Operational ceiling: 15,800ft
Maximum ferry range: 2,510km (1,560 miles)
Normal range: 611km (380 miles)
Accommodation: Pilot and maximum of three passengers
Warload: Weaponry available includes XM27E1 7.62mm machine gun or XM75 40mm grenade launcher to port with flexibly mounted machine gun in door on starboard side
First flown: 27 February 1963 (prototype YOH-6A)
Entered service: September 1965 (first deliveries – to US Army)

DEVELOPMENT

Evolution of the Hughes Model 369 came about at the start of the 1960s, when the US Army formulated a requirement for a new Light Observation Helicopter (LOH). This was earmarked to replace the piston-powered Bell OH-13 Sioux and Hiller OH-23 Raven and key criteria were high performance, turbine power, easy maintenance and low cost to buy and operate. Several companies submitted proposals, with designs by Bell and Hiller being evaluated alongside the Hughes contender. Flying for the first time in early 1963, a handful of development YOH-6As was completed for trials and the Hughes contender was finally selected for quantity production in May 1965, very quickly being nicknamed 'Loach'. Following initial deliveries, it was soon committed to combat in Vietnam, where several hundred were to become battle casualties.

CURRENT SERVICE

Although 1,434 examples of the original OH-6A were produced for service with the US Army, none of them remain active today. However, some examples of the basically similar AH-6 and MH-6 are still on US Army strength, although these are developed from the Model 500 series and are described separately. Of the first-generation Model 369 helicopters, a few are assigned to the US Navy Test Pilot School at Patuxent River, Maryland, these being known as TH-6Bs. In addition, Kawasaki produced more than 200 examples of the OH-6D version under licence for service with both the Japanese Ground Self-Defence Force and the Maritime Self-Defence Force and others remain in service in small numbers, particularly in South America.

SPECIAL FEATURES

The most notable features of the Model 369/OH-6 are its diminutive size and the egg-shaped pod which contains the cockpit and cabin. Extensive use of glazing provides an excellent field of view for pilot and observer. A skid-type undercarriage was also fitted as standard on all helicopters.

VARIANTS

Initial production for the US Army during the 1960s was restricted to just the **OH-6A** derivative, but subsequent modification resulted in the appearance of the **OH-6B**, which first flew in May 1988. Changes incorporated on this model included installation of a more powerful 313.3kW (420shp) T63-A-720 engine, plus 'Black Hole' infrared suppressing exhaust nozzle, undernose FLIR sensor and wire-strike protection. Some were subsequently further adapted for Special Forces use as the **MH-6B**, **MH-6C** and **AH-6C**.

Kawasaki OH-6D Japanese Ground Self-Defence Force

IAI Arava

TWIN-TURBOPROP STOL MULTI-MISSION AIRCRAFT

IAI Arava 202ECM *Israeli Air Force*

TECHNICAL DATA

IAI Arava 201

Powerplants: Two Pratt & Whitney Canada PT6A-34 turboprops
Developing: 559kW (750eshp) each
Driving: three-blade propeller
Span: 20.96m (68ft 9in)
Length: 13.03m (42ft 9in)
Height: 5.21m (17ft 1in)
All-up weight: 6,804kg (15,000lb)
Maximum speed: 326km/h (203mph)
Cruise speed: 311km/h (193mph)
Operational ceiling: 24,000ft
Maximum range: 1,001km (622 miles)
Accommodation: Two crew and 20 passengers or 2,313kg (5,100lb) cargo
Warload: Two forward-firing 12.7mm machine guns can be fitted on the fuselage, while underfuselage pylons may carry up to twelve 82mm rockets.
First flown: 27 November 1969
Entered service: 1973

DEVELOPMENT

The Arava was the first design undertaken entirely by Israel Aircraft Industries to enter series production, having originally been intended as a replacement for the ageing C-47 Skytrains of the Israeli Defence Force/Air Force. An impressive short take-off and landing (STOL) capability was a feature of the design from the outset, allowing for ease of operation from short, unprepared strips by both civil and military operators, while retaining good enough outright performance to allow the type's usage in a variety of other military roles such as maritime reconnaissance. It did however take several years for the Arava to enter full IDF/AF service as a C-47 replacement, not coming into large-scale use until the late 1970s, although three had been leased during the Arab-Israeli war of 1973.

CURRENT SERVICE

In its home country, the Arava is used in two versions by the Israeli DF/AF: the Series 102 for transport and the 202ECM in the electronic warfare role, both with No 126 Squadron. Other operators, all for transport duties unless stated otherwise, are the Bolivian Air Force, Cameroon Air Force, Colombian Air Force, Ecuadorean Army Air Service, Guatemalan Air Force, Honduran Air Force, Mexican Air Force (five 201s for search-and-rescue), Swaziland Air Force (used in a secondary COIN role), Royal Thai Air Force (three 201s for ELINT-gathering) and Venezuelan Naval Aviation, Army Air Service and Civil Guard.

SPECIAL FEATURES

The Arava is of compact design, but retains a plentiful payload for transport operations and other roles. It has a high-wing configuration, with a twin-boom tail unit with a distinctive 'tapering' end to the fuselage cabin area. The rugged tricycle undercarriage is non-retractable. For electronic warfare operations, EW and ESM equipment can be housed in removable panniers or various radomes, with a rearward-facing scanner being mounted on the rear fuselage between the tail booms, which can themselves carry ECM antennae.

VARIANTS

The two civil versions are the **Arava 101** and **102**, the latter having been acquired by the IDF/AF for general transport taskings. However, the majority of production Aravas have been the military **Series 201** and **202**, the latter having been a retrofit update begun by IAI in 1984. In Arava 202 form, the fuselage can carry 30 fully-equipped soldiers and a greater cargo payload, with winglets being added. In the EW role, the type (such as the Israeli **202ECMs** and Thai 201s) can be fitted with the Elta EL-7010 jammer, with its various associated antennae. Machine guns and rocket pods are another option for the type, as used on COIN operations by Swaziland Defence Force aircraft.

IAI Arava 201 Colombian Air Force

IAI Dagger

SINGLE TURBOJET AIR DEFENCE FIGHTER AND GROUND ATTACK AIRCRAFT

Dagger 'Finger A' Argentine Air Force

DEVELOPMENT

The Arab-Israeli Six-Day War of 1967 led to an arms embargo preventing Israel from re-equipping its air force with new French or American combat aircraft, and stopped deliveries of Mirage 5Js from Dassault. To fill this shortfall, Israel Aircraft Industries was tasked with producing an 'indigenous' combat aircraft, and it did so by means of espionage. The new fighter/strike aircraft was an unlicensed copy of the Mirage 5J, using Atar engines which had already been delivered to Israel; drawings were stolen from Dassault in France and the plant in Switzerland engaged in building engines for Swiss AF Mirage IIIs. The 'new' IAI Nesher had its service baptism during the 1973 Yom Kippur War and proved successful, but the type was obsolete by 1977 by which time IAI had developed the improved Kfir. A total of 51 examples of the single-seat Nesher S and 10 two-seat Nesher Ts had been built, of which 43 would eventually be purchased by the Argentine Air Force as the Dagger A and Dagger B respectively.

CURRENT SERVICE

Now updated to 'Finger' standard, the 19 remaining Dagger As and three Dagger Bs are in service with the Argentine Air Force, operated by Escuadrón I of Grupo 6 de Caza at BAM Tandill. Among the aircraft lost thus far were 17 during the Falklands campaign of 1982, in which the type was heavily involved.

SPECIAL FEATURES

The Dagger shares the same basic shape as the Mirage 5 from which its design was copied, being of tailless delta configuration with a slim, pointed nose (albeit reconfigured as a result of the recent 'Finger' upgrade programme) and greater internal fuel capacity than the preceding Mirage III. Indigenous avionics were fitted to the type by IAI, along with provision to carry the 'home-grown' Rafael Shafrir AAMs, though the type's primary role in Argentine service is now anti-shipping strike and ground attack while still being available for air defence duties.

VARIANTS

All the Argentine Air Force's **Dagger As** and two-seat **Dagger Bs** have now been updated under a three-stage programme. This has incorporated avionics similar to those used in the IAI Kfir, necessitating a re-shaped nose – the conversions being known as the '**Finger A**' and '**Finger B**' respectively.

SEE ALSO: ATLAS CHEETAH, DASSAULT MIRAGE III/V/50, ENAER PANTERA 50CN & IAI KFIR

TECHNICAL DATA

IAI Dagger 'Finger A'

Powerplant: One IAI Bedek-built SNECMA Atar 09C afterburning turbojet
Developing: 60.80kN (13,668lb st) with afterburner
Span: 8.22m (26ft 11.6in)
Length: 15.55m (51ft 0.2in)
Height: 4.50m (14ft 9in)
All-up weight: 13,700kg (30,203lb)
Maximum speed: 2,350km/h (1,460mph)
Cruise speed: 956km/h (594mph)
Operational ceiling: 59,055ft
Maximum range: 1,250km (776miles)
Mission range: 685km (425miles)
Accommodation: Pilot only
Warload: Two 30mm DEFA cannon are standard, while a typical weapons load consists of anti-shipping stores or conventional iron bombs. Two Rafael Shafir short-range air-to-air misssiles.
First flown: September 1969
Entered service: 1973

IAI Nesher

IAI Kfir

SINGLE TURBOJET AIR DEFENCE FIGHTER AND GROUND ATTACK AIRCRAFT

IAI Kfir C-2 Ecuadorean Air Force

TECHNICAL DATA

IAI Kfir C-7

Powerplant: One IAI Bedek-built General Electric
J79-J1E afterburning turbojet
Developing: 83.40kN (18,750lb st) with
afterburner
Span: 8.22m (26ft 11.6in)
Length: 15.65m (51ft 4.25in)
Height: 4.55m (14ft 11.25in)
All-up weight: 16,500kg (36,376lb)
Maximum speed: 2,440km/h (1,516mph)
Operational ceiling: 58,000ft
Maximum range: 3,232km (2,006 miles)
Mission range: 1,186km (736 miles)
Accommodation: Pilot only (or two in tandem
in trainer versions)
Warload: Nine hardpoints are fitted to the C-7,
able to carry up to 6,085kg (13,415lb) of stores.
These may include either free-fall or 'smart'
weapons, along with Rafael Shafrir or Python
AAMs or Maverick or Hobos air-to-surface
missiles. Two 30mm DEFA 553 cannon are
standard equipment.
First flown: 19 October 1970 (J79-engined Mirage
IIICJ prototype); September 1971 (IAI-built)
Entered service: 1983 (Kfir C-7)

DEVELOPMENT

The IAI Kfir resulted from the necessity to improve
upon the Israeli Defence Force/Air Force's Mirage fleet
that was heavily involved in the Arab-Israeli conflicts
of 1967 and 1973, but which had suffered from the
outset from various deficiencies. Owing to the high
speeds it needed for take-off and landing, the Mirage
required a long runway, and it possessed somewhat
outmoded avionics, amongst other shortcomings.
However, Western arms embargoes made the purchase
of a replacement impossible, unless an indigenous
programme could be undertaken (as had occurred with
the Nesher/Dagger). Following expertise gained in the
Mirage V-based Nesher programme and an earlier
Mirage III upgrade, both also intended to iron out
some of the aforementioned problems, IAI set to
work on this 'new' machine in the late 1960s, the
Nesher being seen only as an interim aircraft. The
powerplant, made available from stocks obtained
when the IDF/AF had purchased the F-4 Phantom,
was to be the General Electric J79 – the first aircraft
thus powered was a converted two-seat Mirage III
from the original French order, followed in 1971 by
a re-engined Nesher S, and then the first new-build

production run of 27 initial aircraft. Canards were
added when these examples were upgraded to Kfir
C-1 status, after which the improved C-2 and the
corresponding TC-2 trainer formed the majority of
aircraft produced.

CURRENT SERVICE

Naturally, the Israeli Defence Force/Air Force is the
largest Kfir operator with a fleet of some 50 C-7s and
several two-seat TC-7s being split between three
squadrons at Nevatim and Ovda. Other users are the
Colombian Air Force (eleven C-2s/ C-7s and one TC-2),
Ecuadorean Air Force (17 C-2s and TC-2s), and the Sri
Lankan Air Force, which currently flies four C-2s and a
solitary TC-2.

SPECIAL FEATURES

From the Kfir C-2 and TC-2 onwards, large fixed canard
foreplanes were added to the design (small such
canards were used on the now-retired C-1 version).
These give an improved turning radius and take-off
performance, while improving controllability at all
areas of the speed envelope. The optional air-to-air
refuelling probe can be used with tanker aircraft

fitted with either the probe-and-drogue or flying-
boom AAR methods.

VARIANTS

Only the **Kfir C-2** and corresponding **TC-2** operational
trainer, and the further updated **C-7** and **TC-7**, are in
service today. The external distinguishing feature of
the latter variant is the presence of a pair of extra
weapons hardpoints situated under the engine intakes.
The rest of the update programme consisted primarily
of avionics improvements, with a new digital weapons
delivery and navigation system being fitted, and
compatibility with 'smart' weapons. No orders were
forthcoming for the **Kfir C-10** update with a new
cockpit fit, standard refuelling probe and more
modern radar.

IAI Kfir C-7 Israeli Air Force

IAI 1124 Westwind & SeaScan

IAI 1124 Westwind Honduran Air Force

DEVELOPMENT

Rockwell initially developed the basic design as the Model 1121 Jet Commander, but having acquired the design rights, Israel Aircraft Industries successfully put the aircraft into production in 1968 as the 1123 (powered by GE CJ610-9 turbojets) and turbofan-powered 1124 Westwind variants for the civil executive and VIP transport market. From the latter machine, IAI developed the 1124N SeaScan as a maritime surveillance and SAR support platform, with three having been built.

CURRENT SERVICE

Two standard 1124 Westwinds are used in the VIP transport role by the Esquadrón de Transporte of the Honduran Air Force, and are civil-registered. They are operated from Base Aérea Coronel Hector Caraccioli Moncada (La Ceiba). The Israeli Defence Force/Air Force flies the three 1124N SeaScans on behalf of the country's Navy, these being on the strength of No 195 Squadron at Tayeset with Lod Transport Command HQ Bacha 27.

SPECIAL FEATURES

The Westwind and SeaScan share the same basic configuration, the very short undercarriage being an especially notable feature of the type. The twin turbofan engines are pod-mounted on either side of the rear fuselage, just forward of the tailplane. Tip-tanks are a feature of all versions, while the SeaScan has its maritime radar mounted in a bulbous nose radome.

VARIANTS

The **1124N SeaScan**, unique to the Israeli DF/AF, is equipped with a Litton AN/APS-504 search radar with 360° coverage in all weathers. Two pylons mounted on the fuselage sides can carry torpedoes or missiles if desired. The **Westwind**, apart from its role as a VIP transport, has also been equipped for the target-towing role, with the requisite targets being stowed in underwing pods (though the four Model 1124s operated by the civil Rhein-Flugzeugbau concern under contract to the German forces have now been phased out).

IAI 1124N SeaScan Israeli Defence Force/Air Force

TECHNICAL DATA

IAI 1124N SeaScan

Powerplants: Two Garrett TFE731-3-1G turbofans
Developing: 16.46kN (3,700lb st)
Span: 13.16m (43ft 2in)
Length: 15.93m (52ft 3in)
Height: 4.81m (15ft 9.5in)
All-up weight: 10,660kg (23,500lb)
Maximum speed: 872km/h (542mph)
Cruise speed: 741km/h (460mph)
Operational ceiling: 45,000ft
Maximum range: 5,373km (3,335 miles)
Mission range: 2,555km (1,587 miles)
Accommodation: Two crew plus seven passengers

IAI 1125 Astra/Astra SP & C-38A

TWIN-TURBOFAN EXECUTIVE/VIP TRANSPORT

IAI 1125 Astra

TECHNICAL DATA

IAI 1125 Astra/C-38A

Powerplant: Two Garrett TFE731-3A-200G turbofans
Developing: 16.24kN (3,650lb st)
Span: 16.05m (52ft 8in)
Length: 16.94m (55ft 7in)
Height: 5.54m (18ft 2in)
All-up weight: 10,659kg (23,500lb)
Maximum speed: 862km/h (535mph)
Cruising speed: 800km/h (497mph)
Operational ceiling: 45,000ft
Accommodation: Flight crew of two and 6-9 passengers
Maximum range: 5,763km (3,581 miles)
First flown: 19 March 1984; 16 August 1994 (Astra SPX)
Entered service: 30 June 1986; 1996 (Astra SPX)

DEVELOPMENT

IAI's decision to produce an updated version of its 1124 Westwind series resulted in the more advanced 1125 Astra, first flown in 1984. This was a more fuel-efficient, environmentally acceptable development with a new-design aerofoil section wing mounted low on the fuselage (the Westwind's are mid-mounted). The Astra has a higher standard of passenger comfort and a deeper fuselage profile. The cabin is 0.61m (2ft) longer and dual controls are fitted as standard. The latest composite construction technology was used in its design, and it has a swept-wing design rather than the unswept unit of its predecessor.

CURRENT SERVICE

The Indian Air Force operates six Astra SPX versions, used by its Air Research Centre and Analysis Wing at Palam. Designated as the C-38A, two examples of the type are in service with the USAF's 201st Airlift Squadron, Maryland Air National Guard as VIP and staff transports for the ANG Headquarters.

SPECIAL FEATURES

Apart from the swept-wing layout and composite construction, the Astra features many other advances over its Westwind predecessor. The fuselage is slightly wider and some 2ft longer, and the Astra has a taller

undercarriage, though it retains the earlier aircraft's tail unit.

VARIANTS

The **Astra SP** and **SPX** are updated versions of the basic machine, with more advanced digital avionics and improved aerodynamics. The SPX has revised wings with winglets to reduce drag. The **C-38A** is the designation of the Astra in USAF service.

C-38A Astra United States Air Force

IAI/Elta Phalcon

FOUR-TURBOFAN AIRBORNE EARLY WARNING AIRCRAFT

IAI/Elta Phalcon 1 Chilean Air Force

DEVELOPMENT

Many different conversions of the Boeing 707 have been undertaken by Israel Aircraft Industries over the years, including aircraft modified for the tanker and electronic intelligence-gathering roles. The Phalcon AEW platform was developed by IAI and its electronics division Elta, and is available in a variety of individual configurations to suit particular customers. It is important to note that the Phalcon designation refers to the AEW system itself, but this has so far only been incorporated into the Boeing 707, and it is thus this aircraft which is described. An Ilyushin Il-76 was to have been the chosen platform for a Phalcon order from China, but bowing to pressure from the US, Israel subsequently cancelled the order.

CURRENT SERVICE

A single example of the Phalcon 1 is in service with the Chilean Air Force, while a second ENAER/IAI/Elta aircraft is on order. Although unconfirmed, the Israeli

Defence Force/Air Force has probably adopted a form of Phalcon fit on some of its Boeing 707s, and likewise the South African Air Force.

SPECIAL FEATURES

The Phalcon system is based around the Elta EL/2075 phased-array radar, which in its most advanced form has four antenna arrays. Two are housed in either side of the forward fuselage in large cheek fairings, a third in the nose radome, and the fourth can be located under the tail though no aircraft has been seen with this unit as yet. The nose radome has a flattened underside for ground clearance purposes, while the two forward-fuselage antennae are located in flat-sided bulges. Wingtip antennas serve the aircraft's extensive Elint/ESM system. The aircraft can also be operated as an airborne command post.

VARIANTS

In service with the Chilean Air Force, the **Phalcon 1**

TECHNICAL DATA

IAI/Elta Phalcon 1

Powerplant: Four Pratt & Whitney JT-3D/3B turbofans
Developing: 80.07kN (18,800lb st)
Span: 44.42m (145ft 9in)
Height: 12.93m (42ft 5in)
Operational ceiling: 42,000ft
Endurance: 8-10hours
Accommodation: Two crew and around 13 systems operators (unconfirmed)
First flown: 12 May 1993
Entered service: 1994

has 260° coverage provided by the nose and two side antennae. It is not known what fitments other Phalcons that may be in service possess. The second Chilean example will be a dual-role AEW/tanker aircraft.

IAI/Elta Phalcon 1 Chilean Air Force

IAR IAR-99 Soim

SINGLE TURBOJET BASIC/ADVANCED TRAINER AND LIGHT ATTACK AIRCRAFT

IAR-99 Soim Romanian Air Force

DEVELOPMENT

The first indigenous jet design from the Romanian aircraft industry to be put into series production, the IAR-99 Soim originally fell under the auspices of the IAv-Craiova firm, but after the revolution of 1989 all the state aircraft factories were merged into the IAR consortium. Designed as a basic/advanced jet trainer with a secondary light attack role, the Soim has not been produced in the originally intended numbers owing to budget cuts within the IAR concern, but has nonetheless now been in Romanian Air Force service for some 12 years, having initially replaced the ageing Aero L-29 Delfin with the air arm's jet training school.

CURRENT SERVICE

Only the Romanian Air Force operates the IAR-99, with some 15-20 aircraft believed to be currently on the strength of 67 Regiment based at Craiova. Fifty aircraft of a later version are on order.

SPECIAL FEATURES

The Soim is of conventional configuration, having an unswept, low-set wing with the engine intakes situated at the wing root. Its cockpit is pressurised, with the rear seat being raised to improve forward visibility. The fuselage has a distinctive 'hump-backed' shape, and the leading edge of the tail fin is slightly swept back with a small dorsal 'fillet' extension.

VARIANTS

Only one standard variant of the **IAR-99 Soim** has reached series production for the Romanian Air Force, but three further developments have in particular been proposed. The first of these was put forward by IAR itself, and first flew on 22 May 1997, making use of an uprated Viper Mk680 turbojet delivering some 21.7kN (4,870lb st), and which would (like the Mk632 unit used in production Soims) have been built by Turbomecanica in Romania. An export version that was offered by Jaffe Aircraft of the USA, announced in 1991, incorporated Western avionics, with the possibility of a more powerful Viper turbojet being fitted. However, the only Soim upgrade to fly has been the **IAR-109 Swift**, developed in conjunction with Israel Aircraft Industries. This machine, whose prototype was based on an IAR-99, also featured upgraded avionics and remains in existence today for test and trials purposes. However, as with the other planned Soim updates, the Swift has failed to receive any orders as yet.

TECHNICAL DATA

IAR IAR-99 Soim

Powerplant: One Turbomecanica (Rolls-Royce) Viper Mk632-41M turbojet
Developing: 17.79kN (4,000lb st)
Span: 9.85m (32ft 3.8in)
Length: 11.01m (36ft 1.5in)
Height: 3.90m (12ft 9.5in)
All-up weight: 4,400kg (9,700lb)
Maximum speed: 865km/h (537mph)
Operational ceiling: 42,325ft
Maximum range: 1,100km (1,265 miles)
Mission range: 350km (402 miles)
Endurance: 2hr 40min
Accommodation: Two in tandem
Warload: A ventral gun pod can be fitted, containing a 23mm GSh-23 cannon, while four underwing hardpoints may bear up to 1,000kg (2,200lb) of stores in total, such as rocket pods, AAMs, machine gun packs or iron bombs.
First flown: 21 December 1985
Entered service: 1988

IAR-99 Soim Romanian Air Force

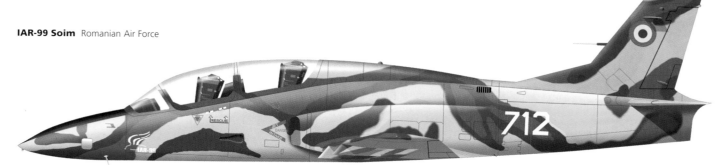

IAR IAR-316B Alouette III

SINGLE TURBOSHAFT ANTI-TANK AND UTILITY HELICOPTER

IAR-316B Romanian Air Force

DEVELOPMENT

As built by ICA-Brasov, later IAR, in Romania, the Artouste-engined Alouette III is basically identical to the SA316B as constructed originally by Aérospatiale in France. The Turboméca powerplants were imported, with production being initiated in 1971, and around 230 are believed to have been built by IAR before the line was closed in 1989. Apart from those which entered military service, the IAR-316B also saw civil use, primarily in Romania.

CURRENT SERVICE

The Romanian military is (unsurprisingly) the biggest current user of the IAR-316B, with 45 in Air Force service and a further five on Navy strength. The Angolan People's Air Force has 35 examples, while six are operated by the Algerian Air Force and a single aircraft flies with the Guinea Republic Air Force.

SPECIAL FEATURES

The basic IAR-316B design is identical to the French Alouette III, having a 'tadpole-shaped' fuselage with fairly extensive cockpit glazing. The helicopter's Artouste turboshaft engine is in an exposed position on top of the rear of the cabin area, just aft of the main rotor head, while the type has a three-blade tail rotor mounted on the starboard side. Below it is a spindly tail 'bumper'. A small tailplane is fitted with rounded-off fin endplates. The IAR-316B itself can be fitted with stub wings for anti-tank duties, in order to carry its AT-3 anti-armour weapons and rocket pods.

VARIANTS

While only the single basic version of the **IAR-316B** was produced, ICA-Brasov/IAR did propose a dedicated, much-modified anti-tank helicopter based upon its licence-built Alouette III. This was the **IAR-317 Airfox**,

with a new fuselage and tail arrangement surrounding the IAR-316B's engine and transmission, and other internal fittings. The fuselage was made slimmer, and the cockpit (which was armoured) modified with a new tandem seating configuration, the pilot sitting in the raised rearward position. 750kg (1,653lb) of stores were intended to be carried, but the Airfox was never ordered by the Romanian armed forces or any other customer, and development was never re-started after the Romanian coup in late 1989.

SEE ALSO: AEROSPATIALE (SUD) SA 316/SA 319 ALOUETTE II

TECHNICAL DATA

IAR IAR-316B Alouette III

Powerplant: One Turboméca Artouste IIIB turboshaft
Developing: 649kW (870eshp)
Main rotor diameter: 11.02m (36ft 1.75in)
Fuselage length: 10.03m (32ft 10.75in)
Height: 3.00m (9ft 10in)
All-up weight: 2,250kg (4,960lb)
Maximum speed: 220km/h (136mph)
Cruise speed: 197km/h (122mph)
Operational ceiling: 10,170ft
Maximum range: 605km (375 miles)
Accommodation: Pilot and six passengers
Warload: Six AT-3 'Sagger' anti-tank missiles and four rocket pods can be carried respectively above and below the type's stub wings, while 7.62mm machine guns are fitted on underfuselage and starboard cabin door mountings.
First flown: 1971
Entered service: 1972

IAR-316B III Romanian Navy

IAR IAR-330L Puma

TWIN-TURBOSHAFT MEDIUM UTILITY HELICOPTER

IAR-330 Puma Romanian Air Force

DEVELOPMENT

As with the IAR-316B Alouette III, Romania's state-owned IAR concern acquired licence-production rights from Aérospatiale for the IAR-330L Puma, equivalent to the standard French-built SA330L in its basic design. Construction began in 1977, the engines this time being licence-built in Romania as well. The intention in building the Puma was to produce a fairly heavily-armed utility helicopter for Romanian military use, and to this end, the provision was made for extensive weapons carriage while retaining the type's cargo-carrying capability.

CURRENT SERVICE

The Romanian Air Force possesses 90 IAR-330Ls for the assault transport role, being operated by eight squadrons within five wings, while the country's Navy flies six more as transports. Other operators of the Romanian-built Puma are the Guinea Republic Air

Force, Kenyan Air Force, Sudanese Air Force and the United Arab Emirates Air Force's element in Dubai.

SPECIAL FEATURES

The main feature of the Romanian Air Force's fleet of IAR-330Ls is their external weaponry. Two 20mm cannon are located in small cheek fittings on either side of the helicopter's nose, while mountings just behind each of the main cabin doors can carry rockets and AT-3 anti-armour weapons, machine guns or bomb attachments. A roof-mounted sight is an optional feature. For naval or coastguard SAR duties and other maritime tasks, IAR can supply the type with flotation gear and an upgraded navigation aid fitment, and has flown a demonstrator Puma thus equipped.

VARIANTS

The basic **IAR-330L Puma** has been sold to military customers in both armed and unarmed derivatives,

and is (as mentioned above) available as an updated maritime helicopter. In addition, the company's **Puma 2000** upgrade, developed in conjunction with the Israeli Elbit firm, provides more powerful engines, night vision capability, a head-up display and other major cockpit enhancements, laser target designation equipment and an increased range of weaponry amongst other improvements. No orders have been received to date.

TECHNICAL DATA

IAR IAR-330L Puma

Powerplants: Two Turbomécanica (Romania) Turmo IVC turboshafts
Developing: 1,175kW (1,575eshp)
Main rotor diameter: 15.00m (49ft 2.5in)
Fuselage length: 14.06m (46ft 1.5in)
Height: 5.14m (16ft 10.5in)
All-up weight: 7,500kg (16,534lb)
Maximum speed: 204km/h (182mph)
Cruise speed: 171km/h (168mph)
Operational ceiling: 19,685ft
Maximum range: 572km (354 miles)
Accommodation: Two crew and 15 fully-equipped troops or 2 tonnes of cargo
Warload: This normally comprises either eight 120mm or sixteen 57mm rockets, four AT-3 'Sagger' anti-armour missiles, four 7.62mm machine guns or four 100kg bombs carried on tube mountings just behind the cabin entry doors on each side, along with a machine gun inside the doors themselves. Two 20mm cannon are fitted in cheek pods on either side of the front fuselage.
First flown: 1977
Entered service: 1978

IAR-330L Puma Romanian Air Force

IAR IAR-823

IAR-823 Romanian Air Force

DEVELOPMENT

When Romania was a member of the Warsaw Pact, with its Air Force commmitted to the 15th Army, it retained an important indigenous aircraft industry. In 1968, this was reorganised within the Ministry of Building Machine Industry. This resulted in some of the Air Force's equipment differing from that which was otherwise standardised throughout the Warsaw Pact countries. The first entirely indigenous primary training aircraft to be produced in Romania, the IAR-823 proved popular as both an *ab initio* trainer

for the Romanian Air Force, with retractable tricycle undercarriage, and as a civil touring aircraft. Design work commenced in the late 1960s and around 100 were produced for the Romanian Air Force in total.

CURRENT SERVICE

The IAR-823's sole military operator is the Romanian Air Force, which today has around 40 (out of the original 100 or so examples delivered) in service as primary trainers with the Boboc-based Institute for Aviation 'Aurel Vilacu'.

SPECIAL FEATURES

One unusual feature of the IAR-823 is its ability to act both as a two-seat trainer, with the instructor and student sitting side-by-side, or as a five-seat tourer. The three additional passengers can sit on a bench-

seat behind the two places up front. It is a low-wing monoplane of conventional design, with an unswept wing and a sizeable canopy glass area with upward opening windows/doors. Practice weapons or small drop tanks may be carried under two wing hardpoints. The two-seater is fully aerobatic.

VARIANTS

Apart from the basic IAR-823, the manufacturer proposed two other improved derivatives, neither of which entered production. The first was the **IAR-825TP Triumf**, with a new, strengthened wing for weapons training, and a Pratt & Whitney Canada PT6A-15AG turboprop engine. This machine appeared in 1982, followed a year later by the **IAR-831 Pelican**, which was identical to the IAR-825TP except for its retention of the original Lycoming piston powerplant of the IAR-823.

TECHNICAL DATA

IAR IAR-823

Powerplant: One Textron Lycoming IO-540-G1D5 flat-six piston engine
Developing: 216kW (290hp)
Driving: two-blade propeller
Span: 10.00m (32ft 9.75in)
Length: 8.24m (27ft 0.25in)
Height: 2.52m (8ft 3.25in)
All-up weight: 1,380kg (3,042lb)
Maximum speed: 310km/h (192.5mph)
Cruise speed: 300km/h (186mph)
Operational ceiling: 18,375ft
Mission range: 1,600km (994 miles)
Endurance: 3-6 hours
Accommodation: Two side-by-side, or pilot and four passengers
Warload: Two underwing pylons for carriage of practice weapons
First flown: July 1973
Entered service: 1974

IAR-823 Romanian Air Force

Ilyushin IL-14

TWIN PISTON-ENGINED UTILITY TRANSPORT

Ilyushin IL-14M Chinese Air Force

DEVELOPMENT

The venerable IL-14 'Crate' was itself developed from an earlier Ilyushin transport design, the IL-12 'Coach', but used a stretched fuselage. Around 3,500 examples of the IL-14 were produced in the USSR, quite apart from sizeable licence production in Czechoslovakia as the Avia 14, and in East Germany where it was named the VEB-14. Many versions were produced, including derivatives used for electronic countermeasures duties and survey work; the Czech Air Force only retired its examples of the latter, the Avia 14FG, in 1993, and the Polish Air Force's similarly-configured IL-14s were finally taken out of service even later. The type has been referred to as something of a (later) Russian DC-3 equivalent, and its longevity and usefulness certainly bears this out.

CURRENT SERVICE

After many years of faithful service with the Warsaw Pact air arms and those of several other Communist nations, only two countries are believed to still operate IL-14s. These are Albania, with Nos 1 and 2 Squadrons at Rinas-Tirana, and the People's Republic of China, whose Air Force of the People's Liberation Army apparently flies 30 'Crates' on transport duties with just one regiment.

SPECIAL FEATURES

The IL-14's two cowled ASh-82 radial piston engines are set forward of the tapering wing, close to the wing root. Its nose is rounded in shape, while the tail fin and rudder are broad and of squared appearance with a dorsal 'fillet' extension. The type, like its IL-12

predecessor, was given a tricycle undercarriage, and the mainwheels retract into the lower part of each engine cowling at a point just forward of the wing. Most IL-14s have seven square cabin windows.

DEVELOPMENT

It is not known exactly which IL-14 variants are still in service with the People's Republic of China – three main transport derivatives were produced. The **IL-14P** strengthened the original aircraft's floor and provided two freight doors, being followed by the lengthened **IL-14M** and finally by the **IL-14T** version, which was a dedicated freighter.

TECHNICAL DATA

Ilyushin IL-14M

Powerplants: Two Shvetsov ASh-82T radial piston engines
Developing: 1,417kW (1,900hp) each
Driving: Four-blade propellers
Span: 31.70m (104ft 0in)
Length: 22.31m (73ft 2.25in)
Height: 7.90m (25ft 11in)
All-up weight: 18,500kg (40,785lb)
Maximum speed: 430km/h (267mph)
Cruise speed: 350km/h (217mph)
Operational ceiling: 24,280ft
Maximum range: 1,500km (809nm)
Mission range: 400km (216nm)
Accommodation: Two crew, up to 28 passengers
First flown: 1952
Entered service: 1954

Ilyushin IL-14M

Ilyushin IL-18, IL-20 & IL-22

FOUR-TURBOPROP PASSENGER/FREIGHT TRANSPORT, ELECTRONIC RECCE AND AIRBORNE COMMAND POST   **USSR**

Ilyushin IL-18 Chinese Air Force

DEVELOPMENT

An Aeroflot requirement for a modern turboprop airliner for services within the USSR and on short-haul international flights led to the IL-18 'Coot', initially a 75-seater aircraft also powered by either Kuznetsov NK-4 or Ivchenko AI-20K turboprops before the latter powerplant was adopted as standard for all aircraft after the first batch of 20 had been produced. Various fuselage stretches were then undertaken, and the 'Coot' was purchased by airlines in many Warsaw Pact and other Communist states, as well as by some of their military air arms. The type was to form the basis of both the IL-20 electronic intelligence-gathering and IL-22 command post/recce military versions, as well as providing the starting-point for the IL-38 'May' maritime reconnaissance platform (described separately).

CURRENT SERVICE

The Russian Air Forces today are believed to operate around 20 IL-18s for communications work, as well as some 25 IL-20s and 20 IL-22s on ELINT and other electronic recce duties; the Russian Naval Aviation arm flies three IL-20s. Unknown numbers of all three types, especially IL-18s, are used in various guises as research aircraft on avionics and other trials duties by

establishments in Russia, such as those at Zhukovsky. A single IL-22 is used by the Belarus Air Force as a command post, and is said to retain Aeroflot colours. Other operators of the IL-18, all for communications or transport work, are the Afghan Army Air Force, the Air Force of the People's Liberation Army in the People's Republic of China, the Kazakhstan Air Force, and the (North) Korean People's Army Air Force.

SPECIAL FEATURES

The basic IL-18 is a low-wing design, with the four turboprops mounted above the unswept wings, driving four-blade propellers. All variants up to the IL-18D had a standard cargo hold in the aft fuselage section, but this was deleted on later production models. The main distinguishing features of the ELINT-gathering IL-20 are its longer nose, numerous large blade antennae above the forward fuselage, and on the underside a long, cylindrical pod probably containing side-looking infra-red (SLAR) equipment, coupled with other blister and antenna fairings behind it. The IL-22 command post and electronic recce platform has a cylindrical fairing atop the tailplane and various antennae positioned above and below the fuselage, but the nose is not extended. Both of

these military variants retain the IL-18's cabin windows.

VARIANTS

After 20 aircraft had been produced, the basic **IL-18** airliner was developed into the 84-seat **IL-18B** with standard AI-20K engines, followed by the **IL-18V** which added an extra five seats, and then the **IL-18D** (formerly the **IL-18I**) which seated 110-122 and used uprated AI-20M powerplants. Standard 'Coots' have been converted into various different trials aircraft for the Soviet and Russian military, many having been on the strength of the LII Gromov Flight Research Institute at Zhukovsky, while a weather-reconnaissance derivative has now been retired. The **IL-20 'Coot-A'** is the ELINT/radar recce aircraft, while the **IL-22** is primarily a command post but also has an ELINT-gathering role. Later, the **IL-38 'May'** was derived from the 'Coot' series but was an entirely new type.

SEE ALSO: ILYUSHIN IL-38

TECHNICAL DATA

Ilyushin IL-18D

Powerplants: Four ZMDB Progress (Ivchenko) AI-20M turboprops
Developing: 3,169kW (4,250eshp)
Driving: Four-blade propellers
Span: 37.42m (122ft 9.25in)
Length: 35.90m (117ft 9in)
Height: 10.17m (33ft 4in)
All-up weight: 64,000kg (141,093lb)
Maximum speed: 675km/h (419mph)
Cruise speed: 625km/h (388mph)
Operational ceiling: 32,810ft
Maximum range: 6,500km (3,508nm)
Mission range: 3,700km (1,997nm)
Accommodation: 75/100 passengers
First flown: 4 July 1957
Entered service: April 1959

Ilyushin IL-18

Ilyushin IL-28 & Harbin H-5

TWIN-TURBOJET MEDIUM TACTICAL BOMBER AND MULTI-MISSION AIRCRAFT

Harbin H-5R Romanian Air Force

DEVELOPMENT

The IL-28 'Beagle' was the first medium jet bomber to see service with the Soviet air forces, and was built in very large numbers for service both in the USSR and with other Warsaw Pact air arms including East Germany, Hungary and Poland. It was developed for other roles as well, and it was for such taskings as target-towing and ECM duties that the last examples in Russian service were largely employed. The Chinese-built Harbin H-5s were produced without a licence under a programme which commenced in 1963 and continued into the 1980s, following the delivery of IL-28s from Ilyushin itself. These 'Beagles' were then overhauled by Harbin, who 'reverse-engineered' the type to produce its successful H-5 copy, which is the

variant that today sees most military service, in spite of now being outmoded. Small numbers were built in Czechoslovakia as the B-228.

CURRENT SERVICE

The People's Republic of China is by far the largest user of the type, some 150 H-5s, HJ-5s and HZ-5s being in service with the Air Force of the People's Liberation Army as the backbone of its bomber force. Another 150 H-5s are used by the Aviation of the People's Navy in the same role. Five IL-28s are operated by the Egyptian Air Force with the ECM Brigade/Tactical Fighter Command at Kom Awshim. The Romanian Air Force retains a mixed fleet of 15, made up of H-5Rs, HJ-5s, IL-28s and IL-28MAs for recce duties with 3/86 Squadron, 86 Regiment de Vinatoare at Borcea-Fetesti, and the Korean People's Army Air Force flies 40 H-5s in the tactical strike role. Albania is also an operator.

SPECIAL FEATURES

The IL-28 and H-5 are of the same appearance, with

the only external differences being between sub-types for different roles. The aircraft has a slightly-swept wing, and the two VK-1A turbojets are mounted in large underwing pods tapering towards the jet pipe at the rear. Its mainwheel units are also located in the lower part of the engine nacelles. All IL-28s and H-5s have a glazed bombardier's nose, and a bubble canopy, with the small rear gun turret being found at the base of the back-swept tail fin with the gun itself at the rear extremity of the fuselage in a rounded fairing.

VARIANTS

IL-28s have been converted as target tugs and ECM aircraft, while several different versions of the H-5 have been produced or converted by Harbin alongside the standard bomber. These include the **HJ-5** operational trainer, and the **H-5R** tactical recce derivative. Some of the Chinese naval examples are also used as either torpedo bombers or target tugs, the latter using a Rushton towed target which simulates anti-shipping missiles.

TECHNICAL DATA

Ilyushin IL-28

Powerplants: Two Klimov VK-1A turbojets
Developing: 26.48kN (5,952lb st)
Span: 21.45m (70ft 4.5in)
Length: 17.65m (57ft 11in)
Height: 6.70m (21ft 11.75in)
All-up weight: 21,200kg (46,738lb)
Maximum speed: 902km/h (560mph)
Cruise speed: 876km/h (544mph)
Operational ceiling: 40,350ft
Maximum range: 2,400km (1,489miles)
Mission range: 1,135km (704miles)
Accommodation: Crew of three
Warload: Two NR-23 23mm cannon in lower forward fuselage, two NR-23 in rear turret. Up to 3,000kg (6,615lb) of bombs or two torpedoes in internal weapons bay.
First flown: 8 July 1948 (Il-28);
25 September 1966 (H-5)
Entered service: 1950 (IL-28); 1967 (H-5)

Harbin H-5R Romanian Air Force

Ilyushin IL-38

FOUR-TURBOPROP MARITIME RECONNAISSANCE AND ANTI-SUBMARINE WARFARE AIRCRAFT

IL-38 'May' Russian Naval Aviation

DEVELOPMENT

The progenitor of the Ilyushin IL-38 'May' is clear from its appearance, being outwardly a maritime reconnaissance and ASW development of the IL-18 airliner. However, there the similarity virtually ends, as the 'May' is a new-build aircraft with only very few directly common components shared between the two types, the main are the AI-20M turboprops. However, the IL-38 is 4 metres (13ft 1.5in) longer than its civil forebear, amongst other changes.

CURRENT SERVICE

Some 36 IL-38s are in service with Russian Naval Aviation. These serve with ASW regiments, based with SF (Northern Fleet) u/i OPAP at Severomorsk and TOF (Pacific Fleet) Vladivostock u/i OLAP DD at Alekseyevka. Three serve with GK AVMF, Moscow at Ostrov. The only export customer for the 'May' has

been Indian Naval Aviation, which has five examples, operated by INAS 315 for long-range maritime reconnaissance/ASW duties based at Goa-Dablomin, but these are now in urgent need of replacement.

SPECIAL FEATURES

Aside from the aforementioned fuselage stretch, the 'May' incorporates other major external changes over the civil IL-18. Most significantly, the wings were moved forward to compensate for the weight of the mission equipment, and the consequent change in the IL-38's centre of gravity. Only a few cabin windows remain (unlike on the military IL-20 and IL-22 'Coots'), and likewise there is only one cabin entry door, on the starboard side. The magnetic anomaly detector (MAD) boom is prominent at the aircraft's tail, while a large underfuselage radome situated just forward of the wing houses the 'Wet Eye' search

radar, and the weather radar can be found in the re-shaped nose. Two large internal weapons bays are sited in front of and behind the wing.

VARIANTS

Only one basic version of the IL-38 'May' has been produced. It is not known if any significant systems upgrades have yet been undertaken, on either the Russian or Indian aircraft.

SEE ALSO: ILYUSHIN IL-20 & !L-22

TECHNICAL DATA

Ilyushin IL-38 'May'

Powerplant: Four ZMDB Progress (Ivchenko) AI-20M turboprops
Developing: 3,169kW (4,250eshp)
Driving: four-blade propellers
Span: 37.42m (122ft 9.25in)
Length: 39.60m (129ft 10in)
Height: 10.16m (33ft 4in)
All-up weight: 63,500kg (139,991lb)
Maximum speed: 722km/h (448mph)
Cruise speed: 611km/h (380mph)
Operational ceiling: 32,800ft
Maximum range: 7,200km (4,468nm)
Endurance: 12hr
Accommodation: operational crew of nine
Warload: Forward and aft internal weapons bays can carry homing torpedoes, sonobuoys and nuclear and conventional depth charges
First flown: 4 June 1957 (IL-18); 1967 (IL-38)
Entered service: 1968

IL-38 'May' Russian Naval Aviation

Ilyushin IL-62

FOUR-TURBOFAN LONG-RANGE TRANSPORT AIRCRAFT

Ilyushin IL-62M Russian Government

DEVELOPMENT

When the IL-62 entered Aeroflot service in the mid-1960s it represented the Soviet Union's first long-range four-engine inter-continental jet transport. It was used on the Soviet national carrier's most important international routes, replacing the turboprop Tu-114. Initial IL-62s were powered by the Kuznetsov NK8-4 powerplant, this being changed to Soloviev D-30KUs when production switched to the longer-range IL-62M. Another change was the provision of additional fuel tankage in the tail fin. It was designed to have the range to fly distances equivalent to Moscow-New York (7,700km/h/4,800miles). Some 245 examples were built.

CURRENT SERVICE

The Kazakhstan Air Force flies an unspecified number of IL-62s on communications duties, while a single IL-62M is on the strength of the (North) Korean People's Army Air Force. The type is also used by the Russian Air Force for communications and VIP/staff transport, ten being on strength for this purpose, and the Russian Government has thirteen IL-62Ms. One example was completed in 1993 as a VIP aircraft for the Russian President.

SPECIAL FEATURES

The IL-62 has a swept wing and a T-tail, with the four engines being pod-mounted (two on each side) forward of the tail assembly. All flying controls are operated manually. Extended-chord 'dog tooth' leading-edge on outer two thirds of each wing and fixed droop on extended-chord outer wings. All tail surfaces are swept back.

VARIANTS

Only two major production versions were produced, namely the standard **IL-62** and extended-range **IL-62M**. However, the Russian Government's aircraft have been modified with the addition of a dorsal fairing containing avionics and satellite communications equipment. The IL-62 was the initial production version with Kuznetsov NK-8 turbofans. The IL-62M is the more powerful version with Solviev engines, increased fuel capacity, and a containerised baggage and freight system. The **IL-62MK** version had strenghthened wings and landing gear for operation at higher gross weights and with seating up to 195 passengers, six-abreast.

TECHNICAL DATA

Ilyushin IL-62M

Powerplants: Four PNPP Aviadvigatel (Soloviev) D-30KU turbofans
Developing: 107.87kN (24,250lb st)
Span: 43.20m (141ft 9in)
Length: 53.12m (174ft 3.5in)
Height: 12.35m (40ft 6.25in)
All-up weight: 165,000kg (363,757lb)
Maximum speed: 900km/h (560mph)
Cruise speed: 850km/h (528mph)
Operational ceiling: 39,000ft
Maximum range: 7,800km (4,841 miles)
Accommodation: Crew of 5 and up to 186 passengers (usually 163)
First flown: 3 January 1963 (IL-62); 1970 (IL-62M)
Entered service: 10 March 1967 (IL-62); Early 1963 (IL-62M)

Ilyushin IL-62M

Ilyushin IL-76

FOUR-TURBOFAN HEAVY TRANSPORT AND MULTI-MISSION AIRCRAFT

Ilyushin IL-76MD Russian Air Force

TECHNICAL DATA

Ilyushin IL-76M

Powerplants: Four PNPP Aviadvigatel (Soloviev) D-30KP turbofans
Developing: 117.68kN (26,455lb st)
Span: 50.50m (165ft 8in)
Length: 46.59m (152ft 10.25in)
Height: 14.76m (48ft 5in)
All-up weight: 170,000kg (374,780lb)
Maximum speed: 850km/h (528mph)
Cruise speed: 750km/h (466mph)
Operational ceiling: 50,850ft
Maximum range: 6,700km (4,160miles)
Mission range: 5,000km (3,103miles)
Accommodation: Crew of seven, plus two freight handlers. Able to carry up to 140 troops or 120 paratroops.
Warload: IL-76 has provision for two 23mm twin-barrel GSh-23L guns in the tail.
First flown: 25 March 1971
Entered service: 1974

DEVELOPMENT

The IL-76 'Candid' has been one of the most successful products of the Soviet and Russian aerospace industry in recent years. Intended as a replacement for the veteran turboprop Antonov An-12 in both Soviet military and Aeroflot service, the 'Candid' has never fully superseded the older type, but has nonetheless seen extremely widespread service in the USSR/Russia, former Soviet republics and many other customers. Ilyushin incorporated many high-lift devices into their sturdy design for ease of operation from short or unprepared runways, and these features have been well-employed. The civilian and dedicated military IL-76s were developed in tandem, though there has been some interchange among different operators, while a number of special missions derivatives have been developed, among them the IL-78 'Midas' air-to-air refuelling tanker (see separate entry). Over 800 of all versions have been built in total, series production having begun at Tashkent in 1975 after an initial pre-production batch had entered service for proving duties a year earlier.

CURRENT SERVICE

The Russian Air Forces are by far the largest single operator of the type, with around 290 IL-76s in current service, augmented by an unspecified number of 'Candids' on the strength of the country's quasi-military Federal Border Guards Service. 170 IL-76s

were inherited by the Ukrainian Air Force, mainly based at Uzin. Other operators are the Algerian Air Force (three IL-76TDs), Belarus Air Force (32 IL-76MDs), Indian Air Force (24 IL-76MDs), the Islamic Republic of Iran Air Force (12 IL-76MDs inherited from Iraq), the Kazakhstan Air Force (IL-76s), Korean People's Army Air Force (two IL-76Ts), the Libyan Arab Republic Air Force (22 civil-registered IL-76Ms, Ts and TDs) and the Syrian Arab Air Force (four IL-76Ms operated by Syrian Air with civil registrations).

SPECIAL FEATURES

The IL-76 has a T-tailed configuration, and the four D-30KP turbofans are pod-mounted under the swept wings. Military IL-76Ms/MDs have a tail gun turret containing two 23mm cannon, while all transport derivatives have a glazed lower nose position for a parachute drop master or navigator, as well as the large clamshell rear doors and a loading ramp able to take up to 30,000kg (66,150lb) of cargo.

VARIANTS

Production began with the standard civil **IL-76**, soon followed by the **IL-76T** with extra fuel capacity, and then the **IL-76TD** which was given uprated D-30KP-1 turbofans. An example of the latter has been converted to support Russian Antarctic operations with the requisite special equipment. All three of these civil variants (also used by military operators) are known

as the '**Candid-A**', as is the **IL-76DMP** fire-bomber, one of which has been converted as a demonstrator. The first specifically military derivative was the **IL-76M**, then replaced on the production line by the **IL-76MD**; these aircraft are equivalent to the IL-76T and TD respectively, and are fitted with the tail turret. Two IL-76MDs have been seen at the Zhukovsky test centre converted to some form of airborne command post, with large dorsal 'canoe' fairings above the forward fuselage as well as numerous blade antennae, and trailing aerials around the rear ramp. The fate of the two surviving Iraqi '**Adnan**' AEW conversions of IL-76s, with a rotodome atop the fuselage, is unknown: one was believed to have remained in Iraq after the 1991 Gulf conflict, with the other having fled to Iran along with several IL-76MDs.

SEE ALSO: ILYUSHIN IL-976/BERIEV A-50

Ilyushin IL-76MD Russian Air Force

Ilyushin IL-78

FOUR-TURBOFAN AIR-TO-AIR REFUELLING AIRCRAFT

IL-78 'Midas' Russian Air Force

DEVELOPMENT

The IL-78 'Midas' is a probe-and-drogue air-to-air refuelling development, which was refined over a ten-year period, of the IL-76 'Candid' transport and was built to replace the Myasischev 3MS2 and SMN2 'Bison' tankers. It is similar to the IL-76 when the additional fuel tanks are removed. A central fuel pod is fitted for the refuelling of large aircraft and the underwing pods are used to refuel smaller types. Refuelling is permitted only in direct visibility.

CURRENT SERVICE

Some 40 are in service – divided between Russia (Long Range Aviation (DA) 22 GvTBAD at Engels) and Ukraine

(7 VTAD 409th Air Tanker Regiment[APSZ] at Uzyn). Some early Ukrainian versions have been converted back to transports and the refuelling equipment removed. Approximately four (possibly six) IL-78MKs are in the process of delivery to the Indian Air Force.

SPECIAL FEATURES

Has a 'T-tailed' configuration and the turbofans are pod-mounted under the swept wings. It is based on the IL-76MD and features two cylindrical internal fuel tanks, which can be removed to allow the aircraft to operate as a freighter. The more developed IL-78M version, has three permanent tanks capable of holding 64,000 litres (14,080 galloms) of fuel – which can be transferred via three Severin/UPAZ-1A PAE refuelling units, one under each wing and one mounted externally on the port side of the fuselage. Fuel can also be transferred from standard tanks in the wing torsion box. The refuelling operator is housed in the

place normally occupied by the tail gunner. It can also be used as a ground refuelling station for four aircraft, if required, on a front line airfield. Lights and ranging radar in the underside rear door, built into the bottom of the upswept rear fuselage, are fitted for night refuelling. A Kupol navigation system and RSBN short-range navigation system is fitted to permit all-weather day/night mutual detection and approach by receiver aircraft from distances of up to 300km (185 miles).

VARIANTS

The IL-78 'Midas' was the initial version, convertible between transport and tanker. The IL-78M is the standard version produced and is non-convertible, having no ramp or cabin doors. The export version is the IL-78MK (Kommerchesky) and the IL-78V has Mk-32B type refuelling pods.

SEE ALSO: ILYUSHIN IL-76 & ILYUSHIN IL-976/BERIEV A-50

TECHNICAL DATA

Ilyushin IL-78 'Midas'

Powerplants: Four PNPP Aviadvigatel (Soloviev) D-30KP turbofans
Developing: 117.68kN (26,455lb st)
Span: 50.50m (165ft 8in)
Length: 46.59m (152ft 10.25in)
Height: 14.76m (48ft 5in)
All-up weight: 210,000kg (462,970lb)
Maximum speed: 850km/h (528mph)
Cruise speed: 750km/h (466mph)
Refuelling speed: 430-590km/h (267-366mph)
Operational ceiling: 29,525ft
Maximum range: 7,300km (4,536 miles)
Refuelling radius: 1,000km (620 miles)
Accommodation: Crew of seven
First flown: June 1983 (IL-78);
7 March 1987 (IL-78M)
Entered service: 1987

IL-78 'Midas' Russian Air Force

Ilyushin IL-976 & Beriev A-50

FOUR-TURBOFAN AIRBORNE EARLY WARNING AND RANGE CONTROL AIRCRAFT

Ilyushin IL-976 Russian Air Force

DEVELOPMENT

The Soviet Union's first operational airborne early warning (AEW) aircraft was the Tupolev Tu-126 'Moss', based on the Tu-114 turboprop airliner, but plans for a replacement (which began in the mid-1960s) were terminated on cost grounds. This programme was later restarted however, and the resulting A-50 'Mainstay' was developed as a variant of the Ilyushin IL-76. It entered service in 1984, and teething troubles were gradually overcome to produce a successful AEW and AWACS platform, albeit one whose interior conditions were inferior to those of the Tu-126: the A-50 is noisier and more spartan inside than the aircraft it replaced. Problems were also encountered during refuelling, as the airflow disturbance caused by the rotodome made the procedure hazardous. However, these had been overcome by the time a pair of 'Mainstays' undertook 24-hour AEW patrols, operating from a Black Sea airfield and supported by Myasishchev 3MS-2 tankers,

during the 1991 Gulf War. When compared with the Boeing E-3 Sentry, the A-50's radar system's range and multiple target tracking capabilities are seen as inferior, but its ability to distinguish between ground targets or low-flying aircraft and general ground features is allegedly better, according to its designers. Beriev undertakes the fitment of the AEW system, either to converted or new-build aircraft, the system's designation being unknown. The IL-976 is a separate rotodome-equipped conversion of the basic 'Candid', used for range control and missile tracking.

CURRENT SERVICE

Fifteen A-50 'Mainstays' are currently in Russian Air Force service, based at Pechora in the polar region. A single example is operated by the People's Republic of China Air Force of the People's Liberation Army, while two more A-50s are on order for the Islamic Republic of Iran Air Force. At least five IL-976s have

been converted, having been seen at Zhukovsky, though their exact Russian military operator or base is not known. They all carry Aeroflot colour schemes, while the 'Mainstays' are in military livery.

SPECIAL FEATURES

Both aircraft share the same basic airframe as the previously described IL-76, the main differences being the rotodomes mounted atop the fuselages of both types. The rotodome fitments of the A-50 and IL-976 appear outwardly similar, but the equipment within is different. On the A-50, the glazed nose of the IL-76 and its derivatives has been covered over, the tail turret is deleted, and a blade antenna-cum-horizontal winglet is fitted on the rear of both mainwheel fairings; the IL-976 retains the nose glazing, and the turret fitment remains, albeit with a bulbous radome covering the guns. The IL-976 also has cylindrical pods on each wingtip, their precise purpose unknown. An air-to-air refuelling probe is standard on the A-50 'Mainstay', the interior of which houses a large display screen for controlling fighters, along with numerous smaller displays covering ground targets and the wider strategic position. It is capable of detecting low-flying cruise missiles, and can control fighters as well as download tactical information to ground stations and fighters automatically.

VARIANTS

Only the basic production versions of both the A-50 'Mainstay' and IL-976 have so far been identified, apart from the improved A-50U, which first appeared in 1995, and features VEGA SHMEL-M radar – with no details forthcoming on any systems upgrade programmes which may have been undertaken or are in the pipeline.

Beriev A-50 Russian Air Force

TECHNICAL DATA

Beriev A-50

Powerplants: Four PNPP Aviadvigatel (Soloviev) D-30KP turbofans
Developing: 117.68kN (26,455lb st)
Span: 50.50m (165ft 8in)
Length: 46.59m (152ft 10.25in)
Height: 14.76m (48ft 5in)
All-up weight: 170,000kg (374,780lb)
Maximum speed: 850km/h (528mph)
Cruise speed: 750km/h (466mph)
Operational ceiling: 50,850ft
Maximum range: 6,700km (4,160miles)
Mission range: 5,000km (3,103miles)
Accommodation: Crew of 15
First flown: 1977
Entered service: 1984

Jodel (SAN) D.140 Mousquetaire/Abeille

SINGLE-ENGINED FOUR/FIVE SEAT CABIN LIGHT AIRCRAFT

D.140E Mousquetaire IV French Air Force

DEVELOPMENT

Like Robin, the Société Aéronautique Normande (SAN), formed in May 1948), was another manufacturer of French light aircraft designed by Jodel. SAN began with the D.117 Grand Tourisme, a two-seat cabin monoplane powered by a 71kW (95hp) Continental C90 horizontally opposed four cylinder engine, of which 259 examples were built. This led to the four/five seat version, the D.140 Mousquetaire. The D.140 had revised tail surfaces and other improvements. Production of the D.140E Mousquetaire IV, with an all-flying tail and modified ailerons, included 18 for the French Air Force. Later the Air Force acquired 14 D.140R Abeilles, which had a cut-down rear fuselage with an improved rearward view canopy together with a glider towing hook. It was also used for banner towing. SAN went into liquidation in 1969.

CURRENT SERVICE

Both the D.140E and R remain in use with the Armée de l'Air for recreation flying and the Abeille for glider towing. They are most numerous with Groupment d'Instruction 00.312 at Salon de Provence.

SPECIAL FEATURES

The D.140 incorporates the typical Jodel cranked wing and has a swept fin, tailwheel configuration and large spats to the main wheels. It can also be used as an ambulance for one stretcher person. There is a large baggage door in the rear fuselage. It can be fitted with UHF radio, VOR, radio-compass and full blind-flying instrumentation.

VARIANTS

The **DR.1050 Ambassadeur** and the **D.150 Grand** Tourisme/Mascaret were produced in the early 1960s. An improved version was produced in the mid-1960s as the **DR.1052 Excellence**, which could have either a Potez or Rolls-Royce Continental engine. The **D.140A Mousquetaire** was the original production version and 45 were produced; the **D.140B Mousquetaire II** had improved brakes and a different engine cowling; the **D.140C Mousquetaire III** had the enlarged swept fin. The **D.140E Mousquetaire IV** had a further enlarged tail, modified ailerons and all-flying tailplane. The **D.140R** was basically a D.140E with cut down rear fuselage which gave improved all-round vision.

D.140R Mousquetaire French Air Force

TECHNICAL DATA

Jodel (SAN) D.140E Mousquetaire IV

Powerplant: One Avco Lycoming 0-360-A2A flat-four piston engine
Developing: 134kW (180hp)
Driving: Two-blade propeller
Span: 10.27m (33ft 8.25in)
Length: 7.82m (25ft 8in)
Height: 2.05m (6ft 8.75in)
All-up weight: 1,200kg (2,646lb)
Maximum speed: 255km/h (158mph)
Operational ceiling: 16,405ft
Maximum range: 1,400km (870 miles)
Accommodation: Pilot plus three or four passengers
Warload: Nil
First Flown: 4 July 1958 (Mousquetaire); mid-1965 (Abeille)
Entered service: Early 1960s (Mousquetaire); late 1960s (Abeille)

Kaman SH-2 Seasprite

TWIN-TURBOSHAFT ANTI-SUBMARINE WARFARE HELICOPTER

SH-2F Seasprite Royal New Zealand Navy

TECHNICAL DATA

Kaman SH-2G Seasprite
Powerplants: Two General Electric T700-GE-401/401C turboshafts
Developing: 1,072kW (1,437shp)
Driving: Four-bladed main and tail rotors
Main rotor diameter: 13.41m (44ft 0in)
Fuselage length: 12.24m (40ft 2in)
Height: 4.58m (15ft 0.5in)
All-up weight: 6,123kg (13,500lb)
Maximum speed: 261km/h (162mph)
Cruise speed: 222km/h (138mph)
Operational ceiling: 20,400ft
Maximum range: 804km (500 miles)
Endurance: 5.3hr
Accommodation: Three crew (two pilots and one sensor operator in cabin). Removal of sonobuoy launcher allows for four passengers
Warload: Up to two Mk50 or Mk46 torpedoes, two Maverick or Sea Skua missiles, eight marine markers/sonobuoys. Small arms mounting for M-60, 0.50in machine guns or 2.75in rockets.
Maximum payload: 2,300kg (5,070lb)
First flown: 2 July 1959 (HU2K-1/UH-2A); 28 December 1989 (SH-2G)
Entered service: 18 December 1962 (UH-2A); 21 March 1990 (SH-2G)

DEVELOPMENT

Conceived to satisfy a 1956 US Navy requirement for a light utility helicopter able to perform SAR and liaison tasks, the Kaman Seasprite has proved a most versatile machine and is still subject to development today, more than 40 years after its first flight. It began life as a single-engined machine powered by the General Electric T58 turboshaft, and a total of 190 examples of the original utility versions (4 YHU2K-1/YUH-2As, 84 HU2K-1/UH-2As and 102 HU2K-1U/UH-2Bs) were built before manufacture ended. Successful adaptation of the Seasprite for the LAMPS Mk1 (Light Airborne Multi-Purpose System) requirement in the early 1970s led to extensive modifications, including the addition of Litton LN 66 search radar, an AN/ASQ-81 magnetic anomaly detector, and the ability to employ active and passive sonobuoys. In this guise, as the SH-2, it gained responsibility for the anti-submarine warfare/anti-ship missile defence (ASW/ASMD) role and was deployed aboard surface combatant vessels.

CURRENT SERVICE

Following replacement by the SH-60B, the Seasprite now equips just two squadrons of the US Naval Air Reserve Force (HSL-84 at NAS North Island and HSL-94 at NAS Willow Grove), each of which has six SH-2Gs on strength. However, it has found favour with several overseas air arms and modest numbers have been purchased by Australia (11 SH-2Gs), Egypt (10 SH-2G/2G(E)s with ASW Brigade at Borg El-Arab) and New Zealand (SH-2F/Gs with Naval Support Flight of No 3 Squadron, RNZAF at Whenupai).

SPECIAL FEATURES

A compact helicopter, noteworthy features of the Seasprite are the externally mounted engine nacelles; retractable twin-wheel main undercarriage units and fixed tailwheel; the towed MAD fitted to the starboard sponson, and the radome located beneath the cockpit.

VARIANTS

With the end of production of the utility versions, further development led to the twin-engined **UH-2C**, and about 40 of the earlier versions were converted to this standard, the first of many modification projects that spawned different versions. These included two specialist rescue derivatives in the form of the armed and armoured **HH-2C** for combat SAR during the Vietnam War and the unarmed **HH-2D**. Thereafter, the Seasprite was adapted for shipborne ASW, initially as the **SH-2D** (20 conversions), but the definitive model was the **SH-2F LAMPS Mk1**. Approximately 100 Seasprites were updated to this standard and the type was also reinstated in production in 1981, with 54 new-build **SH-2Fs** purchased by the US Navy. Following evaluation of the re-engined **YSH-2G** in the mid-1980s, the final version was the **SH-2G** which featured further improvements to the avionics suite; six were built as new, with others being acquired as a result of SH-2F modification.

SH-2G Seasprite Egyptian Navy

Kamov Ka-25

TWIN-TURBOSHAFT SHIPBORNE ASW/UTILITY HELICOPTER

Kamov Ka-25BSh Vietnamese People's Air Force

TECHNICAL DATA

Kamov Ka-25 'Hormone-B'
Powerplants: Two OMKB 'Mars' (Glushenkov) GTD-3BM turboshafts
Developing: 738kW (900shp)
Driving: Two three-bladed coaxial contra-rotating main rotors
Main rotor diameter: 15.74m (52ft 7.75in)
Fuselage length: 9.75m (32ft 0in)
Height: 5.37m (17ft 7.75in)
All-up weight: 7,500kg (16,534lb)
Maximum speed: 220km/h (137mph)
Cruise speed: 193km/h (120mph)
Operational Ceiling: 11,500ft
Ferry range: 650km (404 miles)
Accommodation: Two pilots and up to 12 passengers in utility configuration
Payload: 1,300kg (2,866lb)
First Flown: 26 April 1961

DEVELOPMENT

Arising out of a Russian Navy requirement of the late 1950s for a shipborne anti-submarine warfare helicopter, the Ka-25 was in fact preceded by the Ka-20. Given the code name 'Harp', the Ka-20 flew for the first time in 1961 and was fundamentally a test-bed for the turboshaft engines, gearbox and rotor installation that would ultimately be employed by the definitive 'Hormone' helicopter. Trials of the Ka-25 began in 1963 and lasted for several years, with series production eventually being launched in 1966. Operational deployment of the initial Ka-25BSh 'Hormone-A' ASW version took place in 1967, and manufacture continued until 1975. Approximately 460 examples of three basic models were eventually built.

CURRENT SERVICE

Largely supplanted in Russian service by derivatives of the 'Helix' family, a limited number of Ka-25s are still operational with the Russian Navy in the SAR/Utility role with the Northern, Baltic and Black Sea Fleets. Overseas operators are India, Syria, Ukraine and Vietnam, but the numbers involved are modest.

SPECIAL FEATURES

The most distinctive characteristic of the Ka-25 is the co-axial contra-rotating main rotor assembly, which eliminates the need for an anti-torque tail rotor. Of note are the triple fin arrangement, a radome of varying size according to version under the nose section and the twin-nose/twin-mainwheel undercarriage units.

VARIANTS

In addition to the basic **Ka-25BSh 'Hormone-A'** model which was specifically developed for the ASW mission, at least two other sub-types are known to have been produced, either in new-build form or as a result of modification. One was the **Ka-25K 'Hormone-B'**, which was used for over-the-horizon targeting and relayed guidance data to cruise missiles launched from surface vessels and submarines. This featured a larger bulged radome and lacked the specialised ASW equipment, with some of the space made available being given over to additional fuel for longer endurance. All four legs were retractable in order to raise the wheels out of the field-of-view of the radar. The **Ka-25PS 'Hormone-C'**, a dedicated SAR and utility derivative that also lacked ASW systems, could carry up to 12 passengers or cargo. In the SAR role, 'Hormone-C' featured a winch, searchlight and loudspeaker, while some were also fitted with a homing receiver for aircrew locator beacons.

Kamov Ka-25BSh Russian Navy

Kamov Ka-27, Ka-28 & Ka-32

TWIN-TURBOSHAFT ASW/UTILITY HELICOPTER

DEVELOPMENT

Manufactured for both civilian and military use, design of the Kamov Ka-27 commenced in 1969, with the intention of conceiving an improved helicopter that was compatible with existing Ka-25 facilities, such as hangar accommodation and landing platforms. The result was the considerably heavier but much more powerful Ka-27, which possessed significantly better performance, could carry almost four times the payload and also introduced improved weaponry and avionics equipment. Flown for the first time in prototype form during 1973, the ensuing flight test programme occupied several years before operational deployment of the Ka-27PL 'Helix-A' ASW version followed in 1981. A year later, the SAR-dedicated Ka-27PS 'Helix-D' also entered service with the Russian Navy. In due course, export versions were also developed and offered as the Ka-28, although only a handful of friendly nations received the 'Helix'. Derivatives for civil operation use the Ka-32 designation.

CURRENT SERVICE

Ka-27PL 'Helix-A' and Ka-27PS 'Helix-D' versions serve with the naval air arms of both Russia and Ukraine in reasonable quantities (approx 200), while export customers include China (Ka-28), India (Ka-28), and Vietnam (Ka-28 and Ka-32). Perhaps most surprisingly of all, the US Army has at least one Ka-32 'Helix-C', which is used for threat simulation during combat training exercises.

Kamov Ka-28

SPECIAL FEATURES

Co-axial contra-rotating main rotor blades are the most obvious feature of the Ka-27 family, which also has a neater undernose radar installation when compared with the Ka-25 'Hormone' which it first supplanted and eventually replaced. SAR-dedicated models usually carry a winch above the cabin door on the port side, as well as downward-pointing floodlights. All derivatives have a twin nosewheel and twin mainwheel undercarriage configuration.

VARIANTS

Military derivatives for domestic use are the **Ka-27PL** 'Helix-A' and **Ka-27PS** 'Helix-D', which perform ASW and SAR tasks respectively. The **Ka-28** is the export

equivalent of the Ka-27PL, although it has a different, downgraded, avionics suite. Versions intended for use by civilian operators use the Ka-32 designation, although the distinction between civil and military is sometimes blurred. Variants of the latter include the **Ka-32S** maritime multirole version and the **Ka-32T** utility transport, ambulance and flying crane, both known as **'Helix-C'**. Both were produced for service with Aeroflot, but some ostensibly civil aircraft have actually been military machines and examples of the 'Helix' wearing Aeroflot titles and fitted with radar have been observed operating from Russian warships. More recently, the **Ka-32A** series has appeared, with modified assemblies and systems that meet the latest Russian and US airworthiness standards.

TECHNICAL DATA

Kamov Ka-27PL 'Helix-A'

Powerplants: Two Klimov (Isotov) TV3-117VK turboshafts
Developing: 1,659kW (2,225eshp)
Driving: Two three-blade coaxial contra-rotating main rotors
Main rotor diameter: 15.90m (52ft 2in)
Fuselage length: 11.30m (37ft 1in)
Height: 5.40m (17ft 8.6in)
All-up weight: 12,600kg (27,778lb)
Maximum speed: 290km/h (180mph)
Cruise speed: 270km/h (168mph)
Operational ceiling: 11,480ft
Ferry range: 800km (497 miles)
Endurance: 3hr 30min
Accommodation: Pilot, navigator and observer/hoist operator
Warload: single AT-1MV torpedo or APR-2 ASW missile, or PLAB-250-120 depth charges.
Payload: 3,000kg (6,614lb)
First flown: 24 December 1973
Entered service: 14 April 1981

Kamov Ka-32A7

Kamov Ka-29, Ka-31 & Ka-33

TWIN-TURBOSHAFT ARMED ASSAULT/AEW/UTILITY HELICOPTER

Ka-29TB 'Helix-B'

DEVELOPMENT

Although it shares the same reporting name and evolved from the Ka-27/28/32 series, the Kamov Ka-29 is a radically different machine, being optimised for the assault transport role. Few details of development of the Ka-29TB version have emerged, with this helicopter first being reported in Russian Navy service

TECHNICAL DATA

Kamov Ka-29TB 'Helix-B'

Powerplants: Two Klimov (Isotov) TV3-117VK turboshafts
Developing: 1,660kW (2,226shp)
Driving: Two three-bladed coaxial contra-rotating main rotors
Main rotor diameter: 15.90m (52ft 2in)
Fuselage length: 11.30m (37ft 1in)
Height: 5.44m (17ft 10in)
All-up weight: 12,600kg (27,778lb)
Maximum speed: 280km (174mph)
Cruise speed: 230km/h (143mph)
Operational ceiling: 14,108ft
Range: 520km (322 miles)
Accommodation: Three crew and up to 16 fully-equipped troops
Warload: Includes 9M114 Shturm (AT-6 'Spiral') anti-armour guided missiles, unguided 57mm or 80mm rockets and retractable 7.62mm cannon; alternative loads can include 23mm gun pods and ZAB-500 incendiary bombs, with a torpedo or further bombs contained in internal weapons bay. Four weapon pylons.
First flown: 28 July 1976 (Ka-29); October 1987 (Ka-31)
Entered service: 1995 (Ka-31)

in 1987, when it was observed on board the assault ship *Ivan Rogov*. At that time, it was allocated the code name 'Helix-B'. Development of another, equally radically modified derivative – known as the Ka-29RLD – was begun in 1980, and this airborne early warning version is known to have flown for the first time in 1988, with initial trials being followed by operational evaluation at sea. Development of the Ka-29 series appears to be continuing, with the designation Ka-33 having been assigned to a civilian utility version that was announced at the 1997 Moscow Air Show.

CURRENT SERVICE

The basic Ka-29TB 'Helix-B' assault helicopter is presently in use with the Russian and Ukrainian naval

air arms, which are respectively thought to possess about 25 and 12 examples. The Ka-31 has yet to attain quantity production, but two test machines were evaluated on board the Russian carrier *Admiral Kuznetsov* in 1990 and there are unconfirmed reports that the Indian Navy has ordered three examples of this AEW version.

SPECIAL FEATURES

As with other Kamov designs, the co-axial contra-rotating main rotors are most noteworthy. Amongst the more notable changes is a drastically redesigned forward fuselage and cockpit section, accommodating three crew seated side-by-side and protected by titanium and composites armour. The cabin has also been subject to revision and can now accommodate up to 16 troops and their equipment, or four stretcher patients, seven walking wounded and a medical attendant when used for casualty evacuation.

VARIANTS

The **Ka-29TB 'Helix-B'** assault helicopter is the only version known to have attained quantity production to date, but at least one other variant has been developed and flown. This is the **Ka-31**, originally known as the **Ka-29RLD** (Radiolokatsyonnogo Dozora, or radar picket helicopter), which features a large rotating radar antenna that can be stowed flat under the fuselage when not in use. When deployed, the antenna swivels downward through a 90 degree arc into a vertical position and begins to rotate at six revolutions per minute, with the undercarriage retracting upwards to provide clearance. Plans to market civil versions as the **Ka-33** have also been revealed, but few details have emerged.

Ka-29RLD

Kamov Ka-50 Black Shark & Ka-52 Alligator

TWIN-TURBOSHAFT COMBAT HELICOPTER

Kamov Ka-50 Russian Air Force

TECHNICAL DATA

Kamov Ka-50 Black Shark

Powerplants: Two Klimov TV3-117VMA turboshafts
Developing: 1,633kW (2,190shp)
Driving: Two three-bladed coaxial contra-rotating main rotors
Main rotor diameter: 14.5m (47ft 5in)
Fuselage length: 16.0m (52ft 6in)
Wing span: 7.34m (24ft 1in)
Height: 4.93m (16ft 2in)
Maximum weight: 10,800kg (23,810lb)
Max speed: 390km/h (242mph) in shallow dive
Cruise speed: 270km/h (168mph)
Operational ceiling: 18,040ft
Combat range: 450km (279 miles)
Accommodation: Pilot only (pilot and weapon system operator in Ka-52)
Warload: Maximum of 3,000kg (6,610lb) of external stores on four wing pylons; weapons options include up to 12 9A4172 Vikhr-M (AT-12) tube-launched laser-guided air-to-surface missiles or up to 80 unguided S-8 80mm or 20 unguided 122m rockets. Alternative weapons are UPK-23-250 23mm gun pods, R-73 (AA-11 'Archer') air-to-air missiles or Kh-25MP (AS-12 'Kegler') anti-radiation air-to-surface missiles. Ka-50 also has single-barrel 2A42 30mm cannon, with up to 470 rounds (240 armour-piercing, 230 high explosive) in two ammunition boxes and capable of variable firing rates (350rpm or 550-600rpm).
First flown: 17 June 1982
Entered service: August 1993 (trials unit only)

DEVELOPMENT

This programme was launched in December 1977 as the V-80, with the first of several prototypes making its maiden flight in mid-1982. At that time, it was perceived as a potential replacement for the Mi-24 'Hind', but subsequent progress has been slow, dogged by the loss of the first prototype in 1985 and by a severe shortage of funds.

CURRENT SERVICE

Some development examples of the Ka-50 were assigned to the Russian Army's Aviation Training Centre at Torzhok in August 1993 for trials, with the first four production examples handed over to the Army in 1995-96, at which time plans were laid to order at least 15 more production aircraft. However, despite the fact that assembly of these was underway in mid-1998, work was halted because of insufficient funding.

SPECIAL FEATURES

Unusually for a combat helicopter, the Ka-50 is a single-

seater, although a two-seat version was offered to Turkey in response to their still-unsatisfied 1998 requirement for a new attack helicopter, as well as to China and India. The Ka-52 does have provision for a crew of two, comprising pilot and navigator/weapon system operator, although they are seated side-by-side, rather than in tandem as is usually the case. Both types feature Kamov's trade-mark coaxial, contra-rotating main rotor blades, as well as retractable landing gear and stub wings for the carriage of offensive weaponry. Fixed pods at the wingtips contain the Ka-50's defensive countermeasures equipment, including chaff/flare dispensers and radar warning receivers.

VARIANTS

The basic version is the **Ka-50 'Hokum'** single-seater, with a night-capable derivative known as either the **Ka-50N** or **Ka-50Sh** being fitted with various sensors including low-light-level television, FLIR and an electro-optic sighting system. **Ka-50-2** is the designation allocated to the two-seat version offered to Turkey in 1998, which is basically similar to the **Ka-52**, but

optimised for attack and anti-armour role. The Ka-52 is also a two-seater, for with all-weather day/night attack, that retains 85 per cent similarity with the Ka-50, but has a redesigned front fuselage. In service, the Ka-52 could fulfil a 'battle management' role, whereby it would detect and designate targets that would then be engaged by the Ka-50.

Kamov Ka-50 Russian Air Force

Kawasaki C-1

TWIN-TURBOFAN TACTICAL AIRLIFT TRANSPORT

Kawasaki C-1 Japanese Air Self-Defence Force

DEVELOPMENT

Conceived in response to the Japanese Air Self-Defence Force's C-X requirement which called for a medium-sized transport aircraft to replace the long-serving Curtiss C-46 Commando in the early 1970s, the process of design for what eventually became the C-1 was launched in 1966 by the Nihon Aircraft Manufacturing Company (NAMC). Although NAMC had design authority, manufacture of the aircraft was shared between several Japanese companies, with responsibility for final assembly allocated to Kawasaki, which completed the first XC-1 prototype in the latter half of 1970. Following a successful maiden flight on 12 November of that year, it was subsequently joined by a second prototype in a test programme that was eventually concluded in March 1973, with production examples of the C-1 beginning

to enter JASDF service during the course of 1974. C-1 production ended in 1981

CURRENT SERVICE

Efforts to export the C-1 unfortunately met with no success at all and Japan's Air Self-Defence Force is the only air arm that has ever operated the type, which continues in service today. Attrition has accounted for three of the 31 aircraft that were built during 1974-81, but approximately two dozen examples equip 402 Squadron at Iruma AB and 403 Squadron at Miho AB, while the JASDF test organisation at Gifu AB also possesses two for transport tasks and some test duties. Finally, the unique EC-1 conversion is still in regular service with the Electronic Warfare Training Unit at Iruma.

SPECIAL FEATURES

In common with many of the jet-powered military transport aircraft that were conceived and developed during the course of the 1960s and 1970s, the C-1 has

a high-wing layout with pylon-mounted podded engines suspended from the wing and a T-tail. The sharply upswept aft fuselage section incorporates a rear loading ramp for easy access to the cargo hold.

VARIANTS

Following on from the two **XC-1** prototypes, assembly of another 29 aircraft was undertaken by Kawasaki for the JASDF. All were designated as **C-1s** and the final example was accepted on 21 October 1981. The only other version to see service with the JASDF is the **EC-1**, a modification of the 21st C-1 to be built. Utilised as an ECM trainer, it has been extensively adapted to fulfil this role and has an indigenous TRDI/Mitsubishi Electric XJ/ALQ-5 ECM system as well as bulbous nose and tail radomes and various blister fairings on the fuselage, which contain antennae associated with the electronic equipment. It first flew on 3 December 1984 and was first evaluated by the JASDF's test organisation before being delivered to the Electronic Warfare Training Unit in June 1986.

TECHNICAL DATA

Kawasaki C-1

Powerplants: Two Mitsubishi/Pratt & Whitney JT8D-M-9 turbofans
Thrust: 64.50kN (14,500lb st)
Span: 30.60m (100ft 4.75in)
Length: 29.00m (95ft 1.75in)
Height: 9.99m (32ft 9.25in)
All-up weight: 38,700kg (85,320lb)
Maximum speed: 806km/h (501mph)
Cruise speed: 657km/h (408mph)
Range with 7,900kg (17,416lb) payload: 1,297km (806 miles)
Accommodation: Five crew and up to 60 fully-equipped troops
Payload: 8,000kg (17,640lb)
First flown: 12 November 1970
Entered service: February 1974

Kawasaki C-1 Japanese Air Self-Defence Force

Kawasaki T-4

TWIN-TURBOFAN INTERMEDIATE TRAINER AIRCRAFT

Kawasaki T-4 Japanese Air Self-Defence Force

DEVELOPMENT

The process of development of the T-4 began in September 1981, when Kawasaki was chosen to be prime contractor for the design and assembly of a new intermediate trainer aircraft for service with Japan's Air Self-Defence Force. The resultant T-4 was based firmly on work previously undertaken by Kawasaki with the project designation KA-851, and basic design studies were completed during October 1982. Thereafter, funding for the construction of four flying prototypes, plus two further airframes for static and fatigue testing, was allocated during Fiscal Years 1983 and 1984. Construction of the first XT-4 began in April 1984 and this aircraft was complete by mid-1985, flying for the first time at the end of July. All four prototypes were handed over to the JASDF for test and evaluation between December 1985 and July 1986. By then, an initial order had been placed for production aircraft and the first of these flew in June 1988, with deliveries to the JASDF starting soon after.

CURRENT SERVICE

As with many other indigenous designs, the only customer to date has been the Japan Air Self-Defence Force, which has placed contracts for just over 200 examples of the T-4, this figure including the original quartet of prototypes. In operational use, the bulk of unarmed T-4 production has been for the 1st Air Wing at Hamamatsu Air base, where it replaced the veteran T-33 with two training squadrons and with the 13th Flying Training Wing at Ashiya AB. Other examples are assigned to regional headquarters and combat units of the JASDF, with which they fulfil liaison and communications tasks, while about ten specially configured aircraft have served as display mounts for the *Blue Impulse* aerobatic team at Matsushima AB since replacing the Mitsubishi T-2 in 1996.

SPECIAL FEATURES

Not dissimilar to the Dassault-Breguet/Dornier Alphajet trainer/light attack aircraft in appearance, the T-4 has a mid-mounted wing incorporating slight anhedral. Intake ducts are sited below and forward of the wing assembly, which has the ability to carry two auxiliary fuel tanks or travel pods. Other external stores may be carried on a centreline station, including target-towing equipment, ECM/chaff dispenser or an atmospheric sampling pod. Pilot and student/passenger are housed in tandem, with the second cockpit stepped up slightly to offer a good field of view for the rear occupant. There is also a small baggage compartment in the centre fuselage for use in the liaison role.

VARIANTS

The only variant is the basic T-4 tandem two-seat trainer and liaison aircraft.

TECHNICAL DATA

Kawasaki T-4

Powerplants: Two Ishikawajima-Harima F3-IHI-30 turbofans
Developing: 16.37kN (3,680lb st)
Span: 9.94m (32ft 7.5in)
Length: 13.00m (42ft 8in) including probe
Height: 4.60m (15ft 1.25in)
All-up weight: 7,500kg (16,535lb)
Maximum speed: 1,038km/h (645mph)
Operational ceiling: 50,000ft
Maximum range: 1,668km (1,036 miles) with two external fuel tanks
Accommodation: Two (pilot and student or passenger)
Warload: None, but five pylons (underfuselage one for EW dispenser). Other pods for fuel or equipment
First flown: 29 July 1985
Entered service: September 1988

Kawasaki T-4
Japanese Air Self-Defence Force

Learjet (Gates) 24, 25, 35, 36 & C-21

TWIN-TURBOFAN STAFF/UTILITY TRANSPORT AIRCRAFT

Learjet C-21A United States Air Force

DEVELOPMENT

One of the most successful business aircraft of all time, the Learjet has demonstrated remarkable longevity by virtue of an almost continuous process of improvement since the first example was delivered during the mid-1960s. In consequence, contemporary examples of the family bear only a superficial resemblance to the original small and neat aircraft that began life as the brainchild of Bill Lear at the dawn of the 1960s. In military service, the most widely used version is the Learjet 35A, which achieved FAA certification in July 1974, with deliveries beginning soon after, although it was another decade before the USAF acquired it as the C-21A.

CURRENT SERVICE

The C-21A Learjet is presently in service with the US Air Force and the US Army. In the case of the former, no fewer than 54 of the 78 aircraft on strength are assigned to Air Mobility Command, with which they operate from a variety of locations on communications duties. Other USAF organisations that possess the C-21A are Air Education and Training Command, which has five for pilot training tasks; Pacific Air Forces, with four for communications; and United States Air Forces in Europe, with 13, again primarily for communications.

Finally, the Air National Guard has two. The US Army received three former USAF examples, all of which serve with the Priority Air Transport detachment at Andrews AFB, Maryland. Overseas air arms that utilise the equivalent Learjet 35A are Argentina, Bolivia, Brazil, Chile, Finland, Iraq, Saudi Arabia, Switzerland, Thailand and Venezuela, in some cases operating them alongside other Learjet versions, which are also flown by Japan (36A), Macedonia (25B), Namibia (31A), Peru (25B) and Yugoslavia (25D).

SPECIAL FEATURES

The Model 35A was the first version of the Learjet family to feature turbofan engines, but is otherwise similar to earlier versions, employing a low-wing monoplane configuration with auxiliary fuel tanks mounted at the wing tips (in most cases), although some versions (like the Learjet 31) have winglets instead. All versions also have a T-tail layout.

VARIANTS

The basic military version is the **C-21A** of the USAF, which leased and then purchased a total of 80 aircraft in 1984-85, following up with four more for the Air National Guard in 1987. These are virtually identical to the commercial Learjet 35A. Older versions in

military hands are the **Learjet 24** and **Learjet 25**, which are powered by General Electric CJ610 turbojets, but at least one **Learjet 31** and a few **Learjet 36s** are also military owned. These, like the C-21A, have AlliedSignal TFE731 turbofans.

TECHNICAL DATA

Learjet C-21A
Powerplants: Two AlliedSignal TFE731-2-2B turbofans
Developing: 15.6kN (3,500lb st)
Span: 12.04m (39ft 4in)
Length: 14.83m (48ft 8in)
Height: 3.73m (12ft 3in)
All-up weight: 8,300kg (18,300lb)
Maximum speed: 872km/h (542mph)
Cruise speed: 774km/h (481mph)
Operational ceiling: 42,000ft
Maximum range: 2,235km (1,390 miles) with four passengers
Accommodation: Crew, plus up to eight passengers or cargo
First flown: 7 October 1963 (Learjet 23 prototype)
Entered service: 12 October 1964 (first civil delivery of Learjet 23); April 1984 (C-21A)

Learjet C-21A United States Air Force

LET L410 & L420 Turbolet

TWIN-TURBOPROP LIGHT TRANSPORT AIRCRAFT

DEVELOPMENT

Conceived as a light commuter aircraft, design of the L 410 began at Kunovice in 1966, from where the first prototype made its maiden flight on 16 April 1969. This and the subsequent three prototypes all had Pratt & Whitney Canada PT6A-27 turboprops, as did the initial production L 410A and L 410AF aircraft. Thereafter, a change of powerplant occurred with introduction of the L 410M version in 1976, which featured Motorlet (Walter) M 601 A engines. Further refinement led to the L 410UVP in 1977. Increased span, greater vertical tail area and improvements to the control system were among the features introduced on this model, which was replaced in production by the L 410UVP-E in 1984. Delivery of the 1,000th L 410 took place in November 1990 and approximately 1,100 had been built when production was suspended in 1997. Current marketing efforts are concentrated mainly on the L 420 version, with Western avionics and M 601 F engines, but despite achieving FAA certification in March 1998, no sales have been recorded.

CURRENT SERVICE

Although the majority of aircraft were delivered to civilian customers, a respectable number are in military service with several air arms, most notably in Eastern Europe. Transport and utility versions are presently used by Bulgaria, the Czech Republic, Estonia, Germany, Hungary, Latvia, Libya, Lithuania, Russia, the Slovak Republic, Slovenia and Tunisia. In addition, the aerial survey L 410FG serves with the Czech Republic and the Slovak Republic.

SPECIAL FEATURES

High wing layout with slightly swept fin and retractable tricycle landing gear. Main undercarriage units are

LET 410UVP-S German Air Force

accommodated in fairings on sides of lower fuselage. L 410UVP-E and L 420 versions have reinforced wings with tip tanks for additional fuel.

VARIANTS

Following on from the prototypes, the original production model was the L 410A. As already noted, this had Western engines and all of the 17 examples built were for civil customers, as were three L 410ABs, one L 410AF and 11 L 410ASs. Sales of the L 410M, L 410MA and L 410MU accounted for just over 100 aircraft, most of which went to Aeroflot. In terms of

quantity produced, the L 410UVP and L 410UVP-E models are easily the most numerous, accounting for about 900 aircraft between them, and they are also the most common versions with military operators. Seven of the eight L 410FG aerial survey aircraft were destined for military service with the former Czechoslovakia, while 24 L 410T multi-engine trainers were also completed for Czechoslovakia and Libya.

TECHNICAL DATA

Let L410UVP-E

Powerplants: Two Motorlet (Walter) M 601 E turboprops
Developing: 559kW (750shp)
Driving: Five-blade propellers
Span: 19.48m (63ft 11in) excluding tip tanks
Length: 14.42m (47ft 4in)
Height: 5.83m (19ft 1.5in)
All-up weight: 6,600kg (14,550lb)
Maximum speed: 357km/h (222mph)
Service Ceiling: 19,700ft
Range with max payload: 546km (339 miles)
Cruise speed: 386km/h (240mph)
Accommodation: One or two crew and up to 19 passengers
Payload: 1,710kg (3,770lb)
First flown: 16 April 1969 (L 410); 30 December 1984 (L 410UVP-E); 10 November 1993 (L 420)
Entered service: Late 1971 (L 410); 1986 (L 410UVP-E)

LET 410UVP-T Czech Air Force

Lisunov Li-2

Lisunov Li-2 'Cab'

DEVELOPMENT

Known initially as the PS-84 (Passazhirski Samolet, or Passenger Aeroplane), the Lisunov Li-2 was fundamentally a Douglas DC-3 produced in Russia under license at the GAZ-84 factory at Khimki in Moscow. Acquisition of the license predated WW2 and a key individual in the PS-84/Li-2 project was Boris Lisunov, who spent two years with Douglas at Santa Monica before returning to Russia to oversee the manufacturing programme. The intention was to minimise the number of changes, but it transpired that almost 1,300 engineering changes were to be incorporated and the eventual result differed quite significantly in detail. Notable variations from the original DC-3 included a reduced wing span, a revised door arrangement (with the main passenger door to starboard, rather than port) and different engine installation, and many aircraft were fitted with a front baffle to reduce cooling air flow in winter months. Production began at Khimki, but was evacuated to Tashkent in October 1941 when German

forces approached Moscow; by 1954, when Li-2 manufacture eventually ended, some 5,652 had been built at Khimki and Tashkent, with the overall total augmented by a further 505 from a factory at Komsomolsk-on-Amur. These were widely used by the Russian state airline Aeroflot and by the Red Army until the advent of the Ilyushin Il-12 and Il-14 in the 1950s. Li-2s also served in 14 other countries.

CURRENT SERVICE

Like the DC-3/C-47, the Li-2 has long been regarded as obsolescent, but a few examples may still be active with the People's Liberation Army Air Force (PLAAF) in China and North Korea's People's Army Air Force.

SPECIAL FEATURES

Few special features are incorporated in the basic DC-3 design, but the Li-2 proved almost as versatile as its American counterpart, with suitably modified aircraft undertaking such diverse tasks as bombing, minesweeping, glider towing, mapping and survey

TECHNICAL DATA

Lisunov Li-2 'Cab'

Powerplants: Two Shvetsov Ash-62IR radial engines
Developing: 746kW (1,000hp)
Span: 28.81m (94ft 6.25in)
Length: 19.65m (64ft 5.5in)
All-up weight: 11,279kg (24,867lb)
Maximum speed: 300km/h (186mph)
Service Ceiling: 18,375ft
Cruise speed: 245km/h (152mph)
Range: 1,100-2,500km (684-1,550 miles)
Accommodation: 14-28 passengers
First flown: Late 1939
Entered service: June 1940 (as PS-84)

work, plus a miscellany of transport duties. Provision made for ski undercarriage. Some were fitted with a dorsal gun turret carrying either a 7.62mm or 12.7mm machine gun, while others had a fixed 37mm gun.

VARIANTS

Recorded variants include the basic **Li-2P** passenger transport; **Li-2 Salon** VIP transport version with accommodation for 7-14 passengers; **Li-2D** with auxiliary fuel tanks for greater range; **Li-2G** civil freighter; **Li-2T** military freighter; **Li-2PG** convertible troop transport/freighter; **Li-2VP** for bombing, assault, pure transport, casualty evacuation, minesweeping and glider towing, amongst other duties; **Li-2LP** for forest patrol and water-bombing; **Li-2RP** for fisheries reconnaissance; **Li-2RT** for radio relay; **Li-2SKh** for crop spraying and dusting; **Li-2UT** navigation trainer; **Li-2F** photographic platform; **Li-2FG** mapping/survey version and the **Li-2M** for meteorological research.

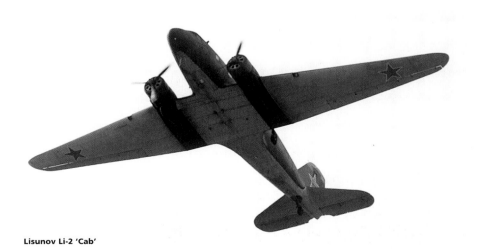

Lisunov Li-2 'Cab'

SEE ALSO: DOUGLAS C-47 DAKOTA

Lockheed T-33

Lockheed CT-133 Canadian Armed Forces

DEVELOPMENT

Easily the most numerous jet trainer of all time, the T-33A came about during the early development of the P-80 Shooting Star when it was realised that a two-seat trainer version of the single-seat fighter would be a useful addition to the USAF inventory. When first proposed, military interest was minimal, but the idea re-emerged in 1947 at a time when attrition of early jet fighters was unacceptably high. Even then, Lockheed had to go it alone and launched the trainer model as a private venture with company funds, although their initiative was soon rewarded with USAF authority to adapt a P-80C into a prototype. This involved lengthening the fuselage slightly to accommodate a second cockpit for a student pilot and the first TP-80C (later redesignated TF-80C, and then T-33A) made its maiden flight in March 1948. Trials with this machine soon confirmed its value, and Lockheed received the first of a succession of contracts in spring 1948, for an initial batch of 20 aircraft. Subsequent re-orders resulted in several thousand more T-33s being built for service with US Air Force and US Navy training units, while licence manufacture in Canada and Japan ultimately raised the final total to more than 6,500.

CURRENT SERVICE

Although no longer active with US armed forces, the T-33 has enjoyed great longevity and a surprisingly large number are still used by about ten air arms. Most have the basic T-33A model, for liaison and support tasks, but some of the armed AT-33 versions and a few RT-33As still fly regularly. Canada will continue to fly eight CT-133 Silver Stars with No 434 Squadron until March 2002 when they will be retired. Other air arms known to be using 'Tee-Birds' in 2000 include Bolivia, Greece, Iran, Japan, Mexico, Pakistan and South Korea.

SPECIAL FEATURES

Two-seat derivative of F-80 Shooting Star, with large auxiliary fuel tanks mounted on wing tips.

VARIANTS

Although produced in vast quantities, only three basic versions appeared in new-build form. Two were specifically intended for training tasks, these being the **T-33A** for the USAF and its US Navy equivalent, the **T-33B** (which began life as the TO-2 and was redesignated as the TV-2 before adopting the T-33B nomenclature in 1962). The only other new-build model was the RT-33A, for reconnaissance tasks and this featured vertical and oblique cameras in a modified nose section as well as having electronic and recording apparatus in the rear cockpit. Later in the aircraft's life, several modified versions appeared, including the **AT-33A** for attack duties, **DT-33A** and **DT-33B** drone directors, **NT-33A** for permanent testing tasks and **DT-33C** and **QT-33A** pilotless target drones. Canadian-built aircraft, which were fitted with the Rolls-Royce Nene 10 turbojet engine, were known as **T-33AN Silver Stars**. A proposal to re-engine the aircraft with two Garrett TFE731 turbofans as the **Skyfox** failed to attract interest, although a prototype was flown in June 1983.

Lockheed CT-133 Canadian Armed Forces

TECHNICAL DATA

Lockheed T-33A

Powerplant: One Allison J33-A-35 turbojet
Developing: 24.02kN (5,400lb st)
Span: 11.85m (38ft 10.5in)
Length: 11.51m (37ft 9in)
Height: 3.55m (11ft 8in)
All-up weight: 6,832kg (15,061lb)
Maximum speed: 966km/h (600mph)
Cruise speed: 732km/h (455mph)
Operational Ceiling: 48,000ft
Range: 2,050km (1,275 miles) with external tanks
Accommodation: Two (instructor pilot and student)
First flown: 22 March 1948 (as TP-80C)
Entered service: August 1948

Lockheed F-104 Starfighter

SINGLE TURBOJET AIR DEFENCE/ATTACK FIGHTER

F-104S ASA-M Starfighter Italian Air Force

DEVELOPMENT

One of the most successful members of the much-vaunted 'Century Series' of American fighters, by virtue of extensive overseas use, the F-104 initially emerged as a pure interceptor, but was never widely used by the US Air Force, which purchased fewer than 250 for Air Defense Command and Tactical Air Command. In the late 1950s, however, the availability of a more powerful version of the J79 engine and the installation of more sophisticated nav/attack avionics systems transformed it into a multi-role fighter with the ability to undertake air-to-air and air-to-ground missions. As the F-104G, the Starfighter was at the heart of the first 'sale of the century', which resulted in more than 1,000 aircraft being manufactured in Europe during the 1960s for service with the air arms of Belgium, Italy, the Netherlands and West Germany. Production was also undertaken in Canada for home and overseas air arms and in Japan, while more F-104Gs (and two-seat TF-104Gs) were built by Lockheed for several allied nations, making it one of the most widely used fighters of the post-war era. Production ended as late as March 1979, with the handover of the 246th and last F-104S to be built in Italy.

CURRENT SERVICE

The only nation that still uses the Starfighter in a front-line role is Italy, which has recently completed a life extension programme that will ensure it remains effective until approximately 2005. Some 49 F-104S

ASA-Ms and 15 TF-104G-M two-seaters were involved, but a number of unmodified F-104S ASAs are also still active. In addition, Japan has adapted a number of Starfighters to serve as unmanned target drones, under the designation UF-104J and UF-104DJ (former two-seater).

SPECIAL FEATURES

The most distinctive attribute of the Starfighter is its extremely thin unswept wing. Combined with the slender fuselage, this soon earned it the accolade of 'missile with a man in it'.

VARIANTS

Following on from the pair of **XF-104** prototypes and 17 **YF-104A** pre-production machines, at least 16 different versions of the Starfighter have existed, although most have long since disappeared from view. Single-seat new-build models were the **F-104A**, **F-104C**, **F/RF-104G**, **F-104J** and **CF-104**, while two-seat equivalents of these were the **F-104B**, **F-104D**, **TF-104G**, **F-104DJ** and **CF-104D** respectively. The **F-104F** was another new-build two-seater (for Germany) and was basically similar to the **F-104D**, although it was fitted with the more advanced avionics of the F-104G. In addition, a number of aircraft were modified for special duties, including the **NF-104A** high-altitude trainer with a Rocketdyne AR.2 booster motor at the base of the fin, the **QF-104A** drone target, and Japan's **UF-104J** and **UF-104DJ** drones.

TECHNICAL DATA

Lockheed F-104S Starfighter
Powerplant: One General Electric J79-GE-19 turbojet
Developing: 52.80kN (11,870lb st) dry, 79.62kN (17,900lbst) with afterburner
Span: 6.68m (21ft 11in)
Length: 16.69m (54ft 9in)
Height: 4.11m (13ft 6in)
All-up weight: 14,060kg (30,996lb)
Maximum speed: 2,333km/h (1,450mph)
Cruise speed: 981km/h (610mph)
Operational ceiling: 58,000ft
Ferry range: 2,920km (1,814 miles)
Combat radius: 1,247km (775 miles)
Accommodation: Pilot only
Warload: 3,400kg (7,495lb) maximum ordnance payload; weapons options can include Selenia Aspide radar-guided air-to-air missile, Raytheon AIM-9L Sidewinder infra-red homing air-to-air missile and bombs or rocket pods for air-to-ground attack. Internal 20mm six-barrel T171E3 Vulcan rotary gun also installed.
First flown: 28 February 1954 (F-104A); December 1968 (F-104S)
Entered service: 26 January 1958 (F-104A); 1969 (F-104S)

F-104S ASA-M Starfighter Italian Air Force

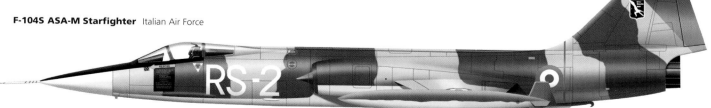

Lockheed C-130 Hercules (Transport versions)

FOUR-TURBOPROP TACTICAL TRANSPORT AIRCRAFT

C-130K Hercules C1 Royal Air Force

TECHNICAL DATA

Lockheed C-130H Hercules

Powerplants: Four Allison T56-A-15 turboprops
Developing: 3,362kW (4,508shp)
Driving: Four-blade propellers
Span: 40.41m (132ft 7in)
Length: 29.79m (97ft 9in)
Height: 11.66m (38ft 3in)
All-up weight: 79,380kg (175,000lb)
Maximum cruise speed: 602km/h (374mph)
Economical cruise speed: 556km/h (345mph)
Operational ceiling: 33,000ft
Range with max fuel: 7,876km (4,894 miles)
Range with max payload: 3,791km (2,356 miles)
Accommodation: Five crew, plus up to 92 troops/passengers
Payload: 19,356kg (42,673lb)
First flown: 23 August 1954 (YC-130);
19 November 1964 (C-130H)
Entered service: 9 December 1956 (C-130A);
March 1965 (C-130H)

DEVELOPMENT

Arguably the most versatile transport to appear since the Douglas DC-3/C-47, the C-130 Hercules originated in response to a USAF requirement issued in February 1951, that called for a new transport aircraft to replace the C-119 Flying Boxcar with troop carrier units of the Tactical Air Command. Four companies were invited to submit proposals by April 1951 and Lockheed's contender was revealed as the winner on 2 July, when the company received a contract for two prototypes. The second of these was actually the first aircraft to fly, in August 1954 and the ensuing test programme, although not entirely trouble free, proved the basic soundness of the design. Deliveries to the USAF began at the end of 1955 and the Hercules has been hugely successful, with more than 2,000 examples having emerged from Marietta, Georgia, where production of the C-130J (see separate entry) continues today.

CURRENT SERVICE

Pure transport variants of the C-130 Hercules are currently in service with air arms in approximately

60 countries around the world, while a number of civilian operators fly the commercial L-100 equivalent.

SPECIAL FEATURES

The basic high-wing configuration and high-set tailplane gives easy access to the cargo hold via a rear ramp. The main undercarriage units are housed in fairings scabbed on to the fuselage side, giving a capacious and unobstructed cargo bay. The aft doors can be opened in flight for air delivery of bulky loads and the side doors may be used to drop paratroops.

VARIANTS

Although a large number of derivatives of the Hercules have appeared, there have actually been relatively few basic variants over the years. The first was the **C-130A**, which saw extensive service with the USAF. The **C-130B** came next and was basically similar, with only detail improvements. The next major transport model was the **C-130E** of 1961, which benefited from more powerful T56 engines, offering better 'hot-and-high' performance as well as greater payload

capability and extended range through adoption of large underwing tanks. The C-130E was also the first version to achieve significant export success, which was improved on by the **C-130H**. Introduced in the mid-1960s, this had new avionics, further improvements to the engines and structural strengthening. Initial production of this version was solely for export and it was not until 1975 that the USAF received any. The C-130H remained the basic production model for more than 30 years, with the 1,089th and last example delivered in January 1998. The **C-130K**, built for the RAF as the Hercules C1, was similar to the C-130H, but incorporated much British equipment.

SEE ALSO: LOCKHEED C-130 HERCULES (SPECIAL MISSION VERSIONS) & LOCKHEED MARTIN C-130J HERCULES

C-130H Hercules Israeli Air Force

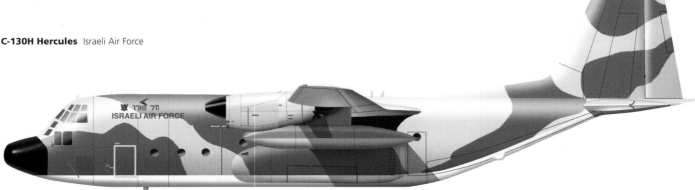

Lockheed C-130 Hercules (Special Mission versions)

FOUR-TURBOPROP AIRCRAFT

EC-130H Hercules United States Air Force

TECHNICAL DATA

Lockheed AC-130U Hercules

Powerplants: Four Allison T56-A-15 turboprops
Developing: 3,655kW (4,900shp)
Driving: Four-blade propellers
Span: 40.41m (132ft 7in)
Length: 29.79m (97ft 9in)
Height: 11.66m (38ft 3in)
All-up weight: 79,380kg (175,000lb)
Maximum cruise speed: 602km/h (374mph)
Economical cruise speed: 556km/h (345mph)
Operational ceiling: 33,000ft
Range with maximum fuel: 7,876km (4,894 miles)
Accommodation: 13 crew
Warload: One GAU-12 25mm cannon with 3,000 rounds of ammunition; one L-60 Bofors 40mm cannon; one M102 105mm howitzer
First flown: 23 August 1954 (YC-130); 20 December 1990 (AC-130U)
Entered service: 1967 (AC-130A operational test); June 1994 (AC-130U)

DEVELOPMENT

Following entry into service with the USAF in the tactical airlift role in the mid-1950s, the basic Hercules transport has proved a most versatile machine, with variants evolving for an assortment of special missions. Many of these came about through modification of standard transport aircraft, but some were purpose built; examples of both types include AC-130 gunships, EC-130s for various electronic roles, KC-130 tankers for aerial refuelling, LC-130 ski-birds for polar operations and MC-130 special operations aircraft.

CURRENT SERVICE

Today, numerous versions of the Hercules remain in service for specialised missions and taskings. The majority serve with the USAF, but some foreign air arms have adapted aircraft for unusual roles. In the case of the US forces, the advent of more modern equipment has resulted in many one-off derivatives having been withdrawn from use.

SPECIAL FEATURES

A basic high-wing configuration and high-set tailplane, as per standard transport aircraft, is common to all

Hercules derivatives. Gunship variants feature weapons mounted transversely in the cargo hold area, all firing to port. Other special mission aircraft have unique equipment, including hose drum units on KC-130 tanker versions; additional antenna arrays on EC-130 elint/communications jamming and battlefield command and control versions; ski undercarriage units on LC-130 versions; FLIR and other sensors on MC-130 special operations versions; and large observation windows on some HC-130 SAR versions.

VARIANTS

One of the first new-build variations on the Hercules theme to appear was the tanker-transport **KC-130F**, 46 of which were built for the US Marine Corps in the late 1950s and early 1960s. Many are still in service today and they have been augmented in Marine Corps service by the **KC-130R** and **KC-130T**, with the broadly similar **KC-130H** being produced in modest quantities for export customers such as Brazil, Israel and Spain. Numerous versions exist or have existed for electronic-related tasks, these almost all originating from modification of pure transport aircraft. This process actually began in the latter half of the 1950s with

the C-130A-II (long since retired) for covert intelligence gathering operations, a role that the Hercules has performed ever since. Today, at least three versions of the **EC-130E** are in USAF service today, these being configured for battlefield command and control (basic EC-130E); for TV/radio broadcast and psychological warfare (**EC-130E 'Rivet Rider'**) and for elint gathering (**EC-130E 'Comfy Levi'**). Other specialised versions with the USAF include those engaged on covert operations (**MC-130E/H/P**), communications jamming (**EC-130H**), search and rescue (**HC-130H/N/P**) and armed attack (**AC-130H/U**).

SEE ALSO: LOCKHEED C-130 HERCULES (TRANSPORT VERSIONS & LOCKHEED MARTIN C-130J HERCULES)

AC-130U Hercules United States Air Force

Lockheed Martin C-130J Hercules

FOUR-TURBOPROP TACTICAL TRANSPORT AIRCRAFT

C-130J-30 Hercules C4 *Royal Air Force*

DEVELOPMENT

Despite achieving considerable success world-wide, with more than 2,150 examples (including over 1,000 C-130Hs) sold by the early 1990s, the basic Hercules design was fundamentally little changed from the original YC-130 prototypes of 1954. As a consequence, Lockheed (which became Lockheed Martin in 1995) elected in 1991 to develop an improved version as a private venture. At that time, it was referred to as the Hercules II, although this name was later dropped. The most visible evidence of redesign concerns the engine installation, with the Allison AE 2100 engine and Dowty Aerospace R391 propeller chosen for the C-130J. Since there was no prototype, fabrication of the first production C-130J-30 began in March 1994. Destined for the Royal Air Force, which became the launch customer when it ordered 25 aircraft in December 1994, this was rolled out on 18 October 1995. In the event, the maiden flight slipped to April 1996 because of problems with the avionics equipment. Further difficulties since then have delayed entry into service, but deliveries to the USAF, RAF and Royal Australian Air Force began during 1999.

CURRENT SERVICE

The C-130J entered operational service with the RAF and RAAF in early 2000. Fifteen C-130J-30 Hercules C4s and ten C-130J Hercules C5s were delivered to Cambridge for storage, pending delivery to the RAF. Australia, which has ordered 12 C-130J-30s, accepted its first in September 1999 and anticipated that it would enter operational service in early 2000, while the US Air Force Reserve Command's 403rd Wing took delivery of six C-130Js at the beginning of 1999. Other customers include the US Marine Corps and the Italian Air Force (20 on order), both of which expect to get their first aircraft during 2000. Kuwait is likely to order four. The USAF plans to order at least 150 C-130Js.

SPECIAL FEATURES

The C-130J is virtually identical to the basic Hercules aircraft as described elsewhere, being a high wing monoplane design with a tricycle undercarriage configuration and having a sharply upswept aft fuselage giving access to the cargo compartment via a rear loading ramp. The most visible difference concerns the propulsion system, with the C-130J having six-blade Dowty Aerospace R391 composites propellers in place of the four-blade units fitted to most earlier versions.

VARIANTS

Two variations of the basic transport aircraft exist, these being the **C-130J** and the stretched **C-130J-30**. As with earlier versions of the Hercules, several derivatives are likely to appear in future, but those which have been identified to date are the **EC-130J** psychological warfare version for the Pennsylvania Air National Guard; the **KC-130J** tanker-transport for the US Marine Corps and the **WC-130J** weather reconnaissance platform for the US Air Force Reserve Command.

SEE ALSO: LOCKHEED C-130 HERCULES (TRANSPORT VERSIONS & SPECIAL MISSION VERSIONS)

TECHNICAL DATA

Lockheed Martin C-130J Hercules
Powerplants: Four Rolls-Royce Allison AE 2100D3 turboprops
Developing: 3,424kW (4,591shp)
Driving: Six-blade propellers
Span: 40.41m (132ft 7in)
Length: 29.79m (97ft 9in)
Height: 11.84m (38ft 10in)
All-up weight: 79,380kg (175,000lb)
Maximum speed: 700km/hr (435mph)
Cruise speed: 658km/hr (409mph)
Operational ceiling: 39,000ft
Maximum range: 5,250km (3,262 miles)
Accommodation: Two flight deck crew plus loadmaster and up to 92 troops
Payload: 18,955kg (41,790lb)
First flown: 5 April 1996
Entered service: 28 January 1999 (initial delivery to USAF for training); 23 November 1999 (RAF)

C-130J-30 Hercules C4 *Royal Air Force*

Lockheed U-2

SINGLE TURBOFAN STRATEGIC RECONNAISSANCE AIRCRAFT

Lockheed U-2S United States Air Force

TECHNICAL DATA

Lockheed U-2S
Powerplant: General Electric F118-GE-101 non-afterburning turbofan
Developing: 84.52kN (19,000lb st)
Span: 31.39m (103ft 0in)
Length: 19.20m (63ft 0in)
Height: 4.88m (16ft 0in)
All-up weight: 18,144kg (40,000lb)
Maximum cruising speed: 692km/h (430mph)
Operational ceiling: exceeds 73,500ft
Maximum range: exceeds 9,650km (6,000 miles)
Endurance: over 14hr
Accommodation: Pilot only (two pilots in TU-2S)
First flown: August 1955 (U-2);
August 1967 (U-2R)
Entered service: 1956 (U-2A); 1968 (U-2R);
1994 (U-2S)

DEVELOPMENT

Developed, tested and introduced to operational service with the Central Intelligence Agency (CIA) in the mid-1950s, the shroud of secrecy that surrounded the Lockheed U-2 remained almost impenetrable until 1 May 1960, when an aircraft piloted by Francis 'Gary' Powers was shot down near Sverdlovsk. Today, almost 40 years on, the U-2 is still a key intelligence-gathering tool, but while the basic designation has not changed, the aircraft certainly has, for it has achieved the rare distinction of being twice reinstated in production. The first time was in the mid-1960s and introduced the much bigger U-2R. Greater size meant additional fuel and payload capacity, but only 12 were built for the CIA and USAF. Subsequently, in the late 1970s, production began of a version for tactical reconnaissance of the battlefield. This was the TR-1 – the new designation indicative of a wish

to overcome the stigma attached to its spyplane reputation. Between 1980 and 1989, 37 aircraft emerged, including some U-2Rs, as well as three two-seaters for pilot training and two ER-2s for NASA. Ironically, the TR-1 designation was dropped in 1992, when the U-2R designation became standard. More recently, adoption of the F118 turbofan has offered major benefits in terms of weight reduction and greater fuel efficiency, and all surviving USAF aircraft have been re-engined as the U-2S, as has NASA's pair of ER-2s.

CURRENT SERVICE

A total of 35 aircraft survive with the USAF, comprising 31 examples of the U-2S and four TU-2S trainers. All serve with the 9th Reconnaissance Wing at Beale AFB, California, from where aircraft are detached to overseas bases in Cyprus, France, South Korea and

Saudi Arabia. NASA's two ER-2s fly from the Dryden site at Edwards AFB.

SPECIAL FEATURES

The most distinctive aspect of the U-2 is its slender wing, which resembles that of a glider. Small outrigger wheels support the wing during take-off, these falling free once airborne, while wingtip skid fittings offer protection for landing. U-2S aircraft are often noted with 'superpods' mounted on the wings; these contain sensors and other equipment. In addition, USAF and NASA aircraft can be fitted with a large dorsal fairing; on the U-2S, this contains 'Senior Span' satellite communications equipment.

VARIANTS

Today, the only military variants in use are the **U-2S**, which is the principal operational model employed by the USAF, and the **TU-2S** for pilot training tasks – all surviving U-2Rs and TU-2Rs having been brought to this configuration. Two **ER-2s** continue to fly with NASA, but all earlier versions have long been retired.

Lockheed U-2S United States Air Force

Lockheed 1329 JetStar

FOUR-TURBOFAN EXECUTIVE/COMMUNICATIONS AIRCRAFT

Lockheed JetStar Royal Saudi Air Force

DEVELOPMENT

Originally conceived to satisfy the US Air Force UCX requirement for a utility cargo aircraft, design of the JetStar began at the start of 1957. Known initially as the CL-329, it would carry up to 14 passengers or 2,268kg (5,000lb) of cargo and featured podded jet engines on the rear fuselage sides. At the outset, it was a twin-engined design and both prototypes had Bristol Orpheus turbojets. Early trials were encouraging, but military spending cuts resulted in the UCX being cancelled, whereupon Lockheed decided to continue with the project as either a twin or four-engined executive aircraft, also offering it to the USAF as the T-40A crew trainer. In the event, the USAF obtained the T-39 Sabreliner and plans to build the Orpheus

under licence also fell through, forcing Lockheed to press ahead with a four-engined version powered by Pratt & Whitney's JT12A. This was the L-1329, which first flew in January 1960 and achieved FAA certification in August 1961.

CURRENT SERVICE

Less than five JetStars are thought to be in military service today. Palestine has a JetStar II which is used as a government executive transport. One is with the Libyan Air Force at Tripoli-Tarrabalus as a VIP transport. Two further examples of the JetStar 8 were delivered to the Royal Saudi Air Force in the mid-1960s and these were still used until quite recently, although they have reportedly been offered for sale.

SPECIAL FEATURES

A low-wing configuration was adopted for the JetStar, with the engines mounted in pairs adjacent to the aft fuselage on production aircraft. Fixed slipper-type auxiliary fuel tanks are located at the mid-span position on the slightly-swept wing, while the fin

and horizontal tail is unique in being an all-moving assembly.

VARIANTS

In its original format, two basic versions appeared, these being the **JetStar 6** with JT12A-6 or JT12A-6A turbojets and the **JetStar 8**, with the slightly more powerful JT12A-8. Subsequent refinement of the basic design took advantage of the quieter and more fuel-efficient TFE731 turbofan, which was fitted to two versions. One was the **JetStar 731**, which was simply a modified JetStar 6 or JetStar 8, while the other was the **JetStar II**, which was a new-build aircraft that also featured revised external tanks. In all, just over 200 JetStars were built, including a few for military operators, primarily as VIP transports. Specifically military versions, none of which remain in use, were acquired by the USAF, which received 16 in 1961-62. These comprised five **C-140As** for navigation aid calibration, five **C-140B** utility transports and six **VC-140Bs** for VIP airlift duties, although the C-140Bs were soon modified to **VC-140B** standard.

TECHNICAL DATA

Lockheed JetStar II

Powerplants: Four AlliedSignal (Garrett AiResearch) TFE731-3-1F turbofans
Developing: 16.5kN (3,700lb st)
Span: 16.60m (54ft 4in)
Length: 18.42m (60ft 4in)
Height: 6.23m (20ft 4in)
All-up weight: 19,844kg (43,750lb)
Maximum speed: 880km/h (547mph)
Cruise speed: 817km/h (508mph)
Operational ceiling: 43,000ft
Range with maximum payload: 5,135km (3,190miles)
Accommodation: Two crew plus up to 10 passengers
Payload: 1,280kg (2,822lb)
First flown: 4 September 1957
18 August 1976 (JetStar II)
Entered service: October 1961

Lockheed JetStar

Lockheed 188 Electra

FOUR-TURBOPROP TRANSPORT AIRCRAFT

L-188E Electra Argentine Navy

DEVELOPMENT

Developed in response to a 1955 American Airlines specification for a four-engine, turbine-powered passenger transport aircraft with the ability to carry up to 75 passengers some 3,220km (2,000 miles), Lockheed's initial proposal met with approval. However, Eastern Air Lines was also in the market for a broadly similar aircraft, but one that possessed greater range, more passenger capacity and a higher cruising speed. Further work on the design resulted in both prospective customers being satisfied and Lockheed secured orders for a total of 75 aircraft even before metal was cut. Construction of the first Electra was completed in just over two years, and this made its maiden flight on 6 December 1957, subsequently being joined by three more aircraft in a successful flight test programme

TECHNICAL DATA

Lockheed 188C Electra

Powerplants: Four Allison 501D-13A turboprops
Developing: 2,796kW (3,750shp)
Driving: Four-blade propellers
Span: 30.18m (99ft 0in)
Length: 31.85m (104ft 6in)
Height: 10.01m (32ft 10in)
All-up weight: 52,664kg (116,000lb)
Maximum speed: 721km/h (448mph)
Cruise speed: 602km/h (374mph)
Operational Ceiling: 28,000ft
Range with maximum payload: 3,540km (2,200 miles)
Accommodation: Crew of five and up to 98 passengers
Payload: 12,020kg (26,500lb)
First flown: 6 December 1957
Entered service: January 1959

that culminated in FAA certification in late August 1958. Deliveries to airline customers began in October 1958, but entry into service was delayed by a pilots' strike until January 1959. Thereafter, three mysterious fatal accidents in the first 14 months of service severely impaired confidence in the Electra at a time when jet airliners were on the verge of becoming commonplace. Despite identification and rectification of the cause of those accidents, the Electra's reputation had been irrevocably damaged and production ended with the delivery of the 170th example on 15 January 1961.

CURRENT SERVICE

Military use of the Electra has been limited to a small number of Latin American air arms. Eight are known to have seen service with the Argentine Navy in a variety of configurations and some L-188Es are still operated by Escuadra Aeronaval 6. They also serve with Escuadrón 712/Grupo Aéreo T1 of Fuerza Aerea Boliviana and one example with Escudrón de Transporte, Furza Aérea Hondureña.

SPECIAL FEATURES

The Electra is a low-wing design with four turboprop engines positioned largely above the wing.

VARIANTS

Two basic versions of the Electra were originally produced by Lockheed, these being the **Model 188A** and the longer-ranged **Model 188C**, both of which were pure passenger transports, numbers built being 116 and 54 respectively. In military service, Bolivia and Honduras employed the Model 188A, but the aircraft obtained by Argentina are a much more complex mix. All eight began life as Model 188As, but subsequent modification has resulted in a number of differing configurations, including the **Model 188PF** convertible passenger/freighter aircraft with a strengthened floor and cargo door, the **Model 188E Exploración** maritime patrol aircraft with Italian SMA-707 search radar in a ventral radome and the **Model 188EW Electrón** WAVE electronic intelligence platform with a suite of Israeli avionics.

L-188E Electra Argentine Navy

Lockheed P-3 Orion & CP-140 Aurora

FOUR-TURBOPROP MARITIME PATROL AIRCRAFT

EP-3E Orion United States Navy

TECHNICAL DATA

Lockheed P-3C Orion

Powerplants: Four Allison T56-A-14 turboprops
Developing: 3,661kW (4,910shp)
Driving: Four-blade propellers
Span: 39.37m (99ft 8in)
Length: 35.61m (116ft 10in)
Height: 10.27m (33ft 8.5in)
Maximum weight: 64,410kg (142,000lb)
Maximum speed: 761km/h (473mph)
Patrol speed: 381km/h (237mph)
Operational ceiling: 28,300ft
Ferry range: 8,950km (5,560 miles)
Mission range: 2,494km (1,550 miles) with three hours on station
Endurance: 17.2 hours
Accommodation: Crew of ten
Warload: 9,072kg (20,000lb) expendable payload, in weapons bay and on 10 external stations. Weaponry includes Mk 46 and Mk 50 torpedoes, depth bombs/destructors, mines, Mk 82 and Mk 83 bombs, Rockeye CBUs, AGM-84 Harpoon anti-ship missile and rockets
First flown: 25 November 1959 (YP3V-1 prototype); 18 September 1968 (YP-3C prototype)
Entered service: 1962 (P3V-1/P-3A); 1969 (P-3C)

DEVELOPMENT

The US Navy's search for a suitable replacement for the Lockheed Neptune began in August 1957, with the release of a type specification calling for a new maritime patrol aircraft. Lockheed was one of several companies to respond, basing its proposal on the L188 Electra airliner. It won a development contract in May 1958, and initial trials were conducted with the third prototype Electra, which served as an aerodynamic testbed for the Orion. Subsequently, in October 1960, the US Navy placed the first of many contracts for production aircraft, which first began entering service in summer 1962. Production was halted in 1995.

CURRENT SERVICE

All three basic patrol aircraft versions of the Orion are still in service, although some are almost 40 years old. P-3A versions are active with Chile (P-3A), Spain (P-3A), Thailand (P-3T/UP-3T) and the US Navy (UP/VP-3A). Examples of the P-3B serve with Australia (TAP-3B), Argentina (P-3B), Greece (P-3B), New Zealand (P-3K),

Norway (P-3N), Portugal (P-3P), Spain (P-3B) and the US Navy (P-3B) in limited amounts. Versions of the ultimate P-3C are used by Australia, Japan, South Korea, Netherlands, Norway, Pakistan and the US Navy, while the Iranian P-3F is basically similar. A number of specially modified aircraft are active with the US Navy, including the EP-3E, which is used for the acquisition of electronic intelligence.

SPECIAL FEATURES

The P-3 is a low-wing monoplane design, with a capacious weapons bay in the forward fuselage and bulged observation windows to port and starboard, fore and aft of the wing. The most notable feature of the Orion is the magnetic anomaly detector 'stinger', which extends aft from the tail cone. The Orion's wing planform is also unusual in having a straight leading edge.

VARIANTS

US manufacture of the Orion totalled about 650 aircraft, of three basic versions. Production opened

with 157 examples of the **P-3A**, before switching to the **P-3B** (144 built) in 1965. This version differed mainly in being fitted with more powerful T56 engines and able to carry and launch the AGM-12 Bullpup missile, some 144 being completed before the advent of the definitive **P-3C** in 1969. By the time Lockheed rolled-out its final example in 1995, a total of 348 P-3Cs and variants had been completed, with ongoing avionics improvements resulting in the appearance of different versions known as **Update I**, **Update II**, **Update II.5**, **Update II.75** and **Update III**, plus Canada's **CP-140** and **CP-140A**. The type's licence manufacture by Kawasaki in Japan added another 110 aircraft to the total, these mostly being P-3Cs. Lockheed Martin is offering a re-engined **P-3C Plus** and **Orion 2000**.

P-3C Orion Japanese Maritime Self-Defence Force

Lockheed C-141 StarLifter

FOUR-TURBOFAN STRATEGIC TRANSPORT

C-141B StarLifter United States Air Force

DEVELOPMENT

Evolution of the Lockheed StarLifter came about in response to a US Air Force requirement of May 1960. This called for a new jet-powered transport aircraft capable of carrying a 27,215kg (60,000lb) payload over 6,480km (4,026 miles) and led to a request for proposals in December 1960. Several US manufacturers responded, Lockheed's L-300 securing a development contract in April 1961. The first StarLifter made its maiden flight from Marietta, Georgia on 17 December 1963, and no fewer than 284 C-141As were eventually built for the Military Air Transport Service (MATS) and its successor, Military Airlift Command (MAC). Entry into service occurred in October 1964, with the first operational mission taking place on 23 April 1965. Deliveries were completed in February 1968. It was subsequently realised that the potential existed to 'stretch' the basic design and incorporate in-flight refuelling capability, so as to gain the equivalent of 90 extra aircraft, while simultaneously boosting their productivity. In 1976, Lockheed was directed to modify a standard C-141A to the YC-141B prototype and this flew for the first time on 24 March 1977. So successful was the idea that 270 aircraft were brought to C-141B standard by Lockheed, with deliveries taking place between December 1979 and June 1982. Many of these remain in service today, but the most recent development has been the installation of modern

C-141B StarLifter United States Air Force

'glass cockpits' on approximately 66 aircraft of the Air National Guard and Air Force Reserve Command. Upgraded aircraft are known as C-141Cs.

CURRENT SERVICE

Delivery of Boeing C-17A Globemaster IIIs to Air Mobility Command means that the StarLifter era is drawing to a close, with aircraft being steadily retired as they are replaced by new equipment. However, a reasonable number are still active with first-line units at McGuire AFB, New Jersey (305th Air Mobility Wing) and McChord AFB, Washington (62nd Airlift Wing) and many more equip second-line Air National Guard and Air Force Reserve Command squadrons, with whom they are expected to remain in use for some considerable time.

SPECIAL FEATURES

High wing, T-tail, upswept aft fuselage with clamshell rear loading doors and pod-mounted engines were all distinguishing features of the first truly effective strategic jet transport to enter service with the US Air Force. Latterly, conversion to C-141B standard added a distinctive hump above the forward fuselage, with this housing the in-flight refuelling receptacle. A small number of C-141Bs feature SOLL (Special Operations Low Level) equipment, which includes a FLIR turret and additional survivability measures.

TECHNICAL DATA

Lockheed C-141B StarLifter
Powerplants: Four Pratt & Whitney TF33-P-7 turbofans
Developing: 93.41kN (21,000lb st)
Span: 48.74m (159ft 11in)
Length: 51.29m (168ft 3.5in)
Height: 11.96m (39ft 3in)
All-up weight: 155,580kg (343,000lb)
Maximum speed: 910km/h (566mph)
Cruise speed: 796km/h (495mph)
Operational Ceiling: 41,600ft
Range with max payload: 4,725km (2,935 miles)
Accommodation: Five crew, up to 205 passengers
Payload: 41,222kg (90,880lb)
First flown: 17 December 1963
Entered service: October 1964

VARIANTS

Almost all of the original short-fuselage **C-141As** had left the USAF inventory by 1982, apart from four aircraft that used the **NC-141A** designation to indicate assignment to test tasks, since retired. Today, the only variants in service are the **C-141B** and **C-141C**, which are externally identical.

Lockheed C-5 Galaxy

FOUR-TURBOFAN STRATEGIC TRANSPORT

C-5B Galaxy United States Air Force

DEVELOPMENT

The C-5 Galaxy had its origins in the US Air Force's CX-HLS (Cargo Experimental – Heavy Logistics System) requirement of 1963, which called for an aircraft with the ability to carry a 113,400 kg (250,000lb) payload over 4,828km (3,000 miles) without the aid of in-flight refuelling. Lockheed's L-500 proposal was eventually chosen and a total of 81 C-5As was ordered for service with Military Airlift Command, with delivery being accomplished between December 1969 and May 1973. The early period of service was not without problems – wing cracks eventually necessitated a major re-winging programme carried out on 77 surviving aircraft between 1981 and 1987. By then, efforts to bolster USAF heavy lift capability had resulted in the Galaxy being reinstated in production as the C-5B. This was basically similar to the C-5A but incorporated some changes and improvements, such as deletion of the complex cross-wind landing gear of the C-5A and inclusion of an improved AFCS (automated flight control system). Delivery of the 50 C-5Bs ordered was accomplished between January 1986 and April 1989, bringing production to an end, although Lockheed Martin proposed building a new C-5D version in the mid-1990s, but this failed to come to fruition.

CURRENT SERVICE

Some 126 Galaxies are currently active with the USAF. C-5As remain in service with the 60th Air Mobility Wing at Travis AFB, California and the 436th Airlift Wing at Dover AFB, Delaware, while a number have been passed to second-line elements of the Air National Guard (137th Airlift Squadron) and the Air Force Reserve Command (433rd Airlift Wing and 439th Airlift Wing). C-5Bs are assigned only to regular force units at Travis and Dover, while the two C-5Cs also fly from Travis. A few C-5As also serve in the crew training role with the 97th Air Mobility Wing at Altus AFB, Oklahoma.

SPECIAL FEATURES

The most distinctive feature of the Galaxy is the upward-hinged visor nose. This can be raised to facilitate loading from the front, while clamshell doors on the underside of the upswept aft fuselage enable loading and unloading from the rear. In addition, it has a high-wing, T-tailed configuration, with pod-mounted engines and passenger cabins on the fore and aft upper deck.

VARIANTS

The **C-5A** was the initial production version and the most numerous derivative, with 81 being built, two of which were subsequently modified to **C-5C** standard, with sealed visor noses and strengthened interiors to accommodate satellites, boosters and other space equipment. The only other version to attain production is the **C-5B**, of which 50 were built in the latter half of the 1980s.

TECHNICAL DATA

Lockheed C-5B Galaxy

Powerplants: Four General Electric TF39-GE-1C turbofans
Developing: 191.27kN (43,000lb st)
Span: 67.88m (222ft 8.5in)
Length: 75.54m (247ft 10in)
Height: 19.85m (65ft 1.5in)
All-up weight: 379,657kg (837,000lb)
Maximum speed: 919km/h (571mph)
Cruise speed: 833km/h (518mph)
Operational Ceiling: 35,750ft
Range with max payload: 5,526km (3,434 miles)
Accommodation: Five crew, plus up to 360 troops/passengers
Payload: 118,387kg (261,000lb)
First flown: 30 June 1968 (C-5A); 10 September 1985 (C-5B)
Entered service: 17 December 1969 (C-5A); 8 January 1986 (C-5B)

C-5B Galaxy United States Air Force

Lockheed L-1011 TriStar

THREE-TURBOFAN STRATEGIC TANKER/TRANSPORT AIRCRAFT

Tristar KC1 Royal Air Force

TECHNICAL DATA

Lockheed L-1011-500 TriStar

Powerplants: Three Rolls-Royce RB211-524B4 turbofans
Developing: 222.41kN (50,000lb st)
Span: 50.09m (164ft 4in)
Length: 50.05m (164ft 2.5in)
Height: 16.87m (55ft 4in)
All-up weight: 244,944kg (540,000lb)
Maximum speed: 806km/h (501mph)
Cruise speed: 890km/h (553mph)
Maximum range: 7,783km (4,836miles)
Accommodation: Crew of 13, plus up to 400 passengers (airline configuration)
Payload: 44,390kg (97,861lb)
First flown: 16 November 1970 (L-1011-1); 9 July 1985 (RAF version)
Entered service: April 1972 (L-1011-1); March 1986 (K1)

DEVELOPMENT

Work on what eventually became the L-1011 TriStar was initiated in January 1966, when Lockheed began a study of future airline requirements for short-to-medium-haul passenger transport aircraft. Initial studies envisaged a twin-engined machine, but a three-engined configuration was eventually chosen in the wake of discussion with potential customers and the Rolls-Royce RB211 was selected to power the new transport. Manufacture of the first aircraft commenced in March 1969, with this being rolled-out in September 1970. A maiden flight followed some two months later. On conclusion of an extensive flight test programme, FAA certification was achieved in April 1972 and entry into scheduled passenger service with Eastern Air Lines occurred shortly before the end of that month. Subsequent development resulted in the appearance of a number of longer-ranged versions for domestic and overseas operators, but competition with the broadly similar McDonnell Douglas DC-10 limited sales and production eventually terminated in June 1985, by which time approximately 250 TriStars had been built.

CURRENT SERVICE

Military use of the Lockheed Tristar is confined to the United Kingdom, with the Royal Air Force having obtained nine former civil L-1011-500s for service with No 216 Squadron at RAF Brize Norton. These perform in-flight refuelling, troop transport and cargo airlift missions. A single example of the L-1011-500 also serves with the Jordanian Royal Flight in civil markings, while the Saudi Arabian government operates two L-1011-500s, which also carry civil identities.

SPECIAL FEATURES

Low-wing design with two engines in pods suspended from wing and a third engine buried in aft fuselage and fed by an air intake duct forward of and faired into the vertical tail surface. RAF tanker versions are fitted with additional fuel cells in the former baggage holds, as well as an in-flight refuelling probe above the cockpit. They also have two hose drum units beneath the aft fuselage section.

VARIANTS

Five basic variants of the commercial airliner were produced, starting with the L-1011-1, which entered scheduled service in April 1972. Further development led to the L-1011-100, L-1011-200 and L-1011-250, all of which were longer-ranged versions. The final derivative, the L-1011-500 extended range model, had a fuselage that was shortened by 4.11m (13ft 6in) but was otherwise identical to its predecessors. All nine RAF Tristars began life with either British Airways or Pan American as **L-1011-500s**, but were extensively modified into four different configurations by Marshall Aerospace during the late 1980s and early 1990s. RAF versions comprise the **K1** tanker/transport (two), **KC1** tanker/cargo aircraft (four), **C2** transport (two) and **C2A** transport (one).

Tristar K1 Royal Air Force

ROYAL AIR FORCE   ZD950

Lockheed S-3 Viking

TWIN-TURBOFAN ANTI-SUBMARINE WARFARE AIRCRAFT

S-3B Viking United States Navy

DEVELOPMENT
The S-3 Viking came about in response to the US Navy's VSX requirement of 1964, which called for a new carrier-based ASW aircraft to replace the Grumman S-2 Tracker. Several companies submitted design proposals, with Lockheed's being adjudged the most suitable and the company was awarded a contract for eight YS-3A test aircraft in August 1969. Trials with these commenced with the maiden flight in January 1972, and Lockheed eventually secured a production contract for 179 aircraft, which were delivered to the US Navy between 1974-78. Introduction to operational service came in 1975 aboard the USS *John F. Kennedy*. After several years of service, an upgrade programme was launched in 1981 that retained the basic S-3A airframe, but incorporated a new avionics suite and enhanced weapons capabilities, prompting adoption of the S-3B designation, with just over 120 of the original aircraft being brought to this standard during the course of the 1980s.

CURRENT SERVICE
With the end of the Cold War, the US Navy's carrier-borne aviation force has been significantly reduced. Several of the squadrons that used the S-3B have been disestablished, but it is still part of the operational inventory and presently equips ten deployable squadrons. The primary mission continues to be ASW, but it also has a secondary role as an aerial tanker for other carrier-borne forces such as the F-14 Tomcat and F/A-18 Hornet, and may also perform bombing and attack missions against sea and land targets. In addition to the front-line squadrons mentioned, the S-3B serves with a permanently shore-based training establishment at NAS North Island, California, which provides air and ground crew to units of both major fleets. One or two S-3Bs serve with test organisations at Patuxent River, Maryland.

SPECIAL FEATURES
Fundamentally conventional in appearance, the S-3 Viking features a high wing with underslung podded engines and also incorporates wing and tail folding to permit stowage in the restricted confines of carrier hangar decks when at sea. Two weapons bays allow for internal carriage of bombs, torpedoes and depth charges. Further stores, including ordnance, fuel tanks and buddy pods, can be carried externally, with each wing having a single pylon located outboard of the engine and adjacent to the wing-fold joint.

VARIANTS
The only variant of the Viking that is still in use is the **S-3B**, but several other versions have served with the US Navy. The most notable of these was the **ES-3A**, some 16 examples of which were obtained in the early 1990s through conversion of the S-3A for carrier-based electronic intelligence tasks (ELINT). These equipped two squadrons but were retired in 1998-99. Six other aircraft were adapted for transport roles (COD) as the **US-3A**, but have long since been withdrawn, while one of the eight **YS-3A** testbeds was adapted as a **KS-3A** tanker, although this version was not proceeded with.

TECHNICAL DATA

Lockheed S-3B Viking
Powerplants: Two General Electric TF34-GE-2 turbofans
Developing: 41.26kN (9,275lb st)
Span: 20.93m (68ft 8in)
Length: 16.26m (53ft 4in)
Height: 6.93m (22ft 9in)
All-up weight: 23,832kg (52,540lb)
Maximum speed: 814km/h (506mph)
Cruise speed: 649km/h (403mph)
Operational Ceiling: 35,000ft
Ferry range: exceeds 5,558km (3,454 miles)
Accommodation: Four (two pilots, tactical co-ordinator, sensor systems operator)
Payload: 3,175kg (7,000lb)
First flown: 21 January 1972 (S-3A); September 1984 (S-3B)
Entered service: 20 February 1974 (S-3A)

S-3B Viking United States Navy

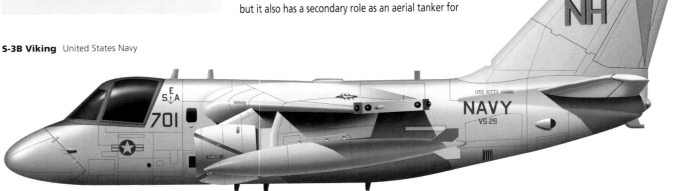

Lockheed F-117 Nighthawk

TWIN-TURBOFAN SINGLE-SEAT LOW-OBSERVABLE 'STEALTH' STRIKE FIGHTER

F-117A Nighthawk United States Air Force

DEVELOPMENT

The two top secret Experimental Stealth Technology (XST) *Have Blue* proof of concept aircraft, designed and built by the Lockheed Skunk Works' Advanced Development Project Office, were first flown at Groom Lake, Nevada in December 1977. Although both XSTs crashed, a production programme (*Senior Trend*) began with the first of five development F-117s being assembled flying from Tonopah, Nevada on 18 June 1981. For the next seven years, all flying took place at night – the project and 59 production F-117As remaining hidden from public view. The 4450th Tactical Group was formed at Tonopah to introduce the 'stealth fighter' into service, receiving its first aircraft on 23 August 1982. In November 1988, the first photographs of the F-117 were released, and the following year it was seen in action, when two F-117s each dropped a 2,000lb laser guided bomb on an army barracks in Panama on 21 December 1989, during Operation *Just Cause*. Popularly known as the Nighthawk, and operated by the 37th Fighter Wing at Holloman AFB, New Mexico, 40 F-117s were deployed to the Gulf in 1991. Flying 1,270 missions after opening the air war, the F-117s dropped nearly one-third of Coalition precision-guided weapons during the conflict. In 1998-99 further deployments were made to the Gulf, and to bases in Italy and Germany for use over the Balkans.

CURRENT SERVICE

52 of the 59 F-117s originally built are currently in service with the USAF's 12th Air Force – the 49th FW (8th & 9th Fighter Squadrons) based at Holloman AFB, New Mexico, and a small detachment of the 53rd Wing for fighter development, at the same base.

SPECIAL FEATURES

The F-117 has a unique multi-faceted (angled flat surfaces) shape to minimise radar returns. Engine gases mix with bypass air and exit through 'platypus' shielded exhausts to dissipate heat emissions and reduce the infrared (IR) signature. The V-shaped tailplane comprises upper section slab 'ruddervators' that combine the functions of rudders and elevators. Key surfaces are coated with radar absorbent material (RAM) and composite materials are widely used to absorb unreflected radar energy. Weapons are carried internally, with the bomb doors only opening momentarily to release the warload.

VARIANTS

No major variants have been revealed, although five stages of up-grade had been completed by March 1997. These have included new flight management system and navigation computers, revised cockpit layout, new infrared warning sensors and improved target acquisition and weapons systems. Further

TECHNICAL DATA

Lockheed F-117A Nighthawk

Powerplants: Two General Electric F404-GE-F1D2 turbofans
Developing: 48.04kN (10,800lb st)
Span: 13.20m (43ft 3in)
Length: 20.08m (65ft 11in)
Height: 3.78m (12ft 5in)
All-up weight: 23,810kg (52,390lb)
Maximum speed: 1,040km/h (646mph)
Cruise speed: Mach 0.9
Mission range: 1,112km (691 miles)
Accommodation: Pilot only
Warload: GBU-10 or GBU-27 Paveway LGBs carried in internal weapons bay, plus conventional bombs of up to 2,000lb (907kg) weight each, typically GBU-10 and GBU-27, up to a maximum load of 5,000lb (2,268kg). Tactical munitions dispensers and missiles including Maverick or HARM can also be carried, along with AIM-9L Sidewinders for self-defence. New weapons include GBU-30s (JDAM) and JSOW.
First flown: December 1977 (XST); 18 June 1981 (pre-series)
Entered service: 23 August 1982

improvements are on-going to enable the F-117 to remain in front-line service until 2015.

F-117A Nighthawk United States Air Force

Lockheed Martin F-22 Raptor

TWIN-TURBOFAN AIR SUPERIORITY FIGHTER

F-22A Raptor United States Air Force

DEVELOPMENT

Expected to begin supplanting the F-15 Eagle as the USAF's premier air superiority fighter in a few years time, the F-22 Raptor has its origins in the Advanced Tactical Fighter requirement of the early 1980s. With potentially lucrative design and production contracts in prospect, several major US aerospace companies submitted proposals by July 1986, with Lockheed Martin and Northrop subsequently being directed to build two prototype aircraft and a ground-based avionics test bed. Following competitive evaluation of the YF-22 against Northrop's futuristic YF-23 in 1990-91, the Lockheed submission was announced as the winner on 23 April 1991, with a contract for the engineering and manufacturing development (EMD) phase being awarded on 2 August 1991. The EMD contract initially called for 11 aircraft, but this was amended in January 1993 to just nine, although this total still included a pair of two-seaters. Subsequent revision of the programme in 1996 resulted in plans for a two-seater being cancelled.

CURRENT SERVICE

The first two EMD F-22s are currently undergoing trials at Edwards AFB, California, where they will be joined by four more aircraft during 2000. Initial USAF operational test and evaluation is currently scheduled to begin at Nellis AFB, Nevada in 2002, with the first

combat-ready unit due to achieve initial operational capability (IOC) in late 2005 or early 2006.

SPECIAL FEATURES

Although not as radical in appearance as the F-117, extensive use of low-observable technology and materials is a key feature of the F-22. Other aids to much enhanced survivability arise from a 'first-look, first-shot, first-kill' capability, hence it being referred to as an air dominance fighter by Lockheed Martin. Stealth attributes include flush and buried antenna to reduce radar cross section, highly contoured air ducts, and internal housing of missile armament – the F-22A having a large ventral weapons bay and two smaller bays in the air intake sides.

VARIANTS

The **F-22A** is the baseline air dominance fighter version, which is currently the only model on order for service with the USAF. Original procurement plans called for a total of 648 aircraft, of which the majority would be F-22As. However, at the beginning of 1994, total planned procurement was reduced to 442 and yet another cut came in May 1997, when the total buy was set at the current level of 348 (including nine EMD machines). At one time, it was intended that two EMD examples and 42 production copies of a two-seat version designated **F-22B** would be acquired, but the

TECHNICAL DATA

Lockheed Martin F-22A Raptor

Powerplants: Two Pratt & Whitney F119-PW-100 turbofans

Developing: In 156kN (35,000lbst) class

Span: 13.56m (44ft 6in)

Length: 18.92m (62ft 1in)

Height: 5.02m (16ft 5in)

Maximum weight: 27,216kg (60,000lb)

Maximum speed: 1,482km/h (921mph)

Operational ceiling: Over 50,000ft

Accommodation: Pilot only

Warload: Full details still classified, but known to include AIM-9 Sidewinder and AIM-120 AMRAAM air-to-air missiles, AIM-9X next-generation AAM and GBU-32 Joint Direct Attack Munition. Also fitted with M61A2 20mm cannon and 480 rounds of ammunition.

First flown: 29 September 1990 (YF-22); 7 September 1997 (first EMD F-22)

Service entry: 2005 (initial operational capability of first combat-ready unit)

development of this model was terminated in July 1996 as part of a series of economies to reduce overall programme costs.

F-22A Raptor United States Air Force

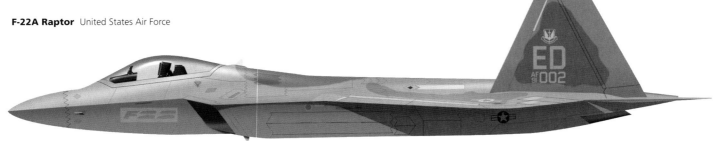

Lockheed Martin (General Dynamics) F-16A/B Fighting Falcon

SINGLE TURBOFAN MULTI-ROLE FIGHTER AIRCRAFT

F-16A Fighting Falcon Belgian Air Force

DEVELOPMENT

Originally conceived as an unsophisticated and uncompromised lightweight air combat fighter, today's F-16 bears only a superficial resemblance to the YF-16 prototype of the early 1970s. The initial impetus for the Fighting Falcon stemmed from the Pentagon's so-called 'fighter mafia', which argued for a small warplane possessing superlative performance to complement the sophisticated F-15 Eagle. General Dynamics faced a formidable challenge from Northrop's YF-17, two examples of each being built for a fly-off. This was won by the F-16, with General Dynamics receiving a contract for six full-scale development F-16As and two F-16B two-seaters. Even then, its future was not assured, but selection in June 1975 to replace

the Starfighter with four European nations was the big breakthrough. Since then, more than 4,000 have been built and production of the F-16C/D versions continues today.

CURRENT SERVICE

With only a few examples still to be delivered to Taiwan, production of the initial F-16A and F-16B versions is now virtually complete. Not surprisingly, the US Air Force was the major customer, buying almost 800, while other air arms that received new-build F-16A/B aircraft are Belgium, Denmark, Egypt, Indonesia, Israel, the Netherlands, Norway, Pakistan, Portugal, Singapore, Thailand and Venezuela. In addition, there are plenty of second-hand F-16s

available, with those that have obtained aircraft from this source being Denmark, Israel, Jordan, Portugal and Thailand.

SPECIAL FEATURES

Arguably the single most distinctive feature of the Fighting Falcon is the location of the air inlet directly beneath the forward fuselage below the cockpit, which gives it a unique silhouette. Other novel aspects are the cropped delta wing planform and the fuselage forebody, which incorporates highly swept vortex control strakes.

VARIANTS

The basic production version is the **F-16A**, of which 1,432 were built. In addition, 312 **F-16B** two-seaters were also completed. Local modification in Holland resulted in the appearance of the **F-16A(R)**, with an Orpheus pod for reconnaissance, while the **F-16(ADF)** that equips the Air National Guard stemmed from a modification project involving a total of 272 Air Defence Fighters to replace the F-106 Delta Dart and F-4 Phantom. Most recently, the Mid-Life Update (MLU) of Belgian, Danish, Dutch and Norwegian aircraft has resulted in the **F-16AM** and **F-16BM** designations being adopted to identify modernised Fighting Falcons.

F-16B Fighting Falcon Royal Netherlands Air Force

TECHNICAL DATA

Lockheed Martin F-16A Fighting Falcon

Powerplant: One Pratt & Whitney F100-PW-100 turbofan
Developing: 65.26kN (14,670lbst) dry; 106.0kN (23,830lbst) with afterburner
Span: 10.00m (32ft 9.75in) with tip-mounted missiles
Length: 15.03m (49ft 4in)
Height: 5.01m (16ft 5in)
Maximum weight: 14,968kg (33,000lb)
Maximum speed: Exceeds 2,124km/h (1,320mph)
Operational ceiling: In excess of 50,000ft
Ferry range: Exceeds 3,891km (2,418 miles)
Accommodation: Pilot only (two pilots in F-16B)
Warload: 6,895kg (15,200lb) including AIM-9 Sidewinder IR-homing air-to-air missiles, AGM-65 Maverick air-to-surface guided missiles; conventional, laser-guided and cluster bombs. Some aircraft, including ADF version, compatible with radar-guided AIM-7 Sparrow AAM and AIM-120 AMRAAM. Single integral Vulcan M61A1 20mm cannon mounted in port wing root, with 511 rounds
First flown: 20 January 1974 (YF-16); 8 December 1976 (first FSD F-16A); 7 August 1978 (first production F-16A)
Entered service: January 1979 (initial deliveries to USAF and Belgian Air Force)

Lockheed Martin (General Dynamics) F-16C/D Fighting Falcon

SINGLE TURBOFAN MULTI-ROLE FIGHTER AIRCRAFT

F-16D Fighting Falcon Hellenic Air Force

TECHNICAL DATA

Lockheed Martin F-16C Fighting Falcon

Powerplant: One Pratt & Whitney F100 turbofan (Block 25/32/42/52) or one General Electric F110 turbofan (Block 30/40/50)

Developing: Typically 129.4-131.6kN (29,100-29,588lbst) with afterburner on latest Block 50/52 aircraft

Span: 10.00m (32ft 9.75in) with tip-mounted missiles

Length: 15.03m (49ft 4in)

Height: 5.09m (16ft 8.5in)

Maximum weight: 19,187kg (42,000lb)

Maximum speed: Exceeds Mach 2

Operational ceiling: In excess of 50,000ft

Ferry range: 4,215km (2,619 miles)

Combat radius: 1,252km (780 miles) with two 907kg (2,000lb) bombs, two AIM-9 missiles and 1,040 US gallons external fuel on hi-lo-lo-hi attack profile

Accommodation: Pilot only (two pilots in F-16D)

Warload: 7,226kg (15,930lb) on Block 52 aircraft; weapon options include AIM-9 Sidewinder or Rafael Python 3/4 IR-homing air-to-air missiles; AIM-7 Sparrow and AIM-120 AMRAAM radar-guided missiles; AGM-65 Maverick air-to-surface guided missile; AGM-88 HARM anti-radar missile; AGM-84 Harpoon anti-ship attack missile; conventional, laser-guided and cluster bombs. New weapons including the Joint Direct Attack Munition, the Joint Stand-Off Weapon and the Wind-Corrected Munitions Dispenser will be used in due course. Single Vulcan M61A1 20mm cannon in port wing root, with 511 rounds

First flown: 14 December 1982 (first MSIP-configured F-16);
19 June 1984 (first production F-16C)

Entered service: 19 July 1984 (initial delivery to USAF)

DEVELOPMENT

With the original production models well established in service in the USA and Europe, attention turned to increasing the already formidable capabilities of the F-16. This process was known as MSIP (Multinational Staged Improvement Program) and began with MSIP I, which concerned the F-16A/B versions, being essentially a retrofit project. In 1984, MSIP II introduced new-build F-16C Block 25 aircraft with revised core avionics, cockpit and airframe changes, while MSIP III began in 1987 and dealt with new systems as they became available. Despite this, the basic F-16C (F-16D for two-seaters) designation was retained throughout, with the different configurations identified by Block number.

CURRENT SERVICE

Although produced in greater numbers than the F-16A/B series, the F-16C/D serves with fewer air arms, recipients being Bahrain, Egypt, Greece, Israel, South Korea, Singapore, Turkey and the US Air Force.

SPECIAL FEATURES

The F-16C and F-16D are readily recognised by virtue of an enlarged dorsal extension to the vertical tail,

from which a small blade antenna protrudes upwards. Many examples also feature special systems housed in pods fixed to the inlet sides. These 'bolt-on' refinements include LANTIRN (Low Altitude Navigation and Targeting Infrared for Night), which allows all-weather precision attack missions to be flown, and AN/ASQ-213 HTS (HARM Targeting System) for the 'Wild Weasel' defence suppression role. Less obvious changes relate to the engine, with Block 25/32/42/52 aircraft using variants of the Pratt & Whitney F100, while Block 30/40/50 aircraft have the General Electric F110. Some Israeli and Singaporean F-16Ds feature a 'big spine' containing additional avionics.

VARIANTS

Approximately 2,300 second-generation Fighting Falcons have been ordered to date. Most are single-seat **F-16Cs**, although there are numerous sub-variants, these being identified by Block number, as indicated elsewhere. The two-seat **F-16D** is similar, albeit less numerous. Ongoing updating efforts have resulted in development of the **Block 50+** and **Block 60**, but there is no guarantee they will be the ultimate Fighting Falcons.

F-16C Fighting Falcon United States Air Force

Lockheed Martin Alenia C-27J Spartan

TWIN-TURBOPROP TACTICAL MEDIUM TRANSPORT

C-27J Spartan

DEVELOPMENT

Lockheed Martin Alenia Tactical Transport Systems (LMATTS) was officially established to develop and produce the C-27J Spartan in November 1996, as a joint venture between Alenia Aerospazio of Italy and Lockheed Martin. The new type was intended as a major development of Alenia's popular G222 tactical transport (already in service as the C-27A with the US Air Force), to create a 'smaller brother' of the C-130J Hercules, using the same AE2100 engines as the larger machine, and numerous common elements of the digital avionics fitment – thus achieving interoperability between the two types – but retaining the proven G222 airframe and dimensions. Under the terms of their agreement, Lockheed Martin are responsible for the engines and avionics, and are providing worldwide marketing resources. Alenia undertook the certification process and are performing flight testing from their

Italian facility (both C-27Js flying as of August 2000 are Italian-registered). It is likely that full Italian civil certification of the C-27J to the European Joint Airworthiness Requirements (JAR) will be achieved early in 2001.

CURRENT SERVICE

The C-27J is yet to enter service, but two prototypes (of which the first is a converted G222, lacking some new systems, and the second a new-build aircraft) are currently being tested by Alenia Aerospazia. It was announced on 11 November 1999 that the Italian Air Force would purchase a dozen of the type as launch customer, to replace ageing G222s, with deliveries to commence in 2001 and continue for three years. Other military orders are awaited, as the C-27J is on the shortlists of several other air arms who require new tactical transports.

SPECIAL FEATURES

A major feature of the C-27J is its short-field performance, with a landing run of less than 500 metres on unprepared strips at maximum take-off weight. The design has been optimised for operation under austere conditions, with no ground support equipment required for loading and unloading, while a 'kneeling' undercarriage making these processes easier on uneven ground and facilitates the boarding of vehicles straight into the hold, via the hydraulically operated door and ramp under the rear fuselage. The cargo hold itself has shown itself in trials to be easily capable of carrying jet engines such as those used by the F-16 and Eurofighter without special handling equipment, and the C-27J can transport military vehicles up to the size of the 'Hummer' with room to spare. In addition, an OH-58 Kiowa helicopter was loaded without difficulty during these tests. The type's airdrop capability is enhanced by the fitment of the advanced new APN-241 search radar and the cockpit's night vision capability. It is fitted with the C-130Js advanced EFIS cockpit displays.

VARIANTS

So far, only the basic **C-27J** transport has been ordered and flight tested, but the manufacturer says that the type is well-suited to other roles as a special missions aircraft. Among these could be as a platform for the US Army's Aerial Common Sensor, an advanced surveillance and reconnaissance system – its ability to cruise at over 20,000ft being an important point in its favour, according to LMATTS.

TECHNICAL DATA

Lockheed Martin Alenia C-27J Spartan

Powerplants: Two Rolls-Royce Allison AE2100D3 turboprops
Developing: 3,458kW (4,640eshp)
Driving: Six-blade propellers
Span: 28.70m (94ft 2in)
Length: 22.70m (74ft 5.5in)
Height: 9.80m (32ft 1.8in)
All-up weight: 30,000kg (66,139lb)
Maximum speed: 487km/h (303mph)
Cruise speed: 440km/h (273mph)
Operational ceiling: 22,000ft
Maximum range: 2,780km (1,727 miles)
Accommodation: Crew of two or three, plus loadmaster. Accommodation for 46 fully equipped troops or 40 paratroopers
Warload: None
First flown: 24 September 1999
Entered service: Due to enter the Italian Air Force inventory in 2001

C-27J Spartan

LTV (Vought) A-7 Corsair II

SINGLE TURBOFAN ATTACK AIRCRAFT

TA-7 Corsair Hellenic Air Force

TECHNICAL DATA

LTV A-7H Corsair II

Powerplant: One Allison TF41-A-400 turbofan
Developing: 64.50kN (14,500lbst)
Span: 11.81m (38ft 9in)
Length: 14.06m (46ft 1.5in)
Height: 4.90m (16ft 1in)
All-up weight: 17,838kg (39,325lb)
Maximum speed: 1,126km/h (700mph)
Cruise speed: 869km/h (540mph)
Operational ceiling: 42,000ft
Ferry range: 4,900km (3,045 miles)
Combat radius: 1,110km (690 miles), hi-lo-hi mission profile with two fuel tanks and eight Mk82 227kg (500lb) bombs
Accommodation: Pilot only
Warload: Varying from 4,309 kg (9,500lb) to 6,804kg (15,000lb) depending on fuel load; weapons options include bombs, cluster bombs, rockets, napalm, AGM-65 Maverick air-to-surface attack missile and AIM-9 Sidewinder IR-homing air-to-air missile. An internal Vulcan M61A1 20mm multi-barrel cannon with 1,000 rounds is also fitted as standard
First flown: 27 September 1965 (YA-7A); 26 September 1968 (A-7D); January 1981 (A-7K)
Entered service: September 1966 (A-7A)

DEVELOPMENT

Originally conceived as a carrier-borne attack aircraft for the US Navy, the A-7 Corsair was subsequently purchased by the US Air Force and saw considerable combat action with both services during the Vietnam War, as well as with the Navy in the Gulf War, shortly before it was phased out. The A-7 was one of several design submissions in response to the 1963 request from the US Navy for a light attack aircraft with a greater range and payload than the A-4 Skyhawk, which it would largely replace. After studying the various proposals, Vought's contender was selected and a development contract was awarded. Progress thereafter was swift, with the first prototype flying in September 1965 and operational introduction following barely a year later. Subsequent development resulted in the TF41 engine being adopted in place of the Pratt & Whitney TF30 on later production versions for the Navy (A-7E) and USAF (A-7D).

CURRENT SERVICE

The Corsair is operational with Greece and Thailand, primarily in the maritime strike role, for which it is well suited. Greece was in fact the first overseas air arm to get the Corsair, receiving 60 A-7H and five TA-7H aircraft in the mid-1970s, augmenting these with a similar quantity of former US Navy A-7Es and TA-7Cs

at a later date. Surplus US Navy aircraft also found their way to the Far East in 1995, when 14 A-7Es and four TA-7Cs were delivered to the Royal Thai Navy.

SPECIAL FEATURES

Resembling the F-8 Crusader, the A-7 Corsair is shorter and squatter, although the basic configuration is similar, with the A-7 having a high-wing and low-set tailplane as well as a nose air inlet duct. There the two types diverge, as the A-7 is optimised for strike/attack missions and has a non-afterburning turbofan engine for maximum economy. Special equipment for carrier operations included a nose-tow link, arrester hook and wing-fold capability.

VARIANTS

Four versions are currently in use. Single-seat **A-7E** and **A-7H** derivatives are tasked with strike/attack duties, while there are also two trainer models, specifically the **TA-7C** and **TA-7H**, both of which are two-seaters with limited strike capability. Equivalent **A-7P** and **TA-7Ps** were used until 1999 by the Portuguese Air Force.

A-7 Corsair Hellenic Air Force

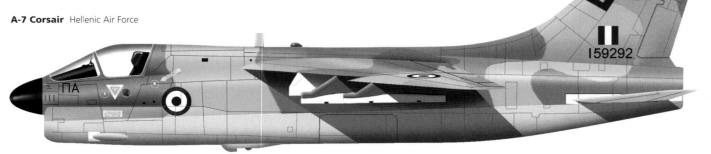

Maule M-7 Series

SINGLE PISTON-ENGINED LIGHT TRAINER/UTILITY AIRCRAFT

Maule M-7

DEVELOPMENT

Maule Air Inc was initially established to produce the M-4, which was basically an improvement on the Piper Cub. Production of the M-4 terminated in 1975 and the Maule name remained in abeyance until 1984, when the present company came into being to build the M-5 Lunar Rocket and M-7 Super Rocket. Based on the earlier M-6-235, the latter type featured an extended cabin with additional windows. Subsequent development has resulted in the appearance of an almost bewildering array of versions, with the M-7 series now available in both tricycle and tailwheel undercarriage landplane form and for operation from water as a floatplane. In 1999, at least 14 different models were actively being marketed.

CURRENT SERVICE

Approximately 700 examples of the M-7 series have been built to date, although relatively few of them were produced for military customers. Nevertheless,

at least three nations are known to use versions of the M-7, with Mexico being the major purchaser, having obtained at least 30 MXT-7-180s for the Air Force and Navy, as well as half-a-dozen M-7-235 for the Air Force. The Royal Thai Army has about 18 MX-7s for pilot training, while the Turkish Coast Guard has a solitary example that was delivered in 1993.

SPECIAL FEATURES

Numerous variants of the basic Maule M-7 series exist, with some having a tailwheel undercarriage, while others are fitted with tricycle landing gear (indicated by 'T' in the aircraft designation, as in MXT-7-180). Various powerplant options also exist, these including a range of piston engines from Textron Lycoming plus a recently developed turbine-powered model, which is fitted with an Allison 250-B17C. In each case, the number in the basic designation indicates the horsepower rating of the installed engine (such as MX-7-180C, which has a 180hp engine).

VARIANTS

The current production versions are the **MX-7-160 Sportplane** four-seater; the **MXT-7-160 Comet** (formerly known as the Maule Trainer); the **MX-7-180A Sportplane**; the **MXT-7-180A Comet**; the **MX-7-180B Star Rocket**; the **MX-7-180C**; the **MXT-7-180 Star Rocket**; the **M-7-235B Super Rocket**; the **M-7-235C Orion**; the **MT-7-235 Super Rocket**; the **M-7-260**; the **M-7-260C**; the **MT-7-260** and the **M-7-420AC**. These variants also differ in many other details, such as accommodation, flap setting option and even the type of wing that is fitted, with tailwheel models having long-span units, while tricycle models have a shorter-span wing. Floatplane versions are also available, although none are believed to be in military service.

TECHNICAL DATA

Maule XT-7-180A

Powerplant: One Textron Lycoming O-360-C4F piston engine
Developing: 134kW (180hp)
Driving: Two-blade propeller
Span: 9.40m (30ft 10in)
Length: 7.16m (23ft 6in)
Height: 2.54m (8ft 4in)
Maximum weight: 1,089kg (2,400lb)
Maximum speed: 248km/h (154mph)
Cruise speed: 217km/h (135mph)
Operational ceiling: 15,000ft
Maximum range: 1,810km (1,125 miles)
Normal range: 804km (500 miles)
Accommodation: Pilot and three or four passengers
First flew: 1968 (M-4); 1975 (M-5)
Entered service: 1984 (M-7 Series introduced)

Maule MXT-7

McDonnell Douglas A-4 Skyhawk

A-4N Skyhawk Israeli Air Force

TECHNICAL DATA

McDonnell Douglas A-4M Skyhawk II
Powerplant: One Pratt & Whitney J52-P-408 turbojet
Developing: 50.0kN (11,200lb st)
Span: 8.38m (27ft 6in)
Length: 12.27m (40ft 3.5in)
Height: 4.57m (15ft 0in)
All-up weight: 11,113kg (24,500lb)
Maximum speed: 1,040km/h (646mph)
Operational ceiling: 38,700ft
Maximum ferry range: 3,225km (2,000miles)
Combat radius: 547km (345 miles) with 1,814kg
(4,000lb) warload
Accommodation: Pilot only
Warload: Maximum ordnance load of 4,153kg
(9,155lb) on five external stores stations;
weapons options include bombs, rockets, air-to-
surface guided missiles and air-to-air missiles;
internal armament consists of two Colt Mk12
20mm cannon in wing roots, each with 200
rounds of ammunition
First flown: 22 June 1954 (XA4D-1 prototype);
10 April 1970 (A-4M prototype)
Entered service: October 1956 (A4D-1);
November 1970 (A-4M)

DEVELOPMENT

Colloquially known as 'Heinemann's Hot Rod' (from its designer, Edward Heinemann) or the 'Tinker Toy Bomber' (a reference to its small size), the Skyhawk originated from Douglas Aircraft in the early 1950s and first flew in Summer 1954. Entering service just over two years later, it became the standard attack aircraft of the US Navy and Marine Corps. Progressive refinement of the basic design allowed it to stay in production until 1979. By then, exactly 2,960 Skyhawks had been built, including several hundred two-seat trainers and many for export.

CURRENT SERVICE

Long since retired from the front-line inventory of the US Navy/Marine Corps, the Skyhawk continued to train aviators for both services until quite recently, with the last TA-4J course being completed in late 1999. Today, less than a dozen TA-4Js still serve with the US Navy in the fleet support role and these are due to be withdrawn by the end of 2000. Overseas, however, a respectable number of Skyhawks are still in first-line service with the air arms of Argentina,

Brazil, Indonesia, Israel, New Zealand and Singapore. In view of this, it will be some time before the last examples are finally retired.

SPECIAL FEATURES

The A-4 is of compact low-wing tailed-delta design with conventional tricycle undercarriage layout and air intakes positioned on the fuselage sides just aft of the cockpit. First installed on the A-4F, many later versions featured a large avionics pack on the upper fuselage, which marred the clean lines and gave rise to a hump-backed appearance. All aircraft have an arrester hook beneath the aft fuselage.

VARIANTS

Quantity production of the Skyhawk began with the **A4D-1** (later **A-4A**). Like the later **A4D-2** (**A-4B**) and **A4D-2N** (**A-4C**), it was fitted with the Wright J65 turbojet engine. With effect from the **A4D-5** (**A-4E**), the J52 became the standard powerplant and all subsequent Skyhawks have used versions of this engine. New-build derivatives included the **A-4F**, **TA-4F**, **TA-4J** and **A-4M** for the USN/MC; the **A-4G** for

Australia; the **A-4H** and **A-4N** for Israel; the **A-4K** for New Zealand and the **A-4KU** for Kuwait. In addition, a number of other versions arose from modification and upgrade projects, including the **A-4L** for the US Navy Reserve; **A-4MB** for Brazil; **A-4P**, **A-4Q** and **A-4AR** for Argentina; **A-4PTM** for Malaysia and the **A-4S** for Singapore. It should be noted that in most cases, two-seat equivalents also exist with overseas air arms.

SEE ALSO: SINGAPORE AEROSPACE A-4SU SUPER SKYHAWK

A-4K Skyhawk Royal New Zealand Air Force

McDonnell Douglas F-4 Phantom II

TWIN-TURBOJET MULTI-ROLE FIGHTER AIRCRAFT

F-4F Phantom II German Air Force

TECHNICAL DATA

McDonnell Douglas F-4E Phantom II
Powerplants: Two General Electric J79-GE-17A turbojets
Developing: 52.53kN (11,810lb st) dry; 79.62kN (17,900lbst) with afterburner
Span: 11.71m (38ft 4.75in)
Length: 19.20m (63ft 0in)
Height: 5.02m (16ft 5.5in)
All-up weight: 28,030kg (61,795lb)
Maximum speed: 2,390km/h (1,485mph)
Cruise speed: 919km/h (571mph)
Operational ceiling: 62,250ft
Ferry range: 3,184km (1,978 miles)
Combat radius: 1,145km (712 miles) on interdiction mission
Accommodation: Pilot and Weapon Systems Operator (WSO)
Warload: Maximum of 7,258kg (16,000lb) can be carried externally, with weapon options dependent upon mission. Air-to-air weaponry includes AIM-9 Sidewinder IR-homing and AIM-7 Sparrow radar-homing missiles, with German upgraded F-4F ICE version able to employ AIM-120 AMRAAM. Air-to-ground ordnance includes bombs, cluster bombs, laser-guided bombs, rockets and guided missiles, including the AGM-65 Maverick and AGM-45 Shrike. Israeli F-4Es compatible with Gabriel anti-ship attack missile. A nose-mounted Vulcan M61A1 20mm cannon is fitted as standard.
First flown: 27 May 1958 (YF4H-1); 30 June 1967 (F-4E)
Entered service: December 1960 (F-4A); October 1967 (F-4E)

DEVELOPMENT

Originally conceived as a shipboard fighter for the US Navy, the Phantom is one of the most successful warplanes of recent times, with over 5,000 built for the US Navy, US Air Force and various allied nations. Progressive improvement led to several versions being developed, with the definitive land-based fighter being the F-4E, which came about as a result of combat experience in southeast Asia. The most significant improvement over previous versions of the Phantom was the addition of an internal gun, and an improved Westinghouse AN/APQ-120 radar fire control system was also adopted. Aerodynamic improvements were made that enhanced manoeuvrability, and it first flew in this guise in June 1967, and entered USAF service later in the year.

CURRENT SERVICE

Pure fighter versions of the Phantom are currently operational with the air arms of Egypt (F-4E), Germany (F-4F and F-4F ICE), Greece (F-4E), Japan (F-4EJKai), South Korea (F-4D/E), Iran (F-4D/E), Israel (F-4E and F-4E-2000 Kurnass) and Turkey (F-4E).

SPECIAL FEATURES

Low-wing monoplane configuration, with marked dihedral on outer panels and anhedral on horizontal tailplanes. Outer wing panels are hinged and can be folded for storage. Twin J79 engines buried in aft fuselage are fed by lateral air intakes that extend forward of the wing leading edge. An arrester hook positioned directly aft of the engine exhaust nozzles is fitted to all versions.

VARIANTS

Three basic fighter versions are currently in service, with the F-4B, F-4C, F-4G, F-4J, F-4N and F-4S models all having been retired. The most numerous fighter is the **F-4E**, which is still used operationally by several air arms, a number of which have funded upgrade projects to extend service life. Basically similar, but unique to Japan, is the **F-4EJ**, a locally-manufactured dedicated interceptor that has recently been brought to **F-4EJKai** standard with a new radar and other avionics improvements. Another version that has been upgraded is the German **F-4F**. Again, it is similar to the F-4E, but lacked Sparrow capability in original form, although the **F-4F ICE** (Improved Combat Efficiency) version can use the AIM-120. Finally, a declining number of cannon-equipped **F-4Ds** still serve with Iran and South Korea, this less capable version predating the F-4E by several years.

F-4EJKai Phantom Japanese Air Self-Defence Force

McDonnell Douglas RF/QF-4 Phantom II

TWIN-TURBOJET RECONNAISSANCE AND UNMANNED TARGET AIRCRAFT

RF-4E Phantom II Hellenic Air Force

DEVELOPMENT

The idea of adapting the Phantom for the tactical reconnaissance role emerged early, and work on the RF-4C was undertaken concurrently with the F-4C fighter in 1962. This provided another chance for the Phantom to demonstrate its versatility and McDonnell wasted no time in converting two Navy F-4Bs into YRF-4C prototypes. The maiden flight took place in August 1963 and less than a year later, the initial RF-4C flew for the first time on 18 May 1964, with deliveries to Tactical Air Command beginning later that year. Over 100 RF-4Es were built for overseas air arms.

CURRENT SERVICE

Although no longer in service with the US armed forces, several air arms operate suitably-configured Phantom variants on reconnaissance tasks. These include Greece (RF-4E), Iran (RF-4E), Israel (RF-4E), Japan (RF-4EJ and RF-4EJKai), South Korea (RF-4C), Spain (RF-4C) and Turkey (RF-4E). In the USA, drone-configured aircraft are still used by the USAF (QF-4E/G) and US Navy (QF-4N/S).

SPECIAL FEATURES

Low-wing monoplane configuration, with marked dihedral on outer panels and anhedral on horizontal tailplanes. Outer wing panels are hinged and can fold for storage. Twin J79 engines buried in aft fuselage are fed by lateral air intakes that extend forward of the wing leading edge. An arrester hook positioned directly aft of the engine exhaust nozzles is fitted to all versions. Reconnaissance-dedicated aircraft have a modified nose housing sensors and cameras; QF-4 versions are capable of unmanned flight for use as target aircraft in weapons training exercise and weapons development programmes.

VARIANTS

The **RF-4C** was the most numerous reconnaissance Phantom, although not the first such version, as the US Marine Corps acquired the **RF-4B** at around the same time and eventually received 46, though these have long been retired. More than ten times that number of RF-4Cs were built for the USAF and over 100 were supplied overseas as the **RF-4E** – a version

similar to the RF-4C that first flew on 15 September 1970. Recipients were Germany, Greece, Iran, Israel and Turkey, while 14 examples of the comparable **RF-4EJ** went to Japan. Two other reconnaissance versions appeared as a result of conversion from the basic F-4E. Three were adapted to **F-4E(S)** standard for Israel, these featuring the huge HIAC-1 Long-Range Oblique Photography (LOROP) camera installation in an enlarged nose, while 17 **F-4EJs** became RF-4EJs in Japan. Finally, the use of unmanned examples of the Phantom as aerial targets by both the US Navy and USAF has resulted in the appearance of several more versions, specifically the **QF-4N** and **QF-4S** of the Navy and the **QRF-4C**, **QF-4E** and **QF-4G** of the USAF.

TECHNICAL DATA

McDonnell Douglas RF-4C Phantom II
Powerplants: Two General Electric J79-GE-15 turbojets
Developing: 48.49kN (10,900lb st) dry; 75.62kN (17,000lbst) with afterburner
Span: 11.71m (38ft 5in)
Length: 19.17m (62ft 11in)
Height: 5.03m (16ft 6in)
All-up weight: 26,308kg (58,000lb)
Maximum speed: 2,348km/h (1,459mph)
Operational ceiling: 59,400ft
Ferry range: 2,816km (1,750 miles)
Combat radius: 1,353km (841 miles)
Accommodation: Pilot and Reconnaissance Systems Operator (RSO)
Warload: Theoretically capable of carrying up to 7,257kg (16,000lb) external load, but usually unarmed, although some aircraft have AIM-9 Sidewinder IR-homing air-to-air missile for defensive purposes
First flown: 8 August 1963 (YRF-4C prototype)
Entered service: September 1964 (RF-4C)

RF-4C Phantom II Spanish Air Force

McDonnell Douglas DC-9/C-9

TWIN-TURBOFAN PASSENGER/CARGO TRANSPORT AIRCRAFT

C-9A Nightingale United States Air Force

DEVELOPMENT

The DC-9 was one of several commercial transport aircraft that originated in the early 1960s, with design work being initiated by the Douglas Aircraft Company in 1963. First flown in prototype form on 25 February 1965, it entered airline service in December 1965 and achieved great success, largely due to its adaptability, which led to the appearance of extended versions with improved engines. Still in quantity production at the time of the company's merger with McDonnell, it became known as the MD-80 series. Manufacture of the MD-80/90 series ended in 1999, but Boeing is continuing to build the broadly similar Model 717 (formerly the MD-95).

CURRENT SERVICE

Almost 60 aircraft have seen military service over the years, and the majority are still in use today. With the US Air Force, 20 C-9As undertake aeromedical transport duties with three units, stationed in the USA (375th Airlift Wing), Germany (86th Airlift Wing) and Japan (374th Airlift Wing). In addition, the C-9C is still employed on VIP missions by the 89th Airlift Wing, although it may soon be phased out. Retirement of US Navy aircraft is also expected in the near future, with the Boeing C-40A (737-700) having been chosen as a replacement. At present, 15 C-9Bs and 12 DC-9 Srs.32/33s equip seven Navy Reserve

transport units (VR-46, VR-52, VR-56, VR-57, VR-58, VR-59 and VR-61) and two more C-9Bs operate with Marine Corps squadron VMR-1. In overseas service, two nations were recently still using this type. Italy acquired two DC-9 Srs 32s for VIP airlift in 1974 and these are based with 306° Gruppo at Ciampino. Kuwait had two DC-9 Srs 32CFs. However, only one Kuwaiti DC-9 still exists with No 41 Sqn at Ali Salim Sabah AB, the other having been destroyed during the Gulf War (but since replaced by an MD-83).

SPECIAL FEATURES

Low-wing design with T-tail and twin engines mounted in pods adjacent to aft fuselage. Specialised C-9A and C-9B military derivatives feature cargo door on port side of forward fuselage.

VARIANTS

Excluding aircraft utilised by Italy and Kuwait, three military versions of the DC-9 were produced for the US Air Force and Navy/Marine Corps. The **C-9A** emerged to replace Douglas C-118A Liftmasters and Convair C-131s in the aeromedical airlift role, being specially configured for transport of litter patients. Known as the Nightingale, production totalled 21. A total of 17 **C-9B Skytrain IIs** was built for the fleet logistics support role with the regular Navy, but most of these mixed passenger/cargo aircraft subsequently

TECHNICAL DATA

McDonnell Douglas C-9A Nightingale

Powerplants: Two Pratt & Whitney JT8D-9 turbofans
Developing: 64.5kN (14,500lb st)
Span: 28.47m (93ft 5in)
Length: 36.37m (119ft 3.5in)
Height: 8.38m (27ft 6in)
All-up weight: 54,885kg (121,000lb)
Maximum speed: 995km/h (618mph)
Cruise speed: 821km/h (510mph)
Operational Ceiling: 37,000ft
Ferry range: 3,669km/(2,280miles)
Range with max payload: 2,390km (1,485 miles)
Accommodation: Flight crew plus up to 40 litter patients and 40 ambulatory patients and five attendants
Payload: 14,118kg (31,125lb)
First flown: 25 February 1965 (DC-9-10); 8 August 1968 (C-9A)
Entered service: December 1965 (DC-9); August 1968 (C-9A)

passed to reserve units. The final purely military model is the **C-9C**, three being obtained by the US Air Force for use as executive transports with 89th Airlift Wing at Andrews AFB.

McDonnell Douglas C-9C United States Air Force

McDonnell Douglas KC-10A Extender & KDC-10

THREE-TURBOFAN TANKER/CARGO AIRCRAFT

McDonnell Douglas KDC-10 Royal Netherlands Air Force

TECHNICAL DATA

McDonnell Douglas KC-10A Extender

Powerplants: Three General Electric CF6-50C2 turbofans
Developing: 233.53kN (52,500lb st)
Span: 47.34m (155ft 4in)
Length: 55.35m (181ft 7in)
Height: 17.70m (58ft 1in)
All-up weight: 267,620kg (590,000lb)
Maximum speed: 982km/h (610mph)
Cruise speed: 908km/h (564mph)
Operational ceiling: 33,400ft
Range with maximum payload: 7,032km (4,370 miles)
Ferry range: 18,507km (11,500miles)
Accommodation: Four crew and up to 75 passengers plus 17 cargo pallets
Payload: 76,843kg (169,409lb)
First flown: 12 July 1980 (KC-10A)
Entered service: March 1981 (KC-10A)

DEVELOPMENT

Based on the wide-bodied commercial DC-10 Series 30CF convertible freighter/airliner, the KC-10A Extender arose in response to a USAF requirement of the late 1970s for a new Advanced Tanker Cargo Aircraft (ATCA). In competition against the Boeing 747, the McDonnell Douglas proposal was eventually declared to be the winner in December 1977, at which time the USAF stated it would purchase a total of 16. With the basic design already well proven in commercial service, testing proceeded rapidly following the maiden flight in July 1980, and deliveries to the USAF for operational evaluation began in March 1981, with the first examples going to Barksdale AFB, Louisiana. Further orders followed during the 1980s and procurement eventually reached a total of 60. Delivery of the last example occurred on 4 April 1990, after this had been used to evaluate underwing hose-reel pods. For several years, the Extender was the only tanker-configured variation of the DC-10, until the Royal Netherlands Air Force purchased two former Martinair DC-10

Series 30CF aircraft which were fitted with a refuelling boom and a remote aerial refuelling operator's station by KLM. After conversion, the first KDC-10 was delivered on 29 September 1995.

CURRENT SERVICE

Some 59 of the 60 KC-10As that were purchased for service with Strategic Air Command remain on the USAF inventory. However, a major reorganisation in the early 1990s eliminated Strategic Air Command and the KC-10As now form part of Air Mobility Command, being concentrated with just two Air Mobility Wings located at McGuire AFB, New Jersey (305th AMW) and Travis AFB, California (60th AMW). The two Royal Netherlands Air Force KDC-10s are assigned to 334 Squadron at Eindhoven.

SPECIAL FEATURES

Broadly similar in appearance to the DC-10, the KC-10A Extender features an in-flight refuelling boom and operator's compartment beneath the rear fuselage,

and is also fitted with a Sargent-Fletcher FR600 hose/reel unit in the starboard aft fuselage side. Following trials with the 60th KC-10A, a total of 20 aircraft has been configured to operate with Flight Refuelling Mk 32B pods mounted beneath the wing tips, which allows the Extender to simultaneously transfer fuel to three receiver aircraft. Loading of cargo is achieved via a large upward hinged door on the port forward fuselage side.

VARIANTS

The **KC-10A** remains the only version in USAF service and this designation applies to all 59 surviving aircraft, even though there are some minor differences in configuration, like the fitting of underwing Flight Refuelling Mk 32B pods on some aircraft. Both Dutch examples are known as **KDC-10s**.

KC-10A Extender United States Air Force

McDonnell Douglas/Hawker Siddeley AV-8A Harrier

SINGLE TURBOFAN STOVL NAVAL GROUND ATTACK FIGHTER

AV-8S Harrier Royal Thai Navy

DEVELOPMENT

In the 1950s and 1960s, a series of high-level reports on the prospects of the British aircraft industry had all agreed that (despite the precedent set by the Martin B-57B Canberra) the possibility of selling military aircraft to the US services could be ruled out. The USAF made it clear that, although the Harrier was technically interesting, they had no demand for an aircraft that could not reach Mach 2. However, the US Marine Corps decided that the aircraft might well have potential in the context of air support for amphibious operations, since it could go ashore much sooner than conventional aircraft. The purchase of a foreign combat aircraft was accepted purely to avoid the delay (conservatively estimated at five to seven years) required for an indigenous design to be ready for service. A batch of 12 Harriers (known by HSA as the Mk 50) were authorised in FY 70. This was then followed by 18 in FY 71, 30 in FY 72, 30 in FY 73 and 12 AV-8As and eight TAV-8As in FY 74 – giving a total of 110 aircraft. All were completed at Dunsfold, where they were test flown before being dissembled and transported to America in USAF aircraft. The Spanish

Navy placed an order (via the US Navy) for 11 AV-8s, and these were designated Harrier Mk 55, or AV-8S Matador. The USMC's AV-8Cs were withdrawn from service in 1987.

CURRENT SERVICE

In April 1997, the Royal Thai Navy commissioned the 11,500 ton carrier *Chakkrinarebet*, primarily as a helicopter platform, but which has a 12 degree ski-jump to suit Harrier operations. In the longer term the RTN Air Division may well acquire the Harrier AV-8 Plus, but as an interim measure the service purchased seven remaining AV-8Ss and two TAV-8Ss from Spain. They are based with No 3 Wing, 301 Squadron at U-Tapao, but are believed to be suffering from a lack of spares.

SPECIAL FEATURES

The AV-8A featured a large tactical UHF antenna over the central fuselage. On delivery to the US, the Martin-Baker Mk 9A ejector seat was replaced (for political reasons) by a US Stencel SIIIS-3 seat. British radios were replaced by Magnavox UHF and UHF

homing, and Sylvania VHF and Tactical VHF. The IFF was changed and a radio altimeter was added.

VARIANTS

The AV-8A equipped the USMC's VMAT-203 training unit, VMA-231 and VMA-542 – all at Cherry Point, North Carolina – and VMA-513 at Yuma, Arizona. Between 1979 and 1984, 47 AV-8As were converted to AV-8C standard (pending availability of a second generation Harrier), being given a Litton ALR-45F radar warning receiver and ALE-39 chaff/flare dispenser in the rear fuselage. This variant also had the lift improvement devices (LIDs) developed for the AV-8B.

SEE ALSO HARRIER GR7, SEA HARRIER, HARRIER T10/TAV-8B, T4/T8 & AV-8B HARRIER.

AV-8S Harrier

TECHNICAL DATA

McDonnell Douglas AV-8A Harrier

Powerplant: One Rolls-Royce Pegasus Mk 150 (F402-RR-401) vectored thrust turbofan
Developing: 95.64kN (21,500lb st)
Span: 7.70m (25ft 3in)
Length: 13.87m (45ft 1in)
Height: 3.63m (11ft 11in)
All-up weight: 10,115kg (22,300lb) for STO; 7,734kg (17,050lb) for VTO
Maximum speed: 1,176km/h (730mph)
Operational ceiling: 40,000ft
Maximum range: 3,428km (2,130 miles)
Mission range: 667km (415 miles)
Accommodation: Pilot only
Warload: Two 30mm Aden guns and AIM-9 Sidewinders on the outer pylons
First flown: 20 November 1970
Entered service: January 1971 (USMC); 1976 (Spanish Navy); September 1997 (Thai Navy)

McDonnell Douglas (Boeing)/BAE Systems AV-8B Harrier II

AV-8B Harrier II United States Marine Corps

TECHNICAL DATA

McDonnell Douglas/BAE Systems AV-8B Harrier II

Powerplant: One Rolls-Royce F402-RR-408 (Pegasus 11-61) vectored thrust turbofan
Developing: 105.87kN (23,800lb st)
Span: 9.25m (30ft 4in)
Length: 14.12m (46ft 4in)
Height: 3.55m (11ft 7.75in)
All-up weight: 14,061kg (31,000lb) in STO mode
Maximum speed: 1,065km/h (661mph)
Ferry range: 3,035km (1,886 miles) tanks retained
Operational ceiling: over 50,000ft
Endurance: three hours
Combat radius: 1,101km (684 miles) with seven Mk 82 bombs, two 300 US gal drop tanks, on hi-lo-hi profile with STO departure and no loiter time
Accommodation: Pilot only (two pilots in TAV-8B)
Warload: Maximum external load of 6,003kg (13,235lb); weapons include laser-guided bombs, slick and retarded bombs, cluster bombs, rockets, AIM-9 and AIM-120 air-to-air missiles, AGM-65 air-to-surface missiles and gun pods. Underfuselage gun pack housing GAU-12A Equaliser five-barrel 25mm cannon, with 300 rounds of ammunition
First flown: 9 November 1978 (YAV-8B prototype); 29 August 1983 (first production AV-8B)
Entered service: January 1984 (first delivery to USMC)

DEVELOPMENT

Although the US Marine Corps was quick to recognise the potential of the V/STOL Harrier and eventually obtained more than 100 AV-8As, it was less than happy with the limited weapons payload, poor range and endurance of the first-generation Harrier and soon began pushing for a more capable version. This was intended to be an Anglo-American venture with British Aerospace as the lead partner, but for various reasons, it failed to reach fruition and the Americans eventually opted to go-ahead independently. The result was the AV-8B, which featured a new carbon-fibre wing as well as a much revised cockpit, including HOTAS controls. McDonnell Douglas modified two existing AV-8As to serve as prototype YAV-8Bs and the first of these made its maiden flight in late 1978. Trials occupied several years and it was not until 1984 that production aircraft began to enter service. Since then, further upgrading has occurred with night attack capability being added in 1989 and radar following in 1993.

CURRENT SERVICE

Production of new-build aircraft has ended, but the US Marine Corps received just over 280 Harrier IIs (including 22 trainers) and is now accepting rebuilt aircraft to the ultimate Harrier II Plus standard. In USMC service, the AV-8B equips seven operational squadrons (VMA-211/214/223/231/311/513/542) and a training unit (VMAT-203). Other aircraft serve with the Italian Navy and the Spanish Navy.

SPECIAL FEATURES

The AV-8B Harrier II is unmistakably descended from the original AV-8A Harrier and retains many of the attributes of that aircraft, including the novel vectored thrust engine. However, changes included adoption of a bigger wing, longer fuselage and addition of leading edge root extensions at the junction of the wing and fuselage. Lift improvement devices were also added beneath the fuselage and additional hardpoints for auxiliary fuel and/or weaponry. Since it entered service, progressive updating has resulted

in the addition of AN/APG-65 multi-mode radar in a revised nose section, and other sensors, including FLIR.

VARIANTS

Production began with the baseline **AV-8B Harrier II** and the designation remains unchanged even though the final aircraft (with AN/APG-65 radar) are known as the **Harrier II Plus**. At least one US example has been allocated to permanent test duties as the **NAV-8B**, while Spanish aircraft are known as the **EAV-8B** and **EAV-8B+**. The two-seat trainer is designated **TAV-8B**.

AV-8B Harrier II United States Marine Corps

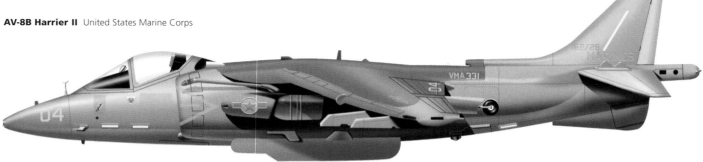

McDonnell Douglas Helicopters (Hughes) MD 500

SINGLE TURBINE OBSERVATION/COMBAT HELICOPTER

MD 500M Defender Royal Danish Army

TECHNICAL DATA

**McDonnell Douglas Helicopters
MD 500MD/TOW Defender**
Powerplant: One Allison 250-C20B turboshaft
Developing: 313kW (420shp) derated to 280kW
(375shp) for continuous operation
Driving: Five-blade main and two-blade tail rotors
Main rotor diameter: 8.05m (26ft 4.8in)
Length, rotors turning: 9.39m (30ft 9.5in)
Height: 2.71m (8ft 10.8in)
Maximum weight: 1,610kg (3,550lb)
Maximum speed: 241km/h (150mph)
Cruise speed: 222km/h (138mph)
Operational ceiling: 4,390m (14,400ft)
Range: 420km (260 miles)
Endurance: 2hr 7min
Accommodation: Pilot and up to five passengers
Warload: Some versions can carry maximum
of four BGM-71 TOW or AGM-114 Hellfire anti-
armour missiles or FIM-92A Stinger air-to-air
missiles or Mk.44 or Mk.46 torpedoes; alternative
armament includes grenade launcher, rocket
pods, M134 miniguns or 7.62mm machine guns
Payload: 590kg (1,300lb) external sling load
First flown: February 1963 (OH-6 Cayuse)
Entered service: 1968 (Model 500M Defender);
1976 (Model 500D)

DEVELOPMENT

Based on the OH-6A Cayuse/Model 369 and virtually indistinguishable from that type, the MD 500 series began life as a primarily civil helicopter. Known at first as the Hughes 500, the military potential was soon recognised and the 500M Defender emerged in the late 1960s. In addition to production by Hughes, it was built under licence by Kawasaki in Japan and by Nardi in Italy. Further development led to the appearance of more potent models, with the ability to destroy armoured vehicles or perform anti-submarine warfare duties.

CURRENT SERVICE

One of the more widely used helicopters, versions of the basic MD 500 are currently operated by air arms in Argentina, Bahrain, Colombia, Costa Rica, Croatia, Cyprus, Denmark, Finland, Honduras, Iraq, Jordan, Kenya, North Korea, South Korea, Mexico, Peru, El Salvador, Spain and Taiwan. Licence-built examples produced by Nardi in Italy are also in service with Italy and Malta. The MD 520MG Defender is less common, serving only with the Philippines, while versions of

the MD 530 are flown by Argentina, Chile, Colombia and Mexico. A number of AH-6 and MH-6 helicopters with US Army special forces are based on the MD 500, but incorporate features of the later MD 520 and 530.

SPECIAL FEATURES

All variants retain the familiar egg-shaped cabin and cockpit, in conjunction with skid-type landing gear. However, the fin assembly was changed at an early stage in favour of the unit that is now standard, this consisting of a t-tail with endplates. Introduced with effect from the civilian Model 500D, it was also used for the 500MD Defender and is a feature of both the 520 and 530 series. Both of the latter have the more pointed nose first used on the commercial MD 500E.

VARIANTS

The basic military model is the known as the **Defender**, although numerous variants exist, including the **MD 500M**, **MD 500MD**, **MD 500MD/TOW** (with missile armament), **MD 500MD/MMS-TOW** (with missile armament and mast-mounted sighting device), **MD 500MD/ASW** (with torpedo armament, search

radar and a towed magnetic anomaly detector 'bird') and **MD 500MG Defender**. Improved versions include the **MD 530MG**, available in various configurations tailored to customer needs, but with provisions for mast-mounted sighting device, FLIR sensors, radar homing and warning equipment and multiple weapon options, including TOW 2 anti-armour missiles, Stinger air-to-air missiles, unguided rockets and a McDonnell Douglas Chain Gun.

SEE ALSO: HUGHES 369/KAWASAKI OH-6 & BOEING HELICOPTERS (MDH) MD520/530 DEFENDER

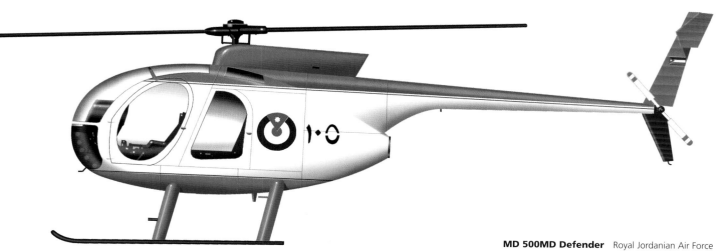

MD 500MD Defender Royal Jordanian Air Force

Mikoyan-Gurevich MiG-15

SINGLE TURBOJET FIGHTER/FIGHTER-BOMBER

WSK SBLim-2A

DEVELOPMENT

Following on from the MiG-9, this was the second jet fighter to emerge from MiG and was infinitely more successful than its predecessor, taking the West by surprise when it was first encountered in battle over Korea. Development had begun some four years earlier, when a number of Soviet fighter manufacturers were charged with conceiving a high-altitude day interceptor. In the event, the UK agreement to provide examples of the Rolls-Royce Nene centrifugal turbojet was instrumental in the success of what became the MiG-15 project, which was authorised to proceed in February 1947. Thereafter, work progressed at a rapid pace, with the first prototype flying by the end of that year. Subsequent evaluation revealed that it was far superior to rival designs, with the go-ahead for mass production being given in August 1948, at the same time as it was decided to proceed with a two-seat trainer version (MiG-15UTI). Service entry followed soon after, with initial deliveries made from October 1948, and the new fighter made its combat debut over Korea in November 1950. In battle, it was generally considered inferior to the F-86 Sabre, but

this had much to do with the fact that US pilots were better trained. Overall, some 5,000 two-seat 'Midgets' were built for operational conversion and advanced training from 1949.

CURRENT SERVICE

Although its Korean War adversary has long since disappeared from the inventories of world air arms, some examples of the MiG-15 or Chinese-built FT-2s are still active with third world nations. Those that remain are primarily used for training, with Albania retaining limited numbers of both the MiG-15bis and MiG-15UTI, while Angola, Congo, Guinea-Bissau, Guinea Republic, North Korea, Mali, Mozambique, Syria, and Yemen were all known to still be utilising the aircraft until recently, although serviceability is probably poor, with spare parts increasingly hard to obtain.

SPECIAL FEATURES

Unique in being the Soviet Union's first swept-wing fighter, the MiG-15 was largely conventional by the standards of the day and similar in appearance to

the contemporary Sabre. Unlike the F-86, however, it employed a mid-wing layout and a high-set tailplane and also featured twin air brakes on the extreme rear fuselage sides, plus a battery of guns in the forward fuselage beneath the air intake ducting.

VARIANTS

Only the MiG-15bis and MiG-15UTI are currently in service, but several other versions of the single-seater were also built. Noteworthy among these was the MiG-15Rbis with AFA-40 photographic equipment for the reconnaissance role, and the MiG-15Sbis escort fighter. In addition, license production of the MiG-15 was undertaken in Czechoslovakia as the S-102 (MiG-15), S-103 (MiG-15bis) and CS-102 (MiG-15UTI) and in Poland as the Lim-1 (MiG-15), Lim-2 (MiG-15bis) and SBLim-1/2 (MiG-15UTI).

TECHNICAL DATA

Mikoyan-Gurevich MiG-15UTI
Powerplant: One Klimov RD-45F turbojet
Developing: 22.26kN (5,004lbst)
Span: 10.085m (33ft 1in)
Length: 10.11m (33ft 2in)
Height: 3.39m (11ft 2in)
All-up weight: 5,400kg (11,905lb)
Maximum speed: 1,015km/h (631mph)
Operational ceiling: 48,640ft
Range with internal fuel: 680km (423 miles)
Ferry range: 1,054km (655 miles)
Accommodation: Two pilots
Warload: Not normally applicable to MiG-15UTI, but one NR-23 23mm cannon or UBK-Ye 12.7mm machine gun can be fitted and there are provisions for 1,588kg (3,500lb) external payload
First flown: 30 December 1947 (S-01 prototype); 23 May 1949 (MiG-15UTI)
Entered service: 8 October 1948 (MiG-15); 1950 (MiG-15UTI)

Mikoyan-Gurevich MiG-15

Mikoyan-Gurevich MiG-17/Shenyang J-5/F-5

SINGLE TURBOJET FIGHTER/FIGHTER-BOMBER

Mikoyan-Gurevich MiG-17

TECHNICAL DATA

Mikoyan-Gurevich MiG-17F
Powerplant: One Klimov VK-1F turbojet
Developing: 25.52kN (5,732lb st) dry; 33.13kN (7,451lb st) with afterburner
Span: 9.63m (31ft 7in)
Length: 11.26m (36ft 11.5in)
Height: 3.80m (12ft 5.5in)
All-up weight: 6,069kg (13,380lb)
Maximum speed: 1,100km/h (684mph)
Operational ceiling: 54,460ft
Ferry range: 2,020km (1,255 miles)
Combat radius: 700km (435 miles) hi-lo-hi attack mission with two 250kg (551lb) bombs and two drop tanks
Accommodation: Pilot
Warload: 500kg (1,102lb) maximum ordnance capacity, including bombs or rockets for attack mission, plus integral gun armament (one N-37D 37mm and two NR-23 23mm cannon); MiG-17PF version was configured for all-weather interception role with RS-2U (AA-1 'Alkali') missile
First flown: 13 January 1950 (SI-2 prototype)
Entered service: 1952

DEVELOPMENT

Bearing a strong family resemblance to the MiG-15, from which it evolved, development of the MiG-17 commenced in early 1949, with the resultant design incorporating a number of improvements intended to eradicate failings encountered with the MiG-15, such as poor handling at high speed. These changes included adoption of a thinner wing of increased sweep angle and greater anhedral, while the aft fuselage was also extended and modifications made to the airbrakes. The tail is taller and the horizontal surfaces have greater sweepback. Flight trials began in January 1950 and were encouraging, with the decision to begin mass production at six factories being taken on 1 September 1951. Delivery of production aircraft got under way in October 1952 and more than 8,000 were eventually built in the Soviet Union and Poland, these including radar-equipped models for all-weather interception and others with camera installations for reconnaissance.

CURRENT SERVICE

The only derivatives still in service are the MiG-17F 'Fresco-C' fighter-bomber, known to be recently active with the air arms of Angola, Cuba, Madagascar, Mali, Mozambique and Syria; and the Chinese-built two-seat versions (Chengdu JJ-5/FT-5) that are also still used in Albania, North Korea and Pakistan. As with the MiG-15, serviceability is likely to be poor.

SPECIAL FEATURES

The MiG-17 has a similar configuration to the MiG-15, with a narrower span wing that features three wing fences rather than two, as on the MiG-15. Triple gun armament is situated in the lower front fuselage below the air intake duct and it has enlarged air brakes.

VARIANTS

Following on from the basic MiG-17, the **MiG-17F** differed by virtue of having an engine equipped with an afterburner and became the principal Soviet version with effect from February 1953. Specialist interceptor models included the **MiG-17P** and **MiG-17PF**; both featured RP-1 Izumrud ('Scan Odd') radar in a revised nose section and both were known as **'Fresco-D'**, although the latter sub-type was much more widely used. Subsequent refinement resulted in the **MiG-17PFU 'Fresco-E'**, which lacked gun armament and was also unique in being the first European production fighter with missile armament, being able to operate with four RS-2US (AA-1b 'Alkali-B') missiles. In addition to production in the USSR, the MiG-17 was built under license in Poland (as the **Lim-5** and **Lim-6**) and China (as the **Shenyang J-5**), with the latter country developing a two-seat version as the Chengdu JJ-5/FT-5 which flew for the first time in May 1966. The only two-seat MiG-17s were built in China.

Mikoyan-Gurevich MiG-17F
Cuban Air Force

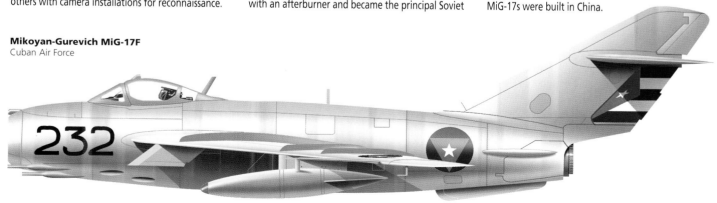

Mikoyan MiG-21F/P/PF/U

SINGLE TURBOJET FIGHTER/FIGHTER-BOMBER

MiG-21PF

DEVELOPMENT

First conceived as a simple lightweight fighter with superlative performance, the MiG-21 was eventually produced in huge numbers for the USSR and many communist nations around the world. Evolution was a fairly complex process and involved trials of swept-wing (Ye-2, Ye-2A and Ye-50 'Faceplate') and delta-wing (Ye-4, Ye-5 and Ye-6 'Fishbed') aircraft before the latter planform was selected for production in late 1958. Thereafter, constant upgrading saw the MiG-21 evolve into a formidable warplane through the adoption of more sophisticated radar, improved engines, additional stores stations and more potent weaponry. In its ultimate MiG-21bis form, although recognisably the same basic type, the resemblance was little more than superficial. Although precise details of the total production are unavailable, it is believed that about 12,500 MiG-21s were produced in the USSR. Variants were also manufactured in Czechoslovakia and India, while China produced several thousand more as the J-7.

CURRENT SERVICE

Although once widely used by a host of air arms, the early versions of the 'Fishbed' are in decline, but the MiG-21PF/PFM and equivalents were recently in service with Algeria, Cuba, Egypt, Guinea Republic, India, Iraq, Laos, Madagascar, Poland, Syria and Yugoslavia.

SPECIAL FEATURES

The most distinctive feature of the MiG-21 is the delta wing planform, married to a conventional low-set tailplane. Early versions had a narrow-chord vertical tail and small air inlet centrebody. However, a broad-chord fin was introduced during manufacture of the MiG-21F-13, which was the first true production model.

Nevertheless, the MiG-21F-13 lacked radar and was thus limited to day air superiority tasks, a shortcoming that was addressed on the MiG-21P, which featured a greatly enlarged centrebody housing a radar.

VARIANTS

Following on from the prototypes, production was launched with the **MiG-21F**, although this soon gave way to the **MiG-21F-13**, which was compatible with the K-13 (AA-2 'Atoll') heat-seeking air-to-air missile. Further improvement led to the **MiG-21P**, which was fitted with a TsD-30 'Spin Scan' radar (later RP-21), with other refinements resulting in the appearance of the **MiG-21PF** in early 1962. A simplified version of the MiG-21PF was built in India as the **MiG-21FL**, while the **MiG-21PFV** was basically a MiG-21FL with provision for use in North Vietnam's humid environment. The last initial series version was the **MiG-21PFM**, which entered production in 1964, with airframe and armament alterations as well as a new two-piece cockpit canopy. The **MiG-21U 'Mongol-A'** is basically a two-seat trainer version of the MiG-21F-13 and flew for the first time in October 1960.

TECHNICAL DATA

Mikoyan MiG-21PFM 'Fishbed-F'

Powerplant: One Tumansky R-11F2S-300 turbojet
Developing: 38.26kN (8,600lb st) dry;
60.57kN (13,613lb st) with afterburner
Span: 7.15m (23ft 5.75in)
Length: 15.76m (51ft 8.5in) including probe
Height: 4.125m (13ft 6.5in)
All-up weight: 9,080kg (20,018lb)
Maximum speed: 2,125km/h (1,320mph)
Operational ceiling: 59,710ft
Mission range: 740km (460 miles)
Ferry range: Exceeds 1,300km (808 miles)
Accommodation: Pilot only, or two in tandem in MiG-21U/UM
Warload: Maximum external ordnance load of 500kg (1,102lb) including bombs, rockets, GP-9 23mm cannon pack and guided weapons such as R-3S (AA-2 'Atoll') IR-homing air-to-air missile, RS-2US (AA-1 'Alkali') semi-active radar homing air-to-air missile and Kh-23 (AS-7 'Kerry') air-to-surface missile
First flown: 16 June 1955 (Ye-4); 9 January 1956 (Ye-5); January 1958 (Ye-6)
Entered service: June 1959 (MiG-21F first delivery)

MiG-21PF

Mikoyan MiG-21 R/S/MF/US/UM

SINGLE TURBOJET FIGHTER/FIGHTER-BOMBER

MiG-21MF 'Fishbed-J' Slovak Air Force

TECHNICAL DATA

Mikoyan MiG-21MF 'Fishbed-J'
Powerplant: One Tumansky/Gavrilov R-13-300
turbojet
Developing: 39.92kN (8,972lb st) dry;
63.66kN (14,307lbst) with afterburner
Span: 7.15m (23ft 5.75in)
Length: 15.76m (51ft 8.5in) including probe
Height: 4.125m (13ft 6.5in)
All-up weight: 9,400kg (20,723lb)
Maximum speed: 2,175km/h (1,351mph)
Operational ceiling: 59,711ft
Ferry range: 1,800km (1,118 miles)
Combat radius: 740km (460 miles) hi-lo-hi attack
profile with two 250kg (551lb) bombs and drop
tanks
Accommodation: Pilot only
Warload: Maximum ordnance load of 2,000kg
(4,409lb) on four underwing pylons and
centreline stores station including conventional
bombs, retarded bombs, cluster bombs, rockets
and guided weapons such as R-13M (AA-2d
'Atoll-D') and R-60M (AA-8 'Aphid') IR-homing
air-to-air missiles; also has integral GSh-23L
23mm cannon with 200 rounds
First flown: Circa 1969
Entered service: 1970 (MiG-21MF)

DEVELOPMENT

Ongoing improvement of the basic airframe resulted in the advent of what is often referred to as the second generation of MiG-21 versions, which had increased internal fuel capacity, greater armament options and ever more complex avionics equipment. This process was launched with the reconnaissance-dedicated MiG-21R 'Fishbed-H', which entered production in the mid-1960s. It was soon joined by fighter-bomber versions, starting with the MiG-21S at around the same time, and culminating with the MiG-21MF.

CURRENT SERVICE

Examples of the MiG-21R remain current with Bulgaria, Egypt, Romania, Yugoslavia and possibly Poland as well, although it is known that the latter country has retired this version from pure reconnaissance tasks. With regard to fighter versions, the MiG-21M still serves with India, Poland, Romania and Yugoslavia, while the MiG-21MF is far more extensively used, currently in operation with Bulgaria, Cuba, Czech Republic, Egypt, Ethiopia, Guinea-Bissau, India, Iraq,

Mali, Mozambique, Nigeria, Poland, Romania (mainly as the upgraded Lancer), Slovak Republic, Syria, Yemen, Yugoslavia and Zambia.

SPECIAL FEATURES

Although still instantly recognisable as MiG-21s, the later versions differed quite markedly from their predecessors. Basic layout was little changed, but several refinements were incorporated, including the provision of two more wing pylons, making a total of four. On the extreme nose section, more alterations were evident, including installation of an angle-of-attack indicator on the port side and movement of the pitot tube from the centreline to the starboard side. However, perhaps the most obvious change of all involved adoption of a deeper dorsal spine that contained additional fuel.

VARIANTS

The first of the second-generation versions to appear was the **MiG-21R**, which was specially configured for tactical reconnaissance, although it could carry armament, including air-to-air missiles for self-defence.

Various types of reconnaissance pod were installed on the centreline, with these configured for different types of intelligence-gathering and employing different types of sensor, including cameras for day or night use, TV, IR linescan and SLAR. Pure fighter versions comprised the **MiG-21S, MiG-21SM, MiG-21M, MiG-21MF, MiG-21MT** and **MiG-21SMT**, of which the latter two were most distinctive in featuring a huge dorsal spine accommodating even more fuel. In recent times, a number of upgrade projects have been marketed, including the **Aerostar/Elbit Lancer** in Romania and Russia's own **MiG-21-93**. Trainer versions comprise the **MiG-21US** (introduced 1966) and **MiG-21UM** (introduced 1971), both being known as the **'Mongol-B'**, despite numerous detail differences.

MiG-21MF 'Fishbed-J' Czech Air Force

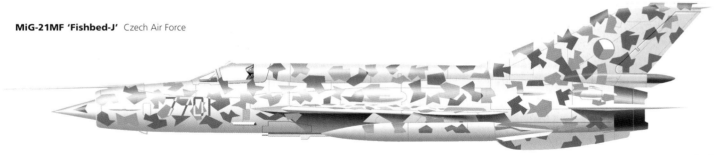

Mikoyan MiG-21bis

SINGLE TURBOJET FIGHTER/FIGHTER-BOMBER

MiG-21bis 'Fishbed-L' Hungarian Air Force

DEVELOPMENT

Easily the most advanced version of the MiG-21 family to be produced in new-build form, the MiG-21bis was also the final version to be produced in the Soviet Union. Development came about primarily as a result of lessons learnt in the heat of battle over Vietnam. That conflict highlighted the need for a more durable airframe with enhanced performance at low to medium altitude, where many air combats took place. The outcome was the MiG-21bis, which also possessed improved air-to-ground capability and which was built in large numbers for Frontal Aviation from 1972, as well as being supplied to numerous friendly nations. India also acquired manufacturing rights and Hindustan Aeronautics produced several hundred examples between 1980 and 1986.

CURRENT SERVICE

Although long since retired from front-line service in its country of origin, the MiG-21bis is still widely used elsewhere. It is also the target for upgrade programmes which should result in it surviving for quite some time

to come. At least 21 air arms were recently known to still be operating MiG-21bis variants, these comprising Afghanistan, Algeria, Angola, Bulgaria, Cambodia, Congo, Croatia, Cuba, Czech Republic, Egypt, Hungary, India, Iraq, Laos, Libya, Poland, Syria, Uganda, Vietnam, Yemen and Yugoslavia.

SPECIAL FEATURES

Broadly similar in appearance to second-generation MiG-21s, the MiG-21bis can easily be mistaken for its predecessors (such as the MiG-21MF) at first glance. However, closer study reveals that the dorsal spine was significantly redesigned to accommodate still more fuel and the fairing with the vertical tail surface now extends much further aft than on the MiG-21MF.

VARIANTS

At least three basic models of the **MiG-21bis** are known to have been built, although external differences appear to be confined to small antennae at the tip of the fin and beneath the nose section. To differentiate between two of them, the code name **'Fishbed-L'**

was allocated to initial production aircraft, while the version with 'Swift Rod' ILS antenna was known as the **'Fishbed-N'**. The third model is the **MiG-21bisN**, which was specifically configured for tactical nuclear strike missions and for which no reporting name is known. MiG-MAPO is offering its upgraded **MiG-21-93**, featuring Russian avionics, a new radar and compatability with current production AAMs.

TECHNICAL DATA

Mikoyan MiG-21bis 'Fishbed-L'

Powerplant: One Tumansky R-25-300 turbojet
Thrust: 40.2kN (9,038lb st) dry;
69.65kN (15,653lb st) with afterburner
Span: 7.15m (23ft 5.75in)
Length: 15.76m (51ft 8.5in) including probe
Height: 4.125m (13ft 6.5in)
All-up weight: 9,800kg (21,605lb)
Maximum speed: 2,175km/h (1,351mph)
Service ceiling: 57,400ft
Range: 1,470km (915 miles) with two AAMs and one 800 litre (211 US gallon) drop tank
Accommodation: Pilot only
Warload: Maximum ordnance load of 2,000kg (4,409lb) on four underwing pylons and centreline stores station including conventional bombs, retarded bombs, cluster bombs, rockets and guided weapons such as R-13M (AA-2d 'Atoll-D') and R-60M (AA-8 'Aphid') IR-homing air-to-air missiles, R-55 semi-active radar homing air-to-air missile and Kh-23 (AS-7 'Kerry') air-to-surface missile; also has integral GSh-23L 23mm cannon with 200 rounds
First flown: Circa 1971
Entered service: early 1972 (MiG-21bis)

MiG-21bis 'Fishbed-L' Hungarian Air Force

Mikoyan MiG-23

SINGLE TURBOJET FIGHTER INTERCEPTOR/FIGHTER-BOMBER

MiG-23BN 'Flogger' Indian Air Force

TECHNICAL DATA

Mikoyan MiG-23ML 'Flogger-G'
Powerplant: One Khachaturov R-35-300 turbojet
Developing: 83.88kN (18,849lb st) dry; 127.5kN
(28,660lb st) with afterburner
Span: 7.78m (25ft 6.5in) swept; 13.965m (45ft
9.75in) spread
Length: 15.65m (51ft 3.75in) excluding probe
Height: 4.82m (15ft 9.75in)
All-up weight: 17,800kg (39,242lb)
Maximum speed: 2,500km/h (1,553mph)
Operational ceiling: 59,055ft
Ferry range: 2,820km (1,752 miles) with auxiliary
fuel tanks
Accommodation: Pilot only (two pilots in
MiG-23UB)
Warload: Up to 2,000kg (4,409lb) of external
stores may be carried, including R-23 (AA-7 'Apex')
IR or semi-active radar homing air-to-air missiles,
R-60 (AA-8 'Aphid') IR-homing air-to-air missiles
and R-3 (AA-2 'Atoll') air-to-air missiles. Integral
GSh-23L 23mm cannon with 200 rounds mounted
in faired pack on centreline and UPK-23-250 gun
pods can also be carried, housing GSh-23L weapon
and 250 rounds
First flown: 10 June 1967 (23-11/1 prototype)
Entered service: 1969 (MiG-23S)

DEVELOPMENT

As had happened with the MiG-21, a twin-track
approach was again employed in development of
the next fighter to carry the MiG name, with flying
prototypes of both projects being built. The Model
23-01 (also known as the MiG-23PD 'Faithless')
featured a delta-wing format and was unusual in
having a primary engine and two lift jets for enhanced
STOL performance. In the event, it was abandoned,
but the alternative Model 23-11 fared better and
was selected as the basis for the new fighter, being
ordered into production as the MiG-23S 'Flogger-A',
in which guise it flew for the first time in May 1969.
Only about 50 examples of the MiG-23S were built
for service trials before the more capable MiG-23M
'Flogger-B' appeared in 1970. Subsequently, further
refinement led to improved air superiority versions
as well as dedicated ground attack derivatives.

CURRENT SERVICE

Although several former operators have retired the
MiG-23, substantial numbers are still in service. Air
superiority derivatives (MiG-23M series designations)
fly with Algeria, Angola, Belarus, Bulgaria, Cuba,
India, Iraq, Kazakhstan, Libya, North Korea, Romania,
Syria, Turkmenistan, Ukraine and Yemen, while
fighter-bomber versions (MiG-23B series designations)
serve with Afghanistan, Algeria, Angola, Bulgaria,
Cuba, Ethiopia, India, Iraq, Libya, Sudan and Syria.

SPECIAL FEATURES

The MiG-23 was a radical departure from previous
bureau designs, dispensing with the familiar nose
intake in favour of twin intakes attached to the
fuselage sides, thus freeing the nose section to carry
the large antenna associated with the Sapfir-23 ('High
Lark') radar. However, the most distinctive feature of
the MiG-23 is its shoulder-mounted variable geometry
wing, which results in excellent performance at high
speed and good handling qualities at low speed.

VARIANTS

The air superiority **MiG-23M** was a full-system aircraft,
whereas the export **MiG-23MS** was downgraded and
relied upon the 'Jay Bird' radar of the MiG-21, thereby
lacking BVR missile compatibility. Other full-system
interceptors were the **MiG-23MF**, **MiG-23ML** and
MiG-23MLD, while strike versions with specialised
nav/attack systems comprise the **MiG-23B**, **MiG-23BN**,
MiG-23BK and **MiG-23BM**. Finally, the **MiG-23UB**
'Flogger-C' is a two-seat trainer derivative that was
built in significant quantities
between 1970 and 1978.

MiG-23 'Flogger' Belarus Air Force

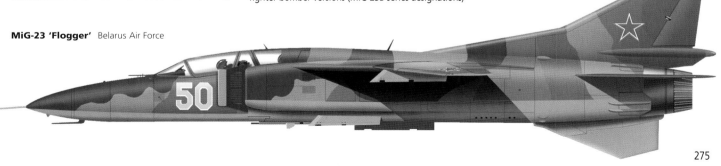

Mikoyan MiG-25

TWIN TURBOJET FIGHTER INTERCEPTOR/RECONNAISSANCE BOMBER

MiG-25PU 'Foxbat-C' Russian Air Force

DEVELOPMENT

Confronted by the USA's B-70 Valkyrie Mach 3 strategic bomber, the USSR launched a crash project at the start of the 1960s to develop a high-flying interceptor with equivalent performance. The outcome was the massive and formidable MiG-25 'Foxbat'. Initially conceived as an interceptor, full-scale development began early in 1962, although it was soon realised that a modified version could perform the reconnaissance role. In fact, the reconnaissance prototype flew first, but the fighter was not far behind, venturing aloft in September 1964. Thereafter, progress with the fighter ran into difficulty, with engine and control problems delaying service entry until 1973, some two or three years behind the MiG-25R reconnaissance derivative.

CURRENT SERVICE

Apart from the USSR, pure fighter versions (MiG-25P series) were delivered to Algeria, Iraq, Libya and Syria, where some are still believed operational. In addition, the break-up of the Soviet Union led to Azerbaijan, Kazakhstan, Russia and Turkmenistan acquiring varying quantities of the MiG-25P series and these are still on charge, although the majority are probably no longer operational. Reconnaissance models (the MiG-25R series) fly with Algeria, India, Libya and Syria in small numbers, while Azerbaijan, Kazakhstan and Russia inherited some in the post-USSR era and the latter two were using them until quite recently.

SPECIAL FEATURES

Twin outward-canted vertical fins and downward-canted wings are the most distinctive attributes of the MiG-25, along with twin cruciform braking parachutes. Interceptor versions usually feature four underwing pylons for missile carriage, while reconnaissance models employ various sensor systems, such as cameras and SLAR. These are usually situated in the nose, occupying space taken up by radar on 'Foxbat' interceptors.

VARIANTS

New-build fighter variants comprise the initial **MiG-25P 'Foxbat-A'** and **MiG-25PD 'Foxbat-E'**, with the latter benefitting from adoption of RP-25 look-down/shoot-down radar and more powerful engines. Surviving **MiG-25P**s were upgraded to a similar standard as the **MiG-25PDS** from 1979, with some gaining an in-flight refuelling probe. The **MiG-25PU 'Foxbat-C'** is a two-seat trainer version, but is not combat-capable, having a second stepped cockpit in lieu of radar. Various new-build or upgraded reconnaissance models have appeared, including the original **MiG-25R** and the **MiG-25RB**, both known as **'Foxbat-B'**, but the latter possessing bombing capability. Further improvement and adoption of different sensors led to the **MiG-25RBK** multi-role bomber/electronic reconnaissance version and **MiG-25RBS** for Elint, both being known as **'Foxbat-D'**, plus the **MiG-25RBT** and **MiG-25RBV** with upgraded Elint systems. Equivalent two-seat trainer

version for reconnaissance units was the **MiG-25RU 'Foxbat-C'**. One other sub-type was the **MiG-25BM 'Foxbat-F'**, for defence suppression using Kh-58 (AS-11 'Kilter') anti-radiation air-to-surface missiles.

TECHNICAL DATA

Mikoyan MiG-25RB 'Foxbat-B'
Powerplants: Two Tumansky (Soyuz) R-15BD-300 turbojets
Developing: 86.2kN (19,378lb st) dry; 109.83kN (24,690lb st) with afterburner
Span: 13.42m (44ft 0.25in)
Length: 21.55m (70ft 8.5in) excluding pitot tube
Height: 6.10m (20ft 0.25in)
All-up weight: 41,200kg (90,829lb)
Maximum speed: 3,000km/h (1,864mph)
Operational ceiling: 68,900ft
Ferry range: 2,400km (1,491 miles)
Range with internal fuel: 1,865km (1,158 miles) subsonic
Accommodation: Pilot only
Warload: 3,000kg (6,614lb) of conventional bombs on six stores stations or single nuclear weapon. Various AAMs.
First flown: 6 March 1964 (Ye-155R-1)
Entered service: 1970-71 (MiG-25R)

MiG-25 'Foxbat-B' Russian Air Force

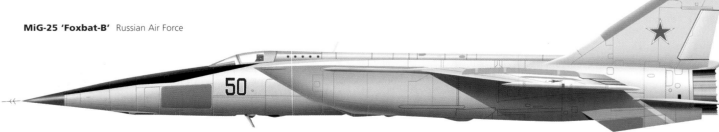

Mikoyan MiG-27

SINGLE TURBOJET TACTICAL FIGHTER-BOMBER

MiG-27 'Flogger-J' Russian Air Force

TECHNICAL DATA

Mikoyan MiG-27 'Flogger-D'
Powerplant: One Tumansky (Soyuz) R-29B-300 turbojet
Developing: 78.45kN (17,637lb st) dry; 112.77kN (25,353lb st) with afterburner
Span: 13.97m (45ft 10in) spread; 7.78m (25ft 6.25in) swept
Length: 17.08m (56ft 0.5in) including nose probe
Height: 5.00m (16ft 4.75in)
All-up weight: 20,300kg (44,753lb)
Maximum speed: 1,885km/h (1,170mph)
Operational ceiling: 45,930ft
Combat radius: 540km (335 miles) on lo-lo-lo mission profile with two Kh-29 air-to-surface missiles and three auxiliary fuel tanks
Accommodation: Pilot only
Warload: Exceeds 4,000kg (8,818lb) on seven stores stations beneath wing and fuselage. Weapon options include free-fall or retarded bombs, napalm canisters, rocket pods, cluster bomb units, gun pods, tactical nuclear stores and Kh-23 (AS-7 'Kerry'), Kh-25 (AS-10 'Karen') and Kh-29 (AS-14 'Kedge') air-to-surface guided missiles, plus R-3S (AA-2A 'Atoll') and R-13M (AA-2D 'Atoll') air-to-air missiles for defensive purposes. Integral armament comprises one GSh-6-30 30mm cannon with 260 rounds
First flown: 1973
Entered service: 1975

DEVELOPMENT

Fundamentally a dedicated strike/attack variant based on the MiG-23BM, the MiG-27 flew for the first time in 1973, and took full advantage of work associated with the earlier attack version. Following a brief development and test programme, it was ordered into quantity production in 1974 and entered operational service the following year.

CURRENT SERVICE

Although formerly used in considerable numbers by Russia's Air Force, the MiG-27 has now been virtually retired from the front-line inventory, but some are still thought to fulfil a secondary training role, with several hundred more in storage awaiting disposition. Russia's naval air arm is believed to retain one regiment (about 36 aircraft), but the main operator is India, with several MiG-27 squadrons. Kazakhstan still operates 41 MiG-27Ms from Taldy Kurgan and Zhangiztobe.

SPECIAL FEATURES

Basically similar to the MiG-23 and using the same 'Flogger' code name, the MiG-27 shares the so-called 'chisel nose' with the MiG-23B series of fighter-bombers, but differs in a number of important details. Foremost among these are the air intakes, which are slightly bigger, but much less complex, by virtue of having fixed-geometry inlets. In addition, to permit carriage of larger stores, the underfuselage pylons were

repositioned beneath the intake ducts, allowing a seventh hardpoint to be added on the fuselage centreline.

VARIANTS

Although only two code names ('Flogger-D' and 'Flogger-J') were allocated to the MiG-27 series, at least five different variations have been identified. Production of the basic MiG-27 'Flogger-D' began in 1974, although this was supplanted in 1975 by the MiG-27K (also 'Flogger-D'), which had PrNK-23K nav/attack avionics and a Fone laser rangefinder/target tracker. The next version was the MiG-27D in 1980, which had extended wing roots tipped with ECM jammers, while the MiG-27M used an RSBN navigation system, but was externally identical, hence both being referred to as 'Flogger-J'. The final version was the MiG-27KR 'Flogger-J2' and this introduced a revised nose shape, with a pimple radome above the chisel and a new undernose fairing that was thought to contain a TV tracker or laser designator. However, 'Flogger-J2' is best recognised by the twin pitot tubes which are set lower on the nose. Indian aircraft are known by the bureau as MiG-27Ls, although Hindustan Aeronautics rather confusingly calls them MiG-27Ms.

MiG-27KR 'Flogger-J2' Russian Air Force

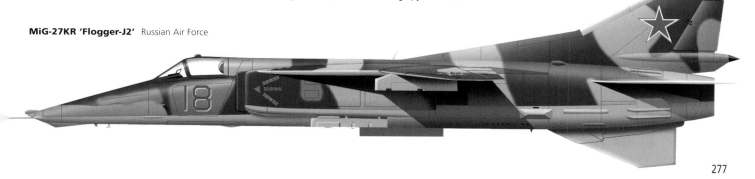

Mikoyan MiG-29

TWIN-TURBOFAN MULTI-ROLE FIGHTER

Mikoyan MiG-29UB Russian Air Force

TECHNICAL DATA

Mikoyan MiG-29S 'Fulcrum-C'
Powerplants: Two Klimov/Sarkisov RD-33 turbofans
Developing: 49.4kN (11,110lb st) dry; 81.4kN (18,300lb st) with maximum afterburner
Span: 11.36m (37ft 3.25in)
Length: 17.32m (56ft 10in) including probe; 16.28m (53ft 5in) excluding probe
Height: 4.73m (15ft 6.25in)
Maximum weight: 19,700kg (43,430lb)
Maximum speed: 2,445km/h (1,520mph)
Operational ceiling: 59,060ft
Maximum range: 2,900km (1,800 miles) with three external tanks
Accommodation: Pilot only (two pilots in MiG-29UB 'Fulcrum-B')
Warload: 3,000kg (6,614lb) on six store stations; weapon options include R-60 (AA-8 'Aphid'), R-73 or R-73E (AA-11 'Archer') IR-homing air-to-air missiles, R-27R1 (AA-10A 'Alamo-A') radar-guided air-to-air missiles, conventional bombs, cluster bombs, napalm and rocket pods, depending on mission. Capability to carry single 30kt RN-40 tactical nuclear weapon also exists but is prohibited under terms of CFE Treaty. Internal armament consists of single GSh-301 30mm cannon with 150 rounds
First flown: 6 October 1977 (prototype 9.01 aircraft); 4 May 1984 (MiG-29 'Fulcrum-C')
Entered service: 1983 (MiG-29 'Fulcrum-A')

DEVELOPMENT

A requirement for a new fighter to replace the MiG-21, MiG-23, Su-15 and Su-17 was formally issued in 1972, with detail design of the MiG-29 commencing in 1974 and leading to a successful maiden flight by the first of five prototypes in October 1977. Nine pre-production aircraft were then completed for factory and state flight testing, but major design changes were necessary before series production began in 1982.

CURRENT SERVICE

Approximately 900 MiG-29s of all variants were built for service with Soviet forces and many remain in use with Commonwealth of Independent States (CIS) air arms. CIS republics that inherited MiG-29s are Belarus, Kazakhstan, Moldova, Russia, Turkmenistan, Ukraine and Uzbekistan, although Moldova has disposed of most of its 34 aircraft. In addition, about 400 were produced for export, to friendly states such as Bulgaria, Cuba, Czechoslovakia (subsequently divided between the Czech and Slovak Republics), East Germany (later inherited by Germany at reunification), India, Iran, Iraq, North Korea, Poland, Romania, Syria and Yugoslavia. More recently, aircraft have been exported to Angola,

Bangladesh, Ecuador, Hungary, Malaysia and Peru, while both Yemen and the USA obtained surplus examples from Moldova, although there is no evidence that any of the 21 aircraft purchased by the USA have flown since delivery.

SPECIAL FEATURES

Mid-wing configuration, with wide ogival leading edge root extensions, twin fins and widely separated engines. A unique attribute concerns the installation of perforated intake doors, actuated by extension and compression of the nose oleo. They remain closed when on the ground to prevent foreign object damage, with engine air also obtained via auxiliary inlets in the upper wing root.

VARIANTS

Almost 850 **MiG-29 'Fulcrum-As'** had been built by 1992, when production virtually ceased. The second version was the **MiG-29UB 'Fulcrum-B'** trainer, which is combat-capable, albeit limited by lack of radar, and about 200 were built by 1991. The third major version was the **MiG-29 'Fulcrum-C'**, which has a slightly deeper 'hump-backed' appearance, with the revised spine containing extra avionics and a small amount of additional fuel. Numerous other models have since appeared, including the **MiG-29SMT** and **MiG-29UBT**. Both have a greatly enlarged spine, although they are most likely to be produced through conversion of existing aircraft rather than in new-build form. In addition, the carrier-capable **MiG-29K** was tested from 1989 onwards and may be purchased by India. A consortium of RSK, Dasa and Aerostar have developed an upgrade programme to take MiG-29As up to the latest SMT standard.

MiG-29 'Fulcrum-A'
German Air Force

Mikoyan MiG-31

TWIN-TURBOFAN FIGHTER INTERCEPTOR AIRCRAFT

MiG-31M 'Foxhound' Russian Air Force

DEVELOPMENT

Similar in appearance to the 'Foxbat', the MiG-31 came about in response to an urgent need to modernise Soviet air defence capability in the early 1980s with a fourth-generation interceptor, when it was clear that new MiG-29 and Su-27 fighters would not be available until mid-decade at the earliest. The outcome was a programme that involved the upgrading of existing combat types such as the MiG-25 and this initially led to the Ye-155M. Intended to examine ways of enhancing performance and range, the Ye-155M served as a testbed for the Soloviev (later Aviadvigatel) engine that powers the MiG-31. Equally importantly, it provided the basis for a new interceptor, which flew for the first time in Ye-155MP prototype form in 1975. At that time, it was intended to use the designation MiG-25MP for production aircraft, but this had changed to MiG-31 by the time the 'Foxhound' entered service in 1982.

CURRENT SERVICE

The principal operator is Russia, which has about 350 with Air Defence Forces Fighter aviation (IA-PVO), while Kazakhstan is believed to possess 30 former Soviet machines. China is reported to have ordered the MiG-31, although none have been observed in service and both Iran and Syria have expressed interest in acquiring the 'Foxhound'.

SPECIAL FEATURES

The MiG-31 bears a strong family resemblance to the MiG-25, but is a very different aircraft altogether. Obvious changes include afterburning turbofans and lengthened tailpipes, provision of a second cockpit for the weapon system operator and twin-wheel main undercarriage units. Less apparent, but no less important, is the Zaslon 'Flash Dance' radar, which was the first electronically-scanned, phased-array type to enter service anywhere, and which can track up to ten targets and engage four simultaneously.

VARIANTS

Production opened with the **MiG-31 'Foxhound-A'**, which was replaced on the line by the **MiG-31B** in 1990. Although basically similar, the latter version introduced improvements to the radar, EW and ECM equipment and also carried upgraded R-33S missiles. Existing MiG-31s adopted the new designation of **MiG-31BS** when converted to the same standard. So far, these are the only variants to enter service, but efforts to improve the type have continued, with the development of the **MiG-31M** from 1984. Mikoyan is proposing an upgrade programme to modernise earlier aircraft to this configuration. Differences include a new multimode Zaslon-M radar, a deeper spine with extra fuel, two more stores stations under the fuselage, digital flight controls and multifunction CRT cockpit displays.

TECHNICAL DATA

Mikoyan MiG-31 'Foxhound-A'
Powerplants: Two Aviadvigatel (Soloviev) D-30F6 turbofans
Developing: 93.1kN (20,930lb st) dry; 151.9kN (34,170lb st) with afterburner
Span: 13.465m (44ft 2in)
Length: 22.69m (74ft 5.25in)
Height: 6.15m (20ft 2.25in)
All-up weight: 46,200kg (101,850lb)
Maximum speed: 3,000km/h (1,865mph)
Operational ceiling: 67,600ft
Ferry range: 3,300km (2,050 miles) with maximum fuel and no weapons
Combat radius: 1,200km (745 miles) with maximum internal fuel and four R-33 missiles
Endurance: 3hr 36min (unrefuelled, with auxiliary tanks)
Accommodation: Pilot and weapon system operator
Warload: Four R-33 (AA-9 'Amos') semi-active radar homing air-to-air missiles, two R-40T (AA-6 'Acrid') IR-homing air-to-air missiles and four R-60 (AA-8 'Aphid') IR-homing air-to-air missiles. Integral armament consists of single GSh-6-23M 23mm cannon with 260 rounds
First flown: 16 September 1975 (Ye-155MP)
Entered service: 1982

MiG-31M 'Foxhound' Russian Air Force

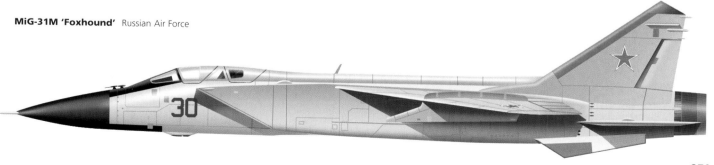

Mikoyan MiG-AT

TWIN-TURBOFAN JET TRAINER/LIGHT ATTACK AIRCRAFT

DEVELOPMENT

Work on design commenced in the late 1980s, with the MiG-AT being chosen in May 1992 as one of two finalists in a new trainer aircraft competition, along with the Yakovlev Yak-130. Initially known as the MiG-ATTA, it originally featured a T-tail layout, although subsequent redesign resulted in a change to the current mid-position tail surfaces. Formal roll-out of the first prototype occurred on 18 May 1995, with taxi trials starting in August, but it did not fly until Spring 1996. Since then, two more prototypes have joined the programme, with the second being to MiG-ATS combat trainer standard, while two further airframes were completed for static testing.

CURRENT SERVICE

Not presently in service, but the Russian Air Force needs 200-250 trainers to replace the Czech-designed L-39 Albatros. Funding for the first ten was requested in late 1996 and an initial batch of 16 aircraft was in production in late 1998, with the first seven then in final assembly. Delivery for evaluation should begin in 2000, but the Yak-130 remains in contention for any follow-on bulk purchases. Export prospects include India, which requires a new trainer, for which a variant of the MiG-AT is being offered.

SPECIAL FEATURES

Generally conventional in layout, the MiG-AT is a low-wing monoplane design with the leading edges of the wing roots swept forward. Its most unusual feature concerns positioning of the engines above the wing roots, slightly aft of the leading edges in order to reduce the risk of ingestion of foreign

MiG-AT

objects. Twin, front-hinged, airbrakes are sited at the extreme rear of the fuselage and all versions can be adapted for carrier landing and launch operations, with optional wing folding, arrester hook and catapult attachment fittings on nose gear.

VARIANTS

The basic trainer variant is the **MiG-AT**, which is available in two sub-variants, specifically the **MiG-ATR** for domestic use with Russian-built engines and avionics, and the **MiG-ATF** with Sextant Topflight avionics from France. A specialist combat trainer version known as the **MiG-ATS** is also available and possesses enhanced weapons options, including the

ability to operate with guided missiles. Lastly, there is the single-seat **MiG-AS**, which is currently still in the concept stage, but which is a dedicated light tactical fighter version with integral gun armament and radar for all-weather operation with air-to-air and air-to-surface missiles.

TECHNICAL DATA

Mikoyan MiG-AT
Powerplants: Two Turbomeca-SNECMA Larzac 04-R20 turbofans
Developing: 14.12kN (3,175lb st)
Span: 10.16m (33ft 4in)
Length: 12.01m (39ft 4.75in)
Height: 4.42m (14ft 6in)
All-up weight: 7,000kg (15,430lb)
Maximum speed: 1,000km/h (621mph)
Operational ceiling: 50,860ft
Ferry range: 2,600km (1,615 miles)
Normal range: 1,200km (745 miles) at Mach 0.5 at 6,000m (19,680ft)
Accommodation: Two crew
Warload: Bombs, rockets and air-to-air missiles may be carried for training or combat applications. Single-seat MiG-AS dedicated attack version has seven stores stations for up to 2,000kg (4,410lb) weapon load, with armament options including R-73E (AA-11 'Archer'), R-77 (AA-12 'Adder'), AIM-9L Sidewinder or Magic air-to-air missiles, Kh-29TD (AS-14 'Kedge') or Kh-31AE/PE (AS-17 'Krypton') air-to-surface guided missiles, Vikhr anti-armour missiles, rocket pods, cluster bombs, conventional bombs and 23mm gun pods
First flown: 16 March 1996
Entered service: (still under development)

MiG-AT

Mil Mi-4

Mil Mi-4 'Hound' Albanian Air Force

DEVELOPMENT

Bearing a strong resemblance to the contemporary American Sikorsky S-55, the Mil Mi-4 'Hound' actually predated the Mi-2. Development was initiated in the autumn of 1951, when Mil and Yakovlev were directed to design, build and fly helicopter prototypes in just one year. The task facing Mil was to conceive a single-engined machine with capacity for 12 passengers and the resulting Mi-4 benefited from a number of design studies previously undertaken by Mil which allowed rapid progress to be made. Ground testing commenced in mid April 1952, but revealed blade flutter that resulted in the maiden flight being delayed until May. Thereafter, few problems were encountered and quantity production was launched in 1953.

CURRENT SERVICE

Few of the 3,000-plus Mi-4s that were built between 1953 and 1964, and operated by 25 nations, remain in service today, but Albania definitely utilises the Mi-4A assault transport and Mi-4S VIP versions, with

1 Squadron, 400 Regiment at Farka-Tirana, and others may still be in limited operation with Afghanistan and North Korea. Chinese-built Harbin Z-5s also survive, primarily with the armed forces of China, although Albania also has some.

SPECIAL FEATURES

Generally similar in appearance to the S-55, the Mi-4 also relied upon a quad landing gear arrangement, with fixed mainwheels and castoring nosewheels. Clamshell doors at the rear of the cabin permitted bulky and outsize loads such as small vehicles to be carried internally, but one of the more distinctive features of some of the military models was a ventral gondola that was used by the navigator/observer; this had provision for mounting a flexible 12.7mm machine gun.

VARIANTS

Like other Mil products, the Mi-4 demonstrated a good deal of versatility and was produced in several variants

for civil and military operation. The majority of the military machines were **Mi-4T** and **Mi-4A** assault transports, but at least one specialised model for maritime tasks is known to have existed, this being the **Mi-4PL 'Hound-B'** for anti-submarine warfare. ASW equipment on the **Mi-4PL** included radar, a towed magnetic anomaly detector, sonobuoys and provisions for anti-submarine depth bombs. Another military derivative known as **'Hound-C'** was adapted for communications jamming duties and the **Mi-4M** was a tactical attack version fitted with a gun turret and also able to use unguided rockets. There were also a number of purely civil versions, including the **Mi-4P** which could accommodate up to ten passengers; the **Mi-4L** de luxe six-seater, and the **Mi-4Skh**, utilised for agricultural tasks such as crop dusting and spraying, as well as aerial fire-fighting.

Mil Mi-4 'Hound'

TECHNICAL DATA

Mil Mi-4 'Hound-A'

Powerplant: One Shvetsov Ash-82V radial piston engine

Developing: 1,268kW (1,700hp)

Driving: Four-blade main and three-blade tail rotors

Main rotor diameter: 21.00m (68ft 11in)

Fuselage length: 16.80m (55ft 1in)

Height: 4.40m (14ft 5.25in)

All-up weight: 7,550kg (16,645lb)

Maximum speed: 200km/h (124mph)

Cruise speed: 160km/h (99mph)

Operational ceiling: 18,045ft

Range: 650 km (404 miles)

Accommodation: Crew, plus up to 12 troops or 1,740kg (3,835lb) of cargo

Warload: Some versions had cannon/machine gun armament

First flown: August 1952; 14 December 1959 (Chinese-built)

Entered service: 1953

Mil Mi-6

TWIN-TURBOSHAFT TRANSPORT HELICOPTER

Mil Mi-6 Russian Air Force

DEVELOPMENT

Conceived for both civil and military applications, development of the Mi-6 began in June 1954, to satisfy Soviet military airlift requirements as well as for use by the state airline, Aeroflot, in more remote regions. The outcome was easily the world's largest and fastest helicopter for several years, but the Mi-6 was also revolutionary in relying on turbine propulsion units, having lifting wings and the ability to undertake the role of flying crane. Flight trials began in the latter half of 1957, paving the way for quantity production before the end of the decade. During the Mi-6's test programme, the helicopter established numerous records for speed and payload capability.

CURRENT SERVICE

Although built in substantial quantities and exported to several friendly nations, the Mi-6 is now in decline, with many having been replaced by the newer and more capable Mi-26 'Halo'. Nevertheless, sizeable numbers are still active with Russia's armed forces (most notably with the Army), and several of the newly independent states like Belarus, Kazakhstan, Ukraine and Uzbekistan inherited examples from Soviet ownership. Other operators that are believed to still

utilise the basic transport model include Egypt, Iraq, Laos, Syria and Vietnam.

SPECIAL FEATURES

Large clamshell-type aft loading doors permit access to the capacious hold of transport-configured Mi-6s. The distinctive stub wings alleviate loads on the rotor during cruising flight, increasing range and payload capability. Most military examples also had provisions for installation of an Afanasayev 12.7mm machine gun in the glazed nose, although this was not always fitted.

VARIANTS

The basic military version and by far the most numerous derivative is the **Mi-6T 'Hook-A'**, intended to fulfil troop transport, cargo airlift and medical evacuation tasks with Soviet forces. Specialised military variants include at least two configured specifically for use as command posts and communications duties on the battlefield, the **Mi-6VKP 'Hook-B'** and **Mi-6AYa 'Hook-C'** (also known as the Mi-22 by the manufacturer). Both possess large amounts of communications equipment and antennae. Other versions also served with Aeroflot, including the **Mi-6A** cargo/passenger transport and the **Mi-6Pass**, an airline version that could carry up to 80 passengers.

TECHNICAL DATA

Mil Mi-6T

Powerplants: Two Aviadvigatel/Soloviev D-25V (TV-2BM) turboshafts

Developing: 4,045kW (5,425shp)

Driving: Five-blade main and four-blade tail rotors

Main rotor diameter: 35.00m (114ft 10in)

Fuselage length: 33.18m (108ft 10.5in)

Wing span: 15.30m (50ft 2.5in)

Height: 9.86m (32ft 4in)

All-up weight: 42,500kg (93,700lb)

Maximum speed: 304km/h (189mph)

Cruise speed: 250km/h (155mph)

Operational ceiling: 14,760ft

Maximum ferry range: 1,450km (900 miles)

Range: 620km (385 miles) with 8,000kg (17,637lb) payload

Accommodation: Five crew and up to 70 troops

Warload: Some have 12.7mm machine gun in nose

Maximum internal payload: 12,000kg (26,450lb)

First flown: 5 June 1957

Mil Mi-6 Russian Air Force

Mil Mi-8, 9 & 17

TWIN-TURBOSHAFT MULTI-PURPOSE HELICOPTER

Mil Mi-8 Russian Air Force

TECHNICAL DATA

Mil Mi-17 'Hip-H'
Powerplants: Two Klimov (Isotov) TV3-117MT turboshafts
Developing: 1,397kW (1,874shp)
Driving: Five-blade main and three-blade tail rotors
Main rotor diameter: 21.29m (69ft 10.25in)
Fuselage length: 18.17m (59ft 7.25in)
Height: 4.76m (15ft 7.5in)
Maximum weight: 13,000kg (28,660lb)
Maximum speed: 250km/h (155mph)
Cruise speed: 240km/h (149mph)
Operational ceiling: 18,380ft
Maximum ferry range: 1,500km (932 miles)
Range at normal AUW: 495km (307 miles)
Accommodation: Two pilots with provision for flight engineer; up to 30 fully-equipped troops
Warload: Suitably configured helicopters can operate with guided anti-tank missiles, unguided rockets, bombs and gun packs; other armament includes 12.7mm machine guns and grenade launchers
Maximum internal payload: 4,000kg (8,820lb)
First flown: 24 June 1961 (V-8 prototype); 2 August 1962 (V-8A prototype); 1975 (Mi-17)
Entered service: 1977 (Mi-17)

DEVELOPMENT

Conceived to replace the Mil Mi-4, design of the Mi-8 began in 1960, and it initially utilised the same main and tail rotor units as its predecessor, as well as the tailboom. However, smaller turboshaft powerplants enabled the engine to be repositioned to a new location above the cabin. This, in turn, offered benefits in terms of simplicity and greater roominess, with the Mi-8 carrying twice as many passengers as the Mi-4. At the outset, the V-8 'Hip-A' prototype was single-engined, but initial flight trials revealed that it was underpowered, and further design led to the twin-engined V-8A 'Hip-B' prototype with Isotov TV2 engines. In this guise, it was far more suitable, and production of the 'Hip-C' began soon after.

CURRENT SERVICE

A hugely successful design, variants of the Mil Mi-8/17 series were supplied to virtually every country in the Soviet sphere of influence. More recently, following the end of the Cold War, it has also been acquired by a few states that were formerly hostile to the Warsaw Pact. Today, examples of the 'Hip' serve with at least 70 countries around the world.

SPECIAL FEATURES

The basic configuration has remained virtually unchanged through almost four decades of production, with the engines situated above the cabin, allowing unobstructed access to the hold via a side door or through the clamshell rear doors. Outrigger units attached to the cabin sides can carry a formidable array of weaponry. Mi-8 variants have the tail rotor mounted to starboard; on Mi-17 variants it is mounted to port and they also have dust filters ahead of the air inlets. Most examples have round cabin windows, but Mi-8P and Mi-8S machines in civil and military service have larger rectangular windows.

VARIANTS

Numerous versions of the Mi-8/17 series exist, with the most common models being generically known as 'Hip-C' and 'Hip-H'. The Mi-8P commercial transport, Mi-8S airliner version and Mi-8T military and civil utility models all use the 'Hip-C' code name, while 'Hip-H' is allocated to Mi-17 models, although rather confusingly those in Russian service use Mi-8MT and Mi-8MTV designations. Also widely used by Russia, the Mi-8T 'Hip-E' was configured for the airborne assault role, while special mission versions include the Mi-8VZPU 'Hip-D', Mi-9 'Hip-G' and Mi-19 command post/relay aircraft; the Mi-8SMV 'Hip-J' ECM jammer; the Mi-8PPA 'Hip-K' and Mi-17PP communications jammer/comint aircraft; and the Mi-171 export equivalent of the Mi-8AMT derivative.

Mil Mi-17H Russian Air Force

Mil Mi-14

TWIN-TURBOSHAFT MULTI-PURPOSE MARITIME HELICOPTER

Mil Mi-14PL 'Haze' Polish Navy

TECHNICAL DATA

Mil Mi-14PL 'Haze-A'

Powerplants: Two Klimov (Isotov) TV3-117MT turboshafts
Developing: 1,454W (1,950shp)
Driving: Five-blade main and three-blade tail rotors
Main rotor diameter: 21.29m (69ft 10.25in)
Fuselage length: 18.38m (60ft 3.25in)
Height: 6.93m (22ft 9in)
All-up weight: 14,000kg (30,865lb)
Maximum speed: 230km/h (143mph)
Cruise speed: 215km/h (133mph)
Operational ceiling: 13,125ft
Maximum range: 1,135km (705 miles)
Endurance: 5hr 56min
Accommodation: Four crew
Warload: Includes torpedoes, nuclear depth bombs and depth charges in an enclosed weapons bay in the lower hull
First flown: September 1969 (V-14 prototype); 1973 (Mi-14PL)
Entered service: 11 May 1976

DEVELOPMENT

A logical follow-on to the Mi-8 'Hip', the Mi-14 is optimised for maritime roles and was designated V-8G when development began in 1966. Flying for the first time in September 1969, the prototype retained the Mi-8 powerplant, but further development resulted in adoption of TV3-117M engines and the VR-14 gearbox. In this guise, a prototype Mi-14 flew during 1973, with deliveries for service evaluation following three years later.

CURRENT SERVICE

The major operator of the Mi-14 'Haze' series is Russia's Navy, which is believed to have about 60, including ten Mi-14PLs and a substantial number of Mi-14PSs. Other air arms with the basic Mi-14PL are Bulgaria, Cuba, Ethiopia, North Korea, Libya, Romania and Syria, while Poland uses Mi-14PS, Mi-14PW and Mi-14PX versions. In addition, the US Army obtained two examples of the 'Haze' for threat simulation, but only one is now thought to be active.

SPECIAL FEATURES

Although it was based on the Mi-8, the Mi-14 differs markedly, with the most significant change being adoption of a boat hull. Other notable features include flotation bags on each side of the fuselage, while the requirement to land and take-off from water made fully retractable landing gear essential.

VARIANTS

The basic ASW derivative and the most numerous model is the **Mi-14PL 'Haze-A'** (known by Poland as the **Mi-14PW**). This normally has a crew of four and is fitted with search radar under the nose section, as well as a Kalmar ASW suite with an OKA-2 retractable dual mode active/passive sonar plus launch chutes for sonobuoys or signal flares. An APM-60 towed MAD is also standard equipment. Refinements to the basic aircraft resulted in the **Mi-14PL 'Strike'**, with provisions to fire the Kh-23 (AS-7 'Kerry') air-to-surface missile, and the **Mi-14PLM**, which had updated equipment including a repositioned MAD and a rescue basket. Fewer examples of the **Mi-14BT 'Haze-B'** mine countermeasures version were produced and most have since been adapted for SAR, largely as a result of poor performance when towing the sled. The only other military version to be produced as new is the **Mi-14PS 'Haze-C'**, which is a dedicated search-and-rescue model that can carry up to ten 20-place life rafts and is also able to accommodate as many as 19 survivors in the cabin. Main differences, apart from the lack of ASW gear, are the retractable rescue hoist that has a basket for up to three people, plus searchlights positioned on each side of the nose and below the boom. In addition, Poland modified one Mi-14PW to **Mi-14PX** standard for SAR training, with conversion involving removal of all portable ASW gear.

Mil Mi-14 'Haze'

Mil Mi-24 Hind

TWIN-TURBOSHAFT ANTI-ARMOUR ATTACK HELICOPTER

Mi-24 Hind Czech Air Force

TECHNICAL DATA

Mil Mi-24P Hind-F

Powerplants: Two Klimov TV3-117MT turboshafts
Developing: 1,434kW (1,923shp)
Driving: Five-blade main and three-blade tail rotors
Main rotor diameter: 17.30m (56ft 9.25in)
Fuselage length: 17.51m (57ft 5.25in)
Wing span: 6.66m (21ft 10.25in)
Height: 3.97m (13ft 0.5in)
Maximum weight: 12,000kg (26,455lb)
Maximum speed: 320km/h (198mph)
Cruise speed: 270km/h (168mph)
Operational ceiling: 14,750ft
Maximum ferry range: 1,000km (620 miles)
Range with internal fuel: 450km (279 miles)
Endurance: 4hr
Accommodation: Pilot and gunner in tandem cockpits; up to eight passengers in cabin
Warload: GSh-30K twin-barrel 30mm cannon with 750 rounds replaces gun turret of earlier models; also compatible with 9M17P Skorpion (AT-2 'Swatter') anti-armour missile, with maximum load of four on twin rails at wingtips. Four underwing pylons may carry assorted rocket or gun pods or grenade launchers, bombs, mine dispensers, flares or auxiliary fuel tanks, up to maximum weight of 1,500kg (3,300lb).
Max external stores payload: 2,400kg (5,291lb)
First flown: 19 September 1969 (V-24 prototype)
Entered service: 1973-74 (Mi-24A Hind-A)

DEVELOPMENT

Almost certainly prompted by the appearance of the Bell AH-1G HueyCobra, development of a Soviet counterpart began in the mid-1960s. In its original form, however, the Mi-24 was fundamentally an armed assault helicopter, with room for up to eight troops, while able to employ rockets, anti-armour missiles and a 12.7mm machine gun. Design work was completed late in the decade, with the first of 12 V-24 prototypes making its maiden flight in September 1969. This featured side-by-side seating for pilot and navigator and service deployment of the broadly similar Mi-24A Hind-A followed in 1973, with a major redesign leading to the Mi-24D Hind-D.

CURRENT SERVICE

Examples of the Mil Mi-24 family are currently in service with more than 40 countries world-wide. Nations known to operate Mi-24, Mi-25 and Mi-35 versions are Afghanistan, Algeria, Angola, Armenia, Azerbaijan, Belarus, Bulgaria, Croatia, Cuba, Czech Republic, Ethiopia, Georgia, Hungary, India, Iraq, Kazakhstan, North Korea, Kyrgizia, Libya, Mozambique, Peru, Poland, Russia, Rwanda, Sierra Leone, Slovak Republic, Sri Lanka, Sudan, Syria, Tajikistan, Turkmenistan, Ukraine, USA, Uzbekistan, Vietnam and Yemen. Limited production of later versions is still believed to be underway at Rostov.

SPECIAL FEATURES

Initial production versions had side-by-side seating for pilot and navigator, with a gunner in the nose, but with effect from the Mi-24D Hind-D, a stepped tandem cockpit was adopted, with the gunner in front. Small stub wings carry armament, while the nose section features sensor equipment and gun or cannon armament. A small cabin has room for up to eight troops.

VARIANTS

About 250 examples of the early **Mi-24A/B Hind-A/B/C** were completed before production turned to the **Mi-24D Hind-D**. This was the first gunship and about 350 were built during 1973-77, by which time the **Mi-24V Hind-E** had appeared. At least 1,000 were built at two factories, making it the most numerous model of the Hind family, but more than 600 cannon-armed **Mi-24P Hind-Fs** were completed during 1981-90. Export Mi-24Ds used **Mi-25** or **Mi-35D** designations, while the **Mi-35** and **Mi-35P** were **Mi-24V** and **Mi-24P** equivalents. Several specialised versions exist, including the **Mi-24RKR Hind-G1**, with a 'clutching hand' device to gather soil samples for NBC analysis, and the **Mi-24K Hind-G2**, with a large camera in the cabin for reconnaissance and artillery fire correction.

Mi-35 Hind Afghanistan Air Force

285

Mil Mi-26

TWIN-TURBOSHAFT TRANSPORT HELICOPTER

Mil Mi-26 'Halo' Russian Air Force

TECHNICAL DATA

Mil Mi-26 'Halo-A'
Powerplants: Two ZMKB Progress (Lotarev)
D-136 turboshafts
Developing: 8,500kW (11,399shp)
Driving: Eight-blade main and five-blade tail
rotors
Main rotor diameter: 32.00m (105ft 0in)
Fuselage length: 33.745m (110ft 8.5in)
Height: 8.145m (26ft 8.75in)
All-up weight: 56,000kg (123,450lb)
Maximum speed: 295km/h (183mph)
Cruise speed: 255km/h (158mph)
Operational ceiling: 15,100ft
Maximum ferry range: 1,920km (1,190 miles)
Range: (with 7,700kg (16,975lb) payload) 500km
(310 miles)
Accommodation: Four crew and up to 80 fully-
equipped troops
Maximum payload: 20,000kg (44,090lb)
First flown: 14 December 1977
Entered service: 1983

DEVELOPMENT

Work on design of what ultimately became the Mi-26 'Halo' was initiated in the early 1970s, when it was known as the Mi-6M. Currently the world's most powerful helicopter, the 'Halo' was intended from the outset to replace the Mi-6 'Hook', which was then the principal heavy lift helicopter with the armed forces of the USSR. However, the new machine would have significantly greater payload capability, increased by between 50 and 100 per cent when compared with its predecessor. Flight tests began shortly before the end of 1977, and involved several prototypes before service evaluation commenced in 1982.

CURRENT SERVICE

The break-up of the Soviet Union resulted in several newly independent nation states inheriting examples of the Mi-26 that were stationed in their territory with the Red Army. Among the air arms known to have acquired Mi-26s in this way are Belarus, Kazakhstan, Russia, Ukraine and Uzbekistan. Mi-26s have also been exported in limited numbers to Cambodia, India and Peru.

SPECIAL FEATURES

Despite its size, the Mi-26 is essentially conventional in design and appearance, although it was the first helicopter in the world to successfully utilise an eight-blade main rotor. The payload capability and size of the cargo hold are comparable to the C-130 Hercules, and the Mi-26 has twin clamshell doors at the rear as well as a downward-hinged lower door with an integral ramp for access to the cargo compartment. Flying crane versions feature a work station for the

sling supervisor, although the location of the gondola varies, some having it below the fuselage aft of the nosewheels, while on others, it is under the rear ramp or on the fuselage side.

VARIANTS

The principal military transport helicopter is the **Mi-26**, which is in fairly widespread service, but numerous other versions have appeared for transport tasks and more specialised duties. These include the **Mi-26T**, which is similar, but intended specifically for civilian use. Other civil variants based on the Mi-26T are the **Firefighting Mi-26**, with internal capacity for up to 15,000 litres (3,962 US gallons) of retardant or 17,260

litres (4,560 US gallons) in an underslung bucket, and the **Geological Survey Mi-26**, with towed seismic apparatus. Several more civil versions exist, like the **Mi-26TM** flying crane and the **Mi-26MS** for medical evacuation. Purely military derivatives identified to date include the **Mi-26NEF-M** for anti-submarine warfare with a towed magnetic anomaly detector and search radar, and the **Mi-26PP**, which is understood to perform radio relay tasks (although this may be known as the **Mi-27**, which is reported to be a command support version).

Mil Mi-26 'Halo'

Mil Mi-28

DEVELOPMENT

Design of the Mil Mi-28 was initiated in 1980, with the first prototype making its maiden flight shortly before the end of 1982. Two prototypes were built for initial trials, with the first having a conventional three-blade tail rotor, while the second was fitted with twin tail rotors. Further development resulted in the appearance of the Mi-28A in 1987 and again, two examples were produced, with the second being to the planned definitive configuration, incorporating a movable electro-optical sensor turret below the nose, revised exhaust diffusers and prominent wingtip chaff/flare dispensers.

CURRENT SERVICE

The Mi-28 has yet to enter service and may never do so, with the Russian Army having expressed a preference for the Kamov Ka-50 in October 1994. Nevertheless, development work has continued.

SPECIAL FEATURES

The Mi-28 conforms to classic helicopter gunship design by virtue of featuring tandem, stepped cockpits for the pilot (rear) and navigator/gunner (front). Small, downward-canted, stub wings each have two pylons for carriage of weapons, with bulbous pods at the extremities containing chaff/flare dispenser units for self-protection. The Mi-28 also has a single-barrel 30mm gun in a turret below the forward cockpit and a tailwheel-type fixed landing gear. The thimble nose radome contains a misile guidance radar and beneath it are two fixed infrared sensors.

VARIANTS

Original two prototypes to basic **Mi-28** standard were followed by two more prototypes, which were given the designation **Mi-28A**. Subsequent modification of the first **Mi-28A** resulted in the **Mi-28N**, unofficially

Mil Mi-28

known as 'Night Hunter' and 'Night Pirate' as it possesses night/all-weather capabilities. In this guise, it began hover trials in November 1995 and transitioned to forward flight for the first time at the end of April 1997. The most visible evidence of change is provided by the mast-mounted millimetre wave radar pod that offers 360° scan, but it also features a new shuttered turret containing laser and optical sensors, including low-light-level TV. Other changes included installation of an uprated transmission and an integrated flight/weapon aiming system with automatic terrain-following and target search/detection capability. Other versions have been conceived for amphibious assault support and air-to-air missions, but there is no evidence that these have progressed to the flight test stage.

Mil Mi-28

TECHNICAL DATA

Mil Mi-28A
Powerplants: Two Klimov TV3-117VMA turboshafts
Developing: 1,636kW (2,194shp)
Driving: Five-blade main and two two-blade tail rotors
Main rotor diameter: 17.20m (56ft 5in)
Fuselage length: 17.01m (55ft 9.75in)
Wing span: 4.88m (16ft 0.25in)
Height: 3.82m (12ft 6.5in)
Maximum weight: 11,500kg (25,353lb)
Maximum speed: 300km/h (186mph)
Cruise speed: 265km/h (164mph)
Operational ceiling: 19,020ft
Maximum ferry range: 1,100km (683 miles)
Range with maximum standard fuel: 460km (285 miles)
Endurance: 2hr
Accommodation: Pilot and navigator/weapons operator
Warload: Four wing hardpoints each able to carry load of up to 480kg (1,058lb), weapon options including maximum of 16 9M114 Shturm C (AT-6 'Spiral') anti-armour missiles or rocket or gun pods. Up to eight 9M39 Igla-V air-to-air missiles may be carried as alternative and Mi-28 also compatible with KGMU-2 mine dispenser. Integral 2A42 30mm turret-mounted cannon, with 250 rounds located under nose section.
First flown: 10 November 1982 (Mi-28 prototype); 1987 (Mi-28A); 30 April 1997 (Mi-28N)

Mil Mi-34

SINGLE RADIAL-ENGINED LIGHT MULTI-PURPOSE HELICOPTER

Mil Mi-34

TECHNICAL DATA

Mil Mi-34C 'Hermit'
Powerplant: One VOKBM M-14V-26 nine-cylinder radial air-cooled engine
Developing: 239kW (320hp)
Driving: Four-blade main and two-blade tail rotors
Main rotor diameter: 10.01m (32ft 10in)
Fuselage length: 8.75m (28ft 8.5in)
Height: 2.75m (9ft 0.25in)
All-up weight: 1,450kg (3,196lb)
Maximum speed: 225km/h (140mph)
Cruise speed: 180km/h (112mph)
Operational ceiling: 16,400ft
Range with maximum fuel: 420km (261 miles)
Endurance: 2hr 26min
Accommodation: One or two pilots and two passengers or cargo in rear of cabin
First flown: 17 November 1986

DEVELOPMENT

Flown for the first time as long ago as 1986, the Mi-34 was originally conceived as a potential replacement for the Mi-2 'Hoplite' light utility helicopter and could well have been built in vast numbers had history taken a different course. Two flying prototypes and a structural test airframe were completed for trials by mid-1987 and during the course of a fairly lengthy test programme, the 'Hermit' became the first Russian helicopter to execute a normal loop and roll manoeuvre. Following completion of flight trials, production was begun during 1993, although financial constraints have had a serious impact on the planned production rate. In consequence, relatively few examples of the Mi-34 have been completed to date, with most of those that have been delivered going to civilian customers or paramilitary agencies, such as the Moscow traffic police.

CURRENT SERVICE

The only country that is presently known to utilise the Mi-34 'Hermit' in a military capacity is Bosnia-Herzegovina, which acquired a single example after the cessation of hostilities with Serbia. It is used for the basic training of pilots of the Muslim-Croat Federation Army Air Force.

SPECIAL FEATURES

A small and light helicopter of largely conventional design, with proven aerobatic qualities, including loop manoeuvre and ability to fly backwards at speeds of up to 130km/h (81mph). Incorporates skid-type main undercarriage, with small skid at base of fin to protect tail rotor assembly. Fin features slight degree of sweep and is mounted on the port side, capped by a T-tail.

VARIANTS

The basic version is the **Mi-34C**, with space for one or two pilots, plus two passengers on a bench seat in the rear of the cabin, although this can be removed to permit carriage of cargo. The specialist **Mi-34P** version is based on the Mi-34C but has been adapted for police work and patrol duty, while the **Mi-34A** is a proposed luxury derivative with an Allison 250-C20R turboshaft engine. One other version is the **Mi-34 VAZ** which is powered by a pair of 164kW (220hp) VAZ-430 rotary engines. This was flown in prototype form during 1993, but does not yet appear to have entered quantity production.

Mi-34A

Mitsubishi F-1

TWIN-TURBOFAN TACTICAL FIGHTER

Mitsubishi F-1 Japanese Air Self-Defence Force

TECHNICAL DATA

Mitsubishi F-1

Powerplants: Two Ishikawajima-Harima TF40-IHI-801A turbofans

Thrust: 22.75kN (5,115lb st) dry; 32.49kN (7,305lb st) with afterburner

Span: 7.88m (25ft 10.25in)

Length: 17.85m (58ft 6.75in) including probe

Height: 4.48m (14ft 8.25in)

All-up weight: 13,700kg (30,203lb)

Maximum speed: 1,700km/h (1,056mph)

Operational ceiling: 50,000ft

Ferry range: 2,600km (1,616 miles)

Combat radius: 555km (345 miles) on hi-lo-hi attack mission with two anti-ship missiles and two drop tanks

Accommodation: Pilot only

Warload: Maximum ordnance load of 2,722 kg (6,000lb) on four wing stations and one centreline station. Weapon options include bombs, rocket pods, radar-guided ASM-1 anti-ship attack missiles and AIM-9L Sidewinder IR-homing air-to-air missiles. Internal armament comprises one JM61 Vulcan 20mm cannon with 750 rounds.

First flown: 3 June 1975 (prototype); 16 June 1977 (first production aircraft)

Entered service: April 1978

DEVELOPMENT

Originally known as the FST-2Kai (signifying modified), the F-1 was a logical progression from the T-2 advanced trainer and shares a good deal of commonality with that type. One major difference is that the F-1 is only a single-seater, with the space taken up by a second cockpit on the trainer being allocated to a much more sophisticated array of avionics equipment. The latter includes a Mitsubishi Electric J/ASQ-1 fire control system and bombing computer, a Ferranti inertial navigation system and radar homing and warning sub-systems. The second and third production examples of the T-2 were adapted to function as testbeds for the F-1 and these flew for the first time just a few days apart in June 1975. Evaluation of both prototypes by the Air Proving Wing at Gifu was completed in little more than a year, culminating in type approval in November 1976, which paved the way for the first production orders.

CURRENT SERVICE

Attrition has been fairly light during more than 20 years of operational service with the Air Self-Defence Force, with barely a handful having been destroyed. However, some of the earliest production examples have now been retired and only about 55 F-1s are still in use, currently equipping two squadrons of the

3rd Air Wing, Misawa AB in Northern Japan and 8th Air Wing at Tsuiki AB in the south.

SPECIAL FEATURES

Similar in configuration to the Anglo-French Jaguar strike aircraft, featuring a shoulder mounted wing arrangement with modest anhedral and downward-canted horizontal tail surfaces. Twin turbofan engines (licence-built Rolls-Royce/Turboméca Adour Mk 801s, as used by the Jaguar) are positioned side-by-side in the aft fuselage and fed by high-set inlet ducts. The F-1 also has a distinctive 'hump-backed' appearance because of the avionics bay situated aft of the cockpit.

VARIANTS

Only one basic variant was built for the JASDF, this being the **F-1**, which entered service in 1978 and remained in production until early in 1987. By then, plans to purchase about 160 aircraft had been greatly curtailed because of financial concerns and only 77 were completed for service with three squadrons. Some have recently undergone a service life extension programme to ensure they remain operationally effective until replaced by the new Mitsubishi F-2, with effect from about mid-2000.

Mitsubishi F-1 Japanese Air Self-Defence Force

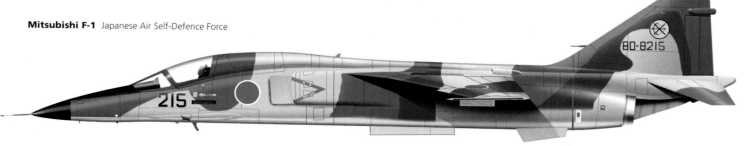

Mitsubishi F-2

SINGLE TURBOFAN FIGHTER AIRCRAFT

Mitsubishi F-2A

DEVELOPMENT

The origins of the F-2 date back to the mid-1980s, when the Japanese Air Self-Defence Force formulated a requirement for a new warplane to replace the Mitsubishi F-1. Known initially as the FS-X, it was decided that a modified F-16C was the best solution and this was formally selected in October 1987. Just over a year later, Mitsubishi was appointed as prime contractor. Lockheed Martin is also closely involved, being chosen to build aft fuselage sections. Contract award followed in early 1989, although concerns over technology transfer to Japan by the USA then caused some delay. Eventually, work on construction of the first of four prototypes began in early 1994 and the initial example of the FS-X was rolled out in January 1995, flying for the first time some ten months later. Trials with the Japan Defence Agency test organisation at Gifu began in March 1996 and have generally gone well, although evidence of flutter when flying with two ASM-2 missiles and the discovery of wing cracks caused a nine-month delay.

CURRENT SERVICE

The Mitsubishi F-2 was still under development at the time of writing, but deliveries to the first operational unit are scheduled to commence around mid-2000. Current plans call for the procurement of at least 130 aircraft (83 F-2As and 47 F-2Bs), with the first recipient being No 3 Squadron of No 3 Wing at Misawa. The next JASDF unit to transition, in 2003, will be No 6 Squadron of No 8 Wing at Tsuiki, followed by No 8 Squadron of No 3 Wing at Misawa in 2005. All three squadrons will be predominantly equipped with the single-seat F-2A versions, while the bulk of the F-2B two-seaters are expected to be assigned to an operational conversion unit.

SPECIAL FEATURES

Basically similar in appearance to the Lockheed Martin F-16 Fighting Falcon, the F-2 incorporates a number of structural modifications, as well as having radically different avionics equipment, much of which is of indigenous design. Alterations to the wing include

greater span, root chord and area, while it also has a tapered trailing edge and an increased-span tailplane. The forward fuselage is also slightly lengthened, to accommodate new radar and other avionics.

VARIANTS

Apart from the XF-2A and XF-2B (two-seat) prototypes, only two versions have been announced to date. These are the production F-2A and its two-seat F-2B equivalent. Both versions are fully combat-capable, although the F-2B will have a lower combat radius as a result of provision of a second cockpit, with some penalty in internal fuel capacity.

TECHNICAL DATA

Mitsubishi F-2A

Powerplant: One General Electric F110-GE-129 turbofan licence-built by Ishikawajima Harima Industries
Developing: 131.7kN (29,600lb st)
Span: 11.13m (36ft 6.25in) over missile rails
Length: 15.52m (50ft 11in)
Height: 4.96m (16ft 3.25in)
Maximum weight: 22,100kg (48,722lb)
Maximum speed: Approximately Mach 2
Accommodation: Pilot only (two pilots in F-2B)
Warload: Includes radar-guided AIM-7 Sparrow and IR-homing AIM-9 Sidewinder air-to-air missiles, as well as ASM-1 and ASM-2 anti-ship attack missiles, bombs, cluster bombs and rockets. One M61A1 Vulcan 20mm internal cannon
First flown: 7 October 1995 (XF-2A prototype)
Entered service: Mid-2000 (first delivery expected)

Mitsubishi F-2A

Mitsubishi MU-2

TWIN-TURBOPROP LIGHT UTILITY TRANSPORT AIRCRAFT

Mitsubishi MU-2R Japanese Air Self-Defence Force

DEVELOPMENT

The origins of the Mitsubishi MU-2 date back to 1959, when the Japanese manufacturer began design of a light, twin-engined, utility transport aircraft with good STOL attributes. The resulting machine was primarily aimed at the executive transport market and achieved considerable success, with well over 800 examples of several different variations eventually being built before the assembly line closed in the mid-1980s.

CURRENT SERVICE

Only four air arms are believed to use versions of the MU-2. Not surprisingly, Japan has always been the major operator, purchasing a total of 53 aircraft of three basic sub-types for the Air Force and Army, but only about 30 are thought to remain active. Mexico's naval air arm has a single MU-2J which is used for light transport duties, the Republic of Congo operates two MU-2JEs and the Dominican Republic has one aircraft.

SPECIAL FEATURES

The basic layout of the MU-2 varies little from version

to version, with all models featuring a neat, high-wing layout, from which two turboprop engines (Astazou on the MU-2A prototype, Garrett TPE331 on subsequent production articles) are suspended. Fixed auxiliary fuel tanks are fitted as standard on most models, with the Japanese Army's MU-2K (military designation LR-1) having provisions for installation of vertical and oblique cameras, as well as SLAR sensors and underwing stores that include rockets, bombs and 12.7mm (0.5 in) calibre machine guns. The SAR-configured MU-2S features additional navigation and communications equipment and also has bulged observation cabin windows and a sliding entry door that can be opened in flight to facilitate the dropping of rafts and other supplies. The most distinctive feature of this version is an extended 'thimble' nose containing Doppler search radar.

VARIANTS

Numerous variants of the basic MU-2 emerged, but only a few were destined for military service. The majority of these were for domestic use with

elements of the Japanese Self-Defence Forces, and only a handful have been sold directly to overseas air arms, as a result of national policy relating to the export of military equipment. The most numerous military derivative was the **MU-2S**, 29 examples of which were produced for the Air Self-Defence Force's Air Rescue Wing, which maintains detachments at major air bases around the country. These perform search-and-rescue duties, but are progressively being replaced by the Hawker U-125. Another JASDF version was the **MU-2J**, which was specially configured for navaid calibration; four were built, but all have been retired from service. The only other pure military version is the Army Self-Defence Force's **LR-1**, 20 of which were built. Most are still employed in the liaison/photo-reconnaissance role.

TECHNICAL DATA

Mitsubishi MU-2J
Powerplants: Two Garrett TPE331-6-251M turboprops
Developing: 496kW (665shp)
Driving: Three-blade propellers
Span: 11.95m (39ft 2.5in)
Length: 12.03m (39ft 5.75in)
Height: 4.17m (13ft 8.25in)
Maximum weight: 4,900kg (10,800lb)
Maximum cruise speed: 556km/h (345mph)
Economical cruise speed: 491km/h (305mph)
Operational Ceiling: 33,200ft
Maximum range: 2,500km (1,550 miles)
Accommodation: Two pilots and up to 12 passengers
First flown: 14 September 1963
Entered service: 1965 (civil operators)

Mitsubishi MU-2S Japanese Air Self-Defence Force

Mitsubishi T-2

TWIN-TURBOFAN ADVANCED TRAINER AIRCRAFT

Mitsubishi T-2 Japanese Air Self-Defence Force

DEVELOPMENT

Unique in being the first aircraft with supersonic performance capability to be designed in Japan, the T-2 was initially perceived as a combat trainer that would serve as a convenient stepping stone between the veteran F-86F Sabre, which performed the combat training role, and the F-104J Starfighters and F-4EJ Phantoms that equipped operational forces. It was also intended to provide the Japanese aerospace industry with valuable experience that could be used to develop and produce an indigenous jet fighter. As it turned out, the T-2 proved doubly significant, for it was adapted into single-seat fighter form as the F-1. The trainer programme was initiated in September 1967, when Mitsubishi was selected as the prime contractor and awarded a development contract. The first of four prototype XT-2s flew in July 1971 and a successful test programme culminated in a go-ahead for full-scale production for the Air Self-Defence Force.

CURRENT SERVICE

Apart from one or two examples that provide trainer support to the F-1s assigned to combat-capable units of the Air Self-Defence Force, T-2s are concentrated almost exclusively at Matsushima, where they equip two squadrons of No 4 Wing. A handful of aircraft

also undertake chase and test duties with the Air Development Test Wing at Gifu, which is also home to TRDI's one-off T-2CCV.

SPECIAL FEATURES

A two-seat trainer with pilots in tandem. Broadly similar configuration to the Anglo-French SEPECAT Jaguar, with a shoulder-mounted wing arrangement featuring modest anhedral and sharply downward-canted horizontal tail surfaces. Twin turbofan engines (licence-built Rolls-Royce/Turboméca Adour Mk 801s, as used by the Jaguar) are located side-by-side in the aft fuselage and fed by high-set inlet ducts.

VARIANTS

Following on from the quartet of **XT-2** prototypes, orders were placed for a total of 92 production aircraft, but two of these were subsequently adapted to serve as prototypes for the F-1 attack aircraft. Of the rest, 28 emerged as **T-2** advanced trainers and 62 as **T-2A** combat trainers, although both versions serve with No 4 Wing. The **T-2CCV** control-configured vehicle incorporates triplex digital fly-by-wire and computer control systems, plus vertical and horizontal canard surfaces. The third prototype XT-2 was selected for modification as the T-2CCV and it flew for the first time in this guise on 9 August 1983; following a brief

TECHNICAL DATA

Mitsubishi T-2

Powerplants: Two Ishikawajima-Harima TF40-IHI-801A turbofans
Developing: 22.75kN (5,115lb st) dry; 32.49kN (7,305lb st) with afterburner
Span: 7.305m (25ft 10.25in)
Length: 17.85m (58ft 6.75in) including probe
Height: 4.39m (14ft 5in)
All-up weight: 12,800kg (28,219lb)
Maximum speed: 1,700km/h (1,056mph)
Operational ceiling: 50,000ft
Ferry range: 2,593km (1,611 miles)
Accommodation: Two pilots
Payload: Maximum ordnance load of about 2,000 kg (4,409lb) on four underwing stores stations, two wing tip racks and centreline pylon. Weapon options for combat training missions include bombs, rocket and AIM-9L Sidewinder IR-homing air-to-air missiles. Integral JM61 Vulcan 20mm cannon also installed.
First flown: 20 July 1971 (XT-2 prototype)
Entered service: 1976

evaluation, it was subsequently delivered to the Technical Research and Development Institute (TRDI) of the Japan Defence Agency. SEE ALSO: MITSUBISHI F-1

Mitsubishi T-2
Japanese Air Self-Defence Force

Morane-Saulnier MS.760 Paris

TWIN-TURBOJET COMMUNICATIONS/TRAINER AIRCRAFT

MS.760 Paris French Air Force

DEVELOPMENT

The world's first business jet resulted from adapting the Fleuret experimental two-seat jet trainer that flew for the first time in January 1953. In revised form, with a greatly enlarged cabin able to hold four people, the Paris met with reasonable success on both civil and military markets as an executive transport and for communications and liaison duties.

CURRENT SERVICE

Military use of the Paris is presently limited to the air forces of Argentina and France. However, numbers on charge have been in decline in both countries, with the French Navy phasing out the last of its examples quite recently. Despite that, the French Air Force still uses about 15 examples for communications tasks and has about a dozen more in storage, with no plans to dispose of any of these aircraft in the immediate future. A handful of aircraft also operate with the

Centre d'Essais en Vol (Flight Research Centre) from various locations. Argentina's Air Force also retains about 15 examples of the Paris IIR at BAM El Plumerillo, Mendoza, although these are mainly used for weapons training and could theoretically undertake light attack duties. Armament capability is extremely limited but they can operate with two 7.5mm machine guns in the nose section and may also carry external ordnance on two underwing hardpoints, with weapon options including up to a dozen 75mm rockets or two 118kg (54lb) light bombs.

SPECIAL FEATURES

Functional in appearance and spartan in cabin layout, the Paris is a low-wing monoplane design, with a T-tail and a tricycle undercarriage arrangement. The twin engines are buried in the centre-fuselage section and fed by small air inlet ducts in the wing roots. Wing tip auxiliary fuel tanks were introduced on the Paris

II and retrospectively installed on earlier aircraft.

VARIANTS

Several basic versions of the Paris have emerged, either in new-build form or as a result of subsequent modification programmes. Production was launched with the **MS.760A Paris I**, fitted with Marboré II engines, although this was soon replaced by the **Paris IA**. The latter variant was basically identical, but performance benefits accrued from the installation of more powerful Marboré VI turbojets. The ultimate new-build version was the **MS.760B Paris II**, which not only had the more powerful engines but also possessed small wing tip tanks, thus raising standard fuel capacity from 1,415 litres (374 US gallons) to 1,870 litres (494 US gallons). In addition, a retrofit project involving replacement of the original engines by the Marboré VI powerplant on the Paris I resulted in the appearance of the **Paris IR**.

TECHNICAL DATA

Morane-Saulnier MS.760B Paris II

Powerplants: Two Turboméca Marboré VI turbojets
Thrust: 4.71kN (1,058lb st)
Span: 10.15m (33ft 3.5in)
Length: 10.24m (33ft 7.25in)
Height: 2.60m (8ft 6.25in)
All-up weight: 3,920kg (8,642lb)
Maximum speed: 695km/h (432mph)
Operational ceiling: 39,370ft
Ferry range: 1,740km (1,081 miles)
Accommodation: Pilot and up to three passengers
First flown: 29 July 1954
Entered service: 1958

MS.760 Paris French Air Force

Mudry CAP 10

SINGLE PISTON-ENGINED AEROBATIC AIRCRAFT

Mudry CAP 10 French Air Force

DEVELOPMENT

Derived from the Piel Emeraude (Emerald) which was originally marketed as a light two-seat aerobatic and touring aircraft for home construction or assembly, the CAP 10 prototype was first flown in the summer of 1968 and achieved French certification in September 1970. It was subsequently manufactured by Avions Mudry at Bernay until it filed for bankruptcy in 1996, by which time some 277 had been built for civil and military customers. Production resumed in 1997, initially as the Akrotech Europe CAP 10 and, since January 1999, as the CAP Aviation CAP 10.

CURRENT SERVICE

More than 50 examples of the CAP 10 were operated as a basic trainer and grading aircraft at Cognac by the French Air Force, which took delivery of its first examples in 1970. These have since been replaced by the Epsilon and only three are thought to still be on charge, with the Equipe de Voltige l'Armee de l'Air display team at Salon-de-Provence. In addition, nine CAP 10Bs (of ten delivered from 1979) are used for

grading at Lanvéoc-Poulmic by 51 Escadrille of the French Navy Air Arm, and the Centre d'Essais en Vol (Flight Research Centre) has at least two for test support tasks. Other military operators include South Korea which received two CAP 10Bs in 1995, and Morocco, which also acquired two for training support of the *Green March* aerobatic team.

SPECIAL FEATURES

A low-wing monoplane design, with tailwheel undercarriage configuration and spatted mainwheel units. Two occupants are seated side-by-side beneath the large aft-sliding cockpit canopy, with space for up to 20kg (44lb) of baggage behind the seats.

VARIANTS

Production was launched with the basic **CAP 10**, but the most numerous version is the **CAP 10B** which features an enlarged rudder and ventral fin. Further refinement has resulted in the appearance of a third version with a new wing structure, incorporating a carbon-fibre main spar, and also

using the same aileron design as the CAP 231. It was first flown in 1999 as the **CAP 222**.

TECHNICAL DATA

Mudry CAP 10B

Powerplant: One Textron Lycoming AEIO-360-B2F flat-four piston engine
Developing: 134kW (180hp)
Driving: Two-blade propeller
Span: 8.06m (26ft 5.25in)
Length: 7.16m (23ft 6in)
Height: 2.55m (8ft 4.5in)
All-up weight: 760kg (1,675lb) aerobatic version; 830kg (1,829lb) utility version
Maximum speed: 340km/h (211mph)
Cruise speed: 250km/h (155mph)
Operational ceiling: 16,400ft
Maximum range: 1,000km (621 miles)
Accommodation: Two
First flown: August 1968 (CAP 10)
Entered service: 1970

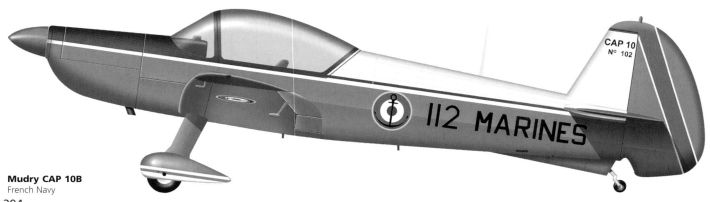

Mudry CAP 10B
French Navy

Mudry CAP 231 & 232

SINGLE PISTON-ENGINED AEROBATIC AIRCRAFT

Mudry CAP 231 Royal Moroccan Air Force

DEVELOPMENT

The Mudry CAP 232 is the most recent example of a line of single-seat aerobatic trainer aircraft that was launched with the Avions Mudry CAP 20 and then progressed via the CAP 230 and CAP 231, both of which featured aerodynamic refinements as well as different powerplant installations. In its latest guise, as the CAP 232, it flew for the first time in July 1994, with French certification following in March 1995. Changes again involved the powerplant and propeller installation, amongst other refinements. Initially, production of the CAP 232 was undertaken by Avions Mudry, but Akrotech Europe took over in the wake of the 1996 bankruptcy. A further name change, to CAP Aviation, occurred in January 1999.

CURRENT SERVICE

Examples of both the CAP 231 and CAP 232 are currently in military use, although the majority of aircraft built have been delivered to civil customers. However, France still has at least two CAP 231s, and the best known military operator is Morocco, which purchased seven. As with the French aircraft, delivery began in 1988 and all seven are still assigned to the *Marche Verte* (*Green March*) aerobatic display team. Turning to the CAP 232, approximately 20 have been built to date, but the only military operator is France, which took delivery of two examples in 1998. Like the older CAP 231, these are flown by the Equipe de Voltige de l'Armee de l'Air aerobatic display unit which is stationed at Salon-de-Provence.

SPECIAL FEATURES

Basic configuration of the CAP 231 and CAP 232 is similar, both being low-wing monoplanes with a fixed tailwheel-type undercarriage.

VARIANTS

Two basic variants are in military use, the **CAP 231** and the **CAP 232**. Differences are mostly concerned with detail improvements and both aircraft rely on the same basic Textron Lycoming AEIO-540 flat-six engine. For recognition purposes, the most obvious difference between the two concerns the propeller, with the CAP 231 having a three-blade type while the CAP 232 employs a four-blade propeller. The CAP 232 is also now the only production model. The **CAP 231EX** (which first flew on 18 December 1991) had Walter Extra-built wings with carbon fibre main spars. Only six were built before the CAP 232, with a new Mudry-built wing of thinner section carbon fibre, was put into production.

Mudry CAP 231 Royal Moroccan Air Force

TECHNICAL DATA

Mudry CAP 232

Powerplant: One Textron Lycoming AEIO-540-L1B5 piston engine
Developing: 224kW (300hp)
Driving: four-blade propeller
Span: 7.39m (24ft 3in)
Length: 6.76m (22ft 2in)
All-up weight: 816kg (1,800lb)
Maximum speed: 403km/h (250mph)
Cruise speed: 269km/h (167mph)
Service ceiling: 4,575m (15,000ft)
Maximum range: 1,200km (745 miles)
Accommodation: Pilot only
Maximum payload: 227kg (500lb)
First flown: April 1990 (CAP 231);
7 July 1994 (prototype CAP 232)
Entered service: 1995 (CAP 232)

NAMC YS-11

TWIN-TURBOPROP MEDIUM-RANGE PASSENGER/CARGO TRANSPORT AIRCRAFT

NAMC YS-11M Japanese Maritime Self-Defence Force

DEVELOPMENT

Unique in being the only indigenous airliner to be manufactured in Japan, development of the YS-11 began in 1957 and was the outcome of a collaborative venture by Fuji, Kawasaki, Mitsubishi, Nippi, Shin Meiwa and Showa under the collective Nihon Aeroplane Manufacturing Company (NAMC) name. Two prototypes were built, with the first making its maiden flight on 30 August 1962. A number of domestic airlines eventually ordered the YS-11, which remained in production until February 1974. A total of 182 examples of several series were built, and a number of these have seen military service.

CURRENT SERVICE

As a home-grown product, it is not surprising that Japan elected to acquire the YS-11 for military service, although the number of aircraft was relatively small, with a total of 23 obtained between 1965 and 1973. Of these 23 aircraft, 13 were destined to join the Air Self-Defence Force (ASDF), with the Maritime Self-Defence Force (MSDF) receiving the remaining ten. All are still thought to be in use, fulfilling a variety of roles including navigation training, calibration,

electronic warfare training of ground-base radar sites, personnel and cargo transport and maritime crew training. Two YS-11ELs are used for ELINT missions. The only other air arm known to have utilised the YS-11A is the Hellenic Air Force, which acquired six former Olympic Airways Series 220s in 1980 for personnel airlift tasks. No more than two remain in service with 356 MTM 'Iraklis' at Elefsis, including one that was subsequently adapted for radar calibration duties.

SPECIAL FEATURES

The YS-11 is generally unremarkable in appearance, being a conventional low-wing design with a tricycle undercarriage layout. However, some JASDF and JMSDF aircraft do feature external additions such as radomes, blister fairings and sundry antennae associated with special missions.

VARIANTS

Aircraft for commercial operations were built in several series, including the initial **Series 100**. This was followed by the **Series 200**, which had a higher gross weight, and the **Series 300** mixed traffic and

Series 400 all-cargo models. Production ended with the **Series 500** and **Series 600**, which were basically similar to the Series 200 and Series 100 respectively, albeit with further increases in gross weight. In Japanese military use, variants identified with the ASDF are the **YS-11C** freighter; **YS-11E** ECM/EW trainer; **YS-11EL** ELINT platform; **YS-11FC** calibration/flight check version; **YS-11NT** navigation trainer; **YS-11P** VIP transport and **YS-11PC** personnel/cargo transport. MSDF variants comprise the **YS-11M** and **YS-11M-A** personnel/cargo transport models and the **YS-11T-A** ASW crew trainer. In addition, the ASDF has one other special mission version, this being the **YS-11E-Kai** ECM/EW trainer, re-engined with locally manufactured General Electric/ Ishikawajima-Harima T64-IHI-10J turboprops and delivered to the JASDF in December 1991.

NAMC YS-11A Hellenic Air Force

TECHNICAL DATA

NAMC YS-11M-A

Powerplants: Two Rolls-Royce Dart Mk 542-10K turboprops
Developing: 2,282kW (3,060ehp)
Driving: Four-blade propellers
Span: 32.00m (104ft 11.75in)
Length: 26.30m (86ft 3.5in)
Height: 8.98m (29ft 5.5in)
All-up weight: 24,500kg (54,012lb)
Maximum cruise speed: 469km/h (291mph)
Economic cruise speed: 452km/h (281mph)
Operatonal Service: 22,900ft
Range with max payload: 1,090km (677 miles)
Accommodation: Three crew and up to 42 troops
Payload: 7,195kg (15,860lb)
First flown: 30 August 1962

Nanchang CJ-6

SINGLE PISTON-ENGINED BASIC TRAINING AIRCRAFT

Nanchang CJ-6

DEVELOPMENT

Used by China in very large quantities, development of the CJ-6 can be traced back to the latter part of 1957, and was originally undertaken by Shenyang, tasked with conceiving an indigenous successor to the CJ-5, itself a licence-built version of the Yakovlev Yak-18 'Max'. The resultant CJ-6 design bore a distinct resemblance to the Yak-18, first flying in August 1958. Early trials with the prototype revealed that the original 108kW (145hp) Mikulin M-11ER powerplant was inadequate, and a further series of flight tests was conducted after it had been adapted to take the 194kW (260hp) Ivchenko AI-14R. Flown in this form in July 1960, the new engine resulted in a marked improvement. Responsibility for the programme was subsequently reallocated to Nanchang and further redesign culminated in a production prototype in late 1961. Following trials with this aircraft, the go-ahead for series manufacture was finally given at the beginning of 1962, with production examples of the CJ-6 utilising the HS6 engine (Chinese-built AI-14R).

CURRENT SERVICE

In addition to widespread use in China, which has received somewhere in the region of 2,100 aircraft, at least 200 examples have been built for export. Some of the latter were delivered to civil customers, but the majority went to several overseas air arms, including Albania, Bangladesh, Cambodia, North Korea, Tanzania and Zambia.

SPECIAL FEATURES

Fundamentally of conventional design, the CJ-6 is a low-wing monoplane, with marked dihedral on the outer wing sections. Among the more distinctive features are the framed 'glasshouse' cockpit that accommodates two occupants in tandem, while the CJ-6 also has a long-legged tricycle undercarriage that results in a 'stalky' appearance when on the ground.

VARIANTS

Following on from the initial **CJ-6** version, installation of the uprated HS6A engine in production aircraft with effect from December 1965, resulted in the advent of the **CJ-6A** and its export **PT-6A** equivalent. This has been the basic model ever since then, but one other derivative is known to have been built in limited numbers, although it is almost certainly no longer in service. Designated **CJ-6B**, it was an armed version and a total of ten examples was completed during 1964-66. Finally, an agricultural model intended for civil use emerged as the **Haiyan A**, although this was only ever flown in prototype form and did not progress as far as quantity production.

TECHNICAL DATA

Nanchang CJ-6A
Powerplant: One SAEC (Zhuzhou) HS6A air-cooled radial piston engine
Developing: 213kW (285hp)
Driving: Two-blade propeller
Span: 10.22m (33ft 6.5in)
Length: 8.46m (27ft 9in)
Height: 3.25m (10ft 8in)
All-up weight: 1,400kg (3,086lb)
Maximum speed: 297km/h (185mph)
Operational ceiling: 20,500ft
Maximum range: 690km (428 miles)
Endurance: 3hr 36min
Accommodation: Two pilots
Warload: Nil
First flown: 27 August 1958 (prototype); 15 October 1961 (production CJ-6)
Entered service: c1962

Nanchang CJ-6 Bangladesh Air Force

Neiva L-42 & U-42 Regente

SINGLE PISTON-ENGINED LIGHT UTILITY/OBSERVATION AIRCRAFT

U-42 Regente Brazilian Air Force

DEVELOPMENT

One of the first products of the Neiva company, design of the Regente light aircraft was initiated in the closing stages of the 1950s. When the prototype Regente 360C made its maiden flight in autumn 1961, it was probably aimed more at civilian customers, but the project received a welcome boost when the Força Aérea Brasileira (Brazilian Air Force) selected it for use as a light utility/communications aircraft. The first military contract covered just 20 examples of the U-42 version, with deliveries commencing early in 1965. Subsequent re-orders added a further 60 U-42s to the total and by the time production of these was running down, Neiva had begun flight testing a new version for observation and liaison duties. This was the L-42, which flew for the first time in 1967 and was eventually the subject of an Air Force order for 40. The Company was aquired by EMBRAER in 1975, who continued the manufacturing programme.

CURRENT SERVICE

Largely replaced in service by more modern types, it is believed that no more than two dozen examples of the Regente are still active with the Brazilian Air Force at Terceira Força Aérea Anápolis Base Flight. About ten U-42s still perform utility transport duties with such organisations as the Centro Técnico Aeroespacial (Aerospace Technical Centre) at São José dos Campos. In addition, a slightly greater number of L-42 observation aircraft remain operational with the 8° Grupo de Aviação (Aviation Group) at Campo dos Afonsos and Santa Maria.

SPECIAL FEATURES

High-wing, strut-braced, monoplane, with tricycle undercarriage layout. Cabin of U-42 utility version has accommodation for up to four people, with dual controls for two pilots; space for baggage behind rear seats which can be removed to facilitate the carriage of light cargo. L-42 observation version normally carries one pilot and one or two observers.

VARIANTS

Two basic military derivatives of the Regente were produced for the Brazilian Air Force. The first and most numerous was the **U-42** utility model, of which a total of 80 was built and delivered during 1965-68. There are reports that the U-42 was later redesignated as the **C-42**, but these aircraft have only ever been seen carrying the U-42 designation on the fin. In 1968, production switched to the **L-42** observation/liaison version. This was fitted with a more powerful IO-360 flat-six piston engine and also featured a cut-down rear fuselage and additional glazing behind the cabin offering enhanced all-round visibility. By the time production ended in 1971, 40 L-42s had been built.

TECHNICAL DATA

Neiva U-42 Regente

Powerplant: One Lycoming O-360-A1D piston engine
Developing: 134kW (180hp)
Driving: Two-blade propeller
Span: 9.13m (29ft 11.5in)
Length: 7.04m (23ft 1in)
Height: 2.93m (9ft 7.25in)
All-up weight: 1,040kg (2,293lb)
Maximum speed: 220km/h (137mph)
Cruise speed: 212km/h (132mph)
Operational ceiling: 11,800ft
Maximum range: 928km (576 miles)
Accommodation: Pilot and up to three passengers
Warload: Nil; L-42 version has wing racks for up to four smoke rockets for target-marking
First flown: 7 September 1961 (prototype Regente 360C); Spring 1967 (YL-42 prototype)
Entered service: February 1965 (first U-42 delivery); June 1969 (first L-42 delivery)

U-42 Regente Brazilian Air Force

NH Industries NH 90

TWIN-TURBINE NAVAL AND TACTICAL TRANSPORT HELICOPTER

FRANCE/GERMANY/ITALY/NETHERLANDS

NH Industries NH 90

DEVELOPMENT

The NH 90 had its origins in a NATO industrial group study undertaken in 1983-84, which paved the way for feasibility and concept definition studies of a new naval/tactical support helicopter for the 1990s. At that time, the project involved five nations, but the United Kingdom withdrew in April 1987, leaving France, Germany, Italy and the Netherlands to carry on. Following further debate, a design and development contract was signed in September 1992 and this provided for five flying prototypes and a ground test vehicle. The first aircraft was rolled out in France in September 1995, making its maiden flight just under three months later. Since then, further prototypes have flown and development is continuing.

CURRENT SERVICE

The NH 90 is not expected to attain operational service until at least 2003, when initial deliveries should be made to Germany (TTH version) and the Netherlands (NFH version), these countries having ordered 205 and 20 respectively. Germany is also to acquire 38 examples of the NFH version, with first deliveries due in 2007. Other customers are France,

which plans to buy 27 NFHs (service entry 2005) and 133 TTHs (service entry 2011), and Italy, which expects to receive 155 TTHs and 64 NFHs, both of which should begin to enter service during 2004. NH Industries also anticipates a healthy export market.

SPECIAL FEATURES

The NH90 has a fully retractable tricycle undercarriage configuration with mainwheels housed in sponsons protruding from fuselage sides. Conventional main and tail rotor layout, with TTH model having aft ramp allowing small vehicles to be driven into cabin and secured for flight. Will also feature 'glass' cockpit and be compatible for operation with night vision goggles.

VARIANTS

The two basic variants that will form the core of production are the **NFH** (NATO Frigate Helicopter) and the **TTH** (Tactical Transport Helicopter). The NFH is primarily tasked with maritime missions, including anti-submarine warfare and anti-surface vessel warfare, plus over-the-horizon targeting for the battle group, vertical replenishment, search-and-rescue and routine transport tasks. The TTH will

mainly function in the Army support role, but will also fulfil other missions, including electronic warfare, airborne command post and VIP airlift. Plans are in hand to develop a **C-SAR** (Combat Search-and-Rescue) version, which will probably have in-flight refuelling capability as well as armour protection and integrated countermeasures, plus FLIR sensors for night/all-weather operations and air-to-air missiles for defence.

TECHNICAL DATA

NH Industries NH 90

Powerplants: Two turboshafts (type dependent upon customer)
Developing: Typically 1,253kW (1,680shp) maximum for continuous operation
Driving: Four-blade main and tail rotors
Main rotor diameter: 16.30m (53ft 5.5in)
Fuselage length: 15.89m (52ft 1.5in)
Height: 5.44m (17ft 10in) overall, tail rotor turning
Maximum weight: 10,000kg (22,046lb)
Maximum cruise speed: 298km/h (185mph) TTH; 291km/h (181mph) NFH
Economic cruise speed: 259km/h (161mph)
Operational ceiling: 13,940ft TTH
Maximum ferry range: 1,204km (748 miles)
Radius of action: 250km (155 miles) TTH with 2,000kg (4,409lb) load
Endurance: 5hr 5min
Accommodation: TTH version has crew of two and will carry up to 20 troops
Warload: NFH will carry torpedoes and anti-ship attack missile armament
Payload: 4,600kg (10,141lb)
First flown: 18 December 1995
Entered service: 2003 (first deliveries due)

NH Industries NH 90

Nord N2501 Noratlas

TWIN-PISTON TACTICAL TRANSPORT AIRCRAFT

N2501F Noratlas Congolese Air Force

DEVELOPMENT

Design of what eventually became the Noratlas began in the latter half of the 1940s and culminated in the first flight of the N2500 during September 1949. Powered by Gnome Rhone 14R engines, this version was not considered suitable for quantity production and Nord undertook further design work that led to the N2501, which was fitted with licence-built Hercules radial piston engines. In this guise, it made its maiden flight in late 1950, with the first production aircraft following suit almost exactly two years later, on 24 November 1952. Formal adoption of the name Noratlas occurred on 9 January 1953, with the first example being officially delivered to the French Air Force in June 1953.

CURRENT SERVICE

Although once extensively used by a number of European air arms (including France, West Germany, Greece and Portugal), the Nord Noratlas is now believed to be active with just one African nation, namely Congo. At least four ex-French Air Force examples are known to have been transferred to the Force Aérienne Congolaise (Congolese Air Force) but only one of the three that survived until quite recently is still believed to be in an airworthy condition.

SPECIAL FEATURES

Similar in appearance to its close contemporaries, the Fairchild C-82 Packet and C-119 Flying Boxcar, the Nord N2501 Noratlas featured a high-wing layout, with twin engines and twin tailbooms culminating in twin fins and rudders. Passengers and cargo were accommodated in the fuselage 'pod', which had rear loading doors and an integral ramp that enabled small vehicles to be driven aboard and secured for flight. Airdrops of bulky and outsized loads could be accomplished, but it was necessary to completely remove the aft loading doors first.

VARIANTS

Numerous versions of the Noratlas were produced by the parent company in France and by a consortium in West Germany, but the two basic models were the N2501F for France and the N2501D for West Germany. A combined total of almost 400 aircraft of these two sub-types was eventually built, while the N2502 with Turboméca Marboré auxiliary turbojets located in wing tip pods was also produced in lesser quantities for service with Israel and Portugal. Other versions that emerged were the N2503, with American Pratt & Whitney R-2800 air-cooled radial engines; the N2506, also with Marborés; and the N2508, with R-2800 radials and Marboré auxiliary turbojets. However, these were not produced in any great quantity.

TECHNICAL DATA

Nord N2501F Noratlas

Powerplants: Two SNECMA-built Bristol Hercules 738 or 758 air-cooled radial piston engines
Developing: 1,559kW (2,090hp)
Driving: Four-blade propellers
Span: 32.50m (106ft 7.5in)
Length: 21.96m (72ft 0.5in)
Height: 6.00m (19ft 8.25in)
Maximum weight: 21,700kg (47,840lb)
Maximum speed: 440km/h (273mph)
Cruise speed: 323km/h (201mph)
Operational ceiling: 24,605ft
Maximum range: 2,500km (1,553 miles) with 4,550kg (10,031lb) payload
Accommodation: Crew plus up to 45 troops or 36 paratroops or 18 litter patients and medical attendants
Maximum payload: 7,400kg (16,314lb)
First flown: 10 September 1949 (N2500 prototype); 28 November 1950 (N2501 prototype)
Entered service: December 1953

N2501F Noratlas

Nord Aérospatiale 262 Frégate

TWIN-TURBOPROP LIGHT TRANSPORT AIRCRAFT

FRANCE

Nord 262E Frégate French Navy

DEVELOPMENT

Design of the Nord 262 was begun in 1961, and the eventual outcome was fundamentally a pressurised, turbine-powered improvement on the earlier piston-engined Max Holste MH250 Super Broussard and unpressurised turboprop MH260, both of which were manufactured in limited quantities. First flown in prototype form just before the end of 1962, civil certification was achieved in July 1964 and the Nord 262 was soon introduced to passenger service with regional operators in France and the USA. Production of the original model and other improved versions continued until 1977, when the 110th and last Nord 262 was delivered to the French Air Force.

CURRENT SERVICE

More than 50 examples of the Nord 262 series have seen service with the French Air Force and Navy in a variety of transport and training roles, although many Navy aircraft have been retired from service within the past year or so. Nevertheless, about 40 are still active, including 24 Frégates with the Air Force. The majority of these are Nord 262D transport aircraft, which serve with ETEC 00.065 at Villacoublay, but five modified Nord 262AENs are used as crew trainers by a navigation school at Toulouse. The remaining 16 aircraft are all assigned to the Navy and comprise three Nord 262A and two Nord 262CS transports, plus 11 Nord 262Es for navigation and flight engineer training. Two other air arms are known to possess the Frégate, although just a handful of aircraft are involved. Both are African states; Burkina Faso and Gabon each use a pair of Nord 262Cs for light transport tasks.

SPECIAL FEATURES

Compact in appearance, the Nord 262 features a conventional high-wing layout, with twin turboprop engines mounted on and extending forward from the wings. It also has a tricycle undercarriage, with the nosewheel retracting forward into a bay below the cockpit, while the mainwheels are stowed in fairings on the lower fuselage sides.

VARIANTS

Versions that have seen military service in new-build form are the **Nord 262A** which was the standard early production aircraft fitted with slightly less powerful Bastan VIC turboprops. The name Frégate is not, in fact, applicable to this model, only being introduced with effect from the **Nord 262C** and **Nord 262D** versions, both of which entered production at the start of the 1970s. The former was primarily aimed at commercial customers, with the latter being similar, but configured specifically for use by the French Air Force as a staff transport. Post-production conversion has resulted in several other sub-types, such as the **Nord 262AEN** and **Nord 262E** navigation trainer models for the French Air Force and Navy respectively.

Nord 262E Frégate French Navy

TECHNICAL DATA

Nord 262 Frégate

Powerplants: Two Turboméca Bastan VII turboprops
Developing: 854kW (1,145ehp)
Driving: Three-blade propellers
Span: 22.60m (74ft 1.75in)
Length: 19.28m (63ft 3in)
Height: 6.21m (20ft 4.5in)
All-up weight: 10,800kg (23,810lb)
Maximum speed: 418km/h (260mph)
Cruise speed: 408km/h (254mph)
Operational ceiling: 28,500ft
Maximum range: 2,400km (1,490 miles)
Accommodation: Two or three crew and up to 29 passengers
Maximum payload: 3,075kg (6,779lb)
First flown: 24 December 1962 (prototype)
Entered service: 1964 (commercial use)

301

North American T-6 Texan

SINGLE PISTON-ENGINED TRAINER AIRCRAFT

Harvard II UK DERA

TECHNICAL DATA

North American T-6G Texan
Powerplant: One Pratt & Whitney R-1340-AN-1 Wasp radial piston engine
Developing: 410kW (550hp)
Driving: Two-blade propeller
Span: 12.81m (42ft 0.25in)
Length: 8.99m (29ft 6in)
Height: 3.58m (11ft 9in)
Maximum weight: 2,404kg (5,300lb)
Maximum speed: 330km/h (205mph)
Cruise speed: 272km/h (170mph)
Operational ceiling: 21,500ft
Normal range: 1,207km (750 miles)
Accommodation: Pilot and student, in tandem
Warload: Normally unarmed, but was adapted for counter-insurgency, forward air control and light attack tasks, operating with bombs, rockets and machine gun armament
First flown: April 1935 (NA-16); April 1936 (NA-19); 1937 (BC-1)
Entered service: 1938 (BC-1)

DEVELOPMENT

Few aircraft ever made a more timely debut than the North American Texan – or Harvard as it was more familiarly known by the Commonwealth nations. Development was undertaken during the late 1930s, with the BC-1 forerunner of the T-6 entering service with the US Army Air Corps in 1938. Further refinement led to the AT-6 series, which was the most widely used basic trainer of World War 2. Ultimately built in huge numbers by North American, it was also manufactured by several licensees that, quite astonishingly, even included Watanabe and Yokosuka in Japan, which between them completed almost 200 for the Imperial Japanese Navy.

CURRENT SERVICE

One of the most widely used trainer aircraft of all time, the Texan and Harvard has only recently ceased to perform this valuable role, with the South African Air Force claiming the distinction of being the last air arm to use it for pilot training. Delivery of the Pilatus PC-7 finally permitted the surviving South African Harvards to be retired in November 1995, but some Texans and Harvards still fly regularly with historical organisations in India, Indonesia, New Zealand, Portugal, South Africa, Thailand and Venezuela. In addition, the veteran trainer still fulfils other useful purposes elsewhere, with one Harvard used as a low-speed chase aircraft by the Defence Evaluation Research Agency at Boscombe Down in the UK, while a T-6H undertakes experimental duties with the Italian Air Force test unit at Pratica de Mare.

SPECIAL FEATURES

The T-6 is of low-wing monoplane configuration, with retractable main undercarriage units and fixed tailwheel. Tandem enclosed cockpits provided for both occupants. The most distinctive characteristic of the Texan/Harvard is the rasping noise emitted while in flight, caused by supersonic propeller tip speed.

VARIANTS

An almost bewildering array of variants of the basic North American design have existed, but the most numerous versions were the **AT-6** series for the US Army Air Corps. In 1948, however, consolidation of trainer designations by the US Air Force resulted in the AT-6 becoming known as the **T-6**, with some aircraft seeing service as **LT-6G** forward air control aircraft in the Korean War of 1950-53. The US Navy **SNJ** series was broadly similar to the USAAC/USAF aircraft, but at least some were fitted with an arrester hook for deck landing training. In both British and Commonwealth service, the T-6 was universally known as the Harvard.

T-6 Harvard South African Air Force

North American T-28 Trojan

SINGLE PISTON-ENGINED TRAINER/LIGHT ATTACK AIRCRAFT

T-28 Fennec Uruguayan Navy

DEVELOPMENT

Conceived and designed as a replacement for the T-6 Texan in the basic and primary trainer role, the first of two XT-28 prototypes of the North American Trojan made its maiden flight in September 1949. Early trials showed promise and the type was ordered into quantity production soon after. Over 1,000 examples were eventually purchased by the US Air Force, from a production run of 1,984, but entry into US Navy service was preceded by a number of major changes.

CURRENT SERVICE

Although once widely used as a trainer by the USAF and US Navy and as a light attack/counterinsurgency aircraft by numerous air arms, the Trojan is no longer operational and the few examples that do still fly in military insignia are operated by units concerned with aviation heritage and history. Thailand still has a handful of T-28Ds with the so-called 'Tango Squadron', while Uruguay's naval air arm retains two T-28 Fennecs that occasionally venture aloft.

SPECIAL FEATURES

Low-wing monoplane configuration, incorporating fully-retractable tricycle undercarriage and tandem layout for pilot and student/observer beneath an extensively glazed canopy.

VARIANTS

Following on from the two **XT-28** prototypes, Trojan production was launched with the **T-28A** for the US Air Force. This had a 597kW (800hp) Wright R-1300-1A engine driving a two-blade propeller and almost 1,200 were completed in the early 1950s, although they were soon replaced by the jet-powered Cessna T-37. The next major version was the **T-28B** for the US Navy, which benefited from having a more powerful engine and three-blade propeller. Just under 500 were built, including a solitary **RT-28B** reconnaissance trainer for the Japanese Air Self-Defence Force. The final new-build version of the Trojan was the **T-28C**, which differed from the T-28B in having an arrester hook and structural strengthening in order to perform

carrier landing training with the US Navy, which received just under 300. Subsequent modification programmes led to the armed and armoured **T-28D**, several hundred conversions being done for use by USAF Air Commando units and a number of friendly nations, particularly in Southeast Asia. Sud Aviation in France undertook a similar programme, resulting in the **Fennec** (Desert Fox) which was extensively used by the French Air Force in Algeria. The **YAT-28E** was a heavily-armed version powered by a YT55 turboprop. Three aircraft were modified for trials in the early 1960s, but the project was not proceeded with.

TECHNICAL DATA

North American T-28D Trojan

Powerplant: One Wright R-1820-56S Cyclone radial piston engine
Developing: 969kW (1,300hp)
Driving: Three-blade propeller
Span: 12.38m (40ft 7.5in)
Length: 10.01m (32ft 10in)
Height: 3.86m (12ft 8in)
Maximum weight: 3,855kg (8,495lb)
Maximum speed: 566km/h (352mph)
Cruise speed: 327km/h (203mph)
Operational ceiling: 35,500ft
Maximum range: 1,900km (1,185 miles)
Accommodation: Pilot and student/observer
Warload: Normally unarmed when used as trainer; light attack versions could carry maximum of 1,815kg (4,000lb) ordnance load on six external hardpoints, with weaponry including gun pods, rocket pods and bombs
First flown: 26 September 1949 (XT-28)
Entered service: January 1950 (T-28A)

T-28 Fennec Uruguayan Navy

North American Rockwell T-39 Sabreliner

TWIN-JET TRAINING AND TRANSPORT AIRCRAFT

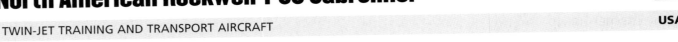

T-39N Sabreliner United States Navy

DEVELOPMENT

Successful in both civil and military markets, the North American NA-246 Sabreliner was developed originally as a private venture. Lack of suitable engines delayed the first flight – this being with two General Electric YJ85 turbojets of 11.13kN (2,500lb st). Thus powered, the prototype completed its US military evaluation test programme at Edwards AFB in December 1958. Military production eventually totalled 213 aircraft (civil production was over 500) and all military models of the T-39 series were certified to civil airworthiness standards. The first customer for the Sabreliner series was the USAF, which took the T-39A communications model, and this was used extensively in Southeast Asia. Rockwell International's Sabreliner Division was then acquired in 1983 by a specially formed Sabreliner Corporation at St Louis. Though continuing to provide product support to all in-use Sabreliners, no further production was resumed.

CURRENT SERVICE

The T-39N serves with the US Navy's VT-86 at NAS Pensacola, equipped with an APG-66 in the nose to allow student back-seaters to learn the intricacies of radar work under one-to-one supervision. VT-86 also operates three T-39Gs, this variant being distinguished by having five cabin windows instead of three. The T-39G provides initial jet familiarisation to prospective navigator students. These are operated under contract with Raytheon Aerospace. It is also in limited service with the USAF and USMC. Other users are Argentina, Bolivia, Ecuador and Mexico.

SPECIAL FEATURES

Low swept wing aircraft with rear podded turbofans. It featured a supercritical wing developed by the Reisbeck Corporation. The US Navy's T-39s have two work stations for student navigators and seats for their instructors.

VARIANTS

T-39A – the first military production aircraft, of which 143 were delivered to the USAF, with a lengthened nose and additional equipment; **T-39B** – six special models for use as trainers for Republic F-105 pilots; **T-39D** – US Navy radar operators trainer (42 built) for training F-8 Crusader and F-4 Phantom crews; **CT-39E** – seven US Navy VIP transport and communications aircraft, similar to the civil Sabreliner 40; **T-39F 'Teeny Weeny Weasels'** – three converted T-39s for the USAF Fighter Weapons School, Nellis AFB, to train pilots and electronic warfare officers for 'Wild Weasel'-equipped F-105G two-seaters; **CT-39G** – 12 built for the US Navy as fleet tactical transports; **NT-39B** – fitted with underwing jamming pods.

TECHNICAL DATA

North American T-39 Sabreliner

Powerplants: Two Pratt & Whitney J60-P-3A turbo jets
Developing: 13.36kN (3,000lb st)
Span: 13.54m (44ft 5in)
Length: 13.34m (43ft 9in)
Height: 4.88m (16ft 0in)
All-up weight: 8,000kg (17,600lb)
Maximum speed: 957 km/h (595mph)
Operational ceiling: 39,000ft
Maximum range: 4,447km (2,763 miles)
Accommodation: Crew of two and up to six passengers
Warload: None
First flown: 16 September 1958 (Civil); 30 June 1960 (T-39A)
Entered service: October 1960

NT-39A Sabreliner United States Air Force

Northrop F-5/CF-5 Freedom Fighter

TWIN-TURBOJET LIGHT FIGHTER AIRCRAFT

F-5A Freedom Fighter Turkish Air Force

DEVELOPMENT

What eventually evolved into the tremendously successful F-5 began life as a private venture, with Northrop undertaking design of the N-156 lightweight fighter in the mid-1950s, partly in response to a US government study of future fighter needs for allied nations in Europe and Asia. Two years later, Northrop succeeded in generating USAF interest in its proposals, albeit for a dedicated N-156T trainer version rather than a fighter. The trainer subsequently evolved as the T-38 Talon, but work continued on the fighter proposal, and three N-156F prototypes were funded under a special research and development contract in July 1959. Following extensive trials, the Northrop machine was chosen for the FX fighter requirement in April 1962 and the first contract for production aircraft was awarded six months later. Like almost all subsequent aircraft, these were supplied to friendly nations under the Military Assistance Program (MAP).

CURRENT SERVICE

A substantial number of Freedom Fighters of varying types are still active with more than a dozen air arms around the world. Countries known to have been operating it recently are Botswana (CF-5A/D), Brazil (F-5B), Greece (F/NF-5A/B), South Korea (F-5A/B, RF-5A), Morocco (F-5A/B, RF-5A), Norway (F-5A/B), the Philippines (F-5A/B), Saudi Arabia (F-5B), Spain (SF-5A/B, SRF-5A), Thailand (F-5A/B, RF-5A), Turkey (F/NF-5A/B, RF-5A), Venezuela (NF-5A/B, VF-5A/D) and Yemen

(F-5B). Canadian-built Freedom Fighters are still in service in Botswana, Greece, Turkey and Venezuela.

SPECIAL FEATURES

Intended to be inexpensive to build and operate, the F-5 was a diminutive machine of low-wing monoplane configuration with twin engines buried in the aft fuselage. It also featured a tail section that could be removed entirely to facilitate engine changes and maintenance. The CF-5 is virtually identical to Northrop-built examples.

VARIANTS

Three basic models of the Freedom Fighter were produced in varying quantities by Northrop, with over 600 examples of the single-seat **F-5A** making it by far the most numerous. Approximately 200 two-seat **F-5B** trainers were also built and Northrop production was completed by just under 90 reconnaissance-dedicated **RF-5As** which featured a camera installation in a modified nose. The F-5 was also manufactured under licence in Canada for the Canadian Forces and the Netherlands. These were fitted with uprated Orenda (General Electric) J85-CAN-15 turbojets. Those for the former comprised the **CF-5A** (89 built) and **CF-5D** (46), while Holland acquired 75 single-seat **NF-5As** and 30 two-seat **NF-5Bs**. Some Canadian aircraft were later transferred to Venezuela as **VF-5As**(16) and **VF-5Ds** (4). Finally, CASA undertook local assembly of 19 **SF-5As**, 17 **SRF-5As** and 34 **SF-5Bs** for the Spanish Air Force.

TECHNICAL DATA

Northrop F-5A Freedom Fighter
Powerplants: Two General Electric J85-GE-13 turbojets
Developing: 12.10kN (2,720lb st) dry; 18.15kN (4,080lb st) with afterburner
Span: 7.70m (25ft 3in)
Length: 14.38m (47ft 2in)
Height: 4.01m (13ft 2in)
All-up weight: 9,379kg (20,677lb)
Maximum speed: 1,487km/h (924mph)
Cruise speed: 1,030km/h (640mph)
Operational ceiling: 50,500ft
Ferry range: 2,594km (1,612 miles)
Combat radius: 989km (558 miles) hi-lo-hi attack mission with two 240kg (530lb) bombs and maximum fuel load
Accommodation: Pilot only (two pilots in F-5B)
Warload: Maximum ordnance load of 1,996 kg (4,400lb); weapon options include bombs, rockets and AIM-9 Sidewinder IR-homing air-to-air missiles; internal armament comprises two nose-mounted M39A2 20mm cannons
First flown: 30 July 1959 (N-156F prototype); 6 May 1968 (CF-5)
Entered service: April 1964 (F-5B); August 1964 (F-5A); 1968 (CF-5); 1969 (NF-5)

F-5A Freedom Fighter Phillipines Air Force

Northrop F-5 Tiger II

TWIN-TURBOJET LIGHT FIGHTER AIRCRAFT

F-5E Tiger II Swiss Air Force

TECHNICAL DATA

Northrop F-5E Tiger II

Powerplants: Two General Electric J85-GE-21B turbojets
Developing: 15.5kN (3,500lb st) dry; 22.2kN (5,000lb st) with afterburner
Span: 8.13m (26ft 8in)
Length: 14.45m (47ft 4.75in) including probe
Height: 4.08m (13ft 4.5in)
All-up weight: 11,187kg (24,664lb)
Maximum speed: 1,700km/h (1,056mph)
Cruise speed: 1,041km/h (647mph)
Service ceiling: 51,800ft
Ferry range: 3,720km (2,314 miles)
Combat radius: 1,405km (875 miles) with two air-to-air missiles
Accommodation: Pilot only (two pilots in F-5F)
Warload: Maximum ordnance load of 3,175kg (7,000lb); weapon options include conventional and laser-guided bombs, cluster bomb units, rockets, AIM-9 Sidewinder IR-homing air-to-air missiles, AGM-65 Maverick air-to-surface missiles and AGM-45 Shrike anti-radiation air-to-surface missiles; internal armament consists of two nose-mounted M39A2 20mm cannons.
First flown: 11 August 1972 (F-5E); September 1974 (F-5F)
Entered service: 1973

DEVELOPMENT

In 1969, the USA issued the International Fighter Aircraft (IFA) requirement for the development of a new lightweight fighter. This was destined to succeed the original F-5A and it was no surprise that Northrop offered an improved version of the successful Freedom Fighter. This was the F-5E Tiger II, which was selected for production in November 1970. Flying for the first time in Summer 1972, well over 1,000 Tiger IIs were produced by Northrop, while it was also assembled in South Korea, Switzerland and Taiwan.

CURRENT SERVICE

Although no longer quite so widely used, the Tiger II is still in active service with a long list of air arms, and upgrade programmes seem certain to ensure it will be around for some time. At present, the basic F-5E fighter serves with Bahrain, Brazil, Chile, Indonesia, Iran, Jordan, Kenya, South Korea, Malaysia, Mexico, Morocco, Paraguay, Saudi Arabia, Singapore, Switzerland, Taiwan, Thailand, Tunisia and Yemen, and as an aggressor aircraft for dissimilar air combat training with the US Navy. Apart from Yemen, all the above also operate the F-5F. Upgrading of Singapore's F-5E and F-5F aircraft has resulted in them being redesignated as the F-5S and F-5T respectively. Finally, modest numbers of the specialist RF-5E Tigereye serve with Malaysia, Saudi Arabia, Singapore and Taiwan.

SPECIAL FEATURES

Broadly similar in appearance to the Freedom Fighter that it replaced, the Tiger II shares the same basic features, but has a modified wing incorporating leading edge root extensions, as well as a dorsal extension to the fin and a two-position nosewheel for an increased angle-of-attack on take-off.

VARIANTS

In new-build form, only three basic variants were produced. The first was the **F-5E** fighter, which was also the most numerous. It was subsequently joined in production by the two-seat **F-5F**, which is primarily a trainer, although it is combat-capable. As with the earlier Freedom Fighter, reconnaissance was eventually undertaken, with the installation of an extended nose containing sensors resulting in the **RF-5E Tigereye**. Several companies have recently offered upgraded versions. In most cases, modified aircraft retain the original designation, although Chilean machines are now **F-5E Plus Tiger IIIs** following updating. In the case of Singapore, however, new designations are used, with the **F-5S** and **F-5T** being upgraded versions of the **F-5E** and **F-5F** respectively. The ultimate version of the F-5 line, the **F-5G** (or **F-20 Tigershark**), did not attract any orders.

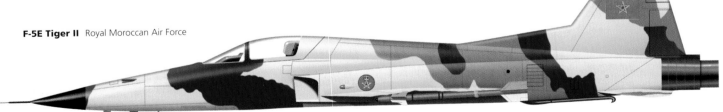

F-5E Tiger II Royal Moroccan Air Force

Northrop T-38 Talon

TWIN-TURBOJET ADVANCED TRAINER AIRCRAFT

T-38A Talon United States Air Force

DEVELOPMENT

Unique in being the first supersonic aircraft to be designed for the advanced trainer role, the origins of the T-38 Talon date back to Northrop's private venture lightweight fighter studies of the mid-1950s. They led to a twin-track development, one path being the N-156F which became the F-5 Freedom Fighter, while the other was the N-156T. It was the latter concept that came to fruition first, with funds allocated in the 1958 Fiscal Year for seven development YT-38s, including one non-flying airframe for ground static tests. The maiden flight occurred in April 1959 and initial trials were sufficiently promising to warrant the US Air Force placing the first of a series of orders for production aircraft later in 1959, with initial deliveries to the 3510th Flying Training Wing at Randolph AFB, Texas following about a year later.

CURRENT SERVICE

As it has been for almost four decades, the US Air Force remains the principal operator of the T-38, with almost 500 aircraft on charge. Most fly with Air Education and Training Command from a handful of bases in the southern USA. However, some also serve with Air Combat Command's elite stealth and reconnaissance outfits in the pilot proficiency role, and others are flown by the US Navy's Test Pilot School at Patuxent

River, Maryland. Overseas service is presently confined to just three nations, namely Germany, Turkey and South Korea, although others (including Portugal and Taiwan) have flown T-38s in the past. In the case of Germany, all 41 of its aircraft are funded to train Luftwaffe pilots, and these are based in the USA (at Sheppard AFB, Texas) and operate in full USAF marks.

SPECIAL FEATURES

Although it possesses supersonic capability, the T-38 is essentially conventional in design and bears a marked similarity to the contemporary F-5 Freedom Fighter. Notable features are the small size and low wing monoplane configuration, with a slender area-ruled fuselage, and raised second cockpit for an instructor.

VARIANTS

Following on from the YT-38, 1,187 examples of the Talon were built before production terminated in January 1972. All were built as **T-38As**, but modification of about 130 aircraft resulted in the **T-38B** (unofficially dubbed **AT-38Bs**) which is used for weapons and fighter lead-in training and can carry an SUU-11 7.62mm Minigun pod or rocket/practice bomb dispenser on the centreline stores station. Looking ahead, an ongoing upgrade project involving the installation of new avionics in at least 425 of the

TECHNICAL DATA

Northrop T-38A Talon
Powerplants: Two General Electric J85-GE-5 turbojets
Developing: 11.92kN (2,680lb st) dry; 17.13kN (3,850lb st) with afterburner
Span: 7.70m (25ft 3in)
Length: 14.13m (46ft 4.5in)
Height: 3.92m (12ft 10.5in)
All-up weight: 5,465kg (12,050lb)
Maximum speed: 1,381km/h (858mph)
Cruise speed: 930km/h (578mph)
Operating ceiling: 53,600ft
Maximum range: 1,700km (1,100 miles)
Accommodation: Two pilots
First flown: 10 April 1959 (YT-38 prototype)
Entered service: 17 March 1961 (operational date)

USAF's Talons will result in the **T-38C**, which is expected to remain in service for several more years. At least two aircraft are known to have been redesignated as **NT-38As**, indicating modification for test duties, while the **QT-38A** and **DT-38A** were drone and drone control versions for the US Navy, although they are no longer in use.

T-38 Talon United States Air Force

Northrop Grumman E-2 Hawkeye

CARRIER-BORNE AIRBORNE EARLY WARNING AND CONTROL AIRCRAFT

E-2C Hawkeye Japanese Maritime Self-Defence Force

DEVELOPMENT

The latest in a line of carrier borne early warning aircraft, the E-2 prototype first flew in October 1960. It was designed exclusively for the AEW task with long endurance, slow approach speeds for deck landings and the ability to carry a large radar antenna clear of aircraft shielding. This resulted in a twin-turboprop aircraft with shoulder mounted high aspect ratio wings, four small vertical fins and a widespan tailplane with considerable dihedral, together with a large rotodome mounted above the rear fuselage. To allow the aircraft below decks, the wings fold and turn parallel to the fuselage and the rotodome can be lowered. The aircraft design has remained almost the same through its 40-year life, but the radar and electronics have undergone constant change such that the present E-2C is a complete internal transformation of the original aircraft.

CURRENT SERVICE

The USN has approximately 98 E-2Cs, many of which are in the process of being modified to the E-2C Group II standard, distributed among the following squadrons: US Navy – VAW 112, 113, 115, 116, 117, 120, 121, 123, 124 and 125, and USN Reserve VAW 77 and 78; Israel – No 19 Squadron with four aircraft; Japan – 601 Hikotai with 13 aircraft; Egypt – EW Squadron with six aircraft; Taiwan – No 78 Squadron with four aircraft; Singapore – No 111 Squadron with four aircraft; France – 4 Flottille with four aircraft.

SPECIAL FEATURES

The E-2C is a force multiplier performing a whole range of tasks. Usually launched first on a strike, the E-2C can provide and increase the battlegroup's detection range out to 555km (300nm). It can detect cruise missiles at 160 miles. surface vessels at maximum range, and via a secure data link send the infomation to the carrier below. The aircraft can also act as an airborne command post for strike aircraft and warn of hostile attacks. Air-to-air refuelling can be directed to ensure efficient refuelling and during mass recoveries air traffic stacking and sequences can be effected.

VARIANTS

Originally designated W2F-1 before the **E-2A**, a total of 59 were constructed and carried the APS96 radar with a hardwired drum memory computer, the aircraft played a large part in carrier strikes in the early part of the Vietnam War. The **E-2B** was a giant leap forward with the introduction of the Litton L304 programmable computer plus other electronic modifications, with 49 E-2As subsequently upgraded to E-2B standards. No E-2As or E-2Bs remain in USN service. The present standard is the **E-2C** which can be distinguished by the large air intake situated above and behind the cockpit. Early E-2s had a variety of radars including AN/AP3-138 and AN/APS-139 and are now known as **Group 0** aircraft. Further new-build and converted Group 0 were modified to **Group I** and later to **Group II** aircraft and use the AN/APS145 radar. The upgrading process, including JTIDS software, continues with all the fleet upgraded to Group II or the export **Hawkeye 2000** standard by the year 2004. Export models are a mix of E-2B converted to E-2C standard and E-2C but with differing degrees of electronic sophistication according to the customer's needs.

TECHNICAL DATA

Northrop Grumman E-2C Hawkeye

Powerplants: Two Allison T56-A-427 turboprops
Developing: 3,803kW (5,100shp)
Driving: four-blade propellers
Span: 24.56m (80ft 7in)
Length: 17.60m (57ft 9in)
Height: 5.58m (18ft 3.75in)
All-up weight: 24,687kg (54,426lb)
Maximum speed: 626km/h (389mph)
Cruising speed: 500km/h (310mph)
Operational ceiling: 38,000ft
Maximum range: 2,854km (1,773 miles)
Accommodation: two pilots plus three systems operators
Armament: Nil
First flown: 21 October 1960; 20 January 1971 (E-2C)
Entered service: 19 January 1964

E-2C Hawkeye United States Navy

Northrop Grumman B-2A Spirit

STRATEGIC 'STEALTH' BOMBER

B-2A Spirit United States Air Force

TECHNICAL DATA

Northrop Grumman B-2A Spirit
Powerplants: Four General Electric F118-GE110 non-afterburning turbofans
Developing: 84.52kW (19,000lb st)
Span: 52.4m (172ft 0in)
Length: 21.0m (69ft 0in)
Height: 5.18m (17ft 0in)
All-up weight: 181,437kg (400,000lb)
Maximum speed: 764km/h (475mph)
Operational ceiling: 50,000ft
Maximum range: Unrefuelled 11,667km (7,245miles)
Accommodation: Two, with provision for a third member
Armament: All of the conventional and non-conventional armaments in the US inventory but with the emphasis on nuclear and precision weapons, including: B83 Nuclear bomb: B61-11 penetrating Nuclear weapon: AGM131 SRAM (Short range attack missile): AGM137a TSSAM (TriService Stand-off Attack Missile): GBU 31: GAM113/BLU113: AGM154JASSM (Joint Air to Surface Standoff Missile): AGM154: Mk 82 Bomb: M117 Bomb: Mk84/BLU109 JDAM (Joint Direct Attack Missile): TMD (Tactical Munitions Dispenser)
First Flown: 17 July 1989
Entered Service: 17 December 1993

DEVELOPMENT

One of the so called 'Black' programmes, the B-2 was designed as a stealthy radar-resistant Cold War bomber – its mission to penetrate Soviet Air Defences and reach the Soviet's ICBM silos. The contract was won in 1981 by Northrop working in association with Boeing, Vought and General Electric to carry out a very extensive programme of computer studies, resulting in a radically different tailless flying wing design. New materials and new techniques were developed, not just in the construction, but in the way the mission was defined and planned. Later known as the ATB (Advanced Technology Bomber) the aircraft was revealed to an invited audience at a 'roll out' in November 1988, and first flew on 17 July 1989, from the manufacture's plant at Palmdale to Edwards AFB.

CURRENT SERVICE

The first operational squadron was the 393rd BS of the 509th BW at Whiteman AFB, Missouri. A B-2A training squadron – the 394th CTS – borrows aircraft to provide ground and aircrew training, and when all aircraft are delivered a second squadron (the 325th BS) will form. The USAF originally planned to acquire 133 B-2s, but with the end of the Cold War this has been drastically reduced to 21, a total that includes the refurbished AV-1 development prototype. B-2s flew combat missions during the Kosovo campaign in 1999, operating directly from the USA.

SPECIAL FEATURES

Northrop's design is totally computer-based with heavy emphasis on radar cross-section resulting in a blended shape constructed of radar absorbent honeycomb structure. Engine inlets have 'S' curves to hide the engines from radar and the outlets are 'V' shaped above the wings to conceal the hot gases from below, any telltale contrails being minimised by injecting a chemical compound. A full glass cockpit diplay is fitted and fly-by-wire controls are standard. An IBM electronic warfare suite is fitted together with the ZSR-62 defence aids system and the AN/APQ181 J-Band radar system for target identification. The whole of the tailless double-W wing is coated in black radar absorbent material, and when seen from in front, behind or the side the shape has no hard edges, but when viewed from above it is formed from 12 razor sharp lines making the double-W shape, with eight flying control surfaces.

VARIANTS

The first six B-2s (1001-1006) were built as prototype/development aircraft, with the production aircraft (1007-1016) built as **Block 10** standard and lacking most of the electronics. The final batch of B-2A Spirits (1017-1021) were built as **Block 20** standard, and along with all the other production and development aircraft, will be brought up to **Block 30** standard by the end of 2000.

B-2A Spirit United States Air Force

Northrop Grumman/Boeing E-8 J-STARS

JOINT USAF/US ARMY BATTLEFIELD RECONNAISSANCE PLATFORM

USA

E-8C J-STARS United States Air Force

DEVELOPMENT

During Vietnam the USAF and US Army recognised that battlefield reconnaissance did not reveal the total picture and that what was required was an all seeing 'electronic eye' over the battlefield. A large airframe was required to carry the equipment and operators for the task, for which the Boeing 707-320 was chosen, with two second-hand ex-airline aircraft becoming E-8A J-STARS (Joint Strategic Target Attack Radar System) prototypes. The two aircraft had commenced a development programme when the Gulf War occurred and both were called up, flying 535 combat hours. They were used to target assembly areas, SCUD launch sites, SAM sites, POL dumps and other military targets. The E-8B production aircraft were to be new airframes fitted with F108(CFM56) turbofans, but closure of the Boeing 707 production line and cost savings meant that the follow-on E-8Cs will again be ex-civil airframes, zero lifed and with the capability of having upgraded engines.

CURRENT SERVICE

Flown during the Gulf War in 1991 with the 4411th Joint Stars Squadron. From October 1996, they were deployed to Europe in support of NATO peacekeeping forces in the Balkans. Production aircraft will be assigned to the 93rd Air Control Wing based at Robins AFB, GA where there will be three squadrons – the 12th and 16th AACSs with E-8Cs, and the 93rd TRS, a training squadron with the two E-8As. The E-3Cs are operated by the USAF on behalf of the US Army. No export of these aircraft is expected for some years. Thirteen are due to be in USAF service by 2004.

SPECIAL FEATURES

The E-8 carries aloft a Norden multi-mode sideways-looking radar, the radar antenna is housed in a canoe shaped fairing behind the nose wheel and extending back to the wing leading edge. The radar radiates to the sides of the aircraft and it therefore flies in an elongated racetrack pattern to look at the area of interest. The radar can operate in a number of modes, each of which can provide different information, including the ability to differentiate between moving and stationary objects. Individual vehicles can be seen out to a range of 100 miles in some modes, or smaller areas can be examined in detail. This information can be used to produce almost photo-like pictures and the whole combined to produce a mosaic of an area. The information is relayed to fixed or mobile ground stations, giving instant targeting data and ensuring that darkness or bad weather cannot protect an enemy.

VARIANTS

The two prototypes are at present different from the production aircraft, carrying only ten operating consoles because of the test equipment, and can be distinguished from the **E-8C** by a teardrop radome behind the rear edge of the wing. Proposed **E-8B** production aircraft based on new airframes with F108(CFM56) turbofans. E-8C production aircraft are converted from zero-lifed ex-civil airliners and will carry 17 consoles plus one for self defence. These aircraft do not have the teardrop radome of the **E-8A**.

TECHNICAL DATA

Northrop Grumman E-8C J-STARS

Powerplants: Four Pratt & Whitney JT8D-3B
Developing: 18,000lb st (80.07kN)
Span: 145ft 9in (44.42m)
Length: 152ft 11in (46.61m)
Height: 42ft 5in (12.93m)
All-up weight: 333,600lb (151,315kg)
Maximum speed: 973km/h(600mph)
Operational ceiling: 42,000ft
Maximum range: 9,270km(5,760miles)
Endurance: 20 hours (with one inflight refuelling)
Accommodation: Three flight deck crew plus 18 mission crew although double crews can be carried for long missions.
Armament: None
First Flown: 22 December 1988 (E-8A); March 1994 (E-8C)
Entered Service: 1990 (E-8A); 22 March 1996 (E-8C)

E-8C J-STARS United States Air Force

Pacific Aerospace CT-4 Airtrainer

TWO-SEAT FULLY AEROBATIC LIGHT TRAINING AIRCRAFT

CT-4A Airtrainer Royal Thai Air Force

DEVELOPMENT

First flown in 1959 as a fully aerobatic light aircraft, the Victa Air Tourer was the winner in a competition held by the Royal Aero Club for such a trainer. The design rights were sold to AESL in New Zealand, now Pacific Aerospace, who re-engineered the design into a two/three-seat military trainer. Now called the CT-4, the aircraft was bought by a number of air forces. A development aircraft has since been flown fitted with a turboprop engine, incorporating minor airframe changes to allow for the smaller and lighter engine.

CURRENT SERVICE

The Royal Australian Air Force's original order was for 48, plus 14 aircraft built for the illegal Rhodesian regime, but not delivered. These are civilian-owned and used at ADFBFTS at Tamworth. The Royal Thai Air Force received 24 aircraft. The Royal New Zealand Air Force has very successfully operated 19 CT-4Bs, colloquially referred to as the 'Plastic Rat', together with the remainder of the four original Air Tourer versions for a number of years, based at the Central Flying School, Ohakea. It has now placed a contract

for its training requirements with industry and will use CT-4E turboprop aircraft. Two other aircraft were in use for some years, one with the Tongan Armed Forces and one with Bangladesh, but are now retired.

SPECIAL FEATURES

A rugged, fully aerobatic training aircraft, side-by-side seating, one piece canopy hinged at rear, and with provision for wing tip tanks. This low cost, locally produced aircraft, has remained popular with these three air forces but will most likely be replaced with turboprop aircraft when funds are available.

VARIANTS

The **CT-4A** was the production aircraft for RAAF and the Thai Air Force, followed by the **CT-4B** with a high gross weight for the RNZAF. The prototype Allison 250-B17D turboprop-powered aircraft was the **CT-4C** and a possible derivative with retractable undercarriage was the **CT-4CR**. An unsuccessful submission for the US Elementary Flying School aircraft was labelled the **CT-4E**. This version is now part of a contract to provide initial flying training to the RNZAF using 13 leased aircraft.

TECHNICAL DATA

Pacific Aerospace CT-4A Airtrainer
Powerplant: One Teledyne Continental IO-360-D flat six piston engine
Developing: 155kW (210hp)
Driving: Two-blade propeller
Span: 7.92m (26ft 0in)
Length: 7.06m (23ft 2in)
Height: 2.59m (8ft 6in)
All-up weight: 1202kg (2,650lb)
Maximum speed: 286km/h (178mph)
Cruising speed: 240km/h (148mph)
Operational ceiling: 17,900ft
Maximum range: 1310km (815 miles)
Accommodation: 2 or 3 persons
Armament: Nil
First Flown: 23 February 1972 (CT-4A); 21 January 1991 (CT-4C)
Entered service: 1973

CT-4B Airtrainer Royal New Zealand Air Force

311

Pakistan Aircraft Company Mushshak

LIGHT TRAINING UTILITY AND COIN AIRCRAFT

PAC Mushshak Pakistan Air Force

TECHNICAL DATA

PAC Mushshak

Powerplant: Textron Lycoming IO-360-A1 B6 flat four piston engine
Developing: 149kW (200hp)
Driving: Two-baded propeller
Span: 29ft 0.5in (8.85m)
Length: 22ft 11.5in (7.00m)
Height: 8ft 6.5in (2.60m)
All-up weight: 1200kg (2,646lb)
Max speed: 238km/h (148mph)
Cruising speed: 208km/h (129mph)
Operational ceiling: 15,750ft
Maximum range: Endurance 5hr 10min
Accommodation: 2/3 seater
Armament: Six under wing hard points capable of taking wire guided Bofors anti tank missiles; machine gun pods; unguided rockets.
First flown: 10 October 1958 (MFI-9); 11 July 1969 (MFI-15); 6 July 1972 (MFI-17)
Entered service: Early 1970s

DEVELOPMENT

The Mushshak is a licence-built version of the Saab MFI-15/MFI-17 Supporter – developed from the MFI-9 Junior/Minicom manufactured by Pakistan Aircraft Manufacturing Factory AMF, first at Risalpur and later at Kamra. Initially, 28 MFI-17s were assembled as kits but 120 were later built, including some for export. The Pakistan aircraft have increased performance and a similar model was exported to the Revolutionary Guard (Iranian Air Force). Further development of the type included a prototype fitted with an uprated Teledyne Continental engine.

CURRENT SERVICE

The Mushshak (Urdu for 'proficient') serves with the Pakistan Air Force and Army in considerable numbers as well as the remnants of the original order of MFI-17 Supporters and the kit-built aircraft. A further 25 Mushshaks were exported to Iran, six to Syria and three to Oman. The Saab-built version of the MFI-15 and -17 serves with a number of air forces (see Saab MFI-15 & 17). Iran still operates Mushshaks with TAB 11 Flying Training School at Tehran-Ghale Morghi; Oman has seven primary trainers; the Pakistan Army Aviation Corps uses the type with Nos 3, 7 and 9 squadrons plus the Aviation School, and six are used as primary trainers with the Syrian Air Force.

SPECIAL FEATURES

Unusual braced, mid-mounted and slightly forward swept wing and rearward hinged canopy. A basic trainer and utility aircraft with limited COIN capability. It has no special features, but has survived in use with a number of air arms, demonstrating its rugged nature, ease of maintenance and low cost.

VARIANTS

The Mushshak is a variant of the Saab MFI-17 Supporter, the only version being a single model with an uprated IO-360 engine.

SEE ALSO: SAAB MFI-17 SUPPORTER

PAC Mushshak Pakistan Army

Panavia Tornado IDS, GR1 & GR4

LONG-RANGE INTERDICTION/STRIKE/ATTACK AIRCRAFT

Tornado GR1 Royal Air Force

VARIANTS

All RAF **GR1s** have been primarily employed in the strike/attack role. However, within the Tornado force certain squadrons have been assigned specialist roles and this will be the case with the **GR4**. The GR1s in Germany have the specialist role of SEAD (Suppresion of Enemy Air Defences) using the BAe Alarm missile. No 14 Squadron has the secondary role of carrying the TIALD designator pod for marking targets for their own and formation aircraft bombs or for other units. The GR1 conversions (**GR1A** & **GR1B**) are dealt with separately.

SEE ALSO: PANAVIA TORNADO GR1A/GR1B & GR4A, TORNADO ECR AND TORNADO F3

DEVELOPMENT

The RAF version of the Tornado IDS is the GR1 with 229 examples delivered, and the Royal Saudi Air Force version of the IDS is almost identical to the RAF GR1. Early aircraft in batches 1 and 2 were not fitted with operational equipment, but these early aircraft went to the Tornado Tri-National Training Establishment at RAF Cottesmore for aircrew conversion. The basic strike/attack GR1 has spawned two sub-variants – the GR1A reconnaissance variant and the GR1B maritime attack variant, and is now itself being upgraded to the GR4 with the aid of an MLU (Mid-Life Update) programme. However, the planned MLU has now been reduced on grounds of cost, although it will still give the aircraft a major upgrade, the various improvements including GPS navigation, MFD cockpit improved weapons systems, TIALD capability, new HUD and under-nose FLIR.

CURRENT SERVICE

From a total of 11 squadrons, the RAF's GR1 currently serves with Nos 9, 14 and 31 Squadrons at Bruggen, Germany; and in the UK with Nos 2 and 13 at Marham (GR1As & GR4As), and at Lossiemouth, Nos 12 and 617 with GR1Bs and No 15(R) (OCU) with GR1s.

SPECIAL FEATURES

The first swing-wing aircraft to enter RAF service, the Tornado has been an outstanding success both as an international collaborative venture and as a military weapon. It has undoubtedly compensated for the lack of standardisation in NATO in respect of air carried weapons. The Tornado is able to carry almost all of them with very few changes required. It performed well in the Gulf War, in Bosnia and more recently in the Balkans carrying out the low-level interdiction role, for which it was designed.

TECHNICAL DATA

Panavia Tornado GR1 (late series)

Powerplants: Two Turbo Union RB199-34R MK103 afterburning turbofans
Developing: 40.48kN (9,100lb st), 71.50kN (16,075lb st) with afterburning
Span: 13.91m (45ft 7.5in) – minimum sweep; 8.60m (28ft 2.5in) – maximum sweep
Length: 16.72m (54ft 10.25in)
Height: 5.95m (19ft 6.25in)
All-up weight: 27,951kg (61,620lb)
Maximum speed: Mach 2.2 clean: Mach 1.8 with stores – 1,482km/h (920mph)
Operational ceiling: In excess of 50,000ft
Maximum range: Ferry 3,890km (2,420miles):
Combat radius: 1,390km (863miles)
Accommodation: Two
Warload: Seven weapons pylons, three under the flat-bottomed fuselage (all plumbed for fuel) and two on each of the moving part of the wing and the pylons move as the wing is moved. The usual location for weapons is the fuselage pylons with fuel on the inner wing pylons and self protection pods on the outer. A pair of 27mm IWLA-Mauser cannon with 180 rounds per gun are located in the forward fuselage. The pylons and aircraft systems can accept most NATO weapons including standard HE bombs, cluster bombs, retard and low drag 'slicks' – plus Sidewinder missiles for self defence on the side of the main wing pylons. The RAF GR1 can also carry the JP233 Airfield Denial Weapon, 454kg (1000lb) free-fall and retard bombs, BAe Alarm anti radiation missiles and TIALD IR/Laser designator pod, plus the Paveway II and III weapon. A typical configuration would be four 454kg (1000lb) plus two Sidewinders, Skyshadow (port outer pylon) Boz 100 chaff and flare pod (starboard outer pylon) plus two drop tanks.
First flown: 14 August 1974 (GR1); 4 April 1997 (GR4)
Entered service: July 1980 (GR1); March 1998 (GR4)

Tornado GR4 Royal Air Force

Panavia Tornado GR1A/GR1B & GR4A

LONG-RANGE INTERDICTION/STRIKE/ATTACK RECONNAISSANCE AIRCRAFT

DEVELOPMENT

The RAF requirement always included provision for recce aircraft but it was considered that the carriage of a pod in the manner of the Phantom, Jaguar and Harrier was too much of a drag penalty. After a number of proposals it was decided to remove both the 27mm Mauser cannons and fit in their place a BAe/Vinton Linescan IR scanner giving horizon to horizon cover and to fit a BAe SLIR (Sideways Looking InfraRed) looking through lower fuselage side windows with a 10° field of view to the sides. The system is a digital filmless video recording system. Results can be viewed in the air and the data will, in the future, be able to be transmitted direct to users on the ground. Some aircraft were converted from Batch 4 GR1s, while others were built as GR1As in

Tornado GR1B Royal Air Force

TECHNICAL DATA

Panavia Tornado GR1A

Powerplants: Two Turbo Union RB199-34R Mk103 afterburning turbofans
Developing: 40.48kN (9,100lb st), 71.50kN (16,075lb st) with afterburning
Span: 13.91m (45ft 7.5in) minimum sweep : 8.60m (28ft 2.5in) maximum sweep
Length: 16.72m (54ft 10.25in)
Height: 5.95m (19ft 6.25in)
Maximum weight: 27,951kg (61,620lb)
Maximum speed: Mach 2.2 clean. Mach 1.8 with stores: 1482km/h (920mph)
Operational ceiling: In excess of 50,000ft
Maximum range: Ferry range 3,890km (2,420 miles);
Combat radius: 1,390km (863miles)
Accommodation: Two
Armament: The RAF GR1A, and hence the GR4A, have both lost the use of the Mauser Cannon and the ensuing space has been used to house the IR based reconnaissance system. Otherwise the aircraft can carry all the weapons carried by the GR1. Likewise the Saudi version has also been seen carrying Alarm missiles indicating it may have a SEAD role. The GR1B can, in addition, carry Sea Eagle missiles.
First Flown: 11 July 1985
Entered Service: 3 April 1987

Batches 5 and 7. The first airframe for the MLU (Mid-Life Update) programme, whereby GR1s are converted to GR4s, was in fact a GR1A conversion to a GR4A. However, the GR1B is a very minimal conversion, being restricted to the fitting of Buccaneer-type pylons to allow carriage of the Sea Eagle and to also allow for the aircraft systems to update the missile through permanently installed links to the aircraft's nav computers.

CURRENT SERVICE

The RAF's GR1A/4As are in service with Nos 2 and 13 Squadrons at RAF Marham; the GR1B is operational with Nos 12 and 617 Squadrons at RAF Lossiemouth.

SPECIAL FEATURES

The Tornado programme, producing a standard – or near standard – aircraft for several nations, has worked well, and the aircraft has proved itself in a number of conflicts. However, each nation has undertaken modifications and changes to its aircraft such that when it came to the MLU there was little chance of a joint programme. The RAF decided to go it alone on its MLU and most of the frontline GR1/GR1As will become GR4/GR4As. The GR1B will be the last to be converted, if at all, as the Sea Eagle may not continue

in service. The GR4/GR4A programme has not lived up to expectations because of budget cuts, but will certainly make improvements to the present aircraft. These include digital map displays, GPS, an upgraded weapons control system, wide-angle holographic HUD, video recorder, new pilots' multi-functional displays and a new fixed FLIR sensor. Although these upgrades do not yet allow the Tornado to fulfil its full potential, they have helped it to become the best low-level penetrator aircraft available today.

VARIANTS

GR1A – conversion of GR1 to the IR recce standard;
GR1B – conversion of GR1 to carry Sea Eagle missile;
GR4A – GR1A having undergone MLU programme, giving it GPS navigation, MFD cockpit, improved weapons systems, TIALD capability, new HUD and under-nose FLIR.

SEE ALSO: PANAVIA TORNADO IDS/GR1/GR4, TORNADO ECR AND TORNADO F3

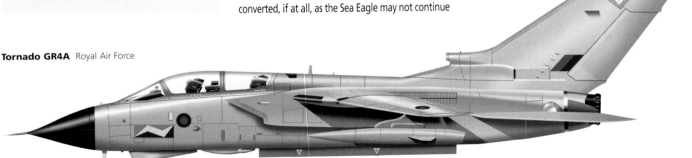

Tornado GR4A Royal Air Force

Panavia Tornado ECR

Tornado ECR German Air Force

DEVELOPMENT

A direct development of the IDS variant, to replace the reconnaissance RF-4E and RF-104G in German service, it was also planned that the Tornado ECR would be operated in the SEAD (Suppression of Enemy Air Defence) role as well. The aircraft was planned for the full SEAD role and was to be equipped with an operational data link to enable the aircraft to carry out electronic reconnaissance missions and data link the information to other aircraft and also to ground stations. Two ECR prototypes were converted in 1988 and although lacking some of the equipment, proved the principle, and 35 aircraft were selected from the German allocation in Batch 7 to be finished as ECR. They incorporate all the refinements of previous batches including digital engine controls for the uprated RB199 MK105, which produce 10% more thrust than the MK103. An Italian Air Force variant of the ECR has also been developed in-house and

incorporates most of the features of the German ECR but using Italian electronic equipment. The aircraft, 20 IDS variants, were converted in Italy and retain the original engines.

CURRENT SERVICE

The Luftwaffe's Jagdbombergeshwader 32 based at Lechfeld is the Luftwaffe's only ECR wing, and the squadrons now specialise in the SEAD role. With the Italian Air Force's 50° Stormo 'Giorgio Graffer', 155° Gruppo is the AMI's SEAD specialist. Although not at full strength, they have operated in the Balkans.

SPECIAL FEATURES

The ECR is the Tornado with the highest rated engines and hence has the best performance. It is the only SEAD dedicated aircraft able to fulfil the full role of locating and striking their own electronic targets without recourse to USAF 'Wild Weasel' aircraft. The

aircraft retains its full ground attack/strike capability with the exception of the internal cannon. Operational experience has shown that the SEAD role and IR reconnaissance are not possible on the same mission and it would be more beneficial for the IR equipment to be carried in a pod by the dedicated reconnaissance squadrons.

VARIANTS

The German ECR has uprated performance over the Italian ECR with carries the same equipment but with standard IDS engines.

SEE ALSO: PANAVIA TORNADO IDS/GR1/GR4, TORNADO GR1A/GR1B & GR4A AND TORNADO F3

TECHNICAL DATA

Panavia Tornado ECR

Powerplants: Two Turbo Union RB 199-34R MK105 afterburning turbofans
Developing: 42.5kN (9,550lb st), 74.3kN (16,700lb st) with afterburning
Span: 13.91m (45ft 7.5in) minimum sweep; 8.60m (28ft 2.5in) maximum sweep
Length: 16.72m (54ft 10.25in)
Height: 5.95m (19ft 6.25in)
All-up weight: 27,951kg (61,620lb)
Maximum speed: Mach 1.4, 2,338km/h (1,453mph)
Operational ceiling: More than 50,000ft
Max range: 3,890km (2,420miles)
Combat radius: 1,390km (863miles)
Accommodation: Two
Armament: Capable of carrying all the weapons used and available to the IDS variant with the addition of HARM (AGM-88). The two 27mm Mauser cannon and associated equipment have been eliminated so that it can carry an internally fitted reconnaissance equipment in the form of an Imaging Infrared System (IRLS or IRS). This has a horizon-to-horizon scan capability and can be supplemented by a passive FLIR turret on the starboard front fuselage, allowing penetration of hostile airspace in the passive mode. Both these infrared information sources can be displayed on either crew member's cockpit displays or the pilot's HUD. The information can also be transmitted to other aircraft or suitably equipped ground stations. Coupled with the IR equipment is a Texas Instrument Emitter Location System (ELS) which allows it to locate, identify, plot and engage enemy threat radars. This makes the ECR a self contained *Wild Weasel* capable aircraft as well as a Recce platform, hence the name ECR (Electronic Combat and Reconnaissance).
First flown: 18 August 1988
Entered service: July 1990

Tornado ECR German Air Force

Panavia Tornado ADV

LONG-RANGE AIR DEFENCE FIGHTER/INTERCEPTOR

DEVELOPMENT

When the MRCA was under review by various NATO member countries, the interceptor role was considered for the aircraft in addition to the IDS version, but was rejected by all except the UK. The requirement for the air defence of the UK was seen as different from that in Europe – an aircraft was needed with long range, all weather capability, and the ability to intercept and destroy at considerable distances from the coast. Hence the ADV was born, and 165 of the total planned build of 385 Tornados for the RAF were the ADV version. The main change was a 1.36m (4ft 5.5in) fuselage plug, providing an extra bay forward of the wing box for a fuel tank and a longer radome. The extra length also allowed the carriage of four Skyflash missiles under

Tornado F3 Royal Air Force

TECHNICAL DATA

Panavia Tornado F3

Powerplants: Two Turbo Union RB199-34R Mk104 afterburning turbofans
Developing: 40.48kN (9,100lb st), 73.48kN (16,520lb st) with afterburning
Span: 13.91m (45ft 7.5in) minimum sweep; 8.60m (28ft 2.5in) maximum sweep
Length: 18.68m (61ft 3.5in)
Height: 5.95m (19ft 6.25in)
Max weight: 27,986kg (61,700lb)
Max speed: 2,338km/h (1,453mph)
Operational ceiling: above 70,000ft
Maximum range: 1,852km (1,151 miles) subsonic; 556km (345 miles) supersonic
Accommodation: Two
Warload: One IKMA-Mauser 27mm cannon fitted starboard side of nose. Under fuselage four BAE Systems Skyflash semi-active radar homing missiles, or four AIM 120 AMRAAM active radar missiles. Up to four AIM 9L or similar Sidewinder, or four ASRAAMS on side of tank pylons on wing. It can also carry the Marconi aerial towed radar decoy and BOL integral chaff/flare dispenser on outer pylons which have been retro-fitted. Italian Air Force F3s are modified to carry Alenia Aspide AAMs under the fuselage.
First flown: 27 October 1979 (F2); November 1985 (F3)
Entered service: 1 November 1984 (F2); 28 July 1986 (F3)

the fuselage. Despite the changes, the ADV retained an 80% commonality with the IDS version. A small batch of ADV aircraft were produced with the same engines as the IDS and were designated as the F2. The F3 had an uprated engine – the Turbo Union RB 199-34R Mk104 – which featured a larger afterburner and required a different fairing at the base of the fin/rudder. Updates to the F3 fleet have been kept to a minimum, as it is expected that they will be retired with the entry into service from 2004 onwards of the Eurofighter Typhoon.

CURRENT SERVICE

The RAF has five Tornado F3 squadrons: Nos 43 and 111 at Leuchars; Nos 11 and 25 at Leeming; and No 5 at Coningsby – together with No 56(R) OCU and the Tornado Operational Evaluation Unit (OEU). Four are based with 1435 Flight at Mount Pleasant, Falkland Islands. The only export order for the F3 came from Saudi Arabia, who received 24 from 1989. The RAF has leased 24 F3s – drawn from Stage One aircraft – to the Italian Air Force. These aircraft underwent an MoD programme at RAF St Athan before going first to 36° Stormo's 12° Gruppo and later to 53° Stormo's 21° Gruppo at Cameri. They will be returned when the Eurofighter Typhoon enters Italian service.

SPECIAL FEATURES

The first swing-wing aircraft in RAF service, the ADV Tornado was to achieve a commonality with the IDS variant. However, it has never been the total success that was hoped, and will be gradually retired as the Eurofighter Typhoon becomes available for service.

VARIANTS

ADV prototypes were built as F2s; the first 18 ADVs were delivered to interim **F2** standard, powered by RB199 MK 103 engines, with no auto wing sweep and without radar. These airframes, with the exception of one at Boscombe Down, were later cannibalised to repair several F3s damaged during maintenance; the **F2A** was a planned upgrade not carried out; the **F3** was the standard ADV Tornado for the RAF. Early Saudi Tornado ADVs were aircraft taken from aircraft then being built for the RAF, and 'redirected' off the production line. RAF Tornado F3s are undergoing the Capability Sustainment Programme (CSP), which equips the aircraft for AMRAAM and ASRAAM missiles, JTIDS and Successor IFF.

SEE ALSO: PANAVIA TORNADO IDS

Tornado F3 Royal Air Force

Piaggio P.166

TWIN-TURBOPROP MULTI-ROLE UTILITY AIRCRAFT

P.166 DL3 Italian Air Force

DEVELOPMENT

First flown in 1957, the P.166 is a direct descendent of the amphibious P.136L, which had a gull wing to keep the pusher propellers clear of the water. A new fuselage and a retractable undercarriage produced an aircraft with a distinct shape and aerodynamic advantages. A military variant was produced as the P.166M, and this was ordered by the Aeronautica Militare Italiana (AMI). This and subsequent versions were piston engined, with a change to turboprops in 1976, and the type still remains in limited production today. The aircraft has found a niche market with the Italian armed forces, and with several quasi-military organisations for maritime and coast surveillance.

CURRENT SERVICE

A number of survivors from the AMI's initial order of 51 aircraft have been upgraded and fitted with surveillance platforms and comprehensive navigation fits. The current P.166 production model is turboprop powered and it carries state-of-the-art surveillance equipment, including IR/UV and radar, and serves with quasi-military Italian organisations as follows: Guardia di Finanza (Italian Customs), 12 aircraft ordered or delivered; Capitanerie di Porto (Coastguard) 12 aircraft delivered and five on order. These aircraft patrol the Italian exclusive economic zone out to 230 miles (370km). A previous order for the piston-engined P.166S for South Africa has now been withdrawn, although some may be stored. Four P.166-DL3s were produced for Somalia, but these were damaged beyond economic repair during the civil war. This leaves 303° Gruppo Autonomo at Guidonia as the principal military operator of the aircraft in the AMI. Some are equipped for photo-survey duties with verical Zeiss cameras mounted in the fuselage.

SPECIAL FEATURES

A simple to maintain and operate, light twin, utility aircraft able to carry a variety of interchangeable sensors to suit the surveillance task in hand. It remains in use with the Italian services as it is locally produced, local training is available and it is cheap to operate, particularly now that it is turboprop-powered.

VARIANTS

The **P.166M** piston-engined variant was the first to see service with the AMI, but a number of variants have seen subsequent use. The current model is the **DL3**, which followed the **DL2** as a specialised platform for a range of sensors used for aerial photography, coastal patrol, environmental control, geophysical survey and counter-insurgency. This version also has the ability to drop up to ten parachutists when freed of the sensor payload.

TECHNICAL DATA

Piaggio P.166 DL3SEM

Powerplants: Two AlliedSignal LTP101-700 turboprops
Developing: 447.5kW (600hp)
Driving: Three-blade propellers
Span: 14.69m (48ft 2.5in) including tip tanks
Length: 11.88m (39ft 0in)
Height: 5.00m (16ft 5in)
All-up weight: 4300kg (9,480lb)
Maximum speed: 400km/h (248mph)
Operational ceiling: 28,000ft
Maximum range: 2130km (1,323 miles)
Accommodation: Two crew plus eight passengers
Armament: Nil
First flown: 26 November 1957;
3 July 1976 (turboprop)

Piaggio P.166 Italian Air Force

Piaggio Douglas PD808

LIGHT JET UTILITY/EXECUTIVE AIRCRAFT

Piaggio Douglas PD808 Italian Air Force

DEVELOPMENT

The PD808 was designed by the Douglas Aircraft Company in association with Piaggio, but when it failed to attract interest in the USA, the project was taken over by Piaggio and construction transferred to Italy. Two prototypes were built which gained FAA certification in 1966, and the prototypes plus the production aircraft were fitted with bulged canopy windows and uprated Viper engines. Production totalled 29 aircraft and ceased in 1979.

CURRENT SERVICE

The Aeronautica Militaire Italiana became the only military customer for the PD808, ordering 25 aircraft – most of which survive to this day, having seen more than 30 years of service. They are now all operated by 14° Stormo and 71° Stormo at Practica di Mare for electronic warfare training, the previous overall grey scheme now having been replaced by a green and blue/grey camouflage.

SPECIAL FEATURES

The PD808 is a light twin-jet transport with good field performance. The aircraft has gained a reputation for being able to carry out its ECM tasks and training with the strike aircraft as part of the package. As with all ECM aircraft, the electronics package carried is tailored to suit the requirements of the mission and could involve radar jamming or providing cover for other aircraft.

VARIANTS

The 25 PD808s ordered for the AMI were produced in several different versions: four VIP aircraft, three electronic countermeasures aircraft, six nine-seater transport and navigation trainers, and 12 airways/navaid checking aircraft. Over the years, the type has been replaced in the VIP and transport role and some have subsequently been converted to the ECM role. At least half the AMI's fleet of PD808s are now active in the role.

TECHNICAL DATA

Piaggio Douglas PD808

Powerplants: Two Rolls-Royce/Bristol Siddely Viper 526s, built under licence
Developing: 1,524kN (3,360lb st)
Span: 13.2m (43ft 3.5in) including tip tanks
Length: 12.8m (42ft 2in)
Height: 4.80m (15ft 9in)
All-up weight: 8165kg (18,000lbs)
Maximum speed: 852km/h (529mph)
Cruising Speed: 800km/h (497mph)
Operational ceiling: 45,000ft
Maximum range: 2,128 Km (1,322 miles)
Accommodation: 2 crew and up to nine passengers
Armament: Nil
First Flown: 29 August 1964
Entered Service: 1965

Piaggio Douglas PD808 Italian Air Force

Piaggio P.180 Avanti

TWIN-TURBOPROP HIGH-SPEED TRANSPORT

P.180 Avanti Italian Air Force

DEVELOPMENT

Designed by Rinaldo Piaggio in 1982 following the example of Burt Rutan and other leading designers, the Avanti soon gained the interest of Gates Learjet, who became partners. However, cutbacks in the executive jet world caused them to drop out again but much of the wind tunnel testing and development of new production processes had already been completed. Major components such as the fuselage are made by Piaggio in the USA along with other composite components, and are shipped to Italy for assembly. Metals and composites, with carbonfibre or Kevlar and epoxy, are used in the construction of the tail and tailcone, nose and canards, outer wing flaps, undercarriage doors and engine fairings. First flight took place in 1986 and certification in Italy and the USA was granted in 1990. The first production P.180 flew in May 1990. In mid-1998 the Turkish holding company Tushav took a 51% shareholding in Piaggio.

CURRENT SERVICE

The Aeronautica Militare Italiana (AMI) was the initial military customer with an order for six Avantis that was followed by a further three in 1999. They are assigned to the three Regioni Aerea and provide VIP, air ambulance and communications support to the AMI. Three were delivered to the Italian Army in the late 1990s and two to the civil protection department. Ultimately the force may take a further 18 aircraft but this is restricted by budget restraints at present.

SPECIAL FEATURES

Probably the only 'triplane' in military service, this futuristic design has taken advantage of some very advanced aerodynamics and produced one of the cleanest fuselages in terms of drag of any aircraft ever built. With a foreplane placed almost at the

nose and a straight wing with twin turboprop pusher engines, it has a very clean laminar flow wing and a variable incidence swept T- tail, plus twin strakes under the rear fuselage. The lift from the foreplane allows the horizontal tail to act as a lifting surface, reducing the wing area and drag. A mid-mounted position for the wing to the rear of the main cabin allows an unobstructed cabin free of a spar and with maximum headroom. The Avanti has near jet performance, noise levels and comfort, but at turboprop prices.

VARIANTS

Later models of the Avanti have an increased all-up weight, which following modification can be introduced on the earlier models, but a six bladed propeller is expected to be retro fitted to all models. A stretched turbofan derivative is under development.

P.180 Avanti Italian Air Force

TECHNICAL DATA

Piaggio P.180 Avanti

Powerplants: Two Pratt & Whitney (Canada) PT6A-66 turboprops
Developing: 1,107kW (1,485hp)
Driving: Five-blade propellers
Span: 14.03m (46ft 0in)
Length: 14.41m (47ft 3.5in)
Height: 3.94m (12ft 11in)
All-up weight: 5,239kg (11,500lb)
Maximum speed: 732km/h (455mph)
Operational ceiling: 41,000ft
Maximum range: 3,187km (1,980 miles)
Accommodation: Two crew and 6-10 passengers
First Flown: 23 September 1986
Entered service: 1993

Pilatus PC-6 Porter/Turbo Porter

STOL UTILITY TRANSPORT

PC-6B Turbo Porter French Army

DEVELOPMENT

Following experience with the Pilatus PC-4, the PC-6 was designed as a STOL utility transport for operations from primitive airfields and temporary surfaces. It required a strong and reliable airframe, good low-speed handling with STOL capabilities, as well as a large cabin with seating for at least seven. The first aircraft flew in 1959, with a 253kW (340hp) Lycoming piston engine, but by 1961 it was apparent that its performance would be considerably enhanced by a turboprop powerplant and the type is now available with a choice of three turboprops. Early PC-6As were powered by 419kW (525shp) Turboméca Astazous. Pilatus then considered that the aircraft would be more saleable with an American engine, and the PC-6B was introduced. In 1965, Pilatus joined forces with Fairchild-Hiller of the USA and 88 Garrett-engined 'HeliPorters' were produced for the US Army as AU-23As.

CURRENT SERVICE

Much of the production of the Turbo Porter has been for military customers, and users of the PC-6A/B/C include the air forces of Switzerland, Angola, Argentina, Austria, Chad, Colombia, Ecuador, France, Indonesia, Iran, Mexico, Myanmar, Oman, Peru, Slovenia, South Africa, Thailand, United Emirates and US Army.

SPECIAL FEATURES

A straight wing fitted with high-lift devices including large flaps, a large and powerful rudder and good handling characteristics. A double loading-door is fitted to facilitate cargo loading. The PC-6 has the ability to take off and land in narrow and confined spaces and is able to operate with normal wheels, large low-pressure tyres or skis, and can operate into STOL strips in extreme locations.

VARIANTS

There are three main PC-6 variants, distinguished by different engines: **PC-6** – Lycoming GSO-480 B1A6 piston engine; **PC-6A** – Astazou turboprop; **PC-6B** – Pratt & Whitney PT6A turboprop; **PC-6C** – Garrett TPE 331-1-100 turboprop of 428kW (575shp). Some have been modified for firefighting tasks. A **PC-8D Twin Porter** flew in November 1987, but did not proceed beyond the prototype.

TECHNICAL DATA

Pilatus PC-6B Turbo Porter
Powerplant: One Pratt and Whitney (Canada) PT6A-27 turboprop
Developing: 507kW (680hp)
Driving: three-blade propeller
Span: 15.87m (52ft 0.75in)
Length: 11.00m (36ft 1in)
Height: 3.20m (10ft 6in)
All-up weight: 2,800kg (6,173lb) on wheels or 2,699kg (5,732lb) on skis
Maximum speed: 280km/h (174mph)
Cruising Speed: 213km/h (132mph)
Operational ceiling: 25,000ft
Maximum range: 1,612km (1,002 miles)
Accommodation: One crew, up to nine passengers
Armament: US licence-built version (Fairchild AU-23A Peacemaker) fitted with underwing strong points for carriage of rocket pods.
First flown: 4 May 1959 (piston); 2 May 1961 (turboprop)

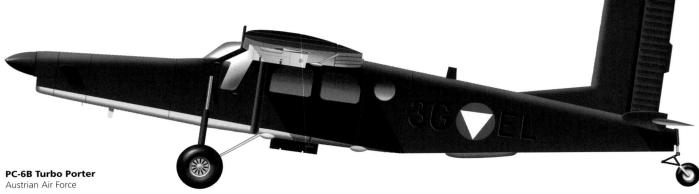

PC-6B Turbo Porter
Austrian Air Force

Pilatus PC-7 TurboTrainer

TANDEM-SEAT BASIC AND ADVANCED TRAINER

PC-7 Turbo Trainer Royal Netherlands Air Force

DEVELOPMENT
The PC-7 is a direct descendant from the Pilatus P-3, a 1950s-vintage piston-engined training aircraft built for the Swiss Air Force. An example of the P-3 was re-engined with a turboprop, but failed to sell initially, and was shelved. The fuel crises of the early 1970s brought renewed interest, and by 1978 the first production PC-7 had flown, aerodynamically cleaned up and with a straight wing, large rearward sliding bubble canopy and tandem seating. Early models were without ejector seats. Since 1992, the PC-7 MkII shares a common fuselage with the PC-9, featuring the same stepped cockpit, the larger cockpit canopy, and Martin Baker ejector seats.

CURRENT SERVICE
Over 500 PC-7s and PC-7 MkIIs have been sold, mostly to military customers for basic, through to advanced flying training. The Turbo Trainer is currently in service with the air arms of Abu Dhabi, Angola, Austria, Bolivia, Botswana, Chad, Chile, France, Guatemala, Iraq, Malaysia, Myanmar, Mexico, the Netherlands, Nigeria, South Africa, Surinam, Switzerland, the United Arab Emirates and Uruguay.

SPECIAL FEATURES
A versatile conventional training aircraft with the ability to take students from basic flying to advanced flying, including full aerobatics, instrument flying, and tactical and formation flying. The MkII featured some of the upgrading of the PC-9 – its bigger, more powerful brother – including a larger tail unit, the stepped cockpit and ejector seats, a more robust undercarriage with nosewheel steering, and the more powerful PT6A-25C engine.

VARIANTS
With its lower-powered PT6A engine driving a three-bladed 7ft 9in propeller, no ejector seats in a level cockpit covered by a rearward sliding canopy, the original **PC-7** is readily distinguishable. The current **PC-7 MkII** is produced on the same production line as the PC-9 and is a more capable aircraft, with the higher power engine and utilising a four-bladed 8ft propeller. The stepped cockpit, with centre frame and side opening, distinguishes it from the earlier version.

TECHNICAL DATA

Pilatus PC-7 Turbo Trainer
Powerplant: One Pratt and Whitney Canada PT6A-25A turboprop
Developing: 410kW (550shp)
Driving: Three-blade propeller
Span: 10.40m (34ft 1in)
Length: 9.78m (32ft 1in)
Height: 3.21m (10ft 6in)
All-up weight: 2700kg (5,952lb)
Maximum speed: 412km/h (256 mph)
Operational ceiling: 33,000ft
Maximum range: 2630km (1,634 miles)
Accommodation: Two
Armament: Underwing hard points allow the carriage of 1040kg (2,293lb) of stores either drop tanks or gun pods/rocket pods/unguided rockets or other ordnance.
First flown: 12 May 1975

PC-7 Turbo Trainer
Royal Netherlands Air Force

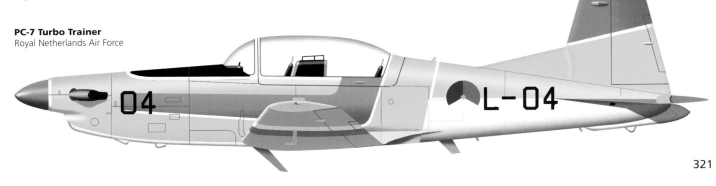

Pilatus PC-9

TANDEM-SEAT BASIC TO ADVANCED TRAINER

Pilatus PC-9 Slovenia Military Aviation

DEVELOPMENT

The PC-9 was designed as a big 'brother' to the PC-7, and when first produced, it had only about 10% commonality with the earlier design, but as both have developed, the PC-7 MkII and the PC-9 now share a production line and a common structure. The PC-9 resulted from the increased cost of jet fuel and was designed to replace the jet trainer in almost all respects but at turboprop economy. The main difference from the PC-7II is the higher powered engine and the equipment fitted as standard, enabling students to make the transition directly from trainer to fast jet. A joint venture by Pilatus and Beech saw a developed version of the PC-9 entered for the USAF/USN JPATS (Joint Primary Aircraft Training System) requirement. Announced as the winner in 1995, the Beech-Pilatus entry has gained the most valuable training contract ever, which should allow production of 711 aircraft for the USAF and US Navy. The aircraft has undergone a number of changes but has finally emerged under the name Texan II (see separate entry).

CURRENT SERVICE

The PC-9 had established itself as a straight-through trainer and was gaining export orders, but these have been overtaken by orders that have now started to

appear as a result of the JPATS order for Texan II. It is in service with the following air arms: Australia, Angola, Cyprus, Myanma (Burma), Thailand, Switzerland, Saudi Arabia, Slovenia, Croatia and Germany (operated under a civil contract for the Luftwaffe).

SPECIAL FEATURES

A straight-through trainer with the economy of a turboprop, but able to accomplish most of the work of a jet trainer. The Texan II aircraft have a one lever (throttle) engine/propeller handling as on a jet, via an electronic engine and fuel control system.

VARIANTS

The **PC-9A** was tailored to Australian requirements for features such as low-pressure tyres and Bendix EFIS. Early aircraft were built from Swiss-supplied kits, with the final 48 being built on-site by Hawker de Havilland. The **PC-9B** is a target towing variant with two winches on wing hard points, supplied to German civilian contractors for Luftwaffe target tasks. The **PC-9 MkII/Texan II** is a very much modified joint project between Beech and Pilatus to fulfil the USAF/US Navy JPATS requirement. The cockpit is pressurised, air conditioned, and has ejector seats covered by a sideways-opening, three-piece canopy. The avionics are digital and include GPS and MLS, and there is

provision for a Head-Up display to give it the capability of a jet trainer, although this is not yet fitted.

SEE ALSO:
RAYTHEON BEECH TEXAN II

TECHNICAL DATA

Pilatus PC-9

Powerplant: One Pratt and Whitney Canada PT6A-62 turboprop
Developing: 708kW (950shp)
Driving: Four-blade propeller
Span: 10.12m (33ft 2.5in)
Length: 10.17m (33ft 4.75in)
Height: 3.26m (10ft 8.33in)
All-up weight: 2250kg (4,960lb)
Maximum speed: 593km/h (368mph)
Operational ceiling: 38,000ft
Maximum range: 1642km (1,020 miles)
Accommodation: Two
Armament: Fitted with six hard points under the wings for carriage of fuel tanks and armanent including gun packs or rocket pods up to 2,239lbs usable load.
First Flown: 7 May 1984
Entered service: 15 December 1984 (Royal Saudi Air Force)

Pilatus PC-9 Slovenia Military Aviation

Pilatus Britten Norman BN-2B Islander/Defender

STOL UTILITY TRANSPORT

Islander A1 British Army

TECHNICAL DATA

Pilatus Britten Norman BN2T Defender

Powerplants: Two Allison 250-B17C Turboprops
Developing: 298kW (400shp)
Span: 14.94m (49ft 0in)
Length: 10.87m (35ft 8in) (may vary according to nose fitted)
Height: 4.42m (14ft 6in)
All-up weight: 3,175kg (7,000lb)
Maximum speed: 315km/h (196mph)
Operational ceiling: 25,000ft
Maximum range: 1,349km (838 miles)
Accommodation: Pilot and up to nine passengers or ten parachutists plus jumpmaster
Armament: Up to four hard points on each wing. Optional weapons include twin 7.62mm gun packs, 250lb and 500lb bombs, rocket packs, missiles and torpedos
First Flown: 13 June 1965 (BN2);
12 May 1984 (Defender)

DEVELOPMENT

The brainchild of the Isle of Wight-based Britten Norman company, the Islander was designed as a light transport for use from primitive and unprepared strips. The first prototype flew from Bembridge in June 1965, and by mid-1967 the orders stood at over 200. Its success outstripped the available capacity and production was transferred to British Hovercraft's premises. Since then, Islanders/Defenders have been under continuous development and have been built in Belgium, Romania and the Philippines. Engine size has varied dependent on customers' requirements. The first turboprop variant flew in 1980 and became available in the Islander/Defender range. A number of aircraft have taken advantage of the type's versatility and load carrying capability to become specialised variants carrying stand-off radars, airborne early warning radars, maritime reconnaissance radar and a number of other surveillance fits.

CURRENT SERVICE

The Islander (unarmed) variant has been delivered to, amongst others; Ciskei, Haiti, Indonesia, Iraq, Israel, Qatar, Somalia, Turkey, Venezuela, Zaire, Zimbabwe,

Netherlands and Cyprus. The Defender (potentially armed) variant has also been delivered to a large number of countries including: Abu Dhabi, Belgium, Belize, Botswana, Ghana, Guyana, Hong Kong, Jamaica, Malagasy, Malawi, Mauritania, Mexico, Oman, Panama, Qatar, Rwanda, Seychelles and Surinam. Specialist maritime Defenders have been delivered to Cyprus, India, Pakistan and the Philippines. The British Army also operates seven Islander A1s and the RAF has an Islander CC2 and a CC2A, both operated from RAF Northolt. A single Islander – an ex-demonstrator of the ASW/ASV variant – is used by the Royal Navy as an underwater weapons trials aircraft.

SPECIAL FEATURES

It is the simplicity of the design and its versatility which has made the Islander/Defender such a success. It has the ability to carry out a large range of tasks at very low cost – both operating and initial costs. The airframe has been adapted or used for a wide range of duties that includes commuter, feeder liner, cargo, executive, transport, ambulance, border surveillance, maritime patrol, urban and rural policing, coastguard and fisheries protection.

VARIANTS

The basic aircraft was the **BN-2**, followed by the **BN-2A** and ultimately the **BN-2B** – with individual aircraft varying according to customer requirements and different role fits. The **BN-2T** is the turboprop-powered version of the current production BN-2B. A specialised surveillance version based on the BN-2T is called the **Defender 4000 (BN2T-4S)** for the export market. Other specialist aircraft fits are named according to the equipment carried such as **Castor Islander** (later Astor) or the **MSSA** an AEW Islander which carries a Westinghouse APG-66SR radar with 360 degree coverage, FLIR and INS.

Islander A1 British Army

ARMY ZG846

Piper PA-18 Super Cub

SINGLE-ENGINED TWO-SEAT UTILITY/TRAINER LIGHT AIRCRAFT

PA-18-150 Super Cub Israeli Defence Force/Air Force

DEVELOPMENT

The simple and economical Piper J-3 Cub is one of the most well-loved light aircraft of all time. The first J-3 flew in 1937 and during World War Two became the L-4 Grasshopper featuring a 50kW (65hp) Continental A-65-1 engine with the US Army. The J-4 Cub Coupe, with side-by-side seating, followed immediately post-war, as did the three-seat J-5 Cub Cruiser. The PA-12 Super Cruiser, with seating for three and a more powerful Lycoming O-235 engine followed, together with the PA-14 Family Cruiser, and these formed the basis for the PA-18 Super Cub – the ultimate

development of Piper's original J-3. The Super Cub remained in production for nearly four decades and over 7,500 were built by 1981, when the type was initially withdrawn. It returned to production, albeit at a low rate, in 1988 but production finally ceased in 1995. Production against US government contracts totalled many hundreds for US Army and Mutual Defense Aid Programs under the L-18 and L-21 designations.

CURRENT SERVICE

Over the years many air arms have used the Super Cub as a liaison, communications, basic trainer and glider tug aircraft for cadet forces. Currently it only remains in service with Argentina, Bosnia (Serbia), Israel, Nicaragua and Uruguay.

SPECIAL FEATURES

Probably the longest running production aircraft of all time, the Super Cub is a low-cost tube and fabric light aircraft, with the classic braced high-wing and fixed tailwheel undercarriage and all-metal wings.

VARIANTS

The PA-18-95 had a 65kW (90hp) Continental C-90-12F or -8F flat-four piston engine; the PA-18-135, which entered production in 1952 had the 100kW (135hp) Lycoming O-290; the PA-18-150 was produced from 1955. The PA-18A was an agricultural version with a hopper in the rear seat and underwing spray bars; the PA-18S was a seaplane version with twin floats; the PA-18-125 became the military L-21A, the PA-18-135 and -150 the L-21B.

TECHNICAL DATA

Piper PA-18 Standard Super Cub 150

Powerplant: One Textron Lycoming (Continental) 0-320 flat-four piston engine
Developing: 112kW (150hp)
Driving: Two-blade propeller
Span: 10.73m (35ft 3in)
Length: 6.88m (22ft 7in)
Height: 2.02m (6ft 9in)
All-up weight: 795kg (1,750lb)
Maximum speed: 210km/h (130mph)
Economical cruising speed: 170km/h (105mph)
Operational ceiling: 19,000ft
Maximum range: 740km (460 miles)
Accommodation: Two, in tandem
Warload: Nil
First Flown: 1949 (PA-18-95); 1954 (PA-18-150)
Entered service: Early 1950 (PAS-18-95); 1955 (PA-18-150)

PA-18-150 Super Cub Uruguayan Air Force

Piper PA-23 Apache/Aztec

LIGHT TWIN PISTON-ENGINED UTILITY AIRCRAFT

PA-23-250 Aztec Spanish Air Force

DEVELOPMENT

First flown as the Twin Stinson, the design was acquired by the Piper Aircraft Corporation in November 1948 and became the PA-23 Apache. It was first flown as such in 1952 and underwent continual development until the model evolved as the Aztec, which had a similar capacity but a more modern appearance. Gone was the round tailplane and short nose, and by 1961 the sharp cut large tailplane and longer nose were introduced. An upgrading of the piston engines allowed increased weights and ranges. The US Navy acquired 20 PA-23-250s in 1960 as UO-1s (changing to U-11As in in 1962) for use in a utility role. A total of 2,165 Apaches and 4,811 Aztecs were built before production was phased out in early 1982.

CURRENT SERVICE

Only small numbers of 'off the shelf' models for use in the liaison/light transport and training role have seen military service. The Spanish Air Force had six PA-23-250 Aztecs (locally known as E.19s) until about 1996, and these are now retired or in storage. A sole Aztec is operated by the Argentinian Gendarmeria Nacional at HQ Campo de Mayo Army airfield. A number of single aircraft continue to operate with third world air arms such as Bolivia, Cameroon, Costa Rica, Madagascar, Mexico and Venezuela.

SPECIAL FEATURES

A cheap, easy to maintain communications and liaison aircraft which is available on the second hand market and fulfils a role with third world air arms, particularly in Central and South America.

VARIANTS

PA-23 Apache – original model with round tailplane and short nose; PA-23 Aztec – later model with swept fin/rudder and longer nose; The Aztec B had a longer nose to incorporate a baggage compartment; the Aztec C had optional turbo-charged TIO-540-C4B5 engines and modified undercarriage; the Aztec D had a longer nose and single-piece windshield; the Aztec F was the final version with cambered wingtips and improved instruments.

PA-23 Apache Geronimo Paraguayan Air Force

TECHNICAL DATA

Piper PA-23-250 Aztec D

Powerplants: Two Textron Lycoming IO-54D-C4B5 piston engines
Developing: 186kW (250hp)
Driving: Two-blade propellers
Span: 11.34m (37ft 2.5in)
Length: 9.21m (30ft 2.5in)
Height: 3.14m (10ft 3.5in)
All-up weight: 2,360kg (5,200lb)
Maximum speed: 348km/h (216mph)
Cruising speed: 332km/h (206mph)
Operating ceiling: 19,800ft
Maximum range: 1,947km (1,226miles)
Accommodation: Pilot plus three/five passengers
Armament: Nil
First Flown: 2 March 1952 (Apache); 1958 (Aztec)

Piper PA-25/36 Pawnee

SINGLE-SEAT AGRICULTURAL AIRCRAFT

PA-25 Pawnee

DEVELOPMENT

The prototype PA-25 Pawnee flew in 1957, a single-seat piston-engined aircraft designed for the crop spraying role from square one and not converted from other uses. It was a development of a design study by Fred Weick (designer of the Ercoupe) of Texas A & M, known as the AG-1, which first flew in 1950. From experience gained with the PA-18A, configured for agricultural use, had shown an encouraging potential market for this category of aeroplane. The pilot was given a high sitting position to ensure an excellent all-round view. Early models had a 111.9kW (150hp) engine, but this was soon upgraded to the 175.2kW (235hp) version in order to provide greater load capability. Even larger glassfibre hopper chemical loads

of 20 cu ft were possible in the later models particularly the Pawnee Brave which has a 224kW (300hp) engine and cantilever wings and a swept tail.

CURRENT SERVICE

A small number of PA-25-235s operate with the Argentinian Institito Nacional de Aviación Civil at Morón Airport. The Policiá Nacional de Colombia has a single PA-36 Pawnee Brave on detachment at Bogatá. PA-36s are also used by the Western Air Command of the Abu Dhabi Air Force Spray Unit at Batin.

SPECIAL FEATURES

Built specifically for the task, the airframe was a rugged tubular structure with crumple zones and a cockpit rollover bar to protect the pilot. This was specially designed to leave the cockpit substantially undamaged in the usual type of low-speed crash associated with agricultural dusting/spraying operations. The fuel

tank was foam filled not only to reduce fire risk but also to cut down fuel surge. The raised glazed cockpit is sealed and force air ventilated both heating or cooling is available to protect the pilot from the spray in use. The hopper, situated ahead of the cockpit, for the chemical spray or dust can be varied according to the load and task, the spray booms are on the trailing edges of the wings visible from the pilot's raised position at centre fuselage.

VARIANTS

PA-25-150 Pawnee – the basic aircraft with Lycoming O-320 111.9kW (150hp) engine; PA-25-235 Pawnee B – an upgrade to the 175.2kW (235hp) engine; PA-25 Pawnee C – further engine upgrade to 193kW (260hp); PA-36-300 Pawnee Brave – a new and larger airframe with cantilever wings and swept tail, plus other improvements, including a 223.7kW (300hp) engine, but this was not as successful as the earlier versions.

TECHNICAL DATA

Piper PA-36 Pawnee Brave 300

Powerplants: One Avco Lycoming IO-540-K1G5 piston engine
Developing: 224kW (300hp)
Driving: three or four-blade propeller
Span: 11.82m (38ft 9.5in)
Length: 8.17m (26ft 9.5in)
Height: 2.29m (7ft 6in)
All-up weight: 1,996kg (4,400lb)
Maximum speed: 238km/h (148mph)
Cruising Speed: 183km/h (114mph)
Maximum range: 740km (460 miles)
Accommodation: One
Armament: Nil
First Flown: 1957 (PA-25);
5 September 1969 (PA-36)

PA-25-260 Pawnee D

Piper PA-28/32 Cherokee

FOUR-SEAT LOW-WING TRAINER/TOURER

PA-28RT-201 Arrow IV Argentine Air Force

DEVELOPMENT

The Cherokee was designed for low-cost production to compete with the Cessna 172, as a single-engined light aircraft suitable for training or for touring. Built in large numbers (over 29,000), it has been subject to progressive development over the years since its first flight in 1960. It has also undergone a series of engine upgrades from the initial 134kW (180hp) to the Turbo Dakota variant with a 149.1kW (200hp) Continental TSIO-360-F engine. The design was so flexible that further variants ranged from a basic two-seater to a high performance business type of aircraft with retractable undercarriage. Each new version, of which there were many (Challenger, Arrow, Archer, Charger, Dakota, to name a few), had minor modifications, changes to wing planforms, tailplanes etc. Later and larger versions (PA-32 Cherokee Six/Saratoga/Lance) were stretched to accommodate six seats with an optional seventh and had turbocharged engines.

CURRENT SERVICE

A number of various models of the PA-28 Cherokee have seen military service, many having now been phased out, but some of those remaining are: PA28-238 Dakotas assembled by ENAER for the Chilean Air Force, Argentina's PA-28-201 Arrows, the Finnish Air Force with Arrow IIs and single aircraft in Columbia, Costa Rica, Tanzania and Turkey (Army).

SPECIAL FEATURES

An off the shelf light communications aircraft, also available for refresher training and maintaining currency for staff officers. The PA-28/PA-32 series is supported by a world wide network of Piper dealers, together with spares back-up – meaning that repairs and maintenance are available around the world.

VARIANTS

PA-28-140/150/160/180 – Cherokee version; **PA28-151** – **Warrior** version with a new wing; the **Warrior II** had a new engine; The **Charger/Pathfinder** has a 175.2kW (235hp) Lycoming engine; The **PA-28-201 Turbo Dakota** has a 149.1kW (200hp) Continental TSIO-360-F; The **PA-32-260 Cherokee Six** and **PA-32-300 Cherokee Six** have the 223.7kW (300hp) Lycoming IO-540-K and the **PA-32-30IT Saratoga** has a turbo-charged engine. The **PA-28-161 Cadet** is a 2+2 trainer version of the Warrior II, powered by a Lycoming O-320-D3G, with reduced trim standard, which was introduced in the late 1980s. The **PA-28R-200/201 Cherokee Arrow** series have the retractable undercarriage.

TECHNICAL DATA

PA-28-181 Cherokee Archer

Powerplant: One Lycoming O-360-A4M piston engine
Developing: 134kW (180hp)
Driving: Two-blade propeller
Span: 10.67m (35ft 5in)
Length: 7.32m (24ft 0in)
Height: 2.22m (7ft 3.5in)
All-up weight: 1,156kg (2,500lb)
Maximum speed: 239km/h (149mph)
Operational ceiling: 13,000ft
Maximum range: 1,074km (667 miles)
Accommodation: Pilot plus three passengers
Armament: Nil
First flown: 10 January 1960 (prototype);
10 February 1961 (production PA-28-160);
17 October 1972 (PA-28-151 Warrior I);
27 August 1976 (Warrior II)

PA-28-236 Dakota Chilean Air Force

Piper PA-31/3IT Navajo

TWIN-ENGINED LIGHT TRANSPORT

PA-31 Navajo Chieftain UK DERA

DEVELOPMENT

When first flown in 1964, the PA-31 was the largest type in the Piper range and designed for commuter/feeder airlines and business use. It proved to be the design basis for all Piper's subsequent large twins. The cabin can be pressurised to provide a 'shirt sleeve' environment for the crew and passengers. The process of improvement was ever present and a number of variants, all with minor changes, continued throughout its production run. Later models had turbo-charged engines and, in common with many other modern twins, had counter-rotating propellers to remove torque problems. The PA-31-350 Navajo Chieftain had the fuselage lengthened by 0.61m (2ft 0in), allowing for a ten-seat interior, and featured a modified nose and cabin. It was powered by 261kW (350hp) TIO-540-J2BD turbocharged engines. Production ended in 1982 and some 2,500 examples of the Navajo series were built. The ultimate model was the PA-31T Cheyenne with 373kW (500hp) Pratt & Whitney PT6A-11 turboprops and increased streamlining.

CURRENT SERVICE

During the lifetime of the PA-31, a number have seen military service. Twelve were in service with the French

Navy until recently and the Finnish Air Force has a fleet of seven Navajo Chieftains for communications. Four Navajo Chieftains (secondhand examples from the civil market) were acquired for MOD (PE) Test and Evaluation and A&AEE use, but these are also in the process of being disposed of. Small numbers, or single aircraft, are still operating with the air forces of Argentina, Bahamas, Chile, Columbia, Costa Rica, Dominican Republic, Guatemala, Mauritania, Honduras, Peru, Sweden, Syria and the US Army.

SPECIAL FEATURES

A low-cost multi-seat transport, useful for crew transport or communication work and has been used for nav training and multi-engine pilot training. World-wide Piper dealerships make servicing easy and provide a spares network within reasonable reach. The piston engines and the cost of Avgas fuel are making these aircraft more expensive to operate than comparative turboprops.

VARIANTS

PA-31 Navajo – original basic version; **PA-31 Navajo Chieftain** – slightly enlarged piston engined variant; **PA-31P** – pressurised, with 317kW (425hp) Avco Lycoming TIGO-541-E1A engines;

TECHNICAL DATA

Piper PA-31-300 Navajo
Powerplants: Two Textron Lycoming IO-540-M piston engines
Developing: 224kW (300hp)
Driving: three-blade propellers
Span: 12.40m (40ft 8in)
Length: 9.94m (32ft 7.5in)
Height: 3.96m (13ft 0in)
All-up weight: 2,812kg (6,200lb)
Maximum speed: 365km/h (227mph)
Operational ceiling: 16,600ft
Maximum range: 2,494km (1,550miles)
Accommodation: Pilot plus six to eight persons
Armament: Nil
First flown: 30 September 1964; 22 October 1973 (PA-31T Cheyenne)

PA-31T Cheyenne – basic aircraft but aerodynamically cleaned up and fitted with 462kW (620hp) Pratt & Whitney PT6A-11 turboprops.

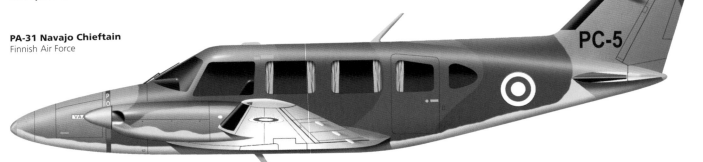

PA-31 Navajo Chieftain
Finnish Air Force

Piper PA-34 Seneca/PA-44 Seminole

TWIN-ENGINED LIGHT TRANSPORT AND TRAINER

PA-34 Seneca Uruguayan Navy

DEVELOPMENT

The PA-34 is basically a twin-engined PA-32 Cherokee Six/Saratoga, and the PA-34T/44 Seminole is likewise the twin-engined version of the T-tailed PA-32T – part of the continuing product improvement from Piper, with retractable tricycle undercarriage and offering seven-seat accommodation. The first Seneca flew in 1968, and since then over 4,500 have been produced, together with almost 500 Seminoles following this model's first flight in 1976.

CURRENT SERVICE

Limited numbers of PA-34 Senecas have seen military service, with the largest group being those of the Brazilian Air Force, an initial order for 12 Seneca IIs being followed by a second batch of 20, all of which

were assembled by Embraer in Brazil. Other countries whose air arms use the aircraft are: Argentina, Bolivia, Colombia, Costa Rica, Guatemala, Haiti, Honduras, Indonesia, Pakistan, Poland and Uruguay. Costa Rica also operates one PA-44 Seminole.

SPECIAL FEATURES

A lightweight transport/communications aircraft with twin-engine safety and part of a world wide aircraft dealership with easily available spares.

VARIANTS

PA-34 Seneca – essentially a twin-engine PA-32; **PA-34 Seneca II** – uprated counter-rotating engines and optional weather radar; **EMB810 Seneca II (U7/7A)** – the Brazilian Embraer-built version; **PA-34-**

200T Seneca II – turbo-charged engines; **PA-34-220T** – penultimate version of the Seneca, with turbo-charged and counter rotating engines, single piece windshield and new instrumentation; **PA-44-180 Seminole** – essentially a twin-engine PA-32T (T-tail). The PA-44-180 Seminole is a light twin developed from the single-engined Arrow, with a pair of 135kW (180hp) Lycoming O-360-E1A6D engines. The Polish firm of PZL Mielec assembled/manufactured the Seneca II for sale in Eastern Europe. Designated **M-20 Mewa**, the first Polish-built prototype flew on 25 July 1979.

PA-34 Seneca Colombian Army

TECHNICAL DATA

Piper PA-34 Seneca II

Powerplants: Two Teledyne Continental TSIO-360-E piston engines
Developing: 149kW (200hp)
Driving: Two or three-blade propellers
Span: 11.85m (38ft 10.75in)
Length: 8.73m (28ft 7.5in)
Height: 3.02m (9ft 10.75in)
All-up weight: 2,073kg (4,570lb)
Maximum speed: 361km/h (225mph)
Operational ceiling: 25,000ft
Maximum range: 1,012km (629miles)
Accommodation: Pilot plus six/seven passengers
Armament: Nil
First Flown: 30 August 1968 (PA-34); May 1976 (PA-44)
Entered service: September 1971

PZL I-22 Iryda

TWIN-JET ADVANCED TRAINER AND LIGHT ATTACK

I-22 M93K Iryda Polish Air Force

DEVELOPMENT

Poland continued to exhibit an independence whilst a member of the Warsaw Pact and did not follow the party line with regard to aircraft purchases, preferring its own designs to the commonly adopted types. The PZL I-22 Iryda (Iridium) was designed as a follow up to the present TS-11 Iskra and first flew in March 1985; however, the prototype was lost in a crash in January 1987. It is an Alpha Jet lookalike except it is a rather more chunky heavyweight and has suffered with a powerplant that lacks thrust. A variety of engines have been tested in early production aircraft but meanwhile only a limited number of production aircraft are being delivered to the Polish Air Force. An avionics upgrade is also under test and several of the engine test aircraft have upgraded Western avionics.

CURRENT SERVICE

The first I-22 entered service with the Polish Air Force in October 1992 at the Deblin Air Academy. Further delivery of the aircraft have continued but later models are fitted with the uprated engine. Exact numbers

are not known, as current aircraft are expected to be returned to the manufacturer to have upgraded engines when it is decided which engine will be used. It is also likely that Western avionics will be fitted.

SPECIAL FEATURES

The design and production of the prototype and early production of the I-22 has been overtaken by changes in international relations and the collapse of the Eastern Bloc. Now that Western engines and avionics are available, the aircraft is capable of being upgraded to a much higher standard, although cost is the stumbling block.

VARIANTS

The range of variants for the I-22 is as follows: **I-22** – the initial production aircraft delivered to the Polish Air Force with the PZL-5 engine; **I-22 M92** – upgraded PZL-15 engine of 17.69kN (3,968lb st); **I-22 M93K** – standard Polish Air Force version with PZL-15 engine; **I-22 M93V** – intended for export, fitted with the Rolls-Royce Viper 545 with 15.0kN (3,370lbs) thrust and also

used as an avionics test bed; **I-22 M96** – a further upgrade fitted with new wing profile, LERXES and a taller tail fin. Also fitted are French (Sextant Avionique) avionics, and this is the standard to which all Polish Air Force I-22s will be modified. There are a number of variants on the drawing board for specialist tasks which would be to the latest upgrade standard, with a supercritical swept wing. These include **Iryda M93M** for maritime recce and attack, and **Iryda M95** – a two-seat ground attack and recce version. Single-seat derivations are also planned and given the designation **M-97** and **M-97MS**.

TECHNICAL DATA

PZL I-22 Iryda

Powerplants: Two PZL Rzeszow PZL-5 turbojets
Developing: 10.79kN (2,425lb st)
Span: 9.60m (31ft 6ins)
Length: 13.22m (43ft 4.5in)
Height: 4.30m (14ft 1.25in)
All-up weight: 6,900kg (15,512lbs)
Maximum speed: 840km/h (522mph)
Cruising Speed: 720km/h (447mph)
Operational ceiling: 36,000ft
Maximum range: 420km (261miles)
Ferry Range: 900km (559miles)
Accommodation: Two
Armament: The aircraft can carry a 23mm GS3-23L twin-barrelled cannon pod under the fuselage centreline and four under wing pylons are each able to take up to 500kg (1,102lb) with inboard pylons plumbed for 380 litre fuel tanks. The maximum external stores load is 1,200kg (2,646lb)
First Flown: 3 March 1985
Entered Service: October 1992

I-22 Iryda Polish Air Force

PZL Mielec (Antonov) An-28 Bryza

LIGHT GENERAL PURPOSE TRANSPORT

An-28/M-28RM Bryza Polish Navy

DEVELOPMENT

A direct descendant of the Antonov An-14, and initially designated An-14M, this light transport was designed and built by Antonov in Russia and first flew in 1969 powered by two TWD 850 turboprops, but it was underpowered and was re-engined with uprated TWD 10 turboprops. In February 1978, a Polish-Russian agreement assigned series production to PZL Mielec, to be built with the designation An-28. Production aircraft bore little resemblance to the prototype, which had a retractable undercarriage, as this was found to be too bulky and unnecessary. The wing is fitted with double-slotted flaps and single- slotted ailerons, and is braced to the fuselage by a single strut. The first Polish built aircraft flew in July 1984, and the aircraft remains in production, with a number of increases in the fuselage length, and fitted with Western engines and avionics.

CURRENT SERVICE

Initial production was mainly for use in the USSR in

civilian roles to replace the An-2, and about 200 had been delivered by 1989, when production ceased. Since then low-rate production has resumed and a number of military versions of the aircraft have been produced, as well as civilian examples. Main user is the Polish Air Force (13th Transport Air Regiment) and the Polish Navy, who have developed a maritime patrol and rescue aircraft. Examples have also been delivered to the air arms of Djibouti and Venezuela.

SPECIAL FEATURES

The aircraft was designed with the training role in mind and is said to be stall-proof, even with extremely rough handling. Its automatic slots and slats, together with spoilers forward of the ailerons, prevent wing drop and makes the aircraft controllable below the stalling speed. Development by PZL Mielec has increased the size of the fuselage, and hence its payload, to make it a useful sized transport/support aircraft. Now fitted with Western engines and avionics, it is expected to produce further sales.

VARIANTS

An-28 (now **M-28**) – standard transport with the PZL TWD-10B engines; **An-28P/M-28P** (Pozarniczy) – paratroop version for dropping fire fighting crews; **An-28/M-28TD** (Bryza) – cargo assault and military transport. Clamshell doors replaced by sliding ramps under the rear fuselage and with increased cargo capacity; **An-28/M-28RM** (Bryza) – sea rescue, maritime patrol, equipped with radar under the fuselage, data transfer systems, and can drop marker buoys and illumination bombs/flares. Has full Western avionics fit; **M-28PT** (Piryt) – Westernised transport version with upgraded cabin and facilities; **M-28 Skytruck PT** – commercial name for export version of M28-PT; **M-28.03/M-28.04 Skytruck Plus** – an enlarged fuselage version to carry 30 passengers, first flown in 1998.

TECHNICAL DATA

PZL Mielec M-28PT

Powerplants: Two Pratt & Whitney Canada PT6A-65B turboprops
Developing: 820.3kW (1,100eshp)
Driving: five-blade propellers
Span: 22.07m (72ft 5in)
Length: 13.1m (43ft 0in)
Height: 4.9m (16ft 1in)
All-up weight: 7,000kg (15,432lb)
Maximum speed: 365km/h (227mph)
Cruising Speed: 335km/h (208mph)
Operational ceiling: 20,340ft
Maximum range: 1,417km (881miles)
Accommodation: Two crew plus 18 passengers
Armament: M-28RM version has racks on the undercarriage to drop marker buoys and illumination bombs/flares.
First flown: 22 July 1984 (Polish-built)
Entered service: 1985

An-28/M-28RM Bryza Polish Navy

PZL Mielec M-18 Dromader

SINGLE-SEAT CROP SPRAYING AIRCRAFT

M-18A Dromader Hellenic Air Force

DEVELOPMENT

The M-18 Dromader is a co-operative project between PZL Mielec and Rockwell International of the USA. The design contains elements of the Rockwell Thrush Commander and was purpose built to meet FAR Part 23 regulations in order that it could be exported around the world. First flown in Poland in 1976, more than 600 of this rugged single-seat crop sprayer have been built. Great attention was paid to pilot safety and the cockpit is protected by a hefty rollover bar, easily opened and jettisoned doors, and is fully sealed and air-conditioned to prevent ingestion of spray.

CURRENT SERVICE

The only known military service of the M-18 Dromader (Dromedary) is a result of an order for 30 aircraft by the Greek Air Force in 1983 to supplement a fleet of Grumman Ag-Cats. They undertake crop spraying, fire-fighting and mosquito control, and the surviving examples of these two types continue in service with 126SM/359 MAEDY at Dekelia.

SPECIAL FEATURES

The Dromader is a basic crop spraying aircraft of rigid construction with some use of corrugated skins,

a tail wheel and the ability to have spray booms or water bombing equipment fitted as required for the task in hand.

VARIANTS

M-18A – the main production variant; **M-18AS** – the designation used when a second seat was fitted in the aircraft to aid conversion. This entailed removing the hopper, so the aircraft was then unable to carry out operational tasks; **M-18B** – proposed upgraded version; **M-18C** – upgraded model with 895kW (1200hp) engine.

TECHNICAL DATA

PZL Mielec M-18A Dromader

Powerplant: One WSK Kalisz Asz-621R radial piston engine
Developing: 721kW (967hp)
Driving: four-blade propeller
Span: 17.7m (58ft 1in)
Length: 9.47m (31ft 1in)
Height: 3.70m (12ft 2in)
All-up weight: 4,200kg (9,260lb)
Maximum speed: 256km/h (159mph)
Operational ceiling: 21,500ft
Maximum range: 970km (603miles)
Accommodation: One
Armament: Nil
First flown: 27 August 1976
Entered service: 1983 (Greece)

M-18A Dromader

PZL Mielec TS-11 Iskra

BASIC AND ADVANCED JET TRAINER

TS-11 Iskra Polish Air Force

DEVELOPMENT

Designed as a contender for the Eastern Bloc's jet trainer requirement to replace the MiG-15UTI at the height of the Cold War, the TS-11 lost out to the Czech Aero L-29, which went on to be used throughout the

Warsaw Pact countries. However, having its own aircraft industry, Poland went ahead with the design, and the first TS-11 flew in 1960, entering production in 1963. It followed the formula of the pod and boom design of early Eastern Bloc jets, but with the tailplane raised well clear of the jet efflux. The aircraft is stressed to -4/ +8g, is capable of inverted flight, and fully aerobatic. Production ended by 1979, when about 500 Iskras had been built, but was restarted in 1982 for a limited run of a reconnaissance variant. The aircraft is now at the end of its service life and is due for replacement.

CURRENT SERVICE

The TS-11 and its sub-variants serve throughout the Polish Air Force as trainers and refresher aircraft, and there are also a number of specialist reconnaissance trainers. The remaining training variants can be found with the 58th LPSZ at Deblin, 60th LPSz at Radon and 61st LPSz at Biala Podlaska, and the Polish aerobatic team the *White Iskras* (White Sparks). The export variant is the Iskra-BisD and this version serves with the Indian Air Academy at Hakimpet.

SPECIAL FEATURES

The TS-11 is a very basic early jet trainer which has been in service with the Polish Air Force since 1963 and the

Indian Air Force since 1975, and in both cases is now becoming expensive to operate and will be replaced by more modern and capable jet or turboprop trainers. There is very little which is now considered special about the aircraft, except its very traditional shape with straight mid-fuselage wing and the pod-and-boom fuselage.

VARIANTS

TS-11 Iskra-Bis A – early production basic two-seat trainer variant with two hardpoints under the wings; **TS-11 Iskra-Bis B** (also called **Iskra 100**) – later upgraded production aircraft, for primary and advanced training with four underwing hardpoints; **TS-11 Iskra-Bis C** – single-seat reconnaissance version with increased fuel capacity and cameras looking out through the floor of the cockpit; **TS-11 Iskra-Bis D** – similar to the Bis B, but able to carry a wider range of weapons, and the version supplied to the Indian Air Force; **TS-11 Iskra-Bis F** – two-seat combat and reconnaissance trainer with the increased weapon capability of the Bis D, plus extra cameras in the intake fairing.

TECHNICAL DATA

PZL Mielec TS-11 Iskra

Powerplant: One Polish-designed IL S0-3 turbojet
Developing: 9.81 kN (2,205lb st)
Span: 10.06m (33ft 0in)
Length: 11.17m (36ft 7.75in)
Height: 3.50m (11ft 5.5in)
All-up weight: 3,840kg (8,465lb)
Maximum speed: 750km/h (466mph)
Cruising speed: 600km/h (373mph)
Operational ceiling: 36,090ft
Maximum range: 1,250km (776 miles)
Accommodation: Two or one, depending on variant
Armament: Fixed forward firing 23mm cannon in starboard side of nose. Up to four hard points under wings. Load includes bombs up to 220lbs (100kg), rocket pods and gun pods (7.62mm).
First flown: 5 February 1960
Entered service: March 1963

TS-11 Iskra-Bis D Indian Air Force

333

PZL Swidnik (Mil) Mi-2

TWIN- ENGINED INTERMEDIATE-SIZED MULTI-PURPOSE HELICOPTER

PZL Swidnik Mi-2R Czech Air Force

TECHNICAL DATA

PZL Swidnik (Mil) Mi-2

Powerplants: Two Isotov GTD-350 turboshafts
Developing: 298kW (400shp)
Driving: Three-blade main and two-blade tail rotors
Main rotor diameter: 14.56m (47ft 9.25in)
Overall length (rotors turning): 17.48m (57ft 4.25in)
Height: 4.50m (14ft 9.25in)
Maximum weight: 3,550kg (7,826lb)
Maximum speed: 210km/h (130mph)
Operational Ceiling: 13,125ft
Cruise speed: 190km/h (118mph)
Maximum ferry range: 580km (360 miles)
Accommodation: Pilot and up to eight
passengers or 800kg (1,764lb) of cargo
Warload: Armament not normally carried, but
some combat-capable versions can operate with
9M14M Malyutka (AT-3 'Sagger') guided anti-
armour missiles, unguided rocket pods, 23mm
cannon and/or 7.62mm machine guns
First flown: September 1961 (V-2 prototype in
USSR); 4 November 1965 (in Poland)

DEVELOPMENT

Conceived as a replacement for the Mi-1 'Hare', but benefiting from the introduction of more reliable and economic turboshaft engines, design and initial development of the Mi-2 was undertaken in the Soviet Union, where two prototypes were test flown in the first half of the 1960s. However, at the beginning of 1964, it was agreed that responsibility for series production would be allocated to PZL's factory at Swidnik, Poland and this facility ultimately built more than 5,000 by the time manufacture terminated in 1991. In the process, it also conceived numerous variations, including derivatives having SAR, utility and combat roles. A number of improvements to the basic design have originated from PZL, including the Kania (Kitty Hawk) which has Allison engines.

CURRENT SERVICE

Numbers have declined in recent years, but despite this, the Mi-2 is still one of the most widely used of all military helicopters, especially with air arms that previously formed part of the Warsaw Pact or were in the Soviet sphere of influence. Countries believed to operate Mi-2 variants are Algeria, Armenia, Azerbaijan, Bulgaria, Cuba, Czech Republic, Djibouti, Estonia, Georgia, Ghana, Hungary, North Korea, Latvia, Lithuania, Mexico, Myanmar, Poland, Russia, Slovak Republic, Syria, Ukraine and even the USA.

SPECIAL FEATURES

Basic configuration is conventional, incorporating a pod and boom layout, with a three-blade main rotor and two-blade tail rotor. A tricycle undercarriage is provided and the cabin may quickly be reconfigured to accept either passengers or up to 700 kg (1,543lb) of cargo. External lift capability is also provided, with the Mi-2 able to carry a maximum of 800 kg (1,764 lb). Twin Isotov turboshaft engines are situated side-by-side directly above the cabin and external fuel tanks are frequently installed.

VARIANTS

Since it had civilian applications as well, the basic **Mi-2** spawned a multiplicity of versions, including those for use in the air ambulance and aerial survey roles, as well as agricultural tasks such as crop spraying. Purely military models are almost as numerous and include the **Mi-2R** for SAR and liaison tasks, the **Mi-2T** with dual controls for pilot training and the **Mi-2US** with 23mm cannon and/or machine guns. More potent combat-capable derivatives are the **Mi-2URN** which combines a 23mm cannon with 57mm Mars 2 rocket pods and the **Mi-2URP**, which is a specialist tank-buster with a maximum payload of four AT-3 'Sagger' anti-armour missiles. Other versions are known to have been evolved for electronic warfare, artillery spotting and maritime missions.

PZL Swidnik Mi-2R Slovak Air Force

PZL Swidnik W-3 Sokól

TWIN- ENGINED INTERMEDIATE-SIZED MULTI-PURPOSE HELICOPTER

W-3A Sokól Czech Air Force

TECHNICAL DATA

PZL Swidnik W-3 Sokól (Falcon)
Powerplants: Two WSK-PZL Rzeszow TWD-10W turboshafts
Developing: 662kW (888eshp)
Driving: four-blade glass fibre/epoxy main rotor with three-blade glass fibre/epoxy tail rotor
Main rotor diameter: 15.7m (51ft 6ins)
Fuselage length: 14.21m (46ft 7.5in)
Height: 3.8m (12ft 5in)
All-up weight: 6,400kg (14,100lbs) (6400kg)
Maximum speed: 235km/h (146mph)
Operational ceiling: 16,075ft
Maximum ferry range: 715km (444miles)
Accommodation: Two crew with 12 passengers (14 troops)
Armament: One GSh-23 23mm cannon pod on fuselage, plus detachable outriggers for ATM pod (4xAT-6 Spiral) or 12x80mm unguided rockets. Armament system can be varied to suit customer requirements.
First flown: 16 November 1979
Entered service: July 1989

DEVELOPMENT

From the same stable as the Mil Mi-2, to which it bears a strong resemblance, the W-3 is in fact a completely new design, having been upgraded and expanded in almost all areas. Initiated in 1978, and with a first flight in 1979, progress has been slow, but since Poland has emerged from behind the Iron Curtain the aircraft is seen as a potential export with Western equipment and engines. Numerous versions to fulfil a variety of tasks are planned, but without firm orders, lack of money prevents production.

CURRENT SERVICE

The Polish Armed Forces and Government Auxiliaries are the main customers so far for the W3-Sokól, with the exception of the government of Myanmar (Burma) who have 12 and may order more, as it has difficulty buying military equipment because of restrictions imposed due to its human rights record. Polish W-3s are operated by the 47th Helicopter Training Regiment at Nowe Miasto and the 36th Special Air Transport Regiment at Okecie in Warsaw. The Polish Navy's 18th Rescue/Communications (Eskandra) flight includes the W-3R Anakonda search and rescue version. Single aircraft are also in use by government agencies, including the fire service at Bemov. A number were supplied to Russia for use by Aeroflot (20) but orders ceased when Poland joined the West. A recent inter-government swap has exchanged 11 W-3As for redundant MiG-29 'Fulcrums'of the Czech Republic.

SPECIAL FEATURES

A low-cost multi-purpose helicopter, which is now adopting westernised avionics and systems to make it an attractive buy for small air arms of non-aligned countries.

VARIANTS

A number of variants have been built or proposed, but not all have found customers: **W-3A** – standard transport, some modified to meet US regulations, with Western equipment; **W-3RM Anakonda** – search and rescue variant, with three flotation bags on each side of fuselage and under the tail. Electronic winch and searchlights; **W-3W Huzar** – low-cost gunship variant for Polish forces, but not yet fitted with ATM. Other proposed variants include the **W-3L (Long)** – stretched version with 14 seats; **W-3U-1 Alligator** – anti-submarine variant; and the **W-3U Salamanda** – the full gunship variant with similar capability to the Mil Mi-24 'Hind'.

W-3RM Sokól Polish Navy

PZL Warszawa PZL-104 Wilga

MULTI-PURPOSE/UTILITY LIGHT AIRCRAFT

PZL-104 Wilga 35A Russian Air Force

DEVELOPMENT

A Polish design to replace the derivative of the Yak-12, the PZL 101 Gowran, underwent a series of updates and revision, appearing in 1962 as the Wilga 3A. A further revision of this simple all-metal high cantilever wing four-seat passenger/liaison aircraft produced the Wilga 35. It can be fitted with skis or floats as well as its normal rough field undercarriage, and has been flown with a variety of engines. The Wilga 35A was the main production version, and the type can be used in a host of roles such as glider towing, club aircraft, pilot training, air ambulance and agricultural usage.

CURRENT SERVICE

A large number of Wilgas are in use in Poland, and in time of crisis would be pressed into service. Fifteen

are currently on charge with Polish Forces as liaison aircraft. They also serve with the Russian Military and the air forces of Egypt, Estonia, Latvia, Lithuania and Ukraine. Ten Wilgas were assembled in Indonesia, and since then the number has risen to 24, distributed between the Indonesian Army and Air Force.

SPECIAL FEATURES

The Wilga is a rugged four-seat multi-purpose aircraft with over 1,000 built, many for export in the private and agricultural and crop spraying markets. Many are now adopting Western engines such as the Continental O-470R to replace the Eastern Bloc radial.

VARIANTS

The **Wilga 1** had a 145kW (195hp) WN-6 engine; the

Wilga 2 was a partial re-dign, with the trailing link main undercarriage; **Wilga 35A** – club aircraft and trainer; **Wilga 35P** – light transport version; **Wilga 35R** – agricultural sprayer with under-fuselage chemical tank; **Wilga 35H** – seaplane version with CAP 3000 floats; **Wilga 35S** – air ambulance version; **Wilga 80-550** – Teledyne Continental IO-550 of 224kW (300hp) for US market; **Wilga 2000** – Textron Lycoming IO-540 of 224kW (300hp) and Western avionics.

TECHNICAL DATA

PZL 104 Wilga (Thrush) 35A

Powerplant: One WSK-Kalisz AI-14RA radial piston engine
Developing: 194kW (260hp)
Driving: two-blade propeller
Span: 11.12m (36ft 6in)
Length: 8.1m (26ft 7in)
Height: 2.96m (9ft 8.5in)
All-up weight: 1,300kg (2,866lb)
Maximum speed: 195km/h (121mph)
Cruising speed: 157km/h (98mph)
Operational ceiling: 13,000ft
Maximum range: 560km (348 miles)
Accommodation: Pilot plus three passengers depending on the fit.
Armament: A special mission Wilga 80 has a UB-16 unguided rocket pod and two Strela-2M AAMs under port wing.
First flown: 21 July 1962 (Wilga I); 11 October 1963 (Wilga II); 17 July 1969 (Wilga 35)
Entered service: 1963 (Indonesia)

PZL-104 Wilga 35A Russian Air Force

PZL Warszawa Okecie PZL-130 Orlik

TURBOPROP BASIC TO ADVANCED TRAINER

PZL-130TC-1 Orlik Polish Air Force

TECHNICAL DATA

PZL Warszawa Okecie PZL-130TC-1 Orlik
Powerplants: One Motorlet M601E turboprop
Developing: 750kW (560hp)
Driving: five-blade propeller
Span: 9.00m (29ft 6.25in)
Length: 9.00m (29ft 6.25in)
Height: 3.53m (11ft 7in)
All-up weight: 2,700kg (5,952lb)
Maximum speed: 560km/h (348mph)
Operational ceiling: 33,000ft
Maximum range: 1,062km (660miles)
Accommodation: Two
Armament: Six under wing hardpoints are located in board and centre ones stressed for loads up to 160kg (353lb), outboard to 80kg (167lb). This permits bombs, 7.62mm gun pods, rocket pods and air-to-air missiles (Strela IR homing). Two pylons are plumbed for the fitting of tanks.
First flown: 8 October 1984 (piston); 16 July 1986 (turboprop); 2 June 1993 (130TC)
Entered service: January 1990

DEVELOPMENT

The Orlik was designed as a piston engine trainer both for civil and military flying and to provide an easy conversion to jets. Difficulties in obtaining the Russian-built nine-cylinder M14PM radial piston engine were experienced, but a turboprop derivative was on the drawing board, and it first flew in July 1986 with a Pratt & Whitney PT6A-25A engine, followed by others using the Motorlet M601E and the Pratt & Whitney PT6A-25A or PT6A-62 engine. The aircraft features a stepped cockpit and Martin Baker CH15A ejector seats under a side-opening one-piece canopy. Following a series of upgrades and equipment changes, the first of the Polish Air Force's Orliks was delivered in January 1990. They are fitted with Czech-built M601E engines and Eastern European avionics, but are being upgraded to include GPS, HUD and transponders. The Orlik represents the first exposure of the Polish aircraft industry's fixed-wing aircraft to world-wide markets and international co-operation. Although

much the same as many other turboprop trainers, it is the most economic option for the Polish Air Force.

CURRENT SERVICE

At present, the Polish Air Force is the only customer for the indigenous Orlik. Early deliveries were to 45 LED at Radon and 60 LPSz at Deblin. The Orlik is the flying component of an overall training system designed by Poles for the Polish Air Force, the other components of which are a ground simulator system and electronic diagnosis and debrief. The Polish Air Force now has an aerobatic team, *Team Orlik*, flying six PZL-130TCs.

SPECIAL FEATURES

Originally conceived as a piston-engined trainer, the Orlik has moved into the turboprop era and now encompasses Western engines and avionics. Upgraded versions are to have a ventral tailfin and turbulizers added to the wingtips and tailplane.

VARIANTS

PZL-130/130TM/130P – prototypes and development aircraft with a variety of engine fits and different avionic equipment; **PZL-130T** – (Developed from the PZL-130TM) fitted with Czech M601E engine driving a four-blade propeller. This was the initial version delivered to the Polish Air Force and had lightweight LFK-F1 ejector seats and a revised canopy shape; **PZL-130TC** – fitted with the PT6A-62 engine, Bendix King avionics, Martin Baker ejector seats and a number of other upgrades; **PZL-130TC-1** – the new standard production aircraft for the Polish Air Force combining all the upgrades, but retaining the Czech Motorlet M601E engine; **PZL-130TD** – fitted with a PT6A-25C engine; **PZL-130TE** – fitted with a PT6A-25, an economy version that lacks much of the equipment carried by the other variants, including ejector seats.

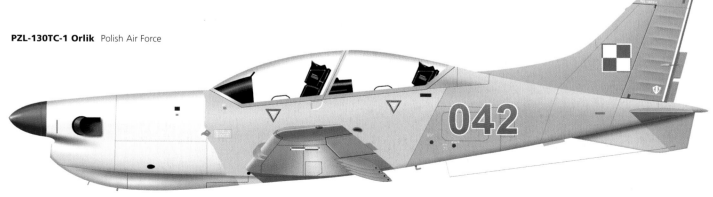

PZL-130TC-1 Orlik Polish Air Force

Raytheon (British Aerospace) Hawker 800

TWIN-ENGINED MEDIUM-SIZED BUSINESS JET

Hawker 800/U-125A Japanese Air Self-Defence Force

TECHNICAL DATA

Raytheon (Hawker) 800

Powerplants: Two Allied Signal TFE 731-5R-1H turbofans
Developing: 19.13kW (4,300lb st)
Span: 15.65m (51ft 4in)
Length: 15.60m (51ft 2in)
Height: 5.36m (17ft 7in)
All-up weight: 12,428kg (27,400lb)
Maximum speed: 846km/h (526mph)
Operational ceiling: 41,000ft
Maximum range: 4,540 km (2,850miles)
Accommodation: Two crew plus eight or nine passengers
Armament: Search and Rescue variant able to drop marker flares and rescue equipment.
First Flown: 26 May 1983 (Hawker 800)
Entered service: 24 April 1990 (C-29A USAF)

DEVELOPMENT

A direct descendent of the de Havilland DH125 (later Hawker Siddeley HS125, then British Aerospace BAe 125) family of business jets, the Raytheon Hawker 800 is a much enlarged and developed version of the BAe 125 800 series. Production of the aircraft was moved to the USA following the acquisition of BAe Corporate Jets by Raytheon. The aircraft are fitted out with sophisticated nav and avionics suites, depending on customer requirements. All aircraft have a large roomy cabin with constant circular cross section and full head height. The model 800 has a new wing and uprated engines, and is almost a new aircraft when compared to some of the early 125 models.

CURRENT SERVICE

A large number of armed forces have models of the DH/HS/BAe125 in their inventory and these include Botswana, Brazil, Malawi, Malaysia, South Africa and the UK. Military customers for the Raytheon Hawker 800 are the Royal Saudi Air Force, which has six for the Royal Flight; the Federal Aviation Authority at Oklahoma City, with six ex-USAF C-29A (Hawker 800s) flight inspection aircraft; the Japan Air Self-Defence Force (JASDF), which initially purchased three Hawker 800s for nav aid calibration and designated them U-125, and subsequently bought 27 further aircraft for search and rescue duties, which were then designated U-125A. The Hawker 800 has also been ordered for the South Korean Air Force.

SPECIAL FEATURES

Undoubtedly the main selling point of the 125 series over the years has been the cabin size, with its full height and constant width. With a clean wing and modern turbofan engines, the aircraft is efficient aerodynamically and capable of long endurance at high speed – ideal for maritime search.

VARIANTS

BAe 125 Series 800 – VIP aircraft, Royal Saudi Air Force; **C-29A** – flight inspection/nav aids calibrator fitted with LTV Sierra research division equipment; **U-125** – Japan Air Self-Defence Force nav aids calibration and inspection version similar to the USAF's C-29A; **U-RSA** – search and rescue equipped, with 360° scan search radar, FLIR, and able to drop rescue equipment, smoke flares and illumination flares.

SEE ALSO: BRITISH AEROSPACE (HAWKER SIDDELEY) 125/DOMINIE

Hawker 800/U-125A Japanese Air Self-Defence Force

29-3041

041

Raytheon T-6A Texan II

TANDEM-SEAT BASIC TO ADVANCED TRAINER

T-6A Texan II United States Air Force

DEVELOPMENT

The Raytheon T-6A Texan II is a direct result of the USAF/USN JPATS (Joint Primary Aircraft Training System) requirement. The company had identified the Pilatus PC-9 as a possible contender, although their already Raytheon-owned Beech Aircraft Corporation had formed a partnership with Pilatus to adapt the PC-9 MkII to fit the specification exactly. Areas of the cockpit and rear fuselage underwent extensive rework in order to meet the wide specification for pilot sizes. The structure of the aircraft has been modified to allow more automated production and easier maintenance. The aircraft is certified to FAA part 23 in the aerobatic category and cleared to +7/3.5g. The engine has been fitted with a full authority digital power management system (PMS) in order to give a single level power control as in a jet. The PMS system controls the engine and the propeller, which is a four-blade variable pitch 8ft Hartzell unit rotating at a constant 2000rpm. The system counteracts the slow response of a turboprop to throttle movements, and through a trim device the rudder is automatically trimmed to compensate for torque from the engine. The aircraft was declared the winner on 22 June 1995, but contracts were not signed until 1996, and the first production deliveries began in late 1998.

CURRENT SERVICE

The first operational Raytheon T-6A Texan II joined the USAF on 23 May 2000. This aircraft was delivered to the 559th Flying Training Squadron, 12th Flying Wing, 19th Air Force, Air Education and Training Command (AETC) based at Randolph AFB, Texas. The USAF expects to acquire a total of 454 T-6As and these will replace the T-37B in USAF service. It is expected to take ten years for the type to fully replace the 'Tweet' in the basic training role. Naval use of the T-6A will be located at NAS Corpus Christie, Texas (TAW-4), NAS Pensacola, Florida (TAW-6) and NAS Whiting Field, Florida (TAW-5) – 328 T-6As have been ordered, with operational use starting in 2003. A number of orders have been placed as a result of the aircraft winning the JPATS competition – the NATO Flying Training in Canada project is receiving 24, to be named Harvard II. Chile has signed a letter of intent and is expected to confirm an order shortly. The first of an order for 45 was delivered to the Hellenic Air Force on 17 July 2000, and the type will be known in Greek service as the Beech/ Pilatus PC-9 MkII. The first 25 of this order are configured similarly to the US T-6A Texan II primary trainer. The next 20 will be in the Greek New Trainer Aircraft (NTA) configuration, which includes a weapons sighting system and ordnance training capability.

SPECIAL FEATURES

A large number of detail changes have been made to this aircraft to ensure that it is a specialised training tool able to train a standard pilot at minimum cost. The aircraft was chosen because of its good handling and stalling characteristics. The PMS gives a turboprop aircraft similar handling to a pure jet and has been modelled on the engines fitted to the J-1A Jayhawk.

VARIANTS

At present the **Texan II** itself is a variant of the Pilatus PC-9, but is liable to become the predominant version, with up to 711 aircraft required to meet USAF/USN training needs. Those for the NATO training scheme, and other air forces, will show minor equipment differences to meet customer needs.

SEE ALSO: PILATUS PC-9

TECHNICAL DATA

Raytheon T-6A Texan II

Powerplant: One Pratt & Whitney Canada PT6A-68 turboprop
Developing: 1,268kW (1,700eshp), but to increase engine life engine flat-rated to 820kW (1,120eshp)
Driving: four-blade propeller
Span: 10.18m (33ft 2.5in)
Length: 10.16m (33ft 2.5in)
Height: 3.26m (10ft 8in)
All-up weight: 2,948kg (6,500lb)
Maximum speed: 500km/h (310mph)
Operational ceiling: 31,000 ft
Maximum range: 1,668km (1,036miles)
Accommodation: Two, in tandem
Armament: The Texan II has six underwing stations and can carry 1400kg (3,080lb) of stores. The aircraft has not yet progressed to the weapons stage of development
First Flown: 15 July 1998 (T-6A)
Entered service: November 1998; 23 May 2000 (first operational aircraft)

Beech/Pilatus PC-9 MkII Hellenic Air Force

Rhein Flugzeugbau Fantrainer

TWO-SEAT PRIMARY AND BASIC TRAINER

Fantrainer 400

DEVELOPMENT

The Fantrainer is a tandem two-seat primary trainer which is unusual in featuring a clean fuselage and wing, with the propulsion supplied by a pusher propeller acting as a ducted fan in its own integral shroud. The design was proposed and developed by Rhein Flugzeugbau (RFB), supported by the German government. The first aircraft was driven by a piston engine, but subsequent aircraft have been powered by an Allison turboshaft. Although an export order was gained, the design has not been a great success, particularly with military customers and no further orders have resulted.

CURRENT SERVICE

The only known military customer for the Fantrainer 400 or the Fantrainer 600 has been the Royal Thai Air Force which ordered 47 – 31 of the 400 version and a further 16 of the more powerful 600 variant. They

were supplied in kit form and assembled in Thailand for use by the Flying Training School/402 Squadron at Kamphong Son. Whilst all are now assembled, they are not as heavily used as expected and are being replaced with the Aero L-39.

SPECIAL FEATURES

Undoubtedly the most striking feature of this aircraft is the position of the engine and the ducted fan propeller. Positioned behind the cockpit it provides a completely clean wing and fuselage and excellent visibility from the cockpit. Much of the construction is from composite materials, but the Thai Air Force aircraft have metal wings.

VARIANTS

The **Fantrainer 400** is the standard aircraft with the Allison 250-C20B turboshaft, whilst the **Fantrainer 600** has a 15cm fuselage stretch, an enlarged canopy

and other minor changes, and is powered by an Allison 485kW (650hp) 250-C30 turboshaft.

TECHNICAL DATA

Rhein Flugzeugbau Fantrainer 400
Powerplant: One Allison 250-C20B turboshaft
Developing: 313kW (420hp)
Driving: Ducted fan propeller
Span: 9.74m (31ft 11.5in)
Length: 9.48m (31ft 1.25in)
Height: 3.16m (10ft 4.5in)
All-up weight: 1,800kg (3,968lb)
Maximum speed: 370km/h (230mph)
Operational ceiling: 20,000ft
Maximum range: 1,186km (737 miles)
Accommodation: Two
Armament: Nil
First flown: 27 October 1977
Entered service: August 1982

Fantrainer 600 Royal Thai Air Force

Robin HR 100

Robin HR100/250 *French Air Force*

DEVELOPMENT

Avions Pierre Robin's first use of metal construction in its light aircraft range was in the prototype DR 253 Regent, which was rebuilt with metal wings. This was powered by a 134kW (180hp) Avco Lycoming O-360. Three production aircraft flew in 1970 and the first definitive version, the HR 100/200, with a 149kW (200hp) Avco Lycoming IO-360 engine appeared in 1971. This had a constant chord wing and did not have the Jodel type cranked wing. It was sometimes referred to as the Royal or Safari. The HR 100 formed the basis for the subsequent HR 100-235 and HR 100-285. The -285 was one of the few production aircraft to be fitted with the new Continental Tiara engine. This powerplant proved troublesome and limited the

production run, and most examples were delivered to the military. Total production was less than 200.

CURRENT SERVICE

Some 14 Robin HR 100s serve with the Armée de l'Air at Centre d'Essais en Vol/EPNER at Bretigny-sur-Orge, Melun-Villaroche, Cazaux and Istres/Le Tube. Only two HR 100s remain with the French Navy and are based with DCAN at Cuers.

SPECIAL FEATURES

Low-wing monoplane bearing a resemblance to the Piper Cherokee, with an enclosed four-seat cabin and fixed tricycle undercarriage. The HR 100-235 and HR 100-285 feature a retractable landing gear.

VARIANTS

The **HR 100/250TR** was fitted with the 186kW (250hp) Avco Lycoming IO-540 engine. One trials aircraft was completed as the **HR 100/320/4+2** to seat four adults and two children, but did not find production. The **HR 100/210** had a 157kW (210hp) engine and 75 examples were built before production ceased in February 1976; the **HR 200** trainer, which first flew in July 1971, was a scaled down version of the HR 100 with a bubble canopy over a two-seat (side-by-side) cockpit – this subsequently becoming the **R.2100** and **R.2160**.

TECHNICAL DATA

Robin HR 100/285

Powerplant: One Teledyne Continental Tiara 6-285 flat-six piston engine
Developing: 213kW (285hp)
Driving: Two-blade propeller
Span: 9.08m (29ft 9.5in)
Length: 7.59m (24ft 10.75in)
Height: 2.71m (8ft 10.75in)
All-up weight: 1,400kg (3,086lb)
Maximum speed: 325km/h (202mph)
Operational ceiling: 18,700ft
Maximum range: 2,130km (1,323 miles)
Accommodation: Pilot plus three passengers
Warload: Nil
First Flown: 3 April 1969 (HR 100/180);
1971 (HR 100/200); November 1972 (HR 100/285)
Entered service: 1971 (HR 100/180); 1975 (HR 100/285)

Robin HR100/250 *French Air Force*

Robinson R22 Beta

Robinson R22 Beta

TECHNICAL DATA

Robinson R22 Beta II

Powerplant: One Textron Lycoming O-320-J2A flat-four piston engine
Developing: 97.5kW (131hp)
Driving: two-blade main and tail rotors
Main rotor diameter: 7.67m (25ft 2in)
Overall length: 8.76m (28ft 9in)
Height: 2.67m (8ft 9in)
All-up weight: 621kg (1,370 lb)
Maximum speed: 190km/h (118mph)
Cruising speed: 177km/h (110mph)
Operational ceiling: 14,000ft
Maximum range: 592km (368 miles)
Accommodation: Two side-by-side
Armament: None
First flown: 28 August 1975
Entered service: 1992

ground level. The helicopter can be moved by hand when fitted with ground wheels on the skids.

DEVELOPMENT

Unit costs of helicopters have always been high in comparison with those of fixed-wing aircraft of similar capacity. In the early 1970s, Franklin D. Robinson, of the USA, formed the Robinson Helicopter Company to design and market a lightweight helicopter (for both civil and military purposes) which would be competitive in price with two-seat fixed-wing aircraft then on the market. It provides comfortable side-by-side accommodation for two in an enclosed cabin. Over 2,000 examples of this lightweight, low-noise and simple maintenance helicopter have been made since its first flight in August 1975. It has full dual controls and is intended for personal transport or training, where it has found a niche at the bottom end of the civil helicopter market. An upgrade after 500 aircraft has increased the weight it can uplift, and upgraded cockpit instrumentation and other minor systems improvements. Although it is fitted normally with skids, it can be fitted with floats and ground wheels.

CURRENT SERVICE

The upgraded R22B Beta was ordered by the Turkish Army Aviation in 1992 for its Basic Training Battalion at Ankara-Güvercinlik, to replace the TH-13T trainer, where ten examples are now in use to train rotary wing pilots. The Argentine government ordered 40 R22Ms, equipped with floats, but these seem to be used mainly by police units such as the Buenos Aires Force, and not strictly military units.

SPECIAL FEATURES

This is a very lightweight, quiet and low-powered helicopter, not the more usual rugged military machine, of typical pod-and-boom configuration with two-blade main and tail rotors. Most of the engine area is open and maintenance is made easy as it is all accessible at

VARIANTS

R22 Beta – upgraded land-based in use by Turkish Army Aviation School; **R22M Mariner** – similar to the Beta, but fitted with floats in place of skids and ground wheels; **R22 IFR Trainer** – for instrument flight training; **R22 Agricultural** - has an Apollo Helicopter Services DTM-3 spraying system.

Robinson R22 Beta

Rockwell Commander/Turbo Commander

TWIN-ENGINE LIGHT TRANSPORT/TRAINER

Turbo Commander 1000 Mexican Navy

DEVELOPMENT

A late 1940s design, the high-wing slender fuselage twin-engined aircraft was part of the resurgence of the American civil aircraft industry after WW2. Initially powered by two Avco Lycoming flat-six piston engines, the aircraft first flew in early February 1952. A few were ordered and tested by the US Services, but it was the civil market where the aircraft had most success. Initially a 5-7 seater, the size and performance was gradually improved during the 1950s and 1960s with designations such as Commander 560/560A, 680, Super Commander/Grand Commander and finally, in 1964, the Turbo Commander 690, a pressurised turboprop with two Garrett AiResearch TPE331s. These were followed by the Jet Commander in 1965, which featured a mid-set wing, with the engines mounted high on the rear fuselage. It had some success with the lower end of the executive jet market. In 1980 the Rockwell Commander line and production was acquired by Gulfstream and the aircraft were then known as Gulfstream Commander Jetprop 840 and 980 – later upgraded to become the Jetprop 900 and 1000. They provided maximum accommodation for a single pilot and up to 10 passengers but were more likely to seat six-seven in some luxury. Production of all variants ceased in 1985, and despite numerous proposals to restart production this has not happened. The elderly design has been overtaken by modern executive aircraft and a large second hand market.

CURRENT SERVICE

A number of countries have employed small numbers of a variety of different Aero Commander models, both the piston-engined variant and more recently the turboprop, but few countries now employ more than a handful of examples and in many cases these are held in reserve or only used for refresher training. Among operators of the Turbo Commander are the air arms of Angola, Bolivia, Columbia, Dominica, Indonesia, Iran, South Korea, Mexico (the remainder of 15), Pakistan, Peru, Turkey, Uruguay and Venezuela. Smaller numbers of the Shrike Commander are in service with Iran, Mexico, and the remainder of 12 with the Argentine Forces; and the final version of the Gulfstream Commander 1000 with Colombia and Guatemala.

SPECIAL FEATURES

A high-wing piston or turboprop aircraft, affording its passengers a good downwind view, the Commander was popular with its operators, but it has become dated and has now been replaced, except in the poorer aviation arms of the world, by more modern transport/communications aircraft that are cheaper to operate.

VARIANTS

Early piston engine variants were: **Aero Commander 520/4560/560A**, with flat-six piston engines; **Aero Commander 680 Super**, with supercharged piston engines; the pressurised **Aero Commander 720 Alti Cruiser**; **Aero Commander Grand Commander**, with two Avco Lycoming 283kW (380hp) engines; **Aero Commander Turbo Commander** fitted with Garrett AiResearch TP331s; **Aero Commander Jet Commander**, with two GE turbojets mounted on the rear fuselage. The **Aero Commander Shrike Commander/Hawk Commander** was the final piston engine variant. The renamed **Gulfstream Jetprop 840** and **980** were the production versions taken over by Gulfstream, with the **Gulfstream Jetprop 900** and **1000** being the final production variants.

TECHNICAL DATA

Rockwell Turbo Commander 690B

Powerplants: Two Garrett TPE 331-5-521K turboprops
Developing: 522kW (700shp)
Driving: Three-blade propellers
Span: 14.22m (46ft 8in)
Length: 13.10m (42ft 11.75in)
Height: 4.56m (14ft 11.5in)
All-up weight: 4,649kg (10,250lb)
Maximum speed: 528km/h (328mph)
Operational ceiling: 32,900ft
Maximum range: 2,522km (1,567 miles)
Accommodation: Two crew plus up to nine passengers
Armament: Nil
First flown: 29 December 1962 (Grand Commander); 31 December 1964 (Turbo Commander 690)

Turbo Commander A695A Colombian Air Force

Rockwell T-2 Buckeye

ADVANCED JET TRAINER

T-2C Buckeye United States Navy

DEVELOPMENT

A mid-1950s design that has survived for more than 30 years, starting initially as a single engined aircraft with a mid wing configuration and tandem seating with the instructor's rear cockpit raised 10in to give good forward and downward visibility. There was no prototype and the first pre-production aircraft flew in January 1958 with the designation YT2J-1, but this was changed in 1962 to T-2A. Production of the T-2A totalled 20 aircraft and it entered service in July 1959

and survived until 1973. Meanwhile two conversions to YT2J-2 were flown with twin engines (initially Pratt and Whitney J60-P-6 turbojets) and this version was selected to succeed the T-2A into production as the T-2B. Only 97 examples were produced before the engine was changed to the General Electric J85-GE-4, producing the T-2C. A total of 231 has been built for the US Naval Air Training Command where it forms the backbone of the training machine, and is used to carrier qualify strike and fighter pilots as well as tactical training, low level formation flying and gunnery. All the survivors of this batch of T-2Cs remain active but will be phased out in the next few years. Export versions of the T-2C went to Greece and Venezuela.

CURRENT SERVICE

US Naval Air Training Command: Only two units now still operate the T-2C, albeit in large numbers: VT-9 (Tigers) at NAS Meridian MS and VT-86 (Sabre Hawks) at NAS Pensocola, Florida. A number of T-2Cs are believed to be still on the strength of the Naval Test Pilot School for spin training. The Greek Air Force has two squadrons, 362 MPE (Nestor) and 363 MEE (Danaos), with the survivors of the 36 T-2E aircraft pooled between them. The Fuerza Aerea Venezolana placed an original order for 24 T-2D Buckeyes; only six now survive and are used in the advanced training role.

SPECIAL FEATURES

A rugged twin-engined advanced trainer, that has withstood nearly 30 years of the rigorous training required for carrier operations. The airframe and undercarriage must withstand the stress of frequent landings and catapult launches from a carrier deck.

VARIANTS

The **T-2A** was the single engine early model, now all retired. The 97 examples of the **T-2B** built, with two Pratt and Whitney J60-P-6 turbojets, have been retired to the AMARC desert storage facility progressively over the last few years. The principal production **T-2C**, is the current model in service with the US Navy's Training Command. It is due to remain in service until 2007, when it will be replaced by the T-45C Goshawk. **DT-2B/Cs** were converted as drone control aircraft. Export T-2Cs were produced for the Venezuelan Air Force as **T-2Ds** and as **T-2Es** for the Greek Air Force.

TECHNICAL DATA

Rockwell T-2C Buckeye

Powerplants: Two x GE J85-GE-4
Developing: 13.1kN (2,950lb st)
Span: 11.62m (38ft 1.5in) (over tip tanks)
Length: 11.67m (38ft 3.5in)
Height: 4.51m (14ft 9.5in)
All-up weight: 5977kg (13,179lb)
Maximum speed: 840km/h (522mph) at 25,000ft
Operational ceiling: 40,415ft
Maximum range: 1685km (1,047 miles)
Accommodation: Two
Armament: Able to carry up to 290kg (640lb) of ordnance, used mainly for an introduction to weapons and in particular air-to-air gunnery.

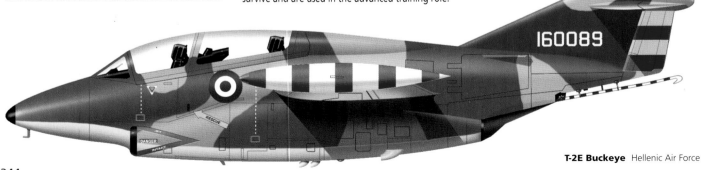

T-2E Buckeye Hellenic Air Force

Rockwell OV-10 Bronco

TWIN-TURBOPROP LIGHT ATTACK/COIN/FORWARD AIR CONTROL AIRCRAFT

OV-10A Bronco Colombian Air Force

DEVELOPMENT

The OV-10 is a COIN aircraft, purpose-built to a 1960s specification for the US Marine Corps but ultimately used by the Air Force, Navy and Marines, particularly in Vietnam. The prototype first flew in July 1965 with a crew of two under a glass canopy, with the capacity to carry two stretchers plus a medic (or five paratroops) in the fuselage pod. It was ordered by the USMC for use as a Forward Air Controller (FAC) and for armed reconnaissance, and was used in a similar role by the

USAF. During the Vietnam War, it was prominent as a helicopter escort and FAC aircraft and provided limited ground support in the absence of tactical fighters. A suitably-equipped OV-10 was thought to be ideal for night FAC and target designation along the trails and roads of Vietnam. Fitted with FLIR and laser designators in the *Pave Nail* programme, they had limited success, but further development was curtailed with the end of the war. OV-10Ds were flown on operations during the Gulf War in 1991.

CURRENT SERVICE

The OV-10 saw service with the USA, US Navy and the US Marine Corps, the last unit (VMO-4) surrendering its last aircraft after 22 years' service. Overseas air arms still use the OV-10, as follows: Colombia – Escudron 311 in the COIN and anti-drug role; Indonesia – a limited number remain as chase aircraft and squadron hacks; South Korea – with the 12th Tactical Control Wing's 237th TAC Control Squadron; Morocco – an unknown number believed to be at Meknes Air Base; Philippines – up to 22 ex-USAF OV-10s delivered to the 16th Attack Squadron; Thailand – 41 Wing, 411

Squadron flies 19 OV-10s (survivors from 32 delivered); Venezuela – with Escuadron 151 on anti-drug and anti-smuggling patrols.

SPECIAL FEATURES

The twin-boom configuration confers excellent downward visibility and was in theory an excellent FAC aircraft, but the advent of the shoulder launched missile and heavily armed ground forces have made the slow and low FAC a sitting target. Much of this type of work is now done by the helicopter gunship or the tactical fighter in the FAC role.

VARIANTS

OV-10A –114 aircraft for the US Marine Corps for the FAC role; 157 aircraft for USAF also for the FAC role; **OV-10B** – six + 12 aircraft for German Air Force as target tugs; **OV-10C** – 32 aircraft for the Royal Thai Air Force (similar to USAF 0V-10A); **OV-10D** – upgraded OV-10A for night operations in Vietnam with USAF; **OV-10E** – 16 aircraft built for Venezuelan Air Force similar to OV-10A; **OV-10F** – the Indonesian Air Force production variant of the OV-10A.

TECHNICAL DATA

Rockwell OV-10 Bronco

Powerplants: Two Garrett T76-G-416/417 turboprops
Developing: 533kW (715 eshp)
Driving: three-blade propellers
Span: 12.19m (40ft 0in)
Length: 12.67m (41ft 7in)
Height: 4.62m (15ft 2in)
All-up weight: 6,552 kg (14,444lb)
Maximum speed: 452km/h (281mph)
Operational ceiling: 24,000ft
Maximum range: 2,298km (1,428 miles)
Accommodation: Two
Armament: Four hard points on fuselage sponsons and a fuselage centreline hard point plus two underwing stations. Able to carry up to 3600lb (1632kg) of external ordnance including napalm, slick and retarded Mk82 500lb (227kg) bombs, unguided 2.75in, 0.5in rockets, machine guns and canon pods, Sidewinder missiles. Four 7.62mm machine guns in underfuselage sponsons. Later models had FLIR and laser target markers and cannon internal armament.
First flown: 16 July 1965
Entered service: October 1968

OV-10E Bronco Venezuelan Air Force

Rockwell B-1B Lancer

FOUR-TURBOFAN STRATEGIC BOMBER

B-1B Lancer United States Air Force

DEVELOPMENT

In the mid-1960s the USA's perceived requirement was for a low-altitude penetration bomber known as the Advanced Manned Strategic Aircraft (AMSA). This requirement was met by the Rockwell B-1A and the first of four prototypes flew in 1974. Cost increases and changes in government halted the programme, save for the four aircraft used as development aircraft. By the 1980s, the thinking had changed and the requirements with it, and the basic design became the B-1B, but to a downgraded specification. It was no longer a supersonic bomber, but a low-altitude high-speed penetrator with fixed intakes. The four crew were now on ejector seats, not in a crew escape capsule. The aircraft's role was a strategic one, but the Gulf War and Balkan (including Kosovo in 1999) crises have changed the concept of air power so that it can now carry almost any US military weaponry. Only 93 B-1Bs were built and these have suffered a protracted period of upgrades and problem solving.

CURRENT SERVICE

Flown by USAF Combat Command: 8th Air Force; 7th Bomb Wing, Dyess AFB Texas – 9th, 13th and 28th Bomb Squadrons; 28th BW, Ellsworth AB, South Dakota – 37th BS and 77th BS; 12th Air Force; 366th Wing, Mountain Home AFB, Idaho – 34th BS; Air

National Guard; 116th BW, Robins AFB, Georgia – 128th BS; 184th BW, McConnell AB, Kansas: 127th BS.

SPECIAL FEATURES

The B-1B is a swing-wing aircraft with a slim fuselage and blended wing roots, with the engines mounted in a pair of engine pods slung below the wing roots. On the B-1B, the inlets were simplified without the need for Mach 2. Initially a nuclear bomber, the B-1B now operates principally in the conventional role.

TECHNICAL DATA

Rockwell B-1B Lancer
Powerplants: Four General Electric F101-GE102 afterburning turbofans
Developing: 64.94kN (14,600lb st), 136.92kN (30,780lb st) with afterburner
Span: 41.67m (136ft 8.5in) at min sweep of 15°. 23.84m (78ft 2.5in) at max sweep of 67° 30'
Length: 44.81m (147ft 0in)
Height: 10.36m (34ft 10in)
All-up weight: 216,365kg (477,000lb)
Max speed: Mach 1.25 at height (1324km/h, 823mph). Low-level (200ft) 965km/h 600mph)
Operational ceiling: More than 50,000ft
Maximum range: 12,000km (7,455 miles)

Accommodation: Four man crew on ejector seats
Warload: As a strategic nuclear bomber, the aircraft is fitted with three bomb bays. It has been adapted to carry almost all of the strategic and tactical weapons in the US arsenal. These include: B28, B61, B83 nuclear bombs and nuclear missiles AGM 69A SRAM A, AGM 86B ALCM, AGM 129A ACM. A full range of conventional and training stores can also be carried including MK82, MK36, MK84 bombs, AM 86C ACM (conventional armament cruise missile). Ultimately the B-1B will be able to carry the full range of smart and precision guided weapons.
First flown: 23 December 1974 (B-1A); 18 October 1984 (B-1B)
Entered service: 7 July 1985

The aircraft has had a long period of continuous development and still more is planned.

VARIANTS

No outwardly distinctive variants. All Lancers will be brought to a common standard of modification and equipment. An upgrade is currently underway to equip the B-1B with precision conventional weapons, principally the JDAM, plus the ALE-50 Towed Decoy system (TDS).

B-1B Lancer United States Air Force

Saab MFI-15 Safari & MFI-17 Supporter

SHOULDER-WING SINGLE-ENGINED TRAINER/ARMY OBSERVATION POST

MFI-17 Supporter Royal Danish Air Force

TECHNICAL DATA

Saab MFI-17 Supporter
Powerplant: One Lycoming IO-360-A1B6 flat-four piston engine
Developing: 149kW (200hp)
Driving: two-blade propeller
Span: 8.85m (29ft 0.5in)
Length: 7.00m (22ft 11.5in)
Height: 2.60m (8ft 6.25 in)
All-up weight: 1,200kg (2,645lb)
Maximum speed: 236 km/h (147mph)
Cruise speed: 208 km/h (129mph)
Operational ceiling: 13,450ft
Maximum range: 1,050km (653 miles)
Endurance: 5hr 10min
Accommodation: Pilot and instructor/co-pilot side by side, with rear-facing third seat.
Warload: Up to 300kg of stores can be carried on six underwing hardpoints.
First flown: 11 July 1969.
Entered service: 1974

DEVELOPMENT

The Saab Safari/Supporter series began life as the Malmö Flygindustri MFI-9 Junior, first flown in October 1958 and built in Sweden and Germany (as the Bo 208 Junior). 256 were built over the following decade. In 1968, Malmö was sold to Saab, at which time the company was involved in developing the MFI-9 into the enlarged MFI-15 Safari basic trainer and army observation platform for the Swedish armed forces. However, despite the Swedish Air Force and Army choosing the Scottish Aviation Bulldog, 52 MFI-15s were eventually built by Saab. It also produced over 70 MFI-17 Supporters, the first of which flew in July 1972. The first military order for the MFI-15 came from Sierra Leone, which ordered four, followed by Pakistan in 1974, which also negotiated a licence to produce the aircraft locally as the AMF (Aircraft Manufacturing Factory) Mushshak. The Danish Air Force ordered 32 MFI-17s in 1975 followed by a batch of 19 MFI-15s for Norway in 1981. Norway ordered four more in 1987 to replace attrition losses. Production of the Mushshak

(see separate entry) began in 1976 at Risalpur, initially using knocked-down kits supplied by Saab, but later progressing to completely indigenous production at Kamra, where production reached 16 a year and is continuing. The improved Shahbaz (Eagle) was introduced in 1989 followed by the Super Mushshak with a more powerful engine in 1997. Pakistan has also sold Mushshaks to Iran, Oman and Syria.

CURRENT SERVICE

Of the 23 Royal Norwegian Air Force aircraft, three have been lost in accidents, and as operations at the flying school at Værnes requires only 16 aircraft, the remaining four have been leased to civilian operators on a reserve basis. The Royal Danish Air Force currently operates 28 MFI-17s under the designation T-17. Some are used for *ab initio* training at the flying school at Karup, and others are attached to Station Flights at front-line bases for liaison and communications duties. Pakistan has more than 200 in service with the Army and Air Force for training and observation,

while the air forces of Iran, Oman and Syria have 25, seven and six respectively, all for *ab initio* training.

SPECIAL FEATURES

Slightly forward swept (5°) shoulder-mounted wing and T-tail. MFI-15s were used in Ethiopia for famine relief in the late 1970s, using canisters carried on four underwing hardpoints. The MFI-17 has six underwing hardpoints. As well as armament, it can carry canisters for air dropping and can also be converted for crop spraying and target towing.

VARIANTS

Externally the MFI-15 and MFI-17 are similar.

SEE ALSO: PAKISTAN AIRCRAFT COMPANY MUSHSHAK

MFI-17 Supporter Royal Danish Air Force

Saab 105

TWO-SEAT SHOULDER-WING JET TRAINER

Saab 105 (Sk60) Swedish Air Force

DEVELOPMENT

Intended as a replacement for the de Havilland Vampire, the Saab 105 was a private venture project, powered by two Turboméca Aubisque turbojets. Swedish governmental go-ahead for development was given on 16 December 1961, with the inclusion of ground attack capability; the first contract for 130 was signed in April 1962, a total raised in August 1965 to 150. Deliveries began in April 1966 to F5 at Ljungbyhed and the Sk60 became fully operational in July 1967. Some 60 standard Sk60A trainers were modified as Sk60B attack versions equipped with underwing pylons, and around 20 others as Sk60C reconnaisance/attack aircraft. As the Swedish Air Force has a strong reserve officer element, a few were modified as four-seat Sk60Ds for airline pilot training with the ejector seats removed and commercial navigation/communications equipment installed. Between 1988-91, a structural modification programme was undertaken to extend operational service life, covering 142 aircraft. A further update during the 1990s involved the installation of Williams-Rolls FJ44 turbofans to 115 aircraft, extending the Sk60's service life to 2015. The sole export customer was Austria, which ordered 20 105XTs in 1968, followed by a second batch of 20 in 1972. The 105XT is powered by General Electric J-85-17B engines and has an increased weapons load of 2,000kg (4,410lb).

CURRENT SERVICE

By the end of 1999, the Swedish Air Force had around 100 operational Sk60s of various models, mainly in use with F10 and F16. The Austrian Air Force continues to operate 27 (out of its original order for 40) in the trainer and liaison roles. Eight serve with FIR 2 for liaison and daytime alert missions, and the remaining 19 are operated by the Ausbildungs und Einsatzstaffel (Training & Operational Squadron) at Linz in a variety of roles including photo-reconnaissance, for which wing-mounted Vinten pods, containing a range of five Vinten 70 cameras, are used. They are no longer used for ground attack missions. Austria intends to keep the Saab 105 in service until 2010.

SPECIAL FEATURES

The Saab 105 is a mid-wing multi-purpose two-seater which is reaching the end of its operational career.

VARIANTS

Sk60A trainer; **Sk60B** trainer/ground attack; **Sk60C** ground attack/reconnaissance; **Sk60D** four-seat version used for airline pilot training for Swedish Air Force reserve officers; **SAAB 105ÖE** for the Austrian Air Force; **Saab 2060** entered for US JPATS competition, but not chosen.

TECHNICAL DATA

Saab 105 (Sk 60C)

Powerplants: Two Volvo Flygmotor RM9 turbojets.
Developing: 12.96kN (2,850lb st)
Span: 10.50m (31ft 2in)
Length: 11.00m (36ft 1in)
Height: 2.70m (8ft 10 in)
All-up weight: 4,500kg (9,920lb)
Maximum speed: 765km/h (475mph)
Cruise speed: 700km/h (435mph)
Operational ceiling: 39,400ft
Maximum range: 1,780km (1,106 miles)
Accommodation: Two, side-by-side.
Warload: Twelve 13.5cm air-to-surface rockets or two 30mm Aden cannon, on underwing pylons. Sk 60C carries Fairchild KB-18 panoramic camera and infrared search unit in extended nose.
First flown: 29 June 1963 (Sk 60)
Entered service: April 1966.

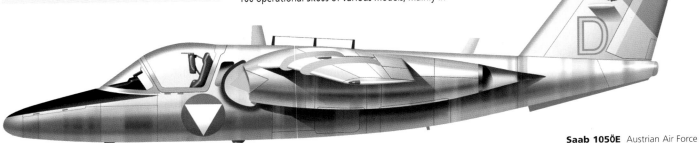

Saab 105ÖE Austrian Air Force

Saab 35 Draken

SINGLE ENGINE SINGLE-SEAT SUPERSONIC FIGHTER/INTERCEPTOR

J35Ö Draken Austrian Air Force

DEVELOPMENT

Designed in late 1940s and early 1950s as a supersonic replacement for the J29 Tunnan with the added requirement for short-field performance. The initial delta wing design was replaced by double-delta in 1953. A 70 per cent scale replica Saab 210 Lill-Draken was used to test the wing shape. The specification

TECHNICAL DATA

Saab J35D Draken

Powerplant: One Volvo Flygmotor RM6C (licence-built Rolls-Royce Avon) with afterburner.
Developing: 78.46 kN (17,637lb st).
Span: 9.42m (30ft 11in)
Length: 15.34m (50ft 4in)
Height: 3.89m (12ft 9in)
All-up weight: 11,000kg (24,250lb)
Max speed: Above Mach 2.0 (2,125km/h, 1320mph)
Cruise speed: Mach 0.9
Operational ceiling: 65,600ft
Maximum range: 2,750km (1,709 miles)
Accommodation: Pilot only
Warload: Up to nine hardpoints below fuselage (three) and wings (three each) and 30mm ADEN M/55 gun in starboard inner wing.
First flown: 25 October 1955
Entered service: March 1960

was fundamentally revised in 1956 with an increase in maximum speed. Deliveries began in 1959 and F13 at Norrköping became the first operational front-line unit. The J35A was later superceded by the J35B which had an improved radar system. The J35D was developed at the end of 1960, and featured a more powerful engine which gave a rate of climb in excess of 49,000ft per minute. The improved J35F, developed from 1959 onwards, offered a major advance in weapons, navigation and air defence systems and entered service in 1965, remaining the Swedish Air Force's main fighter/interceptor until the advent of the Viggen in the early 1980s. The two-seat Sk35C was developed as a suitable trainer. S35Es were unarmed, relying on supersonic low-level flight to evade attackers. Production ended in 1977, when 612 had been produced but during the early 1980s a programme to upgrade 66 J35Fs was undertaken, resulting in the J35J, first delivered in March 1987 to F10 at Angelholm, the only user of the variant. Foreign sales were made to three countries – Denmark (57), Finland (47, of which 35 were ex-Swedish Air Force) and Austria (24, plus a further five for spares in 1999).

CURRENT SERVICE

The Draken is no longer in service with Denmark and only very limited service with Sweden, and is in its twilight years with Finland, where it is being replaced

by the F-18 Hornet. However, Austria's J35Ös, 23 of which are in service with the Surveillance Wing based at Zeltweg and Graz, will be in service until at least 2005.

SPECIAL FEATURES

The Saab Draken is recognisable by its unusual double delta wing plan. It provided the backbone of Swedish air defence until supplemented by the Viggen, but remained in service until the Gripen had become fully operational. An impressive range of weaponry can be carried including the Rb27 and Rb28 Falcon air-to-air missiles, Bofors 135mm unguided rockets and 500lb bombs for air-to-ground operations. Austrian J35Ös carry AIM-9P3 Sidewinders plus two internal 30mm cannon. RWR and chaff/flare dispensers are also fitted.

VARIANTS

Early single-seat Drakens are practically identical externally, varying in engine power. Twenty-six two-seat trainer **Sk35Cs** were built and there were 60 two-seat reconnaissance **S35Es**, of which 29 were converted from **J35Ds**. The **J35F** is distinguished by a bulged canopy. The **J35Ö** is a refurbished J35D fitted with the **J35J's** bulged canopy.

J35F Draken Swedish Air Force

Saab 37 Viggen

SINGLE TURBOFAN SINGLE-SEAT MULTI-ROLE FIGHTER

JA37 Viggen Swedish Air Force

DEVELOPMENT

Initial design work for an attack fighter to replace the Saab 32 Lansen, and eventually the Saab 35 Draken, began in 1952, but proceeded slowly while the development of an afterburner and thrust reversers for the engine were designed and tested. The design was approved in February 1962 and it was formally chosen as the next Swedish Air Force fighter on 28 September 1962. The first of seven prototypes made its first flight on 8 February 1967, and an order for 175 mixed AJ/SF/SH37s was placed on 5 April 1968. The first production aircraft flew on 23 February 1971, with deliveries beginning in June 1971 to F7 at Satenas. The JA37 interceptor was ordered in September 1974. Production ceased in 1990, by which time 330 of various models had been built, all for the Swedish Air Force. Between 1993 and 1997 an upgrade programme for early Viggens was introduced, initially for 115 aircraft, but later reduced due to budget constraints. The major innovation was the introduction of new computer systems to provide integrated attack, fighter and reconnaissance capability. In all 48 AJ37s, 25 SH37s and 25 SF37s were upgraded. At the beginning of the 1990s the Swedish Air Force had 17 squadrons equipped with the Viggen, but this number has dwindled to ten as it is slowly supplanted by the JAS39 Gripen.

CURRENT SERVICE

Around 245 Viggens remain in service with five Wings of the Swedish Air Force: F4 at Östersund (which also acts as the operational conversion unit), F16 at Uppsala and F17 at Ronneby all fly the JA37; F10 at Ängelholm has AJS37s, and F21 at Luleå has a mixed complement of two JA37 squadrons, plus one of AJS37s.

SPECIAL FEATURES

The Viggen has an unusual delta wing and canard planform with flaps on the trailing edge of both. Short-take off and landing capability enables it to operate from 500m (1,640ft) hard strips such as roads. The fin folds to allow operation from underground hangars. The undercarriage is stressed for carrier-type landings, obviating the need for flared landings.

VARIANTS

Surviving **AJ37** first-generation Viggens have now been upgraded to **AJS37** standard. The **JA37** interceptor version has a secondary ground-attack role; it has restressed wings and a small fuselage stretch. The **Sk37** Viggen is used for training and has two separate cockpits, plus a slightly taller fin to compensate for its deeper forward fuselage. The **SF37** version is used for reconnaissance, and the **SH37** for the maritime surveillance and strike role.

TECHNICAL DATA

Saab JA37 Viggen

Powerplant: One Volvo Flygmotor RM8B turbofan (licence-produced Pratt & Whitney JT8D-22) with afterburner
Developing: 73.84kN (16,600lb st)
Span: 10.60m (34ft 9.25in)
Length: 16.40m (53ft 9.75in)
Height: 5.90m (19ft 4.25in)
All-up weight: 20,500kg (45,194lb)
Maximum speed: Over 2,126km/h (1,321mph)
Operational ceiling: 60,000ft
Maximum range: 2,000 km (1,243 miles)
Mission range: 1,000km (621 miles)
Accommodation: Pilot only
Warload: Up to six air-to-air missiles, including Sky Flash, AIM-9L Sidewinder. Integral 30mm Oerlikon KCA cannon. Up to nine pylons under wings and fuselage for up to 6,000kg (14,000lb) of ordnance.
First flown: 8 February 1967
Entered service: June 1971 (AJ37)

JA37 Viggen
Swedish Air Force

Saab 340 & S.100B Argus

TWIN-ENGINED SMALL MULTI-PURPOSE AIRLINER/RECONNAISSANCE PLATFORM

S.100B Argus Swedish Air Force

DEVELOPMENT

Announced in January 1980 as a collaborative project between Saab of Sweden and Fairchild of USA, the initial production Saab-Fairchild 340A was first flown in January 1983 and certified on 15 May 1984, before entering service with Crossair in June 1984. Fairchild withdrew from the project in October 1985, and the aircraft was marketed as the Saab 340 from 1987. The 340QC (Quick Change) freighter was introduced in 1987, followed by the improved 340B version in 1989. The final 340BPlus model was launched in February 1994 with further improvements, a higher take-off weight and improved hot-and-high and short-field performance. In the military sphere, the Swedish Air Force purchased a Saab 340 for VIP transport duties in 1989. After initial selection of the Fairchild Metro

by the Swedish Air Force as an airborne early warning and control platform in 1982, using the Ericsson Erieye radar then under development, trials were carried out in 1986 and 1987 using a dummy radome, but the aircraft was subsequently changed to a Saab 340, and one example ordered for test purposes on 8 January 1993. A further order for five production examples followed. The first flight with a complete working system was made on 1 July 1994 and after completion of trials, the first three aircraft were handed over to the Swedish Air Force in November 1997, followed by the remaining three during 1999. Japan's Maritime Safety Agency ordered a Saab 340 in 1995 and two SAAB 340 SAR-200s the following year. Plans to order a further eight were frustrated by the withdrawal of the type from production. A total of 458 Saab 340s was built before production ended in mid-1999.

CURRENT SERVICE

Around 450 Saab 340s were believed to be in service or stored at the end of 1999, the vast majority in airline service. However, the Swedish Air Force has six S.100B Arguses in the AEW&C role based at Linkoping, and

one Tp100 used for transporting the Royal Family and VIPs based at Bromma-Stockholm. The Japan Maritime Safety Agency uses Saab 340s for search and rescue, and in the auxiliary liaison role. The Greek Air Force has chosen the Erieye system and will operate one of the Swedish Air Force examples for training and development, pending the arrival of four Erieye-equipped Embraer RJ-145s in 2002.

SPECIAL FEATURES

A small airliner with freight and cargo possibilities. Wingtip extensions were offered as the 340BPlus-wt but cannot be retrofitted to non-wingtip aircraft.

VARIANTS

The Swedish Air Force **S.100B Argus** is identified by a 9m (29ft 6in) over-fuselage radome containing the PS 890 Erieye radar system, enlarged ventral fins and a new tailcone housing APU and cooling systems. The **340 SAR-200** has an underfuselage radome that houses APS-143(V) sea surveillance radar and carries markers, flares and a rescue pack, which are dropped through a belly hatch.

TECHNICAL DATA

Saab 340B

Powerplants: Two General Electric CT7-9B turboprops.
Developing: 1,394kW (1,870shp)
Span: 21.44m (70ft 4in)
Length: 19.73m (64ft 9in)
Height: 6.97m (22ft 11in)
All-up weight: 13,155kg (29,000lb)
Maximum speed: 548km/h (340mph)
Cruise speed: 523 km/h (325mph)
Operational ceiling: 31,000ft
Maximum range: 2,865km (1,780 miles)
Endurance: 6 hours on station
Accommodation: Crew of three plus option of two flight attendants. Maximum passengers 37. AEW&C version has three workstation operators.
First flown: 25 January 1983
Entered service: November 1997 (S100B Argus)

Saab 340 Tp100A Swedish Air Force

Saab JAS39 Gripen

SINGLE-ENGINED SINGLE-SEAT LIGHTWEIGHT ALL-WEATHER INTERCEPTOR/ATTACK AIRCRAFT

JAS39A Gripen Swedish Air Force

DEVELOPMENT

Intended to replace the Swedish Air Force's Viggens and the last remaining Drakens, development of the JAS39 began in 1980, and the initial batch of seven prototypes and 30 production aircraft was ordered in June 1982, followed by a second batch of 110 aircraft in June 1992. The prototype first flew on 9 December 1988, but was lost in a landing accident on 2 February 1989. The first production JAS39A, first flown on 10 September 1992, was added to the test programme to replace the lost prototype; the second prototype (the first for the Swedish Air Force) first flew on 4 March 1993 and was handed over 8 June 1993. The official opening of the Gripen Operations Centre at Satenas, home of the first operating unit F7, took place on 9 June 1996. By the end of the year all 30 first-batch aircraft had been delivered and the wing was declared operational in October 1997. Next unit to receive the type was F10 at Angelholm in September 1999, where it replaced the last Swedish Drakens. The two-seat JAS39B Gripen first flew on 29 April 1996, and 14 were funded in the second batch of 110 Gripens ordered. A third batch, ordered in 1997, covers 50 JAS39Cs and 14 JAS39Ds, to be delivered between 2003 and 2006. The Gripen is marketed internationally by BAE Systems, which anticipates a market for up to 250 over the next 20 years. The first export order was placed by the South African Air Force in November

1999, to replace its Cheetahs; nine two-seaters have been ordered with options on 19 single-seat Gripens. Other countries to whom presentations have been made include Austria, Brazil, Chile, Czech Republic, Hungary, Poland, the Philippines and Slovenia.

CURRENT SERVICE

By the end of 1999, the Swedish Air Force had around 80 Gripens in service with two wings, from a proposed buy of 204. The South African Air Force's Gripens will be delivered from 2007 to 2012. In 1999, the Polish Air Force was offered 16 JAS 39s and two JAS 39Bs on loan from 2001-2006, as part of a proposed sale of 60 Gripens to replace Soviet-sourced fighters by 2012.

SPECIAL FEATURES

A light-weight fourth-generation multi-role fighter, the agile Gripen can operate from 800m (2,625ft) runways as part of the Swedish BAS90 dispersed base system, and is fully fly-by-wire.

VARIANTS

The **JAS39A** is the standard single-seat fighter, **JAS39B** the two-seat trainer; **JAS39C** and **JAS39D** are their respective upgraded models incorporating NATO-compatible equipment and a more powerful version of the RM12; **JAS39X** is a potential export version incorporating JAS39C/D upgrades.

TECHNICAL DATA

Saab JAS39A Gripen
Powerplant: One General Electric/Volvo Flygmotor RM12 (F404-GE-400) turbofan.
Developing: 80.5kN (18,100lb st) with afterburning
Span: 8.40m (27ft 6.75in)
Length: 14.10m (46ft 3in)
Height: 4.50m (14ft 9in)
All-up weight: 13,000kg (28,660lb)
Maximum speed: Mach 2.0+ (2,126km/h; 1,321mph)
Cruise speed: Mach 1.1
Mission range: 800km (497 miles)
Accommodation: Pilot only
Warload: 27mm Mauser BK27 cannon in port lower fuselage; AIM-9L Sidewinders on wingtip rails. Six hardpoints (two under each wing plus one on centreline and one below starboard air intake) for missiles including AIM-120 AMRAAM and Maverick, air-to-surface rockets or conventional bomb loads. Reconnaissance pods can be fitted.
First flown: 9 December 1988 (JAS39A);
29 April 1996 (JAS39B)
Entered service: 8 June 1993.

JAS39A Gripen Swedish Air Force

Scheibe SF-25 Falke

SINGLE-ENGINED TWO-SEAT POWERED GLIDER

DEVELOPMENT

The original SF-25A Falke motor glider designed by Egon Scheibe, and based on the Mu-13E Bergfalke II tandem two-seat sailplane, first flew in May 1963 and was powered by a Hirth F12A2C engine. It was followed by the SF-25B and eventually the SF-25C, which version is still in production today, with over 1,200 produced so far. The SF-25C model, introduced in 1971, comes with a choice of engines. It featured an entirely new forward fuselage with an enlarged cockpit and conventional tailwheel undercarriage. Despite its relatively low engine power, it is also used as a glider tug. It has undergone many changes over the years and is quite viable as a long-distance tourer and a very cost-effective training aircraft. The Falke design has also been produced by other manufacturers under licence, including Slingsby in the UK (which produced the RAF's Ventures), Sportavia-Putzer in Germany, Aeronautica Umbra in Italy and Loravia in France. In the 1970s, they were the most common motor gliders to be seen in Europe.

CURRENT SERVICE

The Falke, under its service name of Venture, was for many years a mainstay of the RAF's Volunteer Gliding Schools, whose fleet of 40 gave air experience flights to the UK's Air Training Corps. When the Ventures were declared surplus to requirements, the survivors were sold into the civilian market from 1990 onwards, being replaced by the Grob G109 Vigilant T1 motor glider. However, in addition to hundreds of civilian owned and operated Falkes, the Oman and Pakistan Air Forces continue to use the type both for ab initio training and with military flying clubs.

SPECIAL FEATURES

The Falke's wood, steel tube and fabric construction is relatively cheap to repair in the event of damage while the low-mounted high-aspect wing gives docile handling characteristics. The wings detach for storage and ground transportation. Side-by-side seating aids tuition. The standard undercarriage is one large single under-fuselage wheel, plus outriggers under each wing, giving the Falke glider-like ground handling characteristics, with optional two-wheel main gear. Both nosewheel and tailwheel models are produced.

VARIANTS

Three versions currently available: the **SF-25C Falke 1700** and **Falke 2000** with Limbach engines of various power, and the **SF-25C Rotax Falke** mentioned above. The **SF-28A Tandem Falke** is similar in layout to the SF-25 but has tandem seating under a long canopy. The **SF-25E Super Falke** has a low wing of greater span, which can be folded at mid-span for hangar storage, and is powered by a 48k\w (65hp) Limbach SL.1700EA engine and first flew in May 1974.

SF-25B Falke

TECHNICAL DATA

Scheibe SF-25C Rotax Falke

Powerplant: One Rotax 912A water-cooled piston engine
Developing: 59.7kW (80hp)
Driving: Two-blade propeller
Span: 15.30m (50ft 2.25in)
Length: 7.60m (24ft 11.25in)
Height: 1.68m (5ft 6.25in)
All-up weight: 650kg (1,433lb)
Maximum speed: 190km/h (118mph)
Cruise speed: 180km/h (112mph)
Operational ceiling: 15,000ft
Maximum range: 700km (435 miles)
Accommodation: Pilot and passenger.
Warload: None
First flown: May 1963 (SF-25A); March 1971 (SF-25C)

SF-25B Falke

Schweizer RG-8A Condor & RU-38A Twin Condor

SINGLE PISTON-ENGINED (RG-8A) OR TWIN PISTON-ENGINED (RU-38A) SURVEILLANCE AIRCRAFT | USA

RG-8A Condor United States Coast Guard

DEVELOPMENT

Known by the manufacturer as the Model SA 2-37A, development of the RG-8A was undertaken in the mid-1980s in response to a US Army request for a quiet, long-endurance surveillance aircraft. Based on the SGM 2-37 motor glider, but incorporating a payload bay aft of the cockpit to house sensors and cameras, the RG-8A made its maiden flight in 1986 and entered service soon afterwards. Subsequently, further refinement of the basic concept in the mid-1990s led to the twin-engined SA 2-38A. Known in US military parlance as the RU-38A, this has greater payload and endurance characteristics.

CURRENT SERVICE

At least a dozen examples of the RG-8A are known to have been produced since 1986, although three have reportedly been destroyed. Purely military operators of the RG-8A are Bolivia (one), Colombia (one) and Mexico (two), all of which are believed to be employed on anti-drug interdiction operations in Latin America. In

addition, the Central Intelligence Agency has utilised the type as an airborne communications relay platform to direct long-range reconnaissance unmanned aerial vehicles and for covert surveillance duties. Two former US Army RG-8A aircraft were also operated by the US Coast Guard on anti-drug tasks, but one of these was written off. The survivor has since been modified to RU-38A configuration and is one of two that are earmarked for service with the Coast Guard.

SPECIAL FEATURES

The RG-8A is fundamentally a powered glider and has a tailwheel undercarriage configuration, with a single, heavily-muffled, engine that allows it to operate in so-called 'quiet mode' at low level. In fact, when directly overhead at an altitude of about 2,000ft, it is virtually inaudible, thus making it an ideal vehicle for covert surveillance. It is fitted with a payload bay behind the cockpit that can house a variety of palletised mission equipment, such as infra-red sensors, low-light-level television and conventional cameras for surveillance

operations. The RU-38A derivative employs the same wing structure and forward fuselage, but is slightly larger and has a tricycle-undercarriage, plus twin Teledyne Continental GIO-550A flat-six engines in a pull-push configuration at the front and rear of the fuselage pod. It also has a twin-tailboom layout and slightly increased payload, with FLIR, radar and LLLTV sensors sited in the nose sections of each boom.

VARIANTS

Two basic versions exist, specifically the **RG-8A** and the **RU-38A**, although as already noted, these do differ markedly in physical appearance. Despite this, they are designed for a common purpose, namely that of covert surveillance.

TECHNICAL DATA

Schweizer RG-8A Condor

Powerplant: One Textron Lycoming IO-540 flat-six piston engine
Developing: 175kW (235hp)
Driving: Three-blade propeller
Span: 18.75m (61ft 6in)
Length: 8.46m (27ft 9in)
Height: 2.36m (7ft 9in)
All-up weight: 1,587kg (3,500lb)
Maximum speed: 326km/h (202mph)
Cruise speed: 256km/h (159mph) at 75% power
Mission speed: 130-148km/h (80-92mph)
Operational ceiling: 18,000ft
Endurance: Exceeds 8 hours
Accommodation: Pilot and sensor operator
Payload: 340kg (750lb)
First flown: 1986 (RG-8A); 31 May 1995 (RU-38A)
Entered service: 1987 (RG-8A)

Schweizer YO-3A NASA

Schweizer 269/300 series

Hughes 300C Turkish Army

DEVELOPMENT

Initially designed by Hughes Helicopters as the Model 269 with a triangular tail strut, the 269A version was extensively modified before entering service and the same basic design layout is retained today. The 269B, which was marketed as the Hughes 300, succeeded the 269A in the early 1960s, and the first production 300C made its maiden flight in December 1969. Hughes produced 2,775 of the series, including 792 for the US Army as a basic helicopter trainer (designated as the TH-55 Osage), before production was transferred to Schweizer in July 1983. In addition, BredaNardi built 25 under licence, mainly for the Greek Army. The first Schweizer-built 300C first flew in June 1984 and the company eventually purchased all rights to the design in 1986. Production continues and over 3,500 of all models have been built so far, more than 750 of them by Schweizer. The 330SP is a four-seat development of the 300C that first flew in June 1988. It was unsuccessful in the US Army's 1990 SCAT/NTH competition to find a replacement for the TH-55 Osage.

CURRENT SERVICE

Hughes 269/300s are used mainly in the training role and operators include the Argentine Coast Guard (two); the Greek Navy (26 for training, mainly Italian-built examples); the Indonesian Army (10); the Pakistan Army (10); the Spanish Air Force (13 under the local designation HE20 with Ala 78 at Armilla); the Swedish Joint Helicopter Wing (25 under the designation Hkp5B for training and air observation); and the Royal Thai Air Aviation Division (48 TH-300Cs) for training. The sole military user of the Schweizer 330 so far is the Dutch Navy, which has two for training.

SPECIAL FEATURES

Simple pod and boom layout, with energy-absorbing skids. The engine and fuel tanks are mounted behind the cockpit for ease of maintenance. The Schweizer 330 has an enlarged cockpit and fully enclosed fuselage and tail boom.

VARIANTS

Original civil version was the **Hughes 269**. The US Army evaluated the type as the **YHO-2** and purchased 792 under the designation **TH-55A Osage**. The 'baseline' **300CB** model for training was accounted in 1993 and deliveries began in August 1995. The current military model is known as the **TH-300C** and the Police version is the **300C Sky Knight**; an unmanned version (known as **RoboCopter**) has been developed in Japan and may be offered as a contender for the US Navy's VTOL UAV requirement.

TECHNICAL DATA

Schweizer 300C/TH-300C

Powerplant: One Textron Lycoming HIO-360-D1A piston engine
Developing: 168kW (225hp)
Driving: Three-blade main and two-blade tail rotors
Main rotor diameter: 8.18m (26ft 10in)
Overall length: 9.40m (30ft 10in)
Height: 2.66m (8ft 8.75in)
All-up weight: 930kg (2,050lb)
Maximum speed: 169km/h (105mph)
Cruise speed: 153km/h (95mph)
Operational ceiling: 3,110m (10,200ft)
Maximum ferry range: 360km (224 miles)
Endurance: 3hr 24min
Accommodation: Pilot plus two passengers/observers
First flown: October 1956 (269)
Entered service: October 1958

Hughes 269 Royal Thai Army

Scottish Aviation (BAe/Handley Page) Jetstream

TWIN-TURBOPROP LIGHT TRANSPORT/TRAINER

Jetstream T2 Royal Navy

DEVELOPMENT

The last new design from Handley Page, the Jetstream was a 12- to 20-seat commuter airliner powered by Turboméca Astazou XVIs and was announced in August 1965, partly as a replacement for the DH Dove, conforming to the United States' FAR Pt23 legislation for single-pilot commercial aircraft. The initial military customer was to have been the USAF, which ordered 11 Garrett TPE-331 powered examples under the designation C-10A for its light turboprop transport requirement. However, the order plus four options was cancelled in October 1969 when it became clear that Handley Page could not meet the contract dates. The Astazou-powered Jetstream won the RAF's Varsity replacement competition and Scottish Aviation, which eventually took over production rights, produced 26 under the designation T1, deliveries of which began in June 1973. Production of the early version of the Jetstream totalled 80. The Garrett TPE-331 powered Jetstream 31 was introduced into service in 1982; by October 1993 384 had been sold. The final version was the Jetstream 41, launched in 1988, of which 103 were sold before production ceased in July 1997.

CURRENT SERVICE

Eleven Jetstream T1s are in service with No 45(R) Squadron at RAF Cranwell, part of No 3 Flying Training School, in the multi-engined pilot training role. The Fleet Air Arm has a fleet of nine T2s (former RAF T1s) with 750 NAS at RNAS Culdrose for training observers. The Heron Flight, formerly Yeovilton Station Flight, has four T3s for communications duties which were delivered in 1986. In addition, DERA operates a single T2 from West Freugh for sonobuoy trials. Elsewhere, one of two aircraft supplied in 1986 for Tornado navigator training survives with the Royal Saudi Air Force's No 65 Squadron. The Uruguayan Navy acquired two Jetstreams from the Fleet Air Arm, delivered from Culdrose in January 1999. Finally, the Thai Army has two Jetstream 41s, and two 41s were delivered to the Hong Kong Government Flying Service at Chek Lap Kok in April 1999 to replace its Beech Super King Airs in the maritime patrol/ search and rescue role.

SPECIAL FEATURES

The Jetstream is a low-wing commuter airliner with cruciform tail layout. The engines are mounted on the high aspect ratio wings at approximately one-quarter chord.

VARIANTS

The RAF's **T1** differs from the commercial version by virtue of windows above the cockpit. Royal Navy **T2s**, (which are converted RAF T1s) are identifiable by their thimble noses which house search radar; **T3s** have belly radomes containing Racal radar systems

TECHNICAL DATA

Scottish Aviation Jetstream T1
Powerplants: Two Turboméca Astazou XVID turboprops
Developing: 701kW (940shp)
Span: 15.85m (52ft 0in)
Length: 14.37m (47ft 1.5in)
Height: 5.38m (17ft 8in)
All-up weight: 5,700kg (12,566lb)
Maximum speed: 454km/h (282mph)
Cruise speed: 426km/h (265mph)
Operational ceiling: 25,000ft
Maximum range: 2,224km (1,380 miles)
Accommodation: Two pilots plus four passengers/ students in cabin.
Warload: None
First flown: 18 August 1967 (civilian model)
Entered service: 26 June 1973

but are otherwise basically similar to the Jetstream 31 airliner. The **Jetstream 41** is a broadly similar but larger variant of the earlier Jetstream 31.

Jetstream T1
Royal Air Force

Scottish Aviation Bulldog

SINGLE-ENGINED LIGHT TRAINER

Bulldog T1 Royal Air Force

TECHNICAL DATA

Scottish Aviation Bulldog T1

Powerplant: One Textron Lycoming IO-360-A1B6 flat-four piston engine
Developing: 149kW (200hp)
Driving: Three-blade propeller
Span: 10.06m (33ft 0in)
Length: 7.09m (23ft 3in)
Height: 2.28m (7ft 5.75in)
All-up weight: 1,066kg (2350lb)
Maximum speed: 241 km/h (150mph)
Cruise speed: 222 km/h (138mph)
Operational ceiling: 16,000ft
Maximum range: 1,000km (621 miles)
Endurance: 5hr
Accommodation: Instructor and student side-by-side, with space behind for baggage.
Warload: Four underwing hardpoints can be fitted for practice or active bombs up to 50kg, machine-gun pods, grenade launchers, and air-to-air or air-to-surface missiles. Maximum underwing load 290kg (640lb).
First flown: 19 May 1969 (Beagle prototype); 14 February 1971 (SAL prototype); 30 January 1973 (first for RAF).
Entered service: April 1973 with CFS

DEVELOPMENT

The Bulldog was designed by Beagle Aircraft as a derivative of its successful Pup, but the company was forced into receivership during late 1969, shortly after the prototype had first flown, and the design was sold to Scottish Aviation, which subsequently put it into production at Prestwick. The first customers were Kenya, Malaysia and Sweden who bought a total of 98 Series 100 aircraft. The major customer for the Bulldog was the Royal Air Force, which chose it to replace the Chipmunk in University Air Squadron service. A total of 130 Model 121s, designated T1s, was ordered. Other customers for Series 120 examples were Botswana, Ghana, Hong Kong, Jordan, Kenya, Lebanon and Nigeria. Additionally, there was one demonstrator and a single civilian example for a Venezuelan customer. Production ended in 1983, at which point 325 Bulldogs had been built by SAL.

CURRENT SERVICE

Having served with the University Air Squadrons for a quarter of a century (the first was delivered to London UAS in October 1973), it was announced in 1998 that the Bulldog was to be replaced by the Grob G115E Tutor with the UASs and Air Experience Flights (AEFs), the fleet being operated by Bombardier Services under a Private Finance Initiative. The replacement programme is ongoing and should be completed by July 2001. Additionally, the Central Flying School's Elementary Flying Training Standards Squadron operates Bulldogs under the aegis of No 3 FTS; surplus RAF aircraft are being sold on to other customers, including the Maltese government. Of the other users, Malaysia sold its aircraft to civilian operators in 1997 and replaced them with PC-7s, as have Botswana, Hong Kong and Nigeria, the latter due to financial constraints. Ghana, Jordan, Kenya, Lebanon and Sweden continue to operate the type, the latter for airline pilot training.

SPECIAL FEATURES

The Bulldog is a single-engined low-wing monoplane with fixed tricycle undercarriage. It has a short nose and large glazed cabin area with two windows each side, tapered wings with squared tips, large fin and rudder, and a ventral strake under fin. The oblong tailplane has square tips set at base of fin.

VARIANTS

There is very little external difference between the various models of Bulldog and model numbers were used to differentiate between customers: **Mk 101** – Sweden; **Mk 102** – Malaysia; **Mk 103 & 127** – Kenya; **Mk 121** – RAF; **Mk 122/122A** – Ghana; **Mk 123** – Nigeria; **Mk 125/125A** – Jordan; **Mk 126** – Lebanon; **Mk 128** – Hong Kong; and **Mk 130** – Botswana.

Bulldog Mk 101 Swedish Air Force

SEPECAT Jaguar

TWIN-TURBOFAN SINGLE-SEAT FIGHTER-BOMBER AND TWO-SEAT TRAINER

FRANCE/UK

DEVELOPMENT

SEPECAT was initially formed by Breguet and BAC in May 1966 to develop a high-performance jet trainer to replace the HS Gnat and Hawker Hunter, and to bridge a gap between the Fouga Magister and the Dassault Mirage III. It later evolved into a single-seat all-weather strike/ attack jet, with a secondary two-seat trainer model. Each air arm agreed to purchase 200. RAF deliveries commenced in 1974 and eventually equipped eight front-line squadrons. The first French unit became operational in 1974, in which year the Jaguar International export version was revealed. There have been four overseas customers – Ecuador (ten single-seaters and two trainers), Oman (24 single-seaters and two trainers), Nigeria (13 single-seaters

SEPECAT Jaguar GR1A Royal Air Force

and five two-seaters) and India (116 single-seaters and 15 combat-capable trainers) – where it is known as the Shamsher (Assault Sword). The Jaguar has seen operational service in Africa with the French Air Force, and with the French Air Force and RAF in the Gulf during 1990/1991, and continues to fly peacekeeping duties from southern European bases.

CURRENT SERVICE

Jaguars equip the RAF's Nos 6, 16(R), 41 and 54 Squadrons at Coltishall, and the French Air Force's EC 7 at St Dizier, plus associated British and French test units. The type is also currently in service with Ecuador's Escuadrón 2111, Oman's Nos 8 and 20 Squadrons and India's Nos 5, 6, 14, 16 and 27 Squadrons. The current status of the Nigerian Jaguars is unknown due to the country's financial problems, but they are believed to be for sale.

SPECIAL FEATURES

The first aircraft for the RAF to be designed in metric units, the Jaguar is configured for ease of weapons carriage and stability at low altitude. It has double-slotted flaps along the entire wing length and no ailerons – outer wing spoilers are used instead. RAF versions are identified by Laser Ranging and Marked Target Seekers in the nose and Radar Warning

Receivers fitted in pods slightly below the fin tip. Single-seaters have a retractable refuelling probe fitted to the starboard forward fuselage and some French and Omani Air Force two-seaters have fixed refuelling probes on the extreme nose. Surviving RAF examples are currently being upgraded to GR3/T4 standard with upgraded cockpit, communication and self-defence systems to enable them to carry AIM-132 ASRAAM missiles, with a further upgrade to GR4A/T4A standard once funding is available; 82 surviving RAF Jaguars will also receive upgraded Adour Mk 106 engines. Surviving Ecuadorian and Omani aircraft are also being upgraded to GR3/T4 standard.

VARIANTS

French Air Force single-seat Jaguars are designated **Jaguar A** and two-seat examples **Jaguar E**. The RAF's aircraft are designated **Jaguar S** (GR1, later upgraded to GR1A and GR1B status; survivors now becoming GR3/GR3A) and **Jaguar B** (initially T2, later T2A and now **T4/T4A**). Export Jaguars are identified by two-letter codes: Ecuador ES and EB; Oman OS/OB; Nigeria SN/BN and India IM (maritime), IS (single-seat) and IT (trainers). One **Jaguar M** naval version with arrester hook was produced but was rejected by the French Navy in favour of the single-engined Super Etendard.

SEPECAT Jaguar GR1A
Royal Air Force

Shaanxi Y-8

FOUR-ENGINED HIGH-WING TRANSPORT/FREIGHTER

Shaanxi Y-8 Chinese Air Force

DEVELOPMENT

Basically an unlicensed redesign of the Antonov An-12 'Cub', resulting from detailed inspection of a Russian example and then reverse-engineering it to produce a 'new' design. This work was begun by Xian in March 1969, but the programme was transferred to Shaanxi in 1972. Following completion of two prototypes (the first by Xian, and the second by Shaanxi), production was authorised in 1980. During the mid-1980s the Y-8C version was developed in conjunction with Lockheed, the entire fuselage being pressurised and the length of the cargo area increased by some 2m (6ft 6in). The second prototype was converted to this standard and made its first flight on 17 December 1990. Work on the design continues and the most recent variant to be announced is the Y-8X for maritime patrol duties, of which a prototype has been built, but which has yet to enter full production. The radar installation could be the Racal-Thorn Searchwater, which China purchased in the mid-1990s.

CURRENT SERVICE

Around 60 Y-8s have been produced so far for a mix of civil and military operators. Production continues at the rate of around five per year (albeit with 50 year-old technology). The main military user is the Chinese People's Liberation Army Air Force, which has around 25 for transport duties. Export Y-8Ds have been sold to Myanmar (1), Sri Lanka (2) and Sudan (2).

SPECIAL FEATURES

Designed primarily for military freight operations, the Shaanxi Y-8 is similar in design to the Antonov An-12BK 'Cub', but the Y-8 has a reprofiled nose area reminiscent of the Tu-16 'Badger'. The rear ramp system of the Y-8A and Y-8C has been completely redesigned and is a single downward opening unit.

VARIANTS

The baseline military version is the **Y-8**. Variants include the **Y-8A** helicopter carrier with taller main cargo area

and rear ramp; the **Y-8C** fully pressurised version developed in conjunction with Lockheed; the **Y-8D** export version; the **Y-8E** drone carrier version for the Chang Hong 1 UAV, using trapezes positioned under each wing between the engine nacelles, developed to replace elderly Tupolev Tu-4 'Bulls' used in the same role; the **Y-8H** aerial survey platform; and the **Y-8X** maritime patrol version which has a large undernose radome. The basic civil version is the **Y-8B** with all military equipment deleted; also available is the **Y-8F** livestock carrier, with cages for 350 goats or sheep.

TECHNICAL DATA

Shaanxi Y-8A
Powerplants: Four SAEC (Zhouzou) WJ6 turboprops
Developing: 3,169kW (4,250ehp)
Driving: Four-blade propellers
Span: 38.00m (124ft 8in)
Length: 34.02m (111ft 7.25in)
Height: 11.16m (36ft 7.5in)
All-up weight: 61,000kg (134,480lb)
Maximum speed: 662 km/h (411mph)
Cruise speed: 550 km/h (342 mph)
Operational ceiling: 34,120ft
Maximum range: 5,615km (3,489 miles)
Mission range: 1,273km (791 miles)
Endurance: 11 hr 7 min
Accommodation: Crew of five; up to 96 troops or 80 paratroops in main cabin; alternatively 92 casualties or two lorries plus a jeep
Warload: None
First flown: 25 December 1974 (Xian); 29 December 1975 (Shaanxi)
Entered service: Early 1980s

Shaanxi Y-8 Chinese Air Force

Shenyang J-6/F-6

TWIN-TURBOJET FIGHTER/FIGHTER-BOMBER

Shenyang FT-6 Bangladesh Air Force

DEVELOPMENT

The Shenyang J-6 is the Chinese development of the Russian MiG-19 of the 1950s. Numerically it is still the most important combat aircraft in Chinese military service, fulfilling both the attack and fighter roles.

TECHNICAL DATA

Shenyang J-6

Powerplants: Two Liming Wopen-6 (Turmansky R-9BF-811) afterburning turbojets
Developing: 25.5kN (5,730lb st) dry; 31.9kN (7,165lb st) with afterburner
Span: 9.20m (30ft 2in)
Length: 14.90m (48ft 11in) including probe
Height: 3.88m (12ft 9in)
All-up weight: 10,000kg (22,045lb)
Maximum speed: 1,540km/h (954mph)
Operational ceiling: 58,750ft
Maximum range: 2,200km (1,366 miles)
Accommodation: Pilot only
Warload: Three 30mm NR-30 cannon – one in each wing root and one in lower front fuselage. Four underwing hardpoints. Maximum ordnance 500kg (1,100lb) including AAMs (AIM-9 Sidewinder on Pakistan aircraft), rockets and bombs.
First flown: December 1959
Entered service: 1964

China selected the basic MiG-19S 'Farmer C' for licence production in the late 1950s. Shenyang (and initially Nanchang) were assigned to build the MiG-19, but production was sluggish and quality of a very low order. It was selected for production under the second Five Year Plan. The turbulence of the 'Great Leap Forward' destroyed the carefully-built quality control procedures instituted during the first Five Year Plan. The PLA Air Force would not accept initial deliveries and many were scrapped after failing post-production inspection. The effect of the 'Cultural Revolution' on the J-6 programme was devastating. However, by 1973 the prevailing situation had improved sufficiently for the development of new variants – these included the JJ-6 trainer and JZ-6. Guizhou (GAIC) was responsible for the final variant, the all-weather J-6A. The 1950s-vintage J-6 was produced well into the 1980s, by which time over 3,000 had been built. It was exported in substantial quantities to Albania, Bangladesh, Egypt, Iran, Iraq, North Korea, Pakistan, Somalia, Tanzania, Vietnam and Zambia.

CURRENT SERVICE

No original MiG-19s remain in service today, but the Chinese-built Shenyang J-6 versions are still extensively used in China and continue to operate in Egypt, Iran, North Korea, Pakistan, Sudan, Tanzania and Zambia.

SPECIAL FEATURES

A twin-engined design, with engines positioned side-by-side in the fuselage and fed by a single air intake in the nose. The basic design retained the mid-position wing of the MiG-15/17 series, but the horizontal tailplanes are set much lower.

VARIANTS

The **JJ-6** two-seater trainer first flew on 6 November 1970. The Chinese two-seater owes little to the Russian original – there was no two-seat MiG-19 produced in Russia. The fuselage is stretched by 84cm (33in) ahead of the wing, and the wingroot cannon were deleted to make room for extra fuel. A single cannon was usually retained below the fuselage. Two ventral fins were added below the rear fuselage to maintain stability. Production of the JJ-6 totalled 634 and many were exported under the designation **FT-6** to serve as conversion and continuation trainers for the **F-6**. Pakistan's surviving FT-6s have been extensively upgraded to the same standard as its F-6 fighters. The **J-6X** was a high altitude reconnaissance variant. The **J-6III** had a variable shock cone in the nose. The **J-6A/J-6IV** was a radar-equipped version and the **J-6C** had a repositioned brake parachute. The FT prefix was used for export models.

Shenyang J-6 Chinese Air Force

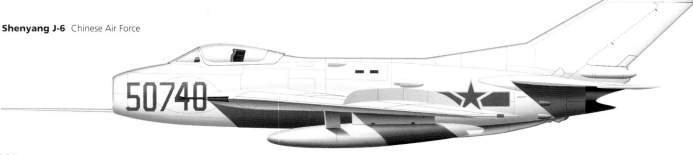

Shenyang J-8, J-8I & J-8II

TWIN-ENGINE ALL-WEATHER MULTI-ROLE FIGHTER

Shenyang F-8IIM

DEVELOPMENT

Originally an enlarged version of the Chengdu J-7, the J-8 was based on the unsuccessful MiG Ye-152A 'Flipper' twin-engined development of the MiG-21. Work on the J-8 programme began in 1964. The first prototype (of two) began flight trials on 5 July 1969, but progress was slow due to the prevailing political atmosphere. It was not until 1979 that pre-series aircraft were eventually ordered, with the first flight of a J-8I taking place on 24 April 1981. Around 50 of the original models were built before production of the J-8I ceased in 1987. The upgraded J-8II made its first flight on 12 June 1984, and in 1985 production of the original J-8 eventually got underway. In August 1987 Grumman and CATIC entered into an agreement to provide an upgrade package using USAF foreign military sales funding. This was cancelled in 1989 following the Tiananmen Square uprising and China has instead chosen to undertake its own upgrade programme under the designation J-8IIM. The J-8IIM's first public appearance was at Air Show China in 1996, where it was displayed with a range of weaponry including PL-9, AA-10 'Alamo' and AA-12 'Adder' air-to-air missiles. The J-8II features a Phazotron Zhuk-8 radar system, which gives improved combat capability.

The Shenyang J-8 has been offered for export under the designation F-8II, with the first mention of this programme occurring in 1994, then followed by the improved F-8IIM. So far no customers have been revealed. Production of the J-8 series is said to be continuing at a low rate as the J-8D, which has an in-flight refuelling capability.

CURRENT SERVICE

In total, four People's Liberation Army Air Force Air Armies (the 1st and 10th with a mixture of J-8Is/J-8IIs and the 7th and 8th equipped solely with J-8IIs) are believed to operate a total fleet of around 100 J-8s, some upgraded from J-8 standard. Unofficial reports suggest that the Navy may also be operating the J-8. The Chinese military forces are believed to have an eventual requirement for 400.

SPECIAL FEATURES

Though it traces its ancestry to the MiG-21 and has suffered from a protracted 30-year development programme, the J-8 (code-name 'Finback') represents China's first truly effective indigenous jet fighter. Distinguished by a thin 60° swept delta wing, in flight the J-8II deploys a ventral fin beneath the tail unit.

Repeated cockpit upgrades have been undertaken in the last ten years.

VARIANTS

The original **J-8** is no longer in service, and several were upgraded in service to **J-8I** standard. It is now the focus of a major upgrade programme, with the Russian radar company Phazotron and missile supplier Vympel involved in the **F-8IIM** project.

TECHNICAL DATA

Shenyang J-8II 'Finback'

Powerplants: Two Liyang (Guizhou) WP13B II afterburning turbojets
Developing: 47.07kN (10,580lb st)
Span: 9.34m (30ft 8in)
Length: 21.59m (70ft 10in)
Height: 5.41m (17ft 9in)
All-up weight: 17,800kg (39,240lb)
Maximum speed: Mach 2.2 (2,338km/h; 1,449mph)
Cruise speed: Mach 0.74
Operational ceiling: 65,615ft
Maximum range: 2,200km (1,367 miles)
Mission range: 800km (497 miles)
Accommodation: Pilot only.
Warload: A total of seven pylons under the wings (three each) and fuselage can carry a maximum of 4,500kg (9,920lb). Normal armament includes PL-2B and PL-7 air-to-air missiles, 57mm air-to-air rocket launchers or 90mm air-to-surface rocket launchers and Kh-31 anti-ship missile. A twin-barrel Type 23-2 23mm cannon is mounted under the fuselage.
First flown: 5 July 1969; 1996 (F-8IIM)
Entered service: Mid-1980s.

Shenyang F-8IIM

ShinMaywa US-1

FOUR-TURBOPROP SEARCH AND RESCUE AMPHIBIAN

ShinMaywa US-1 Japanese Maritime Self-Defence Force

TECHNICAL DATA

ShinMaywa US-1

Powerplants: Four General Electric T64-IHI-10J turboprops plus auxiliary T58-IHI-10-M2 providing blown air for flaps and tail surfaces
Developing: Main engines 2,535kW (3,400ehp); auxiliary 1,014kw (1,360shp)
Driving: Three-blade propellers
Span: 33.15m (108ft 9in)
Length: 33.46m (109ft 9.25in)
Height: 9.95m (32ft 7.75in)
All-up weight: 45,000kg (99,200lb) from land; 43,000kg (94,800lb) from water
Maximum speed: 511km/h (318mph)
Cruise speed: 426km/h (265mph)
Operational ceiling: 28,400ft
Maximum range: 3,815km (2,370 miles)
Typical mission range: 1,110km (690 miles)
Endurance: 6 hours
Accommodation: Crew of four plus up to 20 passengers or 12 stetcher cases with attendants
First flown: 16 October 1974 (from water); 3 December 1974 (from land)
Entered service: 5 March 1975

DEVELOPMENT

ShinMaywa began development of a modern flying boat for the Japanese Maritime Self-Defence Force in 1952, eventually modifying a Grumman UF-1 Albatross to act as a technology demonstrator for its SS-2 design. The modified Albatross first flew on 25 December 1962, using five engines – two standard Wright R-1820 radials, two P&W R-1340 radials, and a General Electric T58 turboshaft mounted in the aft cabin to blow air over the flaps and tail to generate extra lift. The development contract for an aircraft to fulfil the PX-S anti-submarine requirement was awarded in January 1966, by which time ShinMaywa was well advanced with its prototype. This first flew on 5 October 1967 and had four GE T64 engines mounted on the wings, plus a T58 positioned at the fuselage/wing joint to provide blown air for the flaps. After delivery to the JMSDF on 31 July 1968 for trials, type approval was given in late 1970. Eventually 23 were built, including prototypes and pre-production aircraft, and the

survivors were retired by 1989, its role being passed to the Lockheed Orion. The fully amphibious search and rescue US-1 was similar to the PS-1 except for its undercarriage and was soon upgraded with improved engines to US-1A standard – a retrofit programme brought all models up to this standard. Production continues at a low rate. A proposed interim upgrade to US-1Kai standard would include 3,356kW (4,500shp) Rolls-Royce AE2100 turboprops, a pressurised upper hull and composites wing structure. The successor US-X would improve further on the US-1Kai; neither have yet been funded.

CURRENT SERVICE

A total of 18 US-1s had been ordered by the Japanese Maritime Self-Defence Force by FY1999, with another due to be ordered during 2000. Ten are currently in service with No 71 SAR Squadron (Dai 71 Koku-tai) based at Iwakuni AM with permanent detachments based at Atsugi and Iwo Jima.

SPECIAL FEATURES

The world's largest current production amphibian, the US-1 is of entirely conventional design, built of metal throughout. The single-step planing hull has a spray deflector strake and spray suppressor around the nose area, the latter forcing water downwards to reduce the chance of spray reaching the propellers. The T-tail improves low-speed handling. A range of high-lift devices including slats, overwing spoilers and flaps, the inner parts of which can be set at up to 80° of droop, give good STOL characteristics.

VARIANTS

The **PS-1** was the initial anti-submarine amphibian; the **US-1** is the fully amphibious SAR version. The manufacturer's designation is SS-2A.

ShinMaywa US-1
Japanese Maritime Self-Defence Force

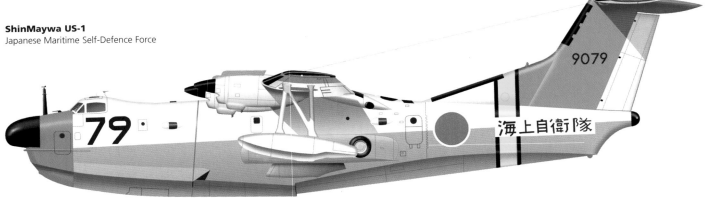

Shorts Skyvan

TWIN-ENGINED SHORT-FIELD UTILITY TRANSPORT

Shorts Skyvan 3M Royal Thai Police

TECHNICAL DATA

Shorts SC.7 Skyvan Series 3M

Powerplants: Two Garrett (now Honeywell)
TPE331-2-201A turboprops
Developing: 533kW (715shp)
Driving: Three-blade propellers
Span: 19.79m (64ft 11in)
Length: 12.21m (40ft 1in)
Height: 4.60m (15ft 1in)
All-up weight: 6,214kg (13,700lb)
Maximum speed: 324 km/h (202 mph)
Cruise speed: 311 km/h (193 mph)
Operational ceiling: 22,000ft
Maximum range: 1,075km (670 miles)
Mission range: 386km (240 miles)
Accommodation: One- or two-pilot operation plus
22 troops in main cabin, alternatively 16 paratroops
plus dispatcher, 12 stretcher cases plus two
attendants, or 5,200lb (2,358kg) of freight.
Warload: None
First flown: 17 January 1963 (piston-engined);
October 1963 (turboprop)
Entered service: 8 June 1966 (civilian)

DEVELOPMENT

Design of the Skyvan started as a private venture in 1959, using as its basis the Miles HDM.105, itself a derivative of the Miles Aerovan. The new design incorporated the results of Miles Aircraft's research into high-aspect ratio wings, with Shorts adapting the Aerovan's wing design for the Skyvan. The design was initially known as the PD.36 but had become the SC.7 by the time the prototype, fitted with piston engines and round cabin windows, first flew. Once a Treasury grant had been procured, the Skyvan went into production and initial aircraft off the line were fitted with Astazou turboprops. Sales of the Skyvan 1 and 2 series reached nine before its replacement, the Garrett-powered Skyvan 3, was introduced in 1968. The prototype military Skyvan 3M followed in 1970, and production continued until 1985, by which time 152 had been built, including prototypes; the last aircraft, for the Amiri Guard Air Wing at Sharjah, was completed at the end of that year.

CURRENT SERVICE

In total 58 Skyvans were sold to military users and those with current fleets are the air forces of Austria, Dubai, Ghana, Indonesia, Oman, Yemen, the Botswana and Guyana Defence Forces, and the Nepalese Army. No longer using the type are the Mauritanian and Singaporean Air Forces; the Argentine Navy; the Ecuadorean Army; Lesotho, Malawi and Thai Police Forces and the Panama National Guard. Among the roles undertaken by Skyvans are paratrooping, supply dropping, troop transport, casualty evaluation, search and rescue, environmental protection and general freight transport. The first military operator of the Skyvan was Austria, which acquired two Series 3s (later upgraded to 3M) in 1969 and these will remain in service until at least 2010.

SPECIAL FEATURES

The Skyvan has a distinctly box-like appearance, as it is built around a 1.98m (6ft 6in) square cargo deck; some aircraft have cargo loading rollers fitted. A high tailplane supports twin fins to provide good clearance over the one-piece rear loading ramp. The high aspect ratio wing is supported by struts from wheel sponsons to wing mid-points. The tricycle undercarriage is not retractable. Its roomy fuselage and a good STOL performance meant that the aircraft was able to take on a variety of military transport roles.

VARIANTS

The main military version is the **Skyvan 3M**. The **Skyvan 3M-200**, introduced in 1982, had a higher maximum take-off weight, but was basically similar. A proposed AEW version of the Skyvan, using a Thorn EMI Skymaster radar housed in a large nose radome and extra tail fins to aid stability, was not produced.

Shorts Skyvan 3M Royal Nepalese Army Air Corps

Shorts 330/C-23 Sherpa

TWIN-ENGINED HIGH-WING TACTICAL TRANSPORT

C-23A Sherpa United States Air Force

DEVELOPMENT

Originally known as the SD3-30 as a replacement for the Douglas DC-3, the Shorts 330 was assisted by a change in American FAA rules that allowed regional airlines to use aircraft up to 30 seats. The Shorts 330 built on the success of the earlier Skyvan, and retained many features, including the latter's 1.93m (6ft 4in) cabin cross-section. Shorts announced in 1982 that it was starting production of the 330UTT, a utility tactical transport; and the Sherpa, a freight version. The first customer for the 330UTT was Thailand, which eventually bought two for the Army plus a further two for the Police. These were followed by a single example for the United Arab Emirates. The Sherpa was successful in a competition run by the USAF for a light transport to undertake its European Distribution System role, defeating the CASA 212 and Dash 7. An order for 18 was received in March 1984, and all were delivered to the EDS hub at Zweibrücken in Germany by the following December; they were returned to the US following the reduction of US forces in Europe. The US Army ordered ten C-23Bs Sherpas to replace some of its C-7 Caribou fleet on 26 October 1988, and these were delivered from 1990, followed by a further six in 1992.

CURRENT SERVICE

The major user of the Shorts 330 series is the US Army, which has 19 C-23 Sherpas (including some transferred from the USAF) on charge for transport duties; the USAF operates at least three in the same role. Further afield, the Royal Thai Border Police Aviation continues to operate two 330UTTs for transport duties; a single 330UTT is used by the United Arab Emirates Air Force Central Air Command, based in Dubai.

SPECIAL FEATURES

The aircraft has a high wing and twin-tailed tailplane plus a box fuselage, designed to simplify the loading of a variety of freight, and a quick-change cabin interior adds flexibility. The Sherpa has a rear loading cargo ramp which can be operated from both inside and outside to allow through loading of freight.

VARIANTS

Basic civilian version were the **Shorts 330-100** and **-200**; utility tactical transport version is designated **330UTT**. The **C-23A Sherpa** is the USAF version without cabin windows; **C-23B** for US Army National Guard has strengthened wings, higher-powered engines and increased maximum take-off weight.

TECHNICAL DATA

Shorts C-23A Sherpa

Powerplants: Two Pratt & Whitney Canada PT6A-45R turboprops
Developing: 893kW (1,198 shp)
Driving: Five-blade propellers
Span: 22.81m (74ft 10in)
Length: 17.69m (58ft 0.5in)
Height: 5.00m (16ft 5in)
All-up weight: 11,612kg (25,600lb)
Maximum speed: 359km/h (223mph)
Cruise speed: 333km/h (207mph)
Operational ceiling: 20,000ft
Maximum range: 1,912km (1,188 miles)
Mission range: 827km (514 miles)
Accommodation: Crew of two plus optional third; main cabin holds 30 passengers, 27 paratroopers, 15 stretchers or two Land Rover-sized vehicles.
Warload: None
First flown: 22 August 1974 (civilian); 23 December 1982 (C-23A)
Entered service: 24 August 1976 (civil); 1985 (C-23A)

C-23B Sherpa United States Army

Shorts Tucano

TWO-SEAT BASIC/ADVANCED TURBOPROP TRAINER

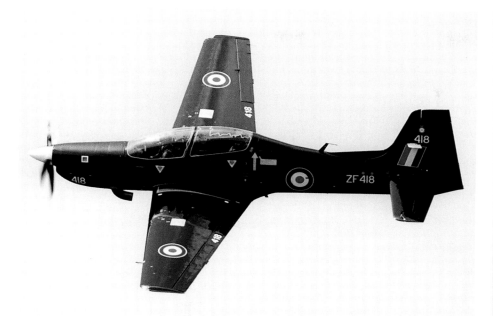

Shorts Tucano T1 Royal Air Force

TECHNICAL DATA

Shorts Tucano T1

Powerplant: One Garrett (now Honeywell)
TPE331-12B turboprop
Developing: 820 kW (1,100shp)
Driving: four-blade propeller
Span: 11.28m (37ft 0in)
Length: 9.86m (32ft 4.25in)
Height: 3.40m (11ft 1.75in)
All-up weight: 3,600kg (7,937lb)
Maximum speed: 513 km/h (319 mph)
Cruise speed: 411 km/h (255 mph)
Operational ceiling: 30,000ft
Maximum range: 3,317 km/h (2,061 miles)
Mission range: typically 1,767 km/h (1,099 miles)
Endurance: 5 hours 12 minutes
Accommodation: Instructor plus student
Warload: Export versions have four optional
underwing hardpoints for total of 1,000kg
(2,205lb). Weapons carried can include 250kg
bombs, LAU-32 and Matra F2b rocket launchers
and FN Herstal 12.7mm machine gun pods.
First flown: 11 April 1986 (demonstrator);
30 December 1986 (first production)
Entered service: 26 June 1987 with A&AEE;
16 June 1988 with CFS

DEVELOPMENT

Developed from Embraer's EMB312 Tucano (which is described separately), in March 1985 the Shorts Tucano won the RAF's AST 412 competition for a replacement for the ageing Jet Provost, for which a heavily modified and rebuilt Embraer example served as prototype. These modifications resulted in only 20 per cent commonality with the Embraer example, and included a higher-powered engine, which provided significantly improved rate of climb and higher low-level speeds; fuselage modifications to extend fatigue life to 12,000 hours; strengthened flying controls and canopy; and upgraded instrumentation. The cockpit layout in RAF examples mirrors that of the BAe Hawk, which follows it in the training syllabus. The first RAF unit to receive the Tucano was the Central Flying School at Scampton. This was followed by No 7 Flying Training School at Linton-on-Ouse where the first course began in December 1989; later recipients were

No 3 FTS at Cranwell and No 6 FTS at Finningley. A review of training procedures has now seen the fleet concentrated with No 1 FTS. Aside from the RAF's order for 130, there were two export customers for the Shorts-built Tucano. The first of these was Kenya, which ordered a dozen T51s in 1988 for use in the weapons training role, with the initial aircraft being delivered on 14 June 1990. The second customer was Kuwait, which ordered 16 for the training role, but the outbreak of the Gulf War before deliveries could take place, meant the aircraft were stored until the cessation of hostilities and reconstruction of air bases.

CURRENT SERVICE

Within the RAF, No 1 FTS currently has a fleet of 78 Tucanos at Linton-on-Ouse, from which the Central Flying School draws aircraft as required. The Kenyan Air Force has 11 T51s based at Laikipia and Kuwait Air Force has 16 T52s.

SPECIAL FEATURES

The Shorts Tucano is superficially similar to the Embraer model, with major visible differences being in the nose area, which is reprofiled to accommodate the engine, an increased tail fillet, and a ventral airbrake. Export Tucanos have optional underwing hardpoints.

VARIANTS

The RAF version is the **T1** and export models are the **T51** (Kenya) and **T52** (Kuwait).

SEE ALSO: EMBRAER EMB-312 TUCANO

Shorts Tucano T1 Royal Air Force

SIAI S.208M

FIVE-SEAT TRAINER AND LIAISON/COMMUNICATIONS AIRCRAFT

SIAI S.208M Italian Air Force

DEVELOPMENT

The four-seat all-metal SIAI S.205 was developed in the early 1960s as a competitor to the Piper Cherokee family, but was larger and could accept more powerful engines up to 224kW (300hp). It made its first flight on 4 May 1965. Fixed and retractable undercarriage versions were both offered, and 'green' S.205s were shipped to the United States where they were finished by Waco Aircraft as the S.220 Sirius; by the time that production finally ended in 1979 (with a late batch of 40 for the Aero Club d'Italia – general production had ended in 1972), 228 had been completed. The improved five-seat, retractable-undercarriage S.208 was introduced in 1967 and contained approximately

60% commonality of parts with the S.205; this later became the standard version and 85 were built. Of these, 45 were for the Italian Air Force under the designation S.208M. The SIAI S.210 twin-engined six-seat development of the S.205 first flew on 19 February 1970; only two prototypes were built.

CURRENT SERVICE

The S.208M continues to fulfil an important liaison role within the Italian Air Force today. No fewer than 11 front-line Stormi operate the type, in each case within a Squadriglie Collegamenti reflecting the Stormo designation (for example, 602ª SC forms part of 2° Stormo). In addition, the Centro Volo a Vela at Guidonia has a fleet of bright orange aircraft which act as glider tugs for the school's large sailplane fleet. Apart from Italy, the only other current military user of the S.208M is the Tunisian Air Force (a traditional user of Italian-built aircraft, with fleets of MB.326s

and SF.260s). It has operated two S.208Ms on liaison, communication and light transport duties for the last 20 years.

SPECIAL FEATURES

The S.208M is a cantilever low-wing monoplane; its constant-chord wings have wing-root fillets. There are no doors on the retractable undercarriage and the nosewheel protrudes slightly. Wingtip tanks each containing 115 litres (25 Imp gallons) of fuel can be fitted for long distance flights. In addition to the starboard-side main door, an optional second door can be fitted on the port side. Aircraft operated by the CVV have been modified for glider towing duties.

VARIANTS

The **S.205** was the initial model from which the **S.208** evolved; unlike its civilian counterpart, the **S.208M** military version has a jettisonable cabin door.

TECHNICAL DATA

SIAI S.208M

Powerplant: One Textron Lycoming O-540-E4A5 flat six-cylinder piston engine
Developing: 194kW (260hp)
Driving: Two-blade propeller
Span: 10.86m (35ft 7.5in)
Length: 8.00m (26ft 3in)
Height: 2.89m (9ft 5.75in)
All-up weight: 1,500kg (3,306lb)
Maximum speed: 320 km/h (199mph)
Cruise speed: 300 km/h (187mph)
Operational ceiling: 17,725ft
Maximum range: 2,000km (1,250 miles)
Mission range: 1,200km (746 miles)
Endurance: 6 hours 40 minutes
Accommodation: Pilot and up to four passengers
Warload: None
First flown: 22 May 1967
Entered service: Spring 1968

SIAI S.208

SIAI-Marchetti SF.260

SINGLE-ENGINED PRIMARY MILITARY/CIVIL TRAINER WITH SECONDARY LIGHT ATTACK ROLE

SIAI-Marchetti SF.260MB Belgian Air Force

TECHNICAL DATA

SIAI-Marchetti SF.260

Powerplant: One Textron Lycoming AIO-540-D4A5 piston engine
Developing: 194kW (260hp)
Driving: two-blade propeller
Span: 8.35m (27ft 5in)
Length: 7.10m (23ft 3.5in)
Height: 2.41m (7ft 11in)
All-up weight: 1,200kg (2,645lb)
Maximum speed: 347km/h (187kt)
Operational ceiling: 19,000ft
Maximum range: 1,490km (926 miles)
Mission range: 148km (92 miles) in light attack role
Endurance: 1hr 25min in light attack role
Accommodation: Crew of three
Warload: The SF.260W has two weapons pylons to carry 300kg (661lb) of ordnance; gun pods, rocket launchers and bombs can be fitted.
First flown: 15 July 1964 (SF.260); May 1972 (SF.262E)
Entered service: 1966

DEVELOPMENT

Designed by Stelio Frati in the early 1960s as the SF.250, the design was taken over under licence by SIAI and initially marketed as an 'upmarket' civilian aircraft. The SF.260E was entered into the USAF EFS competition in 1991 by SIAI and Sabreliner but was not successful, but has since been marketed in both civil and military versions. The SF.260M series is a dedicated military version, with a second letter suffix indicating the operating country, as does the ground attack SF.260W Warrior. Production closed during 1998, with over 850 built, but was restarted in 1999 by Aermacchi (which had acquired the programme on 1 January 1997) to meet new and repeat orders for a further sixty or more aircraft, including examples for Belgium, Italy, Uruguay and Venezuela. The new model has wing refinements, a stronger airframe and a higher all-up weight of 1,200kg (2,645lb); airframe fatigue life has been extended to 15,000 hours. The SF.260TP turboprop first flew on 8 July 1980 and is virtually identical to the standard SF.260 apart from the nose area; it has four underwing hardpoints to carry a similar range of weaponry to that of the SF.260W. Over 60 had been built by 1999 for five air forces and production continues.

CURRENT SERVICE

The Italian Air Force purchased 45 SF.260AMs in 1976 for initial screening and basic training; the survivors now fly with 70° Stormo at Latina. The Irish Air Corps has seven current SF.260WEs from ten delivered in 1977, flying with the Basic Flying Training Squadron at Baldonnel. Other users of the standard SF.260 model include: Belgium (SF.260MB/MD); Brunei (SF.260W); Burundi (SF.260W); Chad (two SF.260WLs survive from the three captured from Libya during border disputes); the Democratic Republic of Congo (SF.260MC); Haiti (SF.260TP); Libya (SF.260WL); the Philippines (SF.260MP/WP); Singapore (SF.260MS/WS); Sri Lanka (SF.260W); Thailand (SF.260MT); Tunisia (SF.260C/WT); Turkey (SF.260D); Uganda (SF.250W); Venezuela (SF.260E), Zambia (SF.260MZ) and Zimbabwe (SF.260M/W/F). SF.260TPs are in service with Dubai, Ethiopia, Haiti, the Philippines, Sri Lanka and Zimbabwe.

SPECIAL FEATURES

The SF.260 offers flexible training and light attack operations and is particularly popular with smaller air forces where it can fulfil several roles from training to ground attack.

VARIANTS

Original **SF.260A/B/C/Ds** were almost entirely used for civilian operations and are out of production, as is the **SF.260M** military version of the **SF.260A**. The basic **SF.260E** (civil version) and military **SF.260F** are currently available and are fully aerobatic primary trainers; **Warrior** nomenclature is applied to light attack models. The **SF.260TP**, powered by a 261kW (350shp) Allison 250-B17D turboprop, is identifiable by its three-blade propeller and reprofiled nose.

SIAI-Marchetti SF.260MD
Belgian Air Force

Sikorsky S-58T

TWIN-TURBINE UTILITY HELICOPTER

Sikorsky S-58T

TECHNICAL DATA

Sikorsky S-58T

Powerplant: One Pratt & Whitney Canada PT6T-6 Twin-Pac turboshaft
Developing: 1,398kW (1,875shp)
Driving: Four-blade main and tail rotors
Main rotor diameter: 17.07m (56ft 0in)
Fuselage length: 14.25m (46ft 9in)
Height: 4.85m (15ft 11in)
All-up weight: 5,896kg (13,000lb)
Maximum speed: 222km/h (138mph)
Cruise speed: 204km/h (127mph)
Single-engine ceiling: 4,200ft
Range: 481km (299 miles)
Accommodation: Two crew and up to 18 troops
First flown: 20 September 1954 (S-58);
19 August 1970 (S-58T)
Entered service: 1971 (S-58T)

DEVELOPMENT

The evolution of the S-58T can be traced back to the original piston-engined Sikorsky S-58 design of the early 1950s. This achieved considerable success with civilian operators and saw widespread service with several branches of the US armed forces, including the Army as the H-34, the Navy as the HSS-1 and the USMC as the HUS-1. Many others were provided to friendly nations under the Military Assistance Program and it also formed the basis for the Westland Wessex, which was built in considerable numbers in the UK, both for home and overseas customers. In the late 1960s, Sikorsky turned its attention to upgrading the basic airframe and conceived the idea of fitting modern and more reliable turboshaft engines. The result was the S-58T, which first flew in prototype form in the summer of 1970. As it turned out, no new-build examples were produced, but following trials with the prototype, Sikorsky successfully marketed the re-engined version and by 1981 had completed almost 150 conversions of existing S-58s for civil and military customers. These initially used the PT6T-3 turboshaft rated at 1,343kW (1,800shp), but later helicopters were fitted with the slightly more powerful PT6T-6. In 1981, however, Sikorsky sold all S-58T rights to California Helicopter International, which continues to support the type today. There remains only two military operators of the type today.

CURRENT SERVICE

The majority of S-58T conversions were delivered to civilian operators, but a handful of air arms around the world opted to modify existing H-34 helicopters. These included Argentina and South Korea, but at the time of writing, the only operators are the air forces of Indonesia and Thailand. Indonesia acquired its first S-58T conversions some 20 years ago and still possesses about 10, while Thailand retains approximately 15, all of which serve with No 201 Squadron at Lop Buri.

SPECIAL FEATURES

The basic attributes of the original S-58 helicopter were retained for the turbine-powered derivative, including the strut-braced main undercarriage units below the cockpit and a single tailwheel beneath the aft fuselage. The change from a piston to a turbine engine installation did, however, result in significant change to the nose contours so as to accommodate twin air-intakes in the extreme forward section, thus giving the type an extended 'chin' that distinguishes this version from the original S-58 design.

VARIANTS

Although the original **S-58** spawned a number of military **H-34** derivatives for such diverse tasks as anti-submarine warfare, troop/utility transport, pilot training and VIP airlift, the turbine-powered **S-58T** has been rather less versatile. Indonesian and Thai helicopters of this type that remain in service have only ever been utilised for general transport tasks, but Argentina did have two for VIP duties by the presidential flight, although they have long since been retired from service.

Sikorsky S-58T

Sikorsky S-61/SH-3 Sea King

MULTI-PURPOSE HELICOPTER

Sikorsky SH-3 Sea King Italian Navy

TECHNICAL DATA

Sikorsky SH-3H Sea King

Powerplants: Two General Electric T58-GE-10 turboshafts

Developing: 1,044kW (1,400shp)

Driving: Five-blade main and six blade tail rotors

Main rotor diameter: 18.90m (62ft 0in)

Fuselage length: 16.69m (54ft 9in)

Height: 5.13m (16ft 10in)

All-up weight: 9,526kg (21,000lb)

Maximum speed: 267 km/h (166 mph)

Cruise speed: 219 km/h (136 mph)

Operational ceiling: 14,700ft

Maximum range: 1,005km (625 miles)

Accommodation: Pilot and co-pilot on flight deck; two sonar operators in cabin; room for 15 paratroops

Warload: Mk 46 or Mk 50 torpedoes to a total weight of 380kg (848lb).

First flown: 11 March 1959

Entered service: September 1961

DEVELOPMENT

Design work on the S-61 began in the mid-1950s. US Navy designation HSS-2 was applied and in the US military rationalisation programme of 1962, this became the SH-3 Sea King. These were joined by the S-61R series, the prototype of which first flew on 31 March 1960 and was the basis for the USAF's HH-3 'Jolly Green Giant' and the US Coast Guard's HH-3F Pelican. Licensed production was undertaken by Agusta and Mitsubishi, as well as Westland in the UK (described separately). Assembly also took place in other countries, including Canada. The Sea King was the US Navy's first all-weather service helicopter and saw action during the Vietnam War, operating with the US Navy in its primary anti-submarine warfare role as well as performing carrier 'plane guard' and combat SAR – it also took part in the Gulf War. The US Air Force also took the HH-3 to both locations for combat SAR versions.

CURRENT SERVICE

US Navy and US Marine Corps jointly have around 115 H-3s of various marks in service in a variety of roles,

including ASW, ASR, utility and VIP duties; other operators of the ASW version include Argentina, Brazil, Canada, Denmark, Iran, Italy, Japan, Peru and Spain, many of which also use them for SAR. VIP versions are flown by the Argentine, Italian and Saudi Arabian Air Forces; HH-3s are used by Italy and Tunisia for SAR and liaison.

SPECIAL FEATURES

Twin engines, mounted above the voluminous main cabin, and good single-engine capability reduce the possibility of ditching, for which the Sea King's boat-like hull and stabilising sponsons provide good flotation. Members of the S-61R/HH-3 series can be differentiated by their rear loading ramp and nosewheel configuration; they also have large aerial refuelling probes mounted on the starboard side of the nose.

VARIANTS

The initial **HSS-2/SH-3A** version was used for anti-submarine warfare; nine were converted to **RH-3As** for mine countermeasures. The improved **SH-3D** was

a refined and enhanced version with improved AN/APN-182 Doppler in place of the older AN/APN-130 unit. Armament was reduced in comparison to SH-3A; an improvement programme started in 1987; the **S-61D-3** is similar. **VH-3D** is presidential/VIP version. The **SH-3G/S-61D-4** of 1970 extended cargo and utility role and increased weaponry. **SH-3H/UH-3H** introduced further equipment for anti-ship missile detection and many other improvements – 163 were produced from existing aircraft. The **HH-3** was used mainly for combat search and rescue. The licence-produced **Mitsubishi HSS-2** was similar to S-61A; the **HSS-2A** was similar to SH-3D and **HSS-2B** is similar to SH-3G. SAR **S-61A/A-1** versions were used on scientific work, and **S-61AH** for SAR. **Agusta AS-61A-4** (of which 35 were licence-built) is a multi-role version; various upgrades have been made.

SEE ALSO: WESTLAND SEA KING AND WESTLAND COMMANDO

SH-3D Sea King Brazilian Navy

Sikorsky S-65/CH-53 Sea Stallion

TWIN-TURBOSHAFT HEAVYLIFT HELICOPTER

USA

Sikorsky CH-53G German Army

Sikorsky MH-53J United States Air Force

TECHNICAL DATA

Sikorsky MH-53J Pave Low III

Powerplants: Two General Electric T64-GE-7A turboshafts
Developing: 2,935kW (3,936shp)
Driving: Six-blade main rotor and four-blade tail rotor
Main rotor diameter: 22.02m (72ft 3in)
Fuselage length: 20.47m (67ft 2in) excluding refuelling probe
Height: 7.60m (24ft 11in)
All-up weight: 19,051kg (42,000lb)
Maximum speed: 315km/h (196mph)
Cruise speed: 278km/h (173mph)
Operational ceiling: 20,400ft
Range: 868km (540 miles)
Accommodation: Four crew and accommodation for up to 50 passengers
Payload: 9,072kg (20,000lb)
First flown: 14 October 1964 (S-65 prototype); 1986 (MH-53J)
Entered service: 1965 (CH-53A); 1987 (MH-53J)

DEVELOPMENT

Conceived to satisfy a US Marine Corps requirement for a replacement for the CH-37 Mojave, the S-65 was one of the largest and most powerful helicopters to be developed up to that time. Flight testing began in late 1964 and such was the urgency of the requirement that production examples of the CH-53A entered service with the Marines in late 1965. They were soon despatched to Vietnam, where they proved to be particularly valuable assets. The availability of uprated engines and other refinements resulted in the CH-53D for the Marines, while other versions joined the USAF for combat search and rescue, quickly becoming known as the 'Super Jolly Green Giant'. More recently, the basic design laid the foundation of the even more powerful S-80 Super Stallion (see separate entry).

CURRENT SERVICE

Examples of the S-65 family are presently flown by the US Air Force (TH-53A and MH-53J/M), the US Marine Corps (CH-53D), Germany (CH-53G), Iran (RH-53D) and Israel (Yas'ur 2000).

SPECIAL FEATURES

Despite its bulk, the S-65 is essentially conventional in layout and incorporates a main rotor and anti-torque tail rotor configuration, although the engines are mounted on either side of the upper fuselage section. It has a retractable tricycle undercarriage, with the mainwheel units housed in sponsons that serve as attachment points for external fuel tanks. Access to the cabin is via forward side doors or a rear loading ramp.

VARIANTS

Numerous versions of the basic S-65 layout emerged during the course of manufacture and post-production modification, but few derivatives remain today, even though many Sea Stallions are still active with the US and overseas air arms. Some Marine Corps heavy helicopter squadrons retain the **CH-53D**, but the original USAF **HH-53B/C** and **CH-53C** versions are no longer in use, with survivors having been transferred to special operations and upgraded to the so-called 'Pave Low III' standard. This work included installation of terrain-following radar, FLIR sensors, additional countermeasures and compatibility with night vision goggles. Upon modification, these were initially designated as **MH-53Hs**, but further enhancement led to the **MH-53J** in the late 1980s and most recently to the **MH-53M**. A few former Marine Corps **CH-53As** are also used for training by the USAF as the **TH-53A**. Turning to overseas air arms, Israel operates the **Yas'ur 2000** version, essentially an upgraded Sea Stallion with enhanced electronic warfare systems, multi-function cockpit displays, a new mission computer and a new autopilot. Co-production in Germany by VFW resulted in the **CH-53G** and most of the 112 delivered are still in service with the Heeresflieger, while Iran may still use a couple of the half-a-dozen **RH-53Ds** delivered for mine countermeasures duties.

SEE ALSO: SIKORSKY S-80 SUPER STALLION/SEA DRAGON

Sikorsky S-70A Black Hawk

TWIN-TURBOSHAFT UTILITY TRANSPORT HELICOPTER

Sikorsky S-70 Hong Kong

TECHNICAL DATA

Sikorsky UH-60L Black Hawk

Powerplants: Two General Electric T700-GE-701C turboshafts
Developing: 1,342kW (1,800shp)
Driving: Four-blade main and tail rotors
Main rotor diameter: 16.36m (53ft 8in)
Fuselage length: 15.26m (50ft 0.75in)
Height: 5.13m (16ft 10in)
All-up weight: 11,113kg (24,500lb)
Never-exceed speed: 361km/h (224mph)
Cruise speed: 294km/h (183mph)
Operational ceiling: 19,140ft
Maximum ferry range: 2,222km (1,381 miles)
Range: 584km (363 miles)
Accommodation: Three crew and up to 14 fully-equipped troops in high-density configuration
Warload: The UH-60 can operate with a variety of weaponry, including AGM-114 Hellfire anti-armour missiles, FIM-92 Stinger air-to-air missiles, M56 mine dispensing pods and unguided rockets; in the troop transport role, it is often fitted with two pintle-mounted 7.62mm Miniguns
Payload: 1,197kg (2,640lb) internally; up to 3,629kg (8,000lb) as underslung load
First flown: 17 October 1974 (YUH-60A prototype); 22 March 1988 (UH-60L prototype)
Entered service: June 1979 (UH-60A); October 1989 (UH-60L)

DEVELOPMENT

The origins of the Black Hawk date back to the mid-1960s when the US Army began contemplating a replacement for the hugely successful Bell UH-1 Iroquois. However, the Vietnam War forestalled serious study for several years and it was not until January 1972 that the Army requested proposals for its UTTAS (Utility Tactical Transport Aircraft System) requirement. Sikorsky responded with the S-70, which was given the Army designation UH-60, while Boeing Vertol's competitor became the UH-61. Comparative evaluation in 1975-76 resulted in the Sikorsky machine emerging victorious, with the initial production UH-60A model entering Army service with the 101st Airborne Division in mid-1979. Newer versions have followed, and production continues today.

CURRENT SERVICE

Versions of the basic S-70A Black Hawk serve with all branches of the US armed forces (see variants) and have been exported to Argentina, Australia, Bahrain, Brazil, Brunei, Chile, Colombia, Egypt, Hong Kong, Israel, Japan, Jordan, South Korea, Malaysia, Mexico, Morocco, Philippines, Saudi Arabia and Turkey.

SPECIAL FEATURES

Although incorporating new technology, the S-70 is conventional in appearance, with twin turboshaft engines situated high on the fuselage sides above the cabin, a non-retractable tailwheel undercarriage and a large variable-incidence tailplane. One particularly noteworthy feature added during production is the external stores support system (ESSS), which allows additional fuel and/or weapons to be carried, while the latest examples embody 'glass cockpits' and digital avionics.

VARIANTS

An array of Black Hawk derivatives have emerged since 1979 and new ones continue to appear. Basic troop-carrying versions with the US Army are the **UH-60A** and **UH-60L**, although an upgrade project is expected to result in the advent of the **UH-60L+** and **UH-60X**. Other US Army versions are the **EH-60A** battlefield ECM detection and jamming system; the **MH-60A**, **MH-60K**, **AH-60L** and **MH-60L** for support of special operations forces; the **UH-60A(C)** for battlefield command and control; and the **UH-60A(Q)** and **UH-60Q** for casualty evacuation. Export equivalents generally use the **S-70A** designation, followed by a suffix number to identify the customer (eg **S-70A-9** for Australia). However, some, like Japan's **UH-60J** and **UH-60JA** and South Korea's **UH-60P**, do not follow this pattern. Variations on the basic Black Hawk theme have also been delivered to the USAF (**HH-60G** and **MH-60G**) for combat search-and-rescue; the US Navy (**CH-60S**) for fleet support transport tasks and the US Marine Corps (**VH-60N**) for executive VIP airlift.

SEE ALSO: SIKORSKY S-70B SEAHAWK

UH-60A Black Hawk
United States Army

371

Sikorsky S-70B Seahawk

TWIN-TURBOSHAFT ASW HELICOPTER

Sikorsky SH-60B United States Navy

TECHNICAL DATA

Sikorsky SH-60B Seahawk

Powerplants: Two General Electric T700-GE-401C turboshafts
Developing: 1,342kW (1,800shp)
Driving: Four-blade main and tail rotors
Main rotor diameter: 16.36m (53ft 8in)
Fuselage length: 15.26m (50ft 0.75in)
Height: 5.18m (17ft 0in)
All-up weight: 9,926kg (21,884lb)
Dash speed: 234km/h (145mph) at 1,525m (5,000ft)
Range: 278km (173 miles) with one-hour loiter time
Accommodation: Pilot and two system operators
Warload: Available weapon options include two Mk 46 or Mk 50 torpedoes and AGM-119B Penguin anti-ship attack missile; is also compatible with AGM-114 Hellfire air-to-surface missile
Payload: 3,629kg (8,000lb)
First flown: 12 December 1979 (YSH-60B prototype); 11 February 1983 (first production SH-60B)
Entered service: 1983 (initial deliveries)

DEVELOPMENT

Based on the S-70A which had been chosen by the US Army as the UH-60A Black Hawk, development of the S-70B Seahawk started in the late 1970s. In 1977, Sikorsky won the US Navy's LAMPS Mk III (Light Airborne Multi-Purpose System) requirement for a new helicopter to deploy aboard surface combatant vessels for ASW and anti-ship missile defence duties. Five development prototypes were ordered and the first of these made its maiden flight in December 1979, with a contract for an initial batch of 18 production examples following in FY82. Subsequent development led to the appearance of variations on the basic theme and a current upgrade programme is expected to result in most US Navy Seahawks being eventually brought to SH-60R standard.

CURRENT SERVICE

The US Navy is the principal operator and currently has some 280 Seahawks. Of this total, about 165 are basic SH-60Bs, which routinely deploy aboard frigates and destroyers, while there are also 75 SH-60Fs, which serve aboard aircraft carriers for close-in ASW protection. Finally, there are 40 HH-60Hs for combat search-and-rescue and special warfare support tasks. Another US operator is the Coast Guard, with a fleet of 42 HH-60J Jayhawks for search-and-rescue. Several overseas navies use the S-70, with Australia, Greece, Spain, Thailand and Turkey all acquiring examples from Sikorsky, while Japan is building the SH-60J version under licence.

SPECIAL FEATURES

Essentially similar to the S-70A, the S-70B incorporates several unique features in order to suit it for the naval role. These include a shortened wheelbase, with the tailwheel positioned much further forward so as to allow safe operation from landing platforms on ships at sea. A total of 25 sonobuoy launch tubes are sited in the port side of the cabin on the SH-60B, although these are not installed on the SH-60F or HH-60H/J versions. Search radar is fitted to the SH-60B, other mission equipment including a towed MAD (magnetic anomaly detector), although this will probably be omitted from the upgraded SH-60R.

VARIANTS

The **SH-60B** being the primary ASW/ASMD model at the present time. The **SH-60F** model lacks the avionics equipment associated with the LAMPS mission, but is fitted with dipping sonar, while the **HH-60H** and **HH-60J** are less complex derivatives optimised for SAR missions. The export equivalents of the SH-60B are generally referred to as **S-70Bs**, again with suffix numbers to identify the customer (eg **S-70B-28** for Turkey). The forthcoming **SH-60R** will combine features of the SH-60B such as search radar and those of the SH-60F, like the dipping sonar.

SEE ALSO: SIKORSKY S-70A BLACKHAWK

Sikorsky SH-60F United States Navy

Sikorsky S-70C

TWIN-TURBOSHAFT UTILITY HELICOPTER

Sikorsky S-70C Taiwanese Navy

DEVELOPMENT

Fundamentally similar to the S-70A Black Hawk and S-70B Seahawk versions referred to in more detail elsewhere, the S-70C emerged in response to very limited demand from civil operators. However, this designation has also been used by a modest number of Black Hawk and Seahawk helicopters destined for military service in areas where political sensitivities are a factor.

CURRENT SERVICE

As far as can be determined, only two air arms are currently operating variations on the S-70C theme, specifically Brunei and Taiwan, and more details of the helicopters supplied to these nations can be found under 'variants'. The People's Republic of China also took delivery of some two dozen radar-equipped S-70Cs in 1984-85, although these were offered for sale in 1992 as a direct consequence of the US embargo on

spares imposed after the Tiananmen Square massacre. There is no evidence that a buyer was ever found and these helicopters are probably no longer operational.

SPECIAL FEATURES

Basically similar to the S-70A Black Hawk and S-70B Seahawk, although many do incorporate nose-radar as standard, in conjunction with other military equipment, such as the External Stores Support System. A luxury VIP cabin is a feature of the two S-70Cs supplied for use by the Sultan of Brunei.

VARIANTS

Versions of the **S-70C** supplied to export customers include the batch of radar-equipped machines that were delivered to the People's Republic of China in the mid-1980s. China's neighbour Taiwan has also received versions of the Black Hawk and Seahawk as the S-70C, these ostensibly civil helicopters being destined for

service with both the Air Force and Navy. Initial deliveries to Taiwan occurred in 1985-86, when 14 SAR-dedicated S-70Cs were received by the Air Force and given the local name **Blue Hawk**. Subsequently, in 1998, a further four were handed over to the Air Force, these radar-equipped S-70C-6s being known as **Super Blue Hawks**. In addition, Taiwan's Navy received 10 **S-70C(M)-1 Thunderhawks** in 1990-91, these essentially being configured for ASW tasks and roughly equivalent to the US Navy SH-60F Seahawk. Another 11 basically similar **S-70C(M)-2** helicopters were ordered by the Taiwanese Navy in 1997. The only other military examples of the type known to exist are two **S-70C-14s** delivered to Brunei in late 1986.

SEE ALSO: SIKORSKY S-70A BLACK HAWK AND S-70B SEAHAWK

Sikorsky S-70C Taiwanese Navy

TECHNICAL DATA

Sikorsky S-70C

Powerplants: Two General Electric CT7-2D turboshafts (or equivalent military T700 turboshafts)
Developing: 1,285kW (1,723shp)
Driving: Four-blade main and tail rotors
Main rotor diameter: 16.36m (53ft 8in)
Fuselage length: 15.26m (50ft 0.75in)
Height: 5.13m (16ft 10in)
All-up weight: 9,185kg (20,250lb)
Never-exceed speed: 361km/h (224mph)
Cruise speed: 268km/h (167mph)
Operational ceiling: 14,300ft
Range: 550km (342 miles)
Accommodation: Two crew and up to 19 passengers in high-density layout
Payload: 3,629kg (8,000lb) externally

Sikorsky S-76

TWIN-TURBINE GENERAL PURPOSE HELICOPTER

Sikorsky S-76C Spanish Air Force

DEVELOPMENT

Sikorsky announced its intention to proceed with the development of its S-76 in January 1975 and flew the first prototype just over two years later, in March 1977. Civil certification was awarded in November 1978, and the type has since achieved considerable sales success. Primarily aimed at the civilian market, further refinement and improvement led to the appearance of the S-76B, which flew in prototype form in 1984, followed by the S-76C prototype in 1990. In addition, two specialised military versions have been produced in modest quantities, firstly as the H-76 Eagle and in naval guise as the S-76N (originally designated H-76N).

CURRENT SERVICE

Approximately 500 examples of the Sikorsky S-76 have been completed since 1979 and production of the latest S-76C+ version is continuing. The majority have been delivered to civil customers, but a limited number of S-76s have been acquired by military services, principally for use in the communications/VIP role. Current operators of basic S-76 versions include Dubai, Panama and the Philippines, each with a single helicopter. Spain has eight S-76Cs for use in the training role with Ala 78 at Granada AB. Purpose-built military derivatives were delivered to the Philippines, which took delivery of around a dozen AUH-76 Eagles for counter-insurgency tasks from 1984, and to Thailand, which received six S-76Ns in 1996 for the Navy.

SPECIAL FEATURES

The S-76 has a conventional main and anti-torque tail-rotor configuration, in conjunction with a fully retractable tricycle undercarriage layout. Military derivatives have provisions for armament and other modifications, including installation of crew protective armour, self-sealing fuel tanks and provisions for pintle-mounted machine guns in the doorways.

VARIANTS

Almost 300 examples of the initial **S-76A** model were completed between 1979 and 1993, these being powered by Allison 250-C30 turboshafts. Production then concentrated mainly on the **S-76B**, which introduced more powerful Pratt & Whitney PT6B-36A engines in 1985, and just over 100 had been built by the time the last one was delivered in December 1997. The **S-76C**, which made its debut in 1991, originally featured Arriel 1S1 engines although these have since given way to the Arriel 2S1. Roughly equivalent to the S-76B, the **AUH-76 Eagle** COIN version is able to operate with armament that includes Herstal 12.7mm machine gun pods and other light weaponry, while the **S-76N** can use Herstal or Maramount M60D machine guns. More formidable ordnance options include rocket pods, torpedoes, mines and guided missiles such as TOW, Hellfire, Sea Skua and Stinger.

Sikorsky SH-76A(GP) Hong Kong Government Flying Service

TECHNICAL DATA

Sikorsky S-76C+

Powerplants: Two Turboméca Arriel 2S1 turboshafts
Developing: 638kW (856shp) for take-off
Driving: Four-blade main and tail rotors
Main rotor diameter: 13.41m (44ft 0in)
Fuselage length: 13.21m (43ft 4in)
Height: 4.42m (14ft 6in)
All-up weight: 5,307kg (11,700lb)
Maximum speed: 287km/h (178mph)
Cruise speed: 269km/h (166mph)
Operational ceiling: 12,700ft
Maximum range: 813km (505 miles)
Accommodation: One or two pilots and up to 13 passengers
Payload: 1,616kg (3,562lb)
First flown: 13 March 1977 (S-76A); 18 May 1990 (S-76C)
Entered service: 1979

Sikorsky S-80/CH-53E Super Stallion

THREE-TURBOSHAFT HEAVYLIFT HELICOPTER

CH-53E Super Stallion United States Marines Corps

DEVELOPMENT

A logical follow-on to the Sea Stallion, what ultimately became the Super Stallion entered development in 1973, when initial funding was appropriated by the US Navy. The first of two YCH-53E prototypes made its maiden flight in March 1974, with a production prototype following suit in December 1975. Progress was slow thereafter and it was not until the summer of 1981 that delivery of production CH-53Es got underway. In the meantime, design of the specialist MH-53E mine countermeasures version had also begun and this first flew in September 1983, with deliveries commencing in late June 1986.

CURRENT SERVICE

US Navy and Marine Corps units currently operate just over 200 examples of the H-53 series. By far the majority are standard CH-53E Super Stallion transport helicopters, of which about 160 equip Marine Corps heavylift squadrons on both the east and west coasts.

The remaining 40 are all MH-53E Sea Dragons, which are principally flown by Navy units on routine resupply tasks as well as mine clearance, but a handful also serve with the Marine Corps training squadron, which provides qualified aircrew to both services. The only export customer is Japan, which accepted its first S-80M in 1988. By 1994, Japan had purchased a total of 11, although one has since crashed.

SPECIAL FEATURES

Basically similar in appearance to the earlier S-65, the S-80 is considerably more powerful by virtue of having a third engine, mounted aft of the rotor mast and fed by an intake on the port side. A seven-blade main rotor is also standard, while both CH-53E and MH-53E versions are fitted with an in-flight refuelling probe, although this is not installed on the Japanese S-80M. As well as being able to refuel in flight, the MH-53E has greatly enlarged fuselage sponsons, which contain extra fuel to extend duration for mine clearance tasks.

VARIANTS

Two basic versions of the S-80 have been built, with production continuing at a low rate for the USMC. The principal model is the pure transport **CH-53E Super Stallion**, which was offered for export as the **S-80E**, although no orders resulted. The second derivative is the **MH-53E Sea Dragon**, which is optimised for mine countermeasures and is able to tow sleds carrying hydrofoil, acoustic and magnetic sensors through water. In practice, however, some of the Navy's MH-53E fleet is used for vertical replenishment missions in support of fleet activities, particularly with the 6th Fleet in the Mediterranean. The export equivalent of the MH-53E is known by Sikorsky as the **S-80M** and was purchased in limited quantities by Japan in the 1980s.

SEE ALSO: SIKORSKY S-65 SEA STALLION

CH-53E Super Stallion United States Marines Corps

TECHNICAL DATA

Sikorsky CH-53E Super Stallion

Powerplants: Three General Electric T64-GE-416 turboshafts
Developing: 2,756kW (3,696shp) for continuous operation
Driving: Seven-blade main and four-blade tail rotors
Main rotor diameter: 24.08m (79ft 0in)
Fuselage length: 22.35m (73ft 4in)
Height: 8.97m (29ft 5in)
All-up weight: 31,640kg (69,750lb) internal payload; 33,340kg (73,500lb) external payload
Maximum speed: 315km/h (196mph)
Cruise speed: 278km/h (173mph)
Operational ceiling: 18,500ft
Maximum ferry range: 2,074km (1,289 miles)
Accommodation: Three crew and up to 55 troops
Payload: 13,607kg (30,000lb) internal; 16,330kg (36,000lb) external
First flown: 1 March 1974 (YCH-53E prototype)
Entered service: June 1981 (initial delivery)

Singapore Aerospace A-4SU Super Skyhawk

SINGLE TURBOFAN ATTACK AIRCRAFT

A-4SU Super Skyhawk Republic of Singapore Air Force

DEVELOPMENT

Singapore first began operating A-4S Skyhawks in 1974. Although refurbished, these represented only a minimal improvement from the basic US Navy A-4B on which they were based. Subsequently, Singapore acquired almost 90 more surplus aircraft and it was these that provided the starting point for a much more sophisticated two-stage upgrade programme. The first stage involved re-engining and produced the A-4S-1, which had markedly improved performance, most notably with regard to acceleration, climb rate and dash speed, as well as reduced fuel consumption

TECHNICAL DATA

Singapore Aerospace A-4SU Super Skyhawk

Powerplant: One General Electric F404-GE-100D non-afterburning turbofan
Developing: 48.04kN (10,800lb st)
Span: 8.38m (27ft 6in)
Length: 12.72m (41ft 8.5in)
Height: 4.57m (14ft 11.75in)
All-up weight: 10,206kg (22,500lb)
Maximum speed: 1,163km/h (723mph)
Cruise speed: 825km/h (512mph)
Operational ceiling: 40,000ft
Maximum range: 3,791km (2,356 miles)
Accommodation: Pilot only (two pilots in TA-4SU)
Warload: Centreline stores station and four wing hardpoints for ordnance including conventional bombs, AGM-65 Maverick air-to-surface missiles, AIM-9 Sidewinder heat-seeking air-to-air missiles, SNEB 68mm unguided rockets, CRV-7 rocket pods and SUU-23 20mm gun pods. Single 30mm cannon also installed in each wing root.
First flown: 19 September 1986 (re-engined aircraft)
Entered service: March 1989 (initial operational capability for re-engined aircraft)

and easier maintainability. Two prototype conversions were undertaken, one a single-seat A-4S-1 and the other a two-seat TA-4S-1. After the completion of successful trials, production conversions emerged, totalling almost 50 by the end of the 1980s. Further updating then ensued, with installation of modern avionics leading to the A-4SU and TA-4SU versions that became operational early in 1992.

CURRENT SERVICE

At present, three Republic of Singapore Air Force squadrons are equipped with the A-4SU and TA-4SU. Two of these squadrons (Nos 142 and 145) are stationed at Tengah in Singapore, along with four aircraft that combine with two F-16s to make up the *Black Knights* national display team. The other unit is No 150 Squadron, which undertakes operational training at the French air base at Cazaux.

SPECIAL FEATURES

Superficially similar in appearance to other examples of the long-serving Skyhawk, the A-4SU Super Skyhawk is actually far more sophisticated, although few of the improvements are readily apparent. Beneath the

surface, however, it has a modern General Electric F404 turbofan engine in place of the original 1950s-vintage Wright J65 turbojet, and it also embodies a completely revamped avionics suite. This incorporates a MIL-STD-1553B databus, head-up display (HUD) and multi-function displays, plus ring laser gyro inertial navigation system and mission computer, with a data transfer module.

VARIANTS

The principal version is the single-seat **A-4SU**, and approximately 50 examples of this Super Skyhawk model are in service both at home in Singapore and in France. Although all have been re-engined and fitted with modern avionics equipment, new capabilities and kit are still being introduced, with one noteworthy recent addition being the GEC-Marconi Atlantic FLIR navigation and targeting pod system. This equipment is most commonly observed on the two-seat **TA-4SU**. About 18 TA-4SUs are in use, primarily for training, but they do have a combat role, hence the provision of full avionics capability.

SEE ALSO: McDONNELL DOUGLAS A-4 SKYHAWK

TA-4SU Super Skyhawk Republic of Singapore Air Force

Slingsby T67M Firefly

SINGLE-ENGINED LOW-WING PRIMARY TRAINER

T-67M Firefly UK JEFTS

DEVELOPMENT

The Firefly is descended from the Fournier RF-6B, which first flew in March 1974, of which 50 were produced by Fournier and Sportavia before production ceased. Slingsby purchased the licence to produce the RF-6B under the designation T67 for civilian (T67A to T67C) and military (T67M) markets, and continues to produce the aircraft; over 260 have been produced to date. The 119kW (160hp) T67M Firefly 2 was the initial military version and is used in the UK by the Joint Elementary FTS for joint service pilot training. The T67M-200, with a more powerful 149kW (200hp) powerplant, was introduced to the range in 1985 and sold to companies operating screening services for air arms. The most powerful military version is the T67M-260, which was successful in the USAF's Enhanced Flight Screener competition to replace its Cessna T-41 Mescaleros and ordered under the designation T-3A; this model is also used by JEFTS.

CURRENT SERVICE

The Joint Elementary FTS based at RAF Barkston Heath has a mixed fleet of 42 Fireflies for all three British services; these are operated by a civilian contractor and have British civil registrations. A similar scheme is operated by Bombardier for the Canadian Forces using 12 T67Cs, again under civil registration. The major purchaser was the US Air Force, which purchased 113 aircraft to replace the Cessna T-41 under its EFS programme; however, the survivors were grounded in July 1997 after three were lost, possibly due to unexplained engine stoppages in flight. The aircraft have remained in storage pending a decision on disposal. The Belize Defence Force Air Wing has one example for training. Dutch, Japanese and Norwegian companies operate Fireflies for initial military pilot screening.

SPECIAL FEATURES

The Firefly has a low wing and prominent bubble canopy to provide excellent all-round vision, and fuel and oil systems engineered for inverted flight. It is made almost entirely from glassfibre reinforced plastics (GRPs), which gives low maintenance costs, improved resistance to fatigue, lower weight and also less drag. Slingsby has long experience of GFRPs in its production of high-performance sailplanes. A wingtip-mounted smoke system can be added for aerobatic display flights. The tricycle undercarriage is non-retractable.

VARIANTS

The basic **Slingsby T67A** series was constructed of wood; the newer **T67C** and **T67M** range is constructed of glassfibre reinforced plastics. The **T67M260/T-3A** has a larger air intake under the nose.

TECHNICAL DATA

Slingsby T67M Firefly 2

Powerplant: One Textron Lycoming O-320-D2A flat-six piston engine
Developing: 119kW (160hp)
Driving: Two-blade propeller
Span: 10.59m (34ft 9in)
Length: 7.32m (24ft)
Height: 2.36m (7ft 9in)
All-up weight: 975kg (2,150lb)
Maximum speed: 281km/h (175mph)
Cruise speed: 235km/h (146mph)
Operational ceiling: 15,000ft
Maximum range: 1,026km (638 miles)
Endurance: 7hr 20min
Accommodation: Instructor and student, side-by-side
Warload: None
First flown: 5 December 1982 (T67M Firefly Mk2); May 1991 (T-3A Firefly)
Entered service: July 1993 (JEFTS)

T-67M Firefly UK JEFTS

SME Aviation MD-3 AeroTiga

SINGLE-ENGINED PRIMARY/AEROBATIC/INSTRUMENT TRAINER

MD-3-160 AeroTiga Royal Malaysian Air Force

DEVELOPMENT

Originated in Switzerland in the late 1960s by Max Dätwyler as a homebuild design, the aircraft was much redesigned later for cost-effective production by MDB Flugtechnik AG in Switzerland. Today, SME Aerospace (originally an aircraft parts manufacturer, and wholly owned by the Malaysian Government) – which provides products and services for defence, aerospace and metal-based products – is manufacturing the MD3-160 with technical support from the aircraft's designer (MDB) and British Aerospace. Production was commenced in Malaysia in 1994 by SME Aviation Sdn Bhd (SMEAv), and 20 have been built for the Royal Malaysian Air Force and a further 20 for the Indonesian Ministry of Communications. It is also being marketed in the USA by SMA Aero, a Florida-based company in a joint venture between SME and Aero Associates. The MD3 was the first aircraft wholly built in Malaysia, to fly.

CURRENT SERVICE

The AeroTiga is used for flight experience and primary training tasks with the Royal Malaysian Air Force's No 1 Flying Training Centre at Alor Setar – tasks which had rather uneconomically been performed by the Pilatus PC-7 following the withdrawal of the RMAF's Scottish Aviation Bulldogs. An order for 20 was placed by the Indonesian Government in 1996, but only five have been seen at Subang, as further deliveries appear to have been put on hold.

SPECIAL FEATURES

Primary structure is of aluminium alloy and the wings are built from a bonded aluminium honeycomb with a single main spar. Optional avionics are available. The MD3 has a fixed nosewheel undercarriage with optional glassfibre fairings. Dual controls are standard. The canopy is forward sliding and jettisonable. There

is space behind the seats for 50kg (110lb) of baggage. Equipment for glider towing is optional.

VARIANTS

MD3-116: powered by a Textron Lycoming 0-235-N2A of 86.5kW (116hp); **MD3-160**: aerobatic trainer and glider tug, with the more powerful 0-320-D2A engine; **MD3-160A**: fully aerobatic version, with AEIO-320-D2B fuel-injection engine and modified fuel system.

TECHNICAL DATA

SME Aviation MD3-160 AeroTiga

Powerplant: One Textron Lycoming O-320-D2A flat-four piston engine
Developing: 119kW (160hp)
Driving: Two-blade propeller
Span: 10.00m (32ft 9.6in)
Length: 7.1m (23ft 3.6in)
Height: 2.92m (9ft 7.2in)
All-up weight: 920kg (2,028lb) – Utility version; 840kg (1,852lb) – Aerobatic version
Maximum speed: 293km/h (182mph)
Cruising speed: 228km/h (142mph)
Operational ceiling: 19,700ft
Maximum range: 875km (543 miles)
Duration: 4hr 10min
Accommodation: Two, side-by-side
Warload: None
First flown: 12 August 1983 (Swiss prototype); 25 May 1995 (SME produced)
Entered service: December 1995 (Royal Malaysian Air Force); October 1997 (Indonesian Air Force)

MD-3-160 AeroTiga Royal Malaysian Air Force

SOCATA (Aérospatiale) Rallye

FOUR-SEAT PISTON-ENGINED LIGHT TRAINER AND LIAISON/COMMUNICATIONS AIRCRAFT

Rallye 235 Guerrier El Salvador Air Force

TECHNICAL DATA

SOCATA (Aérospatiale) Rallye 235 Guerrier

Powerplant: One Textron Lycoming O-540-B4B5 flat-six piston engine
Developing: 175kW (235hp)
Driving: Two-blade propeller
Span: 9.74m (31ft 11in)
Length: 7.25m (23ft 9.5in)
Height: 2.80m (9ft 2.25in)
All-up weight: 1,350kg (2,976lb)
Maximum speed: 275km/h (171mph)
Cruise speed: 245km/h (152mph)
Operational ceiling: 4,500m (14,750ft)
Maximum range: 640 miles
Mission range: 450km (280 miles) in ground support role; 1,010km (627 miles) in unarmed recce role
Endurance: 5 hours
Accommodation: Pilot and passenger/observer; optional bench seat can be fitted
Warload: Four underwing stores pylons can carry a variety of loads including Matra F2 rocket launchers, 7.62mm machine-guns in Type AA52 pods, or 50kg (110lb) bombs. The underwing pylons are controlled by a selection box in the cockpit; all underwing loads can be jettisoned in emergency.
First flown: 1 April 1975 (235T Gabier).
Entered service: Late 1970s

DEVELOPMENT

Initially designed by Morane Saulnier in response to a French government-sponsored competition for a lightweight two-seater, the prototype MS.880 Rallye first flew on 10 June 1959. It proved popular with civil and military markets alike, and over 1,850 of various models with a variety of engines were built. The heavier four-seat MS.890 version was introduced in the mid-1960s, shortly before the company became bankrupt and production was transferred to SOCATA; 1,360 were built before production finally ended in 1983 in favour of the more modern TB series (see Trinidad entry). The unarmed Rallye 235 Gabier and armed Guerrier were the last versions to be produced.

CURRENT SERVICE

The French Navy operates a fleet of Rallye 100S/100STs to give air experience flights to students at the French Navy Officers' School (50S and 51S at Lanvéoc and Rochefort respectively). Two Rallyes serve with the Royal Moroccan Air Force's 'Special Brigade' based at Marrakech. The Central African Republic has a single Guerrier, and Senegal has six for COIN and training

duties; the post-war status of Rwanda's small fleet of Guerriers is not known. Finally, El Salvador has five Rallye 235Gs with the Escuela de Aviación Militar for elementary training, from 16 delivered.

SPECIAL FEATURES

The Rallye's cockpit offers excellent all-round visibility for training purposes; the instructor and student have dual controls; there is also a bench seat in the rear of the cockpit (this is optional on the Guerrier). Full-span leading-edge slats and wide-span flaps allow the Guerrier exceptional short-field and slow-flight performance; its rugged construction and simple maintenance procedures make it ideal for operation in the most spartan conditions.

VARIANTS

Initial lightweight versions include the 75kW (100hp) Continental O-200A-engined **MS.880B Rallye Club**, **MS.885 Super Rallye** with 108kW (145hp) Continental O-300 and **Rallye 180T** with 134kW (180hp) Lycoming O-360; around 400 of these have been used for civilian glider towing duties. The initial heavier **Commodore**

uses the same engine as the MS.885 and engine power increased as production continued, culminating in the 175kW (235hp) version described here. Other roles undertaken by the **Rallye Guerrier** using pods carried on the underwing hardpoints include surveillance using television camera and transmitter, and dropping rescue and medical equipment to ground forces. A single stretcher can be carried behind the front seats for medical evacuation and this space can also be used for the carriage of freight.

Rallye 100S French Navy

SOCATA (Aérospatiale) TBM 700

LOW-WING SINGLE-ENGINED PRESSURISED MULTI-ROLE AIRCRAFT

SOCATA TBM 700 French Air Force

DEVELOPMENT

Initiated as a co-operative venture between the Aérospatiale division of SOCATA and Mooney, and based on the latter's M.301, the prototype (F-WTBM) was followed by two further prototypes. Mooney pulled out of the project in May 1991 and SOCATA elected to continue development as a solo venture. The French Air Force ordered the type to replace the venerable MS.760 Paris in the liaison role; the first unannounced order saw the delivery of six aircraft in 1992 for use with GAEL and ETE 43; a further six, for ETE 41 and ETE 44 (plus the CEAM), were supplied in 1993-94. More have since been ordered; the French Air Force has received funding for 17 aircraft so far. The French Army received its first two aircraft on 13 January 1995, for use in similar roles to those of the Air Force; a third has since been purchased against a requirement for eight. One further French military example has been supplied to the CEV – this was delivered in 1994. Production at Tarbes continues at a rate of around 20-30 per year but this will rise to 35 in 2001; 167 of all versions had been delivered by mid- 2000.

CURRENT SERVICE

The French armed forces are currently the only operators of military TBM700s: the French Air Force has a requirement for 22 in total. Units presently equipped with the type are BA 128 at Metz, BA 106 at Mérignac, BA 114 at Aix and BA 107 at Villacoubly. The French Army has three currently in service with 3GHL at Rennes.

SPECIAL FEATURES

The low-wing single-engined TBM 700 has a high cruise speed and comfortable pressurised cabin with entry via a single port-side door aft of the wing; a port-side crew door is optional. An emergency exit is situated over the starboard wing. The aircraft can be quickly converted to freight configuration due to its reinforced metal floor; tie-down points are optional.

VARIANTS

The baseline model is the **TBM 700**. This is offered in several versions in addition to its more usual liaison role; these include medical evacuation, photographic mapping (through an aperture under the fuselage), navaid calibration duties, maritime patrol, ECM, target towing and freight transportation. The dedicated cargo version is designated **TBM 700C**; this has a port-side cargo door and separate port side cockpit door for the crew; a reinforced floor to take cargo up to 825kg (1,819lb), and the aircraft's maximum take-off weight is increased to 3,300kg (7,275lb). The TBM 700C entered service with civilian operators at the end of 1999.

TECHNICAL DATA

SOCATA (Aérospatiale) TBM 700

Powerplant: One Pratt & Whitney Canada PT6A-64 turboprop
Developing: 1,178kW (1,580shp) flat rated at 522kW (700shp)
Driving: Four-blade propeller
Span: 12.68m (41ft 7.25in)
Length: 10.64m (34ft 11in)
Height: 4.35m (14ft 3.25in)
All-up weight: 2,984kg (6,578lb)
Maximum speed: 555km/h (345mph)
Cruise speed: 450km/h (280mph)
Operational ceiling: 30,000ft
Maximum range: 2,870km (1,783 miles)
Mission range: 1,852km (1,150 miles)
Accommodation: One/two pilots on flightdeck plus up to five passengers in main cabin when operated in transport configuration.
Warload: None
First flown: 14 July 1988
Entered service: 21 December 1990 (civilian); 27 May 1992 (French Air Force)

SOCATA TBM 700 French Air Force

SOCATA TB20 Trinidad

SINGLE-ENGINED LOW-WING LIGHT TRAINER / LIAISON / COMMUNICATIONS AIRCRAFT   **FRANCE**

TB20 Trinidad (Pashosh) Israeli Defence Force/Air Force

DEVELOPMENT

Introduced in 1975, the SOCATA TB family superseded the popular Morane Saulnier Rallye family as a more modern multi-purpose four/five seat light aircraft/tourer. Initially the range was launched with the TB 10 Tobago and lower-powered TB 9 Tampico, both fixed-undercarriage four seat light trainers, and these were joined in 1980 by the TB 20 Trinidad, a retractable-undercarriage version with a more powerful engine. The Trinidad is also produced with a turbocharged engine as the TB 21 Trinidad TC; for commonality all have the same wing. The Aérospatiale TB 30 Epsilon, a derivative of the family, is described separately. Sales

of the TB series have reached over 1,400 to date, of which approximately half are of the TB 20/21 model; the range is currently being developed into the MS series which will use a new family of engines being developed in conjunction with Renault.

CURRENT SERVICE

Although it has been marketed principally as a civilian aircraft, some military users have small fleets of Trinidad variants. The main military operator is Israel, which purchased 22 via the USA, delivered from January 1996 onwards. They are used for liaison and communications work and are known locally as the Pashosh (Lark). The Turkish Air Force bought six in 1995, and Jordan has a single example for VIP duties. The Turkish Coast Guard has two TB 20s for coastal patrol work, and several airline pilot training organisations also use the type. Additionally, the Indonesian Navy has a single fixed-undercarriage TB 9 Tampico for pilot training.

SPECIAL FEATURES

The TB 20 has a low wing and large cockpit windows for all-round visibility; a sharply inclined forward windscreen reduces drag. Entry is via an overwing walkway through gull-wing doors. It has a large fin and rudder with all-moving constant-chord tailplane. The constant-chord wing has 4.5° dihedral and slotted flaps reduce stalling speed and improve low-speed handling.

VARIANTS

The **TB 20** is the baseline version. The **TB 20C** is a medevac/light freight version with a freight door; it has a flat cockpit floor with cargo hooks and a cargo net; alternatively a single stretcher plus attendant can be carried. The **TB 21 Trinidad TC** has a turbocharged TIO-540-AB1AD engine which gives an approximate 15% increase in performance, whilst not increasing the maximum take-off weight.

TECHNICAL DATA

SOCATA TB20 Trinidad

Powerplant: One Textron Lycoming IO-540-C4D5D piston engine.
Developing: 186kW (250hp)
Driving: Two-blade propeller
Span: 9.76m (32ft 0.25in)
Length: 7.71m (25ft 3.5in)
Height: 2.85m (9ft 4.25in)
All-up weight: 1,400kg (3,086lb)
Maximum speed: 310 km/h (192mph)
Cruise speed: 301 km/h (187mph)
Operational ceiling: 20,000ft
Maximum range: 2,052km (1,275 miles)
Mission range: 1,898km (1,179 miles)
Accommodation: Pilot and up to four passengers.
Warload: None.
First flown: 23 February 1977 (TB 10);
14 November 1980 (TB 20)
Entered service: 23 March 1982 (civil)

TB20 Trinidad GT

SOKO/Avioane J-22 Orao/IAR-93

SINGLE-SEAT CLOSE SUPPORT, GROUND ATTACK AND TACTICAL RECONNAISSANCE AIRCRAFT **YUGOSLAVIA/ROMANIA**

J-22 Orao 2 Yugoslav Air Force

DEVELOPMENT

The J-22/IAR-93 Orao (Eagle) was the result of a joint collaboration between Yugoslavia and Romania. Its development began in 1970 to meet both countries' requirements for a multi-purpose aircraft. Construction of prototypes in each country began concurrently in

---

TECHNICAL DATA

Avioane IAR-93B (single-seater)

Powerplants: Two Turbomecanica/Orao licence-built Rolls-Royce (Bristol Siddeley) Viper Mk633-47 turbojets

Developing: 17.79kN (4,000lb st) dry; 22.24kN (5,000lb st) with afterburner

Span: 9.30m (30ft 6.25in)

Length: 14.90m (48ft 10.5in)

Height: 4.52m (14ft 10in)

All-up weight: 10,900kg (24,030lb)

Maximum speed: 1,085km/h (672mph)

Operational ceiling: 44,625ft

Maximum range: 1,900km (1,180 miles)

Mission range: 530km (329 miles)

Endurance: 1 hour 45 min

Accommodation: Pilot only
(two in tandem in two-seater)

Warload: Two 23mm GSh-23L twin-barrel cannon in forward fuselage below air intakes, each with 200 rounds. Four underwing and one underfuselage hardpoints on which maximum of 1,500kg (3,307lb) of ordnance can be carried; typical loads include 500kg (1,102lb) bombs, and 57mm, 122mm and 240mm rockets. Some aircraft are equipped to carry up to eight air-to-air missiles on twin launch rails on underwing stations; drop tanks can also be carried on centreline and inboard underwing points.

First flown: 31 October 1974 (both Romanian and Yugoslavian prototypes);
29 January 1977 (two-seater)

Entered service: 1981 (IAR-93A); 1985 (IAR-93B)

1972 and culminated with simultaneous first flights for both single- and two-seat prototypes. The initial development was hampered by problems in producing a reheat system to complement the licence-built Viper Mk632-41 engines for the type and the fully combat-capable version did not appear until the improved Viper 633-47 afterburner-equipped engine became available. After the construction of batches of pre-production aircraft in each country, full production started in 1979 in Romania and 1980 in Yugoslavia; the latter was ended prematurely by damage to the factory caused during 1992, after which the jigs were believed to have been moved to Pancevo, but Orao production has not restarted. In total, orders were placed for 416 aircraft: 26 single-seat and 10 two-seat IAR-93As and 165 IAR-93Bs for Romania; 15 IJ/INJ-22s, 25 NJ-22s and 165 J-22s for Yugoslavia. Actual delivery figures are not known.

CURRENT SERVICE

Prior to the NATO operations in Kosovo in 1999, the Yugoslav Air Force had around 65 J-22s of various models in service in the attack role, but the exact number currently serviceable is not known. Romania has around 60 attack and 14 trainers in service with four squadrons based at Giarmata, Craiova, Campia Turzii and Caracal-Deveselu.

SPECIAL FEATURES

Differences between the single- and two-seat versions of the IAR-93A include leading-edge root extensions and the removal of ventral fins on the two-seater. Both versions of the IAR-93B and J-22 have wing root extensions. The braking parachute is stored at the base of the rudder in a bullet-shaped housing.

VARIANTS

The initial Romanian single- and two-seaters without afterburner are designated **IAR-93A**, and the identical Yugoslav models **IJ-22** and **INJ-22** respectively; the latter version is also used as a conversion trainer. Later afterburner-equipped models are the **IAR-93B** (both single- and two-seat versions) and **J-22** (single-seat only). The **NJ-22** is a two-seat model, some of which have afterburning, although others from the same production batch do not.

J-22 Orao 1 Yugoslav Air Force

SOKO G-2 Galeb

LOW-WING TRAINER AND LIGHT ATTACK/STRIKE AIRCRAFT

G-2 Galeb Croatian Air Force

DEVELOPMENT

Design work on the Galeb (Seagull) series began in 1957, with construction work beginning in 1959. Full production began in 1963 with orders for the Yugoslav Air Force. The first export order for the Galeb came from Zambia in 1971, and this was followed by an order from Libya. Production ended in 1985 when all export orders had been fulfilled, and the Galeb was replaced by the G-4 Super Galeb (described separately).

CURRENT SERVICE

The main users of the Galeb are some of the breakaway countries that made up the former Yugoslavia. The Serbian part of Bosnia-Herzegovina has a small fleet based at Banja Luka (this force is limited to 21 fixed-wing aircraft in total). Croatia has a few for training and reconnaissance. Yugoslavia's Galeb fleet comprised ten aircraft before the 1999 NATO operations and its current status is unknown. Of the export customers, the Zambian Air Force received six G-2A Galebs, all of

which have long since been disposed of, while it is not known how many of Libya's 80-strong counter-insurgency and training fleet are still current.

SPECIAL FEATURES

The Galeb is a cantilever, slightly-swept low-wing tricycle-undercarriage trainer that bears a passing resemblance to the Aermacchi MB.326. The tandem cockpit is positioned forward of the wing leading edge. Engine intakes are on each side of the fuselage at the wing root. Two machine guns protrude at the top of the nose. Wing tip tanks contain 170kg (375lb) of fuel and can be jettisoned in flight; the fuel system is designed for up to 15 seconds of inverted flight. For photographic reconnaissance a camera can be fitted in the fuselage under the rear cockpit floor – the bomb racks are also used for carriage of flares used for night photography. The target-towing role is accomplished by using the hook situated under the centre fuselage.

VARIANTS

There are two basic versions of the Galeb and both are externally identical. The **G-2A** was the standard version built for the Yugoslav Air Force and was gradually updated during the production run. The **G-2A-E** export version was introduced in 1975 to fulfil the Libyan Air Force order and featured updated equipment compared to the G-2A.

TECHNICAL DATA

SOKO G-2A Galeb

Powerplant: One Rolls-Royce (Bristol Siddeley) Viper 11 Mk 22-6 turbojet
Developing: 11.12kN (2,500lb st)
Span: 11.62m (38ft 1.5in)
Length: 10.34m (33ft 11in)
Height: 3.28m (10ft 9in)
All-up weight:
3,488 kg (7,690lb) in trainer configuration;
4,300kg (9,480 lb) in strike configuration
Maximum speed: 812 km/h (505mph)
Cruise speed: 730km/h (453mph)
Operational ceiling: 39,375ft
Maximum range: 1,240km (770 miles)
Endurance: 2hr 30min
Accommodation: Pilot and passenger in tandem on BAe Type 1B fully automatic lightweight ejection seats.
Warload: Two 0.50in machine guns in the nose, each with 80 rounds. Underwing pylons carry up to 300kg (660lb) in total – this can comprise small (50-100kg) bombs, cluster bombs, four 57mm rockets or two 127mm rockets.
First flown: May 1961;
17 August 1970 (Galeb 3 trainer)
Entered service: 1965

G-2A Galeb Libyan Air Force

SOKO G-4 Super Galeb

LOW-WING TRAINER AND LIGHT ATTACK/STRIKE AIRCRAFT

G-4 Super Galeb Yugoslav Air Force

TECHNICAL DATA

SOKO G-4 Super Galeb

Powerplant: One licence-built Rolls-Royce (Bristol Siddeley) Viper Mk632-46 turbojet
Developing: 17.8kN (4,000lb st)
Span: 9.88m (32ft 5in)
Length: 11.35m (37ft 2.875in) without pitot tube; 12.25m (40ft 2.25in) with pitot tube
Height: 4.30m (14ft 1.25in)
All-up weight: 6,300kg (13,889lb)
Maximum speed: 910 km/h (565mph)
Cruise speed: 845km/h (525mph)
Operational ceiling: 42,160ft
Maximum range: 2,500km (1,553 miles)
Mission range: 1,300km (807 miles)
Endurance: 4 hours
Accommodation: Crew of two in tandem on Martin-Baker Mk10Y zero/zero ejection seats.
Warload: Ventral gun pod (removable) containing 23mm GSh-23L twin-barrel cannon with 200 rounds. Two hardpoints under each wing stressed to 350kg (772lb) inboard and 250kg (551lb) outboard with typical loads including S-8-16 cluster bombs, napalm pods, anti-tank and anti-personnel bombs, 57mm rocket pods or KM-3 12.7mm gun pods in addition to standard high-explosive bombs. The proposed G-4M was to have been fitted with wingtip rails carrying AA-8 'Aphid' and AA-2 'Atoll' AAMs and provision to carry AGM-65B Mavericks on outboard underwing pylons.
First flown: 17 July 1978
Entered service: 1985

DEVELOPMENT

Designed by the Aeronautical Technical Institute of the Air Force & Anti-Aircraft Defence as a replacement for both the Lockheed T-33 and G-2 Galeb, the G-4 programme was launched in October 1973, with construction of the first prototype beginning in May 1975. Apart from the prototype, six pre-production aircraft were built before production got underway in 1983. By the time production was prematurely ended, and the factory at Mostar abandoned as a result of hostilities in 1992, around 136 had been delivered to the Yugoslav Air Force. The jigs were transferred to the UTVA factory at Pancevo and it was claimed that production had restarted in 1993; this appears not to be the case.

CURRENT SERVICE

At the outbreak of hostilities in 1992, the Yugoslav Air Force had received 136 of its planned 150 aircraft requirement. Of the survivors, some 50 remained with the Federal Republic, including the Letece Zvezde (Flying Stars) display team; however, many of these aircraft were destroyed during the NATO campaign in 1999. A small number have been transferred to the Republika Srpska Air Force in Bosnia-Herzegovina. The sole export customer for the G-4 Super Galeb was Burma (later Myanmar), whose armed forces ordered 12, which were delivered in 1991 and 1992; ten remain in service.

SPECIAL FEATURES

The Super Galeb was designed to assist pupils in converting from basic trainers towards more advanced combat aircraft and has good manoeuvring capabilities at high speed (never-exceed speed is Mach 0.9 and

level speed is Mach 0.81). An airbrake fitted to the rear under-fuselage, and single-slotted trailing-edge flaps, provide good handling at lower speeds; a braking parachute container is fitted in the base of the tail unit. The G-4 can also be operated from grass airfields at its normal take-off weights.

VARIANTS

The prototype and pre-production examples were designated **G-4 PPP** and had fixed tailplanes with no anhedral. The second prototype and all production aircraft have all-moving tailplanes with anhedral; a retrofit programme to provide AAMs was to have been instigated before the outbreak of hostilities. The proposed **G-4M** version had revised avionics and increased payload of 1,680kg (3,704lb) with the aim

of undertaking more of the Yugoslav Air Force's weapons training syllabus; however, this proposal was not proceeded with.

G-4 Super Galeb Yugoslav Air Force

SOKO J-1 Jastreb

SINGLE-SEAT LIGHT ATTACK AIRCRAFT

J-1 Jastreb Yugoslav Air Force

TECHNICAL DATA

SOKO J-1 Jastreb

Powerplant: One Rolls-Royce (Bristol Siddeley) Viper 531 turbojet

Developing: 13.34kN (3,000lb st)

Span: 10.56m (34ft 8in); 11.68m (38ft 4in) with tip tanks

Length: 10.88m (35ft 8.5in)

Height: 3.64m (11ft 11.5in)

All-up weight: 5,100kg (11,243lb)

Maximum speed: 820 km/h (510mph)

Cruise speed: 740 km/h (460mph)

Operational ceiling: 39,375ft

Maximum range: 1,520km (945 miles)

Endurance: 2 hours

Accommodation: Pilot only
(two in TJ-21 training variant)

Warload: Three 0.50-inch Colt Browning machine guns are fitted in the nose, each with 135 rounds. Eight underwing hardpoints; the inner two on each side capable of carrying two bombs up to 250kg (551lb) bombs, two clusters of smaller bombs, two 200 litre (44 Imp gallon) napalm tanks, two rocket pods, two 45kg (100lb) photo flares or a smaller mixed load. The outer hardpoints each carry a 127mm rocket.

First flown: early 1960s

Entered service: 1970

DEVELOPMENT

The SOKO J-1 Jastreb (Hawk) is a development of the G-2A Galeb trainer (described separately). Development began concurrently and production ended in 1979 after around 170 of all models were completed.

CURRENT SERVICE

Deliveries to the Yugoslav Air Force totalled 140 – 100 J-1s, 20 RJ-1s and 20 TJ-1s, and these saw service in the conflicts that surrounded the break-up of the country throughout the 1990s. Three Balkan air forces now operate the type: the Republika Srpska Air Force in Bosnia-Herzegovina has a small fleet, based at Banja Luka; Croatia has a few aircraft captured at Udbina in August 1995, and Yugoslavia had a fleet of around 30 before the 1999 NATO operation. Further afield, Libya was a major export customer, acquiring 24 for COIN operations; and in Zambia, two from six delivered in the early 1970s remain, but are unlikely to still be serviceable.

SPECIAL FEATURES

The J-1 Jastreb was developed to complement the G-2A and in most respects retains the two-seater's airframe, with extra strengthening at critical points plus improved hardpoints for extra carriage of stores; the Viper engine is also more powerful. Other changes include improved reconnaissance, electronics and navigation systems and an independent engine start system. The Jastreb retains the same size cockpit as the Galeb, but the rear cockpit area is faired over. The brake parachute is housed in a fairing just below the rudder. Target towing is accomplished using a hook under the centre fuselage.

VARIANTS

The standard attack version for the Yugoslav Air Force was the **J-1**; export versions with updated equipment were designated **J-1-E**. The tactical reconnaissance versions were the **RJ-1** and **RJ-1-E** and these had a Vinten photo reconnaissance system fitted, comprising 360/140A cameras with 3in lenses in each of the tip-tanks, plus a third camera fitted into the fuselage – for night operations a Vinten 1025/527 camera is fitted in the fuselage position; the camera system can be fitted to the J-1 and J-1-E. The two-seat **TJ-1 Jastreb** was used for operational conversion training and first flew in mid-1974; it was only produced in limited quantities. It has a two-seat cockpit but retains the full operational capability of the single-seat model; however, in the reconnaissance mode it has cameras only in the tip tanks.

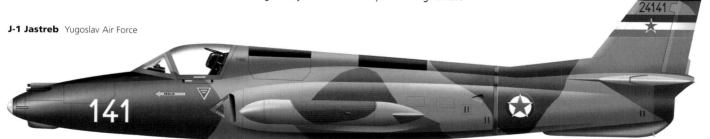

J-1 Jastreb Yugoslav Air Force

SOKO J-20/P-2 Kraguj

LIGHTWEIGHT CLOSE-SUPPORT/GROUND ATTACK AIRCRAFT

P-2 Kraguj

DEVELOPMENT

The Kraguj was Designed by the Aeronautical Research Establishment in Belgrade as an extremely simple to build all-metal lightweight close-support and easy to maintain light aircraft, which was in operation service two years after flight testing of the prototype began. Production was believed to have numbered around 200 for the reserve units of the Yugoslav Air Force. It was rendered obsolete before its service entry by the introduction of the helicopter. It resurrected a concept pioneered by the American Fletcher Defender in the early 1950s. The Kraguj was subsequently mainly used as a weapons trainer.

CURRENT SERVICE

Croatia is the only current military operator of the Kraguj and has a small fleet liberated from Serbian forces at Udbina during Operation *Storm* in August 1995. The aircraft are used for COIN operations and elementary weapons training. The initial operator, Yugoslavia, disposed of its stocks some years ago and several have appeared in the west with civilian users. It was used by all the former Yugoslav forces during the 1990s Balkans conflict.

SPECIAL FEATURES

The Kraguj was designed as an easy to fly aircraft and able to operate from grass strips with a ground run of 120m (395ft) or less, alongside the infantry units with which it was paired. It is a cantilever low-wing monoplane with dihedral only on the outer panels and corrugated skins on the control surfaces.

The undercarriage is non-retractable and the aircraft's nose area is dominated by twin exhausts. Entrance to the cockpit is effected via a rearward-sliding bubble canopy. Manually operated flaps with corrugated skin.

VARIANTS

There was only one variant – the basic **J-20 Kraguj**.

TECHNICAL DATA

SOKO J-20 Kraguj

Powerplant: One Textron Lycoming GSO-480-B1A6 six-cylinder piston engine .
Developing: 254kW (340hp)
Driving: Three-blade propeller
Span: 10.64m (34ft 11in)
Length: 7.93m (26ft 0.25in)
Height: 3.00m (9ft 10in)
All-up weight: 1,624kg (3,580lb)
Maximum speed: 340km/h (210mph)
Cruise speed: 220km/h (136mph)
Maximum range: 600km (350 miles)
Endurance: 2hr 45min
Accommodation: Pilot only
Warload: One 7.7mm machine gun plus 650 rounds is fitted in the leading edge of each wing. Six underwing hardpoints: the inner pair can each carry a choice of 100kg (220lb) bomb, 150 litre (33 Imp gallon) napalm tank or 12-round rocket pack. The outer four hardpoints each carry a rocket of either 57mm (2.24in) or 127mm (5in) calibre.
First flown: 1966
Entered service: 1968

P-2 Kraguj

Sukhoi Su-17, 20 & 22

SINGLE TURBOJET ATTACK/RECONNAISSANCE AIRCRAFT

Sukhoi Su-22M-4 Fitter Czech Air Force

DEVELOPMENT

The origins of the Su-17/20/22 combat aircraft date back to 1965, when design of a variable-geometry derivative of the fixed-wing Su-7 'Fitter' began. Known as the Su-7IG or S-22I, this first flew in August 1966, with a production prototype of the Su-17 following suit in mid-1968. Sufficient Su-17s were built to equip an evaluation regiment in 1970, although the definitive Su-17M did not enter service until 1972.

CURRENT SERVICE

Although no longer used by Russia, variations on the 'Fitter' are still active with almost 20 air arms and are expected to give good service for several years to come, following upgrading that in some cases includes installation of Western avionics. Most operators were within the Soviet sphere of influence and comprise Afghanistan, Angola, Azerbaijan, Bulgaria, Czech Republic, Iran, Iraq, Libya, Peru, Poland, Slovak Republic, Syria, Turkmenistan, Ukraine, Uzbekistan, Vietnam and Yemen. The most common derivative is the Su-17M4/Su-22M4, which equips about half the air arms listed, alongside Su-17UM3/Su-22UM3 two-seaters for training purposes. Other versions in use are the Su-17M3/Su-22M3 and the Su-17M/Su-20, although these are less numerous and are unlikely to survive for much longer.

SPECIAL FEATURES

The Su-17/20/22 series all feature low-set horizontal tail surfaces and a sharply swept mid-position wing, with fixed inboard sections and variable-geometry outboard sections. This configuration permits an impressive array of ordnance to be carried beneath the fuselage and inboard wing panels, with the final production versions having six wing stores stations (including two dedicated to self-defence air-to-air missiles) and two fuselage hardpoints. Another feature common to all versions is the nose-mounted air inlet, with the fixed centrebody on later models containing a Klem laser rangefinder. Late production Su-17M3/M4s can carry the KKR-1 reconnaissance pod, which contains cameras, elint equipment and flare dispensers.

VARIANTS

The Su-17 family differs principally in detail, with progressive refinement of the basic design resulting in the appearance of several sub-types, identified by suffix numbers, as in **Su-17M2**, **Su-17M3** and **Su-17M4**. Export equivalents use the same system, although these are usually known as **Su-22s**. The counterpart of the original **Su-17M** was known as the **Su-20**. Two-seat trainers are identified by the UM suffix, as in **Su-17UM3** or **Su-22UM3**, and are generally similar to single-seaters, although they only have one gun.

TECHNICAL DATA

Sukhoi Su-17M4 Fitter

Powerplant: One Lyulka AL-21F-3 turbojet
Thrust: 76.49kN (17,196lb st) dry; 110.32kN (24,802lb st) in afterburner
Span: 13.80m (45ft 3in) spread; 10m (32ft 10in) swept
Length: 18.75m (61ft 6.25in), with nose pitot tubes
Height: 5.00m (16ft 5in)
All-up weight: 19,500kg (42,989lb)
Max speed: 1,400km/h (870mph) clean at sea level
Operational ceiling: 49,870ft
Combat radius: 1,150km (715 miles) hi-lo-hi profile with 2,000kg (4,409lb) warload
Accommodation: Pilot only
Warload: 4,250kg (9,369lb) ordnance load may be carried, including smart guided weapons such as AS-10 and AS-14 air-to-surface missiles, as well as conventional bombs, sub-munitions dispensers, unguided rockets and gun pods. Russian aircraft were able to deliver tactical nuclear weapons. For self-defence, two AA-8 infrared homing air-to-air missiles can be carried, while one NR-30 30mm cannon is situated in each wing root, along with 80 rounds of ammunition per gun.
First flown: 2 August 1966 (Su-7IG/S-22I prototype)
Entered service: 1972 (Su-17M/20); 1978 (Su-17M4)

Sukhoi Su-20 Fitter
Polish Air Force

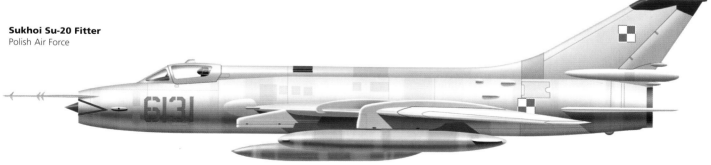

Sukhoi Su-24

TWO-SEAT STRIKE FIGHTER-BOMBER

Sukhoi Su-24MR Russian Air Force

DEVELOPMENT

Developed as a Russian response to the General Dynamics F-111, the fixed-wing T6-1 tactical bomber made its first flight on 2 July 1967. The fixed-wing was discarded in favour of a variable-sweep wing and work began in December 1967, culminating in a first flight for the revised T6-2I on 17 January 1970. Production began in 1971, with the prototype Su-24 flying in December. Initial operational capability was achieved in 1973, but full official acceptance was not given until 1975; it replaced Il-28 'Beagle' and Yak-28 'Brewer' medium bombers. The second-generation Su-24M 'Fencer-D' entered service in 1978 and was followed by the Su-24MR 'Fencer-E' reconnaissance and Su-24MP 'Fencer-F' electronic warfare versions in 1984; only around 20 of the latter were built. The Su-24 made its combat debut in the Afghan War from April until July 1984. They returned to the theatre in 1988 until February 1989. A total of 635 Su-24/24Ms and 130 Su-24MP/MRs were in service by end of the 1980s.

CURRENT SERVICE

Russia operates the bulk of the surviving Su-24s, along with the Ukraine, which has five operational regiments and over 200 aircraft, plus three reconnaissance/EW units. Other countries of the former USSR to operate Fencers include Azerbaijan, Belarus, Kazakhstan and Uzbekistan (which later transferred some to Tajikistan). Other Su-24 operators are Algeria, Iran, Libya and Syria.

SPECIAL FEATURES

As well as strike and attack roles, Su-24M is also employed as an SEAD platform, using a range of anti-radiation missiles including Kh-58/AS-11 'Kilter'. Three underwing pylons are available to carry a wide range of weaponry and pods. The Su-24 is also used in the air-to-air refuelling role, being able to both take on fuel and dispense it.

VARIANTS

The first 14 aircraft were designated 'Fencer-A' by the West, followed by the 'Fencer-B', distinguished by its narrower rear fuselage and relocated brake parachute housing. The 'Fencer-C', last of the Su-24 variants, has radar warning antennae on the engine intakes and near the top of the fin. The Su-24M 'Fencer-D' is the second-generation fighter-bomber, with a longer forward fuselage and drooped radome, simplified nose probe and retractable refuelling probe. The Su-24MR 'Fencer-E' reconnaissance version is based on the Su-24M and has a large dielectric panel on the forward fuselage, no cannon, a large heat exchanger fairing on the spine, plus a comprehensive recce suite. The Su-24MP 'Fencer-F' EW version carries a row of dielectric panels mounted on the forward fuselage, and has large antenna fairings under the nose and on the spine. The Su-24MK is the downgraded export version of the Su-24M 'Fencer-D', and was made available from the mid-1980s.

TECHNICAL DATA

Sukhoi Su-24M
Powerplants: Two Saturn/Tumansky AL-21F-3A axial-flow afterburning turbojets
Developing: 109.83kN (24,691lb st)
Span: Wings open 17.64m (57ft 10.25in); fully swept 10.37m (34ft 0in)
Length: 22.59m (74ft 1.5in)
Height: 6.19m (20ft 4in)
All-up weight: 39,570kg (87,235lb)
Maximum speed: 1,400km/h (870mph)
Operational ceiling: 55,775ft
Maximum range: 2,850km (1,770miles)
Mission range: 1,250km (777miles) with external tanks
Accommodation: Pilot plus weapons systems officer
Warload: Five underfuselage hardpoints take a wide variety of weaponry to a weight of 8,000kg (17,637lb). Weapons include Kh-23, Kh-25 and Kh-58 air-to-surface missiles; Kh-31T and Kh-58U anti-radiation missiles with LO-80 or LO-81 Fantasmagoria pod; R-60 air-to-air IR missiles; or up to six unguided rockets/bombs. The tactical nuclear capability has now been removed.
First flown: 2 July 1967 in original form
Entered service: 1975

Sukhoi Su-24MR
Russian Air Force

Sukhoi Su-25

TWIN-TURBOJET GROUND ATTACK AIRCRAFT

Su-25 'Frogfoot-A' Czech Air Force

a one-inch thick titanium bathtub with armoured glass. Foam-filled fuel tanks are surrounded by inert gas to minimise explosive damage. Its engines can be run on kerosene, diesel or petrol, if necessary.

VARIANTS

Main model is the single-seat **Su-25 'Frogfoot-A'** of which export models are known as **Su-25K**; the two-seat trainer is known as **Su-25UB 'Frogfoot-B'**. Fifty **Su-25BM** target-tugs were built. The **Su-25UTG/UBP** carrier-borne version was basically a two-seat trainer equipped with arrester gear, but the programme was discontinued and the survivors used for land-based duties. The **Su-25T** is the latest version, and Suhkoi is upgrading existing Russian Su-25s to **Su-25TM** standard.

TECHNICAL DATA

Sukhoi Su-25K 'Frogfoot-A'
Powerplants: Two Soyuz/Gavrilov R-95Sh turbojets.
Developing: 40.21kN (9,039lb st)
Span: 14.36m (47ft 1in)
Length: 15.53m (50ft 11.5in) including probe
Height: 4.80m (15ft 9in)
All-up weight: 17,530kg (38,645lb)
Maximum speed: 1,000km/h (620mph)
Operational ceiling: 22,950ft
Maximum range: 1,950km (1,212 miles) with underwing tanks
Mission range: 500km (310 miles)
Accommodation: Pilot only.
Warload: One GSh-30-2 twin-barrelled 30mm cannon mounted in the nose with 250 rounds. Ten underwing hardpoints with maximum load of 4,340kg (9,568lb); favoured weapon is BETA B-250 250kg (551lb) bomb. Adaptor rails enable carriage of AS-7 'Kerry' air-to-air missiles; Su-25T has eight pylons and a wider range of armament.
First flown: 22 February 1975;
26 April 1978 in final form
Entered service: 16 April 1980 for trials in Afghanistan; 18 June 1981 in front-line service.

DEVELOPMENT

The Russian Air Ministry launched a competition in March 1969 for a ground-attack aircraft to counter the Fairchild A-10A Thunderbolt II and to capitalise on lessons learned (the hard way) during the Six-Day War in 1967. Four companies took part, with Sukhoi being successful with the private venture T8 project upon which it had been working for some time. This was developed into the Su-25 'Frogfoot', and an order for two prototypes was issued retrospectively on 6 May 1974, work having begun two years earlier. After successful trials including combat in Afghanistan, the Su-25 was ordered in March 1981. First deliveries were made to the 200th Independent Air Attack Flight in April 1981; this unit was later expanded to full Regiment size. Over 700 have been built so far; construction continues with the Su-25TM all-weather development version, also designated Su-39, in which Bulgaria, Georgia and Slovakia are interested. The Su-25T is based on the two-seater but with pilot only and the rear cockpit area filled with improved avionics; it is identifiable by its humped back and reshaped nose.

CURRENT SERVICE

The main Su-25 user is the Russian Air Force with 195. Russian Naval Aviation has 40, and three former Soviet Bloc satellite countries also have Su-25 fleets – Bulgaria and Czechoslovakia, which later split into the Czech Republic and Slovakia. Small numbers also equip the former Soviet Union territories of Azerbaijan, Belarus, Georgia, Turkmenistan and the Ukraine. Other export countries include Angola, Iran, Iraq and North Korea. As well as seeing service in Afghanistan, where 23 were lost, the Su-25 has been used in combat in the Azerbaijan-Armenian conflict during 1992, in Georgia in 1992-93 and in the guerrilla war in Chechnya. Angola has lost many of its 14 aircraft to the shoulder-launched SAM missiles of the UNITA rebels. Iraq lost at least 30 during the Gulf War of 1991, most of which were destroyed on the ground.

SPECIAL FEATURES

The Su-25 is a simply-designed, highly-manouevrable aircraft capable of operating from semi-prepared strips close to the battlefield. The pilot is protected in

Su-25 Frogfoot
Russian Air Force

Sukhoi Su-27 & Su-30 Flanker

LONG-RANGE AIR SUPERIORITY MULTI-ROLE FIGHTER

Su-27P Flanker-B Ukrainian Air Force

TECHNICAL DATA

Sukhoi Su-27P Flanker-B

Powerplants: Two Saturn/Lyulka AL-31F afterburning turbofans
Developing: 79.4kN (17,857lb st), 122.59kN (27,557lb st) with afterburner
Span: 14.70m (48ft 3in)
Length: 21.94m (72ft 0in) without probe
Height: 5.93m (19ft 6in)
All-up weight: 33,000kg (72,750lb)
Maximum speed: 2150km/h (1,336mph)
Operational ceiling: 59,055ft
Maximum range: 3,650km (2,287miles)
Accommodation: One (two in tandem in Su-27UB)
Armament: Ten or 12 weapons pylons with maximum ordnance of 8,000kg (17,636lb). Single-barrel 30mm GSh-301 cannon. Weapons include up to ten AAMs comprising semi-active radar guided R-27Rs (AA-10A 'Alamo-A'), IR-guided R-27Ts (AA-10B 'Alamo-B'), semi-active radar guided R-27ERs (AA-10C 'Alamo-C'), IR-guided R-27ETs (AA-10D 'Alamo-D'), R-73s (AA-11 'Archer') and R-60s (AA-8 'Aphid')
First flown: 20 April 1981
Entered service: December 1984

DEVELOPMENT

Designed in Russia by Pavel Sukhoi as an all-weather interceptor and long-range bomber escort, the T-10-1 turbojet powered prototype was first flown on 20 May 1977. Re-designed because of control problems, the production standard T-10S-1/Su-27 was airborne in April 1981. After further refinements the heavily armed, very long-range fighter entered service in December 1984. It was given the NATO code-name Flanker. Development has continued, with the Su-27P Flanker-B taking over as the Russian Air Force's air defence fighter. The Su-27SMK multi-role version, of which the Su-30MK is an export variant, has a 4,000kg (8,820lb) bombload. The carrier-based air-defence/ ground attack Su-27K/Su-33 Flanker-D was embarked on the *Admiral Kuznetsov* in 1996.

CURRENT SERVICE

Flankers serve with the Russian armed forces, and in Belarus and Uzbekistan. China has over 75 with three PLAAF regiments and is co-producing 200 more as the J-11. Ethiopia purchased a handful of Su-27s from the Russian Air Force in the late 1990s. Eight were delivered to the Indian Air Force 2nd Wing, 24 Squadron at Pune as Su-30s (essentially two-seat Su-27PUs, built for the Russian Air Force but not delivered). Sixteen were delivered to Syria as air defence fighters, possibly based at Al-Qusayr in the Southern Air Defence Zone. In the Ukraine, some 60 are operated by 831 IAP from Myrhorod. Vietnam received five Su-27SKs and one Su-27UBK during 1995/96, and more are on order.

SPECIAL FEATURES

The Su-27 features a powerful look-down/shoot down and track-while-scan radar, laser rangefinder set, a head-up display and analog fly-by-wire flight control system. It is extremely manoeuvrable for its size and power, with sufficient internal fuel to give an excellent range. Latest versions have more powerful turbofans, canard foreplanes and can carry a wider variety of weapons. The navalised Su-27K has new double-slotted, full-span, trailing edge flaps, the outboard sections of which operate differentially as drooping ailerons at low speeds.

VARIANTS

Su-27 Flanker-B is the standard production version, and **Su-27P Flanker-B** the basic defence version of the same aircraft; **Su-27UB Flanker-C** – a two-seat combat trainer; **Su-27SK** – export version of single-seat Su-27; **Su-30 (Su-27PU)** – two-seat long-range interceptor/multi-role fighter derivative, now in service with the Russian air defence forces and offered for export as the **Su-30MKI**, with thrust vectoring as an option; **Su-32FN (Su-27IB)** – two-seat strike derivative, designed as an Su-24 'Fencer' replacement; **Su-33 (Su-27K) Flanker-D** – shipborne fighter, ordered by Russian Naval Aviation; **Su-35 (Su-27M)** – with canard foreplanes, an advanced air-superiority fighter with ground attack capability; **Su-37** – similar to Su-35, but using thrust vectoring for enhanced manoeuvrability.

Sukhoi Su-30 Flanker
Russian Air Force

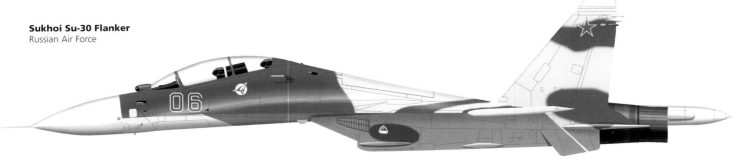

Sukhoi Su-27IB (Su-34), Su-32FN & Su-32MF

LONG-RANGE FIGHTER-BOMBER AND LAND-BASED MARITIME ATTACK AIRCRAFT

Sukhoi Su-32FN Russian Air Force

DEVELOPMENT

The Su-27IB was initially developed as a side-by-side two-seat Su-27 with the aim of replacing the Su-24 and MiG-27 in Russian Air Force service; the first prototype was a converted Su-27UB. Sukhoi has redesignated the aircraft as the Su-34 to emphasise its position as the Su-24's successor, but it is still known as Su-27IB in Russian service and has been unofficially nicknamed 'Platypus'. The Su-27IB first came to the attention of the West when a photograph of it making an approach to the aircraft carrier *Admiral of the Fleet Kuznetsov* was published; it was later exhibited at Minsk in February 1992. Production got underway in 1994 and by 1997 four were under construction, at which time it was intended to have a dozen in service by the end of 1998. This plan has since been abandoned. The Su-32FN export version made its first flight on 28 December 1994 and was exhibited the following year at Paris when it was described as in production to replace the Russian Navy's Su-24s; this programme was suspended before a fully equipped prototype got airborne. Su-32FN is Russian designation; the export version is known as the Su-32MF. The Su-27IB and Su-32MF are to be built in parallel at Novosibirsk.

CURRENT SERVICE

The Su-27IB underwent acceptance trials for the Russian Air Force late in 1999. It is under consideration

for South Korean F-X programme, competing against the F-15K, Rafale and Eurofighter Typhoon.

SPECIAL FEATURES

Compared to the Su-27, the Su-27IB has a new deeper and wider front fuselage which includes a small galley and toilet area for the crew. The wing has extensions and additional foreplanes, plus thicker 'wet' tailfins. There is a new undercarriage and larger diameter tailcone, which has been blended into a spine running from the rear fuselage to the cockpit area.

TECHNICAL DATA

Sukhoi Su-27IB

Powerplants: Two Saturn/Lyulka AL-31F turbofan engines with afterburners
Developing: 79.4kN (17,857lb st) dry and 130.42kN (29.320lb st) with afterburning.
Span: 14.70m (48ft 2.75in)
Length: 23.33m (76ft 6.25in) without probe
Height: 6.50m (21ft 4in)
All-up weight: 45,100kg (99,428lb)
Maximum speed: 1,900km/h (1,180mph)
Operational ceiling: 55,750ft
Maximum range: 4,500km (2,796 miles)
Mission range: 600km (372 miles) low-level; 1,113km (691 miles) at altitude

Endurance: in excess of 10 hours
Accommodation: Pilot and navigator/weapons operator
Warload: One 30mm GSh-301 machine gun in starboard wing root. Twelve underwing hardpoints capable of carrying air-to-surface missiles (such as AS-14 'Kedge' and AS-17 'Krypton') and laser-guided bombs, plus air-to-air missiles such as AA-11 'Archer' and AA-12 'Adder'. Also likely to carry the Vympel R-73 rear-firing missile. The Yakhont anti-shipping missile can also be carried.
First flown: 13 April 1990 (Su-27IB prototype); 28 December 1994 (production aircraft).
Entered service: 1992

VARIANTS

The initial **Su-27IB** was described as a deck trainer, but had no folding wing mechanism or deck arrester hook. Five prototypes were built under the engineering designation T10V. Other proposed versions include the **Su-27R** reconnaissance version to replace the Su-24MR and the **Su-27IBP** to replace the Yak-28PP and Su-24MP. All export versions will be designated **Su-32**; they have a different nose shape.

Sukhoi Su-32FN Russian Air Force

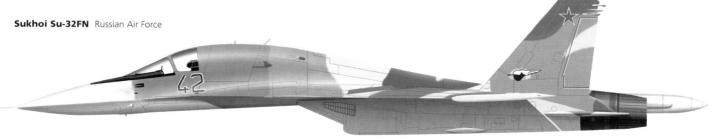

391

Sukhoi Su-27K/27KUB & Su-33/33UB

SINGLE/TWO-SEAT SHIP-BASED AIR DEFENCE AND ANTI-SHIP FIGHTER

Sukhoi Su-27K/Su-33 Russian Navy

DEVELOPMENT

Development began in 1976, using some of the many Su-27 prototypes as its basis, adding naval equipment such as an arrester hook, plus moveable foreplanes. The first development aircraft flew in 1984 and then undertook a long programme of arrester hook and ski-ramp testing. The programme was intensified in

TECHNICAL DATA

Sukhoi Su-33

Powerplants: Two Saturn/Lyulka AL-31K turbofan engines with afterburners
Developing: 74.5kN (16,755lb st) dry; 130.4kN (29.23lb st) with deck-launch boost.
Span: 14.70m (48ft 2.75in)
Length: 21.18m (69ft 6in)
Height: 5.90m (19ft 4.25in)
All-up weight: 33,000kg (72,752lb) on land; 30,000kg (66,135lb) on carrier
Maximum speed: 1,400km/h (870mph)
Operational ceiling: 55,780ft
Maximum range: 3,000km (1,865 miles)
Endurance: Up to 10 hours with in-flight refuelling
Accommodation: Pilot only.
Warload: Twelve underwing hardpoints for a range of air-to-air missiles similar to that carried by other members of the Su-27 family, with the addition of the R27EM to shoot down sea-skimming targets; has also been seen with dummy 4,500kg (9,920lb) 3M80 Moskit anti-ship missile on centreline but this is believed impractical.
First flown: 17 August 1987 (prototype), 1992 (first production aircraft)
Entered service: 1992

1984 and full development of the T10K began, although the first prototype, which did not have folding wings or strengthened undercarriage was therefore unusable at sea. The second prototype made the first landing on a ship on 1 November 1989. Full-scale production began shortly afterwards. Production continues although problems with electronic countermeasures have affected the aircraft in Russian Navy service. The Su-27K was officially renumbered Su-33 on 31 August 1998, when it was also formally accepted into service.

CURRENT SERVICE

Russia took delivery of its first aircraft in 1992. 279th KIAP at Severomorsk, Kola Peninsula has a complement of up to 20, which make shipborne deployments to the *Admiral Kuznetsov*.

SPECIAL FEATURES

As befits a navalised aircraft, compared to the basic Su-27 Flanker, the Su-27K/Su-33 has a strengthened undercarriage with twin nosewheels plus folding

wings and tailplane for shipborne storage. An arrester hook is fitted between the jet exhausts at the rear of the aircraft and the tailcone itself has been shortened to reduce the possibility of deck strikes on take-off and landing during carrier operations.

VARIANTS

From the basic **Su-27K/Su-33** several variants have been developed. The **Su-33 Upgrade** programme was announced in 1999, but has not as yet been funded; this improves the cockpit displays and gives compatibility with a wider range of weaponry. The **Su-27KM** was the proposed ultimate version but does not seem to have been proceeded with; other versions reported to be under development include the **Su-27KRT** reconnaissance and target acquisition model of which a prototype was said to be flying, and the **Su-27KPP** EW command post. The two-seat training version is the **Su-27KUB** and is under private development at present. The **Su-30K-2** two-seat interceptor is based on the Su-33, although its designation is provisional.

Sukhoi Su-27KUB

Sukhoi Su-27M & Su-35

SINGLE-SEAT ALL-WEATHER STRIKE FIGHTER AND GROUND-ATTACK AIRCRAFT

Sukhoi Su-35 Russian Air Force

DEVELOPMENT

Sukhoi's faith in its Su-27 design was such that work began on an advanced version of the Su-27 (designated T10S-70, then T10M and finally Su-27M) in the early 1980s before the main initial version had entered widespread service. An experimental aircraft with foreplanes was flown by the company in May 1985 before it started work on a batch of six prototypes and five pre-production aircraft. Flight testing then occupied the five years until 1993, at which time the aircraft was intended to enter service in 1995 and enjoy a large production run during the following ten years; it would be operational until around 2020 when it would eventually be replaced by the Mikoyan MFI. However, problems with the radar system have led to delays and the aircraft has been challenged by the cheaper MiG-29SMT. The programme seems currently to be in abeyance as far as the Russian military is concerned, although Sukhoi is still chasing overseas orders. Although this model of the 'Flanker'

is still officially known as the Su-27M, in 1993 Sukhoi redesignated this aircraft as the Su-35. In 1995, it allocated the designation Su-37 to the definitive thrust-vectoring version of this design, the first example of which (a converted Su-35) first flew in April 1996. The current engine nozzles swivel through ±15°; Saturn is developing the three-dimensional AL-37PP engine for possible production examples. If production does commence, it will be with this model.

CURRENT SERVICE

At present Sukhoi is looking for orders for the Su-35 and the aircraft is under consideration for the delayed South Korean F-X programme, where it is competing against the F-15K, Rafale and Eurofighter Typhoon.

SPECIAL FEATURES

Compared to it Su-27 predecessor, the Su-27M has the advantage of better flight characteristics – it is lighter and therefore more agile, with new armament

and upgraded flight control systems. Flight control is provided by a digital fly-by-wire system with quadruple redundancy. The tail cone houses a rearwards facing Ryazan radar. A retractable inflight refuelling probe is fitted. The nose has been reshaped to accommodate its Zhuk-27 multimode terrain-following radar. The nose canards are counterbalanced by a larger fin area and the undercarriage redesigned and strengthened.

VARIANTS

The initial **Su-27M** designation has been replaced by the **Su-35**. The **Su-37** has thrust-vectoring engine nozzles which are said to make it even more agile.

TECHNICAL DATA

Sukhoi Su-35

Powerplants: Two Saturn/Lyulka AL-35F turbofans
Developing: 125.5kN (28,218lb st) with afterburning
Span: 15.16m (49ft 8.75in)
Length: 22.185m (72ft 9.5in)
Height: 6.36m (20ft 10.25in)
All-up weight: 34,000kg (74,957lb)
Maximum speed: 2,500km/h (1,555mph)
Operational ceiling: 58,400ft
Maximum range: 6,500km (4,040 miles) with inflight refuelling
Mission range: 1,390km (864 miles)
Accommodation: Pilot only
Warload: One 30mm GSh-301 30mm machine gun with 150 rounds is mounted in the starboard wing root. Up to 14 underwing hardpoints can be fitted for a range of weapons up to a load limit of 8,200kg (18,077lb) – these include AA-10 'Alamo', AA-6 'Acrid', AA-8 'Aphid', AA-11 'Archer' and AA-12 'Adder' air-to-air missiles, AS-10 'Karen', AS-12 'Kegler', AS-14 'Kedge', AS-17 'Krypton' and AS-18 'Kazoo' air-to-surface missiles, plus a full range of rockets and bombs.
First flown: 28 June 1988 (full prototype)

Sukhoi Su-35 Russian Air Force

Sukhoi Su-30M

TWO-SEAT MULTI-ROLE SUPERSONIC FIGHTER

Sukhoi Su-30MKI Russian Air Force

TECHNICAL DATA

Sukhoi Su-30MK

Powerplants: Two Saturn/Lyulka AL-31FP turbofan engines with afterburners
Developing: Each 74.5kN (16,755lb st) dry and 122.6kN (27,557lb st) with afterburning.
Span: 14.70m (48ft 2.75in)
Length: 23.335m (76ft 6.25in) without probe
Height: 6.355m (20ft 10.25in)
All-up weight: 38,000kg (83,775lb)
Maximum speed: 2,150km/h (1,336mph)
Operational ceiling: 57,420ft
Maximum range: 5,200km (3,230 miles) with in-flight refuelling
Mission range: 3,000km (1,865 miles)
Accommodation: Pilot and navigator/weapons operator
Warload: One 30mm GSh-301 machine gun with 150 rounds in starboard wing root. Twelve underwing hardpoints for maximum load of 8,000kg (17,635lb) of stores: these include AB-500, KAB-500KR and KAB-1500KB bombs, B-8M-1 and B-13L rocket packs, S-25 rockets, up to six AA-10C/D 'Alamo' or AA-12 'Adder' AAMs, or two AA-10D and six AA-11 'Archer' missiles. Other missiles carried include AS-14 'Kedge', AS-17 'Krypton' and AS-18 'Kazoo'; plus one Raduga 3M80E supersonic anti-ship missile.
First flown: 1 July 1997 (Su-30MK)
Entered service: 1999 (true Su-30)

DEVELOPMENT

Design work on the Su-30M series began in 1991, the 'interim' prototype (without canards) constructed by converting a Su-27UB two-seat trainer; this first flew on 14 April 1992. The first 'definitive' prototype was constructed during 1993 and displayed the following year. Canards and a thrust-vectoring system were offered as options during 1997 and the 'interim' prototype was tested in this configuration during 1997. The first prototype Su-30MKI was destroyed at the 1999 Paris Air Show. Production began at Irkutsk to fulfil an order for 40 placed on 30 November 1996 for the Indian Air Force, and the first eight, which were delivered in March 1997, were basically to Su-30K (export Su-30) standard. These aircraft, and a further 20 delivered in batches since 1997, will eventually be upgraded to Su-30MKI standard; ten more ordered in September 1998 will be delivered as Su-30MKIs. In November 1999, Sukhoi granted Hindustan Aircraft a licence to to build Su-30MKs; the company expects to build around 100.

CURRENT SERVICE

The first eight of India's 50 Su-30MKIs were delivered in 1997 to No 24 'Hunting Hawks' Squadron at Pune. and are effectively Su-30Ks due to be upgraded later; they had been joined by a second batch of ten by October 1999, the latter being Su-30Ks originally intended for Indonesia, which on 9 January 1998 cancelled the order for eight single-seaters and four two-seaters it had placed four months previously.

SPECIAL FEATURES

Compared to the Su-30, of which it is the multi-role version, the Su-30M has improved combat capabilities due to its more accurate avionics systems. The main visible difference is the addition of canards. The nozzles of the vectored-thrust engine initially developed for the Su-35/Su-37 can be set at angles of ±15° and are set by the flight control system.

VARIANTS

The **Su-30M** is the basic multi-role version. The export version is designated **Su-30MK** and if the Russian Air Force purchases them, it is expected they will be designated **Su-30MKR**. The **Su-30MKI** is being built for the Indian Air Force – four sub-configurations have been disclosed to date; all Indian aircraft will eventually be updated to the same standard.

SEE ALSO: SUKHOI SU-27 VARIANTS

Sukhoi Su-30MKI Russian Air Force

Transporter Allianz C-160 Transall

TWIN-ENGINED TROOP/FREIGHT TRANSPORT

C-160D Transall German Air Force

TECHNICAL DATA

Transporter Allianz C-160F Transall

Powerplants: Two Rolls-Royce Tyne 20 Mk 22 turboprops
Developing: 4,548kW (6,100shp)
Driving: four-blade propeller
Span: 40.00m (131ft 3in)
Length: 32.40m (106ft 3.5in)
Height: 11.65m (38ft 5in)
All-up weight: 51,000kg (112,200lb)
Maximum speed: 536km/h (333mph)
Cruise speed: 495km/h (308mph)
Operational ceiling: 27,885ft
Maximum range: 4,500km (2,796 miles)
Accommodation: Crew of three plus either 93 passengers on canvas seats, 8,000kg (17,637lb) of freight, or 62 stretchers in the casualty evacuation role.
First flown: 25 February 1963
Entered service: 1967

DEVELOPMENT

Initial talks in 1959 between France and Germany resulted in the Transporter Allianz, Europe's first multi-country development programme, with the aim of producing a Noratlas replacement. Three companies were involved: Nord, which built the wing, engine nacelles and landing gear; Hamburger Flugzeugbau (later part of MBB), responsible for the front and rear fuselage and fin; and Weser Flugzeugbau (later part of VFW-Fokker), which produced the fuselage centre sections and undercarriage panniers. The designation of C.160 reflected the aircraft's cargo role and its wing area in square metres. The initial production requirement was 110 aircraft for the German Air Force and 50 for the French Air Force; the prototype made its first flight from Melun on 25 February 1963. Production of the initial version ended in 1972 after 175 had been built, including prototypes. A new generation version of the Transall was authorised in 1977 with upgraded avionics and increased range, due to an extra fuel tank in the strengthened wing. The French Air Force ordered 29, all of which were delivered by mid-1985. Ten are tankers equipped with hose-and-drogue refuelling equipment in the port sponson; five more have this feature and can be rapidly modified; eight more are standard transports; four are Astarté communications relay models and two are C.160G Gabriel electronic

intelligence versions. The only other customer for the second-generation Transall was Indonesia, which received six examples.

CURRENT SERVICE

The French Air Force has over 70 Transalls, including 26 new-generation examples – three aircraft support the French Foreign Legion in the Central African Republic. Germany still has a substantial fleet of 84 aircraft; Indonesia has six (some of which have been operated under civilian guise) and Turkey has 20, purchased from Germany in the 1980s. South Africa, which was the only direct export customer with nine, currently has its Transalls in storage pending a decision on their future.

SPECIAL FEATURES

The Transall's shoulder-mounted wing enables easy loading of freight into the fuselage without compromising propeller ground clearance; the high tail enables tall loads to utilise the rear fuselage; an internal winch assists loading operations. The C-160's undercarriage is mounted within fuselage sponsons, and can be slightly retracted whilst on the ground to facilitate loading. Paradropping is accomplished via a door on each side of the rear fuselage. Double-slotted flaps, airbrakes and spoilers give good short-field performance, including operation from semi-prepared

strips. Wing designed to accommodate auxiliary jet engines if required, but these have never been fitted. Second-generation Transalls are instantly identifiable by their refuelling probes, fitted above the cockpit.

VARIANTS

First-generation French Transalls are designated **C.160F** and German Transalls **C.160D**; there are no obvious external differences between the two; German examples transferred to Turkey are **C.160T**. South African examples are designated **C.160Z** and the four **C.160P** models were mail-carrying versions modified by Air France. The **C.160 Rénové** has upgraded avionics. Two French C.160s were converted as Sigint platforms (**C.160 Gabriel** or **C.160G**) – which have wingtip pods, a blister fairing on the rear port fuselage, a large retractable dome under the forward fuselage and numerous antennas.

C-160T Transall Turkish Air Force

Tupolev Tu-16

MEDIUM-RANGE MULTI-ROLE TWIN-JET BOMBER

Tupolev Tu-16K 'Badger-G'

DEVELOPMENT

Intended as a platform for launching nuclear weapons, and using technology derived from the B-29 Superfortress, three examples of the prototype Tupolev Model 88 were ordered to compete against the Ilyushin IL-46. The Tu-16's success resulted in a production order in December 1952 and it was seen in the West for the first time at the 1954 May Day parade. The first major model to appear was the Tu-16A 'Badger-A' nuclear bomber, of which 700 were built, and this was exported to Egypt, though most of these were lost during the 1967 Six-Day War. Next

to appear was the cruise missile-equipped Tu-16KS 'Badger-B' and this was followed by the anti-shipping Tu-16K 'Badger-C', and it underwent several upgrades to accommodate newer weaponry as it became available. Many reconnaissance versions were also produced and are listed below under 'variants'. The final major Tu-16 version was the 'Badger-G', which appeared in 1968 and was capable of carrying the then-new AS-5 'Kelt' missile and, later, the AS-6 'Kingfish'. Eventually, around 2,000 were produced before the line closed in 1959. The aircraft was also licence-built in China as the Xian H-6 (described separately).

CURRENT SERVICE

The Tu-16 has reached the end of its service career with the Russian Navy, but over 120 remain in use with the Chinese Air Force and 30 with the Chinese Navy. Egypt received 20 Tu-16H 'Badger-Gs' to replace those lost in 1967, and the survivors have now been retired. Iraq's fleet is believed destroyed during *Desert Storm*. Indonesia had 25 Tu-16KS, the survivors of which were retired in the 1970s.

SPECIAL FEATURES

Long thin fuselage and large tail unit. Wings swept back with engines embedded in wing roots. The large

bomb bay gives many weaponry and equipment options. Undercarriage retracts into wing pods.

VARIANTS

The **Tu-16A 'Badger-A'** was the conventional and nuclear bomber version; other models classified by NATO as 'Badger-A' were the Navy's torpedo-carrying **Tu-16T**, the SAR-equipped **Tu-16K Korvet** and the **Tu-16N** tanker version. The cruise missile-equipped **Tu-16KS 'Badger-B'** has a retractable radome and this was followed by the **Tu-16K 'Badger-C'** which had a prominent nose radome and was used for anti-shipping duties. The Tu-16 series was widely used for reconnaissance and intelligence gathering. Under the basic designation **Tu-16R** were the **'Badger-D'** (with nose radome) for maritime reconnaissance and Elint, **'Badger-E'** for photographic reconnaissance using pallet-mounted cameras in the bomb-bay, and **'Badger-F'** for maritime Elint with underwing pods – the **'Badger-K'** undertook the same task but without pods. The most recent reconnaissance conversion is the upgraded **'Badger-L'**. The final major Tu-16 version was the **'Badger-G'**, which appeared in 1968. Two further versions are the **Tu-16P 'Badger-H'** chaff dispenser and **'Badger-J'**, used for active ECM jamming.

SEE ALSO: XIAN H-6

TECHNICAL DATA

Tupolev Tu-16K 'Badger-G'

Powerplants: Two Mikulin AM-3A turbojets
Developing: 85.21kN (19,155lb st) each
Span: 32.99m (108ft 3in)
Length: 34.80m (114ft 2in)
Height: 10.36m (34ft 0in)
All-up weight: 75,000kg (165,350lb)
Maximum speed: 1,050 km/h (652 mph)
Cruise speed: 850 km/h (488 mph)
Operational ceiling: 49,200ft
Maximum range: 5,760km (3,580 miles)
Mission range: 1,800km (971 miles)
Accommodation: Crew of six comprises two pilots, navigator, forward gunner, rear gunner(s) and one or two observers.
Warload: Main weapons are two KSR-11 or KSR-2 (AS-5) 'Kelt' rocket-powered missiles; conventional bombs up to total weight of 9,000kg (19,800lb) in weapons bay. Defensive armament comprises forward dorsal and aft ventral pods each containing two 23-mm AM-23 guns with a further two in the tail.
First flown: 27 April 1952 (prototype)
Entered service: 1954

Tupolev Tu-16K 'Badger-G'

Tupolev Tu-22

STRATEGIC LONG-RANGE BOMBER

Tu-22 'Blinder'

DEVELOPMENT

Work on the Tu-22 'Blinder' began in the early 1950s under the designation Samolet (Aeroplane) 105A, and was intensified following the 1954 entry into service of the Tu-16 'Badger'. The Tu-22 was intended to be a replacement for the Tu-16, and eventually

TECHNICAL DATA

Tupolev Tu-22K 'Blinder-B'

Powerplants: Two Dobrynin VD-7M turbojets
Developing: 156.9kN (35,273lb st) each, with afterburner
Span: 23.65m (77ft 6.75in)
Length: 41.60m (136ft 5.75in)
Height: 10.15m (33ft 3.5in)
All-up weight: 94,000kg (207,231lb)
Maximum speed: 1,510 km/h (938 mph)
Operational ceiling: 43,635ft
Maximum range: 5,850km (3,635 miles)
Accommodation: Crew of three, in tandem
Warload: Main weapon is the Kh-22 (AS-4 'Kitchen') supersonic cruise missile, recessed into the lower fuselage. Alternatively a range of free-fall bombs could be carried within the bomb bay. One NR-23 23-mm cannon in tail turret.
First flown: 21 June 1958
Entered service: 1961

entered service in 1961 in its Tu-22B form, armed with free-fall bombs, both conventional and nuclear. However, this variant was not particularly successful and only 15 were built. The Tu-22R reconnaissance version, which retained its bombing capability and was used for maritime operations, was more successful and 127 were produced, some being fitted with in-flight refuelling. Some 46 trainers were also produced under the designation Tu-22U. It was the USSR's first successful supersonic bomber. By the beginning of the 1960s, the fighter was replaced by the SAM missile as the biggest threat to bombers, and redesign work on the Tu-22 was undertaken to give it a stand-off capability. The result was the Tu-22K, of which 76 were built. These entered service in 1967, and their main weapon was the versatile Kh-22/AS-4 'Kitchen' missile. The last Tu-22s to be built were the 47 Tu-22P electronic warfare versions. By the end of the 1970s, however, the Tu-22M 'Backfire' had begun to enter service and the 'Blinder' was slowly withdrawn from service, although one or two remain in the testbed role. The Tu-22B was exported to two countries and saw operational service with both. Iraq's fleet of Tu-22s was used in operations against Iran in the long-running conflict between the two countries, while those sold to Libya were used offensively against Tanzania (in support of Uganda), Chad and the Sudan. Both countries' aircraft were modified

Tu-22Rs. Closer to home, the 'Blinder' fleet was occasionally used in operations in Afghanistan.

CURRENT SERVICE

The Tu-22 has now been retired from Russian service. Any that survived the Coalition bombing of Iraq during 1991 are unlikely to be operational; a handful remain in Libya. The split of the former Soviet Union gave Ukraine a regiment of Tu-22R reconnaissance versions.

SPECIAL FEATURES

The Tu-22's engines are mounted at the base of the tail unit, thereby improving air flow and reducing the chance of ingesting debris. Its swept-back, thin aerofoil wing provides a high cruise speed, but high take-off and landing speeds led to many mishaps and the aircraft is not easy to fly. Trainer versions have a second cockpit mounted above and behind the main cockpit.

VARIANTS

The **Tu-22B 'Blinder-B'**, the initial free-fall variant, was followed by the **Tu-22K** (also 'Blinder-B') stand-off version. The basic **Tu-22R 'Blinder-C'** reconnaissance versions spawned variants such as the **Tu-22RK** (ELINT-equipped) and **Tu-22RD** (with refuelling probe). The two-seat version is the **Tu-22U 'Blinder-D'** and the **Tu-22P 'Blinder-E'** is the electronic version.

Tu-22 'Blinder'

Tupolev Tu-22M

SUPERSONIC VARIABLE-GEOMETRY BOMBER

Tu-22M3 'Backfire-C' Russian Air Force

DEVELOPMENT

Work on the Tu-22M development began as early as 1959 when plans for a 'Blinder' replacement were implemented. The planned replacement – the Sukhoi T-4 bomber – failed to materialise, and the Tu-22M was developed partly as an insurance policy, which turned out to be a farsighted measure. Although it is designated as the Tu-22M (M for modified), the 'Backfire' is effectively a completely different aircraft to the Tu-22 from which it is purported to derive, incorporating variable-geometry wings to improve fuel consumption and thus endurance. It has the Tupolev model number 145. Production began with the Tu-22M0 and Tu-22M1 initial prototype and pre-production versions, small numbers of which were built. Quantity production really began with the Tu-22M2 'Backfire-B', of which 211 were built and which entered service in 1976. Development then continued with the introduction of the Tu-22M3 'Backfire-C', of which 268 were built. Operationally, the Russians used the 'Backfire' in Afghanistan and, more recently, in Chechnya. In all, 497 were built before production ended in late 1992.

CURRENT SERVICE

Around 150 Tu-22Ms are believed in service with the Russian Air Force and Navy, and they will remain in service as part of Russia's long-range strike capability until at least 2010. 'Backfires' are being modified to carry Kh-SD and Kh-101 cruise missiles; a further

upgrade to M5 standard is in the pipeline. The Tu-22MR reconnaissance version carries a semi-recessed SLAR pod in the bomb bay and has a large dielectric fairing at the root of the vertical fin, plus dielectric fairings on the fuselage. The Ukrainian Air Force has a fleet of 'Backfires' which it acquired at the break-up of the former Soviet Union. They are divided between two regiments at Priluki and Poltava, but current figures for serviceability are not available.

SPECIAL FEATURES

The variable geometry wings of the 'Backfire', which sweep back to 65°, are its most identifiable feature. The two turbofans are mounted in the rear of the fuselage, and the six-wheel main undercarriage units retract into the fuselage. The large fin area is also a distinctive feature.

VARIANTS

The basic **Tu-22M2** has now been superceded by the **Tu-22M3**, which has wedge-shaped air intakes and a reprofiled nose, which improves the top speed of the aircraft. The **Tu-22MP** is an electronic warfare version on which work progresses slowly and the **Tu-22MR** is a reconnaissance variant which carries a semi-recessed SLAR pod located in the bomb bay and has a large dielectric fairing at the root of the vertical fin along with dielectric fairings on the fuselage. Tupolev is working on the **M5**, an upgrade that includes new avionics, radar, EW and navigation systems.

TECHNICAL DATA

Tupolev Tu-22M3 'Backfire-C'

Powerplants: Two side-by-side Kuznetsov/KKBM NK-25 afterburning turbofans
Developing: 245.2kN (55,115lb st) each
Span: 34.28m (112ft 5.75in) fully open; 23.30m (76ft 5.5in) fully swept
Length: 42.46m (139ft 3.75in)
Height: 11.05m (36ft 3in)
All-up weight: 126,400kg (278,660lb)
Maximum speed: 2,000 km/h (1,242 mph)
Cruise speed: 900 km/h (560 mph)
Operational ceiling: 43,640ft
Maximum range: 2,410km (1,495 miles)
Mission range: over 1,500 km (930 miles)
Accommodation: Four (pilot, co-pilot, navigator and weapons systems officer)
Warload: Maximum internal load 12,000kg (26,460lb), with same amount externally on underwing racks; alternatively three Kh-22 (AS-4 'Kitchen') air-to-surface missiles mounted under fuselage and inner wings. Alternatively, six Kh-15P (AS-16 'Kickback') short-range missiles with rotary launcher can be carried internally; other loads include Kh-15, Kh-31 and Kh-35 missiles. GSh-23 23mm twin-barrel cannon in the tail.
First flown: 30 August 1971; 1980 (TU-22M3)
Entered service: 1976

Tu-22M3 'Backfire-C' Russian Air Force

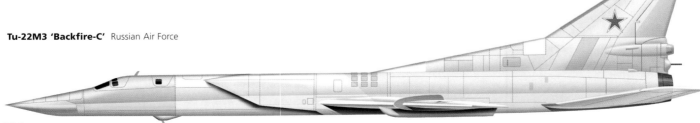

Tupolev Tu-95/Tu-142

FOUR-ENGINED LONG-RANGE STRATEGIC BOMBER

Tu-95MS 'Bear-H' Russian Air Force

TECHNICAL DATA

Tupolev Tu-95MS 'Bear-H'

Powerplants: Four Samara Kuznetsov NK-12MA turboprops
Developing: 11,033 kW (14,795 shp)
Driving: Eight-blade counter-rotating propellers
Span: 50.04m (164ft 2in)
Length: 49.13m (161ft 2.25 in)
Height: 13.30m (43ft 7.75in)
All-up weight: 187,000kg (412,258lb)
Maximum speed: 925 km/h (575 mph)
Cruise speed: 711 km/h (442 mph)
Operational ceiling: 39,380ft
Mission range: 6,400km (3,975 miles)
Accommodation: Crew of seven – two pilots, flight engineer, bombardier, two weapons officers and rear gunner.
Warload: A total of 16 Kh-55 (AS-15A) or RKV-500B (AS-15B) 'Kent' long-range cruise missiles: six in the bomb bay on a rotary launcher; two under each wingroot and three between each pair of engines; later models had external hardpoints removed to meet SALT/START requirements. Maximum weight of weaponry 11,340kg (25,000lb). Two NR-23 23-mm cannon in tail turret.
First flown: 12 November 1952 (prototype); 1968 (Tu-142M)
Entered service: April 1956 (Tu-95); 1972 (Tu-142M)

DEVELOPMENT

Work on a turbine strategic bomber based on the Tu-85 began in 1949, the turbine requirement being dropped in favour of eight piston engines, and the resulting Tu-95 was authorised on 11 July 1951. The prototype was lost during testing and the eight-engine format subsequently abandoned in favour of four turbines. The Tu-95M 'Bear-A' entered service in April 1956 as a nuclear bomber, and around 150 Tu-95s of various marks were built over the next decade. The Russian Navy Tu-142 'Bear-F' dedicated maritime reconnaissance/anti-submarine warfare version was created by mating the fuselage of the Tu-95RT 'Bear-D' (with a 2m (6ft 6in) plug) with a new wing, redesigned undercarriage, uprated engines and new avionics. The Tu-142 was first flown in 1968, entering service in 1972. The longest member of the family was the Tu-142M 'Bear-F Mod III', which entered production in 1975. The Tu-95MS 'Bear-H' was the last version to be built. Based on the Tu-142 without the fuselage plug, it was specifically designed to carry the RK-55 cruise missile. Production began in 1983 and continued until 1994, when the line finally closed.

CURRENT SERVICE

None of the early Tu-95s remain in service. Russia has around 90 Tu-95MSs of two sub-variants in service, and approximately half of these will remain in service in the strike role for the next decade. The Russian Navy has around 55 Tu-142M and 24 Tu-142MR 'Bear-J' models. Former Soviet countries retaining 'Bears' were Kazakhstan, which returned around 40 to Russia, and Ukraine, which returned three and is scrapping a further 24. The sole export user is the Indian Navy, with eight Tu-142Ms in service with INAS312 at Dabolim. A further six Tu-142M 'Bear-Fs' were ordered from Russia in July 1999.

SPECIAL FEATURES

The Tu-95/142 family has a long, narrow fuselage, sharply swept back wings (unique for a propeller-driven aircraft) and counter-rotating propellers. Later models have ventral radomes of various sizes and maritime Tu-142s have longer fuselages.

VARIANTS

The initial model was the **Tu-95M 'Bear-A'**, some of which were converted as **Tu-95U** trainers. Others were modified to carry stand-off missiles as **Tu-95K-20 'Bear-B's** and new-build examples to this standard were **Tu-95KM 'Bear-C's**. The **Tu-95MR** reconnaissance model was initially designated **'Bear-C'**, but later changed to **'Bear-E'**; the **'Bear-D'** was the **Tu-95RT** reconnaissance/surveillance version. Later **Tu-95** models included the modified **Tu-95K-22 'Bear G'**. The **Tu-142 'Bear-F'** is the basic maritime version and the **Tu-142M 'Bear-J'** has a communications role; the **Tu-95MS 'Bear-H'** is the main long-range air force version.

Tu-142 'Bear-F' Russian Navy

Tupolev Tu-134

TWIN-TURBOFAN MEDIUM-RANGE TRANSPORT

Tupolev Tu-134A Aeroflot/Russian Air Force

DEVELOPMENT

Designed to build on experience gained from the Tu-124 'Cookpot', the world's first turbofan short-haul transport, the Tu-134 was initially designated Tu-124A and visually the main difference was the redesigned T-tail configuration; it was only redesignated after 100th test flight of the prototype. The longer-fuselage Tu-134A entered production in 1970, offering extra seating and improved engines. The Tu-134B, with a revised flight deck and no navigator, was introduced towards the end of the production run, and 852 of all models had been completed by time production ceased in 1985. A improved Tu-134M version offering a mid-life update programme including Ivchenko Progress/Zaporozhye D-436T turbofans is currently under consideration.

CURRENT SERVICE

Large numbers were supplied to Aeroflot and these have been redistributed to various smaller airlines within the former Soviet Union territory; the type was also extensively exported, predominantly to East European airlines. Main military user is Russia with up to 180 still in service in various roles, including at least 90 purpose-built Tu-134UBLs, which have Tu-22M nose cones (but no specific avionics) fitted and are

used for Tu-22/Tu-160 pilot training. Other military users include Belarus, Bulgaria, Czech Republic, Georgia, Kazakhstan, Moldova, North Korea, Syria, Ukraine and Uzbekistan.

SPECIAL FEATURES

Twin-engine T-tail layout with engines mounted on each side of rear fuselage. Early Tu-134s identified by navigator's glazed nose cone; this was replaced on aircraft produced from the mid-1970s and solid panels and a different radar system were fitted; this modification was also retrofitted to earlier models.

VARIANTS

The **Tu-134** was the basic model, superceded by the Soloviev D-30 powered **Tu-134A**, which entered service in 1970. Further engine improvements and interior refinement produced the **Tu-134B**. The Tu-134 has proved popular as a testbed, and at least a dozen have been used, under the general designation of **Tu-134LL**, in various programmes including agricultural, ice and pollution surveys (as **Tu-134SKh**), as a support aircraft for the Russian Buran spacecraft project (as **Tu-134BV**) and for astronaut training (as **Tu-134AK**). Russia operates a small number converted as bomber trainers (**Tu-134BSh**). The structurally identical **Tu-135**

is a high command executive transport version, marked up with the Tu-134A designation, but carrying a rear fuselage antenna 'stinger'. The **Tu-134UBL** is a Tu-160 crew trainer featuring 'Blackjack' avionics and radar in a Tu-160 shaped nose.

TECHNICAL DATA

Tupolev Tu-134A
Powerplants: Two Soloviev D-30 Series II turbofans
Developing: Each 66.7kN (14,990lb st)
Span: 29.00m (95 ft 1.75in)
Length: 37.05m (121ft 6.6in)
Height: 9.14m (30ft 0in)
All-up weight: 47,000kg (103,600lb)
Maximum speed: 898km/h (558mph)
Operational ceiling: 36,000ft
Maximum range: 1,890km (1,174 miles)
Accommodation: Crew of three plus up to 84 passengers, depending on cabin layout
Warload: None
First flown: 29 July 1963 as Tu-124A.
Entered service: 9 September 1967 with Aeroflot

Tupolev Tu-134B-3 Bulgarian Air Force

Tupolev Tu-154

THREE-ENGINED MEDIUM-RANGE PASSENGER TRANSPORT

Tupolev Tu-154B Czech Air Force

DEVELOPMENT

Designed as a replacement airliner for Aeroflot's turbojet Tu-104 and Il-18 turboprop fleets, and announced in 1966, the Tu-154 resembled the earlier Tu-134 and drew on the contemporary Boeing 727 and Hawker Siddeley Trident for systems such as leading-edge slats, triple-slotted flaps and triplex hydraulic systems. The initial Tu-154 was later superseded by the higher-powered Tu-154A from 1974, and the increased capacity Tu-154B in 1977. It was designed to have the ability to operate from gravel or packed earth airfields and have a good field performance. Initially designated Tu-164, the Tu-154M was introduced in December 1984 and offered further engine improvements. A twin-engined version, the Tu-154M2 with a 2m fuselage stretch and Perm PS-90 engines was apparently under development in the early 1990s, but has since been abandoned in favour of newer, more efficient models in the Tupolev range such as the Tu-204. Around 1,000 had been built by the end of 1999.

CURRENT SERVICE

The Russian state airline Aeroflot was the major user, with over 600 of all models, and the Russian Air Force still operates a large fleet. Some former Soviet Bloc and East European countries still operate examples for VIP and transport duties, including Belarus, Bulgaria, Czech Republic, Poland and Slovakia.

Another was operated by the German Air Force for Open Skies duties, one of two inherited from the East German state airline Interflug when the two states merged, but was destroyed in a mid-air collision with a USAF C-141 off the African coast in 1997; Germany has one VIP variant still in service. Another military user is the North Korean Air Force. Mainland China has two for electronic intelligence.

SPECIAL FEATURES

Similar in plan view to the twin-engined Tu-134, the Tu-154 represents second-generation airliner design with rear engine T-tail configuration. Its circular fuselage section allows six-abreast seating and extra fuel can be carried in the centre-section (though not used in flight – it is for on-ground refuelling only). Although the Tu-154M is similar to its predecessors, it is the result of a complete redesign with a larger horizontal tail and engine nacelles and earlier models cannot be retrospectively modified to this standard.

VARIANTS

Initial **Tu-154**, **Tu-154A** and **Tu-154B** versions were powered by Kuznetsov NK-8 engines; the **Tu-154M** announced in 1983 had far more economical, quieter and reliable Rybinsk D-30KU turbofans and entered service with Aeroflot in 1984, with 329 produced so far. The **Tu-154C** was a specialised cargo conversion of the Tu-154A/B with a large forward fuselage

freight door. Upgrade and modification programmes offered by Tupolev include uprated D-30KU or CFM56 engines. The cryogenically-powered **Tu-155**, using liquid hydrogen fuel, was tested in 1988 and 1989, and a follow-on **Tu-156**, which will be powered by liquified natural gas, is under consideration.

TECHNICAL DATA

Tupolev Tu-154M

Powerplants: Three Rybinsk D30KU154-11 turbofans
Developing: 104kN (23,380lb st)
Span: 37.55m (123ft 2.5in)
Length: 47.90m (157ft 1.75in)
Height: 11.40m (37ft 4.75in)
All-up weight: 100,000kg (220,460lb)
Maximum speed: 935km/h (581mph)
Operational ceiling: 39,000ft
Maximum range: 3,900km (2,425 miles)
Accommodation: Crew of three or four and up to 180 passengers, depending on cabin layout.
Warload: None.
First flown: 4 October 1968 (Tu-154); 1982 (Tu-154M)
Entered service: Cargo services July 1971, passenger services 9 February 1972 with Aeroflot.

Tupolev Tu-154M Slovak Government

OM-BYO

Tupolev Tu-160

VARIABLE-GEOMETRY LONG-RANGE STRATEGIC BOMBER

Tu-160 'Blackjack-A' Russian Air Force

DEVELOPMENT

Originally designated Product 70, development of the Tupolev Tu-160 began in 1967, but full design work did not start until 1975. By the time the first aircraft were ordered in 1977 its main counterpart in the West, the Rockwell B-1A, had been cancelled. The existence of the Tu-160 first came to the notice of the West in 1981, when one was photographed at the test site at Zhukhovsky. Production of 100 examples of this long-range supersonic strike aircraft was authorised in 1985 and between 40-50 were completed (including the prototypes and pre-production examples) before production ended in 1992.

CURRENT SERVICE

The protracted development programme and various difficulties with the operating systems have resulted in extremely restricted operations. Eight Tu-160s (from a total of 19) were returned by the Ukraine to Russia in November 1999; under the terms of the START treaty the remaining aircraft will be scrapped by 2001. The Russian Air Force is believed to have around a dozen aircraft, of which only half are operational, and possibly as few as two remain combat capable. Finance has also been found for the completion of one of the six part-built Blackjacks at Tupolev's Kazan plant. An interest in three ex-Ukraine Air Force Tu-160s was expressed by the US company Platforms

International Corp of Mojave, and in March 1999 the Ukrainian Government authorised the sale of these for $20 million, to include spares and support equipment, for use for satellite launching. The aircraft will remain at Priluki and be maintained and flown from there by local crews, transiting to customer countries for satellite launches.

SPECIAL FEATURES

The heaviest and most powerful combat aircraft ever built, the Tu-160 resembles the Rockwell B-1 Lancer, but is much larger. The airframe is free from any protuberances, and its four engines are mounted in pairs beneath the inner (fixed) wings. Its variable geometry wings sweep back to 65° and have full-span slats and flaps to improve low-speed handling characteristics; the flight control system is fly-by-wire. The undercarriage has a narrow wheel track and six-wheel mainwheel bogies. The retractable refuelling probe is mounted forward of the cockpit but is not operational, in conformity with the START treaty.

VARIANTS

Basic version is the **Tu-160 'Blackjack-A'**. The **Tu-160P** was a planned long-range interceptor which did not materialise, and the **Tu-160SK** shown at Paris in 1995 with the Buryan rocket launch vehicle beneath it was the result of a Russian/German consortium.

TECHNICAL DATA

Tupolev Tu-160 'Blackjack-A'

Powerplants: Four Kuznetsov/Samara NK-321 turbofans.
Developing: 245 kN (55,055lb st) each, with afterburner.
Span: 55.70m (182ft 9in) fully spread; 35.60m (116ft 9.75in) fully swept
Length: 54.10m (177ft 6in)
Height: 13.10m (43ft 0in)
All-up weight: 275,000kg (606,260lb)
Maximum speed: 2,220 km/h (1,380 mph; Mach 2,05)
Cruise speed: 960 km/h (596 mph)
Operational ceiling: 49,200ft
Maximum range: 14,000km (8,700 miles)
Mission range: 12,300km (7,640 miles)
Accommodation: Four (two pilots, navigator/bombardier and weapons systems officer)
Warload: Two bomb bays can carry either six RK-55 (AS-15) 'Kent' cruise missiles or 12 Kh-15S (AS-16) 'Kickback' defence suppression missiles; will carry Kh-101 ALCMs when available. Defensive equipment includes 72 chaff/flare dispensers under the rear fuselage.
First flown: 19 December 1981
Entered service: May 1987.

Tu-160 'Blackjack-A' Russian Air Force

UTVA-66

UTVA-66

DEVELOPMENT

Designed by UTVA, part of the Yugoslav state aircraft factory system, the UTVA-66 is a direct development of the earlier UTVA-56 design, an all-metal high-wing general duties aircraft produced to meet the needs of civilian flying clubs and the military's requirement for an artillery spotter. The prototype first flew on 22 April 1959 and the new type entered production as the UTVA-60. The improved UTVA-66, with its larger tail, stronger undercarriage and wing slats, was publicly announced in 1968, although a total of four prototypes had been flying for at least a year by then. Production of the UTVA-66 at Pancevo continued until 1976, when it was dropped in favour of the UTVA-75 light trainer.

CURRENT SERVICE

The conflict that raged in the former Yugoslavia for most of the 1990s has probably seen the demise of the larger part of the UTVA-66 fleet, which is believed to have numbered over 80, but around 15 are possibly still airworthy in the communications/liaison role and for 'hack' duties.

SPECIAL FEATURES

The UTVA-66's high wing provides good downward visibility, and its leading-edge slots and large flaps linked to ailerons give it excellent slow-flying handling characteristics, an 80km/h (50mph) stalling speed and a take-off and landing run of less than 200m (650ft). Long undercarriage legs and large tyres give good rough-field capability. The UTVA-66-AM ambulance version has an under-fuselage hardpoint enabling the carriage of a jettisonable parachute pack containing food or medical supplies. Unusually, the rear cabin window is upward hinged to facilitate the loading of stretcher cases and freight.

VARIANTS

The basic **UTVA-66** is a four-seat utility version which can also be used for glider towing. The **UTVA-66-AM** ambulance version carries two stretchers which are loaded through the upward-hinging rear window; a seat for an attendant is provided behind the pilot. The **UTVA-66H** float-equipped version first flew in September 1968 and had BIN-160 floats fitted and a 2,010kg (4,431lb) maximum take-off weight, only one example appears to have been built. The **UTVA-66V** had underwing armament options. The **UTVA-70** was a proposed twin-engined six-seat version using two Textron 220kW (295hp) Lycoming GO-480-G1J6 engines on stub wings. It appears that a prototype said to have been under construction in 1970 was not completed.

TECHNICAL DATA

UTVA-66

Powerplant: One Textron Lycoming GSO-480-B1J6 six-cylinder piston engine.
Developing: 201kW (270hp)
Driving: Two-blade propeller
Span: 11.40m (37ft 5in)
Length: 8.38m (27ft 6in)
Height: 3.20m (10ft 6in)
All-up weight: 1,814kg (4,000lb)
Maximum speed: 250km/h (155mph)
Cruise speed: 230km/h (143mph)
Operational ceiling: 22,000ft
Maximum range: 750km (466 miles)
Endurance: 3 hours
Accommodation: Pilot and up to three passengers.
Warload: An underwing hardpoint under each wing can be fitted with a machine gun.
First flown: Late 1966
Entered service: 1969 with Yugoslav Air Force

UTVA-66 Serbian Air Force

UTVA-75

UTVA-75 Croatian Air Force

DEVELOPMENT

The UTVA-75 was designed and built by UTVA in partnership with Prva Petoletka-Trstenik and two technical institutes as a two-seat trainer and utility light aircraft with a secondary glider-towing role. Work on the design began in 1974 and construction of the prototypes began the following year. Latterly this model was redesignated UTVA-75A2. Around 260 were built for both military and civil use before

production ceased with the outbreak of hostilities in the Balkans during the early 1990s. The UTVA-75A improved version was announced in 1986 – this was a four-seat version with larger cabin doors and the elimination of the rear cockpit windows. A prototype was built and flew in 1986, but production was not proceeded with. One further version of the type was the UTVA-75AG11, an agricultural aircraft which used the same airframe but had a single-occupant cabin and large hopper in the forward fuselage; again, only a single prototype seems to have been built.

CURRENT SERVICE

The bulk of military UTVA-75s in current service are operated by members of the Balkan bloc: Bosnia has four aircraft for communications duties, operating from Zenica and Bihac; Croatia has a fleet of ten for pilot training alongside PC-9s; Slovenia has 11 based at Brnik for training; and Yugoslavia had around 30 trainers, but their current status is unknown following NATO operations in the region during 1999. The sole

UTVA-75 export customer was the Colombian Army, which currently has a fleet of five.

SPECIAL FEATURES

The UTVA-75 has a cantilever low wing with fixed tricycle undercarriage. The control surfaces and fin skins are corrugated/fluted. The upward opening gull-wing cabin doors are jettisonable in emergencies. Construction is of metal throughout, and as well as armament, the military versions can carry 100kg (220lb) cargo containers on their underwing hardpoints; 100 litre (22 Imp gallon) drop tanks can also be fitted.

VARIANTS

The UTVA-75 standard version can be identified by its rear cockpit windows, which were deleted on the UTVA-75A with its larger door. The UTVA-75AG11 has a single cockpit, with a chemical hopper between the cockpit and engine firewall, and a more powerful 224kW (300hp) Textron Lycoming IO-540-L1A5D piston engine, and first flew on 3 March 1989.

TECHNICAL DATA

UTVA-75

Powerplant: One Textron Lycoming IO-360-B1F flat-four piston engine
Developing: 134kW (180hp)
Driving: Two-blade propeller
Span: 9.73m (31ft 11in)
Length: 7.11m (23ft 4in)
Height: 3.15m (10ft 4in)
All-up weight: 960kg (2,116lb)
Maximum speed: 215km/h (133mph)
Cruise speed: 185km/h (115mph)
Operational ceiling: 13,125ft
Maximum range: 2,000km (1,242 miles) with drop tanks fitted to underwing points
Mission range: 800km (497 miles)
Endurance: 8 hours
Accommodation: Pilot and up to three passengers in two pairs of seats.
Warload: Two underwing hardpoints fitted to military aircraft, each capable of carrying a 100kg (220lb) bomb, two-round rocket-launcher or machine gun pod.
First flown: 19 May 1976
Entered service: 1976

UTVA-75 Serbian Air Force

Valmet (Aermacchi) L-90 RediGO

TWO/FOUR-SEAT TURBO-POWERED TRAINER

Valmet L-90 RediGO Finnish Air Force

DEVELOPMENT

Originally designed by Valmet (later Finavitec) of Finland, the L-80TP Turbotrainer first flew on 12 February 1985, but was damaged in an accident soon afterwards. The second prototype, renamed L-90TP RediGO, with a 313kW (420shp) Turboméca TP319 engine, was first flown 2 December 1987. The Finnish Air Force became first customer on 6 January 1989 with an order for ten aircraft to replace Piper Arrows, deliveries of which were completed by late 1993. Other foreign sales were announced at this time, but Valmet announced that it would close its production line after building 30 aircraft. It did so in 1995, having fulfilled orders from Eritrea and Mexico, the latter sold via McDonnell Aircraft Co in the USA to offset Finland's purchase of F/A-18 Hornets. The RediGO was designed to fulfil both civilian and military certification requirements, and is intended to slot into the training syllabus between primary piston-engined trainers and primary jet trainers such as the BAE Systems Hawk. Aermacchi of Italy took over the RediGO programme on 31 January 1996 and aircraft

are being built in Italy under the designation M-290TP RediGO. The civilian-registered RediGo demonstrator has been transferred to Italy but no sales had been recorded by end 1999, although Aermacchi believe that in the next ten years there will be a market for up to 400 aircraft.

CURRENT SERVICE

The Finnish Air Force currently has nine RediGOs in use in the communications role with the Air Force Academy (Ilmasotakoulu) at Kauhava, delivered from 1992 onwards. Other operators are the Eritrean Air Force (eight delivered in 1994 and used for training) and the Mexican Naval Aviation School at Bajadas, Vera Cruz, which has ten for use in the COIN, ground attack and training roles, delivered from 1993.

SPECIAL FEATURES

Of all-metal construction, the L-90 is a low-winged retractable-undercarriage monoplane with tapered wings and electrically operated flaps. Options include operations in the survey role (with a vertical camera

and operator in the cabin); as a target tug with winch gear; on coastal patrols with a radar pod under one wing; in the medevac role with the starboard seats removed and a stretcher in their place, and for search and rescue with a searchlight and survival pods on the underwing pylons.

VARIANTS

The **L-80TP Turbotrainer** was the initial prototype; no variants of the RediGO have been built to date.

TECHNICAL DATA

Aermacchi M-290TP RediGO
Powerplant: One Rolls-Royce (Allison) 250-B17F turboprop
Developing: 336kW (450shp)
Driving: three-blade propeller
Span: 10.60m (34ft 9.25in)
Length: 8.53m (27ft 11.75in)
Height: 3.20m (10ft 6in)
All-up weight: 1,900kg (4,189lb)
Maximum speed: 415km/h (257mph)
Cruise speed: 326km/h (203mph)
Operational ceiling: 25,800ft
Maximum range: 1,203km (748 miles)
Mission range: 370km (230 miles)
Endurance: 5hr 55min in normal operational configuration.
Accommodation: Pilot and passenger in front seats with provision for two removable seats in rear of cockpit.
Warload: A maximum of 800kg (1,764lb) of stores can be carried on six underwing pylons.
First flown: 1 July 1986
Entered service: 1991

Valmet L-90 RediGO Finnish Air Force

Valmet L-70 Vinka/Miltrainer

LOW-WING BASIC MULTI-ROLE AIRCRAFT

Valmet L-70 Vinka Finnish Air Force

TECHNICAL DATA

Valmet L-70

Powerplant: One Textron Lycoming AEIO-360-A1B6 flat-four piston engine
Developing: 149kw (200hp)
Driving: Two-blade propeller
Span: 9.63m (31ft 7.25in)
Length: 7.50m (24ft 7.75in)
Height: 3.31m (10ft 10.25in)
All-up weight: 1,250kg (2,756lb)
Maximum speed: 240km/h (149mph)
Cruise speed: 222km/h (138mph)
Operational ceiling: 16,400ft
Maximum range: 950km (590 miles)
Endurance: 6hr 12min
Accommodation: Instructor and pupil; civilian version offered with four seats
Warload: Four underwing hardpoints can carry a maximum external load of 300kg (661lb); weaponry includes bombs, 37mm or 68mm rockets, flare pods, machine guns; anti-tank missiles.
First flown: 1 July 1975
Entered service: 7 October 1980

DEVELOPMENT

On 23 March 1973, the Finnish Air Force issued a development contract with Valmet for a basic trainer to replace the Saab Safir. The L-70 Miltrainer, which is designated Vinka by the Air Force (named after a cold arctic wind) first flew on 1 July 1975. The aircraft was designed to undertake a wide range of roles, many using cannisters fitted to the underwing hardpoints. Duties include search and rescue, photographic reconnaissance (through an aperture in the fuselage behind the front seats), observation and liaison, and casualty evacuation (one stretcher plus attendant). Alternatively, with a pilot only, light cargo up to 280kg (617lb) can be carried internally. The Finnish Air Force placed an order for 30 aircraft on 28 January 1977 and the first aircraft was delivered on 7 October 1980; deliveries were completed by the end of 1982. Despite extensive marketing abroad, the L-70 failed to achieve any export orders.

CURRENT SERVICE

The sole operator of the L-70 Miltrainer is the Finnish Air Force, which has 28 surviving from its fleet of 30, operated by the Ilmavoimien Koelentokeskus (Air Force Flight Test Centre) at Halli, where pilots start their courses flying the Vinka before progressing to the BAe Hawk Mk 51 (46 of which were licence-built by Valmet). Additionally, each of the four front-line units (three fighter squadrons and a transport/support squadron) have one or two Vinkas on charge for communications and liaison work, alongside examples of the RediGO, PA-28 and PA-31.

SPECIAL FEATURES

The Vinka/Miltrainer has a fixed tricycle undercarriage and is designed for aerobatic or utility use as a two-seater, although for civilian use, four seats can be fitted. Extra strengthening in the Finnish Air Force models means that they have a fatigue life in excess of 8,000 hours. For Arctic operations skis can be fitted. An inverted oil and fuel system enables the Vinka to be used for aerobatics.

VARIANTS

Only the basic version was produced. The company developed a slightly larger version in the early 1980s powered by a 261kW (350shp) Allison 250-B17D turboprop, but this did not reach production. However, Valmet later used the Vinka as the basis for its L-90 RediGO (described separately).

Valmet L-70 Vinka Finnish Air Force

Westland Wessex

TACTICAL AND SEARCH AND RESCUE HELICOPTER

Wessex HC2 Uruguayan Air Force

DEVELOPMENT

In 1953, the Fleet Air Arm issued a specification for a general-purpose shipborne helicopter for use in the ASV and ASW roles. Westland acquired a licence to build the Sikorsky S-58, using a Napier Gazelle turboshaft in place of the S-58's Wright R-1820-24 radial. Following the success of an imported, modified HSS-1N Seabat, contracts for prototypes, pre-production and production aircraft were issued for the HAS1. Eventually, seven front-line squadrons utilised the HAS1 and its successors until August 1979. Many were converted to HAS3 standard in the late 1960s (although three were new-built). The FAA's last main variant was the HU5 for operations in the commando role, serving until 1987 although some were later passed to the RAF for use in Cyprus. Chosen by the Royal Air Force as a troop and equipment transport, the Wessex HC2 became its first twin-engined single-rotor helicopter when it entered service in February 1964. As well as UK operations, it was also active in Aden, Cyprus, Germany, Hong Kong and Singapore. The Royal Flight received two HCC4 VIP transports in June 1969 that served until their retirement in 1998. Overseas customers included Australia, Brunei, Ghana and Iraq; there were also a small number of civilian sales before production ended in 1981, by which time a total of 382 had been built.

CURRENT SERVICE

The RAF continues to use the Wessex at Aldergrove (No 72 Squadron) for transport duties. Abroad, No 84 Squadron at Akrotiri, Cyprus uses the type for various roles, an important part of which is acting as SAR cover for the island. The only other user is Uruguay, which bought two ex-civilian Wessex 60s in 1992 and has since added six ex-RAF HC2s formerly used by No 28 Squadron in Hong Kong, plus five from No 2 FTS at Shawbury. Indonesia has 12 Sikorsky S-58Ts for transport; Thailand has ten.

SPECIAL FEATURES

Tapering fuselage and fixed undercarriage, which consists of large main wheels mounted on struts in front of the main cabin door. Because the engine is mounted in the nose, large exhaust pipes protrude between the cockpit and cabin.

VARIANTS

The single-engined **Wessex HAS1** was the initial Fleet Air Arm version; most were later upgraded to **HAS3** standard. The RAF's **HC2** is twin-engined; the **HCC4** was the VIP version operated by The Queen's Flight (later No 32 (Royal) Squadron). The **HU5** was basically a navalised HC2.

TECHNICAL DATA

Westland Wessex HC2

Powerplants: Two coupled Rolls-Royce (Bristol Siddeley) Gnome H.1200 Mk110/111 turboshafts

Developing: 1,005kW (1,350shp)

Driving: Four-blade main and tail rotors

Main rotor diameter: 17.07m (56ft 0in)

Fuselage length: 14.74m (48ft 4.5in)

Height: 4.83m (15ft 10in)

All-up weight: 6,123kg (13,500lb)

Maximum speed: 212km/h (132mph)

Cruise speed: 196km/h (122mph)

Operational ceiling: 12,000ft

Mission range: 500km (310 miles)

Accommodation: Flight crew of two plus up to 16 troops; for SAR operations a navigator/winch operator is added

Warload: Optional loads could include AS12 wire-guided missiles, 2in rocket pods, and machine guns.

First flown: 17 May 1957 (XL722 development aircraft); 18 January 1962 (HC2)

Entered service: April 1960 (HAS1); February 1964 (HC2)

Wessex HC2 Royal Air Force

Westland Wasp

SHIPBORNE LIGHT ANTI-SUBMARINE HELICOPTER

Wasp HAS1 Indonesian Navy

DEVELOPMENT

The Wasp's origins lay in the Saunders-Roe P.531 of the late 1950s. Westland acquired the Saunders-Roe helicopter division in 1959 and developed the design into the Scout AH1 for the British Army; Royal Navy interest in the design led to an extensive evaluation programme and an order for a pre-production batch of Sea Scout HAS1s, the name being subsequently changed to Wasp. The Wasp differed from the Scout primarily in undercarriage layout, having wheels rather than skids. The Royal Navy placed orders for

TECHNICAL DATA

Westland Wasp HAS1

Powerplant: One Rolls-Royce (Bristol Siddeley) Nimbus 103 or 104 turboshaft engine
Developing: Derated to 529kW (710shp)
Driving: Four-blade main and two-blade tail rotor
Main rotor diameter: 9.83m (32ft 3in)
Fuselage length: 9.24m (30ft 4in)
Height: 2.72m (8ft 11in)
All-up weight: 2,495kg (5,500lb)
Maximum speed: 193 km/h (120mph)
Cruise speed: 177 km/h (110mph)
Operational ceiling: 13,400ft
Maximum ferry range: 488km (303 miles)
Mission range: 435km (270 miles)
Accommodation: Two flight crew plus up to four passengers in cabin; alternatively one stretcher across rear of cabin.
Warload: Two Mk44 or one Mk46 homing torpedo or two depth charges carried between undercarriage legs; or two Nord (Aérospatiale) AS12 wire-guided air-to-surface guided missiles on fuselage sides.
First flown: 28 October 1962
Entered service: 6 June 1963

further aircraft over the coming years and the type remained in service until 1988, seeing action in the Falklands conflict when aircraft from HMS *Antrim*, *Brilliant* and *Plymouth* disabled the Argentine Navy submarine *Santa Fé*. There were some overseas orders for the Wasp, principally from South Africa, which ordered 17 between 1962 and 1972, of which only 16 were delivered. The survivors, believed to number seven, were withdrawn from service in the early 1980s and sold to a Singaporean company; they were later sold on to Malaysia. The Royal Netherlands Navy was another major customer, operating 13. New Zealand received six new examples and purchased further ex-FAA examples; these were operated for many years until the last was retired in April 1998, following the arrival of the SH-2 Seasprite. As the Navy progressively withdrew the type in favour of the Lynx, they were refurbished and sold to foreign operators, including Brazil and Indonesia. In total, 98 Wasps were built.

CURRENT SERVICE

The Indonesian Navy has a fleet of nine Wasp HAS1

helicopters that were purchased second-hand from the Netherlands and FAA, which are operated from frigates and shore-based at Surabaya; these are due for replacement, and due to sanctions as few as two could be airworthy. The Royal Malaysian Navy received six ex-FAA HAS1s in 1988 and later supplemented these with ex-South African examples, plus further FAA machines for spares – they are shore-based with 499 Sku at Lumut, and nominally 12 are on strength.

SPECIAL FEATURES

Fully enclosed fuselage tapering from cabin to give 'tadpole' shape, long undercarriage legs give insect-like appearance. The rear fuselage folds for shipboard storage, and the rear wheels are toed outwards at 45 degrees to give stability whilst on deck. A winch could be fitted to the starboard fuselage side. Unlike the Scout, the Wasp's tail rotor is metal and it also has a horizontal stabiliser on the starboard side of the tail.

VARIANTS

There was only one basic variant, the **Wasp HAS1**.

Wasp HAS1 Royal Malaysian Navy

Westland Sea King

ASW/SAR/AEW MULTI-ROLE HELICOPTER

Sea King HU5 Royal Navy

DEVELOPMENT

Westland entered into an agreement in the mid-1960s with Sikorsky to licence-produce its S-61 Sea King design (described separately), and in October 1966 the first of four pattern aircraft was delivered to the UK. These were used for trials work leading to the production of 56 Sea King HAS1s for the Royal Navy; followed by 13 HAS2s with uprated engines. The RAF then ordered 15 HAR3s to replace the Whirlwind in the SAR role. These were followed by a further eight HAS2s for the Royal Navy, including a prototype HAS5 conversion that introduced the Thorn-EMI Sea Searcher radar; earlier models have since been upgraded to HAS5/6 and HAR5 (Navy SAR) standards. The HAS5/6 became the standard production model from 1980; eventually the Royal Navy ordered 112 ASW Sea Kings and with the purchase of four HAR3 and six HAR3As between 1980 and 1992, the RAF's fleet reached 25 and enabled some Wessex to be retired. The distinctive AEW2 was developed from 1982 to provide AEW cover for the Fleet Air Arm. There was also a healthy overseas market for the Sea King, with seven nations purchasing 100; two more (destined for Germany and

India) were lost before delivery. By the time production ended in 1996, 239 Sea Kings had been built.

CURRENT SERVICE

The Fleet Air Arm has 60 HAS5/6 for SAR and ASW duties with five front-line squadrons shore-based at RNAS Culdrose and one at RNAS Prestwick; No 849 NAS's nine AEW2s are also shore-based at Culdrose. The RAF Sea Kings are stationed around the country; two grey-painted examples serve in the Falklands. Overseas, the Royal Australian Navy has seven in the maritime utility role (the dipping sonar and anti-sub roles were lost during the 1990s). SAR operators are Belgium (5), Germany (21) and Norway (12); ASW operators are the Egyptian Navy (5) and Pakistan (6). India has a mixed fleet of Mk42s for ASW and SAR; Pakistan has six Mk 45s for ASW.

SPECIAL FEATURES

Generally as for Sikorsky SH-3. Twin engines and good single-engine capability reduce the possibility of ditching, for which the Sea King's boat-like hull and stabilising sponsons provide good flotation.

TECHNICAL DATA

Westland Sea King HAS6
Powerplants: Two Rolls-Royce Gnome H.1400-1T turboshafts
Developing: 1,238kW (1,660shp) each
Driving: Five-blade main and six-blade tail rotors
Main rotor diameter: 18.90m (62ft 0in)
Fuselage length: 17.02m (55ft 10in)
Height: 5.13m (16ft 10in)
All-up weight: 9,752kg (21,500lb)
Maximum speed: 226 km/h (140mph)
Cruise speed: 204km/h (126mph)
Maximum ferry range: 1,742km (1,082 miles)
Mission range: 231 km (144 miles) ASW; 185km (115 miles) AEW; 407km (253 miles) SAR
Accommodation: Crew of four for ASW; up to 22 survivors in SAR role
Warload: Up to four A244S or Sting Ray homing torpedoes or four Mk11 depth charges or two BAE Sea Eagle or Aerospatiale Exocet missiles. Mounting on starboard door for machine gun.
First flown: 7 May 1969 (HAS1); 6 Sep 1977 (HAR3); 1 August 1980 (HAS5)
Entered service: Summer 1969 (HAS1); December 1977 (HAR3); 2 October 1980 (HAS5)

VARIANTS

The HAS1 fleet has been converted successively to HAS2 and HAS5 standard and has a large flat-topped radome housing the Sea Searcher radar and enlarged cabin to house the new equipment; the HAS6 has a further improved ASW suite and lighter equipment. The AEW2A is instantly identifiable by its starboard-mounted Searchwater maritime surveillance radar, mounted in an external 'kettledrum'. RAF HAR3s are generally painted bright yellow.

SEE ALSO: SIKORSKY S-61/SH-3 SEA KING & WESTLAND COMMANDO

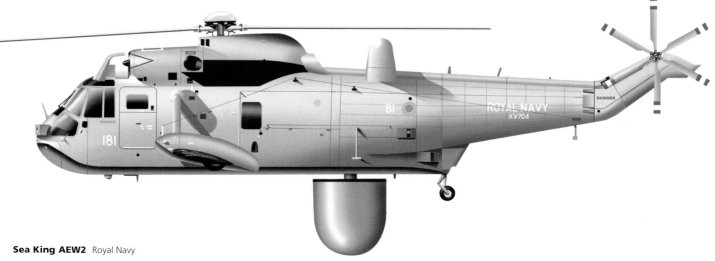

Sea King AEW2 Royal Navy

Westland Commando

TACTICAL ASSAULT HELICOPTER

DEVELOPMENT

With licence production of the Sea King underway in mid-1971, Westland turned its attention to an assault version, not equipped with floats. The Commando, intended for the assault, tactical and general transport roles, did not initially attract interest from the Ministry of Defence and was first ordered by the Egyptian Air Force, followed by that of Qatar. Eventually an order from the Royal Navy for 40 helicopters under the designation Sea King HC4 was placed, and this was followed by orders for a Mk4 for the Empire Test Pilots' School (ETPS) and two for the Defence Research Agency (now DERA). In all, 89 Commandos were produced between 1973 and 1983. Sea King HC4s from Nos 845, 846 and 848 Naval Air Squadrons took part in the Gulf War, flying initially from King Khalid Military City before moving into Iraq as *Desert Storm* advanced, where they were used mainly for medical evacuation and troop transportation, with a secondary mine-hunting role.

Sea King HC4 Royal Navy

CURRENT SERVICE

The Fleet Air Arm currently has three operational units – Nos 845, 846 and 848 NASs – based at RNAS Yeovilton, where they are dedicated to supporting the Royal Marines' 3 Commando Brigade. Secondary roles include SAR, casualty evacuation, ground force suppression and special forces operations; a detachment is deployed to the former Yugoslavia and regular deployments are also undertaken to Norway. The Egyptian Air Force Assault Brigade at Abu Hammad has a mixed fleet of Commando Mk1/2/2B/2E which it uses for transport, VIP and Elint work, while Qatar's eight Mk3 and four Mk2A/Cs are deployed in the ASW and transport roles respectively – serving with No 8 Anti-Surface Vessel Squadron and No 9 Multi-

Role Squadron at No 2 Rotary Wing at Al Udald. At least two Mk3s are equipped to launch AM39 Exocet anti-ship missiles.

SPECIAL FEATURES

Basically similar to the Westland Sea King, but with four underfuselage hardpoints to allow carriage of external cargo up to 3,628kg (8,000lb), the Commando differs principally from its forebear in its lack of floatation bags and sponsons on the main non-retractable undercarriage gear.

VARIANTS

Initial **Commando Mk1** for Egypt was Sea King Mk41 export version of Sea King HAS1; the **Commando 2**

carried more troops and the **Commando 3** version has provision for armament. The **Sea King HC4** is a utility version of the Commando 2.

SEE ALSO: SIKORSKY S-61/SH-3 SEA KING & WESTLAND SEA KING

TECHNICAL DATA

Westland Sea King HC4 (Commando Mk2)
Powerplants: Two Rolls-Royce Gnome H.1400-1T turboshafts
Developing: 1,238kW (1,660shp)
Driving: Five-bladed main rotor and six-bladed tail rotor
Main rotor diameter: 18.90m (62ft 0in)
Fuselage length: 17.02m (55ft 10in)
Height: 5.13m (16ft 10in)
All-up weight: 9,752kg (21,500lb)
Maximum speed: 226km/h (140mph)
Cruise speed: 204km/h (126mph)
Maximum ferry range: 1,742km (1,082 miles)
Mission range: 396km (246 miles)
Accommodation: Crew of two on flight deck and seats for 28 troops along fuselage sides; maximum emergency capacity 45 troops.
Warload: Options include a machine gun mounted in cabin doorway and machine-gun pod on each side of forward fuselage; sponsons can also be fitted to carry one rocket pod each side (including Matra F4, Thomson-Brandt 68-33 and Medusa pods of varying calibre).
First flown: 12 September 1973 (Egypt); 26 September 1979 (HC4)
Entered service: January 1974 (Egypt); November 1979 (HC4)

Sea King HC4 Royal Navy

Westland Lynx AH1/AH7

BATTLEFIELD TRANSPORT AND ANTI-TANK HELICOPTER

DEVELOPMENT

Developed as part of the Anglo-French helicopter agreement of February 1967, the Westland Lynx has proved an extremely versatile helicopter. Westland embodied very many completely new design features in the Lynx, which set it apart from the Sikorsky products. With all-weather avionics, no previous helicopter can equal the type for agility and all-weather, single-crew operation. Westlands solely developed the battlefield and general purpose version of the Lynx for the British Army as the AH1. This was capable of operation as tactical troop transport, logistic support, armed escort of troop-carrying helicopters, anti-strike, search and rescue, reconnaissance and command post duties. Its large cabin and excellent performance attracted British Army interest for anti-tank missions and troop transport to replace the Westland Scout. Initially, 114 were ordered for the British Army and most were subsequently upgraded to AH7 standard. The Lynx was the first helicopter to be rolled – this being demonstated at the 1972 Farnborough SBAC Show.

Lynx AH7 UK Army Air Corps

CURRENT SERVICE

The Lynx AH7 serves widely with the British Army Air Corps and Royal Marines as an anti-armour attack helicopter and for general communications, observation and troop transport. A small number of Lynx AH7s are operated by 3 Commando Brigade Air Squadron based at RNAS Yeovilton – this followed a decision not to proceed with a hybrid Army/RN Lynx AH6 for beach assault duties.

SPECIAL FEATURES

It is distinguished from the naval Lynx in having a skid landing-gear. The key to the Lynx's agility is the forged titanium rotor hub for the four-bladed semi-rigid main rotor. It has a digital flight cntrol system

and all-weather avionics. The AH7 features an IR suppressor on the engine exhaust. The tail rotor is made of composites and rotates in the opposite direction to that of the AH1 in order to reduce the noise output. The more powerful tail rotor improved the ability to hover for extended periods at high weights – an important factor during anti-tank operations. The well-glazed cabin has a deep wrap-around windscreen with large 'eyebrow' windows in the fibreglass roof of the two crew seats.

VARIANTS

The **Lynx AH1** was the original army version, followed by the **AH5** for the British Army – similar to the AH1

but with Gem 41-1 turboshafts. Nine were ordered, but only one example flew as such before the order was switched to the final British Army version, the **AH9**, which is described separately.

SEE ALSO: WESTLAND LYNX HAS3, WESTLAND LYNX AH9 & WESTLAND LYNX HMA8

TECHNICAL DATA

Westland Lynx AH7

Powerplants: Two Rolls-Royce Gem 42-1 turboshafts
Developing: 846kW (1,135shp)
Driving: Four-blade main and tail rotor
Rotor Diameter: 12.80m (42ft 0in)
Length: 13.17m (43ft 2.5in)
Height: 3.66m (12ft 0in)
All-up weight: 4,876kg (10,750lb)
Maximum speed: 259km/h (161mph)
Cruise speed: 130km/h (81mph)
Operational ceiling: 10,600ft
Maximum range: 628km (390 miles)
Ferry Range: 1,342km (834 miles)
Endurance: 2hr 50min
Accommodation: Pilot and co-pilot/observer and can carry up to 12 troops
Warload: Up to eight Hughes TOW air-to-surface missiles; one 20mmm Oerlikon-Bührle KDA cannon; optional pintle-mounted 7.62mm GEC Minigun; two pods each carrying 18 68mm SNEB or other rockets.
First flown: 21 March 1971; 11 February 1977 (AH1)
Entered service: August 1978 (AH1)

Lynx AH7 UK Army Air Corps

Westland Lynx AH9

TWIN-TURBOSHAFT UTILITY HELICOPTER

Lynx AH9 UK Army Air Corps

DEVELOPMENT

Westland's decision to develop a version of the Army Lynx utilising a tricycle undercarriage rather than skids led to its demonstrator aircraft G-LYNX appearing for the first time in this configuration at the 1988 Farnborough Airshow. It was ordered by the British Army Air Corps as the Lynx AH9, and eight previous AH7s were initially converted as the first production examples (the first flying during the summer of 1990). Sixteen completely new-build AH9 models subsequently rolled off the Yeovil production line, and the type is still offered for export by GKN Westland as the slightly-modified Battlefield Lynx.

CURRENT SERVICE

Nos 3 and 4 Regiments of the UK Army Air Corps each has one squadron of AH9s, based at Wattisham.

SPECIAL FEATURES

The Lynx AH9 incorporates the technical modifications which produced the AH7 version from the initial AH1s,

these including a reverse-direction tail rotor, paddle-tipped BERP (British Experimental Rotor Programme) rotor blades of composite construction for improved high-speed performance, TACAN equipment and an uprated gearbox. The AH9's most distinctive feature is the tricycle wheeled undercarriage – rather than skids – that is unique to this Lynx variant. The AH9 does not have TOW capability.

VARIANTS

Only the **Lynx AH9** has entered series production, but the type remains on offer to export customers as the **Battlefield Lynx**. This machine has slightly less fuel capacity than the AAC's AH9, but makes up for this with its increased weapons-carrying ability. GIAT 20mm cannon pods, FN Herstal 7.62mm machine guns, and HOT or Hellfire anti-tank weapons can all be carried by the Battlefield Lynx, which has yet to find a customer. A prototype Battlefield Lynx, known as the **Battlefield Lynx 800**, was tested with the more powerful LHTEC CTS800 powerplant, but did not enter production.

TECHNICAL DATA

Westland Lynx AH9
Powerplants: Two Rolls-Royce Gem 42-1 turboshafts
Developing: 845kW (1,135shp)
Driving: Four-blade main and tail rotors
Main rotor diameter: 12.80m (42ft 0in)
Fuselage length: 13.24m (43ft 5.25in)
Height: 3.73m (12ft 3in)
All-up weight: 5,126kg (11,300lb)
Maximum speed: 255km/h (158mph)
Operational ceiling: 10,600ft
Maximum range: 982km (610 miles)
Endurance: 5hr 40min
Accommodation: Two crew and up to 12 passengers
First flown: 21 March 1971 (Lynx prototype); 1977 (AH-1); 20 July 1990 (AH-9)
Entered service: September 1991 (AH9)

SEE ALSO: WESTLAND LYNX AH1/AH7, LYNX HAS1/HAS3 & WESTLAND GKN LYNX HMA8/SUPER LYNX

Lynx AH9 UK Army Air Corps

Westland Lynx HAS2/3/4

Lynx HAS2 French Navy

DEVELOPMENT

Developed from the original WG.13 concept, the naval Lynx has become one of the foremost medium ship-based helicopters in the world. It was developed principally for ASW hunter-killer duties operating from guided-missile destroyers and frigates. The Lynx is also capable of operations in the air-to-surface and strike, SAR, troop transport, reconnaissance and fleet liaison/communication roles. Various series of upgrades have enabled additional missions to be undertaken and also greatly enhance capabilities. Equipped with the Ferranti Seaspray and dunking sonar and it has a very capable radar system. It made its combat début during the Falklands Conflict of 1982 and has since formed an important part of several NATO Navies. The naval Lynx saw service during the Gulf War and has seen limited service throughout the Balkans campaign.

CURRENT SERVICE

The main user is the Royal Navy. The naval version is also in service with the French Navy (HAS 2 and 4[FN]), Royal Netherlands Navy (Mk27/29 – UH-1A, SH-14B and SH-14C), Brazilian Navy (Mk21), Argentine Navy (Mk87), Royal Danish Navy (Mk80), Qatar (Mk28 and 84), Nigerian Navy (Mk89), Norwegian Navy (Mk86), Portuguese Navy (Mk95) and German Navy (Mk88, shore-based).

SPECIAL FEATURES

It has equipment for a wide range of shipboard missions including ASW, SAR, ASV (anti-surface vessel) search and strike, reconnaissance, troop transport, fire support, communications and fleet liason. Large sliding cabin doors, with a single square window, and tricycle wheeled undercarriage, with castoring action for on-board operations. Folding tail and main rotor to facilitate storage on ships. An advanced automatic flight control system is fitted. The lightweight Sea Spray search and tracking radar is carried in a chin-mounted radome in an extended nose. The nose has been modified to incorporate new passive identification devices, radar aerials and other equipment.

VARIANTS

The HAS3ICE was a downgraded version for utility work on the Antarctic patrol vessel HMS Endurance, for operations in the South Atlantic. HAS3GM – 18 were upgraded to this version with improved cooling for Desert Storm in 1991. Forty-five RN HAS3s are being upgraded to HAS8 standard, with conversion to be completed in 2001. The Lynx Mk2 was for the French Navy, with Alcatel dunking sonar and Omera-Segid ORB-31-W radar. Those supplied to overseas navies have a Mk number appropriate to each country

SEE ALSO: WESTLAND LYNX AH7, WESTLAND LYNX AH9 & WESTLAND GKN LYNX HM.

TECHNICAL DATA

Westland Lynx HAS3
Powerplants: Two Rolls-Royce Gem 42-1 turboshafts
Developing: 847kW (1,135shp)
Driving: Four-blade main and tail rotors
Rotor diameter: 12.80m (42ft 0in)
Length: 11.92m (39ft 1.5in); 10.62m (34ft 10in) with main rotor blades and tail folded
Height: 3.48m (11ft 5in)
All-up weight: 5,000kg (11,300lb)
Maximum speed: 333km/h (207mph)
Cruise speed: 130km/h (81mph)
Operational ceiling: 10,600ft
Maximum range: 630km (392 miles)
Endurance: 2-3 hours
Accommodation: Crew of two (three in ASW and SAR role)
Warload: External pylons for two torpedoes (Mk44, 46 or Sting Ray), two Mk11 depth charges or four Sea Skua anti-ship missiles. An FN HMP 0.50in machine gun can be carried.
First flown: 21 March 1971 (Lynx prototype); 10 February 1976 (HAS2)
Entered service: September 1976 (HAS2); March 1982 (HAS3)

Lynx Mk80 Royal Danish Navy

Westland/GKN Westland/AugustaWestland/Lynx HMA8/Super Lynx

TWIN-TURBOSHAFT MARITIME ATTACK AND UTILITY HELICOPTER

GKN Westland Lynx HMA8 Royal Navy

DEVELOPMENT

In April 1991, a contract was signed to provide Royal Navy Lynx HAS3s with new composite rotor blades, utilising BERP (British Experimental Rotor Programme) technology to deliver increased performance and a longer fatigue life. In addition, numerous significant aspects of the helicopter's avionics and weapons systems were upgraded, in the course of a three-stage programme. Only the completion of all three stages resulted in the full specification being reached, this producing the RN's Lynx HAS8 – later redesignated as the HMA8. One- and two-stage upgrade aircraft were designated as Lynx HAS3CTS. For export customers, two versions of the Super Lynx are produced, with specifications differing depending on the individual customer's requirements.

CURRENT SERVICE

Two Royal Navy squadrons are equipped with the Lynx HMA8, augmenting earlier HAS3 versions – No 815 Naval Air Squadron's Operational Evaluation Unit having been the first unit to receive the type in

the summer of 1992. In addition, the Brazilian Navy, Portuguese Navy and Republic of China (Taiwanese) Navy all operate the Super Lynx; the German Navy has seven new Super Lynxes (to be known as Sea Lynx Mk88As) on order and seventeen Lynx Mk88s being upgraded recently to this standard; likewise, the Royal Danish Navy's Lynxes are in the throes of a Super Lynx refit programme; the Royal Malaysian Navy has six on order; and the South African Navy has ordered the new Super Lynx 300 for its shipborne helicopter requirement.

SPECIAL FEATURES

The Lynx HMA8 (previously HAS8) upgrade programme involves the fitment of a Racal RAMS automated, computerised central tactical management system, tail-mounted magnetic anomaly detector, INS and GPS navigation equipment, Racal Orange Crop ESM and Whittaker Yellow Veil ECM pods and, most outwardly distinctive, a GEC Sea Owl thermal imaging turret. BERP rotor blades using composite technology are another important feature.

VARIANTS

The **Series 100** is equivalent to the Royal Navy **Lynx HMA8** described above, while the **Series 200** uses two LHTEC CTS800 turboshafts delivering 945kW each in place of the Rolls-Royce Gem 42-1s. Finally, the most advanced Super Lynx is the **Series 300**, incorporating a fully-integrated digital cockpit, compatible with night vision equipment, using six flat panel LCD colour displays. South Africa was the launch customer for the Super Lynx 300, in late 1998.

SEE ALSO: WESTLAND LYNX AH1/AH7, AH9 & LYNX HAS1/HAS3

TECHNICAL DATA

Westland Lynx HMA8/Super Lynx 100

Powerplants: Two Rolls-Royce Gem 42-1 turboshafts
Developing: 845kW (1,135shp)
Driving: Four-blade main and tail rotors
Main rotor diameter: 12.80m (42ft 0in)
Fuselage length: 13.33m (43ft 8.6in)
Height: 3.48m (11ft 5in)
All-up weight: 5,330kg (11,749lb)
Maximum speed: 232km/h (144mph)
Operational ceiling: 8,450ft
Maximum range: 982km (610 miles)
Endurance: 5hr 40min
Accommodation: Two crew (pilot and co-pilot/ observer) and up to nine passengers
Warload: Two Mk44, Mk46, A244S or Stingray torpedoes, or two Mk11 depth charges in ASW configuration. For anti-ship operations up to four Sea Skua anti-ship missiles.
First flown:
25 January 1989 (HAS8)
Entered service: 1992 (as HAS8)

GKN Westland Lynx HMA8 Royal Navy

Xian H-6

Xian B-6D

for total production point to over 180 being built before the production line closed in 1989. Work on the B-6D development and export model started in 1975 and its first flight took place on 29 August 1981. Xian has also sold spare parts to the Egyptian Air Force for its Tu-16 fleet, and in 1987 four were reported to have been sold to Iraq, where they joined at least four other Tu-16s. All are believed to have been destroyed during Operation *Desert Storm* in 1991. Some H-6s have been converted for tanker operations and Flight Refuelling Ltd carried out design studies in the late 1980s in association with CATIC for probe and drogue tanker conversions.

CURRENT SERVICE

Around 100 H-6s are believed to remain in service with the People's Liberation Army Air Force and Navy, including several modified for flight refuelling. H-6Ds fitted with chin fairings containing indigenous Chinese radars are also believed to be used as cruise missile platforms.

SPECIAL FEATURES

The relatively elderly Russian Tu-16 design has been updated by Xian, including the modernisation of the cockpit area.

VARIANTS

The original **H-6A** has been progressively upgraded throughout its service career. The **B-6D** was model chosen for export sales.

DEVELOPMENT

A development of the Tupolev Tu-16 'Badger', China received a licence to manufacture the type in 1957 and began by reassembling two Russian-supplied aircraft, the first of which made its maiden flight on 27 September 1959. The H-6 project was the biggest aircraft project undertaken in China at the time, and it was originally intended to be a split Harbin/Xian programme but all the work was transferred to Xian in 1961, leaving Harbin free to pursue its helicopter work. The first entirely-Chinese produced H-6A first flew on 24 December 1968. Production averaged between four and six aircraft per year and estimates

TECHNICAL DATA

Xian H-6

Powerplants: Two Xian (XAE) WP8 turbojets.
Developing: 93.17kN (20,944lb st)
Span: 34.19m (112ft 2in)
Length: 34.80m (114ft 2in)
Height: 10.36m (33ft 11.75in)
All-up weight: 72,000kg (158,733lb)
Maximum speed: 993km/h (616mph)
Cruise speed: 786km/h (488mph)
Operational ceiling: 39,370ft
Maximum range: 4,300km (2,672 miles)
Mission range: 1,800km (1,118 miles)
Endurance: 5hr 41min
Accommodation: Crew of six.
Warload: Six or seven 23mm cannon are positioned in the nose, dorsal, ventral and tail of H-6A; no nose guns on B-6D. Internal bomb bay carries up to 9,000kg (19,841lb) of conventional or nuclear bombs. B-6D can carry two 2,440 kg (5,379lb) C-601 anti-shipping missiles on underwing pylons.
First flown: 24 December 1968 (H-6A)
Entered service: Early 1970s.

Xian H-6 Chinese Air Force

Yakovlev Yak-18/18T

SINGLE PISTON-ENGINED TANDEM TWO-SEAT BASIC/PRIMARY TRAINER

DEVELOPMENT

The design of what became the Yak-18 commenced before World War 2, and was continued after the conflict, based around the wartime UT-2MV design. The new aircraft flew in 1945, and was followed in 1946 by a far more revised layout which entered production in 1947 as the Yak-18. This tailwheel undercarriage tandem two-seat trainer featured a distinctive cowling, with each cylinder of its radial engine being closely cowled. In the mid-1950s, the revised Yak-18U introduced a tricycle undercarriage layout and was followed in 1956/1957 by the improved, tricycle undercarriage Yak-18A (initially sometimes called the Yak-20). This major production version introduced a normal cylindrical cowling and many detail improvements, and it was built in substantial numbers. Production ended around 1967 with some 6,750 of all versions built, many of these serving with military and civilian flying schools in a number of countries. Several single-seat aerobatic models also existed. In 1964, design work began on a completely revised, four-seat tricycle undercarriage derivative of the Yak-18 that led to the Yak-18T. The prototype flew in 1967, and the type was widely produced in a number of versions from around 1973 onwards. Manufacture was resumed in 1993 and the type still remains in production, some 2,000 having been built. The NATO code name for the tandem-seat Yak-18 models was 'Max'; 'Mouse' appears to have been reserved for the single-seat aerobatic derivatives. The Yak-18A has also been produced in China as the Nanchang CJ-5/BT-5.

CURRENT SERVICE

Large numbers of Yak-18s serve within the Russian Federation, most of these being Yak-18T models with the FPS Russian border guards aviation elements, and with the paramilitary aeroclub organisation ROSTO (formerly DOSAAF). Yak-18Ts also serve in Lithuania with that country's national guard. Six were recently ordered by Bulgaria. Earlier Yak-18A models currently

Yakovlev Yak-18T

serve in Afghanistan (status uncertain), Laos, and Mali, for basic or primary training.

SPECIAL FEATURES

Of very simple construction, all Yak-18s have a basically all-metal structure with metal and some fabric covering. The initial, tailwheel undercarriage Yak-18s had the main undercarriage legs attached near to the wing leading edge, retracting backwards under the wings. Some of the earlier tricycle undercarriage Yak-18As had a retractable undercarriage which was almost completely exposed when retracted; the Yak-18T and some later Yak-18As have a more conventional inwards-retracting main undercarriage.

VARIANTS

The initial, tailwheel undercarriage **Yak-18** had a 119kW (160hp) M-11FR (or RF) radial engine. Early **Yak-18A** models featured an Ivchenko AI-14R radial

Yakovlev Yak-18T

of 194kW (260hp), later Yak-18As having the AI-14RF; the standard production **Yak-18T** has a 269kW (360hp) or slightly higher rated VOKBM (Vedeneyev) M-14P radial. Yak-18Ts are produced in a number of variants, including four-seat trainer, four-seat communications aircraft, air ambulance, and light freighter. They have a wider fuselage compared to the Yak-18A, with an overall wingspan of 11.16m (36ft 7.25in). Yak-18As have been operated with a fixed ski undercarriage replacing the normal retractable tricycle units.

SEE ALSO: NANCHANG CJ-6

SEE ALSO: NANCHANG CJ-6

TECHNICAL DATA

Yakovlev Yak-18A

Powerplant: One Ivchenko AI-14RF radial engine
Developing: 224kW (300hp)
Driving: Two-blade propeller
Span: 10.60m (34ft 9.25in)
Length: 8.35m (27ft 4.75in)
Height: 3.35m (11ft 0in)
All-up weight: 1,320kg (2,910lb)
Maximum speed: 300km/h (186mph)
Cruise speed: 259km/h (161mph)
Operational ceiling: 16,600ft
Maximum range: 700km (435 miles)
Mission range: 523km (325 miles)
Endurance: 2 hours
Accommodation: Instructor and pupil pilot in tandem
Warload: None
First flown: 1946 (original Yak-18 prototype)
Entered service: 1947/1948

Yakovlev Yak-38

V/STOL NAVAL STRIKE FIGHTER

Yak-38 'Forger-B' Russian Navy

DEVELOPMENT

Studies that led to the subsonic Yak-38 commenced during the mid-1960s, and drew heavily on experience gained with the Yak-36. Code named 'Freehand' by NATO, the Yak-36 was an experimental VTOL aircraft that pioneered many principles that were later used in the Yak-38. At first referred to as the Yak-36MP, the single-seat Yak-38 (NATO code name 'Forger-A') first flew in 1970 and the Soviet Union's Naval Air Force received its initial examples in the mid-1970s; a first operational cruise for the Yak-38 aboard the aircraft-carrier *Kiev* was made in 1976. The Yak-38 was a less capable and less advanced design than the contemporary V/STOL Harrier. The use of three engines, two of them lift engines situated behind the cockpit that were only used for take-off, landing, and hover, coupled with a small weapons-carrying capability and a simple radar-rangefinder in the aircraft's nose, rendered the Yak-38 very much a first generation vertical take-off machine. Initial production examples did not have a rolling take-off capability, but according to Russian sources this ability came with the improved Yak-38M, which appears to have been operational from 1984. Most Russian sources now quote a final production figure of around 75 Yak-38/Yak-38M: this total including a batch of two-seat conversion trainers (code named 'Forger-B's by NATO). Yak-38s were eventually deployed on the Soviet Navy aircraft-carriers *Kiev*, *Minsk* and *Novorossiysk*, in addition to shore-based trainers. These carriers were, however, decommissioned during the early 1990s. The Soviet Union's break-up saw the newly-independent Ukraine

inherit a significant percentage of the Yak-38/Yak-38M fleet, albeit with no relevant ships to operate them from. A supersonic V/STOL successor, the Yak-141, did not reach production.

CURRENT SERVICE

The operational status of existing Yak-38/Yak-38Ms in the Russian Federation remains in doubt. The Ukraine no longer declares any fixed-wing combat aircraft for its naval air arm under the Conventional Armed Forces in Europe (CFE) treaty; all of its 'Forgers' are believed to be shore-based at Kirovskoye but are quite possibly still airworthy.

SPECIAL FEATURES

Of principally all-metal construction, the Yak-38 series have two vectoring nozzle outlets for the main engine (one on each side of the lower rear fuselage) in conjunction with reaction-control valves at the wingtips and tail for slow-speed/hovering control. Take-off and landing on the Soviet aircraft-carriers was fully automatic and computer-controlled. The outer sections of the aircraft's wings fold for ease of stowage aboard ship.

VARIANTS

Various engine types have been quoted for the **Yak-38** series over the years; the V/STOL-capable **Yak-38M** has a better thrust-to-weight ratio possibly suggesting a change of main powerplant. Upgrades and alterations to the original layout saw such additions as fences on the upper fuselage beside the top fuselage intake

TECHNICAL DATA

Yakovlev Yak-38M

Powerplant: One Tumansky R-27V-300 turbojet (main engine); two RKBM RD-36-35FVR lift engines
Developing: 66.7kN (14,990lb st); 31.9kN (7,175lb st) (lift engines)
Span: 7.32m (24ft 0in)
Length: 15.50m (50ft 10.25in)
Height: 4.37m (14ft 4in)
All-up weight: 13,000kg (28,660lb)
Maximum speed: 1,009km/h (627mph)
Cruise speed: undisclosed
Operational Ceiling: 39,370ft
Maximum range: undisclosed
Mission range: 370km (230 miles)
Endurance: approximately 1.25-1.5 hours
Accommodation: single pilot
Warload: Approximately 2,000kg (4,410lb) on four wing pylons beneath the fixed inner wing sections, including 23mm twin-barrel GSh-23 cannon pods, unguided rocket pods, unguided bombs up to 500kg, two fuel tanks, two R-60 (AA-8) 'Aphid' air-to-air missiles, or (possibly) AS-7 'Kerry' air-to-surface missiles.
First flown: 28 May 1970
Entered service: 1975/1976

for the lift engines, to avoid recirculation ingestion of the downward jet blast from the lift jets. The two-seat **'Forger-B'** trainer has a lengthened, drooped nose to fit the second, tandem pilot's position, and an extended rear fuselage; it has no nose radar or weapons provision.

Yak-38 'Forger-A' Russian Navy

Yakovlev Yak-40

THREE-TURBOFAN SHORT/MEDIUM RANGE PASSENGER/VIP TRANSPORT

DEVELOPMENT

Design work on what became the Yak-40 began in the early 1960s, with a project go-ahead in 1965. Part of the intention was to create a viable short/medium-haul airliner for domestic services within the vast expanses of the Soviet Union, as a potential successor for such types as the Lisunov Li-2 (DC-3). The first prototype, which flew in October 1966, was followed by four prototype/pre-production aircraft. Actual series production began in 1967, and airline services commenced with Aeroflot in September 1968. The type was designed for operation from austere landing strips which were especially prevalent in the remoter parts of the Soviet Union. The Yak-40 proved to be ideal in this role, but the type was also exported comparatively widely to countries within the Eastern Bloc and to Soviet-aligned countries elsewhere in the world. Yakovlev claimed at the time that it was the first Soviet aircraft to be certificated according to Western airworthiness standards. A variety of different versions were planned for the Yak-40 but few, if any, of these reached production, and most Yak-40s were comparatively similar in outward appearance, except in detail areas. Following the break-up of the Soviet Union, a number of proposals for 'westernising' the type existed, including re-engining schemes. About 1,000 production Yak-40s were built between 1967 and 1978, and the type was given the NATO code name 'Codling'.

CURRENT SERVICE

One of the principal current military operators of the Yak-40 is Poland, with as many as 14 in service. The main user is 36 SPLT at Warsaw-Okecie for liaison and VIP operation, and the target-towers of 17 EL at Poznan-Lawica. In addition, military Yak-40s continue to serve in the following countries: Bulgaria, Cuba, Czech Republic, Equatorial Guinea, Ethiopia, Guinea-

Yakovlev Yak-40 Slovak Air Force

Bissau, Laos, the Russian Federation, Slovakia, Yugoslavia, and Zambia.

SPECIAL FEATURES

Designed for operations from grass/semi-prepared airstrips, the all-metal and pressurised Yak-40 has a high-lift, lightly-loaded wing design layout. The type has low-pressure tyres and undercarriage legs with long-stroke shock-absorbers. Main cabin access is by means of an integral ramp/air-stair, in the lower rear fuselage. This allows operation from airstrips where facilities are minimal, and autonomous operation is further achieved with an on-board AI-9 APU.

VARIANTS

Early Yak-40s had an 'acorn' fairing at the fin/elevator leading edge junction, subsequently dispensed with, and a different intake design for the centre engine. Various main cabin seating layouts were possible, or an all-freight interior (albeit carrying small, non-

bulky items), or mixed freight/passengers, or an air ambulance configuration. A clamshell thrust-reverser was included during production for the centre engine's rear fuselage outlet. Some contemporary Polish Air Force Yak-40s are configured for high-speed target-towing. A large number of one-off, special test-bed and research Yak-40s have also existed; some of these have flown in Aeroflot colours, and they include the **Yak-40 Aqua**, and various meteorological and earth-resources research aircraft. In addition, a bizarre four-engined testbed also existed, being operated by the VZLU research and test establishment in the former-Czechoslovakia, with an M-602 engine mounted in its nose.

TECHNICAL DATA

Yakovlev Yak-40

Powerplants: Three Ivchenko AI-25 turbofans
Developing: 14.7kN (3,300lb st)
Span: 25.0m (82ft 0.25in)
Length: 20.36m (66ft 9.5in)
Height: 6.50m (21ft 4in)
All-up weight: 16,000kg (35,275lb)
Maximum speed: 600km/h (373mph)
Cruise speed: 550km/h (342mph)
Operational ceiling: 26,575ft
Maximum range: 1,800km (1,118 miles)
Mission range: 1,450km (901 miles)
Endurance: approximately 3 hours
Accommodation: Normally two-man crew on flight deck; many different passenger seating layouts, including 32-seat high-density arrangement, 27-seat or other layouts including eleven-seat VIP configuration
Warload: None
First flown: 21 October 1966
Entered service: 30 September 1968 (Aeroflot)

Yakovlev Yak-40 Czech Air Force

Zlin Z 42/Z 43 & Z 142/Z 242 series

SINGLE PISTON-ENGINED TWO/FOUR-SEAT LIGHT TRAINER/TOURING AIRCRAFT

CZECH REPUBLIC

Zlin Z 142CAF Czech Air Force

TECHNICAL DATA

Zlin Z 142CAF

Powerplant: One Avia M 337AK piston engine
Developing: 156.5kW (210hp)
Driving: Two-blade propeller
Span: 9.16m (30ft 0.5in)
Length: 7.33m (24ft 0.5in)
Height: 2.75m (9ft 0.25in)
All-up weight: 1,090kg (2,403lb)
Maximum speed: 227km/h (141mph)
Cruise speed: 185km/h (115mph)
Operational ceiling: 14,100ft
Maximum range: 950km (590 miles)
Mission range: 525km (326 miles)
Endurance: 2.75 hours
Accommodation: Instructor and pupil side-by-side (instructor in left-hand seat)
Warload: None
First flown: 29 December 1978 (Z 142)
Entered service: 1981/1982 (Z 142); 1994 (Z 142CAF)

DEVELOPMENT

The continuing success of the trainer and aerobatic Z 226, Z 326 and related models, encouraged Zlin to develop a parallel series of light touring/trainer models. Design work commenced during the mid-1960s on what became the two-seat side-by-side seating dual control Z 42. The prototype first flew on 17 October 1967. A four-seat derivative, the similarly successful Z 43, flew on 10 December 1968. Approximately 320 examples were produced of both types, with series production of the Z 42 stretching from 1970 to the early 1980s. In December 1978, Zlin flew an improved successor, the two-seat Z 142, which had the ability to fly inverted for up to 90 seconds. This model retained a similar basic layout to the Z 42, but a radical redesign with different wing planform and other alterations resulted in the Z 242. This two-seat Lycoming-powered development was intended for the US market and first flew on 14 February 1990. In May 1991, the four-seat Zlin Z 143 was launched, with the first flight on 24 April 1992; again intended for the US market, this model is currently available in its Lycoming-powered Z 143L form, as is the Z 242L. Notable amongst military customers for these types

is the batch of eight Z 142CAF basic trainers for the Czech Air Force. In 1997, Zlin's production facilities were flooded in a major natural disaster, but in mid-1999 the company received a massive boost with an order for 100 Z 242L basic trainers for the Egyptian Air Force. Total production so far of the Z 142/Z 143/Z 242 series (excluding this order) is some 483 examples.

CURRENT SERVICE

The final known military operator of the Z 42/Z 43 series is Hungary, with four Z 43s in service. The Czech Air Force's eight immaculate Z 142CAF trainers serve with the 342nd Training Squadron at Pardubice. Algeria also employs the Z 142, while Z 143 models serve with Egypt and Slovenia. The latter also operates eight Z 242Ls. Four Z 242Ls similarly serve in Macedonia; several of this model have recently been ordered/delivered for service in Peru.

SPECIAL FEATURES

The Z42 and Z43 shared a basically common structure, of mainly all-metal construction with some glass-fibre skinning. The Z 142 and Z 242 are fully aerobatic two-seat trainers with mainly all-metal structure

and some composite skinning. Most Zlins from these series can be used for either glider or banner towing.

VARIANTS

The basic **Z 42** was powered by a 134kW (180hp) Avia M 137A piston engine, while the **Z 43** and **Z 142** have versions of the Avia M 337 piston engine. The Z 42 and Z 142 have slightly forward-swept wings. Avionics in the Z 142, Z 143L and Z 242L are to customer choice and usually of US origin. The **Z 143L** and **Z 242L** are American-powered (175kW (235hp) Textron Lycoming O-540-J3A5 in the former; 149kW (200hp) Textron Lycoming AEIO-360-A1B6 in the latter). They have redesigned wings with no forward sweep; the Z 242L has a completely different nose and cowling shape.

Zlin Z 43 Hungarian Air Force

419

Zlin Z 326 Trenér Master and Z 526

SINGLE PISTON-ENGINED TWO-SEAT BASIC/PRIMARY TRAINER

Zlin Z 526

DEVELOPMENT

Already established as a successful designer and producer of light trainer aircraft, the Czechoslovak Zlin company secured a major order in 1948 for the production of a new primary trainer for the emergent post-World War 2 Czechoslovak Air Force. The Z 26 Trenér that won this contract was the first in a line of successful two-seat basic trainers and aerobatic aircraft designed for military and civilian operation that progressed through the Z 126 to the Z 226 of the mid-1950s and thence to the Z 326 Trenér Master. The prototype Z 326 flew in 1957 and introduced a semi-retractable main undercarriage to the line with many detail refinements. Deliveries began in 1959, with the type subsequently serving as a basic trainer in the air forces of several Soviet Bloc or Soviet-aligned air forces. Like previous and subsequent models, the

Z 326 has an aerobatic-dedicated single-seat derivative (in this case the Z 326A Akrobat), and small numbers of these also served in various armed forces or paramilitary organizations as well. Continuing development led to the Z 526 series, which moved the instructor into the rear seat in its two-seat models and which was available in several versions from the late 1960s, serving a number of military operators. Amongst these was the Czechoslovak Air Force itself. The final versions in the range were the Z 726 family, the first of which flew in 1973. Total production of the whole series from the Z 26 up to and including the final Z 726 models in the late 1970s was at least 1,452 examples.

CURRENT SERVICE

Small numbers of military Z 326 and Z 526 models continue to serve in several locations, although none now operate in military service in its country of origin. Examples of the Z 326 operate in Cuba, Mozambique and Iraq, although the status of all these machines is in doubt. The well-used Cuban Z 326s are based at San Julian in the basic training role, but most are now believed to be grounded. The principal military user of the Z 526 is Egypt, whose air force flies a handful of examples alongside PZL-104 Wilgas for refresher

training, communications and general 'hack' duties. A Z 526 was recently noted in service with the Bosnian Muslim-Croat Federation's armed forces, although its status is now uncertain.

SPECIAL FEATURES

Of simple, mainly all-metal construction with some fabric-covered areas, the single and two-seat members of the Z 326 and Z 526 series were stressed for aerobatic flight although many in military service simply served as primary/basic trainers. The semi-retractable main undercarriage introduced in the Z 326 series allowed the main wheels to project when retracted, to minimize damage in the event of a wheels-up landing.

VARIANTS

Both single-seat **Z 326A Akrobat** and two-seat **Z 326 Trenér Master** models could be fitted with wingtip fuel tanks to increase endurance. Some examples were used for glider towing, with a towing attachment fitted beneath the rear fuselage behind the tailwheel undercarriage member. The **Z 526** series introduced a constant-speed propeller, and had more power with a 134kW (180hp) Avia M 137A piston engine. An Avco Lycoming-powered model was also developed.

TECHNICAL DATA

Zlin Z 326 Trenér Master

Powerplant: One Walter Minor 6-III piston engine
Developing: 119kW (160 hp)
Driving: Two-blade propeller
Span: 10.58m (34ft 9in)
Length: 7.83m (25ft 8in)
Height: 2.06m (6ft 9in)
All-up weight: 900kg (1,984lb)
Maximum speed: 245km/h (152mph)
Cruise speed: 212km/h (132mph)
Operational ceiling: 15,750ft
Maximum range: 650km (404 miles)
Mission range: 322km (200 miles)
Endurance: Approximately 1 hour
Accommodation: Instructor and pupil in tandem (instructor in front seat)
Warload: None
First flown: 12 August 1957 (Z 326); 3 September 1965 (Z 526)
Entered service: 1959

Zlin Z 326

WORLD AIR ARMS INVENTORY

A review of the principal types of aircraft that are believed to be in service with the world's air arms. The aircraft are broadly grouped under four headings: Combat, Combat Support, Training and Miscellaneous. The latter group mainly includes communications, transport and VIP aircraft.

FAMA/FMA IA-58 Pucaras Argentine Air Force

AFGHANISTAN

AFGHAN ARMY AIR FORCE

COMBAT
- Mikoyan-Gurevich MiG-17F 'Fresco'
- Mikoyan MiG-21bis 'Fishbed'
- Mikoyan MiG-23B 'Flogger'
- Mil Mi-24/25/35 'Hind'
- Sukhoi Su-7BM 'Fitter'
- Sukhoi Su-20/Su-22M-4 'Fitter'

COMBAT SUPPORT
- Antonov An-12BP 'Cub'
- Antonov An-26 'Curl'
- Antonov An-32 'Cline'
- Mil Mi-8/17 'Hip'

TRAINING
- Aero L-29 Delfin
- Aero L-39C Albatros
- Mikoyan MiG-21UM 'Mongol'
- Mikoyan MiG-23UB 'Flogger'
- Sukhoi Su-22UM-3 'Fitter'
- Yakovlev Yak-18A 'Max'

MISCELLANEOUS
- Antonov An-2 'Colt'
- Antonov An-24 'Coke'
- Antonov An-30 'Clank'
- Ilyushin IL-18D 'Coot'

ALBANIA

ALBANIAN PEOPLE'S ARMY AIR FORCE

COMBAT
- Chengdu F-7A
- Shenyang F-6

COMBAT SUPPORT
- Harbin Z-5 (Mil Mi-4S)
- Shiziazhuang Y-5

TRAINING
- Nanchang CJ-6
- Shenyang F-2/FT-2
- Shenyang FT-5
- Shenyang FT-6

MISCELLANEOUS
- Aérospatiale AS316/319 Alouette III
- Aérospatiale AS350 Ecureuil
- Bell 222UT

ALGERIA

ALGERIAN AIR FORCE

COMBAT
- Mikoyan MiG-21MF/bis 'Fishbed'
- Mikoyan MiG-23N/MS 'Flogger'
- Mikoyan MiG-25PD 'Foxbat-E'
- Mil Mi-24 'Hind'
- Sukhoi Su-24/MR 'Fencer'

COMBAT SUPPORT
- Antonov An-12 'Cub'
- Antonov An-26 'Curl'
- Ilyushin IL-76MD/TD 'Candid'
- Lockheed C-130H/H-130 Hercules
- Mikoyan MiG-25RB 'Foxbat'
- Mil Mi-6 'Hook-A'
- Mil Mi-8/17 'Hip'

TRAINING
- Aero L-39ZA/C Albatros
- Beech T-34C-1 Turbo Mentor
- Mikoyan MiG-21U/UM 'Mongol'

- Mikoyan MiG-23UB 'Flogger'
- Mikoyan MiG-25RU 'Foxbat'
- PZL (Mil) Mi-2 'Hoplite'
- Zlin 142

MISCELLANEOUS
- Beech King Air C90B
- Beech Super King Air B200T
- Bell 206L LongRanger
- Dassault Falcon 900
- Eurocopter AS355F Ecureuil 2
- Fokker F27-400M Friendship
- Gulfstream Aerospace Gulfstream III/IV
- Kamov Ka-27 'Helix'
- Mil Mi-4 'Hound'

ANGOLA

ANGOLAN PEOPLE'S AIR FORCE

COMBAT
- Eurocopter AS565AA Panther
- Mikoyan MiG-21MF/bis 'Fishbed'
- Mikoyan MiG-23BN/ML 'Flogger'
- Mikoyan MiG-29 'Fulcrum'
- Mil Mi-17 'Hip'

Dassault Falcon 900 Algerian Air Force

- Mil Mi-24 'Hind D/E'
- Sukhoi Su-22M-4 'Fitter'
- Sukhoi Su-25 'Frogfoot'

COMBAT SUPPORT
- Aérospatiale SA342L Gazelle
- Antonov An-26 'Curl'
- CASA C.212-200/-300/-300MP Aviocar

TRAINING
- Cessna 172
- Mikoyan MiG-23UB 'Flogger'
- Pilatus PC-7 Turbo-Trainer
- Sukhoi Su-22UM-3 'Fitter'
- Sukhoi Su-25UB 'Frogfoot'

MISCELLANEOUS
- Antonov An-2 'Colt'
- Boeing 707
- Eurocopter AS565UA Panther
- Gulfstream Aerospace Gulfstream III
- ICA-Brasov IAR-316B Alouette III
- Lockheed C-130K Hercules
- Lockheed L-100-20 Hercules
- Mil Mi-8C 'Hip'
- Pilatus PC-6/B Turbo-Porter
- Pilatus/Britten-Norman BN-2T Islander

421

ARGENTINA

ARGENTINE AIR FORCE

COMBAT
Dassault Mirage IIIE/EA/DA
Dassault Mirage 5PP
English Electric Canberra B62
FAMA/FMA IA-58 Pucara
McDonnell Douglas A-4AR Skyhawk
McDonnell Douglas MD 500D/E

COMBAT SUPPORT
Aero Commander 500
Boeing 707-300
Fokker F27-400/-500/-600 Friendship
Fokker F28 1000C Fellowship
Lockheed C-130B/H Hercules
Lockheed KC-130H Hercules
Lockheed L-100-30 Hercules

TRAINING
Beech T-34C Turbo Mentor
English Electric Canberra T64
Cessna A182
Chincul-Piper PA-A-25-235 Pawnee
Chincul-Piper PA-A-28-236 Dakota IV
Chincul-Piper PA-A-28RT-201 Arrow IV
Chincul-Piper PA-A-34-220T Seneca III
Embraer EMB-312 Tucano
FAMA/FMA IA-63 Pampa
Morane-Saulnier MS760 Paris IR
Sukhoi Su-29AR

MISCELLANEOUS
Aérospatiale SA315B Lama
Bell UH-1H Iroquois
Bell 212
Bell 412
Boeing 757-23A
Boeing-Vertol CH-47C Chinook
Cessna A.182J/K/L
de Havilland Canada DHC-6 Twin Otter 200
FAMA/FMA IA-50 Guarani II
Learjet 35A
McDonnell Douglas MD 530F
Piper PA-31-310 Navajo
Rockwell Sabreliner 75A

Sikorsky S-61R
Sikorsky S-70A Black Hawk

ARGENTINE NAVAL AVIATION COMMAND

COMBAT
Aermacchi MB.326GB
Aermacchi MB.339A
Agusta-Sikorsky AS-61D-4
Dassault Super Etendard
Embraer EMB-326GB Xavante
Grumman S-2A/E/UP Tracker
Lockheed P-3B Orion
McDonnell Douglas A-4Q Skyhawk
Sikorsky SH-3D/H Sea King

COMBAT SUPPORT
Beech King Air 200T
Fokker F28-3000 Fellowship
Lockheed L-188P Electra

TRAINING
Beech T-34C-1 Turbo Mentor

MISCELLANEOUS
Agusta A109A
Aérospatiale SA316B Alouette III
Beech Queen Air B80
Eurocopter AS555MN Fennec
Pilatus PC-6/B2-H2 Turbo-Porter

ARGENTINE COAST GUARD
Aérospatiale SA330L Puma
CASA C.212-300M Aviocar
Eurocopter AS365N2 Dauphin 2
Eurocopter AS565MA Panther
Hughes 300C
Piper PA-23-250 Aztec
Piper PA-28 Warrior II

ARGENTINE ARMY AVIATION COMMAND

COMBAT
Agusta A109A
COMBAT SUPPORT
Alenia G.222
Bell 205A-1/UH-1H
Bell 212
CASA C.212-200 Aviocar

de Havilland Canada DHC-6
Twin Otter 200/300
Eurocopter AS332/B Super Puma
Grumman OV-1D Mohawk

TRAINING
Cessna T-41D Mescalero
Hiller UH-12ET

MISCELLANEOUS
Aérospatiale SA315B Lama
Beech Queen Air B80
Cessna U-17A
Cessna T207A Skywagon
Cessna 500 Citation I
Eurocopter SA330L Puma
Eurocopter AS532 Cougar
Fairchild SA-226T Merlin IIIA
Fairchild SA-226AT Merlin IVA
Rockwell Sabreliner 75A

NATIONAL GENDARMERIE
Eurocopter AS350B Ecureuil
Pilatus PC-6/B Turbo-Porter
Piper PA-23 Aztec
Piper PA-28-236 Dakota
Piper PA-31T Cheyenne II

ARMENIA

REPUBLIC OF ARMENIA AIR COMPONENT

COMBAT
Mil Mi-24P/K/RKR 'Hind'
Mikoyan MiG-25 'Foxbat'
Suhkoi Su-25 'Frogfoot'
COMBAT SUPPORT
Mil Mi-8/17 'Hip'
TRAINING
Aero L-39 Albatros
Aerostar (Yakovlev) Iak-52
MISCELLANEOUS
Antonov An-24 'Coke'
Antonov An-32 'Cline'
PZL (Mil) Mi-2 'Hoplite'
Tupolev Tu-134A 'Crusty'
Yakovlev Yak-40 'Codling'

AUSTRALIA

ROYAL AUSTRALIAN AIR FORCE

COMBAT
General Dynamics F-111C/G
Lockheed P-3C/EP-3C Orion
McDonnell Douglas F/A-18A/B Hornet

COMBAT SUPPORT
Boeing 707-338C
de Havilland Canada DHC-4 Caribou
General Dynamics RF-111C
Lockheed C-130E/H Hercules
Lockheed Martin C-130J-30 Hercules

TRAINING
Aermacchi MB-326M
BAE Systems Hawk 100
Hawker Siddeley (BAe) 748 Srs 228/229
Lockheed TAP-3B Orion
Pilatus PC-9/A

MISCELLANEOUS
Boeing 707-320C
de Havilland DHC-4 Caribou
Dassault Falcon 900

ROYAL AUSTRALIAN NAVY

COMBAT
Kaman SH-2G(A) Super Seasprite
Sikorsky S-70B-2 Seahawk
COMBAT SUPPORT
Westland Sea King 50/50A
TRAINING
Bell 206B-1 Kiowa
Hawker Siddeley (BAe) 748EW
MISCELLANEOUS
Eurocopter AS350B Ecureuil

AUSTRALIAN ARMY AVIATION

COMBAT SUPPORT
Bell UH-1H Iroquois
Bell 206B-1 Kiowa
Boeing Vertol CH-47D Chinook
Sikorsky S-70A-9 Black Hawk
TRAINING
Eurocopter AS350B Ecureuil
MISCELLANEOUS
Beech Super King Air 200
de Havilland DHC-6 Twin Otter

AUSTRIA

AUSTRIAN AIR FORCE

COMBAT
Saab J35OE Draken
Saab 105OE
COMBAT SUPPORT
Agusta-Bell AB212
Bell OH-58B Kiowa
Pilatus PC-6/B2-H2 Turbo-Porter
Shorts Skyvan 3M

Lockheed Martin C-130J Hercules Royal Australian Air Force

Agusta-Bell AB212 Austrian Air Force

TRAINING
Agusta-Bell AB206A JetRanger
Pilatus PC-7 Turbo-Trainer
MISCELLANEOUS
Aérospatiale SA316 Alouette III
Agusta Bell 204B

AZERBAIJAN

AZERBAIJAN AIR FORCE
COMBAT
Mikoyan MiG-21 'Fishbed'
Mikoyan MiG-25PD 'Foxbat E'
Mil Mi-24 'Hind'
Sukhoi Su-15 'Flagon'
Sukhoi Su-17M 'Fitter'
Sukhoi Su-24 'Fencer'
Sukhoi Su-25 'Frogfoot'
COMBAT SUPPORT
Mikoyan MiG-25RB
Mil Mi-8/17 'Hip'
PZL (Mil) Mi-2 'Hoplite'
TRAINING
Aero L-29 Delfin
Aero L-39 Albatros

BAHAMAS

ROYAL BAHAMAS DEFENCE FORCE
Cessna 404
Cessna 421C Golden Eagle

ROYAL BAHAMAS POLICE FORCE
Colemill Panther Navajo

BAHRAIN

BAHRAIN AMIRI AIR FORCE
COMBAT
Bell AH-1E HueyCobra
General Dynamics F-16C/D Fighting Falcon
Northrop F-5E Tiger II
TRAINING
Bell TAH-1P HueyCobra

Northrop F-5F Tiger II
MISCELLANEOUS
Agusta-Bell AB212/412SP
Boeing 727-2M7
Boeing 747SP
Gulfstream Aerospace Gulfstream II (TT)
Gulfstream Aerospace Gulfstream III
Sikorsky UH-60A/L Blackhawk

PUBLIC SECURITY FLYING WING
Bell 412SP
Eurocopter BO105C
McDonnell Douglas MD500MD

BAHRAIN AMIRI NAVY AIR ARM
Eurocopter Super Five (BO105CBS-4)

BANGLADESH

BANGLADESH DEFENCE FORCE AIR WING
COMBAT
Chengdu F-7M Airguard
Mikoyan MiG-29 'Fulcrum'
Nanchang A-5CD 'Fantan'
COMBAT SUPPORT
Antonov An-26 'Curl'
Antonov An-32 'Cline'

Bell 212
Mil Mi-17 'Hip H'
TRAINING
Aero L-39ZA Albatros
Bell 206L LongRanger
Cessna 152
Cessna T-37B
Guizhou (GAIC) FT-7
Mikoyan MiG-29UB 'Fulcrum'
Nanchang CJ-6
Scheibe SF-25C Falke
Shenyang FT-6
MISCELLANEOUS
Lockheed C-130B Hercules
Mil Mi-8S 'Hip C'

BARBADOS

BARBADOS DEFENCE FORCE
Cessna 402C

BELARUS

MILITARY AIR FORCES
COMBAT
Mikoyan MiG-23MLD 'Flogger K'
Mikoyan MiG-29 'Fulcrum C'

Sukhoi Su-24MK/MR 'Fencer'
Sukhoi Su-25 'Frogfoot A'
Sukhoi Su-27P 'Flanker'
COMBAT SUPPORT
Antonov An-12BP 'Cub'
Antonov An-26 'Curl A'
Ilyushin IL-22 'Coot B'
Ilyushin IL-76MD 'Candid'
TRAINING
Mikoyan MiG-23UB 'Flogger C'
Mikoyan MiG-29UB 'Fulcrum B'
Sukhoi Su-25UB 'Frogfoot'
Sukhoi Su-27UB 'Flanker'
MISCELLANEOUS
Antonov An-24 'Coke'
Tupolev Tu-134 'Crusty'
Tupolev Tu-154 'Careless'
Yak-40 'Codling'

ARMY AVIATION
COMBAT
Mil Mi-24V/P 'Hind E/F'
COMBAT SUPPORT
Mil Mi-6 'Hook A'
Mil Mi-24Rkh 'Hind G1'
Mil Mi-26 'Halo'

BELGIUM

BELGIAN AIR FORCE
COMBAT
General Dynamics F-16A/B Fighting Falcon
COMBAT SUPPORT
Airbus A310-225
Boeing 727-29C
Hawker Siddeley 748 Srs 288
Lockheed C-130H Hercules
TRAINING
Dassault/Dornier Alpha Jet B
Fouga CM170R Magister
SIAI-Marchetti SF.260MB/D
Piper PA-18 Super Cub

F-16B Fighting Falcon Belgian Air Force

423

AMX International AMX Brazilian Air Force

MISCELLANEOUS
Aérospatiale SA316B Alouette III
Dassault Mystere 20E
Dassault Falcon 900B
Fairchild Merlin IIIA
Westland Sea King Mk 48

BELGIAN ARMY LIGHT AVIATION GROUP
COMBAT
Agusta A109HA
COMBAT SUPPORT
Agusta A109HO

GENDARMERIE
Aérospatiale SA318C Alouette-Astazou
Aérospatiale SA330H Puma
Cessna 182Q/R
McDonnell Douglas MDH900 Explorer
P/B-N BN-2T Turbine Islander

BELIZE

BELIZE DEFENCE FORCE
P/B-N BN-2B-21 Defender
Slingsby T.67M-200 Firefly

BENIN

PEOPLE'S ARMED FORCES OF BENIN
Antonov An-26 'Curl'
de Havilland Canada DHC-6 Twin Otter
Dornier Do 128-2 Skyservant
Eurocopter AS350B Ecureuil
Rockwell Commander 500B

BHUTAN

BHUTAN AIR ARM
Dornier 228
Mil Mi-8 'Hip'

BOLIVIA

BOLIVIAN AIR FORCE
COMBAT
Canadair AT-33AN Silver Star
Pilatus PC-7 Turbo-Trainer
Lockheed T-33SF Shooting Star
COMBAT SUPPORT
Basler Turbo 67
Bell UH-1H Iroquois
Convair 580
Douglas DC-8-54CF
Fokker F27-400M Troopship
IAI Arava 201
Lockheed C-130A/B/H Hercules
Lockheed 188A Electra
TRAINING
Aerotec A-122 Uirapuru/A-132 Tangara
Beech 36 Bonanza
Cessna 152 Aerobat
Cessna U206C/TU206G Stationair
MISCELLANEOUS
Aérospatiale SA315B Lama/HB315B Gaviao
Beech B36 Bonanza
Beech B55/B58 Baron
Beech King Air F90
Beech Super King Air C200
CASA C212-200 Aviocar
Cessna 210/Robertson STOL 210
Cessna 402B
Cessna 421C
Fokker F27-400 Friendship
Gates Learjet 25/35
Piper PA-32 Cherokee Six
Rockwell Sabreliner 60
Rockwell Turbo Commander 680E/1000

BOLIVIAN ARMY/NAVY AVIATION
Beech King Air C90
CASA C.212-300M Aviocar

BOSNIA-HERZEGOVINA

ARMY AIR FORCE (Muslim Controlled)
Bell UH-1H/V Iroquois
Cessna 550 Citation
Mil Mi-8MTV 'Hip'

SERBIAN REPUBLIC AIR FORCE
Soko J-21 Jastreb
Soko J-22(M) Orao 2
Soko NJ-22(M) Orao 2D
Soko P-2 Kraguj
Soko/Aérospatiale SA341L
COMBAT SUPPORT
Bell UH-1H/V Iroquois
Mil Mi-8 'Hip'
Soko/Aérospatiale SA341H Partizan
TRAINING
Soko G-2 Galeb
Soko G-4 Super Galeb
MISCELLANEOUS
Cessna 172
Piper PA-18 Super Cub
UTVA-66
UTVA-75

MILITIA (Serbian)
Antonov An-2 'Colt'
Soko P-2 Kraguj

BOTSWANA

BOTSWANA DEFENCE FORCE AIR WING
COMBAT
Canadair CF-5A Freedom Fighter
COMBAT SUPPORT
Airtech CN.235
Bell 412/412SP
CASA C.212-300 Aviocar
Lockheed C-130B Hercules

P/B-N BN-2A-21 Defender
TRAINING
Aérospatiale AS350 Ecureuil
Canadair CF-5D Freedom Fighter
Cessna A152 Aerobat
Pilatus PC-7 Turbo-Trainer
MISCELLANEOUS
Cessna O-2 Skymaster
Eurocopter AS350B Ecureuil
Gulfstream Aerospace Gulfstream IV

BRAZIL

BRAZILIAN AIR FORCE
COMBAT
AMX International AMX
Dassault Mirage IIIE/EBR
Grumman S-2E Tracker
Northrop F-5E Tiger II
COMBAT SUPPORT
Bell UH-1D/H Iroquois
Boeing KC-137 (707-320C)
de Havilland Canada DHC-5A Buffalo
Embraer EMB-110/K1/P1K/P1A
  Bandeirante
Embraer EMB-111B Patrulha
Embraer EMB-145AEW/EMB-145 RS/SA
Hawker Siddeley (BAe) 748 Srs 200
Lockheed C-130E/H Hercules
Lockheed KC-130H Hercules
TRAINING
Aerotech T-23 Uirapuru
AMX International AMX-T
Bell OH-13 Sioux
Dassault Mirage IIIBE/DBR
Embraer EMB-312 Tucano
Embraer EMB-326 Xavante
Eurocopter HB350B
Hughes OH-6A Cayuse
Neiva T-25N Universal

Northrop F-5B Freedom Fighter
Northrop F-5F Tiger II
MISCELLANEOUS
Bell UH-1H Iroquois
Bell 206A/B JetRanger
Boeing 737-2N3
British Aerospace 125 Srs 3B/RC
British Aerospace 125 Srs 400/403
Cessna 208 Caravan I
Embraer EMB-110/110A/110B/110P-L
Bandeirante
Embraer EMB-120RT Brasilia
Embraer EMB-121A/E Xingu
Embraer EMB-201R Ipanema
Embraer EMB-810C Seneca
Eurocopter AS332M Super Puma
Helibras HB355M Esquilo
Learjet 35/36A
Neiva N-591 Regente

BRAZILIAN NAVAL AIR FORCE
COMBAT
Agusta-Sikorsky SH-3D/H SeaKing
McDonnell Douglas A-4 Skyhawk
Westland Super Lynx HAS21A
COMBAT SUPPORT
Eurocopter AS352M Cougar
TRAINING
Bell 206B JetRanger III
McDonnell Douglas TA-4 Skyhawk
MISCELLANEOUS
Helibras HB350BA Esquilo
Helibras HB355F2 Esquilo II

BRAZILIAN ARMY AVIATION
COMBAT
Eurocopter AS550A2 Fennec
Helibras HB350L1 Esquilo
COMBAT SUPPORT
Eurocopter AS565AA Panther
Sikorsky S-70A Black Hawk

BRUNEI

ROYAL BRUNEI AIR FORCE
COMBAT
British Aerospace Hawk 200
Eurocopter BO105CB
COMBAT SUPPORT
Airtech CN-235M/MPA
Bell 212
Sikorsky UH-60L Black Hawk
TRAINING
Bell 206B JetRanger III
British Aerospace Hawk 100
Pilatus PC-7
SIAI-Marchetti SF.260W Warrior
MISCELLANEOUS
Bell 214ST

Embraer EMB-110 Bandeirante Brazilian Air Force

Eurocopter BO105CBS
Sikorsky S-70C Black Hawk

BULGARIA

BULGARIAN MILITARY AIR FORCES
COMBAT
Mikoyan MiG-21PFM/MF/bis 'Fishbed'
Mikoyan MiG-23BN/MF/ML/MLD 'Flogger'
Mikoyan MiG-29 'Fulcrum A'
Mil Mi-24D/V 'Hind'
Sukhoi Su-22M-4 'Fitter'
Sukhoi Su-25K 'Frogfoot'
COMBAT SUPPORT
Antonov An-24 'Coke'
Antonov An-26 'Curl'
Mikoyan MiG-21R 'Fishbed'
Mil Mi-8T/17 'Hip'
TRAINING
Aero L29 Delfin
Aero L39ZA Albatros
Mikoyan MiG-21UM/US 'Mongol'
Mikoyan MiG-23UB 'Flogger'
Mikoyan MiG-29UB 'Fulcrum B'
Sukhoi Su-22UM-3 'Fitter'
Sukhoi Su-25UBK 'Frogfoot'
MISCELLANEOUS
Antonov An-2 'Colt'
Antonov An-30 'Clank'
Bell 206 JetRanger

Let L-410UVP Turbolet
PZL (Mil) Mi-2 'Hoplite'
Tupolev Tu-134A 'Crusty'
Yakovlev Yak-40 'Codling'

BULGARIAN NAVAL AIR ARM
COMBAT
Mil Mi-14PL 'Haze A'
COMBAT SUPPORT
Mil Mi-14BT 'Haze B'

BURKINA FASO

BURKINA FASO AIR FORCE
COMBAT SUPPORT
Hawker Siddeley 748 Srs 320
Eurocopter SA365N Dauphin
Mil Mi-8/17 'Hip'
Nord 262C-50P/65 Fregate
MISCELLANEOUS
Beech King Air 200
Cessna F172N
Cessna F337E
Eurocopter AS350 Ecureuil

BURUNDI

BURUNDI NATIONAL ARMY
COMBAT
Aérospatiale SA342L Gazelle

SIAI Marchetti SF.260C/TP/W
TRAINING
Reims Cessna FRA 150L
MISCELLANEOUS
Aérospatiale SA316B Alouette III
Dassault Falcon 50
All operated by the air element of the Army.

CAMBODIA

ROYAL CAMBODIAN AIR FORCE
COMBAT
Mikoyan MiG-21bis/UM 'Fishbed'
Mil Mi-24 'Hind'
COMBAT SUPPORT
Antonov An-24RV 'Coke'
Harbin Y-12
Mil Mi-8 'Hip'
Mil Mi-17 'Hip'
Mil Mi-26 'Halo'
P/B-N BN-2A Islander
TRAINING
Aero L39ZA Albatros
Tecnam P92 Echo
MISCELLANEOUS
Beech Super King Air 200
Dassault Falcon 20E
Eurocopter AS350B Ecureuil
Eurocopter AS365 Dauphin 2
Fokker F28-1000 Fellowship

Tupolev Tu-134A 'Crusty' Bulgarian Air Force

425

Airbus CC-150 Polaris Canadian Forces

BAE Systems Hawk 115 Canadian Forces

ENAER T-35 Pillan Chilean Air Force

Lockheed CP-140 Aurora Canadian Forces

Eurocopter AS350B Ecureuil

CHAD NATIONAL FLIGHT

COMBAT

Pilatus PC-7 Turbo-Trainer

SIAI-Marchetti SF.260WL Warrior

COMBAT SUPPORT

Lockheed C-130H/H-30 Hercules

MISCELLANEOUS

Aérospatiale SA316 Alouette III

Antonov An-26 'Curl'

Pilatus PC-6B Turbo-Porter

Reims Cessna FTB337

CHILE

CHILEAN AIR FORCE

COMBAT

Cessna A-37B Dragonfly

Dassault Elkan (Mirage 5MA/MD)

ENAER A-36B Halcon

ENAER Pantera C

Northrop F-5E/F Tiger II

COMBAT SUPPORT

Beech 99A

Bell UH-1H Iroquois

Boeing KC-137

Boeing 707-351C

CASA C.212-100 Aviocar

de Havilland Canada DHC-6-300

Twin Otter

IAI/Elta Phalcon 1

Lockheed C-130B/H Hercules

Sikorsky UH-60 Black Hawk

TRAINING

Cessna O-2A (337)

Bell 206

Dassault Mirage 50DC

ENAER T-35A/B Pillan.

CAMEROON

CAMEROON AIR FORCE

COMBAT

Atlas Impala 1/2

Dassault/Dornier Alpha Jet MS2

Fouga CM-170 Magister

COMBAT SUPPORT

Aérospatiale SA342L Gazelle

de Havilland Canada DHC-5D Buffalo

Dornier 128-6MPA Skyservant

IAI Arava 201

Lockheed C-130H/H-30 Hercules

MISCELLANEOUS

Aérospatiale SA318C Alouette II

Aérospatiale SA319B Alouette III

Aérospatiale SA330C Puma

Bell 206L-3 LongRanger III

Boeing 727-2R1

Eurocopter AS332L Super Puma

Eurocopter AS365N Dauphin 2

Gulfstream Aerospace Gulfstream III

Piper PA-23 Aztec

CANADA

CANADIAN FORCES – AIR COMMAND

COMBAT

Lockheed CP-140 Auroa

McDonnell Douglas CF-188A/B Hornet

Sikorsky CH-124A/B/U Sea King

COMBAT SUPPORT

Airbus CC-150 Polaris

Bell CH-146 Griffon

Bell CH-118 Iroquois

Boeing-Vertol CH-113 Labrador

Canadair (CL-600S) CC-144/CE-144/

CP-144 Challenger

de Havilland Canada CC-115 Buffalo

Lockheed CC-130E/H Hercules

Lockheed KCC-130H Hercules

Lockheed L-100-30 Hercules

Lockheed CP-140A Arcturus

TRAINING

Civil T.67M Fireflies and King Air C90As

are used at the CATC for pilot training.

Beech King Air C90

Beech CT-145 Super King Air 200

Bell CH-139 JetRanger

BAE Systems Hawk 115

Canadair CT-114 Tutor

Canadair CF-116A/D Freedom Fighter

Canadair CT-133A Silver Star

de Havilland CC-142/CT-142 Dash 8

Raytheon CT-156 Harvard II

MISCELLANEOUS

de Havilland Canada CC-138 Twin Otter

CAPE VERDE

CAPE VERDE AIR FORCE

Antonov An-26 'Curl'

COAST GUARD

Dornier 228-201

CENTRAL AFRICAN REPUBLIC

CENTRAL AFRICAN FLIGHT

Aérospatiale Rallye 235GS Guerrier

Dassault Falcon 20C

Cessna O-2A Chilean Air Force

ENAER T-36 Halcon
MISCELLANEOUS
  Aérospatiale SA315B Lama
  Beech 99A
  Beech King Air 100
  Beech King Air B200
  Boeing 737-58N
  Cessna O-1 Bird Dog
  Eurocopter BO105CB-4/CBS
  Eurocopter/Kawasaki BK117B-1
  Extra 300
  Gulfstream Aerospace C-20B
    Gulfstream IV
  Learjet 35A
  Piper PA-28-236 Dakota

CHILEAN NAVAL AIR COMMAND
COMBAT
  Eurocopter AS332B Super Puma
  Eurocopter AS532SC Cougar
  Lockheed P-3A Orion
COMBAT SUPPORT
  CASA C.212A-100 Aviocar
  Embraer EMB-110CN/
    EMB-111 Bandeirante
  Lockheed UP-3A Orion
TRAINING
  Bell 206B JetRanger
  Cessna O-2A
MISCELLANEOUS
  Cessna Citation I/II
  Dassault Falcon 200
  Eurocopter BO105S/LSA-1/CBS-5

CHILEAN ARMY AVIATION
COMBAT
  McDonnell Douglas MD 530F
COMBAT SUPPORT
  Aérospatiale SA315B Lama
  Aérospatiale SA330F/L Puma
  Airtech CN-235M-100
  CASA C.212A-100/300 Aviocar

Cessna 337G
Eurocopter AS332B/1 Super Puma
TRAINING
  Cessna R172K Hawk XP
  Enstrom 280FX
MISCELLANEOUS
  Bell 206
  Beech Baron
  Beech King Air B90
  Cessna 208

CHILEAN POLICE AIR UNIT
Bell 206L3 JetRanger
Cessna 182Q
Cessna U206G Stationair
Cessna 210M Centurion II
Eurocopter BO105CBS/LSA-3
Piper PA-31 Navajo
Swearingen SA-226TC Metro

CHINA (People's Republic of China)

**AIR FORCE OF THE
PEOPLE'S LIBERATION ARMY**
COMBAT
  Harbin H-5/HJ-5
  Nanchang (NAMC) Q-5 'Fantan'
  Shenyang J-5/5A
  Shenyang J-6/6C &
    Guizhou J-6A/B
  Shenyang J-7 &
    Chengdu/Guizhou J-7 I/II/III
  Shenyang J-8 I/II 'Finback'
  Sukhoi Su-27SK 'Flanker'(J-11)
  Sukhoi Su-30MKK
  Xian H-6
COMBAT SUPPORT
  Antonov An-26 'Curl'
  Beriev A-50
  Harbin HZ-5
  Harbin Y-11
  Ilyushin IL-18 'Coot'

Ilyushin IL-76 'Candid'
Lisunov Li-2 'Cab'
Shaanxi Y-8
Shenyang JZ-6
Tupolev Tu-154M/D
Xian Y-7
TRAINING
  Chengdu JJ-5
  Guizhou (GAIC) JJ-7
  Nanchang (NAMC) CJ-6
  Nanchang (NAMC) K-8 Karakorum
  Shenyang J-4
  Shenyang JJ-6/C-6
  Sukhoi Su-27UB 'Flanker'
MISCELLANEOUS
  Antonov An-30 'Clank'
  Canadair CL-601 Challenger
  Harbin Z-5
  Shijiazhuang (SAP) Y-5

ARMY AVIATION CORPS
COMBAT
  Aérospatiale SA342L-1 Gazelle
Combat Support
  Eurocopter AS332L1 Super Puma
  Harbin Z-5
  Mil Mi-8/17 'Hip'
  Sikorsky S-70C-II Black Hawk
MISCELLANEOUS
  Changhe Z-11 (Fennec)
  Harbin Z-9/9A

AVIATION OF THE PEOPLE'S NAVY
COMBAT
  Beriev Be-6 'Madge'
  Changhe Z-8
  Chengdu/Guizhou J-7 I/II/III
  Harbin H-5/SH-5
  Harbin H-6
  Harbin Z-9/9A
  Kamov Ka-28 'Helix'
  Nanchang Q-5 'Fantan'

Shenyang J-6/JJ-6
Sud SA321Ja Super Frelon
Xian H-6/H-6 III
Xian JH-7
COMBAT SUPPORT
  Xian Y-7
TRAINING
  Shenyang J-5A
MISCELLANEOUS
  Harbin Z-5
  Shijiazhuang (SAP) Y-5

**HONG KONG GOVERNMENT
FLYING SERVICE**
All HKGFS aircraft are civil registered.
Beech B200C Super King Air
Sikorsky S-70A-27 Black Hawk
Sikorsky S-76A+/C
Slingsby T.67M-200 Firefly

COLOMBIA

COLOMBIAN AIR FORCE
COMBAT
  Cessna A-37B/OA-37B Dragonfly
  Dassault Mirage 5COA/COR/COD
  Douglas AC-47
  Embraer A-27 Tucano
  FMA IA-58A Pucara
  Hughes 369D/E/F/HN/HS/M
  Hughes 500/OH-6A Cayuse/530FF
  IAI Kfir C-7/TC-7
  Rockwell International OV-10A Bronco
COMBAT SUPPORT
  Airtech CN.235
  Bell UH-1H Iroquois
  Bell 205A-1
  Bell 212
  CASA C.212-300 Aviocar
  Douglas AC-47T Skytrain
  Fokker F28-3000C Fellowship
  IAI Arava 201

Lockheed C-130B/H Hercules
Sikorsky UH-60A/L Black Hawk
TRAINING
Beech T-34A/B Mentor
Cessna T-37B/C
Cessna 310R
Cessna T-41D Mescalero
Embraer T-27 Tucano
Enstrom F28F
MISCELLANEOUS
Beech B80 Queen Air
Beech Baron
Beech King Air C90/300
Bell 206L-3 LongRanger
Bell 412
Boeing 707-373C
Cessna 206 Stationair
Cessna 208 Caravan I
Cessna 210 Centurian
Cessna 402/441
Cessna 550 Citation II
de Havilland Canada DHC-2 Beaver
Embraer EMB-110P1A Bandeirante
Fairchild Dornier 328-100
Fokker F28-1000 Fellowship
Hawker Siddeley (BAe) 748
Piper PA-23 Aztec
Piper PA-31 Navajo
Piper PA-31T Turbo Cheyenne II
Piper PA-34 Seneca
Rockwell Turbo Commander A695A
Rockwell Commander 980
Schweizer SA 2-37A

COLOMBIAN NAVAL AIR ARM
Beech King Air
Eurocopter BO105CB
Eurocopter AS555SN Fennec
Piper PA-28 Cherokee
Piper PA-31 Navajo
Rockwell Commander 500

COLOMBIAN ARMY AVIATION
COMBAT SUPPORT
Mil Mi-17 'Hip'

MISCELLANEOUS
Beech Super King Air 200
Cessna U206G Stationair
Convair 580
Piper PA-28 Cherokee
Piper PA-31 Navajo
Piper PA-34 Seneca
Rockwell Commander 500/1000
Sikorsky UH-60L Black Hawk
UTVA-75

COMOROS ISLANDS

COMOROS MILITARY AVIATION
Eurocopter AS350B Ecureuil

CONGO

PEOPLE'S REPUBLIC OF THE CONGO AIR FORCE
COMBAT
Mikoyan-Gurevich MiG-17F 'Fresco'
Mikoyan MiG-21MF 'Fishbed'
TRAINING
Mikoyan-Gurevich MiG-15UTI 'Midget'
MISCELLANEOUS
Aérospatiale SA316 Alouette III
Aérospatiale SA365 Dauphin
Antonov An-24 'Coke'
Boeing 727

CONGO (FORMERLY ZAIRE)

DEMOCRATIC REPUBLIC OF CONGO AIR FORCE
COMBAT
Aermacchi MB.326K
Dassault Mirage 5M
COMBAT SUPPORT
Aérospatiale SA330C Puma
de Havilland Canada DHC-5D Buffalo
Douglas C-47 Dakota
Lockheed C-130H Hercules
TRAINING
Aermacchi MB.326GB

Reims Cessna FRA150M
SIAI-Marchetti SF.260MZ
MISCELLANEOUS
Aérospatiale SA316 Alouette III
Boeing 727-100
Britten-Norman BN-2A Islander
CASA C212-200 Aviocar
Eurocopter AS332L Super Puma

COSTA RICA

COSTA RICA PUBLIC CIVIL GUARD
Cessna O-2A Super Skymaster
Colemill Panther PA-31 Navajo
de Havilland Canada DHC-4A Caribou
McDonnell Douglas MD500E
Mil Mi-17 'Hip H'
Piper PA-34 Seneca
Soloy (Cessna) U206G Stationair

CROATIA

CROATIAN MILITARY AIR FORCE AND ANTI-AIRCRAFT DEFENCE
COMBAT
Mikoyan MiG-21bis 'Fishbed'
Mil Mi-24D/V 'Hind'
Soko IJ-21 Jastreb
Soko P-2 Kraguj
COMBAT SUPPORT
Airtech CN235M
Antonov An-32B 'Cline'
Mil Mi-8P/S/T/MTV-1 'Hip'
TRAINING
McDonnell Douglas MD500
Pilatus PC-9
Soko G2-A Galeb
UTVA-75
MISCELLANEOUS
Antonov An-2 'Colt'
Bell 206B-3 JetRanger III
Canadair CL-215/CL-415
Canadair CL-601-3A Challenger
Cessna 172
Cessna T210N

Dornier Do28D Skyservant
McDonnell Douglas MD500D
Piper PA-28 Warrior
Piper PA-36 Pawnee Brave
PZL (Mil) Mi-2 'Hoplite'
Rockwell Sabreliner 75A

POLICE AIR WING
McDonnell Douglas MD500D
Mil Mi-8MTV-1

CUBA

CUBAN REVOLUTIONARY AIR FORCE
COMBAT
Mikoyan-Gurevich MiG-17F 'Fresco'
Mikoyan MiG-21PFM/MF 'Fishbed F/J'
Mikoyan MiG-21bis 'Fishbed L'
Mikoyan MiG-23MF/MS 'Flogger'
Mikoyan MiG-23BN 'Flogger H'
Mikoyan MiG-29 'Fulcrum A'
Mil Mi-14PL 'Haze A'
Mil Mi-24D 'Hind D'
COMBAT SUPPORT
Antonov An-24 'Coke'
Antonov An-26 'Curl'
Antonov An-32 'Cline'
Mil Mi-8/17 'Hip'
TRAINING
Aero L-39C Albatros
Mikoyan-Gurevich MiG-17F 'Fresco'
Mikoyan MiG-21UM/US 'Mongol'
Mikoyan MiG-23UB 'Flogger C'
Mikoyan MiG-29UB 'Fulcrum B'
Zlin 326
MISCELLANEOUS
Antonov An-2 'Colt'
Antonov An-30 'Clank'
PZL (Mil) Mi-2 'Hoplite'
Yakovlev Yak-40 'Codling'
Zlin 142 Scout

CYPRUS (GREEK)

CYPRIOT ARMY AVIATION
COMBAT
Aérospatiale SA342L-1 Gazelle
COMBAT SUPPORT
P/B-N BN-2B-21 Maritime Defender
TRAINING
Pilatus PC-9
MISCELLANEOUS
Bell 206L-3 LongRanger
McDonnell Douglas MD500
PZL Swidnik Kania

POLICE
Bell 412SP
Pilatus/B-N BN-2T Turbine Islander

Rockwell Commander 1000 Colombian Army

Sukhoi Su-25K 'Frogfoot A' Czech Air Force

Mikoyan MiG-23ML 'Flogger' Czech Air Force

Mil Mi-17 'Hip' Czech Air Force

430

Antonov An-30 'Clank' Czech Air Force

CZECH REPUBLIC

CZECH AIR FORCE AND AIR DEFENCE

COMBAT
Aero L-159 Albatros
Mikoyan MiG-21MF 'Fishbed'
Mikoyan MiG-23ML 'Flogger'
Mil Mi-24D/V 'Hind'
Sukhoi Su-22M-4K 'Fitter'
Sukhoi Su-25K 'Frogfoot A'

COMBAT SUPPORT
Antonov An-24 RV 'Coke'
Antonov An-26 'Curl'
Let L-410M/T/UVP Turbolet
Mil Mi-8PS/PPA/T 'Hip'
Mil Mi-9 'Hip G'
Mil Mi-17

TRAINING
Aero L-29 Delfin
Aero L-39C/MS Albatros
Aero L-59T
Aero L-139
Mikoyan MiG-21UM 'Mongol'
Mikoyan MiG-23UM 'Flogger'
Mil Mi-24DU 'Hind'
Sukhoi Su-22UM-3K 'Fitter'
Sukhoi Su-25UBK 'Frogfoot B'
Zlin 142 CAF

MISCELLANEOUS
Antonov An-30FG 'Clank'
Let L-410FG Turbolet
PZL (Mil) Mi-2 'Hoplite'
PZL Swidnik W-3A Sokol
Tupolev Tu-134A 'Crusty'
Tupolev Tu-154B-2 'Careless'

CZECH REPUBLIC POLICE AVIATION
Bell 412HP
Eurocopter BO105CBS-4
Mil Mi-8P 'Hip'
PZL (Mil) Mi-2 'Hoplite'

STATE FLYING SERVICE
Canadair CL-601-3A Challenger
Ilyushin IL-62M 'Classic'
Let L-410UVP-E20C Turbolet
Tupolev Tu-154M 'Careless'
Yakovlev Yak-40/40K 'Codling'

DENMARK

ROYAL DANISH AIR FORCE

COMBAT
General Dynamics F-16A/B-10/15/15 OCU
Fighting Falcon

COMBAT SUPPORT
Lockheed C-130H Hercules

TRAINING
Saab T-17 Supporter

MISCELLANEOUS
Canadair CL-604 Challenger
Gulfstream Aerospace Gulfstream III
Sikorsky S-61A-1/5 Sea King

NAVAL FLYING SERVICE
Westland Lynx HAS80A

ARMY FLYING SERVICE
Eurocopter AS550C-2 Fennec
Hughes 500M

DJIBOUTI

DJIBOUTI AIR FORCE

COMBAT SUPPORT
Mil Mi-8 'Hip'

MISCELLANEOUS
Antonov An-28 'Cash'
Cessna U206G Stationair
Cessna 402C
Dassault Falcon 50
Eurocopter AS355F Ecureuil
PZL (Mil) Mi-2 'Hoplite'

DOMINICAN REPUBLIC

DOMINICAN REPUBLIC AIR FORCE

COMBAT
Cessna A-37B Dragonfly

COMBAT SUPPORT
Bell UH-1H/205A-1
Cessna O-2 Super Skymaster

TRAINING
Cessna T-41D Mescalero
ENAER T-35 Pillan

MISCELLANEOUS
Aérospatiale SA316 Alouette III
Beech Queen Air 80
Beech King Air 90
CASA C212-400 Aviocar
Cessna P210N
Eurocopter SA365H Dauphin 2
Eurocopter AS350B Ecureuil
McDonnell Douglas MD369
Piper PA31 Navajo
Rockwell Commander 680

DOMINICAN ARMY
Cessna 207 – operated by the Dominican
Air Force on behalf of the army.

ECUADOR

ECUADOREAN AIR FORCE

COMBAT
BAC Strikemaster 89/89A
Cessna A-37B Dragonfly
Dassault Mirage F1E/JA
IAI Kfir C-2/TC-2
SEPECAT Jaguar International ES

COMBAT SUPPORT
de Havilland Canada DHC-5D Buffalo
de Havilland Canada DHC-6-300
Twin Otter
Hawker Siddeley (BAe) 748 Srs 2A
Lockheed C-130B/ Hercules
Lockheed L-100-30 Hercules

TRAINING
Beech T-34C Turbo-Mentor
Cessna T-41D Mescalero
Dassault Mirage F1JE
Lockheed AT-33 Shooting Star
SEPECAT Jaguar EB

MISCELLANEOUS
Aérospatiale SA316B Alouette III
Bell UH-1B/H Iroquois
Bell 206B JetRanger

Sikorsky S-61A Sea King Royal Danish Air Force

Bell 212
Boeing 727-17/134/230/2T3
Cessna 150L
Fokker F28-4000 Fellowship
Rockwell Sabreliner 40R/60

ECUADOREAN NAVAL AVIATION
TRAINING
Beech T-34C Turbo-Mentor
MISCELLANEOUS
Airtech CN.235M-1001
Beech Super King Air 200/300
Bell 206B JetRanger
Bell 222
Bell/Helidyne 412
Cessna Citation I
Cessna 320E Skyknight

ECUADOREAN ARMY AIR SERVICE
COMBAT
Aérospatiale SA342K/L Gazelle
COMBAT SUPPORT
Aérospatiale SA330L Puma
Airtech CN.235M
de Havilland Canada DHC-5D Buffalo
Eurocopter AS332B Super Puma
IAI Arava 201
TRAINING
Cessna 172G
MISCELLANEOUS
Aérospatiale SA315B Lama
Beech King Air A100/200
Beech Super King Air 200
Bell 214B
Cessna 550 Citation II
Eurocopter AS350B Ecureuil
Learjet 24D
Pilatus PC-6B Turbo-Porter
Rockwell Sabreliner 40R

EGYPT

ARAB REPUBLIC OF EGYPT AIR FORCE
COMBAT
Aérospatiale SA342L Gazelle

Boeing AH-64A Apache
Chengdu F-7A/B
Dassault Mirage 5E2/SDE
Dassault Mirage 2000EM/B
Dassault/Dornier Alpha Jet MS2
General Dynamics F-16A/B Fighting Falcon
General Dynamics F-16C/D Fighting Falcon
McDonnell Douglas F-4E Phantom II
Mikoyan MiG-21PF/PFM/MF 'Fishbed'
Shenyang F-6
COMBAT SUPPORT
Aérospatiale SA342K/L/M Gazelle
Beech 1900C
Dassault Mirage 5SDR
de Havilland Canada DHC-5D Buffalo
Grumman E-2C Hawkeye
Lockheed C-130H/Elint Hercules
Meridonali CH-47C/D Chinook
Mikoyan MiG-21R 'Fishbed'
Mil Mi-8/17 'Hip'
Westland Commando 1/2
TRAINING
Aero L-39ZO Albatros
Aero L-59E Albatros
Dassault Mirage 5SDD
Dassault Mirage 2000BM
Dassault/Dornier Alpha Jet MS1
Embraer EMB-312 Tucano
Mikoyan MiG-21UM/US 'Mongol'
Shenyang FT-6
MISCELLANEOUS
Agusta-Sikorsky AS-61
Airbus A340-212
Dassault Falcon 20E-5/20F-5
Gulfstream Aerospace Gulfstream III/IV/
    IV-SP
Heliopolis Gomhouria 6/8R
Hillier UH-12E
Sikorsky UH-60L Black Hawk
Westland Commando 2B/2E

EGYPTIAN NAVY
Aérospatiale SA342L Gazelle
Kaman SH-2G Super Seasprite
Westland Sea King 47

SALVADOREAN AIR FORCE
COMBAT
Bell UH-1H/M Iroquois
Cessna A-37B Dragonfly
Cessna O-2A Skymaster
Douglas AC-47 Dakota/Turbo Dakota
Fouga CM-170 Magister
McDonnell Douglas MD500MD Defender
COMBAT SUPPORT
Basler Turbo 67
Bell UH-1H Iroquois
TRAINING
Cessna T-41D Mescalero
ENAER T-35B Pillan
Fouga CM170 Magister
Hughes 269
MISCELLANEOUS
Arava 201
Douglas DC-6B
Fairchild Merlin IIIB
Gulfstream Commander
McDonnell Douglas MD500D
SOCATA Rallye 235GS

EQUATORIAL GUINEA NATIONAL GUARD
Antonov An-32 'Cline'
Dassault Falcon 900

ERITREAN AIR FORCE
Mikoyan MiG-29 'Fulcrum'
Mil Mi-8/17 'Hip'
Mil Mi-35 'Hind'
COMBAT SUPPORT
Harbin (HAMC) Y-12 II
TRAINING
Aermacchi MB-339FD
Aermacchi L-90TP RediGO
Dornier 228
Mikoyan MiG-29UB 'Fulcrum'

ESTONIAN ARMY AVIATION
Antonov An-2 'Colt'
PZL Swidnik (Mil) Mi-2U 'Hoplite'
ESTONIAN BORDER GUARDS
Let L-410UVP Turbolet
Mil Mi-8S/8T/8TB 'Hip'

ETHIOPIAN AIR FORCE
COMBAT
Mikoyan-Gurevich MiG-17F 'Fresco'
Mikoyan MiG-21MF 'Fishbed'
Mikoyan MiG-23BN 'Flogger'
Mil Mi-24 'Hind'
Sukhoi Su-27A/U 'Flanker'
COMBAT SUPPORT
Antonov An-12BP 'Cub'
Antonov An-32 'Cline'
Lockheed C-130B Hercules
Mil Mi-8/17 'Hip'
TRAINING
Aero L-39C/ZO Albatros
Mikoyan MiG-21UM 'Mongol'
Mikoyan MiG-23UB 'Flogger'
SIAI-Marchetti SF.260TP
MISCELLANEOUS
Aérospatiale SA316 Alouette III/IAR-816B
Mil Mi-14PL 'Haze'
Yakovlev Yak-40 'Codling'

ETHIOPIAN ARMY AVIATION
Cessna 401
de Havilland Canada DHC-6 Twin Otter

FIJI AIR WING
Eurocopter AS355F2 Ecureuil
Eurocopter SA365N Dauphin

FINNISH AIR FORCE
COMBAT
McDonnell Douglas F/A-18C/D Hornet
Saab J35FS/S Draken
COMBAT SUPPORT
Fokker F27-100 Friendship
Fokker F27-400M Troopship
TRAINING
British Aerospace Hawk T51/51A
Saab Sk 35CS Draken
Valmet L-70 Vinka
MISCELLANEOUS
Learjet 35A
Piper PA-28R-180R Arrow II

Piper PA-28RT Cherokee Arrow IV Finnish Air Force

Saab J35 Draken, BAe Hawk T51 & Valmet L-70 Vinka Finnish Air Force

Dassault Mirage F1CR French Air Force

Dassault Mirage 2000N French Air Force

Piper PA-28RT Cherokee Arrow IV
Piper PA-31-350 Chieftain
Valmet L-90TP RediGO

FINNISH ARMY
Hughes 500D
Mil Mi-8P/T 'Hip'

BORDER AND COAST GUARD
Agusta-Bell 206A/B JetRanger
Agusta-Bell 412HP
Dornier 228-212
Eurocopter AS332L/L1 Super Puma

FRANCE

FRENCH AIR FORCE
COMBAT
Dassault Mirage 2000C/D/N
Dassault Mirage 2000-5F
Dassault Mirage F1C/CT
Dassault Rafale
SEPECAT Jaguar A
COMBAT SUPPORT
Aérospatiale SA330Ba Puma
Aérospatiale AS532UL Cougar
Airbus A310-304
Airtech CN.235-100
Boeing C-135FR/KC-135R Stratotanker
Boeing E-3F Sentry
Dassault Mirage F1CR
Dassault Mirage IVP
Douglas DC-8-53 Sarigue
Douglas DC-8-72CF
Lockheed C-130H/-30 Hercules
Transall C.160F/R/NG
Transall C.160G Gabriel
Transall C.160H Astarte
TRAINING
Dassault Falcon 20SNA

Dassault Mirage F1B
Dassault Mirage 2000B
Dassault/Dornier Alpha Jet E
Embraer EMB-121A/AA Xingu
Embraer EMB-312 Tucano
Mudry CAP 10B/20/231
SEPECAT Jaguar E
SOCATA TB30 Epsilon
MISCELLANEOUS
Aérospatiale SA316 Alouette III
Aérospatiale SA330B Puma
Aérospatiale AS332C/L/L1 Super Puma
Aérospatiale AS355F1 Ecureuil
Aérospatiale AS555AN Fennec
Dassault Falcon 20C/E/F
Dassault Falcon 50
Dasssault Falcon 900
de Havilland Canada DHC-6-200/300
   Twin Otter
Jodel (SAN) D.140E Mousquetaire IV
Jodel (SAN) D.140R Abeille
Morane-Saulnier MS.760 Paris IR/IIR
Nord N 262AEN/N 262D Fregate
SOCATA TBM700

FRENCH NAVAL AIR ARM
COMBAT
Dassault Atlantique 2
Dassault Super Etendard
Dassault Rafale M
Westland Lynx HAS 4(FN)
COMBAT SUPPORT
Breguet Br.1050M Alize
Dassault Falcon 50
Dassault Falcon 20G Gardian
Grumman E-2C Hawkeye
Nord N 262A/CS/DA Fregate
Sud SA321G Super Frelon
TRAINING
Dassault Falcon 10MER

Dassault Super Etendard French Navy

Embraer EMB-121AN Xingu
Mudry CAP10B
Nord N 262E
SOCATA Rallye 100S/ST
MISCELLANEOUS
Aérospatiale SA316 Alouette III
Eurocopter AS365F/N Dauphin 2
Eurocopter AS565MA Panther
Robin HR100-250
Sud SE3130 Alouette II
Wassmer CE43 Guepard

FRENCH ARMY AVIATION
COMBAT
Aérospatiale SA341F Gazelle
Aérospatiale SA341M/342M Gazelle/HOT
COMBAT SUPPORT
Aérospatiale SA330B/H Puma
Aérospatiale SA341F Gazelle/Athos
Eurocopter AS532UL Cougar
Eurocopter AS532UL Cougar Horizon
TRAINING
Aérospatiale AS555UN Fennec
Aérospatiale SA341F Gazelle
MISCELLANEOUS
Aérospatiale SA361H Dauphin
Pilatus PC-6/B2-H4 Turbo Porter
Reims Cessna F 406 Caravan II
SOCATA TBM700

GENDARMERIE NATIONALE
Aérospatiale SA319B Alouette III
Eurocopter AS350B/B-1 Ecureuil
Eurocopter/Kawasaki BK117
Sud SE316B Alouette III

FLIGHT RESEARCH CENTRE
Aérospatiale SE3160 Alouette III
Aérospatiale SA330Ba Puma
Aérospatiale SN601 Corvette100
Airbus A300B2-103
CASA C-212-300 Aviocar
Cessna 310
Dassault Falcon 10
Dassault Falcon 20C/E/ECM/F
Dassault Mirage IIIB/E/R
Dassault Mirage F1CR
Dassault Mirage 2000B/C/D/N
Dassault Mirage 2000-5
Dassault Rafale B/C
Dassault/Dornier Alpha Jet
Eurocopter AS365N Dauphin 2
Eurocopter AS555U2 Fennec
Jodel D140R Abeille
Morane-Saulnier MS760 Paris
Mudry CAP10/10B
Nord 262 Fregate
Pilatus PC-7
Reims Cessna FTB 337F

Reims Cessna F411
Robin HR.100-250TR
SOCATA TBM700
Transall C.160F
Wassmer CE43 Guepard

GABON

GABONESE AIR FORCES
COMBAT
Dassault Mirage 5G2/5DD/5DG
COMBAT SUPPORT
Airtech CN.235M
Embraer EMB-110P Bandeirante
Lockheed C-130H Hercules
Lockheed L-100-20/-30 Hercules
Nord N 262C Fregate
MISCELLANEOUS
Bell 412SP
Dassault Falcon 900EX
Gulfstream Aerospace Gulfstream IVSP

PRESIDENTIAL GUARD
ATR ATR 42F
Beech T-34C-1 Turbo-Mentor
Embraer EMB-110P Bandeirante
Eurocopter AS355 Ecureuil

ARMY AVIATION
Aérospatiale SA330C Puma
Aérospatiale SA342L1 Gazelle

GENDARMERIE
Aérospatiale AS350B Ecureuil

GEORGIA

REPUBLIC OF GEORGIA AIR FORCE
COMBAT
Mil Mi-24 'Hind'
Sukhoi Su-25/TM 'Frogfoot'
COMBAT SUPPORT
Mil Mi-8 'Hip'

Panavia Tornado ECR German Air Force

TRAINING
Aero L-29 Delfin
MISCELLANEOUS
Antonov An-2 'Colt'
PZL (Mil) Mi-2 'Hoplite'
Tupolev Tu-134 'Crusty'

ABKHAZIAN REBEL AIR FORCE
Aero L-39 Albatros
Aerostar (Yakovlev) Iak-52
Sukhoi Su-25 'Frogfoot'

GERMANY

GERMAN AIR FORCE
COMBAT
McDonnell Douglas F-4F Phantom II
Mikoyan MiG-29 'Fulcrum A'
Panavia Tornado IDS
Panavia Tornado ECR
COMBAT SUPPORT
Airbus A310-304
Bell UH-1D Iroquois
Transall C.160D
TRAINING
Cessna T-37B
Mikoyan MiG-29UB 'Fulcrum'

Northrop T-38A Talon
MISCELLANEOUS
Canadair CL-601 Challenger
Eurocopter AS532U2 Cougar
Let L-410UVP(S) Turbolet

NAVAL AIR ARM
COMBAT
Breguet Atlantic 1
Panavia Tornado IDS
Westland Sea Lynx 88/88A
COMBAT SUPPORT
Breguet Atlantic KWS
MISCELLANEOUS
Dornier 228-212/1(LM/LT)
Westland Sea King 41

ARMY AVIATION
COMBAT
Eurocopter BO105P (PAH-1)
COMBAT SUPPORT
Bell UH-1D Iroquois
Eurocopter BO105M (VBH)
Sikorsky CH-53G Stallion
TRAINING
Eurocopter EC 135
Sud SE3130 Alouette II

GHANA

GHANA AIR FORCE
COMBAT
Aermacchi MB.326F/KG
Aermacchi MB.339A
COMBAT SUPPORT
Fokker F27-400M Troopship
Fokker F27-600 Friendship
Pilatus/B-N BN-2T Turbine Islander
Shorts SC-7 Skyvan 3M
TRAINING
Aero L-29 Delfin
Scottish Aviation Bulldog 122/122A
MISCELLANEOUS
Aérospatiale SA316B Alouette III
Agusta A109A
Agusta Bell 212
Fokker F28-3000 Fellowship

GREECE

HELLENIC MILITARY AVIATION
COMBAT
Canadair NF-5A Freedom Fighter
Dassault Mirage 2000EG/BG
Dassault Mirage F1CG

McDonnell Douglas F-4F Phantom German Air Force

PZL Mielec M-18A Dromader Hellenic Air Force

General Dynamics F-16CG/DG Fighting Falcon
Lockheed P-3B Orion
McDonnell Douglas F-4E Phantom II
Northrop F-5A Freedom Fighter
Vought A-7H Corsair II

COMBAT SUPPORT
Douglas C-47A/B Dakota
Embraer RJ-145 AEW
Lockheed C-130B/H Hercules
McDonnell Douglas RF-4E Phantom II
Northrop RF-5A Freedom Fighter

TRAINING
Cessna T-37B/C
Cessna T-41D Mescalero
Northrop F-5B Freedom Fighter
Rockwell T-2E Buckeye
Vought TA-7C/H Corsair II

MISCELLANEOUS
Agusta-Bell AB.205A
Agusta-Bell AB.206A JetRanger
Bell OH-13H Sioux
Bell 47G-3B
Bell 212
Canadair CL-215/CL-145
Dornier Do 28D-2 Skyservant
Grumman G-164C Super Ag-Cat C
NAMC YS-11A-300
PZL Mielec M-18A Dromader

HELLENIC NAVY
COMBAT
Agusta-Bell AB212ASW
Sikorsky S-70B-6 'Aegean Hawk'
COMBAT SUPPORT
Agusta-Bell AB212EW
MISCELLANEOUS
Aérospatiale SA319B Alouette III

HELLENIC ARMY AVIATION
COMBAT
Bell AH-1P HueyCobra

McDonnell Douglas AH-64A Apache
COMBAT SUPPORT
Agusta-Bell AB205A
Bell UH-1H Iroquois
Boeing-Vertol CH-47D Chinook
Cessna U-17A/B
Sikorsky UH-60A Black Hawk
TRAINING
Bell TAH-1P HueyCobra
Nardi-Breda NH300C
MISCELLANEOUS
Agusta-Bell AB212
Beech King Air 200
Rockwell Commander 680L

COAST GUARD
Cessna 172RG Cutlass
SOCATA TB20 Trinidad

IAI Arava 201 Guatemala Air Force

GUATEMALA

GUATEMALA AIR FORCE
COMBAT
Cessna A-37B Dragonfly
Pilatus PC-7 Turbo-Trainer

COMBAT SUPPORT
Basler Turbo 67
Bell UH-1H Iroquois
Bell 212
Fokker F27-400M Troopship
IAI Arava 201
TRAINING
Cessna T-41D Mescalero
ENAER T-38B Pillan
MISCELLANEOUS
Beech Super King Air 300
Bell 206B-3 JetRanger
Bell 206L-1 LongRanger
Cessna U206G Stationair
Cessna T210M Centurion
Piper PA-31-350 Navajo Chieftain
Sikorsky S-76 Spirit

GUINEA-BISSAU

GUINEA-BISSAU AIR FORCE
COMBAT
Mikoyan-Gurevich MiG-17F 'Fresco'
COMBAT SUPPORT
Antonov An-24RV 'Coke'

TRAINING
Mikoyan-Gurevich MiG-15UTI 'Midget'
MISCELLANEOUS
Aérospatiale SA313B Alouette II
Aérospatiale SA316B Alouette III
Dassault Falcon 20

GUINEA REPUBLIC

GUINEA REPUBLIC AIR FORCE
COMBAT
Mikoyan-Gurevich MiG-17F 'Fresco'
Mikoyan MiG-21PFM 'Fishbed F'
COMBAT SUPPORT
Antonov An-14 'Clod'
Antonov An-24RV 'Coke'
TRAINING
Mikoyan-Gurevich MiG-15UTI 'Midget'
MISCELLANEOUS
Aérospatiale SA342K Gazelle
Eurocopter AS350B Ecureuil
IAR-316 Alouette III
IAR-330L Puma
Ilyushin IL-18 'Coot'
Yakovlev Yak-40 'Codling'

GUYANA

GUYANA DEFENCE FORCE AIR COMMAND

COMBAT SUPPORT

Pilatus/B-N BN-2A-2 Defender

Shorts SC-7 Skyvan 3M

MISCELLANEOUS

Bell 206B JetRanger II

Bell 412

Mil Mi-8 'Hip'

HAITI

HAITIAN AIR CORPS

COMBAT

SIAI-Marchetti SF.260TP

Cessna O-2/337

COMBAT SUPPORT

Douglas C-47 Dakota

TRAINING

Cessna 150/172

MISCELLANEOUS

Beech B55 Baron

Beech King Air

Cessna 402B

HONDURAS

HONDURAN AIR FORCE

COMBAT

Cessna A-37B Dragonfly

ENAER A-36 Halcon

Northrop F-5E/F Tiger II

COMBAT SUPPORT

Bell UH-1B/H Iroquois

Bell 412EP

Dassault Super Mystere B2

Douglas C-47 Dakota

IAI Arava 201

Lockheed C-130A/B Hercules

Lockheed L-188A Electra

McDonnell Douglas MD 500D

TRAINING

CASA C.101BB Aviojet

Cessna T-41D Mescalero

Embraer EMB-312 Tucano

Hughes TH-55A Osage

MISCELLANEOUS

Cessna 182/185

Cessna 310

Cessna 401

IAI 1124 Westwind

Piper PA-31-235 Navajo

Piper PA-42 Cheyenne III

Rockwell Commander 690B

HUNGARY

HUNGARIAN AIR DEFENCE GROUP

COMBAT

Mikoyan MiG-29 'Fulcrum A'

Mil Mi-24D/V 'Hind'

COMBAT SUPPORT

Antonov An-26 'Curl'

Mil Mi-8P/S/S/TB 'Hip'

Mil Mi-9 'Hip'

Mil Mi-17/PP 'Hip'

TRAINING

Aero L-39ZO Albatros

Aerostar (Yakovlev) Iak-52

Mikoyan MiG-29UB 'Fulcrum B'

MISCELLANEOUS

Zlin Z43

ICELAND

ICELANDIC COAST GUARD

Eurocopter AS332L1 Super Puma

Eurocopter AS365N Dauphin 2

Fokker F27-200 Friendship

INDIA

INDIAN AIR FORCE

COMBAT

Dassault Mirage 2000H

English Electric Canberra B(I)58

Mikoyan MiG-21bis 'Fishbed'

Mikoyan MiG-21FL 'Fishbed'

Mikoyan MiG-21M/MF 'Fishbed'

Mikoyan MiG-23MF 'Flogger B'

Mikoyan MiG-23BN 'Flogger H'

Mikoyan MiG-27ML 'Flogger'

Mikoyan MiG-29 'Fulcrum A'

Mil Mi-24/35 'Hind'

SEPECAT Jaguar IS/IM

Sukhoi Su-30MK/MKI

COMBAT SUPPORT

Antonov An-32 'Cline'

Gulfstream Aerospace Gulfstream III

HAL (Dornier) 228-201

Hawker Siddeley (BAe) 748 Srs 2

Ilyushin IL-76MD 'Candid'

Mikoyan MiG-25R 'Foxbat'

Mil Mi-8/S 'Hip'

Mil Mi-17 'Hip'

Mil Mi-26 'Halo'

TRAINING

Dassault Mirage 2000TH

English Electric Canberra B(TT)58

HAL Chetak

HAL Cheetah

HAL HPT-32 Deepak

HAL HJT-16 Kiran I/IA/II

Hoffman Super Dimona

Mikoyan MiG-21U/US/UM 'Mongol'

Mikoyan MiG-23UB 'Flogger C'

Mikoyan MiG-25RU 'Foxbat C'

Mikoyan MiG-29UB 'Fulcrum B'

PZL Mielec TS-11 Iskra

SEPECAT Jaguar IB

MISCELLANEOUS

Boeing 707-320C

Boeing 737-2A81

Eurocopter SA365 Dauphin

Gulfstream Aerospace Gulfstream III

HAL ALH

Learjet 29

Antonov An-26 'Curl' Hungarian Air Force

BAe Sea Harrier FRS51 Indian Navy

Kamov Ka-28 'Helix' Indian Navy

INDIAN NAVAL AVIATION

COMBAT

British Aerospace Sea Harrier FRS51
Ilyushin IL-38 'May'
Kamov Ka-25 'Hormone'
Kamov Ka-28/31 'Helix'
Tupolev Tu-142 'Bear F'
Westland Sea King Mk 42/42A/42B

COMBAT SUPPORT

HAL (Dornier) 228-101
Pilatus/B-N BN-2A/B Defender

TRAINING

British Aerospace Harrier T60
HAL HPT-32 Deepak
HAL HJT-16 Kiran 1/2

MISCELLANEOUS

Aérospatiale SA319 Alouette III/
HAL Chetak
HAL ALH

INDIAN ARMY AIR CORPS

HAL ALH
HAL Cheetah
HAL Chetak

INDIAN COAST GUARD

Dornier 228
Fokker F27-100
HAL ALH
HAL Chetak

INDONESIA

INDONESIAN NATIONAL DEFENCE
– AIR FORCE

COMBAT

British Aerospace Hawk 109
British Aerospace Hawk 209
Douglas A-4E Skyhawk

General Dynamics F-16A/B-15 OCU
Northrop F-5E Tiger II
Rockwell OV-10F Bronco

COMBAT SUPPORT

Aérospatiale SA330J Puma
Airtech CN.235M-100
Boeing 737-2X9 Surveiller
Fokker F27-400M Friendship
IPTN (CASA) NC.212-100/200 Aviocar
IPTN (Eurocopter) NAS 330L Puma
Lockheed C-130B/KC-130B/H/H-130 Hercules
Lockheed L-100-30 Hercules
Sikorsky S-58T
Transall C.160NG/P

TRAINING

Beech T-34C-1 Turbo-Mentor
British Aerospace Hawk T53
Cessna T-41D Mescalero
FFA AS 202/18A-3 Bravo

Northrop F-5F Tiger II
SME Aerospace MD3-160

MISCELLANEOUS

Boeing 707-3MC1
Cessna 401A/402
Fokker F28 1000/3000R Fellowship
IPTN (Bell) 412
IPTN (Eurocopter) NAS332L1 Super Puma
IPTN (Eurocopter) NBO105CB
McDonnell Douglas MD500MD
Pilatus PC-6/B Turbo-Porter
Shorts Skyvan 3M

NAVAL AVIATION SERVICE

COMBAT

IPTN (Eurocopter) NAS332F Super Puma
Westland Wasp HAS 1

COMBAT SUPPORT

Airtech CN.235M

438

ASTA Nomad N22B/N22S/N24A
de Havilland Canada DHC-5 Buffalo
IPTN (CASA) NC.212-100/200 Aviocar
IPTN (CASA) NC.212-200 Elint/MPA
IPTN (Eurocopter) NAS332B Super Puma

TRAINING
Aérospatiale SA313 Alouette II
Beech F33A Bonanza
Piper PA-34 Seneca
Piper PA-38-112 Tomahawk
Rockwell Lark Commander 100
SOCATA TB9 Tampico

MISCELLANEOUS
IPTN (Bell) 412
IPTN (Eurocopter) NBO105CB/S

ARMY AVIATION SERVICE
COMBAT
IPTN (Eurocopter) NBO105C/CB

COMBAT SUPPORT
Bell 205A-1
de Havilland Canada DHC-5D Buffalo
IPTN/Bell 412HP/S
IPTN (CASA) NC212-200 Aviocar

TRAINING
Bell 206 JetRanger
Schweizer-Hughes 300C

MISCELLANEOUS
Aérospatiale SA316B Alouette III
P/B-N BN-2A Islander
PZL-104 Wilga 32
Rockwell Commander 680FL

NATIONAL DEFENCE – POLICE FORCE
Beech Super 18
Bell 206B JetRanger
Cessna U206

de Havilland Canada DHC-5D Buffalo
IPTN (Eurocopter) NBO105CB
IPTN (CASA) NC 212M-100 Aviocar

ISLAMIC REPUBLIC OF IRAN AIR FORCE
COMBAT
Chengdu F-7N Airguard
Grumman F-14A Tomcat
Lockheed P-3F Orion
McDonnell Douglas F-4D/E Phantom II
Mikoyan MiG-29SA/UB 'Fulcrum'
Northrop F-5E/F Tiger II
Shenyang F-6
Sukhoi Su-20/22M-2 'Fitter'
Sukhoi Su-24MK 'Fencer'

COMBAT SUPPORT
Antonov An-74 'Coaler'
Bell 214A/C
Boeing 707-3J9C
Boeing 747F-131/200
Fokker F27-400M/600 Friendship
Ilyushin IL-76MD 'Candid'
Ilyushin IL-76 'Adnan'
Lockheed C-130E/H/RC-130H Hercules
McDonnell Douglas RF-4E Phantom II
Meridonali CH-47C Chinook

TRAINING
Beech F33A/C Bonanza
Embraer EMB-312 Tucano
Lockheed T-33
PAC Mushshak
Pilatus PC-7 Turbo-trainer

MISCELLANEOUS
Agusta-Bell 206B JetRanger
Agusta-Bell 212

Dassault Falcon 20F
Dassault Falcon 50
Dornier 228
Harbin Y-7
Harbin Y-12
Lockheed JetStar 8/II
Pilatus PC-6/B Turbo-Porter
Rockwell Aero Commander 690

ISLAMIC REPUBLIC OF IRAN NAVY
COMBAT
Agusta-Bell 212AS
Agusta-Sikorsky SH-3D Sea King

COMBAT SUPPORT
Sikorsky RH-53D Sea Stallion

MISCELLANEOUS
Agusta-Bell 205A
Agusta-Bell 206B JetRanger
Dassault Falcon 20E
Rockwell Aero Commander 690

ISLAMIC REPUBLIC OF IRAN ARMY
COMBAT
Bell AH-1J SeaCobra

COMBAT SUPPORT
Agusta-Bell 205A-1
Agusta-Bell 206A/B JetRanger
Bell 212
Bell 214A/C
Meridionali CH-47C Chinook

MISCELLANEOUS
Cessna 185A
Dassault Falcon 20E
Rockwell Commander 690/A

IRANIAN GENDARMERIE
Rockwell Commander 690A

IRAQI AIR FORCE
COMBAT
Aérospatiale SA321GV Super Frelon
Aérospatiale SA342L Gazelle
Chengdu F-7
Dassault Mirage F1EQ/BQ
Mikoyan MiG-21PF/MF 'Fishbed'
Mikoyan MiG-21U/UM 'Fishbed'
Mikoyan MiG-23BN/ML 'Flogger'
Mikoyan MiG-23UB 'Flogger'
Mikoyan MiG-25PD 'Foxbat'
Mil Mi-24 'Hind'
Sukhoi Su-20/22 'Fitter'
Sukhoi Su-25 'Frogfoot'

COMBAT SUPPORT
Aérospatiale SA330F Puma
Antonov An-12 'Cub'
Antonov An-26 'Curl'
Bell 214ST
Ilyushin IL-76 'Adnan 1'
McDonnell Douglas MD500D
McDonnell Douglas MD530F
Mil Mi-6 'Hook'
Mil Mi-8/17 'Hip'

TRAINING
Aero L-39ZO Albatros
Embraer EMB-312 Tucano
FFA AS 202/18A Bravo
Pilatus PC-7 Turbo-Trainer
Pilatus PC-9

MISCELLANEOUS
Aérospatiale SA316C Alouette III
Agusta-Sikorsky AS-61TS
Eurocopter BO105C
Eurocopter/Kawasaki BK117A/B

BAe Hawk 109 Indonesian Air Force

Beech Super King Air 200 Irish Air Corps

IRELAND

IRISH AIR CORPS

COMBAT SUPPORT
Aérospatiale SA316B Alouette III
Airtech CN.235MP
Cessna FR 172H/K

TRAINING
Aérospatiale SA342L Gazelle
SIAI-Marchetti SF.260WE Warrior

MISCELLANEOUS
Aérospatiale SA365F Dauphin 2
Beech Super King Air 200
Gulfstream Aerospace Gulfstream IV

IRISH NATIONAL POLICE FORCE
Eurocopter AS355N Squirrel
Pilatus/B-N BN-2T-4S Defender 4000

ISRAEL

ISRAELI DEFENCE FORCE – AIR FORCE

COMBAT
Bell AH-1G/AH-1S HueyCobra
Douglas A-4H/N Skyhawk
General Dynamics F-16A/B-10/15 'Netz'
General Dynamics F-16C/D-30/40
  'Barak/Brakeet'
IAI Kfir C-7
McDonnell Douglas AH-64A Apache
McDonnell Douglas F-4E Phantom II
McDonnell Douglas F-4E Kurnass 2000
McDonnell Douglas F-15A/B Eagle 'Baz'
McDonnell Douglas F-15C/D Eagle 'Akef'
McDonnell Douglas F-15I Eagle 'Ra'am'

COMBAT SUPPORT
Agusta-Bell 212
Beech RU-21A
Beech RC-12D/K

Bell UH-1
Boeing 707 R'em
Boeing 707-320 Tavas
Boeing EC-707 Chasidah
Boeing KC-707 Saknayee
Boeing RC-707 Barboor
Douglas C-47 Pe're
Douglas RC-47 Barvaz
IAI Arava 201
IAI Arava 202ECM
IAI 1124N SeaScan
Lockheed C-130E/H Hercules
Lockheed EC-130 Aya
Lockheed KC-130H Hercules
McDonnell Douglas RF-4E Phantom II
McDonnell Douglas F-4E(S) Phantom II
Sikorsky S-65 Yas'ur 2000
Sikorsky UH-60A Black Hawk

TRAINING
Beech Queen Air B80
IAI Kfir TC-7
IAI Tzukit (CM 170 Magister)
Piper PA-18-150 Super Cub

MISCELLANEOUS
Aérospatiale HH-65A Dolphin
Agusta-Bell 206B JetRanger
Beech U-21A
Beech Super King Air B200
Bell 206L LongRanger
Dornier Do 28B-1
SOCATA TB20 Trinidad

ITALY

ITALIAN AIR FORCE

COMBAT
Aeritalia (Lockheed) F-104S-ASA/ASA M
AMX International AMX
Breguet BR 1150 Atlantic
Panavia Tornado IS
Panavia Tornado IT
Panavia Tornado ITECR
Panavia Tornado F3

COMBAT SUPPORT
Alenia G.222TCM/VSELINT
Boeing 707-382B

Boeing 707-3F5C
Lockheed C-130H Hercules
Lockheed C-130J Hercules
Piaggio-Douglas PD-808GE1/E2

TRAINING
Aermacchi MB-339A/B/C/CD
AMX(T)
Lockheed TF-104G Starfighter
Nardi NH500E
SIAI-Marchetti SF.260AM

MISCELLANEOUS
Aermacchi MB-326
Aermacchi MB-339PAN
Agusta-Bell 212
Agusta-Sikorsky AS-61A-4
Agusta-Sikorsky HH-3F Pelican
Airbus A319CJ
Alenia G.222RM/PROVIV
Dassault Falcon 50
Dassault Falcon 900EX
Gulfstream Aerospace Gulfstream III
McDonnell Douglas DC-9-32
Piaggio P.166M/DL-3
Piaggio P.180 Avanti
Piaggio-Douglas PD-808/RM/ECM
SIAI-Marchetti S.208M

ITALIAN NAVAL AVIATION

COMBAT
Agusta-Bell 212ASW
Agusta-Sikorsky ASH-3D/H Sea King
McDonnell Douglas/BAe AV-8B Harrier II +

TRAINING
McDonnell Douglas/BAe TAV-8B Harrier II

ITALIAN AIR CAVALRY

COMBAT
Agusta A129 Mangusta

COMBAT SUPPORT
Agusta A109A/AT/CM Hirundo
Agusta-Bell AB205/205A-1/B
Agusta-Bell AB206A-2/C-1 JetRanger
Agusta-Bell AB212

McDonnell Douglas F-4E Phantom Israeli Defence Force/Air Force

Agusta-Bell AB412
Dornier 228-212
Meridionali CH-47C/C+ Chinook
MISCELLANEOUS
Cessna O-1E Bird Dog
Piaggio P.180 Avanti
SIAI-Marchetti SM 1019E

PORTS AUTHORITY
Agusta-Bell 412HP
Piaggio P.166DL-3/SEM

MILITARY POLICE
Agusta A109A/A-II
Agusta-Bell 206A-1/B-1
Agusta-Bell 412SP

CUSTOMS
Agusta A 109A-II/A 109C
Agusta-Bell 412HP
ATR 42-400MP
Nardi NH500M/MC/MD
Piaggio P.166DL-3/SEM

IVORY COAST

IVORY COAST AIR FORCE
COMBAT
Dassault/Dornier Alpha Jet C
TRAINING
Beech F33C Bonanza
MISCELLANEOUS
Aérospatiale SA330H Puma
Beech Super King Air 200
Cessna 401
Cessna 421 Golden Eagle
Eurocopter AS365C Dauphin 2
Fokker 100
Gulfstream Aerospace Gulfstream III/IV

JAMAICA

JAMAICA DEFENCE FORCE AIR WING
Aérospatiale AS335N Ecureuil
Beech King Air A100
Bell UH-1H Iroquois
Bell 206A/B JetRanger
Bell 212
Bell 412EP
Cessna 210M Centurion
Pilatus/B-N BN-2A Defender

JAPAN

JAPANESE AIR SELF DEFENCE FORCE
COMBAT
McDonnell Douglas F-4EJ-Kai Phantom II
McDonnell Douglas F-15J/DJ Eagle
Mitsubishi F-1

McDonnell Douglas AV-8B Harrier II+ Italian Navy

Kawasaki-BV 107 Japaneses Self Defence Force

Mitsubishi F-2A/B
COMBAT SUPPORT
Boeing E-767
Grumman E-2C Hawkeye
Kawasaki C-1/EC-1
Kawasaki-BV CH-47J Chinook
Kawasaki-BV 107
Lockheed C-130H Hercules
McDonnell Douglas RF-4E/EJ Phantom II
NAMC YS-11C/E/P/E-Kai/EL
Sikorsky UH-60J Black Hawk
TRAINING
Beech T-400
Fuji T-1A/B
Fuji T-3
Fuji T-7
Kawasaki T-4
Mitsubishi T-2
NAMC YS-11NT
MISCELLANEOUS
Beech Queen Air 65
Boeing 747-47C
British Aerospace 125-800B (U-125)
Gulfstream Aerospace IV-SP (U-4)
Mitsubishi MU-2J/S

Mitsubishi(Lockheed) UF-104J/DJ Starfighter
NAMC YS-11FC
Raytheon Hawker 800 (U-125A)

JAPANESE MARITIME SELF DEFENCE FORCE
COMBAT
Lockheed P-3C UII.5/U.III Orion
Sikorsky HSS-2B Sea King
Sikorsky SH-60J SeaHawk
COMBAT SUPPORT
Lockheed (Kawasaki) EP-3D/UP-3D Orion
NAMC YS-11M/M-A
Sikorsky MH-53EJ Sea Stallion
TRAINING
Fuji T-5
Kawasaki-Hughes OH-6D/DA Cayuse
Kawasaki (Lockheed) UP-3C Orion
NAMC YS-11T-A
MISCELLANEOUS
Beech King Air LC-90/UC-90
Kawasaki BK117
Learjet U-36A
ShinMaywa US-1A
Sikorsky UH-60J Black Hawk
Sikorsky S-61A/AH

JAPANESE GROUND SELF DEFENCE FORCE
COMBAT
Bell AH-1S HueyCobra
COMBAT SUPPORT
Bell UH-1H/J Iroquois
Kawasaki OH-1
Kawasaki-Boeing Vertol CH-47J Chinook
Kawasaki-Hughes OH-6D/J Cayuse
Kawasaki-Vertol 107 Sea Knight
Mitsubishi-Sikorsky UH-60JA
Black Hawk
MISCELLANEOUS
Beech LR-2 Super King Air
Eurocopter AS332L Super Puma
Mitsubishi MU-2C (LR-1)

JORDAN

ROYAL JORDANIAN AIR FORCE
COMBAT
Bell AH-1F HueyCobra
Dassault Mirage F1CJ/EJ
General Dynamics F-16A/B-15 OCU (ADF)
Fighting Falcon
Northrop F-5E Tiger II

Lockheed C-130H Hercules Royal Jordanian Air Force

COMBAT SUPPORT
Airtech CN.235
Bell UH-1H Iroquois
CASA C.212-100 Aviocar
Eurocopter AS332M-1 Super Puma
Lockheed C-130H Hercules

TRAINING
CASA C.101CC Aviojet
Dassault Mirage F1BJ
McDonnell Douglas MD500D
Northrop F-5F Tiger II
Scottish Aviation Bulldog 125/125A

MISCELLANEOUS
Aérospatiale SA316 Alouette III
Canadair CL-604 Challenger
Extra 300
Gulfstream Aerospace Gulfstream III
Lockheed L-1011 Tristar 500
Sikorsky S-70A-11 Black Hawk

KAZAKHSTAN

KAZAKHSTAN AIR FORCE AND AIR DEFENCE
COMBAT
Mikoyan MiG-23M 'Flogger'
Mikoyan MiG-25PD 'Foxbat'
Mikoyan MiG-29 'Fulcrum'
Mikoyan MiG-31 'Foxhound'
Mil Mi-24 'Hind'
Sukhoi Su-24 'Fencer'
Sukhoi Su-27C 'Flanker'

COMBAT SUPPORT
Antonov An-12BP 'Cub'
Antonov An-24 'Coke'
Antonov An-26 'Curl'
Mil Mi-6 'Hook'
Mil Mi-8/9/17 'Hip'
Mil Mi-26 'Halo'
Sukhoi Su-24MR 'Fencer'

TRAINING
Aero L-29 Delfin
Aero L-39C Albatros
Mikoyan MiG-23UB 'Flogger'
Mikoyan MiG-25RU 'Foxbat'
Mikoyan MiG-29UB 'Fulcrum'
Sukhoi Su-27UB 'Flanker'

MISCELLANEOUS
Antonov An-2 'Colt'
Antonov An-24V 'Coke'
Antonov An-30 'Clank'
Boeing 757-2M6
Dassault Falcon 900/B
Tupolev Tu-134 'Crusty'
Tupolev Tu-154B-2 'Careless'

KENYA

KENYA AIR FORCE
COMBAT
British Aerospace Hawk 52
Hughes 500MD/TOW Defender
Northrop F-5E Tiger II

COMBAT SUPPORT
Aérospatiale SA330G Puma
de Havilland Canada DHC-5D Buffalo
de Havilland Canada DHC-8-103 Dash 8
ICA-Brasov IAR-330L Puma
McDonnell Douglas MD500ME

TRAINING
Hughes 500D
Northrop F-5F Tiger II
Scottish Aviation Bulldog 103/127
Shorts Tucano T51

MISCELLANEOUS
Dornier Do 28D-2 Skyservant
Eurocopter BO105CBS
Fokker 70ER
Harbin Y-12

KOREA (NORTH)

KOREAN PEOPLE'S ARMY AIR FORCE
COMBAT
Harbin H-5
Mikoyan MiG-21PF/PFM 'Fishbed'
Mikoyan MiG-23ML 'Flogger'
Mikoyan MiG-29A/U 'Fulcrum'
Mil Mi-14PL 'Haze'
Mil Mi-24 'Hind'
Nanchang Q-5 IA 'Fantan'
Shenyang F-5
Shenyang F-6/FT-6
Shenyang F-7
Sukhoi Su-7BMK 'Fitter'
Sukhoi Su-25K 'Frogfoot'

COMBAT SUPPORT
Antonov An-24 'Coke'
Hughes 300C
Ilyushin IL-76T 'Candid'
McDonnell Douglas MD500D/E
Mil Mi-8/17 'Hip'
Shijiazhuang (SAP) Y-5

TRAINING
Aero L-39C Albatros
Mikoyan-Gurevich MiG-15UTI 'Midget'
Mikoyan MiG-21U 'Mongol'
Mikoyan MiG-23UB 'Flogger'
Mikoyan MiG-29UB 'Fulcrum'
Nanchang CJ-5/6
Shenyang FT-5
Sukhoi Su-25UBK 'Frogfoot'

MISCELLANEOUS
Ilyushin IL-14 'Crate'
Ilyushin IL-18D 'Coot'
Ilyushin IL-62M 'Classic'
PZL (Mil) Mi-2 'Hoplite'
Tupolev Tu-134 'Crusty'
Tupolev Tu-154B 'Careless'

KOREA (SOUTH)

REPUBLIC OF KOREA AIR FORCE
COMBAT
Cessna A-37B Dragonfly
General Dynamics F-16C/D-32/-52
Fighting Falcon
McDonnell Douglas F-4D/E Phantom II
Northrop F-5A Freedom Fighter
Northrop F-5E Tiger II

COMBAT SUPPORT
Airtech CN.235M
Boeing-Vertol CH-47D Chinook
Cessna O-1A/E Bird Dog
Cessna O-2A Super Skymaster
Lockheed C-130H/H-30 Hercules
McDonnell Douglas RF-4C Phantom II
Northrop RF-5A Freedom Fighter
Raytheon/Hawker 800RA/SIG
Rockwell OV-10D Bronco

TRAINING
British Aerospace Hawk 67
Cessna T-37C
Cessna T-41B Mescalero
Lockheed T-33A Shooting Star
Northrop F-5B Freedom Fighter
Northrop F-5F Tiger II
Northrop T-38A Talon

MISCELLANEOUS
Bell 212/412
Bell UH-1H Iroquois
Boeing 737-3Z8
de Havilland Canada U-6A Beaver
Hawker Siddeley (BAe) 748
Rockwell Commander 520/560F

REPUBLIC OF KOREA NAVY
COMBAT
Lockheed P-3C UIII+ Orion

CASA C.101CC Aviojet Royal Jordanian Air Force

General Dynamics F-16C Fighting Falcon Republic of Korea Air Force

Cessna A-37B Dragonfly Republic of Korea Air Force

McDonnell Douglas F/A-18C Hornet Kuwait Air Force

McDonnell Douglas MD500MD/ASW
Westland Lynx HAS99
MISCELLANEOUS
  Bell 206B JetRanger
  Grumman S-2A/E Tracker
  Reims-Cessna F 406 Caravan II

REPUBLIC OF KOREA ARMY
COMBAT
  Bell AH-1F HueyCobra
  McDonnell Douglas MD500MD/TOW
COMBAT SUPPORT
  Bell UH-1H Iroquois
  Boeing-Vertol CH-47D Chinook
  McDonnell Douglas MD500MD
  Sikorsky UH-60A/L/P Black Hawk
MISCELLANEOUS
  Aérospatiale AS332L Super Puma

KUWAIT

KUWAIT AIR FORCE
COMBAT
  Aérospatiale SA342K Gazelle
  Eurocopter AS532AF Cougar
  McDonnell Douglas F/A-18C/D Hornet
COMBAT SUPPORT
  Aérospatiale SA330H Puma
  Lockheed L-100-30 Hercules
TRAINING
  British Aerospace Hawk 64
  Shorts Tucano T52
MISCELLANEOUS
  Douglas DC-9-32CF
  McDonnell Douglas MD-83

KYRGYZTAN

REPUBLIC OF KYRGIZIA AIR ARM
  Aero L-39C Albatros

LAOS

LAO PEOPLE'S LIBERATION ARMY AIR FORCE
COMBAT
  Mikoyan MiG-21PF/U 'Fishbed'
COMBAT SUPPORT
  Mil Mi-8/17 'Hip'
  Mil Mi-6 'Hook'
TRAINING
  Mikoyan MiG-21U 'Mongol'
MISCELLANEOUS
  Antonov An-2 'Colt'
  Antonov An-24 'Coke'
  Antonov An-26 'Curl'
  Kamov Ka-32T 'Helix'
  Yakovlev Yak-40 'Codling'

LATVIA

AVIATION AND AIR DEFENCE FORCE
  Antonov An-2 'Colt'
  Let L-410UVP-T Turbolet
  PZL Swidnik (Mil) Mi-2R/S/U 'Hoplite'

LATVIAN ARMY AVIATION
  Antonov An-2 'Colt'

LATVIAN NATIONAL GUARD
  Antonov An-2 'Colt'
  PZL-104 Wilga

LEBANON

LEBANESE AIR FORCE
COMBAT
  Aérospatiale SA342L Gazelle
  Hawker Hunter FGA70/70A
COMBAT SUPPORT
  Aérospatiale SA330L Puma
  Agusta-Bell 212

Bell UH-1H Iroquois
TRAINING
  Fouga CM 170 Magister
  Hawker Hunter T66C
  Scottish Aviation Bulldog 126
MISCELLANEOUS
  Aérospatiale SA316B Alouette III
  Dassault Falcon 20F
  Sud SE3130 Alouette II

LESOTHO

LESOTHO DEFENCE FORCE
  Agusta-Bell 412SP/EP
  CASA C.212-300 Aviocar
  Cessna 182Q
  Eurocopter (MBB) BO105S
  Soloy-Westland-Bell 47G-3B-1

LIBERIA

LIBERIAN ARMY AIR UNIT
  Dassault Falcon 20
  de Havilland DHC-4 Caribou
  Cessna Caravan I
  Cessna 172/185
  Cessna 337G
  IAI 101B Arava

LIBYA

LIBYAN ARAB REPUBLIC AIR FORCE
COMBAT
  Dassault Mirage F1AD/BD/ED
  Dassault Mirage 5D/DE
  Mikoyan MiG-21bis 'Fishbed'
  Mikoyan MiG-23MS/BN 'Flogger'
  Mikoyan MiG-25PD 'Foxbat'
  Mil Mi-24D/V 'Hind'
  Sukhoi Su-20/22M-2 'Fitter'

Sukhoi Su-24MK 'Fencer'
  Tupolev Tu-22A/U 'Blinder'
COMBAT SUPPORT
  Aeritalia G.222T
  Antonov An-26 'Curl'
  Dassault Mirage 5DR
  Ilyushin IL-76M/T/TD 'Candid'
  Lockheed C-130H Hercules
  Lockheed L-100-20/30 Hercules
  Meridionali CH-47C Chinook
  Mikoyan MiG-25RB 'Foxbat'
  Mil Mi-8 'Hip'
TRAINING
  Aero L-39ZO Albatros
  Dassault Mirage 5DD
  Fouga CM170 Magister
  Mikoyan MiG-21UM 'Mongol'
  Mikoyan MiG-23UB 'Flogger'
  Mikoyan MiG-25RU 'Foxbat'
  PZL (Mil) Mi-2 'Hoplite'
  SIAI-Marchetti SF.260WL Warrior
  SOKO G-2A/E Galeb
  SOKO Jastreb J1E
  Sukhoi Su-22U/UM 'Fitter'
MISCELLANEOUS
  Aérospatiale SA321GM Super Frelon
  Agusta-Bell AB212
  Boeing 707-320
  Dassault Falcon 50
  Let L-410T/UVP Turbolet
  SOCATA Rallye 235GT

LIBYAN ARAB REPUBLIC NAVY
  Mil Mi-14PL 'Haze A'
  Sud SA321GM Super Frelon

LIBYAN ARAB REPUBLIC ARMY
  Aérospatiale SA316B Alouette III
  Aérospatiale SA341L Gazelle
  Agusta-Bell AB205

444

Agusta-Bell AB206A JetRanger
Cessna O-1E Bird Dog
Meridionali CH-47C Chinook

LITHUANIA

MILITARY AIR FORCES
COMBAT SUPPORT
Antonov An-26RV 'Curl'
Let L-410UVP Turbolet
Mil Mi-8T/TV 'Hip'
TRAINING
Aero L-39C Albatros
MISCELLANEOUS
Antonov An-2 'Colt'
Antonov An-26 'Curl'
PZL (Mil) Mi-2 'Hoplite'

LITHUANIAN NATIONAL GUARD
Aerostar (Yakovlev) Iak-52
Antonov An-2T 'Colt'
PZL-104 Wilga
Yakovlev Yak-18T

MACEDONIA

MACEDONIAN ARMY AVIATION
Antonov An-2 'Colt'
Beech Super King Air 200
Bell UH-1H Iroquois
Eurocopter BO105
Mil Mi-8/17 'Hip'
Zlin 242

MADAGASCAR

MALAGACHE AIR FORCE
COMBAT
Mikoyan MiG-21MF 'Fishbed'
COMBAT SUPPORT
Antonov An-26 'Curl'

TRAINING
Cessna 172M
Mikoyan-Gurevich MiG-17F 'Fresco'
Mikoyan MiG-21U 'Mongol'
MISCELLANEOUS
Cessna F337
Douglas C-47 Dakota
Hawker Siddeley (BAe) 748
Pilatus/B-N BN-2A Defender
Piper PA-23-250D Aztec
Yakovlev Yak-40 'Codling'

MALAWI

MALAWI ARMY AIR WING
COMBAT SUPPORT
Aérospatiale SA330J Puma
Basler Turbo 67
Dornier 228-201/202K
MISCELLANEOUS
British Aerospace 125 Srs 800B
Cessna 421B Golden Eagle
Eurocopter AS332 Super Puma
Eurocopter AS365N Dauphin 2
Eurocopter AS350B-1 Ecureuil

MALAYSIA

ROYAL MALAYSIAN AIR FORCE
COMBAT
British Aerospace Hawk 100/200
McDonnell Douglas F/A-18D Hornet
Mikoyan MiG-29N 'Fulcrum A'
Northrop F-5E Tiger II
COMBAT SUPPORT
Airtech CN.235M
Beech King Air B200T
de Havilland DHC-4A Caribou
Lockheed C-130H/-30/H-MP Hercules
McDonnell Douglas A-4PTM Skyhawk
Northrop RF-5E Tigereye

Sikorsky S-61A-4
TRAINING
Aermacchi MB.339A
British Aerospace Hawk 108
Mikoyan MiG-29NUB 'Fulcrum B'
Northrop F-5F Tiger II
Pilatus PC-7 Turbo-Trainer
MISCELLANEOUS
Aérospatiale SA316/316B Alouette III
Agusta A109C
Agusta-Sikorsky AS-61N
Bombardier Global Express
Cessna 402B
Dassault Falcon 900
Fokker F28-1000 Fellowship
IPTN (Eurocopter) NAS332L Super Puma
Sikorsky S-70A Black Hawk

ROYAL MALAYSIAN NAVY
Westland Wasp HAS1

ROYAL MALAYSIAN ARMY
Aérospatiale SA316/316B Alouette III

MALDIVES

MALDIVES DEFENCE FORCE
HAL (Dornier) 228-212
Mil Mi-8T 'Hip'

MALI

MALIAN REPUBLIC AIR FORCE
COMBAT
Mikoyan MiG-21MF 'Fishbed'
COMBAT SUPPORT
Antonov An-24 'Coke'
Antonov An-26 'Curl'
Mil Mi-8 'Hip'
TRAINING
Aero L-29 Delfin

Yakovlev Yak 11 'Moose'
Yakovlev Yak-18A 'Max'
MISCELLANEOUS
Antonov An-2 'Colt'
Basler Turbo 67
Eurocopter AS350B Ecureuil

MALTA

ARMED FORCES OF MALTA
Aérospatiale SA316B Alouette III
Agusta-Bell AB47G-2
Nardi-Hughes H-369M
Pilatus/B-N BN-2B-26 Islander
Scottish Aviation Bulldog T1

MAURITANIA

MAURITANIAN ISLAMIC AIR FORCE
de Havilland DHC-5D Buffalo
Harbin Y-12 (II)
Pilatus/B-N BN-2A Defender
Piper PA-31T Turbo-Cheyenne II
Reims Cessna FTB 337F
SIAI-Marchetti SF.260E
Xian Y-7

MAURITIUS

MAURITIUS COAST GUARD
Aérospatiale SA316B Alouette III
HAL (Dornier) 228-101
Pilatus/B-N BN-2T Maritime Defender

MEXICO

MEXICAN AIR FORCE
COMBAT
Lockheed AT-33A Shooting Star
Northrop F-5E Tiger II
Pilatus PC-7 Turbo-Trainer
COMBAT SUPPORT
Boeing 727-14
Cessna 182S
Douglas C-47 Dakota
Fairchild Merlin II/III/IV
Lockheed C-130A Hercules
TRAINING
Beech 23 Musketeer III
Beech F33C Bonanza
Maule MX-7-180
Northrop F-5F Tiger II
MISCELLANEOUS
Aérospatiale SA330F Puma
Beech King Air A90/C90
Beech King Air 200
Bell UH-1H Iroquois
Bell 206 JetRanger
Bell 206L LongRanger

British Aerospace Hawk 208 Royal Malaysian Air Force

Airtech CN.2325M-100 Royal Moroccan Air Force

Bell 212
Boeing 737-247/33A
Boeing 757-225
Convair 580
Eurocopter AS332L Super Puma
Eurocopter AS355F2 Ecureuil
Gulfstream Aerospace Gulfstream III
IAI Arava 201
Lockheed JetStar
McDonnell Douglas MD530F
Pilatus PC-6B Turbo Porter
Rockwell Commander 500S
Rockwell Turbo Commander 500/680
Rockwell Sabreliner 60/75
Schweizer SA 2-37A
Shorts SC-7 Skyvan 3
Sikorsky S-70A-24 Black Hawk

MEXICAN NAVAL AVIATION
COMBAT SUPPORT
Beech King Air 90
CASA C.212-200M Aviocar
Cessna 152
Cessna 182
Cessna 206 Stationair
Cessna 210
Cessna 337G
Cessna 402B
Cessna 404
Cessna 421
de Havilland Canada DHC-5D Buffalo
Mil Mi-8MTV 'Hip'
Piper PA-23-250 Aztec
Piper PA-31 Navajo
Valmet L90TP RediGO
TRAINING
Beech F33C Bonanza
Beech B55 Baron
Maule MX-7-180
McDonnell Douglas MD500E
MISCELLANEOUS
Aérospatiale SA319B Alouette III
Antonov An-32 'Clank'

Bell UH-1H Iroquois
Eurocopter AS365 Dauphin
Eurocopter AS550 Fennec
Eurocopter BO105C/CB
Fairchild-Hiller FH-227
Learjet 24D
Mitsubishi MU-2F/J
Rockwell Sabreliner 60
Rockwell Commander 695

MOLDOVA

MOLDOVA AIR FORCE
Antonov An-2 'Colt'
Antonov An-24 'Coke'
Antonov An-72 'Coaler'
Ilyushin IL-18 'Coot'
Mil Mi-8 'Hip'
Tupolev Tu-134 'Crusty'

MONGOLIA

AIR FORCE OF THE MONGOLIAN REPUBLIC
Antonov An-2 'Colt'
Antonov An-24 'Coke'
Antonov An-26 'Curl'
Harbin Y-12
Mil Mi-8 'Hip'
Mil Mi-24V 'Hind'

MOROCCO

ROYAL MOROCCAN AIR FORCE
COMBAT
Aérospatiale SA342L Gazelle
Dassault Mirage F1CH/EH/EH-5
Northrop F-5A/B Freedom Fighter
Northrop F-5E/F Tiger II
Rockwell OV-10A Bronco
COMBAT SUPPORT
Aérospatiale SA330C Puma
Agusta-Bell 205A
Airtech CN.235M-100

Dassault Falcon 20ECM
Dassault Falcon 50
Dornier Do 28D-2 Skyservant
Lockheed C-130H/KC-130H Hercules
Meridionali CH-47C Chinook
Northrop RF-5A Freedom Fighter
TRAINING
Beech T-34C-1 Turbo-Mentor
Cessna T-37B Tweet
Dassault/Dornier Alpha Jet
FFA AS 202/18 Bravo
Fouga CM170 Magister
Mudry CAP10B
MISCELLANEOUS
Agusta-Bell 206B JetRanger
Agusta-Bell 212
Beech Super King Air 200/200C/350
Boeing 707
Cessna 560 Citation V
Gulfstream Aerospace Gulfstream II/III
Mudry CAP231

ROYAL GENDARMERIE AIR SQUADRON
Aérospatiale SA316B Lama
Aérospatiale SA330C Puma
Aérospatiale SA342K Gazelle
Eurocopter AS365N Dauphin 2
Sikorsky S-70A-25/26 Black Hawk

MOZAMBIQUE

MOZAMBIQUE AIR FORCE
COMBAT
Mil Mi-24 'Hind'
COMBAT SUPPORT
Antonov An-26 'Curl'
CASA C212 Aviocar
Mil Mi-8 'Hip'
TRAINING
Zlin 326
MISCELLANEOUS
Cessna 152/172
Piper PA-32-300 Cherokee Six

MYANMAR (BURMA)

AIR DEFENCE FORCE
COMBAT
Chengdu F-7M Airguard
Nanchang A-5M 'Fantan'
COMBAT SUPPORT
Bell 206 JetRanger
Fokker F-27F Friendship
Mil Mi-17IB 'Hip'
PZL (Swidnik) W-3 Sokol
Shaanxi Y-8D
TRAINING
Guizhou (GAIC) FT-7
Pilatus PC-7 Turbo-Trainer
Pilatus PC-9
SOKO G-4 Super Galeb
MISCELLANEOUS
Bell 205A-1
Cessna 180
Cessna 550 Citation II
Pilatus PC-6/B Turbo-Porter
PZL (Mil) Mi-2 'Hoplite'

NAMIBIA

NAMIBIAN DEFENCE FORCE
Cessna O-2A Super Skymaster
Dassault Falcon 900B
HAL SA 316B Chetak
Learjet 31A
Reims Cessna F 406 Caravan II
Sikorsky S-61L

NATO

NATO AIRBORNE EARLY WARNING FORCE
(Aircraft are registered in Luxembourg)
Boeing E-3A Sentry
Boeing 707-320C/329C

NEPAL

ROYAL NEPALESE AIR FORCE
COMBAT SUPPORT
Aérospatiale SA330C/G Puma
Shorts Skyvan 3M
MISCELLANEOUS
Bell 206L LongRanger III/IV
Hawker Siddeley (BAe) 748-2A
Eurocopter AS332L/L1 Super Puma
HAL SA 316B Chetak

NETHERLANDS

ROYAL NETHERLANDS AIR FORCE
COMBAT
General Dynamics F-16A/AR/B
Fighting Falcon

Dassault Falcon 900B Namibian Defence Force

Fokker 50 Royal Netherlands Air Force

Agusta-Bell 412SP Royal Netherlands Air Force

Aermacchi MB.339CB Royal New Zealand Air Force

Pacific Aerospace CT-4E Airtrainer
Royal New Zealand Air Force

McDonnell Douglas AH-64A Apache
COMBAT SUPPORT
Boeing-Vertol CH-47D Chinook
Eurocopter BO105CB/DB
Eurocopter AS532U2 Cougar
Fokker 50U
Fokker 60
Lockheed C-130H-30 Hercules
McDonnell Douglas KDC-10
TRAINING
Pilatus PC-7 Turbo-Trainer
MISCELLANEOUS
Agusta-Bell 412SP
Gulfstream Aerospace Gulfstream IV
Sud SE3160 Alouette III

NAVAL AVIATION SERVICE
COMBAT
Lockheed P-3C Orion

Westland SH-14D Lynx
TRAINING
Beech Super King Air 200

NEW ZEALAND

ROYAL NEW ZEALAND AIR FORCE
COMBAT
Kaman SH-2F/G Seasprite
McDonnell Douglas A-4K Skyhawk
Lockheed P-3K Orion
COMBAT SUPPORT
Bell UH-1H Iroquois
Boeing 727-22QC
Lockheed C-130H Hercules
TRAINING
Aermacchi MB-339CB
Beech King Air B200
Bell 47G-3B

McDonnell Douglas TA-4K Skyhawk
Pacific Aerospace CT-4E Airtrainer

NICARAGUA

NICARAGUAN ARMY AIR FORCE
COMBAT SUPPORT
Antonov An-26 'Curl'
Mil Mi-17 'Hip H'
TRAINING
Cessna T-41D Mescalero
Piper PA-28 Cherokee
MISCELLANEOUS
Antonov An-2 'Colt'
Cessna 180
Cessna U-17B
Cessna 404

NIGER

NIGER AIR SQUADRON
Antonov An-26 'Curl'
Boeing 737-200
Dornier Do 28-2 Skyservant
Dornier 228-201
Lockheed C-130H Hercules

NIGERIA

NIGERIAN AIR FORCE
COMBAT
Mikoyan MiG-21MF 'Fishbed'
Mil Mi-35P 'Hind'
SEPECAT Jaguar International SN/BN
COMBAT SUPPORT
Aeritalia G.222
Aérospatiale AS330H Puma
Dornier Do 28D-2 Skyservant
Dornier Do 128-6 Turbo-Skyservant
Eurocopter AS332B Super Puma
Eurocopter BO105D
Lockheed C-130H/H-30 Hercules

TRAINING
Aermacchi MB.339A
Aero L39ZO Albatros
Dassault/Dornier Alpha Jet N
Mikoyan MiG-21U 'Mongol'
Pilatus PC-7 Turbo-Trainer
Schweizer-Hughes 300C
MISCELLANEOUS
Boeing 727-2N6
British Aerospace 125 Srs 1000B
Cessna Citation II
Dassault Falcon 900
Dornier 228-100/212
Gulfstream Aerospace Gulfstream II/IV

NIGERIAN NAVY AIR ARM
Westland Lynx HAS89

NORWAY

ROYAL NORWEGIAN AIR FORCE
COMBAT
General Dynamics F-16A/B Fighting Falcon
Lockheed P-3C U.III/N Orion
Westland Lynx HAS86
COMBAT SUPPORT
Bell 412 SP
Dassault Falcon 20ECM-5
Lockheed C-130H Hercules
TRAINING
Northrop F-5A/B Freedom Fighter
Saab MFI-15 Safari/MFI-17 Supporter
MISCELLANEOUS
de Havilland Canada DHC-6 Twin Otter
Westland Sea King HAS43/A/B

OMAN

ROYAL AIR FORCE OF OMAN
COMBAT
British Aerospace Hawk 203
SEPECAT Jaguar International OS

SEPECAT Jaguar GR

COMBAT SUPPORT
Agusta-Bell AB205A
Agusta-Bell AB212
BAC One-Eleven 475GD
Bell 214
Lockheed C-130H Hercules
Shorts SC-7 Skyvan 3M

TRAINING
British Aerospace Hawk 103
FFA AS 202/18A Bravo
PAC (AMF/Saab) Mushshak
Pilatus PC-9M
Scheibe SF.25C Super Falke
SEPECAT Jaguar OB/T2

MISCELLANEOUS
Bell 206B JetRanger
Boeing 747SP-27
Eurocopter AS330J Puma
Eurocopter AS332C/L1 Super Puma
Gulfstream Aerospace Gulfstream IV

OMAN POLICE AIR WING
Airtech CN-235M-100
Bell 205A-1

Boeing 727-22QC Royal New Zealand Air Force

Bell 214ST
Dornier 228-100
Pilatus B/N-2T Turbine Islander

PAKISTAN

PAKISTANI AIR FORCE
COMBAT
Chengdu F-7P Skybolt
Dassault Mirage IIIEP/B/OD
Dassault Mirage 5F/PA/PA2/PA3

General Dynamics F-16A/B Fighting Falcon
Nanchang A-5-III 'Fantan'
Shenyang F-6
COMBAT SUPPORT
Dassault Falcon 20F
Dassault Mirage IIIRP
Lockheed C-130B/E Hercules
Lockheed L-100-20 Hercules
TRAINING
Cessna T-37B/C Tweet
Dassault Mirage IIIBE/DP/OD

Dassault Mirage 5DPA2
Guizhou (GAIC) FT-7
Lockheed T-33A Shooting Star
Nanchang Karakorum 8
PAC (AMF/Saab) Mushshak
Shenyang FT-5
Shenyang FT-6
MISCELLANEOUS
Aérospatiale SA316/319 Alouette III/
IAR-816B
Beech B55 Baron

General Dynamics F-16B Fighting Falcon Royal Norwegian Air Force

BAC One-Eleven 475GD Royal Air Force of Oman

Beech King Air
Boeing 707-340C/351C
Boeing 737-33A
Cessna 172N
Cessna Citation V
Dassault Falcon 20E/EW
Fokker F-27-200 Friendship
Harbin Y-12
Piper PA-34 Seneca II

PAKISTAN NAVAL AVIATION

COMBAT
Breguet BR 1150 Atlantic 1
Lockheed P-3C Orion U.II.75
Westland Lynx HAS3
Westland Sea King HAS45/45C
COMBAT SUPPORT
Aérospatiale SA316 Alouette III
Fokker F27-200/400M Friendship
Pilatus/B-N BN-2T Maritime Defender

PAKISTAN ARMY AVIATION CORPS

COMBAT
Bell AH-1F HueyCobra

COMBAT SUPPORT
Aérospatiale SA315B Lama/IAR-315B
Aérospatiale SA316B Alouette III/IAR-816B
Aérospatiale SA330J Puma
Agusta-Bell AB 205A-1
Bell UH-1H Iroquois
Bell 206B JetRanger II
Cessna O-1E Bird Dog
Harbin Y-12
Mil Mi-17 'Hip H'
PAC Mushshak
TRAINING
Bell 47G
Schweizer-Hughes 300C
MISCELLANEOUS
Cessna 421
Gulfstream Aerospace Commander
690/840

PALESTINE

PALESTINE AUTHORITY
Lockheed L-1329 JetStar
Mil Mi-8 'Hip C'

Mil Mi-17 'Hip H'

PANAMA

NATIONAL AIR SERVICE
COMBAT SUPPORT
Airtech CN235M
Bell 205A/UH-1H
Bell 212/UH-1N
CASA C.212-200/300 Aviocar
Pilatus/B-N BN-2A Islander
TRAINING
ENAER T-35D Pillan
MISCELLANEOUS
Boeing 727-44
Piper PA-31T Turbo Cheyenne
Piper PA-34 Seneca I

PAPUA NEW GUINEA

PAPUA NEW GUINEA DEFENCE FORCE
COMBAT SUPPORT
Airtech CN.235M-100
ASTA N22B Nomad

ASTA N22SB/SL Searchmaster B
Bell UH-1H Iroquois
MISCELLANEOUS
IAI Arava
IPTN NBO105

PARAGUAY

PARAGUAYAN AIR FORCE
COMBAT
Embraer EMB-312 Tucano
Embraer EMB-326GB Xavante
Northrop F-5E Tiger II
COMBAT SUPPORT
Bell UH-1B/H Iroquois
CASA C.212-200 Aviocar
Douglas C-47 Dakota
TRAINING
Aerotec A-122 Uirapuru
ENAER ECH-35A/B Pillan
North American AT-6 Harvard
Northrop F-5F Tiger II
MISCELLANEOUS
Agusta A109HO
Beech Baron
Beech King Air 90
Boeing 707-321B
Cessna T-41D Mescalero
Cessna 185
Cessna U206C
Cessna 210 Centurion
Cessna 402B
Cessna 550 Citation II
de Havilland Canada DHC-6-200
Twin Otter
Helibras HB 350B Esquilo
Hughes 300
Piper PA-32R Lance
PZL-104 Wilga

ASTA N22B Nomad Papua New Guinea Defence Force

PARAGUAYAN NAVAL AVIATION

TRAINING

Bell OH-13H Sioux

Cessna 150M

MISCELLANEOUS

Cessna U206A

Cessna 210 Centurion

Cessna 310

Cessna 401B

Helibras HB350B Esquilo

Hiller UH-12E Raven

PARAGUAYAN ARMY AVIATION

Beech Baron

Cessna 206

Cessna 310

de Havilland Canada DHC-6-200 Twin Otter Paraguayan Air Force

PERU

PERUVIAN AIR FORCE

COMBAT

Cessna A-37B Dragonfly

Dassault Mirage 5P

Dassault Mirage 2000P/DP

English Electric Canberra
B(I)12/B62/T4/T54

Mikoyan MiG-29C 'Fulcrum A'

Mil Mi-24 'Hind D'

Sukhoi Su-20 'Fitter F'

Sukhoi Su-22M-2 'Fitter J'

Sukhoi Su-25 'Frogfoot'

COMBAT SUPPORT

Antonov An-32 'Cline'

Antonov An-74 'Coaler B'

Bell UH-1H Iroquois

Bell 212

Boeing 707-323C

Boeing 737-500

de Havilland Canada DHC-6 Twin Otter

Harbin Y-12 II

Lockheed C-130A Hercules

Lockheed L-100-20 Hercules

Mil Mi-8T/8MTV/17 'Hip'

TRAINING

Aermacchi MB-339AP

Cessna T-41A/D Mescalero

Dassault Mirage 5DP

Dassault Mirage 2000DP

Embraer EMB-312 Tucano

Eurocopter AS 350B Ecureuil

Ilyushin IL-103

Mikoyan MiG-29UB 'Fulcrum'

Sukhoi Su-22UM-3 'Fitter G'

Sukhoi Su-25UB 'Frogfoot'

Zlin 242L

MISCELLANEOUS

Beech Queen Air A80

Beech King Air C90

Beech Super King Air 300

Bell 214ST

Bell 412HP

Dassault Falcon 20F

Douglas DC-8-62CF

Eurocopter BO105CBS

Fairchild Metro III

Fokker F28-1000 Fellowship

Learjet 36A

Mil Mi-6 'Hook'

Pilatus PC-6/B2-H2 Turbo-Porter

PERUVIAN NAVAL AIR SERVICE

COMBAT

Agusta-Bell AB212AS

Agusta-Sikorsky AS-61D/ASH-3H

Embraer EMB-111 Bandeirante

COMBAT SUPPORT

Antonov An-32 'Cline'

Beech Super King Air B200T

Fokker F27-200 Friendship

Mil Mi-8/8T/17 'Hip'

TRAINING

Beech T-34C-1 Turbo-Mentor

Bell 206 JetRanger

MISCELLANEOUS

Cessna 206

de Havilland Canada DHC-6 Twin Otter

Embraer EMB-120 Brasilia

PERUVIAN ARMY AVIATION

COMBAT

Agusta A109K2

COMBAT SUPPORT

Antonov An-32B 'Cline'

Mil Mi-6 'Hook'

Mil Mi-8/17 'Hip'

Mil Mi-26 'Halo'

MISCELLANEOUS

Aérospatiale SA315B Lama

Bell 412

Cessna 150/172

Cessna U206G

Enstrom F28F Falcon

PERUVIAN NATIONAL POLICE

Antonov An-32 'Cline'

Beech King Air E90

Bell UH-1H Iroquois

Bell 212

Cessna 172

Cessna 182N

Cessna U206/G Stationair

Convair VC-131H Samaritan

Eurocopter BO105LSA-3

Eurocopter/Kawasaki BK117B-1

Fairchild C-123K Provider

Harbin Y-12

Hughes 369D

Lockheed C-130 Hercules

Mil Mi-17 'Hip'

Pilatus/B-N BN-2A Islander

Piper PA-31 Navajo

Piper PA-34-200T Seneca

Rockwell Commander 695A

Sikorsky S-76 Spirit

PHILIPPINES

PHILIPPINE AIR FORCE

COMBAT

McDonnell Douglas MD520MD

Northrop F-5A Freedom Fighter

Rockwell OV-10C Bronco

Sikorsky AUH-76 Eagle

COMBAT SUPPORT

Bell UH-1H Iroquois

Fokker F27-200/200MPA Friendship

GAF Nomad N22 Searchmaster L

GAF Nomad N22B Nomad Missionmaster

Lockheed C-130B/H Hercules

Lockheed L-100-20 Hercules

TRAINING

Cessna T-41D Mescalero

Northrop F-5B Freedom Fighter

SIAI-Marchetti S.211

SIAI-Marchetti SF.260MP/TP

MISCELLANEOUS

Aérospatiale SA330L Puma

Bell 412

McDonnell Douglas MD500 Defender Philippine Air Force

451

Cessna T210 Turbo Centurion
Eurocopter BO105C
Fokker F28 Fellowship 3000
Sikorsky S-70A-5 Black Hawk
Sikorsky S-76

PHILIPPINE NAVAL AVIATION
Eurocopter BO105C
P/B-N BN-2A-21 Islander

PHILIPPINE POLICE SERVICE
Eurocopter BO105C
P/B-N BN-2A Islander

POLAND

**POLISH AIR DEFENCE
AND AVIATION FORCE**
COMBAT
Mikoyan MiG-21M/MF/PFM 'Fishbed'
Mikoyan MiG-21bis 'Fishbed'
Mikoyan MiG-23MF 'Flogger'
Mikoyan MiG-29 'Fulcrum'
Sukhoi Su-22M-4K 'Fitter'
COMBAT SUPPORT
Antonov An-26 'Curl'
Mikoyan MiG-21R 'Fishbed'
Sukhoi Su-20R 'Fitter F'
TRAINING
Mikoyan MiG-21UM 'Mongol'
Mikoyan MiG-23UB 'Flogger'
Mikoyan MiG-29UB 'Fulcrum'
PZL I-22 Iryda
PZL M-93K Iryda
PZL Mielec TS-11 Iskra
PZL (Swidnik) S-1RR

PZL (Swidnik) W-3W/WA Sokol
PZL Warszawa-Okecie PZL-130TB/TC-1 Orlik
Sukhoi Su-22UM-3K 'Fitter'
MISCELLANEOUS
Antonov An-2/TD 'Colt'
Bell 412HP
Mil Mi-8S 'Hip'
PZL Mielec (Antonov) An-28TD 'Cash'
PZL (Mil) Mi-2 'Hoplite'
Tupolev Tu-154M 'Careless'
Yakovlev Yak-40 'Codling'

POLISH NAVAL AIR ARM
COMBAT
Mikoyan MiG-21bis 'Fishbed'
Mil Mi-14PL 'Haze'
COMBAT SUPPORT
PZL Mielec (Antonov) An-28RM/TD 'Cash'
PZL Mielec TS-11 Iskra R
TRAINING
Mikoyan MiG-21UM 'Mongol'
PZL Mielec TS-11 Iskra
MISCELLANEOUS
Antonov An-2 'Colt'
Mil Mi-14PS 'Haze'
PZL (Mil) Mi-2R 'Hoplite'
PZL (Swidnik) W-3 Sokol
PZL (Swidnik) W-3RM Anakonda

POLISH ARMY AIR FORCE
COMBAT
Mil Mi-24D/V 'Hind'
PZL (Swidnik) W-3W Sokol
COMBAT SUPPORT
Mil Mi-8P/T/Mi-17 'Hip'
PZL (Mil) Mi-2 'Hoplite'

INTERIOR MINISTRY
Bell 206B JetRanger III
Mil Mi-8P/S/T 'Hip'
Mil Mi-17 'Hip H'
PZL (Antonov) An-28TD Bryza
PZL (Mil) Mi-2
PZL -104M Wilga 2000
PZL Kania
PZL M-20 Mewa
PZL (Swidnik) W-3/3A Sokol
PZL (Swidnik) W-3RM Anakonda

PORTUGAL

PORTUGUESE AIR FORCE
COMBAT
General Dynamics F-16A/B-15 OCU
Lockheed P-3P Orion
Reims Cessna FTB 337G
COMBAT SUPPORT
Aérospatiale SA330C Puma
CASA C.212-100A/ECM/300 Aviocar
Lockheed C-130H/H-30 Hercules
TRAINING
Aérostructure RF10
Dassault/Dornier Alpha Jet A
de Havilland Canada DHC-1 Chipmunk T20
SOCATA TB30 Epsilon
MISCELLANEOUS
CASA C.212-100B Aviocar
Dassault Falcon 20D
Dassault Falcon 50
Sud SE316B Alouette III

NAVAL AVIATION
Westland Super Lynx HAS95

QATAR

QATAR EMIRI AIR FORCE
COMBAT
Aérospatiale SA342L Gazelle
Dassault Mirage 2000-5EDA
Dassault/Dornier Alpha Jet C
Westland Commando 3
TRAINING
Dassault Mirage 2000-5DDA
MISCELLANEOUS
Aérospatiale SA342G Gazelle
Airbus A340-211
Boeing 707-336C/3P1C
Boeing 727-2P1
Boeing 747SP
Dassault Falcon 900
Westland Commando 2A/C

ROMANIA

ROMANIAN MILITARY AVIATION
COMBAT
Avioane IAR-93A/B Orao
Bell AH-1RO Dracula Helicopter
Mikoyan MiG-21PF/PFM/M/MF/Lancer
Mikoyan MiG-23MF 'Flogger'
Mikoyan MiG-29 'Fulcrum A'
COMBAT SUPPORT
Antonov An-24 'Coke'
Antonov An-26 'Curl'
Harbin H-5R/HJ-5
ICA IAR-330L Puma
Ilyushin IL-28/IL-28MA 'Beagle'
Lockheed C-130B Hercules
Mikoyan MiG-21R 'Fishbed'

General Dynamics F-16A Fighting Falcon Portuguese Air Force

Dassault Falcon 50 Portuguese Air Force

Mikoyan MiG-29 'Sniper' Romanian Air Force

Mikoyan MiG-29UB 'Fulcrum' Russian Air Force

Kamov Ka-29 'Helix-B' Russian Forces

Aero L-39C Albatros Russian Air Force

Mil Mi-8P/17 'Hip'

TRAINING

Aero L-29 Delfin
Aero L-39ZA Albatros
Aerostar (Yakovlev) Iak-52
Avioane IAR-99 Soim
ICA IAR-823
Mikoyan MiG-21UM/US 'Mongol'
Mikoyan MiG-23UB 'Flogger'
Mikoyan MiG-29UB 'Fulcrum'

MISCELLANEOUS

Aérospatiale SA365N Dauphin
Antonov An-2/TP 'Colt'
Antonov An-30 'Clank'
ICA IAR-316B Alouette III

ROMANIAN NAVAL AIR ARM

ICA IAR-316B Alouette III
ICA IAR-330 Puma
Mil Mi-14PL 'Haze A'

MILITARY AIR FORCES
TROOPS OF AIR DEFENCE

COMBAT

Mikoyan MiG-21 'Fishbed/Mongol'
Mikoyan MiG-23M/UB 'Flogger'
Mikoyan MiG-25 'Foxbat'
Mikoyan MiG-27 'Flogger'
Mikoyan MiG-29 'Fulcrum'
Mikoyan MiG-31 'Foxhound'
Sukhoi Su-15 'Flagon'
Sukhoi Su-17 'Fitter'
Sukhoi Su-24 'Fencer'
Sukhoi Su-25 'Frogfoot A'
Sukhoi Su-25T 'Frogfoot'
Sukhoi Su-27P/S 'Flanker'
Sukhoi Su-30
Sukhoi Su-32FN
Tupolev Tu-22 'Blinder'
Tupolev Tu-22M-2/3 'Backfire'
Tupolev Tu-95K-22 'Bear G'
Tupolev Tu-95MS 'Bear H6/H16'
Tupolev Tu-160 'Blackjack'

COMBAT SUPPORT

Antonov An-12 'Cub C'
Antonov An-12BP 'Cub'
Antonov An-22 'Cock'
Antonov An-24 'Coke'
Antonov An-26 'Curl'
Antonov An-32 'Cline'
Antonov An-72/74 'Coaler'
Antonov An-124 Ruslan 'Condor'
Beriev A-50 'Mainstay'
Ilyushin IL-20 'Coot A'
Ilyushin IL-22 Coot B'
Ilyushin IL-76 'Candid'
Ilyushin IL-78 'Midas'
Mil Mi-8 'Hip'
Tupolev Tu-126 'Moss'

TRAINING

Aero L-29 Delfin
Aero L-39C Albatros
Mikoyan MiG-29UB 'Fulcrum'
Sukhoi Su-25 'Frogfoot B'
Sukhoi Su-27UB 'Flanker'
Tupolev Tu-134UBL 'Crusty'
Yakovlev Yak-130

MISCELLANEOUS

Antonov An-2 'Colt'
Antonov An-30 'Clank'
Gulfstream Aerospace Gulfstream II
Ilyushin IL-18 'Coot'
Ilyushin IL-62 'Classic'
Ilyushin IL-80 'Maxdome'
Ilyushin IL-82
Let L-410UVP Turbolet
PZL (Mil) Mi-2 'Hoplite'
Tupolev Tu-134 'Crusty'
Tupolev Tu-154 'Careless'
Yakovlev Yak-40 'Codling'

NAVAL FORCES

COMBAT

Ilyushin IL-38 'May'
Kamov Ka-25PL/PS/TS 'Hormone'
Kamov Ka-27PL/PS 'Helix'
Kamov Ka-29 'Helix B'
Mikoyan MiG-29/UB 'Fulcrum'
Mil Mi-14BT/PL/PS 'Haze'
Sukhoi Su-24MP 'Fencer'
Sukhoi Su-25/UB 'Frogfoot'
Sukhoi Su-27/UB 'Flanker B/C'
Sukhoi Su-33 'Flanker D'
Tupolev Tu-22 'Blinder'
Tupolev Tu-22M-2/3 'Backfire'
Tupolev Tu-95RT 'Bear D'
Tupolev Tu-142 'Bear F'

COMBAT SUPPORT

Antonov An-12BP 'Cub'

Antonov An-12 'Cub B/D'
Antonov An-24 'Coke'
Antonov An-26 'Curl'
Beriev Be-12 Tchaika ('Mail')
Ilyushin IL-20 'Coot A'
Kamov Ka-31
Mil Mi-8/17 'Hip'
Sukhoi Su-24MR 'Fencer E'
Tupolev Tu-16 'Badger'
Tupolev Tu-142MR 'Bear J'

TRAINING
Sukhoi Su-25UTG 'Frogfoot'

MISCELLANEOUS
Antonov An-2 'Colt'
Tupolev Tu-134 'Crusty'
Tupolev Tu-154 'Careless'
Yakovlev Yak-40 'Codling'

GROUND FORCES

COMBAT
Mil Mi-24D/V/P 'Hind'

COMBAT SUPPORT
Mil Mi-6/VKP/Aya 'Hook'
Mil Mi-8/VZPU/K/SMV/PPA 'Hip'
Mil Mi-9 'Hip G'
Mil Mi-24K 'Hind'
Mil Mi-24RKR 'Hind'
Mil Mi-26 'Halo'

MISCELLANEOUS
PZL (Mil) Mi-2 'Hoplite'

FEDERAL BORDER GUARD SERVICE
Antonov An-2 'Colt'
Antonov An-26 'Curl'
Antonov An-72P 'Coaler'
Ilyushin IL-76 'Candid'
Kamov Ka-27P/Ka-29 'Helix'
Mil Mi-8 'Hip'
Mil Mi-26P 'Halo'
Yakovlev Yak-18T
Aerostar (Yakovlev) Iak-52

RWANDAN AIR FORCE
Eurocopter AS355F Ecureuil
Eurocopter AS365CS Dauphin
Mil Mi-8MTV 'Hip'
Mil Mi-24 'Hind'

ROYAL SAUDI AIR FORCE
COMBAT
McDonnell Douglas F-15C/D Eagle
McDonnell Douglas F-15S Eagle
Northrop F-5E/F Tiger II
Panavia Tornado ADV
Panavia Tornado IDS

Antonov An-30 'Clank' Russian Air Force

Tupolev Tu-134A-3 Russian Air Force

COMBAT SUPPORT
Agusta-Bell 205A
Agusta-Bell 212
Boeing E-3A Sentry
Boeing KE-3A
Eurocopter AS532A2 Cougar II
Lockheed C-130E/H/H-30 Hercules
Lockheed KC-130H Hercules
Northrop RF-5E Tigereye
Panavia Tornado IDS(R)

TRAINING
British Aerospace Hawk 65/65A
British Aerospace Jetstream 31
Cessna 172G/H/M
Northrop F-5B Freedom Fighter
Pilatus PC-9
Reims Cessna F172G/H/M

MISCELLANEOUS
Agusta-Bell 206A JetRanger
Agusta-Bell 412EP
Airbus A340-200
Airtech CN.235M
Boeing 707-138B/368C
Boeing 737-268
Boeing 747SP-68
Boeing 747-3G1
Boeing 757-200
British Aerospace 125-800B
Gulfstream Aerospace Gulfstream III
Learjet 25/35A
Lockheed VC-130H Hercules
Lockheed L-1329 JetStar 8
Lockheed L-1011 TriStar 500
McDonnell Douglas MD-11

ROYAL SAUDI NAVY
COMBAT
Eurocopter AS532SAL Cougar
Eurocopter AS565SA Panther
COMBAT SUPPORT
Eurocopter AS532UC Cougar
Eurocopter AS565SC Panther

ROYAL SAUDI LAND FORCES
COMBAT
McDonnell Douglas AH-64A Apache
COMBAT SUPPORT
Bell Model 406CS Combat Scout
Sikorsky S-70A-1/1L Desert Hawk

SAUDI ARMED FORCES MEDICAL SERVICES
Bell 212
Gulfstream Aerospace Gulfstream II/III
Learjet 35A

Lockheed C-130H/H-30/L-100-30 Hercules

SENEGALESE AIR FORCE
COMBAT
SOCATA R235A Guerrier
COMBAT SUPPORT
de Havilland Canada DHC-6-300MR
Twin Otter
Fokker F27-400M Friendship
TRAINING
Fouga CM 170 Magister
SOCATA Rallye 160ST/235E Guerrier
MISCELLANEOUS
Aérospatiale SA318C Alouette II
Aérospatiale SA341 Gazelle
Boeing 727-2M1
Britten-Norman BN-2T Islander

Scottish Aviation Jetstream 31 Royal Saudi Air Force

SEYCHELLE ISLANDS

SEYCHELLES COAST GUARD
Beech 1900D
Cessna A150T Aerobat
Pilatus B/N BN-2A Islander
Reims Cessna F 406 Caravan II

SIERRA LEONE

SIERRA LEONE MILITARY FORCES
Mil Mi-8 'Hip'
Mil Mi-24V 'Hind'

SINGAPORE

REPUBLIC OF SINGAPORE AIR FORCE
COMBAT
Eurocopter AS550A2/C2 Fennec
Fokker 50MPA Maritime Enforcer 2
General Dynamics F-16A/B-15OCU
  Fighting Falcon
General Dynamics F-16C/D Fighting Falcon
McDonnell Douglas A-4SU Skyhawk
Northrop F-5E Tiger II
COMBAT SUPPORT
Agusta-Bell 205A
Bell UH-1H Iroquois
Boeing KC-135R Stratotanker
Boeing-Vertol CH-47D Chinook
Eurocopter AS332M/UL Super Puma
Eurocopter AS532UL Cougar
Eurocopter AS550C/A-2 Fennec
Fokker 50UTA-B
Grumman E-2C Hawkeye
Lockheed C-130H/KC-130B/
  KC-130H Hercules
Northrop RF-5E Tigereye
TRAINING
McDonnell Douglas TA-4SU Skyhawk
Northrop F-5F Tiger II
SIAI-Marchetti S.211

SLOVAK REPUBLIC

SLOVAK AIR AND AIR DEFENCE FORCE
COMBAT
Mikoyan MiG-21MF 'Fishbed'
Mikoyan MiG-29/SE 'Fulcrum'
Mil Mi-24D/V 'Hind'
Sukhoi Su-22M-4 'Fitter'
Sukhoi Su-25K 'Frogfoot'
COMBAT SUPPORT
Antonov An-12BP 'Cub'
Antonov An-24B 'Coke'
Antonov An-26 'Curl'
Let L-410MA/OVP Turbolet
Mil Mi-8PPA/P/T 'Hip'
Mil Mi-17 'Hip H'
TRAINING
Aero L-29 Delfin
Aero L-39C/MS/V/ZA Albatros
Let L-410T Turbolet
Mikoyan MiG-21UM/US 'Mongol'
Mikoyan MiG-29UB 'Fulcrum'
Mil Mi-24DU 'Hind'
Sukhoi Su-22UM-3K 'Fitter'
Sukhoi Su-25UBK 'Frogfoot B'
MISCELLANEOUS
PZL (Mil) Mi-2 'Hoplite'

GOVERNMENT FLYING SERVICES
Mil Mi-8P/PS 'Hip'
PZL (Mil) Mi-2 'Hoplite'
Tupolev Tu-154M 'Careless'

Yakovlev Yak-40 'Codling'

SLOVENIA

SLOVENIA MILITARY AVIATION
COMBAT
Pilatus PC-9
COMBAT SUPPORT
Bell 412EP/HP/SP
Let L-410UVP Turbolet
TRAINING
Bell 206B-3 JetRanger
Zlin 143L
Zlin 242L/272
MISCELLANEOUS
Cessna Citation I

Pilatus PC-9 Slovenia Military Aviation

Learjet 24D/35A
Pilatus PC-6 Turbo Porter
UTVA-75

SOUTH AFRICA

SOUTH AFRICAN AIR FORCE
COMBAT
Atlas Cheetah C
Atlas Impala II
Dassault Mirage F1AZ
COMBAT SUPPORT
Aérospatiale SA316B Alouette III
Atlas Oryx
Atlas CSH-1 Rooivalk
Boeing 707-320B
Douglas C-47TP Dakota
Lockheed C-130B/E Hercules
Sud SE3160 Alouette III
TRAINING
Airtech CN.235M-100
Atlas Cheetah D

Atlas Impala I
CASA C.212-100/200 Aviocar
Pilatus PC-7/II Astra
MISCELLANEOUS
Beech Super King Air 200C/B200C
Beech Super King Air 300
Cessna 185A/D/E
Cessna 208 Caravan I
Cessna 550 Citation II/SP
Dassault Falcon 50
Dassault Falcon 900
Eurocopter/Kawasaki BK117A-1/3
Pilatus PC-12M

SPAIN

SPANISH AIR FORCE
COMBAT
Dassault Mirage F1C/CE/EE/EDAS
Lockheed P-3A/B Orion
Lockheed P-3B TACNAVMOD Orion
McDonnell Douglas EF-18A/B Hornet

COMBAT SUPPORT
Airtech CN.235-10/100
CASA C.212A-1/AA-1/AV-1/200DE Aviocar
Dassault Falcon 20D
Fokker F27-200MPA Friendship
Lockheed C-130H/H-30/KC-130H Hercules
McDonnell Douglas RF-4C Phantom II
TRAINING
Beech F33C Bonanza
Beech B55 Baron
CASA C.101EB Aviojet
CASA C.212E/E-1 Aviocar
CASA-Northrop SF-5A/B/SRF-5A
 Freedom Fighter
Dassault Mirage F1B/BE/DDA
ENAER T-35C Pillan
Hughes 300
Sikorsky S-76A Spirit
MISCELLANEOUS
Aérospatiale SA330H/J Puma
Boeing 707-331/368
Canadair CL-215T

CASA C.212-100/AB-1/200S-1/B-1 Aviocar
Cessna 560 Citation V
Dassault Falcon 20E/F
Dassault Falcon 50
Dassault Falcon 900
Dornier Do 27A4
Eurocopter AS332B/M Super Puma

SPANISH NAVAL AIR ARM
COMBAT
Agusta-Bell AB212ASW
McDonnell Douglas EAV-8B/B+
 Harrier II/II+
Sikorsky SH-3D/G Sea King
Sikorsky S-60B Seahawk
COMBAT SUPPORT
Sikorsky SH-3 AEW Sea King
TRAINING
Hughes 300
McDonnell Douglas TAV-8B Harrier II
MISCELLANEOUS
Cessna 550 Citation II

ARMY AIR-MOBILE FORCES
COMBAT
Eurocopter BO105ATH
COMBAT SUPPORT
Agusta-Bell AB212
Bell UH-1H Iroquois
Boeing Vertol CH-47D Chinook
Eurocopter AS532UC/UL Cougar
Eurocopter BO105GSH
TRAINING
Bell OH-58B Kiowa
Eurocopter BO105CB

CIVIL GUARD
Eurocopter BO105C
Eurocopter/Kawasaki BK117

ENAER T-35C Pillan Spanish Air Force

SRI LANKA

SRI LANKAN AIR FORCE
COMBAT
FMA IA-58 Pucara
IAI Kfir C2/TC2
Mikoyan MiG-27 'Flogger'
Mil Mi-24V 'Hind'
COMBAT SUPPORT
Antonov An-32 'Cline'
Bell 212
Harbin Y-12
Hawker Siddeley (BAe) 748 Srs 2A
Lockheed C-130B Hercules
Mil Mi-17 'Hip H'
Shaanxi Y-8D
TRAINING
Cessna 150L
Chengdu FT-5
Guizhou (GAIC) FT-7
SIAI-Marchetti SF.260TP/W Warrior
MISCELLANEOUS
Beech King Air B200T
Bell 206B JetRanger
Bell 412
Cessna 421C Golden Eagle
HAL Chetak

SUDAN

SUDANESE AIR FORCE
COMBAT
BAC Strikemaster 90
Chengdu F-7B
Eurocopter BO105CB
Mikoyan MiG-23BN 'Flogger H'
Mil Mi-24 'Hind'
Shenyang F-5/Chengdu FT-5
Shenyang F-6/FT-6
COMBAT SUPPORT
Agusta-Bell 212
Dassault Falcon 20/50
de Havilland Canada DHC-5D Buffalo
ICA-Brasov IAR-330L Puma
Lockheed C-130H Hercules
Mil Mi-8 'Hip'
Shaanxi Y-8

Piper PA-28 Cherokee

SWEDEN

SWEDISH AIR FORCE
COMBAT
Saab AJS/AJSF/AJSH/JA 37 Viggen
Saab JAS 39A/B/C Gripen
COMBAT SUPPORT
Gulfstream Aerospace Gulfstream IV-SP
Lockheed C-130E/H Hercules
Saab 340 AEW&C Argus
TRAINING
Saab Sk 37 Viggen
Saab Sk 60A/B/C/D/W
MISCELLANEOUS
Beech Super King Air 200
Gulfstream Aerospace Gulfstream IV
Rockwell Sabreliner 40
Saab 340B
Scottish Aviation Bulldog 101

SWEDISH NAVY
COMBAT
Agusta-Bell AB206A JetRanger
Kawasaki-Vertol KV107 II
COMBAT SUPPORT
Aérospatiale AS332M Super Puma

MISCELLANEOUS
de Havilland Canada DHC-6-300
Twin Otter

SURINAM

SURINAM AIR FORCE
CASA C212-400 Aviocar
Cessna 172
Cessna 310

SWAZILAND

SWAZILAND DEFENCE FORCE
Aérospatiale SA316 Alouette III
IAI Arava 201

CASA C.212-200 Aviocar
MISCELLANEOUS
Piper PA-31-350 Navajo Chieftain

COAST GUARD
CASA C.212-200 Aviocar
Reims Cessna FA 337G

SWEDISH ARMY FLYING SERVICE
COMBAT
Eurocopter BO105CB
COMBAT SUPPORT
Agusta-Bell AB204A/AB206B
Agusta-Bell AB412
TRAINING
Hughes 300C

SWITZERLAND

SWISS AIR FORCE
COMBAT
Dassault Mirage IIIS
McDonnell Douglas F/A-18C/D Hornet
Northrop F-5E Tiger II
COMBAT SUPPORT
Aérospatiale SA316B/SE 3160 Alouette III
Dassault Mirage IIIRS
Eurocopter AS332M Super Puma

Agusta-Bell AB204A Swedish Army

Gulfstream Aerospace Gulfstream IV-SP Swedish Air Force

Aérospatiale SA316B Alouette III Swiss Air Force

McDonnell Douglas MD500MD Defender Taiwan Navy

TRAINING
British Aerospace Hawk 66
Dassault Mirage IIIBS/BS
Northrop F-5F Tiger II
Pilatus PC-7 Turbo-Trainer
Pilatus PC-9
MISCELLANEOUS
Dassault Falcon 50
Learjet 36
Pilatus PC-6/B Turbo-Porter

SYRIA

SYRIAN ARAB AIR FORCE
COMBAT
Aérospatiale SA342L Gazelle
Mikoyan MiG-21PF/MF/bis 'Fishbed'
Mikoyan MiG-23MF/ML/MS/BN 'Flogger'
Mikoyan MiG-25PD 'Foxbat E'
Mikoyan MiG-29 'Fulcrum'
Mil Mi-24 'Hind'
Sukhoi Su-20 'Fitter F'
Sukhoi Su-22M-2 'Fitter'

Sukhoi Su-24MK 'Fencer D'
Sukhoi Su-27 'Flanker'
COMBAT SUPPORT
Antonov An-24 'Coke'
Antonov An-26 'Curl'
Ilyushin IL-76M 'Candid'
Mikoyan MiG-25RB 'Foxbat B'
Mil Mi-6 'Hook'
Mil Mi-8/17 'Hip'
TRAINING
Aero L-29 Delfin
Aero L-39ZA/ZO Albatros
MBB Flamingo
Mikoyan-Gurevich MiG-15UTI 'Midget'
Mikoyan-Gurevich MiG-17F 'Fresco'
Mikoyan MiG-21U/UM 'Mongol'
Mikoyan MiG-23UB 'Flogger'
Mikoyan MiG-25PU 'Foxbat C'
Mikoyan MiG-29UB 'Fulcrum'
PAC Mushshak
Sukhoi Su-22U/UM-3 'Fitter'
MISCELLANEOUS
Dassault Falcon 20F

Piper PA-31-310 Navajo
PZL (Mil) Mi-2 'Hoplite'
Tupolev Tu-134B-3 'Crusty'
Yakovlev Yak-40 'Codling'

SYRIAN ARAB NAVAL AIR ARM
Kamov Ka-25Bsh 'Hormone A'
Mil Mi-14PL 'Haze A'

TAIWAN

REPUBLIC OF CHINA AIR FORCE
COMBAT
AIDC Ching-Kuo A/B
Dassault Mirage 2000-5Ei/5Di
General Dynamics F-16A/B-20
Northrop F-5E/RF-5E Tiger II
COMBAT SUPPORT
Boeing 727-100
Douglas C-47 Dakota
Fokker 50
Grumman E-2T Hawkeye
Lockheed C/EC-130H Hercules

TRAINING
AIDC AT-3 Tzu-Chung
Beech T-34C Turbo-Mentor
Northrop F-5F Tiger II
Northrop T-38A Talon
MISCELLANEOUS
Boeing 737-800
Sikorsky S-70C-2 Black Hawk

REPUBLIC OF CHINA NAVAL AIR ARM
COMBAT
Grumman S-2T Tracker
McDonnell Douglas MD 500MD Defender
Sikorsky S-70C(M)-1/2 Thunder Hawk

REPUBLIC OF CHINA ARMY AIR ARM
COMBAT
Bell AH-1W SuperCobra
Bell OH-58D Kiowa Warrior
COMBAT SUPPORT
Bell UH-1H Iroquois
Boeing Vertol 234MLR Chinook
TRAINING
Bell TH-67 Creek
Hughes 269/TH-55A

TAJIKISTAN

TAJIKISTAN AIR ARM
Mil Mi-8MTB 'Hip H'
Mil Mi-24 'Hind'

TANZANIA

TANZANIAN PEOPLE'S DEFENCE FORCE AIR WING
COMBAT
Chengdu F-7A
Shenyang F-5
Shenyang F-6
COMBAT SUPPORT
de Havilland Canada DHC-5D Buffalo
Harbin Y-12(II)
TRAINING
Shenyang FT-2
MISCELLANEOUS
Aérospatiale SA316B Alouette III
Agusta-Bell 206B JetRanger
Beech King Air A100
British Aerospace 125-700B
Cessna 402/404
Fokker F28-1000 Fellowship
Piper PA-28 Cherokee

TANZANIA POLICE AIR WING
Agusta-Bell 206L LongRanger
Bell 47G-3B2
Cessna U206 Stationair
Eurocopter BO105CBS

Northrop F-5A Freedom Fighter Royal Thai Air Force

Rockwell OV-10C Bronco Royal Thai Air Force

Bell UH-1H Iroquois Royal Thai Air Force

460

Cessna U-17B Royal Thai Army

ROYAL THAI AIR FORCE

COMBAT
Aero L39ZA Albatros
Fairchild AU-23A Peacemaker
General Dynamics F-16A/B-15OCU
Northrop F-5A/B Freedom Fighter
Northrop F-5E Tiger II
Rockwell OV-10C Bronco

COMBAT SUPPORT
Alenia G222
Basler Turbo 67
Bell UH-1H Iroquois
Cessna O-1A/E Bird Dog
GAF N22B Nomad
Hawker Siddeley (BAe) 748 Srs 208
IAI Arava 201
Lockheed C-130H/H-130 Hercules
Northrop RF-5A Freedom Fighter

TRAINING
Bell 206B-3 JetRanger
Cessna 150H
Hoffman H36 Dimona
Northrop F-5F Tiger II
Pacific Aerospace CT-4A/B Airtrainer
Pilatus PC-9
RFB Fantrainer 400/600

MISCELLANEOUS
Airbus A310-324
Bell 412
Boeing 737-2Z6/4Z61
Cessna T-41D Mescalero
Eurocopter AS332L2 Super Puma 2
Fairchild Merlin IVA
Learjet 35A
SIAI-Marchetti SF.260MT
Sikorsky S-58T

ROYAL THAI NAVY AIR DIVISION

COMBAT
Bell 212ASW

McDonnell Douglas AV-8A(S) Harrier
Fokker F27-200 Maritime Enforcer 1
Lockheed P-3A Orion
Sikorsky S-70B-7 Seahawk
Summit Sentry 0-2/337
Vought A-7E Corsair II

COMBAT SUPPORT
Bell 214ST
Bell UH-1H Iroquois
Cessna O-1G Bird Dog
Dornier 228-212
GAF N24A Nomad Searchmaster L

TRAINING
McDonnell Douglas TAV-8A(S) Harrier
Vought TA-7C Corsair II

MISCELLANEOUS
Canadair CL-215
Cessna U-17A/B
Fokker F27-400M Troopship
Grumman US-2C/F Tracker
Lockheed UP-3T Orion
Sikorsky S-76N

ROYAL THAI ARMY

COMBAT
Bell AH-1F HueyCobra

COMBAT SUPPORT
Bell UH-1H Iroquois
Bell 206A/B JetRanger
Bell 212
Boeing-Vertol CH-47C/D Chinook
CASA C.212-300 Aviocar
Cessna O-1A/E Bird Dog
Shorts 330-UTT

TRAINING
Cessna T-41B Mescalero
Cessna U-17B
Maule M-7-25 Super Rocket
Schweizer 300C/TH

MISCELLANEOUS
Beech 1900C-1
Beech Super King Air 200

British Aerospace Jetstream 41
Robinson R-22

ROYAL THAI BORDER POLICE
Airtech CN235-200
Bell 205A-1
Bell 206B JetRanger
Bell 206L LongRanger
Bell 212
Bell 412/SP11
Bell UH-1H Iroquois
Fokker 50
Pilatus PC-6/B Turbo Porter
Shorts SC.7-3M-400 Skyvan
Shorts 330-UTT

ROYAL THAI AGRICULTURAL AVIATION
Airtech CN235
Bell 206B JetRanger
CASA C.212-100/200/300
Cessna 180
Cessna U206
Cessna 208 Caravan
Cessna 310Q
Enstrom F28F
Eurocopter AS350B
Fletcher FU-24-954
McDonnel Douglas MD500
Pilatus PC-6B

Pilatus/B-N BN-2 Islander
Schweizer H-300

TOGOLESE AIR FORCE

COMBAT
Dassault/Dornier Alpha Jet
Embraer EMB-326GB Xavante

COMBAT SUPPORT
de Havilland Canada DHC-5D Buffalo
Fouga CM170 Magister

TRAINING
SOCATA TB30 Epsilon

MISCELLANEOUS
Aérospatiale SA315B Lama
Aérospatiale SA319 Alouette III
Beech Super King Air 200
Boeing 707-312B
Dornier Do 27A-4
Eurocopter AS332L Super Puma
Fokker F28-3000 Fellowship
Reims Cessna F337E

TONGAN DEFENCE SERVICES AIR WING
Beech G18S
Champion Citabria

GAF N22B Nomad Royal Thai Air Force

Agusta-Bell AB204B Turkish Army

TRINIDAD AND TOBAGO

**TRINIDAD AND TOBAGO
DEFENCE FORCE WING**
Cessna 172M
Cessna 310R
Cessna 402
NATIONAL HELICOPTER SERVICES
Eurocopter BO105CBS
Sikorsky S-76A Spirit

TUNISIA

TUNISIAN REPUBLIC AIR FORCE
COMBAT
Aérospatiale SA341 Gazelle
Aermacchi MB-326B/K/L
Northrop F-5E Tiger II
COMBAT SUPPORT
Agusta-Bell 205A
Let L-410UVP Turbolet
Lockheed C-130B/H Hercules
TRAINING
Aero L-59T Albatros
Aermacchi MB-326B
Northrop F-5F Tiger II
SIAI-Marchetti SF.260CT/WT Warrior
MISCELLANEOUS
Aérospatiale SA316B Alouette III

Agusta Bell HH-3E Pelican
Alenia G222
Eurocopter AS350B Ecureuil
Eurocopter AS365 Dauphin
SIAI-Marchetti S.208A
Sud SE3130 Alouette II

TURKEY

TURKISH AIR FORCE
COMBAT
Canadair/Northrop NF-5A Freedom Fighter
General Dynamics F-16C/D Fighting Falcon
McDonnell Douglas F-4E Phantom II
Northrop F-5A Freedom Fighter
COMBAT SUPPORT
Airtech CN.235M
Boeing KC-135R Stratotanker
Lockheed C-130B/E Hercules
McDonnell Douglas RF-4E Phantom II
Northrop RF-5A Freedom Fighter
Transall C.160T
TRAINING
Canadair/Northrop NF-5B Freedom Fighter
Cessna T-37B/C
Cessna T-41D Mescalero
Northrop F-5B Freedom Fighter
Northrop T-38A Talon
SIAI-Marchetti SF.260D

MISCELLANEOUS
Beech King Air 200
Bell UH-1H Iroquois
Cessna 550 Citation II
Cessna 650 Citation VII
Eurocopter AS532AL Cougar
Gulfstream Aerospace Gulfstream IV

TURKISH NAVAL AVIATION
COMBAT
Agusta-Bell AB 212ASW
Sikorsky S-70B Seahawk
COMBAT SUPPORT
Agusta-Bell AB 212EW
Airtech CN.235MPA Persuader
TRAINING
SOCATA TB 20 Trinidad
MISCELLANEOUS
Agusta-Bell AB 204AS

TURKISH COAST GUARD
Agusta-Bell 206B JetRanger
Agusta-Bell 412
Airtech CN-235
Maule MX-7

TURKISH ARMY AVIATION
COMBAT
Bell T/AH-1P HueyCobra

Bell AH-1W SuperCobra
COMBAT SUPPORT
Agusta-Bell 205A
Bell UH-1H Iroquois
Bell OH-58B Kiowa
Eurocopter AS532UL Cougar
Sikorsky S-70A-17 Black Hawk
TRAINING
Agusta-Bell 204B
Agusta-Bell 206B JetRanger
Bellanca 7GCBC Citabria
Cessna T-41D Mescalero
Hughes 300
MISCELLANEOUS
Agusta-Bell 212
Beech King Air 200
Beech T-42A Cochise
Cessna U-17B
Cessna 421B Golden Eagle

TURKISH GENDARMERIE
Agusta-Bell 204B
Agusta-Bell 205A-1
Agusta-Bell 206A JetRanger
Agusta-Bell 212
Beech King Air B200
Dornier Do 28D Skyservant
Mil Mi-17V 'Hip H'
Sikorsky S-70A-17 Black Hawk

TURKMENISTAN

TURKMENISTAN AIR FORCE
COMBAT
Mikoyan MiG-21 'Fishbed'
Mikoyan MiG-23M/U 'Flogger'
Mikoyan MiG-25/U 'Foxbat'
Mikoyan MiG-29/U 'Fulcrum'
Sukhoi Su-7B/Su-17M/UM 'Fitter'
Sukhoi Su-25 'Frogfoot'
Mil Mi-24 'Hind'
COMBAT SUPPORT
Antonov An-12 'Cub'
Antonov An-24 'Coke'
Mil Mi-8 'Hip'
TRAINING
Aero L-39 Albatros

UGANDA

UGANDAN AIR FORCE
COMBAT SUPPORT
Agusta-Bell 412SP
Mil Mi-8/17 'Hip'
Mikoyan MiG-21MF/UM 'Fishbed'
TRAINING
Aero L39ZA Albatros
FFA AS 202-18A Bravo
SIAI-Marchetti SF.260W Warrior

McDonnell Douglas F-4E Phantom Turkish Air Force

Sukhoi Su-27 'Flanker' Ukrainian Air Force

MISCELLANEOUS
Bell 206 JetRanger III
Gulfstream Aerospace Gulfstream III

NATIONAL POLICE AIR WING
Bell 212
de Havilland Canada DHC-6 Twin Otter

UKRAINE

MILITARY AIR FORCES
COMBAT
Mikoyan MiG-23M 'Flogger'
Mikoyan- MiG-29 'Fulcrum A/C'
Sukhoi Su-17M 'Fitter'
Sukhoi Su-24M/MP/MR 'Fencer D'
Sukhoi Su-25 'Frogfoot A'
Sukhoi Su-27 'Flanker'
Tupolev Tu-22R 'Blinder'
Tupolev Tu-22M 'Backfire'
Tupolev Tu-95 'Bear A'
Tupolev Tu-95MS 'Bear H6'
Tupolev Tu-95MS 'Bear H16'
Tupolev Tu-160 'Blackjack'
COMBAT SUPPORT
Antonov An-12BP 'Cub'
Antonov An-24 'Coke'
Antonov An-26 'Curl'

Antonov An-72 'Coaler'
Antonov An-74 'Coaler B'
Ilyushin IL-22 'Coot'
Ilyushin IL-76MD 'Candid'
Ilyushin IL-78 'Midas'
Mil Mi-6 'Hook'
Mil Mi-8/17 'Hip'
Sukhoi Su-24MP 'Fencer F'
Sukhoi Su-24MR 'Fencer E'
TRAINING
Aero L-39 Albatros
Aerostar (Yakovlev) Iak-52
Mikoyan MiG-23UB 'FloggerC'
Mikoyan MiG-29UB 'Fulcrum B'
Sukhoi Su-17UM 'Fitter'
Sukhoi Su-25UBK 'Frogfoot B'
Sukhoi Su-27UB 'Flanker C'
Tupolev Tu-134UBL
MISCELLANEOUS
Antonov An-2 'Colt'
Antonov An-30 'Clank'
Tupolev Tu-134A3 'Crusty'
Yakovlev Yak-40 'Codling'

NAVAL AVIATION FORCE
COMBAT
Kamov Ka-25 'Hormone'
Kamov Ka-27 'Helix'

Kamov Ka-29 'Helix'
Mil Mi-14PL 'Haze'
COMBAT SUPPORT
Antonov An-12 'Cub D'
Antonov An-26 'Curl'
Antonov An-72P 'Coaler'
Beriev Be-12 Tchaika ('Mail')
Kamov Ka-29 'Helix'

UKRAINIAN GROUND FORCES
COMBAT
Mil Mi-24D/V/P 'Hind'
COMBAT SUPPORT
Mil Mi-6 'Hook'
Mil Mi-8PPA 'Hip K'
Mil Mi-8T/TB 'Hip'
Mil Mi-24K 'Hind G2'
Mil Mi-26 'Halo'
PZL (Mil) Mi-2 'Hoplite'

UNITED ARAB EMIRATES

UNITED ARAB EMIRATES AIR FORCE

ABU DHABI
COMBAT
Aérospatiale SA342L Gazelle
Dassault Mirage 5A/R/D/E
Dassault Mirage 2000E/R/D
Dassault Mirage 2000-9
Eurocopter AS565SA Panther
General Dynamics F-16C/D Fighting Falcon
McDonnell Douglas AH-64A Apache
COMBAT SUPPORT
Aérospatiale SA330C/F Puma
Airtech CN.235M/MPA
CASA C.212-200 Aviocar
Dassault Mirage 5RAD
Dassault Mirage 2000RAD
Eurocopter AS332L Super Puma
Eurocopter AS532UC/SC Cougar
Lockheed C-130H Hercules

TRAINING
British Aerospace Hawk 63/100
Eurocopter AS350B Ecureuil
Grob G 115TA Acro
Pilatus PC-7 Turbo-Trainer
MISCELLANEOUS
Airbus A300-620
Beech Super King Air 350
Boeing 747SP
British Aerospace 146-100
Dassault Falcon 900
Eurocopter BO105CBS

DUBAI
COMBAT SUPPORT
Agusta-Bell 205A-1
Agusta-Bell 412
Bell 214B
ICA-Brasov IAR-330L Puma
TRAINING
Aermacchi MB.326KD/LD
Aermacchi MB.339A
British Aerospace Hawk 61
SIAI-Marchetti SF.260TP
MISCELLANEOUS
Bell 206B JetRanger
Bell 206L-1 LongRanger
Bell 212
Boeing 747SP
Eurocopter AS365N1 Dauphin 2
Eurocopter BO105CBS
Gulfstream Aerospace Gulfstream II/IV
Lockheed C-130H/L-100-30 Hercules
Pilatus/B-N BN-2T Turbine Islander
Shorts SC7 Skyvan
Shorts 330-UUT
Sikorsky S-76A

DUBAI POLICE AIR WING
Agusta A109K2
Agusta-Bell 212
Agusta-Bell 412EP

Antonov An-72 'Coaler' Ukrainian Air Force

Bell 206B JetRanger
Bell 212
Eurocopter BO105CBS

Ras Al Khaimah
Cessna 500 Citiation I

Sharjah
Bell 206B JetRanger
Boeing 737-2W8

Umm Al Qaiwain
Bell 222UT

UNITED KINGDOM

ROYAL AIR FORCE

COMBAT
British Aerospace Harrier GR7
Hawker Siddeley Nimrod MR2
Panavia Tornado GR1/A/B
Panavia Tornado GR4/4A
Panavia Tornado F3
SEPECAT Jaguar GR1/3/3A/4

COMBAT SUPPORT
BAC VC10 C1K/K2/K3/K4
Boeing E-3D Sentry AEW1
Boeing-Vertol Chinook HC2/2A/3
EH Industries Merlin HC3
English Electric Canberra PR9

Lockheed Martin C-130J Hercules C4 Royal Air Force

Hawker Siddeley Nimrod R1
Lockheed Hercules C1/C3
Lockheed Hercules C4/C5
Lockheed L-1011 Tristar K1/KC1/C2/C2A
Westland Puma HC1
Westland Wessex HC2

TRAINING
Bell 412EP Griffin HT1
British Aerospace Hawk T1/1A

British Aerospace Harrier T10
English Electric Canberra T4
Eurocopter AS350BB Squirrel HT1
Grob G109 Vigilant T1
Grob 115 Tutor
Hawker Siddeley Dominie T1
Scottish Aviation Bulldog T1
Scottish Aviation Jetstream T1
SEPECAT Jaguar T2A/4

Shorts Tucano T1
Slingsby T67M Firefly

MISCELLANEOUS
British Aerospace 125 CC3
British Aerospace 146 CC2
Eurocopter AS355F1 Twin Squirrel HCC1
Pilatus/B-N Islander CC2/2A
Westland Sea King HAR3/3A

ROYAL NAVY

COMBAT
British Aerospace Sea Harrier FA2
EH Industries Merlin HMA1
Westland Lynx HAS3/HMA8
Westland Sea King HAS5/6

COMBAT SUPPORT
Westland Gazelle AH1
Westland Lynx AH7
Westland Sea King AEW2A/HC4

TRAINING
British Aerospace Jetstream T2
British Aerospace Harrier T8
British Aerospace Hawk T1/1A
Grob G 115 Heron
Westland Sea King HAS5/HAS5U

MISCELLANEOUS
British Aerospace Jetstream T3
Eurocopter AS365N-2 Dauphin 2

ARMY AIR CORPS

COMBAT
Westland Lynx AH1/7
GKN Westland WAH-64 Apache Longbow

COMBAT SUPPORT
Agusta A109A
Bell 212
Pilatus/B-N Islander AL1
Westland Gazelle AH1
Westland Lynx AH9

TRAINING
Eurocopter AS350BB Squirrel HT2

British Aerospace Sea Harrier FA2 Royal Navy

GKN-Westland WAH-64 Apache Longbow Army Air Corps

SEPECAT Jaguar GR1A Royal Air Force

BAC VC10 K3 Royal Air Force

Hawker Siddeley Nimrod MR2 Royal Air Force

DEFENCE EVALUATION AND RESEARCH AGENCY (DERA)

BAC One-Eleven
Beagle Basset CC1
Boeing-Vertol Chinook HC2
British Aerospace Harrier T4 VAAC
British Aerospace Harrier GR7/T10
British Aerospace Hawk T1
English Electric Canberra B2(TT)
Gloster Meteor D16
Hawker Hunter T7
Hawker Siddeley Andover C1/C1(PR)
Lockheed Hercules W2
North American Harvard T2b
Panavia Tornado GR1/F2
Piper PA-31-350 Navajo Chieftain
Scottish Aviation Jetstream T2
SEPECAT Jaguar GR3
SEPECAT Jaguar T2/T2A
Shorts Tucano T1
Westland Gazelle HT2
Westland Lynx
Westland Sea King

UNITED STATES OF AMERICA

UNITED STATES AIR FORCE

COMBAT

Boeing B-52H Stratofortress
Fairchild A-10A Thunderbolt II
General Dynamics F-16A/B Fighting Falcon
General Dynamics F-16C/D Fighting Falcon
Lockheed AC-130H/U Hercules
Lockheed F-117A Night Hawk
McDonnell Douglas F-15A/B/C/D Eagle
McDonnell Douglas F-15E Strike Eagle
Northrop-Grumman B-2A Spirit
Rockwell B-1B Lancer

COMBAT SUPPORT

Alenia C-27A Spartan
Bell UH-1N Iroquois
Boeing EC-135C Stratotanker
Boeing KC-135D/E Stratotanker
Boeing EC-135N Stratotanker
Boeing KC-135R/T Stratotanker
Boeing RC-135S/U/V/W/X Stratotanker
Boeing EC-135Y Stratotanker
Boeing E-3B/C Sentry
Boeing E-4B
Boeing E-8 J-STARS
Fairchild OA-10A Thunderbolt II
Lockheed C-5A/B Galaxy
Lockheed AC-130 Hercules
Lockheed C-130E/H Hercules
Lockheed EC-130E Hercules
Lockheed EC-130E(CL)/H Hercules
Lockheed EC-130E(RR) Hercules
Lockheed MC-130E Hercules
Lockheed HC-130H(N)/N/P Hercules

Boeing RC-135W United States Air Force

McDonnell Douglas AV-8B Harrier II United States Marine Corps

Lockheed LC-130H Hercules
Lockheed MC-130H/P Hercules
Lockheed C-130J Hercules
Lockheed C-141B/C Starlifter
Lockheed U-2/T2
McDonnell Douglas C-9A Nightingale
McDonnell Douglas KC-10A Extender
McDonnell Douglas C-17A Globemaster III
Northrop-Grumman E-8A/C J-STARS
Sikorsky MH-53J Pave Low
Sikorsky HH/MH-60G Pave Hawk

TRAINING

Beech T-1A Jayhawk
Boeing C-18
Boeing TC-135S/W Stratotanker
Boeing T-43A
Cessna T-37B Tweet
Cessna T-41D Mescalero
de Havilland Canada UV-18B Twin Otter
Lockheed TU-2
Northrop T-38A/B/AT-38 Talon

MISCELLANEOUS

Beech C-12C/F Huron
Beech C-12J

Boeing EC-18B/D
Boeing C-22B
Boeing VC-25A
Boeing C-32A
Boeing C-135B/C/E/OC-135B Stratotanker
Boeing NKC-135E Stratotanker
Boeing WC-135W Stratotanker
Boeing VC-137B/C
Boeing EC-137D
Boeing CT-43A
de Havilland Canada E-9A Dash 8
General Dynamics NF-16A/D Fighting Falcon
Gulfstream Aerospace C-20A/B/C
  Gulfstream III
Gulfstream Aerospace C-20H Gulfstream IV
IAI C-38A Astra SPX
Learjet C-21A
Lockheed NC-130A/E/H Hercules
Lockheed WC-130H Hercules
Lockheed WC-130J Hercules
Lockheed NC-141A Starlifter
Lockheed YF-117A Night Hawk
McDonnell Douglas VC-9C Nightingale
McDonnell Douglas QRF-4C Phantom II

McDonnell Douglas QF-4E/G
Rockwell NT-39A/B Sabreliner
Shorts C-23A Sherpa

UNITED STATES NAVY & MARINE CORPS

COMBAT

Bell AH-1W SuperCobra
Grumman F-14A/B/D Tomcat
Kaman SH-2F/G Seasprite
Lockheed P-3A/B/C Orion
Lockheed S-3A/B Viking
McDonnell Douglas F/A-18A/B/C/D/E/F
  Hornet
McDonnell Douglas/BAe AV-8B
  Harrier II & II+
Sikorsky SH-3D/G/H Sea King
Sikorsky SH-60B Seahawk
Sikorsky SH-60F Ocean Hawk

COMBAT SUPPORT

Bell UH-1N Iroquois
Bell-Boeing V-22 Osprey
Boeing E-6A/B Mercury
Boeing-Vertol CH-46D/E Sea Knight
Grumman EA-6B Prowler

McDonnell Douglas/BAe T-45A Goshawk United States Navy

Beech C-12J United States Air Force

Boeing C-17A Globemaster III United States Air Force

de Havilland Canada E-9A Dash 8 United States Air Force

Grumman E-2C Hawkeye United States Navy

Grumman C-2A Greyhound
Grumman E-2C Hawkeye
Lockheed KC-130F/R Hercules
Lockheed LC-130F/R Hercules
Lockheed TC-130G Hercules
Lockheed KC-130J Hercules
Lockheed TC-130Q Hercules
Lockheed C-130T Hercules
Lockheed KC-130T/T-130 Hercules
Lockheed EP-3E/J Orion
Lockheed ES-3A Viking
McDonnell Douglas C-9B Skytrain II
McDonnell Douglas DC-9-32/32F/CF
McDonnell Douglas DC-9-33RC
Sikorsky CH-53D/E Sea Stallion
Sikorsky RH-53D Sea Dragon
Sikorsky CH-60
Sikorsky HH-60H Black Hawk

TRAINING
Beech TC-12B

Beech T-34C Turbo-Mentor
Beech T-44A Pegasus
Beech U-21J
Bell TH-57B/C SeaRanger
Boeing TC-18F
Grumman TE-2C Hawkeye
Lockheed TP-3A/EP-3J Orion
McDonnell Douglas/BAe T-45A Goshawk
McDonnell Douglas/BAe TAV-8B Harrier II
Northrop F-5E/F Tiger II
Northrop T-38A/B Talon
Raytheon T-6A Texan II
Rockwell T-2C Buckeye
Rockwell T-39N Sabreliner

MISCELLANEOUS
Beech UC-12B/RC-12F/UC-12F/UC-12M/
  RC-12M Huron
Beech NT-34C Turbo-Mentor
Bell UH-1N/HH-1N Iroquois
Boeing-Vertol HH-46D/UH-46D Sea Knight

Douglas EC-24A
Fairchild SA-226AC Metro III
Grumman NA/NEA-6B Prowler
Grumman NA-6E Intruder
Grumman NF-14A/B/D Tomcat
Gulfstream Aerospace C-20D/G
  Gulfstream III
Lockheed DC-130A Hercules
Lockheed RP-3A Orion
Lockheed UP-3A/B/VP-3A Orion
McDonnell Douglas NTA-4F/J Skyhawk
McDonnell Douglas QF-4N/4S Phantom II
McDonnell Douglas NF/A-18A/C/D Hornet
McDonnell Douglas/BAe NAV-8B/
  NTAV-8B Harrier II
Rockwell CT-39E/G Sabreliner
Schweizer X-26A/B
Sikorsky VH-3A/UH-3A/VH-3D/UH-3H
  Sea King
Sikorsky MH-53E Sea Stallion

Sikorsky UH-60A Black Hawk
Sikorsky NSH-60B Seahawk
Sikorsky YSH-60F Ocean Hawk
Sikorsky VH-60N White Hawk

UNITED STATES COAST GUARD
Aérospatiale HH-65A Dolphin
CASA C.212-300 Aviocar
Dassault HU-25A/B/C Guardian
Grumman VC-4A Gulfstream I
Gulfstream Aerospace C-20B Gulfstream III
Lockheed HC-130H Hercules
Schweizer RU-38A Twin Condor
Sikorsky HH-60J Jayhawk

UNITED STATES ARMY
COMBAT
Bell AH-1E/F/P/S HueyCobra
Boeing Helicopters/Sikorsky YRAH-66A
McDonnell Douglas AH-6G/J Little Bird
McDonnell Douglas MH-6H/J Little Bird
McDonnell Douglas AH-64A Apache
McDonnell Douglas AH-64D
  Longbow Apache
COMBAT SUPPORT
Beech RC-12D Improved Guardrail V
Beech RC-12G 'Crazyhorse'
Beech RC-12H Guardrail
  Common Sensor (Minus)
Beech RC-12K/N/P Guardrail
  Common Sensor
Beech RC-12Q Direct Air Satellite Relay
Bell UH-1H/V Iroquois
Bell OH-58A/A+/-58A(N)/-58A(R)/C Kiowa
Bell OH-58D/-58D(II) Kiowa
Boeing-Vertol MH-47D/E Chinook
de Havilland Canada RC-7B/EO-5B

Sikorsky CH-53E Sea Stallion United States Marine Corps

McDonnell Douglas AH-6J/MH-6J
Shorts C-23A/B/B+ Sherpa
Sikorsky UH-60A/L Black Hawk
Sikorsky EH-60A Black Hawk
Sikorsky MH-60K/L Black Hawk
Sikorsky YUH-60Q Black Hawk

TRAINING
Bell TH-67A Creek

MISCELLANEOUS
Beech VC-6A King Air
Beech C-12C/D/F/L/R Huron
Beech JC-12C
Beech T-34C Turbo-Mentor
Bell JAH-1F/JEH-1H/JUH-1H
Bell NUH-1H/QUH-1M/NAH-1S
Bell JOH-58A/C/D/D(I)
Boeing-Vertol JCH-47D
Cessna UC-35A Citation V Ultra
Cessna O-2A Skymaster
Cessna 182
de Havilland Canada UV-18A Twin Otter
de Havilland Canada OE-5/5A/RC-7 Dash 7
Fairchild C-26A/B Metro III
Fokker C-31A Friendship
Gulfstream Aerospace C-20J Gulfstream II
Gulfstream Aerospace C-20E/F Gulfstream III
Gulfstream Aerospace C-20F Gulfstream IV
Learjet C-21A
McDonnell Douglas JAH-64A
McDonnell Douglas QF-4 /QRF-4
Pilatus UV-20A Chiricahua
Piper PA-31T Turbo-Cheyenne II
Sikorsky JUH/NUH-60A
Sikorsky YEH-60B
Sikorsky EH/JUH-60L
Shorts JC-23A

URUGUAY

URUGUAYAN AIR FORCE

COMBAT
Cessna A-37B Dragonfly
FMA IA-58 Pucara

COMBAT SUPPORT
Bell UH-1H Iroquois
Bell 212
CASA C.212-200 Aviocar
Embraer EMB-110C Bandeirante
Fokker F27-100 Friendship
Lockheed C-130B Hercules
Westland Wessex HC2

TRAINING
Beech T-34A/B Mentor
Cessna T-41D Mescalero
Pilatus PC-7U Turbo-Trainer

MISCELLANEOUS
Beech Queen Air A65
Cessna 172
Cessna 182A/D

Beech RC-12K Guardrail United States Army

Cessna 206
Cessna 210
Embraer EMB-110B1 Bandeirante
Eurocopter AS365 Dauphin
Piper PA-18 Super Cub
Rockwell Commander UR-4B

URUGUAYAN NAVAL AVIATION

COMBAT
Grumman S-2A/G Tracker

COMBAT SUPPORT
Beech Super King Air 200T
Scottish Aviation Jetstream T2
Westland Wessex 60/HC2

TRAINING
Beech T-34A/B Mentor
Beech T-34C-1 Turbo-Mentor
Piper PA-34-200T Seneca II

MISCELLANEOUS
Cessna 182H/J/K

UZBEKISTAN

UZBEK AIR ARM

COMBAT
Mil Mi-24 'Hind'
Mikoyan MiG-29A 'Fulcrum'
Sukhoi Su-17M 'Fitter'
Sukhoi Su-24MR 'Fencer'
Sukhoi Su-25 'Frogfoot'

Sukhoi Su-27P/UB 'Flanker'

COMBAT SUPPORT
Antonov An-12/12PP 'Cub'
Antonov An-26/-26RKR 'Curl'
Mil Mi-6/-6BUS 'Hook'
Mil Mi-8/17 'Hip'
Mil Mi-26 'Halo'

TRAINING
Sukhoi Su-17UB 'Fitter'

MISCELLANEOUS
Antonov An-24 'Coke'
Ilyushin IL-76 'Candid'
Tupolev Tu-134 'Crusty'

VENEZUELA

VENEZUELAN AIR FORCE

COMBAT
Canadair N/VF-5A/B Freedom Fighter
Dassault Mirage 50EV
General Dynamics F-16A/B Fighting Falcon
Rockwell OV-10E Bronco

COMBAT SUPPORT
Alenia G.222
Bell UH-1B/H/N Iroquois
Bell 214ST
Bell 412SP
Eurocopter AS332B Super Puma
Eurocopter AS532UL Cougar
Lockheed C-130H Hercules

TRAINING
Beech T-34A Mentor
Canadair NF-5B Freedom Fighter
Dassault Mirage 50DV
Embraer EMB-312 Tucano
Rockwell T-2D Buckeye

MISCELLANEOUS
Aérospatiale SA316B Alouette III
Beech King Air 200/200C
Bell 214ST
Boeing 707-320C
Boeing 737-2N1
Cessna 500 Citation I
Cessna 550 Citation II
Dassault Falcon 20F
Gulfstream Aerospace Gulfstream II/III
Learjet 24D
Mil Mi-17 'Hip'
Pitts S-2B Special

VENEZUELAN NAVAL AVIATION

COMBAT
Agusta-Bell AS 212AS

COMBAT SUPPORT
CASA C.212-200/-200ASW/400 Aviocar
de Havilland Canada DHC-7 Dash 7-102

MISCELLANEOUS
Beech King Air E90
Beech King Air 200
Bell 206B/L JetRanger

Beech T-34C-1 Turbo-Mentor Uruguayan Navy

Gulfstream Aerospace Gulfstream III Venezuelan Air Force

Cessna 310R
Cessna 402C
Eurocopter AS355F-1 Ecureuil
Piper PA-23-250 Aztec
Rockwell Commander 695

VENEZUELAN ARMY AIR SERVICE
COMBAT SUPPORT
Agusta-Sikorsky AS-61D
Bell 205A-1
Bell UH-1H Iroquois
IAI Arava 201/202
Pilatus/B-N BN-2A-6 Islander
TRAINING
Bell 206B JetRanger
Cessna 182N
MISCELLANEOUS
Agusta A 109A/A-2
Beech Queen Air B80
Beech King Air E90/200
Bell 206L LongRanger
Cessna 172L
Cessna U206G Stationair
Cessna T207A

VENEZUELAN CIVIL GUARD
Beech Queen Air B80
Beech King Air E90
Beech King Air 200C
Bell 206B JetRanger
Bell 206L LongRanger
Bell 214ST
Cessna U206G Stationair
Eurocopter AS355F-2 Ecureuil
IAI Arava 201

VIETNAM

VIETNAMESE PEOPLE'S ARMY AIR FORCE
COMBAT
Kamov Ka-25Bsh 'Hormone'
Kamov Ka-28/32 'Helix'

Mikoyan MiG-21MF/bis 'Fishbed'
Mil Mi-24 'Hind'
Sukhoi Su-22M-3 'Fitter'
Sukhoi Su-27 'Flanker'
COMBAT SUPPORT
Antonov An-26 'Curl'
Mil Mi-6 'Hook'
Mil Mi-8/17 'Hip'
TRAINING
Aero L-39C Albatros
Mikoyan MiG-21UM 'Mongol'
Nanchang CJ-6
Sukhoi Su-22UM-3 'Fitter'
Sukhoi Su-27UB 'Flanker'
Yakovlev Yak-18 'Max'
MISCELLANEOUS
Antonov An-30 'Clank'
Yakovlev Yak-40 'Codling'

YEMEN

REPUBLIC OF YEMEN AIR FORCE
COMBAT
Mikoyan MiG-21MF/bis 'Fishbed'
Mikoyan MiG-23ML 'Flogger'
Mikoyan MiG-29A 'Fulcrum'
Mil Mi-24 'Hind'
Northrop F-5E Tiger II
Sukhoi Su-22M-2 'Fitter'
COMBAT SUPPORT
Agusta-Bell AB212
Antonov An-12B 'Cub'
Antonov An-24 'Coke'
Antonov An-26 'Curl'
Lockheed C-130H Hercules
Mil Mi-8 'Hip'
TRAINING
Aero L-39C Albatros
Mikoyan-Gurevich MiG-15UTI 'Midget'
Mikoyan MiG-21UM 'Mongol'
Mikoyan MiG-23UB 'Flogger'
Mikoyan MiG-29U 'Fulcrum'

Northrop F-5B Freedom Fighter
Sukhoi Su-22UM-3 'Fitter'
Yakovlev Yak-11 'Moose'
MISCELLANEOUS
Agusta-Bell AB206B JetRanger
Ilyushin IL-76 'Candid'
Shorts SC7 Skyvan

FEDERAL REPUBLIC OF YUGOSLAVIA (Serbia & Montenegro)

AIR FORCE AND AIR DEFENCE
COMBAT
Mikoyan MiG-21PFM/MF/bis/R
Mikoyan MiG-29A/B 'Fulcrum'
Soko G-2A Galeb
Soko G-4A Super Galeb
Soko I-22/IJ-22 Orao/
J-22(M)/NJ-22(M) Orao 2
Soko J-1/RJ-1 Jastreb
Soko/Aérospatiale SA342L Partizan
COMBAT SUPPORT
Antonov An-26 'Curl'
Mil Mi-8/17 'Hip'
Soko/Aérospatiale SA341H Partizan
TRAINING
Mikoyan MiG-21UM/US 'Mongol'
Mikoyan MiG-29UB 'Fulcrum'
UTVA-75
MISCELLANEOUS
Antonov An-2 'Colt'
Dassault Falcon 50
Learjet 25B
UTVA-66/H
Yakovlev Yak-40 'Codling'

ZAMBIA

ZAMBIAN AIR FORCE AND AIR DEFENCE COMMAND
COMBAT
Mikoyan MiG-21MF 'Fishbed'

Shenyang F-6/FT-6
Soko J-1E Jastreb
COMBAT SUPPORT
Agusta-Bell AB205A
Agusta-Bell AB212
Antonov An-26 'Curl'
de Havilland Canada DHC-5D Buffalo
Harbin Y-12 (II)
Mil Mi-8 'Hip'
TRAINING
Aermacchi MB-326GB
Hongdu/PAC K-8 Karakorum
Mikoyan MiG-21UM 'Mongol'
Nanchang CJ-6
Saab-MFI-17 Supporter
SIAI-Marchetti SF.260MZ
MISCELLANEOUS
Agusta-Bell 47G
Dornier Do 28D-1 Skyservant
Hawker Siddeley (BAe) 748 Srs 265
Yakovlev Yak-40 'Codling'

ZIMBABWE

AIR FORCE OF ZIMBABWE
COMBAT
Chengdu F-7 II/IIN Airguard
Hawker Hunter FGA9
Mil Mi-35 'Hind'
Reims Cessna FTB 337G
SIAI-Marchetti SF.260TP
COMBAT SUPPORT
Aérospatiale SA319 Alouette III
Agusta-Bell 412SP
CASA C.212-200 Aviocar
Pilatus/B-N BN-2A Islander
TRAINING
British Aerospace Hawk 60/60A
Hawker Hunter T81
SIAI-Marchetti SF.260M/W/F
MISCELLANEOUS
Eurocopter AS532UL Cougar

PHOTOGRAPHS

The photographs in *The Directory of Military Aircraft of the World* have been supplied by the individual photographers listed below and printed on the pages indicated.

Peter J Cooper 159

Ben Dunnell 29, 160, 219 & 380

John Dunnell 79 & 125

Brian Elliott 359

Graham Finch 39, 91, 198, 399, 442, 444, 449, 457,463 & 464

Peter R Foster 9, 18, 23, 25, 34, 35, 55, 56 (x2), 57, 66, 107, 108, 109 (x2), 113, 114, 117 (x2), 119, 120, 145, 153, 155, 179, 181, 182, 202 (x2), 212, 213, 220, 221, 222, 225 (x2), 237 (x2), 262, 289, 291, 296 (x2), 298, 303 (x2), 304, 324 (x2), 329, 330, 338, 343, 345 (x2), 355, 363, 373 (x2), 376 (x2), 388, 421, 425, 426, 428, 429, 443, 450, 451, 457, 458, 459, 461, 462 & 469 (x2)

Paul A Jackson 378 (x2)

Malcolm Lowe 440

Andrew P March 10, 68, 125, 157, 158, 176, 183, 204, 226, 248, 267, 285, 293 (x2), 302, 344, 357 & 375

Daniel J March 23, 27, 31, 37, 47, 58, 75 (x2), 76, 77, 83, 84, 88, 92, 101, 104, 123, 126, 129, 130, 132, 139, 143, 154, 167, 178, 189, 197, 206, 216, 229 (x2), 240, 243, 252, 253, 255, 260, 264, 295, 305, 306, 314, 319, 321, 331 (x2), 347, 350, 353, 393, 401, 422, 427, 434 (x2), 435, 440, 446, 447, 453, 458, 462, 463, 466 & 467

Keith Saunders 186

Rod Simpson 11, 12, 18, 25, 41, 46, 54, 87, 110 (x2), 111 (x2), 112, 118, 136, 141, 144, 172, 173, 181, 182, 184, 187, 188, 192, 197, 211 (x2), 221, 222, 223, 231, 291, 298, 325, 327, 338, 341, 360, 379, 407, 419, 421, 432, 436 (x2), 441, 447 & 451

Kevin Storer 148, 301, 315 & 349

Brian S Strickland 21, 103, 159 & 414

Joanna Strickland 232

Katsuhiko Tokunaga 38, 82, 150, 180, 290 (x2), 362 & 404

Jim Winchester 46, 60, 137, 299, 450 & 461

Brian Pickering/Military Aviation Photographs, **Gordon Bartley**/BAE Systems (together with **Phil Boyden**, **Geoff Lee** and **Chris Ryding**), the Royal Air Force and the Royal Air Force Benevolent Fund have provided a significant number of the photographs printed in the pages of this Directory.

In addition, photographs from the following manufacturers have been used in the Directory: Aérospatiale, Aerostar, Boeing, Bombardier, Dassault, Embraer, ENAER, Eurocopter, GKN Westland, Gulfstream Aerospace, Lockheed Martin, MBB, McDonnell Douglas, Raytheon and Saab.

All remaining photographs **Peter R March**/PRM Aviation.

GLOSSARY

The following abbreviations, titles and terms have been used in this book:

AAC	Army Air Corps	B-V	Boeing-Vertol	FAC	Forward Air Controller
AAM	Air-to-Air Missile	BAC	British Aircraft Corporation	FADEC	Full Authority Digital Engine Controls
AAR	Air-to-Air Refuelling	BAe	British Aerospace plc	FBW	Fly By Wire
ABNCP	Airborne National Command Post	Be	Beech	ff	first flight
ACC	Air Combat Command	BG	Bomber Group	FFA	Flug und Fahrzeugwerke AG
ACF	Avion de Combat Futur	BOAC	British Overseas Airways Corporation	FG	Fighter Group
ACW	Airborne Control Wing	BS	Bomber Squadron	FGA	Fighter Ground Attack
ACW	Advanced Combat Wing	C-SAR	Combat Search-and-Rescue	FH	Fairchild-Hiller
ACX	Avion de Combat Experimentale	CAC	Commonwealth Aircraft Corporation	FLIR	Forward Looking Infra-Red
ADF	Advanced Tactical Fighter	CAF	Canadian Armed Forces	Flt	Flight
AEF	Air Experience Flight	CAS	Close Air Support	FMA	Fabrica Militar de Aviones
AETC	Air Education and Training Command	CASA	Construcciones Aeronautics SA	FMV	Forsvarets Materielwerk
AEW	Airborne Early Warning	CFE	Conventional Armed Forces in Europe	FOD	Foreign Object Damage/Debris
AFB	Air Force Base	CFS	Central Flying School	FRA	FR Aviation
AFFTC	Air Force Flight Test Center	CFT	Conformal Fuel Tanks	FS	Fighter Squadron
AFRC	Air Force Reserve Command	CIA	Central Intelligence Agency	FSTA	Future Strategic Tanker Aircraft
AFSC	Air Force System Command	CIS	Commonwealth of Independent States	FTS	Flying Training School
AG	Airlift Group	cm	centimetre	Fw	Focke Wulf
AGM	Air-to-Ground Missile	Co	Company	FY	Financial/Fiscal Year
AHIP	Army Helicopter Improvement Programme	COD	Carrier On-board Delivery	GAF	Government Aircraft Factory
AIDC	Aero Industry Development Corporation	COIN	Counter Insurgency	GAIC	Guizhou Aviation Industry Corporation
ALAT	Aviation Legére de l'Armeé de Terre	comms	communications	gal	gallon
ALCA	Advanced Light Combat Aircraft	CV	Chance-Vought	GD	General Dynamics
ALH	Advanced Light Helicopter	D-BA	Daimler-Benz Aerospace	GE	General Electric
AMC	Air Mobility Command	D-BD	Dassault-Breguet Dornier	GKNW	GKN Westland
AMD-BA	Avions Marcel Dassault-Breguet Aviation	DARA	Defence Aviation Repair Agency	GPS	Global Positioning System
AMI	Aeronautica Militare Italiana	DERA	Defence Evaluation and Research Agency	GR	Ground Attack Reconnaissance
AMRAAM	Advanced Medium Range Air-to-Air Missile	DGPS	Differential Global Positioning System	GRP	Glass fibre Reinforced Plastic
AMW	Air Mobility Wing	DH	de Havilland	HAL	Hindustan Aeronautics Ltd
AMX	Partnership of Aermacchi, Alenia and Embraer	DHC	de Havilland Canada	HAP	Hélicoptère d'Appui et de Protection
An	Antonov	Do	Dornier	HAR	Helicopter Air Rescue
ANG	Air National Guard	DPA	Defence Procurement Agency	HARM	High-speed Anti-Radiation Missile
ANGOSA	Air National Guard's Operational Support Aircraft	DVI	Directive Voice Input	HAS	Helicopter Anti-Submarine
ANGOSTA	Air National Guard Support Turboprop Aircraft	EC	Escadre de Chasse (Fighter Wing)	HMA	Helicopter Maritime Attack
ARIA	Advanced Range Instrumentation Aircraft	ECM	Electronic Counter Measures	HMS	Her Majesty's Ship
ARL	Airborne Reconnaissance Low	ECM	Electronic Combat and Reconnaissance	HOT	High speed, Optically-tracked, Tube launched
ARS	Air Refueling Squadron	EE	English Electric	HOTAS	Hands On Throttle And Stick
ARW	Air Refueling Wing	EFIS	Electronic Flight Instrumentation System	HP	High Performance
ASCW	Airborne Surveillance Control Wing	EFS	Enhanced Flight Screener	HP	Handley Page
ASM	Anti-Submarine Missile	EHI	European Helicopter Industries	hp	horsepower
ASM	Air-to-Surface Missile	ehp	equivalent horsepower	HQ	Headquarters
ASMD	Anti-Ship Missile Defence	Elint	Electronic intelligence	HS	Hawker Siddeley
ASRAAM	Advance Short Range Air-to-Air Missile	EMD	Engineering and Manufacturing Development	HUD	Head-Up Display
ASTA	Aerospace Technologies of Australia	ENAER	Empressa Nacional de Aeronautica de Chile	IAA	Indian Army Aviation
ASTOR	Airborne Stand-Off Radar	EP	Enhanced Performance	IAF	Israeli Air Force
ASW	Anti-Submarine Warfare	eshp	equivalent shaft horsepower	IAF	Indian Air Force
ATA	Advanced Trainer/Attack	ESM	Electronic Measures	IAI	Israeli Aircraft Industries
ATB	Advanced Technology Bomber	ESM	Electronic Surveillance/Support Measures	ICBM	Inter-Continental Ballistic Missile
ATR	Avions de Transport Régional	ESSS	External Stores Support System	ICE	Improved Combat Efficiency
ATS	Advanced Training System	ETOPS	Extended-Range Two-Engined Operations	ICH	Improved Cargo Helicopter
Avn	Aviation	ETPS	Empire Test Pilots' School	IDF	Israeli Defence Force
AWACS	Airborne Warning and Command System	EW	Electronic Warfare	IDF	Indigenous Defence Fighter
		FAA	Fleet Air Arm, Federal Aviation Administration	IDS	Interdiction/Strike

IFF	Identification Friend or Foe	MRTT	Multi-Role Tanker/Transport	SEPECAT	Société Européenne de Producyion de L'avion Ecole de Combat
INA	Indian Naval Aviation	NA	North American		
INAS	Indian Navy Aviation Squadron	NAEWF	NATO Airborne Early Warning Force	shp	shaft horsepower
IOC	Initial Operational Capability	NAMC	Nihon Aircraft Manufacturing Company	Sigint	Signals intelligence
IR	Infra-Red	NAS	Naval Air Station	SIVAM	Amazon Surveillance project
IR/UV	Infra-Red/Ultra Violet	NASA	National Aeronautics & Space Administration	SLIR	Sideways Looking Infra-Red
IRCM	Infra-Red Countermeasures	NATO	North Atlantic Treaty Organisation	Sm	Smaldeel (Squadron)
JAR	Joint Airworthiness Requirement	NAWC	Naval Air Warfare Center	SMURFS	Side-Mounted Unit, horizontal tail Root Fins
JASDF	Japan Air Self-Defence Force	NEACP	National Emergency Airborne Command	SNCASE	Société Nationale de Constructions Aéronautique du Sud-Est
JbG	Jagdbombergeschwader (Fighter Bomber Wing)	NFATS	Naval Force Aircraft Test Squadron		
JEFTS	Joint Elementary Flying Training School	NFH	NATO Frigate Helicopter	SOCATA	Société de Construction d'Avions de Touisme et d'Affaires
JGSDF	Japan Ground Self-Defence Force	nm	nautical mile		
JJ	JianJiao	NOTAR	No Tail Rotor	SOS	Special Operations Squadron
JMSDF	Japanese Maritime Self-Defence Force	NTA	New Trainer Aircraft	Sqn	Squadron
JPATS	Joint Primary Aircraft Training System	NTH	New Training Helicopter	SRIM	Service Radio Installation Modification
JSTARS	Joint Surveillance Target Attack Radar System	OCU	Operational Conversion Unit	SRR	Short-Range Recovery
JTIDS	Joint Tactical Information Distribution System	OEU	Operational Evaluation Unit	ST	Stretched Twin
KAF	Kenya Air Force	OPTEC	Operational Test and Evaluation Command	st	static thrust
kg	kilogramme	P&W	Pratt & Whitney	STOL	Short Take-Off and Landing
km/h	kilometres per hour	P&WC	Pratt & Whitney Canada	SUPT	Specialised Undergraduate Pilot Training
km	kilometre	PAC	Pakistan Aeronautical Complex	SYERS	Senior Year Electro Optical Relay System
kN	kilonewton	PAF	Pacific Air Force	TACAN	Tactical Air Navigation
KPAAF	Korean People's Army Air Force	PBN	Pilatus Britten-Norman	TAI	Turkish Aerospace Industries
kW	kilowatt	PDLCT	Pod de Dèsignation Laser & Camèra Thermique	TARPS	Tactical Air Reconnaissance Pod System
l	litre			TDS	Towed Decoy System
LAFT	Light Aircraft Flying Task	PFI	Private Finance Initiative	Telint	Telecommunications intelligence
LAMPS	Light Airborne Multi-Purpose System	PGM	Precision Guided Munition	TFS	Tactical Fighter Squadron
LANTIRN	Low Altitude Navigation Targeting Infra-Red Night	PLAAF	People's Liberation Army Air Force	TFW	Tactical Fighter Wing
		PMS	Power Management System	TFX	Tactical Fighter Experimental
lb	pound	PR	Photo Reconnaissance	TIALD	Thermal Imaging Airborne Laser Designator
LGB	Laser Guided Bomb	PRU	Photographic Reconnaissance Unit	TJS	Tactical Jamming System
LOH	Light Observation Helicopter	PV	Private Venture	trans	transport
Loran	Long range navigation	PWR	Passive Warning Receiver	trng	training
LOROP	Long-Range Oblique Photography	PZL	Pañstowe Zaklady Lotnicze	TT	Target Towing
LTV	Ling-Temco-Vought	QC	Quick Change	TTH	Tactical Transport Helicopter
M	Mach number	R-R	Rolls-Royce	TTTS	Tanker/Transport Training System
m	metre	RAAF	Royal Australian Air Force	TVS	Thrust-Vectoring System
Mach	Mach Number	RAF	Royal Air Force	TWR	Threat Warning Radar
MAD	Magnetic Anomaly Detector	RAM	Radar Absorbent Material	UAE	United Arab Emirates
MAP	Military Assistance Program	RDA	Radar Development Aircraft	UHF	Ultra High Frequency
MARPAT	Maritime Patrouillegroep (Maritime Patrol Group)	recce	reconnaissance	UK	United Kingdom
		RJAF	Royal Jordanian Air Force	UN	United Nations
MBB	Messerschmitt Bolkow-Blohm	RM	Royal Marines	US	United States
MD	McDonnell Douglas	RN	Royal Navy	USAF	United States Air Force
Met	meteorological	RNAS	Royal Naval Air Station	USAREUR	US Army Europe
MFD	Multi-Function Displays	RNethAF	Royal Netherlands Air Force	USCG	United States Coast Guard
MFI	Malmö Flygindustri	RNorAF	Royal Norwegian Air Force	USMC	United States Marines Corps
mg	machine gun	RNZAF	Royal New Zealand Air Force	USN	United States Navy
Mk	Mark number	RQS	Rescue Squadron	UTT	Utility Tactical Transport
MLU	Mid-Life Update	RSV	Reparto Sperimentale Volo	V/STOL	Vertical/Short Take-Off and Landing
mm	millimetre	RW	Reconnaissance Wing	VAAC	Vectored thrust Advanced Aircraft flight Control
MMSA	Multi-Mission Surveillance Aircraft	RWR	Radar Warning Receiver	VHF	Very High Frequency
MOD	Ministry of Defence	SA	Scottish Aviation	VIP	Very Important Person
mods	modifications	Saab	Svenska Aeroplan Aktieboleg	Vne	Maximum speed, never exceed
MPA	Maritime Patrol Aircraft	SAAF	South African Air Force	VTA	Military Transport Aviation
mph	miles per hour	SAI	Singapore Aircraft Industries	VTAS	Voice Throttle and Stick
MPLH	Multi-Purpose Light Helicopter	SAL	Scottish Aviation Limited	WS	Westland
MR	Maritime Reconnaissance	SAR	Search and Rescue	WSO	Weapons System Officer
MRCA	Multi-Role Combat Aircraft	SEAD	Suppression of Enemy Air Defences	WW2	World War Two
MRT	Multi-Role Transport	SELL	Special Operations Low Level	XST	Experimental Stealth Technology

INDEX

POWERPLANTS